p²·⁵

p·²⁵²

THE IRISH TROUBLES

BOOKS BY J. BOWYER BELL

Besieged Seven Cities Under Attack

The Long War: Israel and the Arabs Since 1946

The Secret Army: The IRA Since 1916

The Myth of the Guerrilla: Revolutionary Theory and Malpractice

The Horn of Africa: Strategic Magnet in the Seventies

Transnational Terror

On Revolt: Strategies of National Liberation

Terror out of Zion: The Irgun Zvai Leumi, LEHI, and the Palestine Underground, 1929–1949

A Time of Terror: How Democratic Societies Respond to Revolutionary Violence

Assassin: The Theory and Practice of Political Violence

The Gun in Politics: An Analysis of Irish Political Conflict, 1916–1986

IRA Tactics and Targets: An Analysis of Tactical Aspects of the Armed Struggle, 1969–1989

THE
IRISH
TROUBLES

A Generation of Violence
1967–1992

J. BOWYER BELL

ST. MARTIN'S PRESS

NEW YORK

Again and still, this troublesome text is dedicated
to my Kerry wife
NORA BROWNE
who has made my
troubles few and my delights many.

Mo ghrá thú

Contents

Foreword

Almost my entire life has been involved with Ireland, the Irish, but never by intent. I never planned on Ireland. I never foresaw an involvement in Irish matters. In 1965 I came to write one book, spend a pleasant summer by the Barrow River, have a family vacation, and enjoy the country. That was to be all. Instead I could not get away, ever.

Attracted by the possibility of a work on the contemporary Irish Republican Army, I was lured back the next year. I arrived, did the research, wrote a history of the secret army. That was to be all, the end. I, of course, grew fond of the Irish, made friends, traveled all thirty-two counties, had adventures. That should have been the end, but Ireland has never been easily discarded nor swiftly won. The island was not finished with me.

Even with Ireland soon in the news, my secret army not so secret, the country filled with anxiety and journalists, I had other interests, other wars. I never planned on writing on a generation of troubles. I could not have *imagined* a generation of troubles. No one could. No one did. And during the years of turmoil, I had no intention of ultimately producing a work on an Irish tragedy in endless acts.

Any Irish prologue is as indeterminable as has been my Irish involvement, slow but in retrospect inevitable. My own analytical concerns as a scholar were the dynamics of the covert, the workings of rebels. In the beginning with the IRA I never foresaw years spent in the company of gunmen in a variety of alien arenas or an observer's place in contemporary insurrections. In fact I anticipated time at a university desk filled with books, journals, conventional sources. I had no intention of having my career evolve into repeated tours through the garden spots of terror or my concerns those more often described in thrillers and adventure films than in academic journals. Yet there I was in Beirut or Khartoum, still, as in Ireland, in the company of gunmen. And there, then, I had no plans to return to an Irish war. Yet I ended up, year after year, on the island. And certainly, I had no intention—no more than did the others—of returning to an Irish war or observing a time of turmoil close up and personal. Still I found myself year after year back again. Ireland does many things for different people and thus the island changed my life as well as my times.

I spent more time in Ireland, not always underground, chatting up the secret army, not always on matters of the political moment, or always focused on unpleasant and violent matters at all. The major attraction, however, was the trouble on the island, and my asset was access to the militant republican movement. So I observed the IRA's armed struggle from close up, often too close up. I was shot at on occasion, always without effect, gassed, pursued, followed: what I had come to expect in times of turmoil. All became merely an increasingly unromantic obstacle to the pursuit of reality. Such nasty wars are not romantic in any case but dreadful and dangerous even for visitors. Standing at the bottom of a dark lane waiting for a source who will arrive armed and suspicious is no less nerve-racking off the Falls as it is in Beirut or Khartoum. Without the taste of cordite, the feel of fear, the reality of the danger that often marks another day underground, I found it hard to write realistically about an armed struggle. It was hard to understand the dynamics that would later be reduced to journal articles and seminar presentations without personal contact with the involved with those active on one side or the other.

So in Ireland I talked to those I could reach, on one side always and sometimes on the other. I was still disinterested if well-connected and so contacted all and sundry, my gunmen and the democratic politicians, the police, the solicitor's clerk, and the barman at my local. I attended riots when I might well have stayed home, went along with the doubtful or the dubious when I should have stayed home. In fact, Ireland had, without my noticing, become another home. I was not the first transient trapped by the Celts.

Ultimately, the Irish Troubles evolved into a primary interest. Even my treks through some most unsavory arenas, often far from the island, led to Irish information. Mostly, of course, the important events were on the island, the people concerned there. Sometimes, however, the Troubles splattered out into far places: three volunteers killed in Gibraltar, arms smuggled out of Boston or Tripoli, debates at Westminster, less visible events. There were, too, the retired to be found in the Bronx and City offices in London, but mostly the Troubles stayed in Ireland—and when I could, so did I stay as close to events as possible.

Over the years I watched the bombs being made, a most uncomfortable experience, and saw them go off, often even more distressing. I kept on talking and began to take notes. And I watched the landscape change and watched even the indomitable Irish change. As I changed. Gradually, like everyone else, I was transmuted by the years on the edge of a war without victories, with only victims, a long, long war. There were so many funerals, so many betrayed, so many broken hearts. There were children I had seen in strollers who grew up to carry .38 revolvers and the weight of Tone's Republic. And there were so many innocent dead, forgotten maimed, so many idealists corrupted and so much good gone wrong.

I grew old in Ireland. My other wars, my other analytical interests, offered perspective, if rarely hope, for the Irish events. Those other wars mostly ended.

The Irish conflict went on and on, longer than those in Eritrea or Angola, much, much longer than the classic campaigns of Begin or Grivas, the FLN in Algeria or the *focos* in Latin America. In time those dreadful Irish events became one of the premier armed struggles of modern times. It was a drama no one claimed to have authored and few enjoyed performing.

Ireland of the Troubles is not all of Ireland or Irish politics, often only background music to more pressing matters like local elections, the unemployment rate, the rise of U2, or the scandal of the moment. Ireland of the Troubles is not even all of my Ireland. True, the Troubles bleed over into all Irish life, appear in poems and songs, on election agendas and in the display of statistics and grievances, but Ireland, the island, is not simply and often not mainly an arena for gunmen and bigots. This particular work, however, is so focused. It is not even political history but an analysis of the evolution of the gun in Irish politics since 1967.

This, the recourse to physical force by the committed and involved, has produced the spectacular and the awful and always the interesting, if not always the significant. It has often been a nasty, dreadful time. All armed struggles are squalid, brutal, ruthless, but few others have taken place in such public view. Ireland is an arena inhabited by the articulate, an arena littered with printed and conventional sources—programs and reports and election results are filed—and an arena seemingly with built-in klieg lights for the media eager for the latest photogenic outrage. For a generation of Troubles, however exaggerated or mis-reported, has been an intractable, fierce political conflict. And I have concentrated on the violence, the troubles, the turmoil. There is much else to write about Ireland, about Irish politics and Irish virtues, even much less interesting, perhaps more interesting, but this text is focused on the Troubles, on a generation that has often revealed the worst in all those involved. Sadly, so sadly, even the decent have rarely accomplished much good and have at times contributed to the turmoil.

The Troubles have troubled all sorts. Long ago my friend Professor Richard Rose said that the problem was that there *was* no solution. So far he has proven correct. Every initiative has been tried from cunning political formulas to larger bombs. Nothing has produced an accommodation, much less a solution. And after all this time few have hopes beyond the amelioration of the horror. Certainly, my Irish exposure has eroded much of the hope and optimism that are usually integral to Americans, ever eager to reason together, to compromise. Certainly, my Celtic concerns have exposed me too often and for too long to the violent and unrepentant and too often to the repetition of error.

Everywhere amid the Irish tumult there is the evidence of malice and the institutionalized injustice that edges out the decent and honorable. And the horrors occur in a small place where names are known. There, in a lush country-side or in tidy, small towns, a dirty war is especially horrid, especially in a country where most are kindly and decent. They, the Irish and the others, can be and often are violent, sometimes in plain sight at Harrods's door in London or on Nassau Street next to Trinity College Dublin or on Royal Avenue in Belfast. And worst of all, such violence at times seems without resolution.

Each trip to the island offers a backlog of recent atrocities, new grievances, and the prospects of more of both. And there has always been more, easily seen on the evening television news in Dublin or Kerry or New York, or even, less expectedly, watched far away but still live in a house on the Gaza Strip. The Troubles have long supplied hard news, spectacular news, mostly bad news.

Irish life goes along as always—the horses run, the milk comes in the morning, the plants open or close, and the wrong team wins. Still, the times have not been good for the Irish, all the Irish or any of the Irish, the Protestants or the Catholics, the poor, the nationalists and the unionists, those involved and even those innocent of all but bad luck. Times have been hard, but then in the past they were often thought no better. This is largely illusion. Ireland for two centuries has been a largely peaceful arena of dispute. The famine was the great catastrophe—and emigration—not great wars, invasions, or massive pogroms. The present violence is real enough but often exaggerated. The Troubles kill few and involve only a small minority in the politics or the armed struggles. Much of the island, even much of Northern Ireland, is mostly peaceful at least on the surface. Few, if still too many, live on the dangerous edge. The rest have adjusted. There has been atrocity, killing, but no general slaughter. Belfast, center of the Troubles, is not Beirut, and Ireland is not a combat zone.

Long ago when I was innocent of Irish matters and mostly of secret wars and guerrillas, Ireland, part real, part imagined, was merely a small island on the margin of events, green fields and poets, mostly in exile, and an old war not quite concluded. Much of that Ireland has changed, not all for the bad. I changed. And the world's perception of the island changed. It was no longer home of poets. The gunman had returned. And this, for the innocent and the victims, was very bad news. For those ambitious or determined, for those curious or professionally concerned, such news of political turmoil can be useful. Ireland troubled became not only a vortex of violence but also a case study, a stop on the terrorist tour, a cover story for the newsmagazines, a tick on every television producer's list. Ireland was not simply a green land of legend, home of Joyce and Yeats and Guinness and Blarney, but also now spectacular news, bombs and murders and troops on the streets. The island or at least Northern Ireland was a stage for a cast thrust into the television lights by planning or through bad luck, by necessity or with enthusiasm. It was a stage also crowded with the innocent, the vulnerable, the everyday people who often wanted no part of the drama, only peace and quiet. There were other players who had suddenly tasted power who had awakened ambitions. There were those responsible for order, for justice, for the schools or the roads. Most of those involved in the Troubles were decent, but some were malevolent. All had roles none had foreseen. It was a grand and deadly and fascinating drama.

Ireland was suddenly awash with authors and analysts. The journalists rushed in first but were followed, closely followed, by academics and the involved, by transients and tourists. The toll in books and articles, serious books, serious articles, as well as trash and froth, runs into the thousands. During the early years the chattering classes on tour, the carrion birds of the social sciences, the media magnates, those with real concerns and those simply attracted to bombs, circled the island. Some of those attracted were serious, compassionate, others less so. As the years passed so did the urgency of the event and so quietly good, sound, often conventional works appeared, some not even on the turmoil but on island politics and economics, some on the policy or programs related to violence. Eventually every discipline became involved. The analysts and the writers have never left entirely. In fact, a new generation has arrived that came of age during the Troubles. And Ireland is still an attraction.

This new Ireland of the Troubles reported by the media has been fashioned out of real conflict. It is composed of real people, has grown from deep roots and blossomed when least expected. It is an Ireland rewarding, if to no other, to the analyst of political violence. Ultimately as the years passed, my notes and clippings and interview cards piled up: The prospect of a history began to emerge. It would this time be a history of all the turmoil, not simply the dynamics of the secret armies. The focus would be on a generation of spectacular and often novel events that had generated an enormous literature but not a single history. I had consumed much of this enormous literature along the way, just as I had talked with the involved, or taken note at chance meetings in far places. And gradually as others grew exhausted with the endless turbulence without prospect of a final chapter to the drama, I felt that the time had come to detail the long war. The existing stalemate was in a sense a last chapter of sorts.

Much that I had accumulated I had yet to publish, for I would then undoubtedly have lost many sources who assumed that their perception of the last generation was exact, the absolute truth, hard-edged revelation and not to be adjusted by alien interpretation. So I had waited to publish in detail on Irish matters. Still, it was time: I might fall in front of a bus with all the Irish details still unwritten. And, too, I had grown old with the Troubles so that once a text was published, I could focus again on more distant matters. So with the help of two most congenial and understanding American sponsors, the Harry Frank Guggenheim and Smith-Richardson Foundations, I undertook a history of a generation of Irish distress. The project devoured more time than I had imagined. But then most Irish matters usually do.

The text is long and in sources somewhat unusual. For a generation, as noted, I have been involved in accumulating, sometimes unwittingly, the material that winnowed became in the book history and analysis. There were tens of thousands of hours of interviews, many before the book was conceived. Some of the interviews were formal, many not, some occurring as might be expected in Dublin or London offices while others often took place far from the scene—the Commissioner of the Metropolitan Police Sir Robert Mark in a Philadelphia hotel after we spoke to a conference of editors; arms merchants in the Middle East pursuing clients; journalists in Italy who long before had rushed to Derry or Belfast to see real revolution that soon came to Rome or Milan during the Italian years of lead. I met functionaries in southern Africa or Israel, talked to officials in Washington and London, met those concerned with the island in all sorts of places. Impressions, the gradual analysis of motives and hidden agendas, attitudes and assumptions, are difficult to footnote, but much of this work's analysis arises from the interviews, from the involved and observant, from people.

On the other hand, a good deal of what is included in the text is not only easy to find but also obvious as to source—the daily Irish and British newspapers quoted the officials and spokesmen, often at length, printed organizational statements, often intact, printed government bulletins, included as well as the specific comments of the victims, the involved, the impressions of the staff. To cite each quotation as is the academic convention would mean, quite literally, hundreds upon hundreds, thousands upon thousands of footnotes citing the press of the day. Hence quotes without notes unless otherwise obvious are from the daily press. Beyond a simple chronicle, the newspapers are important to contemporary history. Journalists, given the chance and despite the brief half-life of their work, accumulate all sorts of vital and useful information. Many journalists in Belfast, Dublin, and London became at least for a time specialists on the Troubles. The good newspapers, especially the *Irish Times*, supply more than just a chronicle of events and are the sources in the text of most direct quotes that have no footnotes.

Even then for the concerned, there is a shortcut. Only professionals read a generation of newspapers. There are now not only published bibliographies but chronologies as well, in particular the massive three volumes of *Northern Ireland: A Chronology of Events* by Richard Deutsch and Vivien Magowan. This material came mostly from the splendid *Fortnight* magazine in Belfast, which still publishes a chronology. And from Albany, New York, the small Northern Ireland News Service issues a weekly news service that includes quotations amid the daily survey of the events of the week.

In any case, the limited citations, as sparse as possible, aid in keeping the text within reasonable bounds. As it is long, the Irish conflict has engendered here a long book. Those Troubles have also produced an entire library of work from primary sources through the ephemeral party presses and on to academic analysis of the paintings on the gable ends of terraced houses in Belfast or Derry. The extent of this massive literature on the Troubles is briefly surveyed in my "Sources." As it is, I have already published four bibliographical articles that cover only works published before 1972. The literature is not only massive—over seven thousand *serious* items in English alone—but it is graced with splendid analytical works, good journalism, fine memoirs, and excellent journal articles. The shelves also are stuffed with all the flood of print that a spectacular and novel crisis inevitably engenders—instant books, bad books on fascinating subjects, special pleading, all the pages that an advanced society engenders on serious matters. For the serious scholar even the more obscure journals with one issue or the proclamations of ephemeral groups can often be found in Belfast's Linenhall Library, repository of almost every source.

Beyond the problem of indicating, much less citing, the sheer quantity of the printed sources, there are several minor but specifically Irish problems in any text on the Troubles. Words in Ireland, especially in relation to the Troubles, tend to mean more (or sometimes less) than conventional definitions. Many want the North to be a direction, not, as do the unionists, a place. Ulster for the loyalists has six counties, not the historic nine, and so its use often implies British Ulster, Our Ulster. Just as the Irish nationalists point out that parts of the Republic are further north than the North, they want the loyalist Ulster labeled the Province of Northern Ireland but often call it the North. In turn, for the unionists and most loyalists, Ulster is British despite the fact that Great Britain is another island entirely. On the Irish island for militant republicans, the IRA, there are the six counties—the Province of Northern Ireland—and the Free State, an entity that has not existed since December 1937. Since April 1949, there has been the Republic of Ireland but not the Republic of Tone or the IRA. Members of the Dublin establishment never refer to their Republic as the twenty-six counties and until the Troubles hardly recognized that there *were* six lost counties. While nearly every Protestant in those six counties is loyal to the British connection, the Crown, many are not Unionists, members of the Unionist Party, but unionists or even loyalists. Most loyalists are unionists, but some, those who, if need be, to keep their way of life, have advocated independence and thus are neither loyal to the Crown nor advocates of the union. Generally, "loyalist" is used for the most militant unionists, often those Protestants willing to introduce or to excuse or at least to tolerate the gun in politics. Mostly the context makes clear the use of the words, but satisfying all of the concerned is not possible. For many unionists and all loyalists, Londonderry is Londonderry, forever, just as it remained Derry for all the nationalists and not a few unionists. There will always be those who want the text to match not just their perceptions but their usage as well. And that usage may change with the years: John Stephenson, born in England, evolved into Seán Stephenson as his commitment to Ireland grew, and he finally emerged as Seán Mac Stiofáin of the Provisional IRA—Chief of Staff Seán Mac. Dave O'Connell—to his old friends—became Dáithí O Conaill in public, in the republican movement. Usually the proper public name is in the text. Sometimes the Seans use an accent, Seán, sometimes not, and often are called John. Consistency is not Celtic but at least sought in the text.

Whatever the Irish may want on matters of usage and spelling, they have over the years been willing to suffer inquiry and relay the truth as discerned. For me, for more than most since my concern has been often, if not always, mostly focused on the covert and illicit world of the IRA, people have been the prime sources. Many of them will be disappointed in the text, in the wording, in my failure to see their reality clearly or accept their interpretation whole. Many expected no less. Others knowing my connection with the militant republicans will seek—often find whether present or not—bias, yet an enormous number of people on and off the island have helped me, knowing I would use North instead of Northern Ireland, fail to understand the Unionist position or the restraints on various political initiatives. Some suspected that I would underestimate the obstacles to effecting real change through political means while retaining political power. And yet their responses have enriched what could otherwise have been chronicle. It is the people involved who have supplied the basis of the text. They have taken me at my word, accepted that I am in the heel of the hunt alien, disinterested, not really part of the problem, even if my published work has inclined to become involved.

There have been all sorts of people. People met by chance or cunning, people deeply involved and those utterly without interest in politics of any sort. All sorts of friends and allies, passing strangers and those officially so instructed have helped along the way, all too aware that eventually the result would appear in print and probably in a form opposed to the truth as they perceived it. Lots, nearly all, helped anyway. And some will find their contribution misused. They had not so much given up hope as given up explaining.

Over a generation those colleagues and friends and congenial officials who have also helped me grew to legion. They were only slightly less helpful than those involved in pursuing their campaign cr their killing. So it was not only those intimately and immediately involved, from the gunmen to the conciliators, who were more forthcoming than might have been imagined. The vocation of the historian, at least in Ireland and across the Irish Sea in Britain, still found friends and so did I. Colleagues helped, of course. Even those who never spoke in public and rarely in private on serious matters often made exception. But some, especially in Britain, had simply had too much of Irish matters.

The end result has been thousands of hours contributed by others without prospect of return. Many would prefer not to be mentioned. Some would feel even more strongly. The long war is still active. These sources include a remarkable number of those actively or recently involved: most militant republicans, many British and Irish officials and politicians, fewer fundamentalist loyalists or active security people. And there have been a great many everyday people, some who were present at one disaster and many who have learned of the Troubles only through the telly. It is about the mix one might expect and I thank them all, even those who politely declined to help.

In nearly every case the first contact was made with someone's aid and comfort, and so this is thanks to all of those who at some point over the years offered that aid and comfort, different people at different times. There were scores of officials and scholars and transients. And there were those who came to hear me propound on Irish matters, often those scholars who knew far more about the long Irish chronicle than I did or would. There were especially and always on call a few of the most faithful of all, such as Oliver Snoddy, first at the National Museum, for some time president of the Gaelic League, and more lately under various guises including that of my publisher in Irish. There were as well some of my old—or aging—republican friends, whose names might better be sought in the index than in the foreword.

To find a sponsor for an analytical interest in Ireland has not always been easy. After a time the Irish Troubles lacked the draw of transnational terrorism or the collapse of the Soviet empire. These Celtic troubles that have gone on and on out on the margin of Europe seemingly lack application in policy matters. They have rarely been at the top of anyone's list of major concerns. Sometimes even the Irish preferred to consider other, less divisive matters. I thus have been fortunate that my two American foundations with headquarters in New York City have been generously supportive as the project continued. The Harry Frank Guggenheim Foundation beginning in 1987 awarded me four fellowships to pursue Irish matters. Their program officer Karen Colvard and the staff have been most supportive. The foundation has sponsored seminars, made contacts, kept in touch, and tolerated digressions. Substantial support has been offered by the Smith-Richardson Foundation, with three research grants largely focused on Irish political violence. There first William Bodie, presently at the Institute for National Security Studies at the National Defense University in Washington, and later Devon Gaffney Cross have kept the faith with my convictions. Foundation support for research in a less than trendy subject, often undertaken using less than savory sources, has made possible this text. In fact, this text on the Troubles may tell my sponsors even more about Ireland than they felt necessary, and worse, offers no single villain, no easy solution, in fact no prospect that pleases at all, only a litany of errors best avoided and pretensions best discarded.

The Irish Troubles are, after all, a special and particular failure as distressing to the Irish, to the involved and responsible, as to the victims and the innocent. So in a sense Ireland of the welcomes has no welcome for the gun in politics, nor for that matter do many involved. Thus, all aid and comfort was and is doubly welcomed, not just from the Murphys of Harold's Cross and the Brownes of Ballybunion, but all the others. In New York my agent, Tony Outhwaite, of JCA has been a constant comfort and at St. Martin's my editor, Tom Dunne, shrewd, adroit, and keen, has been tolerant of a massive and often convoluted text and a manuscript that often proceeded but slowly through the Celtic twilight under the detailed line editing of Adam Goldberger. And, as always, much of my long trek in troubled times was eased by the presence of my only real Irish connection, my Kerry wife Nora.

J.B.B.

New York
Dublin
New York

1965–1992

Ireland

1. Derry
2. Antrim
3. Tyrone
4. Fermanagh
5. Armagh
6. Down
7. Donegal
8. Leitrim
9. Sligo
10. Mayo
11. Roscommon
12. Longford
13. Cavan
14. Monaghan
15. Louth
16. Meath
17. Westmeath
18. Offaly
19. Kildare
20. Dublin
21. Wicklow
22. Carlow
23. Laoighis
24. Kilkenny
25. Wexford
26. Waterford
27. Tipperary
28. Galway
29. Clare
30. Limerick
31. Cork
32. Kerry

Northern Ireland

N

Portrush

Ballycastle

Limavady

Derry

Dungiven

ANTRIM

DERRY

Ballymena

Larne

Strabane

NORTHERN IRELAND

Magherafelt

Antrim

Carrickfergus

Castlederg

Cookstown

Lough
Neagh

BELFAST

Bangor

Hollywood

Omagh

TYRONE

Newtownards

Dungannon

Lisburn

Irvinestown

Clogher

Aughnacloy

Lurgan

Hillsborough

Lower
Lough
Erne

Enniskillen

Portadown

DOWN

FERMANAGH

Armagh

Downpatrick

Newtown
Butler

ARMAGH

Keady

Newry

Crossmaglen

Warrenpoint

IRISH
SEA

miles

0   10   20   30

0 10 20 30 40
kilometers

Derry City

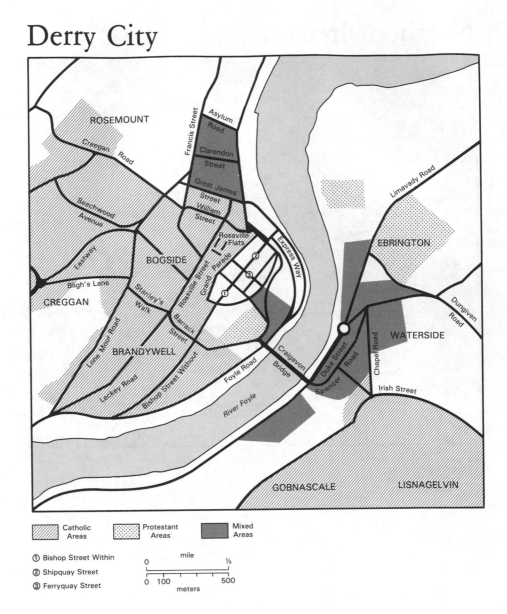

ROSEMOUNT

Francis Street

Asylum Road

Clarendon Street

Creggan Road

Great James Street

Beechwood Avenue

William Street

Rossville Flats

Limavady Road

Eastway

BOGSIDE

Rossville Street

Grand Parade

Express Way

EBRINGTON

Bligh's Lane

② ③ ①

CREGGAN

Stanley's Walk

Dungiven Road

Lone Moor Road

Barrack Street

Craigavon Bridge

Duke Street

WATERSIDE

BRANDYWELL

Leckey Road

Foyle Road

Spencer Road

Chapel Road

Bishop Street Without

River Foyle

Irish Street

GOBNASCALE

LISNAGELVIN

| | Catholic Areas | | Protestant Areas | | Mixed Areas |

① Bishop Street Within
② Shipquay Street
③ Ferryquay Street

mile
0   ⅓
0   100   500
meters

Inner Belfast

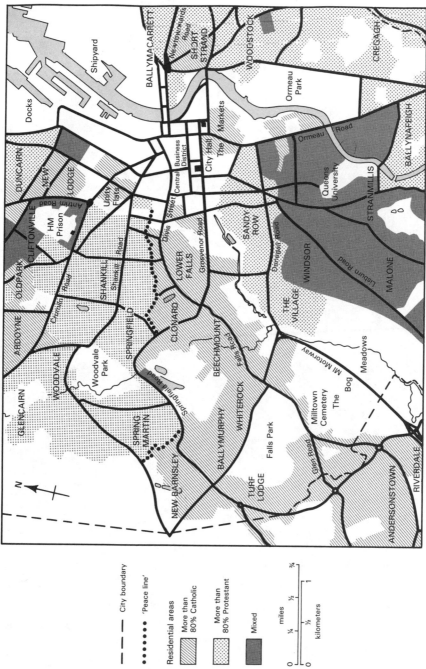

Shipyard

Docks

BALLYMACARRETT

Newtownards Road

SHORT STRAND

WOODSTOCK

CREGAGH

Ormeau Park

DUNCAIRN

NEW LODGE

The Markets

City Hall

The Markets

BALLYNAFEIGH

Central Business District

Ormeau Road

Ormeau

CLIFTONVILLE

Antrim Road

Unity Flats

Central Street

Queens University

STRANMILLIS

HM Prison

Divis

Grosvenor Road

SANDY ROW

OLDPARK

Shankill Road

LOWER FALLS

WINDSOR

MALONE

Lisburn Road

ARDOYNE

Crumlin Road

SHANKILL

Donegall Road

Falls Road

CLONARD

BEECHMOUNT

THE VILLAGE

WOODVALE

SPRINGFIELD

Woodvale Park

M1 Motorway

GLENCAIRN

Springfield Road

WHITEROCK

BALLYMURPHY

Milltown Cemetery

The Bog

Meadows

SPRING MARTIN

NEW BARNSLEY

TURF LODGE

Falls Park

Glen Road

ANDERSONSTOWN

RIVERDALE

N

*"Killing a man is murder
unless you do it to the
sound of trumpets."*
—Voltaire

Prologue: Belfast Spring, 1967

Who controls the past controls the future.
Who controls the present controls the past.
George Orwell, *1984*

As Easter 1967 approached, William Craig, Minister of Home Affairs for the Province of Northern Ireland, on March 7 announced a ban on the newly organized Republican Clubs. They were, he said, merely a front for Sinn Féin. And Sinn Féin, as all sound Northern Unionists knew, was the political creature of the Irish Republican Army. For decades the IRA volunteers had sought to subvert the lawful authority of the Crown and establish a united Ireland, a nationalist Ireland, and a Catholic Ireland by resorting to physical force: the gun. They had bombed and murdered in Ireland and England. They had shot down policemen on their appointed rounds and killed innocent people on the streets. They had burned and boasted, blasted and defied all authority. They were wicked, evil men. Their last campaign had ended in 1962, only five years previously; they were not repentant, and would not recognize the reality of contemporary Ulster, the six counties safely embedded within the United Kingdom.

Because 1967 was the hundredth anniversary of an Irish Republican rising, the great Fenian revolt, Craig and his colleagues felt it only prudent to take appropriate measures to ward off any provocative displays. Ireland was a country for provocative displays arising from past events. Easter was always a difficult time in Northern Ireland and had been so the previous year. In memory of the Easter Rising of 1916 that led to the Tan War, the Irish Free State, and the division of the island, the subversives marched across the whole province, commemorating the old martyrs and promising sometime, perhaps sooner rather than later, to complete the job—unite the island as the Irish Republic. At Easter there was always a series of displays with the rebel tricolor, treasonous speeches, and even a statement from the IRA Army Council on the state of the movement. This 1967 Easter at least treason would not be fashioned into Republican Clubs by Sinn Féin or into open defiance with a Republican commemoration. It was common sense and, of course, good politics to ban the subversive Republican Clubs that hardly anybody but the police had even noticed.

In Northern Ireland history was a ready tool of politics, a myth made real by contradictory commemorations and marches recalling ancient battles, arcane dates, old triumphs that were elsewhere relegated to minor historical texts. In

1

Ireland and in Ulster, historians were always doubly engaged, possessed of powers denied their academic colleagues elsewhere. The past mattered a great deal. So did symbols. There could be defiance in a Celtic tune or a rebel song, treason in a tricolor banner carried on a wet spring morning, oppression in an Orange Masonic drum pounded until knuckles bled on a mild July day. The province, loyal or rebel, Orange or Green, wore a hard heart not on a sleeve but on a banner displayed to provoke, intimidate, and maintain the faith. And so this Ulster, if often tranquil, feared the worst during any marching seasons—a thousand Orange marches and too many Green. The authorities feared first and particularly any provocative display by the nationalists, the others.

The majority unionists, a million strong, despised the minority nationalists, outnumbered two to one in the province but a majority on the island. The unionists cherished their Protestant past and so feared for the future. For nearly fifty years those within the ruling establishment had husbanded their six-county Irish enclave, their faith, and their British connection, which were so alien to the others: the papists, the Celts, treacherous with ambition. So the Republican Clubs were banned to prevent treasonous rebel history being publicly revered. There was never a time to surrender: No Surrender was a heritage of the past now deployed by Craig.

Such a course was congenial to all proper, patriotic unionists and was most congenial to Craig, a bland, pink, well-shaven, plump-faced man, confident, ambitious, assured if provincial, one of his own. On the rise in the Unionist Party, he was not without guile or talent and was a key part of the apparently seamless structure of the establishment: Unionist and Protestant, the institutions of the state and the Orange Masonic orders, mutual interests and a net of friendships. All the establishment were apt to be conservative in habit, determined on defense, and magnanimous rarely. And so too Craig. At home he might be kindly, congenial in conversation, at ease with his equals and intimates, a hale fellow; yet, like all his own, he could be crude and cruel in defense of his province, hard won from history, a haven, not some example from a good government textbook. So smooth and absolutely confident, elegantly tailored and crudely composed, he had no intention of catering to the democratic fashions and fantasies of his and the system's critics.

Craig took pleasure in giving not an inch in full knowledge that the ban on the Republican Clubs would be not just prudent but also popular. Keeping the Fenians down was as personally satisfactory to him as it was politically wise for the Unionist Party. Craig gave the impression of a man who enjoyed coming down with a polished, elegant boot. Power is to be used. Times, as rumored, might be changing, but not much in Northern Ireland as far as the Minister of Home Affairs was concerned. The old ways were safe and sure. And the old ways were founded on fear: fear of the island majority, fear of change, fear of the cost of past Orange arrogance so necessary to maintain present power. In a seemingly soft and easy land the Orange system felt brittle to those protected by it. Change could shatter the old assurance, the effect of ritual intimidation, the habits of all that had given the island fifty years of peace if not prosperity. The cement that allowed the Unionist Party to rule Northern Ireland was loyalist-unionist fear.

The Protestants feared the other Irish, the Fenians, the IRA, the entrenched

Republic in the twenty-six counties beyond their own six. They feared the indomitable, devout Catholic Irish. They feared today and tomorrow and so focused on preserving the immediate past—that was the purpose of politics. Nothing else mattered as much as the constitutional issue—the security of the majority in the six counties to maintain their traditions. Nothing else often mattered at all, not class nor caste, not everyday differences, not personalities, not the usual bread-and-butter issues. Fear had permitted, had encouraged, the formation of a sectarian state within the United Kingdom, a political relic ignored by London, detested by Dublin, unknown elsewhere, and a marvel to its supporters.

Many Protestants, who were mostly plain, often poor children of their own history, were also prejudiced practically from birth, decent folk but fearful of the alien. The system began by teaching toddlers differences, superiority, and privilege. Thus, most were bigots, some simple and gentle, others nasty and if need be brutal. The year before, emboldened by provocative sermons, several simple loyalists had gathered together, appropriated the old title of Ulster Volunteer Force used by the faithful to resist home rule with arms in 1912, and gone out into the Belfast streets to kill. A great many Protestants were contemptuous of the tinsel splendors of the other faith and of the other feckless, foolish, irresponsible Irish. That was a world of plaster saints, dictatorial and ignorant priests, large families and lax habits, drink and incense. They were inferior and so dangerous. Only a very few loyalists might kill (and the new UVF killed two innocent Catholics and by error an elderly Protestant woman), but a great many understood the reasons, not twisted at all but traditional reasons, that led to the murders. The system needed defenders.

Protestant order in the province was imposed by law. Justice could be seen to be done when the system moved through the courts, where judges were not bought with bribes but were controlled by mutual assumptions founded in fear of subversion. For the courts, the police, the local councillor, and the prison warder, the system need only work without recourse to the mob to assure continuity. Debate need not be tirades nor sermons, screeds. The establishment, the wellborn, the rich and the connected, the educated, the proper, even the poor mostly kept rein on outrage, ignored the few dissenters among them, tamed their wild men, and watched the minority warily. They would give them no personal offense, speak of the weather and the distant past, but give them no access to means that might be turned against the system.

William Craig consequently sought gain at the expense of the alien others, a net gain in the provincial zero-sum game over the weak but dangerous by displaying the power of the provincial assembly located in Belfast at Stormont. He sought means to protect his own from an imagined and from a real Irish Republican threat, from nationalist subversion, ultimately from Irish Catholicism that controlled the rest of the island. It would be a very small gain, but they added up over the years. Most of all he intended to display power. Whatever else is the purpose of power but to use, to impose, to display? And such display reassured him and his that their tomorrow would be like yesterday. Tomorrow might be poor and mean for many Protestants, who had a shabby life in a poor

3

province, but *their* clubs were not barred from marching to the drums inherited from the past.

All the peculiarities and rites of Ulster were considered provincial peculiarities, not worthy of concern. They were a provocation that Dublin ignored, a lapse in fair play that London ignored. No one cared about Republican Clubs, not in 1967. At Westminster the affairs of Northern Ireland were filed in the General Department of the Home Office and left to the clerks along with ceremonial functions, British summer time, the protection of animals and birds, the administration of state-owned pubs—the odds and ends. And at the end of an odd Ireland Ulster belonged and stayed for nearly fifty years. The Channel Islands, the Isle of Man, the Charity Commissions, and Northern Ireland could be found in one subsection run by a staff of seven with only a single civil servant from the administrative class to manage such peripheral matters. It remained the convention not to discuss Northern Irish matters at Westminster, and Labour attempts in the mid-sixties to raise questions of unemployment and civil rights had been discouraged by succeeding Speakers and by the protests of Northern Ireland Unionist members. The Unionists wanted London to make up any fiscal shortfalls—the province was not self-sustaining and so dependent on an imperial contribution—and to allow the Stormont government to rule the province unchallenged and unchecked. And for nearly fifty years the arrangement had worked.

The new Northern Irish Prime Minister was Captain Terence O'Neill. He was a mild, seemingly moderate man, chosen by his own on March 25, 1963, who like his predecessors discouraged any visits by the British Home Secretary. An occasional royal visit was welcome but any hint of political interference was resented. So the Unionists had their heart's desire, filed next to state pubs, money from the imperial contribution, and no ministers arriving on the boat train. In Great Britain, Ireland had returned to the mists with the Anglo-Irish Treaty, which set up the Free State and the Government of Ireland Act, given royal assent on December 23, 1920, which set up the devolved Province of Northern Ireland. Most remained bemused about Irish matters and it was still possible over sherry in Kensington or Tunbridge Wells to find elegant people who assumed that all the Irish were somehow still British, if quaint. No one except the odd Labour agitator cared about Ireland.

Recognizing their special problem, the Unionists knew that this was just as well. Democracy had been adjusted to need and a system evolved that protected the majority. O'Neill and Craig and the rest were not leaders of some unruly mob; they were no up-country fanatics, associates of hooded killers or racist theorists. They were decent men, smooth, well-tailored, properly educated men of the West, provincial leaders, welcome at Westminster, easy in their career. They were all elected officials within the United Kingdom, answerable to Crown and country and often to the cabinet in London. O'Neill spoke like the officer and gentleman he was, a landowner, a responsible citizen, a decent man, quiet, serene in an electorate that could be crude. He was not reactionary but progressive, keen on technology, capital investment, and prosperity. He was ever polite, mild in a system admittedly built on defamation and domination. He and many of his allies felt that if the others had an Irish Catholic state in the south, no less sectarian, surely the Unionists were entitled to have a British Protestant province of their own: fair play.

The Orange establishment at play in 1967 went mostly unnoticed to the south in Dublin, capital of the Irish Republic, home of the IRA headquarters. The banning of the Republican Clubs and Fenian ceremonies simply did not matter to those concerned with local political interests and the lure of prosperity. Beyond ritual orations and patriotic bobs to the past, the Dublin establishment had no interest in the national issue or in the tribulations of the militant republicans, avowed enemies of the Dublin government in Leinster House. There the elected Dáil met. There the Prime Minister, the Taoiseach, directed the system. The Taoiseach was Jack Lynch, a veteran of the Irish system: a mix of democracy, clientele politics, bureaucratic power, and influence of the *nouveau riche*. Partition had faded as a useful grievance and no one in the government knew much of the contemporary IRA or cared about the North. The police special branch might watch the IRA, but no one watched the six counties. Neither the television, increasingly an important factor of Irish life since the establishment of Telefís Éireann in 1961, nor the press seemed alarmed at the banning. No one sensed a scoop. From all other indicators, pub gossip to pulpit statements, the Irish seemed singularly unmoved by any militant republican problem. That was the stuff of yesterday. More discussion would arise over a Kerry loss at football. The Republic had settled into a limited, ill-distributed, parochial prosperity that was nonetheless more interesting than Fenian doctrine.

Ulster largely existed for both Dublin and London as never-never land—never visited, never noticed. The province had been chopped off from the whole of Ireland with the Government of Ireland Act of 1920, which gave the Protestants, until then advocates of continued union for all thirty-two counties, something of their own. Isolated, they had used the devolved power to fashion a loyal province that was resented by the impotent government in Dublin. For those in the twenty-six counties, this national issue had been reduced to assurance that history would someday unite the island, but in the meantime such an aspiration appeared only in rebel songs and election speeches, except for the very faithful and very few of Sinn Féin and their secret army. These militants had never accepted the Irish Free State that had come out of the Anglo-Irish Treaty of 1921, never accepted their former leader Eamon de Valera's 1937 Constitution for an Éire-Ireland with its withdrawal from the Commonwealth and an end of the oath of allegiance to the Crown. The militants felt, then and later, that the declaration by the Coalition government in 1948 that the "nation" was a republic, was sophistry.

For those in power the begrudgers were irrelevant—if unity was to come, it would do so because the Irish Republic had grown prosperous, attractive to those in British Ulster. Meanwhile the North was far away, a part of the nation to be sure, as the 1937 Constitution still made clear. Time would heal the division, somehow, without sacrifice and without the need for physical force as proposed by the rump of the IRA. The Old IRA had gone home in 1922 after defeating the irregulars—the other, defeated IRA—who followed de Valera into the Dáil. This new IRA was a fragment of the old dream, no more. It was a time for other dreams, other men.

Until quite recently the island had to its people appeared enormous, a grand site of saints and scholars who had transformed the Western world, converted the barbarians of Europe and tutored their poets and playwrights by example. Even those Irish without art had formed for over a century a vast global diaspora across the seas, built others' railways and canals, built whole countries, staffed the schools, maintained distant churches, fought others' wars, sometimes prospered in a grand exile. Both the historical role and the existing distribution of the race gave great dimensions to the fewer than 5 million on the island and just over 3 million in the Republic. The home island was famed for the piety of its ways, and to most who walked those ways it was, as always, a great, grand country, not just broad in beauty, in sanctity, in learning, wit, and creativity, but also in area.

The distance from Cork to Tralee was enough to turn visitors from one into foreigners in the other, with its different ways and accent and nature. Ireland felt big to people used to walking, where a bike was a real boon and none but the comfortable could get to Dublin on the train. Dublin was huge and different, lure and threat, and a long way off. And those north of the Liffey knew little of the Dublin south of the river, and in the country each townland was special and ample. Loyalties were deep and local and concerns narrow. No one traveled much, except to annual holidays for the sea and the baths at Ballybunion or the Irish and the scenery in Connemara. In 1967 every place in Ireland was still a long way from Tipperary. So not only did time run more slowly in Ireland, but also Ireland was grand in perception, diverse to the inhabitants if homogeneous to outside observers.

Thus, Northern Ireland was far away, far even and especially from Dublin, far from the particular concerns of the day, a part of history seldom considered but as cartoon. The loyalist province was a political abomination, six counties cut off by force from the historic nine-county Ulster and held hostage by the British. It was, however, a distant abomination and after eight hundred years the Irish had learned to live with abomination. The Northern counties had always been distant. The people there, Catholic and Protestant, shared a harsh accent and hard ways, however diverse they might seem to each other. In the six counties the Protestants often seemed rabid, primitive, fundamentalist, not like the genteel West Britons, colonels and bankers and even proper working folk, to be found in the Republic. And then no one loved Belfast but those caught there. It was a rough industrial ruin, mean streets filled with hard men who worked by the hour and women who worked by the piece. And the rest of the North country and the Ulster people were hard as well, even the Catholics, tidy minds and tight lips, a nod and at best the wry word, difficult to understand. Few from the South knew them, few had ever been to Londonderry, a site and symbol of Protestant domination, where Catholics lived beneath the walls in the Bogside ghetto, or to the small hill farms of South Armagh or mid-Tyrone, where a poorish existence could be scraped out by families long on the land.

The Catholic difficulties and grievances, and they were legion, had faded away in the consciousness of Dublin as the years passed and nothing could be done. Better forget than remain guilty over impotence and an unwillingness to sacrifice. Those who did care in Sinn Féin seemed to spend much of their time engaged in the theological discussions of blame for the movement's endless schisms and feuds, the universal pastime of the revolutionary. These faithful seemed a mix of embittered old women, unrepentant gunmen, and a scattering of very idealistic men with limited education and towering pretensions.

Ireland divided might never be at peace, but by 1967 no secret army was going to unite the island. Times had changed. Dublin had a skyscraper on the Liffey, a new and elegant bus terminal, traffic problems, and a feel of bustle. The country had new roads, even a short segment of a superhighway south from Dublin toward neighboring Naas. There were new cars to use the new roads. Ireland was going places. There was the television, more jobs to slow emigration, and even a nod to the North. On January 14, 1965, Taoiseach Seán Lemass met Prime Minister Terence O'Neill at Stormont and a month later on February 9 in Dublin—a recognition of the reality if not legitimacy of the Northern Ireland government. The pragmatists were in power in Dublin, and as long as the rising prosperity continued, they were likely to dominate the agenda.

The sadly reduced Irish republicans recognized the direction of events and saw how close to the edge of irrelevance they stood. Some of their own did seem little more than cranks, historical anachronisms unable to move beyond old quarrels. And their best and brightest, the stayers after the campaign years, had little to offer. No one in the new Ireland wanted to hear of the old days. The physical force men, the gunmen as soldiers, had seen their guerrilla campaign flounder and end in 1962, leaving the movement without any military assets, any military role, or any direction at all. For the five years since the campaign ended, the subversives whom Craig claimed to fear had sought only to hold together the Dublin center—general headquarters (GHQ), Sinn Féin, and the monthly newspaper, the *United Irishman*—and look for a way forward. Some wanted to wait until fashions changed and the next generation could take the gun off the shelf. Some wanted no more guns but a radical party. Many simply drifted away. No one wanted a split, so matters moved from week to week, mostly on credit.

Given the limited numbers and narrow talents of the remaining IRA activists, a few hundred idealists without funds who had a few thousand friends without much commitment, just to put out the newspaper and pay the bills was an accomplishment. What was wanted was an opportunity to do *something*. So the IRA burned a few foreign, capitalist barns, threw stones at Irish traitors, destroyed the wrong kind of monumental statues, and even fired a shot at a visiting British gunboat. Not much.

The IRA radicals felt that perhaps Craig's ban would open a way to play a political card. The civil rights campaigns of disobedience were fashionable abroad. Craig and O'Neill and the rest of the Orange establishment did not even play by democracy's rules but twisted the system unfairly in Northern Ireland so that there were legitimate popular points of pressure inside the "artificial" entity. This prospect was already under exploration. In Dublin Anthony Coughlan of Trinity College and a member of the Wolfe Tone Society, a republican creation open to all, had written an article proposing pressure on the Stormont government to wrest concessions from the system. On August 13, 1966, there had been a Wolfe Tone conference at Maghera, Derry, attended by Cahal Goulding and Roy Johnston from the IRA, along with liberals like Coughlan and the Northerners Conn and Patricia McCluskey, who had started to agitate without allies. The Northerners found Coughlan's ideas extreme, but the next day all agreed to begin a civil rights crusade under a more general banner than that of the Wolfe Tone Society. Since the IRA did not have guns or the will to use force in 1967, this initiative had led to the formation of the Northern Ireland Civil Rights Association (NICRA) on January 29, 1967. It included republicans, trade unionists, Communists, moderate reformers, and one Young Unionist. Their agenda had six points: (1) one man, one vote in local elections; (2) an end to gerrymandered election districts; (3) laws against discrimination by local government; (4) housing allocated on a fair points system; (5) an end to the Special Powers Act; and (6) disbandment of the B-Specials (the part-time police militia) of the Royal Ulster Constabulary (RUC). This was the nationalist wish list, the minimum of the radicals and what any decent Englishman would support. It was a sound agenda, though NICRA had no means to act beyond petition and parade.

In Dublin at republican headquarters, 30 Gardiner Place, a dirty and decaying Georgian house off Mountjoy Square on the unfashionable north side, the leadership decided to protest and hold a banned meeting in Northern Ireland. A banned meeting would be a positive and provocative act, not a petition, and thus more militant. It fit the movement's needs, the times, and paralleled the new direction pushed by Johnston and others. It required neither money nor gear nor great resources. It was a relatively easy decision to take in Dublin. Decisions at Gardiner Place were easy to make in that the "movement" was dominated by six or seven harried men. In fact the republican movement, the IRA, and Sinn Féin largely consisted of this same handful of harried men dependent on their own limited resources. They could raise a few bob, the loan of the odd pound, a subscription. The army was run in the spare time of a painting contractor, Sinn Féin, was directed by an accountant from the Electricity Supply Board (ESB), and the two or three full-time people were never sure of pay at all. The rest dropped by after hours.

To hold a banned Republican Club meeting would be an act, generally popular and without great risk. There would be a formal, announced meeting of the Belfast Republican Club to be attended not just by the members, all Sinn Féin as Craig suspected, most IRA as Craig insisted, but also by other radicals concerned with civil liberties: a united front for democracy. It was true that radicals were thin on the ground, likely to be middle-class solicitors or housewives dubious of associating with the barely disguised members of the Falls Road IRA. And the practicing radicals knew too well that the IRA, possessed of the absolute truth, made bad company as an ally.

In Belfast, beyond the real republicans were nationalist voters for the Republican Labour Party of Gerry Fitt and Harry Diamond and even some in the conservative Nationalist Party who might want to protest discrimination. There were a scattering of sympathetic teachers and lecturers, the usual provincial radicals, a few nonsectarian labor leaders, the middle-class Catholics who wanted the system to work. Some were already members of NICRA. It was not a very promising base. Most Northern radicals were unsympathetic to republican pretensions and limitations, seeing the republicans as pious bigots, not real Marxist-Leninist revolutionaries, members of a closed fraternity of gunmen who spoke Irish badly, went to mass regularly, and often drank not at all: puritans without politics. Still, the others had no place to go either—so unimportant that they had not been banned. So it would be a united front protest, a step away from republican isolation, and one of the first such attempts since the depression.

All of the plans looked good on paper. All the radical organizations in Belfast tended to be staffed by the same people, who were fascinated by paper ideas, not action. At most the organizers could hope to collect a hundred or so people including the radicals: Communists, lecturers, solicitors, Republican Labour, maybe a Nationalist or two, some of the foolishly curious, and a sprinkle of Dublin people. Beginnings were always difficult and everyone involved knew that provoking the Orange machine, however gentle the prod, was risky. At Gardiner Place it was decided to send as representative from Sinn Féin, legal in the Republic, Tom Mitchell, who had been captured in October 1954 during an arms raid on Omagh barracks and so imprisoned during the 1956–62 campaign. Mitchell was well known in the North because from his cell in A-Wing, Crumlin Road Prison, Belfast, he was twice elected as an abstentionist candidate to the Westminster Parliament in May and again in August 1955. He only lost his seat at the third election on May 8, 1956, when a Nationalist candidate split his vote. The "Mitchell affair"—elected, disqualified, reelected, redisqualified, almost elected—made him and his presence provocative. Most of the Sinn Féin activists in Dublin had campaign records and often prison records as well. Tony Meade, editor of the *United Irishman,* who would drive Mitchell up as part of the Dublin delegation, had also been captured, after a bombing attempt on an RUC police barracks in Armagh, and imprisoned in Crumlin Road. Other Dublin protesters would travel separately, like Anthony Coughlan, not from Sinn Féin but from the republican Wolfe Tone Society. The Sinn Féin people would drive up to Belfast in Meade's white estate wagon. They decided to include an American historian working on a book about the IRA so that he could see history made, and also give a lift to Malachy McGurran, still another active campaign veteran but from the North and so often unwelcome. They would drive across the border on the main road to Belfast, often left open, drop McGurran at his parents' home in Lurgan, then drive on into Belfast just in time for the meeting.

None of the three Sinn Féin people looked like a romantic's idea of an IRA gunman. Mitchell was blond, pink of face, more Norse than Celt, a clerk in real life, dedicated to the Republic in private but hardly charismatic in public. McGurran was short, dark, sharp, with quick eyes, a touch of the North in his tongue, and no innocent in the risks of the six counties. Meade was taller, thin, freckled, boyish, with untamed hair and a quick, often cynical, tongue, who was learning a journalist trade on the job after his years in Crumlin prison. (To his horror, he had been caught hiding in a confessional booth in Armagh Cathedral, no place for a devout republican, given the long animosity between the church and the movement.) The IRA volunteer was often pious, but the movement was nonsectarian and often the target of the conservative hierarchy's criticism of physical force.

They were the IRA's rising generation. The old stayed home. The young were not attracted to the old dream. So there were only the campaign people. The three men in the white car were like the younger Catholic radicals in the North, who were eager, arrogant, cynical, and rebellious, some their families' first at the university, almost all unwilling to tolerate another generation of the Orange system; they were different in that prison had made them both older and kept them young. At least they had not lost hope that the movement could act on events instead of commemorating the past.

In 1967 in Ireland the worldwide rebellion of the young was almost invisible. Elsewhere there were sit-ins and monster rallies but not in Ireland. The Cold War froze protest—too radical, perhaps Communist—even if the Republic was neutral. Society was conservative and inflexible, protest vulnerable to economic pressure and general disapproval. What was the use of protest anyway? The Church was content that North and South and the Protestants made no waves. The governments North and South were cozy and easy with the system as structured. Dissenters could emigrate or be still. There had been enough change during the Tan War and the Troubles. The most that might happen were farmers blocking traffic with tractors, demanding more money, or a few flash strikes soon over. Politics was voting. Politics was marching and commemorating, listening to speeches and going to funerals: symbols and votes.

In Belfast the banned meeting would bring out Craig's enemies in real life: Sinn Féin, the IRA, and the dreaded Marxists. They would appear on an unchanging Northern stage. There in front of Saint Mary's Church Hall off Divis Street were the ubiquitous RUC Special Branch in civilian clothes that only emphasized their role as watchers, along with the RUC constables in their long overcoats and side arms. They stood about waiting. Nothing started on time in Ireland except one race meeting held on the beach at Laytown, County Meath, which was of course dependent on the tide. Waiting was part of the meeting. So everyone waited: the police, the little crowd, the children attracted to any action, a few curious. Not many all told. Nearby were a few new houses but still the rows of old ones, back to back. A new highway, the M-1, pushed almost into the city center, but still the tiny lanes off Divis Street and the Shankill Road were the same; fugitives from the Tan War would find the same safe houses, the Catholics on their lane and the Protestants on theirs. Belfast was still Belfast. The North seemed immutable, Stormont stone, waiting for the meeting near Saint Mary's, the oldest Catholic church in the city. There was no sense of a beginning or of an era ending. All that occurred was the usual: the wait as prologue to a ritual that was probably futile and hardly important.

Inside Saint Mary's Hall, the meeting drew, almost reluctantly, the expected radical fringe of Irish political life. The faithful could have been a prayer group, mostly men, mostly ill-dressed and poorly kept, neat, decent, working class. Their guests were a few militants: Betty Sinclair, notorious Belfast Communist; the new civil libertarians of NICRA, Communists and republicans mostly; and for the Wolfe Tone Society Anthony Coughlan from Dublin, whose articles had frightened the moderates. There was Alderman Gerry Fitt, now Westminster MP elected for West Belfast in 1966 and a Stormont MP since 1962 from the Docks; and Maghera republican Kevin Agnew, increasingly concerned about pushing the civil rights issue. The rows of folding chairs filled up from the back bit by bit with the local protesters. A gray, heavy cloud of cigarette smoke began to gather in the dim light over the protesters, who shifted on the hard seats, unsure of their role. It was not just another dreary protest meeting but an act of defiance—or so the organizers said.

The meeting was hardly a big draw; most people had other things to do on a Sunday afternoon with no rain and no work. There was one Dublin journalist and hardly anyone else—BBC-TV was reported to be on the way. James Kelly, the correspondent from the *Irish Independent,* was seen at the edge of the group, interviewing no one. Protest seldom inspired enthusiasm. Why get arrested for consorting with a Red? Others might ask, Why hold a meeting when a bomb was needed? The O/C of the Belfast IRA, Billy McMillen, was lurking outside. He could produce on demand only his few activists, like Jimmy Sullivan and a few old veterans who would appear at any republican gathering, however strange. The other Belfast republicans, three generations of militants, had no interest in politics. And there were not too many middle-class liberals or ideological radicals who wanted to travel into the Falls under the RUC Special Branch eye to little purpose, just to spend an hour sitting on hard seats in a dank hall on a cold Sunday afternoon.

So the small audience sat and muttered in the chill hall, neat in their Sunday clothes. Mostly they were republicans and so sat as secular duty, spoke to their own, whispered about the visitors, the latecomers, the lads up from Dublin, commented on the numbers of the police, always the police, parked outside, standing outside, waiting. The radicals were especially uneasy in such alien company. The police at least gave meaning to the event, even if the protest would not involve a traditional parade, the provocative display of banners, or even the illegal shots over a grave: the comforting old ways. At best it was an outward and visible sign that the GHQ in Dublin had not forgotten Belfast. For the few radicals the prospects in their narrow and often incestuous world would be brighter—the republicans again and properly were showing an interest in "politics" and might be captured for the cause at some future date.

Despite the hard times, the republicans did have a broad all-Ireland constituency, thousands of friends and allies far beyond the scope of a Leninist study seminar. A united front maneuver indicated that the IRA leadership was giving up the old Fenian ways and moving into the socialist future. And for Fitt of Republican Labour, concerned with power and votes and reform programs, a Sinn Féin–IRA concern with real life was to be welcome. All told it was a very short meeting—the police concentrated everyone's mind. Fitt spoke. Betty Sinclair pointed out the historic obstacles of cooperating with the republicans, who even more than her Communists felt they possessed the one true guidebook on the way forward. The words had all been heard before. The causes were shopworn. Then, their duty done, the radicals broke for the door, heading for home before police patience evaporated. There was a TV camera crew outside, but hardly anyone noticed and it was soon gone as the crowd began moving along toward tea.

If the republicans could have their little provocative display, the RUC had decided on its own response, nothing spectacular, nothing dramatic, merely a reminder of the real power. When the Dublin delegation of three came out the door, Mitchell stayed a moment to talk with friends. Meade and his American walked on around to the white estate wagon, got in, and drove back to pick Mitchell up for the drive back to Lurgan and Dublin. As the car crept toward the little crowd in front of Saint Mary's, there was a flurry. Mitchell was being arrested, stuffed into a police car, and taken to the nearby Queen Street RUC station. Meade accelerated past the arrest, took a sharp turn, and stopped next to Billy McMillen at the far edge of the crowd. McMillen got the word, turned to scatter his volunteers in case there was to be a wide police net, then disappeared. So did the known IRA people and so did Mitchell. Meade drove off with the American, uncertain as to the immediate future: Was the sweep general? Were the people up from Dublin on the want list? Should McGurran be warned? What was the charge against Mitchell?

Actually the RUC had very little in mind. The police, seeing Mitchell, thought a little display of authority would not be amiss. Mitchell would do nicely, one they had had before. A few hours in Queen Street would worry him and his, be his due, and indicate the penalty of provocation. So it was not a serious arrest but a new ritual in reaction to a new form of trouble. The RUC knew just how unhappy Mitchell would be back in police hands no matter how or why. Actually he was even more unhappy than they imagined. First, he was one of those who really did not want to do more time, even a little more. Second, he knew that he was more vulnerable than just your average protest attender. Anyway, Mitchell was sweating in the Queen Street station as the RUC chatted him up. The few remaining IRA volunteers were visiting friends and neighbors; Fitt, Agnew, and Sinclair were at dinner or on the train to Dublin. Radio Telefís Éireann (RTE) was putting some film on the air, and Meade was left driving his American around Belfast in the recognizable white estate wagon.

Meade decided that the only way to help Mitchell was to pursue matters conventionally: complain through channels. The only channel seemed to be Gerry Fitt. His Republican Labour Party, a vehicle for nationalist working-class voters in Belfast, mainly consisted of Fitt, Diamond (the founder and a Stormont MP from the Falls), and a few young men like Patrick Kennedy interested in politics despite the bleak prospects. The party was legal and both Fitt and Diamond were in Stormont—a channel, if scorned by the Unionists. In Britain Fitt would have been a hard-core Labour man focused on issues not ideas. Unremarkable in presence, witty in conversation, cheerful of feature, with horn-rimmed glasses, a former merchant seaman, he looked like half the workingmen in Belfast. The others seemed to be shorter, round and red, built like beer kegs. Fitt lived up the Antrim Road with his wife and five daughters—he called them the Miss Fitts, famed throughout West Belfast—and was as working-class respectable as imaginable despite his rebel songs and appeal to republican voters. Many of the plain folk of Belfast might be sound on the national issue like Fitt, more republican by inclination than nationalist, but there was also a focus on labor issues, wages or benefits or houses, class issues, where the community, the minority did not get fair shares. They voted their interests and their heart but no more. Their lives were innately conservative and they were on most matters pious, prudish, narrow, and amenable to parish rules. In Britain such voters produced Labour leaders who focused on union matters not national purpose, sought contracts not authority from the general will, men who were often suspicious of ideas and ideals, especially within the party, the fancies of Oxbridge. The difference in Belfast was that Fitt and Diamond voters were getting a bad deal not simply because of their class but also because they were Catholics, Irish Catholics, people actually or potentially disloyal to the system. The constitutional issue colored everything and even determined Fitt's campaign song, a rebel ballad shaped to electoral use, a ballad to rouse the spirits of those with no faith in rebellion and not much in the Republic. They voted Republican Labour as protest and Fitt went to London and protested to his ilk in the Labour Party or to Stormont and protested to the unheeding Unionists. He was the voice of the minority in the province. And so Meade felt that Fitt, who had been at the meeting, was the obvious place to begin—or end. Knocking unannounced on the door, he was welcomed.

Gerry Fitt was always gregarious, ready with a new story as well as a kind word. On the platform he had a hard tongue when it was needed, as it was often in Belfast, but in private he was merry. What he really wanted in his city and in Northern Ireland was an end to the shoddy life dealt out to his own and, then, no less patriotic than the next, some day, some way, a united Ireland, grail if not goal. When he appeared at the banned meeting, it was to protest not so much the system itself as the inequalities within it. So Fitt did what he could for Meade. He made the telephone calls that tracked down Mitchell, let the police know that a member of Stormont and Westminster was concerned—and that was that. A few of his lot gathered in the front room to hear what the two chaps, obviously the IRA, had to say about faraway Dublin. The one with Meade was actually wearing a trench coat, an American model, but still the unofficial costume of the gunman. Everyone was very discreet. There was not much to say. Fitt put on his campaign song—a rebel ballad to rouse the spirits of those with no faith in rebellion. Meade was not amused.

Kevin Agnew arrived to collect the two Dublin chaps for a late-night Chinese meal. He had spent much of the last year working on the basis of a civil rights movement. Essentially still a republican prone to absolutes and abstentionism--to take a seat in Belfast, Dublin, or London would recognize the legitimacy of partition—he, along with many in the North, felt that the system was vulnerable. There need not be a wait for another military campaign that would fail as well. In 1967, although all nationalists believed in the reality of the IRA, most thought any guerrilla war ridiculous. So Agnew, like Kennedy and Fitt's young men, was interested in Dublin GHQ's views on the future, on new directions, on prospects. Meeting over an Irish-Chinese takeout on a Belfast back street while the police were cruising the main roads looking for a white estate car, they realized that the prospects did not look good. Neither Fitt nor Agnew, the two points of potential protest, had much leverage. No Catholic did. There was no word from Queen Street, but no word on further arrests.

Meade cruised by a few well-known republican houses to find that there had been no sign of police interest. It was time to go home to Dublin and hope for the best at the border. McGurran, who might still be on any RUC wanted list, would have to be left safely in Lurgan. And so the journey south began, a little over an hour to the border, another world away. Meade and his Yank historian drove south. There was no trouble along the way: the front of all the RUC barracks dim with a single blue bulb, no patrol cars on the road, no one at the border, no problem. Eight hours on the run with no one chasing them, hardly anyone the wiser, an adventure that seemingly ended just past the closed custom post on the Dublin road.

Being on the run, even briefly, even vicariously, creates a curious atmosphere.

There is no romance, no background music or dull parts left on the cutting-room floor. The runner is prey, vulnerable, uncertain, a fugitive beyond comfort, with only suspicion as companion. There may be no safe house, even in Belfast filled with republicans already on police lists. Chance seems to play an enormous role—which way someone will look, whether an old friend will help, whether there will be an unexpected checkpoint. Covert politics makes communication difficult. Fear is a constant: fear of an accident, a mistake, the sudden flash of recognition in the eyes of a traffic warden. Just getting around Belfast for no real purpose is difficult, but in a real underground the man on the run must run to special places, carry messages, move arms, give orders. Just running alone, staying free, spends assets without bringing success any closer. Such a career is enormously costly in energy, a matter for the young who believe in their luck. And at the end there is no romance in playing the hare. You are often tired, frayed, dirty, often frightened, never at rest while the others easy in uniform and authority search in eight-hour shifts and tick the result on file cards. Most people on the run end up like Mitchell—in a cell.

As soon as the border was crossed, at least in March 1967, the running stopped and a relieved Meade drove on into Dundalk, the first stop on the main road to Dublin, still worried about Mitchell but without much hope that there was news yet. It was late. Dundalk, however, was a republican way station, and Mark's Pub was an oasis at any hour. No matter what the licensing laws, Mark always welcomed transient volunteers, orators off the back of trucks, old soldiers on the way to commemorations, and transients on the Belfast-Dublin road. Ireland was splotched with safe houses and old friends, some known to the authorities and some not. A map of republican Ireland would not resemble the everyday map put out by Rand McNally or sold by Esso for sixpence. Much could be left off as barren, while tiny villages would loom large. In some parish lands in South Armagh or West Kerry, nearly every home is safe and in West Belfast any home off the Falls might do. And so Mark's in Dundalk would be one dot among many on the mental map carried by all IRA organizers: those sent out on the Irish roads in search of money and enthusiasm, sent to calm quarrels and explain policy, organizers who ended their allotted rounds in a borrowed bed or friendly back room. In Dundalk everyone, friend or foe, knew of Mark's, an everyday pub off the main road, the walls hung with historical mementos and the floors thick with Sweet Afton butts and spilled pints. Day or night the light was dim, the long room almost sealed in amber, the air stained with cigarette smoke and smelling of wet tweed and Irish beer. There was no polished brass or plastic benches, just hard wood and Guinness ashtrays and rebel songs later in the evening. Everyone knew Mark and so did not always watch him too carefully. He broke no rules, a republican who did not harm; he was no gunman, stored no gelly—explosives—nor constructed devices in a back room; Mark was an advocate of the cause but not a threat to daily order. He just welcomed his own even in the bleakest of times and times were usually bleak for the IRA, nearly as bad in 1967 as 1962, when the campaign ended.

The news Meade brought into Mark's was hardly cheerful: Mitchell held by the police and no word at all. He could be held still longer without charge or accused of all manner of offenses—the meeting had been banned—or simply moved about

RUC barracks in Belfast. So far there was no word from Fitt or the others and it was almost closing time. Then the door rattled, nearer to opening time than closing time, so it was no late local surely. And there in the door was Mitchell himself with Patrick Kennedy of Republican Labour, both making the first stop in the Dublin trail, both down from Queen Street RUC station in a surprise package. Mitchell was free and clear, released after verbal harassment and general police amusement, uncharged, not even searched, warned by ritual but hardly any worse for wear.

But Mitchell had been shaken. As soon as the police grabbed him in front of Saint Mary's, he realized that he still carried in his coat pocket the IRA's weekly financial statement for the Dublin unit. This despite the fact that Meade and the American had stopped the car short of the border on the way up and insisted that everyone check to see if any "papers"—even the *United Irishman*—were about. IRA volunteers were notorious for carrying "papers" that on arrest assured conviction. The American even insisted that they carried such papers *only* before being arrested, a form of inverted efficiency. In fact no covert revolutionary organization is efficient. The underground is shaped to allow persistence at the cost of effectiveness—secrecy, for example, assured continuity at an enormous cost: Absolute secrecy guarantees absolute chaos. This was theory. Mitchell had in fact gone through the car but not his own pockets. And anyway, why worry on a public trip by an almost official delegation of a party legal in the Republic? So for hours he had been sitting at Queen Street waiting to be told to dump out his pockets and then to be moved to a cell, charged with membership in an illegal organization. The fact that IRA records were carried up from Dublin to the banned meeting by the "legal" representative of the legal party would be ample evidence of the IRA's fine hand behind Sinn Féin, behind the Republican Clubs, behind any civil rights protest. Craig—arrogant, assured—would be proven right. It had not been a pleasant few hours.

But the overconfident RUC had neglected standard police procedure. What they were doing was not standard police work but defense of the sectarian system against potential subversion. In their pursuit of symbolic domination they had arrested a symbol—Mitchell—kept him as symbol, not as suspect, and released him as a lark. It had clearly been, as everyone knew, an exercise in ritual politics, not in police procedure, and thus had failed. It was not as clear that the system's response to even the mildest provocation, a hundred uneasy people meeting in a church hall for a few minutes, could open the way for a civil disobedience campaign. Even when the American circulated his analysis of the prospect of using such a campaign to engender future violence, the wisdom of the GHQ staff was that protest as protest—show how evil Stormont was—could be an avenue forward. In sum fact, Agnew's work, and the impact of the American civil rights campaign tended to convert the IRA to nonviolence. Few saw any possibilities in using a nonviolent appeal as a means to launch an armed campaign.

So Mitchell had walked out untouched and Kennedy had driven him and the "papers" down to Dundalk and had stopped as required at Mark's. They were received with vast enthusiasm by the pub's remaining late-night republicans. Still shaken, Mitchell was doused with brandy and port, the deadly Irish medicine of last resort for flu, funerals, and the frailities of life. Certainly Mitchell felt frail enough, since even a few months more in a cell was a shattering prospect; and the brandy and port convinced him to spend the rest of the night on a cot at Mark's and go down to Dublin the next morning. Kennedy drove back to Belfast and Republican Labour, and the American on down to Dublin at dawn, a mere twelve hours late, nearly prompt by republican standards.

There was another barely noted protest meeting in Dublin in front of the General Post Office (GPO). A few unknown men in cheap suits and serious faces with a bullhorn on a truck harangued the crowds moving on to their shopping. No one cared about Sinn Féiners or Belfast or protest. The big news in Dublin was that Jammet's Restaurant was going to close, and the poet Patrick Kavanagh—"disheveled with shoes untied"—had married; also, the proposed arrival of Jayne Mansfield at the Mount Brandon Hotel in Tralee, County Kerry, was canceled amid clerical criticism of this attempt "to besmirch the name of our town for the sake of filthy gain." It was an unfair smear, said the accused, a Catholic, sole support of her five children. This was the stuff of Ireland—poets and scholars and a little imported scandal. The banned meeting, scruffy, ill-attended, quiet, was nothing. It had been briefly noted in Belfast and on the RTE News and then forgotten. No one stopped to hear Tomás Mac Giolla, president of Sinn Féin, in front of the GPO on O'Connell Street, a traditional site for protest meetings, with the scars of 1916 still visible on the Post Office facade. There were too few to protest. No one could have imagined thousands making a special trip in a couple of years to hear about civil rights. No one took that sort of lark seriously. The IRA was history. Even the RUC had not taken them very seriously.

The IRA was merely a symbol in the Irish political equation. In Belfast without guns or gunmen, Billy McMillen was able only to run when menaced. Mitchell and Meade and McGurran, the few other activists in Dublin, they were the IRA, the real IRA, down at the heel, the tag end of legend now without money, without gear, with uncertain direction and yet a fierce commitment. The rest was nostalgia, patriot songs in pubs like Mark's, safe houses for men with no reason to run, the memories of old soldiers. The real movement had been torn by the bitterness of recent splits, the squabbles after the campaign, the debts, confusion. Having shed many traditionalists and some of the faithful, they finally moved toward radical political action. Belfast in 1967 was the first public indicator of the secret army's priorities.

The IRA was barely secret and no longer in the army business, merely a subversive splinter overseen by Cahal Goulding, the chief of staff, and a few friends in Dublin. The IRA had become a branch of a small painting-and-decorating concern, an army run by men, young felons, recognized by no one but Special Branch detectives. They toured on bicycles, slept with friends, and kept the faith. There were a few good men left from the campaign years, young, hard, energetic men like Meade, Mitchell, and McGurran. There was Séamus Costello, who sold cars at the Ford dealers Walden Motors on Parnell Street, and Seán Garland and Mick Ryan, both from the ragged inner city of North Dublin, running headquarters on tea and borrowed pounds.

Out in the country, Rory Brady—Ruairí O Brádaigh—was teaching school in Roscommon and active while his campaign colleague Dave O'Connell—Dáithí O Conaill—teaching woodwork at Ballyshannon in Donegal, was less involved.

He felt that Dublin was adrift from the military tradition he had favored. There were a great many like O Conaill who had doubts; some would help Dublin and some would wait, while many would drift on to their own parochial interests, republicans still but silent. The Dublin GHQ was then a few good men on endless rounds of make-do, begging for money, attending meetings, keeping the newspaper alive and spirits up, running on the last dregs of hope and the indomitable persistence of the republicans. They had kept the movement alive but not much more.

No revolutionary movement's prospects ever look very hopeful in the prologue of the play. Indeed, most rarely get to the first act. The republicans were different in that their history had been one of snakes and ladders, up to the shooting and back to the drawing board for nearly two centuries. In 1967 all knew that good times might follow bad—after all, things had not looked very good after Easter Week 1916. Always to the observer, however, the glass seems half-empty, not half-full as it does to the rebel. Always there are debts to the printer and the landlord, the light runs on borrowed coins, and the gas and the tea are brought from home. The unheated office is filthy, the cups crusty and unwashed, last week's unsold broadsheets are piled on those from last month in the corner. The deadlines are past, the tattered banners furled in a corner after a canceled parade. The walls are unpainted, dark, water-stained, and pinned with old notices. Dues are unpaid, the copier is broken, the telephone file is lost, only the dream remains.

Even Lenin at the Finland Station in Petrograd in 1917, with Russia in chaos, the government discredited, the army mutinous, and the people on the street— even then he spoke for a tiny band with only a dream for an asset and so looked a loser: charismatic, dramatic, but a loser. And there was no Lenin off Mountjoy Square. So there the Irish radicals inhabited offices not unlike those used by most rebels. Marx and Bakunin and Trotsky had had such offices, often exile offices, wretched, watched rooms, always small, always paper-strewn, unsavory, rank with cabbage or curry, always in the wrong part of town, rooms with overdue rent. James Connolly, icon of the Irish left, had known penury in such rooms. Garibaldi had made candles on Staten Island and met his Italian republicans in such rooms. And although Marx wrote books in the public reading room of the British Museum, his Communists could be found above pubs, deep in the dialectic. The Africans in London had argued the end of imperialism in bleak halls and gone back in their cheap suits to bed-sitters and cold beans on toast after the exhilarating hours. In rooms without views or water, the world has regularly been won with words. And these were revolutionary exiles who at least had rooms for the party, for the cause. Ho Chi Minh worked in hotel kitchens, shoveled snow in New York City. He had no party and so had no mean room for his dream. Others met at a single Cairo cafe table or at a special park bench.

All looked like losers and most were. Bakunin ended gross and betrayed and Marx marginal, famous only among his own. Che died in Bolivia. At times the streets of Algiers were filled with would-be presidents of unknown nations yet to be liberated, Namibia and Zimbabwe, names unknown even to stamp collectors. And even in the glory days of anti-imperialism, a steady stream of new nations of the month, there were more leaders than followers, more rebels than rebellions. Only a few came into power. It was the few in power that mattered, not the drab rooms. Times were always hard for hard men out of power, for ideologues without patrons, for rebels without funds. So selling Ford Zephers like Costello or collecting insurance premiums door to door like Ryan or even painting pubs like Goulding had precedent if no charm.

At Gardiner Place, the seat of the movement, Meade and Denis Foley turned out the *United Irishman* while the supreme agitator Séamus O Tuathail (not even a member of the republican firm) waited in the wings for his chance. There Goulding stopped by between decorating jobs and Garland stayed in residence. There all republicans still in favor stopped by in time. Meade ran informal tea seminars and pamphlets were sold and files misplaced and at times the Army Council met when no one much was watching. The guttering out of the Republican Clubs' protest hardly dissuaded the dedicated. Mac Giolla was always ready to speak to anyone or no one from the back of a truck. He and his wife sold the newspaper in pubs on printing day, political waifs, one step up from panhandlers, given silver by those who thought them cranks. They all were cranks since they believed the movement had a future. No one else thought so—not even at times the American, who was still, after all, a historian, an analyst of the past. And the IRA was not the Communist International, and Garland and Mac Giolla were not Garibaldi or even Connolly. No one in Ireland wanted to bother about republican ideals but focused on new jobs, new houses, new consumables, not the old politics and old feuds. The old times were represented by the unveiling of the real door to 7 Eccles Street immortalized by Joyce in *Ulysses* in the new Bailey Restaurant in Dublin's Duke Street. That was Ireland—ban most of the man's books, take an artifact as relic from a good house gone to ruin, turn it into profitable history as decoration in a trendy Dublin pub off Grafton Street. Anyway, they were taking the books off the censored list—five thousand to go the very next month—and a flash pub showed that the country was on the move. Unlike Joyce, it seemed, the IRA was simply an artifact without commercial value, without political value, without a future.

In Ulster, the Province of Northern Ireland, history was a little more awesome, though not much. By 1967 the police had shown that the republicans were not a serious matter. Banned meetings in church halls were diversions not really worth shutting down. The protesters had not even demanded fair shares, only the right to exist. The Unionist choreographers for Northern political dramas had almost out of habit sketched in a ritual role for the IRA gunmen, a symbolic role played briefly Sunday evening by Mitchell. The Orange state was having trouble rationalizing a defense without a valid enemy, so the IRA could not simply be ignored. Yet no one could really challenge the system. Certainly all the beneficiaries accepted the returns, assumed the establishment immutable, held their tongues at the raw expressions of majority arrogance. The proper felt that there was nothing to be done about bigots. They would die out in time. No one really could or would challenge the system from inside or out. In London no one had noticed the province for years, and in Dublin only the most occasional condemnation of partition could be found. Resentments had grown cold, even vengeance held no charms if sacrifice was necessary. From the South Premier Seán Lemass had met Captain Terence O'Neill, the Prime Minister of Northern Ireland, and what harm? The government had no wild ambitions. The schoolbooks ended in 1916 and so did history. The claims of the 1937 Constitution were just that, claims made by de Valera, not to be discarded, but not a matter of priority. In truth the North, Ulster, had hardly even been threatened by the IRA guerrilla campaign of 1956–62 and certainly any new challenge would be giggled off the street. There was no room on the island for the trendy urban guerrillas à la Che Guevara, darlings of Western university students elsewhere. In Ireland university students demonstrated about high fees and went to church on Sunday like everyone else. This supposedly volatile pool of rebellion had remained quite placid during the Republican Club event in Belfast.

On hearing of the ban, the students at Queen's University Belfast had hurriedly formed their own Republican Club. The new grouping immediately organized a parade where the coffin containing the body of democracy was carried out to Craig's home. Then it was carried away and the members returned to traditional inactivity. Getting in to Queen's was an enormous step for most of the Catholics; staying was vital. That a Derryman like Eamonn McCann would risk expulsion by his left-wing activity was not example but warning. Some would have liked to take up politics, follow the international fashions, but nothing appealed and nothing stirred real commitment. One of the militant new members of the Republican Club, Bernadette Devlin from Cookstown (sound nationalist-republican territory in North Tyrone), soon quit in boredom: What did a Republican Club actually do? The student club members were not even perceived as a threat by the authorities, who asked only that the club name be changed. No one bothered, and the police had other priorities. Devlin joined several Catholic societies who did good, did something, visited the old and sick, offered a practical alternative, gave an outlet to energy not spent on classes.

In the province the threat to the British way of life in the previous two years had seemed to arise not from IRA gunmen or civil rights demonstrations but from Orange militants running wild in defense of a system that really needed no defenders. These loyalists felt and so made clear that any mood of toleration was a dangerous first step. They were worried not by the IRA or the Queen's students but by their own Unionist leader, O'Neill, who as Prime Minister was consorting with Dublin. Meeting Lemass was a mistake, a dreadful, perhaps treasonous mistake. Treason was sought everywhere by the true believers, surrounded as they were on the island by a Catholic majority. For decency's sake O'Neill, a decent man, might let the Protestants down, might surrender all that had been gained by giving the first inch. For form's sake, for skewed priorities, even Craig would not pursue the ban with arrests, would not go beyond his leader. So Craig, well-tailored, well-spoken, kept well in mind the entire loyalist constituency—not just the proper, the golfers and mill managers and rugby club salesmen, but also the raw and simple folk with fundamentalist beliefs. Craig and his friends knew that O'Neill, their leader, elegant in accent and accomplishment, was too much the Ulster squire, too *English,* more fitted to Westminster than Stormont. He was risking a great deal for decency's sake in meeting Lemass and getting nothing in return but kind Catholic words. Despite the lack of visible opposition, the province was uneasy, any change was suspect, and O'Neill was increasingly seen as change.

Those neither polished nor properous but fanatical in defense of the system spoke in biblical anger, continuing the stress on the threat of the Roman Church, the dangers of the Irish Republic, the prospect of traitors within. The more traditional Unionists had listened to such concerns from the moment O'Neill arrived. Harry West, Brian Faulkner, John Taylor, and Austin Ardill were not men of the streets—all dapper, comfortable, even elegant—but all sensed a need for militancy. Two of the most uncompromising loyalists, Desmond Boal and John McQuade, had made little secret of their dislike of O'Neill. They felt a tremor in the solidity of the party as protector, and so an opportunity.

One of the reasons for the tremors was the growing power of another of Belfast's endless series of Protestant divines fearful of the power of the Pope and the persistence of Irish nationalism. The vocation of the cleric is in part to make the invisible real and awesome. In 1967 in Belfast no man could more effectively evoke the hidden fantasies of the plain, Protestant people than the Reverend Dr. Ian Paisley, militant Protestant and defender of the Orange faith from Ballymend. Paisley, like so many zealots, seemingly emerged from no place, a man unknown, without credentials, possessing only a mission and a gift for publicity. Actually, like the other Ulster militants before him, he emerged from a rich midden of fear and hate, an arena long splattered by the overswill of historical reality, general fancies, and popular terror. The sludge at the bottom of many Protestant minds encouraged self-righteous anger, delusions, hate in a good cause, bigotry, and faith. A different sludge had accumulated in Catholic minds that produced just as wild a result but one fit as well on grievance and one more closely related to the concerns of the twentieth century.

Paisley saw Rome as the first foe and the Irish nationalist as the Pope's legions. The IRA was merely the secret army of the alien faith. He had presence. He was a predator, a man intimate with biblical verse and his people's history, capable of a dynamic sermon or an intimate argument. He proved to be that rarity—a bigot with wit, with a ready mind, largely self-trained, with an honorary doctorate from Bob Jones University, a Christian college far away in South Carolina in the United States. He had as well the Northern gift of a harsh tongue. He spoke for his own and often more clearly than the men at Stormont.

There was no better sign that the banned meeting lacked charisma than the absence of Paisley eager to exploit any sign of the establishment failure to take up arms against the others. If civil disobedience was to work in the classical way, provocation was required, and the Orange loyalists were easy to provoke. For Paisley, without surety of tenure, a family business, or a safe seat in Stormont, the faith must be constantly defended. His congregation and the other fundamentalists so believed. The proper, the vicars of the Church of Ireland related to those who would talk to the vicar at Rome, the comfortable in the Methodist and Presbyterian pulpits, the established churches—they could let the people down. Paisley's own Free Presbyterian Church, established in 1951, reorganized in 1966, had a congregation born again in the true faith. And none was more righteous than Paisley, who had been eager to cause trouble and preach resistance. Gusty Spence of the new UVF, imprisoned for murder on Malvern Street, said, "I am sorry I ever heard tell of that man Paisley." Paisley had not preached murder and had condemned the killing. But his career had revealed to all the mix of faiths that made the system work. And the system worked through repression and close to the narrow edge of violence, since it had always been under threat of force. In 1967 the system seemed to have worked well, reducing traditional threats, the sermons of self-made divines, the ambitions of Unionist politicians, even the example of the previous year's sectarian murders, to froth on the great Orange stream. The system worked and so needed no Paisley, no UVF, not even Craig and Faulkner and the rest in control.

In the spring of 1967, with the first, light green leaves showing on the long row of trees stretching through the silver ground fog on and upward to the massive, marble parliament buildings of Stormont, there was a tangible atmosphere of stability. The great, elaborate building had been put up to survive the last Pope, intimidate the others, stand witness to the new Ulster. The fanaticism and fancies of the fundamentalists seized on old anxieties or misunderstood history faded away. Usually, except at election time, the endless rows of terrace houses off the great Protestant streets of the Shankill and Crumlin, which cut through the heartland, could be forgotten. And so faded the urgency of republican threats. This "subversion" was merely the residue dream of the poor and disinherited, often unemployed, standing about in tattered mufflers without money for a pint, much less arms for a rising. Stormont was real, the ultimate Unionist fortress, huge, obvious, defiant. It was a bastion of already-dated, imperial architecture, the ground great and neat, manicured, the trees old and the guards at the gates courteous. It appeared structured for the ages.

Inside the great building was found still the mean and petty politics of the system made up of the locals, village solicitors, farmers without scope or sophistication, ignorant and innocent merchants, a few company directors, many often decent but rarely deep, never questioning, easy next to the bigots. On the outside, at least, no sign could be found of the raw, crude, cruel politics of domination. The writ of arrogance rarely had to be shown. Here was only a large, impressive—if crude—building fit for the Indian raj, ready for a governor-general. Here was a great building in a green, green park, the outward and visible sign of an Ulster arrogance that still in the end was founded on fear. To counter the fear, felt by everyone from Paisley to the proper people in Malone Road drawing rooms and country houses, domination had to be displayed. Stormont was the most expensive example; the most recent of Paisley's displays was the most raw. The Orange system, the state, the power easily displayed in marble and institutions, so unchallenged, isolated, and sufficient, still had to be reinforced over and over. Meetings were banned, parades were run through nationalist districts, council houses were denied, pain was inflicted, domination was tested and retested by those who felt under a yet intangible constant threat.

The challenge of a few dozen disreputable and discredited IRA men—badly dressed, badly educated, narrow, bitter, and futile—holding a banned meeting in a back street attended by a few incorrigible radicals and the odd nationalist idealists was a minor matter. The IRA went back to Dublin, and in Belfast weekly meetings were badly attended. The students at Queen's did not stay the course, and their Republican Club closed. The radicals recruited no one new and found talk of forceful action upsetting. The nationalists were content with petitions. Nothing had seemingly changed. The people of Ireland had other priorities. The real was to be found in the marketplace, in shop windows, in matters available for credit or time payments.

There was no point in the nationalists tolling the rosary beads of old wars. Even the IRA had discarded explosives as a solution to Stormont: The building was too grand for their secret army. In 1967 there was no point in a secret army anyway. There was no point even in Paisley's fulminations or loyalist plots. Tomorrow would be a better day, everyone so believed: a better day that did not require sacrifice or change or risk, only a charge account or a better job or a certificate of skills won. Romantic Ireland, North or South, was long gone in 1967. And tomorrow would find the gray, marble mass of Stormont rising unchanged above the mist—solid, arrogant, smooth to the touch, hard to move, impossible to destroy, an apt symbol of a system constructed for the long run. Stormont was a Protestant palace for a Protestant state built to control the direction of history. The Stormont parliament building loomed over the fading quarrels of Irish history, permanent and provincial, an enormous monolith of stability. The system had the past in hand and so what mattered? Seldom had quiescence been as easily mistaken for stability.

1

The Irish Arena, Progress Delayed: 1962–1968

History is made by those who say no.
André Malraux

In British Ulster, fifty years after the Irish Easter Rising of April 1916, little had seemingly changed but the local control of the Unionists. The twenty-six counties of the Irish Republic to the south might have changed, fashioned a pious local nationalism, set up a state, printed stamps, held elections, forced the old language on a lethargic people; but none of this had slopped over onto the six counties of Northern Ireland. There, within the United Kingdom, each year was much the same despite the flurry of local politics, the getting and spending, the momentary attractions. The pillar boxes were red and the stamps bore the Queen's portrait. Times might be hard, but they were always better than in the Irish Republic. These six counties, claimed as Ulster, were British, and British Ulster was as cold, as gray, as dour as any chilly March morning, as stern as the pediments of Stormont. And the province, content, was turned against change. The Protestants, aliens planted there since Stuart times, had stayed, opposed over the years by many, but most of all and at the end only by the others, the Catholics, the island-bound nationalists. As Protestants the Unionists had opposed concession, home rule as Rome rule, and, betrayed in 1920, as they had always feared, had been left to establish their own Ulster. They were besieged, to be sure, but it was a small, grand country for the faithful. Power had devolved onto the province from London and so a parliament had been established at Stormont, a system of control fashioned with the assets to hand, and a fortress against the Celtic, Catholic nationalists on the island secured.

The rest of the island retained unrequited nationalist ambitions and sought a unity to be imposed against the wishes of the province. There had been murder and arson, campaigns of violence, campaigns of propaganda and subversion, a subversion many loyalists felt disguised as moderation and goodwill and foolishly encouraged by those Protestants in power who should know better. Moderation, consensus, toleration of disputation might do elsewhere, might do in Great Britain; but in Ulster eternal vigilance was needed to protect the loyal. The majority system, the Unionist Party, the devolved government, and the Protestant institutions, public and private, were defense, assuring the faithful that they would remain within the United Kingdom. Many fundamentalists, those not so proper and with fewer options, were loyal to their needs first, loyal not to Westminster or perhaps even the Queen but to a British Ulster perpetually under threat. Their British Ulster must be defended against history, against Rome and Dublin, even against London if need be, but mostly against them, the Irish Catholics.

The threat was always there from this alien other, had always been there from those with a different culture, unpalatable values, a foreign religion. Those others had strange ways, strange rebel songs, subversive, even strange, clumsy games: a wild, often ignorant and savage people hued over by a shallow gentility. They were the Gaelic-Irish, always defeated, never dispersed. They persisted in fact and in fantasy, persisted on the edge of daily consciousness, unrequited and unredeemable, a vaporous dreamy people capable of great violence. They haunted the Ulster of the loyalist, haunted Craig and Paisley and even O'Neill. Eternal vigilance was needed to maintain the union, to protect, to defend it. For loyalists, for the Unionists less militant but no less faithful, for the majority, for nearly all Protestants, history was no more than a chronicle of defense against this alien force. This was not popular with innocent moderates abroad, often not popular with visiting journalists or academic critics. Sectarian states were not fashionable.

But British Ulster was not unique. The Irish Free State was a religious state, a Roman Catholic state. The great Republican leader Eamon de Valera had said so directly during his broadcast to the United States on Saint Patrick's Day, March 17, 1935: "Ireland has been a Christian and a Catholic nation. All the ruthless attempts made through the centuries to force her from this allegiance have not shaken her faith. She remains a Catholic nation."* And in the 1937 Constitution, when Éire-Ireland emerged, he had made this clear: The Roman Church had a special, dominant position. But not in Ulster, where the system assured a Christian but not Catholic province secure within the United Kingdom. This did not mean necessary injustice for the minority tradition, only that proper precautions be taken that the Unionists, loyalists, Protestants did not suffer the same fate as their Southern colleagues, where the number of Protestants was halved between the Easter Rising of 1916 and the 1960s. That Rising had brought in time the decay of the Protestant minority, alien in their own land. In order to save their own, the Unionists had devised the Ulster system. Many of the proper, especially the middle class, did find the rantings of the populist orators, the sermons of the more dreadful fundamentalists, the overt bigotry of some of the crude loyalists, even the fulminations of too-ripe Unionist grandees deeply embarrassing. All societies had such embarrassments, patriot orators, narrow bigots, and the foolish protecting interest with prejudiced logic, even if Ulster seemed particularly and unfortunately rich in the dreadful. The two traditions

---

*From the radio broadcast printed in the *Irish Press*, March 18, 1935, cited in Conor O'Clery *Phrases Make History Here, A Century of Irish Political Quotations* (Dublin: O'Brien, 1986), p. 96, but not found in *Speeches and Statements by Eamon de Valera, 1917–1973* (Dublin and New York: Gill & Macmillan and St. Martin's Press 1980), edited by Maurice Moynihan, nor in the authorized biography *Eamon de Valera* (Dublin: Gill & Macmillan, 1970) by the Earl of Longford and Thomas P. O'Neill.

had long had raw, rasped edges, had often skittered on the edge of pogrom and riot. All this, however, need no longer be the case. Bigotry and the inequalities of the system were increasingly irrelevant and ultimately, surely, unnecessary. A new Ulster no longer needed the raw, old prejudices but needed only to move with the times to assure permanence, prosperity, and a proper place in the new postwar Europe.

The decent people perceived an Ulster quite at odds with the existing institutionalized injustice. Much that appeared to be oppression to the innocent eye had become mere rituals and so could easily be attuned to modern mores once treachery no longer threatened. The Unionist political system had by necessity evolved in isolation because the minority refused to participate, because Dublin could do nothing and London did nothing. It had evolved admittedly to reassure the threatened. The social and economic distinctions were of long standing, spun from friendships and associations as elsewhere, and were parallel to minority practice. Like attracted like. Friends accommodated friends and so Protestants hired Protestants, gave them preference through provincial agencies, houses and preferment and exception. Many Protestant males were involved in several major Masonic-style orders, of which the Orange Order was the largest and most important, which had evolved into defenders of the system, crucial factors in Unionist politics, Protestant social organizations at times, defenders of the British connection always. The Orange Order was merely an outward sign of the long, historic Protestant tradition; the rituals were outings; the men of influence were no different from those nets of old boys elsewhere. There were inequities, but they were amenable to adjustment. There were lasting prejudices, some justified; there were bigots, some in power. Hate was spoken from political rostrums, but this was everywhere the case and often with less cause than could be found in Ulster. Many of the Catholic minority were subversive in mind if not manner. Basil Brooke, an Ulster grandee in the Stormont cabinet, spoke for many in 1934: "I recommend those people who are Loyalists not to employ Roman Catholics, ninety-nine percent of whom are disloyal. . . ."* And there could be no denying thirty years later that many were still disloyal. It was an Ulster fact.

The moderate and proper members of the majority were humiliated by hatred as political program, by preachers who were often versed in little more than memorized biblical texts, rude Christians all, who slandered the Roman Church, mocked the Pope, and demonstrated against any ecumenical gesture however mild. The bigotry of a Basil Brooke was at least expressed in patrician tones for the gentry still directing the province. Such sentiments were not those expressed by the rough and venomous pastors on the sidewalks of East Belfast. The Paisleys had no friends along Malone Road in middle-class Belfast or in the big country houses running to seed. His ilk simply made the necessary adjustments to the system difficult. Perhaps in a fundamentally conservative province where the faith mattered, where history imposed prejudice and suspicion, where a threat to the constitutional system remained, the six counties could not be as tranquil as Kent. In Ulster faith still mattered and so an English pluralist system was only a distant

---

*One of Basil Brooke's often-cited pronouncements on Catholics, the quotation can be found first in the *Londonderry Sentinel*, March 20, 1934.

possibility. In Ulster there were still killing differences just behind the sermons and nods on the back lanes. Nevertheless, the proper Protestant defenders felt that the system was basically sound, the inequalities were aberrations, the future safe and promising. So said they all, the bankers and the big farmers, the solicitors and many of their clerks, the proper people, the families with newspaper subscriptions and savories at dinner. Prejudice—founded though it was on the visible evidence of Irish Catholic failings and inferiority—must be discreet.

The provincial system was always vulnerable. It was obviously also true that Irish republicans, a conspiracy of wicked, evil men, still existed, tolerated or encouraged by Irish nationalists North and South. Craig was no fool. To monitor their every move was common sense, to prohibit their displays prudent, to suspect their friends and neighbors but rational and crucial. For the Orange faithful, the loyalists, even for the decent and decorous, the IRA was far beyond moderation. The IRA had not changed agendas nor denied its intentions and so could not be wished away by novel reforms, seminars, or position papers. The new IRA was as dangerous as the old, and might use the new moderation as means to undermine the system. The IRA was the epitome of Irish Catholic nationalism—the enemy incarnate—and so the great enemy.

The secret army of loyalist nightmares, that Irish Republican Army, was a descendant of Irish rebellions stretching back to the eighteenth century. It had been the core of the Easter Rising and provided the guerrillas of the Tan War. The republican movement had fifty years before played a real role in the establishment of the Irish Free State, opposed by republican purists who wanted the whole island and the ideal of Easter 1916. This Free State evolved into the Irish Republic on April 18, 1949, but was also denied as the real dream by republican purists. From Dublin this Irish Republic's writ ran in only twenty-six counties and not at all in militant republican hearts loyal to the real army of the real Republic. Decade after decade the secret and subversive IRA remained fixed on the goal of a united Ireland. And decade by decade the IRA saw fewer volunteers, less enthusiasm, a decay of prospects, and an erosion of capacity.

Armed campaigns proved futile—bombing in the North, bombing in Britain, raids along the border, and finally the last guerrilla campaign that sputtered out almost unnoticed in 1962. All that was left were recriminations and those few exhausted young men without money or modern arms or a means to act on the future. The last crusade had left behind a few memories, a ballad or two, and men still in British prisons. The great, secret army of subversives, rebels in trench coats, rebels with Thompson guns, gunmen in the Celtic mist, madmen carrying sputtering fused bombs—they had simply become a film director's cliché. The IRA was more likely to be found in a thriller than in real life. Yet in Ulster the IRA was around the next corner, always there, never seen and so all the more real. For the loyalists, the secret republican army arose real and awesome in populist sermons, the pub gossip of Orange men, and the florid oratory of militants. They would not have accepted the real IRA as real. In Belfast there remained a handful of middle-aged former felons, the few survivors of the last campaign, and the old ones who had never changed their minds. They could not alone fill the hall at Saint Mary's. And in the country there were only a few more who never gave up on the Republic. The real IRA had almost vanished. The secret army was secret because it was not there. It had almost closed down five years before the banned meeting in March 1967.

On the evening of February 24, 1962, Ruairí O Brádaigh, a recent graduate of University College Dublin and a schoolteacher, was a wanted man. He was sincere, convinced, and had the duty of writing the epitaph to his generation's failure. The volunteers would disappear before spring, the assets were already spent or lost, and the friends grown cold. The future was bleak and there was no one to blame. Beyond the Army Council of seven there were only a few young men and some old-timers, nearly as few, just as poor. Irish republican history had ended, at least for now and perhaps for good, no matter what the Ulster bigots thought, no matter what the Ulster politicians needed to keep their system going.

The movement had come to the end of history. Since Wolfe Tone in 1798, the Irish republicans had relied on physical force to break the connection with England, the source of all ills. With the aid of the French, Tone had led the failed attempt to establish an Irish republic based on the ideals of the Age of Reason, the French example, and Irish needs. His example and his works became the foundation for the Irish republican movement, and his grave in Bodenstown, County Kildare, became a sacred site. In his ending was the beginning for Irish republicans.

The Fenians had won the right to wage war for an Irish Republic that they believed was all but established in the hearts of the people. The martyrs of 1916 had given example in arms that the IRA in the Tan War transformed into a partial triumph. And since then, despite dwindling numbers, the movement had persisted in seeking means to wage war. And now there were none.

History for the republicans was largely a tale of confrontation, persistence, grievance, betrayal, and recourse to force. The Irish people had suffered and survived, lost their lands, their customs, and their language; they had been penalized for their faith and their dreams. And they had survived, absorbed many of the aliens—Protestants at times found a home in Irish republicanism, too. When possible, the republicans had risen in arms—1803 and 1848 and 1867, again and again—fighting against absorption by the greater island. They were beaten down, again and again, but remained unassimilable. This long chronicle saw the evolution of an Irish nation always denied by the British center, always under threat of arms, and threats of cultural extermination, always harried, restricted, and, worse, lured by the foreign. And always the real Irish had persisted—their great gift—and maintained the faith. Millions had been driven from the island. Millions had lost their Celtic ways and their Irish language. Many had succumbed, become Castle Catholics—pro-British—or had refused to become Irish. Most who stayed Protestant had remained unassimilated, planted, alien corn, yet if not more Irish than the Irish still Irish. Many became Anglo-Irish, the Ascendancy if rich (with large estates, big houses, often titles) and simple Protestant if poor; but others, especially those outside the Church of Ireland, were militant and fundamentalist Protestants considered Irish only by those living elsewhere. So the Protestants scattered across the island were Irish and were not, some few rebels and most content with the link to the Crown. The others, the Irish-Irish, supplied most of the separatists' recruits. Through it all—famine, war, co-option, plantations—the faith in the Church but most of all

27

in the nation had remained, freshened by martyrs' sacrifices, by repeated examples of resort to physical force—the pikes at the rising of the moon or the gunman down the lane.

This was history for republicans, the Church's role eroded a bit and the prospects of Protestants in the long crusade enhanced as ideology required but little changed over the years. Irish history was mostly a tale of resistance to the English, a splendid chronicle of heroes and martyrs and villains. For Irish republicans, history was a bright, shining chronicle that turned failures into bench marks of progress. It was a history not about defeats, which were legion, nor humiliation and despair and oppression, all blotches on the story of the race, but a history of resistance of a people's determination to be a nation once again. It required not scientific historians, whose findings contradicted much of the revealed truth, but faithful readers eager to write a final chapter. Irish republican history, memorized not only by gunmen but also by schoolchildren, was almost dialectic—a chronicle of opposites clashing. There had been the long clash of Marxian-like thesis and antithesis, oppressor and rebel, Brit and Celt, producing for each generation a new model rebel for the morrow. Failure in the field meant but a refinement and purification of the faith, a necessary stage. The mysterious Irish nation was the product of each failed generation overcome by new means of oppression, new betrayals, new lures for the apostates. History was inevitable conflict that maintained the nation.

The conflict engendered a rich variety of means, rebellion, coups, revolution, agitation, and mobilization, sparked land leagues and conspiracies, boycotts, night riders, mass movement, monster meetings, cabals, parties, and guerrillas. The conflict had thrown up strategies of national liberation, strategies of confrontation and conciliation, some partially successful in the amelioration of grievance and others flawed and failed. History was conflict, defeat, and persistence. In 1962 only the last remained and for what purpose no one knew.

Modern history for the republicans began, more or less, with Wolfe Tone in 1798 and merged the ideals of the Age of Reason and the French Revolution to the historical currents of island national separatism. The single great event that shaped the future was the famine brought by the potato blight in September 1845. It was not the first potato famine nor did misery come unknown to an island overcrowded, filled with beggars and poverty. The Irish nationalists blamed not the invisible fungus *Phythophthora infestans* nor the times nor the oppressing class nor the structure of society, but rather the British for permitting the famine. This catastrophe brought devastation of the land and enormous loss of population, a drain that continued generation after generation, the ruin of a people. In the newly reinforced Irish diaspora, Irish nationalists turned again to physical force as the best means to reclaim their island and so ignored the great revolutionary ideologies of class fashioned by Marx, Engels, Bakunin, and the other new socialists as they did the more placid dreams of utopians, social democrats, and simple reformers.

The militant nationalists, mostly republican, who properly saw the United Irishmen of 1798 and Young Irelanders rebels of 1848 as precursors, spurned the Ireland that evolved within the British Empire after the Act of Union in 1800, which ended the Irish Parliament. This Ireland moved gradually forward from an era of bandits and beggars, faction fighters and rural agitators. It was not an Ireland with an Ascendancy, planted Protestants, and with a vast population of Catholic poor nursing ancient and justified grievances. It was a new Ireland, increasingly modernized in attitude and institutions, and one that moved into a new imperial role. The old inequalities were removed, the Roman Church not just recognized but increasingly partner in modernization. The land issue was solved and the Ascendancy's excesses curbed. This new Ireland was scheduled to have home rule, since the island was different from Britain, and so, thought London, best served by local institutions. For decades the Irish issue—home rule—troubled British politics, parliamentary majorities, and party priorities. Once home rule had been fashioned to British satisfaction, it was assumed that the Irish would disappear from Westminster's agenda. There would be an end to Ireland of the sorrows. There would even be a final end to inequality. In the new, imperial Ireland, divisive faith and social schisms were to be swallowed up by spreading prosperity—a prosperity increased by a declining population and an eroding cultural separation. Moreover, the very scope and responsibilities of the empire offered an opportunity for talent, for ambition, for the parochial to act on a grander stage than the Irish parish.

At the end of the nineteenth century the British system had survived repeated Fenian campaigns of violence, from frontal invasions of Canada, when Irish rebels carried out formal raids from the United States, to bombs in London that required the establishment of the Special Branch of the police. Home rule had been postponed because of enormous Conservative resistance founded in large part on Irish Protestant fear and British imperial loyalties. When Britain entered World War I in 1914, the Irish, Catholic and Protestant, volunteered for service in enormous numbers. Ireland from London seemed nearly as British as Scotland or Wales, different but no longer the seat of subversion. The last desire of Irish Catholic nationalists seemed to be the home rule that in some form would come after the war.

The Fenians, however, believed that the Irish Republic was all but established in the hearts of the people and that this legitimized their campaigns of physical force. As the Fenians faded, their ideas, for some, did not. It took more than red postal boxes and cheers for the royals to make Ireland truly loyal. Romantic Ireland was not dead and buried with the last of the Fenians. Republican Ireland simply waited to be awakened. And there were abroad republican conspirators, the Irish Republican Brotherhood (IRB), who from the moment war was declared saw the conflict as Ireland's opportunity and theirs, if not to snatch a republic at once, at least to rise and so inspire another generation to succeed.

In a very real sense the culmination of a millennium of Irish history as fashioned by nationalists, mainly organized as the Irish Volunteers, came on Monday morning, April 24, 1916, when the Irish Republic was proclaimed from in front of the General Post Office, Sackville Street, Dublin, by the rebels—the IRB, the Irish Volunteers, the socialist Irish Citizen Army, the unreconstructed dreamers. The conspirators who had planned and would direct the Easter Rising—and with a few notable exceptions would be executed for so doing—represented all the long and tangled skeins of the new nationalism. There were poets, felons, teachers, agitators, and conspirators who, in their proclamation declaring the Republic, summoned the "Irishmen and Irishwomen: in the name of God and of the dead generations . . . to her flag." So there were the few, rebels, mostly young men with no name and fame to come, touched by the litany of grievance and the dream, all sorts and conditions of rebel. There was an old Fenian, Tom Clarke, the Marxist James Connolly, and the poet and teacher Padraig Pearse, who was to be provisional president. There were Protestants and Catholics and Marxists, devotees of Gaelic nationalism and Irish speakers, those without politics but a taste for adventure and a rifle. There were not many to challenge a great empire, but all felt the call of history, their history.

During the next week the republicans did transform the drama to fact, sacrificed in blood, added Easter 1916 to the litany of Irish risings. And like all those previous risings, the rosary beads of the nation, the Easter volunteers failed. The leaders were executed, Eamon de Valera the only Dublin commander to avoid the firing squad, and he and the volunteers marched through hissing crowds to boats that would take them to an internment camp in Wales. He felt that the rising had done better than anyone might have imagined, given the confusion and the odds. If only the people had come out, come out even with just knives and forks. But the people had not and now spat at the prisoners. But this rising was different, special, for the hidden Ireland had been outraged at the executions, James Connolly of the Irish Citizen Army dragged wounded to be bound to a chair and shot, the others dispatched as quickly as possible by Englishmen in anger, Pearse shot and his brother, Tom Clarke shot, all of the leaders shot. The irresponsible foolishness of the Easter Rising itself was forgotten in the face of yet another example of British arrogance.

The Irish nation stirred once again to feel Irish, felt the slain leaders martyrs. Those who resented their executions were largely Catholic, for the Protestants of Ireland thought Connolly, Pearse, and the rest were traitors during wartime. They had done untold harm. July 1916 in France in a real war had seen the fearful Irish sacrifice of the Ulster Division at the Somme, more killed in minutes than the toll of the Rising, more killed in days than in all the Irish rebellions. In France there had been more Irish sacrifices than could be imagined in the poetic musings of Pearse. That was the real world, the real war. It did not matter to the republicans—not all Catholics—who turned the defeat of the Easter Rising into victory by launching a guerrilla campaign on the wave of nationalist emotion that had been unleashed. As far as can be told, Ireland was by no means a nation once again. Many supported the campaign of the Irish Republican Army, but far more had no opinion and some bitterly opposed the IRA. Still, enough helped (or most important did not hinder) so that by 1918 the IRA did not have to wait for the next generation to renew the struggle. Most rebels can make do with the people's passivity and write in their support in postwar histories. The IRA became the archetype for all future national liberation campaigns, as did the Tan War; it became also the archetype for the divisions, recriminations, and internecine war that followed.

Many of the people proud to be Irish did not rush to join the rebels, but they did not report the lad down the lane to the Royal Irish Constabulary. And those who normally would do so had second thoughts. The remaining conspirators, their political party Sinn Féin, their IRA guerrilla army did not thus have to wait for a generation. Suddenly the Easter sacrifice had been authenticated by the British firing squads. An ocean was created for the guerrilla fish: Toleration was assured; sufficient recruits were gathered from all classes to make rebellion work; and an ideal opponent existed—dedicated to justice and fair play but not at imperial expense, a foe divided from the start regarding means and ends. And rebels always know the three great things: what is wrong, what is wanted, and what must be done. Britain was what was wrong, the republic the goal, and the means to that end the deployment of physical force. The Tan War that followed, the Glory Years of the IRA, then rested on a foundation of agreed historical memory. It was a patriot's history, the recollections of old ways and loyalties and most of all old judgments concerning the nature of order imposed on the island. In a real sense the Irish touched by nationalism withdrew their consent to be governed by London. Even those who abhorred rebel violence seemed to feel a new mandate was necessary.

In the 1918 Westminster elections, used by the Irish nationalists as a plebiscite, the Sinn Féin candidates, united only in their loyalty to Ireland rather than the Crown, received massive support. Only the Protestant minority still favored the historic British connection. What the Sinn Féin voters favored was not certain except a different Irish arrangement. How many of the majority favored a republic is still unknown. After 1922 the winners claimed all that did not oppose them in arms, but that was the patriot history being written. The old gunmen skipped over the unpleasant parts, the murdered innocents of the dirty war, the betrayals and lies, the Irish Catholic people who would have preferred a British connection, and the Troubles that followed the Anglo-Irish Treaty, when old friends murdered each other. All that was clipped out of the great film of *A Nation Once Again* and left in the waste bin of history for later scholars to rummage about when it no longer mattered.

In theory for the republicans the movement was based on firm nonsectarian principles that

> To unite the whole people of Ireland, to abolish the memory of all past dissensions, and to substitute the common name of Irishmen in place of the denominations of Protestant, Catholics, and Dissenter—these were my means.

This call to unity by Tone, in three resolutions for the United Irishmen, core of the 1798 rebellion, can be found repeatedly in republican publications, still the theoretical rock of the movement.* Tone's call to unity did, briefly, almost uniquely, produce a general resistance, the United Irishmen. Gradually, however, Irish and Catholic become synonymous in the nineteenth century. The Protestants, except for a few nationalists, had mostly become militant in their sectarianism, preferring the advantages offered the loyal to the charms of island nationalism. The Easter Rising and the IRA guerrilla war had not united the Irish but had intensified their religious division. No matter; the concept remained a

*A recent republican discussion may be found in Seán Cronin, *Irish Nationalism: A History of Its Roots and Ideology* (Dublin: The Academy Press, 1980), pp. 40–64.

basic part of republican ideology and was taught to the new IRA recruits, almost all Catholic.

In the Tan War these volunteers were found in the lower middle class: solicitors' clerks, poorly paid schoolteachers, parish priests, provincial pub owners, small-town editors, students, salesmen, and some small farmers. Mostly they were found in the cities, Dublin, Cork, Limerick (not many in divided Belfast), or clumped in country towns, especially in Munster and the Midlands. Those from the wilder reaches, where survival was difficult, as well as the rich and the very poor, had other priorities. Most in the IRA were simple people of no property. Some had ambitions for more, some looked for a main chance, many felt the new nationalism filled old hungers. Many showed up when victory was in sight and some went directly into the Free State service against the IRA irregulars. And in the end the old IRA won twenty-six of the thirty-two counties for a Free State and gave rise to the purists who as the IRA wanted the dream not the reality.

The reality was the new Ireland. It was not the nation of the republican dream. It was also not the Ireland dominated by the big houses of the Ascendancy and the elegance of the Georgian rows in the cities, not the Ireland of the Castle Catholics who daily went to move paper in British offices, not the Ireland of the imperialists or the Orange men. Those Protestants who had sacrificed on the Somme returned to a different country, two Irelands. In the six counties of British Ulster they went back to Masonic lodges, parades of domination, and limited opportunities that were still better than those offered to the majority in the other Ireland. Protestants with homes in the new Free State had been bypassed by history and become irrelevant: They were only 6 percent of the population. There were then several Irelands, none satisfactory.

The rebels had dreamed of turning all or almost all the Unionists into Irish in their united Ireland. It would be Irish-speaking Ireland. Few but those on the fringe could speak the old language any more but that could be changed. It would be pious Ireland. It was certainly already a devout, churchgoing island, even though each faith was exclusive and suspicious. And the new Ireland would play Gaelic games, be home to saints and scholars as of old, a Christian Ireland replete with poets and playwrights, a new Ireland altogether. It was a thousand-year-old Ireland, bucolic, separate, parochial, peaceful, choreographed by patriot historians, epic poets, by special pleading and by enthusiasts and buffs, made real by faith and fearful by the Rising. It was an Ireland that never existed except in badly written, poorly printed books. A few Irish Americans might believe in such an Ireland, but soon even the children who read the patriotic primers did not. The country that emerged after 1921 was make-do, truncated, a beginning or a betrayal depending on the perspective. The nationalists had to make do with only twenty-six of the thirty-two counties; the Protestants got the rest of the northeast as consolation prize, a Protestant province for a Protestant people. There was a hateful oath to the Crown, and British bases, and a governor-general. For republicans it was not Irish, not free, and not a state. History had been miswritten.

Over the next generation those in power sought to close down the republicans. The enemies of the idealists were the new institutions of the nation, the owners of property, the priests, the prim and trimmers, the easily led, those for the easy life, and those who believed more could be gained in time without sacrifice. Their enemies were idealists and purists moved by the great incandescent dream that could not be found in the clumsy government in Dublin, in a truncated nation, in the real world.

Those republicans who did not flee to the diaspora or despair were led by de Valera, the survivor of 1916 and still president of the Provisional Republic. For some he was the dream personified, an icon to equal Michael Collins, killed in a 1922 ambush by a republican sniper. Then de Valera took his troops out of Sinn Féin, giving up the policy of abstentionism, and entered the new oath-bound Dáil Éireann as Fianna Fáil, Warriors of Destiny. Dev put his name down to enter Parliament but still insisted, "You must remember I am taking no oath." So Fianna Fáil had deserted the long crusade and for the *real* republicans was no more than a creation of apostasy, not as awful as the old Free Staters but nearly so. They kept to Sinn Féin, which faded away, and then placed their loyalty with the Army Council of the IRA—the real government of the real Republic.

These republicans remained underground, existing on memories and the hope of a new campaign, and focused on the evil government in Dublin rather than the British overlord. When de Valera finally arrived in power in 1932, there was a brief IRA honeymoon, but the purists remained unmoved by his avowed faith in the Republic, his tinkering with the terms of the hated treaty, and his old rhetoric; and by the time he produced the new 1937 Éire-Ireland Constitution, the break had come and republicans were being arrested again. They insisted that the second Dáil, not de Valera, was the real government of Ireland—a constitutional legitimacy important to very few that was passed along to the Army Council by the Dáil survivors in 1938 to justify the IRA bombing campaign against the British in 1939–40. By then the IRA's history was replete with resignations and withdrawals, and futility as time and Fianna Fáil reforms eroded the faith. As for the bombing in England, many of the unrepentant saw no need or purpose in a murderous gesture without hope of changing history. During the war de Valera, fearful for Irish neutrality, interned the republicans, executed a few, and let hunger strikers starve to death if they chose. There proved no harder man than the reconciled republican, a fact in 1922 when the Free Staters summarily executed seventy-seven "irregulars," and a fact when Fianna Fáil came to power, and a fact when during World War II the de Valera government interned the suspect, imprisoned the active, executed those guilty of capital crimes, and allowed an IRA adjutant general to die on a hunger and thirst strike. In Northern Ireland the Unionist government took an even dimmer view of the unrepentant republicans and had most in prison ships or jail cells for the duration. When the gates opened in 1945 and 1946, the world was seemingly different. Most of the released went home to lead quiet lives. A few changed their minds, but most saw an end to the great crusade. And the few who did not had to begin at the beginning—marginal, scorned, without assets or even membership lists, only the illumination of the dream undiminished by the years locked away and forgotten.

The practical had formed their own republican party (Clann na Poblachta), joined in the government with the hated Free Staters, and seen a republic declared at last on April 18, 1949. It was not the real Republic, that messianic shimmering grail that had cost so many lives, but was just a government, a matter of law and budgets and twenty-six counties. It was not at all what the faithful had in mind. The Irish Republic, printed on stamps, on currency, on revenue labels, mentioned in the Dáil from time to time, was a shoddy matter of words. Ireland was not a nation once again but a disappointment, a failure.

The new Republic contained a pious, parochial, rural society, a green land of narrow roads, men in cloth caps, pints and parish priests and dancing on the crossroads. There was a frugal comfort for many if never for all, a decent democratic government, more talented than fewer than 4 million deserved, but one still dominated by the issues arising from the civil war. Men did not speak, families passed in silence, politics remained in the shadow of betrayal and death and lies. Political novelty was suspect, reform unwanted by many, grudges and vengeance long delayed. A generation that had grown up in hatred drove away the young. There was a feeling that local time ran slower than elsewhere, than in England—the near center of the bustling world—or in far-off Europe and America, the edges of the universe.

Dublin was clotted with bikes, clerks in wrinkled tweed suits, women in last year's London styles, and dray carts of Guinness. It felt dated and quaint. The pubs were still out of Joyce, easy for him to have recognized. The manners were genial, the ideas small, the discourse arcane on matters of language and faith, the morals narrow. A religious vocation was a prize worth any price and so sold in the schools and byways. Physical pleasure was suspect, a wife was a luxury, and ease was found in drink. There was no raucous new music, no Hollywood morals, no industry, no pollution, no artistic angst; but there were lots of priests. Christian Brothers ran schools and Protestant Trinity College endangered Catholic souls (although somehow it had a republican lecturer in Irish in Máirtín O'Cadhain). There were few saints and few productive scholars, and the writers were censored and the painters painted like the English had once. The Church fought progress that came with a new country dance hall and American pop music. Still they were all Irish failings. The sophisticated and the creative might complain, but the nation was neither very sophisticated nor concerned with creativity but mostly content after troubled times with what had been won.

The sixties saw extensive changes in the Irish Republic, beginning with the television broadcast of Telefís Éireann in 1961 that brought the outside world first into the pubs. A magnetic, blue box glowed above the evening pints, the long rolling black hills and narrow roads were dotted with a single blue window. Then there were more windows blue as it moved into the homes. The outside could come inside. Taoiseach Seán Lemass was one of the youngest of the old ones. He had served at sixteen in the GPO on Easter Week, eventually replaced de Valera in Fianna Fáil. He sought change, prosperity not just continuity, not the frugal comfort preached by his mentor, not just what the others had accomplished but a modern Ireland, competitive and progressive. Thus, with de Valera in the president's house in Phoenix Park in 1959, Lemass oversaw the first Programme for Economic Expansion, approved in 1958 and followed by a second, both drawn up by the Secretary of the Department of Finance, T. K. Whitaker. The plans injected capital into production in order to stimulate exports, and vitalized and transformed first the Irish economy, then Irish society, far more than had the gun or the nationalist dreams of rebels. The key was money. There was at last money in Ireland. The long flow of emigrants began to dry up—there were jobs at home. For the first time since the famine, the tide of emigration ebbed and the population began to stabilize. The bicycles began to be replaced with automobiles. The crossroads dancers were deserted for dance halls filled with the Elvis Presley clones and local showbands. Trendy ideas were discussed on Gay Byrne's television chat show. "Censored in Ireland" became a bad joke rather than a curate's boast.

The old Ireland was going, replaced not by saints, scholars, or republicans in power but by devices that plugged in and did the wash, by cars that could be exchanged for better in a year, by gadgets that glittered and lit up and could be replaced by the newer and even more trendy. There was better medicine and real dentists and school buses for children and new houses and new roads and novel fertilizers and special feed for the stock. On the edge of the cities little houses lit by electricity had cars in front and employed fathers inside. The houses might be tacky and the cars cheap but it was all a net gain to a people long impoverised and oblivious to the cost of pollution or the meaning of architectural taste. First things came first in the new Ireland. The ITGWU (Irish Transport and General Workers' Union) built the horrid steel-and-glass Liberty Hall skyscraper on the Liffey; below, in the city, fashionable bars served gin and tonic, often with an ice cube. Times were a changin' and seemingly the Irish with them. A new middle class appeared, not interested in cheap cars or tacky little houses but proper possessions. There were new suburban houses to be built, Mediterranean villas and English Tudors in Bray and on Howth Head. The new mohair suits and men without caps were on the streets. The old ways did not seem as important. Everyone still went to Mass, but the homilies were updated and the vision of the Legion of Mary went down market. Everyone still voted for the same party, but the quarrels of the old soldiers increasingly seemed irrelevant.

The conservatives, and the island had an ample supply, might not like Elvis or the traffic around Stephen's Green, but it was hard to argue against prosperity or the improvement in the general health of the people. It was even hard to argue against the happiness of a people who could now stay in Ireland, buy things, eat well, go to shows. Money is very democratic and, when well spent, can perform wonders. Government investment and public skills during the coalition government under Health Minister Noel Browne had ended tuberculosis, a white plague so fearful that its very name was often avoided in the countryside, a historic scourge that had seemingly come with the island and the faith. And now all at once it was gone, leaving empty fever hospitals and Noel Browne without a medical speciality. He retrained as a psychiatrist, assuming perhaps that the Irish would always need this sort of medical intervention. Government investment and commitment promised general and free secondary school transportation under Education Minister Donogh O'Malley. And where the government faded away private enterprise—new men with accounting degrees or simply ambition— appeared. But Irish enterprise that still faced intransigent peasants, books kept in ink, the old ways, great charm and courtesy as curtain for incompetence.

The begrudgers and pious and incompetent fought a rearguard action. Special targets were the visible signs of change: the new music, the new books and plays, the new styles. The censorship board was still at work; there were few advocates for divorce; many were attracted to birth control but none urged legalizing abortion. What no one could easily see was the degree to which money could buy out loyalties, national and ethnic assumptions, historical agendas. How much was Ireland actually changing and how much was glitter and gadget?

Much of the change was limited to those concerned with ideas, to those living in Dublin, the freshly rich and the newly liberated. No one could deny the changes, and there was no way prosperity could be put back into a pious bottle. In fact there seemed little that could be done to keep prosperity from ruining Dublin. Lack of money had meant not only the prevalence of old diseases and decayed buildings but the preservation of a great city locked almost as if in amber after 1921. Now money allowed the salvaged treasures to be ravished in the name of progress: grand new *Irish* buildings to replace the Georgian of the Ascendancy—the old Irish rebels victors as new Irish speculators. The new money meant scattering ugly white villas on every coast, slashing the countryside with new roads, and turning ancient pubs into plastic palaces serving odd drinks to women on their own: progress. Money, in Irish terms lots of money, engineered all matter of change, change without experience or limits imposed by taste or by law. The times for Ireland were heady; once a bike had been a dream, high wheels, sturdy over the mud and ruts, a possession for a lifetime, and now there were to be Fords made in Cork and sold to the likes of everyone!

Nearly every journalist, nearly every commentator, the university seminars and the weekly reviews' analysis, all the common wisdom agreed on a New Ireland. New was better, had to be. New was inevitable, had to be. The country would be prosperous, sophisticated, tolerant, fresh, invigorating, exciting, no longer mired in old feuds, old sureties, old ruts. The new model priests were on the telly and the old begrudgers pushed to the back of the pub, regulars no more. It was the new common wisdom and who could deny the reality, North or South? The man in the cloth cap was disappearing to be replaced by sleek men, flushed with deals and mergers, eager for Mediterranean holidays and the admiration of city bankers. Those ignored in the rush to a new prosperity—the urban poor, the marginal farmers, the old, the young on welfare, the untrained and undereducated—were forgotten, just like the old gunmen.

The founding fathers were moving on, time at last at work: Dev was old and blind and sitting in the park; the famous guerrillas and patriots were dying out—Tom Barry quiet in Cork, Seán McEntee retired, and even Seán MacBride was out of politics; General Richard Mulcahy, epitome of the Free Staters, had left the Dáil; and in the North, O'Neill was in Stormont instead of the old bigots. Seán Lemass was a pragmatist and his successor, Jack Lynch of Cork, would come from a new generation. His competitors would be even younger, with no memory of the Glory Years. The old IRA rebels had for the last fifty years been keeping new men away from power, letting them grow old, retired without prospects. But the next generation, who had not been burned by the Troubles or exhausted by the old men's longevity, was thus on the lip of power.

Far to the north of Dublin, at the end of a ninety-minute drive, lay the rest of Ireland, the six counties of the "Ulster" province of the United Kingdom—the

North that was not as far north as parts of Donegal. British Ulster had only some of the old counties. It was a province that the real Irish did not recognize or often consider. After nearly fifty years, it was little known to the citizens of the Republic except through slogans, patriot history, and unchallenged assumptions, prejudices reinforced by the political currency of the times. It was supposedly just like the other twenty-six counties except that it had more Protestants and was more thoroughly contaminated by Britain. Some of the nationalists played games or came to Dublin on business but hardly any of the Unionists had Irish interests or connections beyond Trinity College and Protestant friends along the border. So the six counties were not supposed to be different but were surely isolated from events in the Republic. To read a Northern, particularly Northern Protestant, newspaper was to enter a different world that hardly related to events in Cork or Sligo: a journal with different priorities filled with different holidays, different sports and political priorities, different heroes, pages more suited to an English reader. But in the Republic no one knew this. No one then or later purchased Northern newspapers except for a few Catholic provincial weeklies. The Black North was more symbol than place for those in the South.

To the innocent eye British Ulster seemed little different from Irish Ireland. It was as green, cursed or blessed by the same endless rain and mild winds, as neglected and isolated as the South even if touched with the red of Royal Mail pillar boxes and the bustle of industrial Belfast. Perhaps the fields were neater, certainly the roads were better, but Guinness was as popular, cloth caps were worn, and the same golden greyhounds were walked down twisting country lanes. There was the same quiet but a grating accent, not soft at all. There were more kinds of churches, seemingly one on each corner of every small town, but the same large crowds on Sunday. It was a churchgoing country. There were Union Jacks, often all year round, a touch of the mainland British in the postage stamps and automobiles with different license tags and different makes and a muddle of currency, Ulster sterling and British and Irish notes and coins, any would do. The Belfast newspapers properly, then, reported on a province not at all like Munster or Leinster. All these visible differences, however, were part of the surface gloss; for, even putting aside the peculiar institutions and forms of government established to defend the remnant of the all-Ireland minority, the new Ulster was a divided society. It was divided out of sight of the transient who saw only Irish on the street in dowdy styles, all speaking with a hard nasal twang, all apiece.

There were two Northern Irelands. The Protestant one, Ulster and Orange, in theory a part of the British main, was loyal to the Crown. That Ulster was patriotic, thrifty, abstemious, proudly Protestant, little different it was said than Northumberland. The children went to government schools, learned of the empire, were taught Victorian virtues and history, and the names of kings. And everyone—Anglican, Presbyterian, Methodist, fundamentalist—went to chapel on Sunday and pursued the Lord's work the remainder of the week. These were the skilled workingmen in tidy suits and bowler hats, linen merchants with big Derry houses, the country gentry self-shaped to an English model; these were the proud clerks, small farmers, and tidy mechanics not yet up to bowlers, the everyday people and their betters. When questioned they responded that they were British or Irish, or from Ulster; for, however loyal, they were not sure. They were not sure *exactly* the focus of their loyalty: Britain? The United Kingdom? The Crown? Ulster itself? Their Orange system? They were not sure they were truly British— certainly the British thought them Irish.

Their ancestors had been on the island since the seventeenth century, too long to have real roots on the mainland, where the real British lived. The direction of Irish nationalism had moved out on a Catholic tide, abandoning the Protestants, the Anglo-Irish, the West Britons, those who saw no need to create a new history or new loyalties. They were determined not to speak Irish or accept ancient myths and Celtic heroes as their own. They were quite happy with the rituals and benefits of a United Kingdom, an empire and then a commonwealth. After three hundred years the Protestants had become less Irish without doing a thing but persisting as Protestant, as loyal as when planted, maybe more so. They were more loyal, more devoutly Protestant, more virtuous, more disciplined, even more productive than their Protestant neighbors in the Irish Republic. There Catholicism ruled if not in name. Each year there were fewer Protestants in the Republic. There Rome's writ in morals and attitudes ran and so the Northern Protestants saw the inevitable and undesirable amalgamation of Irish Catholic nationalism in the Free State. It was neither their way nor their state, not free and a different kind of Irish—parochial, narrow, exclusive, and aggressive. Such an ideology required constant Unionist defense to protect the liberties of the province.

Those Roman Catholic were surely nationalists, Irish by choice, not British. They were thus subversive to the system in the six counties and were above all different. They might not look different, but they were. That came from another tradition, that other Ireland, consolidated to the south in the Republic. These others were committed to a Celtic language, a Celtic heritage alien to Britain, and to the future of the Dublin system. Poorer but as proud, these Irish nationalists, outnumbered two to one, had few doubts: In time partition would be undone, the island united, a nation once again; justice would be done, history redeemed and fulfilled. So they had different heroes, played different games, hurling and Gaelic football, on different days, Sunday not Saturday, looked not to the Somme in 1916 but to Easter and the Rising, flew the tricolor and walked each Sunday to Rome's church. They read Dublin newspapers, went to the great Gaelic Athletic Association (GAA) All-Ireland Finals at Croke Park, looked to Fianna Fáil or the others for aid and comfort—and were mostly forgotten in a Republic with more pressing priorities.

To Dublin, the nationalists were as parochial and irrelevant as the loyalists were to London, distant provincial people now settled in place by the Anglo-Irish Treaty that had ended the great Irish question: Let Ulster dance to Ulster's tunes. Into the small space of the six counties the two traditions fit uneasily. All the other conventional divisions—class and culture, politics and variant religions— were overshadowed by a focus on the constitutional issue. Was the state, the Stormont system, transient or forever? Was a united Ireland ruled from Dublin the intended end product of history? Was geography history?

Yet, there was little room for hate without risk of violence. There was always the need to avoid offense on a personal level while maintaining either dominance or resistance on a societal one. Some villages or districts could manage without recourse to humiliation or anger, while other areas revealed at the slightest rub raw emotions or hate, suspicion, distaste, arrogance, and fear seething beneath a placid surface. Over many years the North had become a divided society that permitted life to be led without constant friction. The key was the elimination of much contact and the easing of what remained with civility, real or assumed. The province played to rules not stated and seldom visible that allowed differences to be displayed only at ritual moments.

Neighborhoods were segregated. Businesses, clubs, pubs, games, churches, hospitals, schools, all the institutions and arenas of society existed for either tradition but rarely for both. Big stores and central cinemas catered to money, but elsewhere there were Catholic pubs and Protestant tailors, deep in areas of their own. In small towns, in the mixed countryside, in the border neighborhoods, a constant, never-ending dance of delicate adjustment took place so that offense need not be given nor intimacy encouraged. The other was identified by proffered clues—a name, a school attended, a reference, or a word—and so the contact could be shaped to form. There were those who crossed the divide, pursued poetry or Marx in the company of believers not Protestant or Catholic. There were exceptions, the token Catholics in Protestant shipyards or constables in the Royal Ulster Constabulary, token Protestants in a Catholic office or both kinds on a committee to secure a university for Derry. In the main, each, whatever might be the public position, pursued a life isolated from the other in constant Brownian motion to avoid contact. It was thus easy to hate the general—Catholics or Unionists—but difficult to fault the specific—Murphy's lad or old Wilkinson from Mackie's.

Yet all public displays were intended to reinforce the virtues of tradition, the rituals of the tribe. They were not only to encourage one's own but to challenge, intimidate, and threaten the other. Ulster had civility among individuals and left intimidation and hate for the mass. The great Orange parades, festival and display, parade and party, political declaration and holiday, were plotted to pass Catholic districts with a thundering beat of the giant Lambeg drums to stress domination. The gatherings of the militant nationalists and the republicans on holiday of renewal and dedication took place under the tricolor. The ceremonies were designed to appear subversive, and often were. The pale faces in the crowd agleam with the ritual words of an IRA manifesto looked to the statement as ammunition against those in unjust power. Such commemorations preserved the faith of the minority, the neglected and abandoned of the North. They defied the system, sectarian tyranny with a democratic face, injustice living on borrowed time. The mystical IRA would rise again—note the circle of fearful RUC at every ceremony, evidence of the defenders' fear. Both tribes and traditions could coexist only with the constant and unarticulated personal adjustment that let private life get on with the day while the great differences clashed in ritual combat. The system worked for fifty years. This was no small triumph.

Getting on with the day, living a normal life in Northern Ireland, was not an easy matter. Both traditions accepted that the future was not certain, history had not quite ended, not yet, perhaps not ever. Vigilance and persistence were crucial. Both the nationalists and loyalists could not imagine that they played any but a zero-sum game, one's advantage was the other's violent ideas hallowed by use, justification for physical force, for murder, for a state with special powers and vigilantes paid and unpaid. There was a long history of conflict and so there were long and exacting memories of real grievance. In a parochial society these were husbanded for lack of competition, retold, fondled, and passed on so that history moved slower: Many could easily remember danger and humiliation before their grandparents' time. There was little mutual trust, little real understanding of the alien other, not politically and so not personally. Empathy was rare. To the involved, everything about the other seemed different and undesirable.

The province had crushing economic problems as well as the fundamental schism. There was massive and permanent unemployment, urban decay, miserable housing, limited social services, a tax base no larger than that of the city of Leeds, an aging industrial base in linen and shipbuilding, and a rural backwater replete with misery and dim prospects. Yet things at first glance did not look so bad. The countryside was green and tidy; Derry was quaint, with a ring of walls, and Belfast had the great Edwardian City Hall, a splendid commercial center, and the cranes and scaffolding of the famous shipyards. One had to look just a bit harder to see the hovels in the country, the misery of the squalid Bogside below Derry's walls, the unemployed on the Belfast street corners, and the red figures at the bottom of ledger columns in the stale offices within the ornate buildings built during past prosperity. The province was and would remain the most difficult of all in the United Kingdom, indeed in Europe: a small, decayed, postindustrial slum with green fields on the margins of the continent. It was a laboratory that simultaneously demonstrated the failures of capitalism, the welfare state, and postindustrial society. At least the tribal bickering diverted attention from the institutionalized misery of the six counties beyond remedy of quick-fix economic solutions or the injections of social reform popular in the capital.

Beyond each problem lurked a sectarian solution, a class of interests intensified by perpetual division. There were more Protestants unemployed but a higher Catholic percentage, nothing would change this—both were aggrieved at the others' figures, nothing would change this. It was the others' fault as well as the system's. There were more council houses built by percentage than on the mainland, but the Protestant council favored their own—in large part to maintain the sectarian voting strengths—and what choice did the Unionists have but to favor their own, maintain the power to prevent subversion from being reward? The others would have done no less. And if the Catholics complained about the limited social grants, the Protestants were quick to point to the size of Catholic families, feckless and irresponsible, children at Rome's bidding to be paid for by Protestant taxes. So they pointed in public oratory, but never pointed where a Catholic neighbor stood, nice old Mrs. O'Day and her shoe full of bairns. And so it went with every conventional problem, economic or social. Each response, each plan or proposal, engendered dissent arising from the great divisions, both real and perceived.

The actual resorts to violence since the establishment of Northern Ireland had been both rare and limited, if brutal. At times of great stress there had been pogroms in Belfast, where the two sides were crammed at critical mass next to each other, and there had been some rural, almost traditional trouble. Mostly the troubles were those found elsewhere. There had been rural stagnation, the great depression, a world war. The small, divided society had coped. It might be unfair, bizarre, eccentric, directed by limited provincials, ignored by London and by

Dublin; but the province trundled along as best it could. Remarkably, the people, rich and poor, rural and urban, both traditions, loved their corner of the island, the best wee country.

To rule that wee country, the Stormont system, the Orange state, had been created amid violence and Protestant fears of betrayal by concessions to Dublin granted by the government in London. Anguish, fear, desperation, and anger hardly led to a model of toleration and goodwill as government. What the loyalists wanted once they were Unionists was a provincial devolved government that protected their interests, their families and future, their traditions and property, their own and if need be, and it often was, at the expense of the minority Catholics. The Unionists felt power could not be shared nor allotted by a federal system or special voting arrangements, for power ceded would somehow be used against the majority. There was fear that any concession would lead to surrender.

It was accepted, if often unstated, by the Unionists that the ultimate control of the planned Orange state lay in London, where a harassed and uncertain postwar cabinet might opt for conciliation or might simply neglect or ignore safeguards desperately needed to protect the faithful on the frontier of the Roman Catholic state in the other twenty-six counties. What was needed and what was sought and achieved was local dominance that assured a sound defense if London let well enough alone. The Unionists proceeded to structure a provincial government that would govern the province, see to the roads and rates, encourage agriculture and manufacture, fund schools and hospitals, regulate the use of intoxicating liquor, and above all maintain the British way. Division on all the other matters— economic differences, social priorities, conventional political agendas—usually had to be foregone to assure this defense. And this defense of the division was extended to all other matters.

In theory the system was for all—all the loyal—whatever their persuasion. The fact was, according to Sir Basil Brooke, that even a Catholic newspaper had identified Catholics as 100 percent nationalists. They all wanted the destruction of Ulster. Loyal Catholics could be treated loyally, if found. But the disloyal man—plotting to destroy the country—would not be tolerated. Since all Catholics were nationalists and all nationalists disloyal then the founders and directors of the Province of Northern Ireland had to depend solely upon their own, fashion a Protestant state for a Protestant people, a loyalist state for loyalists. And so they did.

The provincial government that moved to the great marble hulk at Stormont, where on November 16, 1932, the Prince of Wales opened the parliament, was an elaborate device for so small a country. The six counties extended over 5,237 square miles and in the 1926 census had 1,256,561 inhabitants scattered over northeast Ireland. There was as well as the big parliament at Stormont an excess of local councils. Ulster would be an overgoverned province, dependent on limited and parochial talent, a dull, conservative, unsophisticated, plain province novel only because of its recourse to authoritarian measures and sectarian purpose. Many able and sincere civil servants would serve it well, many decent men would hold office, most would find reasoned explanation for the inequities: After all, Ireland was different.

The Stormont parliament of two chambers was first elected by proportional representation. That was ended for the May 1929 election in order to eliminate the prospect of seats for the Independent Unionists and the Labour Party and so to establish a clear Unionist majority and Nationalist minority. The Unionists wanted no seats lost, even to other Protestants. The Protestants must be politically united and absolutely in control of all provincial power. Not only did the established, constitutional forms of the province have to be crafted to maintain the Union; but also the players—the parties and organizations and groups—had to be kept in proper place, in line, inside the tent. Consequently, the parliament was structured as an arena for the Unionist Party to legislate what the loyal within and without the bureaucracy had deemed necessary and expedient. The opposition, the Nationalists, were there not to oppose, not even to play a small role, but merely on toleration of the majority. They only attended in order to guarantee funds for Catholic schools, were not a real opposition. They could not be a loyal opposition if they were not loyal and if they were they would be Unionists and all Unionists were Protestants and all Catholics were Nationalists and so disloyal and around the circle went. In fifty years, one piece of Nationalist legislation—an act on wild birds—became Northern Irish law.

The danger was not the maneuvers of the minority within the Stormont system—they were kept out even while they were inside Stormont—but the wildly divisive needs of the loyal—those who might be tempted by their economic interests or their fundamentalist religious views or by simple ambition to desert the Unionist Party. Real politics, then, took place outside Stormont, within the Unionist Party, where interests were balanced and differences compromised or fudged. And with the Unionist Party, the interests of those most skilled, the rich, the wellborn, and the finely educated dominated. They manipulated the less capable, used mirrors and wires and arrogance to maintain control of the majority, wrote the agenda, made the laws, received just compensation and saw the crumbs properly allocated. One-party rule functioned because of the perceived threat of the nationalists, the long history of threat and response that made traditional political gain less important. No issue was worth the risk of division that would permit or encourage nationalist advantage and the beginning of the end. Thus the parliament and the local councils were not as much units of governance as the outward forms and internal rewards of the Unionist Party's decisions.

In a tiny state with a three-to-two Protestant majority, control by simple election based on fair representation would seemingly produce no real problem nor any desperate need for institutionalized injustice. A little patronage might be lost but considerable legitimacy gained. Matters, however, were not so simple. All competitors in the democratic, political game are inclined to want more—landslides, huge majorities—and tiny, miserable, ineffectual opposition. The Christian Democrats want this in Italy, the Republicans in America, everyone from Alabama to Athens wants to win big. The Unionists were no different, especially since all such opposition from the nationalists was really treason, not just a political option. Secondly and most important, the nationalist Catholics were unevenly dispersed, assuring them plague spots of local Nationalist Party domination if all were fairly done. Fair as fair would have given the Nationalists control of certain local councils, where untold damage might be done to the stability of the province. There was an east-west religious division in Ulster with

71 percent of the east being Protestant and 60 percent of the west being Catholic. And even in Protestant-dominated areas like Belfast, there was, in West Belfast, a solid and major Catholic district. To further complicate matters, some of the nationalist local majorities were in symbolic loyalist areas. This was especially true in Londonderry. There on the Foyle in 1689 the Protestant faithful, loyal to William and Mary, had held out in the besieged town against the Catholic forces of James II. The siege was a legend for there the Apprentice Boys had shut the gate on the Catholic advance, there the traitor Lundy had sought to sell out the loyal, and there the suffering Protestants had persisted and won and bested the papists. This was Londonderry.

The city had been founded by London speculators, who sought a Protestant bridgehead in the Irish turmoil. It was always a historic loyalist city, a shrine. In a Northern Ireland this symbol was endangered in any local election by a two-to-one Catholic majority. This majority might be eroded over time by limiting housing for the nationalists, restricting jobs for them, making Derry life difficult. But something was needed more quickly. The solution was twofold: reduce the number of Catholic votes by a restricted franchise that also rewarded Protestants, and gerrymander the three election districts to waste the Catholic majority by concentrating it in one. From time to time fine-tuning was necessary, but in 1966 the Londonderry strategy still worked after forty years. It kept the symbol in Protestant hands and inevitably was an affront to democratic purpose if a triumph of loyalist logic. In Derry, by adjusting the suffrage to advantage, the Unionists gave no sign of moderation as the decades passed; rather, refinement instead of reform remained the rule. Time had no effect on loyalist assumptions— there was no New Ireland visible in Derry. In 1966 the adult population was 30,826: 20,102 Catholics and 10,724 Protestants. First, restricted suffrage for local urban—corporation—elections reduced the Catholic majority to 14,429 against 8,781 Protestant. Second, the city was not craftily but blatantly divided into three wards to secure a Unionist majority.

South Ward	North Ward	Waterside Ward
11,185 voters	6,467 voters	5,549 voters
10,047 Catholics	2,530 Catholics	1,852 Catholics
1,138 Protestants	3,946 Protestants	3,697 Protestants
8 Nationalist coun- cillors	8 Unionist coun- cillors	4 Unionists coun- cillors

The system was to be found many places except the massively Catholic towns of Newry and Strabane, and the system once imposed was beyond challenge; in fact, so irrelevant was any challenge that most seats went uncontested. In 1955, 96 percent of rural council, 94 percent of county council, and 60 percent of urban and borough council contests were not fought. Pools of potential Nationalist voters were thus gerrymandered into irrelevance.

A restricted franchise for local election of rate payers—those who paid suffi-cient taxes—and wives was further limited in a 1946 "reform" that removed lodgers, a tactic to reduce the potential number of Independent Unionists and Labour voters as much as Nationalists. There was as well extended suffrage, multiple voting for those likely to belong to the system by giving company directors up to six extra votes. Not surprisingly, Catholics were rare in the ranks of company directors. Once the Irish question had been "settled" with the triumph of the Free State over the IRA irregulars in 1923 and Dublin's subsequent and hasty acceptance of the finding of the Boundary Commission that left the six counties as the Province of Northern Ireland, London showed almost no interest in island events. In the House of Commons all queries were turned aside by the Speaker as not relevant to business. The bureaucracy at Whitehall buried Irish matters within the Home office. Seemingly as long as there was apparent quiet, the Unionists had a free hand.

The Unionists were all too aware that the traditional alternative left to their system of domination was conspiracy or violence. Democratic opposition by Catholics remained halting and uncertain, always on the edge of abstention. The old United Irish League under Joe Devlin was formally restructured in Saint Mary's Hall, Belfast, on May 28, 1928, as the national League of the North; but the new party had a minimal impact on events and found no Unionist toleration despite the party's inherent conservatism and willingness to play a Stormont role as opposition. The Unionists felt no need for a token Catholic acceptance. They focused, rather, on Protestant defections either to the Labour Party and the Left or to often momentary coalitions around issues and symbols that were of fundamentalist Christian concern. The political danger for the Unionists, often Anglican landed gentry, would be a failure to subsume class and caste interests—particularly those of populist Protestantism, often evangelical poor—within the party of defense. The few nationalists around Joe Devlin were no threat and not even worth co-opting with parliamentary courtesy or patronage scraps; but there always lurked the threat of subversion, even armed subversion, by the minority. Burning houses, assassinations, gunfire in the streets, murder from the ditch were not faint historical precedents, but accurate descriptions of a recent reality that had shaken the North during the Tan War and after.

The Irish republicans, emboldened by their success in the South, had most assuredly not put the gun on the shelf. Their secret army was known to drill out of sight, and their Army Council's statement was read at Easter. The real system, Unionist domination, required real protection beyond the jury-rigged of a democratic establishment. That Stormont system monopolized conventional politics and patronage, denying them to the minority; it could not monopolize the gun.

On April 22, 1922, the Civil Authorities (Special Powers) Act was passed by the new parliament, followed on May 31 by the Constabulary Act. The first indicated the powers of the state in defense and the second established the police means to ensure that defense. The special powers enumerated were the most extensive of any democratic state, permitting the government to ignore almost all legal restraint so dearly accumulated by centuries of struggle and practice. In order to defend democratic government the government was given the power to destroy it. In effect the Minister of Home Affairs could do nearly as he pleased according to the very first sentence that was thereafter elaborated in detailed powers:

The Civil Authority shall have power in respect of persons, matters and things within the jurisdiction of the Government of Northern Ireland to take all such steps and issue all such orders as may be necessary for preserving the peace and maintaining order.

There was a death penalty for a variety of offenses, flogging for others—this in 1922—and the almost total limitation on a suspect's rights at the minister's pleasure.

Arrests could be made without warrant, inquests prohibited, and individuals interned solely on signature, without reason or appeal. Men could be put away for years as a result of a stamped form, a name scrawled on the dotted line, and the authorized signature. And if the whole range of police powers given to the minister or his delegates proved for some reason insufficient, a final provision had been included:

If any person does any act of such a nature as to be calculated to be prejudicial to the preservation of the peace or maintenance of order in Northern Ireland and not specifically provided for in the regulations, he shall be deemed to be guilty of an offense against the regulations.

The bill allowed the Minister of Home Affairs or his delegate to do as they saw fit. It was so extreme that in April 1963, during his introduction of a new Coercion Bill in the South African parliament, the South African Minister for Justice B. Johannes Vorster (no civil libertarian) noted that "he would be willing to exchange all the legislation of that sort for one clause of the Northern Ireland Special Powers Act." Not that in Unionist eyes the act was ideal. As in the case of suffrage, refinement was made: The Public Order Act was passed in 1951 and renewed in 1969; the Flags and Emblems Act was enacted in 1954. These further strengthened Stormont's powers and limited nationalist expression.

There were as well all the residues of the past to scavenge if present need was discovered: A group of IRA men arrested in Belfast on April 25, 1936, were tried under the Treason Felony Act of 1848 for they "together with divers other evil disposed persons, feloniously and wickedly did compass, imagine, invent, devise and intend to deprive and despose Our Lord the King from the style, honour and royal name of the Imperial Crown of Great Britain, Ireland, and of the British Dominions beyond the Seas. . . ." Again the Unionists felt no need to explain: The IRA did exist, sought to destroy the United Kingdom, and had long been involved in treason. Certainly the Irish government in Dublin had equally draconian security laws—laws first used against Irish republican militants and then used by republicans who, once co-opted by the system, doubly detested those who remained pure in heart and unrepentant. None in the Republic was more bitter, more eager to punish, more outraged at provocation, than former republicans faced by their own. In the North the reality of the IRA, always the enemy, made internment, curfews, censorship, banning organizations, and withdrawing rights seem conventional. The laws and the courts that oversaw their implementation had been shaped to defend the new system. The judge might be learned and fair, but he was also Protestant, except for the odd token Catholic, and an agent of the Crown.

Most necessary of all was the system so empowered: the police, the courts, and the prisons. During the Troubles the police, the Royal Irish Constabulary and then the RUC, by history and by necessity a paramilitary force, had been supported by three groups of auxiliaries: The A Specials, 3,553 full-time constables disbanded after the boundary settlement had ended the threat of a confrontation with the new Dublin government; the B Specials, a provincewide Protestant militia that was particularly effective in the countryside during any emergency; and the part-time C Specials, disbanded in 1935 as the North moved toward normalcy. The B Specials, down to 8,500 in 1968, remained on call until disbanded in 1969. The core of the police was the RUC, established in 1922, with a membership of three thousand, with one-third Catholics to allow transfers from the old RIC. Only four hundred Catholics chose to remain and their number eroded over the years although a certain number could be found up until 1969, when everything changed. The RUC by necessity was sectarian, an instrument of the majority, not an everyday police force at all.

The police were increasingly a well-trained, well-armed, highly motivated Protestant force, but one that sought to be fair—all criminals being equal game if the IRA remained all Catholic. The B Specials had been shaped to defend against the IRA and made no pretenses at being fair: They were a Protestant militia to defend the Protestant system. The Hunt Committee on the Reorganization of the Police in Northern Ireland noted in 1969 that "while there is no law or official rule that precludes any person, whatever his religion, from joining the Ulster Special Constabulary the fact remains that, for a variety of reasons, no Roman Catholic is a member." During the Tan War and beyond, the Specials roamed their districts at night under arms, harassing, threatening, burning homes, and at times killing suspect Catholics and imposing British order by terror. After the end of the Troubles, the neighbor down the lane as B Special could be intimidating and arrogant at the roadblock, if not violent and lethal, just as a return to civility occurred in town the next day. Thus, the B Specials were one of the province fault lines between private toleration and public arrogance. The RUC men might be less crude but stood as armed symbol as well as competent police, the system's armed force complete with military structure, automatic weapons, armored cars, and machine guns. They could be approached normally by Catholics in matters of crime—unlike the B Specials—and yet were seen as institutionalized enemy at the same time. There they stood in couples on the corner in their peaked caps and long, dark green overcoats, guns shouldered at ease, a presence not at all like one expected in a British provincial city.

There was, in fact, no real point in pretending that Northern Ireland, increasingly Ulster in Unionist usage, was Kent or Sussex or that there was a role for unarmed Bobbies. Ulster might be British, but it required very different policing methods to go with the laws. The laws were interpreted by a largely Protestant judiciary that sent the convicted to prisons run by Protestants. The end of the security system that began with Special Branch detectives ended in a prison cell. Thus, the prisons were in loyal hands. Warder, clerical staff, civil servants, and governors were all Unionists, a few token Catholics but mostly all Protestants. The entire law enforcement—judicial system was a major defensive work thrown up and refined first to defend the Orange state and second to oversee law and order. Few Unionists saw any difference in the double tasking.

The rewards, as well as the responsibilities, of the province were also unevenly distributed. If at all possible the loyal were rewarded, if not materially, and this was often the case, then symbolically. And if neither was possible, then at least costs and damage were revealed to fall disproportionately on the others. There was no trouble about the system being "unfair," for treason need not be given free tea, vacations, or small comforts. The problem remained that there were not enough comforts to go around even for the loyal. No matter how the minority might be stinted, the best that often could be done was to humiliate them. Displayed domination had to do instead of decent housing, assured employment, and social benefits. For much of the history of Northern Ireland, the problems appeared beyond solution, beyond the competence of the locals, beyond even the capacity of London. It was a small province with limited talent. Without vision, with limited skills, traumatized by the turmoil of the Tan War and the Troubles, fearful of London's intentions, battered by the great undertows of the world depression, the government was hardly able to affect events locally. The government at Stormont was dull, dour, uninspiring, often bigoted by choice as well as circumstances. It struggled through the grim, dark twenties, through the depression interrupted by the sacrifices of the war and replaced by the Labour austerity that followed on the years of stagnation. Many good and competent people were involved in this long haul, talented and faithful civil servants, modest and thoughtful consultants and advisers, but the record of devolution was not a happy one. Yet the crucial complaint—penury—was not really related to bigotry or the divided society, only to the remedies proffered to ease the misery: Shame the minority with domination of the majority.

One of the most persistent factors present in the history of Northern Ireland from the beginning until the present was the great British disease, unemployment. There was no solution. Northern industry, a golden Victorian triumph that shaped Belfast and to a degree Londonderry, was founded on shipbuilding and linen, passing fancies as the twentieth century moved along. The wee yard Workman, Clark and Co. was swallowed by the larger Harland & Wolff, symbol of Belfast prosperity—for Belfast was once prosperous, especially relative to an impoverished Ireland. And with prosperity Belfast was arrogant. That arrogance and that prosperity did not survive World War I. And added to the difficulties of an aging plant and unfashionable manufacture, Northern Ireland was particular prey to the costs of the depression and to the price of the Dublin-London economic war as de Valera sought unsuccessfully to break the British connection and achieve local, economic independence by deploying local and ineffectual remedies. There were no advantages to being an isolated six of thirty-two counties often ignored even in Irish matters by the London cabinet. Although agriculture did well in the North, nothing else worked to advantage and so unemployment was endemic.

As the depression took its toll, the official numbers increased: 35,000 in 1929, 72,000 in 1930; 76,000 in 1932. Because there were more Protestants than Catholics there were more Protestants unemployed than Catholics—a sore and dangerous point for the Unionists. The percentage of unemployed was nearly everywhere and by any criterion higher than that of the Protestants, as was the number of their internal and external emigrants. A Catholic was more likely to be without a job and to travel to Britain or abroad to find one. The patronage of the local councils and the positions within the control of the provincial government were deployed to ease loyalist anxieties. Protestants thus had more jobs and stayed in the province to maintain the system. Except for token Catholics and a few prominent symbols, jobs always went to Protestants—loyalists. Sir Basil Brooke, he of the hard word and then Minister of Agriculture, assured the Derry Unionist Association in March 1934 that criticism of sectarian hiring was pointless. "I recommend those people whom are Loyalists not to employ Roman Catholics, 99 percent of whom are disloyal. . . .* He had already appealed to loyalists to employ good Protestants. And so his colleagues in government, in the bureaucracy, in the councils did. As late as 1969 only 13 Catholics were employed out of 209 in the technical and professional grades of the civil service, 23 out of 319 in the higher grades. No matter what disparity in qualification the numbers indicated real and continuing discrimination. Comparable figures could be found in almost all Protestant-controlled businesses from Harland & Wolff or Mackies down to the shop assistants and barmen. Brooke noted publicly that "he had not a Roman Catholic about his own place"; nor did many Protestants. The Catholics did the same, except the Catholics had few jobs to give their own, controlled few companies and fewer local councils. It was necessary, both felt, to take care of one's own especially. The Unionists felt that this was especially true in hard times— and the province had never had any other under Stormont—when the unwary loyalists might be attracted to the call of class. There had to be a defense against radical solutions proffered by those who felt socialism a cure to all the ills of the province and the kingdom as well. The Unionist establishment thus must reward its own when possible, cherish every job—no room for token gifts—as calculated response against both the nationalists and the radicals who might make an appeal across cultures. The ensuing resentment of the Catholics was if anything a net asset. Only briefly and haltingly did the radical seem a viable prospect in Belfast.

The class conversion of the Unionists never came. Dissent was as likely to focus on fundamentalist Christian aspirations or symbolic Orange issues, neither tinder for contemporary revolution, a revolution that found no takers in the Republic either. The island was religiously and socially conservative, suspicious of alien remedies, and seized on more popular political conflicts: The national issue mattered, not class. The result was that the government under Sir James Craig, Viscount Cragivon, trundled along, the numbers were awful, emigration high, income low. The Imperial Contribution, the province's tax to the center, so to speak, dribbled away to a mere ten thousand pounds by 1934–35. The figures on the costs of the province were always open to speculation but the common wisdom has been that Northern Ireland was a remittance state. Agriculture was not bad. Most other indicators were bad. Manufacture declined and no new industries developed. Employment was low and housing appalling. This was the worst problem of all.

*Michael Farrell, *Northern Ireland: The Orange State* (London: Pluto, 1983), pp. 90–91.

The construction of small council houses for the poor produced the greatest resentment. The state controlled houses for the poor. And the houses, like all else, went to Unionists. Many Catholics felt that if houses could not go to Protestants, they simply would not be built. Without a house the Catholics would go away, thus strengthening Unionist majorities. With a house the Catholics would stay and put the gerrymandered districts to threat. So there were few houses for Catholics. Between 1945 and 1967, 1,048 were built by local authorities in County Fermanagh, and 853, 82 percent, went to Protestants even though Catholics, who were poorer, needed them more. The minority did not get houses or jobs or votes or a congenial police or anything but few little dribble-down benefits, often through United Kingdom policies, not those of Stormont. They did not, because as Brooke said, "ninety-nine percent were disloyal."

The Catholics were really not so disloyal. Aspiration for a united Ireland had little founding in expectation. No one really expected much or worked for deliverance. The minority might not be "loyal" to the system as shaped by the Unionists, but they did not oppose it because they could not. Anyway, most people, most of the time, are not interested in politics, the getting and spending of power by others, but only in their immediate priorities, the welfare of the family, a job, a house, even a single luxury, and so a tomorrow not unlike yesterday. Most Catholics had made peace with a harsh reality that was not a special fabrication of Stormont, for much that happened in the province arose from distant economic problems beyond the reach of the Unionists and apparently of the cabinet in London. Certainly the inequities, discrimination, and intimidation arose from majority intentions but in a divided society much humiliation could be avoided, much discrimination blunted or ignored. Catholics, except in places in the country or along district edges, lived in segregated areas. These might be tiny but were homogeneous—one parish or a single tangle of city streets. In many districts, urban and rural, there was a separate Catholic world. There with Catholic schools and hospitals, nationalist clubs and sports, neighborhood associations and friendship, life could be lived without friction and almost without contact with the others. In the country and small towns isolation was more difficult but for serious matters the others were not touched; weather might be discussed but no more. Any intimacy that might have existed as children, and there was often little, disappeared with age, with different schooling, different churches, the pervasive division of all aspects of society. Proximity did not breed familiarity but contempt or suspicion for the others in mass and ignorance of the individual.

The province revealed all sorts of patterns of division, degrees of discrimination and contact, but everywhere division. The big divisive issues of state—whether to limit investment to the area east of the Bann, the Protestant heartland, as the expense of the West, where the need was greater but where more Catholics lived or the details of state aid to the Mater Hospital—were left to the educated Catholics concerned with such matters. The everyday Catholic, sullen about housing, fearful of unemployment or already a victim, often humiliated by B Specials in the country and everywhere by the Orange marches during the summer season, simply accepted the reality of domination, a domination in a small corner of the island where a minority, through the power of the Crown, had remained besieged majority. There were two undiscussed factors that buttressed this reality. First the British, not simply the Ulster Protestants, assumed that the Irish—this usually meant all Irish in London and Catholics in Belfast—were innately inferior by culture if not by birth. In 1971 a majority study on race and intelligence by a British psychologist claimed that the Irish were an inherently and intellectually inferior racial group. No scholar would so publish until he knew the conclusions if not welcome would not be mocked. Many in Great Britain and Northern Ireland believed that the Catholic Irish were a group apart, lacking in intelligence, stupid, lazy, untamed, dirty, wild, inherently prone to violence and drink, requiring civilization.* Some in Britain would include all the Irish, but in Northern Ireland Irish meant Catholic. If Irish Catholics were lesser, then there was rationale for the Stormont system. Second, many, perhaps most, Catholics in Northern Ireland accepted that they *were inferior*. Whether this was by birth or not scarcely mattered; they had less education, less capital, poorer prospects, worse leaders, and none of the signs of success. They were inferior and felt so; if they were not loyal they were at least resigned to their fate.

The purpose of the Stormont system of ritual politics was to reinforce the two assumptions that made all else possible: The minority must acquiesce and the majority must assume domination as a right and responsibility made manifest in ritual. Much of the politics of the province was not about the distribution of power but about the allotting of prestige that often came without any other benefit.

The great Orange ritual came during the marching season, when various Masonic orders marched to commemorate past loyalist victories. The season culminated in the grand parades on July 12 in honor of Protestant King William's triumph over Catholic James II at the Battle of the Boyne in 1690. Then a good time was had by all, a good show given to all—even Catholics, said the decent and moderate. After all, many of the vendors were Catholics, as were at least a few of the spectators. What harm did it do to troop around Londonderry's walls and past Catholic neighborhoods in market towns? What real harm did a few drunken anti-papist songs do? It was merely exuberance and bad manners. The Catholics who watched the pennies thrown from Derry's walls skip and bounce into the mean streets of the Bogside might not agree, but then they did not count but as audience to arrogance. So the ritual parades went on, ignored if possible by the nationalists, tolerated by the elegant and powerful, beloved by the common folk as splendid spectacle in a dour year.

The men, one lodge after the other, came draped in elaborate Orange sashes— the one my father wore and the good Sunday suit topped by a bowler, symbol of the skilled prewar Belfast craftsman now co-opted as costume. Banners proclaimed loyalty and location and the chosen lodge hero. Huge, elaborate standards rippled in the wind, held aloft by straining clerks and farmers on holidays. And there were the bands, all accordion bands or fife-and-drum bands, and the huge

---

*A report by Séamus Taylor, a research and development officer with the Equality Unit of Haringey Council in London, indicated that the 1991 Irish stereotype in Britain had become in particular "the terrorist," and there was still ample evidence of a general British anti-Irish feeling. *Irish Times*, March 18, 1991.

Lambeg drums, and pipes and more fifes, all in tune after a year of practice with the same old songs, Orange hymns from a shared history. They marched on, and passed curbs painted red, white, and blue, passed Union Jacks and Ulster's flags waving from every window, passed giant murals of King Billy and the Siege of Londonderry, then their proud families and their kith and kin—all British and loyal—and passed as intended by the marshals, passed each and every year the shuttered, sealed, undecorated houses of the others, where there were no crowds, no cheers, no notice given, in some streets not even a dog let out in the front garden. It was, after all, their country so they could march where they chose. So there was something for everyone. The end came with the arrival of the field and the patriot oratory of redemption and renewal. It was a grand day, always a grand day, a moment in the sun, weather permitting, children exhausted, marchers footsore and the assembly ground scattered with candy wrappers and slumped celebrators and picnicking families. Old men met their friends, old soldiers, not many from the Somme anymore but those from North Africa and even back from the British Army of the Rhine, young soldiers in toy costumes and teenage boys playing football or the fool for the girls. The instruments were in a heap covered by discarded lodge banners and at the edge of the green was a lone piper playing for himself. It hardly summoned up a real battlefield or represented harsh domination—or so said those of goodwill.

The Catholics knew the meaning behind the exercise. The great drums beat out defiance and domination, drowned out any dialogue, summoned the faithful to one more annual victory over the traitors at the gate. The drums, the banners, the bowlers, the flags, were props in ritual politics. This was the outward and visible face of the Orange system: defiant, sectarian, closed, violent if crossed, ever on guard of conspiracy, sensitive to criticism but immune to conciliation. It was a system founded on historical grievance, possessed of the truth, fed on an inherent superiority threatened by pure numbers of the island's Catholics. The leaders could not offer the usual returns of a modern state and so had recourse to more visceral and more addictive awards. The system had transformed secondary benefits into primary.

To counter the Orange system centered in Stormont, a system displayed during the marching season as symbol and the rest of the year as mean and petty discrimination, the Catholics, almost all nationalists, had no conventional recourse. The Protestants were, of course, rarely receiving conventional rewards, jobs, decent housing, higher welfare payments, access to dental care; but they constantly had recourse to symbolic benefits. The Catholic recourse, too, was to unreal politics, mostly republican dreams and in a few cases Marxist-Leninist analysis, equally unrealistic; but mostly their dreams were expressed in an affection for the symbols and rituals of an Irish nationalism too distant to require sacrifice, too impotent to inspire hope, too real to forget—a short drive would allow a letter to be posted in a green pillar box with a stamp bearing portraits of the 1916 heroes. For practical politics their only hope appeared to be an appeal beyond the Orange system to London. In Commons a few Labour MPs had listened to Gerry Fitt's complaints about the denial of civil liberties. There were few converts to Irish matters like Paul Rose and Jack Stallard. Kevin McNamara had Irish roots and needed no conversion. Interest increased once Fitt, on March

31, 1966, won a seat in the general election in West Belfast from James Kilfedder—the other eleven seats went to Unionists.

Until Fitt's win in West Belfast nationalist politics of protest had been very local, hardly visible. In 1963 the Homeless Citizens League had been set up to call attention to the housing problem. Stormont paid no attention. On January 17, 1964, Conn and Patricia McCluskey founded their Campaign for Social Justice (CSJ) in Dungannon "to collect data on all injustices done against all creeds and political opinions." It was a Catholic front group for decency dominated by a few middle-class people who were preparing if all else failed, as was likely, to present a grievance-case to the Commission for Human Rights at Strasbourg and to the United Nations. No one paid any attention.

Conventional provincial politics had no interest in minority grievance, real or imagined, detailed at Stormont or sent to London. All the big moves had, as always, favored hard-core Protestant attitudes. The report on urban growth had proposed the linkup of Portadown and Lurgan as a necessary new city—a new city to the east of the Bann, a new city of Protestants that would invigorate not provincial growth but Orange advantage. The great Catholic push had been made to secure the second university for Derry. The arguments were seemingly obvious and overwhelming and until almost the end supported by Londonderry Unionists, who had much to gain. In 1965 the Lockwood report despite all the Londonderry logic urged Coleraine as the site, a site in the Protestant heartland rather than in vulnerable Londonderry, desperately poor and undeveloped Londonderry far to the west on the border with the Republic, a Protestant symbol but a Catholic city. So Catholic provincial politics had not worked out well. Fitt would instead attempt to take the nationalist grievances to Westminster and use the traditional road of parliamentary protest, making friends, influencing people, working from the bottom of the Labour party up. In Northern Ireland the CSJ would seek publicity and support in an international arena and thus work outside the conventional politics that had failed with the new city and the Derry university. Hardly anyone paid any attention.

The failure of politics was not altogether a failure of Unionist vision, for the Catholics, like the Protestants, were forced into symbolic displays, one remove from apparent power. Most of the Catholics' organizations, like the Ancient Order of Hibernians, were poor copies. The AOH had none of the attractions of the Protestant Masonic orders—*their* parades were real ritual not copies any more than the Dublin Saint Patrick's Day parade was the equal of New York's, one a Catholic diaspora display and the other a tatty clone. The rituals of protest in the North were largely republican, not the official comings and goings of the Dublin government's little ceremonies of remembrance or low-budget diplomatic display but the rites of a covert and secret army. The great march every June in County Kildare to Wolfe Tone's grave was, like the Orange Parade on July 12, the great formal occasion—one that promised recourse to physical force to achieve the real Republic that also ended with the faithful scattered on the grass with picnics and war banners furled. In the North the republican route was posted with signs commemorating the patriot dead—Easter being the great holiday. In violent times the great ritual was the IRA funeral with the illegal shots fired over the coffin draped in tricolor by an illegal section of the IRA. Since conventional politics had died inside Stormont, for the republicans, for many nationalists, politics was recourse to commemoration that transformed the dead into martyrs and promised those who would bar the march of a nation that the gun still had a part to play in Irish politics. Once the IRA campaign had ended in 1962, symbolic republican politics became nearly as futile as petitions or polling.

In fact, to observers, it seemed that the politics of protest was largely within the loyalist community. The militant Unionists had been concerned about O'Neill's staying power almost since he was chosen—rumors of plots were a constant by those who doubted his cunning and steel. More distressing to the hard men in and out of Stormont, Craig and those on the back benches, Ian Paisley in his Free Presbyterian pulpit or the pages of his new *Protestant Telegraph,* first published in April 1966, knew that just beyond politics waited the mob. Fear of a Catholic rising was the ultimate weapon in the Orange armory. It was the legitimacy of even illicit force as a means of Orange defense that had worried the civil rights people in NICRA. So many thought Coughlan's articles were ill-advised, that they might provoke loyalist violence.

During the general election campaign in September 1964, Ian Paisley had emerged as an Orange spokesman as well as Protestant divine when he made an issue of an Irish tricolor flown at Republican Labour headquarters on Divis Street. He demanded it be removed or he and his would do so. The RUC tried to remove the flag despite the presence of a crowd of two thousand republican supporters. They broke into the office with pickaxes and took down the banner, emerging to three days of rioting, and this was even before Lemass and O'Neill met in January of the following year, 1965. Paisley held a mass to protest *that*. His protests, like the one in January 1966 in London at Westminster Abbey against the Church of England's proecumenical policies or the one in Rome in March 1966 over the visit of the Archbishop of Canterbury to the Pope, were often seen as fundamentalist displays mainly to gain personal attention—his Free Presbyterian Church was as far from Canterbury as the Pope. He had always had his eye on the media and so a Republican flag was as good as a Pope. Increasingly the political issue offered more opportunity—not that his distaste for Catholicism lessened. And so in February 1966 he warned that the fiftieth anniversary of the Easter Rebellion in April would bring subversive demonstration. All that happened was a splinter republican group blew off the top of Nelson Pillar in O'Connell Street in Dublin on March 7, 1966, on the second attempt, using American money and local talent. This was nothing novel in Belfast. No matter, on March 1, 1966, Paisley spoke at a rally of the newly formed Ulster Protestant Volunteers (UPV). All of this visible militancy at a moment that moderation seemed on the rise inhibited nationalist ambitions. Stormont was closed. Fitt was isolated in Westminster. The Orange militants were again emerging from the shadows.

After the passing of the republican marching season in April, on May 21, 1966, a public statement from the unknown Ulster Volunteer Force stated that "from this day on we declare war against the IRA and its splinter groups." The response was not so much to any IRA activity—there was none—but to the O'Neill-Lemass meetings. Betrayal from within was as great a fear of the Orange mind as a frontal attack. On May 27 John Scullion, a Catholic, was stabbed as he walked along the Falls Roads. The attackers escaped by car. On June 11 Scullion died in a hospital, the second political death of the year; an elderly Protestant lady, Mrs. Martha Gould, had died of injuries caused by a petrol bomb tossed at a Catholic-owned pub in Belfast on May 7. The bomb missed and landed on her porch next door. It was labeled a wanton but individual act. Scullion's stabbing seemed more ominous. Then on June 26 four Catholic barmen were walking home after work down Malvern Street of the Shankill Road in Belfast. Gusty Spence, leader of the UVF, and the others had started out to kill the well-known republican Leo Martin but could not find him. Returning home disappointed and frustrated, they discovered the four barmen walking home—any Catholic would do—and so they opened fire. Two were injured and Peter Ward, eighteen, was shot dead. It was a blatant and seemingly unnecessary act. The police acted swiftly.

On the night of June 27–28 five Protestants, including Gusty Spence, were arrested. Two were charged with the murder of Peter Ward and three with the death of John Scullion. They were tried and convicted. Minister of Home Affairs Brian McConnell under the Special Powers Act banned the UVF, which had existed mainly in the mind of Spence and his friends. In Stormont, O'Neill then attacked Paisley for thanking the UVF for their support and called the organization "this evil thing in our midst." The Prime Minister, the Unionists, the RUC felt no need for self-appointed UVF defenders. It was, of course, not the system's fault, for in Stormont in December O'Neill during the debate on the Queen's speech blamed the tensions of the Easter commemorations that "flaunted before our people the emblems of a cause which the majority of us abhor." He also, "on the other hand," criticized those self-appointed defenders who "see moderation as treason and decency as weakness."

These defenders were elusive especially in 1966–67. The contacts were informal, individuals met with similar disasters and prejudices, a collection of the like-minded and bloody-minded who had to meet. In 1966 Noel Doherty, a printer and a B Special, an Orange man, a hard man, had suggested both the Ulster Constitutional Defense Committee and the Ulster Protestant Volunteers as good people to his friend Paisley. Paisley approved of militancy but would not advocate violence. On March 1 he had appeared at the UPV rally but no more. So Doherty simply put the Shankill people labeled, rather than organized as the Ulster Volunteer Force, into touch with others so inclined at Loughgall who were members there of the Ulster Protestant Volunteers. The men in the country had explosives and those on the Shankill had targets. Both sets, as would almost all future Protestant paramilitaries, felt a need to react to provocation. The provocation, just as in the O'Neill-Lemass meeting, might be beyond reach but local Catholics never were. In any case matters in 1966 went no further. Doherty and his friends in Loughgall were arrested during the Malvern Street murder round-ups. Two received sentences for possession of firearms and Doherty was given a two-year sentence. The Ulster Protestant Volunteers disappeared. The UVF as an organization disappeared as well, but the name was too redolent, too powerful to discard entirely. For the moment the paramilitaries were removed from the board, but the killings had been evidence that primitive responses were still just under the surface of moderation and decency.

This latent anger and resentment had slowed the nationalists' search for an alternative avenue to affect events. Fitt was making slow if real progress at

Westminster. The Nationalist Party was shut out of Stormont politics and the politics of petition lacked drama and probably realism. The idea that the aggrieved might follow the American example of nonviolence had evolved from the Wolfe Tone Society, Coughlan's articles, and the Maghera meeting in August 1966 and so culminated in a meeting on November 28, 1966, in Belfast with John D. Stewart as chairman. Kadar Asmal, an Indian exile from South Africa teaching at Trinity College Dublin and intimate with the problems of entrenched injustice, was speaker. After the meeting the organizers decided to go ahead and launch the formal Northern Ireland Civil Rights Association the next year. So at the International Hotel in Belfast on January 29, 1967, NICRA brought together all active dissent: Kevin Agnew, Betty Sinclair, Joe Sherry of the Republican Labour Party, Conn McCluskey from CSJ, Paddy Devlin of the Northern Ireland Labour Party, a few unattached radicals, someone from Queen's, a Liberal, and other republicans. Tony Smythe from the British National Council of Civil Liberties was present as observer, in effect representing Fitt's friends in Westminster. The NICRA that emerged was dominated by the cautious, not the least the republicans, united only in a desire to go beyond witness, to do something.

This is why Craig's ban on the Republican Clubs proved so tempting. Something—an act of civil disobedience—could be done out of sight off Divis Street that would not unleash the Belfast Orange mob but would—well, might— attract attention in the right quarters, in London. So the meeting was held and Mitchell arrested and released, the Queen's University students marched to Craig's house and back, and Tony Smythe went home to London with his firsthand report. And nothing else happened. There were no more UVF killings, nothing was left but the nostalgia of the name. Cahal Goulding at Bodenstown in June played down physical force, to be used only when "demanded and supported by the people." The Queen came to Ulster in July and a woman threw a bottle at the royal limousine as it was driven through Donegall Square in Belfast, and in Great Victoria Street a brick was dropped from a building under construction and hit the hood. Perhaps a mistake, perhaps not. In October Roy Johnston urged a civil rights movement that involved both Catholics and Protestants—no future in the province for civil liberties for republicans. On December 11 the new Irish Taoiseach, Jack Lynch, met with O'Neill, and the ubiquitous Ian Paisley helped pelt his limousine with snowballs near the statue of Lord Carson while his Protestant clergymen supporters yelled, "Keep Ulster Protestant!" It was a distinct improvement over the brick on the hood of the Queen's limousine not to mention the UVF murders of 1966, a touch of farce in a province most serious.

Nothing else happened. For a year nothing changed. On Monday, March 25, O'Neill reviewed his five years of office hoping for further improvements in community relations "to remove the balance of hatred which is hereditary to us all." He felt sure that the Catholics appreciated the improvements of the last five years. Most of the improvement consisted of O'Neill performing a few visible rites of moderation—a visit to a Catholic school and enthusiasm for investment and industrial technology—and keeping a civil tongue. Nationalist leader Eddie McAteer of Derry sourly noted that nothing had been done but talk. The Catholics felt no gratitude. Talk had done them no visible good. The Protestants of Paisley's ilk felt that there had been too much talk. On December 12, 1967, a national opinion poll noted that 90 percent of the province would choose O'Neill as leader over Paisley, so Orange agitators did not seem to have many takers at the end of 1967; but then neither did any reforms in the system: Fifty-two percent opposed legislation against discrimination and 50 percent opposed new legislation on housing. The majority wanted no change.

The Unionists' Minister of Home Affairs in April banned both a loyalist parade and a republican parade in Armagh—evenhanded repression. The republicans marched anyway. NICRA held a meeting to protest the bans. A week later NICRA held another rally to protest the government's ban on Republican Clubs the previous year. This appeared much ado about matters of interest only to the involved; but the militant loyalists responded to the NICRA-republican provocative maneuvers traditionally. On the way back from a meeting of the Woodvale Unionist Association at Craven Street Hall in Belfast, O'Neill's car was the target of a volley of stones, eggs, and flour. The disloyal were acting as expected, but the Unionist Prime Minister was not. Still no one cared. And no one cared to remember the Malvern Street murderers now safely in Crumlin Road Prison. In London the new Labour Home Secretary listened to Paul Rose on the province but promised nothing. Ulster was not on Labour's agenda, not even on Dublin's wish list. O'Neill thus felt no urgency.

Historically reform of a static and discriminatory system engenders the most serious problems, inspires a rising demand for change far beyond the capacities of the system to grant, far beyond the toleration of the threatened to contemplate, especially if such concessions come out of their bit of the pie. Incremental improvement is spurned by the eager and opposed by the entrenched, who are reluctant to start such a process of erosion. What is needed is a determined and dedicated constituency, and this O'Neill did not have. What was wanted was a leader both cunning and adamant, one lucky as well as charismatic, and this O'Neill was not. He was exactly what he seemed, a decent man who felt a few words had moved mountains of bigotry. He lacked any real empathy for the minority and brought to bear on the problem of reform most modest political talents. He could not reason with his own nor offer acceptable symbols as part payment to the minority. And real reforms not only would be in some cases at majority cost but not to his own political advantage: The more he took from the majority, the more the minority would want—and when they received O'Neill would not. He was not taking from Peter to pay Paul, he was dismantling the temple that sheltered him. And the Unionist temple also sheltered those who did not want repairs on the roof even discussed, much less the roof removed to be put on someone else's chapel.

Paisley sensed this crucial weakness not just in O'Neill's position but the Unionist establishment's position: Any reform was suicide on the installment plan. And O'Neill's colleagues, less astute, sensed a weakness in the Prime Minister's political base, a critical flaw for any politician, in that he could not sustain a majority for the reforms. That there might be reforms with a Labour government in London could not be ignored by O'Neill, but those Unionists and Paisley were out of power, lacked responsibility, and so could allow ambition free play. There was thus little room for O'Neill to maneuver had he been so inclined, had he felt any urgency, had he read the backbenchers properly, taken Paisley seriously, sensed the resentment of the minority. Like most politicians, however, he had short views and a handy stock of genial aspirations as policy.

In Stormont, Austin Currie, a Nationalist MP from East Tyrone, raised the question of unfair housing allocations with a specific case to hand. O'Neill felt no need to transform the Catholic claim of discrimination into a useful cause to push fairer means of allocation housing. He in fact had so far never felt the need to transform wishful thinking about a better day into specific law. So the system did not, would not, compromise. John Taylor of the Unionist hardliners, who had lost patience with O'Neill, scathingly attacked Currie and defended the local Dungannon Rural District Council dominated by his own strong, uncompromising Unionists. If a beginning were to be made on reform, Currie had a good case. O'Neill let Taylor do the running. Currie was outraged by Taylor's defense, threw his notes at the Unionists. The Speaker ordered Currie to leave the House for improper conduct. Within Stormont there seemed no possibility of concession. And Taylor would get the credit for the defense and O'Neill the blame for creating conditions that made one necessary. Currie was a natural parliamentary type, ambitious for power gained through elected office in a system that presented no such career option. For him, for the Nationalists, despite all the talk, all O'Neill's meetings, pirouettes, and press releases, there seemed no hope in Stormont, merely a forum for Unionist display and a means to allocate Unionist patronage. It was not a parliament at all. And for the Unionists there should be none. There would be no change: not an inch nor a council house nor a kind word. Nothing. There was no more history to be made, nothing more to say. There was no place even to say no that was not owned by the establishment or protected by the hard men. And someone had to find a way to say no without provoking carnage, only a tide toward reform. The system would not take no. The future was as the past, just emerging but no different.

2

Confrontation, the Long March Begins: January 1968–March 1969

No man has the right to fix the boundary of the march of a nation.
Charles Stewart Parnell

The march of the human mind is slow.
Edmund Burke

One of the most painful aspects of systemic discrimination in Northern Ireland has always been the allotment of housing. The single most fearful scourge—unemployment—could in part be seen as a general ill, imposed by international conditions and alleviated by like helping like through sectarian hiring. It was unfair for the Protestant state to favor their own unemployed, but somehow tolerable. In the matter of council-built housing, however, all not only were not equal, but also painfully not equal when it came to houses, all assigned by the Unionists. These were assigned seemingly solely to reward the faith, to maintain the majority and punish the minority. Need did not matter. Catholic need was simply denied. Protestants were moved to the head of the list; Protestants took precedent over large Catholic families living in a hovel. Each house so allotted to the undeserving created frustration and anger in the denied. With a house one could live decently even without a job and without prospects.

Nothing much could be done about unemployment. There were, percentages aside, more unemployed Protestants than unemployed Catholics. Nothing much could be done about the implications of a Protestant state for a Protestant people. Those in power had too much power and those not in power had none. Politics was politics, the winners took all. Something, however, should be done to house the desperate whose only hope of shelter was public building. No matter what the rationale of the system, no matter what the charts and graphs said, no matter how many Protestants were poorly housed, the Catholic poor felt that they were imprisoned in miserable terrace houses without sufficient room, without plumbing—dank, cold, dark, tiny hutches for huge families. In the urban ghettos, the Bogside under the Derry walls or off the Falls in Belfast, there were row after row of structured misery, nasty dwellings even when built. Reform had taken the shape of monstrous bunkers of high-rise flats in the midst of the city. Unity Flats and Divis Flats were huge, cold piles at the mercy of hooligans, disasters as social planning imported from British bad examples that generated delinquency and ruined lives. In the country, matters were often worse, if not as visible. Whatever the radicals might propose on civil rights, it was jobs and housing that mattered. And if nothing much could be done about jobs, something should be done about housing. Thus, two years before the first civil rights organization, the Campaign for Social Justice, had been founded in Dungannon, the Homeless Citizens League had started up over houses.

Even as the NICRA people were contemplating more militant action in March 1968, the Derry Housing Action Committee had been announced. Then in Caledon, County Tyrone, the local Republican Club was urging Catholics to squat in newly built council houses that would otherwise be allotted to Protestants. The people squatted. In June 1968 the people were evicted, as expected. But something had to be done by someone. In 1968 the Nationalist MP Austin Currie took up the cause of his Tyrone constituents in their complaints against the Unionist Dungannon Rural Council. At Stormont, where Nationalists had traditionally simply been ignored and so acted less as an opposition than as a Celtic chorus of grievance, Currie had been expelled. He was still outraged: But there the matter would undoubtedly end—or so the Unionists and the Tyrone people assumed. There matters had always ended. Times, however, had changed just that little bit.

Currie felt that the injustice was too egregious. Miss Emily Beattie, a single girl of nineteen, secretary to the solicitor to the council in Armagh, was to have a house, instead of a needy Catholic family, instead of a "priority tenant." It was blatantly unfair: A whole family was to continue to be miserably housed while one wee, well-connected girl had a whole house. It was the way things had always been done. But on June 20, 1968, Currie took possession of the house at Caledon—a sit-in in defiance of the law. The law arrived in the form of the RUC, including the constable brother of Miss Beattie, and removed Currie and the others. On July 5 there was a sit-down on the bridge in Derry by 150 members and friends of the Derry Housing Action Committee. Seventeen people were arrested and two elected to go to prison rather than be bound over to keep the peace. During the summer of 1968 there was a slowly increasing number of militants, often out of touch with one another, who felt there should no longer be peace unless there was justice too. Most people paid little attention—Currie's sit-in was a nine-day wonder, the Derry Housing Action Committee was the momentary enthusiasm of young local radicals, the NICRA efforts were proper, decent, but futile of course. No matter—the Campaign for Social Justice decided on a march from Coalisland to Dungannon to protest the housing allocations, to renew interest in the problem, to act instead of just complaining. It would be the first civil rights march and all the like-minded were invited. NICRA accepted.

The march was scheduled to begin at six o'clock in the evening on August 24, and the organizers soon discovered the draw was more attractive than anticipated. No one ever expects a public event to begin on time in Ireland, and few do, but on that sunny evening the start point was jammed long before time. Not only did most of Coalisland, a strong republican town, appear, but so did nearly twice as many potential marchers as expected. When the parade finally began at seven o'clock there were 2,500 people, a scattering of banners from the Young Liberals and Young Socialists out of Belfast, uninvited but still welcome and eager to march, several bands, drums and brass and the pipes, and a cheerful crowd singing as they walked. They sang what they knew, rebel songs like "Who Fears to Speak of '98" and the great anthem of Catholicism, "Faith of Our Fathers." It was not so much a radical, civil rights march, despite the young radicals and support for the cause, as a movable summer festival, part nationalist, part republican, very Catholic, with a dash of radicalism and a mix of children's accordion bands and politicians. Marchers popped into pubs, dropping out for a pint and running to catch up. The parade watchers stepped in behind the marchers making up for the drinkers who never caught up. The crowd moved into Dungannon to find a police cordon across the road. Paisley's Ulster Protestant Volunteers had announced a counterdemonstration in the center of Dungannon. The police immediately banned the civil rights march from the center of Dungannon. They insisted that the civil rights march detour into a Catholic neighborhood. The marchers' good humor began to evaporate. The organizers with a large, grumbling crowd belatedly realized that many of their own were republicans and most were waiting for something to happen.

A truck was rounded up, a microphone found, a meeting created: Something was going to happen. Currie spoke. Gerry Fitt threatened to lead the marchers through the police line, but moderation triumphed. Betty Sinclair, who represented NICRA and had been at the banned Republican Club meeting, got up on the back of the truck, grasped the microphone, and insisted that this was a "nonpolitical, peaceful demonstration. Anyone who wants to fight should get out and join the IRA." There was a cheer for joining the IRA. Before matters got out of hand, she ended the march and asked the crowd to sing the civil rights anthem "We Shall Overcome." Having hardly understood the nature of civil rights or civil disobedience, innocent of any anthems but their own, the crowd soon drowned her out with "A Nation Once Again." Fitt, Currie, Sinclair, and the satellite politicians left for home, duty done, demonstration done. Deserted, the crowd sat down in the road for a sing-along and informal demonstration of disobedience. An hour later everyone, marchers and police, went home, each with a lesson learned.

Paisley had intervened and stopped the march. The local RUC, following his lead, had cordoned off the march, revealing a hard face despite a personal intimacy with many of the marchers—that was personal, this was political. Undoubtedly "they"—Paisley and the RUC—had absorbed lessons at Dungannon: Use the system to stop the Croppies—Fenians, Catholics, Teagues, them. The nationalist politicians had certainly grasped that the techniques and tactics of nonviolence had much to offer if at some risk of violence. The radicals like Bernadette Devlin felt that the old politicians had proved irrelevant and that power was to be found in direct demonstrations involving the people. Nothing much the students were doing at Queen's had seemed as promising. A civil rights campaign could be used effectively by those without power. And the republicans present, if traditional, felt nothing but physical force—armed power—would move a police cordon. Some republicans elsewhere might have hope for disobedience, but most committed republicans did not feel that the RUC would be amenable to playing by the new rules imported from America. Still, they had marched along. Nevertheless, the marchers, the opponents, the observers, the press and the everyday people were only momentarily attracted to a passing distraction on a long summer's evening. After all, nothing much had really happened. Participants, sitting in council houses, walking country roads, waiting in the confusion of the smoke at Waterloo, do not always recognize famous battles.

Impressed with the size of the crowd and the general enthusiasm, the conventional in NICRA on Monday, September 2, after considerable debate, decided on another march, this time in Derry. The agenda of issues to be raised was extended from houses, a sure winner, to include the other nationalist grievances: unemployment, local government reform, and the right of free speech and assembly. The last could be tacked on after events in Dungannon had shown that the RUC would not be tolerant even in small matters. Derry was an obvious target if the civil rights campaign was to continue marching instead of analyzing and petitioning. All the nationalist problems were crammed into one small, unhappy city on the edge of the province. There the gerrymandering that produced a Unionist local government was blatant, an example for political science textbooks on how to turn one-third of the votes into two-thirds of the council seats. There the Catholics were housed in the most dreadful conditions. There the unemployment was permanent, general, and seemingly irreducible, condemning most to idle penury or emigration. Partition had cut the city off from the country, time had destroyed the old industries, Unionist politics had ignored the city's needs or interests, seeking only to hold Londonderry as symbol, as *theirs*. In Derry protest was futile. The Nationalists under Eddie McAteer were simply going through the motions. McAteer, whose brother Hugh had been chief of staff of the IRA, had held his party together and kept hope alive but had failed to dent the system. The few Derry republicans were only the usual suspects any time the RUC needed to sweep up subversives. There, more than anyplace in the province, the Protestants seemed to delight in domination—marching in the Apprentice Boys' parade each August 12 along the walls of the old city to Orange airs, tossing pennies at the Fenians down below in the slummy Bogside. The marchers in bowlers and Masonic gear were easy in their superiority, militant, arrogant, cruel, and crude, bussed into the city to intimidate and celebrate.

> *Slaughter, slaughter, holy water,*
> *Slaughter the Papists one by one.*
> *We will tear them asunder*
> *And make them lie under*
> *The Protestant boys who follow the drum.*

And they did, all those trapped and futile and deprived, lay under the drumbeat of Orange superiority. The triumphant marchers were better housed, better educated, better in their own eyes, more readily employed, more mobile, more skilled. They were on their wall beyond any imaginable papist challenge. They were superior to a feckless, dirty, undisciplined, riotous clan, genial at best, senselessly violent at worse, violent with drink, violent with passion. The Irish Catholics were without discipline or capacity. And so the drumbeat, the music of arrogance, grounded in the evidence of Protestant eyes sweeping across the misery of the Bogside, a Fenian fen.

But Derry was not simply a dreary statistic made visible or a symbol of Protestant domination, but also a real home with real streets and real neighborhoods. People lived there and loved the city—the core around the Diamond behind the famous walls, the edges spreading out into the countryside, the Foyle estuary, the bridge and the churches. Many might be poor but would, if possible, live no place else. In a sense the most disheartening recent event for the city, for the divided community, for those who had some hope for the system or faith in a better future, had been the 1965 Lockwood report's decision not to build the new university in Derry. All the practical arguments had led to a Derry site, much of the Londonderry Unionist community agreed; but logic had not prevailed. The Unionist majority centered at Stormont had not written in a part in their play for the Catholic others, did not need them, would not risk putting down a marker in faroff Londonderry, even if the city were the symbolic home of Protestant resistance to Catholic domination. As the Unionist Minister of Education Harry Midgley had stressed ten years before, "All the minority are traitors and have always been traitors to the Government of Northern Ireland."* And so they still were. There would be no university. A better Londonderry might attract the others, Irish Catholics, traitors: so, nothing for Londonderry. There never had been much for Derry, where Catholics lived on the margins with a small middle class scrambling to hang on and with a large working class that rarely worked and where the Protestants, often only marginally better off, were arrogant and fearful.

In Derry both traditions, but especially the Catholics, had long been devastated by unemployment. There went no new jobs. There had never really been any jobs within memory by 1968. School leavers might find employment briefly as messengers, delivery boys, helpers, clerk assistants; but in a few years, like their elders, like their parents, they went on the dole, replaced by other young lads. And you went on the dole forever unless you emigrated or struck it lucky. In Derry the only ways out, the only hopes, were either the pennies on the pools, a bet on the races, gambling the odds or glasses of porter, mean vices arising from a need for hope and assuring only the certainty of misery. To be drunk was a triumph not a curse. To back the right horse made the month. Nothing else did. Meals were small, monotonous, and unhealthy, sweets were a child's only savory, tea was a universal balm, and holiday dinners were a dreadful economic challenge. Everyone seemed pale, scrawny, cursed with bad teeth, threatened until very late with nineteenth-century diseases. Almost everyone was cursed by eroding idleness, purposelessness, the certainty that nothing would change. Long ago the Glory Days of the Tan War had come and gone and nothing had changed. Consequently, only the young and innocent in Derry believed that their action—an imported nonviolent protest—would have an effect. The rest knew that nothing had an effect, nothing changed the system, nothing at all had worked to nationalist advantage, and so they watched with a jaundiced eye the enthusiasm of the militants clotted around the new protests. Radicals, revolutionaries, republicans

*Portadown Times, February 15, 1957.

had come to naught in the Black North before and this lot was relying on weakness to win: no hope there.

Derry, being small, only had so many enthusiastic militants to go around, hardly enough to enliven any one organization. The republicans adrift after the end of the campaign had a few people and there was the odd radical, such as John White, inclined toward the republicans, Liam Cummins and Finbar Doherty. The last was a tiny lad with enormous glasses and barely bottled energy. There was Eamonn McCann, sent down from Queens in Belfast as incorrigible, nearly as small as Doherty and possessed of an even more extensive anti-Imperialist vocabulary. There were a couple of others from the Northern Ireland Labour Party, one or two thrown up by the Housing Action Committee, and the odd drifter. Radical Derry: They were both leaders and followers, signing their own petitions, clapping their friend's speech, the same crowd at every venue. Mostly their elders were watchers: Seán Keenan, local dean of the republicans, Eddie McAteer of the Nationalist party (who had invested a lifetime in Nationalist politics to no great returns for him or the Nationalists), and the chairman, James Doherty. Ivan Cooper of the Northern Ireland Labour Party and John Hume, unattached but prominent in the Credit Union Movement, were deeply concerned but very cautious. Hume had refused to run for Stormont in 1965. Much of the new militant activity seemed to be stunts, spontaneously organized by young men with little to risk—and mostly this was the case. The young saw that the Unionist machine, long comfortable, had grown rigid, might be vulnerable to stunts, was too staid to cope with new energy.

In July Doherty created the James Connolly Commemoration Committee, planned a march, and after it was banned, put on a rally attended by about a thousand with Gerry Fitt as speaker. After the Coalisland-Dungannon march in August, the locals in Derry were determined on a march. NICRA sent a delegation to meet with the potential organizers in a room above the Grandstand Bar on William Street. They innocently agreed to a march that would move from Duke Street across the Craigavon Bridge over the Foyle River through the city walls and up to the Diamond in the center of the city. The Diamond was the most sacred ground to the Orangemen. Territorial imperatives were vital in Northern Ireland. To march down in the Bogside was one thing, but to march inside the walls was invasion, a denial of domination. NICRA did not know. Every organization except the Unionists was to be invited, an ad hoc civil rights committee was established, and October 5 chosen as the date.

The moderates did not join the ad hoc committee. A march into the Diamond was hardly a nonviolent venture. Those who disagreed with caution, White of the Republican Clubs, Eamonn Melaugh of the Housing Action Committee, Doherty with his Connolly Society, Dermie McClenaghan from the Young Socialists, and Brendan Hinds from the Labour Party, tended to represent themselves. They placarded Derry with radical posters hardly relevant to civil rights: Class War, Not Creed War. Not unexpectedly their elders were annoyed and the Civil Rights Association people back in Belfast were concerned. The Derry people did not care about the CRA. The Dungannon game was to be replayed but over symbolic Orange ground. After delaying, which greatly worried the march organizers who wanted confrontation, William Craig late on the afternoon of October 3 banned the march. On Tuesday, October 1, the Apprentice Boys of Derry had given notice that their "Annual Initiation Ceremony" would march from Waterside to the Diamond on a route not unlike that of the civil rights march. No one had heard of the "Annual Initiation" but no matter; now both marches could be banned. Craig informed McAteer that the civil rights march was a nationalist-republican parade: Unionists often professed to see no difference between the two. McAteer insisted that the Nationalist party was not involved in the affair. Craig refused to change his mind. There would be no marching by anyone.

The NICRA people were inclined to avoid any confrontation if possible. Derry sounded dangerous. At a meeting with the Derry organizers, held in the City Hotel on Friday night, October 4, NICRA learned that the march was going to go ahead despite Craig. McCann, Doherty, and company were, in fact, delighted with the ban and the caution of their elders. They wanted trouble. NICRA still wanted no march. James Doherty of the Nationalists and John Hume had already refused to sign a necessary document notifying the police. At the end NICRA reversed its stand after Frank Gogarty, a Belfast member, announced that if the Derry people were marching then he was marching. There would be three MPs from Westminster: Russell Kerr, Anne Kerr, and John Ryan of the Labour Party would be brought along by Gerry Fitt. He had rounded them up at the Labour Blackpool conference and brought them along to see Ireland firsthand. So the whole civil rights establishment decided to march, to appear, Ivan Cooper, John Hume, Austin Currie, Betty Sinclair, Eddie McAteer and the Nationalists—the whole lot marching.

Four thousand were rumored to have marched to Dungannon, and the Derry people expected more—the ban would bring them out. If you want a crowd in Ireland, ban a crowd. On Saturday, October 5, the marchers began to assemble at Duke Street. There were not thousands. Driving by on the way to the new semester at Trinity in Dublin, one Derry transient felt a twinge of disappointment that he could not join up. It was important but it was not *very* important. Trinity called him and more pressing matters called to much of Derry. The organizers waited and still no thousands showed. Dr. Raymond McClean, a political innocent later deeply involved in the civil rights movement, picked up his daughter in the center of the city just as the marchers gathered. He remembered the foreboding silence and got away.

But finally a start had to be made. There were only about four hundred marchers emerging from a crowd of about a thousand standing at the Waterside station. The demonstration parade was led off by Fitt, McAteer and company, the famous. They were not to go far without a confrontation. The RUC had blocked the route with a cordon of police and tenders at the bridge about three hundred yards from the starting point. The marchers were involved in a banned parade. The marchers plodded up to the cordon. There was a pause. The RUC had seldom had to deal with banned parades. Suddenly the police began to baton the first row. There was no special reason, no particular catalyst, no incitement by the marchers shuffling about in front of the constables, no excuse given then or later. The parade was illegal and provocative and one and then all the front row of the RUC started. One of the first hit, one of the most handy, was Gerry Fitt. His head broken open. He stumbled back dripping blood and was taken off to the hospital.

Another police cordon had appeared behind the parade. The demonstrators milled about for a couple of minutes. The police seemed to be finished. Betty Sinclair made a speech thanking everyone for being nonviolent and then urged them to disperse. So did McAteer and so too Cooper. Austin Currie was less specific about the virtues of peace in his talk. The crowd was angry and loud. Then Eamonn McCann gave his speech, which the magistrate's court later characterized as "incitement to riot." Actually he told the crowd that they could go home, sit down, or march into the police. The demonstrators then argued tactics in the middle of the street—the organizers feared that if the old fogies and honored guests had their way nothing would happen. The police, however, were not finished. The cordon squeezed around the marchers and the police began clubbing people to the ground. They were led by District Inspector Ross McGimpsey, chief of the local RUC, who showed real enthusiasm in responding to provocation as tradition required. He was not a young man but determined to make his baton felt, not leave the work to plain constables, all of whom were equally busy smashing heads and chasing demonstrators. The marchers were hunted down, batoned, scattered, chased through the lanes and alleys, most a long way from home, until at last they became too distant a target and the constables dropped back. Nearly a hundred reappeared for treatment at the Altnagelvin Hospital: ninety-six according to the *Irish Times,* seventy-seven plus eleven police according to the later Cameron report. The others found their way back to nationalist areas. Sporadic rioting and stone throwing continued through the evening and into the night while many of those who had been on the front row met again at the City Hotel to review the day. No doubt about it, all agreed, the police had run amok.

Not even the militant, eager for the police to overreact, had anticipated a police riot. And no one, least of all, Inspector McGimpsey, William Craig, and the police had anticipated that off to one side the Telefís Éireann cameraman Gay O'Brien would take a few hundred feet of film of the police smashing the head of Gerry Fitt, member of Parliament, peaceful civil rights marcher, Catholic, father, and decent fellow. Police brutality on the printed page from a small provincial city might have passed unnoticed in Great Britain, had passed unnoticed in the past; but film, action film, was gobbled up not just in Britain but worldwide by television producers eager for hard news violence—and Derry offered hard news violence where the good guys and the bad were easy to recognize. The bad guys were Protestants in police uniforms or the Protestant officials in tailored suits who soon appeared not to apologize but to explain why whacking Catholics was necessary. The good guys were the Catholics in scruffy clothes running from the police, middle-aged politicians and young kids who didn't have to explain why they were running and were soon given a chance to explain why they were marching. The mainland British were stunned, mostly by the blood and violence and soon by the nationalists' grievances. Nothing was going to be quite the same in Northern Ireland ever again.

For a generation scholars and analysts and the television industry itself have focused on the nature of the impact of the violence on the viewers. There is no doubt that seeing *real* violence, seeing it live, personal, close up in the living room, even seeing it in replay (many viewers do not recognize the difference in any case) does have a far greater impact than the printed page, than word of mouth, than "knowing" about the horror. Seeing is believing. One strip of film can and did have an enormous impact. Seeing is to gain, even secondhand, often at a remove of thousands of miles and across a huge cultural gap, a sense of the dreadful: Gerry Fitt on the evening news reeling under the batons made Derry real, Derry grievances real, Derry important. Suddenly on the screen Ireland lived as a problem, a crisis. The film made the everyday people and certainly the television producers avid to see more of Northern Ireland, see more film, have more explanations, be exposed to more reality. More, everyone wanted more, maybe not more violence but more, maybe more violence.

This new curiosity, decent or dreadful, accelerated and exaggerated real events. After a long time the producers and the audience would grow immune to Irish horror, but in the autumn of 1968, Ireland, for many in Britain, was a lost, green island of mists, quaint accents, and sheep-dotted hills. There had been no news from Ireland in half a century. There had been no Irish issue in British politics since the Troubles were tidied up in 1921. No one knew anything about Ireland. No one *cared* anything about Ireland. Few could find Derry on a map or had heard of Fitt. And then in one evening there was Ireland again, an issue, a crisis, a focus for television's eye and the ensuing instant analysis, a hot subject—replay of the American civil rights campaign, replay of the May events in Paris 1968. The province became the next regular stop on the traveling media circus. First the television teams out of London, then the Continent, and soon the big groups from the U.S. networks. As a consequence Irish politics was not only utterly changed but also minutely observed.

Saturday night at the City Hotel the survivors were, as they had been previously, divided on all matters: the virtue of the police attack, the validity of hooligan violence, the next move, the last move. Marx and Connolly were dragged about, scuffed and used in previous confrontations, old Irish saws were sold as wisdom, the feuds of yesteryear were retailed. It was the last such discussion in isolation, where everyone knew the proper role. The Irish were about to lose monopoly possession of Ireland. The others—often more expert than the locals on Marx or Marcuse or even the Fenians, often absolutely innocent, snatched from an office in Los Angeles or Milan and dispatched with a guidebook and expense account—were coming. The journalists appeared with the new week, seeking color and comment. They wanted the reaction of the "typical unemployed person" and the views of the police, the politicians, the responsible and radical. They wanted all this today and in short Celtic bits. They had come to the right place: Every Irishman was an actor, an expert, profound, poetical, wry, and passed from hand to hand to fill the needs of eager editors and producers.

In Belfast on Sunday Craig held a press conference and accused the civil rights movement of being involved with the IRA—he had photographs of prominent IRA men in the Derry march—praised the police, denied that there had been any brutality. This had been good enough in the past. But he forgot the RTE film. He forgot he was not talking to the locals. He did not yet understand the power of television. When a group of student protesters arrived at his home, some straight from Derry, to protest about the police and the cover-up, he called them "silly, bloody fools" on camera live. That film was broadcast just like his denial of brutality, his praise of the police, his Pavlovian response regarding IRA involve-ment, all this to an audience who had seen the Derry footage. Just as the RUC had not been prepared for civil disobedience and so followed the script prepared by the demonstrators (and here enter police brutality) so too Craig and those Unionists at Stormont were unprepared for the television era where real could be made realer.

Coming down with the boot, arresting dissent and riding out the brief storm, had always worked in the past. Now, however, there was television, and replace-ments for those arrested or beaten into hospitals, and escalating protest, and so coverage and so protest. No end was in sight. The province's splendid isolation had ended and the authorities were ill-prepared for the change. They had a bad case to sell and no skills at selling. Fifty years would rust any machine, erode all reflexes, encourage the growth of self-righteousness and arrogance previously sold as confidence in a grand wee country. Times were not so much a changin' as suddenly changed between one news program and the next. The time for new men had come just as the new crop of idealists had moved to manipulate the television eye by action. Ireland became for a while an existential stage cluttered with the decrepit stage sets (Stormont, the National Party and the Unionists, the gentry and the Orange Order) of a play that had closed after a long run. Some old men would adapt, learn to manipulate the television, shape new roles in a new play. Others would withdraw. The future, whatever else, would not be the past replayed in isolation.

The two groups least able to adjust to the transformation in the Northern arena were the hard men in Stormont and the radicals on the GHQ of the IRA. The former grasped an opportunity to discard O'Neill (business as usual); the latter consumed by their reform of the republican movement, were unable to give adequate time to the distant Northern disturbances, trouble unrelated to their immediate needs. Both were willing to use the demonstrators but would have preferred to get on with the job in peace. O'Neill was, as always, perfectly aware of the discontent on his right. The removal of Harry West as Minister of Agriculture in April 1967 because of his secret interest in the Saint Angelo Airport near Enniskillen, which he wanted the government to reopen, had generated backbench grumbling. It was not so much that Harry had been ill done by as O'Neill had done it. So any trouble in the province was trouble for the Prime Minister. In Dublin the IRA GHQ was almost innocent of the implications of the civil rights campaign in that it supported the initiative since it was political rather than military. Volunteers were permitted to participate. Some in Dublin were sincerely concerned but the real focus was to wrest the republican movement from the old traditionalists. The demonstrators did not want to be smeared as an IRA pawn, thus making O'Neill and Craig victims of a plot. There were, in any case, real plots against the Unionist establishment.

On the far side of the Stormont system, Paisley and his friends, still confident of their future despite the UVF fiasco, had no hesitation in going all out for O'Neill now that he was vulnerable. If he moved toward concession under attack from London and the media, he could be harried as weak. On Wednesday, October 9, Paisley met with William Craig, who was filled with growing ambition and had a read on the situation not unlike Paisley's, and Paisley later announced that "the Ulster people have expressed their point of view. No surrender. No comment." On the same day in Belfast, students from Queen's University held a three-and-a-half-hour sit-down in Linenhall Street for a list of demands: one man, one vote; repeal of the Special Powers Act, the Public Order Act, and the Flags and Emblems Act; the introduction of a parliamentary commissioner; a human rights bill to be made law; the introduction of a points system for housing allocation; electoral boundaries to be redrawn fairly; an impartial inquiry into police brutality in Derry; and jobs to be allocated on the basis of ability. They wanted everything and they wanted it at once.

What made this more than student piffle was the nature of the demands—most people in Britain thought everyone in the United Kingdom already had all that. Certainly everyone should have all that. Why was Northern Ireland different? Was the vote unequal, the housing unfairly assigned, the system crooked or partisan or sectarian? The students were apparently not demonstrating as a gesture. After the sit-down, those involved—Bernadette Devlin, Michael Farrell, Kevin Boyle, and the others—returned to Queen's and put together their organization. It was soon called People's Democracy as a result of a printer's addition to their first poster—it had to be called something. They wanted action—all the decent demands first and then the big stuff, socialism, revolution, all the wonders that the French students had scrawled on Paris walls. In the meantime there were enough tangible grievances and humiliations to go around, to attract even the most conservative nationalist, even the Catholic without politics.

In Northern Ireland the students, particularly the Queen's University students, would play a major role in the unfolding drama. At the core, not unexpectedly, were Catholic students, many, nearly all, the first of their family at a university, a possibility opened by the Educational Act of 1947. There were not actually that many Catholic students, fewer than subsequent lay analysis would assume, and fewer still working-class families; but they made up for the lack of numbers with enthusiasm: A few Eamonn McCanns can go a long way, usually too far for most. Unlike their parents and their friends, they had not yet been crushed by the pervasive hopelessness of the nationalist community. The students, unlike many of their generation, had not spent their last five years idly, fruitlessly seeking work or, if working, underutilized and often living under the fear of dismissal. And the students, unlike their parents, had spent their conscious adult life in pursuit of improvement, in expectation of more: They had a future. They had no sense of the possible. Anything was possible. Everything was possible. And, as students, they also possessed the time—the employed have no time and the unemployed too much. The students were of an age filled with energy and they lacked immediate responsibility. They had the absolute convictions of the young that would help drive the demonstrations. And they had as example the Paris May 1968 events, the other European anti-Vietnam demonstrations, the American civil rights movement of civil disobedience. They felt that they could play a part in larger events. They *knew* what they were doing was important—the presence of the media, the whirr of cameras, the interviews by correspondents with strange accents and strange credentials indicated that. They were convinced that what they did mattered. And their drive generated enthusiasm at home, pulled along the older and the cynical, gave example to the idle and stoic. What good would a protest do if no one came, or a parade if no one marched? Few paid much attention to their new, radical ideas; elaborate ideological explanations were filtered out along with their revolutionary agendas and militant labels. It was the impact of the escalating campaign against authority that the followers noted. They were causing trouble where trouble was due.

Almost all of those involved in the civil rights campaign were quite aware of the target and intimate with just grievance but were almost wholly innocent of the principles and practice of nonviolence. What the demonstrators sought was to provoke the system, thus revealing institutionalized injustice. Then it would be possible to broadcast, often through slogans, the appropriate and democratic demands of all those denied by the Unionist-Orange-Stormont system. The theory and practice of nonviolence developed in India and exploited in the United States and elsewhere was more validation than tutor. In fact the real idea of nonviolence was to violate unjust law and thus provoke violence by those in power, which would undermine the system's legitimacy and lead to reform. In Northern Ireland the system had always run on the imposition of violence in reality or through symbolic display. Only the slightest provocation was needed to assure an overreaction. Previously the dominated Catholics had not responded in kind because of justifiable fears. In theory the situation was ideal. In 1968 there was no doubt that the system would respond as before, so the students were not educating the system or their own but staging a drama for an audience that might demand or impose reform, a world audience and a British audience. Nonviolence in India had depended on a response in London, in America on a response from Washington: The locals would do as they chose if there were no intervention. What counted was that at first the system did as it had always done. Only later, maybe, if the people felt their power, was there a risk that the wrong actor might opt for violence and spoil the message. Strategy, however, was no one's strong suit; the students spent an enormous amount of time on definitions and theory and everyone else almost no time at all—action was everyone's heart's desire. Essentially the students did the old marching in a new way to conform to international practice. Everyone else acted as was the wont of the province.

In the case of Northern Ireland, the target of the civil rights campaigners, then, from the very first was to make trouble. They were not happy with Betty Sinclair, satisfied with the existence of a demonstration, nor with William Craig suddenly willing to allow such a demonstration. Their game plan called for Catholics causing Protestants trouble. Fortunately few paid attention to those who wanted to march home and the Unionists acted as always. The system had no flexibility; could not imagine any other role than the one written intuitively by the demonstrators; would, given the right cue, respond as history indicated. The Unionist psyche was graven with Not An Inch. The fundamental loyalists regarded any evidence of minority opposition as a terminal threat. With or without orders, regardless of any central Stormont strategy, all devout Orangemen—and such were most of the police, the system's first line of defense—would respond to provocation with violence. And so they did. And so they would continue to do.

What frustrated and enraged the Unionist community was that the provocation was so unfair, so cunning, so beyond their conventional power. Everyone knew, fair or no, that the British public, just like the international media representatives, would take the side of the demonstrators. The majority knew that the target—the British establishment—neither understood nor liked them, the Unionists, the Protestants, their province or their institutions. Desperate to be British, devoted to the Crown, in their heart of hearts they had no faith in the fatherland. Promises would be made, at least by the Tories, but in the end not kept, certainly not by Labour. Even worse, most understood why: The Orange state was founded on domination displayed. They believed that this domination arose from the inherent superiority of the Protestant society still under threat. In a divided society, when the disloyal minority had access to an island nationalist majority, power could not be shared nor could the authorities afford concession, compromise, or conciliation without arousing dangerous hungers. Dominance in all matters at all times was crucial if one tradition, the lesser, were not to swallow the better, as had already happened on the rest of the island. "Fair" played no part in provincial politics. The issue was survival. Justice was the province of the dominant. It was not disinterested. It was not to be dispensed with an even hand but rather used as a weapon in the siege.

Those distant and secure in London and, most particularly, all those outside agitators with television cameras and irresponsible, pious opinions did not, would not, understand Ulster reality. The ruling society was at war to protect the faithful from absorption and so dispersal in Irish Catholic society. Publicly one might argue for the rights of the majority, for the Protestants were a majority in the six counties; but privately the goal was the domination by the majority—a domination that not only was affected by the distribution and exertion of actual power but also by the necessity of having those acts symbolically demonstrated. The minority must not only be powerless but also made to feel powerless.

Perhaps they need not actually live in hovels below the Derry walls and be target for the Apprentice Boys' pennies but in some form the Catholics must be made to *feel* powerless. The alternative was not, as O'Neill and the moderates assumed, better housing and no parades. That would not turn the minority into loyalists but only undermine the existing power structure, whet appetites, cause real trouble. The minority would still be Catholics. No true loyalist could see the majority tradition functioning unless it remained within the province of the dominant tradition. And since dominance, implying as it did inferiority imposed by the system, was incompatible with democratic practice, no argument about "majority" rights would convince the distant. Catholicism was inherently aggressive. Without defense the province would be lost to Rome and degradation.

The critics who bothered to examine the Unionist assumptions at all felt no such argument could be acceptable. A defense that required the corruption of Western values meant that such a society was not worth defending—assuming such a defense was necessary at all and not some fantasy of the locals. The critics felt that the system at heart was wrong, immoral, undemocratic. And it was—no one knew so more than those who had fashioned it so. What else could they have done? What else could they do? Even O'Neill's "progressive" gestures, the speeches on development, the ecumenical moves, the visit to a convent, the talk with Lemass, could not cover the continuing reality. O'Neill could not manage to hide his own unwitting arrogance and majority assumptions, for he like the others had little exposure to a dissenting, suspicious public.

> It is frightfully hard to explain to Protestants that if you give Roman Catholics a good job and a good house, they will live like Protestants, because they will see neighbors with cars and television sets. They will refuse to have eighteen children, but if a Roman Catholic is jobless and lives in a most ghastly hovel, he will rear eighteen children on National Assistance. . . . If you treat Roman Catholics with due consideration and kindness, they will live like Protestants and in spite of the authoritative nature of their Church.*

No one much but O'Neill believed that a job and a house would turn a member of the minority into a member of the majority. Why should it? The Catholics did not want to *be* Protestants. They might, indeed, want a nice house, a car and television sets, even fewer children; but they wanted to be Catholics. For many Unionists, Catholics not dominated by Protestants must want to dominate Protestants. They might say not, but they marched behind the banners of revolution and the Irish Republic, sang rebel songs, had rebel hearts. Their cause in the province was pretense, their goal unification, their pieties specious.

As a majority in the Republic to the South, the Catholics had not needed, as had the Protestants under threat in the North, institutionalized injustice. All that was needed was to wait—and year by year the number of Protestants declined, their political power evaporated, their economic power decayed. The time would come when there were more Jews—three—in the Dáil than Protestants—one. The children went off to England to school, stayed and married in Britain, while on the island their churches were empty, closed, mute monuments to the implications of exclusive Irish nationalism. The Protestant population of whole counties could meet in a room. The big houses had been burnt or sold off. The flags of British regiments and British victories at Saint Patrick's Cathedral grew tattered and the Anglo-Irish a historical curiosity. Irish Catholicism was insatiable, the threat absolute. In this sense the issues of the Reformation were alive and well in Northern Ireland. The province could not for long be both free and pluralistic. Many Protestants felt the Catholics unleashed would, with a majority in the island, take over their Ulster.

A television set was not going to change the tide of Irish history, nor would concessions nor kindness: only dikes could be built and manned. And dikes can be destroyed by a single small, unplugged leak. The province was filled with those who had the skill but not the wit to pull that bung. It was crucial to keep Catholics' heads down and minds elsewhere. Every reformer was a drill or worse a drill sergeant for an army unassembled. Every civil rights demonstrator with a banner was a lethal and intolerable threat to be beaten back—not dissuaded with kindness, not rerouted by logic, but beaten back, an act of comforting to the defender as painful to the potential rebel. And the novelty beyond comprehension

Belfast Telegraph, May 10, 1969.

was that the radicals seemed to place themselves in harm's way. They wanted to be attacked, wanted trouble. The students—"silly, bloody fools"—were more dangerous than they knew or their elders imagined. Only very gradually did the astute realize that the Unionist community was trapped in the planned ambush: They *must* act but in ways that assured the intervention of those who would force concessions opening the way for defeat.

The nature of this defeat sought by the demonstrators was defined with varying degrees of reality. The moderates sought to harness the students, who assumed the road to revolution had opened up. The radicals resisted. Still, on the same Wednesday Ivan Cooper was elected chairman of the newly formed Derry Citizens Action Committee and John Hume vice-chairman, new men, capable, moderate reformers eager to push on but not to bring the nationalist people to anti-Imperialist barricades and so ensure unnecessary violence. The moderates tended to see nonviolence as desirable for both sides. Fitt had recognized soon after he had been dragged from the scene bleeding that some violence had advantage. The less the better thought those who attended protest meetings in suits and ties—there was much to be lost. At the meeting in the City Hotel the four "original organizers" present were outmaneuvered and the new organization under Cooper and the moderates established to replace the radical few. The radicals had met the previous night to plan strategy, to call for action, to launch another march. They saw revolution down Duke Street. McCann, who had the chair as first organizer, could not even convince his own radicals to boycott the new leadership, for in division there did not seem to be strength. He stormed out slamming the new Citizens Action Committee as "middle-aged, middle-class, and middle-of-the-road." He was not entirely inaccurate. The committee postponed both immediate marches and thus the revolution, instead calling for a sit-in at the Diamond.

The new committee was conscious of the factors in Northern politics not amenable to the radical analysis of the young. The committee members could see the risks as well as the opportunities, had something to lose, were concerned to harness rather than unleash the enthusiasm of the youth, and were doubtful about the mobilization of a "risen" people. They had reason to worry. Neither the young nor many of the subsequent converts to the cause cared greatly for the niceties of nonviolence or the charms of pacifism. Many wanted action, their own back, the system at bay—and their rights, of course. They would parade behind the banners and if offered an opportunity would throw stones at the police in good cause. Why not? They could afford little other entertainment. The police were hereditary enemies, order was no advantage, and riot was a release. These marchers might not frighten the police, who were equally eager for an opportunity to use their batons on the trespassers, but they always frightened the march organizers, the committees, the leadership constantly fearful that the violent extremists would tread on their moderate heels, use the nonviolent banner poles as pikes, and cause irredeemable trouble. If there was going to be violence, let the system be responsible, not the aggrieved.

O'Neill, the moderate on the other side, recognized from the first his difficulty. The London center with a Labour government wanted reforms that would bring the province in line with democratic norms. O'Neill was not averse to moving under such pressure and securing the necessary reforms; but to do so, even under pressure, would probably result in his eventual removal as Prime Minister by the conservatives in Stormont, who would accept the benefits but not the responsibility of giving a few inches to save the whole. And there was no doubt that outside Stormont and his party he would immediately be savaged by the hard men like Paisley, who would prefer to go down with the ship rather than give the first inch. He felt he could count on the moderates in the province to ease the transition. He soon found most Unionist moderates stayed off the streets. They murmured in their sitting rooms or in clubs or societies but could not be found in Stormont, much less organizing demonstrations. A few might write a letter but only a few. What was needed, according to O'Neill, was sanity: ". . . unless this province returns to sanity, future progress is gravely at risk." The minority who had so far seen progress only as photo opportunities for the Prime Minister knew the real truth: no trouble, no progress. The Nationalists withdrew from Stormont as Official Opposition on October 15. "The crisis demands a bigger and more statesmanlike approach," McAteer insisted. For the very first time the Stormont system was in trouble. The Unionists could not count on Westminster; rather the reverse. Prime Minister Harold Wilson spoke not only for his party when he said on October 15 that "I do not think anyone in the House is satisfied with what has been done." He spoke also for Great Britain. And Wilson and London had no time for those loyalists opposed to any and all O'Neill reform: They were "thugs." London, ignorant by choice of the Stormont system, the Orange state, had little idea of the power of those thugs, the weakness of any moderate current, or the assumptions of those who operated in the province. London anticipated that the decent, necessary thing could be done because it was decent and, if need be, necessary. Injustice did not have to be an aspect of a system that prevented greater injustice: the triumph of Irish-Catholic-republican nationalism.

Wilson's innocence was matched by that of the Dublin establishment. Secure in their reading of recently written patriotic history, they knew all about the North, an area seldom visited: The problem was partition. In London on October 30, Jack Lynch told Wilson so, told him that the street violence was a result of partition. The march of Irish history had been interrupted by the division of the island in 1921. Now this aberration was causing trouble. History must be served. The Dublin solution was simple: a united Ireland, if not now, then sometime in the future. All the complexities of Northern Ireland, the power and intentions of the loyalists, who read justice, equality, and history differently, had as yet no relevance in Dublin. Lynch, his republican Fianna Fáil Party, and most of the Southern Irish had always evaded the Northern reality. They read history as a long struggle against an alien British suzerain fought by all the Irish that had been thwarted in 1921. Now was the time to complete the job. Geography was destiny, so all the island was Ireland, republican Ireland. That was it. The six counties should not have been snatched away, and once they were returned all would be well. The nearly million Orange dissenters might not be so easy to absorb, might be united geographically but on an island thus merely divided on different lines. Ireland so united could never be at peace. But this had not occurred to those in Dublin.

Dublin waited not, as London did, for Stormont to reform, but for justice to prevail. There was little hope for O'Neill from beyond the province or understanding from within. There was opposition to any forced concessions by the majority and insistence on more and visible concessions by the minority. He had no card to play but the threat that any competitor would be given the same hand and less time to play—a threat that has never dissuaded those eager for the deal.

On November 4, O'Neill, Craig, and Brian Faulkner, Minister of Commerce and a growing Unionist power, met for four hours with Wilson, his Home Secretary, James Callaghan, and Alice Bacon. Labour wanted immediate and extensive reforms. Delay would be of no benefit. Adamancy would serve no one in the Stormont cabinet or without. The next day Wilson indicated that if the extremists overthrew O'Neill then the British government would reappraise its relations with Northern Ireland. Good, as defined by London, was to be done, by Stormont or by London. The loyalists had suspected all along that their faith in Britain was unrequited, yet the province would still not be moved. Many truly felt the first step was the last. Some, like Craig, began talking of independence as a potential option. Others felt the need for a strong man as Prime Minister, not a reform man: Let London deal with an Orange man. And the marches and demonstrations went on, harried by loyalist militants and even at times by the police.

On November 16 the seriousness of O'Neill's dilemma became clearer. Many watched the escalating political crisis, the parliamentary maneuvers, and the trial balloon of independence—UDI, a Unilateral Declaration of Independence not unlike Rhodesia's in November 1965. There were the displays of Paisley and his movable feast of protest and always the clatter of street politics. Some sensed the almost certain prospect of serious street violence that might not be contained within the rituals of the march or the sit-in or even, when it came to that, the bounds of ceremonial riot. Killing politics had appeared before. Politics played out in Northern streets was not simply an everyday democratic phenomenon, not an organized witness to injustice, not a people's play or a student rag, but very possibly a prologue to the gun. The distant optimists in London, the equally distant republican traditionalists in Dublin, and many of the activists in the North with short memories did not think so, were too focused on their own reality to take a cool look ahead or parse the past. They pushed on down the road into thickening resentment.

On November 16, in Derry, there were not a few hundred demonstrators, easy prey for the RUC, but fifteen thousand faced by a sullen, reinforced police cordon and kept orderly by hundreds of stewards hard-pressed to pen up the bottled aggression of the huge crowd. The march had been banned by Craig and was stopped by the police at the entrance to the city walls. For some of those present it was a silent and powerful moment of confrontation. The future was now. Then quietly a symbolic few passed by the cordon and the crowd slowly followed, drifted on up to the Diamond as individuals and sat down. The moment had passed but the nationalists, the Catholics, had been mobilized, or at least gathered in one place for a specific purpose. Standing before the thin cordon of police, the people had power. This had an enormous impact on the radicals, who saw a risen nation before their eyes as theory had predicted. It distressed the authorities, who saw student pranks transformed into mass subversion. Both sides had eased away from confrontation. But if that power had been responsibly or at least cautiously used on Saturday afternoon, there was still no guarantee that sooner or later someone would move unwisely. An uneasy, growing anxiety had come to the province. What if a brick had been thrown, what if a constable had struck out, what if?

Simultaneous with the escalating protests came reform proposals by London and reluctantly shaped by those Unionists responsible. The Londonderry Corporation voted a points system for housing. O'Neill announced a five-point reform program: points for housing, an ombudsman, abolition of the company vote in local elections, a review of the Special Powers Act, and a Londonderry Development Commission. A week later the reform electoral law was more than just promised, it was passed. The difficulty was that hardly any nationalists paid attention to what a year before would have been considered revolutionary concessions. The action had moved into the streets. On Saturday, November 30, three days after the electoral law passed, Armagh was the site of a confrontation between five thousand civil rights demonstrators and one thousand Paisley supporters who had been rushed into the city. The police failed to clear away the Protestant crowd but kept the two sides largely apart. A Paisley group attacked the press, broke a BBC television camera, and exchanged stones with the civil rights people. They in turn at the end of the day attacked the buses moving the Paisley people out of town. The RUC then baton-charged the stone throwers. No one came out of the matter very well, but at least everyone did come out largely undamaged. Real violence had again been avoided—but only barely. Minds were again concentrated all over the province.

On Monday, December 2, the Northern Ireland cabinet met on the political situation. It was becoming clear that Craig could no longer be contained in the orthodox Unionist tent. That evening in Ulster Hall, Belfast, he claimed the civil rights movement was bogus, composed of "ill-informed radicals" and that the democracy of the Republic of Ireland was of a lesser standard than that of the province. When Phelim O'Neill called for Craig's resignation at Stormont on Wednesday, the members of the Unionist Parliamentary Party dissociated themselves from his statement: Some wanted Craig kept in the tent and others seemingly saw him as a means to push O'Neill out of the same tent. All active Unionists were always in the tent. Outside was retirement or neglect, the margins of politics. Inside was action. Craig repeated his Ulster Hall speech at Clogher in County Tyrone on December 5. The tent was going to have to be made bigger or smaller. On the following day the Unionist Party approved O'Neill's five-point program. But he had first to give assurances that there would be no further changes: Five points was more than enough for some.

Paisley, along with his new ally, Major Ronald Bunting, a retired army officer and former reformer turned hard-line loyalist, had been issued a summons for taking part in an illegal assembly at the Armagh troubles on November 30. The law would take its course with those who chose the streets outside. The hard men did not seem to have matters their way yet. A Craig challenge might be premature. As O'Neill pointed out, both Wilson as Prime Minister and Conservative Party leader Edward Heath had made it clear that any reversal of the promised reforms would be unacceptable. In a speech on Monday, December 9, O'Neill insisted that justice must be done—"Ulster stands at the crossroad"—

and if justice were not done Westminster might act "over our heads." With London's support, both Labour and Conservative, with the five points promised, and most of all with the prospect of serious civil violence made clear, the responsible nationalists should now respond with a campaign for moderation, a breathing period, calm. There was no need to keep up the demonstration pressure. The moderate Unionists agreed. A judicious pause was needed.

The *Belfast Telegraph,* a sound Protestant newspaper, substantial and judicious, carried coupons to be clipped and mailed in to support the Prime Minister. Civic leaders, many Unionist officials, the nationalists, all sorts and conditions wrote or wired their support: Over one hundred thousand people thus acted for moderation and reform. Good men were not standing idly by doing nothing, letting the worst filled with passionate intensity prevail. NICRA and the Derry Citizens Action Committee called for a truce. The marching season was over. The Unionist Party rallied around its leader as his potential rivals praised his reforms. All rallied, that is, but Craig, who continued his attack until O'Neill called for his resignation as Minister of Home Affairs on December 11. The following day the Unionist Parliamentary Party gave O'Neill a massive vote of confidence—the only four negatives were from Harry West, John McQuade, Desmond Boal, and William Hinds, the Unionist mastodons. By Monday, December 16, it was reported that 120,000 had filled in newspaper coupons backing the Prime Minister's Ulster-at-the-crossroads speech. The governments in Dublin and London had expressed their hopes for the reforms and their faith in O'Neill. McAteer, Hume, and the rest of the minority political leadership in the province expressed great hope. The *Derry Journal* felt reforms were on the way and the nationalist *Irish News* that there was thus no reason there should not be steady progress. Only a few like Craig of the orthodox Unionists and men like Paisley and Bunting wanted to exploit the moment.

Most observers had simply ignored those outside the Nationalist tent. There was dissent from the People's Democracy, but what did a handful of radical students really matter? Their efforts had always been harassed by the police and their analysis was quite different from the reaction of the middle-class politicians. They had scorn for the trimmers and neoimperialists, those who take a slice, not the whole loaf, and thank the giver. They and theirs wanted *real* change, not a system reformed, not adjustments for capitalist Catholics hiding behind a refurbished facade. Their socialist analysis required a real transformation. They had seen a risen people and continued to see police oppression. So on December 26, Boxing Day for the British, St. Stephen's Day for the Irish, they called for a march from Belfast to Derry beginning on January 1.

Since the handful of student radicals represented only themselves, no real Irish tradition, led no constituency, had never worked at politics—had never worked at all, some Nationalists would point out after being stung at the label Fascist and reactionary—then no one was concerned much about their intentions. No one but Major Bunting, as commandant of the Loyalist Citizens of Ulster, whatever they were. On the very next day, December 27, he warned the PD not to march through loyalist areas. No one was concerned about Bunting's warning for he had no vast constituency either. What Craig and Bunting, the PD and the radicals sensed was that the old tents had been folded, provincial politics could not be moderated by formulas and adjustments. Their causes had nothing to gain and much to lose if Unionism coped: One or the other had to be smashed—superiority reinforced or denied.

In Dublin, on Sunday, December 29, the *Sunday Independent* named Captain Terence O'Neill Man of the Year. Craig seemingly had overplayed his hand. The ill-advised, if not ill-informed, radicals of the PD and reactionaries like Bunting with his Orange mob, the two tips of the political spectrum, were alone in opposing the general Irish consensus. All they had to offer was new myths or old grievances. The system could adjust, could be reformed. O'Neill without charisma, even without enormous convictions or any real empathy for the minority, could do the job—had largely *done* the job.

At 9:00 A.M. on Wednesday, January 1, 1969, a tiny band of forty or fifty bundled-up and cheerful PD marchers got under way at the Belfast City Hall. A few latecomers rushed to catch up, so that once the march was truly under way, there were about a hundred regulars and many others along for a while. Some would drop out—or be driven out—along the way, but other sympathizers would link up as the march progressed; but there never was a crowd, only a straggle with a few banners unfurled for photographers. The exercise resembled a charity march. As the faithful straggled out toward Antrim under a One Man One Vote banner, Major Bunting and his supporters appeared on schedule waving their Union Jacks and Ulster flags, jeering. It almost made the march worthwhile—someone cared. For Bunting and his friends these radical Catholic students were nearly as bad as republicans and free to trek through Ulster streets: intolerable. The march was provocation and affront: evidence, in fact, that the Fenians had not been intimidated as the security of the system required. Even a few of the bold were too many. Bunting promised that the loyalists would "troop the colours" along the PD route. There would be no post-Christmas stroll for subversives and traitors. What others saw as an isolated band of scruffy students, many loyalists saw as the point of the Roman lance probing the first inch. They might look like students but only to the innocent eye.

All along the route, colors trooped aside, there were many eager for a go at the marchers, taken as an outward and visible sign of treason by university Catholics, which made it worse—an affront to the system by the young and privileged and intellectually arrogant. There was thus to be no easy passage allowed. And there was not. Regularly loyalists appeared across the line of march, blocking progress, screaming, shouting, pounding a Lambeg drum or holding sticks. This forced long delays. The police dithered, sought alternative routes, delayed instead of clearing away the blocking crowds, showed no enthusiasm in providing cover for those they disliked. Gradually it became clear that the RUC were willing to let the marchers walk into hails of rocks before suggesting alternative routes that would assure still more trouble, bigger ambushes, more dangerous showers of stones. The way to Derry became one long gauntlet of Protestant militancy, a march with a police presence but almost no police protection. In effect the RUC joined in the harassment. It was clear that they felt the PD people deserved what they were receiving and although no one liked the stones and the mobs the PD had sought them.

The word spread that the march was running into trouble. Telephone calls to friends, rumors, local reports, all led to a media presence lured in by the mobs and confrontations. The province was interested and the event long-lived. More marchers would appear to make up for those who dropped out. People began to drift up to Derry in order to meet the PD march when it arrived on Saturday. The trouble continued. All over Ireland there was growing concern. On Friday evening, January 3, Paisley and Bunting spoke at the Derry Guildhall. Windows were broken while they talked and a riot developed. A car, supposedly Bunting's, was burned. Among some, perhaps many, Catholics in Derry and throughout the province, nonviolence had no takers.

On Friday night Bunting had called for his supporters to meet the next day near the bridge at Burntollet outside Derry. On Saturday morning the police warned the marchers that a safe route could not be guaranteed. The PD column knew this translated into "would not be offered." The police had no intention of protecting them; nevertheless, off they went on Saturday morning, over a hundred strong; some had come all the way from Belfast. They were led by Bernadette Devlin, Farrell, and McCann, and included those unknown to observers, like Dolours Price from a republican family, and those known to the police, like Gery Lawless. All were bedraggled and tired but determined on the last push. The RUC mingled with the mob, advised wrong turns, delayed progress, all without attempts at guile, revealing just how unredeemable the Stormont institutions were. The PD could still thus count on the system as ally. At Burntollet Bridge the PD marchers were ambushed by two hundred Protestants, many of them off-duty RUC B Specials, carrying clubs, sticks studded with nails, and heavy stones. They had come to hurt, not harass. They beat the students into the road.

The eighty RUC present did nothing, watched, later on chatted with the attackers. They revealed once more that they were part of the problem, so arrogant in the old ways that they ignored the photographers unless they were aggressive. All the aggression came from the loyalists who chased the marchers. Some huddled flat on the road. Others were driven off into fields or a small stream, dripping and bloody in mud over their boots. Gery Lawless was last seen being chased over a ditch by four loyalists. Some marchers kept on dragging the injured down the road with them still on the way to Derry. Bernadette Devlin was knocked down, hit by a stick with two nails at the end. Loyalists stood about thumping at those lying on the road until more tempting targets showed up. Someone lifted Devlin up. The loyalists chased fleeing demonstrators through fields and into the woods. A few constables were sympathetic once the blood flowed. Most simply watched. Eighty-seven people ultimately ended up in the Altnagelvin Hospital.

Somehow the PD formed up on the road as the stones arched in about them and the loyalists rushed about on the edges hitting out at the isolated and vulnerable. They started to march. The battered band was joined by people rushing out of Derry who formed up behind the survivors. There were, suddenly, two thousand marchers outside Derry. Some were taken off to the hospital. As they moved on, they were attacked and stoned at Irish Street. Petrol bombs landed among them but fortunately rarely exploded. Michael Farrell was hit by four stones and fell to the road. Along with Farrell a dozen more of the original marchers had to be taken off to the hospital—and the end was not in sight. Tom McGurk, PD's moderate, felt the march should be stopped—but how does one stop in the midst of a riot?

The demonstrators reached Spencer Street, where more Protestants waited with stones. They had tried singing "We Shall Overcome" and then the "Internationale." The end was in sight. The RUC suggested the members wait—so they would be a better target. The marchers rushed past the police and the stones and came out at last into Guildhall Square and safety. The long march from Belfast was over at last. There in the square was a huge, anxious crowd, deeply angry at the reports of the long trail of violence, the complicity of the police, the unrepentant system. The loyalists had by their own efforts from Bunting to Spencer Street made the march a triumph. The survivors spoke to the crowd. Farrell had a bandaged head. Devlin had a hard word for Unionist Derry— "capital city of injustice." Frank Gogarty, chairman of NICRA, called the police inept, a reactionary tool of Unionism. As Devlin noted later, "It is impossible to describe the atmosphere. . . . The war was over and we had won; we hadn't lifted a finger but we'd won."* Again there was no doubt that it was a famous victory; people recognized Devlin on the street, Farrell kept his bloodstained coat about for years, and the number who had marched to Derry grew in recollections.

The PD had choreographed not just a scene but an insight into the nature of the Orange system, indicating just how immutable it had become to the "reform" all the moderates seemed to feel would transform reality. They had provoked the system to violence by a most minor action and thus had revealed the nature of systemic oppression. They had written in a part for the Orange militants and to their delight found that the RUC wanted a role as well. And once unleashed, the violent response was, of course, difficult to control but not lethal. The loyalists felt righteous, indignant, angry with the silly, arrogant Catholic students for causing trouble. They were unable to act other than was their habit; any denial of domination must be met.

That the RUC had been revealed as a sectarian force complicit with Orange violence was bad enough. Alone it would have shaken the system because of the rising distaste in all British political circles and because of the concomitant escalation of minority anger. Worse was to come, and once again from the RUC. After the Guildhall Square meeting the RUC had driven many of the crowd back from the city center through Fahan Street, Rossville Street, and William Street into the Bogside. This was merely a minor indignity explained as crowd control. Some of the constables then celebrated in drink a job well done. At two o'clock Sunday morning a crowd of constables, many obviously drunk, all angry, surged out through the Butcher Gate, rushed down Fahan Street into Saint Columb's Wells and Lecky Road shouting:

> *Hey, hey, we're the monkees,*
> *And we're going to monkey around*
> *Till we see your blood flowing*
> *All along the ground.*

*Bernadette Devlin, *The Price of My Soul* (New York: Alfred A. Knopf, 1969), p. 149.

They were out to get the Taigs—the Catholics, them. Derry had a police riot as burly, red-faced men in uniform, caps askew, batons in hand, pounded down doors, beat up anyone they found, broke windows, and roamed up and down shouting and singing. After an hour they left. Behind was the last remnant of the RUC's cover as a normal police force.

The following day temporary guards with sticks and iron bars protected the edges of the Catholic quarters. District Inspector Ross McGimpsey was told that the RUC would be kept from the area until the guilty constables were punished. Organizers organized. Barricades were set up establishing a no-go zone where Stormont's writ did not run. John "Caker" Casey appeared with paint and brush and carefully printed on an entire gable end of a terrace house on Saint Columb Street, easily visible to all, an enormous notice: YOU ARE NOW ENTERING FREE DERRY. In time it would be one of the great icons of the Troubles, familiar to a worldwide television audience and touched up with fresh paint from time to time to maintain the image. That night a radio transmitter installed in a flat on the eighth story of the Rossville Street flats let Eamonn McCann and the radicals speak over Radio Free Derry, the Voice of Liberation. Although John Hume had addressed a rally urging them to defend the area, no one had envisioned barricades, Free Derry, and McCann and company on the radio. All this was a gift from the RUC. Yet Derry was not really ready for a revolution. After a heady week the barricades came down on Friday night after speeches by Hume, Cooper, and Michael Canavan of the Citizens Action Committee. The moderates had been assigned the task of sweeping up after the chaos and the action people had gone home. By then, the center of action had shifted again.

Inside the Unionist establishment the response to the PD march had not been outrage at the Burntollet-Derry violence but outrage that the PD had marched, had been encouraged by a train of events easily traced to flexibility at the core, to O'Neill. The system had given space to the PD to provoke. This was the crucial error—giving way. The Prime Minister, a man of his party, recognized this response as the first serious challenge. Nothing was possible without the toleration of his own. They must be made to see that absolute intractability would not succeed while limited concession could. On Monday, January 5, he issued a statement.

> The march to Londonderry planned by the so-called People's Democracy, was, from the start, a foolhardy and irresponsible undertaking. At best those who planned it were careless of the effects which it would have; at worst they embraced with enthusiasm the prospects of adverse publicity causing further damage to the interests of Northern Ireland as a whole. . . .
>
> Some of the marchers and those who supported them in Londonderry itself had shown themselves to be mere hooligans ready to attack the police and others. And at various places people have attempted to take the law into their own hands in efforts to impede the march. These efforts include disgraceful violence offered indiscriminately both to the marchers and the police who were attempting to protect them.

Of course those who were responsible for this violence were playing into the hands of those who are encouraging the current agitation. Had this march been treated with silent contempt and allowed to proceed peacefully the entire affair would have made little mark. . . .

Enough is enough. We have heard sufficient for now about civil rights; let us hear a little about civic responsibility.

This was then and later the moderate Unionist posture. Northern Ireland was under attack, not the system or the party or the Prime Minister. The attack sought violence that, although understandable, was counterproductive. The institutions, the police, were not at fault; the people, the Unionists, were misguided; the fault lay not in their own but in them and their alien allies. O'Neill, as he had so often, missed the point and alienated all. Of course, the PD was provocative—the interests of Northern Ireland were not theirs but those of the Unionists, even probably those of the Nationalist Party and the Catholics of property. Of course, silent contempt would have worked if the march had been in Britain, not in Ulster, where the dominant must dominate and be seen to do so. Many loyalists received no other return from "their" Northern Ireland but the psychic pleasure of visible domination. Fashioned over generations, with attitudes and assumptions cultivated over centuries, the militant Orangeman would stone his own police in order to exert his right to display domination. Such violence was not a matter of tactics but of principle. Contempt, as detailed by O'Neill on that Monday was insufficient for the implacable. Contempt did not work unless the victim felt contemptible—as would a loyalist forced to stand and be stoned; but somehow it only made the Catholic victim more arrogant. Contempt was too elegant a weapon and O'Neill too soft a man to understand the realities so obvious to the angry farmer beating a young woman demonstrator into the road. Yet urging contempt as means only indicated to Catholics that even reform Unionism was of a piece. O'Neill was only more elegant, only offered more subtle tactics in defense of his Northern Ireland.

So hardly anyone liked the speech or the direction that O'Neill had taken at the Derry crossroad. There was neither evidence of the kind of civic responsibility O'Neill had demanded from the minority nor support from the Unionists that the speech was largely intended to pacify. The PD and the rest intended to keep up the pressure and so ensure that the Orange militancy would continue to be displayed. And the Orange militants were all too eager to smash the next display in defense of *their* Northern Ireland. On Saturday, January 11, there was a demonstration in Newry that turned into a riot, apparently to the delight of the watching police, who felt the radicals had thus revealed their real intent. Ten constables were injured and twenty-eight civilians. The PD later met and voted to raise money to compensate the traders of Newry and the RUC. The riot had been a tactical disaster. NICRA and the moderates were appalled. Hume condemned the violence. Captain William Long, who had replaced Craig as Minister of Home Affairs, called the PD attack brutal, an attempt to cause civil strife. A campaign that required unstructured mass support was not easy to organize—the mass, ignorant of the advantages of both new ideas and organization, tended to respond traditionally.

Matters got no better. The foreign media, quite innocent of Irish matters and traditional responses and attitudes, had appeared on schedule once trouble began—again photogenic trouble articulated by Irish wit. And a flood of real outside agitators, equally innocent of Ireland, appeared to monitor the evolving revolution. Tariq Ali, fashionable agitator out of the British hard left and the *Black Dwarf,* spoke in Belfast on the revolutionary situation in the province. Free-lance ideologues and itinerant *teoretiki* began to arrive off student flights, more when violence was on European television, fewer in the pauses while the demonstrators planned the next move. The Year of the Guerrilla produced revolution-groupies who now had to check off Belfast and Derry to be acceptable in Berlin or Turin.

The civil rights people called for another demonstration, this time to stress the unemployment rates in Strabane—in 1969, 27.7 percent, the highest level of male unemployment in the province. Again Major Bunting responded with a promise to show the Union Jack to the town of Strabane, too Catholic to be truly loyal. Matters were not going to improve. No rush to civic responsibility was apparent. The pattern was set: provocative demonstration before a sullen police and aggressive counterdemonstrators that led at least to scuffles and at times to riot. What shifted was not this pattern but rather, as O'Neill had predicted in his January 5 speech, Unionist consensus. Many loyalists, many Unionists, felt that the fault lay with a Prime Minister who had let the camel in the tent and lacked the determination to kill the beast or drive it out. O'Neill was at fault. After all there *must* be a fault not in the system but in the personnel.

Day by day O'Neill's support began to dribble away, a loss easily calibrated by the defections of his backbenchers and the rise in the aspirations of his rivals. They need only oppose him, need not offer constructive alternatives: It was the fault that was to be jettisoned. On January 15 O'Neill appointed the Cameron Commission to investigate the recent disturbances. The minority thought the move too late; but Harry West felt it an unnecessary concession. Craig on the outside continued to speak against the Prime Minister. His leadership prospects were mixed: He was too eager, too limited, too ambitious. The most viable of O'Neill's rivals was Brian Faulkner, who resigned from the cabinet on January 23. He was now ready for the mantle when it was time. Nothing was going right for the Prime Minister. Bunting and Paisley were in jail—if briefly—for their part in the Armagh riot. Crowds howled at O'Neill, "Protestants go to prison and thugs go free!" In London, Wilson pointed out that the Unionists had not gone the whole way yet to reform the province. They had gone much too far for many in Stormont. On January 30, twelve dissident Unionist MPs signed a document urging a change in leadership. The four dissenters from the December vote of confidence, West, McQuade, Boal, and Hinds, were joined by Craig, John Taylor, a young, smooth hard-liner, John Brooke, who had some hopes for O'Neill's job, Captain Austin Ardill and four others. Faulkner and William Morgan had both resigned from the cabinet. O'Neill's days were numbered despite his determined vow: "I will not trim my sails. I will do my duty." On Sunday Craig and Brooke repeated the dissident demand that O'Neill step down. No one paid much attention to Edward Heath in London, who urged a moderate policy of political advance.

Moderation had few political takers in Ulster. The competition was between two intransigent societies. Militancy paid better returns, always had, especially negative militancy. Saying *no* was the nature of Northern Ireland politics. What was needed within the Unionist Party was a consensus. O'Neill decided on the unusual step of asking all the voters to arrive at such a consensus instead of persuading the Unionist members of Parliament. On Monday, February 3, O'Neill met with the governor-general, Lord Grey. The next day Parliament was dissolved and a general election called on February 24. It would be a strange election, not so much to choose members to Stormont—that outcome was easy to predict—but rather to decide on the leadership of the Unionist Party.

O'Neill could look back to what should have been a commendable record. He had arrived in office at a moment of severe recession and low provincial spirit. Almost all the economic indicators had been poor. Unemployment had gone up steadily over the previous decade. The average worker's weekly earnings were only 78 percent of those in Great Britain. Housing had been miserable, with 19.3 percent of the homes with no water and 22.6 percent with no flush toilets. There had been too few yearly housing starts, six thousand instead of the ten thousand planned, and too few building starts of any kind. There was potential weakness in the old agricultural sector and a general despondency. Times had been bad. Now, there was still unemployment and economic difficulties, poorish wages, shortages in new houses, and agricultural problems; but much had been accomplished. Progress was visible.

His technocratic solutions that sought new industry, new growth points, a modern infrastructure, and a liberal investment climate had, O'Neill would claim, turned the province around. New industry had been brought into Ulster—Michelin, DuPont, ICI, Goodyear, Enkalon, Courtaulds—Northern Ireland was the center of the new artificial fibers industry, a British manufacturing bright spot. The opening to the South, the meetings with Lemass and Lynch and the end to the IRA campaign, had put the constitutional threat on the shelf and validated the Stormont system. The new O'Neill congeniality toward the Catholic community, a tone of decency, indicated the direction of future reforms. These reforms had to come slowly, of course, after careful preparation to calm loyalists' fears, but not so slowly, of course, as to antagonize London.

The habits and prejudices could not be discarded overnight nor the system transformed at the request of reckless and radical critics or even London Labour ministers. Not only had there been vast and beneficial change in the province, but also most of those who opposed O'Neill's reforms did so under the stained banners of the discredited ultra-Orange. Paisley, Bunting, and the others were voices from the past. Such diatribes had led to the violent confrontations with the civil rights marchers. Such opponents should have been a political asset. The Stormont politicians like West, Craig, and Faulkner were vindictive and ambitious, concerned with their own future, old grievances, personal matters, not the issues. They offered no valid alternatives, only said no. Thus, O'Neill could face the election with some political equanimity, for it was the only means to put down the hard men in and out of Parliament by translating the December wave of support for moderation and decency into votes.

So in the province all attention was shifted to electoral matters in what would be one of the few significant contests in provincial history. Once Unionist hegemony had been established elections had been tribal; all Protestants voted Unionist and Catholics did not. The differences within the Protestant community rarely engendered "politics" outside the Unionist Party. Usually in the past the Unionists had settled most differences in private and kept the elections as referenda on the national issue—the tribal vote that left as the only open question the division of the few other seats. Those few other Catholic seats were of little real use to anyone. In 1965 only thirty-nine of the fifty-two seats had been contested and most of the results even then were a foregone conclusion. This election would be not a vote of confidence on Ulster as established but on O'Neill as leader. In 1969 there were two kinds of Unionists. Some, like Paisley running against the Prime Minister in O'Neill's Bannside district, were not really Unionists but loyalists. Some Unionists like Craig or Brooke or Faulkner or even O'Neill's cousin Major James Chichester-Clark had personal ambitions and varied political attitudes. The Nationalists would send out the usual candidates to keep the tribal vote. They would in a sense be O'Neill votes but ones that would do him little good. The new people thrown up by the crisis, however, were interested in issues, not the Unionist leadership problem or the Nationalist ritual. Michael Farrell as PD candidate would run against both Paisley and O'Neill. The moderates like Hume could run in safe Nationalist constituencies and win seats. The PD wanted a stage as much as a seat they were unlikely to win.

The result of the general election, announced on February 26, should have settled the matter of O'Neill but somehow did not. Seemingly little had changed.

	1965	1969
Unionist	37	39
Nationalist	9	6
Independent	0	3
Northern Ireland Labour Party	2	2
Republican Labour	2	2
National Democratic	1	0
Liberals	1	0

This was not the case. Paisley as a Protestant Unionist, had polled 6,331 votes to O'Neill's 7,745, with 2,310 for PD's Farrell. It was a symbolic disaster for the Prime Minister in his own Bannside. Paisley's vote was the crusher; the others were discounted as mere Catholic votes. Paisley's partner, Major Bunting, did not do as well, trailing badly in Belfast-Victoria, but then he was not Paisley, the Big Man. And Paisley had almost run Captain O'Neill into the ground and may have run him out of politics.

Elsewhere the new faces thrown up by the civil rights crisis indicated change not continuity: Bernadette Devlin (PD) polled 5,812 in South Derry against Major Chichester-Clark; John Hume and Ivan Cooper won in Derry (Foyle) and Mid-Derry, not unexpectedly, over Nationalist candidates. Hume and Cooper and some others would soon need a new party to go with their voting appeal. Paddy Devlin won a new seat in the Falls for the old NILP. McCann had come in a respectable third for the Derry Labour Party with 1,993 votes in Derry, trailing

Hume and McAteer. And Paddy Kennedy won in Belfast Central for Gerry Fitt's Republican Labour, although both parties only stayed even in Stormont seats. There were only so many Catholic votes to go around and no evidence of a tribal shift bringing in extra votes. What it all translated out to in Northern Ireland terms was a continued erosion of O'Neill's position. Those at the top who do not win, lose.

In the twenty-three constituencies where an O'Neill Unionist candidate faced an anti-O'Neill candidate, the totals were 141,914 votes and eleven seats for the Prime Minister and 130,619 votes and twelve seats against. The old Unionist Party had been divided; some had left it to vote against O'Neill and many of those who stayed waited for him to go. O'Neill had his Bannside seat but not his vote of confidence. He had lost. He was not alone. The Nationalists had lost three seats and the future to Hume and Cooper, who had both won as independents, Hume defeating the Nationalist leader Eddie McAteer. The NILP had seen its militants drift into PD or the civil rights movement and would see Paddy Devlin, who beat Harry Diamond of Republican Labour, go as well; like the Nationalists, events had passed them by. They addressed issues no longer thought crucial. Outside Stormont the militants took over NICRA and on March 16 four of the old members of the executive, including Betty Sinclair, resigned in protest. On the other end of the spectrum, Paisley and Bunting, emboldened by the Bannside vote and the Unionist divisions, were eager for more action. The list of results looked the same but everything had changed.

On February 28, at Stormont, O'Neill received twenty-three Unionist Parliamentary Party votes, so cast without enthusiasm; Faulker was opposed, with Craig abstaining. Faulkner obviously wanted to be Prime Minister and was first in line now, with Craig eager on the sidelines, looking for allies and an opening. Ten O'Neill opponents walked out of the vote and three of his supporters were not in the Unionist Party. Nothing was thus decided by the election. O'Neill was still there but on toleration. Yet much had changed. The new people were validated by their own: Devlin and Farrell, Hume and Cooper, Paisley and Craig. The question still remained, as Hume underlined in his maiden speech in Stormont, whether politics was going to remain on the streets or be fought out at Stormont. Yet there was no real majority for moderation in the Parliament and so no effective leadership that was not open to attack from the militants in various ways. There was nothing new that O'Neill could do.

There was no effective way to keep the streets cleared by either an appeal to responsibility of Hume's civil rights activists or to old Unionist loyalties represented by O'Neill. Few militant loyalists would now heed the Stormont cabinet, a coterie of losers. There was no way to drive the demonstrators and their opponents off the streets that was not counterproductive. There was no way to fashion any real consensus inside or outside of politics. There was no consensus. And so far the province had been wracked only by politics, inside Parliament or outside in the street, unruly, loud, now and then splattered with blood, but politics still—agitation, demonstration, ritual, and riot. Despite loyalists' suspicions and fears, no IRA had appeared, there had been no return to the gun by the hidden republicans. And despite Catholic concern, there had been no murderous Orange pogroms or repeats of the Malvern Street murders.

It was cold comfort as the province faced an uncertain future, a future filled with opportunities for action, good and bad, and so a future boding danger and disaster as well as hope. Those who wanted change were still euphoric if they counted no cost and deeply concerned if they did. Those who wanted a return to the past increasingly found the present unpalatable and the future dangerous. They too felt action necessary. For those whose only weapons were reason and restraint, those in the Unionist establishment, those moderate nationalists, those without politics but only a desire for peace, there was fear that trouble, serious trouble, was possible—was probable. There was a long, nasty record of anxiety coalescing in violence in Northern Ireland. Rituals of revolt and domination might no longer serve. Recourse to old legitimacies in new and troubled times was possible. Recourse to new methods, ideas, and initiative might not produce the desired adjustment to present reality. No one knew whether tomorrow would be like yesterday. The power of the past brooded, capable of inspiring those who might march to a different and more deadly drummer. The past in Ireland, like men's minds, changed ever so slowly, if at all. Prediction of the future had just become very difficult in Northern Ireland.

3

Passage to Chaos:
March 1969–March 1970

It's to hell with the future and live on the past.
May the Lord in His mercy be kind to Belfast. . . .
Ballad to a traditional refrain
Maurice James Craig

For those not intimate with the dynamics of the Stormont system, politics seemed to move along as before once O'Neill had been confirmed by the provincial election and the Unionist Party. This was not the case. For a Prime Minister to go to the general public to solve Unionist divisions during a major crisis, when the system was under assault, was unknown and for many unforgivable. And to many Unionists the crisis seemed to have been O'Neill's doing, arising from his meetings with Lemass and Lynch, his amenability to reform suggestions, and his advocacy of "progress" that the province could not afford and did not need. Ian Paisley's 6,331 votes were an intolerable affront to the Prime Minister. Moderate Unionists felt him an extreme sectarian agitator, a Free Presbyterian symbol of the worst Not An Inch bigots. He was crude, not of the gentry, not a proper person at all—and he had received 6,331 votes; or rather O'Neill had not received them. O'Neill did not have the trust of his people.

The question at Stormont was when he would go. And an equally important question was whether he would be replaced by Brian Faulkner, merchant not gentry, no Eton and Irish Guards, stolid, ambitious, too militant, a nonstarter—but in contrast to Paisley, proper. Could such as Faulkner fashion a Unionist majority in Stormont? Craig, too ambitious and too militant, was a far outside runner. Who else was there that offered change and a defense of the system but Faulkner or the likes of Craig? Critics of the system, less intimately concerned with Stormont maneuvers, simply saw weakness, division, and movement for the first time in fifty years. Militant defenders saw the same weakness, division, and movement—but movement the wrong way. For them O'Neill was a traitor like Lundy of Londonderry, who would have opened the gates to Catholic James II, seeking to regain his throne, in the crucial year of 1689. They would close the gate. All those years ago it had taken thirteen apprentice boys; in 1969 a handful in Stormont would do. People in the province sought historical example, a world shaped by patriot historians often more real than the world beyond the window.

Lundy lived and the Young Irelanders and Carson, who had opposed home rule, and Connolly and Pearse, who had risen in 1916, and all the rest. They were real, looming over the present. So the loyalists summoned up the past in defense of the present. Beyond the agitation of Paisley and Bunting the really hard men increasingly felt the time had come to act, that historical citation was not sufficient for the defense of the system. So far, however, the men at the top had kept the play to themselves. The few hard men in Stormont tended to act as a political magnet for the uncertain Unionists, finding defense in a change at the top, not in recourse to violence.

O'Neill was aware of the drift of Unionist sentiment but felt he must persevere as long as possible. In response to the growing civil disorder, distasteful to the moderate Unionists and even worrisome to moderate Catholics, the new Public Order Bill was introduced. The minority opposition felt that the bill was intended to impose order on their people, not on the province, and resisted not only with parliamentary tactics—forty amendments were offered—but also with techniques lifted from the civil rights movement: Nine members sat down on the floor of the House singing "We Shall Overcome." Outside, the civil rights movement was failing to overcome its own problems. The movement was riven by those of the new Left who avowedly sought socialism and revolution, often with the slogans of the European radicals on Irish banners, and the moderates, who feared the very same socialism and revolution and feared even more the potential official reaction by a system quite capable of real repression. The new radicals did not seem to know that in the Orange state revolution would not be a dinner party. Still, provincial matters moved on: demonstrations for and against O'Neill, for revolution, for civil rights, against the Public Order Bill. Marches took place without incident. Marches and demonstrations were banned, postponed, announced, and canceled. There was a cottage industry in posters and proclamations. There were scuffles and confrontations and late-night seminars.

On Sunday, March 30, in Belfast, the Castlereagh substation electricity transformer was wrecked by an explosion with the damage later estimated at £500,000. Relatively little attention was paid to the explosion because most observers were fearful that the riots might escalate into a Catholic rebellion in the streets or Protestant sectarian pogroms or a civil war. One bomb did not mean much. So far, despite all the turmoil and shouting, the broken heads at Burntollet and the batons before the bridge at Derry, there had still been no recourse to lethal force. There had been no call for a renewed campaign by the IRA or for the Protestants to burn out the Catholics. In fact, Unionist fears aside, the IRA in the province turned up as peacekeeping stewards, more converts to nonviolent demonstrations than representatives of a secret army. The IRA was in fact not manipulating the civil rights people but joining them. And, given all, the Stormont system had adapted, adjusted, eschewed real repression—and so had the majority who might have acted outside the system to defend it. If politics were not normal, politics went on. The debate on the Public Order Bill moved into April, Paisley urged that O'Neill go and the Minister of Home Affairs, Robert Porter, banned a People's Democracy march and meeting. In fact, because of a by-election in Mid-Ulster, politics dominated the news despite another explosion, at the water installation at Dunadry, County Antrim. That bomb was blamed on the IRA by the militant Orangemen and on the militant Orangemen by everyone else. Then attention switched back to the coming by-election for the Westminster parliament, made necessary by the death of the sitting candidate for Mid-Ulster.

In Mid-Ulster the opponents of the Stormont regime faced an uncertain opportunity: a Westminster district that had a Catholic majority, easily lost if the Nationalist vote was split by two candidates. A unity Nationalist candidate would almost certainly win but there was no unity. The republicans felt particularly possessive about the district. This was where IRA man Tom Mitchell had run for the seat three times during the border campaign from his Crumlin Road Prison cell. This was where all the excitement had been when he won the first time, was disqualified, won the second time, was disqualified, and finally lost the third election because the vote was split by an independent Nationalist, a betrayal that still rankled. This was the district where the dogs had even been dragged off the streets of republican villages when the man campaigned so that he spoke to none but his own. Mitchell was still available or, if need be, Kevin Agnew, with his deep republican sympathies, who had been involved in the civil rights movement from the very beginning. It was a republican, not a Nationalist, seat, or so thought they. On the other hand the ambitious Austin Currie, who was by now credited with beginning the civil disobedience campaign with the sit-in at Caledon, Tyrone, wanted to run for the Nationalists. If elected the republican would not sit in Westminster and the Mid-Ulster people and the Nationalist minority in the province would have one fewer spokesman. Currie wanted to speak not only for Mid-Ulster but for Ireland. And the Nationalist Party was still the vehicle of the minority tradition. Those involved in the civil rights movement, in particular those clustered around the People's Democracy, wanted their own, wanted no part of the Nationalist vehicle, which they considered a husk, a Green Tory repository of the comfortable lace-curtain Catholics, soon to be discarded by a risen people. And so much for Currie and the IRA as well, old gunmen and narrow men in trench coats and with obsolete ideas, as irrelevant as Tom Mitchell's old campaign. They would not use the seat and the new Left knew the value of standing on a chair instead of obeying one. They wanted someone of their own.

The young, the protesters and proclaimed revolutionaries, shrewdly suggested no ideologue but Bernadette Devlin from Cookstown, a strong republican area, for she had almost respectable, republican views on the national issue. That issue had divided the small Irish Left for a century and had produced their one great hero-totem, James Connolly, who inexplicably came out on Easter Week 1916 with the pure nationalists and ended wounded, tied to a chair in front of a British army firing squad as another martyr for Ireland. Devlin was both nationalist and socialist and so not as alien as some of the bearded orators of the PD who advocated revolutionary theories or the concept of dual power or seemed eager to reproduce the Paris *événements*, events a long way from the hills of Tyrone and the lanes of Cookstown. Her socialism could be taken as youthful enthusiasm by her elders. As a Westminster candidate she would be remarkably young; but she was impressively articulate, physically brave, had a gift for hard work, and gave evidence of a soft heart. So very young, very sincere, often widely out of touch with the tradition-encrusted electorate, she was accepted by the republicans because she did not look like a stayer in Mid-Ulster politics, backed by the civil rights movement because she symbolized all the idealism of the young, accepted by the traditionalists because she was sound on the national issue, and endorsed by Austin Currie because he had no other choice.

She ran as if pursued, spoke formally sixteen different times in ten different places, never stopped talking over tea, in the car, in front of doors, alongside the road, at wee meetings and grand. She shook hands, stood firm on socialism, and benefited, perhaps, from speeches by the PD—Kevin Boyle and Bowes Egan and Michael Farrell and Fergus Woods showed enthusiasm and confidence. That she frightened the others—she was a rebel woman, a Catholic Castro in a miniskirt—was enough for some of the people on the hillsides who suspected change and opposed any revolution that might benefit them. She became a symbol to thrash the system. She certainly entranced the media, tired of sincere men in business suits deploring violence and evasive spokesmen of the old parties repeating themselves. She attacked the system, attacked O'Neill, suggested the abolition of Stormont, caused as much trouble as she had on the streets of Derry. Devlin was good copy, a wee miniskirted girl crying revolution into the winds of Ulster and offering a happy end for the mass audience. She won.

Bernadette Devlin was elected on April 17, 1969, in a poll of 92 percent; with a margin of over 4,000 votes—33,648 to 29,437—over a Unionist lady, Anna Forrest, widow of the former Unionist member and so in Ireland heir to the seat, who had neither the charisma nor a split in the Catholic votes. Some of those Catholics would have voted for a yellow dog as long as it belonged to the tribe, but in this case they had been delighted to give that vote to the wee lass. Devlin thus became the youngest member of the House of Commons since William Pitt, taking her seat on her twenty-second birthday. The television cameras followed her to London for her maiden speech, and there she proved as newsworthy as she had been in the hills of Ulster. She had lunch with the government chief whip, took her seat, and an hour later gave her speech. Not since the days of F. E. Smith had the House listened to such an electrifying speech said Conservative MP Norman St. John Stevas. Then she rushed for dinner with Lord Longford, her photograph appeared in the evening papers and her views in the editorials of the more proper journals. She was crafted as an Irish rebel come to London. At the top of the lanes and in the small villages the people might not be socialist but, as Devlin noted, they now had a socialist representative, and one sound on the national issue, one of their own.

The Mid-Ulster by-election had momentarily drawn attention away from the accelerating decay of O'Neill's position. Hers was a Catholic seat and so a Catholic had won, no penny on the Unionist scale. But that scale was slipping. In public and in private, support for O'Neill was dribbling away. The Cameron Commission met on Friday, April 18, for the first time. For the militant loyalists it was a sad day and so too for the Derry civil rights people whose demonstration was banned: "The Stormont Government has surrendered the authority of Parliament to the bully boys who now appear to rule this country." On Saturday and Sunday there was a confrontation in Derry between the civil rights people and Paisley supporters that degenerated into rioting. Altnagelvin Hospital had 165 riot casualties, including 86 police. Samuel Devenney of the Bogside collapsed when the police broke into his house for unknown reasons. He later died—a victim, said the nationalists, of police brutality. There were more demonstrations planned. More demonstrations would ensure more riots, more casualties, more risks of escalation—and O'Neill had no answers. On Sunday, April 20, an explosion broke the water pipeline between Silent Valley Reservoir and Belfast, and another under an electricity pylon at Kilmore cut the terminal link built in a joint scheme with the Irish Republic. The loyalist militants blamed the IRA and everyone else blamed the loyalist militants. Everyone tended to blame O'Neill. He was still Prime Minister.

There were grumbles across the Irish Sea as well: O'Neill had apparently used up all credit. In London, Home Secretary James Callaghan noted that "what we seek is equality of rights, privileges, and responsibilities for all citizens in the UK."* He had already referred to Bernadette Devlin's brilliance. He was no friend to Ulster. He wanted to ruin Ulster with reforms. The Orange militants assumed at Stormont the nice, proper Captain O'Neill would do the job for London. On the same day in the House, when Devlin spoke not "about one night of broken glass but of fifty years of human misery," the tide seemed to be flowing against the Union. The only misery that the hard men could see was the fault of a Prime Minister who had let matters drift, let rebels march, watched the power and glory of the system come under assault—even by a girl in a miniskirt talking nonsense in Westminster. It was O'Neill's doing. Even his allies knew the truth: His doing or no, the blame settled on him. On Wednesday, April 23, Major James Chichester-Clark, Minister of Agriculture and O'Neill's cousin, resigned, technically over the one-man-one-vote issue—he felt it was too soon for such a move—but actually to position himself in the leadership stakes.

Two days later an explosion severed the main water pipeline at Annalong carrying much of Belfast's water supply. On the weekend, with water largely cut off, Belfast depended on water wagons and standpipes. O'Neill was being bombed out of office by his own. Unionist politics, thwarted by events and a democratic system, turned to a violent defense. In the spring of 1969, O'Neill generated bombs that concentrated minds on Stormont. On Monday, April 28, O'Neill resigned. He spoke to the province in a farewell message thanking the people who had supported him as he tried to do right—"morally right, political right, right for our country and all who seek to live in peace within it." His loyalist opponents by April 1969 felt that he had been wrong, wrong to try at all to change a tested system, and so had destroyed the peace. They withdrew their support. A few constructed bombs. His nationalist opponents felt he had been too late in seeing the wrong, slow in reform, had not tried hard enough, and worse, had been inept in political maneuver. Somehow, decent or no, he had been the wrong man and so almost everyone watched his departure with equanimity.

O'Neill had lacked sufficient conviction; more important, he had lacked the energy to impose his will. Without charisma, without empathy, without a commanding presence, with all the limitation of his class and caste and but a narrow vision of progress, he had alienated his own without converting the others. He was a decent, kind, often gentle man, not easy in Ulster politics; he had been

*James Callaghan, in *A House Divided: The Dilemma of Northern Ireland* (London: Collins, 1973), gives the English Labour reaction to the Irish crisis.

articulate under pressure; but he was not a man for this season in Northern Ireland. He meant well. He tried, where no one had tried before. It was not enough. He was discarded, bombed out of office by Orangemen who would not give an inch or spare him a kind word, who wanted only the old days and the Catholics miserable. And so he left, was awarded with a title by the British establishment who appreciated his virtues, and found a job in a London merchant bank. He would not be redeemed by events, by historians, or by history. He could not set the crooked straight and so withdrew, leaving the six counties in the hands of a man who felt it too soon to give each man a vote. It was a sad going and hardly noticed as the quarrelsome and determined deployed for further engagements.

To the amazement of all, that cousin, Chichester-Clark, a major not a captain, pipped the apparent heir Brian Faulkner at the post. The new man was also Eton, also Irish Guards, also country family and properly bred and decent, and was sufficiently cunning to win within the Unionist Party seventeen votes to sixteen, O'Neill's last vote was against the new man Faulkner, the shrewdest and most ambitious of them all. The gentry held the hill long lost elsewhere in the United Kingdom. The province might be at the lip of civil turmoil, but the new men, the merchants and money men, would have to wait longer and, it would seem, the minority would have to wait forever. No equal votes for them, no vast reforms. Faulkner was Minister of Development, where he could display any new progressive ideas about development, money, and investment and remain avid for office. The new Prime Minister—taciturn, orthodox, unexpectedly ambitious—hoped that with his cousin gone he could move the province back to normal. That was all most of his own wanted: to be normal, as always. He could stress what had been done to bring the province into line with British practice, normal practice now, let bygones be bygones, especially those matters that might penalize the system. As for the rest, he had no ideas, and never had.

On May 6, he announced an amnesty that covered most of the offenses arising from the demonstrations, including charges against the RUC. Everyone was to get a clean sheet. Paisley seemed content and Michael Farrell and the PD unmoved, which was just as well for the new cabinet: Paisley's toleration and PD's opposition marked a good beginning. The weeks passed without great violence except for continued disturbances around Hooker Street in Belfast, where serious confrontation had been avoided. Derry had been the main arena. On May 21 Chichester-Clark met with Harold Wilson and James Callaghan at Downing Street and returned optimistic about his program and prospects. Matters moved on apace into the summer: assurances to the police and support of the Public Order Bill, progress on one-man-one-vote apparently suddenly ripe with the new times, development plans, social reforms. Paisley was off in Switzerland demonstrating against the Pope, back to the old tricks that did not readily lead to riot. The IRA was burning farms owned by Germans, foreign capitalists, in the Republic, back to their old, mostly symbolic tricks, which did not readily disturb Northern Ireland. There were no more explosions in the province. A few demonstrations took place, there was lots of recrimination; and slowly concern rose about the impact of the Orange summer marching season.

A few months of relative quiet did not assure permanent stability. Maybe it was too quiet. All the players were still on stage, still possessed the same contradictory assumptions, had the same priorities and predilections that had previously led to trouble. On June 16 Roy Bradford, Minister of Commerce, announced in London that even the vacationers (each tourist was a vital asset to the hard-pressed Northern economy) were at ease. "Ask any of the thousands of visitors now enjoying the wonderful colors of June and they will tell you that the North of Ireland is essentially a peaceful place. The tourist has just about as much chance of being molested as he has of being knocked over by a runaway camel."* The residents ran somewhat greater risks.

On June 28 at Strabane a civil rights demonstration and an Orange parade at Dungiven went off quietly, did not spark violence despite counter demonstrations. In fact, increasingly the civil rights people appeared divided between the radicals, McCann and Devlin and the PD, and the reformers like Austin Currie, the Nationalist party people or the moderates who had "sold out." This gave the Unionists, in turn, the opportunity to focus on their own problems. John Taylor told the Young Unionists that there had been a sinister trend during O'Neill's tenure that had now apparently been corrected. Others were not so sure. On July 5, back from Switzerland, Paisley called for the removal of O'Neillites from the government. The provincial pace quickened. The violence that followed a PD march in Armagh on Monday, July 7, indicated that the marching season might again polarize the North just as politics seemed to be easing into the traditional splits, recriminations, and denunciations, the old speeches without rocks and riots.

There was no way, however, to postpone or deflect the traditional Orange marches scheduled for Monday, July 13, to celebrate once again Protestant William's triumph over the Catholic King James II at the Battle of the Boyne in 1690. It would be the 250th anniversary of this sacred Orange event and nearly one hundred thousand were to demonstrate before the Catholic minority their continued faith in combination. Marching to the thudding of the giant Lambeg drums was in troubled times even more necessary, to cow the others and reassure one's own. Cancel and risk riot or permit the march and risk riot seemed the options. And a Unionist government was not about to cancel, not this year nor next nor ever: It was a right that must be exercised to be effective, a right to be seen, to be dominant.

The results on July 13 were not as bad as some had feared but dreadful enough. Paisley spoke to five thousand at the Diamond, Loughgall, County Armagh, with venom but without violence. In Derry heavy rioting began with attacks by the young Catholics on the RUC that lasted deep into Monday morning. At one point several police fired shots into the air to get clear of a cul-de-sac. Two civilians were taken to the hospital with bullet wounds from such "warning" shots. Twenty police were injured. Buildings were burned. There was also trouble in Dungiven, where a police baton charge was apparently the cause of the death of Francis McCloskey, a sixty-six-year-old Catholic. There was trouble in Lurgan and trouble in Belfast in the Crumlin Road area along the Catholic-Protestant divide.

*Richard Deutsch and Vivien Magowan, *Northern Ireland, 1968–1973: A Chronology of Events, Vol. 1, 1968–1971* (Belfast: Blackstaff Press, 1973), p. 30.

More ominously, the rioting in Derry was renewed on Monday. Violence was no longer a weekend matter.

Porter as Minister of Home Affairs announced that several hundred Ulster Special Constables were to be called up for standby duty: The B Specials were back, bringing with them a largely justified reputation as a sectarian force, bigots in state uniforms, armed to intimidate Catholics. For years a Protestant neighbor might pass the time of day, shop across the same counter, borrow a spade and lend tea, but once in a B Special uniform he grew cold, and hard-eyed, and all social warmth froze. It was an amazing transformation, and once seen it was never forgotten. As B Specials, Protestants served their system. The Unionists saw it as a necessary and appropriate service: If not the loyal, then who else would defend their way of life? Porter felt that the police were being hard-pressed throughout the province and the issue was order not old grievances. He had only three thousand constables to control a province of five thousand square miles, to protect a million and a half people. It was not now enough. The RUC was understaffed and overextended and needed the aid and comfort of the B Specials.

The B Specials were untrained in crowd control, unprepared for more than roadblocks and guard duty. They were shaped as a symbolic shield against the mythical IRA that had in 1920 been real enough to summon forth such a citizens' army. For fifty years the minority had regarded the force as a means of intimidation. The Specials were everything that the Catholics detested. Their presence, however logical to the Unionists in Stormont, however helpful to a hard-pressed police, was likely to be counterproductive in changing times. If the Specials moved near action, moved near militant demonstrators or moved within sight of the now constantly present cloud of young Catholics eager for violence, the whole provincial powder keg might go up. The Specials could unite troublemaker, demonstrator, and the conventional as one, all opposed to the pasts reestablished by legal vigilantes. Fortunately for Porter, the Derry disturbances began to die out on Tuesday before the B Specials could cause an escalation.

In London the Labour government, and Callaghan and the Home Office especially, had watched the evolution of the Irish problem with a wary but largely innocent eye. The London establishment—civil servants, politicians, editors, bankers, the trade union leadership, the BBC producers, the dons and bishops— was almost totally divorced from Ireland. These people knew nothing much of the island and cared less. The Irish problem in British politics had been settled in 1921. There was nothing to be gained in Ireland, nothing anyone wanted to learn, nothing to attract attention except good fishing, golf clubs, and the surety for the Tories of the Unionist votes in Westminster. Northern Ireland matters were not discussed, by agreement in Commons, by choice elsewhere.

In 1921 Ireland had disappeared into the Celtic mists and, North or South, had emerged only as a subject when Éire had not only failed to join the Allies but had also been suspected (falsely) of harboring German U-boats; in fact de Valera regularly violated Dublin's neutrality to British advantage. Still, Éire had not signed up like the other little countries, so there was a legacy of popular suspicion to go with a continuing unstated prejudice against those Irish: Protestant or Catholic, they were Paddies all until they became in Finchley or Leeds indistinguishable, English too, British actually. So there were the stage Irish, feckless blunder and drink; the emigrant Irish, Celtic until transmuted into British; and on the other side of Saint George's Channel was the little island, once full of poets and saints, that surrounded the salmon rivers and golf links.

No one in Britain had ever really understood the Irish or wanted to; in fact, no one even *liked* the Irish as long as they stayed Irish, no matter whether rich or poor, Catholic or Protestant, here or there. If, like Captain Terence O'Neill, Eton and Irish Guards, one could circulate in the clubs of the establishment as the country gentleman, then the Irish connection was immaterial: Many Irish titles had always had English holders. If this were not the case, as was true with almost all on the island, then the establishment and the public harbored a bias largely hidden even from themselves. The Irish, having refused to be British, and showing no interest over the centuries in the charms, disciplines, and priorities of the United Kingdom, were an irritant. A 1413 English law indicated the attitude of the English for the past five centuries: "All Irish men, Irish clerks and beggars be voided out of the realm." The sentiment was sufficiently popular to be reincorporated in a 1629 law. But though the British barely recognized their own prejudice, they did see that Irish matters never had been easy. In 1807 an Englishman, Sydney Smith, a rare exception, had noted this one great flaw in British political acumen, in British cunning, and so was cited down through the decades:

> The moment the very name of Ireland is mentioned, the English seem to bid adieu to common feeling, common prudence, and common sense, and to act with the barbarity of tyrants, and the fatuity of idiots.*

Fair or not, in 1969 it was accurate to say that no one in Britain wanted an Irish problem, few knew anything about a real Ireland, and fewer wanted their acquaintance broadened.

Sitting in London, Callaghan, a Celt by birth if not inclination, had as much as any British politician showed an interest in Northern Ireland and a concern with economic development; but he, like most others, had been drawn to the issue only by the rising chaos. Around him within the establishment, the ignorance on Irish matters was vast. Few knew the map, few had visited the island, fewer knew any Irish history, late or soon, and almost no one in London could grasp the enormous differences in the institutions and attitudes of the two islands. The island was thought not really foreign: a play state in the South and a bit of the United Kingdom in the North; a vacation land, rather as if Cornwall were crossed with the Congo.

In point of fact within the establishment clumps of specialists on South Arabian tribes or the history of the Hittites could more easily be found than those conversant with Irish politics. Thus, the London center, not just at the beginning but for a very, very long time, could grasp the island problems only by analogy, by the misapplication of experience, by institutionalized assumptions all warped by

*The citation from *Letters of Peter Plymley*, 1807, is regularly quoted—in Ireland, at least, and more rarely in despair in Britain.

inarticulated prejudice. And beyond the center, the British people were in large part moved by an even greater ignorance and deep distaste made more complex and more serious because it went unrecognized. America knew that the nation had been racist, was still largely racist, and was engaged in a difficult struggle to transform this legacy; but the British knew only that they were a fair and just and decent people, no bigots they (at least not until the Commonwealth immigrants, black and brown and various shades of amber, began to appear in great numbers). They might not like foreigners, but then who did? They did not always accept Jews readily, but this was a minor matter for the English at least. The Irish were—well, should not be—different. Since almost all were different, they were tacitly assumed lesser. What all in Britain really knew, from historical analogy, from folk memory, from the application of common sense, was the virtue of prudence: Ireland offered no rewards. The result of these assumptions and considerations was that in July 1969 in London there was on Ireland a general agreement. And Callaghan received the word: "The advice came to me from all sides was on no account to get sucked into the Irish bog."*

In the summer of 1969, from London at least, Irish matters could be viewed, when there was time, with detachment if not absolute objectivity. Consequently, the pattern of British response was relatively easy to see between June and September. In one variant or another the reaction would be repeated for a generation. First, no one knew much about Ireland, except that secretly they did not like the Irish. Second, there was no gain to become involved, to learn more, or even to act. Third, if acting was required the easy move was to try familiar means from parliamentary commissions to royal visits: Send the usual over to Ireland and get on with other matters. And so year after year the same innocence and ignorance and distaste shaped British actions. As is the case with most governments and certainly with the British, those who make real decisions are pressed for time and have limited information. Vision is short, response hasty and shaped in part to coarse political need.

In the summer of 1969 Callaghan had other, more pressing, more interesting, more important problems: There was legislation on race relations where reform faced severe obstacles; there was a bill on gambling; there was a problem with Kenyan Asian immigrants; and there was always the full in-box, crammed with day-to-day responsibilities. All of these matters, large and small, had political ramifications for Callaghan, not unmindful of his own career; for the government, individually united on the need for a further period of office; and so for the Labour Party, facing the prospect of a general election. The cabinet and especially Prime Minister Harold Wilson had other policy and political problems even more pressing than gambling and Kenyan Asians, who like the Irish represented no voting bloc. A long view was rare even on those issues that had evolved into permanent considerations: the strength of the pound, the special relationship with the United States, the aspirations of the trade unions. There was little time for minor matters. In time there would be a few Irish specialists, a few civil servants who had lasted the course, a few who served with great enthusiasm on

*Callaghan, p. 15.

Irish matters. But Ireland would become a central concern only when it was almost too late and the government was urged to act by the latest atrocity. If at all possible, the natural inclination in London was not to act, or to act hastily, distressed that lethargy had not paid dividends. In July Callaghan noted that "for the time being we decided we would wait."*

The reluctance to act except through the existing system, which had proven ineffectual, was a constant. Police could not be sent instead of the army because there was no precedent, no legal machinery, no energy; sending the army was easier. Just as the rules of the House of Commons had been fashioned to prevent discussion of Northern Ireland and so to allow the members, whatever their party, to do nothing, so the system explained the inaction that many found congenial. Always the government would find pressing and convincing legal and procedural reasons why something could not be done, why initiatives that were easy for the laity to advise were somehow impossible. There was no sense of urgency until the next crisis, the next atrocity, until the evening news, until an outraged British public demanded something be done. So in the very beginning of the Irish Troubles, Callaghan's first choice—the British choice—was to do nothing. Like Scarlett O'Hara, he would think about Ireland another day. For Scarlett the film ended with a slammed door. For Callaghan and a long parade of successors, the door would remain open on the Irish bog.

Actually, Callaghan had taken thought on Irish matters, as would many over the years. The British tendencies to inertia and innocence, ignorance and bias were not absolute. In real life there were those who understood the Irish, understood with affection, gave serious and early consideration to Irish matters. Callaghan, who arrived in the Home Office to find Ireland pigeonholed next to wild birds, had considered various options if Stormont ran into really impossible problems. If order had to be imposed, it could not simply be done with the forces to hand in the province. The RUC was already stretched and the British army consisted of the Thirty-ninth Infantry Brigade, two infantry battalions, and one armored car regiment. The officers in the province were inclined to think that the armored cars could prevent any Irish army intrusions (and in the summer of 1969 everyone was doing a rethink on an uncertain future), but that if sectarian war began a great many more troops were going to be needed on the ground. In London too consideration had been given to the implications of any such dispatch of the army to maintain order. For a time, if Stormont failed, there would be the need to rule the province directly. How rule? How long? At what cost?

The early work was done in isolation from the establishment in general and the cabinet in particular, but it was done. Often splendid contingency work done down the power pyramid is forgotten during the crisis, but in this case the Home Secretary had been interested and had come to several far-reaching conclusions. If dispatched, their army would have to stay in the province and would have to answer to London, not to Stormont: The Unionists had few friends in Labour. This would probably indicate the irreversible erosion of the Unionist system. The army, then, could not and would not be sent in and snatched out; and while in the

*Callaghan, p. 15.

province the army could not be allowed to act for Stormont or even be seen to act for Stormont. Once Stormont so lost control over the province, once the disorder in the streets had knocked the system off the wall, the Queen's men would not want to put it back together again. The disappearance of the Stormont system would produce few regrets within the Labour Party. Although some in the party thought of the Irish crisis as an undesired new responsibility, Callaghan and others were determined to act on Irish events if the turmoil grew to eliminate present grievances. The turmoil might not grow, Stormont might creep through aware of the necessity of reform after the close call. Restraint by all and good luck might ease everyone through the crisis. So there matters stood when the Belfast violence began on August 4.

Chichester-Clark, first by telephone, then by letter, and finally in a direct meeting with Callaghan on August 8 in London, explored the implications of a future deployment of the British army. The Unionists thought of it as their army (Chichester-Clark a major, O'Neill a captain). There was no cheerful news from Callaghan, who stressed that along with the army would surely come political intervention. Chichester-Clark was asked to look down the road and see the end of Stormont. Obviously he did not like the view. For many Unionists an end of Stormont would mean the beginning of the inevitable absorption of the province in the Irish Republic, an unmitigated, irreversible disaster, the end of history. Once moving down that road there was no coming back; in that beginning was the end. Yet the province could not be allowed to collapse into anarchy, and would not be so allowed by London. So Chichester-Clark left London with only the authority to use CS gas if the troubles escalated and the realization that the intervention of the British army would be the beginning, not the end, of his troubles. Stormont was wedged between two rocks.

In the province the Unionist community shared Chichester-Clark's anguish. In less than a year their world had been turned over by the use of the most special of Northern Ireland rituals: the parade. This time the parade was little more than a Catholic mob pretending to protest but seeking to provoke violence, to harass the police, to cause trouble that would be visible in London. And this time the civil rights parades had done just that and in the process distorted the reality of the Unionists. They felt that their image had been distorted and then dispatched to the world by a media eager for hard-edged villains. Worse, the Unionists had not been defended in London, where almost no one within the establishment, not even within the Conservative Party, seemed to understand or care about their fears and anguish or recall their service and sacrifice and loyalty. The world and Britain too sided with the others, the traitors, the mobs in the streets.

Most responsible Northern Unionist opinion was willing to accept reasonable reforms, if not for justice's sake then at least to bring the province into line with British practice. Many of these reforms were under way, others had been promised, all would surely come in time. The street demonstrations were thus not for the reform but for the ruin of the province. In any case the reforms had been oversold. The grievances were not really so acute. The Catholics exploited or at least used the social services, wanted as right new council houses, kept to their own institutions, schools, and Mater Hospital by choice. Huge families were kept on welfare and every granny wore health service glasses. They hired only their own, went only to their own pubs, played their own games. They wanted separate but more—to have their own and the state's as well. Anyway, the sensible Catholic could now see that the system was going to adjust in certain matters. Much had always been made of little; even the Orange parades were social occasions, enjoyed by all. The bad old days, if they had ever existed but in Catholic imagination, had gone. That was history. The present was a prosperous, orderly province, a grand, wee country. But this side of the argument had no listeners, was turned into bigotry—which did not seem to be so to those who had been bred on the vices of the feckless Catholics.

Increasingly the Unionists felt that all or most of the Catholics had encouraged rampant violence in the streets. The civil rights leaders urged peace and profited by chaos. The Catholics all profited by the chaos. And proper Catholics then made this recourse to violence legitimate by their willingness to vote for a socialist student in a miniskirt as long as she was a *Catholic* socialist student in a miniskirt. No one cared about Protestant rights. Who paid the taxes? Who had to keep order? No one would admit that Catholic Ireland was bigoted too, that Southern leaders had created a priest-ridden society that each year saw fewer Protestants, fewer freedoms—books were still banned and films and legislation too paraded past the priests. Everyone knew it but no one in the media bothered to cover it.

So the grievances went on and on, repeated to the faithful, recounted at club and pub. No one would admit that the civil rights banners flew over an army disciplined by IRA stewards and filled with communists, anarchists, agitators, all encouraged from abroad, all eager to destroy democracy as well as Stormont. No one recalled the province's loyalty past and present, the province's accomplishments. The BBC television readers, the newspaper editorial writers, the foreign correspondents, and the London columnists smeared the whole province, made every Unionist an Orange bigot, exaggerated the admitted failings and atypical extremists. The province was not crafted in Paisley's image. In London every single newspaper but the conservative and somewhat cranky *Daily Telegraph* sympathized with the demonstrators, urged further and faster reform, and in sudden and ignorant concern lectured and hectored and insulted. BBC was obviously biased. The whole world's media was biased and only added fuel to the province's fires. No one had a kind word. No one noticed the hectic pace of reforms under Chichester-Clark. Certainly, the minority showed no sign of gratitude, gave no hint that the majority was responding generously, that the Unionists were not also Orange fanatics. The majority did not feel at fault, was committed to fair shares, wanted only a respite for themselves, for the RUC, for the province.

Instead of a respite came more trouble in Belfast, the most dangerous arena of all, where tens of thousands of volatile working people, many unemployed, most with countervailing fears and prejudices, lived in abutting districts and estates, the edges mingled and many of the other persuasion on the wrong ground. In Belfast violence might easily erupt into a general pogrom, a fear that had already led to a trickle of population exchange as the odd family moved back to live with their own or away from the boundary of the other community. Those deep in the wrong enclave began to pack, mentally at least. On Saturday, August 2, Protestants from a Junior Orange parade backed by two hundred members of the

Protestant Shankill Defense Organization tried to attack the Catholic Unity flats, one of the Belfast horrors, huge and bleak, a misguided attempt to house workers in the center city. The police attempting to turn back the attack ran into trouble from both sides: The Protestants threw stones, the Catholics petrol bombs. The violence continued Sunday and Monday, with the police hard-pressed, at one point breaching Protestant barricades with an armored vehicle and a water cannon. When peace settled in on Tuesday after the worse communal violence in thirty years, the RUC inspector general, Anthony Peacocke, still felt that his police could handle the crisis without the aid of troops. Those who could remember—and many could since fifty years is as nothing in Irish memory—even recalled the street battles of the Tan War in 1920–21. And there had been no renewed war. The RUC had stood firm, won through—and once again been denied credit. It would be a continuing refrain.

Chichester-Clark had not been as sure about future prospects and so had flown to London for his talks with Callaghan. The Belfast weekend had boded ill for the scheduled Apprentice Boys' parade in Londonderry on August 12. On that Tuesday, a week away, some thirty thousand Orangemen would journey to Catholic Derry to march along their traditional routes so that the Fenians could watch and listen to patriot speeches: Once more the Orangemen would display their domination. It was likely that this would be one parade too many, one provocation too many for an increasingly truculent and resentful audience. The Derry Catholics had been soured on generations of insults and grievances, many beyond legal reform to ameliorate, the grievances of the spirit. And that spirit had been emboldened by the season of protest. To parade dominance one must be assured of the intimidated.

In the province all the responsible people recognized the dangers inherent in the Derry parade. From the first the Orangemen had felt that they must march if for no other reason than that not to would probably assure violence by the truculent minority and by their own in any case. Dr. Russell Abernethy, governor of the Apprentice Boys, said on August 1 that every reasonable measure had been taken to avoid giving reason for interference with their parade. It was, of course, the very fact of the parade that gave reason. The Ministry of Home Affairs indicated that the traditional march would be permitted. Banning would surely lead to trouble and the parade was a *legal* display and so must be protected. And for a week politicians and spokesmen for both traditions urged peace and moderation and restraint. On Sunday, August 10, prayers for peace were offered in all Derry churches. The republican Seán Keenan, chairman of the Derry Defense Association, told a crowd of a thousand amid appeals for peace that since no one wanted sectarian strife, he hoped no group would even remotely consider marching through the Bogside. Eddie McAteer, John Hume, Ivan Cooper, and the other Derry people worked overtime urging moderation. Minister of Home Affairs Robert Porter asked "everyone in the days ahead to bear themselves with dignity and restraint" in an appeal on the eve of the parade. At midnight on Monday, August 11, Roaring Meg, a siege gun used by the Protestants to defend the city in 1689 against the Catholics, roared out over Derry in the annual salute. Bonfires were lit in Protestant areas. All over the province Orangemen were set to move on Londonderry (not Derry), their city, as was their right, and practice; their demonstration was legal as well as traditional. Who would say them nay? So the flash point would come on the following day when the drums rolled.

To the enormous relief of practically everyone, the parade, some fifteen thousand bedecked and bannered Orangemen, moved along to the band music with a minimum of fuss. The potential Catholic stone throwers below the walls at Waterloo Place on the edge of the Bogside were kept at a distance by the police. The Protestant crowds limited themselves to shouting back insults. The police (seven hundred were available in the city) for some time had no great difficulty in maintaining order, keeping the parade going, and penning the Catholics in the Bogside.

The RUC was focused on what was assumed to be the major problem: keeping the Catholics in the Bogside away from the center of town. On their part, for weeks the Catholic spokesmen of all persuasions had indicated that their fear was an invasion of the Bogside, and few made any secret of their fear that such an intrusion would have either the cooperation or the participation of the police. Some Orange militants were not averse to such a foray, but many wanted only to walk the route, meet their friends, perform their duty, and go home. And many did just this despite the increased stone throwing along Waterloo Place. For two hours there was almost no trouble. Some 150 coaches filled with Orangemen and drove out of the city. But then an RUC-Catholic confrontation grew more likely as the police pushed into the streets around Waterloo Place to keep the Bogsiders from moving out. The Bogsiders, feeling the pressure, in turn pushed back to keep the invading RUC out. Efforts to calm everyone had mixed results. McAteer spoke. Hume asked that the police move the Protestants who were crowding behind the RUC lines a little further back but in sight of the Catholics. The Catholics saw a line of RUC moving forward, followed by a Protestant mob. The RUC saw Catholics pushing forward to get at the Protestants.

Robin Chichester-Clark, a Westminster Unionist MP, tried to help calm the crowd. Then, eventually and disastrously, the RUC perceived the Catholics as threatening. The police thus became part of the problem. They charged, just as the Catholics had feared, and were followed by two hundred or so Protestant scavengers, just as the Catholics had feared. The worst Catholic scenario had occurred. Despite everything, despite all the conciliatory efforts from republican Seán Keenan to Unionist Chichester-Clark, despite everyone's pleas and warning, the police were determined to baton their way into the Bogside at the head of a Protestant mob.

The rationales of the RUC differed from Catholic perception. The Orange parade was traditional, legal, and for most policemen desirable. The Bogsiders behind their provocative barricades threw stones, caused trouble, and were responsible for any disorder. In a well-run, well-policed city, there was no excuse for barricades, nor for truculent crowds eager for combat. In Londonderry there was going to be no revolt of the minority as long as the RUC could act, and so act they did once revolt was perceived. The long months of criticism, the indigestible provocation of Catholic actions (IRA man Seán Keenan as peacemaker was an added insult), and the habits of a career led to the baton charge to beat the Fenians back if not into the ground. Once the fighting started there was really no longer a police agenda, no real attempt at peacekeeping or even scattering resistance by wile or maneuver. What the police wanted was direct confrontation: to smash a resistance that in the end, probably in the beginning, was an attack on the integrity of the state and the system. Such an insult could not be controlled by the judicious use of police techniques, even had they been available, but only by a resort to violent intimidation.

The police surged into the barricades and were stopped. They tried again. The confrontation developed into a pattern until six in the evening, when RUC Sergeant Pendleton drove a Humber armored car equipped with a protective grid into the major Rossville Street barrier. There police penetration ground to a halt because of the increasing hail of Molotov cocktails, petrol-filled milk bottles prepared over the weekend and distributed to key defense points. The supply was topped up by those too young to fight at the barricades. The center of the Bogside resistance became the nine-story Rossville flats building, farther in from Waterloo Place, at the entrance to the old Bogside and not far from the FREE DERRY sign, which had been touched up by a professional for visitors and tourists. From the roof of the flats young men kept up a barrage of the petrol bombs, and even with the barricade momentarily in ruins they turned back the RUC and the trailing Protestant mob. Unable to force a way into the Bogside and suffering considerable losses from the fighting, the police withdrew from the more exposed positions to William Street on the edge of the district. There fighting continued into the night and the next day.

Finally, after a telephone call to Porter at the Home Affairs Ministry, the RUC began firing CS gas canisters into the Bogside on Monday night just before midnight. Coughing, eyes streaming, the defenders wrapped their faces in wet cloth and smothered the spitting canisters as they landed; the defenders would not be moved. The low-lying Bogside was soon shrouded in a gas cloud, but those on the top of the Rossville flats were largely untouched. The few canisters that reached the roof were kicked off or doused. From there the battlefield spread out below. The crowds piled more junk on the barricades, pried up stones to throw, ran and watched. Down below were the burning buildings set on fire by the petrol bombs—the bakery, the courthouse, several houses beyond reach of the fire fighters—all sending up churning clouds of smoke to mingle with the CS gas. The police lines engaged in repeated baton charges and sent a constant rain of gas shells, popping and cracking above the din of the crowd. This panorama of a community in revolt was filmed by those on hand, and was a magnet to the media rushing to the scene before the action ended.

There was no end of action, no rest in Derry for the RUC nor in the province for anyone. Derry people began to phone their friends all over the province. Ireland was soon linked up to the barricades. To divert the authorities from what they defined as an unwarranted invasion of Catholic Derry by a police mob, Catholics attacked RUC stations in Coalisland, Strabane, and Newry. The RUC in Derry should not have reinforcements. Control was slipping away from Stormont, from all authority. On Wednesday the fighting in Derry continued running down RUC strength, using up hundreds of rounds of tear gas, never much moving from the edges of the Bogside. The RUC could—someday—go home; the Catholics were home. Their energy levels were higher. The barricades held. In Belfast RUC stations came under attack as barricades went up in West Belfast to seal off the area from both the police and the Protestants. There would be no RUC reinforcements for the Bogside from Belfast. There were reports of trouble in Armagh, Dungannon, Lurgan, Newry, Dungiven, and Enniskillen. From Stormont the province appeared on the edge of open revolt. The RUC, stretched way too thin, suddenly felt besieged, more at risk than any time since 1922. A policeman's uniform was no protection, rather the reverse. With limited intelligence, uncertain leadership, and no understanding of the mood of the Catholics or the nature of the disorder, the RUC did not know how to respond other than with baton charges. If the Fenians could not be shot and would not be intimidated, what then?

Two British police officers, Robert Mark and Douglas Osmond, sent on August 16 as observers, would later find the RUC critically ill-prepared:

> The police, they said, were on the defensive. Sentries had been armed with machine-guns at the stations; there were large numbers of men sitting around in poor accommodation waiting for something to happen . . . one country police station [was] shuttered, bolted and barred . . . and nothing could be seen except the smiling Irish afternoon. They found the station covered in litter and cigarette stubs and the vehicles and other equipment. The men were just sitting there waiting for a non-existent attack to be made on them. Mark and Osmond went back there three or four days later and found things in exactly the same disorganized and dirty state.*

The RUC was as much a paramilitary force as it was a police force. By inclination and by training, the RUC in August 1969 expected an attack from those who had ample reason to attack. They felt no need to go out into the Catholic heartland to impose the will of the system—just being in uniform did that; but the RUC had always felt an urgency to act on provocation, on their own ground, on the defense. The best defense was to intimidate the others. If that didn't work, and it always had but might not always do so, then one gave not an inch.

The RUC in Derry had felt the need to intimidate by their own march into the Bogside. When the Catholics resisted, the police wanted to impose a penalty on them. They did not want to get into the Bogside and run riot, as the Catholics feared, but rather to impose their will, punish, dominate. They did not try to outflank the Bogside defenders—symbolic ground, not real ground, was what the battle was about.

What was unfolding on Wednesday was a police state running out of police.

---

*Callaghan details this report in *A House Divided*, pp. 56-58. Douglas Osmond, Chief Constable of Hampshire, would be taken along to the Downing Street conference held on August 19 to add evidence for existing anxieties. Robert Mark, then Deputy Commissioner of the Metropolitan Police, Scotland Yard, would later reappear, first during Lord Hunt's examination of the Royal Ulster Constabulary and then as Commissioner of the Metropolitan Police during the IRA's first extensive English campaign, and then emerge on the far side of the Troubles as Sir Robert Mark, symbol of the revitalized British police, honored at home and abroad.

The dominant majority had always needed to have force to dominate and suddenly that force was being eroded. The first line of defense was going. In Belfast large Protestant crowds had gathered spontaneously and begun to push at the edge of the Catholic districts. They felt that they must defend their own by striking the vulnerable. In Derry the siege continued. The Citizens Defense Association now wanted the RUC out, wanted Stormont out. The defenders, including Bernadette Devlin, caught by a news photographer lifting stones for a barricade, were encouraged by reports of trouble elsewhere. But they were also exhausted and fearful of a reinforced police attack. Chichester-Clark, who had recalled Parliament, broadcast that the B Specials would be used but "not for riot or crowd control but to relieve the regular police. . . . We want peace not vengeance. If the rioters withdraw peacefully to their homes and observe the law no attempt will be made to exploit the situation." The Catholics did not believe him. The barricades stayed, and would stay for nine weeks, keeping the others out of Free Derry. The police were rioting, at fault, attacking. They should go home. The B Specials had never been other than a Protestant mob. They were untrained and their deployment would announce a pogrom in uniform. They existed to terrorize and this is what Chichester-Clark was pretending to hide with his promises. Already there were reports of the mobs at the heels of the RUC in Belfast as well as Derry.

All day Wednesday the situation deteriorated. Callaghan in London had at least made some preparation. The army awaited word if Chichester-Clark called or even if he did not. In London, however, the general response was horror and surprise. Things could not be allowed to get much worse. As the *Times* noted that Wednesday, "Stormont will have failed and it will be the turn of Westminster to renew its acquaintance with the Irish Question—a prospect that any sensible politician must pray he will be spared." This was the common wisdom and would largely be untouched by a generation of trouble.

In Dublin, Taoiseach Jack Lynch, too, wished that the cup would pass him by, pass by his party, Fianna Fáil, triumphant with a victory in the June general elections, pass by the state. The state, the party, and the Taoiseach lacked power. Everyone seemed to feel responsible for the minority, some passionately; and heated by fears of pogrom, they renewed their neglected patriotism. Everyone wanted something done. And Jack Lynch, moderate, cautious, pragmatic, shrewd, knew what others chose not to consider, did not want to know: The Republic had no assets, no force to deploy, no goodwill in London, no leverage at Stormont, and no one to call in the North. Lynch was going to have to make do with words—and he had always been a quiet man.

Below all the swirling general anguish, the slogans of old, and the atavistic emergency of the national issue in the midst of the new Ireland, the few cold and analytical people doubted there was a foundation for action. They noted that the Republic no longer held a risen people but an easy society unable to imagine real sacrifice for the faraway Northern nationalists, unwilling to act but adamant that the nation must act. The Irish in the South had been led falsely to believe that the whole people had made great sacrifices in the glory years of the Tan War, and now they wanted results. Lynch not only had no assets but also could anticipate a rising militancy. He would have to be seen to act without so doing. On Wednesday evening in a radio-television broadcast he indicated that he could not stand by while innocent lives were lost.* Stormont was no longer in control. He ordered Irish army field hospitals set up at points along the border and requested the United Nations to send a peacekeeping force.

The speech was a shrewd maneuver, keeping his markers within the Irish borders and out of British Belfast and overleaping all with an appeal to the U.N. in New York. Chichester-Clark was outraged: Stormont was on Wednesday night at least still in control and Lynch had no right to tinker in the province for political purpose. It was for Stormont an "incredible, irresponsible intervention—a treacherous back stabbing."† London decided that the United Nations ploy could be ignored and deflected while the Irish army was safely out of the way setting up Red Cross tents. Dublin played no great role in British thinking. The Northern Catholics, however, paid attention to Dublin, despite the long record of failure to aid them in times past, and so assumed that real relief was on the way. The Irish troops were not going to stop at the border. The United Nations would appear forthwith in the Bogside or Belfast. Certainly by Wednesday night aid was needed as the Protestant mobs fought to break into Catholic districts in Belfast and the Derry siege continued.

On Thursday, August 14, Chichester-Clark first attacked Lynch: "We must and we will treat the Government which seeks to wound us in our darkest hour as an unfriendly and implacable government. . . . " He then called out 8,500 B Specials. It was a dangerous and potentially explosive move but there seemed no choice. Television film showed the RUC constables in Derry sprawled on the curbside, exhausted, unable to return to beating at the Catholic barricades. But he reluctantly had accepted the view that many would see the B Specials as part of the problem rather than a solution. The B Specials could not be activated alone. The British army, whatever the implications might be in the long run, was the only immediate option open to take away the taste of the Specials and to spell the RUC. The British were aware that the time for the army had come. Stormont had been given too much time already.

Callaghan, not unaware of the rewards of power and crisis, telephoned Harold Wilson that a personal meeting was essential on Irish matters. He flew to meet his Prime Minister at Saint Mawgan RAF Station in Cornwall. Wilson, after the discussion, flew back to his holidays in Sicily and Callaghan back to London to manage the crisis. Ten minutes in the air he received Chichester-Clark's radio request for army intervention. He scribbled in pencil on a signal pad, "Permission granted." What was the point of being Home Minister if one's purvey is limited to wild birds and Asian immigrants? The burdens of power might be great, but the exercise leaves a pleasing tang. Relayed by Gibraltar and on to the Home Office, the scrawl released General Ian Freeland's troops, already on call, to relieve the RUC in Derry, and released the Irish ogre from provincial captivity. Irish

---

*When, as was inevitable, the season of recriminations came, it was claimed that Lynch said "stand idly by" in his speech: "It is clear also that the Irish Government can no longer stand by and see innocent people injured and perhaps worse." Although his script said "stand idly by," his teleprompter transcript showed "idly" to be missing. Many swore to have heard the words, many believed that he had said them.
†Brian Faulkner, *Memoirs of a Statesman* (London: Weidenfeld and Nicolson, 1978), p. 62.

matters moved on to a different and less confined stage, there to trouble the many.

The British army was deployed just in time for those in Derry, because the first element of the armed B Specials had arrived, with all that might have meant. The British army moving on Derry with prudent haste (the military vehicles waited at each red light) reached the barricades just in time. In fact for a time the Specials even mixed with the four hundred men of the first Battalion Prince of Wales Own Yorkshire under Lieutenant Colonel W. Todd. Still the Bogsiders were jubilant at the failure of the RUC to break the siege and so ignored the Specials until they could be moved away. By not losing, the Bogsiders had won. In fact, in their relief and euphoria, the Bogsiders showed every evidence of delight in the arrival of the British army. The Derry Citizens Defense Association negotiated a perimeter agreement; there were kind words all around; tea was reputedly handed out. This was too much delight in an imperial army for republican Keenan, but that was another matter, for another day. For the moment the Bogside was safe.

Elsewhere in the province matters did not go so smoothly. In Armagh a Catholic, John Gallaher, was shot dead when B Specials fired into a crowd. In Dungannon shots were also fired but without casualties. In Belfast, where tempers and distaste had only been aroused by the violent outbreaks in July and August, not sated, there was general expectation of future trouble—and in the supercharged atmosphere of Belfast shots might well spark serious trouble. The loyalists, including and especially the RUC, feared the IRA, old or new, knew that the Belfast republicans were armed subversives, would shoot to kill if they could. The police hated the long year of Catholic provocations, if not all Catholics, and so wanted if not vengeance at least no minority provocation, no encouragement for the gunmen. The Catholics, in turn, were fearful that with the B Specials mobilized and at large on the Belfast streets, the police would oversee a Protestant pogrom.

Thus, as Derry eased, Belfast tensed. After a year that had savaged the Stormont system, the Catholics would not wait idly by to be beaten into the ground. They had been out stoning the RUC stations. They, like the loyalists, expected worse trouble, and in both cases there were those who sought it. There were crowds of hard men out of the pubs, the idle accumulating near the flash points. There were lots of young men eager for action, for excitement, high on danger and often on stout, without work in the morning or without thought of morrow. The RUC, concerned about the promise of traditional violence, which in Belfast would be far more serious than the baton charges of Derry, felt that the great threat to order would be the secret army of the Republic, a hidden, shooting IRA simply waiting for an opportunity to strike the RUC. So the Catholics mostly feared the pogrom that the Protestants were willing to instigate while the RUC sought the rooftops for an invisible IRA. One illusion fed another; perception was more real than real, as every stimulus awakened old reflexes.

The IRA that loomed so large in the fears and preparations of Belfast did not exist and had never existed. The real Belfast IRA had only a few scattered active volunteers under their commanding officer, O/C Billy McMillen, a collection of veteran republicans in reserve who were largely alienated by recent GHQ attitudes and actions, and almost no arms. The old IRA men probably had more arms hidden away, than did the active unit: Politics was the new direction, not war.

There were no great hidden dumps, no automatic weapons, only odds and ends that McMillen had kept or uncovered when he had found earlier in the summer only one old submachine gun and a pistol as the total quartermaster general supply. More had trickled in and more would show up the closer trouble came, but there was very little when needed. The total on hand the night of August 14 came to two Thompson submachine guns 1921 vintage, one Sten, one Lee-Enfield rifle, and nine handguns. Goulding, the IRA chief of staff, had told the Army Council not to worry, and they hadn't—but neither had he. Nothing was on the way from GHQ in Dublin because there was nothing much in Dublin either. All this meant that there would be no outside help to turn back what appeared to be a Protestant invasion. And this invasion was made, if anything, more likely by the new militancy of the young tossing stones across the invisible boundary lines, made brave by protest, made bold by Derry, assured that *their* army was behind them. None could have imagined that their army was a couple of dozen radicals, some middle-aged gentlemen, and some ancient mismatched weapons: a force that could parade in a pub.

On their side the Protestants knew the IRA lurked deep inside the Catholic heartland but anticipated freedom of action for a while at the edges—and *their* army and *their* police would see to their safety. The loyalists waiting all along the foot of the Shankill Road saw the Catholics moving up Divis Street, ready to cause trouble, ready to attack. They were not to be given an inch. Both sides were fearful and aggressive, unled and unrestrained, high on the news out of Derry. Clusters in pubs drank, which fueled aggression as well as habit. The crowds built up because there were crowds. Someone tossed a petrol bomb and then another. There were flames suddenly pouring out of the Catholic Arkle Bar (all Belfast pubs were either Catholic or Protestant in ownership, custom, and common knowledge). Everyone, everything, belonged to one tribe or the other: pubs, playgrounds, occupations, or schools. In legend and often in reality, one was either a Protestant Jew or a Catholic Jew in Belfast, in Northern Ireland. There were only two tribes and in August they rasped across the edges of their difference. As the Arkle Bar burned, Catholics began showering RUC vehicles parked in the side streets with bricks, petrol bombs, and concrete blocks from the roof of new housing near the Hastings Street RUC station. The trouble had begun. It would soon be recognized as the Irish Troubles.

There was fighting on Dover Street, where a Protestant crowd behind a screen of B Specials tried to get through Divis Street. A bingo hall and several houses began to burn. No one seemed to set fires, they just started. All along the dividing line of Divis Street there was trouble. In Cupar Street RUC head constable Rooney led a baton charge against the Catholics—Catholics being the greater danger to order for the police, who soon heard three revolver shots from the crowd. Armed resistance was expected. Constable Elliot saw a man step out of the crowd, drop on one knee, and fire at him. The marksman missed but these were the first IRA shots in Belfast, in the renewed Troubles, shots fired from a hastily dispatched, poorly armed, untrained volunteer in the midst of a riot. The first shots were only heard that night on Cupar Street but they had been expected. In Cupar Street the RUC-IRA exchange wounded five people: three Protestants, one Catholic, and a policeman.

In Divis Street IRA men firing from the direction of Gilford Street hit and killed Herbert Roy, a twenty-six-year-old Protestant. He had been peering around the corner of Dover Street when he was hit in the chest by a single .38-caliber bullet. Three policemen were wounded. The RUC responded to the IRA attack with three heavy Shorland armored personnel carriers armed with .30-caliber Browning machine guns, easily capable of shooting through the walls of a house. No matter, it was a war against the IRA. With the Shorlands rumbling up and down the streets firing at suspected targets, firing blind, the situation deteriorated rapidly. One Browning round cut through the wall of 5 Saint Brendan's Path and killed nine-year-old Patrick Rooney in his bed. With *their* police in action against the IRA, Protestant mobs began pushing into Catholic streets, burning down each captured house. Refugees staggered out of burning streets, trying to reach safe Catholic districts. The fighting surged and stopped, began someplace else. Long lines of red tracers coming from across the Shankill road, like deadly fireworks, sprayed across the sky for a while and stopped. Looters and arsonists operated, often freely, trailing behind the mobs. Those from the outside media who had managed to reach the city saw the unimaginable: war in a city within the United Kingdom.

At Saint Comgall's School, which controlled further entry in the Divis Street area, a small IRA group with only petrol bombs for weapons was joined by several older IRA men from the 1940s who were armed with a Thompson, a .303 rifle, and four pistols. Together for ninety minutes firing into the street, they kept the loyalists back, wounding as many as eight. It was one of the few organized acts of armed resistance. The IRA that the RUC fought, that the mobs feared, did not exist. Neither the IRA nor the local vigilantes had made any real contingency plans. In May a defense committee had been set up after a brawl in the Catholic Ardoyne isolated just off Protestant Crumlin Road, but the locals wanted no part of the founders, republicans Joseph Graham and Anthony Cosgrove, once they had heard their militant views. The locals wanted protection, not a war. In July a republican veteran, Frank McGlade, recreated local vigilant patrols but interest had tended to taper off along with the threat. Thus, in August Catholic Belfast was left with McMillen's handful of IRA volunteers scattered over the city, the old IRA men who opposed McMillen and GHQ, and their own devices. The old IRA men emptied their stockpiles and the activists had the little on hand— scrapings and the obsolete in both cases. At least the Catholic crowds showed determination in each area. In the Ardoyne the same pattern developed that had occurred off the Falls: mob clashes; loyalist crowds running loose on the edges of the Catholic district; the RUC, fearful of the IRA, turning their attack on the Catholics—"the greater danger"—and so encouraging the Protestants, who were met with a small, split, virtually unarmed IRA unit. A few older men with hidden weapons, veterans of the British army instead of the IRA, held the line in the Ardoyne. Heavy RUC fire killed Samuel McLarnon, forty-seven, in his front room on Herbert Street, and then Michael Lynch, twenty-eight, as he was walking along the street. Ten other Catholics were injured, eight by police bullets.

By the middle of the morning, on Friday, August 15, with a great pall of smoke hanging over the city, with thousands of refugees in transit, with the mobs still on the street and the crack of bullets audible most places in the west of the city, there was no hope left that the RUC could impose order. All sorts of people rushed about throwing up barricades and forming committees. It would be more than two months before the barricades came down, and in a real sense they never did. The frightened people governed as best they could behind burned cars and heaped rubbish. In Ballymurphy a young republican barman, Gerry Adams, was involved not with the IRA but the Saint Bernadette's relief committee. Across the way on the New Barnsley side of the Springfield Road, a young Protestant, Andy Tyrie, was active in organizing relief. Everyone wanted to do something. Everyone felt threatened. In the Catholic areas there was real doubt that the RUC could keep the loyalists and B Specials away from the Catholics, or that they wanted to. Vulnerable, Catholics began to think that the IRA would be needed. Something was needed if Belfast was not to collapse into chaos.

Belfast had not been like Derry. Derry was a small and intimate place. Many knew their neighbors if not well at least by sight, knew the RUC constable. There had been a neat symbolic line between the Bogside and the city, where the contestants could use limited means in a real but symbolic battle fought by rules none could have named but all followed.* Belfast was too big, too diverse, too crude, and so too dangerous for limited displays. There were dozens of mixed streets, vulnerable and isolated districts, hostage families living in the wrong place, different traditions abutting back to back. People lived in their own parish, without need of contact with others, without such contact. The others were often an unknown mass, object of all sorts of fears and fancies. Yet it was Ireland and small, so there was just sufficient familiarity to breed justified anger, which was erected on example and expectation and applied in mass. Everyone—innocent, ignorant, or experienced—tended to see what had been expected. And the worst had been expected.

The RUC saw an armed and deadly IRA everywhere. In Derry everyone knew Seán Keenan was the IRA but in Belfast the IRA was every Catholic or to Catholics every other Catholic. The Protestant crowds, driven wild by drink and fury, by the long summer of civil rights provocation and the general and unending criticism of them and theirs, were determined to use the opportunity to get their own back, smash the others in righteous anger, and in so doing save the system. Rioting had its own charms, and arson and looting were not limited by

---

*In Derry the rules of engagement were tacit, had evolved through a year of riots and held for most of the province, including Belfast. Stones were thrown without targets, batons wielded reluctantly, heads were not smashed nor constables burned as often as such eventualities should have occurred statistically. This might not have seemed the case to the policeman felled by a brick or the rioter dragged bleeding to a cell, but an examination of the television footage indicates over and over a dance of provocation and response that in the province was canceled once the gun was introduced in Belfast. In Beirut, where a weapon is associated with manhood and power, these lethal dances did not escalate when the shooting started—again, thousands upon thousands of shots were fired to little effect unless you were the statistical oddity that ended in the morgue. In Beirut the walls were pocked with thousands upon thousands of spent rounds, as the streets in Derry or Belfast were covered in bricks and broken glass. In Ireland stones were integral to protest, but guns meant rebellion and so came under different rules. In any case, what worked in Derry, a violent but moderated form of civil disobedience, fell apart under the strain in Belfast, where the confrontation could no longer escalate under the fragile and tacit rules of the previous summer's game. Belfast as arena imposed war rules.

religious persuasion. The Catholics, however, felt they were the violated once the first stones had been exchanged. The mobs had been let out by Stormont, drunken hard men without qualm or moderation mixed with armed B Specials, bigots with a badge. They were backed up by the paramilitary RUC with armored vehicles, heavy weapons, and no restraint. The time between a bonfire on the Falls and gunfire along Divis Street was a few hours, a few hours at the end of generations of anxiety, institutionalized hatred, and mistrust that Derry would have found alien: Their Protestants were often bigots, too, rude and coarse, but not killers; after all, Catholics had the numbers, if not the law. Derry was site of a nice old morality play but in Belfast no one kept to the script, everyone believed in a lethal conspiracy and so rushed to arms.

It did not matter greatly who was to blame; what was going on was going on, and could not be denied. Belfast was burning. By August 15, even the inspector general of the RUC, Anthony Peacocke, knew that the monster of civil war could not be put back into the bottle by policing, intimidating the Catholics, and herding the Protestants back from the brink. He did not have the resources. And no policeman, whatever his inclinations and attitudes, could permit the city to be given over to mobs. In Belfast, as in Derry, the state had run out of policemen.

In Belfast at 4:30 on the morning of August 15, Harold Wolseley, the commissioner of police, accepted that the RUC could not manage any longer and asked for the army to be sent into the city. His request arrived at Stormont, where an embittered Northern Ireland cabinet accepted the inevitable and dispatched a request to the waiting Home Office in London. Callaghan gave immediate approval. He had already spoken with Fitt, who wanted the troops despite Lynch's statement in Dublin that they would not be welcome. They would be welcome along Divis Street, as Lynch must have known; but then his constituency and Fitt's differed. Callaghan had earlier spoken with Chichester-Clark, who placed his last hopes in the B Specials; Stormont knew they had run out of chips by Wednesday night: The Specials were part of the problem, as everyone had insisted. So the end had come. The British army would be responsible for order and security. Now London would be the new part of the problem.

In fact no one could even agree on what the old problem had been. Inspector General Peacocke had in fact already indicated the main challenge as he perceived it.

> Information is to hand from a reliable source that an infiltration of members of the Irish Republican Army is about to commence from Eire into Northern Ireland. It is the intention to escalate the degree of control over inward bound traffic and to this end assistance in the form of patrols by armored cars is also requested. The information indicates that the infiltrators will be armed and the support of mobile armored units, which I cannot supply, would be of material assistance in countering these subversive activities against the Government and people of Northern Ireland*

*United Kingdom, *Violence & Civil Disturbances in Northern Ireland in 1969 (The Scarman Report)* (Cmd 566), April 1972, 2 vols.

Peacocke believed in the IRA, as did many in the RUC, at Stormont, and throughout the province. The RUC wanted it clearly understood that the Belfast violence was not to be blamed on the authorities but on active conspirators: "It is of paramount importance that the public should know that the police did not open fire in Belfast last night until they themselves had come under heavy gunfire attack almost simultaneously in several parts of the city." The RUC, putting theory into practice, arrested twenty-four people under the Special Powers Act, including Billy McMillen and Frank Card. Jim Sullivan took over command of the regular IRA unit and no one took over for Card in the Clonard district. The RUC had at least found twenty-four subversives, which was more than the Catholics had found when they looked around for the IRA. The unionists, however, saw what they saw. Whatever had happened in Derry, Belfast had revealed an armed conspiracy beyond the capacity of the civil authorities. The IRA had been too strong. Even then Chichester-Clark had held off on his request to London in hopes that a peace meeting at the huge and largely Protestant-manned H&W shipyard might cool off loyalist resistance to the perceived threat. It was too late by then and only London was left. At five in the afternoon, five hundred troops of the Third Battalion Light Infantry with fixed bayonets took positions in various parts of Belfast. In other parts of the city barricades were still being constructed, arson being done, shots being fired.

After Frank Card's arrest, Billy McKee had set up the Clonard defense with a handful of IRA men armed with shotguns and .22 rifles. Catholic Bombay Street off the Falls Road was burned out while the troops were still moving in a few streets away. While helping families move out of the burned street, a republican Fianna youth, fifteen-year-old Gerald McAluley, was shot dead at 4:00 P.M. in an exchange of fire with the loyalists. The boy was the first IRA casualty. In the Ardoyne a loyalist RUC–B Special crowd fought with Catholics. One Protestant was shot and killed and the Catholic Brookfield Street burned. Not until the next day were sufficient British troops dispersed between the two communities to assure stability. This time there was no doubt that many Catholics felt the army had saved their lives, their homes, their community. Tea and biscuits were dispensed. And there was a pause. The British army had a honeymoon moment of peace and quiet; but as the new commanding general, GOC Lieutenant General Sir Ian Freeland, said on August 18, "Honeymoons can be very short-lived."

The threatened IRA invasion out of the South did not materialize. The B Specials were pulled back out of sight to guard key points. The barricades were still growing. The air reeked of burning buildings. The toll stayed at seven dead and 750 injured. The British army was run up to strength. The Second Battalion Queen's Regiment, the First Battalion Royal Hampshire Regiment, and the Third Battalion Light Infantry were flown in from Lyneham and deployed about the city. The First Battalion Royal Green Jackets at Tidworth had their leave canceled and were put on standby. In a couple of days an order was issued canceling the leave of the First Battalion Royal Hampshire Regiment. General Freeland, who had only been in the province a few weeks, wanted to be sure that the army could do the job. He now had six thousand men to support the three thousand RUC constables. On Saturday, August 16, sniping in Belfast during the day tapered off. In Armagh five thousand people without incident attended the funeral of John Gallaher, shot dead on Thursday. The crisis had eased. The interpretations, explanations, and implications began to be distributed.

The Unionist establishment and many loyalists believed that the 1968–69 civil disobedience demonstrations and civil rights parades had been orchestrated by an IRA-radical conspiracy aimed at the system. The system, operating on an island with a Catholic majority, could only operate with stringent defense measures, seen elsewhere as sectarian measures. These measures could have been reformed if the system had been given time. Loyalists had always suspected, often with good cause, the existence of radical outside agitators eager for trouble, eager to attract media attention. For those who cannot defeat their own demons, outside agitators, illusive and invisible, are often summoned up as the cause of trouble. As early as October 6, 1968, Craig had noted that Gery Lawless of the Trotskyist Irish Workers Group had rushed into the scene in Derry. He had later been at the confrontation at Burntollet Bridge and made no secret of his advocacy of revolution. Tellingly for Craig he had been an IRA man whose case before the European Court of Justice in Strasbourg had attracted considerable legal interest and produced heavy tomes of published evidence. And Lawless was hardly alone as an example of the Republican-radical mix, although anyone exposed to Lawless recounting the wisdom of the Fourth International in the bar of the City Hotel in Derry would have few fears of revolution.

The Unionists' fear of the Irish republicans was real enough and the republicans wished to be frightening. Seán Keenan in Derry had been behind a barricade with his IRA friends like Neill Gillespie: They made no secret about their intentions. And in Belfast there had been Thompson guns and the old felons out on the streets joining the new subversives of McMillen. In the Republic the IRA GHQ had claimed that their Northern units had been defending the nationalist areas. On August 17, some units had launched an attack, albeit abortive and ineffectual, against the RUC barracks at Crossmaglen in South Armagh. To those long nurtured on giving not an inch, always living in a siege state, it was easy to find conspiracy—republicans, radicals, troublemakers.

All the unionists thus again felt misunderstood by the British establishment, who neither rewarded loyalty nor believed in conspiracy. The unionists again felt misunderstood by the media, including the British media, who neither accepted their explanations nor believed in conspiracy. In fact the unionist plaint, repeated again and again, boring observers and convincing few of the disinterested, appeared in 1969, as it would for years, a whine not an analysis. The democratic state had been under attack. The police had showed remarkable restraint, been heavily assaulted, depended only on batons and CS gas in Derry, come under fire in Belfast. Neither Wilson nor Callaghan seemed moved and yet the unionists had been there, had seen the provocation, had the hospital reports of constables shot in the streets. Most hurtful was the universal criticism by the British media—*their* media. From the supposedly dispassionate and disinterested BBC through the conservative press (the *Daily Telegraph* excepted) and on to the nasty liberal columnists and Labour Party hacks, no one had a kind word for Stormont. The foreign observers were even more cutting, reducing the complexities of Northern Ireland to good guys and bad guys, brave demonstrators and bigots. Even the Pope, no friend of the Orangemen, had a comment. Everyone had a comment, a hard word. Bernadette Devlin photographed on a barricade was still a heroine and the exhausted police were villains, monsters. It was not fair. It was, however, not unexpected. The Unionists suspected all but their own. They had hoped that their own would include if not Labour then the Conservatives, but no one had a kind word, no one. So Faulkner spoke for all the Unionists, all unionists, those loyalists back from arson listening in their local pub, the isolated Protestant farmer in Tyrone, all those threatened:

> The Stormont Government, struggling to maintain order, under pressure politically, with limited resources, and consisting largely of men more experienced in administration than in publicity, had little chance of making its voice heard above the chorus of comment.*

They were misunderstood, misrepresented, their failures exaggerated and their virtues past and present denied—denied by their friends, denied by the media. They were pilloried, and promised only that radical change would be imposed. Such a recital of grievances won few hearts. Real grievances to the Unionists sounded like rationalizations to almost all others.

The minority, if not exactly jubilant at the August events that had led to the arrival of the British army, certainly felt enormous relief that the community had escaped serious harm. This was soon accompanied by a renewed confidence in their own mobilization that had shaken the Stormont system, thrown up the barricades, defended the edges of the community. They now knew all too well there was no IRA conspiracy, no secret army to help them. The IRA in Derry was not represented by Keenan; it *was* Keenan and his few old friends. In Belfast the IRA had done so little visible that the slogan "IRA—I Ran Away" was scrawled on walls and the chief of staff, Goulding, in Dublin was accused of being militant in speech but not in action. On August 18, with Goulding's army, the IRA that no one had seen in years, on full alert, the chief of staff had announced that the Army Council had sent "a number of fully equipped units to the aid of their comrades in the Six Counties." No one in those six counties had seen them. There had been only the few isolated clumps of locals like that of Billy McKee in Clonard. The Dublin GHQ had done nothing. Goulding, who few in Belfast had met, had been off in the Dublin Mountains with a television team during much of the crisis and had sent only communiques, not arms. There were no arms. Goulding had suddenly appointed Mick Ryan quartermaster general, QMG. This produced no arms but some order. All sorts of people stopped by Gardiner Place bringing word of this shotgun or that old cache so that Ryan collated his finds and shipped the results north in furniture vans—too late. The IRA's only real effort had been the attack on the RUC station at Crossmaglen and that had been organized independently by Seán Mac Stiofáin and so had upset GHQ in Dublin.

As for the Communist conspirators, the radicals had as always fallen into quarrels, schisms, and splits. And there were hardly enough radicals to make up the sides. The new hard Left attacked the old generation and the new civil rights

*Brian Faulkner, *Memoirs of a Statesman* (London: Weidenfeld and Nicolson, 1978), p. 63.

leadership with equal venom. Betty Sinclair of the Belfast Trades Council was a Communist right enough but an apparatchik without an apparatus, a Stalinist vestige. She was a major force for moderation not at all eager for confrontation. She was also irrelevant. The Fourth International was irrelevant and Gery Lawless and his mysterious Fourth International were irrelevant. The new people in the summer of 1969 represented only themselves, clones of the advocates who had arisen the previous Year of the Guerrilla. Thousands might vote for Bernadette but despite, not because of, her socialist politics. Hundreds from the schools might attend a march but then go home to do their lessons—accountants would always be needed. Only a few—Gery Lawless, Michael Farrell, Eamonn McCann, each standing almost alone under a special personal ideological banner—had dreams of a revolution, a radical change, a new society around the corner. What most Catholics suspected was around the corner was neither Republic nor revolution but an Orange bigot.

What the vast majority of the Catholics, nearly all nationalists, wanted was reform at once, ideally an end to Stormont, the great, practical dream; and for vengeance's sake, consternation in the faces of the unionists, the loyalists, them. In theory many would opt for a united Ireland, which was not an immediate or viable proposition and so was beyond sacrifice except by the republicans, a minority of true believers. The Catholics opposed with as much rigor as the fundamentalist Orange divines and Unionist gentry the radical ideas of the new Left. Social issues in the province focused not on divorce or abortion or the redistribution of wealth but on swings locked on the sabbath or the ritual paths of provocative marches. On the moral issues Catholics and Protestants were almost as one: Not an inch should be given to secularism, the sins of the flesh, or the appeals of the godless.

Within the Catholic community, however, the small group of IRA people (not all men—wives were important and often more militant) sensed in 1969 a possibility for action. The old felons who had been quiescent after—and often during—the campaign that had ended in 1962 now found a role in the defense of the nationalist community. Few of them had seen any point in nonviolence, and yet the protests appeared to have opened a window of opportunity for the eventual use of physical force. Certainly loyalists seemed inclined to force. During the previous year there had been a troublesome surge toward sectarian violence, a defiance of order and restraint, by many young Catholics. In theory republicans were nonsectarian and in theory the radicals were nonviolent.

In practice each demonstration attracted a fringe, a halo of young men looking for trouble. Each confrontation had generated instant mobs, stones and petrol bombs at the ready, eager for action. They were not interested in the tactics of restraint, the pleas of the steward or the peacemakers; they were not amenable to priest or politician. They cared nothing for the vote or the Easter Republic. They were held back from attack only by the direction of the day, the low cunning of the responsible, and insufficient mass. Once there was a crowd in action, a mob moving, fueled by drink, hidden by dark, legitimized by the political slogans on the trampled banners and the personal recollection of insult, they would run riot until exhausted.

And down the lane in Belfast the same process had generated an Orange potential for even more lethal violence. The loyalists, high on drink and hatred, fed by a different but compelling list of grievances, could not always be kept to the allotted routes, kept in line by the old Lambeg drum. In Belfast their own police, the RUC, and if they hampered their action, their very own B Specials, could not restrain their rage, a blunt determination different only in degree from that of the RUC in Derry clubbing Catholics at the barricades. There, as with the Catholic mobs even in Belfast, there was restraint, tactics, rules; but the new loyalists numbered not just the very young eager for action but older and more brutal elements, very hard men, blunt, coarse, and fierce.

Thus, August had released two mobs—the nationalists wanton and destructive and the loyalists lethal. The mobs saw the Troubles as opportunity and challenge, not like unionists as conspiracy or like the nationalists as an opportune crisis. In August 1969 free-floating violence had come to the province, mobs seeking a target, mobs without banners. Some in each would be captured and institutionalized by secret armies; some would grow older, cautious, and find other pursuits; some would in violence discover a vocation: Almost all would cause trouble. And this was only just apparent at the end of August 1969. Even at first, however, some in Britain had recognized that the trouble, if it came, might not be simply Orange and Green. Richard Crossman, editor of *The New Statesman*, insisted on August 17 that "once the Catholics and Protestants get used to our presence, they will hate us more than they will hate each other."* The problem seemed intractable, with warring tribes remaining in place. No one could imagine, however, another round of the 1918-22 Troubles, although the threats and fears and explanations were as thick on the ground as thrown rocks and broken petrol bottles.

The most immediate and visible result of the August violence was neither the flood of recriminations, accusations, and rationalizations nor the fleeting glimpse of anarchy but the efforts of Stormont, the Home Office, Downing Street, and the British army to restore order. The responsible wanted the province on the track of reform—even the Unionists recognized the urgency—so as to tie up the frayed ends of the tapestry before some loose thread allowed the whole thing to unravel. Urban order, so conventional within the United Kingdom as to be unnoticed, had in Northern Ireland proved fragile. One loose thread—and there seemed lots— might do the trick so haste was not amiss. This sense of urgency, sharpened by the sound of automatic weapons fired in anger within the United Kingdom, even existed in London. On August 19, a Tuesday, Chichester-Clark arrived in London for a meeting with British officials concerned with the province. Present in the Cabinet Room at 10 Downing Street were Brian Faulkner, Robert Porter, and three experienced civil servants, Sir Harold Black, Ken Bloomfield, and B. R. Cummings. With Wilson and Callaghan were Michael Stewart, Denis Healey, Lord Stonham, General Sir Geoffrey Baker, Chief of the General Staff Sir Philip Allen, and Sir Burke Trend. Northern Ireland had come a long way from the pigeonhole in the Home Office next to wild birds.

All began on an unexpectedly conciliatory note when Chichester-Clark indi-

---

*Richard Crossman, *The Diaries of a Cabinet Minister* (London: Hamilton and Cape, 1977), vol. 3, p. 620.

cated without expectation of concession that General Freeman as GOC should take over control of all security forces—just what the British wanted and what they had intended to impose and had suddenly been presented free of charge. Chichester-Clark had wisely decided to concede what he could not prevent from being taken. He and his were still uncertain just how much Wilson, a Labour man, had in mind to take from Stormont. In fact, Callaghan and Wilson had in mind a precise readjustmen of the Stormont system. They would make explicit matters of provincial reform that had so far been implicit and in so doing reassure the Unionists that the province was not being abandoned. Rather the reverse was the case: Northern Ireland was going to be made British, the Stormont system was going to be adjusted through reform to British practice. The camel's nose of reform was to be yanked so that the camel was in the tent. The pace of change and reform, the rationales and explanations, the responsibilities for details were matters of negotiation, but for Callaghan the camel was in the tent, the writing on the wall, whatever: Stormont had to shape up.

If Chichester-Clark did not want to pet the camel, fine, but sooner rather than later his Unionists would have to accept the inevitable: Ultimate power lay in London, the army was in place in the province. What was needed on August 19 was a joint communique. So they hammered out the seven basic points of the Downing Street Declaration, which set out the pace and nature of reform. Momentum would be maintained as local government franchise, revisions of local government areas, allocation of houses, creation of a Parliamentary Commissioner for Administration, and machinery to consider citizens' grievances against other authorities were hurried to fruition. As well, the B Specials would be removed from duties in the cities and RUC Inspector General Peacocke, harshly criticized by Callaghan's two police observers, Mark and Osmond, would have to go.

For the British the key was that Stormont would now have to accept British standards. Provincial independence would be circumscribed as the sectarian system was quickly phased out. The August troubles thus had for Labour a salutary effect. And the province was reassured that the constitutional link would be maintained—so much for Lynch and the United Nations. The troops controlled by London (sent, it was recalled, at Stormont's request) would stay only until law and order were established. Economic development would be vital for social stability, a Labour plug, but this was expressed as an aspiration, not a program. In fact, the agenda for Stormont was suddenly very full. Callaghan could foresee his key aim secured in that "every citizen of Northern Ireland is entitled to the same equality of treatment and freedom from discrimination as obtains in the rest of the United Kingdom irrespective of political views or religion." *

Wilson, Callaghan, and the rest knew what the Declaration really meant: an end to all the legal sectarian practice. It would be an end to a paramilitary RUC intimidating Catholics, an end to B Specials as an Orange militia, and the multivoting in local elections to Protestant advantage, and biased housing allocations, and gerrymandering away the little Catholic advantage that did exist. It would be an end to all the nasties recently revealed, all the long-ignored

---

*Joint Declaration of August 1969's point five.

practices, awful out of context, awful even in a Northern Irish context, all patently, obviously archaic, undemocratic, and so finished—by Labour fiat. Or else. Or else direct rule. The Declaration, of course, did not read this way. British politics is far more elegant. The Declaration was filled with reassurance, praise, and quiet agreement that should convince all good men and true that both sides had reasoned together, found common ground. Both Downing Street and Stormont would go forward together with the agreed Declaration, with economic development and without the B Specials at the bottom of the lane. The problem had been properly addressed by the cabinet, by Labour, by the government. The problem, however, was Ireland, and not so easily solved as writing out Declarations.

The Stormont delegation was still at Downing Street, still at the table with the Declaration not yet released, when the nature of British innocence and arrogance was revealed. At the end of the day, Harold Wilson and Chichester-Clark went off to appear on television while the others waited at Downing Street until showtime. Then they crowded into a small room off the Cabinet Room and there followed the event. In a reply to a query Wilson noted that B Specials would be "phased out" of their present role. "We now want to see the B Specials phased out. Their disarming is entirely a matter for the GOC." In the little room Callaghan exclaimed in an exasperated voice, "I told him not to say that." But he had. And what an impact that casual, innocent aside produced. No matter that he *meant*, the B Specials would be moved to different duties, no matter that the cabinet *intended* but had not revealed that the B Specials later would be phased out not only of their present role but also altogether: He said "phased out" and was taken by all the Unionists to have announced the end of the Specials. The British had barely a clue of what Wilson had so casually done; for, after all, the B Specials were only being moved out of the center of the cities. But phased out for Northern Ireland meant disbanded, not withdrawn, and also meant that Chichester-Clark's packet of reforms was seen as a poisoned gift from the British cabinet. The Prime Minister would return to a Unionist Party in shock and disarray.

The Unionist delegation should have known that "reform" by a Labour government was not merely a painless declaration and a few hasty laws. The Unionists muttered among themselves but did not mention what Wilson had said when he returned to the Cabinet Room. And, they recognized now, at last, that as Callaghan later indicated, "Our side of the table was quite clear that the B Specials would ultimately be phased out."* The Unionists realized that to do so might destroy moderate Unionism and even more surely would produce violence in the streets. Both might be necessary to transform the province, but this had been ignored in London, where "phasing out" was a matter of wording and timing. The Unionists thus returned to their province to explain to their own that they had misheard, the B Specials were not to be phased out. Faulkner insisted the next day that "there is absolutely no suggestion the USC [B Specials] will be disbanded. Let me make that crystal clear." What had to be done was to focus all Unionist energies on enacting the promised reforms fast enough to remove

*Callaghan, p. 63.

117

minority grievances but suavely enough not to concentrate majority minds. In other matters Wilson often had a ready formula to make the indigestible eatable, but this time he had blundered. The English simply did not understand Irish politics or sensitivities, majority or minority, Northern Ireland, or the Republic.

With the ruins of the burned-out Catholic terraces still warm, the knitting up of the raveled ends began. The Catholics, with the army in place and the B Specials gone, were defended but awaited the substantive changes promised that would cause majority anger. The British in New York maneuvered behind the scenes to see that the Irish Republic's efforts to internationalize the problem at the United Nations were thwarted. The less said about Northern Ireland, the better—a lesson Wilson's slip underscored. In turn in Dublin, fearful of being outflanked on the nationalist issue, Lynch made it clear that the IRA would not be allowed to usurp power. On August 19, the Taoiseach publicly criticized subversives—obviously the IRA. He criticized, as well, those who had rioted in front of the British embassy protesting the collapse of Northern order, calling the riot "lawless behavior by a small minority." Despite considerable pressure from within Fianna Fáil by those who felt something must be done beyond speeches and diplomatic ploys at the United Nations, Lynch could really do no more than fend off the appeal of the IRA, fend off his own ultranationalists eager for "something," and go through the motions of the U.N. appeal. This U.N. appeal as all anticipated led nowhere. On August 20 the Security Council adjourned consideration of the Republic's request, thus letting down Dublin easily. In London, with no outside interference and the Downing Street Declaration in place, Callaghan announced that he and Lord Stonham, Minister of State in the Home Office, would go to the province for a three-day weekend tour to show support for moderation and Chichester-Clark.

As Callaghan prepared to fly in, flying out was Bernadette Devlin. She arrived in New York on August 22 to explain her view—a radical Irish view—to the Americans and so raise money for NICRA. For many in Ireland, America remained the promised land, where crucial funds and vital support could be had for the asking. She was immediately followed by a delegation of Unionists to undo the harm that her partisan speeches might do. Ulster did not stay home. In a modern electronic society crisis cannot be homebound however much those in London might have wished for isolation. The ripples of crisis had spread out to New York and Chicago. Everyone seemed at work to undercut the others.

In fact, the only certainty about "solutions" included in the Downing Street Declaration was that hardly anyone paid attention to the contents. It was too much too soon, or too little too late, or too much trouble to read. Action was what was needed and to our agenda not theirs. Craig wanted Chichester-Clark to resign. On August 23 Paisley led a motorcade to Stormont to protest against "military dictatorship" in the province. When Chichester-Clark set up the Hunt Committee to examine the police, the militant loyalists felt sure that the B Specials were truly to be phased out and the RUC maimed by reform, while the nationalists assumed the reverse, that the B Specials were never to be disbanded. The Stormont cabinet assumed that unless changes were made after the Marks-Osmond report that had convinced Callaghan, after the evidence of RUC armored cars machine-gunning Belfast Catholic districts, after the media reports of the RUC at work in Derry, something had to be done or all would be lost. Something in British practice and so Northern Irish experience was a commission—so in came Hunt with his powers and budget and advisers and civil servants. At least Cardinal Conway, Catholic primate of Ireland, blamed all the troubles not on the RUC, as did many other nationalists, but on the mobs armed with submachine guns who had invaded Catholic quarters. The cardinal had already warned that delay in introducing reforms was dangerous. Everyone expected something. The barricades were still up, the defense committees still functioned; the police were leashed, the army was in the street, and the orators were without moderation. The advocates of revolution could preach sedition in the Catholic no-go zones and the supporters of pogroms organize still in Protestant pubs. All told it was not a happy prospect for Chichester-Clark or even for Callaghan.

The Home Secretary was a practiced politician, exuberant, enthusiastic in public, domineering in private, ambitious to act and to be seen to act; his trip across the still stunned province on his Irish weekend was a media extravaganza. He was welcomed by Catholics in the Bogside and Belfast and by the Protestants along Bombay Street and the Shankill Road. It was an excellent photo opportunity that brought good news back to London: English common sense at work. There would be an investigation of the outbreak by Mr. Justice Scarman to go with the Hunt investigation, and reports and investigations were far better than rocks and petrol bombs. There were explanations of the proposals for the Northern Ireland cabinet: The text sounded better with a cheerful gloss once the shock had worn off and the B Special slip was filed as old history. Callaghan met government ministers, met Seán Keenan in Derry, met old ladies and photogenic children, talked to this one and that, spoke to all, was "captured" by the television camera in the process. He met with Paisley at the Conway Hotel in Belfast. He tossed out a platitude: "You know, Mr. Paisley, we are all children of God," and received a smashing Ulster return, "No, we are not, Mr. Callaghan. We are all the children of wrath."* Still it was not wrath's weekend but Callaghan's. He listened to grievances, nodded and smiled, issued a joint communique with the government on Friday, August 29, detailing the measures being taken to accelerate the reforms indicated in the Downing Street Declaration.

Already, everyone was told, Lord Hunt's Committee on the police and the Scarman Tribunal on the violence were done deeds. An immediate grant of £250,000 was on the way to relieve present distress. All could look forward with optimism to his plans, his government's plans, the future. And on invitation, he would return to discuss the conclusions of the various working parties on housing allocations, discrimination in public employment, and prohibition of incitement to religious hatred in another tour in mid-October. The province was not to be forgotten. Then it was back to London for Callaghan and Lord Stonham, leaving behind Oliver Wright and Alex Baker, senior British civil servants, to work with Chichester-Clark's office and that of Minister of Home Affairs Porter.

The province was hardly normal despite Callaghan's enthusiasm and opti-

*Callaghan, p. 82.

mism. Stormont's writ no longer ran unchallenged; in some areas it didn't run at all. And Stormont's beneficiaries, mild, moderate, and extreme Unionists, loyal to a system suddenly in transformation, were shaken and unsure. Stormont was no longer the hub of the wheel but a blur at the center. Callaghan had been caught on television shouting through a bullhorn in a Bogside window that he was with *them*—the Catholics—"I am not neutral. I am on the side of all people who are deprived of justice" just as everyone had long feared. Wilson had said the B Specials would be phased out and no subsequent explanation had come from London or from Callaghan or even from Faulkner. "Mr. Wilson was *not* talking about standing them down," reassured the loyalists. Paisley immediately responded, "If you want to destroy a government you pull its teeth. . . . Faulkner should tell the truth. The B Specials will be destroyed and our line of defense with it." Every defense was needed.

The Hunt Committee would be a means to snatch away law and order from Unionist control just as the Scarman Commission would surely exonerate the rioters and smear the police and the Protestants. The majority felt betrayed. As the weeks passed and the barricades stayed up in the Catholic districts, the past could not be recaptured. In Derry the British army even painted a white "peace line" down the edge of the street, "on one side of which lay 'Free Derry' and on the other side of which lay Her Majesty's territory." And now the IRA was awakening. Pirate radio stations in Derry and Belfast were broadcasting treason. And although there were Protestant barricades, Protestant vigilantes, Protestant radio stations broadcasting "Incitement to religious hatred," the loyalists were far more concerned with the minority usurpations and pretensions than with parallel loyalist responses. Increasingly the everyday Protestant felt that somehow the Catholics had learned to play the new game, summon up assets unknown in previous Northern politics, generate orators and agitators and no-go zones and attract the media, capture Callaghan and the London establishment, leaving the Orange militants behind. They could only imitate the new Catholics ineffectually—even Paisley was no longer the most prominent agitator—who could have imagined a girl in a miniskirt? Six Conservative MPs had toured the province and told Paisley that their advice was to "shut up." The Protestants' lifelong assumption of their natural ethnic ascendancy had begun to erode. Everything was changing and so too the arrogance of the bold. The result was that out of sight within much of the fundamentalist loyalist community frustration and anger and now fear were seething.

On the surface the government drove ahead with reform. Many of these had long been under consideration and would have come about without any Downing Street Declaration. And a great deal had already been done to remove grievance. In fact, the Unionist cabinet felt ill used, rushed along by the bullying of Callaghan and Labour, criticized by the media, attacked by an insatiable minority eager to hurt, and finally, now, by their own, crying, "What about the B Specials?" One of the costs was an erosion of the first enthusiasm for governing and thus the energy to do so. Ministers crisscrossed the countryside selling the new look to the old, to those who only wanted to be let alone, explaining to those who were about to be discarded, the constables or councilmen from the little towns, that they—the heart of the party and the system—were still cherished at

Stormont. No one at Stormont was really sure the reforms would be enough to save the system or that the old loyalties could ever again be recognized, much less rewarded. All that could be done was persevere in a world they hardly recognized and which they could not accept had emerged from their own past policy. They had bought the *Titanic,* a Belfast ship, failed to make proper payment, and were now in charge as the vessel sank. What was the point of being captain, of being Prime Minister at Stormont? Still, duty insisted, and much progress was made at modernizing and reforming, turning one man into one vote by law, reorganizing local government, setting up local council districts, going forward with the Greater Belfast Urban Area Plan. The ship might not sink after all, made sound with a new coat of paint. Belfast had once built well and might again, yet.

The most immediately visible result of the August violence was the no-go zones in Derry and Belfast. The local defense committees, Protestant and Catholic, oversaw the barricades, set up guard rosters, sat on central committees, and soon could listen to the pirate radio stations churning out the flavors of the moment, some quite unpalatable. The advent of turmoil gave meaning to the lives of many underutilized men. Unemployed, unemployable, they found a career at the barricades, a late vocation in protest politics and later in subversion. The shift to local control and advantage had been insidious and steady as Stormont weakened. Very quiet no-go zones had existed for nearly two years in the central Catholic districts of Belfast and Derry, where the RUC avoided provocation. The new creations with guards and banners drew in the media and thus sparked the outrage of those who saw, properly, the challenge to the state. Protestants, grudgingly recognizing Fenian example, copied the provocation, since no one else was "defending them." Over the month of September complex and confused negotiations went on as barricades went up to replace those removed, promises were made, and accusations flew at the tricks of the others. During much of September barricades went up and came down between riots and alarms.

Callaghan and the British felt that the solution, other than a return to the norm, was for the army, guardian of order, to erect authorized barricades: a peace line to separate the two communities, thus ending a need for no-go zones edged with upended and burned-out buses, ruined stolen cars, heaps of paving stones, and jumbled rubbish. If you cannot bulldoze them, then build them proper.

> The strategy that evolved during September while the battle to remove the barricades swayed to and fro—some down one day and others up the next—was that we let it be known that we would not remove barricades that were designed for protection until we had persuaded the people behind them that the troops were present in sufficient numbers to look after them, and that they had nothing to fear. On the other hand, we said, barricades erected simply as a form of protest would have to come down. . . . The third point in our strategy was that the Army should build our own barricade along the principal frontline between the two communities so that all the other

barricades could come down automatically. This became the so-called peace line, which still stands.*

In fact, the peace line, as much as any visible artifact of the new Troubles, indicates the implacable division of Northern Irish society. It became permanent, irreversible, visible sign of the inability of reason and goodwill to erode the integrity of the quarrel. There had always been no-go zones in Irish minds, divisions in society that allowed two radically different peoples to share a single habitat as if one.

As a new structure of division the government's wall began first as a white painted line. The army announced on September 9 that a peace line would be built. And so came a hurried construction of sheet metal between posts topped with barbed wire, raw and ugly as the riots. Finally came the civil servants and the urban planners and ultimately an elegantly landscaped, architecturally designed wall, the height carefully scaled in consideration of the missile tosser and the arc of petrol bombs and the siting cunningly drawn to permit the control of the unruly. At the back of new housing estates it formed more a backdrop than a wall, blended in, became part of everyone's mental architecture—and kept out the others. The peace line not only reflected the divisions of local society and in so doing inculcated them, but also revealed the center's intention to control that society.

The new walls may not have made bad neighbors; but they did indicate, if not impose, what misguidedly those original painted lines had sought to erase: divisions of desperation, erected on fear, ambition, in competition and hate, in hope. The government's wall was erected in more tangible if less permanent materials than the old ethnic walls and indicated London's unarticulated intentions and priorities of the time. The countryside is crisscrossed with military fortifications scattered long ago, monastery walls tumbled by Henry VIII's edict, tiny hand-built fences pierced by sheep and sloth, the tumbled heaps in front of burned big houses, tag ends of Anglo-Norman fortified homes, and even the ruins of the times. So there are the other walls of the Troubles as well, the rebuilt gable end of Free Derry, the ruins of Bombay Street—soon tidied—the deserted houses left by fearful refugees. Belfast could trace the Troubles in walls, peace walls, gable walls covered with murals, ruined walls.

Behind the Catholic barricade walls, the new student Left saw in plain view a revolutionary situation: no police, no law, no control, no stopping a risen people ready to be organized. For all intents and purposes, PD had broken with the moderates within the civil rights movement, seen as old, stale, stolid reformists, and opted instead for the trendy radical ideas floating out of the continent and America. The young were moving with the times and the fashions, a little slowly, a little out of sync, as was provincial Ireland's wont, but moving. Society had to be transformed, revolution encouraged. Elsewhere in wartime American or Italian regional universities, there might be issues to be exploited, masses to be unleashed by example and exhortation, but in Ireland the radicals had seen not an

*Callaghan, p. 110.

agenda but a risen people, marched in front of tens of thousands, and now had seen the police driven from the streets. They had seen the means into the future and it worked. They had tasted the tang of cordite, choked on CS gas, been surrounded by a real, not imaginary, working-class resistance. The formal ideas of the rebels' short shelf of heroes, Fanon and Marcuse, black liberation and Lenin revisited, had been made real in the streets, at the barricades. In Belfast all seemed possible, at least for a few days. Michael Farrell felt that they now had "credibility with the working class and peasantry." They had made the long march to Burntollet, fought in the streets of Derry and Belfast, and now would organize the people.

They were, however, only ten or twelve PD members behind the barricades, and the people with other priorities and assumptions showed no interest in the call of socialism or the charms of Left revolution. Starting out on their long march, the students neither humbled by life nor aware of their limitations epitomized for many in Ireland resistance to injustice. The students and radicals knew, as did all, the deprived, the poor, the old and young, the reality of grievance. They discovered to the amazement of all but a few the means into the future—the adaptation of the provincial ritual of the march. What they proposed for that future, however, had few takers in a provincial island with a pious and deeply conservative society. The radicals seemed important, then and later, because not only had they been the point of the protest lance but also because they wrote the books, made the speeches, gave voice to the inarticulate. They did not make a revolution or even come close. The young lions grew older, the flower children faded, a few in Germany and a few more in Italy would opt for terror as a means to achieve everything. Most could recall with pride that something had been achieved: the end of the Vietnam War, finally, the humiliation of de Gaulle, civil liberties for many black Americans, the rise of the women's rights movement, a new environmental sensitivity. Lots had emerged from the new Left but not a new Ireland. In Ireland the everyday people tended to keep to the allotted ways. The struggle for radical reform was overshadowed in time by the national issue, by ethnic solidarity, by psychological grievances generations in the building, by other agendas entirely. It was revolution enough that the people had followed the students into the streets, that they had been converted to the possibility of change, without expecting that they, too, the men of no property and few rights would, against their inclinations and convictions, be converted to the fashionable solutions of the times. But in youth hope is fresh and in the autumn of 1969 it was still very much alive.

In an effort to tighten up the PD organization instead of continuing with the amorphous appeals of the civil rights movement, the members met on October 11 in Saint Mary's Hall to become one more small, if famous, schismatic radical group. The violent summer had led to an end of relevance for the PD, not a beginning of revolution for the radicals. They were without a future. Less than a dozen agitators with the wrong agenda joined by their university friends, kith and kin, and the odd transient did not create a vanguard movement, did not offer leadership to the proletariat or to the "peasant" found mostly in books or even to the familiar Catholics out beyond Saint Mary's. History had captured the PD instead of the reverse, although the orators did not yet note the fact.

The other Catholics behind the barricades with a program ready were the orthodox republicans. They had, unlike the students, struggled through the crisis without rising enthusiasm, without the necessary assets to play much part, with only a growing resentment that their leadership had so gravely erred and so left them and their people vulnerable. The purpose of the republican movement was to wage war and GHQ had been otherwise engaged. Jim Sullivan in Belfast and Seán Keenan in Derry with their defense committees knew that except for a few aging IRA men, their people wanted no part of the republican dream and no new campaign of physical force. They did not even in most cases see Britain as a tyrant or the British army as an invader. Thus, the republicans came out of the struggle for the barricades determined but realistic, set on a stage strategy that could lead to the destruction of the Stormont system. Many of the Northern republicans and their friends in the Republic wanted to wage war. First they needed to shape a defense. From this they could escalate. There were enormous obstacles, not the least GHQ in Dublin. Unlike the radicals who had imported foreign ideas to graft on local means, the traditional republicans depended on old habits and old means to seek the Republic. In the autumn of 1969 they were desperate men united only by the need for the gun in politics. This proved ample to effect the course of events.

The radicals misread objective reality, mistook the shock of political awareness within the minority as mobilization. A risen people, if such existed, did not want alien ideas and did not want crusaders for the ultimate republic. They might need defenders, even with the British army, and so would tolerate such a role for the IRA—at unexpected later cost. What most of the minority wanted was a little peace and quiet, security from fear, and as much else as they could get. Usually peace and quiet have most takers even if the banners bear more militant devices. On the Catholic side of the barricades during the autumn of 1969, the population kept a sharp watch: Would they be defended, would their grievances be ameliorated, should they be quiet?

London and Stormont were eager for quiet and wanted the minority to feel they were getting reforms, change for the better, serious attention, the lot. McAteer and the Nationalists, even Gerry Fitt, had complained that the Unionist establishment never treated them like a *real* opposition, paid any attention. Now everyone was paying attention. All of this—Chichester-Clark's professed program, Callaghan's statements and visits, the Downing Street Declaration, the phasing out of the B Specials—could not have been imagined a year previously. The minority should have been on a triumphant high; but as the Unionists were quick to notice, they wanted still more, indicated little gratitude, and criticized any concession to loyalist sentiment. In fact, after a fifty-year drought of privation, humiliation, and arrogance bravely borne, the minority had a seemingly unquenchable thirst for more. What London had arranged, what Stormont was constructing, could be read and enacted and touched. What the minority wanted was an emotional satisfaction not easily found in the long, gray subsections of a local government bill or a shift in the age of majority. For the Catholics, what the loyalist mobs attempted to do in Belfast, what the police had done in Derry, indicated how shallow was the majority commitment to reform. There was thus little real evidence of a change in the nature of the Orange beast. Why should the minority show gratitude for concessions that were only delayed justice? So, once the barricades were down, the radicals and republicans off tending their agendas in isolation, the Catholics watched the struggle within the majority between reluctant decency and the stirring of the Orange mob. The Catholics like the Protestants tended to see the province as stage for a zero-sum game where the gain for one meant a corresponding loss for the other: Nothing had mutual benefit. This meant each reform was a net Catholic gain that still did not assuage the demand for more and was seen as another loss by the Protestants. The necessity of continuing the reform process was obvious, even to the Unionist establishment; the question was, How fast and how much?

The Northern Ireland cabinet, hardly in the past the seat of charisma or new directions, had been transformed by the reform challenge. There were almost constant reports of work in progress beginning in September. The Public Protection Authority, a novel idea, announced receiving six hundred complaints between September 9 and 16. The Cameron report on the first round of the Troubles was published, and criticized the failure of provincial leadership. On September 18 the first meeting of the Economic Mission to Northern Ireland, a project announced on August 29, took place. Out in Belfast Bombay Street was to be rebuilt, new walls for old. Faulkner and Fitt met on the matter on October 1. There was work on reforming local government reported on October 2. To balance off the hustle of the bureaucrats and ministers, on Saturday, October 4, Protestant violence broke out along Belfast's Woodstock Road and trouble there and later along Shankill Road continued for five hours. Both Paisley and Desmond Boal appealed for the crowd to disperse, without much effect. On the following day a crowd of five thousand shouting, "Army out!" attempted to march to Paisley's church on Ravenhill Road. They were led by John McKeague, who was increasingly the center of Belfast fundamentalist Orange anger. A narrow, venomous bigot who had a small shop and curious tastes, he had a gift for the bitter word and no aversion to violence. Still, when Callaghan arrived on Thursday, October 9, for his promised visit, he was greeted only with enthusiasm. Matters were progressing. The barricades were coming down. The reforms were going up. The minority had paused in the midst of army-imposed peace and the majority had not run amok; their resistance would surely fade.

Chichester-Clark, Faulkner, and the rest of the Unionists took Orange resistance more seriously than did London or Callaghan. Their countryside did not like the B Specials going. Their people did not like the proposed elimination of many local government posts without due honor to the involved or replacement of the local patronage and petty power. Their people often did not like Catholic pleasure in the reforms. Stormont understood all too well but could only explain, argue, plead necessity and reason. There were, however, a great many unreasonable fundamentalists about the province and in Belfast now found in the streets. In fact there seemed to be a division between Unionists who sought the future of the province through Stormont and so London and those loyalists who gave first priority to their own wee province and past domination. They were loyal to their own.

On Friday morning, October 10, the government announced the resignation of the RUC inspector general, Anthony Peacocke, who had joined the force as a cadet in 1932 and reached the top of the pyramid only in February 1969. A decent man but no administrator, a local unprepared for the turmoil of the times, he had, as the Scarman report would indicate, failed to cope. His successor, Sir Arthur Young, was chosen in part because Harold Wilson felt his experience in the antiterrorist campaign in Malaya might be useful, but instead he tended to follow a more reasoned policy of going softly, leaving anti-insurgency to the army. Peacocke, whatever his limitations, had been Ulster's own; Young, whatever his qualifications, was London's choice: a sign of the times. This might have slipped by on another day but the government also published the Hunt report on the same morning; in retrospect this was not judicious timing. Within hours seven thousand copies had been sold, a record for bureaucratic papers from Her Majesty's Stationery Office (Belfast). No matter what was intended, the report was read as betrayal, if read at all rather than spread by rumor through the Protestant districts: The Specials would go—disbanded just as predicted—and security would be handled by the military. And these were facts, not rumor, the worse for being expected.

The Shankill Defense Association, set up by loyalists in May, wanted the government to resign. Unionists leaders outside the inner circle called for Chichester-Clark to go. Worse was the praise of Austin Currie, Frank Gogarty of NICRA, and Eddie McAteer. Jim Sullivan felt that Peacocke's going was "very good news." By evening large crowds were roaming the Shankill Road beginning to shape a riot. There were attacks toward Catholic districts, dashes down connecting streets, stones and threats. Then the army was attacked. Unknown snipers opened up at random throughout the troubled area. The army and RUC replied with CS gas. By Sunday morning casualties had reached three killed and sixty-six injured, with thirty-seven of those by gunshot wounds, including fourteen soldiers, three RUC, and twenty civilians. Paisley blamed drink (which had certainly been taken), and Hunt insisted that it was not the report, although few bureaucratic reports have ever had such a reception: seven thousand copies and sixty-nine casualties. Callaghan, subdued, continued his Northern Ireland tour. In the land of the children of wrath, matters were not as they ought to be, as they had been seen from London; and they were not amenable to simple goodwill or a walking tour. Returning to London he reported that rioting had reached a most serious turning point. It had come to murder in the city. A Protestant sniper shot down and killed an RUC constable, Victor Arbuckle, on the Shankill Road. Even and especially the RUC was not sufficiently loyal—being a Unionist, even being in the RUC, was no longer enough.

After the weekend, peace of a sort returned. The troops were jeered on the Shankill Road. Protestant barricades were up in Sandy Row and at the Boyne Bridge. In contrast army-RUC patrols into the Bogside were cheered or teased. Craig, in Larne, said Ulster stood at the brink of civil war, an analysis some felt was not political but rhetorical, another step in his campaign for the top of the pyramid. Alcohol sales for the weekend were restricted. Chief Constable Young toured the Shankill Road area on Saturday. Nothing happened. The army reported on Sunday, October 19, "the quietest weekend since the troubles started in August." Protestant violence, then and later, was mostly structured by emotion, by events, by the contingent and unforeseen, not by a conspiracy or godfathers of violence. While politics hardly returned to normal, the focus was switched to the legal complications arising from the previous violence: Who would be charged or convicted or even jailed for past violations? And the reforms continued. The minority concentrated on the potential dangers of the newly proposed Ulster Defense Regiment that London felt would shift security from a Stormont-controlled paramilitary, sectarian police to a British-controlled non-sectarian military force. Many Catholics saw it as a move to recreate the B Specials under another name. Serving in such a UDR would have few charms; provincial police vocations had attracted only token Catholic interest and the UDR was merely to be a provincial security militia. This argument about the UDR took place through conventional forms, not by riot. Arguments over the other reforms—the Police Bill and the Public Order Bill; the Northern Ireland Community Relations Commission under Chairman Maurice Hayes, a Catholic; the Age of Majority Act (Northern Ireland), which reduced the voting age to eighteen—passed largely unnoticed in December.

By December 1969 there were all sorts of other hopeful indicators to those who wanted to be hopeful. There were no riots after the post-Hunt confrontation. No Protestant backlash to the reforms appeared. There were no barricades, no civil rights confrontations, no sign of the PD revolution, no sign of an IRA campaign, no sign of the IRA in fact. In Dublin, on December 9, Jack Lynch said his government did not intend to use force to end the partition of Ireland. In Britain and by some in the Republic, it was thought a welcome sign of maturity, a move away from traditional inflammatory oratory. On the same day John Hume suggested preservation of the houses on Lecky Road, where the FREE DERRY sign had become a great tourist attraction, familiar from a thousand photographs, from the images dispatched by every television crew stopping by Derry on the tour of troubled spots.

Having watched the province skirt so close to the edge of chaos, London's man at Stormont, Oliver Wright, who had served as Wilson's representative in Rhodesia and as ambassador to Portugal, felt that Ulster had managed to pass the most dangerous corner. There was not so much euphoria as relief. Matters could have been so much worse. Nothing but the odd bomb, mostly directed against Fenian targets, had disturbed the peace since the Belfast riot of October 12. The restrictions on by-elections, marches, public demonstrations, and the use of any firearms, together with the reduction of licensing hours and the speeches on moderation, had worked. Matters might be returned to normal in the new year. The legal troubles of both Bernadette Devlin and John McKeague had not led to violence. The province seemed less volatile. So Christmas passed and on December 28 the *Sunday Independent* in Dublin chose Bernadette Devlin as "Man of the Year"—civil rights were thus institutionalized in conservative Irish opinion. On January 1, 1970, Captain O'Neill was made a life peer—he would be Lord O'Neill of the Maine. It seemed an appropriate start for a new year and a new Ulster era.

In the next six weeks only the very perceptive felt uneasy. Factors for stability had increased. Optimists felt that the Catholics were likely to be satisfied with reforms and the Protestants with the continuation of Stormont. There was still indignation and agitation but no mobs. Craig and Paisley and Bunting, however hard, were not gunmen nor advocates of riot. And those who might be so inclined, like McKeague or the revived covert Ulster Volunteer Force (UVF), had few followers. This meant that the Unionist cabinet and much of the party held the center of the stage, with a reluctant but real supporting cast of moderate Nationalists. The center felt time was on their side; if a "solution" was illusive then an accommodation was not—it was possible, for democracy was about the possible.

The weeks passed. Bombay Street was to be rebuilt. The new UDR attracted recruits, some Catholics but not many. No charges would be pressed against the sixteen police cited in the investigation by County Inspector Henry Baillie of the Burntollet-Derry riots. Let sleeping dogs rest. The Public Order Act was passed at Stormont and thirty students staged a peaceful sit-in protest at Queen's on Thursday, February 5, the first of many demonstrations planned. The minority seemed content, as did most Unionists. The security forces could hardly be sanguine, however, for a new menace appeared in a wave of symbolic bombings. Small explosions occurred at a Catholic taxi company, an army post at Brown Square barracks near Shankill Road in Belfast, outside the house of Sheelagh Murnaghan, a former Liberal MP. These were disclaimed by the UVF, which did take responsibility for a "token protest blast." By February 25, there had been twelve explosions, most apparently by militant loyalists, since the beginning of the year. In Belfast on February 26, a bomb in Belfast at Carlisle Circus knocked down the statue of the Reverend Hugh Hanna, a Protestant divine known as Roaring Hugh, hardly an Orange target like the Saint Agnes Parochial Hall in Anderstown bombed at almost the same time. This mostly Protestant militancy was reflected in the refusal of the Unionist hard men—Desmond Boal, John McQuade, William Craig, Harry West, and Dr. Norman Laird—to support a motion of confidence in the government.

Mostly people in the province assumed that this was Unionist politics back to normal, minds concentrated on by-elections in mid-April. The bombs would probably dribble away in the coming search for Unionist votes. In the meantime many were united in delight when a Derry singer, Miss Rosemary Brown— "Dana"—won the Eurovision song contest for Ireland. A province cannot live by crisis alone and, in fact, most people hardly paid attention to such politics. Chichester-Clark had said that 1970 would be a year of rethinking and rebuilding—a Come To Ulster Year. And why not come to the tune of a Eurovision song instead of a Lambeg drum or a rebel ballad? Why not, times were a changin' and not all to the bad.

4

The IRA Divides:
February 1962–January 1970

*There is a tide in the affairs of men, which taken at the flood,
leads on to fortune . . . .*
William Shakespeare, *Julius Caesar, act 4, scene 3*
quoted by Ruairí O Brádaigh, 1972

February 1962 was the darkest moment in over a generation for the Irish
republican movement, aground in the shallows, bound in miseries. On February
5 the IRA Army Council at last formally voted to end the campaign, so long in
planning, so spectacular at first, and finally so hopeless. Nothing remained but a
few activists along the border, the old, mismatched arms, and a reluctance to face
the reality that the end to the dream had come for now, surely an end for a
generation. There would still be the faithful, of course. There would never be an
end to the Irish republican faithful, never had been an end since the Rising of
1798. On the evening of February 27, 1962, at 7:40, this part of republican
history ended when Ruairí O Brádaigh released the public statement indicating
that the end had come. The campaign had failed in large part because of "the
attitude of the general public, whose minds have been distracted from the
supreme issue facing the Irish people—the unity and freedom of Ireland."*
The general public had in truth been so distracted for forty years. The IRA
campaign had at first largely been ignored and then later opposed as imposition
and provocation.

At the end, as always, there were republican begrudgers: those who wanted to

---

*J. Bowyer Bell, *The Secret Army, The IRA 1916–1979*, (Dublin: Poolbeg, 1989), p. 334. The
tribulation of the IRA during this period can be followed in *The Secret Army* and in Tim Pat
Coogan's *The IRA* (London: Fontana, 1980), as well as in Henry Patterson's *The Politics of
Illusion, Republicanism and Socialism in Modern Ireland* (London: Hutchinson, 1989), but a
detailed account does not exist. The IRA was merely a small group of marginal subversives,
and interest has tended to focus on the origins of the split between the Officials and
Provisionals rather than on the republican movement in general. During the period there was
little public coverage and the *United Irishman* monthly, while interesting, reveals little of the
inner working. Various works have been promised, but as yet there is neither a detailed account
of the 1962–1970 years or of the convoluted journey of many republicans from the IRA
through the Officials to Sinn Féin-Workers Party and on through the Workers Party to the
1992 split and the new Democratic Left.

continue, those who said that they did, those who would criticize any position—those with little responsibility and those with only their "eternal hostility to the British forces" as an asset. This had not been enough, not for those responsible. The actives trickled home. O Brádaigh would stay on as chief of staff only until he could be replaced—he wanted to teach away from the Dublin center, at home in Roscommon. Cahal Goulding of Dublin, who had missed much of the campaign and the feuding while in an English jail for an arms raid with Seán Mac Stiofáin on Felstead School, could replace him. Nothing seemed likely to replace the failed military campaign. At least the prisoners, North and South, could hope for an early release. Later in 1962, as expected, thirty-four were gradually released in Northern Ireland. The last four in Crumlin Road Prison in Belfast came out on December 16, 1963. The others, the faithful, the old felons in Belfast, the mountain men in Kerry, the ragtags of what had been a glorious resistance to an empire, were left with only the past to cherish and the present to criticize. Goulding would have to begin again as he had in 1946 to find a means into the future, a means toward the elusive Republic.

Despite the February statement that the Irish resistance movement looked "forward with confidence" to the final phase of the struggle for full freedom, there seemed little future even for those determined to remain active. Many soon felt that there was nothing to be carved from the rotten wood of the movement and so drifted away into private life. An active member of the republican movement rarely has a private life, the dream comes first. And that was all that Goulding and the rest had. The physical force faction had no visible role. Politics in the Irish Republic, that residue of the dreams of Easter Week 1916, had no lure for most people in the twenty-six counties, who seemed concerned only with rising prosperity, the pub, or the Sunday parish sermon. For a generation republicans had seen no need of politics beyond the support the small Sinn Féin party gave the armed struggle. Since the days of the Fenians, the central purpose of the movement had been to fashion conditions that would permit the waging of war. War, not politics, powered the IRA. So there was to be no more war and yet no peace of mind. The begrudgers complained on and on: The Army Council should not have quit, should have quit sooner, should have followed some other course. The new Army Council thus inherited only failure and recriminations, bitter assets. It was not a happy time.

From this unhappy time the tiny core of the determined in Dublin GHQ, with no guidance, no money, with no use for the few old weapons, with no resources of any sort but what they could borrow or steal, haltingly forged another republican movement, the same of course but different. They made bricks by inventing straw and constructed a dwelling for hope, for radical ideas, for a new generation. Mostly young, without property, with limited education, with narrow views, unsophisticated, parochial in all but their own history (and there narrow too), they possessed enormous energy. They revitalized Sinn Féin under Tomás Mac Giolla, an employee of the Electric Supply Board and a bookish man and (as was often the case in Ireland) in a niche far below his potential capacities. The party was open to politics, not just propaganda; it was no more at first than a scattering of the loyal who met once or twice a month and a few branches where the past was savaged and a future sought. The men in Dublin produced the muckraking *United*

Irishman (UI) under Denis Foley, then Tony Meade, and then Séamus O Tuathail. The paper combined the old in-house patriot reverence for the past with scathing attacks on present political, social, and economic injustice. The GHQ now showed an interest in society beyond that of the covert republican world. Goulding was eternally optimistic, year after year, even after Michael Ryan returned from an extended bicycle tour around the island to report that there was no republican movement out there no matter the excitement in Dublin. Except for the Dublin center in the years after the end of the campaign, the movement atrophied. Dublin persisted. The GHQ, the new Sinn Féin, and the *UI* produced a spectrum of action options, target points within the system dominating the tight little island—an island not united, not free or fair, not republican, an island of sorrows and proven failures. The patent failures of the government alone should attract recruits to a radical vision.

For the transients, the visitors, the returned emigrants, for those lured by tales of an unspoiled paradise by *Bord Failte*—the Irish Tourist Board—for scholars of Wilde and Yeats and O'Casey, for the rich and comfortable on the island, the country was a special and wondrous place, a gentle island where time had stopped. There were the soft green fields, spectacular scenery seldom blotched by new buildings or cut by highways. There were wide, empty beaches, romantic white cottages under a haze of peat smoke, and long, long rows of tall, amber Georgian houses in the capital. There was a splendid racing season with the best of the famous Irish horses on display, a grand export item. There were pubs unchanged since they were patronized by Joyce and more recently patronized by Brendan Behan, darling of the West End and New York's Broadway, a living, drinking Irish rebel. There was real Irish spoken in the west for the linguists and the Aran Islands were almost untouched since Synge's *Riders to the Sea*. It was a land where the people were articulate, genial, slow and gentle in manner, pious, quick in wit, kind to aliens. There were more sheep on the roads than cars, more time given to talk than to getting and spending; everything moved slower; it was not so much a backwater as a land beyond the demands of time.

On the edge of Europe, the country was truly all the travel brochures promised—brochures that neglected the seamy side of Ireland: the economic stagnation that made the cities home to bicycles (the whisper of the narrow tires meant no cars), that transformed the elegant ruins into the hovels of the poor, without proper plumbing and decent heating or even space for all those crammed into each room, and that drove the unemployed to emigration. Forty thousand each year left the island not to return, mostly young, new citizens of the old diaspora. Each was a sign of failure ignored by the fortunate who stayed home. Home also meant a cultural hegemony of butchers and Irish-speaking teachers, publicans and priests that institutionalized censorship, assured the propagation of patriot history, made novelty suspect. And there were the hidden slums, the rural penury, the costs of aging, the diseases long vanquished elsewhere. All these were the dreary price of surface tranquillity. Ireland had failed, somehow, to capture the promise from the glory days of the Tan War, failed to fashion a real Republic.

Much had been accomplished. A democratic government had been formed, law and justice assured, a national bureaucratic center created, even daring semistate industries (socialism was anathema) established: the milk board and the peat board, fish and power and even the horses organized. The Shannon had been tamed, the country electrified, peat turned to energy, new airplanes bought for Aer Lingus, and homes financed. If the government could not cope, then de Valera's party or friends did, set up a newspaper in the *Irish Press* or the New Ireland Assurance Company. The Abbey Theatre had Irish national drama on display, the school system had Irish in the curriculum, and the country was a nation once again. Ireland lived not in some romantic twilight as sold to the tourists but in a real world, not a world as dynamic as the continent but still a developing world of small industries, small gains, and small returns in a secure and democratic society. It contented those who could remain, who were satisfied with modest gains, with the pieties of the parish and the intimacy of the familiar, with limited bounds. Ireland, a small, isolated, politically divided island, inhabited by only a few million, well out of the beaten track of European concerns, hardly touched by the clash of postwar ideas beyond clerical concern with communism, was fascinating to scholars and the successful emigrants but to few others. Ireland drifted along forgotten, a beautiful land untroubled by the complex technologies and expanding transnational themes of Western life, untouched in truth by most contemporary themes.

This isolation and tranquillity, albeit paid for in prospects and material rewards, was all the better for the many who rested content with the old ways, the comfort of past quarrels and present pieties. In his Saint Patrick's Day address a generation previously in 1943, de Valera had wished for just such a world, if one slightly more comfortable, more fluent at least in Irish, and more secure from the drain of emigration than was the case even in the sixties. He wanted and many wanted a romantic Ireland sprung from martyrs' graves.

> That Ireland which we dreamed of would be the home of a people who valued material wealth only as the basis of right living, of a people who were satisfied with frugal comfort and devoted their leisure to the things of the spirit—a land whose countryside would be bright with cozy homesteads, whose fields and villages would be joyous with the sounds of industry, with the rompings of sturdy children, the contests of athletic youths and the laughter of comely maidens, whose firesides would be forums for the wisdom of serene old age. It would, in a word, be the home of a people living the life that God desires that man should live.*

It would be and was also a life without intellectual turmoil, urban stimulation, heavy industry, or divergent faiths, without the challenge of change, a life where morality was determined by the orthodox and penury by economic innocence. A

---

*Maurice Moynihan, editor, *Speeches and Statements by Eamon de Valera, 1917–1973* (Dublin and New York: Gill & Macmillan and St. Martin's Press, 1980), p. 466. It is wise to consider that Ireland—so narrow in its limits to the diverse, the creative, the ambitious, and the talented, to the radicals and all the chattering classes, mostly in Dublin—was and is by no means uncongenial to many who live on the island, not saints or scholars, but a people easy with island horizons, whose very presence is a triumph over emigration.

generation later, for the provincial nationalists in power, for the orthodox and the pious, for those with some material wealth that allowed right living, secondary school for the children, and access to a dentist for the family, such a bucolic Ireland seemed a reality. One had only to ignore the statistics of social scientists, the carping of the bookish, the fancies of the Communists, and occasionally the evidence of one's eyes. All was often right with the banker or the publican, the general practitioner, the big farmer, the schoolteacher and the estate agent. The view from the hill out of the doctor's door or from the good farm's front window was splendid—the tip of the new church to the right, the long roll of the hills, and the mist on the mountain to the left—Ireland not of sorrows but of our dreams.

Neither the rural idealists nor the policies of the government could address the contemporary ills that clamored for attention, most especially in the cities. In Dublin, Cork, and elsewhere the beautiful old buildings, were decaying and dangerous, damaged by dry rot and two centuries' use; and the miserable council housing was small, grim, and mean. This Ireland was as old as de Valera's dream, the Ireland of the very poor, those struggling to stay proper and decent, those on the edge, those often badly fed, living crammed in miserable houses, untutored and often ill, without hope of any comfort but charity. This was the ignored Ireland, the Ireland that could be found as well beyond the clatter of the cities hiding beyond the green hills in the countryside. There the old, dead hand of rural poverty and the inherited wisdom of the ignorant unchallenged by reform or by revolution remained. The Ascendancy was gone, many of the big houses were burned-out ruins, the Protestants' charity and skills were spent elsewhere, and neither their manners nor their monuments were maintained. The small farmer, the casual laborer, the last clerk hired lived on fear and potatoes. The rural poor, too, dreamed not of frugal comfort but of a scavenged ticket on an emigrant boat. This unhappy, hidden Ireland, urban and rural, was largely what the IRA volunteers first found once the campaign had run its course in 1962.

The IRA volunteers, mostly moving into their late twenties, realized that little had changed. Ireland was not a republic, not united, and also not a green and pleasant land. Even the government's successes had been constructed on English example and practice. All the new national edifices from Aer Lingus to postage stamps, the judges' wigs,* the forms for insurance, the whole outlook of the clerks and solicitors made the country merely a West Briton province studded with branch offices of London firms where goods could be dumped for higher prices and the bright attracted away from an economy just barely ticking. de Valera was a native governor ignorant of the real sinews of British power. Material rewards were scant. Government initiative and ambitions were limited regardless of party, hedged about by orthodox economics out of discarded texts. The country was focused on self-sufficiency in an interrelated world and on ancient political quarrels once more passed to another generation. Nothing had changed. Ireland for fifty years had been stalled.

The only new wave was Lemass's hope of manufacture for the export market

---

*In 1992 the Irish judiciary was still debating the propriety of wearing wigs with as yet no firm consensus.

now absorbing drink and improved handicrafts, Guinness and Waterford glass, tweed caps and whiskey. The country was still dominated by agriculture, by the premises of small farm towns. The farmer still ruled, shipping bacon and butter, beef on the hoof for others to slaughter and profit, smoked salmon for others to eat. Too many farmers ruled in the old way, suspected their neighbors' gains, the logic of new methods, the advice from the center: There was bovine tuberculosis in the herd after years of eradication. Industry had always been in Belfast and Derry, in the North, a different sort of country, and even there, despite imperial preference and London subsidies, by the sixties it was in serious trouble: Linen or ships were often better produced elsewhere and nothing had been done to change. In the Republic there was not even dying industry and so no real money: no money for health care, no money for continuing education, no money to keep workers from emigrating, no money for repairs, for investment, for the old, for the young, for the future. And who was to blame for poverty centuries old?

The Ireland the volunteers found in the countryside was almost as bleak and gray as that of the grim depression years of the thirties. There might be changes in Dublin, neon and American pop tunes and a few new model British cars, but the real Ireland was the country never covered in the coffee-table books on horses and castles. Rather is was an Ireland of small towns where the houses needed paint, the little shops were tatty, the people intimate, and old family circus posters remained tattered on walls year after year. The films changed once a week and the pubs were all down the main street: Twenty-six in Graiguenamanagh in County Kilkenny with only twelve hundred people and one church, too few Protestants for a church. There were more and more too few Protestants for a church and always the mean pubs, a room dim as porter, narrow and dirty with a hidden snug or two, filled at drinking time with silent men in ill-cut suits, suits never cleaned, never pressed, and older men in caps and long raincoats, rawboned farmers straight from the fields who made a pint last. These were men with old stories and narrow lives who had at least stayed and grown old, unlike the emigrants. And it seemed always to rain in the country. Lives were damp, rooms cold, in icy winter, with a thin electric bar glowing orange. In the evening the bulbs were dim, the turf fire low. The water was seldom heated for a bath, the diet was monotonous, tea was a staple and the radio a luxury. Some out in the country were republicans, republicans still, often very still.

The country, if not romantically bucolic, was not simply dismal. The farmers' sons played hurling and Gaelic football, watched the girls who had stayed in the parish, listened to the radio, and enjoyed the sun when it came; but they were still cut off from even a touch of elegance, singing last year's songs. Scattered out in the county were the ugly, square dance halls, often the only bright spot for awkward men with red faces and clumsy haircuts, a neutral ground to meet in an agony of misgivings the ladies and lassies in fashions based on English magazines and the Sunday matinees growing old as the bachelors waited to be an heir, waited to be sure, waited in a long row on one side for the music, for another dance, for courage. The most famous idol, Brendan Bowyer, took his showband to Liverpool and had an unknown local combo called the Beatles lead off. Back in Ireland they preferred the old tunes.

All Europe could be ruined by a great war, whole nations disappear and millions gassed, the world could be divided by ideologies and engaged in a cold war fought in strange distant countries all without unduly disturbing those in a midland town or a village on the Donegal coast. There men planted the swedes in the morning and imagined the Third World as the black golliwogs on the coin box on the bar counter. There children had to go to school, perhaps for the Irish, certainly because of the law, and there the women went to Mass and, if comfortable, to the meeting of the Irish Countrywomen's Association. Little had changed.

The North was no different, at least for Catholics: The countryside was made tidy by Protestants but still ragged for the others, with small farms, mean offices for rural solicitors or country doctors, and the same dirty pubs. The cities had the same miserable ghettos, British not Irish—there wasn't even the pride of possession. The Catholic Ancient Order of Hibernians—proper, pious, respectable—attracted only 3 percent of the population in contrast to the Orange Orders' 19 percent. Survival was more important than competition or defiance. They were tenants in their own land with the Queen on their postage stamps and the neighborhood bigot for a policeman in his B Special constable's uniform to remind them that here the Tans won. So in Ulster the island was as dank and dour but the pillar boxes were red, the police were the enemy, and the Catholics were exiles inside the last great bastion of biblical Protestantism in Europe. There was for the minority neither money nor hope nor a residue of pride from the glory days after Easter even if the innocent still had faith in Dublin or Dev. In the Republic at least politicians could hire their own so that the old IRA had found small returns from their patriot service. Not in British Ulster. At least the Republic showed that the Irish could run a country: collect taxes, if not make all prosperous; afford an army, if not unite the island; be a nation once again. And there was even hope for better times.

This, too, was not the real Ireland, only the flip side of de Valera's dream of frugal comfort. When the IRA came stumbling home Ireland had begun to change. One had only to look and see the future sweeping across the island. First there was Dublin. In the sixties there was not simply promise of change but real change, the hope of prosperity that would sweep away the stale damp with new money. Only a few *wanted* to be frugal. Piety had takers, but not poverty. The long years of stagnation had not suffocated hope, had in fact brought to fruition a new generation filled with ambition and possessed of a trained eye for the main chance. The future had been released by Lemass and T. K. Whitaker, who accepted the new orthodoxy of investment in export industries rather than persisting with programs for an autarkic Ireland that could support only some and only then poorly. It was not time to discard Buy Irish but to Sell Irish. Export meant jobs and jobs meant a new kind of Ireland, a better Ireland. There would be, there were, opportunities where none had been foreseen, capital where there had been none, domestic investment that generated profit to be reinvested. Times were a changin' and a few German motors began to edge their ways through the fleets of bicycles swishing around Stephen's Green, ministerial Mercedeses parked in splendid glory. Soon it was no easy matter to park a Rover or a Renault in front of the Shelbourne or find a bike about Stephen's Green.

Ireland, especially urban Ireland, was not quite the same and no matter where the observer looked in the sixties the scene shifted. The *Irish Times* became a modern newspaper and no longer spoke for the lost Ascendancy that had somehow melted away in both reality and perception. The Protestants even as presence were going: The big houses were sold for hotels or schools, the children married abroad and did not return, the fashions were set in Hollywood, not by the banker's daughter. So they disappeared into small parish churches and into golf and tennis clubs where the others seldom ventured, stayed on the board but would be replaced by one of the others. There would be no Protestant replacements. The Republic of Ireland, first proposed by a Protestant, that had as first martyr a Protestant, William Orr, hanged in 1797, and that had in the long struggle been sought by various means by Protestant nationalists and republicans, was still anathema to the Protestants of the North. No matter if a free Ireland had Protestants as presidents and Protestants as advocates, for the unionists it was still a truly Catholic country, orthodox in belief and practice, merely superficially tolerant. Nothing was more triumphant than the Church's *Ne Temere* that assured mixed marriages would produce only Catholic children. In another twenty years much of Georgian Dublin was gone, the Ascendancy was neutered, and there was one Protestant in Dáil. The new Ireland was filled with the new rich in ascendancy and there was no time even for recriminations or reflection, only for advantage and display. Then the people would make clear there was no need to adapt to other customs, other values, for had not they kept the faith and been no worse for it?

Like the Ascendancy, elegant people in elegant houses living on old capital and off old silver, the old Irish country world idealized by de Valera, too, melted away year by year in theory as well as assumption. The countryman was drawn to Dublin by opportunity and so no longer left forever to find a position in Birmingham or in Boston and, as important, no longer stayed on wretched in Leitrim or West Kerry. Dublin was the lure, the new glass box Dublin choked with traffic and opportunity, filled with offices and pubs with carpets. It was all so sudden. The factories opened in the countryside and towels were made for sale in Italy and electronic components assembled for shipment to Germany. The Common Market would put Limerick and Cork in the big picture and Japanese investors could already be found taking notes in Mayo. There was the installment plan and money to buy things crafted in plastic and Day-Glo colors. Ice came to the pubs and trendy priests to television.

In 1967 Donogh O'Malley's reform brought free education to everyone up to eighteen and brought the children to the school if need be in yellow buses— eighty thousand in the transportation program in 1968. So the children came to school in yellow buses along with ice to the pubs and jobs to the lucky or skilled. And more people came to the doctors and more to the building societies for home loans. Emigration came down to twelve thousand by 1967, and not all of those were driven away by poverty; some were ambitious or simply curious. On the island the price of good acres rose and some of those acres near the cities were soon planted in houses. Dublin crept out beyond the old suburbs. The look of Ireland was changing for the first time in fifty years.

The transformation in the sixties was swift, irreversible, for some traumatic, for most unexpected, even perhaps for those in power who had bet on Sell Irish. Nearly everyone approved of the new: the slackening of emigration, the money to be spent, the children in schools, the new houses, the new in general. How could you not? There was a sudden spate of new books on the new Ireland and each glittered with optimism about the future, detailed with delight the changes of the immediate past. Tim Pat Coogan's *Ireland Since the Rising* displayed a photograph of the new Liberty Hall glass headquarters on the dust jacket and inside, noting the unfortunate residue of the old, praised this new Ireland emerging from decades of isolation. The new Ireland also emerged from over forty years of analytical silence. The universities had produced little of relevance, a reluctance to write was still a foolish academic fashion, nor had the schools taught the present. By agreement history ended in 1921. Children could go through school and not know the British still ruled six counties or that the Irish killed each other over the treaty. There were no new university disciplines, certainly not in the alien social sciences. Ireland was even without a standard history—Coogan's *Ireland Since the Rising* was the first cut. All that immediate past was too raw and too contentious. So the state and nation had been kept out of sight and out of mind and now could be ignored altogether in the new and prosperous times.

Year Zero would be 1966 and all good things would now flow, things that could be consumed, spent, displayed, and enjoyed at last. The newspapers—the *Irish Press* of Tim Pat Coogan and Fianna Fáil and the *Irish Independent* for Fine Gael, the *Cork Examiner* for its own and the *Irish Times* for the elite—found little fault with the direction of events. There were those who worried that a few valuables might be destroyed by progress and prosperity but adjustments could be made. Some Georgian houses could be saved, no truly pornographic magazines would be imported, the encouragement of Irish could go forward with new money, and poverty was not crucial to poetry.

Not only was there money to be spent, an end to emigration, funds for education and public health and new roads, but also, most important, the bad old quarrels, the historical rancor and malice of the past rivalries, could go. The bad past could truly be forgotten. There would be a new positive history. Dev was already president in Phoenix Park rather than in power. Lemass, the most flexible, the youngest, the most modern of the old lot, would soon give way to a new Fianna Fáil generation already crowding on stage. There were even radical conservatives within Fine Gael bearing famous old names and new priorities. There had been an end to the IRA's foolish campaign, a reminder of priorities better forgotten. These few were not so faithful as foolish, the misguided with the wrong agenda for a new Ireland. There was as alternative the Lemass-O'Neil 1965 meeting that indicated a way ahead, cautious and slow, without the gun or the sound of trumpets. Most in the Republic had given little thought to the direction and development of Northern Ireland, assuming that in the fullness of time the island would be united. Derry and Tyrone were a long way away. Time, the logic of history, and now the prosperity of the country made unity inevitable. Gunmen weren't needed. For the first time since 1921 the island seemed to look ahead with enthusiasm.

Some few looked ahead with horror because the past had been discarded, the established pieties were no longer absolute, and the common wisdom was without takers. These were the rock-hard conservatives, some in the church, some even in the republican movement, to be found saying nay in the pub or at party meetings. Some others, a great many more, were, on the other hand, delighted that so much had been discarded but still foresaw the future as horror. The orthodox feared any change while the radicals feared that this change would institutionalize the real orthodoxies in an even more conservative society: The rule of the consumer would clash with both the old ways and the proper new ones. The horrible old Ireland was to be replaced by an even more dreary prospect: a bad, new Ireland, jerry-built on quick profits, slick promotions, and the exploitation of the many. One set had hated the dance hall because it corrupted morals and the other because it was ugly and distracted the youth from the social evils around them. Within the IRA and republican movement the conservatives who might be suspicious of any threat to social conventions of the past were less important than the new men in Dublin GHQ who opposed the evils that came with the new.

The fear by radicals, including many active IRA people, was that Ireland would be a mass society for the manipulated consumer, deadened to real injustice or the possibility of created lives. The Irish people, so long denied even the basics, would be bribed by things tawdry and cheap, easily purchased but with a fearful ultimate price. The people would become wage slaves, competing for trinkets and bemused by television images and regular employment. de Valera had at least cherished the spirit, the language, the old national dream, even if he had given up on reality and justice and the six counties. The new men, however, let in the door by Lemass, cared nothing for youths and maids except as customers to company advantage. They cared neither for things of the spirit nor the triumph of the poor. In the Dáil and out, sleek, plump, arrogant, they cared only for building permits, access to political favor, rising dividends, and very expensive motor cars; they cared only for the main chance, no matter at whose expense. The poor, the people, meant nothing to men on the make—what had the people done for Ireland lately to equal the lure of easy money? The money men's new Ireland was one of growth statistics. It was an Ireland of golf clubs, yacht clubs, and thoroughbreds purchased for thousands at Kildare horse auctions. It was an awful, newly rich Ireland, crude, effective, harsh, arrogant and ignorant, shaped before the very eyes. It was a country that had leaped from small farms to big deals. And what was to be made of all this?

The island was no longer without vitality, devoid of creativity, the site only for old quarrels, but was a productive engine, a part of Europe, a tale of success. The people approved—every indicator including the election to enter the Common Market so agreed. The establishment approved. The parties and the prelates were as one. The poor were being housed in great estates on the edges of the cities, some stacked in high rises, most provided with the basics. They were being offered jobs in the export industries. They were amused by the new culture of the consumer, strengthened by those who would have gone abroad—and what if the housing was cheap, the facilities limited, the jobs poorly paid, the consumer culture vapid? What if the managers and manipulators made quick fortunes at the expense of the many, depleted the resources of the past, destroyed the gracious for a quick turnover and a highway through the party's heartland? Progress must be served and for most in Ireland, the *reality* of the present canceled out all else. New money was never pretty and seldom acquired by the reflective. Time would erode the raw edges and education would advance the horizons of the poor. So much was gained. The old, the past had engendered quarrels and malice and grievances beyond bearing. The glass boxes in Dublin were, if not beautiful, *Irish*: Irish built, Irish designed, Irish inhabited. The jobs in the Dutch component assembly plant and the Japanese factories were *Irish* jobs. There was now at last, money in Ireland and all that money could buy. Fair shares and taste and restraint could wait. Dublin could not be rebuilt in a day in any case although it seemed that the speculators were trying.

Ireland thus had somehow moved from the village, romantic in oratory and literature if nasty in experience, directly into the postindustrial world while the IRA had been first playing at guerrillas along the border and then seeking an agenda in the draughty rooms of Gardiner Place. That the country was not united, not free, not republican, not fair, not just, and surely, not the proper end product of the patriot dream seemed to mean little beyond Gardiner Place. The countryside, if not Dublin and Cork, still had traditional republicans, slow men but sound on the national issue who lived as always at the end of the land with a barn to be used and a fiver for the lads in hard times, but increasingly they seemed relics from another world. The Tan War seemed fought by men in ancient costumes. A whole generation had grown up innocent of the Tan War martyr Kevin Barry as anything but a song.

The real action was in the cities, where new ideas about society spun about in the wake of the new money. There were some radical Labour Party members and a few free-floating intellectual militants like Roy Johnston and Tony Coughlan who influenced the republicans. Johnston, an Irish physicist who had been a member of the English Communist Connolly Association, was an avowed Marxist-Leninist. He signed up with the republicans where Coughlan did not. A few aging radical republicans from the thirties, such as Peadar O'Donnell (novelist and agitator), George Gilmore (dissenter), and Máirtín O Cadhain (lecturer in Irish at Trinity College, Dublin), all once important IRA soldiers and theorists, had an influence on new directions after a generation of isolation. They had sound ideological reasons why the New Ireland was unappealing. The young and still uncertain republican movement, dominated by men of no property, was fertile ground for these radical ideas. In the sixties, without prospects or resources, in an Ireland set up for capitalist consumption, on an island still divided and exploited, the little group at GHQ instinctively had responded with distaste to the Ireland dominated by the men in mohair suits and then found reason in the experience of their own and in the ideas of their class.

Any such radical Irish dissent faced the almost insurmountable obstacle of fresh money in many hands. All the old forces—the established church, the exhaustion of the people, the national conservatism arising from endless hard times, the fear of class analysis—still sat cemented into place as well. Those most apt to complain could not: the very old neglected in cold attics on tiny pensions eking out life and the very young in families without fires or funds or skilled friends. All of them, the inarticulate in the ghettos, the miserable way up the rural lane beyond thought and the services of the state, the marginal and the unorganized, had been touched by good times. They had seen the new television, been encouraged by President John Kennedy's visit, touched by the sight of money down the street. The poor had their hopes too that the rising tide would lift even their poor holed boat. And protest had long been dangerous: A move toward heresy, an insult to the system sanctified by the proper and orthodox, perhaps

139

would be taken as communism, an ill-defined concept but like Satan always a danger to Holy Ireland. No one loved a live rebel, not the church, not the state, and not the boss. What could radicals offer but ideas instead of money? Who would hire a Red? And then what? Even the conventional unions and the proper Labour Party had adjusted to the system despite the hopes of a few radical recruits. They would be tamed as had been each new generation of Labour people. What, indeed, could the IRA offer but even more dangerous associations, even less structured complaint, even greater risks?

The intense men of the GHQ were, in fact, not at all sure what to offer. Most were at best self-educated, often open to conversion by the reasoning of one book, the logic of one speaker. They were unsure in the clash of ideas and uneasy in the pubs around Trinity or University College Dublin (UCD), where the privileged students played with theories for three years before reading law or going into accounting. The IRA men were fascinated with the ideas that seemed a long way from the border war. The students in turn were fascinated with IRA gunmen but not as mentors. There had always been in Ireland a radical tradition, a socialist dream that many felt could be woven into the national issue; but since the failure of Jim Larkin's great strike in 1913, the mainstream Labour Party, North and South, had been dominated by the most conservative officials. Union bureaucrats, pious whether Protestant or Catholic, socially at one with their neighbors, they were deeply suspicious of ideas, much less revolution, and were dedicated to entitlements, adjustments, and accommodations within the system. Let students, briefly neo-Marxist, stumble around the national and class issues; the purpose of their movement, their party, and their unions was hours, wages, and holidays.

But this conservatism led the men at GHQ to believe there was a niche for them. The left of the political spectrum was unoccupied. GHQ thus made a beginning. In June 1964 the Wolfe Tone Society was organized to discuss such radical matters. The Sinn Féin–*United Irishman* offices became the site of informal seminars on prospects and issues.

There were those, especially in the country at the end of the lane, who from the first found such city ideas sterile and often took a more violent course without recourse to the GHQ agenda. For them the movement was clumped around an army, and an army had a duty to wage war. A monument was bombed at a cost of one IRA life, shots authorized by GHQ were fired at the British torpedo boat *Brave Boarder* visiting Waterford. Then more shots were fired without authorization by the same unit emboldened by action. The kind of action GHQ really wanted was linked to issues—not a bomb to protest a royal visit (which was done), but arson during labor disputes (which was done), and armed agitation. This concept had hard going since most of the IRA still wanted a military career and most Irish republicans, except for the agitators from the thirties, were radical only on the national issues. So many of the physical force people drifted away. The IRA seemed to be running down not gearing up.

At the Bodenstown commemoration in June 1966 the entire Belfast unit under Billy McMillen and Jim Sullivan arrived in Kildare in a hired minibus. This was the Belfast Brigade, fearsome ogre in the Orange mind, staunch defender in the perception of the threatened nationalists: two officers and not enough troops for a football team. The elders and the traditionalists wanted to hear no more of social issues, fishing rights, economic programs, class analysis. They might have no agenda of their own but they were sound on the national issue and knew the purpose of an army.

The need for some sort of action had taken the form of an explosion at 1:32 A.M. on March 7, 1966, that tore off the top of Nelson Pillar in Dublin's O'Connell Street, a national landmark now truncated above heaped rubble. The tiny group of schismatics who had broken with the IRA in June 1956 had solicited American money and on the second try celebrated the Easter Rising their way. The celebration was not only in a way most Irish republicans understood but also effective propaganda of the deed. In America *The New York Times* gave first-page coverage and in Ireland the event was a nine-day wonder as the other army, the Free Staters, proved less deft in the use of explosives than the republicans. From Gardiner Place the official republican movement indicated no interest in such stunts. The problem for many republicans, many not simply aging reactionaries or schismatic rivals, was that the GHQ had nothing desirable to offer instead of stunts. Even armed agitation in economic and social matters would not bring the Republic closer and this had always been the engine driving the movement.

Out in the country, even in Belfast, there gradually grew a feeling that Dublin had embarked on an alien course, probably wrong but more important not really republican. In the past, others, including O'Donnell and Gilmore, had taken a similar path, produced schism, weakened the movement, and disappeared. Others, like Seán MacBride, had formed Clann na Poblachta, and after initial success— the party carried ten seats in 1949 and MacBride became Minister for External Affairs in a coalition government—it also disappeared. The Irish republican has a long memory. One of the factors for an old and often traditional movement is that history is littered with precedents. So in the mid-sixties many in the movement had doubts. Nearly everyone liked the new chief of staff, Cahal Goulding, a charmer over a pint, a friend of Brendan Behan, a republican since birth who had as a lad during World War II spent time interned in the Curragh prison camp. His father was a republican who had been out in 1916 and his grandfather a Fenian and he had served his time in an English prison. Goulding was a droll and decent man engaged in an impossible job, running the republican movement in the time left over from his painting and decorating business. And the rest in GHQ had paid their dues. Seán Garland had been wounded at the Brookeborough RUC barracks attack in January 1957, when the campaign's one national hero, Seán South, was killed. The others—Mick Ryan, Séamus Costello, Tony Meade and Denis Foley at the *UI,* Malachy McGurran from the North, Tom Mitchell —had all been campaign volunteers, served in the North, often spent prison time, long time in several cases; they could not be faulted. They had stuck with the campaign to the end and knew what a secret army was but somehow had started down a road that shimmered of politics and compromise. Yet, there remained no clear alternative; so a hard-core purist like Seán Mac Stiofáin, who had served his time in prison for the arms raid with Goulding under the English version of his name, John Stephenson, felt no qualms about his colleagues or their policy. With physical force smashed, what other policy was there? Politics did not mean accepting the imposed imperial system, only seeking an advantage by other means.

Standing above his farm on a hillside in Kilkenny overlooking the Barrow River, twisting brown below, Paddy Murphy, a campaign man, a countryman, a man of property, too, had no time for the newly rich capitalists who were buying power in Fianna Fáil through their contributions, no interest in the new getting and spending; but he felt no pull toward the new direction. What were the old Ascendancy salmon fishing rights to him or him to salmon rights? What was his IRA doing picketing miserable housing in Dublin or reduced to arson in the Midlands to demonstrate against exploitation? What was the point when Ireland's ills arose from British imperial control, not fishermen or foreign investors. Others were uneasy, some poor, some comfortable, all dedicated. Some would have been outraged at anything but a repeat of their futile careers: It was the new generation's time to fail, ruin their lives in turn. Some others were deeply embedded in the reactionary milieu of rural Ireland, adamantly opposed to "communism" as described by the parish priest who had opposed the IRA as well. Some in Belfast, more intimate with both communism and the empire, felt the movement was off course, led by young men corrupted by alien ideas. Everywhere within the covert republican world was a fear that politics might lure the movement into accepting the institutions of the state. They looked at de Valera and then the mistakes of O'Donnell and Gilmore, and the failure of MacBride and Clann na Poblachta. Dev and his Justice Minister, Gerry Boland, had ended by hanging republicans, the thirties radicals had ruined the IRA for nothing, and MacBride had simply called the Free State a Republic and no more. For many of the physical force men, *any* nonmilitary investment was unwise: Politics was like a scarlet woman, intriguing but sinful and dangerous, not worth the risk. For many, politics meant propaganda for the IRA or voting for abstentionist candidates, not advocacy of revolution. GHQ had so far kept what was left of the movement from splitting because the doubters had little to seize and no place to go. The new ideas would only matter if they generated power and movement.

For the republican critics there was a natural tendency to focus on those involved in the new direction who had neither Fenian grandfathers nor campaign scars. Some were new men, attracted by what repelled the conservatives. One was emblematic of all that the traditionalists suspected: Roy Johnston. As a member of the James Connolly Society and an avowed Marxist he was in many parts of the country anathema, for Irish society was socially and often economically conservative, confused about the details of communism but certain that it was alien, ungodly. Mixing with communism would be ruinous to the IRA's image of pure nationalist dedication. So Johnston was suspect on principle. He was also a technocrat, highly educated, who believed in the reality of the written word over events, a computer specialist who spoke in the tongues of contemporary thought and hence soon had a profound effect on the Dublin center, innocent of such ideas and such skills. For the suspicious he was a glib outsider surrounded by memos and outlines and bits of paper, too quick with words, too fast with explanations.

Johnston was just what Goulding felt was needed: a fresh voice, a trained mind, a man with analytical tools, a real recruit instead of one more solemn plowboy out for a Thompson gun. Goulding was told that Johnston might be all of that, decent, well-meaning, a gentleman, but dialectic policies and paper resolutions were not going to unite the country. He would smear the movement as Communist, thus complicating an already difficult situation. He would turn the center from military matters. He would disrupt. And he was not one of them but an import. No one at GHQ cared to listen. The man had much useful to say, went on training camps, lectured on diet as well as Lenin. And in Johnston they had found someone who could put down on paper the inarticulate certainties held by the leadership. The nation could be united but in three stages adapted from Marxist theory. At the moment there was no need for an army; later, at another stage, military force would be needed and by then history would have erased many of the obstacles snagging the republicans' path, including the historical opposition to Irish unity by the Protestant working class.

This was a most attractive analysis given the military weakness of the IRA. The few arms had been scattered and no more had been found. The few trained volunteers had drifted away and training camps were rare. The IRA six years after the campaign was weaker militarily despite the gain in politically active volunteers and the excitement at Gardiner Place. And by 1968 there was movement in the North that dovetailed with Dublin theory: The civil rights demonstrators would drive the Stormont system toward democracy, a necessary stage, and thus could be fully supported both in means and professed aims. Johnston wrote internal papers on the prospects. The IRA was thus captured by the forces of nonviolence. Stormont had to be transformed before it could be replaced—a nicety lost on some republicans, who joined the demonstrations to cause trouble for Stormont in a new way although they would have preferred guns to placards. When they became too troublesome, it was IRA marshals who imposed nonviolent discipline. In fact in Dublin both in theory and in practice Northern events had a tendency to intrude on the organizational concerns of the GHQ. The civil rights demonstrators were interesting but a diversion. At Gardiner Place the leadership grew isolated from any but those committed to the new course.

Those who did not follow the new line were scorned. Fears of the movement violating principle and giving up abstentionism seemed irrelevant, a difference on technical matters that could be sorted out. Fears of any end to the military role seemed foolish—what role? What military? Increasingly GHQ revealed a remarkable lack of gratitude for old republican service or for what was offered as well-meant criticism by those opposed to change. Many old IRA men translated any novelty into old arguments. Everyone at Gardiner Place, except the dissidents, grew tired of old grievances, old quarrels, old postures. Some made this clear to the old faithful: Best put out to pasture in changed times. For GHQ these critics were suspicious of everything. They condemned Johnston's "Three Stooges" theory out of ignorance. They discovered "Communists" everywhere. And they tended to appear only at funerals. They offered the rosary at commemorations but not money or service to the movement. They were rosary republicans. Johnston, in fact, wrote a letter to the *UI* suggesting that saying the rosary at commemorations was sectarian and thus a violation of Wolfe Tone's dictum. The conservatives or at least those who heard about it were horrified. Mac Stiofáin, born in London with an English father and once an English name, at least knew that no Communist from Dublin should be telling the Irish when to pray and stopped distribution of the newspaper in Cork and Kerry. He received a six-month suspension reduced to two.

GHQ on the road to the future was increasingly immune to other sensitivities as the movement shed consensus, the invisible binder for a covert organization. The women's organization Cumann na mBan was particularly recalcitrant. Republican women had long been ideologically most pure, most militant. They sniffed out politics and opposed it. Why had so many died? Not for politics. Joe Cahill from Belfast spoke to Sinn Féin president Mac Giolla during a commemoration about the growing alienation. His comments about old Belfast republicans had little weight—McMillen and Sullivan were the coming men, not the old gunmen. Even the radical students in the North had demonstrated the value of new ways. What had the felons to offer but old war stories?

The new direction was, thus, finding hard going in most places. The enormous changes spreading across the country in the sixties meant in part that Dublin events came closer to the country, so that GHQ ideas could reach out and convert a few but also be displayed to the secret republican world that had changed little. Put a physical force man in a new car, with new boots and a new leather jacket, but his mind is often still set as before. Thus, the faster events moved in Dublin the more truculent the republican elders grew and the more irritated grew GHQ. Only Mac Stiofáin—he had moved up from Cork to Navan in July 1966 and became GHQ intelligence officer—showed a sensitivity to the rising dissent, in part because his republican work carried him about the country asking questions and in part because he was sympathetic to the concerns of the dissenters. Ruairí O Brádaigh in Roscommon (and on the Army Council) appeared only once a month or so and then when he indicated concerns that were not those of GHQ he was ignored. Dissent was not welcome. Dublin expelled those who protested too much, whole units if that became necessary, famous old names if need be.

The old veterans in the North were eased out of power or disciplined. Billy McKee had been replaced in 1964 as O/C of Belfast by McMillen, who was younger, more open to radical ideas, and if he was a simple man, still he was not as narrow as some of the other felons of the forties. In February 1967 John Joe Rice in Kerry and his people had been expelled. The most famous of the felons, Jimmy Steele of Belfast, who had spent seventeen Christmas Days in prison, finally answered back for all the discarded on July 6, 1969, at Mullingar cemetery, from a commemoration platform that Goulding had sought to close to him. For Steele the movement was being stolen by alien influences in Dublin. He was expelled. And there were others, not frightened of "communism" or even political concerns but simply in favor of physical force as first option. The real purpose of the movement was to break the connection by force, and the real means was a secret army made legitimate by history and by the refusal to recognize the existing and imposed authorities in Dublin, Belfast, and London. Abstaining—not taking seats even if elected—for many republicans was a matter of principle. And, anyway, the IRA was an army dedicated to physical force. If Goulding wanted to do something else, wanted something else, then he should not warp the movement to that purpose. Increasingly in 1968 it became clear that GHQ intended not simply to shift direction but also to transform the movement, discard the past for a course already proven futile, raze the IRA and use the rubble as a foundation for something alien. No one in Dublin seemed to realize that legitimizing the existing institutions by taking seats in puppet parliaments would eliminate the movement's capacity to act in the name of Ireland in a just war. Dublin could no longer imagine a war. So no one in the GHQ cared about the IRA. No one in Dublin seemed concerned with the military options that the civil rights movement opened up, concentrating instead on the need to reform Stormont. No one in Dublin even seemed to realize that the protesters might provoke a pogrom that would require military defense.

Instead, largely ignoring Northern events, the GHQ moved to a point of no return: a nine-point proposal drawn up by Seán Garland that would permit an end to abstentionism. The Army Council had in the Kildare Army Convention in the autumn of 1968 been increased from seven to twenty, so diluting opposition to GHQ. The centers of opposition in the country had been expelled or ignored so that when delegates were selected for the crucial IRA 1969 Army Convention the GHQ-center would dominate. Yet even then the revisionists could not be assured of a constitutional majority to change Sinn Féin rules. Nor was anyone certain that a split was inevitable. In fact, of course, the split had already occurred.

It had long been apparent that if there were to be a division it would come on the question of abstention. There were always divisions within the republican movement. A revealed truth, even a revealed political truth, guarantees divisive interpretations, many gospels, several roads into the future, quarrels over escalation or persistence or even personalities, quarrels over strategy and tactics that turn on principle. The republicans had experienced all of these from the disruptions of charisma to the dreaded charms of co-option and compromise. Since the republican world has almost always been covert, these divisions have been exacerbated by secrecy, and the sixties proved no exception, even though the underground world had dwindled from the hidden nation of 1921 to a few thousand acolytes in 1969, many no longer active. By 1969 GHQ felt that the time had come. Delay was alienating many of their own who were tired of waiting. As early as 1965 in Tyrone Seán Caughey had resigned and formed his Irish Union to pursue politics; and the delay was convincing none of the traditionalists; rumors had some few already organizing secretly. Still, many, even some like Mick Ryan on the GHQ who were convinced of the new direction, felt that a split could be avoided. Mac Stiofáin was sure if Goulding could only be made to see reality, all could be worked out. Some simply counted on their fingers and felt the necessary revisionist majority could not be achieved for the present. No one pushed for a split, only for his policy. The small 1969 Army Convention would be a microcosm of the clash between the forces unleashed in the new Ireland and the persistence of old values and agendas. It did not seem so to the delegates hidden away in their narrow covert world. In the meantime that secret world was invaded by a real and different world in 1969 before the convention could meet.

The collapse of order in Derry and Belfast in August 1969 accelerated internal republican events. The Belfast walls scrawled with "IRA—I Ran Away" graffiti shattered the Northerners who chose to blame Dublin GHQ. They, like their Catholic neighbors, should have known that there was no secret army. This was not Dublin's fault but reality: The IRA was a giant monster for the Stormont system and in hard times for nationalists a mythical comfort. The Belfast IRA did not even have the potential to become a real factor within the city before 1969. It was illusion shaped by fear and hope. And in August there had been no comfort, no hope, and that other army, the British army, a real army, had been sent into the streets to protect the Catholics. There had not even been an IRA to run away.

In the North, in many parts of Ireland, there were suddenly republicans determined to see that such did not happen again, that next time there would be a real secret army. There was an enormous sense of urgency but an urgency limited after the first burst of enthusiasm mostly to Northern Ireland. In Dublin old republicans showed up seeking arms, seeking to offer their services, seeking a role. There was nothing for them at GHQ. Most drifted away alienated and uneasy, blaming GHQ. They did not blame their own lack of involvement in the movement or events in general. Gardiner Place had not been prepared. When the men from the country grew uneasy about an Orange backlash, when O Brádaigh brought it up in an Army Council Meeting, Goulding insisted that there was no problem. But there had been.

There were various immediate rationales out of Dublin: The arrival of the British army would protect the nationalists, would lead to the Stormont reform needed by the three-stages doctrine, was thus objectively a good thing. The paucity of military resources was not Dublin's fault and after all the present critics had done little to prepare for trouble and much to cause dissent in the army. No one had foreseen August, so no one could have been prepared. Ireland, as analyzed in Gardiner Place, had not changed greatly simply because the British army was in the streets instead of the barracks, so GHQ priorities remained much the same even while some sort of expedient military response was organized. So Ryan was made quartermaster general to find arms. The movement had no foreign friends and no likely suppliers. Cars were sent out into the country to collect bits and pieces. Volunteers were accepted for uncertain purpose since there was as yet no gear, no training program, and no military agenda. In a real sense GHQ sought to maintain the direction of events—and this meant a focus on the reforming proposals contained in Garland's report and not on the prospect of war in the North. Dedicated to the concept of revolution, none was prepared for a revolutionary situation where real power might flow from guns. After decades of failure they doubted the gun as the main means to act on history. Most of those at GHQ wished for an accommodation in the North that would allow the real agenda to be followed.

Others in Irish politics were actually more concerned than the IRA GHQ. The vulnerability of the Northern Catholics rekindled concern in many circles, especially Fianna Fáil, by law the only republican party in the country. After decades of impasse, history was seen to be moving. If not everything, then something was possible. For the Dublin politicians, the IRA, just as it did in the six counties, possessed a reality belied by reality. Many people who should have known better assumed that not only was there a secret army but also that in recent years the leadership had moved far to the Left amid Communists and anarchists. Heretofore of interest only to historians and the police Special Branch, the IRA might have a role to play because it was a secret army, because it was illicit but legitimate, because there was seemingly very little conventional that those in the Republic could do beyond resort to private anguish and public threats. Something should be done but with what tools? The Irish Republic had no effective army, no leverage, no influence.

Jack Lynch was in fact cunningly cutting his limited cloth to cover the real options, thus calming his party critics and the public concern. He would shift responsibility onto London. There would be no thanks given to a British army that was vital to the minority's survival. Others less perceptive and responsible, more bellicose or more daring, wanted to act. Like the volunteers on the steps of Gardiner Place, they were driven by urgency but offered little of value. What they did offer was taken by the IRA GHQ with alacrity. After August certain republicans found that the comfortable were willing to sign checks or pass over cash or even discuss military options although only as private citizens. Members of Fianna Fáil privately became involved, as donors, as go-betweens, as self-appointed legates. A few in conventional politics felt that the IRA could be purchased as conduit and the "Communists" discarded in the deal. This would open up an armed intervention in the North that could be plausibly denied and simultaneously corrupt the radical republicans. Those so afflicted by this late-summer madness assumed the IRA was real and the "Communists" a threat. More telling, they assumed that money so spent would buy a piece of the action. Goulding accepted both an automobile and a cash donation.

The ultimate focus was on Northern republicans who would have to deploy for defensive purposes. Some of these had come to the conclusion that for practical purposes the movement had split. Goulding would use the money for politics and not for gear. They did not want GHQ in control of a military response. Private preparations began to be made to channel resources and prospects away from GHQ. Mac Stiofáin discovered that a large contribution he had accepted for aid to the North might instead be added to the general fund. Money given for defense was, as others suspected, to be spent on political maneuvers in the twenty-six counties. Mac Stiofáin told his donors to hold off awhile. Others eager to help were put on hold as well. The Belfast people began opening contacts with old friends of similar persuasion in the Republic. Liam Burke of Belfast was reported meeting with Ned Dempsey in Carlow even before August. Northerners like Harry White living in the South, long-quiet physical force people alienated from GHQ, were sighted abroad. The Irish-Americans were reported in turmoil within hours of the August events. Those far from the center of the circle, those expelled or dismissed, those dedicated to physical force and an underground army, began to clump together either to seize the shell of the movement or to reestablish a proper republican movement. Many could not but imagine that all good republicans, Goulding and Garland and the rest, would support the steps necessary to protect the Northern nationalists.

A few had quiet doubts. GHQ had shown no signs of making hasty amends. Few people from the center went North regularly. Ryan, as QMG, was an exception. Yet, Dublin was *still* talking about stages and reforming Stormont and getting gear later. There had been gunfights along the Falls already. Gear was needed, not reforms. Even Seán Keenan in Derry when tea was still being given to British soldiers had called the British army in August the first target. Keenan was not alone, just more bold. The island had been turned upside down in a week and

Gardiner Place could not or would not adapt. Sill, even those most opposed to GHQ, hoped that a split could be avoided. So too did those at the center.

When everything had collapsed in August, the IRA unit was not ready. The veterans had to go to long-hidden dumps, had to come out on the streets without direction or orders, had barely protected their own. And then there was still no flood of aid from Dublin. August was the last straw. Old IRA people in Derry and Belfast appeared first on street defense committees and then like Keenan out of the Bogside and Albert Price off the Falls had taken a visible part in citywide defense. John Kelly, who had broken his leg escaping from Crumlin during the border campaign and then retired to private life in Belfast, had been one of the first to make contact in Dublin to arrange arms supplies. Making contact with Gardiner Place seemed pointless. Mick Ryan had no real gear except what had been rounded up and trucked north too late. And it was too varied to be the basis for the future. Other IRA people began to put matters right without going through McMillen. Among them were Billy Kelly, a seaman and John's brother; Séamus Twomey, a veteran of the forties known only to his own, a quiet bookmaker with a wry sense of humor; Joe Cahill, who had escaped the noose; the young barman Gerry Adams, a hereditary republican, old Gerry's son, Dominic Adams's nephew; one of the few active young republicans, Jimmy Drumm; and Jimmy Steele. They made contacts, particularly in the South, particularly in their positions as members of defense committees, with those unsympathetic to the Dublin GHQ or outside the republican circle altogether. No more than Goulding were they loathe to take money or arms from any donor. All they wanted was that the takings were used for the North.

On September 22 the military dissidents effectively took control of the Belfast IRA. McMillen had called a unit meeting—the whole Belfast Brigade might run to two dozen volunteers with no more than a few available at any time. As usual with republican meetings, everyone was late—in fact, only three volunteers appeared at all. Then the door flew open and into the room burst sixteen armed men including Steele, McKee, the Kellys, and Twomey. Since there were sixteen of them, all apparently armed and angry, and only his three regulars, McMillen accepted a compromise: There would be no communications with Dublin GHQ for three months, and the local money, about £3,500 collected since August, would be used not for "relief" but for guns and would be spent quickly. If Dublin did not shape up, then an independent Northern Command would be set up in the six counties, long a Northern IRA aspiration. They would send no delegates to Goulding's extraordinary Army Convention in December, where the abstentionism question contained in Garland's report would be discussed. Usually a chief of staff could have discussions at an Army Convention produce the desired majority, and Belfast suspected that this was what Dublin intended. More than just a Belfast or Northern reform was necessary—the entire IRA needed a new agenda.

The key figure at this meeting was not a Belfast man but Daíthí O Conaill, who as a Southerner with traditional views gave the Belfast takeover broader implications. In 1969 he was still a hero of the campaign years. At eighteen he had been at Brookeborough with Garland and Seán South. He had spent time in the Curragh, escaped with Ruairí O Brádaigh, and later been badly wounded in an

RUC ambush in Tyrone. Captured then, he had ended the campaign in Crumlin Road Prison. His presence made it clear that those in opposition to McMillen had greater ambitions. But McMillen had no intention of honoring a deal made at gunpoint.

Other deals were being made (or more accurately were thought to be in the making) as Northerners of all ilks spread out over the island seeking aid, comfort, and arms from any source. In Dublin an informal committee was established by Harry White, Joe Collins, Jack McCabe, and others from the North. McCabe went to America in February to look for arms and money. In the Republic the Northern defenders, most allied with the potential IRA dissenters, got a ready hearing from nationalists, money and promises of money from many, and had intimate talks with Irish army officers, sitting politicians, provincial potentates, and cabinet ministers. Everyone was concerned about the vulnerability of the Northern nationalists. A general assumption was that the IRA people would know the ground. They certainly made no secret of their needs. Others might want funds for the destitute, for relief after the pogroms, for needy victims; the hard men wanted guns. As John Kelly would indicate later, there was no mystery: "We did not ask for blankets or feeding bottles. We asked for guns and no one from Taoiseach Lynch down refused that request or told us that this was contrary to Government policy. . . .*

Anything seemed possible. Everyone was involved. The logjam of Irish politics seemed to have broken. Stormont was shaken, perhaps fatally. The army was in the streets. The North wanted justice, expected justice, and the republicans sensed an end to the old imposed settlement. But when they flocked to Dublin GHQ, not only did they find little gear but also little sense of the change. GHQ seemed blind to the turmoil and opportunities, and refused to become properly involved. Goulding would take from Fianna Fáil a car and the odd quid, but would not take the meaning of the deal: The government was running scared. Mick Ryan would run himself ragged as quartermaster general rounding up arms in the twenty-six counties and shipping them north in furniture vans but he hadn't the time to arrange a really big shipment.

Everything was changing. Half the people in Ireland seemed to be searching for guns for the other half to tote north. There was real money to be had, money in the thousands, not the grudging fiver of a year before. There was soon a real government promise to train defenders—Dublin would secretly train those the IRA sent to learn. There was a riptide running everywhere but only the old eddy over the drain at Gardiner Place. Discussions in the Army Council still showed no grasp of the implications of the August events. Johnston did not understand practical reality. He believed in bits of paper, ideas, resolutions, concepts. Written agendas for him were more real than the fires along Bombay Street. He knew that "we don't have a revolutionary situation." Bombay Street didn't fit the model. Even Goulding knew matters were more serious than that. Yet those converted to the new direction saw the trouble in the North not as an opportunity

*Taken from Kelly's speech at the arms trial in October 1969 and widely quoted to indicate the involvement of the Fianna Fáil government, although the defendants were found innocent.

but as an unwanted responsibility. Defense of the nationalists would lead no place useful.

The real republicans with the IRA as vanguard would move forward into politics, into a reality unwarped by the irrelevant tradition so dear to the old veterans and the purists like Mac Stiofáin, like the Belfast gunmen, like O Conaill. Instead of a return to Tan War priorities, the Army Convention could vote to form a National Liberation Front, a trendy title in 1969, that would include the other radical and revolutionary groups, including the Irish Workers Group, a handful of Moscow-orthodox ideologues meeting in a garage in Pembroke Lane in Dublin 4 dominated by Mick O'Riordan, a popular if ineffectual Communist veteran of the Spanish Civil War. This would involve the new radicals who had been on the margins of 1969 the International Year of the Guerrilla, the anti-Vietnam War rallies, and the protests of popular causes. None of these new people to be brought into the fold had either military assets or a concern with the national issue beyond what Marx or Lenin had written on the matter. All were alien in thought, dress, and assumption to much of Ireland and to most of the republican movement. Each would be marked by a subversive label that would draw police interest, priestly scorn, and popular distaste. Why associate with proven losers with alien ideas unless those ideas were to become dominant? Why call the IRA something else unless it was to be something else? And if this were not troublesome enough, why discard abstentionism, a principled stand for many that when voided had led to republican apostasy: de Valera had gone into Leinster House and the Dáil, and later even executed his old comrades; O'Donnell and Gilmore had gone into the Republican Congress and disappeared; MacBride had become a minister and declared a Republic no one could find. What was the point of denying principle to play at politics? And why play with irrelevant leftists without prospects? Yet no one doubted that the new policy might have a majority, the GHQ would see to that, and so the Army Council sent along the proposals by a vote of twelve to eight.

The IRA center had traditionally determined the outcome of an Army Convention by educating the units and adjusting representation, overlooking potential dissenting delegates, and then controlling the agenda. Conventions were not so much fixed as determined by those already in control. Some who disagreed were no longer active and most volunteers were inclined to go with those in power. When the IRA met in the extraordinary convention on a grim, cold, rainy night in December in an isolated venue, Knockvical House hidden in the country, the split was obvious, beyond patching. With a show of hands the resolutions passed, passed by too many delegates from Tyrone and none from Belfast, by delegates escorted to their seats by friends of the staff, by delegates who had neglected to collect Mac Stiofáin's dissidents still waiting in the country for their ride, by thirty-nine votes to twelve. GHQ had won a future free of the old strictures and limitations better interred with romantic Ireland, a future free of the old soldiers and endless commemorations. Mac Stiofáin rose and said, "You are now no longer in the IRA . . . we no longer regard you as such and we will take no further part in these deliberations." He turned and left the room, followed by the determined dissidents on the way to order the faithful into a real IRA. He stepped out of the door into a waiting car and was driven through the night directly to Belfast, where he met with some twenty hard men of like mind. They agreed to call a provisional Army Convention of real republicans to sort out the movement and set the IRA on a proper course. This hurriedly organized Provisional Army Convention met before Christmas, again in an isolated house in the midlands, and confirmed what was decided in Belfast. There was now a Provisional IRA—the Provos—intent on waging an armed struggle, not on moving into a political future as a party allied to irrelevant radicals.

As the IRA constitution requires, the Army Convention elects first a twelve-man Army Executive, a conclave usually of elders and those who had been or soon would be members of the Army Council. The IRA Executive then chooses the seven-man Army Council, which controls the entire republican movement. The Army Council, embodying the very power to govern Ireland (as granted by the survivors of the second Dáil on December 8, 1938) chose secretly the chief of staff. He in turn chose his own staff: adjutant general, sometimes an operations officer as well, a quartermaster for arms, an intelligence officer, a finance officer, a publicity officer, and any needed aides. These were all attached to the GHQ and mostly located in Dublin. The Army Council seldom met even in peaceful times and the Army Executive had at best an oversight commission meeting a few times a year at most. The Army Council was the key and in the past it had been dominated by from one to three individuals, always including the chief of staff. This would continue to be the case over the next generation. The first Provisional Council that met in December 1969 was chosen so as to represent the whole Irish republican world, not just those active in its formation. It was rightly assumed that many long-inactive republicans would come into the fold and many new people, eager for a role in nationalist defense, were waiting to be scooped up out of the hands of the National Liberation Front. In the meantime the first Army Council was selected at the first Army Convention to appeal to the whole movement.

Seán Mac Stiofáin was the obvious first choice, not only as a member but as chief of staff. He had the singleness of purpose, the energy, and the proper views, had been involved from the first in resisting the new departure, had stayed to the last, and was the only member of the GHQ staff to break with Gardiner Place. He lived at Navan, halfway between Dublin and the North. As intelligence officer he knew the republican world well. And despite or because of his English background and accent he was more rigorous in his republicanism than most: a born-again rebel, self-educated in his faith and the necessary military tools. Ruairí O Brádaigh was a former chief of staff, a longtime member of the Army Council, and an experienced Sinn Féin functionary. Originally from Longford but long based across the Shannon in Roscommon, he knew the world away from Dublin well. He was short and looked much the schoolteacher that he was. Reflective, a forceful speaker, he would hardly have passed as an advocate of armed struggle who had soldiered through both the campaign and prison on his way to his teaching career. He would become president of Provisional Sinn Féin and a constant on the Army Council. O Conaill, O Brádaigh's campaign colleague, was the very picture of an IRA soldier-gunman: tall, sallow, with a lean and hungry look and a cigarette in his hand. He was eager to debate strategy and tactics, and was good with the media. He was often on the Army Council and always a vice president of Sinn Féin. Belfast was represented on the first Army Council by Leo Martin and Joe Cahill. Martin, whom the UVF Malvern Street killers had missed, was theoretically the new officer commanding the Northern IRA but practically for years the best-known West Belfast republican. Joe Cahill, who had his death sentence in 1943 commuted, had emerged from Crumlin still faithful if not very active. Other Belfast people were either on Mac Stiofáin's staff or involved in creating a new brigade largely from scratch. The last two places on the Army Council went to two sound Southern republicans: Seán Treacy, from Leix, who had been the republican organizer (another of the "official" republicans attracted), and Patrick Mulcahy, from the Dublin Road, Limerick, who would be secretary. The Army Council was very much provisional in that room would have to be made for others later, but for the moment the call was for a 1970 Army Convention to authorize the Army Council. Then the IRA could pursue agreed policies: a military strategy, an effort to arm, oversight of a political program, and recruitment to a real IRA. What the involved wanted was to exploit the turmoil so as to launch an armed campaign.

The republican leadership, on and off the Army Council, were men of no property, seldom men with access to those of property. A few like O Brádaigh had an education, a few like O Conaill had scrambled up into the middle class, but mostly they were everyday people with at best a skilled trade: carpenters, bookmakers, foremen, bartenders, plumbers, haulers. Many were irregularly employed; none was very comfortable. In personality they were very different. Some were taciturn, others glib and articulate; most on matters that counted were solemn. They were not always friends but were always bound by their loyalty to the Republic and their sacrifices for the faith. Many had come from republican families or through neighborhood example; more after 1969 would bear psychic scars from the police and army rather than recommendations from another generation. Whatever the original motive—pride, a desire for a gun, hatred, romance, love of adventure, or lure of power—those who stayed the course seldom strayed. When the Provisional IRA grew grand over the next years, took in all and sundry for a time, the band of brothers became a great militia for a while, with their faith defused among many along for the ride. Mac Stiofáin, born John Stephenson in Leytonstone, Northeast London, felt at home with the lifelong felons from the Falls, Cahill and Twomey, or Harry White in Dublin, or the farm boys from Kerry, or the Roscommon schoolteacher O Brádaigh with a Swiss Protestant family connection. He shared with them the transcendental faith in the Republic, Tone's Republic. Politics had become the central flame of their lives, the guiding principle that was beyond compromise, beyond the adjustment to the times or the practices that Dublin felt essential. To adjust would be to betray. And when the faithful strayed, as seemed to be the case with the Dublin center, the shock was severe even though republican history was littered with apostasy and heresy from Dev down to the most recent informer. On principles they agreed. Then and later the Army Council would disagree on little that mattered.

At the first formal Provisional Army Council meeting in January 1970, the driving sense of purpose went beyond recruitment, competition with the other, "official" IRA, or even the defense of the North. Everyone involved in the entire enterprise wanted to adjust to events in such a way as to guarantee a real military campaign. This time—unlike the last time—the people would be mobilized; they were in fact largely mobilized already by the campaign of civil disobedience and by the Protestant backlash. On this foundation, on the Republican faith, on a reading of the tides of the history, the IRA would focus first on a period of defense, moving on through provocation and cunning to a posture of retaliation that would assure a final offensive stage as the British army reacted as was the wont of the orthodox and the arrogant. Armies were apt when stoned to act like armies, not take names but take aim. The military had manuals of anti-insurgency but little training in peacekeeping and little enthusiasm for peace. The experience of the Irish was that the British would act in Ireland as they always had, as they had within the empire—but this time to IRA advantage.

So there the seven sat, men moving well beyond youth, rumpled, inelegant, unsophisticated, poorly read, without funds or trained minds, unknown but to the police; they sat in a cold room over hot tea, determining the stages to free Ireland, preparing to make war on an empire. Criminal optimism is a requirement for the rebel, commitment beyond reason, persistence without proper foundation; so they were well prepared. That night the seven men knew their minds and, unlike Johnston and now Goulding, their own people. They had from books and experience read Irish history backward, seeking in the past rationalization for present intentions and assumptions. And it was to be a patriotic Irish rebellion against the traditional British enemy. They knew what was wrong in Ireland: not an undemocratic Stormont to be replaced in another stage, not a bad 1921 Treaty, not fundamental Protestant arrogance and militancy, not partition itself or all the grievances that flowed from it, but rather simply the British connection. This was, according to Tone, to the seven, to all republicans, "the never-failing source of all our political evils." The seven too knew what they wanted, as had Tone: "to unite the whole people of Ireland, to abolish the memory of all past dissensions, to substitute the common name of Irishman in the place of the denominations of Protestant, Catholic, and Dissenter." And thus they knew the necessary means for such an undertaking—a military campaign.

The path to changing history would begin with defense, move to retaliation, and then blossom into war, a war that the British could not win nor the Irish lose, a war fought over the perception of reality, a war fought by an IRA fueled by Irish will, by a risen nation, a war that no matter how protracted could have but one end. They had waited all their lives for such an opportunity. And on the dark, cold night with the rain beaded on the window, without resources that could be weighed and measured, without a gun or a poster, with only their own, they were sure that they had caught a tide in the affairs of men. They set their secret Ireland on a course to win fortune.

They had hardly been alone in sensing new tides in Irish history. In fact, only the official IRA in Dublin had deployed wishful thinking about the nature of Ireland rather than test the real waters of 1969, suddenly hot to the touch. The great crowds of nationalists in the North from 1968 on had felt mobilized, had felt the earth tremble, had believed anything possible: the end of Stormont, the unity of the island, the institutionalization of justice, the revolution. They believed for the moment that all roads ran downhill. Standing before tens of thousands shouting, "We shall overcome," how could one not be overcome by optimism and enthusiasm? Wasn't this the mobilization of the masses? And in this they shared a conviction with the loyalists, who feared that the British would desert them, feared their proper leaders would sell them out, feared that the first inch had been given, that crying, "No surrender" into the wind might not save the day. And so, as always, they had struck at the vulnerable—the Romans, Fenians, Taigs—rather than at the power in London. As in the past, the rough and angry loyalists expressed the core of their tradition, the right of domination, by recourse to arson, intimidation, and murder. While their Catholic neighbors on the other side of the street were excited by change, fearful of retaliation, stirred by movement, the loyalists, their curbs painted red, white, and blue, were maddened by anxiety at change unanswered, excited to retaliation.

And then the proper in London, Belfast, and Dublin responded to the rising August violence with concern at the sacrifices that the turmoil might require. Some might hope that good would result, but all suspected the cost would be high. London might imagine reforms in Northern Ireland arising from a long involvement. The proper Unionists might, albeit reluctantly, accept the necessary reforms so imposed as a price of continued power in a system that would then be immune to further criticism. In Dublin the practical could hope for little but they were not so unwise as to admit this publicly. They knew that the voice of Ireland, the voice of the Republic, came from a toothless mouth. London could act, Stormont could be driven to act, but Dublin could do nothing. And the people for the first time in decades felt that action was needed on the national issue.

The fact was that the Dublin establishment could urge reforms on the North but not impose them, that violence in the North could be deplored but not prevented, that intervention in any meaningful way was beyond the capacity of the state and probably beyond the desire of the people. The most apparent need to many seemed the defense of Northern countrymen, nationalists, Catholics. The most disturbing factor for others in the South was that the troubles would spill over into the Republic, divisive, lethal, and open-ended: They feared doing anything for risk of worse. Some in the South, however, felt that something must be done, somehow could be done, for the nationalists, for Ireland. And so a few acted during a brief, bright period of midsummer madness when the tides of change were seen to race, when Belfast burned and the Bogside became battleground.

Unlike the IRA with their texts, most Southern nationalists had no ready analysis of what was wrong in Ireland. Nearly everyone assumed that a united Ireland was good and inevitable, but still not quite an immediate prospect. Some were content with Stormont reforms for now. These now included even the Official IRA hurriedly distancing Gardiner Place from the Provisionals. Some dreamed of an entirely new treaty settlement undoing the errors of 1921. Few had any idea of how this could be accomplished although all recognized it would be at the expense of the Unionists. Many wanted not only defense but change; few wanted violence; and none wanted a war by the Provisionals. How could individuals, parties, clans, and groups best effect events to advantage if a military "solution" beyond arms for self-defense was a chimera? Even one as astute as Jack

Lynch, who had to weigh the Republic's needs, not those of the whole island, did not want yesterday to be reconstructed as tomorrow once order was restored, even if he had no plan for an alternative tomorrow.

No one had a blueprint. In London the establishment apparently felt the Irish jinni could be put back in the bottle if the shape of the container was molded for contemporary practice. The conventional in the North, most Unionists and a few Catholics, wanted few changes. The Unionists hoped that little would change. There should be no interference from the Republic and only enough reform to calm the minority and so London. The Protestant way of life, the loyalist establishment, the essential shape of Stormont would emerge once the waters had calmed, solid rocks beyond the erosion of history. Some loyalists would not be so content. They wanted not only to run history backward but also to punish those Catholics who had aroused new anxieties since 1968. With each passing crisis week, however, the prospect of proper punishment and a return to the golden era before the marches became subsumed in the struggle to defend what was left.

On the other side of the divide, the nationalists too were uncertain of direction. Most thought that they wanted to be one with the Republic but this seemed far down a practical menu. Many wanted the end of Stormont and almost all reforms that would bring the province into British practice. There were those who wanted to enter some sort of socialist regime as painted by European theorists and the radical activists, a few thirsted for revolution, while the many wanted to gain at least systemic power and symbolic vengeance. All the nationalists wanted and felt it only right to have more: more control, more rights, more things, and more say, more. Those who knew their own mind, knew what they wanted, how to get it, and who as enemy would oppose them, had great power. Thus, the handful of students had shaken the system and the hidden gunmen of the IRA could do so again.

The Republic was clouded with illusions, the nationalists in the province diverted by orators and action of the streets. The IRA was in turmoil, the radicals in constant confrontation with all and with each other. The Stormont establishment and their British overlords knew what they wanted, if not why this would be impossible: a decent, reformed society integrated and legitimate that hushed loyalist fears and indefinitely postponed the nostalgic desire for unification. Such a society should, must, be self-monitoring, not imposed. To arrive at such an end in a reformed polity would require time, patience, the assurance of order, the rule of law, and thus stability and contentment. This sensible goal and consequently any and all strategies to that end were also illusion. The unstated assumption was that the province of Northern Ireland was if not English then British, where all deadly quarrels had long ago been solved—and by the English, not the Irish. It was rather like a view of man that excluded original sin, a heresy and one that could only lead to misunderstanding, disappointment, and anger. The British and especially the English always found it difficult to accept those with other agendas, other priorities; they insisted that the world be like them, play the game. The Irish game was different.

The core of loyalist desire, certainly that of fundamentalist loyalists, was the visible exercised domination of the minority and that of the nationalists was an unyielding desire for justice shaped as revenge for that domination. Both might have secondary aspirations, often held as absolute by the conservative and conventional whose class or education had shifted priorities; and these aspirations might be addressed by a strategy of decency. Those less delicate, the Christian fundamentalists, the country Orange men, the Belfast republicans, the student radicals, the militant and unrepentant, could not so easily be incorporated in a reformed society. As for Dublin, the nationalists stretched from those content with a reformed Stormont at no cost to those who could see a united Ireland just as Easter 1916 had projected on the morrow. Opinions and attitudes in the Republic had been shaped in isolation from Northern reality, neglected the entire Unionist community as artificial and irrelevant, and arose from bad history and self-deception. In time Dublin would find various formulas—unity without violence was a continuing structure—that would allow influence without cost, interference without responsibility, while the complexities and nature of Northern Ireland filtered into the consciousness of Southern nationalists.

As long as the Northern population sat before a zero-sum game, every nationalist gain turned into a Unionist loss, then the IRA determined on a war had enormous power because that lethal game in republican theory at the end would absorb both players into one: The Irish loyalists would become Irish and the Irish rebels no longer rebellious. The IRA could claim a desirable endgame. Protracted war would impose a new reality on the separatist Irish Protestant tradition by eroding the charms of domination as policy, by revealing the alien nature of the other island across the Irish Sea, by offering in a united Ireland the only safe haven for all. The IRA war would be focused on the enemy of all, the British Empire, not on the Protestants, Irish all, unless they enlisted in the Crown's forces. This empire had corrupted the Protestants' national and class loyalties with the bribe of provincial domination. This domination was maintained only be imperial power. When Britain lost the will to war and withdrew, then the formerly loyal would find their historical destiny in a united and new Ireland. It did not matter, of course, that this reading of history required a peculiar blindness to the nature and history of the Irish Protestants, and a text patched from grievances, hidden agendas, skewed experience, and a corrupted past. The republicans believed the analysis was valid and Irish history they had learned was real. It certainly did not matter to the Provisional Army Council in the first meeting in January 1970; they knew what they knew. They would do what they intended, easily and without argument, do it *naturally*, without need for proclamation or position paper. They would defend, retaliate, provoke, and pursue the subsequent armed struggle until British will broke and Ireland was a nation once again. The Official IRA, on the other hand, had entered a world filled with position papers, resolutions, seminars, and study groups as the leadership sought to ease the movement out of the republican rut so congenial to the Provisionals into a posture fit for a Marxist-Leninist party of the vanguard. It was not natural but was increasingly the goal of Gardiner Place.

The illusions of the Provisional IRA permitted audacity. Those of London and Stormont and later the militant loyalists assured frustrations. The illusions of the nationalists in the Republic led to foolishness and futility or moderation and resignation. In August 1969 Dublin still saw Northern Ireland through ideological glasses that had been prescribed in 1921: It was assumed that all that need be done was to remove the border and Ireland would be a nation once again. There had been no "Protestant Problem" in the Irish Free State, in Éire-Ireland, in the Republic. There was no need to foresee one in a thirty-two-county Ireland. So no one did—see one—in the Republic or in the projected united Ireland. The province was thus ignored—six more counties—and so too the perceptions and intentions of London. The British establishment was little known and little understood, successors to the oppressors. History was written for patriots and ended in 1921. The future complexities suggested by nearly a million Protestants, many long steeped in bigotry, often violent, rarely aware they were Irish until they arrived in Britain, suddenly entering an all-Ireland polity, were hardly considered. Unity was not immediate and so illusions could run.

There was a new generation in power in Dublin. Jack Lynch, everyone's other choice, was Taoiseach. He had six Gaelic Athletic Association All-Ireland medals that had made him famous, a safe seat from Cork, a calm and quiet manner. He had opted first for the civil service, a sure job, a safe job, an Irish job, the gift of the new state and the dream of the bad years. Then as a barrister he revealed conventional aspirations and found a comfortable role in his safe Dáil seat. He had been a cunning man on the hurling field and so flourished within Fianna Fáil. He seemingly had none of the eager ambition of his more urbane colleagues who grasped the new, who were pleased to be thought technocrats, who had an eye for the main chance and fretted at the pace of advancement. He was calm and cautious.

Lemass and the elders thought that Lynch, even over Lemass's son-in-law Charles Haughey, would satisfy, would move by consensus, would not risk the party and the nation while the others matured. Old rebels move with great caution, having learned the vulnerabilities of entrenched power in their youth. And so Lynch would have, if the prosperity of the sixties had not encouraged the next generation in Fianna Fáil, that of Haughey, all different, all articulate, well educated, superficially sophisticated, and undoubtedly competent. Haughey, George Colley, Brian Lenihan, Kevin Boland, Neil Blaney—the new men— found quiet Jack Lynch not only an obstacle to ambition but also vulnerable, if for no other reason than that he had not been in the GPO or sat on Dev's right hand. Two in his first cabinet would be shuttled off to the presidency in the park: Erskine Chiders, son of a Protestant IRA martyr, and Dr. Patrick Hillery. Kevin Boland, nephew of Harry Boland, another dead IRA hero, would be driven from the fold and many of the rest would compete over the years for Lynch's job, Dev's place, their generation's by time and talent. Thus, Lynch's arrival in 1966 cut short only briefly the leadership stakes as within both major parties a new generation came to power amid the reopened national issue that had for so long existed in the form inherited from 1921. With the arrival of the Northern marches in 1968, Irish politics for the first time in years revealed options not based on formulas. The party, the Republican Party, Fianna Fáil, the party comfortable with power, de Valera's creation—and Dev was still alive and shrewd—had been left by Lemass to the custody of Lynch as leader.

Leading on the Northern Ireland issue had proved to be a problem; where was the parade to go? Those most eager to act were members of the party with strong republican feelings. Neil Blaney from Donegal in the north knew, as many in

Dublin chose not to know, the indignities imposed on the nationalist population and the dangers that arose from the marches. The presence of the British army did not mean an end to the provocations or the protests or the danger. Haughey seemed at the other end of the Fianna Fáil spectrum, a UCD accountant who had married Lemass's daughter, made money and rich friends, fashioned a bloc within the party and touched people without, a smooth one on the way up with none of Blaney's countryman virtues. He was the epitome of the new man in the mohair suit, the Irish tribe of the Mercedes. Yet he, too, had Northern ties, was not divorced either from Northern realities and needs and never from ambition. Some of those most concerned about the nationalists were less easy to place, neither risen stars nor traditional nationalists. The Minister for Local Government, Kevin Boland, was the son of Gerry Boland, an old IRA man who as de Valera's Minister of Justice had been responsible for crushing the IRA, stashing the volunteers in the Curragh Camp. He oversaw the hanging of Charlie Kerins, the IRA chief of staff, and waited out the death of Seán McCaughey, the IRA adjutant general, kept in the most squalid conditions, who died on a hunger and thirst strike in Porlaoise Prison in 1946. Kevin Boland was not his father's son but an increasingly intense republican moving even beyond Fianna Fáil's caution in urging action that he found obviously necessary because the party *was* republican. Many individuals in various parties or identified with none did what they could immediately. They contributed to the defense committees, met with the defenders, fretted in public and in private. Some were willing to see an IRA revived but most were focused on any means to protect Northern nationalists. And many did not think the British army would do a thorough job. The army and the loyalists wore the same colors, the police were uniformed bigots, and Stormont ran the judges and prisons and had friends in London. Something else must be done and all understood the strength of the militant republican stain in Ireland, in Irish politics.

Jack Lynch, quiet and moderate and decent, was no fool. He led Fianna Fáil because he was a party man. He had to speak to his constituency, his party and his people, as well as to the facts. The main fact was that Ireland had no chips to play in a power game with Britain. The Irish army was ill-trained, ill-armed, antiquated in uniform and equipment and mission, more a symbol of sovereignty than an armed force. Only the equestrian team in Sam Browne belts, jodhpurs, and polished boots was world class. The RUC and B Specials could probably keep out an Irish military intrusion; the British thought a few armored cars would suffice. The Irish financial and economic structure was enormously vulnerable to any British maneuver. And furthermore, the shrewd seriously doubted whether there was any commitment by the public to sacrifice for Northern nationalists beyond charitable gifts and pub ballads. They would surely not back an adventure in 1969, whatever the patriot orators said—they had no compelling sense of grievance. Northern Ireland, the Black North, was a distant land, alien and foreign, that roused great emotions but briefly. Nearly everyone wanted something done. Some would not stand idly waiting to be asked but most looked to Lynch. Not the IRA Provos, of course; they were responsible only to themselves and ultimately the Irish people. And Lynch and others were aware of the lasting power of patriot oratory, the ballad as aspiration, the long years of Irish national history as revealed truth that prevented the government from doing nothing, saying nothing, even offering the truth.

On August 13, in Dublin, Lynch's government responded officially to the crisis. There was to be an information effort run separately under the journalist Séamus Brady. There was to be a Northern committee from the Cabinet including three border men, Neil Blaney, Joseph Brennan, Minister for Labor, and Padraig Faulkner, Minister for Education, along with Haughey. That Wednesday night in his television address to the nation Lynch indicated that Ireland would *not* stand by, that an appeal would go to the United Nations, that the British troops were unacceptable, that reunification was the only possible permanent solution. This was the official high point. Soon £100,000 was earmarked for relief (and propaganda) in the North, but even then plausible denial was assured by covering the funds with false names in two accounts. The contacts with the Northern defenders, including those known to Captain James Kelly of Irish Army Intelligence, undertaken with the knowledge of his superiors and, it was understood, the Minister of Defense, James Gibbons, went ahead. Provisions were made to train some of the Northern defenders in Irish army camps over the border—a process interrupted in the case of the Derry men in Fort Dunree, Donegal, on October 3, when the prospect of newspaper revelation arose and put an end to the arrangement.

All this time the defenders were, as John Kelly had noted, seeking arms without anyone saying nay. October 4–5 there was a meeting between Captain James Kelly and representatives of the Northern Ireland Defense Committees. The meeting was secret, but from the contacts evolved the plan to move purchased arms secretly through Dublin to the North. Some defense committees were soon getting Southern money to pay auxiliaries and protect the threatened. And most committees were soon dominated by old or new IRA men exploiting their assumed military experience. Some Irish army arms had already been moved to border towns; the sale of others was stopped for fear that these guns might actually end in the hands of Northern loyalists. Subsequently, the problem was who knew what and when—questions never properly answered. In and out of the government, those then acting to aid the North assumed then and later that they did so legally and with the authorization of the appropriate authorities. Lynch would contend he knew little until very late—as would the Special Branch police, their administrative head, Peter Berry, Secretary of the Department of Justice, and Minister for Defense James Gibbons. Only later in a courtroom under oath, in what became known as the Arms Trial did Gibbons indicate knowledge of the early maneuvers and some "vestigial" knowledge of an actual shipment planned to arrive in Dublin in the spring. And by the spring Irish matters had changed, certainly in perception.

As early as September 20, in a speech at Tralee, Lynch had indicated that, of course, unification must come peacefully. Subsequently he refined his rhetoric to satisfy many of his patriots without shifting from a position that in effect gave Northern unionists a veto. And, more important, he could not be outflanked on his nationalist side by the IRA using illicit violence or by his own supporting inappropriate violence. For all practical purposes there could not be voluntary unification without a transformation in the loyalties of the Unionists. For a century radicals had waited for the loyalists to be converted to class interests, and now Lynch placed unity on their national convictions, heretofore the very essence of their commitment to division. And despite the "unacceptable" presence of the British army, no one except the IRA wanted the British army to be withdrawn. So as long as the army *was* there matters looked different. What need was there for arms in the hands of Catholic defenders? What need was there for defenders who took Dublin money and Dublin legitimacy and used it to organize the new IRA? What were these people—Fianna Fáil ministers, army officers, and men from the North—doing but subverting authority and legitimacy? What was their authority?

Gibbons made it clear in private and at his trial that despite evidence given to the contrary he would not accept responsibility for trying secretly to arm the defenders; and, of course, neither would his Taoiseach, Jack Lynch. Instead, on May 1, Captain James Kelly was arrested. On May 4, Michael O Moráin, Minister of Justice, resigned from the cabinet on grounds of ill health. Haughey and Blaney were dismissed from the cabinet two days later and Kevin Boland, Minister for Local Government, and his parliamentary secretary, Paudge Brennan, resigned in opposition to Lynch's position. That evening the Taoiseach told of receiving information concerning an effort to import arms illegally. Whatever those involved had thought they were doing, whatever the effect of the excitements of August, Lynch had pulled the plug. There would be no secret arms shipment, no tracks leading to the government's door, and no pardon for those involved.

The revelations on May 6 led in time to two arms trails involving Captain James Kelly, John Kelly of the Belfast defenders, Albert Luykx, an Irish national involved in the European purchase, and Charlie Haughey.* Charges against Blaney were too weak to stand. The two trials gravely damaged Gibbons's credibility. Swiftly declared innocent by the jury on October 23, the accused felt vindicated that the arms shipment from the first had been authorized and that the appropriate individuals knew of the plan. No matter, Lynch had solidified his position, confounded the potential rebels from his Republican Party, and seemingly removed Haughey as a potential rival. The midsummer madness was dead, the stake of party loyalty and personal interest driven through its heart. Haughey might, as he did, rise from the political dead, but militant Republicanism within Fianna Fáil and hence within conventional Irish politics was no more. Haughey remained in the fold but could no longer pursue vindication. The arms scandal would never have a satisfactory coda, rather, it went in the grave with the shadow of the gunmen.

The attraction of Tone's Republic, the Fenian legacy, the physical force tradition, had in any case really eroded away long before 1969. The Republican party, Fianna Fáil, might still send a small delegation to Bodenstown on the Sunday to lay a wreath—well out of sight of the real IRA republicans massing in the field near Sallins—but it was a dead ritual, a dash in and a few words for the next day's newspapers and off to the real world. Only the turmoil in the North had

---

*In February 1992 when Charles Haughey finally resigned as Taoiseach and therein from active Fianna Fáil politics, the Dublin *Sunday Tribune* indicated that he had been less than candid about his part in the arms importation operation.

sparked the momentary revival in the Republic and led to tinkering with the system imposed in 1921. Lynch had turned his head to miss the dogs of war as they ran loose when war might be needed; when peace was assured he found, surprisingly, that he must curb those who had dashed out of the house of the law. What could he do but act within the law, punish those who had not, restore stability? Lynch's masterful control of both the machinery of the system and the emotions of his own meant that Dublin could largely divorce the country from the Northern Ireland crisis except for any future spasm of indignation and concern. The new orthodoxy would insist on nonviolent union, which meant no union at all unless the unionists and British endorsed it—as they should, of course; as they would not, of course. And since they would not the real republicans in the Provisional IRA would resort to violence to see that they did so. As the Provos had known all along Fianna Fáil and the rest of Dublin would be no hope in troubled times, rather the reverse—no reactionary so vicious as a new generation in power under false pretenses, comfortable in three-piece suits, state limousines, and the exchange of favors. So the Provos went ahead with their money and their future bet on war while their official IRA rivals opted for the class struggle and seats in the Dáil. The Provos thought them fools for they could feel the tide of events moving Ireland forward for the first time in generations. And they, not the other republicans in or out of government, had caught that tide, could afford to take the trip into the future.

5

The Rise of the Provos:
January 1970–February 1971

Northern Ireland is at war with the Irish Republican Army Provisionals.

Prime Minister James Chichester-Clark, February 7, 1971

Those in the Provisional IRA who had kept the faith in 1969, kept their IRA away from Gardiner Place's class politics and out of the hands of classy Fianna Fáil politicians, had always suspected both alien ideas and the conventional people safe in the system. Pure, iridescent nationalism compatible with the church (no matter what the hierarchy said), the old ways, and the countryside supplied almost a secular vocation that did not need the divisions of class that had proved so attractive elsewhere. Ireland had largely avoided the Industrial Revolution, which hit only a patch in the northeast. It had avoided even commerce and office employment, except in Dublin, a city of neither industry nor commerce but of clerks. The appeal of Marx and Bakunin and Lenin, the wonders offered by Jim Larkin or James Connolly, did not naturally attract. The militant republicans had no love of property but no feel for class politics either. And as for the orthodox within the system, Irish-speaking or Ascendancy bred, they were hindrance and danger. The men of property, the large farmer with a checkbook open for the defenders, the Fianna Fáil councillor who knew the words to "Kevin Barry" or even "Seán South of Garryowen" but had forgotten those interned or imprisoned by his party and his friends in Dublin could not buy the Provos. How can you buy a dream? The other IRA might think the Provos invented, summoned up by Fianna Fáil to play a defender's role and ruin the new Gardiner Place radical departure, but this was wishful thinking—and by those who had taken the money first. No, from the first the Republic had been betrayed by the politicians, first those who took the Treaty, partition, the oath, the lot, rather than retain the faith; and then by Dev himself, discarding Sinn Féin and going into Leinster House under the oath. Each desertion left or right, Peadar O'Donnell and the Republican Congress or Seán MacBride and his Clann na Poblachta, had weakened but never destroyed the movement. So when John Kelly and the others were making their rounds all but in public, in private the Provos took what was offered and went their own way.

The Provos were created out of opportunity for the committed, not out of the tinkering of Fianna Fáil as some of the Officials chose to believe and even as a few of the tinkerers claimed. They had not so much the needed skills to be defenders as an inherited legitimacy, the proper banner, and a willingness unhampered by any practical considerations. At first the Provos actually augmented a British army that, however welcome in August 1969, was soon a mixed blessing even to those Catholics without politics. Historically for all nationalists the British army had been the oppressor, friend of the Orangemen. The troops on the street obviously would be no friend to any republican, subversives all, just as they would see the Unionists under the Union Jack as their ally. The Provos were thus assumed needed by many with no concern for unity, partition, or even civil rights, and would so be considered for many years. And so the Provos were needed, wanted, and flooded with volunteers eager to "defend" and anxious for a slot in the secret army of their illusions. The Provos and their agents could not at first in Ireland and then in England and soon in America find sufficient gear to make an underground army a reality, even to make recruit classes realistic. There were only so many salvaged Lee-Enfields or even shotguns to hand. Other than the B Specials, Ireland was not an armed camp; farmers and hunters had a few civilian guns and almost no one else possessed more than the relic or souvenir. Many volunteers could be shunted into Provisional Sinn Féin, soon to be set up with O Brádaigh, who had left his teaching position in Roscommon, as president. Others had to be put on standby or assigned makeshift "military" duties or made to wait through long recruit classes that from the first Army Convention were a clone of the old IRA before Goulding had enlarged the Army Council.

The traditionalists organized the movement as easily and naturally as some creatures produce new shells. The old IRA, the Official IRA, was for them a discarded husk. An Army Council was more than a name and numbers. Goulding and Garland and the others might have both but they lacked allegiance to the Republic. At first the new Provisional IRA was mainly shadow and aspiration. Those at the center knew all and the quarrels of the republicans faded as one moved out into the countryside, where few knew or cared. The ideological battleground at first was Belfast and Dublin. And in Dublin, with Belfast support, the Provisionals set up the new in the same form as the old. Sinn Féin was identical, filled first with the discarded, the rebels, and gradually with many of the old and many of the new, some directed to empty old branches, cumann, or to new branches with new names. Fresh martyrs were memorialized. There were soon Provisional commemorations for those martyrs—Sundays at Bodenstown and elsewhere would have to be staggered or shared because of the excess of true republicans. There was a new Cumann Cabrach dedicated to the welfare of republicans, in particular prisoners and the families of those on the run, both categories likely to need attention if the plans of the Army Council had effect. There was a Cumann na mBan for women—pleasing to the traditionalists in the country who liked the old ways but irrelevant to many women who would soon be on active service, not on auxiliary duty as in the past. There was a Fianna Éireann, a youth organization matched by a similar group for the girls. They would be both feeder for the IRA, first-level indoctrination units, and for some, especially in the Republic, simply a scouting opportunity. Two newspapers appeared: *An Phoblacht,* edited by Eamonn MacThomais, and in Belfast *Republican News,* whose first issue appeared on June 30, 1970, with Jimmy Steele as editor until his death on August 11. Both were house organs, preaching to the converted, memorializing past and present sacrifices, giving snippets of history, revealing the appropriate policies. In time the traditional editors were replaced by members of the generation of 1969, such as Danny Morrison in Belfast, who had little interest in old quarrels, and (after her active service period) Rita O'Hare, equally as radical, in Dublin. The weekly papers would merge but essentially remain party journals that rarely indicated the workings of that party. Thus, in Ireland the movement had the three corners of the republican trinity in place, the army, the party, and the paper, all comfortably like those of the recent past, all capable of expansion. The key was the capacity to expand.

Nothing could happen without military supplies. As might have been expected, official and semiofficial sources had evaporated almost at once, with John Kelly standing on the dock waiting for a shipment that did not arrive. There was only so much to be harvested within the Republic and less prospect of finding things in Britain to bring over to Ireland. The key was America. There an American support organization, Northern Irish Aid (NORAID), had been formed by O Conaill and three veteran Tan War IRA men: Michael Flannery, a retired insurance salesman, Jack McGowan, Clare IRA, and Jack McCarthy, Cork IRA with union contacts. Flannery was typical—pious, kindly, a paragon of domestic virtues and religious piety; his republican faith and outlook had not eroded during his long residence in America. NORAID would in time contain several generations of Irish-Americans, all with absolute conviction that could not be eroded by the arguments of the Dublin government, the suspicions of American law enforcement agencies, or the course of Irish events. Contributions went up and down and NORAID never raised over the years what a few rich Zionist businessmen could manage one morning over the telephone, nor managed to exploit their assets as did the Greeks over the Cyprus issue, but the involved persisted and substantial sums reached Ireland. The money was collected and sent to overt republican institutions. A newspaper, the *Irish People*, published those segments of *An Phoblacht* likely to appeal to Irish-Americans, who were more conservative than their IRA militants. Money was collected as well, often at the same time, often by the same people, to go to IRA GHQ for more military uses. It would be some time and not through NORAID that American gear began to flow in predictable amounts into the IRA. Until then individuals did their best. In any case the American structure was created; and while it was no competitor to the support given the Fenians or the old IRA, it was an enduring comfort to those in Ireland.

All of these organizations had to be put together at once, almost always by part-time republicans, often harassed by the authorities, North and South and abroad, and criticized by those other republicans from Gardiner Place. In many parts of Ireland, the traditionalists became known as "Kevin Street," from their Dublin headquarters in the top two floors of a dingy Edwardian town house off Wexford Street, not far from Stephen's Green, on the south side. One went past the pub on the corner, into an obscure door with a brass Sinn Féin mail slot, inside by a ground-floor dry cleaner redolent with steam, and up a narrow, worn staircase, to reach the revolution in rooms far smaller than the other republicans' but just as bleak.

There, in one of the two rooms on the top floor, day in and day out, Tony Ruane would meet and greet the arrivals: locals by for tea, the eager in from Tipperary or Meath, Italian journalists, German radical students, stringers for the London newspapers, Irish-Americans seeking the heart of the matter, those who wanted publicity handouts or Sinn Féin T-shirts, a farmer with a bit of gear in the car and no contact. In no time Kevin Street turned into the archetypal revolutionary office, with unsold party papers stacked in the corners, banners and rolled flags leaned against the walls, unwashed teacups, spilled ink, smeared reports, soiled paper (a revolution still moves on paper), and the few chairs filled with the faithful and the followers. The Sinn Féin Executive met in the next room; Irish Republican Publicity Bureau statements were available—the usual means with which the IRA, among others, would make known the news of the moment, often by means of a telephone call from the floor below. In fact Ruane's role often changed depending on which phone he answered. It was possible for a journalist sitting in the back room to ring a mystery telephone connection and find Ruane across the desk at the other end of the line. Technical progress was slow—even the police Special Branch electronic bug, a very early model, fell off the underside of a table in the meeting room onto the floor with a thud. Besides the steady stream of pilgrims and scribes, the war came to Kevin Street when a book-bomb detonated on a table, giving Ruane a bit of a burn and a considerable scare. In the same series Mac Stiofáin opened his and for some weeks wore a striking black eye patch as a result; while across town Goulding used a stick to open his package and suffered no ill effects. Mostly only the curious and enthusiastic showed up at Kevin Street, not the war. Except when closed Kevin Street was the visible center, watched by grumpy policemen in plain clothes, bugged one way or another, the telephone traffic monitored; but there were simply too many strange people in and out to keep track of everything.

In time the Officials found their title sat uneasily as the organization sought to move away from the hard republican position, out from under the implications of being "Official" Sinn Féin in a drive to run a workers party. On the other hand, there were still many official republicans and few who wanted to abandon the name Sinn Féin—or anything else of value—to the Provos. So the name changes, like the shift in emphasis, came slowly. And they were soon renamed in spite of themselves. Gardiner Place had the same stream of visitors. Mick Ryan kept a list of all and sundry. Who knew who would come in handy in an uncertain future. There was one early change in Official procedures that had a long, lasting effect, unimportant but telling: The Easter lily paper medallion, sold without license for funds and as a mark of support on the streets during Easter Week, was backed by gum instead of affixed by pin.

For fifty years republican sellers in defiance of the law had pinned on Easter lily patches and often ended in jail for a few days. It was a tradition. Now, tradition aside, the seller could simply stick the lily on the lapel; still traditionalists, the Provos continued to pin theirs. Reputedly Gery Lawless, prominent and self-proclaimed Irish radical out of an English Trotskyist stable and once a Dublin republican, who saw both sets of nationalists as equally misguided, called one set Stickies and the other Pinheads. Provos was too good a name to discard, even if the leadership was eager to discard any implications summoned up by provisional, and so remained the Provos, Kevin Street. And now the Officials, Gardiner Place became for all the Stickies, the Sticks, long after the Easter lily had been forsaken for the red flag. The split did not follow previous divisions, with one small group plodding on toward the Republic and the other absorbed into the norm or isolated on a side road, because both little groups attracted great numbers of new recruits. Not all of the eager knew the difference in the two movements or cared, but collectively they assured persistence of what would be two options and so two rivals. Despite the very different potential constituencies, not at first apparent to the involved, covert revolutionary quarrels can turn lethal and from the first the Stickies and the Provos made no secret of their abomination of each other, recent friends and colleagues suddenly deadly and dangerous enemies.

For much of 1970 the Provisionals sought to create an official republican movement to prepare for war while the Official republican movement sought only a provisional military mission in their search for an official radical political form. No wonder the potential volunteers often ended at Gardiner Place instead of Kevin Street and the watching analysts needed programs. By the end of the year, the Provos had largely succeeded in their task and only partly at the expense of their IRA rivals. The Officials, harried by Northern turmoil and old habits, had moved more cautiously toward a workers party. Gardiner Place would have to wait through years of internal proselytizing before Sinn Féin could first be hyphenated with the Workers Party and finally dropped altogether, signifying the almost complete transformation of the movement into a legitimate radical party, supported secretly by a ghostly and vestigial IRA, as bodyguard and sometime money-raiser, that offered the new members a whiff of cordite without responsibility or risk. For the time being many in the movement did not foresee either the disappearance of the IRA or the erosion of the republican ethos by class interests; they saw instead the Provos as prime challenge.

The overt split had come on January 11, 1970, at the Sinn Féin Ard Fheis, the annual party conference, at the Intercontinental Hotel in Ballsbridge, Dublin 4, an American-designed glass box for the New Ireland that was a world away from the traditional seedy hotel meeting rooms of past conferences. There a vote on abstention carried but without the required two-thirds majority; rather, the resolution had been simply to accept the Army Convention's position from the December meeting that had produced Mac Stiofáin's walkout. It was considered a trick by the traditionalists, unfair, illicit, a violation of the Sinn Féin constitution, and only to be expected. Those at the center had grown tired of delay. A few hoped until the end to keep most of the delegates. Some did not care. The dissenters—O Brádaigh, O Conaill, and the rest—walked out into an already hired hall to set up a Provisional Sinn Féin. There were, then, formally, two republican movements, with the convictions of difference stiffening and positions hardening. A number of attempts to achieve reunion to fashion a middle position were tried and failed. Inevitably a certain number involved withdrew in disgust or anguish, but because of Northern conditions not many and not for long. Assets are always lost, betrayed, or hidden for a better day. This was crucially true for gear: Who gets the guns is a killing question in splits. These feuds are always blamed on the other, no matter who fired first, and further alienate the moderates, the involved, and observers. If the rivals are competing over a single ideological niche, time usually reveals the fitter and the grave receives the loser, for there is room for but one revealed truth in the underground. In 1970 only some of these factors came into play. The reality was that the republicans, regardless of specific ideological stance, and strategy had to cope with an influx of volunteers rather than the reverse: Every door had a line, contributions were to be had, gear was offered. The outside world did not care which IRA was which. Goulding and Mac Stiofáin faced not a narrowing niche, as had been the case so often in revolutionary splits, but, seemingly, a risen people clamoring to be organized. No one wanted to be moderate or join a third force or stay home. Even the conventional widening of differences, the inevitable canker and venom, the hardening of attitudes, even shots exchanged, did not disrupt the growth of both organizations. In fact even old republicans found the split difficult to fathom and the new volunteers were unaware that there was now a republican choice. They had knocked at the handy door.

Behind their door on Kevin Street the Provos had everything to do: organize an entire movement, pursue a defensive policy for the moment, find gear and train new volunteers, and in so doing respond to Northern events. There was hardly time to send emissaries around the country to explain what had happened to the movement with the North on the boil. In a real sense these Northern events remained an intrusion for the Officials as much as an opportunity. They might have an organization in place but all of their volunteers had to be made aware of the political implications of each act while the Provos had only to be taught to shoot. GHQ did not want to shoot. For many at the Official center, cut off from the traditionalists, still in theoretical control of many of these country units, the six counties remained alien, filled with harsh-voiced, dour, overly devout men impervious to novelty, soldiers with ideas inclined to old grievances and older patriotism. Yet the two great reservoirs of republican strength in 1970 remained the rural faithful in Ulster and the Belfast Catholic working class. The Provos swept in the city gunmen almost at once and then began organizing the countryside. The Officials went slower, educating their volunteers before arming them, perhaps instead of arming them. Not all took to novel ideas, especially in the countryside.

The Northern Catholic country folk in the six counties and along the border were not easy to understand. They were often sly and shy, no talkers and seldom in town. Their faith in the Republic had arisen in the long struggle against an ascendancy that could be moved only by physical force. The country was filled with hidden fault lines, disputed margins, and unmarked frontiers both scattered about the hills and in the minds of men and women. The two traditions existed in the same land on mutual sufferance, avoiding contention, keeping to trails that never crossed and to subjects that caused no quarrels. There had been too many quarrels for too many years to risk a wrong word. The past killings were never quite past. The IRA in South Armagh or the hill villages of Tyrone came down from the old night riders, men who burned ricks and barns, maimed cattle, murdered land agents, who took oaths to secret orders, appeared after dark to protect their own or to harm the system, and then disappeared into the silence of a silent country.

The country poor were often very poor, often beyond the reach of the welfare state or the concerns of welfare workers, well beyond the new laws. There were little old men, the last on the land, who lived in wretched penury in stone hovels without water, without electric light, often without washing or a diet beyond the potato. They might be seen in their stiff, shiny suit at Mass or at a grim public house that was nothing but a front room, dark from smoke, where pints were served across a deal table. Others, equally dour and pious, had bigger farms but the same mind, the same grievances. Mostly the farmers stayed in the hills, kept to the land and to themselves, came to fairs, sold a little, bought less. They would put up those on the run, move bits across the gorse-covered hills, and in the old days take a shot if shots were to be taken. Many were the residue of the Irish peasant, shattered by the famine and in most of the island long since eased into frugal comfort. Not all of these lived so close to the margin but most, even those in the village with the pub or the petrol station, were of an ilk. In the North, the hill farmers (if successful) often turned a profit, had a car, were wired to radio and television, had subsidized piped water, were familiar with agricultural grants and artificial fertilizer. They were not usually as rich as their Protestant neighbors or as sophisticated as the Dublin man, but they were no longer the ragged rebels in hill hovels from the last century. Yet life remained much the same, even with BBC Ulster on the telly. Ideas stayed the same, attitudes were stolid, and the law was alien. Such people had survived by ceding under threat all but the hill land and dreams of vengeance. For them, for many in the country, piety, confession, and the sermons of the priest were part of the environment, like the land and the weather. And there too was the Republic cherished in Pomeroy and Coalisland and Crossmaglen in a way not so in Dublin or Cork.

The Republic was glory with the promise of power, quick and bright, the one marvel in a life parish-bound, limited by the furrow and fate. The Republic was an icon without agenda or details that yet demanded soldiers and sacrifice, a vocation for those without talent or education, without prospects, with ten acres, gnarled hands, and a single suit. The hill men rarely came to Dublin, the Free State, once a decade to a GAA match or once a lifetime to see the Pope or Dev's funeral in 1970, to a cell in Mountjoy if arrested on the border. The publican and his son, the solicitor's clerk, the proper with lace at the window and Sunday suits were only more articulate, not so land-bound but no softer. And for them, too, Dublin was another country, and Dublin came rarely to them. There was an oration at an Easter commemoration, a soft-spoken man from a city saying magic words on a gray day with snow in the air, and for the rest it was a local man up the boreen with a *United Irishman* and a request for a bit of money not there and a wave on the way back to the real world to count the Republic's gain over a pint. This world was not open to political excursions and so the Provos slowly began to exploit the old loyalties. Once awakened and given form, the hills would become a rock that the British patrols, the appeals of other decent Catholics, and the excesses of a nasty war could not erode.

All of the Officials' urban concerns focused on class and social issues not yet come to the countryside. They should have attracted Catholic victims of industrialism, living lives stunted by an imperial, capitalist system maintained by sectarian bigotry. In theory these ideas should have attracted the sectarian bigots as well, misled by their masters; but neither private overtures nor public pleading produced more than a few inconclusive discussions with a Protestant working class without loyalty to Marx's prescriptions or Lenin's remedies, preferring the secondary benefits of inherited domination. So, whatever the theory, the Officials competed with the Provos in appealing to the Catholics. Many of these were lifelong republicans and felt no great need for additional ideas and analysis. The Belfast faithful were narrow, pious, and proper, tied to their dark, smoky city and grim terrace houses as was the countryman to his hill. They might be soft among their own, easy over a pint, might laugh in their own kitchen; but they had for the politicized Dubliner limited vision and no real politics, only the hard word in a harsh voice. They were often dour, conservative men, proper, proud of their denials and nation, patriotic to excess, Catholic to a fault, hard, black Irishmen tempered in a local bigotry. They, like the black Protestants, believed in family virtues, the church, and the customs of the tribe. They, like the country rebel so far off and so different in manner, could scarcely credit abortion or divorce, the three stages of revolution, the Dublin radical agenda, or a commemoration without the rosary. They seemingly lacked humor, an affection for discourse and display, a soft side. Instead, they exhibited a seriousness of purpose, a dedication that allowed no deviation, a ready recourse to physical force used not only against the traditional foes but also against their own, the weak, the foolish, the unfaithful—Belfast was a hard city and the republicans were pure. In their way, like all republicans, they sought not simply service but sacrifice, would do hard time, would undertake the difficult but not as display. They had titles and pretensions but only within the army. In time the Belfast radical tradition might touch that army but not at first, not when the people needed defense. Most of all, they maintained an inexplicable pride in their city, the rewards of its rigors, the challenge of its urban dangers.

Belfast has for a century been ruled by Protestants, Orange bigots in robes and police patrols in the streets. Yet the republicans loved their city: It offered the comfort of their own wee district, their chapel, the true Church, offered their old friends, the special lanes, the same faces, offered a whole life, was the still point of a turning world. They went south only to Tone's commemoration at Bodenstown and, if prosperous, for holidays they went west to the cold Atlantic resorts of Donegal—north but not in the North. Few were ever very prosperous or for long. Jimmy Steele was a baker's roundsman with one holiday in his whole life, and yet he was buried an IRA lieutenant general with over ten thousand mourners at the funeral. The Republic was for them transcendental, a grail for those who had signed on the crusade for life. They were as far from Dublin, a soft, ruined Georgian city dreaming on the Liffey, as from the gnarled farmers in the parishes of Down or up the Glens of Antrim. In the six counties all suffered the arrogance of the Orange zealot and spoke with an accent as harsh as their secular faith. In Belfast the lad next door was a *pure* republican, a real republican, no pub dreamer, no country lad parading in a pasture, no theologian of the Left but a hard man without quibbles or moderation. The man from the Falls or the Bone was a pilgrim with the proper badges, the round gold Fianna pin of the Irish speaker and the Pioneer pin that indicated lifelong denial of alcohol, awards of denial, temperance, cultural separatism that went with the proper attitude, with a gun and a savage heart. He, too, made the Officials in Dublin uneasy, too near the flip side of the Orange fundamentalist for comfort. Not so the Provos, for there he was one in conviction and the faith in the power of the gun.

The melding of the two traditions, the man who had never set foot on sod or seen a cow with the lad who found the traffic in Strabane unnerving, would in time form the strength of a secret army. And the Provos sought not the comfortable but an army—and as quickly as possible. Like all revolutionaries they did not so much seek talent as faith—winnow through the many for converts and let talent come later. In the meantime many existing republicans had to make choices. The split came first where Dublin GHQ had the greatest control: Dublin, Belfast, Cork, or a rural unit that had stayed together and in touch. Many individuals in 1970 assumed in fact that they were IRA members but remained unknown to GHQ or the passing organizer. If there were no war, why show up for the parade? At one time in Dundalk, no mean town, no great distance from Dublin on the main road to Belfast, three different volunteers, each innocent of the other's rank, assumed he alone held the command of the Dundalk unit, a unit that never met for there was no need. Even in a small city like Derry, the young in 1970–71 might not realize that the movement had split. Many of the young in the North had no understanding or interest in the issues that seemed so vital in Dublin. In 1970 potential recruits wanted the means of defense, a place in a secret army. That at least the Provos and the Stickies could grant, for the moment, even if that army came without weapons, uniforms, or battle plans.

During much of 1970, throughout the island, both IRAs were inundated with recruits, a stream that grew thicker as the turmoil increased and the presence of the British army on the streets proved a mixed blessing. The nationalists could not be sure the British would defend them. So who was to do it? Not Dublin. Where had Dublin been in August 1969 but standing idly by? Not the United Nations or the United States or a united Europe. So it had to be the IRA, reinvented by necessity. The single great problem for both the IRAs was that despite the enthusiasms of the many, despite toleration and support and the creation of support groups in the United States, arms could only be found in dribs and drabs. Mostly the bits were still coming from attics and old dumps and from over the farmer's fireplace. The constant searches for arms produced a remarkable mixed collection, but it still left more recruits than guns. In the case of the Provos, the QMG did not limit the sweeps to firearms but began bomb production almost as soon as the Army Council took command. In fact in Dublin the new QMG Jack McCabe, one of many IRA veterans living in the city, began the production of explosives in a garage in Santry—a contribution that ended on December 30, 1971, when he was mortally injured in a black powder explosion possibly caused by his use of a metal shovel in the bulk production demanded by the needs of the Northern units.

Self-made explosives would take a fearful toll of IRA volunteers over the years because of chemical errors, awkward handling, faulty detonators, unstable ingredients, hasty construction, and often foolish behavior. No wealth of skill or years of practice can undo one lit cigarette end on cordite, one clock hand jiggled, one bare wire brushed against another. There is a roar and a military funeral with closed coffins, a volley of honor, and one more example to be taught to the next engineering class. Accidents or not, the explosives problem was amenable to self-taught skills, local materials, improvisation, reference books, imported bits and pieces, and the simple purchase of chemicals, petroleum, by-products, household staples, and industrial materials. There would always be bombs and the involved did not have to look beyond the island for the ingredients.

The only real solution to the lack of guns was imports. A decade later the IRA would finally construct, in addition to various bomb containers and grenades, an effective mortar, but all of these were adjunct to the real thing: guns, lots of guns, real guns, military weapons with military ammunition. And here a continuing republican problem occurred. The Provisional IRA was a working-class movement, with only a sparkling of the lower middle class, a few teachers and pub owners, a very few small businessmen or clerks. The new volunteers were almost all young men, for the mature could play little direct part in an underground and were shunted into subsidiary tasks, often deadly dangerous tasks that carried the risk of long prison terms but not on the front line. The Provos were thus an army without special skills, often without any skills, school leavers or the habitually unemployed of the Catholic North and their Southern counterparts.

As men of no property the IRA at all levels possessed none of the technological and managerial capacities required to run a contemporary war, even a guerrilla conflict, and they had few of the contacts with those who could be persuaded to help. There were contacts—Ireland is a small country—but few of these could be counted on in troubled times and fewer would risk prison for sentiment or out of nostalgia. And since few of the skilled and educated were of the overt republican faith, institutionalized suspicion remained: In Ireland, for any skill, any advice, often any purchase, one turns first to one's own, seeking familiarity and kinship, not competence or a bargain. This was the case in skills and capacities that lay outside the republican circle: Could those, even those eager to help, really be trusted? And even beyond trust the Provisionals had to accept that they needed help and advice. An underground revolutionary army wants arms first, then money, and advice last; help comes with strings, and the secret army would rather use the familiar if possible, even deny the validity of the alien. Thus, a grasp of illicit import-export procedures, the acquisitions of arms, the transmutation of guns into paper and back to guns, the intricacies of customs and inspectors and bills of lading was lacking. At first lucky amateurs simply moved gear into the country, and later the QMG would succeed from time to time with tactics so crude as to be overlooked by the cunning opponent: money walked past customs in a paper bag, Semtex explosives and machine guns dropped off small boats, rifles carried in golf bags, and ammunition shipped as screws. Much could be made good in time but the fact remained that in 1970 the Provos were hardly ready for a role as defenders much less ready to move over to retaliation. They, as well as the Officials, especially in the North, instead sought to control the old assets, attract new volunteers, and move forward. The Stickies aimed at armed agitation and the Workers Party while the Provos sought an armed struggle and ultimately the Republic.

The key to the future was Belfast, where the Protestant threat was the greatest, the British army was most visible, and where more Catholics, mostly working class, mostly poor, mostly alienated, existed in one place. There the Provos set up a brigade staff—Belfast had always been more attracted to the use of the old Tan

War forms and titles than the rest of the country and maintained the habit even when the units had dribbled away to squad size or disappeared entirely. Billy McKee was first O/C, had led the armed resistance to the Protestant intrusions in August, a good man in a hard spot. Small, slight, unprepossessing, he was a daily communicant, a conservative man insistent on discipline and order but without political concerns or radical interests. His A/G was Séamus Twomey, an unknown bookmaker. He often wore dark glasses, and was taciturn like his colleagues, although he had a gift for a good story and the wry word; he was more open to the new. He did not bother to invent a soldier front. Leo Martin was intelligence officer and one of the best-known republicans in the city, so much so that the Malvern Street killers in 1966 had him as first target. Seán McNally was quartermaster, a thankless job of begging, borrowing, and pleading with the Army Council for more. Tommy O'Donnell, a first-rate bookkeeper, tidy and precise, was finance officer. Seán Murphy was in charge of training. Joe Cahill, Jimmy Drumm, Jimmy Steele, and several of the other old felons were on the staff. Belfast had given few volunteers to the recent campaign although several, like Ivor Bell, reappeared to help out, a few stayed with the Officials, and the others were gone. Some like John Kelly made their way south to argue for support and stayed—Kelly as GHQ finance officer. Only one or two of the next generation like Gerry Adams with family connections were about at the beginning although hundreds were at the door. The Provos staff organized the city into three battalion areas, drawing a map that would for two decades represent reality: First Battalion covered the Upper Falls, Ballymurphy Estate to the north and Andersonstown to the west; Second Battalion covered the Lower Falls, Clonard, and the new Divis Flats nearer the city center; and Third Battalion took in the outposts of the Ardoyne and the Bone off Crumlin Road and the Short Strand cut off on the east bank of the Lagan River. In time the battalion areas would take on local pride, in the clubs drinkers roared rebel songs waving one or two or three fingers in the air, in the streets the people followed their lads like a match, the locals, the neighborhood unit, the battalion.

Scattered across the three battalion areas were nineteen Provo units depending on demand—and the demand increasingly was dependent on the response of the authorities to the continuing turmoil. The more trouble, the more volunteers, and the more problems of organizing and integrating for the Provos. Everyone needed to work twenty-five hours a day, spend enormous personal resources, rush to keep up with events. There was at least a little money, but there were never enough arms or trained instructors. But the enormous asset, the elixir coursing through the Provisional organization, was optimism: The old pessimism had been shaken first by the protests and then by the collapse of order and the arrival of the British army. The ground had moved. The faithful knew what to do and what, therefore, was going to happen. And as the weeks passed the future unfolded as predicted: The British army was beginning to alienate the Catholics. How could it not? It was an army, it was British.

By the end of March 1970, the exciting news seemed to come from outside Belfast, even outside the North. On March 24 Bernadette Devlin met with Prime Minister Wilson in London to press an investigation into the death of Samuel Devenney of Derry during an RUC intrusion into his house in July 1969. London wanted no part of a local police matter in far-off Derry. The next day in Dublin the customs officials at the port intercepted arms being illegally imported—a forerunner of the excitement to be generated in May with the Arms Case scandal but in March only an indication that the Republic was not, despite what Protestants often insisted, in collusion with Catholic gunmen and that, as everyone suspected, those gunmen were importing the tools of their trade for the next round. The local Belfast gunmen met at the Easter 1970 commemoration at Milltown cemetery. There were two speeches, two sets of republicans since the Provos had not accepted Jim Sullivan's official offer for a joint celebration: The Officials were not official and the sooner forgotten the better. There was trouble with the police and then with a Protestant mob both on Easter Sunday and the following Monday despite the presence of five hundred soldiers and six hundred RUC. The real trouble, however, began on Tuesday, March 31, with rioting along the Springfield Road by the Ballymurphy housing estate. The rioting continued the next night and the Royal Scots Regiment resorted to CS gas that once used floated through the narrow streets of Ballymurphy, alienating the inhabitants of each house in turn. One family angry, two families angry, a neighborhood resentful, and a net gain for the Provos. This first use of gas in Belfast, the fighting that injured thirty-eight soldiers, the failures of the Stickies to fight back—Jim Sullivan urged the nationalist crowd to disperse—was all grist to the Provo mill: Everyone played the assigned role.

The army after the Ballymurphy riot was increasingly seen as opposed to nationalist interests, so that more volunteer defenders began to turn to the Provos, who defended, unlike the Stickies, who talked politics. Even without arms or gear there was no doubt in Belfast that the Provisionals were militant, military, seeking war not revolution. The countryside might not be sure about the two IRA roads but soon in Belfast every dog in the street knew the contradictory attractions. Sullivan and the Officials felt that the Provos were provoking the security forces in Ballymurphy to riot in part to embarrass their republican rivals, who had a wiser more cautious policy. All that this "wisdom" got the Stickies was further feuding with the Provos: fights over the distribution of the *UI,* confrontations in pubs and on the streets, charges of "kneecapping"—shooting a selected victim in the leg as punishment—and at the end of April, worse. Some Provos fired thirteen shots at a group of Stickies standing around Billy McMillen, who was hit and slightly wounded. It had been only a matter of time until the feud turned ugly. There was retaliation, a patched-up truce, provocation, and more shooting on the Lower Falls.

On the other side of the uncertain peace line, the competition between the Unionists was as real if not yet as violent. Once again there was general Unionist unease at concessions. On Friday, April 17, the results of two Stormont by-elections in Bannside and South Antrim were announced. Paisley won the first over the Official Unionists (7,981 to 6,778 with 3,514 for Northern Ireland Labour) and his ally W. J. Beattie took the second by a majority of 958 in an electorate split four ways. The decay of orthodox Unionism continued. On April 24, despite cheers and a big personal vote for Chichester-Clark, the Unionist Party voted against the reform housing policy 281 to 216, a policy the government at Stormont intended to pursue despite such hesitation. Chichester-Clark's eroding control was in direct contrast to that of Lynch in the South, who on May 6 had won a unanimous vote of confidence from his Fianna Fáil Party regarding the Arms Case dismissals and resignations. Then an unexpected United Kingdom general election was called for June 18 by Harold Wilson on May 18. In the province this would test the relative strength of the various Northern Ireland currents when a pause might have been of more use to the moderates. Irish priorities were hardly noted in London. Wilson saw a seeming Labour opportunity and took it—the Northern Ireland politicians could, as usual, fight in their own corner.

This election there would be more varieties than usual. The Unionist moderates of the now ancient O'Neill era had already been transmuted into Chichester-Clark supporters. The real moderates, Oliver Napier, John Hunter, Robert Cooper, and David Corkey, had founded the Alliance Party on April 21 as a nonsectarian alternative favoring reform and union, too, with support from all six counties. Their new party would prove a stayer in the complex provincial political world. All varieties of moderates were increasingly uneasy at the rapid growth and appeal of Paisley's fundamentalist Protestant Unionist Party, whose every vote made reform more difficult, the militant loyalists more truculent, violence more likely, and the proper aspirations of the Alliance or Unionists less probable.

On their side of the barricades the militants within the republican movement showed little interest in elections: The conventional might still support the old Nationalists and the vocal radicals back a civil rights nominee like Bernadette Devlin, but in 1970 most Catholics focused on escalating provocation, not on parties. What good had parties ever done them? The action, the prospect of real power was in the streets, not in voting booths as a perpetual minority. The Provos had begun their still "secret" bombing campaign carried out largely by a Belfast special operations unit that had by the end of June detonated over forty devices. This was real power. Adding to the turmoil, Saor Éire, a small covert group, revolutionary in name but criminal in most practice, had seized upon armed robbery as a means of toppling the system or at least keeping some of the more active members in funds. On May 7, Saor Éire had taken responsibility for a payroll robbery in Strabane, Tyrone, that netted fourteen thousand pounds and generated an intense police and military search, since there had been forty thousand pounds stolen in ten raids in Northern Ireland in the previous eighteen months. Some, perhaps many, were the work of Saor Éire. A key indicator of a revolutionary situation is the disappearance of the demarcation line between simple crime and political crime; arson can be propaganda by the deed or a way to collect insurance on a failing business or both. Those involved with Saor Éire, some with dubious records, could believe that personal advantage was a reward for political risk: Rob from the state and drink the proceeds in the most primitive terms. Saor Éire was a true sign of the times and not a comforting one for the authorities.

Despite the Saor Éire armed raids and the unclaimed bombs exploding as a result of the Provos' special unit, much militant republican activity went unnoticed. The Provo-Stickie competition was rarely visible as the traditionalists in Belfast won over both the potential volunteers and the Catholic population eager for a sure defender. They did not win everything, for many good republicans appeared in official colors and many more were attracted by the rising political commitment of the Sticks in contrast to the gun hunger of the Provos. In the countryside even less was to be seen as the Stickies tried to hold on to their own and the Provos sent out organizers—if there were no guns yet from America, there was at least money for full-time people. What was most worrisome for the authorities was the general decay of order, the rise of conditions far worse than those of August 1969 despite the presence of the British army. No one believed it was because of the presence of the British army. An additional sign of troubled times is the rise in the numbers of the authorized armed—police, army, militia, party shock units, whatever—that indicates to the rebel his own importance. The more troops the more effective the rebellion, and the more difficult, so that the rebel must work harder to ensure more troops, which makes his task still more difficult: a constant circle of escalation that at the end leaves a huge army with decreasing effect as the cycle shifts to rebel advantage. In fact the British military presence was increased in response to the approaching Westminster elections when a contingent of Royal Marine commandos arrived on June 2. Eight thousand soldiers would be in Northern Ireland for the elections on June 18 and no one in Stormont or London was sure that these would be enough if matters turned sour. The arena was still viewed as one threatened by sectarian disorder (which was true enough) and not by a republican armed struggle, which was increasingly likely.

When the election results for Northern Ireland came in on Friday, June 19, they crudely reflected sentiment on the ground. Such elections have nothing to do with United Kingdom issues or politics; they are either straight tribal votes or else award the prominent in either camp. The big news in Britain was that Wilson had blundered—the Conservatives and Heath were winners. This was not the news in Ireland at all. The Unionists lost two seats, one to Paisley, more loyalist than they, and one to a nationalist, Frank McManus, running as an Independent with republican connections, who took a nationalist seat that could be lost to the Unionists if the nationalists split. Both Gerry Fitt and Bernadette Devlin kept their seats in strong nationalist districts. What the new MP lineup did not reflect was the prospect of violence instead of votes: Paisley, in particular, even if a political man and not a general of a secret underground, was symbol of loyalist anxiety and anger.

The loyalists had no secret IRA, no friendly Republic to the south, no sympathetic media praising their violation of the law in protests for good causes. No organization, neither the Orange Orders nor the Unionist Party, seemed adequate for the emergency. Nothing and no one truly represented them. These were the fundamentalists, the hard-core working-class loyalists who now suspected the old gentry and the new rich as inadequate in defense of the realm. And most dreadful of all for these loyalists, bedecked in Union Jacks, resplendent with past patriotic sacrifices, old campaign ribbons or miniature medals on every middle-aged lapel, old regimental ties for the proper and old war songs for all, was that the British army, *their* army, did not take their side in the provincial divisions. Heretofore the loyalists had felt authority, as manifested by the Unionists, the RUC, and the B Specials, was theirs; but by the summer of 1970 the Unionists were split, the RUC shamed and disarmed, the B Specials disbanded, the Orange lodges good only for parades, and the system ruined by reforms. Some few determined men had decided to act secretly, to retaliate; but for them, for all loyalists, the overriding problem was a lack of institutional practice. Others had always led and the most fundamental seldom went far from the street corner or pulpit.

Since 1969 militancy beyond mere riot had taken the form of brief vigilante excursions by neighbors or a few bombs planted almost instinctively by a tiny group of fundamentalists. There was no Protestant secret army, but there was throughout the province during much of 1970 a rising anxiety to match the rising optimism of the Provos. The inherent superiority of the Protestants came suddenly into question: Their numbers on the island had always been inferior and their favor in London had always been problematical, but now their competence to defend was under unexpected siege by the old ogre, the IRA, in new form. Even the elections—Devlin, McManus, and Fitt at Westminster—seemed to indicate that radicalization of the minority politics paralleled that of the majority. The elections had edged out moderates, increasing Protestant fears and Catholic aspirations.

In London there was no general agreement or intense interest in the results from Northern Ireland. Those who paid any attention at all to Irish matters sensed no direction of events, noted only news of the continued rioting that wracked Belfast (as it did again in July). What had counted was the changing of the London guard, not the squabbles on another island, but now Reginald Maudling as Home Secretary would have to devise a response to balance incompatible interests to ensure order. And as was true of every Home Secretary, other matters were pressing. The province often had to suffer through United Kingdom general elections at unfortunate moments and sometimes by-elections as well that at times had an exaggerated importance as a result of peculiarly Irish circumstances. There were also the elections for Stormont and the local elections and even occasional referenda, each with results usually easy to foretell and each likely to further divide a divided society. Elections in Northern Ireland were often as much a ritual (like an Orange parade or an Easter commemoration) as a means to office.

The vote of the two religious communities was very nearly a constant no matter what the election or the issues involved within the province or within the United Kingdom. Most efforts to find a nonpartisan way had an unhappy history—the Northern Irish Labour Party or class-based efforts attracted a tiny Belfast minority and so far the Alliance party had netted mainly, if not entirely, moderate Unionists. Each election, if nothing more, indicated and reinformed the religious divide. Within the two constant blocs, increasingly after 1969, there were severe divisions that a public vote often intensified, to the advantage of the more militant, thus complicating any push toward moderation. Before 1969 militancy had been hidden within the whole as each side assumed a changeless society, but after 1969 the future was offered to the bold—and the most bold soon were on the streets or buying guns.

As far as the Westminster elections went, Ireland was a marginal national issue—there were no Irish districts in Britain, very little Irish vote, only a few concerned with any Irish issue, no political gain for a concern with the province, no need to invest time in fashioning a novel Irish policy. Generally, both Labour and the Tories wanted most of all an end to the Irish intrusion, law and order, peace and quiet, at worst an acceptable level of violence with a continuing military presence with the odd atrocity; at best they wanted an accommodation that would cork the bottle. The Anglo-Irish Treaty of 1921 had corked that bottle once, corked it for fifty years; and what was needed, nearly everyone in London felt, was another such accommodation: the return of Lloyd George, not more Black and Tans. London always sought conciliation, institutionalized compromise, an end to the crisis, but only when that crisis escalated. Then, with the mob on the street or the gun in politics and this month's disaster in the headlines, reluctantly, the British establishment looked for an out. There were no real differences between the Tories and Labour as the Irish problem dragged on. The Conservative and Unionist Party obviously, as its formal name indicated, had a link with the provincial Stormont establishment, but it was vestigial and fragile. Perhaps the Conservative support of order more than law was more apparent than that of Labour, with its hard Left faction's support of Irish nationalism. But both those in the Conservative party who were concerned Unionists and those in Labour who were active advocates of the minority were few and unrepresentative. Thus, after any party change in London there was no new Irish policy. The only change was the dispatch of a different set of administrators, often most reluctant administrators, Ireland being exile even if the office was in London. So there was a switch in nameplates in the bureaucracy and a continuation of the same lethargy.

The Irish assumed that their fate was, if not high on Britain's list of priorities, at least on the urgent list. It never was. Only the passing of the years and the presence of Irish members in the House gradually revealed how far from London events in Belfast or Derry could be. Ireland engendered boredom or outraged indignation, no more. So Maudling went on his obligatory whirlwind tour and found the North a "bloody awful country." It was a ritual only Callaghan had enjoyed. The trip indicated to Irish observers that there would now be a Tory Irish policy that everyone there assumed would be promilitary, hard-edged, less critical of the Unionists. Instead the Tory policy was one with Labour: drift.

However, instead of an easy return to British matters, London found that all during the summer the Irish were in the headlines and on the television news. Beginning on Friday, June 25, there were three nights of very serious rioting along the edges of the nationalist areas of Belfast and Derry. Matters had been complicated when a parade of Orange Lodge No. 9 District in the Whiterock area of Belfast ended with stone throwing and ultimately shooting on Saturday. There had been no respite on Sunday, June 27, and by the end of the weekend the army had fired 1,600 cartridges of CS gas in Belfast. It was this first use of CS gas in Belfast that had alienated many Catholics untouched by other issues. The disinterested army barging through their little streets, acting as an army not as policemen, rapidly dissipated the gratitude accumulated the previous August.

Protestant mobs began to move against the isolated Catholic Short Strand district across the Larne. There was no sign of the British army. Billy McKee arrived with a small group of Provos and took up positions in the churchyard of Saint Matthew's, the core of the quarter, where six thousand Catholics were threatened. The IRA fought on through the night: darkened streets, howls and flickering lights from fires, the crack and whine of bullets, confusion and fear and no sign of authority. Three Protestants and an IRA volunteer, Henry McIlhone from the Third Battalion, were killed and Billy McKee slightly wounded. The mobs were driven back and there was little doubt that the Provos had won— "revenge is sweet" and no thanks to the other army, the British army, *their* army.

The Provos immediately began to reap the full reward: a new wave of recruits eager to defend. The Central Citizens Defense Committee had evolved into a publicity office for grievances leaving street defense to the British army or the expanding Provos. The Officials, still set on converting the Protestant working class to their radical ideas, found the role of Catholic guardian unappealing, Billy McKee and his Thompson gun under Saint Matthew's an awful example. The Provos insisted that they would soon have the gear and already had the intention of protecting their own, protecting them against the Orange mobs, of course, against the British army, if need be. And the June riots (with seven killed, two hundred civilians injured, fifty-four by shooting, and ten British soldiers taken off to a hospital) proved to be only an overture.

Maudling had come to Belfast, looked about, reassured Stormont, announced the new Tory Irish policy, and departed. On Friday afternoon, July 3, the army searched a house on Balkan Street in the Falls and found, as their informer had indicated, a cache of nineteen weapons. The Officials who dominated the Markets area could do nothing. The guns were gone, lost to the army. A few local lads began stoning the troops as they left an hour later, nothing vicious, just the reflex response of idle hands. Then the small Provo unit added to the din with nail-bombs—dynamite and shrapnel devices taped together for use against personnel. The army tried to move back into the Markets and the Officials felt that they had to defend their own—the Lower Falls was the hard core of their support. The rioting escalated. Lieutenant General Sir Ian Freeland sent in three thousand troops backed by helicopters and armored cars and announced a total curfew while house-to-house searches began. This time provocation would be shut down with a flood of force across the whole area. The Great Falls Curfew confrontation was under way. House by house the soldiers smashed down front doors, tore away walls and floorboards, looking for arms or documents or something, smashed by accident and by design the furnishings, insulted the owners, who insulted them, cursed their lot and the people, who cursed them, took advantage and took liberties. Farther along, at the edge of the continuous moving riot, great clouds of CS gas swirled, shots were occasionally heard, and the lanes rained stones, nail-bombs, flaming bottles of petrol, bricks, and ball bearings. The storm and the danger drove the army troops to further excess. The Officials, with over eighty men in the area, fought a delaying action against the troops in open gun battles. Four civilians were killed and some sixty wounded. One civilian was crushed by a Saracen armored car. Except for a brief respite, the curfew remained in force until Sunday morning at nine.

By then the Falls had been pacified, the terraces ransacked and searched, but the gas still tainted the entire neighborhood, the streets were littered with rocks and debris, and the houses were pockmarked by bullets. The army found in total fifty-two pistols, thirty-five rifles, six automatic weapons, fourteen shotguns (included in this total were the original nineteen weapons found on Balkan Street) as well as ammunition, explosives, homemade bombs and two-way radios. The resistance had been smashed. Those Stickies who had escaped the sweep were hiding elsewhere. The army press officers were well pleased and drove journalists and two triumphant Unionist ministers, William Long and John Brooke, around to view the pacified Falls. *Their* army driving them around the ruins. The Black Watch and the Life Guard regiments, the regulars, had promptly and effectively responded to irregular attacks and IRA provocation, according to army sources. A job well done, according to army sources. A job obviously done for the Orange system or else why drive the Unionists about? according to those who watched the army's doings. That army, the regulars had alienated not only the entire Markets area but also much of Catholic Belfast. Obviously, if you were a Catholic, Maudling had given the army the order to move with a free hand and then let them display the results to his Unionist friends. This was the new Tory policy. The Falls Curfew proved an enormous boon to the Provos, who had not participated in the defense of the area but had none of the Stickie qualms about a defender role. Recruitment was up immediately and so too retaliation: The secret bombs were further justified, the provocations upped, and the sniping more pronounced. In the drift toward the war the Provos sought, the Falls Curfew was a steep upward jag in the needed alienation of the Catholic community, the discovery of the British army as enemy.

Actually the militancy of the new recruits eager to move faster than mere defense had to be tamed. Even after the Falls Curfew, the Provos felt that they had neither the gear nor the support of the population to escalate. The emphasis was on training and arming, not fighting. In Belfast a parallel policy was to postpone open confrontation with the British army and keep operations secret, unclaimed. For the moment conciliation was the public Provo face. In fact, a group of the Belfast GHQ staff—McKee, Martin, Frank Card, and Liam and Kevin Hannaway—met regularly with British officers to avoid trouble, to ease old problems, and to keep the army away from the organization. The British thought they were getting an insight on the IRA and the IRA thought they were preventing that, so everyone was happy for a while. Meanwhile the Army Council assumed that the next step would depend on the same kind of reasonable but costly error that General Freeland had made on the Falls. With Maudling in the Home Office such errors were sure to come, but the summer of 1970 was too soon to expect too much. The Provos did not want the British army to play the part of oppressor too soon, before the volunteers were ready. In their innocence most volunteers thought they were ready if only they had more arms. And the gear was not available. Bits and pieces had shown up in the North smuggled in through air and sea express packages. Some seventy weapons stockpiled in America after the end of the 1962 campaign were sent over by summer. These were mostly United States Army M-1s and Garands that took .300 ammunition that was as hard to find as the .45-caliber ammunition needed for the few remaining Thompsons. So both kinds of ammunition had to come from America as well. There would be more gear on the way for in the spring Cahill and O Conaill had met with NORAID people and less visible friends. An earlier emissary had already been in touch with the IRA's old supplier George Harrison with his friend Liam Cotter. They had sent the campaign weapons and were so obviously suspect that the American law enforcement authorities actually tended to overlook them. In time there would be more

NORAID money, more weapons, more disciplined recruits; but as yet the Provos could not cope with a real shooting war.

To many who had been a long way from the Markets during the Falls Curfew, Belfast events seemed close enough to war to require an urgent response. To the South anxiety again led to the transmission of mixed signals by the government. These were read by the loyalists and many in London as provocative, and by the militant nationalists as encouragement. These were sent, however, largely out of anxiety and frustration about what Dublin could not do and what Dublin should do. President Patrick Hillery made an unannounced trip to Belfast—a provocation to the entire spectrum of British and Unionist authority as well as to all loyalist feeling but also an exercise without great purpose. Why cause trouble? What sort of claim was being made? To whom was the flag being shown? What did Dublin want? Dublin did not know. On July 11, Jack Lynch in a radio address indicated that the crisis was an Irish quarrel. Again further "interference" came with his unilateral announcement that his government would be the second guarantor after the British government to govern the six counties wisely and well. Lynch had already publicly indicated that the Irish quarrel could only be settled by agreement with the Unionists, that in fact Irish unity could not, would not be achieved by force but only by agreement with the Northern Unionists. Since this was unlikely, all Lynch really wanted was that the British government act sufficiently wisely and well to restore real law and order and so remove the North from the political agenda. The decent Dublin position was that in theory Britain's presence was an imposition if in practice it was crucial and that Irish unity could come peacefully but not soon.

Neither London nor Belfast paid much attention except to his public truculence. Any Dublin statement about the internal affairs of the United Kingdom slightly annoyed London, even if the political need was understood, and outraged Stormont, since political intention was assumed. The degree of London-Dublin common interest was simply not apparent. Both wanted peace and quiet for the moment; both suspected that the IRA was a potential danger to stability; both found the Orange establishment unsavory and perhaps unnecessary; but neither could imagine common purpose, having so long assumed conflicting interests. The anxiety in Dublin was higher—Irish events could hardly be ignored by the Irish government—and yet the British could soldier on, ignoring Irish affairs, repeating yesterday's policies quite isolated from provincial events. This British isolation from the crisis was often a matter of concern by those consumed in that crisis. It was almost unimaginable that the British did not care, should not care. In a singular act, James Anthony Roche threw two CS gas containers into the House of Commons on July 23: "How do you like that, you bastards? Now you know what it's like in Belfast!" But, of course, they didn't. Neither symbolic CS gas drifting through the chamber nor the memory of Belfast rioting on the television did more than distract: the revolting Irish again. Hardly anyone noticed that there had been seventy explosions in Northern Ireland as a result of the secret IRA bombing campaign. Rioting began every weekend and carried on into the next week with gas, baton charges, shots exchanged, and the damaged filling hospital emergency wards while BBC began to report it as the weather:

storms and riots over Northern Ireland, some light truculence in Derry and Strabane, more expected on the morrow—and on to cricket.

In July there were attempts against the lives of the prominent: William Craig, the Reverend Martin Smyth, Grand Master of the County Grand Orange Lodge of Belfast, and Lord Justice Curran. And on the last day of the month an unknown young man, a Catholic, Daniel O'Hare, was shot and killed by the army for, it was claimed, carrying a petrol bomb. And yet there seemed no appropriate government response to the dangers for the famous and the unknown. London was hence lethargic: What was to be done? Dublin was reduced to pieties about the arrival of 1,500 refugees and recycled patriot oratory. The Stormont government, as always under attack by loyalists for being too meek, had no real program. The nationalist politicians were busy attacking each other and agreed only on the need for more reforms unless they spoke of an end to partition—and why reforms if that led to dissolution of the state? And on the edge of the stage the Provos waited for war.

As the riots continued on through the first week of August, the British hope that reform would be sufficient, justice could come with order, bring order, gave those involved little satisfaction. Even justice seen to be done seemed only to encourage the tumultuous. All the rumors of militant Unionist plots to replace Chichester-Clark with a hard man continued to float across the province. Out with O'Neill. Out with his cousin? In with someone. There were lots of someones who waited on the bridge of the seemingly sinking Stormont ship. On August 8, William Craig returned to politics, supported by Harry West, and in a radio interview called for internment. Internment was a good ploy, show the disloyal rascals business was meant, come down with the boot on *them*. Joined by Ian Paisley and a few of the militant Unionists, the ultras called for a new, *firm* Prime Minister—Craig offered himself. All signs indicated constant plotting and a steady erosion of the room for maneuver left to the Stormont government.

One continuing problem for the reluctant reformers around Chichester-Clark was both a failure in perception by the nationalists and the persistence of past contention unrelated to present reality. First, the Catholics did not seem to grasp the nature of the extensive reform program. Much had been done, much was being done, more would be done. It was as if they not only wanted more, no matter what was offered, but also visible humiliation of their enemies: Revenge is sweet. The detailed and turgid items and subitems, advisory clauses and addenda that meant legislative reform, reform creeping through normal Stormont procedures all the while under attack from the Orange hard men, did not satisfy the nationalists, the Catholics. Second, the events that began in 1968 had not been neatly cut off: The nasty and often unnecessary results of legal responses to provocations and parades and demonstrations long forgotten in the whirl of continuing events suddenly reemerged as court cases or reports to add to contemporary confusion. The thrown stones often produced legal ripples that disturbed other waters long after the original riot. Bernadette Devlin had to go to jail; the Samuel Devenney case dragged on to RUC disadvantage; and Orangemen in turn went to jail for their protests. Stormont had no time to explain, no experience catering to Catholics, no control over the past reemerging.

Instead, the cabinet fretted as the other Unionists plotted: on Wednesday,

August 26, the hard man John Taylor became Minister of Home Affairs when Robert Porter resigned. Perhaps necessary for Unionist purposes, the appointment outraged the nationalists—as it was in part meant to do, since their concern would assure loyalist delight. The less than loyal Catholic opposition had been largely consolidated on the previous Friday, August 21, in a new Social Democratic and Labour Party led by Gerry Fitt and including Paddy Devlin, Austin Currie, John Hume, Ivan Cooper, and Patrick O'Hanlon, Stormont MPs, and Senator Patrick Wilson. It was a mixed group united by religion, opposition to the unionists of all flavors, self-interest, and impatience with the old Nationalist party. As an early act, the SDLP expressed the "utmost concern" at Taylor's appointment. Beyond the conventional SDLP the quarrels went on. The People's Democracy, on the margins of events, attacked NICRA, whose spokesmen in turn attacked the new SDLP, also the target of the residue of Fitt's Republican Labour Party, which was left behind in the move to the new group. And Provisional Sinn Féin seized on the national issue, unlike the SDLP, and Office Sinn Féin seized on class, unlike the SDLP. All, however, wanted more, more reforms, more action, more power: less for *them*. Only the Provos, almost irrelevant in conventional political terms, intended to take what they wanted.

The result was that 1970 dribbled away not so much in rising violence as in continuing uncertainty. No public positions changed. Heath and Lynch met at the United Nations session in New York without results. The plots against Chichester-Clark continued as did the movement toward reform. Some few, those involved in adjusting the system, were satisfied with the results. The Northern Ireland Community Relations Commission was at work urging the removal of offensive slogans from provincial walls—an endless and thankless task, for graffiti was a traditional art form, vicious, satirical, and often in its more elaborate presentation splendidly romantic: King Billy on His Horse at one end and Up the Provos at the other with the inevitable splatter of the obscene dripping down the gable ends. Still hate was being whitewashed. Faulkner at Stormont moved that the new Central Housing Executive be confirmed as a public authority and was praised by John Hume: reform at work, reform seen to be done. Sir Arthur Young, criticized by all in a thankless task, resigned and departed on Friday, November 13, where on Monday in London he praised his RUC: "No British bobby going to Ulster could see any difference in the force, except for the color of the uniform. No force has changed so much so quickly." Young may have believed in such a bobby, such a force—many Unionists did—but neither the Catholics nor the disinterested believed in him. His comment was another in what was destined to be a long history of proclamations that the leopard had, at last, changed its spots, now smaller, now going, always still to be found. His replacement as chief constable, Graham Shillington, was welcomed by Craig and Paisley and so viewed as an ominous sign by the defenders of the CCDC, the PD, the Nationalist Party, and a variety of minority spokesmen. A certified angel would have awakened the suspicion of many Catholics if appointed as chief constable. In this and many matters a lifetime of habits could not easily be undone, certainly not by accepting on faith the fact that the Orange machine was consuming itself at Stormont, nibbling away privilege and spitting out concession. The Catholics found it hard to believe even when demonstrably the case.

There were some welcome signs of moderation. Bernadette Devlin on her release from jail indicated that she would advise against riot even if she did appear on the same platform in Paris with Séamus Costello of the Officials, along with a NICRA speaker. Her quibble made no Unionist heart beat faster: She was a foolish and irresponsible child of the times, lethal and dangerous. In the degree that the minority enjoyed her adventures so did the majority find her objectionable—sand in the gears still grated even if the grains were finer. Moderation could not be imagined from Devlin. The Northern Ireland Labour Party expelled Eamonn McCann. With the creation and expansion of the SDLP and the gradual disappearance of the Nationalist Party, the conventional had found a party to compete with the Unionists, to pursue electoral politics, to gobble up the practical from the radicals and the reasonable from the militant nationalists. The SDLP made no pretense of universality, was a confessional home for Northern Catholics of all varieties and so by necessity moderate. Inside were the conventional politicians still not used to being a loyal opposition, still unversed in responsibilities of governing—how could it be otherwise? Outside were the independents like Devlin or McCann or McManus in Fermanagh, South Tyrone, the radicals and the odd republican like Patrick Kennedy of the Republican Labour remnant in Belfast, and of course the men of violence. As yet the Provos were not interested in "politics." Sinn Féin was not a conventional party but a way station for some on the way to war, a cheering section for the campaign, a means of acting on nonmilitary events. It did not entail running in elections or governing in irrelevant or illicit bodies. The party thus provided mostly a forum for republican rhetoric despite Ruairí O Brádaigh's efforts to shape a more effective instrument. The Officials' Republican Club ventures in class politics in the six counties were equally limited and only cost them wider nationalist support. On October 18 Goulding unexpectedly contended that the establishment would not let his lot achieve their ends unless they resorted to violence; but this bellicose posture was seen to be one of his off-the-cuff policy statements rather than evidence of a commitment to an armed struggle. As the Officials moved gradually away from the gun there were many zigs and zags to come, many necessary resignations and defections. For the time being, conventional politics of the minority in Northern Ireland was a mix of the SDLP and the odd independent, and was seen by many Unionists as more of the same: agitation for minor change that would erase the Union for nationalist advantage. Nationalist politics was thus assumed by the more fearful loyalist to be not about regional advantage, practical matters, but about unification, ideal matters.

This was hardly the case. The only nationalists who put the national issue first were the Provos. Beginning with nothing, they had, despite the limitations imposed by scanty resources, come a very long way by the autumn of 1970—much further than most observers assumed. They felt strong enough on September 8 to hold a formal IRA funeral for Michael Kane, a father of five, killed on September 4 when his clothespin detonator went off prematurely while he was trying to blow up an electric pylon on the outskirts of Belfast. The Provos were still operating with awkward, unstable explosive devices constructed with uncertain elements by self-trained engineers: Such trials would often produce errors, usually lethal, always spectacular, and leading to ceremonial military funerals for such "killed on active duty." Such solemn ritual funerals permitted for one brief moment the transcendental Republic to be made real. At Kane's funeral three pistol volleys were fired over his coffin, an honor that made it clear the Provos were doing the bombing. This indicated that the nationalist population would tolerate bombs if not gunmen, funerals if not yet murder.

In fact, the Provos' campaign had escalated to the point that the end-of-the-year figures indicated very substantial costs to the establishment. During the year there had been 153 explosions, forcing a larger, more visible, and more intrusive security presence. On December 30 the Northern Ireland Auditor General report on government expenditures indicated that the cost of the 1969–70 disturbances was almost £5 million. But this was still only money—no member of the army had been killed and only three RUC constables—two by a Crossmaglen car-bomb trap. Still, there had been the 153 bombs in 1970 and regular attacks on customs posts that involved country units and showed the six-county capacity of the IRA. It was the most action since the Tan War. The nationalists seemingly tolerated the bombs, did not disown the Provisionals. There had been no significant shift in the political spectrum to Provo disadvantage; instead, the moderate Unionists were still under attack, the Stickies' class politics pushed by the Republican Clubs and the *United Irishman* had not sold, and the SDLP simply replaced the old Nationalists as a Stormont party—a fatal weakness as the minority population grew more militant, more ambitious, more republican. And so it was not a bad Provo year at all. The IRA recruited, trained, filtered out undesirables—often not a minute too soon—and even deployed most of the new tide of volunteers. Times had changed.

There were those who sought peace not war, accommodation not militancy; some, maybe most, wanted simply peace and quiet. And some would organize for peace and quiet. On November 30 the proper people—the decent, the middle class—had announced the Movement for Peace in Ireland, an opinion-forming organization, in contrast to most of the other more active peace sector, where on the same day the Community Relations Commission funded for two thousand pounds a project to investigate children and conflict. Both efforts on November 30 foreshadowed a long series of projects and proposals and organizations dedicated to peace and conflict resolution: a whole new subfield in academic and analytical studies. Many of the exercises were too amorphous, too academic, ill-conceived or irrelevant, however well-meaning. They all tapped a general desire for tranquillity, a desire that indicated proper sentiments but often required no great sacrifice and returned professional benefits to some. This did not deter a great many from becoming involved in efforts to use analytical tools, particularly of social science, to ameliorate the violence. Doing good, however, proved far more complex than causing trouble. Doing good in an effort to erode the foundations of violence might in time prove worrisome to the men of violence but not at the end of 1970. These were early days for peace work and peace studies. Not so early, however, that many in far places had failed to pencil in Northern Ireland as an example, soon one of the crucial stops on any tour of divided societies, societies under stress, societies of interest to the specialists in troubled times.

As the year closed, the problem for the Provos was not peace but controlling the volunteers who wanted instant war. Then and later the Provos would hardly be aware of the considerable investment in conflict resolution, having dedicated their lives to and risked their lives for the armed struggle. For them 1970 had been a good year. No other player had done as well as the Provos, made as much with as little. No other player had proved an unexpected threat to them.

The Officials in 1970 had gradually hardened their hearts against the Provisionals, out-of-date, men of simple violence, whose tactics—they had no strategy or analysis—were endangering the ultimate goals of the movement. The Officials did not believe a revolutionary situation existed in Ireland and said so. The Officials, in order to deny the Provisionals, became, day by day, more radical, more orthodox Marxist, less republican. Gardiner Place attacked those within republican ranks who attacked them, gave up the old agendas, concentrated on all-Ireland analysis, on other priorities, on lesser realities than the day-to-day events in Northern Ireland. A few militant speeches were made, like Goulding's in October 1970, and many committed republicans would remain dedicated both to physical force and the Easter Republic for many years, but the tides were beginning to run other ways. Few in Dublin GHQ went to the North regularly. A few operations were ordered out of Dublin but mostly the Northern units ran their own war, with GHQ imposing bounds rather than encouraging the militant. The view from GHQ remained very much a view from Dublin adjusted to minimize the Northern developments. Dublin was slowly becoming attuned to scientific socialism, democratic centralism, dialectic analysis. In such an atmosphere the national issue was to become an irritant not an inspiration.

In fact Official Sinn Féin stayed Sinn Féin because the new departure had arisen on the ruins of the old republican movement, because many were still and would continue to be republicans in many traditional ways, because the very words had legitimacy and historical context that could not easily be left behind especially to the Provos, who GHQ saw as neo-fascist. Beyond the ideological division, which was not a shooting matter, a split in two armed bands of the faithful almost inevitably would lead to shooting. The divisions on the ground, where the war was fought and where recruiting took place, abraded—in Dublin an Official might not see a Provo for years, mutually acceptable funerals were often the only common ground, with the two sets of mourners on separate sides, older and wiser and avoiding the others' eyes. So in Belfast a three-man committee of "neutral" republican veterans was established to ease tension and to monitor incidents, one more indication that whatever happened to the republicans had happened before, so that even as the distaste for the other was institutionalized in training sessions, over pints, in the homes of the dedicated, the leadership sought to avoid gunfire in the streets. For the Provos in 1970 the Officials in many ways represented the greater danger: They had kept the name and the headquarters, they had their own republican truth, their own secret army. They might compete and for some time seemed to do so. What persuaded the Provos of the threat was the new direction from Gardiner Place that attracted some radicalized volunteers and radicalized some innocents who had arrived at the door but could compete with the appeal of the Provos' physical force. The Sticks would not stay the course—they said so themselves. The Provos assumed, however, that nationalism would attract more volunteers than socialism; physical force and armed defense more than radical ideas. The Provos' focus was on the British army. And that army was assumed from the first to be a given, would act the part as assigned, would be an IRA asset.

The Provo assumption would have been ridiculed by the British army leadership in Northern Ireland. That leadership included General Freeland (who was to be replaced briefly in February 1971 by Lieutenant General Erskine Crum); Major General Anthony Farrar-Hockley, commander in chief of land operations; and Brigadier Frank Kitson, the military's leading theoretical expert on insurgency and a veteran of Kenya, Malaya, and Cyprus. They saw the IRA not as a secret army but as incompetent gunmen extorting compliance from the fearful Catholics. The British were aware that matters could not be allowed to get out of hand. Many of the involved, not Kitson alone, had long exposure, some firsthand, to anti-Imperial rebels. Most knew the nature of an armed struggle and the damage that a few incompetent rebels might do. It was clear to these officers that there could not, in fact should not, be a military solution. The army should be neutral, opposing the IRA with visible decency, fair play, and lack of provocation while waiting for the reforms to go through Stormont. That was what the book said. Keep order and wait. The major immediate difficulty was that fair play and decency seen to be done to the minority only enraged the majority militants into riot and violence. The Protestants continued to think the army their own, and so however outrageous majority behavior was at times no one could imagine a real Orange armed campaign against the military. This was not the case with the other side. The minority belonged to a different nation and might have a different agenda—certainly it hid two rebel IRAs. The army often had to intervene in Catholic areas, opening an opportunity for IRA provocation unrelated to specific grievances, unlike Orange militants, who came into the streets only because of perceived grievances. This in turn required a hard British army response in order to be fair to the majority, in order to punish provocation and restore stability. Army intervention was inevitably heavy. An army is an army, not a police force. With the best will in the world the military response was crude, painful to innocent civilians, and often violent. The soldiers were not bobbies, would not suffer stones and petrol bombs with equanimity. No one in the Catholic areas ever seemed grateful or fair or forgiving once they did intervene. And if they did not intervene the IRA would run the city.

The problem was that if the army was to continue to be an army and impose order, that imposition assured that normal law could not operate in areas under military occupation. Kitson, whose views were not significant within the British army in 1971 as they were assumed to be by those on the outside, where observers credited him with imposing an anti-insurgency policy that violated democratic norms, had recognized both the problem and the failure of the army's efforts to de-escalate the conflict and erode IRA support: "In the end the IRA were making more headway than we were."* One overriding reason for this headway was

---

*During his tenure as chief of staff, Seán Mac Stiofáin was quite conscious of previous British military actions in recent anti-colonial campaigns. He had a copy of Kitson's *Low-Intensity Operations,* and his own memoirs, *Revolutionary in Ireland* (Edinburgh: Gordon Cremonesi, 1975), cite Kitson a dozen times. It was the Aden example, however, that most influenced

simply that the British army deployed for anti-insurgency—sought to *impose* order rather than keep the peace as the police might do—and so, no matter how elegant and astute the formation of military policy, engendered a rush to insurgency. Treated as insurgents, the IRA could so become. And what else could an army do? The dilemma was fatal and not fully recognized: A decade later army officers still complained that the police were insufficiently aggressive, did not push the limits, did not stay on top of the situation—that is, did not fight a war.

The Provos, then, had the British army as ally that could be counted a constant along with assured loyalist provocation. They had limited competition from the Officials, had the toleration of the Catholics that could be deepened, and had an analysis based on two hundred years of republican practice. They had limited military materiel, untrained volunteers, a paucity of skills, and a very narrow base of support in the Republic—but they had the essentials. There was no single moment when the IRA moved to an irreversible armed struggle. As everyone had slipped easily into the assumptions of the year before in the very first meeting, so little to discuss and so much to do, so, too, did the organization slip easily into war. In January 1971 the Provo Army Council recognized that provocative retaliation against the British army was in progress without any crucial decision needed. The Army Council rarely made any crucial decisions, rarely had to vote: Consensus ran the Provos. After January 1971 some singular incident would become an excuse to make retaliation the norm in public. Billy McKee as Belfast O/C was simply pushing ahead. He had one hundred active-service people diversely armed and backed up by one thousand auxiliary volunteers. There were continual riots; the army conducted arms searches as order decayed; and the republicans practiced their trade. Even Chichester-Clark on January 18 spoke of internment as a means to end disorder.

Craig, Paisley, and the other hard men were still on his heels. They could hear the bombs and drive past the riots. The very day, January 27, that the Prime Minister's party at Stormont with twenty-nine votes to seven easily turned back an amendment condemning the government for its "consistent and deplorable failure to appreciate and adequately deal with the origins of subversion in the community," an RUC constable in Belfast was stabbed in Upper Liberty Street and there was an explosion in Sandy Row. There was now a bomb a day going off in the province. The security forces knew where the IRA was—safe in the Catholic quarters of Belfast and Derry. Why didn't Chichester-Clark act? On February 3 serious rioting broke out in the Kashmir Road and Clonard areas of Belfast. Troops were attacked with Claymore bombs, rocks, steel darts, acid bombs, nail-grenades, regular grenades, and flaming petrol. Then the army-RUC patrols came under submachine gun fire. Military patience was exhausted. This was not simple riot. The next day General Farrar-Hockley held a press conference and revealed publicly that the IRA men who had been meeting with the military—and he named them—McKee, Martin, Frank Card, Kevin and Liam Hannaway—were responsible for the rise in terrorism. And this was quite true.

---

him. Generally, Provisionals looked mainly to Irish history for example, not to theory and texts or even to British practice elsewhere.

And because it was true, the loyalists were outraged: Why had their army been meeting with gunmen? Why wasn't the army shooting avowed rebels instead of taking tea with them? And for the Provos, the British giving out the names was a sign that they had moved into the next stage, milked the military innocence dry. It also indicated that the army felt that they could no longer tame the Provos with kind words while Stormont ground out reforms, no longer isolated the Provos from nationalist support by relying on future reforms and army good behavior, and so no longer dissuade them from making war. In this the army was right. The time for war had come. John Taylor said to the *Times*, "We are going to shoot it out with them. It is as simple as that."

On the next night, Friday, February 5, there was, as could be expected on the weekend, serious rioting in Belfast, more regular than rain. In the Ardoyne petrol bombs set an army Saracen armored car ablaze and the confused troops opened fire on the mob of stone throwers. They hit and killed a young Sinn Féin member, Barney Watts. One of the Ardoyne IRA men moved up to the neighboring Bone, the enclave off the Crumlin Road, to see if the unit there would open up and create a diversion. He then moved on down to New Lodge and asked Billy Reid for help. Reid had no weapons but the locals rushed about and found a grenade and a Sterling submachine gun. The first would not cause much trouble and he did not know how to use the Sterling. Still, he moved off to try. When his chance came, the volunteer emptied the Sterling's magazine in one long burst and immediately withdrew without waiting for any response. On Lepper Street one soldier, Robert Curtis, a twenty-year-old gunner with the Ninety-fourth Locating Regiment of the Royal Artillery, slumped to the ground and curled up without a sound, apparently stunned. Someone put a cigarette in his mouth. It did not glow. He lay there unmoving with the cigarette dangling in the dim and flickering light of Lepper Street. A policeman crouched down beside him and discovered that he was dead, hit under the armpit by a single slug that had left almost no entrance wound. Sprawled on the Belfast street, victim of the Second Battalion, Provisional IRA, Curtis was the first soldier to die in Ireland since the Tan War fifty years before.

The killing was not over. The Provos lost a volunteer at almost the same time Curtis was hit. James Saunders, the twenty-two-year-old O/C of the Bone, was shot dead in the Oldpark area of West Belfast by the British army. The gunfire continued along the Shankill Road. Another civilian was killed. There was rioting that night in Derry as well, shops were set on fire and burned through the night. Dawn brought further riots and then again the sound of gun battles along Leeson Street. West Belfast is largely flat, low-lying buildings, endless terraces of small houses, with a few tall public buildings or developments. Sound carries. Everyone could hear the sound of high-velocity weaponry cracking and echoing over the city. Later, during the morning, Chichester-Clark, pale, his face drawn and his voice heavy, declared on television that "Northern Ireland is at war with the Irish Republican Army Provisionals." The Provos had their war.

6

The Armed Struggle Escalates: February 1971–August 1971

*For we hold that a nation has no right to surrender its
declared and established independence, and that
even a minority has a right to resist that surrender
in arms.*

Robert Erskine Childers, speech at his court-martial by the Irish
Free State on November 18, 1922, which passed a death sentence,
carried out on November 24

At two o'clock on Monday morning, February 8, a controlled explosion at the northeast corner of Saint Stephen's Green in Dublin severely damaged the statue of Wolfe Tone. The bombers, Northern loyalists knew all too well the cause of Ulster's distress: the Catholic Republic's malevolent ambitions. The men of the IRA had brought war to their province, in large part because the proper guardians of the system in London had lacked the will to stop them. Worse, not only the suspect British Labour Party but also the old ally Tories still seemed bemused at demands for unnecessary reforms and remained immune to provocation by the disloyal. No one in power or out in Great Britain, certainly none of the trendy media people attracted like carrion birds to Northern violence, understood Ulster reality, grasped that the IRA not only intended war—was waging war—but would also destroy all that had been cherished and defended over the centuries. The IRA wanted a thirty-two-county Republic, Tone's Republic. They saw only civil disorder. The British army saw merely armed agitation. The Orange establishment admitted a need to adjust, to reform; but there was a limit. And what did the IRA care?

What did the gunmen care of agitation and reform and issues? What did they care of civil rights or even fair play? They wanted everything. Murderers and bombers, they often ignored their own government in Dublin, conveniently for Dublin. The gunmen often ignored their own Catholic hierarchy at Maynooth, conveniently for the Roman church. They ignored the qualms of their own Northern people, ignored civilized standards, ignored all restraint. They were intent on imposing their will on the whole island and Ulster first: to the advantage of Dublin, to the advantage of the Roman Catholic Church, and to the advantage of Northern nationalists. A bomb at Tone's feet in Dublin indicated symbolically their analysis.

Look what had so far been accomplished in the name of the renegade Tone, Protestant and French officer but an Irish rebel and a republican and so a traitor to history. War had come to Ulster, a war waged by the IRA cunningly and with provocation, with recourse to brutality and terror, a war waged regardless of the costs, waged by those beyond shame or compromise. The IRA monster was, as feared all along, real. And what was to be done? One bomb in the Republic, in Dublin, in front of Tone was a beginning, would sharpen political minds.

Amid the clamor of Irish politics as the first year of the armed struggle continued, voices crying to prevent a wilderness created by Provo bombs and Provo intentions, had lacked purpose. All the loyalists recognized the threat, even some of the nationalists feared the gunmen. There was no consensus on a response, not from loyalists or the British, not from Northern nationalists or the Dublin establishment. Only the Provisional Army Council and the faithful within the republican movement seemed to know *exactly* what was to be done. The IRA military campaign would escalate just as fast as the arms and men became available. Volunteers were hurriedly trained and deployed. Gear was rounded up and brought to the North. The intended beneficiaries—the Irish—could be persuaded to legitimize operations as necessary that would have horrified them a short while before. Increasingly, intensity meant eroding moderation and rising toleration, true in small, dirty wars as in large, total ones. There was no way that either the Stormont reformers or the British political establishment could fashion a package of concessions sufficient to lure nationalist support without alienating the loyalists to the point of open rebellion. And such a loyalist rebellion would only add to the turmoil that operated to the advantage of Ulster's foes, only erode British military capacities to IRA advantage, only alienate London, would only make matters worse. And if, as seemed likely, the British authorities finally saw the light and chose repression, it might be too late. The IRA could simply go further underground, assured of the support of the nationalists in the North and the current of rising sympathy of the people, perhaps even the politicians, in the South. If matters continued the province was endangered by British sloth; if matters were taken in hand the province would still be riddled with war and subversion. Everything seemed to favor the IRA—even Tone's statue had not been badly damaged.

Dublin, amid the complexities of the Arms Trial did not want further involvement in the Northern problem. London had a new cabinet, other priorities, found Irish matters distasteful, tended to lethargy, and unlike their men in place at Stormont or Lisburn military barracks outside Belfast, felt no sense of urgency. Inside Stormont most energy was expended on internal maneuver, recriminations, and rationalizations, while inside British military headquarters at Lisburn, the army concentrated on the limited options available in the novel Irish arena. The British army's policies had been shaped in the Third World, and were more suited to Oman or Kenya. At least the military and police persisted with the problems of imposing order. They had to act. The provincial politicians of all varieties simply argued the pace of moves already futile.

What had occurred in Ireland since the seven, unknown men of the IRA Army

Council had sat about a table in January 1970 planning a war to be won without assets was a remarkable triumph of revolutionary will. For once the IRA had got it right: Keep applying the formula of faith and eventually it fits the facts. The seven had known in their heart of hearts what was wrong with Ireland, what needed to be done, and what the results should be. The analysis could be complex but it could also be shouted out by a man on the back of a truck, sewn on banners, understood by the dim and limited. And so it was. Every new volunteer was so indoctrinated and most believed.

The IRA wanted above all else to wage war and so every commander and every volunteer had acted to that effect. For two hundred years republicans, conspirators, Fenians, bombers and assassins and volunteers, members of the secret army, had sought to wage war, a war legitimized by the toleration of the Irish people. And now again an opportunity arose. Decisions within that secret army now evolved easily from events, from habit, from the actions of the British army, from the contingent and unforeseen, from the state of play, but always from a reading of reality that indicated cause, means, and intent. Each decision was taken without thought and was in no real way a part of a master plan. Each decision was taken within the context of historic republican analysis: A grand strategy was simply to seize any means to wage a war of national liberation.* At the beginning of 1971, when the Army Council authorized a move from retaliation to offensive operations, such an acceleration had already been undertaken by those on the spot in Belfast. Belfast until later remained the key and was always the core of the Provisionals. The Army Council was more than anything simply legitimizing a stage that could only be seen as separate by those analysts inclined to the tidy. The IRA campaign moved along by jumps and starts, incorporated more lethal means when available and appropriate, evolved from a primitive hasty defense to the low-intensity but real war of February 1971. This war was sufficiently effective to drive the loyalists to bomb in Dublin. In the Irish arena this was a sure sign that the loyalists sensed change and threat.

The great boost to the direction of events foreseen by the IRA came, first, from the British counter-responses to provocation, and second, from the mix of factors that led to the alienation of much of the nationalist population from remedial politics. The IRA felt it knew the British and knew the futility of reform. In the first case, the IRA played a major part, cunningly fashioning tactics to prod the British army into acting as an army. Politicians who sent armies out to act as police are regularly disappointed at the unexpected zeal soon displayed by those who often direct traffic from an armored car. In the second case the perception of the IRA and the ideas of Irish republicans had more takers, proved not unrelated to reality and to British events and British army practice, stoked the general nationalist impatience and disappointment. This hardening alienation allowed

---

*Real armies, academicians, and analysts tend to focus on their concern with structured strategy, tactical options, and the nature of deployment, while gunmen with less time and at great risk (unless the conflict escalates into an irregular war) rarely do more than accept the grand strategy expressed in rebel slogans and concentrate on the techniques of persistence. *Cf.* J. Bowyer Bell, "An Irish War: The IRA's Armed Struggle, 1969–90: Strategy as History Rules OK," *Small Wars and Insurgencies,* Vol. 1, No. 3, December 1990, pp. 239–265.

the move from Catholic defender to secret army. The move was tolerated by most nationalists and supported by some.

What made the IRA war work was the deployment of the republican dream in a way congenial to the recruits without alienating the nationalist base. This was possible in large part because of the attitudes, priorities, and loyalties that the IRA could manipulate. The core of the Official IRA did not want such a war and pursued policies that would in time make participation impossible. GHQ had already by February 1971 made life difficult for their Northern units by imposing ideology over perceived reality. A loyalist gunman looked more like the gunman he was than a working-class mate that he was suppose to be. The Provos treated such gunmen as British imperial agents and defended the nationalists: a petty bourgeois, sectarian nationalist response according to the ideologues; sensible according to most of the threatened. The Stickies were reading themselves out of the play, leaving the major role to the Provos. Many in the Gardiner Place headquarters did not *want* their politics disturbed by war and those who advocated a role for a secret army also agreed with such politics and so could be edged away from the center. The Stickies' political center could only hold the ideologically converted volunteers in the North. Their ranks began to thin.

For the Provos there was a need to turn away volunteers. Many arrived as believers. The others soon became republicans. For the Provos the whole process of escalation had been so *natural* and predictable as to be beyond comment. That was the key to their strategy. No one had to be converted to read reality—the British army was at the front door and the Orange bigot on display. Nothing had to be imported, nothing fashioned by ideologues, nothing sold to the people, nothing rationalized because of events.

Although the Provos had their war, the arena largely remained in Belfast, along the fringes of the nationalist ghetto. Only those on bombing missions, also largely within Belfast, penetrated hostile areas; but this they did with increasing regularity as the campaign accelerated. Elsewhere organizers or local sympathizers moved with less dispatch. Even the notoriously republican territory of South Armagh produced few activists and little action until Joe Cahill, on a building site in Belfast, complained to his fellow workers from near Crossmaglen. Many of the six-county units, long atrophied, simply met and then waited to see what developed. Some remained technically loyal to the Dublin Official GHQ, largely because they were not contacted by anyone. Everywhere, however, units were coming back to life. Sometimes a unit was no more than a few old men meeting in a back room in Leitrim or Monaghan. In Derry Seán Keenan, who had been dismissed from the IRA by Goulding, ostensibly for his association with the *Voice of the North* propaganda project out of Dublin but mainly because he was an opponent of the new departure, was associated in the revival with three middle-aged republicans, Tommy Carlin, Joe Coyle, and Tommy McCool. Derry had always been a nationalist rather than a republican area; and after August 1969 almost all local attention remained focused on defense of the area and not on armed struggle.

At first the British army was seen neither as enemy nor alien and Keenan consequently sounded old-fashioned. In Derry and elsewhere the shifts of the Provos, first from Catholic defenders that the nationalist population had innocently assumed them to be in 1969 to a military militia, and then to a secret army opposed to the British, had to be gradual. Keenan could not tell the Derry people to oppose the British army as they opposed the Orange militants—they had to be inspired, day by day, by the core of the revived IRA, by the tactics of provocation, by the acts of the British army, and finally by the direction of events. In the meantime defense was the key. In the United States during the organization of NORAID and other republican groups, Keenan would highlight the need for defense while stressing the British army as the ultimate enemy. In Derry, where most of the nationalist people sought defenders, not a secret army engaged in a guerrilla war against the British, the Provos had to move cautiously, defense being the key—and compete as well with the Officials, who had only class war plans, ideological dreams quite unlike the Provo agenda.

The local Official unit in Derry under John White was quite visible. White was much younger than the Provo leaders, more articulate, pleasingly radical, a part of the entire thrust of the 1969–71 agitation. He had charisma and they had old slogans. And White didn't bother with the details of the split. He simply explained to his IRA unit that Dublin was reorganizing, and few of the new recruits cared much about any split or even what Keenan's old Provos were doing. Many of the young Stickies, mobilized by the civil rights demonstrations, felt closer to White's radicalism and the ideas out of Dublin that filtered through to the North. They had joined the IRA to defend and were content to discover that they were revolutionaries as well, volunteers with ideas and soon guns. None had the traditional grounding in republican ideas and attitudes that seemed to come with the Belfast turf. None had any of the experience of rural dissent and violent protest that had been absorbed by republicanism in parts of the countryside. They were for the moment content in the Official IRA.

In the summer of 1970 the Derry Provos suffered a profound loss when on Friday evening, June 26, a bomb detonated prematurely in Tommy McCool's house in the Creggan housing estate. He was killed, as were his two children and both Carlin and Coyle. The Derry Provos were almost eliminated. Their marginality was poignantly indicated when McCool's IRA funeral was hardly noted outside the city and little understood by those who watched the procession. The rite seemed from another time and place. As late as October 1970, Martin McGuinness, one of the more militant of the growing number of alienated young people, sought to join the IRA by signing up with the Officials. There was no serious Provo presence. Those left from the Carlin group clustered about Phil O'Donnell, a former British paratrooper who could pass on his military experience but had no arms and hence could advocate no immediate armed struggle. Arms were crucial to the Provos, less so to the Stickies, who in Derry were stocked with young talent and radical ideas. In time McGuinness and his friends found John White and the Stickies insufficiently militant, more a radical political organization than a secret army in the making. They left White and met with Keenan and then with Mac Stiofáin and O Conaill. They moved into the organization but not until the end of the summer in 1972 did the parallel O'Donnell group disappear. Gradually the Derry unit under McGuinness became a rival to White. The Derry Stickies, however, unlike the Officials in Belfast under McMillen, remained a major factor for some time.

Elsewhere the Officials in the North were denied the defender role by the Provos, seldom guided by Dublin GHQ (Mick Ryan was the only member of GHQ regularly in the North), and so tried with diminishing success to pursue ideologically sound ideas that in practice assured advantage to the Provos, whose role played on nationalist prejudice and need. Almost until 1972, however, the republican situation was not clear, certainly not to those who were involved in the clang and chaos of events. Those involved often did not feel that Stickie ideas precluded the gun or else that Provo faith was simple Green nationalism.

One of the results of the new direction of the Officials and the schism was that the competition for control and influence could not be limited to the clash of ideas. Many observers predicted the rivalry would end in a feud. In Belfast by 1971, the two groups of poorly controlled, armed young men scattered over the same territory would argue. They would compete over the territory and ideas and prestige and often over the same arms. They would focus on their close rivals rather than the British. Some felt the most dangerous enemy to be heretical republicans.

The Stickies had a dozen units scattered through the city but were strong only along the Falls and in the Markets in Belfast. The Provos had fourteen units that emerged as the three battalions of the Belfast Brigade, an IRA larger and even better armed than at any time since the Tan War days. And the Provos could only be effectively challenged by competition in a war Official GHQ did not want or on the ground in a feud that neither leadership wanted but both suspected was inevitable. There was room for only one secret army, and the Provos intended to be it. In turn the Stickies felt that they and their ideas represented the future, that the Provos were relics of an unfortunate, sectarian past, Green Fascists whose campaign was alienating the Protestant working class and prolonging the unnecessary violence. The Stickies assumed the Provos had been left behind by evolution and would fossilize.

Whatever the assumptions, the clash of visions was unavoidable and so too was recourse to force. There had been fights over the distribution of the *United Irishman* in Provo areas, threats made, and in April 1970 those first shots had been fired in Anderstown that had wounded McMillen slightly. A truce had been arranged. The further up the republican totem pole the less the leaders wanted to fight each other—they might abhor their old comrades but they saw no need for gunfights; each assumed history would vindicate the faith. But throughout 1970 both sides accumulated grievances as well as new volunteers who knew little of the old days of a single movement. The continued recriminations in the pages of the *UI* and *Republican News*, at pubs and on the street, produced the scuffles and confrontations in January 1971 that led to the formation of a three-man committee of older republican neutrals to arbitrate any disputes. The necessity for exclusive possession of the faith is, however, not amenable to committees and compromises: Either you possess the way into the future or they do. In 1971 the route was still blurred, the Officials still republicans, the competition potentially lethal. In March 1971 the truce collapsed.

On Friday, March 5, the Officials attacked the British army troops billeted in Henry Taggart Memorial Hall in Ballymurphy. The local Stickies had decided to have a go without McMillen's and GHQ's permission. GHQ often found out about Northern events from the radio news. And with no one to say no, the volunteers had opened up on the British. No one in nationalist Belfast at least could fault an attack on the British army—except, in this case, the Provos. Ballymurphy was the Provo heartland. A Stickie attack was provocative. The next day they snapped up the Stickies' Ballymurphy O/C who had ordered the attack and pistol-whipped him. The remainder of the weekend was given over to an escalating feud that included shootings and kidnappings. On Leeson Street on March 8, the British army, making no effort to intervene, watched the shoot-out from the sidelines with considerable glee. There was no one to say no or rather say no effectively.

On Monday evening a Provo team decided not to shoot the number-two Official, Jim Sullivan, in front of his wife but instead burned down a pub around him. The Provos then shot up the Cracked Cup pub where McMillen was drinking with other Stickies. None were hit in the barrage. Billy McKee, meanwhile, was rounding up Official hostages. McMillen, once out of the Cracked Cup, ordered the assassination of eleven Provo commanders in response. The immediate result was that Charlie Hughes, O/C of the Provos' D Company in the Lower Falls, a popular young commander who had aided the Officials the previous year, was shot and killed while standing on a front porch on Cyprus Street off the Falls. Many minds were then concentrated and a cease-fire was called. The truce did not come into effect before Joe Cahill's brother Tom, a well-known Provo from Ballymurphy, was shot several times by three Stickies while he scrambled around on his milk float trying to put a magazine in his pistol. The truce survived, as did Tom Cahill, but the police found his magazine when he could not and so a court sentenced him to two years for possessing ammunition, thus adding insult to severe injury. The ill feelings cankered rather then disappeared, especially as the Provos moved into a dominant position on the ground by pursuing policies that the Officials felt were not simply wrong but massively counterproductive, alienating the Protestant working class. The political conversion of the Protestants was for the Officials the ultimate key to Ireland future. They felt that the Provos were not only corrupting the nationalists with an atavistic appeal but resisting the natural, dialectical flow of history. Provo commander Billy McKee machine-gunning Protestant workers with his Thompson from a position in the yard of Saint Matthew's Catholic church was symbol and sign of everything the Officials abhorred. It was just that image that paid the Provos returns in much of Belfast: an aggressive defense by true nationalists not only against loyalists acting as the Crown's surrogates but also against British security forces that had by February 1971 alienated much of the minority population.

Many safe middle-class Catholics and many nationalists isolated in the country wanted nothing more than peace and quiet and a chance to exploit the reforms engendered by the civil rights marches and demonstrations. They felt less need of defense, and opposed IRA action as provocation. In fact the establishment of the SDLP gave those Catholics inclined to political solutions a vehicle more relevant and more inclusive than the old Nationalist Party, which was gradually disintegrating.* The new SDLP, as the name indicated, included all sorts and condi-

*Cf. Ian McAllister, *The Northern Ireland Social Democratic and Labour Party, Political Opposition in a Divided Society* (London: Macmillan, 1977).

tions, from Fitt and Paddy Devlin, the Belfast republicans, workingmen, to Derry's John Hume out of Maynooth, a Derry teacher with a small-business career. There were radicals and old country nationalists, solicitors and farm laborers. Mostly there were middle-class activists and Catholic voters. The party did not have universalist pretensions, no Northern Ireland Labour Party class ideas nor Alliance dream of a cross-community mutuality of interests, no class politics, no Catholic ideology, political or social, not much interest in big ideas.

The SDLP was constructed as a confessional party, most closely resembling the Christian Democrats of Italy, a party that encompassed a wide spectrum of social and economic interests cemented with Catholicism. In Italy there were the Communists to cement Catholic solidarity and in Ireland there were the loyalists. In the Irish Republic all the parties were in a sense Catholic, even and at times especially the Labour Party because everyone was a Catholic. In Northern Ireland the SDLP was Catholic because the majority parties, Unionist all, were closed, focused as every loyalist organization on a defense of the Protestant way of life. So the SDLP from the first appealed only to the minority. Not only did the SDLP swiftly supplant the Nationalists, it also revealed a change in the nature of Northern Ireland Catholic society: younger, better educated, somewhat more skillful, questioning and optimistic. The distant purpose of the party may have been to oversee a transformation in the island's political structure, but the prime focus was on the local rewards that electoral politics could bring to the involved and to those they represented.

A new generation had come of age during a time of miserable postwar austerity that had ended with the escalation of hope engendered by the 1968–69 civil rights campaign. The Nationalist Party could not incorporate the new, in some cases the hardly tried, and so appeared stodgy, compliant, and irrelevant, a clutch of aging men about the parish pump ineffectually whinnying about just grievances. Tumultuous protest had replaced denied petitions and sullen boycotts. The old Nationalist Party had, as would any passing generation, sneered at the young radicals filled with ideas and presumptions. Then unexpectedly the Nationalists, failing to tame the radicals or watch its conservative flank, had been bustled offstage by new men. The new men, some not so young, shared a faith in electoral politics and a belief in incremental reform. They wanted a piece of the action. They saw no point in seizing the Nationalist Party—there was little to seize anyway but old debts and old feuds. They were shrewd, capable, intimate with their own, and doubtful of grand ideas. Few would have had trouble in Leeds or Liverpool or Dublin Central or even Brooklyn. As Irish politicians all wanted justice, dignity, a bit of their own back, unity some day but mostly a decent part of what was to be had at the moment.

Their primary problem, other than those accruing to any new party replacing an old one, was to fashion a means to act on events. There were two huge obstacles: first, their inevitable minority standing in the province as a whole, and second, the competition of the romantic and lethal republicans within the minority. And all the while the thunder and turmoil of violence continued to alienate the majority and encourage the republican minority. At birth the SDLP had to appear relevant. The Nationalists had not. The republicans claimed they were. The loyalists were in disarray and uninterested in the problems of moderate Catholics. The SDLP was on its own.

Some political benefits could be reaped from the disorders. The Provos cared little for conventional politics. The Officials, fewer on the ground, were involved in on-the-job training in radical politics with ideas that alienated much of the minority, deeply conservative about most social and many economic issues. Thus, the SDLP could gain office, move into the new reform bureaucracies, present effective petitions, perform visible service, gain some of the benefits spent to ensure civil order, and thereby find a vital role that would be rewarded by votes and office. And office—local, provincial, national—was power and power made parties work. This would be possible if the people were not distracted by the gunmen, by the lure of great gain promised but not yet delivered, the attraction of the secondary benefits of vengeance achieved and malice rewarded. If the SDLP could sell bread now and let the honey wait, then appetites would grow for the supplies at hand. All the SDLP in 1971 needed to do was organize and wait, grow by increments, and pay with reasonable promises—and hope that the violent din would ease so that the voice of reason could be heard.

The SDLP was a Catholic party and made no real effort to seek votes or support among Protestants. The leadership was mostly middle class except in the inner cities and most conventional and conservative; solicitors, pub owners, salesmen, clerks, small shopkeepers, the lace curtain Irish with unpaid mortgages and children to educate. Could one party lashed together with the old faith do for the whole lot? The only complex ideological question the SDLP members chose to face was their attitude toward the political space between the immediate goal of reforming the province—where agreement with some of the majority was surely possible—and the dream of that distant, vague, ultimate goal of a united Ireland—where agreement with none of the majority was conceivably possible. After reform, what then? Would the lure of unification draw the party away from provincial politics? Could the SDLP be a loyal opposition in a province dominated by loyalists who tended to see each reform as part of a unification agenda? Did the SDLP even want to be such an opposition? How could the party calm majority fears and hold to the dream of the nationalists? How compete with the republicans, who sought all now with a gun?

While the SDLP leaders might feel their organization and agenda vital, a major player in 1971, hardly anyone else in the province paid them equal attention. Events in Belfast were too violent, too dramatic, too dangerous to divert concern from what appeared to be an urban guerrilla war within the United Kingdom: an armed struggle in a modern western state. On February 11, 1971, the Ministry of Defense noted that since July 1970, 743 pounds of explosives, 8,070 yards of fuse, 2,618 detonators, 282 assorted weapons, and approximately 40,000 rounds of ammunition had been discovered and 171 persons charged with unlawful possession. The next day a law was signed making it obligatory for persons with knowledge of deaths or injuries caused by gunshot or explosive devices or offensive weapons to inform security forces. The authorities knew that the republicans using all those weapons also had access to secret medical treatment, to advanced communications, to safe houses, and to all sorts of aid and comfort. Matters had gone beyond petrol bombs and the occasional sniping of the past.

The fundamentalist loyalists had long known this. What they found increasingly difficult to understand was why the security forces did not act effectively. Why did not the army clear out the traitorous ghettos? Why weren't obvious suspects interned? Internment, in fact, became the favored means of Orange hawks, even some Orange moderates, to stop the drift toward open rebellion. Something surely had to be done. Stormont was under threat and Chichester-Clark dithered. On February 20 Terence O'Neill had indicated a preference for direct rule from London—an overt betrayal that confirmed the militants assumptions about him. All Stormont needed was that the British army put the boot in. Throw the gunmen and their friends into internment camps and there would be no more trouble. There had not been in the past. Why now?

In Dublin, on the same day that O'Neill called for direct rule, Lynch suggested adjusting the Republic's laws so that a new kind of Irish society might be created equally agreeable to North and South. This only confirmed the unionist assumptions about him and the South's unchanging ambition for a united Ireland. Papist, Republican Ireland was hardly going to become attractive by tinkering with the constitution: It was a way of life that was at stake in Ulster. Ulster was at stake. After all on BBC's "Panorama" ten days later on March 1, the Taoiseach noted that Dublin's claim on the six counties was fundamental and he would not abandon it. And yet there was no feeling of urgency in those responsible for the Stormont system. No call went out for defenders. In fact, Chichester-Clark had welcomed Lynch's Dublin speech, had met with Cardinal Conway on "community relations"—the first such contact in fifty years—and on March 2 announced that the RUC would not be rearmed. On March 4 Maudling came to Northern Ireland, spoke vaguely at Stormont, and went home with the sound of gunfire still to be heard in Belfast streets. No one seemed to care.

On Saturday, March 6, after two days of rioting, including the Officials' attack on the army at Henry Taggart Memorial Hall, Chichester-Clark told a press conference that there was full agreement on security matters with London. He had no other initiatives to report. The only cheerful news for the loyalists had been the reports of the British army standing idly by on March 8 when the Provos and Stickies fought it out on Leeson Street. That gunmen were free to use Belfast streets as their arena was a sign of the times.

Then on March 9, a Tuesday, all the horror that an armed struggle implies became very real—urban guerrilla war, even waged with great restraint, even waged with far more control than McKee or McMillen could exert, was always a dirty, ruthless, brutal business. And so it proved in Northern Ireland—again. Early that evening Paddy McAdorey and two other Provos while drinking in Mooney's Bar in the center of Belfast struck up a conversation with three young, off-duty soldiers from the Royal Highland Fusiliers, Joseph McCraig, eighteen, his younger brother John, seventeen, and Douglas McCaughey, twenty-three. The six moved on to another pub and later drove out toward Ligoneil to a "party." At about seven-thirty the car stopped. The three young Scots got out, still clutching beer bottles, to relieve themselves in the roadside ditch. They were each shot in the back of the head and killed. The three were soon found on Whitebrae Road: The two brothers were sprawled together and McCaughey was propped up on the embankment, his beer glass still in his hand. The general response was horror, horror at murder, horror at the murder of three young men, horror at murder under the guise of friendship and horror by many republicans that the cause had come to this, wee boys on a lark shot in the back. The Officials and the Provos both denied responsibility. Two of the three IRA men were questioned but never charged. McAdorey was later shot dead in a gunfight with troops on August 9 in Jamaica Street in Ardoyne. The British army announced that all the under-eighteen troops would be withdrawn from the province. Ulster was once again different, too dangerous for boy soldiers. Maulding condemned the killing and said the army would not be forced into retaliating. Jack Lynch in Dublin condemned the killers as "enemies of the Irish people." Everyone in authority, nearly everyone in Ireland, was stunned and horrified.

Twenty years later, after thousands of deaths and horrors unimaginable that summer, the three young Scots are still remembered. A poem begins starkly, "Filled with Irish beer and bullets." The three young Scots have a place in the long litany fashioned from atrocity, dreadful deaths, and spent lives. Even some of the Provos were taken aback since the killings had broadened the rules of IRA engagement restricting attacks to troops on duty. Increasingly the rules of Provo engagement had been broadened, greater risks were taken with innocent lives— already nine civilians had been injured in a pub bombing in County Down and a woman bringing a child back from school had been hit in a sniper attack. And already, especially after the three Scots, the realization began to spread through the Provos that their offensive campaign would be tolerated, even if it proved dangerous to the innocent, the transient, and the unlucky, and brutal in execution. Public nationalist horror would not mean private betrayal. The gunmen could operate and the streets of Belfast and Derry were no longer safe.

The loyalists wanted the province made safe, the streets secure, the countryside tranquil —as under Stormont, as in the olden days. They wanted the suspects interned and the activists killed and vengeance taken. On March 12, four thousand shipyard workers called for internment at a mass meeting. Lord Hunt, who had authored the first report on the RUC, urging reforms, indicated to a Scottish newspaper that internment should be seriously considered. On March 16 Chichester-Clark flew to London for talks with Heath, Maudling, and Defense Secretary Lord Carrington. Lieutenant General Sir Harry Tuzo (GOCNI), military commander of the province, was present. Something had to be done. Even Chichester-Clark's moderate Unionists wanted action. Terror was loose in the streets. Chichester-Clark flew back to tell Stormont on March 19 that reinforcements would be on the way—another 1,300 soldiers, bringing the total for the province to 9,700. This was not enough, not for the militants but, more important, not for much of the Unionist Party. O'Neill had introduced reforms that shattered the assurance of the system and he had been discarded to stop the decay. Instead his cousin Chichester-Clark had dithered while the decay continued, while the IRA organized and took to the street. A gawky, well-meaning man perhaps but lurching about without result, the Prime Minister could not persuade the British government to make a serious move. A strong, immediate response was necessary—not a penny packet of soldiers.

Chichester-Clark knew he had let the side down in not forcing London's hand. They would not listen, so he would resign. General Tuzo, the British army commander, appealed to him to stay. He would not. Then a personal appeal came from Heath. He would still go. Lord Carrington suddenly arrived with General Sir Geoffrey Baker on Saturday, March 20, to try his hand. Having at last displayed firmness, Chichester-Clark would not be moved.

At ten on the same day, as the arguments went on at Stormont, six women dressed in combat jackets and black berets, the paramilitary uniform of the Provos, marched from Oldpark to the Ardoyne to protest internment by remand—keeping suspects in prison without charges for long periods. The paramilitaries not only controlled their street but also those who would march on them. Increasingly protest and parades were focused on issues arising from the Provos' armed struggle and subsequent security response. No one heeded the NICRA marches or the radicals' dedication to immediate social change. Everyone could see that the Provos had the initiative. They had in their way run off Chichester-Clark.

On the evening of March 20 the Prime Minister resigned because he "saw no other way of bringing home to all concerned the realities of the present constitutional, political, and security situation." On Tuesday, March 23, Brian Faulkner was elected Prime Minister twenty-six votes to four, opposed by William Craig, by Paisley and his fundamentalists, by Harry West, and it was assumed by some of his own votes. Faulkner was outside the traditional Ulster elite of landowners with plummy British accents, military titles, and membership in the proper London clubs. Faulkner's family was in trade; though successful, skilled, and comfortable, he was not gentry. In a more progressive society, even in England long before, he would long ago have been accepted and integrated into the proper and powerful. He was rich and intelligent, familiar with the world, competent and shrewd. He was also a member of the Grand Orange Lodge, very much a straight-arrow Unionist; yet his rise to power a few years before would have been considered both revolutionary and a triumph of an expanded establishment. Now it was inevitable. The center of gravity at Stormont had moved to the right; and beyond were the fundamentalists and street-corner bigots.

In 1971 Faulkner was a last effort to make Stormont work before the unacceptable face of Unionism in the form of Craig and West or even Paisley destroyed all credibility in London and all legitimacy in the province. For years considered a hard-line Unionist tempered only by ambition, he now became the smiling face of Stormont, the last station before the end of the line and the mob's men in power. Once he would have been the mob's man but times had changed. Now he had become, without moving, a moderate. The ultraloyalists had moved on and they knew exactly what they did not want—essentially the events of the past four years—but not how to turn back the clock. Faulkner was from the first at risk. His parliamentary competence, his past record of bringing industry to the province, his firm Unionist position on security issues, his support by the British Tory government, all so important in London, were at best frail support given the capacity of the ultras to maim anyone who did not produce appropriate results.

The results that they most desired were quite beyond any one politician's capacity. Who could turn back time? Even if the IRA jinni could be put back into the bottle, it would be a different bottle, a different cork, a different world. Stormont could not be restored. Even the necessary order and the rule of law—the IRA and Catholic pretensions confounded—was no easy matter. Many in and out of the establishment, the British army, the London center, believed that *in time* all the paramilitaries could be isolated and their support eroded by the benefits of peace and prosperity. Everyone, including the IRA, believed that *in time* someone would win. Paisley and Craig cared nothing for winning in that long run. They and theirs had short views, wanted immediate results, order now, law later, annihilation not attrition. And those short views had great power to exert on the responsible. Although Faulkner's Stormont ship was far from sinking, the vessel in a rising, raging sea required cunning handling and perhaps oil on the waters.

Increasingly the oil that most loyalists sought would be supplied by the introduction of internment under the Special Powers Act. Like much else in Northern Ireland, internment meant more than a simple dictionary would indicate. Internment was an outward and visible sign that the system could resort to any appropriate means to defend the Protestant province, to crush the pretensions of the disloyal, to display as well as possess power. Internment, thus, was not simply the capacity to jail suspects who could not be processed by the judicial system in an ordinary way because of the special circumstances. Internment was also a means to humiliate the minority. And in so doing the act would reassure a majority perpetually in need of reassurance. The problem was that coupled with the great symbolic power of internment, a power only loosely understood outside the province, were many nasty details. In the old days the RUC could sweep up the potential gunmen and their friends. Republicans were known, available, and rare. Internment could work. By 1971 it might not.

The loyalists, especially the fundamentalists, wanted a victory over the present, over the direction of events, over history; and in the end this could only be achieved if the minority accepted such a victory as inevitable and unavoidable. In the prevailing conditions in Northern Ireland, the minority could not be forced to be humble in their hearts because the kind of power necessary to *make* them humble had to be founded on the assurance of timeless domination and absolute capacity to punish. This power no longer existed.

The excitement of confrontation had thrown up the new. The old republicans were easy, but what of the new? And there were radicals like Bernadette Devlin and Michael Farrell and Eamonn McCann. Were they proper targets? What of the even more conventional figures like Hume and Ivan Barr, chairman of the NICRA executive, and Paddy Devlin, Fitt, and the independent MP Frank McManus? They were not like the old nationalists but not gunmen either—and not even very radical except in their refusal to accept the system. These visible agitators were a constant source of majority anguish. Their loyalist opponents on the streets of Ulster, Ian Paisley or Major Bunting, or in the Parliament at Stormont, Craig and West, felt them to be little more than front men for treason. Should such treason hidden under reform banners be permitted? Certainly the treasonous gunmen, the Provos and Officials, were still on the streets. Why were they loose? What was happening to the province?

In fact it was not only the loyalists who had difficulty with the new cast but nearly all observers. In 1968 and 1969 everything had seemed clear to the London of the Labour Party or to the newly arrived television camera crews. The young people were wearing white hats and faced a sectarian police in dark caps serving a bigoted system. The Unionists were bigots and Stormont an anachronism and the

IRA gunmen the bogeymen of the majority. The radicals were right, the streets belong to reform, and the loyalists were without merit—history's losers at last. All this external assurance had dribbled away in gunshots and bombs and atrocities until in 1971 Northern Ireland remained hard news but without heroes. The IRA was real enough, the British army were no saviors, the loyalists were unpleasant and unrepentant, and the young radicals from 1968 had become irrelevant. Their march was over, and there were gun battles and political impasse and unimagined horrors.

The young radical heroes found it more difficult to be irrelevant than it would have been to be real villains. They did not want to march offstage any more than their elders in the SDLP accepted their minor role once the gun had entered politics. The heady days of the student movement—the Italian school strikes of 1967, the barricades of Paris in 1968 and Danny the Red, Tariq Ali and Rudy and the riots in Berlin, the huge antiwar demonstrations in American universities—had vanished. There was instead twilight and exhaustion. Che Guevara was dead in Bolivia and there had not been One, Two, Three Vietnams: In fact the Vietnam War dragged on even with LBJ out of the way. The Year of the Glorious Guerrilla had come and gone, along with the next year and the next. People power had not prevailed on the campuses or in real life. All the flowers were wilting. Ulster, one more stop on the media tour, had become complex, increasingly attractive to combat photographers and war correspondents rather than visiting radicals and theorists. Behind the famous FREE DERRY sign lurked gunmen, not ideas. The wall became not harbinger but a tourist attraction, soon to be free-standing when the old tier of terraces was gutted and gone in another urban clearance scheme. And as a carefully maintained facade before the combat arena, it became a symbol of the civil rights movement to be read in various ways. Still many kept the faith. On Sunday, February 21, 1971, Devlin met with Angela Davis, Communist and black power militant, in a jail near San Francisco, a long way from the Bogside. The day before hardly anyone had noticed a NICRA march back in Ireland between Coalisland and Dungannon, where the long trek had first moved onto the road back in 1968. Devlin in San Francisco and NICRA barely in the news and the great campaign was a relic like the Derry wall.

Conditions in the province continued to make uncertain both the very considerable progress that the radicals had made and also the prospect that—with continued pressure from London and, perhaps, the street—real change would be institutionalized. Every step had been resisted by militant loyalists inside and outside Stormont with very public howls of indignation and threats to resort to alternative and forceful means of defense to protect the majority way of life. Those who could delay the direction of events did so up to the very last second. Magnanimity was singularly lacking in the politics of Unionist reform. All was grudgingly ceded and only because there was no alternative. O'Neill's initiatives had been directed at attracting outside investment that otherwise would have been repelled by the system. His successor, Chichester-Clark, had continued the reforms but concentrated on holding together the Unionist coalition and imposing order in the streets. He pushed only what the Unionists had to tolerate in order to legitimize restriction of demonstrations.

The real and perceived pace of reforms simply fell further and further behind the demands of the minority and the requirements of the situation. The Unionists did not care about the first and did not want to know about the second. The Tory establishment's reluctance to focus on the province or intervene in Unionist affairs allowed the Stormont system to soldier on into rising chaos. By the time Faulkner took office, the unremitting dissent of the extreme loyalists expressed in the most violent language, the continued bad grace of the establishment, the slow pace of reform (the first public prosecutor, Barry Shaw, QC, did not take office until April 1972, three years after the office was first proposed), and the habitual arrogance of those in power had largely discredited any Stormont regime. The courts, the police, the new Ulster Defense Regiment, the local councillors and the implacable loyalist bureaucrats alienated the minority day after day. The British army too, still largely innocent of Northern politics, imagining an insurrection, increasingly under attack, responded as armies tend to and further eroded the tainted legitimacy of order. And Faulkner came to power not only on the wave of loyalist suspicion and nationalist distaste but also with a reputation for duplicity, conniving against his own, plotting for advantage at all times. He was regularly accused as treacherous and devious by his own party: no Mr. Clean to sweep the province into the future but a shrewd survivor determined on office even as, even if, the system disintegrated. The result, not in Catholic eyes alone, was not a pretty picture.

When the minority had mobilized for justice, what they had wanted was not only a swift transformation in the structure and function of the system; more important, they implicitly demanded that the system concede on every level past error and so in small part compensate for fifty years of misery. Even without the implacable hostility of the Orange militants, all of this was impossible. The majority did not really feel at fault and except for a few did not really want adjustments to appease the minority. Reforms would come at all for fear of London, not from the heart. Thus, what the civil rights movement had accomplished could largely be found written as slogans on their march placards. They had ensured reforms, reforms that would in time enhance social and economic equality, and yet no new just, democratic institutions could be devised for the province, despite repeated efforts. The movement had not even produced immediate results and could not make bigots into friendly neighbors or tolerant of the minority's faith and agenda. And the marchers could not change history or heal invisible psychic wounds. The movement did erode the old system, force London to take action, mobilize many nationalists. So the civil rights movement was a success of a sort but simply not the kind of success really wanted. Of course, there was no socialist, revolutionary Ireland. All that had been ignored by the Catholics. Of course, there was no reformed system, for that system was the outward and visible face of a fearful and defensive majority determined on domination as the only alternative to defeat.

There was a growing concern among activists and political observers focused on error. What had gone wrong with the campaign of civil disobedience so that the long march had led not to a transformation of the sectarian system but rather to violence in the streets that left no role for the demonstrators? Most of the immediate analysis and much that was to come was shaped by rationalization and special pleading. No one accepted fault, anyone could find the culprit, usually within the alliance, really an alignment for reform. The Provisionals were to blame because they had used the movement as cover to organize an armed struggle. The Officials were to blame because their radical republicanism had contaminated the movement and because they, too, had not been converted to nonviolence. The middle-class and moderate nationalists were to blame because at bottom they wanted peace and quiet and so would not push on to an ultimate confrontation. The students and the radical fringe were to blame for their revolutionary rhetoric, which had alienated the British in London and the moderates, Protestant and Catholic alike, all over the island. Someone or everyone was at fault that civil disobedience had not unfolded as promised, as predicted, as such a strategy had apparently done elsewhere.

Everyone had failed to realize that political mobilization—the crowds on the streets—had to be institutionalized to be effective, and so no coherent reform vehicle had been created. Perhaps none could have been created, since the protesters had little in common politically but a singular distaste for the system. They represented a rainbow of Catholic interests allied to a very few Protestant idealists like Ivan Barr. Each individual or small group had a particular agenda that went beyond specific reforms and those simple issues of the street (one man one vote or fair shares in housing) that could in time actually be translated into detailed and dull laws with committees and procedures and lists.

Mostly the demonstrators and their allies and supporters wanted pride and often at bottom vengeance. The psychic wants of the minority became more real than the demands for houses and fair votes and jobs and an end to legal intimidation and exclusion, most of all a legal end to the whole unionist system. This was the overt and uniting agenda: an end to Stormont. And this was largely accomplished as early as 1971 because of pressure from Westminster. Inequities would remain, some for a generation; the unionist thrust for domination, though blunted, would remain, even after a generation, but within a very short time there had been real and radical change. Stormont had been shaken, mortally damaged. Many nationalists no longer felt inferior, powerless. The psychic accomplishments of the movement, however, were slow to mature and by 1971 could no longer be achieved in the streets. Effective, traditional politics that offered steady but not spectacular returns was the answer and that took time and time had largely run out. The minority wanted more. The returns of the street had been addictive. And there were no more immediate political highs on offer. In that sense the movement had ceased to move in visible and satisfactory ways toward a general goal, could not supply practical returns to satisfy psychic aspirations nor psychic returns from practical action. Action in the streets as order eroded was not practical.

In other places civil rights demonstrators had seemingly had more clear-cut triumphs. Why hadn't the Irish? The American blacks had smashed segregation, seen Martin Luther King's dream move toward reality, taken and used very real power. In India Gandhi had driven out the British once disobedience, founded on a moral commitment, indicated that the cost of staying was too great. The antiwar demonstrations in the United States had resulted in a national questioning, in moves toward withdrawal even with the delaying tactics of President Nixon and his adviser Henry Kissinger. The students in Paris had started de Gaulle down the road to retirement. And yet, in Ireland the undeniably just movement had blundered into a low-intensity war. Why?

All the right parts had seemingly been there, if unnoticed until 1968. The ruling majority was, in fact, a minority on the island and, most important, a tiny, antidemocratic, sectarian minority within the United Kingdom. The London center, like Washington during the struggle for desegregation, could intervene in good cause, could impose justice if the locals refused. The avowed standards of the nation were being violated in the province and reforms could be ordered from Westminster. The demonstrations had almost always been nonviolent, had almost always had enormous impact on the center, whether in Belfast or London, and on the general public through the media. The cause was just, the means had been properly applied locally, the Stormont opponent had played the part as expected, reforms had started—and a war. The end should have been a transformation, a triumph. The analogies with the other successful civil rights campaigns were, for Ireland in 1970, faulty. Ireland was special. It was gradually emerging from the confrontation between majority and minority in the province, between British commitments and assumptions and those of the Irish, between the compelling psychic needs of all those concerned on and off the island. This led to a bleak conclusion: The problem had no solution—that was the problem.

The other cases of disobedience campaigns were not relevant or only partially so. Nonviolence used properly against an empire with neither the will nor the resources to resist had produced concessions in the past. When used against an unyielding center, powerful and morally immune, the story had often been different and so had been less noted in Ireland. In South Africa the demonstrators had been shot off the streets at Sharpeville in 1960. The Afrikaners, a people chosen by God to rule a land redeemed by blood, had the convictions and power to impose apartheid. A generation or so later both capacities would have eroded and the power of protest escalated, but after Sharpeville opposition for a very long time was muted and ineffectual. And nonviolent opposition to an efficient, authoritarian state—Soviet Russia, Communist China, Nazi Germany, even Francoist Spain or some of the Latin American military dictatorships—was largely futile. Ireland was not exactly like either the United States or the authoritarian regimes, and like all political strategies, civil disobedience is not everywhere an ideal fit.

In Ireland the marching campaign between 1968 and 1970 had been a success as a reform movement. The London center had no need to be brutal and so responded to the newly perceived situation with pressure for provincial reforms. Stormont was persuaded to offer what others in the United Kingdom had long possessed. But everyone involved in Ireland wanted more. The loyalists wanted more of the same and the reforms were taken as visible indicators of betrayal, not just laws. And for the minority just reforms were only laws, not compensation for history's humiliation. So the loyalist community, as a psychic entity, like the Afrikaners, could not concede their assumed superiority so swiftly or at all. The campaign assaulted their basic assumptions, awakened their old fears, and so permitted a defense of their way of life by those less moderate or decent who were quite willing to deny the legitimacy of the institutions in favor of the right of the majority to dominate. In Ireland the threatened center could concede through pressure from the top only those adjustments that did not give the minority the psychic victory.

And in Ireland not only could the center at Stormont not concede psychic advantage to the minority; that minority also could not find a means to more. Devlin and McCann and Hume did not want to *be* unionists or Protestants; they sought a road into a future that might be variously defined but that would not be shaped to maintain the majority way of life, certainly not through the domination the majority so long felt crucial. The minority in their heart of hearts wanted history rewritten so that Ireland, their Ireland, would triumph—a psychic option painted over with political and economic analyses by the Provos and Stickies, an option that the majority assumed was primary, an option that could only erode as time passed and the costs became obvious. In 1971 the strategy of nonviolence could achieve what were essentially secondary benefits at great cost to the majority and at great risk to the minority. This in the midst of the alarms of 1971 was not easy to see.

The Irish experience, then, while not typical in that the imported strategy had worked curiously, mysteriously, was judged by most practical standards a success. The involved might not think so but the distant did. The demonstrators revealed the nature of an unfair, sectarian system in dramatic confrontations. They persuaded London to take action and many in the majority accepted those actions as necessary, perhaps valid. They mobilized a lethargic minority, found a means to act on events when conventional politics were denied, and brought pride and confidence to the denied community, as well as jobs and votes and houses. In turn the majority, if only in part, was driven to question the nature of their way of life, their superiority; and so, if only in part, they adjusted to changing power relations in the province, to a different London, and even to the great, outside world. A great many specific reforms were passed that did not end prejudice and bigotry any more than the end of segregation in America had ended racism. But they were reforms. And some produced very tangible results: new electoral rules, new jobs in the bureaucracy, a different police force, another name for Londonderry.

The reforms were not simply cosmetic but gave hope to many of the hopeless Catholics. Those with long views, especially those who could ignore the sound of gunfire, could see the gradual normalization of the province. The form that this might take proved elusive and the disappearance of the divide in the population was unlikely, but the province was no longer a painful political anomaly. The province, however, had become a different sort of anomaly because the struggle for reform had released long-dormant psychic hungers that proved as vital.

By the spring of 1971 civil rights campaigns would play a far lesser role in Northern events and more often than not would arise not from the grievances of the fifty years of Stormont but from the clash of aspirations unleashed by the success of the Provisional IRA. Civil libertarians, reformers, advocates of the Catholic cause increasingly found that the issues of concern arose from the security of the province, the efforts to impose order even at the cost of justice, increasingly by recourse to armed force. Thus, the nodes of discord involved the complexities of an undeclared war.

The IRA in Belfast organized republican military funerals for volunteers: a procession, a flag-draped coffin with black beret and black gloves, an honor guard, often of IRA men, masked or in sunglasses, in paramilitary camouflage uniforms and also with black berets and black gloves, a slow march of the thousands of mourners to the graveyard trailing behind, turning the cortege into a parade. At the graveyard in the republican plot, often with a marker incised with the name of the patriot dead stretching back to William Orr in 1797, there would be a volley of honor fired from smuggled pistols or even rifles. Intimidating, effective, it was a provocative ritual with no role in a campaign of reform. The loyalists were outraged at this symbolic defiance by gunmen, by a ceremony that sought to turn treasonous criminals into martyrs. The British army, often stationed along the route, was at first bemused: For all visible purposes they were present at a military event, a military funeral arising from an undeclared war that had just begun to touch the army. Some British soldiers even saluted as the first IRA coffin passed, a bizarre if understandable reaction that also enraged the loyalists. The loyalists understandably wanted the authorities to do something— at once.

So began a round of attempts to restrict such displays, ban paramilitary uniforms, end provocation. This produced protests from republicans and others who then demonstrated in uniforms. The Provos sent women in berets and combat jackets to confront the authorities; more cases for the courts. The loyalists, unable to wait, appeared in the streets. There were soon other complaints as the problems escalated. There were complaints when IRA representatives appeared on BBC—recognition of gunmen—and a call for more legislation. There were complaints about RUC forms finding their way to loyalist politicians. There was a campaign to reject census forms. There was concern in and out of Stormont by the SDLP about the number of firearms licenses held in the province—the majority, including many ex–B Specials, had legal guns but the minority did not. New security legislation to restrict IRA provocations was introduced but many loyalists felt that the only real solution was internment: Get them all off the streets, use the law on the books, stop diddling around.

Even as the emphasis shifted to the harsh edges of security and the provocations of the republicans, there was still the impression of reform action: David Bleakley, Minister of Community Relations, held talks about removing anti-Catholic slogans from the walls of Saint Matthew's Church in Ballymacarret; the Ulster Teachers' Union called for integrated education; the members of the new Housing Executive were announced and a week later on May 13 they held their first meeting. Erasing slogans not bigotry, advocating mixed education supported by a tiny number of parents and none of the churches, naming commissions and holding meetings, had no visibility and no general impact: The media preferred women in black berets or interviews with bigots. At the end of May, the Minister of Development, Roy Bradford, indicated that the differences between Stormont and the British system had been progressively eliminated. The majority had thus given enough. The minority was hardly moved. On May 31 Hume called for Westminster to declare a willingness to create a new system in the province without sectarianism and with the participation of all sections of the community. The majority was appalled—they had a satisfactory system if given a chance. The minority wanted more. Everyone wanted more even if more of the same.

Few in either community had the patience or the interest in the details of reform politics by the late spring of 1971. The community had become mildly addicted to sensation. There were still provocative marches, still riots, and more important, still an escalating IRA campaign bringing more bombs, more ambushes, more country areas under threat each week. And the escalating British army response to the conflict brought only minimal security returns. Frank Card and Billy McKee were arrested on April 15 on explosives charges. Joe Cahill took over as the Provisional IRA O/C of Belfast and the campaign continued to escalate since, if anything, Cahill's enthusiasm for action was greater than McKee's and his interest in controlling the units less. There were now sometimes four or five bomb explosions in Belfast on a bad night. There were fewer good nights as the Provos moved in materiel that had been stolen or donated throughout the island. Although Faulkner spoke in May about what he claimed really mattered—the economy—everyone else assumed that what really mattered to Faulkner, to the loyalists, and thus to London, apparently still committed to the Stormont system, was the decaying security system and the IRA.

Faulkner from the first had realized that he and the system could survive only if the streets came under the control of the security forces. His own, the majority, almost all decent people, could not long tolerate a government that could not respond to rebel siege. Once he had been acceptable to militant Unionist dissent, as a more cunning Craig and a less raucous Paisley, but once Prime Minister, he alone became responsible for the tumult. The British army seemed to feel that a sly mix of coercion in the case of the IRA coupled with concession in the case of the Catholics in general would separate the fish and the ocean; but the militant majority was in turn apt to respond with violence when there was too little coercion and too much concession. Worse, some extremists attacked any vulnerable Catholics, often openly and occasionally not distinguishing between their targets and those like the British army who protected them. The army was not to be given a clean board to run out an anti-insurgency chess game. Concessions to the minority simply assured violence by the majority. And the army alone had few concessions to offer beyond the press office and a cheerful manner. The remaining option was coercion—always a firm favorite with any military.

Faulkner wanted internment. Internment had worked during the 1939–45 war and later during the IRA 1956–62 campaign. Whether it "worked" as a security measure in 1971, it was one of the few remaining unplayed cards that would hush militant Unionist criticism, calm the majority with a symbolic triumph, and so give him and the system time. It would damage the opposition in the streets, with luck cripple the treasonous long enough for the army and the RUC to impose order, allow a recess for reasonable reform, and keep the Orangemen off the streets. Times had changed so that he could not simply act. London had to buy internment.

London dithered still. In the province the army was not keen. Internment might taint the disinterested army with an Orange brush. Much more important than symbols, many did not think internment would work. The army commander, Lieutenant General Sir Harry Tuzo, exposed to the reality of the streets and the capacity of the RUC, doubted that it would have the needed security impact. The RUC, quite aware from any constable up that internment had a dual function, was in general much less reluctant to have a go but no longer any better prepared than the army. The army only knew a few IRA people, spokesmen and visible types. The RUC had old lists of their enemies, a new list of the articulate radicals, and often knew the locals but not as well as they imagined. They, like the army, had the names of the few but felt this would do. The RUC felt that the army simply did not know the country, which was true; the army felt that the police did not recognize that the country had changed and did not know their new enemies, which was true. Faulkner was not interested in the details, especially in the army's pragmatism. If not one new gunmen was lifted, stashing the old favorites and the new radicals would have the effect on its own that he wanted. He needed internment and so did the system and from day one he made this clear in Belfast and in London.

The army at least hoped the politicians would accept a small internment, known gunmen, the leaders—some of whom British officers knew personally, others who had appeared on public platforms. The RUC had a far more inclusive enemies list, spanning the spectrum of troublemakers, and this was what Faulkner wanted: the whole lot behind bars, the minority cowed, the majority assured. The Director of Military Intelligence found that the Special Branch was adamant, as was Faulkner. Maudling and the cabinet in London, again lethargic, would have preferred delay or a more appealing, less risky option, but nothing was available. All Tuzo could offer was opposition and no promise of imposing order but only, as he noted on June 8, a gradual ascendancy over the IRA. He could try and push a short list but the RUC and Faulkner balked at this; and in the end, since they knew their own, Tuzo had to go along with civilian leadership.

The bombing continued. Armed troops were ordered to guard RUC stations on June 11. Five hundred more troops arrived. On June 22, the fiftieth anniversary of Stormont, Paisley again criticized Faulkner, whose dithering was endangering the system. The next day Craig claimed the government was moving toward Irish unity, the ultimate horror. The bombs continued. At the end of the month it was announced that an additional 900 soldiers would arrive, bringing the total to 11,800. Beginning on Monday, July 5, there was serious nightly rioting in Derry. There, early on the morning of July 8, the British army shot dead Séamus Cusack of Creggan. Later in the day soldiers shot and killed another Catholic, Desmond Beattie. Cusack was reported to have raised a rifle against troops of the Royal Anglian Regiment and Beattie to have been hit as he threw a nail bomb. Witnesses in the crowd reported that both had been unarmed, both had been shot intentionally, both had been murdered by the army. Violence in Derry escalated at the news. John Hume demanded an investigation.

On July 11 the SDLP began a boycott of Parliament. Hume proposed an alternative assembly. The next day at a press conference, Hume indicated an end to toleration: "There comes a point where to continue to do so is to appear to condone the present system. That point, in our view, has now been reached." Without the SDLP Stormont would be isolated, a loyalist establishment under siege, protected by military force amid rising turmoil. It would only incidentally be a parliament. Faulkner had on July 9 already telephoned Heath and insisted that the only option was internment. And Heath, with no cards of his own, agreed that Faulkner and Tuzo should go ahead with a preliminary sweep as a trial. Internment would be the Orange card next played, dealt reluctantly from London and anticipated on July 12 when the SDLP withdrew the minority's consent to be governed by Stormont.

On Friday, July 23, 1,800 members of the security forces carried out the planned trial dawn raids and arrested in Belfast and nine other towns a total of forty-eight suspects. In the previous two weeks the provincial situation had grown no more stable. Paisley announced that he should be leader of the loyal opposition in Stormont since Hume and company, followed by Paddy Kennedy and the Republican Labour Party, had withdrawn from participation. He was recognized as loyalist but hardly loyal. Only the Alliance was left to urge moderation. There was no prospect of an inquiry into the Derry killings once Hume had delivered his request as an ultimatum, so the SDLP was out for the foreseeable future. Rioting and bombing and sniping continued. The only good news was the safe passage of the Orange parades on the Glorious Twelfth with no violence. Everything was grim. Paul Johnson of the *New Statesman* even urged "absolute and unconditional British withdrawal from Northern Ireland." Discounting his Leftist political posture in Britain, discounting the SDLP's new extralegal assembly, discounting Paisley and the truculence of the militant Orangemen, Faulkner waited for internment and salvation. The British government, far from withdrawing, had persisted in a Stormont salvage operation.

On July 24 Faulkner stated that the use of the military to stamp out the wave of violence would be resolute and there was no need of private enterprise to protect the system. This was meant to calm the fundamentalist Protestants, who had grown uneasy, wanted to defend their own. No one else seemed to be doing so. There were more army dawn raids but few significant arrests. The IRA's private enterprise had led them to the conclusion that internment was imminent and their commanders had gone on the run. There was a feeling that time was running out—Paisley announced he would not shrink from the duty of becoming Prime Minister. Army searches continued in Belfast and Derry. In the Westminster debate on Northern Ireland, Callaghan announced that his party favored a Council of Ireland that would include members of the Irish Dáil; while this was not the unilateral withdrawal of the *New Statesman*, it was a serious Labour Party proposal that indicated the future of the province was debatable.

Faulkner flew to London for a meeting with Tuzo and Heath. All that was announced was an extra one thousand troops on the way to the province. Chichester-Clark had left on the heels of just such an announcement. And in the province the IRA from a commandeered bus attacked an army post on the Springfield Road in Belfast with a machine gun. No one could pretend that Belfast was simply a British provincial city, an everyday part of the main. Any reporter could stand in front of the Europa Hotel and listen to the crump of the nightly IRA bombs, watch the army and police fully armed rush, often in armored cars, to each new emergency, and so feel an exposure to a war zone that could be elaborated later at the bar.

Yet neither Belfast nor Northern Ireland *was* a war zone. Machine-gun attacks aside, most Provo activity was a crude bombing campaign, mostly in Belfast and Derry, and stray shots fired at the security. Much of the countryside was tranquil. Much of Belfast and Derry—almost all of the loyalist areas—was peaceful. The occasional attacks on security forces came at the fringes of the nationalist ghettos—a few shots fired, little damage done. In the previous four months only four members of the British army and four civilians had been killed, and no member of either the police or the Ulster Defense Regiment. The bombing had not seriously disrupted the economic life of the province. And many felt the economy was the key. Unemployment was still the great shadow, with the Ministry of Health and Social Services reporting 10.1 percent male jobless and 5.4 percent female—a total of 45,000 and an increase of 5,715 since July 1970, a year before. The total was the highest in nineteen years—and as usual the Catholics were disproportionately represented. The housing situation remained grim despite promises and programs. Little new investment was visible in the province and few reforms yet touched the ghettos. The conventional felt that once this happened the machine guns would disappear.

In a sense the bombs and riots were a distraction from the inherited and inherent economic and social problems. At least on the political scene there was now action. And the action, while not simply symbolic, was not very deadly. Ten thousand troops watched twenty-two thousand supposedly violently alienated Orangemen parade peacefully across the province on July 12. Except for some early morning symbolic bombs along the route of the Belfast parade to Finaghy, there was no trouble. Even when there was trouble, it had become ritual trouble. The riots, despite the deaths of Beattie and Cusack in Derry, had much of ceremonial form—the street mob structured itself to display rather than to harm. The political boycott of Stormont was little different than previous Nationalist Party withdrawals; moreover, the civil rights movement had first discarded the radicals and by the summer of 1971 reached an impasse. Yet, those who feared violence could easily find it, see it in the streets, hear it with the detonation of the Provo bombs, watch it on BBC Ulster each evening. The fearful saw a crisis, the Orange militants were sure it was upon the province, the Provos were straining to make this certain, the orthodox felt isolated from the tide of events.

Everyone involved in Northern Ireland from the gunmen through the politicians on to the watching media perceived crisis, heard the explosions and the rumble of change and movement and danger. Tomorrow might not be like yesterday. And this is deeply disturbing, especially in a static, rigid society. In contrast to the quiet, old days when Stormont's writ ran, when the minority endured, when one year, one parade season, was like the last, now the province seemed aflame. These flickering flames had everywhere been magnified by the observers who had turned their telescopes about and now saw grand what once had been insignificant. For the loyalists internment became the means to douse the flames, reverse the telescope.

The rising loyalist pressure for internment had at last forced London's hand. Armies would prefer to avoid using the troops trained, risking what had taken years to create, a spiffy peacetime army. And even Northern Ireland presented a risk of escalation. Still, within the British military establishment there were those who felt that the long haul through the end of empire had given them a peculiar grasp of what Kitson now called low-intensity conflict. Even if occasionally neglected or, as in 1971, forgotten institutionally, Palestine, Malaya, Kenya, Cyprus, and Aden were appropriate preparation for any threat posed by the IRA. Few then or later within the British military stressed that somehow the insurgents were now running those countries or that military counterinsurgency techniques had often led to political and ethical disasters: dreadful concentration camps, murderous sweeps through the countryside, torture, and in the end, withdrawal. All was shifted in recollection to a memory of craft and new techniques. The British army consequently felt the RUC was ill prepared for insurgency, modern subversion, and internment. And the British army was quite right. Rural intelligence was haphazard and faulty, especially with the disappearance of the B Specials, and the IRA homelands in Belfast and Derry were impenetrable to the police. The British military also felt they had the skills to compensate for this problem. And the British army was quite wrong.

The Chief of the Imperial General Staff, General Sir Geoffrey Baker, accepting the criticism that the RUC did not even know how to interrogate, sent the Director of Intelligence, Dick White, to Northern Ireland. He in turn recommended that the police be given special training in army methods. These methods descended from those used by the Communists in the Korean War—former Northern Ireland Commander of Land Forces Major General Anthony Farrar-Hockley had been so questioned. Such methods induced, it was believed, an effective prisoner response. From shaping this response the British army intelligence had devised a more antiseptic interrogation method. Cunning mistreatment produced answers. When tried out in Aden, however, the practice led to allegations of torture, an investigation by Labour Defense Secretary Denis Healey, and an adjustment in the rules. The army had adjusted and kept deep interrogation in the manual. Essentially such deep interrogation made use of techniques of disorientation including "self-inflicted" pain (standing against a wall in an awkward position) and sleep deprivation. All this led to sufficient pliability in the prisoner to allow effective questioning. Such interrogation was thought to be much more elegant than the traditional RUC reliance on questions, threats, and rough treatment, with the process repeated until the prisoner talked or collapsed with exhaustion. Putting in the boot lacked subtlety while forty-eight hours squatting against a wall somehow seemed more rigorous, more fitting.

In April 1971 RUC people were brought over to the British Intelligence Centre, Maresfield, Sussex, and taught army techniques. These new skills would hardly transform the Northern Ireland situation if only because the training was limited to a few skilled interrogators who would have a go at the few prime suspects. It was a step in modernizing the RUC and one that indicated the limitations of all involved.

Still something had to be done about the RUC. The police still had no modern intelligence apparatus, no broad monitoring program beyond the obvious police routines, no exposure to contemporary special operations or even modern dirty tricks. And contact with the army was often grating. The army despaired of all RUC intelligence. In fact, the army suspected all other intelligence gatherers—including MI5 and MI6, the competing civilian agencies whose tasking and arenas overlapped with each other, with the military, with the police. Ulster was both national and international, a counterintelligence field and a focus for the regular foreign intelligence of MI6, not to mention an opportunity for the quick-witted who were eager to push disinformation or deception, to sponsor informers, or to explore covert options. By 1971, in intelligence matters broadly defined, the army had to worry about its own as well as its bureaucratic competitors and all its Ulster allies. And it worried most, as far as internment was concerned, about the RUC's faults and intelligence.

The army did the best possible with the existing organizational priorities and the visible political structures. They took photographs, circulated patrols, talked to everyone, used the other involved agencies, assigned the few useful books on the IRA and Ireland, bought some data and discovered other, and began experiments with plainclothes special operations. So did the RUC (with or without elegant training in mistreatment of suspects); so did MI5 and MI6, rediscovering, if ineptly, Ireland after fifty years. All moved in isolation amid intensified bureaucratic mistrust, with the police and the army riding point: Their mistakes were visible. Two years after the army had arrived on the streets of Northern Ireland, the end result as far as the prospects for internment went was that the police and the army still operated largely in the dark. The army knew this; those in the RUC who also knew largely discounted it. The great sweep in July, the dry run, had focused mostly on Official republicans and had produced little hard information. The army hope was that internment, designated Operation Demetrius, would depend upon interrogation methods: Sweep up the first wave, squeeze them dry, and move on to those pinpointed as a result of disorientation. The police intention was to get the prime benefits of intimidation through internment and consider a selection of the guilty ample secondary reward.

The bottom line was that practical internment would depend upon RUC lists, and such lists, made no more inclusive by recent experience, were haphazard and specifically sectarian—not a single Protestant was thought subversive by the police. Maudling in London had suggested to Faulkner that a few Protestants might be taken as tokens, but nothing was done. Stormont wanted the disloyal intimidated, not an exercise in community relations. So the police and the army were primed to cause the maximum damage to those relations: the RUC as willing creatures of bigotry and the army as advocates of torture. Nothing had been learned from all that experience, fifty years isolated in an Ulster where no one had investigated bigotry, and a generation within the military bureaucracy where few understood the priorities of politics or the power of the media. The politicians at least should have known the risks.

To Faulkner it seemed the only choice, and a congenial one. Anything else remained unthinkable: Paisley or concession to the Republicans. For London it had been the easy choice: Let Faulkner cope, it was his province, let the army cope, it was their job. And with a remarkable lack of imagination Heath turned to more pleasant matters. In Dublin there was no choice at all. No one had managed to fashion a way to influence Northern events. Lynch had indicated the means to avoid the commitment, and Haughey and company the danger of involvement. For generations all they had needed to do was cry against one more injustice in partition and proceed with more practical matters. The only shift that could be made was to expand the grievances and urge action on those held responsible. Few paid attention, certainly not outside the country. In Northern Ireland Hume and company had taken the SDLP out of Stormont and so, like Dublin, could only watch and add up the costs of the inevitable. No one knew what to do (but the Provos) and so everyone had done what was habitual and easy: Choose internment, tolerate internment, evade responsibility if possible. And ever so briefly it was possible. All the other options required enormous adjustments of reality and perception and agenda.

7

The Province at War, Internment to the Failure of Stormont: August 1971–January 1972

Acts of Injustice Done
Between the Setting and the Rising Sun
In History Lie Like Bones, Each One.
W. H. Auden

On Saturday, August 7, Northern Irish reality began the slide to chaos that many observers had fearfully predicted. At 7:30 Harry Thorton, a building worker from Newry, and a friend were driving by the Springfield Road barracks. Their van backfired. Soldiers instantly opened fire on the van. Thorton was killed outright. The passenger, covered in blood, was dragged into the street and beaten by frightened and enraged police constables and soldiers before being taken away to the Mater Hospital.

The incident instantly attracted the Catholics of nearby Clonard into the streets. Experienced in the urban turmoil, they realized what had happened before the army had time to put out a rationale. Troops were attacked along the Falls as well as in the Ardoyne, New Barnsley, and Ballymurphy area as the story spread of the army murder. The British army counted at least eight incoming gunshots. That evening a crowd of three hundred attacked the Springfield Road RUC, with IRA volunteers firing into the building.

The violence died down briefly but then on Sunday a soldier was shot and killed at Farringdon Gardens, Ardoyne. On the edges of the Catholic districts, rioting began again and spread throughout Belfast. Again there was gunfire. There was an explosion at the home of Resident Magistrate William Millar, an army patrol was ambushed in Lurgan by the IRA, an RUC station was attacked at Coalisland, and three heavy explosions hit the Ballylumford Power Station near Larne. Faulkner did not want to wait for more. For him Belfast was already in chaos and the province under attack by the IRA. At his request the Northern Ireland government under Section 12 of the Special Powers Act introduced internment early on the morning of August 9, twenty-four hours before Tuzo had planned to begin his Operation Demetrius. The army would go in just before dawn on Monday.

Few tactical initiatives to achieve effective change have ever been taken in Ireland by participants so wary of the result. Tuzo and the army thought it a distasteful weapon and a blunt weapon at that, with 450 suspects on the list of the day. The police felt the list would do but the army would ruin the operation and shift the blame to the RUC, as would Faulkner and all the politicians. Faulkner knew the risks but felt he had no option. And the few disinterested British observers in the province had no power, no say, and little understanding of the risks. No matter, the order was given, and at 4:30 in the morning with a promise of faint light soon and a long day of riot ahead, the police and army moved into Catholic areas—and only into Catholic areas.

A major blunder was thus made in ignoring even the mild advice of Maudling to add a few Protestants to the list: Internment was demonstrably sectarian. No Protestant would do, even as token. And soon blunder two became clear: Any difficult Catholic would do. The list had been stitched up from old lists, fallout from the dry-run raids of the army, and a hit list of critics, some from the civil rights people, some from old grievances, some simply handy radicals. The 450 names represented not the core of the gunmen but the dregs of bad intelligence. Here an inactive republican was arrested—a terror, even a terrorist, thirty years before, but now only a grandparent; there a student speaker or a transient photographed next to him at a rally was snatched; and from this street a man with the wrong name was hustled off to prison. The errors were compounded on the spot. Relatives were taken, or the wrong Murphy, this Seán, not that Seán. Finally, after all the ancients and innocents were weeded out, it became clear that almost no gunmen were arrested. The fish had swum to other oceans long before.

It is difficult to imagine why anyone thought internment would be a surprise. Every Unionist politician had discussed the prospect for months, every militant loyalist had urged such an action sooner rather than later. Everyone, even Tuzo, had talked about it in public. The dry-run raids came on top of obvious and ineffectual army and police intelligence efforts to label gunmen. The Provos had been on the run for months, moving beds, staying with innocent friends and never for long. Those few caught had simply chosen the wrong bed, the wrong night to visit home, the wrong house as safe. A few were even lifted quite by error, as were relatives taken in lieu of the wanted, uncles instead of nephews, the wrong brother, an old man instead of a young one: and Catholics all, every one. And even with a willingness to make do with anyone, only 342 were taken out of a list of 450. Most of those lifted went first to an army barracks and then on to Crumlin Road Prison or to two new internment camps, one the *Maidstone* prison ship, the other tin huts surrounded by wire at Magilligan on the north Derry coast.

The isolation of the internees meant that the details of the errors were momentarily hidden in the din of the moment. All these errors might have been anticipated, even the major strategic blunder of an all-Catholic sweep; most had actually been discussed at various levels. In London and Belfast, the realists and pessimists had anticipated nearly everything: Mistakes would happen, the list was faulty, the loyalists' nationalist enemies were likely to be more vocal than dangerous, the liberal media would not like even a smooth Operation Demetrius, nor would Labour, nor many in London and Dublin, nor would the Catholic minority. Everyone had been warned but had felt that there were no options. And all the predictions had been accurate. What had not been foreseen was that the minority anger would give the militants an opportunity to harness outrage. Catholic crowds stoning the withdrawing security forces during a day of riot had been foreseen. The province descending into open insurrection had not. The Orange card had been played and burst into flames that blistered the hand that had held it. Faulkner could savor nothing, his move turned to ashes in his mouth.

Enraged at the provocation of internment, enraged at the brutality of the army and police during the arrests, enraged at the implications of such a ritual so late in the game—Croppies Lie Down—emboldened by the pride three years in the making and the power that lies in cobblestones and the possession of justice, the crowds did not go home. The security forces had to answer not only for a mess of their own making but also for years of grievances and resentment not yet placated by reforms and concessions. This time the sullen resentment, still not defused by access to power or tangible returns, and exacerbated by loyalist arrogance was now intensified by the ignorant arrogance of a Tory establishment in London. The Conservatives clearly preferred catering to their Unionist friends in Stormont to taking the trouble to right wrong. London let the system chastise its critics with its army and their laws. This time the IRA did, indeed, have a war.

There was resistance and riot everywhere the arrests were made. Again the core was Belfast, where the minority was massed and the Provos ready. The troops, still new to urban, irregular warfare, arrived in the Catholic ghettos to find women and children filling the streets, which were ill-lit with flashlights and the flickering light of burning buildings. They were almost overwhelmed by a fearful din.

> As I stood in the cold at 5:15, watching the black coils of smoke wind upwards into the fine eggshell blue morning sky, I could hear from the west a distant cacophony, a metallic rattling, faintly musical, an urban alarm signal of the crisis North.
>
> Up close it was a huge sound. Women, young girls, small boys in dressing gowns and housecoats or hastily pulled on jeans and sweaters knelt in their hundreds on the corners of Catholic side streets, holding in one hand the metal lid of their dustbin, and crashing it again and again on the concrete flags below.*

The sky rained missiles, Belfast confetti—cobblestones broken from the street, bricks, loose rocks, discarded tins and bottles. As the soldiers and police moved into the little lanes, petrol bombs followed the stones, making sputtering red arcs in the dawn sky before the pop and crash that added more flames. There were no streetlights—most had been smashed to provide riot cover—so there was only the

---

*Simon Winchester, *In Holy Terror* (London: Faber & Faber, 1974), pp. 163–64.

flicker of the burning petrol for guidance. And there was always the noise, rising and falling, waves of clattering lids, streams of curses, the snap and crackle of fires, ricocheting stones bouncing off walls and clunking into vehicles. There were crowds down every street, women who spit, children who cursed, and then the echo of shots and the echoes from anyplace, from no place. The doors were barred and barricades were going up. The soldiers had to stumble on the edge of the crowds, past women and girls cursing and shrieking, past men and boys heaving cobblestones, to find a strange address in the dark. Then they battered down the door, ransacked the house to find a man to go with a name, dragged the suspect out through an angry family into a violent crowd under a red-orange sky. They had to rush the man down a street covered in broken glass and loose cobblestones under a hail of missiles to the relative safety of a Humber tender, an armored personnel carrier (APC), appropriately called a Pig. The din continued inside these APCs with the stones rattling on the sides. And there were more names on the list, more narrow streets, more crowds to come, more stones, more hate and spit and maybe shots. Frightened and angry soldiers got their own back on the prisoner, old or young, guilty or innocent, now handy and vulnerable. And when the tenders finally reached the first stop, the army barracks, more time could be given to vengeance.

> I was forced to run over broken glass and rough stones to a helicopter without shoes. I spent only fifteen seconds in the helicopter and I was then pushed out into the hands of military policemen. I was forced to crawl between these policemen, back to the building. They kicked me on the hands, legs, ribs, and kidney areas.*

Even before the suspects were all swept up the British army had compounded the errors of internment by using violence as a policy. Select suspects were put through deep interrogation—standard operating procedure. This military addition to internment would require years of explanations and rationalizations to argue away the charge of torture—and torture that produced intelligence of the most limited value. The army would continue to resent that deep interrogation, a standard operating procedure in some cases, could engender such a response. The military assumption remained that such criticism was hypocritical and ill-informed. The critics could not have found a more vulnerable institution supposedly quite innocent of politics, public opinion, or the power of the media, or protected by the isolation of the military establishment from other norms and other notions.

Internment not only opened the province to a real irregular war and the British army to obloquy, fair or no, but also led to the opinion among Catholics that the authorities had divorced order from justice. Before August 1971 the minority had

*This is from a signed statement by Henry Bennett lodged with the Association for Legal Justice and quoted in Danny Kennally and Eric Preston, *Belfast, August 1971: A Case to Be Answered* (London: Independent Labour Party, 1971). A more general treatment of internment can be found in John McGuffin, *Internment!* (Tralee: Anvil, 1973).

anticipated the possibility that London could and might impose a justice long denied by Stormont. The republicans knew that London would not do so except as a tactic. For the IRA the republicans, and many Irish nationalists, the existence of the province as a province, divided from the main, assured the institutionalization of injustice. The loyalists were, on the other hand, fearful that London might, indeed, concede away their way of life as "justice." And in a sense London seemed to feel that justice *had been* ceded, just not fully applied—the most dangerous illusion of all.

After internment the loyalists were reassured, the republicans were vindicated, and the nationalist minority for the time being accepted as a given that the British in whatever form were one with the Orange system. And the injustice of internment—sectarian, arrogant, meant to intimidate the Catholics and reassure the Protestants, imposed with violence, accompanied by torture—brought the angry into the August streets and would henceforth play a major role in the continuing legitimacy of the minority's proclaimed defenders. In time the minority might grow tired of anger and confrontation, might seek concession and co-option, turn to conventional politics, no longer support or even tolerate the gunmen of the IRA; but many, some children in 1971, would never recover from the impact of the Orange card.

Other horrors and impositions would reinforce this posture, but internment was the key. The siege of the Falls or the deaths of civilians rationalized away by the army or the police, the symbolic incidents from Burntollet Bridge to the murder of the three young Scots, were signposts on the road to war but there was always a way back: The minority, except for the IRA and the most militant in a few neighborhoods, operated within the system. After internment there was no way back for many and only the end of Stormont held any attraction for most. Stormont could no longer hope to win back the alienated. James Callaghan would later suggest that he had been inclined to close down Stormont if Labour had gone ahead to win in the general elections that brought the Conservatives to power. In retrospect the idea had charm, as it did from the moment in 1969 that London belatedly and reluctantly realized that something had to be done about Ulster. Once in power Heath and Maudling had ample time to watch the province move toward open conflict, since they did no more than tinker and delay. Then, as the pressure built up, they allowed Stormont access to a card that could not reverse the tenor of the game—even if a miracle had happened and a good and effective internment had been organized, Stormont would only gain more time to delay. To blunder in the execution of the play of the Orange card, to compound matters by adding injury to insult with the army's deep interrogation technique, to lie about the results and the event, to make all the mistakes available was an incredible boon to the republicans and an enormous boost to chaos. The intensity of that chaos after August 9, as the violence spread and escalated, indicated how stable the province had really been—not in contrast to the good old days, not in contrast to England, but in contrast to what would happen when the shooting started. And with the shooting came the lies.

The lies of the authorities, those at Stormont or British army press conferences, those in London, had to begin immediately. The lies were delivered by spokesmen who wanted to believe what they read or said, may have believed what they read or said: Internment, swift, surgical, and effective, had transformed the province, assured order, and need not be questioned further. No damage had been done. No complaints could be countenanced. No apologies or excuses or explanations were needed. And all the while the sky was lit with fires and the streets were filled with mobs. The soldiers fought gun battles across the province. All this was quite visible to the assembled media. Faulkner announced that over three hundred people had been arrested and might be interned and that parades had been banned for six months. Faulkner had, he announced at 11:15 A.M., been driven to this distasteful action: "I have taken this serious step solely for the protection of life and the security of property. . . . We are, quite simply, at war with the terrorists, and in a state of war many sacrifices have to be made, and made in a cooperative and understanding spirit." During the day the disorder was momentarily contained and there was some hope that the system would scrape through. As evening came the violence was renewed and the security situation began to slip out of hand as the IRA moved into the streets. By that evening the IRA controlled large areas of Belfast and Derry, gunfights were within the hearing of Stormont and went on before the cameras of the avid television crews. Faulkner had a war against terrorism but one he had created, one that did endanger life and property as the violence against the security forces spread to Newry, Strabane, and Armagh, as the fault line between Protestant and Catholic burned as well. The toll of the gunmen and security forces began to come in from the hospitals: By November thirty soldiers would be dead, eleven members of the RUC and UDR, and seventy-three civilians, few of these from the IRA. Faulkner's decision to do something rather than nothing, to risk all to keep control in proper hands, had been a disaster. No one gained but those who were to be punished.

On Monday the army had to adjust to the unexpected reality of serious provincial violence. And they resented that they had been asked to impose a sectarian policy and then were blamed for the results. The army felt that there was no sympathy for the soldiers' restraint, given the risks and provocation, no understanding of the army's basic decency or the procedures of interrogation or the prepared press office statements read to those fed on atrocity stories. Spokesmen noted that no other army would have behaved as well—a moot point if one of yours had been beaten and dragged out of the house at dawn to be beaten again by frightened soldiers in a tender and then again by less frightened soldiers on arriving at a military barracks so that at the end a cell seemed a refuge. The British public, like most publics, tends to believe their own, their army, their lads; but this time, the men had been sent into homes in the United Kingdom on a shoddy mission and in full view of an unsympathetic media. Neither the media nor the Irish Catholics, North or South, were interested in other examples or polished rationalizations.

Belfast was burning and the IRA was active. Any reporter had access to events: Thousands of innocents, Catholics and Protestants, were fleeing their vulnerable homes, homes often already on fire; the nationalist areas were no-go zones protected by IRA guns; the casualty toll was going up by the hour. On Tuesday in Belfast alone eleven people, including Father Hugh Mullan, a priest shot while administering the last rites to an injured man in Ballymurphy, were killed. The first IRA man to die was Patrick McAdorey, a twenty-five-year-old sniper from the Ardoyne, shot dead behind a garden wall in Jamaica Street. Two hundred forty houses were burned out—and in the Ardoyne troops had not been available to protect the Catholics who came under fire from armed Protestants. There were similar horror stories (and nothing lost in the telling) from other nationalist areas in the province. The IRA was reported out in some areas of the countryside—a UDR man was shot dead on the Tyrone-Fermanagh border.

The fires burned all Monday night and into Tuesday. Word came from the Republic that five relief camps had been set up near the border for Catholic dependents of internees. On Tuesday, August 10, NICRA called for an immediate campaign of civil disobedience as a protest against military terrorism. Foreign Minister Patrick Hillery flew to London to meet Maudling. By evening the death toll since the beginning of internment had reached seventeen. Rioting continued in Derry. In Belfast, a gunfight initiated by the Officials led by Joe McCann around the Inglis's Bakery in Eliza Street lasted most of the night. Another 550 troops were flown in, bringing the total in the province to 12,500. They were overstretched: on the streets under barrages of rocks, vulnerable to snipers hour after hour, back to the barracks for a few hours, and then again on the streets. On Wednesday the riots continued unabated. The death toll rose. Some seventy internees were freed and others moved to the Magilligan Camp on the north coast or the *Maidstone* in Belfast harbor. Both centers were cramped bleak, without proper facilities. And as the internees moved in those released reported on army brutality.

There was no letup in international fascination with the television clips of Belfast burning or with the horror stories: torture, murder, the British army at play. Heath flew back from Plymouth to London. Hillery returned to Dublin. Hume and Fitt flew to London to see Maudling. No one seemed happy except the official spokesmen and Faulkner's friends. Faulkner announced that "the security forces and the government feel that internment is working out remarkably well. It has exposed the gunmen." Many of these exposed gunmen could be heard firing on RUC and army patrols in West Belfast. Security officials nevertheless insisted that internment had been a success and that 70 percent of the suspects sought had been arrested, among them a high proportion of the IRA leadership, and that 116 suspects not in the IRA had been released.

The primary basis for these statements was not intelligence but wishful thinking. The army and RUC had known only a few IRA names and most of those had gone on the run. Kevin Hannaway and Francis McGuigan, Belfast Provos, had been lifted but the Belfast structure was quite intact and the rank and file hardly touched. Lots of the famous republican names reactive since 1969 were missed as well as the new volunteers. In Derry, where the unit was filled with the middle-aged and so known, the army did better, arresting Seán Keenan and Phil O'Donnell, and so their Derry unit was no firm competition for John White's Officials. White, young and unknown, had evaded arrest. Generally the next day was little better for the army. The death toll in the province rose to twenty-two. Accusations of brutality were made by the conservative Catholic Defense Committee. Fitt and Devlin called internment sectarian. In London, Crossman in the *New Statesman* called for withdrawal from the province in twelve months—"come what may." Some hints of a return to normality were seen when Paisley led marchers to Stormont to call Faulkner a traitor, and in Derry the Apprentice Boys managed to march without incident. It was about the only good news except that the rioting was tapering off as a result of exhaustion.

There was a brief return to politics. Paisley went to London to complain to Maudling. David Bleakley, Minister of Community Relations, noted that "the military and police had been given very emphatic instructions to deal" with intimidation, so indicting that order could be imposed. The flight of refugees to the South tapered off although eighty Protestants arrived in Liverpool—evidence of a sort of evenhanded chaos. Perhaps Faulkner and the army might scrape through. Then a massive public relations disaster struck. There was not going to be a return to everyday politics, not at least for some time. In Belfast, despite the evidence to the contrary, some in the British army felt that Operation Demetrius had been more or less successful just as planned, just as the spokesman had contended. Two hundred or so nasties were behind the wire, so the IRA had been ruined. Not knowing who to lift, the army was pleased with those in the bag: Keenan and the Derry people, Hannaway and McGuigan from Belfast, many from the RUC republican lists. And the professionals were even more pleased that the sweep had driven the IRA gunmen into the open—the army was returning fire and there were reports of twenty or thirty firm hits even if there were neither bodies nor admissions to hospitals. And the quick releases would cover up the unavoidable errors. Séamus O Tuathil from Dublin, where he was a famous editor of the *United Irishman* and well-known agitator, was not arrested on merit but because he was staying in the house of Billy McMillen, the Officials' O/C. This was a dreadful error, for O Tuathil smuggled out brutality reports on scraps of paper and thus appeared as a scoop in the *Irish Times*. Oliver Kelly was lifted because his family was republican and his brother John was mixed up with the Provos. Other subversives included John McGuffin, who wrote a book on the event, a personal gain and another net loss for an army anxious to forget, and Liam Mulholland, who was seventy-seven and charmed to be thought dangerous. Faulkner personally released many of these as soon as the blunders became clear—too late of course. At least news of the deep interrogation had not leaked out since that was ongoing and secret. So matters could be worse. And the army preferred to focus on the real gunmen in captivity. Any charges about internment could and would be answered cogently and fairly by military spokesmen: The well-planned, carefully and fairly executed, and successful operation had crippled the IRA. The army called a press conference to reveal this.

On Friday, August 13, an army spokesman, before a large group of newspapermen, television reporters, cameras, and observers read a statement claiming that the IRA had suffered a major defeat. The troops had killed twenty or thirty gunmen and wounded as many more: a body count without bodies. The leadership of the IRA had been lifted (no names mentioned) and their ranks decimated, with three hundred suspects interned. The army professed contentment. Unfortunately for the army at almost the same time Patrick Kennedy, the Stormont MP for Republican Labour, called a counterconference at Saint Peter's School in Whiterock, up the road from the army event. He introduced Joe Cahill, Belfast O/C of the Provos, a small, bald man, often under a porkpie hat, who had taken over for McKee. He appeared quite unlike anyone's image of either a gunman or an IRA man but he had been one of the key Provo players from the beginning. A lifelong IRA man who had barely escaped the gallows that had claimed Tommy Williams in 1942, he was well known in the city and by many of the media people invited by Kennedy. And there he was up the Falls Road from the army, in the open, cameras rolling, questions answered: the Provos at play. Ammunition was running low and so he could use aid from the Republic, but generally matters had gone as anticipated. Internment was no surprise. Only two Provos had been shot in the fighting and only thirty interned. So the IRA was in good shape. He closed the conference and, his cover destroyed, made his way south to Dublin, where the Army Council sent him to America to raise money now that he was a most recognizable figure.

The media people had rushed back to their hotels to transmit the fact that matters were not going as the British army claimed. The Provos were holding press conferences in broad daylight. All reports indicated that the army should have been humiliated by Cahill's coup. Nearly everyone but diehard army spokesmen agreed that internment had been a disaster. Army statements were still a disaster. On August 13 the British army spokesman, Brigadier Marston Tickell, at the end of the two-hour press conference, felt he could not answer the question as to who was winning the propaganda war—the army or the IRA. Few attending had much doubt.

Despite everything, Tuzo felt that the decision for internment had been a reasonable one, that the failure of intelligence was largely the police's fault, and that the rising charges of brutality were excessive and misinformed. There was thus no real need for the army to adjust either its posture or its propaganda. On Sunday, August 15, he warned that petrol bombers would be shot. This strategy was ill-advised in a city where petrol bombs were as common as rocks and, though more spectacular, less dangerous. By Sunday petrol bombers were no longer the province's main problem.

The minority had essentially withdrawn their toleration of the Stormont right to rule: Fitt announced a rate and rent strike and no-participation policy by the SDLP. The other minority groups began to follow suit. Paying neither rent nor taxes as a nationalist duty had enormous and immediate charm in many quarters, even if the strike was never as extensive as claimed. The SDLP was boycotting Stormont anyway, so the political response merely tagged along behind the gunmen who were firing on the British at the bottom of a garden. The shift in emphasis was that politics, protest, civil disobedience, ritual, and riot were now directed not against the inequities of the system but at the system itself, any British system for the militants and the visible one for the others. Except for a few Castle Catholics (the token, usually middle-class, conservatives co-opted by the system) the minority had been absolutely alienated. The Provos began to broaden their targets and put the volunteers on a war footing. The next stage had been reached all over the six counties. The graffiti "I Ran Away" could be forgotten. In Derry, Martin McGuinness, one of the new wave of 1969 volunteers who had transformed the movement elsewhere, took over the unit as O/C. Everywhere there was massive support and general toleration, a toleration that spread throughout the South.

There Lynch, once more pushed by events, had called for an end to Stormont two days after internment Monday but had made no other move other than opening the refugee camps. Dublin had to continue to play softly or else be caught by the turmoil and with an army that the knowledgeable felt would not have gotten to Newry in 1969, much less in 1971, with the British army up to seventeen thousand men in Ulster. In the Republic, however, both republican movements found their door, often labeled Sinn Féin, besieged again with eager volunteers. North and South there were new people, new money, but the same old problems with training and gear—little of the former and less of the latter. The good men were in action and could not be spared for the classroom, and even their operations were limited by the mismatched arms available on a carefully policed island for a secret army with few foreign friends or contacts. The Provos, at least, felt as Cahill had said, that they were in good shape.

There were in Northern Ireland still signs of normality, if street protests, sit-ins, alarming reports of the cost and chaos and the return of the refugees could be considered normal. The Derry barricades were to come down—for a while at least. What was truly not normal was the level of the IRA campaign, for their war had now become extended, more intense, tolerated or supported by a huge number of nationalists, North and South. The parallels drawn by the republicans with the Glory Years of the Easter Rising and Tan War were not missed by many. And, as in all previous campaigns from the Fenians to the more recent failures along the border in 1956–62, the struggle within the prisons played a prominent role. In a unconventional war the rebel seeks to push on all fronts even as the military absorbs most assets, often leaving little for politics or propaganda. There is no difference in serving in prison, pasting posters, or bombing on active service. In real wars, conventional campaigns, prisoners are lost and forgotten; but in an armed struggle prisoners are soldiers on a different front, their service no less important, their presence never forgotten. Those lost to the first sweep would be transmuted into assets. This was done first by ballads, a crucial symbolic indicator. The most popular in 1972 was a hastily written song based on the Belfast sweep and called "The Men Behind the Wire." It was written by Pat McGuigan, who on January 6, 1972, would be interned himself—most said for writing the song in the first place, the song that became the anthem of internment:

> *Armored cars and tanks and guns*
> *Came to take away our sons*
> *But every man will stand behind the*
> *   men behind the wire.*
> *Through the little streets of Belfast*
> *In the dark of early morn*
> *British soldiers came marauding*
> . . .
>
> *Heedless of the crying of children*
> *Dragging fathers from their beds*
> *Beating sons while helpless mothers*
> *Watched the blood pour from their heads*
> . . .

Not for them a judge or jury
Nor indeed a crime at all
Being Irish means they're guilty
So we're guilty all.

If lacking in subtlety or elegance, McGuigan's ballad yet indicated just what the impact had been and why. Those sons and fathers had been transmuted to patriots and, for the IRA, soldier-prisoners. The Crumlin Road Prison in Belfast had long been a home for Northern republicans, interned or imprisoned, who kept to their own, elected officers, organized escape committees and education classes, and invested enormous amounts of time in looking for a way out of prison and/or a means to improve the movement. Such time was duty tour and, if not an honor still a mark of distinction. All such prisoners were, in their own eyes and the eyes of the system, quite different from the normal criminal population, whatever the establishment rhetoric of the moment. Even isolated singly in English prisons, one among ordinary criminals, they were treated differently by the authorities and by the criminals. Northern Ireland had always been a relatively crime-free society, the prisons were few and unpleasant, and in 1971 obviously inadequate for a considerable levy of subversive detainees.

As was the case during World War II, a ship was pressed into service—the *Maidstone*—but it was clear from the first that the vessel was without adequate room or facilities and that some sort of camp would be necessary. Long Kesh, two miles south of Lisburn, a British army headquarters just southwest of Belfast, was hastily built over the runways of an abandoned RAF airfield: fifteen-foot wire fences, watchtowers, twelve main buildings to house the internees, toilet blocks, and buildings for guards. It was a replica of prisoner of war encampments world-wide. Miserable and bleak, with the most limited amenities, search-lights burning twenty-four hours a day, mud or dust, squalid and nasty, the Kesh was notorious, an IRA battle honor, a symbol and a school. Another camp, Magilligan on the bleak northern coast twenty-four miles east of Derry, with four cages and the huts inside, opened in January 1972 to handle the overflow from the Kesh. Just as grim, it lacked the notoriety of the Kesh. When the British decided to phase out internment and criminalize the paramilitaries, the Kesh was replaced a few years later with a whole new complex of enormous, sterile, escape-proof buildings, designed in an H-shape and erected next to the old camp. The Kesh became Her Majesty's Prison the Maze except in common usage. The *Maidstone* and Magilligan in Derry had been closed, so Long Kesh and the women's prison at Armagh were raised to star status along with Crumlin. Thus the Kesh, Crumlin, and Armagh became laden with meaning, names of battles.

The prisons of Northern Ireland, and often those in the Republic, are a special IRA world with habits and attitudes descending from the Fenians. Over ten thousand men and women would pass through this world; a few would remain for most of their adult lives, and even those who did short time, would be changed. This new Ulster archipelago had not existed before August 1969, for most of the militants during the marching seasons—Devlin or Gogarty, Bunting or Paisley—came and went through the conventional prisons and regular court season at speed, as part of the march. Until the summer of 1971 the security forces had barely begun the process of arresting, trying, and sentencing suspected paramilitaries, particularly republicans. This was in fact ostensibly the major factor in introducing internment: The RUC could not fill the jails with gunmen because normal means were ineffectual. By mid-August 1971 the jails were crammed, if not always with gunmen.

The most controversial of the new holding pens had been set up in a British military barracks to allow for the special deep interrogation techniques that had evolved from those lessons learned by the British army in previous colonial insurrections. That the military felt such a procedure to be standard given the conditions indicates what the British military thought those conditions were. Only a few senior commanders knew that the RUC had been trained in such techniques or that the army planned on applying them to IRA suspects. Thus, the internees assumed to possess vital information would receive carefully monitored maltreatment. The interrogators sought to disorient a dozen or so selected prisoners whose revelations would open up the IRA underground. These men were hooded, kept without sleep or normal hours while listening only to white noise, erratically fed, harassed, kept for long periods in painful positions, and so made amenable to query. Adaptation to previous civilian complaints during colonial campaigns had assured the army that these methods, now refined, would be satisfactory in Northern Ireland—given the circumstances. When, as was inevitable, news leaked out, first the army and then London insisted there was no cause for alarm: Such interrogation was standard and carefully managed. After that it was all downhill.

Northern Ireland was not just another colonial insurrection, nor were internment's critics easily pacified: Injustice was seen to have been done through internment, used as a sectarian tool, and torture seen to have been done in the use of deep interrogation. The army had arrested innocent suspects with brutality. The army had taken them to barracks and made them run the gauntlet—beaten them all, beaten them after the frightful and frightening time during the arrest, beaten them as revenge or as policy. This leaked out almost at once, as well as the rumor, later proved accurate, that suspects arrested later were being brutalized even as the news of earlier maltreatment was disclosed. Soon, the hidden maltreatment of the select few through deep interrogation also leaked out. London's response, as often was the case in Northern Irish matters, was to appoint a committee to investigate the methods of interrogation. The three commissioners, Lord Parker, Lord Gardiner, former Labour lord chancellor, and John Boyd-Carpenter, were not announced until November 30, the same day that the Irish government in Dublin announced its intention to place the allegations of brutality before the European Court of Human Rights at Strasbourg. A great deal of time had passed by then and attitudes had hardened. The late British response appeared at best grudging and self-serving. In time the majority report of Lord Parker and Boyd-Carpenter exonerated the army: "We have come to the conclusion that there is no reason to rule out these techniques on moral grounds and that it is possible to operate them in a manner consistent with the highest standards in our society."

There was thus no maltreatment, or rather no torture and brutality, and so no need to worry. There had been only recourse to unpleasant means to acquire indispensable information. Lord Gardiner in his minority report felt quite differently.

> The blame for this sorry story . . . must lie with those who many years ago decided that in emergency conditions in a colonial-type situation, we should abandon our legal, well-tried and highly successful wartime interrogation methods and replace them by procedures which were secret, illegal, not morally justifiable and alien to the the traditions of the greatest democracy in the world.*

When these opinions became public in March 1972, events had moved on and positions long hardened, as was often the case with such reports. For the minority in the province, for Dublin, for much of Western public opinion alerted by an eager media, British brutality if not torture during internment was taken as a given. A commission of elegants reporting six months later was irrelevant to the first impressions and unconvincing in the bargain.

The loyalists were not concerned about the rights of gunmen and had no sympathy for media postures or with any protest: Order had to be restored. Internment was needed. Deep interrogation was a minor irrelevance seized on by the guilty and the silly to hide gunman reality. John McKeague, speaking for the Shankill Defense Association, promised that there would be Protestant retaliation unless the army sorted out the terrorists. Dr. George Simms, the Church of Ireland primate, said in an RTE interview that internment was horrible and repugnant and a hateful decision but was the lesser of two evils. Only Paisley, perceptive as usual, feared that once used internment would in time be deployed against Protestants. Like many of the majority, Paisley recognized that the last and perhaps best defense of the system might be extralegal—at least as far as the government in London was concerned if not the Queen. The other Orange militants saw only the confusion of their historic foes. Not only did the loyalists defend internment and deep interrogation but so also did members of the British establishment and much of the army. Even years later it would be claimed that it had produced "vital information from evil men."† Still, the Conservative government, taking heed of Lord Gardiner's comments and the extensive media coverage, announced that interrogation procedures would be changed.

In the summer of 1971 internment was not going to work. Those responsible did not want to know. Whether replaying the past with the same cards might have worked in Northern Ireland if tried much earlier, before the Provos had become an intractable factor, was moot. With a mobilized minority and a revitalized republican movement, albeit in two parts, and with Stormont unable

---

*On March 2, 1972, Prime Minister Heath announced the findings of the three privy councillors contained in the *Parker Report* (Cmd 4901, March 1972). Much in the mind of the three was the memorandum submitted to them by Amnesty International quoted in McGuffin, *Internment*, pp. 197–215, and European opinion generally. The Prime Minister indicated that the five controversial techniques—hooding, wall-standing, subjection to noise and deprivation of food and sleep—would not be used again.

†Lieutenant-Colonel Michael Dewar, *The British Army in Northern Ireland* (London: Arms and Armour Press, 1985), p. 55.

to coerce opposition alone, common sense would have suggested that internment would be counterproductive. In Belfast, Tuzo and the army, obeying orders and without sure alternatives, had grave practical doubts. There should have been more than doubts. The army did not know whom to arrest, where even those on their makeshift list might be, or how to operate within the Catholic areas if there was serious resistance. Technically, the army would go in blind. But no officer likes to admit incapacity, especially after over a year of exposure to the terrain, especially after a month of dry runs, and most especially with a feeling that their RUC police ally was arrogant, cynical, and incompetent. Public opinion and politics were secondary considerations. So the army accepted that a good effort was better than none and if a good effort was difficult they would do the best possible. It was a gross mistake. Yet what could an army do but indicate doubts and then obey orders?

The RUC, the Unionist establishment, the men at Stormont, the hard men in the terrace houses in East Belfast would all gain from internment no matter how flawed the exercise or how many fish slipped the net: The Lambeg drum did not have to be in tune to intimidate. Internment would indicate Protestant power still existed, could still be used, this time by the army, their army, the British army sent in by London to defend them. The general anxiety of the whole majority would be assuaged even if no traitor was actually caught. The decay of order was worrying to the decent as well as to the dreadful. The London cabinet, the army, the British might and probably would come up empty; order might not be restored and probably would be damaged if only in the short run; but the ritual would be performed and so a success—the loyalists would have reassurance, which in the summer of 1971 was more necessary than effective intimidation.

The Unionists, too, were wrong. Internment would fail doubly: fail to work and fail to reassure. The majority could no longer afford the price of reassurance because the minority could and did raise the cost. The British had waited so long that internment was no longer an effective option and the loyalists had waited too long for the ritual to be a symbolic ritual. Instead the minority revealed new boldness and capacity, redoubling the majority's insecurity. In two years the minority players had changed. Their psychic grievances could no longer be rebottled or smashed and worst of all could no longer be accommodated simply by serial concessions. The minority did not feel inferior and so wanted justice. Justice may be variously defined but up to the moment of internment could be largely achieved by specific steps toward fairness. After internment the newly outraged minority wanted *more*. What exactly was ill-defined, except by the IRA, but not easily ceded. A major initiative that transformed the province and included the end of Stormont was the last viable option, which London had postponed until the last Orange card had been played. The postponement meant that an end of Stormont would not end the game. Britain had with internment risked not just a practical failure (nearly assured, as Tuzo knew) but a symbolic failure that just getting rid of Stormont might not recoup. The name of the game had changed.

Internment would guarantee for the minority a general commitment to change, an emotional mobilization against the past fifty years. This determination was so firm that the center would be able for years to find no solution that would placate the minority without alienating the majority. This determination would permit the IRA's armed struggle no matter the subsequent decay of support and toleration. For the republicans, the province should not exist. For most other nationalists the minimum demand was a new form leading to ultimate unity of the island. The IRA wanted unity now and the others later, perhaps much later, but in the meantime a new and just provincial system. For the majority the disorder following internment shaped all the old fears. Thus, with their fears justified, the hope in the present was as the hope in ages past: No surrender. The majority was riven by suspicion that some, some at Stormont, some with pretensions of moderation, might give an inch to save a foothold and so lose the whole. And those in London would not understand, would not grasp Ulster reality, and so could not be trusted. No one could be trusted.

So it is strange that no one responsible foresaw the disasters that were bound to occur if internment was introduced. The army was quite unprepared. Of course, property was ruined, innocent people hurt, the wrong men taken. Of course, the suspects were mauled by frightened and angry young soldiers. What had been expected? Of course, the mobs were out. Given the riots for less cause over the years, what had been expected? Certainly the army must have considered that the IRA would exploit the event, resist arrests that could not all be simultaneous and a surprise. The internment sweep would be clumsy, brutal, at times ineffectual, and but the first step.

What did the army imagine the media would make of what came next? Hundreds of men were beaten and then jammed into cells or on board a makeshift prison ship, without charges. There would be families howling at the gates, solicitors with papers, demonstrators through the British Isles, questions in Parliament, and hectoring editorials, and the whole thing on television—no letup and the army blamed as well as Stormont and the RUC. To this the army as standard procedure added deep interrogation, a public relations death wish at work.

Nothing was likely to remain secret for long and the explanations had to satisfy beyond the establishment and the military. And no explanations were prepared, not for failure, not for the inevitable excesses, and of course not for special interrogation techniques. No one had given revelation much thought, so eager were the involved to try out the techniques and so removed were the commanders from the real world. Interrogation opened everyone concerned to waves of outrage at this scientifically applied, carefully monitored ill treatment based on research in pain and imposed as standard procedure. The assumption that suspects could be selectively brutalized in an authorized program for maltreatment in the United Kingdom in 1971 without scandal was profound folly.

In fact, criticism started immediately within the army as Brigadier Kitson gave a withering indictment of the whole affair. "I think he was jolly nearly sacked for what he said. He told them that it had been done in the wrong way, at the wrong time and for the wrong reasons. Didn't seem to go down terribly well."* It did not

---

*Desmond Hamill, *Pig in the Middle, The Army in Northern Ireland* (London: Methuen, 1985), p. 64. Kitson's subsequent publications on low-intensity conflict were used as theoretical works by those ultra-conservatives within British society who foresaw not subversion but revolution, with no one firm at the helm. The result was an atmosphere conducive to

go down well because the army still was inclined to feel that much had been accomplished, albeit at some unanticipated cost. And an army's priorities were hardly those of the politicians who had authorized Operation Demetrius. The officers believed that twenty or thirty IRA gunmen had been hit. Why not believe their soldiers? The army assumed that out of three hundred arrests, many must have been gunmen. Why believe Joe Cahill and not their own intelligence? Many in the army found all sorts of rationalizations. Why, then, be upset at Left journalists and bleeding-heart liberals? Why not look on the bright side and tidy up the techniques? So Kitson was ignored in 1971.

All that the London establishment learned from internment week and the ensuing fallout was that caution would pay, that force in order's name could be used but only discreetly. The fact that latent and not so latent anti-Irish sentiment existed throughout Britain was a help. The Irish were different, in many ways lesser if amusing and if not amusing often violent, and so could be treated differently. This British prejudice was often curious in that unlike American racism or Japanese exclusiveness it went unacknowledged: All a chap need do is be like us. And when the Irish refused to be English, there was universal resentment. And most certainly the situation in Ulster was different, Irish not English, not even British. Consequently, toleration existed for extraordinary methods, especially after any particularly distressing Irish event, among all classes and parties. In 1971 and afterward it was a help in London that the critics of the system in place, any system in place, could be labeled terrorists. And such a label was hardly inappropriate, hardly the result of prejudice.

Never again after internment was the media treated so ineptly. The army learned how to manipulate these observers with cameras or notebooks: briefings, special lunches, treats in London, tours and leaks and detailed kits were all ready. And there was intervention at a higher level if there was reluctance to follow the going line.* The basic assumptions of the British view were thus rarely questioned and even the more egregiously unpleasant policies found sympathetic ears. That lesson, at least, was learned.

Most of all the British reputation for justice and fair play paid interest in Ireland year after year. Commissions were appointed, trials held, investigations authorized, strict orders enforced; and if the government faltered, British society produced critics who found adequate forums. This, coupled with the visible incompetence and ruthless brutality of some of the players in the province, helped create a pool of sympathy for the responsible. Psychopathic Orange killers, Marxist-Leninist IRA terrorists, greedy and bigoted politicians, criminals and mad dog killers were on parade. All of them were fomenting communal strife, murdering and robbing for dubious reasons, causing the trouble that only the disinterested presence of the dutiful British kept in bounds. So said a generation of press officers, army spokesmen, academics, television readers, editorial writers, foreign journalists in for a week, and producers of news documentaries after a visit

---

reactionary subversion, muttering of coups and private armies, not the first time that Ireland has inspired the British military to contemplate armed resistance to the government.
*Cf. Jo Thomas in "Bloody Ireland," *Columbia Journalism Review*, May/June 1980, pp. 31–37, reviewing her trouble in covering Northern Ireland for *The New York Times*.

to Lisburn barracks. And most of the British and the foreigners did so sincerely, believing they spoke the truth. They believed. And given the cast of the drama in Ulster it was easy to believe.

Few in Britain wanted to believe the worst of the army, of the government, of the system. (This is hardly peculiar to the British.) So, many would rally no matter what the charge. Many simply refused to accept any Irish criticism, any defense even of the victims: London would not lie nor would the army brutalize. Thus, much unpleasant news from Ireland was filtered out, not simply by the awful jingo evening papers or retired Blimps in London clubs but by the British in general. There was the practice of generations of filtering out Ireland, adjusting the fanciful grievances of Celtic reality to British common sense. This quite fanciful British common sense was always a net asset to a government seeking to cope with a most distressful province, a province gripped by a protracted, intractable level of violence.

The maltreatment of prisoners that arose in response to that violence seen as colonial rebellion did not suddenly disappear once revealed. As a result the nationalist population was outraged with a series of revelations through the year and on into 1972 as those responsible adjusted. Over this period news leaked out very swiftly, was spread first by the involved (easily denied), then usually by the Irish newspapers (easily ignored), and finally through the British media, where it reached a wider public (easily distracted). The authorities after explanations and rationalizations appointed several formal investigators at some level and had the responsible adjust procedures.

The most immediate acts were those that took place during the arrests of August 9, visible to a great many Catholics but excused as the result of inexperienced troops under pressure. The rough treatment proved harbinger not aberration. Between August 9 and 11 the internees were taken to Ballykinlar and Magilligan army camps, to the *Maidstone* and Crumlin Road Jail and the Girdwood army barracks near Crumlin. At Girdwood the prisoners were forced to run the famous gauntlet of soldiers to and from a helicopter. In many cases the brutalizing of internees appeared systematic and organized—someone in authority had prepared or tolerated such treatment. Within a few days news of these events had seeped out into Belfast and down to Dublin. By the time Séamus O Tuathail's smuggled account of his experiences appeared in the *Irish Times* on August 19 a second stage of maltreatment was under way.

The notorious deep interrogation took place between August 11 and 17. Coupled with this more elegant approach, beginning on August 23 and continuing on into 1972 in various internment centers, but particularly in Palace army barracks, the army and police continued more traditional harsh methods of interrogation. This low-tech violence could not be hidden for long either; but despite spreading publicity it was not discontinued.

By the end of the year the nature of the exercise was generally known and would, at the instigation of the Dublin government, come before the European Court of Human Rights at Strasbourg on November 30. This was merely one of many initiatives arising from the British methods, ranging from an effort by Gerry Fitt in New York on August 25 to involve the United Nations in the memorandum of Amnesty International to the Parker committee and the Dublin government for an impartial investigation. The response of the British authorities had at first been to ignore or to fend off such interference, claiming their actions were necessary, if harsh, security procedures. The Unionists never had doubts. Faulkner felt the Republic's attitude was one of "cant and hypocrisy" and Taylor urged Dublin to introduce internment to cut off the IRA bases in the South. In time the rising volume of complaints and the evidence from released prisoners forced the authorities to appoint committees to investigate, but these inquiries were not exactly impartial.

To some degree the British public's toleration of the security measures in Ireland coupled with the most optimistic analysis of the effectiveness of the arrests eroded any acute sense of urgency in London. Resentment at ill-informed critics of all sorts edged the responsible into a defense of the initiative that subsequent events and revelations did not seriously shake. Internment may not have worked, but at least something had been done. What had been done in Northern Ireland, however, was to erode restraint. The nationalists now tolerated the IRA going over to the offensive. The SDLP and others who wanted no part of the gun in politics had to find a role beyond ritual protest and rationalizing murder by the Provos and Stickies. On August 14 Bernadette Devlin called for a one-day strike and then the nonpayment of rent and rates as a protest. Not paying taxes as a patriotic duty had a compelling charm. The next day in Belfast Gerry Fitt, after a meeting of nine opposition Stormont MPs, called for a campaign of civil disobedience. Amid the protests and demonstrations, the revelations of the mistreatment of the internees, and the huge media buildup, the IRA added to the din with shooting and bombing. This armed struggle, which showed no signs of abating, further assured the republicans of nationalist toleration: The British army was now enemy, and who but the IRA was left to defend them? This armed defense, merging into the Provos' long-sought offensive stage, simultaneously outraged the loyalists. There seemed little room for conciliation, little prospect of building on the order that internment had promised and failed to produce. In fact, by the end of August, the weeks before internment began to seem very orderly, and prospects for an orderly autumn began to seem faint.

Robert Cooper of the Alliance Party felt that the Protestants were being driven into Paisley's arms and Paisley and the militant loyalists were in turn organizing behind the back of the Unionist Party. At Stormont a core group suspected that Faulkner might betray Ulster, as had O'Neill, might desert Ulster, as had Chichester-Clark. Then the meeting in September in London of Faulkner, Heath, and Lynch awakened all the old loyalist doubts. Why Lynch? What had been promised the Irish Republic? Paisley, Craig, Boal, the Reverend Martin Smyth, head of the Belfast Orange Order, and a few others formed a Unionist Alliance in September. On September 29, when the Ardoyne Provos bombed the Four Step Inn on the Shankill Road, killing two people and injuring twenty, Paisley used the moment to snatch leadership. He rushed from a Unionist Alliance meeting in Belfast at the Grand Central Hotel in Royal Avenue to the ruins of the Four Step Inn to announce that he was forming the Democratic Unionist Party. Fundamentalist loyalism would have its own political vehicle—or, as it developed, Paisley would have a political party to offer a home to all militants, not simply his own Free Presbyterian flock. Thus, the IRA campaign engendered not only competi-

Prime Minister of Northern Ireland Captain Terence O'Neill meets with Taoiseach Seán Lemass at Stormont on January 14, 1965.

Seán Lemass, Jack Lynch, and Charles Haughey of Fianna Fail.

Republican Commemoration at Bodenstown in June 1967. In conversation are Cathal Goulding, chief of staff of the IRA, Seán Mac Stiofáin, later chief of staff of the Provisional IRA, and Séamus Costello, later chief of staff of the Irish National Liberation Army.

Civil rights demonstrators clash with the army in Derry in 1969.

Burnt-out Catholic street in the Ardoyne, Belfast, in August 1969.

Meeting of Provisional Sinn Féin Executive Committee, Kevin Street, Dublin.

Séamus Twomey, Provisional IRA O/C of Belfast, at a Brigade Staff meeting.

Above and below: Car bomb in Derry, March 1972.

Above and below: Car bomb in Derry, March 1972.

Ruairí O Brádaigh, president of Provisional Sinn Féin.

Tomás Mac Giolla, president of Official Sinn Féin, later the Workers Party.

DAVID GIFFORD

British army in Belfast.

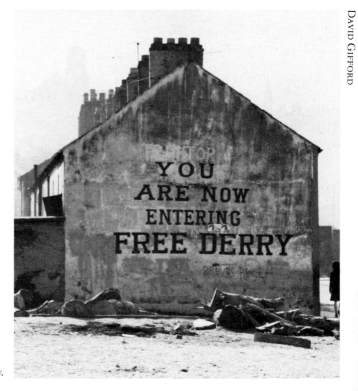

DAVID GIFFORD

The entrance to the No-Go Zone of Derry.

Long Kesh, Maze Prison, outside Belfast before the construction of the H-Blocks.

Bloody Sunday, January 30, 1972, in Derry, when thirteen protesters were shot dead by the British paratroop regiment during a civil rights demonstration.

William Craig of the Ulster Vanguard Movement and Billy Hull
of the Loyalist Association of
Workers, LAW, directing a loyalist protest immediately after the
Northern Ireland parliament
at Stormont was prorogued and
the instigation of Direct Rule
from London was announced on
March 24, 1972.

Provisional IRA leaders on June 23, 1972. Left to right: Martin McGuinness, Dáithi O
Conaill, Seán Mac Stiofáin, and Séamus Twomey.

Seán Garland and Mick Ryan of the Official Republican movement at Gardiner Place, Dublin.

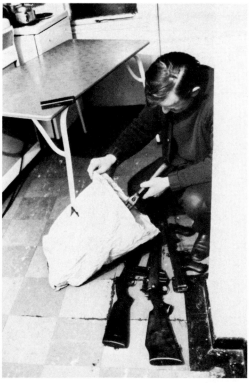

Provisional IRA volunteer transporting arms.

Announcement of the formation of the Northern Ireland Executive. Unionist leader Brian Faulkner, Northern Secretary William Whitelaw, Alliance Party leader Oliver Napier, and SDLP leader Gerry Fitt.

Belfast children in nationalist district.

Belfast children in loyalist district.

Car bomb on May 17, 1974, on South Leinster Street off Nassau Street, next to Trinity College, Dublin. The four almost-simultaneous car bombs in Dublin and Monaghan killed thirty-one people and injured fifteen.

Gerry Adams, president of Provisional Sinn Féin and Westminster MP, and Danny Morrison, Provisional Sinn Féin Director of Publicity, outside party offices on the Falls Road, Belfast.

Northern Secretary Merlyn Rees with security force during an inspection of security barriers in the Belfast city center in 1976.

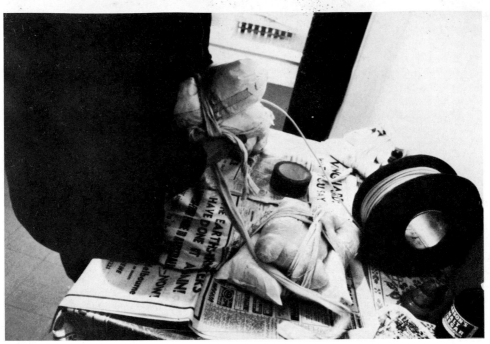

Above and below: Provisional IRA bomb being constructed.

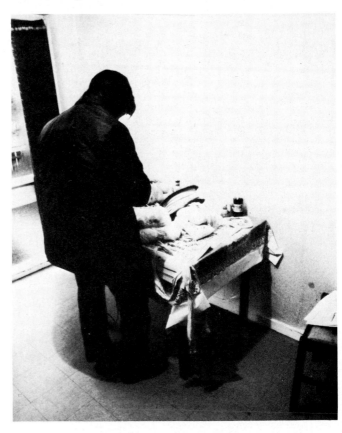

tion within the nationalist community to give a lead to outrage but also the division of the Unionist monolith into competing militancies.

Politics in the province were being crowded off the front pages by the bombs. The effort by the SDLP and the radicals to rush into the arena once the fallout from internment had blown off was hardly an unqualified success. A rent-and-rates strike or another march lacked the spectacular. At least the strike involved many nationalists in nonviolent options and in time resulted in Stormont passing the Payment for Debt Act (Emergency Provisions) that allowed the government to dock welfare payments for nonpayment of rent and taxes. The move that hit the poorer Catholics was seen by the nationalists as vindictive—it did not even make good the losses—and so further alienated the minority. Paisley's new DUP had little immediate impact; organizing a new party takes place out of sight, a process of little appeal to Paisley.

Mostly the turmoil arose from the Provos' armed struggle, abetted by the Officials, who were more discreet in their target selection. The Provo snipers were active in both the towns and countryside, turning the province into a free-fire zone. Armed bank robberies to raise funds became more common, more blatant, and more attractive to marginal groups or common criminals. The Provos began extensive bombing, theoretically to destroy the "artificial economy of the six counties" but in large part because explosions were possible and spectacular and might blow away the system if not the Brits. So explosions became the norm; no night was complete without a detonation within earshot. For Belfast and Derry the constant rumble soon became habitual. The Provos' explosive factories in the Republic and in the countryside turned out a variety of matériel that made possible larger and larger explosions. The makers used commercial fertilizers, some easily available chemicals, various household additives, and petroleum products. Detonators were stolen or shipped into the country piecemeal. Commercial explosives were stolen both in Ireland and abroad. Some were to say that a certain percentage of the construction explosives intended for New York City's third, giant water main ended instead in Ireland. Factory-produced Irish cordite and gelignite used with the homemade explosives produced a massive detonation from an admittedly bulky bomb. The self-taught engineers began to reduce the bulk, improve the intensity, and thus transform the bombs from devices akin to the cartoon anarchists' smoking, black cannonballs of the nineteenth century to more adaptable and effective modern constructions primed and run off batteries or with clocks. In August there were over one hundred IRA explosions, many of them massive, all drowning out any political dialogue.

Stormont struggled on. The withdrawal of the nationalists was partly hidden by the advent of Paisley's DUP as a formal opposition. What else was to be done except respond to the rent and rate strike or urge harsher security measures no one seemed to know. There were 196 explosions in September. Internment had not worked. The figures just grew more depressing. In the four months before Operation Demetrius four soldiers had been killed, no policemen, and four civilians. In the four months afterward, thirty soldiers, eleven policemen, and seventy-three civilians were killed. The army continued to pick up and intern suspects so that by mid-December 1,500 individuals had been taken into custody. And one thousand had been released, each a martyr to intelligence incompetence, each an ink blot of alienation along with the family and friends. It did no good to blame the Provos.

The meeting in Munich on September 4 between Heath and Lynch had been little more than cosmetic. Lynch could do nothing. Heath still wanted to do nothing. And Faulkner in Belfast could only soldier on. Mostly the Official Unionists waited, watched the militants drift toward Paisley and the new DUP, plotted against or for Faulkner, unable to influence the British Tories, who many suspected wanted to opt for direct rule, discarding Stormont. The Unionist government was at work on a proposal for the future government of the province but without great enthusiasm and without a radical vision. No one seemed interested in Unionist hopes. Mostly it was Unionist fears that counted. On September 23 a debate on Ulster at Westminster revealed what had always been suspected: Harold Wilson and the Labour Party wanted to dismantle Stormont even as they supported the Conservatives' handling of the situation. It might be only a matter of time before the Conservatives accepted Wilson's advice. No one in the province was happy except perhaps the Provisional IRA with the bombs going off all night in Belfast and their men making the country roads unsafe. They at least had an armed struggle.

The Northern Irish crisis had escalated into the new Troubles without an immediately visible or viable solution. Radical change appeared just as dangerous to London as doing nothing: British withdrawal, rarely discussed, would apparently produce civil war, while imposing order with unrestrained military force was unacceptable in a democratic society. In the middle, even reforms did not seem to produce promised results. If reform was to work, reform had to be seen to work. Then the rising support of the IRA would be eroded among the minority. Reform had not been seen to work—internment wiped out all that had gone before, all that had seemed so radical to the majority—and so the IRA campaign had escalated. More was needed. On Friday, August 20, the Northern Ireland government had issued a White Paper called "A Record of Constructive Reforms" that listed acts implementing equality since 1969. It went unread by those for whom the reforms were supposedly crafted. There was a war. There were five hundred men interned on suspicion. There were Paisley and Craig and the rest eager for a return to the old days, the old sectarian ways that were still all too present. If London were to reduce the war, marginalize the IRA, and so fashion time for the minority to perceive the new direction, then the security forces would have to be effective. But to be effective, as the army had pointed out to the politicians, assured that the minority would be alienated. It was a no-win situation.

Internment was only the most visible example of a security measure that undermined security. Those who worked on the ground, searching for explosives, generated anger and distaste among those whose houses were ransacked or whose neighbors were harassed. There seemed no means of amelioration much less a viable solution. Even those British politicians innocent of Ireland could see the results on the television if not in their constituency concerns. The province had turned into a war zone and in the autumn of 1971 no one in London or Belfast could see just where a wrong turn had been taken or where to turn to reach an accommodation of interests. All roads led downhill into the smoke from the bomb blasts. All yesterday's options had vanished with internment. There seemed little to replace internment but direct rule, which offered only the certainty that London would be blamed, could no longer keep responsibility at one remove. And direct rule would alienate the majority with no guarantee of making the minority happy. So there it was, as everyone during 1971 in Britain had feared: The Irish question had reentered British politics and again brought no easy options but only wrath and violence.

This time at least the Irish question did not bring this dissent and division into Westminster, into the very structure of the state, as had the old Home Rule quarrel. This time the Troubles were a provincial matter. This time Irish votes did not matter in the Commons. This time another Ireland centered in Dublin might be brought into the problem as a benign presence. This time the Irish question was awful but not vital. The fifty-year recess with Ireland reduced to neighbor and province, amusing, site of golf courses and fishing waters, a vacation spot, had come to an end in 1968. The sectarian system out of sync with British practice and norms in a small, distant, unimportant province run by Tory cousins could, it was assumed, be adjusted and matters returned to normal. It was a small matter and so an intimate crisis even in 1970. The RUC truly knew all the republicans. NICRA could fit into a room. The students on the marches knew one another's first names. For a generation most of the involved had names and postures. When they were joined after 1968 by a new cast, the players had names as well. At the edge of events were potential volunteers, recruits, followers, mobs in waiting, secret armies that began to filter into the arena in 1970. There were thus the new names like John Hume and Bernadette Devlin and the old gunmen like Joe Cahill and Seán Mac Stiofáin; the new Prime Minister was the old Faulkner and the new DUP leader was the old Paisley. By 1971, with a few exceptions, those first seen reacting to the new opportunities would remain regular members of the cast. In this sense the Irish Troubles were to remain intimate. Names were added as power shifted in London and Dublin, names were added as the new came of age, but always the familiar ones were at the top.

The stage became crowded with recruits and volunteers and camp followers as the structures grew large. The Provisional IRA's campaign involved thousands of volunteers, unit commanders, newspaper editors, mural painters and safe house caterers, legates sent abroad, grandfathers of violence activated and kept at home, messengers and drivers and active service people in Manchester and Antwerp and the hills of Kerry. After a generation there would be more dead volunteers listed in the IRA's *Last Post* than there had once been in the army. In time the loyalists would involve thousands in their secret armies and structured conspiracies, all new and often faceless as well. On such a small stage where everyone in theory knew everyone, contacts across the divided were few, one group knew little about the other and not even in detail. Intelligence was poor except about media-famed leaders and in time resulted in repeated and lethal mistakes. A divided community knows only its own and the others' dead. And there would be many of these in the years to come, littering even the small stage.

Every organization spawned by the crisis or inherited from more peaceful days tended to grow grand if it was relevant to the integrity of the quarrels. New parties were founded—not only the SDLP and DUP, with old cores and a large constituency, but novelties with a short half-life like Eamonn McCann's Socialist Resistance Group founded in the Derry Bogside on August 17, 1971, or Kevin Boland's Aontacht Eireann founded in Dublin a month later. There appeared to be all sorts of change and yet much stayed the same. Paisley's fundamentalists had long been abroad and Ireland had always had a few radicals, even a few radicals in the IRA. The media, of course, magnified all these emerging figures and forms.

Even the major players grown grand in a small province were not very grand elsewhere—especially in London. Mostly, particularly after 1972, the Irish names in the Irish Troubles would remain remarkably stable. London was always ready to discount the parochial concerns in six small counties and the capacities of the local leaders, often bigots or gunmen or both, seldom of Churchillean stature, rarely sophisticated, and never English. London felt it not only knew the Irish but after years knew them all too well. The crisis, then, retained a certain intimacy and for the British a certain familiarity as well as time passed. It could be slotted into a file with the famous names underlined. The result was that although the problem seemed to have no solution it never had to be understood or solved, only ignored or in moments of emergency cosmetically adjusted. There was nothing else to be done and no real cost in doing nothing.

If the Irish crisis from London's reverse telescope appeared small, a nasty scene directed by limited men without a sense of the possible or even a grasp of the present, then a different perception was offered to everyone else by the power of television. A bomb on the evening news, perhaps in color as such sets spread, but always live and personal and close up, exaggerated the problem. The problem and the violence it generated were hardly either intimate or small except in its ranking on the British political agenda. The international media came back to the province in search of hard news, visible news spread out scenically beneath the highrise windows of the Europa Hotel in Belfast. With internment and the bombs and nightly riots, the North was hot again. Everyone was interested. Everyone had an opinion. The newsmen and women producers and stringers sent from London even knew now whom to ask. This was a crisis rerun with violence added. Everyone wanted Irish news. The Pope was concerned. American politicians were outspoken. Radicals in Italy or Germany appeared in the Bogside or off the Falls to savor revolution in action, a revolution that had petered out in Paris in 1968 and by 1971 had seemingly been thwarted in Rome and Milan but seemed alive and well in Ulster.

The immediate response by the Unionists in particular and the majority in general had been resentment of the media. Robin Chichester-Clark complained of his disgust with BBC coverage in a telegram to the director. At least what tales were being sent abroad to Frankfurt or Los Angeles did not appear on BBC Ulster. What worried the loyalists was that Dublin or, worse, Heath would exploit the image to impose an unwanted reality on the province. It was hard to claim internment had worked while Belfast burned on the telly and it was hard for the cabinet in London to move on to more important matters when reporters wanted to know about Ireland.

After an initial attempt to ride matters out after internment week, ignore Parliament and chastise Dublin for interference—cogenial rituals—Heath had accepted that something had to be done. So Parliament was recalled on the Irish matter. After various Labour suggestions that appeared wise on paper and appalled the loyalists in Northern Ireland, the government's handling of the matter was supported by all but sixty Labour votes. The consensus was, Let Heath handle it; and Heath's intention still was to do as little as possible. The Irish mistakenly assumed that their problem was urgent. The loyalists were sure that Wilson would cede the province to Dublin. The republicans were sure that he would not. Dublin still wanted peace and quiet. Heath made his second cosmetic move by holding an Irish summit, once again raising fears in the province unrelated to reality. Lynch was invited to meet with the prime minister and Faulkner in a September conclave. The three agree that it was a good idea to end violence, internment, and other emergency matters as soon as possible. Faulkner and Lynch went home and Heath moved on to more pressing concerns.

In Northern Ireland Paisley was already off the Stormont ship. Neither Faulkner nor the other Unionists had any idea if his DUP would be viable. Paisley had an attraction, alas, but did not seem a party man. Yet any break in the system was worrisome, for heretofore dissent had been structured as coups and cabals hidden on the Unionist back benches. Now Paisley was the official opposition. Paisley's ally John McQuade had resigned from the Unionist Party and was elected to a seat on the Belfast Corporation for his Shankill Ward with 5,710 votes to the official Unionist Mrs. Winnifred Whinton's 450 votes. This boded ill for moderate Unionists. Faulkner had the seemingly impossible task of maintaining the Stormont system by placating British distaste with Irish matters and the Unionist establishment, by placating the Catholics with the impression of movement, and by placating his own by refusing to give in to the minority demands and simultaneously cementing the British Tory connection. The arrival of the DUP meant that those really his own were fewer; the arrival of Hume's alternative assembly meant that those of the other persuasion were beyond accommodation. The result was the government's Green Paper issued on October 26 that did little more than tinker with the system, ruled out proportional representation, and made no provision for any power sharing. Faulkner had arrived at a position that in chess is called zugzwang, where any move loses.

On the same day the Green Paper appeared, the nationalist Assembly of the Northern Ireland People met at Dungiven Castle to discuss the serious problems facing the community. John Hume was elected president of what was largely a propaganda exercise rather than a revolutionary assembly. The SDLP looked to London for action, to Dublin for encouragement, to the Catholics for support and solidarity. The members also looked irrelevant because the IRA was making the running on their side of the divide and the uncompromising loyalists of Paisley and company on the other. And neither would be interested in writing in a role for Hume, Fitt, & Co. On the next day Faulkner announced that G. B. Newe, a Catholic, would serve in the cabinet with the rank of Minister of State in the Prime Minister's Office, a token Catholic, the very first appointed in a Northern Ireland government—a token without a Stormont seat or any political base, a token so long delayed as to have no advantage. The appointment was thus ignored by the British, spurned by the Catholics, and detested by the Protestants: a move without any advantage. It appeared especially to the minority that Faulkner was more concerned about his Unionist opposition than reforming the system. And the Stormont system seemingly faced a cunning minority deploying various means for the same end. The refusal of the Catholics to hold office, to participate in the Stormont political system, to go home or to forgo demonstration, the refusal of the Catholics to pay rents and rates, to consent to be governed collectively, meant that the system was not governing. None of this political action or inaction had the visibility and impact of the Provos' armed struggle, augmented by the Officials and at times by the crowd. Bombs did not entirely drown out politics but certainly made dialogue difficult and the news from the province unbalanced.

What the bombs did not seem to do was concentrate the minds of those responsible for the maintenance of the system. Faulkner and the old Unionists felt that they must struggle on. They had no options. Internment had been necessary and had some benefits. London was not happy but still London had not shut down the system—after all what else was there but the Unionists as buffer to keep Paisley and Craig in the wings? So Faulkner held on. His most active opponent remained the IRA. At the Provisional Sinn Féin's Ard Fheis, the annual convention, Mac Stiofáin even called for more civil disobedience and an extension of the nonpayment campaign to motor tax, installment plan payments, and mortgages, again an enormously popular suggestion for many of those long strapped by payments, who could now be patriotic and plush for the time being. What the republicans wanted, what they had always wanted, was to make Northern Ireland ungovernable and thus to bring down first Stormont and then the British connection. And the tides of history seemed to be flowing their way. Self-proclaimed friends from Europe appeared at the door of Kevin Street Sinn Féin in Dublin as well as at Gardiner Place, where the new rhetoric was more familiar to radicals. Major journalists and producers and documentary makers were becoming old friends. Tours had to be arranged, explanations given; the spokesmen spoke at all hours to all comers. The world was interested at last, if not London. The Irish-American politicians had acted in reflex to the nightly news: Brits Out. Senator Kennedy, a specialist in Irish matters, was surprised that the British government felt this was unwarranted interference in an internal matter.

Week after week, amid the bombs and shooting, the revelations of maltreatment of prisoners, the protests and parades, the British government itself made no effort to intervene in the province's internal affairs. Nothing happened. Nothing changed. The Provos put forth a five-point plan on September 5 that included the abolition of Stormont and the creation of a nine-county Ulster within a federated Ireland. It was largely the work of O Brádaigh and O Conaill and was to form the basis of Eire Nua, the program of Provisional Sinn Féin for a decade. The plan attracted as much interest as Stormont's earlier Green Paper. Harold Wilson on September 12 had a more complex, less drastic twelve-point plan that was essentially a reform of the existing system that in no way diminished loyalist suspicions that Labour wanted to destroy Ulster. And Ulster kept right on running without any changes. The Unionists' greatest concern was that "in the last resort" the British government would opt for direct rule. This would end devolution and their control of events. Any loss of control was still seen by many as prologue to unification. The years of turmoil had only eroded some of the unionists' expectations. Most were increasingly alienated by the decay of order and the discussion of treason. Most suggestions for change of any serious sort simply fed unionist paranoia. And nothing made a conspiracy against Stormont more likely than the escalating violence that London seemed to tolerate.

The numbers made very unpleasant reading for all but the IRA. The Army Council's bombing campaign, the offensive wedge that gradually evoked toleration by the Catholic population, had slowly accelerated before internment:

January 1971	12 explosions
February	28
March	33
April	37
May	47
June	50
July	91

The sniping and ambushes had attracted less attention than a few of the Provo spectaculars. On July 16 a five-man team wearing white coats had raided the Royal Victoria Hospital in Belfast and freed a wounded volunteer from two RUC guards. On the next day a large bomb destroyed the plant of the British *Daily Mirror* in Suffolk, causing a loss of £2 million and one hundred jobs. It was another loss chalked up to the artificial economy of the six counties, a target for a generation despite the spin-off losses of jobs, investment, and profit that often hurt the IRA's constituency. In a war everyone must sacrifice, even those not asked who could be injured by the bomb, shot by mistake, or martyred by oversight.

After internment all the numbers had gone up. As noted the first seven months of 1971 in retrospect no longer seemed as violent as they had at the time. The piecemeal deployment of British army reinforcements did little to blunt the Provo offensive. Intelligence was poor, tactics and equipment were often inappropriate, targets were diffuse and beyond hard protection, cooperation with other agencies, especially the police, was often poor, and there was no centralized command, with Faulkner isolated at Stormont and the cabinet in London otherwise occupied. The new Ulster Defense Regiment was still being put together and the RUC being reorganized. MI6 was still competing with MI5, the police Special Branch, and the agencies of army intelligence. Soldiers were shot and killed by booby-trap bombs. Banks were robbed at gunpoint. The RUC constables were killed on duty and off and the UDR murdered at home and at work. On September 26 the IRA introduced antitank rockets in Belfast—one of MacStiofáin's missions abroad to find new weapons had borne violent fruit. Arson, malicious mischief, unchronicled riots, stones tossed at random, windows broken, theft, ritual confrontation (every afternoon in Derry at Williams Street after the boys left school, a riot was arranged)—all became the pattern of Northern life. Soldiers had to patrol through Catholic districts amid clanging bin lids, screaming women and children, the threat of ball bearings shot from slings, the certainty of rocks, the possibility of gunshots, and a miasma of hate.

Each day had a chronicle of incidents. On Saturday, October 16, two RUC officers were shot and wounded in Madrid Street in East Belfast, Protestant territory patrolled by a Protestant RUC police force. In Derry a soldier was killed by an IRA sniper. Sniping was becoming institutionalized in Derry city, the Catholic children even knew which brick the IRA man would remove to give him a line of fire, what time the shooting would likely take place, what the odds were. In time the British under fire would know at what shadow to aim, which brick was likely to disappear and when. A loser only meant the game would begin again the next day with different players, same rules, same risks, ultimately similar results. In Belfast's Short Strand, the Catholic enclave, automatic fire was directed against troops until two in the morning, pinning the British down in the streets. A dead civilian was discovered later in Sheriff Street, maybe IRA, maybe no, unlucky either way. There was rioting in Derry as usual. Four buses were burned in Belfast, another black mark for public transportation that ultimately had to be discontinued. The Arts Theatre in Belfast closed because the audience would not brave the disturbances. And the Dutch police at Amsterdam's Schiphol Airport seized a DC 6 loaded with arms, including bazookas, destined for the Provos, an indicator that the Army Council was preparing for more, not less, violence as the year moved on.

On November 5, at Westminster in the Commons, a government spokesman indicated that the total weight of explosives in all bomb incidents in the province was estimated at 2,292 pounds in September and 2,381 pounds in October. Figures released in Belfast four days later indicated that since the beginning of the year the army had dismantled 418 bombs (the IRA had used 9,940 pounds of explosives for such devices), found 62,121 rounds of ammunition, searched 411 cars, while 1,757 people had been arrested for riotous behavior. In fact, between August 9 and November 6, 882 people had been arrested and 476 released, 278 interned and 112 kept under detention order, with 16 under Section 10 of the Special Powers Act. And the numbers, no matter how large, gave no indication of the tangible signs: the army patrol in the countryside appearing along the winding road like a lost war-movie crew, the Ferret army cars spinning around the corners of central Belfast, the dull shudder that indicates a heavy bomb, and the small children throwing rocks almost too heavy to lift at soldiers too bemused to move. It was a province at peril; only the middle-class suburbs and the all-Protestant areas of the countryside appeared immune—and Stormont, where Faulkner tried to run the business as usual, isolated on the green hill at the end of the great entry road, almost but not quite beyond the sound of the explosions.

Nearly everyone was against this IRA violence, even those who had much to gain by the chaos. Technically even the IRA was against violence, choosing physical force only to secure justice, only to counter the greatest force of the British, only because there was no other way. This IRA force meant that most moderate nationalists, most Catholics, could accept the reforms that would be generated without contamination, could still oppose violence and accept its rewards. The conservative and conventional always felt that the violence should now end, end with the last bomb, the previous bomb; the need was now over, the point made. It was time to reap the rewards, not blow away the state. The radicals understood the reasons and even the need, especially for defensive violence, could explain at length, but shot no one, made no bombs. They wanted revolutionary change without charge. Let the Provos, the Stickies, the gunmen make the running. Everyone from both sides of the divide deplored the murderous mistakes, the civilians maimed and slaughtered by premature explosions, by explosions too near the innocent, by explosions that detonated before an effective warning could be received, by chance and error and stupidity, by the contingent and unforeseen: the girl shot down on the corner in the midst of an ambush, the child who walked in front of a getaway car, the old man who turned into a lane at the wrong moment. Ruairí O Brádaigh explained that the death of Angela Gallaher, seventeen months, during an exchange of gunfire during an IRA attack on a British army patrol in Belfast on September 3 was one of the hazards of urban guerrilla warfare.

Such details were a concomitant part of the IRA campaign despite the effort to avoid civilian casualties. Some civilians were claimed as targets, others killed in bombings that were both indiscriminate and sectarian but either denied or claimed as military actions against loyalist paramilitaries. Mostly the mistakes, which were legion, arose from incompetence, sloth, fear, anxiety, bad intelligence, feckless planning, and inexperience. War, any war, is not tidy. Mistakes killed volunteers one after another as their bombs detonated too soon. Mistakes killed the transient and unlucky. Mistakes seemed intregal to the armed struggle. All these IRA mistakes and all the predictable blunders and spin-off costs in a guerrilla war were deplored by politicians, by prelates and the public, by the decent who focused on first causes: the gunmen and bombers. The IRA had few friends within the Roman Church, few who edited newspapers or lent money, few who belonged to the chattering classes or even few who attended universities and wrote essays. Those who had possessions and potential deplored such violence on moral grounds with honest and justifiable horror. For them murder was not worth the cost in suffering.

Yet within the nationalist community, even within the church, there were those who, while opposing the excesses and mistakes of the IRA and often the continuing campaign, were more ambivalent about the armed struggle. Some blamed the British or the loyalists for the conditions that generated violence, others found excuses and rationales. Many, even those violently opposed to both the IRA and their tactics, still felt an atavistic attraction to British confusion. There were those, of course, who felt not only a distant tug but a real tie to the IRA campaign. Many of the Catholic politicians, in any case, opposed all the things that the IRA opposed, came from similar backgrounds, and were in effect involved for the time being in common cause for the removal of the grievances of Stormont and history. To attack the IRA would be to attack their own. Nevertheless, with a few exceptions, like Patrick Kennedy of Republican Labour, who tended to support the Provisonals, they saw no need for the gun. The minority politicians were dedicated to politics and political reward. They understood voting and organizing and discussing. They were comfortable with accommodation and compromise, hoped for power and responsibility, and so found the crystalline belief of the republicans—a faith unshaken by hardship, failure, time, or reason—alien. Even as the British imposed compromise to the roar of bombs, the politicians wanted the bombing ended. Less than their people, they did not feel a need for an IRA defense; more than their people they wanted real politics. Temporarily they could only use the streets in protests that added turmoil to the

Provo's campaign. Increasingly they wanted the IRA irrelevant, off the scene, a part of history as soon as possible, so that when the British made an offer they would be the beneficiary.

Thus, there arose gradually two nationalist constituencies. There was the first, smaller but more intense, of the republicans, especially the Provos, concentrated in hard-core areas like West Belfast or South Armagh but to be found everywhere. The second constituency consisted of those dedicated to more conventional politics who, as the years passed, tended to discard their faint sympathy, then their ambivalence, for determined opposition to the gun in politics. Eventually they condemned the IRA and largely voted SDLP. The radicals split on the national issue, with some on the republican fringe, not unlike Bernadette Devlin or the People's Democracy, and the others seeking socialism first and thus moving away at an accelerating rate into class politics. The Provos' original ideological competitor, the Official IRA, would distance themselves as much as possible. The moderates, those not attracted to the Catholic party, the revolution, or the war, had always opted for conciliation and so opposed violence from the start.

The Provos assumed that in time the people would no longer be deluded by the offers of peace now or the promise of politics as usual. There was, for them, evidence in the toleration and often support of their campaign that this time their Irish were willing to support the war. Thus, the opposition of the conventional politicians was hardly a surprise and not really important. Where could Hume or Fitt or Devlin go? What could they do? Street protest was to IRA advantage. The Stormont boycott by the SDLP took them out of even the fringe of power. And on their part, looking beyond the moment, the SDLP could see that present violence by the IRA would in time pay real dividends to the SDLP when the British began to offer concessions. These could be accepted with clean hands because the SDLP could abhor IRA violence without effect. They could advocate civil disobedience knowing that such provocation led to riot and violence that in turn was exploited by the IRA just as it was by the party as evidence for need of change. Mostly, however, they were honestly and deeply opposed to violence even if it did pay. With the passage of time, their criticism would grow louder and more direct, especially those originally close to the gunman. Thus, Fitt, who once led the Republican Labour Party and in 1971 still focused on British shortcomings, would increasingly be alienated by the Provisionals. The same was true for many. And these were not the only ones increasingly willing to criticize IRA violence.

One of the most persistent and vocal of all Provisional IRA critics remained the Roman Catholic hierarchy. The republicans had, after all, arisen from the anti-clerical rationalism of the eighteenth century, and during the nineteenth century had competed for the loyalty of the emerging native Irish, natural constituency of the Church. Worse, the Fenians, the old IRA and the new, simply opposed the hierarchy, not the faith (a dangerous distinction), did not believe that waging war would deny them heaven, and hence ignored the bishops just as they ignored the politicians. The Church had only tolerated the IRA during the short years of the Tan War, 1918–1921, when their communicants tolerated or supported physical force used in their name, but once the Free State was established, the hierarchy in the South supported only the legitimate political establishment, whatever the title or form. In the North the Church was especially sympathetic to grievance but never to the gun. As the IRA was wont to point out the gun might eliminate the need for the Church as protector in the North and puppet master in the South. Thus, the legions of Rome, so fearful in loyalist myth, were at one with them on the dangers of the IRA.

On September 12 Cardinal Conway and six Catholic bishops issued a statement telling the IRA they were bringing shame and disgrace on a noble and just cause. And they pointed out the lack of logic in putting at risk lives by trying to bomb a million Protestants into a united Ireland. For the IRA those Northern Irish Protestants were merely misguided, open to conversion as Irish to the national cause. When the IRA campaign succeeded, the Northern Protestants would accept unity. The Catholic hierarchy was mistaken. The IRA rolled out as argument the Protestant converts of times past, from Wolfe Tone to Erskine Childers, even if in 1971 Protestant Provos were rare indeed. In any case, the Church had no effect on the republicans, long inured to what they saw as self-serving attacks. They had their own faith; and with such a conviction a million Protestants, a Dublin establishment in power for fifty years, an Irish population long loath to sacrifice for the national cause, opposition from both Church and the parties, from the conventional and powerful, from the British Empire, meant nothing. Rebels are and must be criminally optimistic or else they would never begin. The IRA was nothing if not persistent. And this time it appeared that persistence had paid real dividends: Why else were the bishops concerned?

For the Roman Catholic Church, supposed patron of the IRA, there was rather in real life a long history of opposition to the pretensions and arrogance of the militant republican movement, an opposition stretching beyond Fenian times. The Church did not love a rebel, especially one who could not be disciplined by the weapons available to the hierarchy. The new armed campaign was at least familiar and the bishops used more cunning than in the past, all too aware that a direct confrontation, the threat of excommunication, the denial of the sacraments, the worst that could be done had proven insufficient in the past. This time the Church, sympathetic to the grievances of their six-county flock, most at the hands of Protestant bigots, urged moderation, reform, accommodation, and looked to London and Dublin for relief. The republicans, certain of the eventual conversion of the Irish Protestants into Irish nationalists, simply ignored the Church. After all, the Church was nicely positioned in the twenty-six counties as all but a state religion, deeply embedded in the written constitution and more so in the hearts and priorities of the politicians, and nicely positioned in the six counties as defender of the minority. Everywhere the Church controlled the schools, the faith, and morals of the people. Those 1 million Protestants in a united Ireland would erode this comfortable arrangement and might insist on a pluralistic state that would not tolerate Roman hegemony. So republicans no more listened to the threats of the Church than to the anguish of the innocent. Opposition to violence was assumed to arise from interests not from ethics. Revolutionary national violence was not to the taste of everyone, even those who silently accepted the returns.

On the other side of the divide there was no such ambiguity. Everyone opposed the IRA. Everyone assumed that any IRA gain was their loss. Such violence was damned on every ground from pragmatic (a criminal and subversive threat), to theological (a murderous crusade by Catholics). There was no need for analysis, no sign of understanding or sympathy or momentary empathy. The IRA, a subversive and criminal conspiracy of wicked, evil men, was engaged in a ruthless and barbaric adventure, tolerated if not encouraged by the entire minority community and by the Republic. And perhaps it was part of a vaster conspiracy—Rome, Moscow, the liberal press, outside agitators, them.

The Protestant militants, like their coevals across the divide, understood very little about the nature of the other tradition. The IRA believed that the Protestants were Irish confused by generations of British propaganda and thus open to conversion to the nationalist faith. For the Protestants the IRA were the legions of the Pope who would bring a sectarian Catholic state to the whole island, duplicating the results of the Tan War in the twenty-six counties in Ulster.

Nearly everyone in Northern Ireland but the IRA was concerned about the direction of events—or the lack of direction. Nothing new politically seemed to be happening during the autumn of 1971—only more talk from the radicals, more protests, more press releases from the SDLP. Everyone was waiting for the inevitable move from London, the coming concession that would transform the arena. And nothing made this clearer than one more atrocity. On the night of December 4, 1971, a fifty-pound bomb detonated in McGurk's Bar, a Catholic public house in North Queen Street Belfast, bringing down the building into a heap of smoldering rubble and injured survivors. Rescuers worked all night removing the trapped people. By Sunday morning the numbers were totaled: fifteen killed and eight injured; and by then hours of rioting had seen three policemen, one soldier, and three civilians wounded by gunfire and still others hurt by thrown stones and missiles. On that Sunday, December 5, the unknown Empire Loyalists claimed responsibility for the atrocity. Unable to strike at the IRA, the loyalists had turned against the available and vulnerable local Catholics. But the actual targets were not the victims or their invisible defenders but, on one hand, the British cabinet, vacillating, insufficiently loyal to the Protestant cause; and on the other their own endangered psyche, fearful of betrayal, that required the constant reassurance supplied by the ritual use of power. They could kill so they still existed. They could be disloyal to prove their loyalty. They would kill again but McGurk's, a name to be added to the major atrocity list, a list not even fairly begun, indicated the deep confusion of the province.

Nothing was to change for the better. In London on December 6, Faulkner told Conservatives that military success came before political advances. As Faulkner spoke the most intense fire yet in Belfast was gutting a carpet warehouse on the Dublin Road and Munton's shirt factory's top floors. In Derry twenty gelignite bombs were thrown at the enemy. The week continued with the death of UDR men in Tyrone and Belfast, patrols ambushed, and an armed raid on a branch of the Northern Bank in Belfast. The only novel security response was overseen by John Taylor: a program, of cratering cross-border roads, visible evidence of the authorities' long-held illusion that the IRA in the North was an artificial entity kept alive only by transfusions from the South. For the loyalists the IRA was both native ogre embedded in the entire Catholic community and a band of gunmen kept alive by support from the Republic. For many in the British establishment, intimate with colonial examples where the rebels had foreign aid and articulated foreign ideas, the IRA was assumed similar, a force crafted by outside agitators exploiting local grievances and supplied abroad. Cut off like the Mau Mau or the Malayan Communists, the IRA would wither. That the border could not be sealed with the resources available and that the IRA was not artificial could more easily be ignored from the Carlton or Anthaneum clubs of London than from Newry or Enniskillen.* Still, Taylor and the other Unionists liked the feel of some action being taken—and it did ease some loyalist anguish, at the small cost of inconveniencing those who crossed the border to visit the next-door farm or to move up IRA explosives. It was not really a change for the better as much as a sign of the times.

In Stormont, where the Official Unionists won a vote of confidence twenty-three to five, the loyalists nattered on about the security issue. Desmond Boal felt that Harold Wilson's statement that there must be an end to violence before a political solution was unrealistic. This was the position of not only Faulkner but also much of the loyalist community: Stomp on the gunmen first then talk. To have Wilson on their side was odd; and to have the Protestant and quite independent Boal urging an attempt to find a political solution before an end to disorder was quite disturbing. Most Unionists, most loyalists, felt that the IRA terror could be defeated, especially if London felt a greater urgency. Close the border, punish Dublin, crush the gunmen, root them out, send in the tanks. The details were dim, the expected results quite clear, and the advocacy strident. And nothing was done, a few holes dug in country roads, and so the litany of disorder, bomb blasts and shots at night continued.

On December 12, three days after the Thursday Stormont debate, an Official IRA unit attempting to burn the house of Senator Jack Barnhill at Strabane, County Tyrone, killed him by error and then bombed the house and withdrew. Another error. As Bernadette Devlin noted, "Senator Barnhill was a bigot of the first-class order but he did not represent British Imperialism and was not a threat to the IRA" so he was not a "legitimate target." John Hume had no concern about the legitimacy of targets in his statement. The young radicals might play with revolution yet, weighing some men as targets and others not, but not Hume, who called the act "callous, cold-blooded murder." On the other side of the divide, the entire spectrum of loyalist opinion was outraged. McGurk's was largely forgotten in the excitement. Barnhill's assassination too would be forgotten as the atrocity roll grew.

Violence by December seemed endemic. In fact, again to the horror of many loyalists, Home Secretary Reginald Maudling after his meeting with Unionists at Stormont told a press conference on December 15 the London view of matters: "I

---

*In time when the IRA attacks came to London, the physical impact of the bombs were included in histories and anecdotal descriptions of the clubs along with the damages of the blitz, the disappearance of certain artifacts, and the results of various restorations. Cf. Anthony Lejeune, *The Gentlemen's Clubs of London* (London: Dorset, 1980), p. 167, for mention of the destruction of the main bar of the Army and Navy Club—an appropriate target, assumed the relevant IRA active service unit—in December 1976 when a four-pound gelignite bomb studded with six-inch nails was tossed in from Piccadilly.

don't think one can speak of defeating the IRA, of eliminating them completely, but it is the design of the security forces to reduce their level of violence to something like an acceptable level." The loyalists did not want "acceptable" violence, they wanted no violence at all, the perpetrators punished, and their order restored. And they wanted this now. Faulkner immediately made clear to the media that he believed that the British government was determined absolutely to end the campaign of violence by the IRA. But Maudling, in a message to Faulkner the next day, reiterated the London belief that the security forces could only be expected to reduce violence to an acceptable level. This would not do. And as 1971 came to a close, McGurk's had made clear what would happen if Faulkner could not produce or London continued without clear direction.

In fact, by the end of the year, a constant was that British policy had no direction. A decision had been made on internment and after that nothing. The only option was a willingness in the last resort (whatever that might be) to consider direct rule (whatever that might bring). In the meantime at least IRA violence tapered off during the Christmas season, although no truce was declared. In many ways the armed campaign remained parochial: Bombing was stopped for tea, the young volunteers without jobs did not rise early so that the operation fell into patterns, just as deadly but as time passed regular, or as regular as Irish time permits. It was not acceptable but predictable. The end of the year figures indicated just how far from an acceptable level was a province with regularized bombing.

On Wednesday, December 29, a British foot soldier on patrol in Foyle Road in Derry was shot and killed, bringing the total of soldiers in 1971 to 43. Five members of the UDR, 11 policeman, as well as 61 civilians and 52 IRA volunteers, had been killed as well. The army reported 156,728 rounds of ammunition, 605 firearms, including 26 submachine guns and 243 rifles, 105 hand grenades, and 1,531 nail bombs seized, mostly from IRA volunteers or stockpiles. The IRA was moving from the old Lee-Enfield to the American military M-1 and Garand carbines as well as a few SLR NATO rifles but mostly the armory remained a hodgepodge scavenged on the island or smuggled in odd lots. The totals were still impressive.

Besides the military indicators, the number of more revolutionary signs appeared. Each month in 1971 some £303,787 was stolen in armed raids. Some was stolen by decent common criminals, some was stolen by private enterprise masked for a political purpose, like Saor Éire, who tended to rob banks to destroy capitalism and spent the gains for more immediate needs; a bit was taken by Protestant militants; and much was looted by the units of the IRA, especially the Provos. A revolutionary war needs guns and money. The Provos needed more. The campaign gobbled the funds that could be acquired by passing buckets after rallies at the GPO in Dublin or trekking through the pubs on Friday night, by the dues from Sinn Féin, by the welfare money raised by NORAID, and by the illegal contributions smuggled in tote bags and coat pockets over to Ireland by Irish-American tourists. This was a real war and it had to have more money, more guns to replace those lost, more explosives to replace those that were blowing away the six counties.

The most visible evidence of that real war had been explosions, still very low-tech, although the QMG had improved the detonators, now set with timers, and the quality of the home-produced explosives. The demand was enormous because the security defense was so porous that the IRA volunteers could detonate all the bombs they could make. As noted, on Thursday, December 30, in Santry, North Dublin, the Provisional QMG Jack McCabe was mortally injured in the Santry garage. The urgency of the campaign was indicated by the fact that the QMG was using a metal shovel on a concrete floor of the garage to move explosives. Elsewhere the haste regularly produced what the British began to call "own goals"—volunteers killed by mishandled explosives, by inferior or old chemicals, by premature detonation, by accidents, by faulty timers, by careless-ness and ignorance and bad luck. Despite the very considerable cost, the Provos continued to bomb away a very vulnerable society. They were learning on the job. Each month in 1971 between two hundred and six hundred pounds of explosives were dismantled by the British army and the total exploded was estimated as equal to that of the French resistance in World War II.

Thus, 1972 began without promise of peace. Just after midnight there were eight explosions in Belfast to welcome in the new year. Later in the day Maudling's New Year's message to Brian Faulkner hoped for an end to violence, an end to internment, and the participation by majority and minority commu-nities in public affairs. Everyone wanted an end to violence, even the Provos after they had won, even the loyalist members after they had restored the past. Everyone from the British army to the Official IRA assassins was involved only in defense and only until justice was done. But to see that justice was done, even on the vague terms noted by Maudling, more than hopes would be needed as the days dribbled away leaving behind ashes, ruined buildings and lives, fresh graves.

The conventional tried to keep up the pressure on London and on January 2 at an anti-internment rally in Belfast five thousand demonstrators appeared at the Falls Park. NICRA leaders said they were going back to the street. Actually, the IRA hoped that the demonstrators would come out again, provoking the British army and providing a high din level. The IRA could not lose. The British army seemed determined to treat street protest like insurrection and the Irish neigh-borhoods like Mau Mau zones. And even the complaints of the church had no effect in January 1972—no vulnerable Catholic wanted to see his only defender sent home gunless. Dr. Cahal Daly, bishop of Ardagh and Clonmacnoise, an adamant local opponent of the armed struggle, on January 1 insisted that it was morally wrong for Catholics to be members of the IRA, an illegal organization that acted in contravention of the democratic institutions of the state. The IRA ignored him. Stormont was not democratic; and had not the Church acted illegally when it suited the Church's purposes? The Church, the politicians, the conventional, the government in Dublin would have to wait on the war. No wonder they complained. The war was not paying them dividends, was whittling away their capital.

The IRA, both the Provisionals and Officials, now played a crucial role in the disintegrating Northern society, offering the minority security, offering the majority an Irish role that the unionists did not want, offering the British violence until they declared an intention of withdrawing, offering the Dublin government example and their own republican opponents nothing. The war would bring leverage to the politicians but with risks and not right away and the long view has few takers in public life. The war already brought the returns of vengeance to the mean minded and the truculent and offered more. And the war brought the Protestants, all too aware of the threat to their very identity, to despair: threatened again, and bereft of spokesmen to explain and convince, again at risk, always at risk.

Thus January came and 1972 offered various and contradictory futures to all in the province, promising or desperate but strange; it offered enormous risks, assured violence and a limited selection of political options. The only real promise was that tomorrow would not be like yesterday, and this in a society that until 1968 had been frozen in place. The winds of change in 1971 had torn and tattered the old flags, but they still slapped and crackled over the same armies, some secret and some regular, all driven by a history of quarrel and grievances. All in the province were apparently engaged in a zero-sum game, not ready for trust, none ready for the easy life. The new alignments and fresh banners of 1971 were only decoration for the old causes. The new year promised only to be different, not better.

8

Bloody Sunday: January 1972

The Milder Forms of Violence Earn
Nothing But Police Neglect.
Thomas Kinsella, "Butcher's Dozen"

A visitor in January 1972, one without any special Irish experience or local access, saw a curious arena for the complexities of the Troubles. There seemed to be no war zone. There were few signs of terror or turmoil to be found in the six counties without a search. Despite the low, gray skies, the curtains of cold rain sweeping through almost daily, the ground fogs and taste of smoke in the air, the country was as always still beautiful. Still green, the land rolled on in neatly farmed squares, cut by bending, narrow rivers and in the west pocked by lakes, large and small. Most of the province still resembled a travel poster.

Driving out of Belfast, south toward the Mountains of Mourne or north along the coast to the Glens of Antrim, driving down any country road, passing through tiny market towns or past isolated pubs, there appeared out of a car window the island of legend—misty, soft, verdant, caught out of time: no neon, little glitter or chrome, no giant signs or novel buildings, no fast foods mass-produced and sold next to large, purpose-built parking lots by American chains or even as in Britain in small shops along the high streets by Pakistani immigrants. There was not much variety in the shops in the small market towns. The small local stores might be good on bottled Guinness, tinned beans, and root vegetables but had no olives or red wine or much in the way of fresh fruit.

So far Tyrone or Down, indeed the whole province, had been largely missed by consumer culture except for the ubiquitous television. And even telly the blue box that had imposed adjustments in hours and interest, had as yet wrought few changes in manners, morals, or the pace of events.

Time did truly move slower and so too did service, if not the charm of delivery. The plumbing and the heating had not caught up with the century, nor had manners deteriorated. And as far as the Irish were concerned, this was all to the good. There was a comfort and ease in old habits and the strictures of the past. The province might be a divided society but for most it was their own and they cherished it. The old ways still ran, the parish priest or the minister had much to say on many matters, the new was suspicious, not alluring. The country was still country—woolly dogs at heel, sheep in the road, milk cans at the gate—and so content.

This country contentment was troubled by the unanticipated intrusion of the new nationalist ambitions, ambitions that were as invisible from a car window as the divisions of the society. From the cars of the media the province was bucolic and tranquil, from a past lost elsewhere in the West with industrialization, the arrival of great cities and the circle of suburbs, with progress.

It was true that Belfast and Derry and the larger towns were and had always been different, urban industrial centers not touched with rural green. There, long before the present Troubles, demand for Irish products, ships, tobacco, linen, had eased, prosperity had vanished, and decay had come. Time in the cities, too, ran slower but without any great charm. For visitors the Northern cities, unlike Dublin or Cork, seemed hard, the accent harsh, the people without grace or the Celtic wit found in the pubs of the Republic.

The people in the North were apt to warm slowly, involved in their own divided world. Even with the splendor of the natural setting of Londonderry or Belfast, even with the harsh edges blurred by morning mists, the two cities were decaying industrial sites fallen on hard times. Still, for most of the time, however fast or slow that time seemed to run in the province, there was little evidence of a war that had increasingly attracted international interest.

Yet by 1972, in certain small areas, a glance even from a car window indicated that the old innocent calm had long passed. In West Belfast throughout the Catholic areas and along the fault line with the Protestant districts, in central Londonderry and in the Bogside and Creggan estate, on the high street of a few of the provincial towns, the presence of the British army and the RUC was apparent; uniformed men, automatic weapons, armored cars, all heretofore alien in the United Kingdom. There was as well evidence of riot and arson; the husks of burned cars, blackened, pockmarked walls, often the ruins of barricades, broken bottles and dirty streets.

There were as well bright, new reminders of turmoil. There was the graffiti on the walls, political slogans, often in Belfast elaborate murals of dissent or domination, not the admonitions to the local football team or the rude pornography of the poor. The murals would become a worldwide cliché, along with the children throwing stones, Free Derry corner, and the British soldiers under hastily painted admonitions to support the IRA. Even more impressive, if not always to the cameramen, the new and necessary military posts and reinforced RUC stations had become forts, draped in nets, surrounded by wire, guarded by wary and serious young men from Manchester and Birmingham stationed on the border of hostile Indian territory rather than in regimental camps outside cities in Great Britain.

This Belfast was the battleground for a war that foreign correspondents had come to report. This was what made Northern Ireland *foreign* for the distant. A slow tour down the Falls Road in January made the heart grow cold. At the best of times West Belfast appeared to all but the locals, who as one loved their grand, wee city, as a blighted dead end, a used industrial slum for workers without prospects. Spread out beyond the Falls Road and the Shankill, Catholic and Protestant arteries, the mean little streets and tiny terraces without amenities seemed more attuned to the world of Charles Dickens than of Harold Wilson, with his ideal of a great technological kingdom, prosperous, sleek, infused with the glitter of the future. Neither Terence O'Neill's dream of development nor that of Wilson had imposed any visible change. Instead Belfast was appropriately bleak for the television camera: dour, closed ghettos under a great haze of smoke, the huge praying mantis cranes of the shipyards to the east and the soft mountains to the west. It was a used-up city of old industries, old stores, old houses, and old ways without takers. Even the pubs were old. Some bars were still resplendent with Victorian glass and polished mahogany from the glory days; but most of the old pubs were not antiques but quite unattractive establishments, narrow, dark, dirty, reeking of stale Sweet Aftons and sour drink, their snugs stained with spilled beer, their floors worn, their counters badly used by generations of elbows. These were the locals for the poor—club, meeting hall, game palace, an escape from limited lives. What glitter existed had moved away to the newer roadhouses in the suburbs, sanctuaries for the proper. The inner city was increasingly left to the Troubles. And this was the troubled Belfast of the media: a city weighted by problems, as short on solutions as amenities.

Correspondents did not go to the zoo, visit the garden suburbs, drink in the new pubs, visit along Malone Road, attend the drama festivals, or range much beyond the bounds of riot. In much of Belfast people went to work as usual, received their mail and milk on time, worried about the children's teeth and the school fees, lived everyday lives, and, like those in Dublin or Coventry, read of the riots and deaths in the newspapers. The middle class had begun to shop outside the city center, chose not to hear the increasingly regular crump of IRA bombs, resented the implications that their province was a combat zone inhabited by religious bigots. Their Belfast was much as it had always been, a pleasant, British provincial city with conventional economic problems and a few local peculiarities.

The Belfast of the media was somehow constructed out of bits and pieces only for the television. The international cameramen, the American television producers, the foreign correspondents from Stockholm or Milan had invented a battleground. Their Belfast, seen from the top of the Europa Hotel, was a city of police briefings, a city defined by army information officers, barricades, crayon lines on military maps, and the disturbances of the moment in the riot zones. Their Belfast ran to no normal clock, existed as backdrop to contrived tragedy and atypical incident, slandered the everyday, the decent. The media seldom find friends among those who seek the conventional and abhor violence.

Londonderry, very small, hardly worth more than a day's visit from the Europa, was much the same. A scenic, walled town on the Foyle, it was merely a nexus of key flash points, the army on patrol in narrow streets, a long pan to show the misery of the Bogside with the world-famous FREE DERRY gable end sign, and a voice-over tolling the statistics of unemployment and discrimination. During troubled times editors and producers want scenic trouble all the time, not balance, local pride, or chronicles of the orthodox. The media expected and found a war, an unconventional war, fashionable, photogenic, a campaign of low intensity, true, but still a war with the daily crump of explosions in Belfast, with the British army under fire while on patrol, with the afternoon, after-school riot at William Street in Londonderry.

Ireland as the newest stop of the crisis tour—Vietnam, the Middle East, Latin

American guerrillas, Euroterrorists—had special charms. Belfast was a short plane-hop from London, the locals spoke English, and both the authorities and the rebels were forthcoming, articulate, and quite conscious of the importance of the media. There were lots of statistics, lots of briefings, all the background necessities. On arrival the correspondents found an articulate and quotable population, eager official information officers and spokesmen; they easily discovered access to the underground world of the paramilitaries. A producer could arrange to film a secret interview, a correspondent could interview a commander of a secret army, and an academic expert could find informed aid in fashioning a poll of attitudes or holding a conflict resolution seminar.

Many armed struggles are almost invisible and truly secret—conspiracies within closed societies or firefights in the wilderness. A production team might hike for weeks through most unpleasant bush only to have the promised attack take place in the dark or too quickly to film. Rural wars are a hardship without certain returns. Even the urban guerrillas seldom perform on schedule: Bang and they are gone, leaving a sprawled body and no eyewitnesses, adequate but not visually compelling. Ireland was different. Ireland offered instant communications, regular flights for film and rushes, rational actors and sensible issues, combat easily interpreted by skilled locals and reporters after a quick study, and most of all, visible action. The industry demands meant for those actually involved in the crisis, the IRA or the RUC or the British government, that all action was exaggerated and distorted and most of all public. Northern Ireland could not heal or find accommodation in private or even suffer in silence as the nationalists had in the long decades after the establishment of the Stormont system. Editors and producers and even academic chairmen wanted the late, late news. So there must be news. And, of course, often there was.

There were marches, those afternoon riots in Derry, the burning buildings and bomb sites in Belfast. British soldiers in combat gear could be filmed in incongruous settings, amid the children they claimed were used as cover by the IRA. There they regularly were for the camera, real soldiers, creeping along on full alert beneath sprayed and splattered Republican graffiti—"Brits Out! Join the IRA!"—while their eyes kept swiveling, their guns ready, moving on down normal streets past shoppers and women pushing prams through rush-hour crowds and by chattering old ladies: photogenic, edgy targets.

British patrols could be filmed, as well, in the gorgeous Irish rural outback, moving through green fields instead of rice paddies, the squaddies with faces blackened, fingers tense. And the war in the Irish countryside was only an hour's drive from the Europa, not even a day trip. Sometimes the IRA even laid on transient patrols of masked volunteers brandishing Thompson submachine guns.

It all made for great visuals and easy reporting with a dash of adventure. The thud of the Provos' bombs could be heard in the pubs and lounge bars: "A fifty-pounder, I judge, out toward Royal Avenue. . . . Not to worry, only a couple of nail bombs tossed around the corner, they do it every night." The lobby of the Europa Hotel at times appeared to be the site of an international journalists' convention, crews babbling in various tongues and recent arrivals briefed by those coming through the province for the second time. The Europa joined those other grand hotels that the media had used to watch the closing of the British

Empire, the Lydra Palace in Nicosia or the King David in Jerusalem, the Palace in Aden, the old Stanley in Nairobi. Everyone in the trade had to put in some Irish time.

The result was one more crisis, one more trouble spot on the foreign news pages of the elite papers, one more bit of action film to fit in the evening television news. The Irish Troubles had become an agenda item but one on almost no government's agenda, not even very often London's. Northern Ireland, for all the coverage, was not a major crisis or an event with great ramifications. The fate of the West was not to be decided nor did great armies seem likely to clash, whatever the results. It was not a flash point or even a symbol. And by 1972 it no longer offered, as once had been the case, easily identifiable heroes and villains.

Still, the confrontation and violence could be filmed and could be discussed not only by the experts but also by all sorts and conditions whose interests, values, assumptions, and faiths could find Northern Ireland parallels. The Troubles were what one could make of them, a crisis amenable to varied and contradictory interpretations, an event magnified by observation, a very modern event fashioned mainly with quite ancient materials.

In January 1972 the Troubles seemed to have reached an impasse. What more could happen? The British army would sooner or later end IRA escalation, but what then? More of the same seemed likely, tomorrow like yesterday. For many observers, then, January hardly seemed harbinger for the most eventful Irish year since 1921 but only another dour month in an increasingly repetitive plot. Most Irish news, day after day, focused on the impact of the continuing IRA armed struggle that in the North at least involved both republican organizations. The Provos bombed away at the artificial economy of the six counties, sectarian targets as far as the Officials were concerned. The Officials, like the Provos, were involved in shootings, armed robberies, trap-mines and culvert bombs, all the deadly techniques of a still-escalating irregular war. The newspapers and television news reported soldiers shot, suspects arrested with arms, nail bombs, IRA men lifted and held on suspicion, detained for interrogation, gunmen raiding banks and army patrols coming under fire. The army was obviously not on top of the situation yet.

There was still optimism in January 1972—a headline in the *Belfast Telegraph* on Saturday, January 1, announced, "The IRA Is Beginning to Lose the War." But as the month progressed there were repeated IRA attacks, attacks on RUC stations or military targets, and then army sweeps through dangerous neighborhoods, a UDR soldier shot here, a sniper reported there, and always the bombs, the punctuation marks of the Irish story. Despite official optimism, there seemed no end in sight. There was, however, no big story. There was still no sign of political development, no shifting of priorities in London or at Stormont, no sign of movement, initiative, or direction. On January 1, Maudling had sent a message to Brian Faulkner, reported in the *Belfast Telegraph* as "My wish is peace," and indicated his desire to end the violence, to end internment, and to reach an agreed means to achieve these. The Irish crisis seemed stabilized despite the escalating IRA armed struggle.

Everyone continued to act as predicted. Even in America the Irish-Americans and their friends in politics added to the clamor. Groups appeared worldwide but especially in the Irish diaspora and particularly in America to support the Irish republicans, to aid the victims, to pressure the Congress in Washington to pressure the British. Senator Ted Kennedy along with Senator Abraham Ribicoff on October 20, 1971, had introduced into the Senate a resolution urging President Richard Nixon to seek an end to the violence and calling for the withdrawal of British troops. Kennedy had criticized internment and the Compton Report on the brutality of the security force* as "sheer hypocrisy," and speaking in favor of the October resolution, he suggested that "Ulster is becoming Britain's Vietnam . . . no American who loves Ireland or who remembers her proud and noble history can stand silent in the face of the tragedy and horror now unfolding in Ulster."

London was, of course, unmoved and Prime Minister Faulkner was outraged: The Irish-American card had been played before in the patriot game. The responses were traditional: politically motivated intervention in a British domestic matter. What more could anyone expect from ignorant and innocent Irish-Americans living in the past. It was simply one more actor speaking a part.

In London there seemed little to do but attempt to impose both an acceptable level of violence and a sense of political reality on the divided province. That was London's responsibility in a province that during 1971 had been far from another Vietnam if still a distressing and so far intractable problem. Ireland had nearly always been a distressful and intractable place for the British authorities. Despite the rising violence during 1971, there was still no sense of Tory urgency. If London accepted that action must sooner or later be seen to be taken, it was, apparently, still Stormont's to take. What action and when was still moot. And Faulkner, besieged as usual by Paisley, by Craig, by his own, sincerely felt that reform had been done and the key was to impose order, to crush the IRA, an IRA that London took less seriously than did the majority of Ulster.

As the days passed, the new year seemed much like the old. No one but the IRA wanted another year as violent, but no one except the IRA seemed to have a viable strategy. London gave no hint of maneuver. Dublin had been quiet during the holidays and was quiet after the holidays. The militant Protestants from Craig down to the lad on the corner were eager to organize and defend their own—to what exact political purpose was not clear. The myriad of official Northern spokesmen had nothing to say beyond the war news. Regularly Stormont or the British army announced that the worst was over, the IRA on the run, either driven to some new outrage because of desperation or exhausted if momentarily quiescent. It did not matter one way or the other that the *Belfast Telegraph* had announced, "The IRA Is Beginning to Lose the War"—the war continued. And for the media it was a war, so far not a Vietnam War, not even another Lebanese conflict but still a war and in a very small place. And as long as war was news the media went on reporting Ireland.

On Sunday, January 16, a typical day, shots were fired at troops in Belleek on the border and in Newry two explosions destroyed an electricity transformer and

---

Report of the Enquiry into the Allegation Against the Security Forces of Physical Brutality in Northern Ireland, Arising out of Events on the 9th August 1971 (The Compton Report Cmd 4823), London, HMSO, November 1971.

a vacant house. Demonstrators attacked British army troops in Derry, nail bombs were tossed and shots fired. The army responded with CS gas. Gelignite bombs were thrown but as usual in a few hours the confrontation dribbled away, an item for tomorrow's newspaper. The demonstrators felt that the army had been unfairly harsh but then demonstrators tended to take such views of authority. In Belfast a paint firm on York Road and a public house on Albertbridge Road burned down. Fifty prisoners held on the *Maidstone* were transferred by Royal Air Force Wessex helicopters to the newly opened Magilligan internment camp, which was more pleasant than the new, purpose-built Long Kesh south of Belfast. The move seemed to indicate that the British thought the crisis likely to last. A great many people, Protestant and Catholic, active and passive, continued to hope that the crisis was a momentary matter, amenable to adjustment. No one wanted to think in the long term. After fifty years of relative tranquillity, if sullen on the part of the nationalists, most people assumed that stability and accommodation could be found, must exist around the next corner.

All during the autumn and winter of 1971–72 there had been speculation about a radical British move in relation to Stormont. Irish journalists constantly read English tea leaves, assuming that matters could not continue. The most optimistic of the IRA commanders assumed that their armed struggle would win (however that was defined) sooner rather than later, perhaps in 1972. Mac Stiofáin was counting the British military deaths with an eye on the losses in Aden, where the British had withdrawn precipitately. No one imagined that matters could continue. And now with Long Kesh and Magilligan violence was being institutionalized like the suspects.

By mid-January there were nearly six hundred internees and the new camp at Magilligan was being used not only for the overflow but also, seemingly, to make visitation difficult. Magilligan was in any case taken as one more affront to the nationalist population. On the previous Friday, January 14, Faulkner had insisted that without internment "vast numbers of gunmen and would-be murderers" would still be on the street. And 168 men had been arrested by the army during the previous week. The total of suspects no longer on the street continued to vary from day to day and remained large by Irish standards despite the sporadic releases of suspects and internees.

Not just gunmen but also all sorts of troublemakers, real and potential, were swept up; even the ultra-loyalist Major Bunting's son Ronald, a member of NICRA, was lifted in January. Most if not quite all of those arrested were suspected republicans or their friends. Gradually the simple radicals were being weeded out of police lists but there seemed no end of potential gunmen. By 1972 there were a great many of these in confinement. The camps and prisons were jammed, prison guards difficult to recruit—two hundred Scottish police officers volunteered for short duty spells to help out.

In fact, governance in Northern Ireland seemed to be focused almost solely on responses to the growing emergency: more troops moved into the province, more prison guards needed, more prison space needed, more searches and seizures and incidents. The various spokesmen always had the figures at hand, for this was a technologically advanced emergency. Between November 30, 1971, and January 9, 1972, 1,183 houses and flats in Belfast had been searched and in 47 of them arms, ammunition, and radio equipment had been found. In many of the others disgruntled and angry families were left to clean up after the security exercise.

The numbers told nothing of the alienation that seeped in after the searches, arrests, seizures, and incidents, no matter how necessary, no matter whose fault. The authorities were in authority and thus responsible. Long Kesh was a miserable place. The *Maidstone* was a disgrace and Magilligan a means to make relatives trek to the far reaches of Derry instead of visiting near Belfast. There seemed no end to internment despite the general outcry. Unionists felt they should be immune, since they were loyal, and nationalists felt penalized because they were not unionists. On Sunday in Derry, Eddie McAteer said that it would be simpler to throw a ring of barbed wire around the whole of the six counties.

Many of those threatened—and most loyalists felt very threatened, with their bad dreams become real in the thump of rebel bombs—felt that he had a point: The IRA had run loose, probably with the connivance of those in the South as the arms trials had indicated, surely because the politicians at Stormont had dithered, certainly because London had been weak, even dismantling the police under the rubric of reform; and thus more barbed wire, lots more, seemed a very good idea. Craig, Paisley, and the Orange militants wanted more effective security measures, more visible repression. So authority was eroded from both sides. The North appeared to be sinking into a chaos that required ever more stringent emergency measures that would assure even more violent alienation.

Certainly, as January drew to a close, the news from the province remained hard. On Monday, January 17, seven detainees held on board the *Maidstone* slipped overboard into Belfast harbor and swam to shore, escaping into the freedom of the Markets area after hijacking a bus. They would appear at a Dublin press conference two weeks later, IRA heroes. Two days later an army statement said that since January 1, forty IRA officers and fifty-nine volunteers had been detained. If so, the detentions seemingly had no effect on their armed struggle. During the same week there were the continuing bombs in Belfast, four explosions in Newry, a soldier killed by a land mine near Keady in Armagh.

Then on Saturday, January 22, the civil rights people held still more demonstrations, and produced, as if on schedule, confrontation, tumult, stones, CS gas and rubber bullets, and allegations of army brutality. It appeared a replay of the glory days of movement without the old expectations of immediate change. It also appeared that the demonstrators faced a more aggressive army response. That night two car bombs exploded in Belfast. It was, more than anything else, as an alternative to such bombs that the civil rights advocates demonstrated. Those advocates of political change, radicals, politicians, the decent and the fearful, felt that there must be some other road into the future, some means to power other than the gun, and so repeated their tactics of the immediate past and took to the streets. They found neither welcome nor understanding. Their leaders were arrested, tried and sentenced, a process dragged out by appeals and the assumption that no one would actually go to jail but that the authorities were punishing the peaceful. And the peaceful could not negotiate, return to Stormont as petitioners. Gerry Fitt of SDLP noted, "If we talked now we would be representing nobody." They could, however, march. To them it seemed counterproductive for London to allow the army to smash peaceful demonstrations, thus turning the wavering toward IRA violence.

On that Saturday afternoon the demonstrators, led by Ivan Cooper and John Hume, targeted Magilligan, took to the long, deserted strand on a cold, bleak afternoon under rain clouds driven by Donegal winds. A couple of thousand people, mostly from Derry, appeared and the Royal Green Jackets offered buns and tea. The offer was turned down and the column straggled up the beach to the wire manned by eighty Green Jackets, eighty men of the First Battalion Parachute Regiment trucked up from Holywood Barracks near Belfast for the confrontation, and fifty or so RUC constables. Teatime was over. Some fifty demonstrators tried to outflank the wire by slipping around the sea end in the ebbing tide. The paratroops opened fire with gas guns and a volley of rubber bullets. The battle was joined and the army and police smashed any resistance with batons, truncheons, and rifle butts, firing rubber bullets at short range directly into the crowd.

The crowd, limping and stunned, some bleeding, all angry, stumbled back to their bus park. On the way home a few demonstrators burned down the Golden Slipper ballroom, owned by a local man who had helped build the new camp. It was the only protestor-initiated violence during an afternoon in which the army seemed determined to come in with the boot. Simon Winchester of the *Guardian*, who had brought along his family, was stunned, having anticipated a response more in keeping with his British experience. He called it the "brutal act of an arrogant military, which upheld, in as unpleasant a manner as possible, the powers of the Stormont government to lay claim to the beaches and the seas that surrounded the country." The authorities in the army at Magilligan, in Stormont, in London felt that duty had been done. After all, marches had been banned again by Prime Minister Faulkner on January 18. The civil rights demonstrators, no friends or provincial authority, had always anticipated arrogance and a certain level of brutality from the RUC but somehow not from the British army. They assumed that the British army would not act as an army but as a surrogate police authority. The soldiers would be open to riotous attack by angry civilians but somehow would not retaliate and certainly would not act as an army under attack. Throwing stones at an RUC constable would lead to a baton charge, but this ought not to be the case with the army. Not many empathized with an army under covert attack by gunmen and bombers of the IRA advocating many of the same causes as the civil rights demonstrators. And even the IRA anticipated that the British army would always be on best behavior, live up to their own press officers' praises. Through the dismantling of the British Empire the rebels had always held the British army to the highest standards. British justice was assumed and any deviation engendered outrage.

The broken heads at Magilligan—unnecessarily bloodied, it seemed to the demonstrators—had come as a most unpleasant harbinger. Perhaps the British authorities were not so different from those at Stormont—certainly the Irish republicans had blamed Britain for all Ireland's troubles, but had heretofore never convinced the nationalists. The authorities, certainly many in the army, increasingly saw such NICRA confrontations not as an alternative to the gun but as allied to it, the disobedience arrow in the rebel quiver. Such rituals indicated to the army the visible disloyalty of the supposedly responsible nationalist leadership. The long-held Protestant view that there was not an overlap of interests but a single ultimate purpose of the Catholics, the Irish nationalists, and the republicans had more takers. The Catholics might want British reforms but were not averse to ultimate unity with the South nor willing to deny the IRA's use of force. All were rebels, even the avowedly nonviolent.

The paratroops, trained as soldiers not as peacekeepers, hard, arrogant young men innocent of politics, isolated in their barracks, simply tended to see the protests as direct challenge by the friends of gunmen. And to the skeptical eyes of the British officers in particular, many with the most conservative politics, and of the police in general, the "moderate" leadership appeared dominated by radicals and demagogues. These protesting nationalists were politicians who would ride to power on the murders of gunmen directed by the Marxists who pulled the strings. The soldiers at the receiving end of the stones had little time for such political analysis. They wanted their own back whatever the tactical virtues of toleration—no buns and tea but baton rounds and bullets if it came to that. Army "brutality" to them seemed no more than self-defense.

Across the entire spectrum of players in the Northern Ireland drama, each read reality as the next chapter of a familiar book. The loyalists having anticipated rebellion for decades felt their fears and warnings justified: The IRA had struck at their state under cover of the civil rights movement, a facade for treason. What was needed was force, terror crushed and a return to former securities, albeit with some reforms to quiet British critics. The unionists, moderate or extreme, whatever class, assumed that the crisis had arisen because the responsible had not been sufficiently strong. Few believed that reforms, justifiable or no, would transform nationalist hearts.

The nationalists in turn felt that the unionists and their state had grown irrelevant, an obsolete system opposed originally by the threat of force in 1921 and no longer viable. The question was timing and tactics. The proper and moderate could see most gradual reform, even unity by persuasion. Most would have preferred swift progress toward a united island but were not willing to support the IRA's armed struggle. Nearly all assumed that a united Ireland was possible, whether immediately or after great changes in hearts, minds, and institutions. Few nationalists even spoke against unity now, only about their doubts about recourse to violence. Although most nationalists and the few radicals seemed willing to accept the benefits that arose from the IRA campaign, their avowed politics offered a peaceful and gradual entry into a united Ireland to the loyalists who, despite all, because of all, remained clumped under the banners of NO SURRENDER.

The radicals might speak of revolution but they wanted no guns, depending on the conversion of the working class, not the murder of British soldiers. This was a posture that increasingly attracted even the core of the Official IRA in Dublin. The most orthodox radicals, even the Official IRA in most cases, those who according to the British establishment would turn Ulster into Cuba, were in matters of violence one with London if for quite different reasons. The other republicans, the Provos, felt that only through the armed struggle would unification be possible. The unionists, proper or fanatical, loyalists, British proxies, would resist it and imperial interests would assure London's adamant opposition as well. Ireland had been divided by force and would be united by force.

London, despite the intense level of violence, continued to shape the Irish problem as United Kingdom politics. There was seen a need for concession and compromise in the province, a need to forget the past, and a real prospect of attracting the support of the decent nationalists while eroding the IRA's capacity and support with firmness and reform. These reforms, many all but accomplished, would not alienate the reasonable unionists. Anyway, the loyalists would have no place to go, would have to accept the reality of the day even if with bad grace: Institutionalized bigotry was over. Thus politics and reason would win out, creating if not one society in the province at least an accommodation to the inevitable. London had short views founded on British practice and interpreted experience that did not allow Northern Ireland to be an imperial event and so the site of a real armed struggle or an arena for revolution or even alien to normal procedures. Ireland might be different, always had been different, but was to be treated as an unruly Wales or a divided Scotland.

London would find the means to balance the interests of both sides of the divided province and in the process impose order. This was assumed to be a natural responsibility of governing the United Kingdom. There was a great deal to governing the United Kingdom beyond the problems of Northern Ireland; still, the province had a spot on the London agenda. At worst an accommodation would be found for the Irish, Protestant and Catholic, despite their resistance, a resistance that London knew was not in their best interest, short or long term. London over the centuries had often known what was the best for the Irish—and therein often lay trouble.

In Dublin the drift away from the charms of immediate or even ultimate unification was private but real. The traditionalists, the easily patriotic, the in-house republicans might, like the nationalists in the North, feel that given recent events, timing was the key; but those at the center, those with real power and a grasp of the possible, recognized only danger from the North, not fulfillment, not justification, not vengeance achieved. They noted that even after half a century the divisions in Southern society arising from the 1921–23 Troubles had not fully healed and further chaos in Northern Ireland could only be divisive in the Republic. Who would pay for unity and in what coin? What could be done with a million angry and alienated Protestants? What would happen to their small, stable state, to the delicate arrangements within an establishment still vulnerable to schism, to the satisfactory Catholic society created with such trouble and sacrifice? The resources, all sorts of resources, to adapt to such a transformation were not at hand. Dublin could do little to defend the Northern nationalists and less to placate their aspirations for unity.

The Dublin government and the establishment had to lead their own people, ever so slowly, away from the easy sureties of the parish pump oratory of the last fifty years. Simple pub patriotism could poison the waters of the state. Ireland could not be a nation once again by wishful thinking, much less by shooting British soldiers or by alienating Northern Protestants or by supporting or tolerating a new IRA. That new IRA, official or provisional, was a danger not only to society in general but also to the state in particular. And as for the Northern nationalists, they had become orphans of the storm. Dublin seemingly could do nothing in the short term, unlike London, and hence must take long views, hold firm until the dangers of the dream of unity became clear to the many, became a reality at the parish pump and in the pub. Partition might have been unjust, imposed by force; the appeal of unity might be undeniable; but the world had moved on. Someday, somehow a united Ireland might be possible but in the meantime and for the foreseeable future what was needed was social and political justice in the North and an end to violence. Only gradually would this analysis become public policy and reluctantly accepted.

Elsewhere everyone felt vindicated. In Westminster or Washington, at Stormont, within the commands of the IRA paramilitaries and the Protestant defenders, for NICRA and the unionists, for the old Nationalists and the new radicals, among all the various party committees, protest groups and covert cadres, in the hearts of most of the six counties, the events had vindicated history and bias. The past had been prologue. No one outside of a few in Dublin had learned anything and none had forgotten anything. All the Irish knew their history and if there were changes to be made let others make them. Such comfort in old reasons and rationalizations, often expressed in shorthand or code, was insufficient for observers, especially those abroad, particularly those who came fresh to Ireland and the new Troubles. They wanted explanations for the Irish violence. Why the Irish? Why now? What were the roots, the implications, the prospects, the lessons? What, indeed, was going on? By 1972, four years into the play, there should be answers.

Unexpected turmoil anyplace produces in the West the explainers who spread out from the crisis in almost predictable waves from the first journalists to the ultimate historians. The Irish Troubles were no exception. The very first of the media observers, innocent of Ireland, tended to find models in their own past or in the immediate newsworthy milieu. So the civil rights demonstrators were the good guys, related either to similar American events or to the wave of radical student demonstrations then sweeping Europe and America. The Stormont establishment was archaic, unjust, authoritarian, and doomed. Dublin was ignored and London admonished for not acting sooner or with dispatch to bring the province into the present.

The British media contingent might have been somewhat more circumspect about London's role but there was little real sympathy for Stormont or special understanding of Irish issues. The innocence of the British media about Irish matters was to remain a constant. Their public wanted no part of Ireland and so there were, as in politics, no careers to be made in specialization. Innocence and traditional bias would do. Innocence and traditional bias were, in fact, the usual form for most who arrived at the Europa. All that the media seemed to need was their self-made scorecard and an army briefing. This was often sufficient base for some very moving descriptions, vignettes and stories, an NBC television documentary on the children in a divided society or a French film on the whole crisis with long, telling interviews.

There was little effort to discover what would happen next or what had happened before—the present was too present, the news too hard. Only gradually did some observers, those who stayed around, those who returned, note the intractability that arose from a divided society, the uncompromising ambitions of both republicans and militant loyalists, and the distressing fact that history was far from dead on the island. There was to be no happy ending, not even a final chapter, a summing up before moving on to the next hot spot. There began to be fewer heroes if still plenty of villains.

Ireland grew more complex even for these transient observers, even for the television audiences. Some observers became addicted, came again and again, even if most did not. Some made friends, all sorts of friends, learned from the locals, honed contacts and sources, grew sensitive to the province. Some on the island realized that they as much as the outlander had painted the North in clichés and began anew. At the end of a story they did not go back to London but home; if they could overcome the prejudices of youth, they could follow the details of the slowly evolving tragedy better than anyone. A few disinterested specialists had always been watchers in the six counties if never suspecting that tomorrow would be so different from yesterday.

The result was that there developed both real and instant experts on Irish matters with the bad being driven out not by excellence but often by other stories elsewhere. Increasingly there developed a pool of competence, the news became more difficult to manipulate, heroes to sell, lies to tell. The result in a few cases was a journalist book, each beginning deep in Irish history, often hastily learned from sincere if scanty research that permitted the requisite academic scaffolding, each growing detailed during the focus on the turmoil after 1968, and each ending with a moral, an admonition to moderation, usually foreseeing, if dimly, a united island, sometime, somehow. All the concerned wrote of their fascination at Irish events for the book, for their papers or producers, for themselves, for the mythical common reader. The reason that reforms could not be put in place and everyone go home seemed to be the legacy of the past and the solution—everyone had a conviction that a solution was possible, especially the Americans—would emerge in time.

As time passed, one set of observers—the conservatives, who included most British observers, and those most focused on the divided society—saw a Protestant-Catholic conflict with the British intervening to establish order. Another set—everyone else—saw instead a vestigial, discredited political structure without logic that should be first reformed and then, sooner or later, absorbed into a united Ireland. The republican sympathizers and many innocent Americans and some radical Europeans simply saw no need of intermediate reforms: unity first. The reforms, however, were acceptable to all but the most militant loyalists.

The nature of the divided society became increasingly obvious even to the IRA and ultimately they alone felt that unity would eliminate the problem. This union of the island appealed to most of the Irish and their friends, to many radicals and liberals if not to some pragmatists, to no unionists, and to only some in London. Unity was simple and logical and impossible except as a word on a map: IRELAND written over warring tribes on a larger island area. Unity was thus a future prospect stirred into the final chapter as the determination of the loyalists became clearer. Everyone but the British establishment agreed that the present was intolerable.

Despite their haste and limited research, most of the early returns of the journalists and observers were reasonably solid. In particular this was true with Max Hastings of the *Evening Standard* in *Barricades in Belfast* and Martin Wallace of Radio Telefís Éireann with *Drums and Guns: Revolution in Ulster*. Patrick Riddell's *Fire Over Ulster* gave the rarely presented views of the decent Unionists to counter the far more popular efforts of authors personally involved, like Bernadette Devlin in *The Price of My Soul* or the more academically concerned and quite splendid if very uneven *The Sins of Our Fathers: Roots of Conflict in Northern Ireland* by Owen Dudley Edwards. As the years passed, Edwards would grow far more conservative in Irish matters than his indignant and hurried entry in the first round of analysis might have predicted, while Devlin, who fashioned a career on the Irish nationalist left, remained faithful to the early commitments. The journalists tended to come and go and then tire of the Irish pace so that a new wave would appear and, too, feel compelled to explain—each explanation more complicated by the passage of the years but eased by the growing library on the Troubles, a library filled with scholars' works as well as the recollections of the committed, the reports of committees, the experiences of transients.

Almost from the first the analysts and academics crowded into the arena, an arena elsewhere often left to the specialists of the media but in the Irish case too tempting to ignore. Northern Ireland was small, accessible, beneficiary of the statistics of a modern state, and filled with appropriate examples. Some of the first academics to address the problem in a book were R. F. P. Elliot and John Hickie in *Ulster, a Case Study in Conflict Theory,* a harbinger of a process, already well under way, that for many analysts transformed the province for years to come into a social science laboratory for theories and models. Northern Ireland became a site for survey research, for conflict and peace theory, for psychological testing, and often merely an example to deploy in distant academic arguments.

Like most of the printed responses of the media representatives, the early academic returns were hasty, partial, determined by methods and agendas brought to the scene. As in the case with journalists only a few analysts had been on that scene before the eruption of general concern. They had been working virgin ground mainly because modern Ireland, North or South, was marginal to most fashionable academic interests, inspiring investigation only as example for grander concerns. Some early works like Rosemary Harris's *Prejudice and Toleration in Ulster, a Study of Neighbors and Strangers in a Border Community,* long in the writing, did more to reveal the nature of the problem than the hurried books addressed directly to recent events. Thus Richard Rose, an American with a chair at Strathclyde University in Scotland, who was interested in applying survey research in British politics, had in *Divided Ulster,* published in 1970, given everyone polling results taken before the marches began. The work provided a badly needed base line unhampered by the subsequent polarization and the inevitable special pleading of the involved: Many scholars were soon involved, some pleading special causes, not all analytical.

The first wave of analysts, often with disinterested approaches, had special agendas. Many simply explained that the Irish cast was acting out the roles of history or playing parts assigned from afar by Marx or the 1916 martyrs or the strictures of academic modeling. No one really explained to general satisfaction why Ireland, why now, and certainly not what was to be done. Lenin or Trotsky was vindicated and/or Wolfe Tone and all the other Irish patriotic ancestors. Thus the Irish national heroes, Robert Emmet, the Young Irelanders and the Fenians for the republicans, or Daniel O'Connell and Charles Stewart Parnell for the decent Dublin democrats, and so on through all the idols of the various island tribes, many academic, most political, were called in to explain the present. No one cared, as yet, to dissect the old myths, myths that easily served for the present as well as they had in the past to firm up conviction and to flay opponents.

The same was true for most new visitors to the island, encumbered with their comfortable baggage, their vision focused through selected spectacles. And they, too, found the scene rewarding, their baggage appropriate, their previous conclusions validated, their favored methods effective. Many academics and analysts never managed a visit but included the island in their survey. This was especially true for academic advocates of special political action, the scholars engagé who had emerged from the university turmoil of the late sixties, many students having arrived on the faculty just in time to incorporate Ireland into their interpretations of history and their aspirations for the future. Their ideological opponents, found not only within faculties but especially within those institutions under threat, found different conclusions arising from the events after 1968. Ireland truly offered something for everyone, academics and analysts included.

What made Ireland especially fashionable was that most theories could be vindicated or validated on site without recourse to exceptions or convoluted explanations. The Irish crisis was amenable to most explanations. All the theoretical approaches from advanced neo-Marxist through radical feminism to behavioralism uncovered the expected. The IRA campaign, for example, could be seen, not unreasonably, as the last anti-imperialist liberation struggle, one with Kenya and Cyprus and Algeria. It could also be seen as a resurgence of a primitive nationalism that would enslave the very people the movement defended. Marx or Lenin or James Connolly would have been appalled at the Provos or pleased depending on the choice of evidence marshaled. There was lots of evidence, more each month. The Official IRA in the North, many republicans, in and out of the Provisional movement, all felt *they* were the true heirs of Connolly, were engaged in a radical liberation struggle, would have had the blessing even of Lenin. Many Provos kept such matters from many of their more conventional American supporters. And many Provos supporters felt Marx need have nothing to do with anti-imperialism or their armed struggle.

Certainly, the British increasingly spoke of Ireland as a potential Cuba and the IRA as Marxists and not always as a simple smear, an exercise in disinformation, but because ultraconservatives so believed. Amid the pressures of the cold war many in Britain as in the United States found Reds under most unlikely stones. And such Irish stones were not completely unlikely. Many IRA volunteers, Provo and Official, certainly in interview sounded Red enough for anyone—same slogans, same programs and promises. It was thus possible to be a neo-Marxist and find the Provos proper—even the most proper, as one visiting Italian radical insisted, because they were so dedicated to the violence necessary to change history. They were bombing away imperialism in the judgment of the extraparliamentary Left in Rome, more so than the talkers of the Officials. What was so attractive for neo-Marxists was that a revolutionary situation appeared to be evolving in the heart of western Europe along lines not alien to theory. Italy had suffered a hard autumn and Paris a spring rising, there were elite radicals underground in Germany and Italy, but in Ireland the masses seemed on the move. The Marxists were entranced; many took student flights to see for themselves; others wrote from a distance.

Much the same was true for all the ideologically dedicated, just as was the case with the analysts concerned with violence and political modernization or social mobilization or the psychology of childhood trauma. Peace Studies departments, political scientists, those concerned with civil disobedience or conflict studies or small-group relations or game theory, all had cause to be interested. No academic journal was complete, it sometimes seemed, without an Irish article. And in time whole issues would be dedicated to nothing else. Everyone had a special perspective, a special methodology, an ox to gore. The advocates of the Fourth International and political deconstructionism were as one. Ireland offered each vindication and opportunity.

What Ireland did not offer toward the end of January 1972 was a predictable future except for the theorists whose predictions were mostly wishful thinking. All the involved threatened and warned. Specific actions dear to the heart of the Cassandra involved must be taken or terrible war would result; civil strife and chaos were certain unless a particular agenda was accepted. All the ideologues could read the direction of history but not next week's events. All the analytical models gave the big picture, not tomorrow's headlines. None of the observers, the English journalists, American academics, French television producers, no matter the empathy, the local access, or the breath of experience, could grasp the direction of events. And events were about to crest.

At one moment at Magilligan there was the prospect of tea and buns under a cold gray sky and the next moment there was a violent melee, broken heads, the grisly thunk of rubber bullets, and the screech of frightened gulls and lost children. There was out of nowhere or at the end of a long trail of abuse a riot on the damp sand. Should they have anticipated that the soldiers would not tolerate further provocation? Should they have assumed that the soldiers would, given the opportunity, retaliate? Should someone have been able to see a few minutes ahead?

What would happen the next time, next Sunday in Derry when NICRA would try again? Not what should happen next, what theory insisted, but what actually would occur to real people? What then? What would have been learned and to whose advantage? Could the mood be tasted and tested? What did Faulkner want, or London? What would the army do, or the demonstrators? Some said the IRA wanted a major gun battle in the Bogside. Others said that a replay of Magilligan would serve the cause, would hasten the seemingly inevitable end of Stormont, would end the lethargy of London. Some few felt that the loyalists would move back to the street while others reported intensive organization efforts by the Orange militants clumped around Craig that would add a new and dangerous dimension to the crisis. Would the loyalists play a Derry role?

Everyone knew something. No one knew what to expect. Everyone feared trouble, but no one knew what kind of trouble or to whose advantage it would be. Certainly the political events of the week as prologue to Derry gave not even cold comfort. The NICRA in Derry announced that the Magilligan violence "strengthens the will of the people of Derry to march in peaceful protest on Sunday next." Paisley, as usual, was outraged, insisting that, as usual, "the government had capitulated to the policy of terror. Today, the IRA had won." He demanded that Stormont stop the parade; and Craig, who proposed a censure motion against the government at Stormont for banning parades, was supported by Paisley along with W. J. Beattie, Norman Laird, Captain Robert Mitchell, and John McQuade, the Orange hard men increasingly frustrated with IRA violence. Craig also and tellingly predicted that the IRA's plan to move protest to the streets—for Craig the IRA and NICRA were one with Bernadette Devlin and even Hume and Barr—would produce violence that would further alienate Catholic opinion. Out of office but still in Stormont, he could have it both ways by attacking the government for banning parades, forecasting disaster when the ban was enforced, and all the while insisting that "IRA parades, legal or illegal, banned or tolerated, undermined the state."

The other violent events were a constant during the week as they had been in past months. The bombs continued: the Mobil Oil Depot at Gamble Street Belfast, the Orpheus Inn in York Street, the Harbour Commissioner's boat, a garage on Victoria Street, and a building in Corporation Street. The biggest bomb ever found—two hundred pounds of gelignite in two milk churns—was defused at Silverbridge on the border near Newry. Two telephone exchanges in County Tyrone were hit. There were two explosions inside the Holywood Barracks perimeter fence, four explosions in Castlewellan, County Down, and more explosions in Newry—fourteen bombs detonated on Wednesday, January 26. An IRA volunteer was killed while handling his device: another "own goal." A co-op was robbed and two armed raids occurred in Belfast. Army posts were attacked, an RUC Reserve constable kidnapped, an RUC off-duty constable shot and killed— the seventeenth police fatality.

Perhaps most indicative of the continuing decay of order was a wild, two-hour gun battle at Forkhill in County Armagh near the border between British troops and eight IRA volunteers out of Dundalk in the Republic directed by Martin Meehan and Anthony "Dutch" Doherty, two of the most wanted Provo gunmen in the North. Some one thousand shots were exchanged.

The countryside and later Dundalk were in a frenzy of excitement—if this was not war, war like the Glory Days of the Tan War, then what was it? The loyalists in the North were outraged, especially at the IRA firing from the Republic. The IRA GHQ was nearly as outraged as the authorities North and South at the waste of IRA ammunition and the highly visible use of the Republic as base. The IRA most certainly did not need wild Belfast cowboys shooting up the countryside but GHQ was reluctant to criticize enthusiastic aggression openly. The bold arrogance of the volunteers led immediately to Southern retaliation. Seven, including Meehan and Doherty, were arrested in Dundalk by the Gárda Síochána, the Irish police, and charged under Section 15 of the Firearms Act with possessing arms and with intent to endanger life. The gun was all too obviously a factor in Irish politics.

The next day, Saturday, the focus shifted to NICRA, with a demonstration march from Dungannon to Coalisland that produced confrontation, rubber bullets, CS gas, and many of the participants huddled in the rain inside the walls of a brickyard, with the angry British army at the gate. It had not been a good day: wet, cold, nasty, an unforgiving confrontation, no tea, no buns, no compromise. The army was provoked, angry, and the demonstrators determined. Still, it was not a replay of Magilligan or an escalation in violence. Derry, however, seemed likely to be a greater risk the next day. The symbolic value of the site was high. The IRA, although supposedly withdrawn from the city, remained a possible factor. The crowds were certain to be larger than at Dungannon. And the Protestant militants might not be content with the army using the boot.

So, once more, the media went on the road to Londonderry, cameras packed, reservations made at the City Hotel, long-distance calls placed to reserve space on the evening television news or the front page: There was likely to be hard news from Derry. The NICRA people were determined and a big crowd, no matter the weather, was assured. The army, especially the paratroops—the Paras—had reportedly lost patience and would be delighted to use the boot according to a Catholic deserter from a Belfast family, Peter McMullen, a cook from the paratroops who had opted to change sides. He had left behind a couple of ineffectual bombs and moved south to sign up with the other army, the IRA. And as for Derry on Sunday, that other army, the IRA, could hardly lose. The more violent the confrontation the more alienated the nationalists. And by Sunday morning, January 30, nearly everyone involved anticipated a confrontation, probably traditional violence, CS gas, broken heads, rubber bullets, outrage and arrogance, but possibly something more, something worse, but possibly a simple ritual, a tea-and-buns parade and then at the end of the day home to watch the rally on television.

By 1972 civil rights demonstrations had been, like the Orange parades or the republican commemorations, shaped to ritual. First came the marshaling by stewards, the border collies of civil parades, harrying all into form. Then began the formal march to confrontation, when, point made, the pacifist leaders urged movement to a reviewing stand. There, on the back of a lorry equipped with loudspeakers and appropriate banners, the performing cast waited. The withdrawal by the crowd to the speakers' corner was often covered by the alarms and excursions of the young who had come not to listen but to toss stones at the police or, if present, the Protestants, often there for similar purpose. This ritual could escalate or dribble away in a cautious retreat to the main body of demonstrators circled about the speakers. Finally came the last, drawn-out act, the crowd's ultimate, long stand. They largely ignored the familiar interminable speeches, orations heavy with grievance and short on flare or even the hard word. Then, patience exhausted, the end came.

Everyone made for home through the gathering gloom and damp to see if they had appeared on the evening telly news. The dangerous moments came at confrontation with the security forces or along the flash zones near truculent Protestants. Real trouble was almost always guaranteed by the inevitable swirl and flurry of those young men who had come to riot. For them a demonstration was an opportunity to stone the police, as for some of their elders it was an opportunity to curse authority. Matters then could escalate out of hand into a different final act of chase and charge, riot and run, until exhaustion ended the rite.

Thus, at Derry on Sunday, January 30, events would appear ominous depending on the point of focus. Most demonstrators had come to be witness, to march a bit, listen a bit, and go home, having defiled Faulkner's ban, having maintained the pressure. They would hear their Bernadette Devlin, the girl with the hard word, and the English Lord Brockway, an elderly, anti-imperialist liberal, long dedicated to good causes, and suffer through the usual collection of NICRA people and Northern politicians, Hume and Barr and the others. They were the tea-and-buns crowd. The youth brigade, hooligans of the rising generation, had come to throw stones and run away to agitate another day. Rumor also had it that the others, the army and the police, if anything wanted a hard confrontation, expected trouble. The Paras, proud of their elite military role, were eager for a go at the elusive IRA. The stone throwers of the rising generation should in any case provide ample irritation. Thus some in the media awaited trouble and others a dull day in the rain. Prediction is always difficult.

It had been clear from the first to the NICRA organizers that the army was not about to let an illegal parade stomp out of the Bogside and into the city proper, so the intention was to march behind the sound lorry up to the wire barricade, manned by the army and police, and then withdraw with the lorry, finishing up at a distance from potential trouble. And so matters developed. The parade of several thousand straggled up to the wire, made their point, and began to withdraw, past the Rossville Flats and Derry City walls on one side and by the Glenfada Park houses in the Bogside on the other, toward Free Derry Corner.

The security forces had feared that some twenty-five thousand might show up and instead found a far smaller group of aggressive "hooligans" remaining at the wire, tossing stones, fire grates, and metal rods, howling and spitting. The army replied with the usual rubber bullets and then with a water cannon spraying great gouts dyed purple over the agitators. At about five minutes before four in the afternoon, matters seemed to be in hand. The greater part of the crowd had moved on Derry Corner and the lorry to listen to the speakers.

The troublemakers were still scattered about in front of the army barricades, but were no longer a threat to the soldiers. As the official tribunal report on the events by Lord Widgery later noted, "The Army had achieved its main purpose of containing the march and although some rioters were still active in William Street they could have been dispersed without difficulty."

Dispersal, however, was not punishment nor clear indication of authority's triumph as far as some of the Paras were concerned. The commander of the Eighth Infantry Brigade, Brigadier A. P. W. MacLellan, MBE, the officer who had been put directly in charge by Major General R. C. Ford, CBE, commander of land forces in Northern Ireland, had the authority to extend the holding action and had so prepared a plan in case of need. His brigade order envisaged a potential sweep if conditions warranted it. The brigade commander, isolated from the area and dependent on incomplete information relayed by an officer in a helicopter, decided that such a sweep operation was in the interests of security.

He authorized the decision on the spot to be made by Lieutenant Colonel Derek Wilford, Commanding Officer One Paras. "It was a decision made in good faith by an experienced officer," the investigator Widgery would later decide. Thus, the Paras, to sweep up as many of the rioters as possible, would go beyond the barricades and snatch up the men beyond the wire.

After a most detailed inspection of the existing records and memories of those involved doubts remained about the orders and exact intentions of those involved.* Everyone saw the troops move out past the barrier at a few minutes past four. After that there is no consensus. The British troops involved, their spokesmen, and associates insist that the Paras came under direct and telling fire from snipers. A variety of those involved, often operating in isolation, reported various incidents. Certainly many of those rushing past the barricades after the rioters soon acted as if they were under fire and lives were in danger. The soldiers later insisted that they heard shots or saw snipers or fired at nail bombers and gunmen. One soldier claimed, falsely or mistakenly, that he had fired nineteen times at a sniper in a window. The soldiers involved would claim that they fired to protect their own lives and as their yellow card of instructions demanded. They fired, as required, only aimed shots and those shots were aimed at armed IRA opponents, not civilians. There was no British army panic, said the investigation. No disinterested witness heard sustained or, in fact, any returned IRA fire; but then none had much experience in combat. It later became clear that the Paras were not very experienced either. Certainly over the next twenty minutes everyone agrees that British firing continued and that one after another civilians fell to the ground. Some of these civilians were hit. Some on the ground were merely fearful.

---

*Twenty years later, in 1992, there was a general review of events, various articles and recollections and a book, *Bloody Sunday in Derry: What Really Happened?* by Eamonn McCann (with Maureen Shiels and Bridie Hannigan) published in Dingle (Kerry, Ireland) by Brandon Press. Several television specials made the greatest impact and revealed in some cases new perspectives. BBC's "Inside Story Special" included the Paras' company sergeant still serving in the regiment in uniform, speaking with British army permission, saying that "I feel in my own heart that all those people were innocent." Britain's Channel Four showed a documentary *Secret History: Bloody Sunday* as well as the film *The Bloody Sunday Murders,* coproduced by Margo Harkin and Eamonn McCann and presented by Maureen Shiels, who was two years old in 1972. These were shown on RTE in Ireland. RTE's own "Secret History" indicated that there had been two Official IRA volunteers with guns in the vicinity of the march ten minutes before the shooting and that Denis Bradley, then a priest who was kneeling over one of the dying victims, indicated that one had fired twice with a handgun at the Paras during the incident, a statement confirmed by Bishop Edward Daly on March 13, 1992. Prime Minister Major felt that there was no need of an additional inquiry into Bloody Sunday, and that the compensation paid the relatives of the victims indicated that they were innocent of any claims that they had been carrying firearms. The paratroopers' commander, Derek Wilford, now retired, regretted the confusion of the orders that led to the shooting but could not accept that his soldiers had killed the innocent "because that would be to accept that my soldiers were wrong" (Nell McCafferty in *The Sunday Triune* [Dublin], February 2, 1992). He does indicate that the Paras intended to cross the barricades into the civil rights crowd in order to draw out IRA gunmen and put a forceful end to the ritual of rioting. Most unexpected of all, Wilford feels that the best British policy now would be withdrawal from the province.

And the shooting was taking place at various places out of sight of many witnesses. No one at the time was sure of everything that was happening. Each was hemmed into a narrow world by the tumult and so limited to a montage of impressions.

Most significant historical events produce a chronicler, a perceptive and articulate witness to visualize the crux of the matter, an observer at a battle who saw it whole—a lieutenant who watched the last great charge of Confederate General George Pickett at Gettysburg or a German artillery observer in his dugout on the morning of D day watching the Allied fleet emerge from the night. Still later this evidence and other would be fashioned by a scholar into a real history. Someone almost always sees the big picture and writes it down. The very civil rights crisis itself produced the few hundred feet of RTE camera footage taken at Derry on October 5, 1968. Sometimes, however, reality is slurred and masked, a matter of many impressions, none satisfactory.

At Bloody Sunday, despite the extensive media coverage, the intimacy of the arena, the cameras, private and commercial, despite the presence of those with cause to recall in detail, no one grasped then or later the whole. Even years later Bloody Sunday brings back for many the image of a priest waving a handkerchief beside a sprawled body. Later there would be small black flags placed on each fatal spot, a deadly crop of thirteen poignant memorials scattered across waste ground by housing projects, with meaning only to the aware.

During the crucial twenty minutes on Sunday afternoon, no one was aware of the event as a whole, not the British soldiers firing at "gunmen," nor the victims, nor the others rushing away from the barricades. The television coverage later broadcast, the pictures by professionals and amateurs, the recollections of the involved, presented no compelling image. The time that stretched out endlessly for the vulnerable and passed in a flash for the men firing did not generate a historian. History as it happens was, as always, a matter of shreds and patches, recollection and perception; and not all the instant replays or stop-action cameras of memory could fashion it whole again. Bloody Sunday remained a frozen kaleidoscope and only meant what the various eyes chose to recall, what the involved made out of the images. It was thus for the perceptive a lesson in the construction and application of Irish history. At the time, however, all was partial, a matter of fragments and fear and a great uncertainty.

Wherever they were, however, those civilians closest to the advancing British soldiers knew that firing was taking place and that they were in danger. Still no one, then or for some time later, had an overall picture of the events. No one realized a major disaster was in progress. Each witness was limited to an often dreadfully dangerous bit of the whole. Many were on the ground or behind cover. No one could readily tell who had been shot, who was shooting. A priest with a white handkerchief waving in the air tried to reach one of the victims and had to withdraw, seemingly under fire. Some of those crumpled awkwardly on the ground must be at least wounded. No one knew or could risk moving while the firing continued. There would be more victims than even the observers cowering in passageways and behind gable ends could imagine.

In a little over twenty minutes the Paras' arrest operation had been transformed into a debacle that neither subsequent rationales and explanations nor official declarations could transform. For the entire Irish nationalist community, including most of the people in the Republic, for many disinterested observers and for the millions upon millions who learned of the events on the late evening news, Bloody Sunday in Derry was a massacre. The Paras had run amok and murdered innocent civilians because they had protested, because they were there, because they were Irish. The dead empire came alive offering example and precedent: the Amritsat massacre in India in 1919, Cyprus and Aden and Palestine, all lived again on the evening news and in newspaper headlines.

The skills and resources of a major state could not undo the twenty minutes, could not persuade, and at the end could barely contain the damage of Bloody Sunday. In fact, subsequent official reasoning and the ultimate Widgery *Report of the Tribunal* only convinced still more that the Paras were guilty of government-condoned murder. Some insisted that the murders had been planned in advance. Some, any evidence aside, did not believe that there had been any provocation. As time passed, fewer believed the soldiers' claim that they had returned fire. Almost no one outside the British army and the Tory establishment accepted that at the moment the soldiers may not have acted wisely. A great many people in Derry and beyond simply accepted that the British Paras had seen their opportunity to kill and seized it with enthusiasm.

In twenty minutes 107 high-velocity 7.62-mm. shots had been fired at the demonstrators, killing thirteen and wounding eighteen, one a woman. No member of the IRA was a casualty. There was no convincing evidence of guns or bombs. And nail bombs had been planted on dead bodies by someone who had realized soon enough that the killing was going to be difficult to justify. Forensic evidence was scanty, satisfactory only to those who wanted to believe in gunmen and bombers. The report of the subsequent tribunal only indicated that there was "strong suspicion" that some of the dead had been firing weapons or handling bombs and other victims "closely supporting them"—whatever that might mean. The actual evidence was unconvincing—because there was no real evidence beyond wishful thinking.

The details of the report were elsewhere unconvincing, everywhere self-serving, often contradictory or highly selective. The British, nevertheless, continued to maintain that the Paras had been fired upon and this justified everything. There is no reason to doubt that some soldiers so believed—they certainly swore to that effect during the investigation. There is not even reason to doubt that the British establishment and large segments of the British public so believed—they were hardly the first to take the word of their own as fact. For these, the marchers had been provocative and the IRA the key factor.

Many of the witnesses denied that there had been any IRA shooting. The two well-disciplined IRA units in Derry, the Officials under John White and the Provos under Martin McGuinness, denied any of their volunteers had been involved. They might have lied. And independent gunmen might have fired in any case. Most witnesses, however, had not heard any provocative shots or noted any gunmen. The origin of fire in such an arena, an echo chamber with no one possessed of a commanding view, would be difficult to determine even for the calm, disinterested, and experienced. Few on the ground on January 30 were calm then or disinterested later. One British sergeant, for example, with ten years' experience, subsequently swore that he had fired three rounds and at least wounded his target, a gunman who was definitely shooting a pistol at the soldiers from behind a car in the Rossville Flats courtyard. The sergeant also noted that during the exchange the incoming fire was intense as any he had seen in Northern Ireland.

In the end, however, none of the dead or wounded was proven to have fired shots. And no one else had noted any heavy incoming fire. Even sergeants with ten years' experience can be confused in the midst of action. So even if, as was quite possible, there had been fire against the Paras, it had no visible effect on the British soldiers, nor was it sustained long enough to be noted by anyone else, nor did it leave visible evidence. Under fire or not, the Paras had reacted without discipline and without restraint, shooting recklessly at obviously fleeing men and women, shooting at those crouched on the ground, shooting at movement and possible or potential or suspected gunmen. The result was that twenty minutes after the Paras went past the barricades at 4:20 in the afternoon, they had shot dead a baker's dozen of the innocent and wounded eighteen more.

One soldier among four Paras in the courtyard of the Glenfada Park houses fired twenty-two shots, even pausing to change magazines, and neither he nor the investigators could account for nineteen of his shots. He claimed to be firing at a gunman in a window of a house inhabited by an elderly couple, safe in another room, but not one bullet mark could be found near the window. He did not know where he had fired or why. He had fired repeatedly and apparently at random in a closed residential area. Yet this only bordered on the reckless, the official reported. There in Glenfada the four soldiers, who claimed they were returning fire, were instead shooting into a small crowd seeking desperately to escape. Four young Irishmen were killed. The incident ended only with the arrival of the Para platoon commander to find twenty or thirty survivors cowering in what had become the killing ground of the courtyard. All were immediately arrested as hooligans.

Elsewhere the victims and the vulnerable, drenched with purple dye, cowering and dazed, could hardly understand what was happening. Simon Winchester of the *Guardian* was on the scene, too close at first to the action to get any clear picture. Like everyone else his Bloody Sunday was a montage of impressions. At the end of the vital twenty minutes he was too shocked by the gunfire and results to understand what had happened.

> It was all over in less than twenty minutes. By about 4:20, it was clear that firing was now sporadic enough for me to walk down into Rossville Street once more, and I took off, looking desperately for familiar faces. Remnants of the crowd that had been listening to Lord Brockway, and had taken off and fled when the firing started, were coming back to view the carnage. . . . We watched with numbed shock as bleeding men were bundled into a fleet of cars and makeshift ambulances that had been driven into Lecky Road. No one seemed sure how many had been killed: there seemed to be about seven badly

injured and perhaps as many as five or six dead. . . . I left the area, still very shaken and frightened."*

Not until later that evening were the actual totals known and the implications of the incident apparent. BBC even split its news coverage of Bloody Sunday so that the impact in Northern Ireland would be less provocative than the more detailed reports broadcast in Great Britain. This was a traumatic policy violation that meant the system was not simply reporting the news but attempting to prevent further violence by censoring coverage.

Even those who had thought the Paras' sweep a good show and accepted the first, cherry briefing of the army had by midevening realized that all was not well. And soon there could be no doubt that there was a crisis of monumental proportions that would remain a grim bench mark in the Troubles for years to come.

> *Here lies one in blood and bones,*
> *Who lost his life for throwing stones.*
>
> *. . . . .*
>
> *This lesson in our hearts we keep:*
> *Persuasion, protest, arguments,*
> *The milder forms of violence,*
> *Earn nothing but polite neglect.*
> *England, the way to your respect*
> *Is via murderous force, it seems;*
> *You push us to your own extremes.*

So wrote Thomas Kinsella, a peaceful poet grown angry, in "Butcher's Dozen." As John Hume noted, for many in Derry it was a united Ireland or nothing, and few would now say no to the men of physical force. The IRA had been proven right once again. And the Irish in Derry were not alone. In horror and condemnation, they were joined by many apolitical people who had so far been inured to the North or to the patriot game.

For many in Ireland the simple attraction of ancient distaste and old patriotic prejudice called anew. Years of patriotic verities, Christian Brothers classes, Easter orations, and unchallenged historical assumptions suddenly came alive: The old men at the Post Office in 1916 lived again. Perfidious Albion openly ruled their illicit bit of the island with the gun and the lie. The British were unrepentant, as arrogant and smooth as Reginald Maudling on the following day in the House of Commons, chiding the paratroops' enthusiasm, as callous as those Tories who still felt Derry a jolly good show by troops unfairly criticized. A wave of atavistic Irish patriotism pulsed out of Derry by the time RTE signed off that night.

In Great Britain, Ireland remained, even for those sympathetic to nationalist views, even for those congenial to a united island some day, essentially a political

*Simon Winchester, *In Holy Terror* (London: Faber & Faber, 1974), p. 200.

issue within a democratic context, a problem of civil governance complicated by unnecessary resort to violence by a tiny minority of those within the province. It was a United Kingdom issue. Almost no one knew any Irish history or cared about Irish events. That should not matter. Everyone meant well—the British people, the establishment, the institutions of the state, the parties, everyone. That should matter, not old grievances and ancient wrongs. All in Britain wanted an accommodation, an agreement satisfactory or tolerable to all. This was a responsibility. This was everyone's intention. Bloody Sunday was an aberration, a momentary matter. And to this there was almost no dissent.

The British believed in their heart of hearts that their nation was decent and their aims just. The Irish, whatever their charms and varied virtues, had often been ungrateful in the past, parochial, unforgiving, marginal people, angry in the heat of emotion, misled by events, unable to appreciate British responsibilities and decency. So the British understood the anguish that Bloody Sunday had caused thus: Irish national angst was translated as emotional concern at an unfortunate and unintended technical disaster.

The British people and the politicians simply could not understand that the Irish, even those most sympathetic to London, felt the British inherently unfair, institutionally dishonest, determined on national gain disguised as general justice, and so willing to encourage or to tolerate the most brutal oppression when crossed. The British, the English, knowing what was good for the Irish, would tolerate no opposition. They must achieve what was just, fair, inevitable, and best by the necessary means. London would then label such state violence as fair and just and necessary as well. What else could be done? If there was criticism it was basely motivated or an emotional response or arose from willful misunderstanding. Hypocrisy was the cardinal English vice and nowhere was it more obvious than in the rationales for Irish policies, offered as disinterested gifts to the province but in reality vessels for British advantage, real and psychological.

Not understanding, irritated or outraged by criticism less than disinterested, the British had never seen the need to explain or apologize or trim a single sail, not in the past, not in Cyprus or Palestine or Kenya, not in Derry. Lieutenant Colonel Derek Wilford was named an OBE nine months later for service in Northern Ireland: Why not? He deserved it. As a Conservative Minister, Alan Lennox-Boyd, had said about an incident in Kenya in 1959, a "certain amount of indiscriminate violence is inevitable." The Paras had not thrown the first stone nor would Wilford be the last soldier honored in dubious Irish battle.

The vast differences between Irish and British reality became apparent to disinterested eyes in the House of Commons on Monday, January 31, when Reginald Maudling, the Home Secretary, rose in a tense moment to explain Derry, explain his government's intentions regarding what was already called Bloody Sunday. Elegant, slightly rumpled, suave, a large man, Maudling, well briefed, well prepared, well spoken, responded without surprises. He announced an impartial investigatory tribunal (fair is fair) and defended with considerable conviction the Paras. He was calm, untroubled, spoke in the rotund tones of his class and education, presented a picture not of a government at bay but of a Conservative enormously confident in manner and posture. He was at home in the House, comfortable with his assignment, assured of his views, a man clearly untroubled by the unfortunate Derry events, best filed and forgotten while everyone moved forward toward a necessary accommodation.

To Bernadette Devlin, sitting in an alien House as a party of one, denied the right to speak on Derry events by the Speaker, Maudling, with his plummy tones and gloriously elegant figure, was a sleek, arrogant fraud, a spokesman for murder. She rushed across the chamber to the horror and amazement of all and began to pummel him, scratching at his face, pulling his hair, screaming that he was a "murdering hypocrite." Dragged away from the shaken but soon suave Maudling, she was severely reprimanded by the House, criticized by the British in and out of the media, who could not imagine why form had to be violated and the House disrupted by Irish hooliganism in a miniskirt. Why could they not be like us?

In Ireland the response was quite different; many on the island, not all of them Catholics, long and deeply indignant at English airs and graces, felt that Devlin had acted quite properly. An arrogant and portly gentleman, member of the proper clubs, sporting a proper tie, was not the one to read wake over thirteen Irish dead. The killing ground of Derry demanded not elegance and grace or even a poem but recognition in London that the province required a major initiative, not more of the same. Maudling was more of the same, delivered, albeit inadvertently, with disdain, and taken by Devlin and most of the Irish as racist arrogance: Britain was right and the Irish must adjust. That is, after all, what Maudling and the Conservatives, the entire establishment, the whole of the British Isles, wanted in 1972 and had wanted for centuries: the Irish to act like them. And yet they would not, Protestant or Catholic, gunman or poet, they persisted in their island ways—and on that Monday this brought them into that most English of clubs, the Commons, to violate the center with rude and personal violence.

The scuffle within the House was briefly visible evidence of the enormous cultural gulf between the two islands, usually hidden by the seeming ease of communication in nearly the same language. The British could not imagine how their good intentions could be questioned, their system be at fault, their definition of justice disputed. For most of the Irish, Bloody Sunday was the response of that system to fair but unwanted criticism. The hard, unnatural union, imposed by force on the island, was not an imperial success and was certainly not the proper end of Irish history. When such a system was defended by British power, the result was more of the murderous force foreseen by Thomas Kinsella's "Butcher's Dozen." Devlin's display of raw bad taste, a grave sin in London, only encouraged the ruling establishment to stay the course. Devlin was rude and wrong. The Irish were volatile and mistaken. British justice would be done for Ireland despite the Irish.

The British appointed the impartial tribunal under the Right Honorable Lord Widgery. He was, more exactly, Baron John Passmore, Lord Chief Justice and former member of the British army, a piece of the main not less elegant than Reginald Maudling and so received by Irish opinion. An investigator of his own people, he was expected to produce in time and at some length, perhaps in great and apparently disinterested detail, a rationale that would be labeled *Report*. This neatly bound and stapled report would be completed after all general interest had long faded. It would then join the others on bureaucracy's shelf: the green paper or the white paper, a blue book or a green. It would have the usual dreary cover, close-set type, the product of Her Majesty's Stationery Office. Such reports by clerks and commissioners transformed blood and bone, fiscal anguish or diplomatic crisis, into the dry material for future historians. Such reports had become traditional for Northern Ireland matters. And as anticipated, Widgery produced in April a report on the incident. To turn what was perceived as a massacre into a forgotten incident, dead civilians into possible IRA gunmen, and an aggressive military foray into conventional peacekeeping went beyond his capacity. Still, he tried.

By then Bloody Sunday had generated millions of words, film documentaries, tracts, books, collections of photographs, all the massive coverage of contemporary crises. And events had moved on. There had been other spectaculars, if not as bloody, other alarms and events. Thus, by the time the report was published in April, nearly everyone concerned had long ago decided on what had happened that gray afternoon in Derry. Widgery simply contributed to the dispute and not to British advantage. He chose in every case to believe the soldiers, to accept the views of the British officers as given, to support the positions of the authorities, and to construct the best official explanation available. And when these sources proved faulty or inadequate, he rationalized or simply evaded unpleasantries. The orders for the foray beyond the barricades supposedly came from Brigadier MacLellan and were passed by Lieutenant Colonel Steel to the O/C Paras—an all-planned, fully authorized, quite necessary operation—except the proper record seemed to have been lost. And he concluded that some victims could have been using guns and others might have abetted the suspected, unfound gunmen. The existing evidence did not prohibit complicity and gunmen even if there was no positive proof. What served the British army's rationalizations could be and was construed from the existing evidence by Widgery.

The army had done the best it could and was not to blame. No one was to blame except perhaps the victims, who had been involved in an illegal march and had provoked the soldiers. Even on its own terms, it was a faulty exegesis usually ignored even by army apologists, who in the end had to rest the case on the undiscovered IRA gunmen. To fire haphazardly into *any* Catholic crowd in Derry and hit thirty-one people but not a single member of either IRA was in itself a remarkable feat.

No matter, by April 1972 all knew what they believed. And no matter what the closely reasoned arguments of the law or the suave rationalizations of the London establishment, long before the Widgery *Report* on Monday morning, January 31, everyone had decided what had happened, shaped the shooting to experience and need, written out yesterday for tomorrow's purpose. So Maudling spoke and Devlin reacted and neither paid the other more than passing and irritated interest. So Widgery's *Report* was not simply forgotten but became grist to the mill and the judge judged. Everyone except the mourners reacted to Bloody Sunday as symbol not event.

9

The End of Stormont:
February 1972–April 1972

Which, If Not Victory, Is Yet Revenge.
John Milton

One of the first to react to Bloody Sunday had been Prime Minister Brian Faulkner, who recognized that London, not recognizing blame, would fault Stormont, just as the Unionists, unable to attack London, habitually turned on the Catholics when feeling betrayed. The Conservative government would admit nothing publicly but would privately savage the Unionists because Bloody Sunday was a disaster; not London's fault, Ireland's fault. Faulkner had previously hoped that Stormont could survive even the rising level of the IRA campaign because dissolution offered the British only further responsibilities without scapegoats or local allies.

All the Irish Catholics were now absolutely alienated, North and South. No consensus for reforms could be constructed in the immediate future. Stormont probably could no longer be saved by the piecemeal defeat of terrorism coupled with a program of gradual reforms. The nationalists, the Catholics, even the most anti-IRA, would be alienated, perhaps irretrievably: Even the poets would look to murderous force.

Faulkner was Irish. He knew his own and no British explanation or investigation or rationalization would serve. Only violence by the state was left. And Stormont once again lacked sufficient counterforce unless London was willing to ante up the troops. And London would want fewer, not more, after Bloody Sunday, a blunder that would, no matter the fault, be laid by the Tory cabinet at Faulkner's door. So Faulkner, as early as possible Monday morning, met with the media to nail the colors to the mast: so far and no further. His statement was clear:

> It is clear now, as a result of the weekend shooting, that campaigns are being mounted in Northern Ireland and the Republic to achieve a United Ireland without the consent of the Unionist majority. We in the Unionist community will not tolerate such a proposal. We are more than ready to discuss how the institutions of Northern Ireland may be framed on a renewed basis of general consent. We are more than ready to develop the most friendly and co-operative relationship

with our neighbours to the South, if and when they manifest a matching good will. But there it ends.

Haggard and hard eyed, Faulkner had no intention of surrendering the principles of his party or his faith: The province was a legitimate part of the United Kingdom. London must understand that there could be no diluting the constitutional reality and denying majority rights. He knew what Bloody Sunday implied well before the news was being deciphered in London drawing rooms or Dublin pubs. London would put the screws to the Unionists at Stormont, where a culprit for Bloody Sunday could most easily be reached. Always during the Troubles the vulnerable, not the guilty, paid.

On February 4 Faulkner went to London to meet Heath with nothing more in his Stormont reform basket than the limited Green Paper of the autumn, a failure at the time, and his efforts to attract token Catholic support, now lost by the Derry disaster, with even the most conservative and conventional resigning any government connection. The fact that Bloody Sunday was a British army event, not a Stormont one, was irrelevant. The Protestants, now doubly on the defensive, would in response grow more militant, turn on the most vulnerable Catholics, the local innocents, as surrogates for the IRA, for the Irish Republic, and ultimately for the disloyal London establishment. The vulnerable would pay. The center—or more important, Stormont—might not hold. Time was on no one's side. Nothing boded well for the remainder of the year.

Elsewhere the response to Bloody Sunday was as predictable as the rain. The international media and its customers were horrified at the massacre and predicted IRA retaliation, the end of Stormont, general disaster. In response Northern Ireland as the hottest, hardest news attracted a new wave of camera teams, free-lance hopefuls, London-based correspondents, and the attention of those editors and producers previously slow to follow island events. Along with the media came the crisis groupies, Italian radicals, students still high on the years of the guerrilla, the concerned from the Irish diaspora, declared revolutionaries on the world circuit, and the analysts of opportunity. On the following Sunday, when the protest movement met in Newry, the thousands could hear Tom Driberg, former Communist, hard Left Labour member of Parliament, shout from the platform, "I don't think the British army will be here much longer. The real terrorists are in Stormont or Westminster!"—and see him finish with a clinched-fist salute of solidarity. Standing next to Bernadette Devlin, he personified the fashion of the moment. His ilk in and out of the media crowded into not only the City Hotel in Derry and the available hotel rooms in Belfast, once the Europa had overflowed, but also into Dublin, a far more congenial headquarters than a Northern base. The poorly connected or the stringers settled into rented rooms and bed and breakfasts. And there was instant news, an expanding crisis.

In New York the Secretary-General of the United Nations, Kurt Waldheim, offered his aid in response to a request from the Irish government—an offer made known at a news conference on February 7. To the south, Dublin sought not so much solution as an expansion of responsibility. In Washington a considerable number of American senators and representatives had public suggestions only in part arising from the anguished concern of their Irish-American constituents.

Senator Kennedy and Conservative Senator James L. Buckley of New York on February 2 separately called on the American government to urge withdrawal. Secretary of State William Rogers, however, felt such action would be inappropriate. Thousands of Irish-Americans did not and demonstrated in front of British government consulates and offices. In Australia there were similar demonstrations in Sydney and Melbourne.

In Europe the radicals instead of Irish emigrants led parades protesting British policy—Ireland was considered a key battleground in the struggle against imperialism by the entire spectrum of neo-Marxists. These and other radicals and reformers had gained entry to Irish events through the extensive media coverage and a variety of ideologically skewed reports coming from the growing pool of observers. At times it seemed that most of the articulate European Left had taken a cheap flight to Ireland with carefully prepared minds and limited budgets. All supported the demonstrators and most were attracted to the Officials, who were not only engaged in an armed struggle but also claimed to be Marxists. With less ideological charms because of their simple nationalism and their commanders' conservative social views, the Provos had fewer champions but even then there were those beyond the parliamentary Left who were attracted simply by their volunteers' dedication to the bomb and the gun. After the collapse of most European protest and the end of the years of the heroic guerrilla, Ireland offered much to the hard European Left, especially hope that all was not over.

It was not simply neo-Marxists but also various analysts who found Ireland fascinating. The wonder of a working-class revolutionary movement captivated even those more conservative, who rented better rooms, took notes, and did not want to appear on the barricades. Some came in disappointment that their dream of nonviolence had shattered and others to watch the new data being made by the involved. They, like nearly everyone else attracted to the island, had come to see history made if not changed.

In Britain the Conservative government would have preferred to have missed the acceleration of Irish history, not to have lived in interesting times. Northern Ireland should be a matter of internal politics, not an international crisis manipulated by anyone or everyone. Mostly the British felt misunderstood and unfairly criticized. The Labour opposition demanded some speedy response and that security responsibility be transferred from Stormont to the British government; but Labour, for the moment, did not go further. In real life there was no speedy response that did not involve either dangerous concessions to those at fault—the demonstrators and their constituency—or an impossible resort to harsher methods. Labour wanted action and there was for the moment little effective action to be taken. Wilson might accuse Maudling of "dragging his feet" but the Home Secretary had no place to go, fast or slow. And Labour had no novel suggestions.

Essentially, however, as had been the case since the first signs of trouble from the civil rights campaign, the various party responses to Irish matters were neither divisive within British politics, nor was the opposition, Conservative or Labour, eager to propose revolutionary steps. The more primitive Tories and the hard Left might care about Irish matters but hardly anyone else did. Prime Minister Heath insisted in a speech to the Young Conservative Conference at Harrogate, Yorkshire, on February 6 that the constitutional position could not change without majority consent and that Britain's responsibility was to maintain order.

Nothing new and in fact seemingly nothing at all was going to happen, despite Bloody Sunday. A wave of protest demonstrations quickly swept through Britain. In one, ninety people, including four policemen, were injured on February 5 when a crowd of five thousand tried to get thirteen coffins through to Number Ten Downing Street. But the protests had no noticeable impact on the government's attitude. Britain had already been inoculated against such radical demonstrations. And after all, as Maudling had pointed out during the emergency debate in Commons on February 1, the organizers of the march bore "a heavy responsibility" for subsequent events. The Conservative government tended to see, again, as always, that the Irish were at fault.

Particularly annoying, again, as always, was the response of the Irish government. Dublin had apparently forgotten nothing, learned nothing, forgiven nothing, and criticized without responsibility in matters best neglected, matters beyond Dublin's jurisdiction, whatever their constitutional or national pretensions. For this traditional and congenial misreading of Irish reality the British would over the years pay heavily. Condescension would have its costs, as would the almost universal desire to find outside agitators as culprits.

The real Irish government bore only marginal resemblance to London's view of militant nationalists in cloth caps reciting old grievances, scruffy rebels with rosary beads in one hand and a Thompson gun in the other. The Irish government, the entire Irish establishment, had been deeply shocked by the events of Bloody Sunday. All had hoped that somehow the Northern crisis might ease, and so evasion had taken the place of policy. Many in Dublin might still be moved by old ambitions and old loyalties but almost all had become realists. The passage of time tended to erode the general, simple ambitions even of the voters, who were increasingly exposed to the real world not found in patriot histories or holiday orations. Then came Bloody Sunday.

To some observers, such a confrontation had seemed more rather than less likely. Certainly within the IRA command circles the prospect of a British army atrocity of some sort had been examined. After all there was a colonial record of force and an army engaged in on-the-job peacekeeping is bound to overreact to provocation. The Irish government, however, as always influenced by wishful thinking and a paucity of power, had hoped that the crisis would ease over time.

The more violent Northern events, the more obvious was Dublin's quiescence—a posture no authority relishes. Now Bloody Sunday required a national response that the people would accept as sufficient. And there was no ammunition to hand. The ambassador, Dr. Donal O'Sullivan, was recalled from London in protest, according to the Irish government, of the "unprovoked attack by British troops on unarmed civilians in Derry." Airport and dock workers refused to handle British carriers or cargo. There was to be a national day of mourning. Everyone seemed to want to do something.

Then, after two days of protests and sporadic arson attempts, a crowd estimated at twenty-five thousand angry people besieged the British embassy, located in an elegant Georgian town house on Dublin's Merrion Square, on Wednesday, February 2, as part of Ireland's official day of mourning. In the crowd were several extremist Republicans with firebombs. When the crowd surged forward against a quickly dissolving police line, they began tossing Molotov cocktails against the front door. Evacuated two days before and isolated by the crowds, the embassy caught fire, burned briskly, and gutted out, fortunately before the entire side of the square caught fire as well. Some in the crowd felt that the wrong target had been chosen. The crowd should have gone to the other side of the square and attacked Leinster House, where the Irish Dáil and Taoiseach Jack Lynch had not only sat idly by but had also authorized the arrest of the IRA people in Dundalk the previous week.

In fact the wise in the Irish establishment realized that the arson in Merrion Square had reduced pressure on the government enormously for "something" that could be seen on the evening television news had been done. Foreign Minister Patrick Hillery might still talk of Britain's "lunatic policies" in the North, appear on American television talk shows with broad and radical proposals, but the worst was over. His appearances in Washington and at the United Nations did not change matters. As usual London did not grasp the community of interests between the two governments. London, unwilling to blame their army, unable to strike at a Northern Irish culprit, whether the victims or the IRA or Stormont or the Irish in general, could at least turn on the pretensions of Dublin. Speeches like Hillery's coming on top of the "outrage" at the Merrion Square riot were doing "lasting damage" to bilateral relations.

London failed to grasp that the Irish establishment was under attack not only from the IRA, Provo or Official, not only from those outraged by British security policies and the Stormont system, but also from a historical anomaly that made it necessary for the government to defend, even to prove, the legitimacy of the democratic institutions of the Irish Republic. The great Irish dream had been a united Ireland, free and Gaelic. Although unwilling to sacrifice for Irish unity, a great many Irish citizens might well tolerate others acting in their name, pursuing revenge for Bloody Sunday, ending partition with the gun. The IRA claimed to speak for the nation and to be the real government. And in time of chaos many might well see the republican movement as true heir to 1916, to the pure dreams of the nation's founding if not yet an alternative government. Much of Ireland failed to grasp their government's dilemma as well.

There was no power to unite Ireland. There was, worse, no mythical Irish to be united by the abolishing of the border. An Ireland without a border would be an Ireland wracked by civil war, an Ireland even further from real unity than ever. No government could achieve unity by force and no government could easily explain this to the people, had they risked trying. The Irish would have to find out on their own, over time.

The political establishment had increasingly felt a rising Irish reality about the meaning of unity, about the irrelevance of a partition line on a map or an island colored green, and that such acceptance had begun to arise from the direction of events. Those seduced by the old slogans, the imperishable dream, were being edged out of the center of the circle, as Kevin Boland had been edged out by his Fianna Fáil colleagues during the Arms Crisis. The realists like Charles Haughey, however, would make their peace with the intractable facts of modern Ireland even if limited loyalties remained viable. The responsible were not so much giving up a dream as defining its reality, a painful process often without visible profit. Bloody Sunday had simply touched all the old, comfortable, atavistic sureties of the patriot game, brought a huge, angry crowd spontaneously onto the Dublin streets—an almost unique Irish political event—and activated the banked spark of militant nationalism in many. Realism was on the defensive.

The arson at the embassy apparently had satisfied those eager for gesture. The passive police, the release of the IRA volunteers arrested at Dundalk through normal court procedures, and the militant speeches of various spokesmen had calmed many potential but pliant nationalists. For much of the week after Bloody Sunday, Dublin seethed with rumor and gossip. The diners at the elegant Russell Hotel on Stephen's Green talked politics instead of horses and so did the waiters and the guests. Everyone, not just the media people, whispered politics in the corners. Politics, substantive politics beyond the getting and spending and electing of the usual clientele arrangements, had come to the Republic. Bloody Sunday was killing politics, worse than the communal violence of August 1969 or the trauma of internment, and largely unwelcome. Beyond protest there seemed little that could be done; before, the rules had been wrong, but this time the rules had imposed a fearful penalty.

Not always consciously, those at the center of the power circle intended to wait out the immediate crisis by doing nothing, by saying the minimum, by biding their time. It never seemed to have occurred to the British that if the Irish government had wanted to make common cause with the IRA and the militants in the North then swift and tumultuous escalation would have been the result. There would have been a real war in the North and protracted turmoil spreading out from an ungovernable province. Matters very quickly could have been very much worse, almost unimaginably worse. Instead, by the time Hillery appeared on the NBC "Today" television show in New York, he asked for no more than the withdrawal of British troops from Catholic ghettos in the North and expressed a desire to talk with the Protestants. This was what the British establishment chose to see as doing "lasting damage." The same increasingly intractable establishment missed Lynch's criticism of the IRA as a small minority that would "under the cloak of patriotism seek to overthrow the institutions of this state."

The twenty-five thousand angry people surging back and forth in front of the burning British embassy as the Gárdaí stood idly by had concentrated minds in Leinster House. The IRA in February 1972 seemed a far greater danger to their democratic Dublin government than to the British control of Northern Ireland. For any government the base is legitimacy, and Northern events had put that issue again into the political arena. That the IRA was a Fianna Fáil target was made clear at the Ard Fheis in February. Less than a month after Bloody Sunday the Gárdaí arrested Cahal Goulding, Official IRA chief of staff, and six of his colleagues. As first target the alien Marxists were more vulnerable than the congenial Provo nationalists, but the message should have been clear. Not everyone noticed. Not in Ireland and certainly not in Britain. The British with their own Irish problems had no time for the subtleties of Irish politics. This was a costly oversight.

Bloody Sunday was obviously not a political disaster for everyone. The Irish republicans, who had benefited from all the British problems as well as many of the British assumptions about the island, had clearly gained the most from

Bloody Sunday. The media had accepted that neither Derry IRA unit was responsible for provoking the Paras with gunfire. Even the most reluctant Northern nationalists seemingly had at last been converted to the view that it was unity or nothing. Even the most conservative, even the token Catholic appointees, had become nationalists and, if nationalist, assumed unity was desirable and on the way. And to the south in the Republic, there had been an enormous surge of sympathy as Bloody Sunday generated or renewed specific commitments to the IRA. Mostly the Provos benefited, but even the Officials had more recruits and offers to help than could easily be absorbed, particularly since GHQ remained ambivalent about the Northern campaign.

Certainly both IRAs had promised immediate vengeance for the thirteen deaths. Despite the nonsectarian foundations of both movements, reinforced in the case of the Officials by Marxist tenets on nationalism and class, most members responded as Catholic to the plight of "our people." So the Provo O/C of Derry, Martin McGuinness, for the record said that "we will avenge every death in Derry today." This was considered by republicans justice, not sectarian vengeance. The unionists saw their analysis that, Catholic in fact equals IRA, vindicated once again.

A week of steady-state IRA violence followed but no spectaculars occurred. Major guerrilla operations take a lot longer for a secret army to organize than do press statements. In fact in most armed struggles, including that waged by the IRA in Northern Ireland, military operations tend to lag behind events, sometimes by weeks, so that observers tend to find connections that do not exist. The Provos, in any case, had no need to do more than their active service units had scheduled: the usual menu of sniping and ambushes, bombs and arson, Claymore mines exploded and police and military facilities attacked. Similar fewer attacks were carried out by Northern Official IRA units. The British sent over five hundred more troops to bring the total to fifteen thousand.

In February 1972 the Provisional IRA had achieved a position almost unimaginable by its commanders and advocates even a year previously. For the Army Council the organization had never been as strong and probably the resources and capacities of the Provos and Stickies in the six counties was stronger than during the Tan War. In fact the assets of the Provos alone were impressive and growing. Several events in February reinforced Provos feeling that matters were well in hand.

There was no division at the top. Séan Mac Stiofáin dominated his GHQ staff and discovered no dissent on the Army Council. The mix of fifties people and the young hawks of 1969 worked in practice. The intrusion of radical ideas, especially by some of the young, could easily be tolerated by the conservatives, given the level of military activity. Command was in place and control continued to expand, bringing in the new areas, reviving neglected fields, and restricting the despised Stickies to a few core areas. Belfast was Provo except for the Markets and one or two small areas still loyal to McMillen. John White had as many volunteers as Martin McGuinness in Derry but had to operate at the end of a long, often unused, line from Dublin. Elsewhere the Official IRA GHQ did not push the mobilization of military potential, so competition with the Provos in IRA activity actually began to decline by 1972. Increasingly the Dublin military connection became

Mick Ryan as the other campaign veterans in the center of the circle—Garland, Goulding, McGurran, and sometimes Séamus Costello—concentrated on politics.

Both military organizations' desire for gear and arms remained constant, and it was a problem never effectively solved by the Officials. Ryan, as QMG or Director of Operations, had little Dublin/GHQ help, only the odd international contact, and few of the assets of an American diaspora. The various Officials could amass local oddments but neither trips to the continent nor American friends produced the kind of shipments that the Northern units needed. The Officials did get a shipment of a dozen AK-47s acquired in America and managed through Canada, and they benefited from some small-scale smuggling, but there was nothing more. Here too the Provos came out on top, just as they had with twenty-six county recruiting. The Provos managed a variety of connections that should have been productive but in the end came down to what anyone would have expected: the Irish-American diaspora. There the Provos found means to bring into Ireland a steady stream of American military and civilian weapons that with other purchases and discoveries fueled the armed struggle for a decade.

In the crucial armed struggle the active service units had adequate military supplies if not the tools for escalation. In some cases, particularly detonators and explosives, the staff had to learn from the ground up and could only improve capacity to a certain point. Many IRA lives continued to be lost to accidents arising from on-the-job training. Not until the end of 1972 did improvement mean a decline in the number of accidental deaths, an increase in the explosive options of the units, and a growing technological capacity. IRA bombs might still fail orthodox standards but had grown very dangerous, very effective, indeed. Every rebel always wants more but in the matter of money and arms the Provos had solved most of their problems by 1972. The IRA was the key and the IRA had never been stronger.

The real Provo problems were simply not apparent to the Army Council, who could see the effect of their bombs each evening on the news, who could tally the rising curve of British military casualties, who saw all around them the international media avid for a statement, who remembered the old bleak days, the last campaign where in six years less damage was done than the Belfast unit now inflicted over a weekend. Once the movement had lived on borrowed five-pound notes, the charity of friends, and the comfort offered by a few obsolete Thompson guns inherited from the previous generation. And now . . .

For the first time since 1923 the republican world had emerged from underground. In both Derry and Belfast IRA volunteers controlled the Catholic working-class districts, the no-go zones where no security forces ventured and republican word was law. This permitted very safe houses, training sites, secure local planning and communication, a sense of ease behind the lines, and enormous publicity. For the first time in years some commanders did not need to worry about the knock at the door. In a sense the Republic was made manifest in these little but vital acres.

Within them the republicans extended their concerns, became involved in local law-and-order and welfare issues, housing and petty crime and places in schools, the problems of old age and female militancy. The underground army became socialized by responsibility. An underground army lacks both experience and talent in such endeavors, so there were the errors of on-the-job organizational training, the irritations of soldiers transformed into welfare workers, and the unavoidable alienation of some who had a visible and local villain to blame for an unsolved housing problem or a son tarred and feathered for shoplifting.

The degree of IRA control of the population, then and later, produced as many problems as benefits. The most obvious was that without jails the IRA was limited to repeated warnings, often ineffectual, or physical punishment, always brutal. A young man shot in the leg and left bleeding and crippled in the lane is a quite different matter from a young man serving three to five in Crumlin Road Prison for the same crime. IRA legitimacy and humanity were at risk when the organization extended its control. A traitor or informer could be shot or even killed with more legitimacy than could a girl be tarred and tied to a lamppost for dating a British soldier. The first act is military, traditional, explicable; the second is novel and unpleasant. On the other hand, if the IRA was to control a no-go zone then there must be order imposed and most certainly the local commanders had every intention of exploiting their areas, extending their control, and fashioning parallel governing institutions; and so they had to pay the cost.

Beyond the immediate costs and returns, the IRA gain of enormous general publicity from the zones meant an unexpected escalation of the struggle without military effort. Television crews arrived and were escorted through IRA territory; their cars were stopped by IRA patrols; their reporters were introduced to active service units, whose stories of life in the IRA zone were dramatic. These stories were eagerly awaited back in New York and Paris. And of course the British were outraged and the Protestants frantic at this visible evidence of lax security or IRA power or both. What did London intend?

For several years the consensus within the core of the IRA was that victory in the form of a British declaration of intent to withdraw could be achieved through the use of physical force. The Provo analysis was based almost entirely on basic republican ideological principles concerning the nature of reality and the direction of Irish history, enhanced by all the events since 1968 that simply reinforced these assumptions. Much of this was not wishful thinking or the conventional criminal optimism of revolutionary leaders.

The IRA, trusting in the lessons of the past, had moved from strength to strength. The only quibble seemed to be just how much strength was necessary, not what kind. And the IRA Army Council felt confident that their capacity would be adequate, since there was so much more to hand than had been the case for fifty years. The leadership of the IRA neither had nor felt a need for more than a narrow, provincial view of reality. Republican experience was adequate. Republican principles were sound. They felt they knew the British, the nature of the Dublin establishment, the limitations of the Irish people, and, if to a lesser degree, the nature of the unionists. For nearly five years events had done little to change IRA minds.

The British response to Bloody Sunday indicated the unchanging nature of the imperial presence in Ireland. The Arms Trial debacle simply stressed again in the Republic the priorities of Dublin. The expansion of the IRA and the arrival of a new generation reinforced the experience of past generations: The true Republic renewed its own, cycle after cycle, a helix of faith and sacrifice. Such faith and sacrifice were necessary because the people in general were hardly bold. They would tolerate action on their behalf, but because of the centuries of oppression these same Irish people were not interested in involvement in physical force politics.

In contrast, almost all of the Northern unionists remained adamant, opposed not only to republican, Irish ideals but often to their own best interests. The militant loyalists made no distinction in their analysis, so that the majority was enemy to the republicans and Catholic Irish—no interest in dividing and conquering. Most loyalists were willing to be politically active and, if not involved in paramilitary activities, were often tolerant of them. A backlash consequently remained an IRA concern. Sufficient precautions concerning Protestant militancy—a form or front of British imperialism as far as republicans were concerned—were taken, although volunteers were reluctant to admit the depth of the majority alienation. The unionists, Irish all, should not be loyal but Irish. The intensity of loyalist resistance to unification, contrasting markedly with the Southern Irish tepid support, tended to be fudged in IRA analysis of progress toward real victory.

Things had gone better than many had expected for the IRA, better than even some IRA people could have imagined: The future seemed in hand. No one noticed, so entranced with the Irish turmoil, that British attention had only been sporadically attracted and that British assets of all sorts were enormous. No one chose to consider the resilience and legitimacy of the elected Dublin government nor the ultimate attitudes of vital actors not committed to republican ideals: most of the population of the Republic, much of the Irish diaspora, all international opinion. Too true, men with guns can cause vast turmoil, build an underground; but the IRA had neither understanding nor as yet assets for any broader struggle. The capacity to do harm lay in Irish streets. The IRA had gained by deploying that capacity, almost to the extent that the security forces had responded. And then the British army in Derry had simply added to that advantageous violence. So in the weeks after Bloody Sunday the IRA ran free.

Haunting the IRA (Provo and Official) armed struggle even during the exhilarating times after Bloody Sunday and often disastrously as time passed was the inherently brutal nature of irregular war. Compounding IRA difficulties was the fact that many of their volunteers were ill equipped, poorly disciplined, and barely trained; some were crude and primitive even if not cruel and vindictive. Many of the volunteers embodied qualities immutable to tutelage, for they arose from a careless, imprecise, narrow, and often slovenly society. It is not only time that runs differently in much of Ireland but maintenance is poor and hope often replaces proper planning. Fashioned as racism the lack of social discipline has long been a weapon of those who find the Irish distasteful, ignoring both the other side of the coin of character and the historical reasons for imprecision. Rationally there were often few rewards for those on the island without resources when they opted for the disciplined mores of the middle class. The capitalists, the Church, the institutions of governance had over a century sought to erode the old habits but except for the creation of a small middle class had not been successful.

The Irish tended to be an easygoing, lax, often hopelessly optimistic people of enormous charm and manner, but there were no easy recruits within their society to rigor and order. Elsewhere in the British army, in the marketplaces of America or Australia, as wild geese or within institutions from the Christian Brothers to the staff of great hospitals, they adapted and succeeded, good soldiers, good Christians, makers and doers and movers. But the commanders of the IRA, themselves self-trained had continuing difficulties installing the habits of real soldiers on the volunteers of a covert, illegal army operating inside Irish society. Any covert armed struggle is in any case inefficient, trading cover for competence.

The result for the IRA was a long train of error: mistakes in timing, in degree, mistakes in interpretation and in placement, mistakes in mechanical devices and planning, often a lack of common sense, a failure to grasp the possible and the probable. Some of these difficulties were those of the individual, some were of the immediate society, some surely arose from the character of a people often unfairly maligned with stereotypes, and most important, all of these local and special difficulties were compounded by the fact that every covert army is inherently inefficient.

Revolutionaries, facing enormous obstacles, must be unduly optimistic or they would never undertake an armed struggle. And once engaged they seek not professionalism, not skills at the trade, not a career, but passage through to power. Thus, secret armies, even long-lived ones like those that appear in the Irish republican world, are institutions of transition, not worth perfecting. Within this temporary world, the ecosystem of revolution, the imperatives of the underground impose inefficiencies that allow persistence and occasionally escalation but at enormous cost. Secret communication, command and control, strategic analysis, tactical flexibility, all are won at a cost paid not only by the volunteers and their constituency but also by the innocent. It is the nature of irregular war to harm the innocent. For some gunmen and bombers there are no innocent people. This was hardly the case in Ireland, but errors, technical, tactical, even strategic, resulted in random casualties, unintentional, awful, unavoidable if the struggle is to continue.

That the official and orthodox opponent, the state, is often quite as brutal, just as deadly, without the excuses arising from underground requirements, is no matter. Some of the state centers so threatened pursue brutality and horror intentionally, but all engaged in an unconventional war have recourse, reluctantly or no, to unsavory means and dreadful by-products of order. It has this century always been accepted that the British aspire and often achieve a higher standard in such conflicts; certainly the guerrillas of Cyprus or South Arabia or Malaya expected such and were thus, only partly for their own purpose, quick to point out lapses. Other nations under threat would deploy the awful as expected but everywhere the guerrillas expected the British to be better. This was true in Ireland even as the rebels tolled the litany of grievances, massacres, starvation, cruelty, torture, exile, the Black and Tans, the lash, the prison ships, the emergency laws, the dead civilians and burned homes.

All of these British brutalities, often real enough, often repeated in part after 1969 and the arrival of British troops, were recalled but did not essentially change the fact that all irregular wars are dirty, nasty, often long, and always brutish. To engage in such a war is to accept responsibility in large part for the horror. And during 1972 the horror would grow as added to the traditional opponents, the soldiers and the gunmen, came the Protestant backlash, massively reducing the number of accepted innocents in the province. The war would grow worse as the IRA campaign continued.

What gave the IRA armed struggle its particularly unsavory taste was that there were a great many errors that always seemed to penalize the innocent, errors that could not be easily foisted on the British or excused because of flaws in Irish society or habits. The IRA was thus brutal, as are all rebels, and incompetent, as are all rebels, and both in full view of the international media and without the capacity to explain or to learn. Then, too, the Irish errors, the bombs without warnings, the men shot by mistake, the operations guaranteed to maim and kill, the technical and tactical blunders, all still seemed, even in a nasty and inefficient business, egregious.

In 1972, even within the republican world, the euphoria of escalation slowly began to be eroded by the costs, even when the costs were disguised as the result of British policies. As yet the secrecy surrounding any Protestant backlash kept that cost potential instead of real. The IRA did not want there to be a backlash and so strove to ignore not simply warning signs but also, if possible, murder. There was little secrecy, on the other hand, surrounding IRA activities—in fact, extensive publicity, evidence of chaos and turmoil, was integral to the IRA hope to make the province appear beyond governance. Thus, the IRA had to accept both the credit and the blame for the turbulence. The armed campaign might be understood and tolerated, but the mounting evidence of error and brutality was less enthusiastically accepted as useful or even valid. There was increasingly such evidence.

On January 18, without consulting with Brigade GHQ, the IRA Ballymacarret unit on the Short Strand agreed that Sidney Agnew, a Protestant living in the loyalist Mountpottinger district of East Belfast, should not give evidence against three local volunteers charged with hijacking a bus. That evening a man and a young woman were sent to Agnew's house, knocked on the front door, and when he opened up, shot and killed him in front of his wife and children. They withdrew from amid a fundamentalist Protestant neighborhood, leaving his children howling and his wife screaming, and Agnew heaped in a pool of blood, slaughtered because he was willing to tell the truth.

The Protestants were outraged at this sectarian murder. The Catholic neighbors near and far were stunned at the calculated and callous brutality, the presence of a young girl as a killer, the bereaved family. The "operation" had horrified Belfast and the province and eroded IRA credibility. It was murder simply to prevent the possible conviction of three men for a dubious hijacking where even their conviction would not lead to the most severe penalties. To the local unit the shooting had seemed logical. The power to remove the witnesses existed and no one thought further than that. The rationale had not seemed sectarian; the deed was necessary, the impact irrelevant.

The Ballymacarret IRA people had not only acted precipitately, murdered a bus driver for expediency's sake, but also had done so in a particularly brutal manner and in an operation that would obviously be seen by the Protestant community as sectarian. They had felt no need to ask permission so that, not for the first time, the margins of the movement determined direction, not the center.

They had assumed only that they could kill as they chose and had as a result produced damning if "logical" horror.

The lesson that was learned, however, was not that horror did not pay but that horror did not penalize. There would be more and worse brutal murders and like the killing of the young Scottish soldiers, each would produce outcries of rage and horror. Each would be damned as brutal or sectarian or both. Each would be forgotten sooner rather than later, buried in subsequent tragedies. Bloody Sunday came at the end of the month and no one remembered Agnew. Only a very few particular horrors had a long half-life in a province increasingly wracked by such abominations.

The Official IRA provided two particularly telling examples of the dynamics of brutality. The operations did in fact have a sobering effect on the Dublin GHQ but not on most of the Northern commanders or the military types within the Officials. The military militants, especially in the North, were all willing to pay the price of continuing—or more precisely were willing to have others pay it. To wage unconventional war is nasty and one crucial facet must be a command acceptance of the ensuing casualties, particularly the innocent, for at the end of the day all responsibility cannot be shifted onto the government, in many cases little responsibility can be denied. The Officials in the North would accept this along with the radical political views dispatched from Dublin, but in turn Dublin increasingly did not want to be entangled in an armed struggle, did not want to absorb the political costs.

On Tuesday, February 22, an Official operation long in the planning and unrelated to Bloody Sunday took place at the regimental headquarters of the British paratroops at Aldershot in England. Using information acquired the previous year, a bomb was placed in the barracks and detonated. The result of the blast was disastrous: one Roman Catholic padre killed and six cleaning ladies killed and one gardener killed and no paratroops killed at all. Early reports that had no details of a bomb in the Paras' barracks produced some delight in nationalist circles at vengeance received for Bloody Sunday, but the whole story unleashed a general wave of condemnation that swamped evidence of any early satisfaction. The Stickies had blundered. And only three weeks after Bloody Sunday such a blunder in Britain eased both conscience and implications of the Paras' killings. It was a costly blunder.

Then, three days later, on Friday, February 25, the Officials in Armagh on their own authority carried out an attack on the militant Minister for Home Affairs, John Taylor, just as he got into his car after leaving his father's office in Armagh City.

> There was an almighty roar that made me think that I had been booby-trapped and a bomb had gone off and my left leg was paralyzed immediately. . . . My left leg was full weight on the accelerator and the engine was roaring like mad and I couldn't in any way release it. I had lost all power. . . . Then I realized that I wasn't bombed at all but that I was being shot. At that stage blood was gushing out and I collapsed back into the seat with the result that out of the seventeen bullets only seven went through my body. Five went through the head

and jaw and the other ten went past my nose and through the far door.*

The IRA volunteer had from close range sprayed Taylor with a Thompson submachine gun, smashing his face, but by the time he had been moved from Armagh City Hospital to a Belfast hospital he was "out of immediate danger." In fact, he was soon back in political action. The Official IRA Northern Command took responsibility for the attack. The Dublin GHQ learned of the event on the radio. Some were satisfied that a man they felt was a militant unionist of some importance had been hit while others less military were uncertain Taylor had been a proper target and were increasingly unwilling to accept unpleasant military surprises. Elsewhere the criticism was complete. The majority saw the attack as sectarian, an affront to democratic institutions and individuals, a view shared by all segments of the British public and substantial portions of the Irish, including the nationalist politicians with most to fear from any Protestant backlash since they—the people and the politicians—not the secret IRA were visible and so vulnerable.

For most people the three operations seemed to indicate the evil of escalation. Agnew and Taylor for different reasons should not have been targets, and the bomb at Aldershot, right or wrong, indicated only that the innocent would pay as well. A bus driver, a politician, a Roman Catholic padre, a gardener, and cleaning ladies, dead and maimed, were not going to win a glorious victory. And so many were horrified, including the Official leaders in Dublin, but the IRA commanders were mostly truculent in their continued convictions. War was war. And so the armed struggle, Official and Provo, proceeded apace.

For the Provisional IRA, despite and to a degree because of the horrors, 1972 would continue to appear a very good year for some time to come. As the crisis intensified and escalated, the IRA would require further stakes to continue play even at the same level. Militarily the IRA was limited by the available arms and the capacities of the volunteers. On-the-job training, especially in explosives, had proven costly but would gradually be effective. The bombs were more sophisticated, opened more targets, made the security forces' job more difficult. Yet, urban activities had tended to reach a plateau. Any volunteers lost could easily be replaced but the level of intensity remained static. In the country commitment and capacity after 1969 had moved out from republican centers more slowly, but by 1972 some rural areas were enormously dangerous for anyone but the IRA, had become bandit country, rural no-go zones. The Republic of South Armagh with a capital at Crossmaglen was only the most prominent of the territories that formed this IRA bandit country. Again the British army response had met but not reduced this rural activity. Week by week the level of violence remained high but stable as the British deployment of troops and techniques kept pace with the IRA. And no matter how poorly British security coped in this period, astute observers doubted that the IRA had the assets to match those available to the security forces: Time would tell. The IRA, on the other hand, increasingly felt time was on their side and that their assets were ample for the task.

*Patrick Bishop and Eamonn Mallie, *The Provisional IRA* (London: Heinemann, 1987), pp. 142–43.

What the IRA lacked for a modern, high-tech armed struggle with a strategy focused on the nature of British perceptions was quite simply understanding of British political realities or the world beyond their Ireland. The Provos were a working-class movement of ill-educated, marginal, and parochial volunteers with scant understanding of the world beyond the Falls or the fields of South Armagh. Their armed struggle could expand but not really escalate and would have to seek softer and more distant targets as the British closed down the local military options. As time passed, the IRA could only adapt to the expanding British counterinsurgency capacity, not effectively counter it. Brave, bold, intimate with the immediate arena, absolutely dedicated, the volunteers lacked not only the vision and strategic insight the struggle required but also the technical skills to operate in a tiny, exposed battleground with a very limited constituency and no allies of note.

None in the IRA knew how the British system actually worked, what moved a Heath or a Thatcher or a Maudling, what the London establishment valued or distrusted, even what the English people were actually like. None really knew much of the world at large beyond the reports of the Irish diaspora. Few had modern skills crucial to modern war, even low-intensity war. There were no chemical engineers, computer programmers, import-export specialists, no fiscal entrepreneurs or advertising executives, no media consultants, no senior bureaucrats or experienced diplomats, no retired generals, no accountants or merchant bankers.

Many revolutionary groups tend to draw from limited strata; for a time, for example, it appeared that the Italian terrorists were all university sociology students. Most have a special appeal to their own, to Moslem or Christians in Ethiopia, to certain ethnic groups like the Tamils in Sri Lanka or the Ibo of Biafra. Some, like the Italian Fascists, based on ideology not ethnicity, draw from particular segments of society, often otherwise hostile. Many national liberation movements are composed of the middle class leading the poor or one tribe dominating the others or the chosen speaking for all. It is unusual to find a movement spanning the entire national spectrum. It is, however, still more unusual to find a revolutionary movement limited to the working class alone.

In the Glory Days of the Tan War, the militants represented a far wider spectrum, typical of most liberation movements then and later. Irish nationalism in 1921 varied in strength geographically, with Munster particularly strong; it held the wealthy Catholics tenuously and could not organize the very poor or appeal to any but a few token Protestants since most were unionists violently opposed even to regional devolution, particularly in the northeast of the island. Yet, despite the opposition of the Protestants and the varying draw of the dream, the Irish-Irish, rich and poor, urban and rural, trained and not, were all involved.

The resistance movements against the Nazi German occupation were often fully representative except when old ethnical rivalries as in Yugoslavia split an already divided nation. Usually, however, whether it was the People's Will in nineteenth-century Russia or the Euroterrorists of the 1970s the rebels' effective constituency and makeup is narrower than the ideal: The nation may be there to be liberated but many want no part of the process. By 1972 in Ireland, seemingly only those involved in the IRA sought liberation. At most the others, the people, the Irish, would tolerate unification. The Provisional movement of 1972 was novel only in that its support was working class or more properly the urban unemployed and the rural poor. The rest of the nation North and South stood aside or opposed the republicans. The Provos discovered and encouraged talent that had been denied, but still the movement lacked educated skills that cannot come simply through opportunity or self-help. A general or even an editor may learn on the job, often quickly, often effectively, but not a linguist or a brain surgeon or an economic analyst.

Most of the available, newly hatched middle-class radicals in 1968–69 remained within the spin-off movements of the civil rights organizations or in time found their way to Official Sinn Féin after Dublin GHQ closed the Stickies' armed struggle later in 1972. Some joined more conventional organizations, North and South. In the Republic very few trained people appeared at the Provos' Kevin Street and only a few at the Stickies' Gardiner Place office. The conservatives and comfortable found the Provos uncomfortable and unaccommodating. Some with money would still give money but seldom their time and never their children. The Provos in the North could hardly penetrate the tiny Catholic middle class, narrow, pious, deeply conservative, always on the edge of anxiety concerning economic disaster. In the South from the Arms Trial on, they found that the comfortable and learned, the skilled nationalists, would not risk much, were alienated by the brutalities of physical force and the rather simple and often shrill appeals of the movement.

Within their catchment area the IRA discovered a wealth of denied talent and unexpected capacity, and the driving ambitions in the service of the dream that permitted the organization to operate, often very effectively. They turned working-class housewives into articulate public speakers, school dropouts into editors, provincial schoolteachers into welcome guests on television chat shows of the international media circuit. They could not, however, fashion high-tech skills or sophisticated experience. More important, the center of the circle was barely aware of the lack.

Most would remain innocent of the value of such talent in a postindustrial world because most could see the enormous power that accrued to those with bombs and guns and a righteous cause. In the weeks after Bloody Sunday these assets looked like winners. The whole movement was confident, the beneficiary of compensating errors, resplendent in fresh skills from running a press conference to constructing a car bomb, eager to display power. And the available evidence tended to support the Provo position: 1972 was an IRA year and no greater evidence was available than the anguish and growing militancy of the Protestants. They clearly realized their way of life was in jeopardy. They, like nearly everyone else, felt matters could not simply continue.

Unexpectedly, even unexpectedly for many IRA commanders, Mac Stiofáin called a seventy-two-hour truce on Friday, March 10, beginning at midnight. The IRA demanded in return the withdrawal of British forces, the release of IRA prisoners, and the end of Stormont. There was no Provo IRA activity during the truce—putting paid to the argument that there was no control from the center— nor was there a British response. That weekend former Prime Minister Harold Wilson was in Dublin, where he met with members of the Provisional IRA. This meeting could be and was construed as the reason for his "fact-finding trip" to the Irish capital, not discussions with the government, and was the first step in real negotiations. Labour for the first time and unexpectedly seemed to be moving away from the usual nonpartisan response to Irish matters. Before, only individuals had sought contact with the IRA and London had shown little interest in such initiatives. Now Wilson was a player.

The Provos obviously felt that real negotiations would have to be with their Army Council. While Wilson's descent was unofficial, it was a real beginning and at a level most comforting to the Army Council. A former prime minister, a leader of the opposition, in Dublin to see them was no small coup. The Irish government, once Wilson's meeting was known, was stunned to have been cover for contact with men considered little better than criminals. The IRA felt, however, that Dublin and the Conservative government in London would soon have to face the new Irish reality. The three demands would have to be met sooner or later. And Wilson and the truce were major steps.

If the future immediately after Bloody Sunday seemed golden for the militant republicans and ominous for everyone else in Northern Ireland, those most determined not to wait idly while a dreadful future was imposed were the most militant and often least capable Protestants. As provincial violence escalated after the failure of internment and neither the institutions of Stormont nor the British army seemed able to cope, there was fear that London would lose patience, sell out the loyalists for peace and quiet. The terms of such a betrayal, one of the perpetual anxieties of the loyal, remained uncertain; but for a great many any diminishing of the Stormont system of control was all but equal to absolute withdrawal of the crown.

The slogan "Not an Inch" exactly conveyed the faith in a total, implacable, historically valid, morally justified, permanent, ordained society that would yet shatter at the first chip: almost a contradiction in terms. The North was a mighty fortress always under siege, implacable and just, but a fortress that could be betrayed from within at any moment. Northern dominance was always Janus-faced, arrogant and fearful. By the autumn of 1971 even the Pollyannas of Unionist politics accepted that change was likely. On October 3, 1971, Paisley publicly suggested that direct rule from London was to be imposed. This was denied but thereafter became a prospect to consider. For some this would be unmitigated disaster, since they remained deeply loyal to the Stormont system as an inviolate outward and visible sign of their society, as bulwark against Irish nationalism and Catholic expansion, as guarantor of the majority's way of life. Paisley, far from the primitive pictured by his nationalist opponents, felt that direct rule would more effectively guarantee that way of life and would maintain an everlasting separation between the vulnerable flock and the aspirations of Dublin.

This view was closely attuned to that of the province's great, if unwilling founder, Edward Carson, opponent of home rule, advocate of integration, but had no common currency until the civil rights crisis. Paisley, indeed, did not take an irrevocable stand on the matter. Certainly his and Desmond Boal's opposition to internment as potentially dangerous to Protestant options indicated that his analysis was not simpleminded nor was his response founded on the limited if real pleasures of domination. If Stormont were to go, direct rule was a valid option. If loyalists had to take to the streets to maintain the connection, then internment would be a burden. The more conventional hard men in or out of Parliament, William Craig, sitting in opposition to the official Unionists of Faulkner, or Billy Hull, who had helped organize the Loyalist Association of Workers, preferred not absorption into the main but a maintenance of devolution to the loyalists— Stormont retained. They, as did many loyalists, assumed an identity with Stormont the Parliament and Stormont the system both maintained by the British connection.

In fact, by January 1972, the loyalists had to contemplate a variety of options. The everyday people, the little loyalists, long content to let their betters think, found this novelty as distressing as did their betters. After fifty years of orthodox, Unionist control, maintained through a maze of institutions and attitudes, the basics were no longer apparent, even if the system seemingly remained intact. The future was debatable. There appeared for the first time real alternatives, few appealing. There were, logically, certain exclusive options for the future—and logic had never played a crucial role in Northern politics. Still, gradually the possibilities became political fodder. The province could be absorbed into the United Kingdom, returned to a reconstructed Stormont, governed by a reformed devolved system, abandoned to Irish nationalism, find a role as an independent entity, or discover common ground with both societies or with Dublin or both. Perhaps there was a combination, perhaps there was a satisfactory accommodation to be imposed by London, perhaps the province could return to the past. What had become novel was that such matters were at issue.

Essentially the province could become part of the United Kingdom, perhaps with the kind of regional local government suggested for Wales and Scotland, perhaps with six counties no different than East Anglia or Sussex. Then the Unionist Party might even disappear into the Conservatives and branches of Labour arrive in Belfast and Lurgan, and the six counties be an indivisible part of a united Kingdom. Although such integration would permanently deny the ambitions of Dublin, frustrate both the Catholic Church and Irish nationalism, Orange domination would almost certainly end as well. The historic rationales for the system of domination would no longer exist. If Antrim were as Anglesey, then Antrim would be so structured. In theory this was grand but in practice less so. The province was not part of the main but part of Ireland. How would integration *really* work? There was, however, no evidence that London intended to treat the Irish province as if it were English; nor was there, beyond Paisley, any deep enthusiasm for permanent direct rule. The majority, both the everyday, average unionist and the educated and elite, wanted Stormont, the Pre-O'Neill Stormont if possible and if not that of Faulkner but not an inch further down the road of reform and toleration if truculence could be made to work. There was a general feeling among the proper as well as the crudely militant that ample reforms had been made, that minority grievances were endless and increasingly a cover for unification. What was needed was time for the reforms to be properly perceived and peace and quiet for that process achieved through, if need be, draconian security measures. This seemed self-evident, reasonable.

After Bloody Sunday, most knew there was no more time and obviously no prospect for further or immediate repression. Reluctantly, the majority began to accept that because London was fainthearted, Stormont would have to be transformed, perhaps even discarded. In a reformed Stormont the change that would satisfy the British might be achieved by laws, negotiated or imposed, that would guarantee minority aspiration. In a Northern context, however, laws could probably never remove minority grievances embedded in nationalist history and memory. Seemingly what the Catholics wanted from the maimed system was "more" that would assure vengeance. Stormont as a system was beyond reform, beyond redemption, could not in traditional form evoke acceptance by the minority. Stormont was for Catholics not just the outward and visible symbol of the implacable majority but also the system of oppression fashioned by hereditary enemies. Neither Protestant nor Catholic referred to Stormont as a governing institution readily diagramed in civics books but used the term as a label for a system of domination that to function had to be employed.

The system was absolute, a mix of institutions and organizations, the criminal justice system and housing allotments, Orange orders and fundamentalist churches. It was a blend of attitudes and assumptions expressed in terms of class and station, with decency and decorum or with the raw power of the street-corner evangelists. In the end all aspects were as one, producing a child of history, complete, intractable, and effective. Stormont, the loyalist way of life, might be tidied, made decent, cut could not be dismantled until the adhesive myths collapsed and the bonds of belief separated.

Heretofore attack had only strengthened the structure, which needed an enemy to defend against. This defense was founded on a sense of righteousness. Thus, in any real sense Stormont could not be reformed, certainly not from London. It might be destroyed by the use of overwhelming force but certainly such force did not exist or was not contemplated. What had come under attack was the relevance of the system in a different age. A stalwart and faithful defense could not be mounted against time, and the loyalists feared that their time was running out. This was what impelled the direction of events, indicated that London would require updating, suggested that Stormont must be adjusted. Increasingly, therefore, the majority, the Protestant people not just their unionist leaders, recognized that at the very least the visible Stormont structure, the institutions housed in the great palace outside Belfast, were in jeopardy.

More disturbing, perhaps even the actual, if largely invisible, system of dominance that had been under open siege since 1968 was no longer viable. The rising tide of IRA violence and the decay of the institutions of defense was real enough. The direction of the government in London, Labour or Conservative, was equally clear. The isolation of the system in a Western world, represented by the assumptions of the visiting media, with opposing values, was obvious.

Most important of all, the defenders faced not only time as an enemy, societal irrelevance, not only the reformers and radicals with written agendas, not only the IRA and the Tory cabinet, but also a far more dreadful threat. The forces from the outside might be met, might be turned away or exhausted, might even be ignored; but it was the threat from within, a threat still denied even in most private counsels, a threat most deadly of all, that most sharpened loyalist anxieties. The great, grave danger was the erosion of their own inviolate certainty of superiority, expressed through exercise.

The system might be saved by transforming the long-proclaimed loyalty from the Crown to the province: Declare independence as had the Rhodesians. However revolutionary this might appear, the London establishment, the elegant clubmen or the Labour barons of union or university, had always slighted Northern Ireland, a dim, provincial place, crudely ruled by unpleasant people. Maudling or Callaghan had been condescending and unsympathetic, so why not defect? The practical difficulties—Northern Ireland was a tiny, remittance state without assets or prospects—hardly troubled the early advocates of a unilateral declaration of independence (UDI). Nor did the need of the Crown's acquiescence trouble them. In a province dominated by dreams or nightmares reality had never determined reality. The liberating charm of the concept of UDI was sufficient for some advocates. A few suggested that to be realistic an accommodation would have to be made with the minority and/or Dublin. Most of those interested could hardly imagine approaching accommodation with the historical enemy or moving beyond slogans. Slogans had always done before in the province. Slogans had always had takers. UDI if sold would be sold as slogan, not as a hard-edged program with subsections and an attached budget.

UDI was often and repeatedly to be, then, professed with a lack of realism: today a province, tomorrow a dominion, a federal solution or a seat in the United Nations. If UDI was to be practical, the minority must be involved. What could London say then? And however improbable, such a UDI alliance might not be impossible. The Northern Catholics did, increasingly, feel abandoned by Dublin, alienated from their fellow Catholics who were content to watch their anguish without offering more than Southern haven. So perhaps a deal could be made, Dublin bought off and London, facing a united province, willing to acquiesce. Yet, the whole argument remained somehow theoretical, unconvincing even to its loyalist advocates.

Independence, however crafted, did not seem a reality but rather a threat or a debating point that retained some appeal within the majority community because it responded to English arrogance. Nothing was more distasteful to an Orange loyalist on an English street to be hailed as Paddy, mistaken for alien, labeled Irish through arrogance by those who had sacrificed less, who had not fought on the Somme or held the line against the IRA. UDI, if no more than bruited, would serve as spiteful riposte, an instrument of minor vengeance, and thus it would be a useful club in the North's political bag.

The loyal, however, found it difficult to change their Orange spots. They continued to lift a glass in the local to the Queen's portrait and, teary eyed, sing the proper patriotic songs. The presence of the British army in loyalist neighborhoods led inevitably to tension and even serious riot but not to a general desire for separation from the Crown. A stone tossed at a British soldier at the end of a Shankill riot, even a shot fired in anger at the army, was thus aberration, not foundation for UDI. Their army was not the enemy.

For there to be loyalists there had to be those disloyal, beyond the pale, fenced in Protestant minds by experience and rumor validated by desire. For generations the others had been limned as alien, their society repellent, their ideas appalling, and the prospect of their control the rationale for all else. What would there be to talk about with a legate from a priest-ridden society dominated by harlot Church, by gunmen in cabinet offices, by advocates of everything alien to the majority? Even the educated and sophisticated, the professional people and gentry, could not easily imagine the other. Most polite Northern society, rich or poor, was constructed so that offense would not be given nor intimacy allowed no matter how regular and close the contact. Paisley might look like a Kerry County councillor, have an accent little different from the IRA O/C of Belfast, hold views on abortion and divorce, the arrogance of English politicians, and the workings of democracy that would have differed hardly a jot from those of the Roman Catholic archbishop of Dublin; but he was a child of the Reformation. The Fenians were Antichrist, the Catholics were Fenians, the IRA was evil. If UDI depended on a deal with evil, then the idea was anathema.

Quite unlike the militant republicans, most Irish nationalists and the many shades of neo-Marxists, who felt that common ground existed for all on the island, as Irish, as workers and peasants, as heirs to a joint past, and as residents bound to a common future, the Orange man really had nothing to say to the others. Not only would "six into twenty-six not go," but no one wanted to go into the twenty-six simply to talk. There was nothing to say. From time to time a spokesman tentatively suggested crossing the divide or an agent arrived to probe the others. Gusty Spence of the UVF, the first paramilitary of the crisis, talked with the IRA. Few others had his credentials or even his interest.

Most loyalists saw no need of contact or conversation but increasingly saw the need to take some action, to divert the inevitable. Only a very few sought to move out of conventional paths. On February 18 Phelim O'Neill resigned from the Unionist Party, and with two other Stormont MPs, Tom Gormley, an independent Nationalist, and Bertie McConnell, a pro-O'Neill Unionist, joined the Alliance Party. Most of his former colleagues saw the step as quixotic; whatever good intentions the Alliance Party had as a third way, the three had taken a road into a political wilderness. Those on the back benches who opposed Faulkner wanted to lead traditional action, another kind of crusade altogether. Their potential pilgrims, the majority voters, had grown increasingly uncertain at the hesitation and defections. For the first time there was no one to present a single and satisfactory program, to explain away the other options, to make the choices. There were too many choices and no organization to give a single lead.

There were by March 1972 all sorts of Protestant organizations that had evolved out of the crisis when the capacity of the orthodox to cope faltered. While the Unionist Party was apparently monolithic, maintaining the hegemony of the Protestant majority over the Catholic minority and the propertied and professional classes over the others, there had been dissent in the past. This movement had forced swift adjustment. The Unionist leaders had responded to division by policies that undermined the prospects of Labour. At times they also made adjustments at Stormont to placate populist opinion on social if not economic issues. In 1969 the vast majority of voters assumed that the system, the Unionist Party, their Orange lodge, the pastor and the owner, their betters, would manage matters. Protestant Ulster was a tight and largely contented class structure. The unionist edifice was maintained by reliance on the glue of the constitutional issue.

This assured that the secondary rewards of psychic domination would be primary to all loyalists. In return the system would assure the maintenance of that domination.

To feel superior was bought as ample benefit. The establishment took care of all else to their advantage. After 1969 the elite, however, seemed unable and often unwilling to guarantee the system by recourse to effective and compelling force. The responsible after 1969 were responsible for devaluing the returns assured to a majority with only the most limited other societal assets. And the elite then sought to buy off the disgruntled not with different benefits or a return of the old but with excuses. The elite, O'Neill and his cousin Chichester-Clark and finally Faulkner, the rich and proper, did not pay the promised dividends but put the system at risk. Some Unionists had even gone over to the Alliance. And the majority saw a rising danger to their way of life. The unfaithful Prime Ministers became lords or stayed leaders and they, the loyal, were left behind, at risk, undefended.

Reluctantly but inevitably, those most at risk began to respond, jealous that their Catholic coevals across the lane had the IRA to defend them, had the Dublin government to defend them, even had the media to defend them. They, the others, had even learned to defend themselves, had practice at speaking in public and making their grievances clear, could organize marches and con the television teams and London journalists. The Protestants, the majority, the loyalists, had no one to do for them, not in London, not at Stormont, and certainly not along the Shankill. They had to do for themselves and so haltingly and often ineptly they did.

> Being convinced that the enemies of the Faith and Freedom are determined to destroy the State of Northern Ireland and thereby enslave the people of God, we call on all members of our loyalist institutions, and other responsible citizens, to organize themselves *immediately* into platoons of twenty under the command of someone capable of acting as sergeant. Every effort must be made to arm these platoons, with whatever weapons are available. The first duty of each platoon will be to formulate a plan for the defense of its own street or road in cooperation with platoons in adjoining areas. A structure of command is largely in existence and the various platoons will eventually be linked in a coordinated effort.

This letter appeared in August 1971, in the *Loyalist News,* and was then distributed as a flier in the Protestant heartland: Shankill, Sandy Row, and East Belfast. It said it all. The Protestant way of life was under open siege. The loyal institutions and the responsible had not responded. The appropriate response was paramilitary, extraconstitutional, local, and defensive. This was the fundamental response, traditional, only novel in that trustworthy leadership seemed to be lacking. So the people of God must act for themselves.

Two or three gathered together under the aegis of the strongest or the loudest or the old sergeant or the new pastor, under the skilled and the experienced and even at times under the previously empowered, like John McKeague, who had put together the Shankill Defense Association in 1969. In September 1971 these local defenders with additions had come together in the new organization, the Ulster Defense Association, the UDA. A few of the hard men, the known, like Craig and Paisley, and the new, like John Taylor, sought to structure the need in conventional ways. The short-lived Unionist Alliance was transformed into Paisley's Democratic Unionist Party, which provided a provincial political umbrella for his expanding activities and influence. Taylor had as yet made no commitment when he was temporarily removed from the scene as the result of the unsuccessful Official IRA assassination attempt on February 25. Craig and the backbenchers, emboldened and hemmed about by their Stormont presence, rivals to Faulkner, took no immediate institutional steps until January 1972, when the Prime Minister's staying power appeared to dissolve. Then Craig decided to go ahead with a new loyalist structure that would make all other efforts unnecessary. The new vehicle would be founded as a broad front, the Vanguard movement, a vehicle that had places for all defenders but would be dominated—of course—by Craig and like-minded Unionists. By February such a broad front seemed necessary because the seamless garment of Unionism had been irrevocably torn. The splits had not arisen from class or national issues, as the neo-Marxists or Irish nationalists had always hoped, but over the means to maintain the system. The more populist the Protestant, the more fundamental in belief, the greater the suspicion of parliamentary politics or in some cases "politics" at all. Vanguard run by politicians would thus surmount such suspicions.

In a sense violence was not at issue or even treason. The means to defend would not be an issue. In some manner most of the establishment had always indicated that the system had to be defended at all costs, even that of confronting the Crown. Recourse to covenants of rebellion, to secret armies and conspiracies, were not so much treason as means to achieve what should be London's ends had the individuals and interests concerned not been led astray. In Northern Ireland it was almost conventional to be more loyal than the royalists of England. Thus, any means to maintain the connection were valid, legitimate, even necessary.

After August 1969, Shankill Defense Association, under the leadership of John McKeague, crudely articulate, charismatic, hard, gave example for a multitude of similar groups. Craig hoped to bring these under his Vanguard umbrella, but by February 1972 the structure of loyalist society was changing. Not only political groups emerged but also all sorts of self-help community groups. Everything seemed up for organization once the whole Stormont system fell into doubt. The active faithful, mostly adult male from the Protestant heartlands, with their army model, with the hated example of Catholics' secret army, with their need to "defend," naturally evolved paramilitary structures. The Ulster Volunteer Force, largely moribund since Gusty Spence had been dispatched to Crumlin Road Prison, was revived in Belfast. Another option was visible by 1972 in the Tartan Gangs, which were neighborhood teenagers transformed into defenders by the addition of tartar scarfs and the slogans of the day: "We are here to defend. They are not letting us live like men. If we can't live like men, then we can die like men." They disappeared with the rise of more mature paramilitaries but indicated the climate of the times. The UDA, the UVF, Red Hand Commandos, Ulster Freedom Fighters, all sorts of organizations appeared in Belfast and were often reflected in the towns and countryside among hard men there. Craig's unstated assumption was that these defenders needed leadership. Vanguard would supply it.

The UDA and the others fulfilled an urgent need for many Protestants to participate in events in a congenial and meaningful way but they did not provide a coherent vehicle for mass militancy. What the UDA did from the beginning was to reflect the nature of the militant Protestant community, neighborhood based, working class, mostly males of military age, and without appropriate organizational experience. The members in UDA and the various smaller but similar groups were eager to maintain the system but not Stormont and not the old elite. The new defenders wanted a system that returned the past and the old benefits.

Most of the members were a mirror image of their Irish republican rivals, whose organizational assets, ideological foundation, and underground experience were far greater. Northern republicans could build on fifty years of clandestine work and seemingly an aeon of national history and experience, even if the builders were as class-bound as the Protestants. The essential difficulty for the Protestants would be that they never managed to find an overt, effective form for their dream or the disinterested discipline an underground requires. The UDA with its military ranks, ersatz uniforms, and command areas was often no more than a clearinghouse for neighborhood vigilantes or hurriedly assembled posses or small groups of hard men meeting in rural pubs, Belfast clubs, or Protestant workplaces. There was certainly idealism at first and often in subsequent years, at least for young members, and there was especially a desire to serve, but what and how could not be made clear.

The great emotional core of the system—to display publicly the domination of the local minority—could not be admitted, since it was a negative posture and because as the years passed it was no longer true in that the minority no longer felt inferior or even dominated by the majority. An RUC reserve constable stopping a suspected minority car was as frightened as the occupants, unlike the old B Special days. The end result was that the existing idealism in time was corrupted by those who would use "the organization" for their own purposes and without ideological or structural challenge. A thief using an IRA identity risked swift retaliation from the local unit, but a thief with a UDA calling card had no effective central command to fear, only rivals competing for the returns of militancy. The UDA and the other fundamentalist paramilitaries never became purely criminal organizations, never were merely covers for psychopathic killers or elegant titles for posses or vigilante murders. But most assuredly, the Protestant paramilitaries, as organizations and as repositories of opportunities, housed criminals and psychopaths and vigilante gunmen without effective internal challenge or serious loss of basic support. Early on, once the campaign of purely sectarian killings began, the paramilitaries lost nearly all respectability. Again Vanguard, however extreme in declaration, was respectable and would have to compete with the attractions of ground-level militancy hardly recognized by the Stormont elite.

The UDA was working class and often working class at its most primitive and unappealing: crude, violent, greedy, harsh, and brutish, with a drinking problem and a short attention span. The noble workers appeared few on the ground when left to their own devices—and the UDA at times flew very strange devices. Their leaders became apologists not simply for vigilante murder rationalized as a military campaign but also for torture, extortion, violent crime, petty misdemeanors, and most horrifying of all serial sociopathic killers. The problem in the very beginning and the problem that remained unsolved for two decades was a working-class membership that lacked the compelling and luminous power of a dream. There was not any inherent majority attraction toward violent criminal or pathological behavior. Defending the indefensible was simply not a viable faith.*

The positive aspects of the Protestant way of life, often cited with justifiable pride, needed no defense. It was the enormous psychological benefits of displayed domination that reinforced the assumptions of superiority, a domination that assured that the others would not prosper and so engendered justifiable loyalist fears of minority vengeance that needed defense. Yet, no one but the warped and embittered, the maladjusted, would long sacrifice for the right to make others miserable. Every society has a few so warped but seldom fashions about them the institutions or order—the visible system that in Northern Ireland had come under siege in 1968. Some Protestant paramilitaries would take risks to impose suffering but more was needed to structure an underground. The Protestants had to organize around a negative, the fear of the others, the guilts and dangers of a domination unearned and unjust and unfashionable. They could not adequately define what it was they defended for in the end they were addicted to the indefensible.

Whatever difficulty the Protestants may have had about exactly what they were defending beyond their rights as a people of God, there was never any doubt about what they were against. The minority had not only spurned their historical role as the justly dominated but had, it was assumed, been transformed by an unsavory alchemy into aggressive, psychopathic killers enlisted in a bloody revolution spearheaded by the IRA. This was the enemy of the UDA and this was the enemy Vanguard would seek to confront more effectively. And there was ample evidence that this enemy was as despicable as painted. It was not just Agnew shot down before his family or Taylor machine-gunned in his car but the bombs blasting away the center of the province and endangering day by day the innocent Protestants.

On Saturday afternoon, March 4, one of the worst Belfast atrocities of all occurred. Saturday was downtown shopping day and the center of the city was crowded with women and children. At 4:30 many were packed into the Abercorn

---

*The structure and history of the loyalists during the Troubles has been uncongenial to conventional methodologies—as well as offering the challenges of a subject both illicit and covert. It has been approached from the two ends of the analytical spectrum by David Boulton, a television documentary producer, with The UVF 1966–1973: An Anatomy of Loyalist Rebellion, (Dublin: Torc Books, 1973), which indicates the obstacles rather than reveals the reality, and by Sarah Nelson in her splendid and scholarly Ulster's Uncertain Defenders: Loyalists and the Northern Ireland Conflict (Belfast: Appletree Press, 1984), which is especially good on attitudes and assumptions, and by necessity attempts no authoritative history. Such a history is especially difficult because increasingly the lethal loyalists were so few, so haltingly structured, so transient and inarticulate, and thus, almost always beyond analytical reach. In fact, a loyalist history is one of the few lacunae in the literature of the Troubles. This problem was again—and effectively—addressed by Steve Bruce in The Red Hand: Protestant Paramilitaries in Northern Ireland (New York: Oxford University Press, 1992).

Restaurant when a bomb detonated in the dining room. The effect was horrendous, the force of the explosion driving broken glass across the room, inflicting the most dreadful injuries on many of the 130 wounded and killing 3 people. The detonation tore people apart, the shards of glass sliced away limbs and maimed a room of people. The wounds were fearful, beyond repair or forgiveness. Television coverage showed the shattered, dripping blood, still in shock, carried one after another from the ruins. The reports were awful; two sisters shopping for a wedding gown each had both legs amputated, others had been frightfully maimed. Why? What conceivable reasons could there be to detonate a bomb in a crowded restaurant at tea time? Why intentionally, coldly, without warning, slaughter women and children, some Protestant, some Catholic, none guilty of anything, none about to testify, none in politics, none in a military installation? Irregular war was brutal but such callous cruelty was not war and could help no one.

Understandably no one claimed responsibility although the assumption was that the Provos had been involved. The RUC knew that a one-minute warning had been telephoned in from a box on the Lower Falls. The authorities and most of the loyalists simply assumed that the IRA was responsible. Then and later the most educated guess was that the IRA First Battalion had undertaken the bombing and neglected to leave sufficient time to call a warning. Belfast Brigade denied then and ever after that they had any evidence to support this. They also had no evidence to deny it privately and the involved never came forward even within the movement. This hardly mattered—the Provos were blamed despite their denial. In the Commons Maulding spoke for most and especially for Northern Protestants when he said that "these crimes are the work of psychopaths. I would not think there was any concerted plan, but there is a new pattern of uncoordinated bombing by psychopathic killers."* Such a community of killers could only be made with compelling and coercive force. The movement to organize had barely come in time.

What Craig and Vanguard proposed was to incorporate all facets of the organized majority into a single organization of defense, to give an opportunity for action, if only ritual, to intimidate the minority, to dissuade London from deserting the ship, and to replace the existing Unionist establishment. They, the experienced elite, would supply the needed leadership, be in the vanguard of Vanguard. From the first there were those, most prominently Ian Paisley, who

---

*There were, indeed, psychopath killers in Northern Ireland as elsewhere and some would use the Troubles as cover, even as rationale, but the horrified in London and elsewhere were inevitably mistaken to see madmen behind most violent acts. Those responsible might have been ruthless, brutal, indifferent to the risks to innocent life, but they were purposeful. Many killed those defined as legitimate targets and others killed the innocent by mistake, through incompetence, as a by-product of authorized operations. And all were indignant that spokesmen for states capable of strategic bombing of civilian targets or individuals, who saw war as an appropriate response to provocation, considered rebels or defenders or members of a secret army to be mad or terrorists or both—outrageous hypocrisy. And such an analysis repeated over the years in London and elsewhere by the responsible did little to shape an effective policy or to make explicable Irish violence. A growing psychological literature on motivation and rationalization, not only in Ireland but also elsewhere, resulted in no change in the repeated assertion even of the informed that such violence was mad.

saw the last rationale as the core: another Unionist establishment takeover of the province, a takeover on the backs of the people. Paisley felt *he* spoke for the little people, the workers and farmers and decent Christians. The Vanguard elite discounted Paisley as a local phenomenon, too parochial for big-time politics.

But the concept of Vanguard faced severe obstacles. How was a brand-new organization without guns going to intimidate an awakened minority led by gunmen who murdered the British army on the streets? The IRA shot Unionist politicians with impunity, bombed away the cities, and already ruled parts of Derry and Belfast and the bandit zones in the country. What action could there be but civil war without proper preparation and against British interests and forces? What good was organizing just to organize? What point parades and covenants and militant speeches that led only to frustration later? The other means were still apparently unappealing to the elite leadership. The pogrom, tolerated or encouraged, would evoke British army intervention. And random vigilante killing, murder of the others to reassure the many, was unsavory. What new was to be done?

In other words, even before Craig and the others had come up with a name, the doubters assumed that Vanguard was a tool for establishment use. It seemed a means to hack out power for the dissenters within the old Unionist system by displaying the numbers, militancy, and faith of the masses. These innocent masses seemed eager to be counted if not sure for what. The new men who had found opportunities in "organizing" wanted more than to be counted. Might not be willing to challenge the old but still represented the new, the raw, and the brutal. They suspected that Vanguard was a means to step in front of the parade that the risen Protestant people were organizing out of desperation.

These suspicions were firmly based in reality. The old system was dead and the hard men wanted to control whatever emerged from the wreckage. And why not? They were one with the people, uncontaminated by Stormont responsibility, enemies of O'Neill and Chichester-Clark and Faulkner, competent, experienced, eager, justifiably ambitious, neither crazy themselves nor unable to control those who were. Who else could lead an increasingly militant majority and intimidate a minority no longer capable of being purchased by reforms? Who else indeed? And what other means than those tried and true in Northern Ireland, the rituals and rites, revived and enhanced? These ceremonies had served so well for so long and would, thus, be particularly effective with the masses, who hungered after reassurance. As for action, why would not threat and the odd individual atrocity suffice, as they had in the past? Vanguard was unusual business as usual. On the evening of Wednesday, February 9, 1972, the leaders of Vanguard held a press conference to announce their umbrella movement. Craig was very much the leader. He had assembled what at the time seemed a spectrum of the uncompromising.

There was the Reverend Martin Smyth, county grand master of the Orange Order for Belfast, representing the marching institutions and indicative of similar support from the Londonderry lodges. Billy Hull, chairman of the Loyalist Association of Workers (LAW) stood for the workplace, home of loyalist legitimacy. Captain Austin Ardill, a slim, balding, elderly ex-Unionist MP for Carrick who was a long-time, bitter opponent of the reforms of O'Neill and Chichester-

Clark and Faulkner in particular and of unnecessary change in general. There was George Allport, a prospective Unionist candidate for Bangor, and Brian Smyth of the Young Unionists as representatives of the next Unionist generation. There had been no sign then or later of Paisley and company or the inchoate fundamentalist movements assembling under the Ulster Defense Association banner. Neither had any time for Craig as competitor, late convert to fundamentalism.

Vanguard, a smallish umbrella held by establishment hands, was really an attempt to institutionalize majority anxiety for elite benefit as much as for policy purpose. Vanguard would be sold to the majority as panacea, used to intimidate the minority with threats, and manipulated as a large bargaining chip with the London center. Vanguard would be an army of defenders, a posse in waiting, a risen people steadfast in their rights. And the leader, William Craig, offered the people reassuring fare: marches and rallies, rallies and marches, a whole series to culminate in Belfast's Ormeau Park on March 18.

The first event at Lisburn on Saturday, February 12, would have been easy to categorize as quaint, like the Orange marches or gable end murals of William of Orange, if the province had not been in turmoil. On a fine afternoon some one thousand had gathered. Craig arrived in a vintage limousine escorted by outrider motorcycles, stepped out and forward, and moved down the ranks of Vanguard supporters, bowler hatted and medal bedangled. Stiff and properly suited, he inspected the loyal as a leader in mufti. He read a long intricate Ulster Covenant reminiscent of the 1912 anti–home rule document, and asked those present to assent to the document. There were three roars of "I do!" And then Craig threatened those who would stand in the way: "We are determined, ladies and gentlemen, to preserve our British traditions and way of life. And God help those who get in our way." Many of the foreign observers did not know what to make of the scene. Was Craig a miniature Duce, an actor in a comic opera, or a suave demagogue authorizing murder? What was going on? Depending on the angle of vision, Vanguard was farce or serious threat, neo-Fascism of Craig's bluster given traditional Ulster form. His speech in any case grew harsher as the provincial order deteriorated daily.

On March 5, the day after the rally at Bangor, in answer to a question by Liam Hourican, Northern correspondent of RTE, he indicated that killing all the Catholics in Belfast might not be necessary: "It might not go so far as that but it could go as far as killing. It could be similar to the situation in the 1920s where Roman Catholics identified in republican rebellion could find themselves unwelcome in their places of work and under pressure to leave their homes." And for the record he announced that he intended to liquidate the IRA. Paisley and Bunting had no time for a competitor outflanking them with the hard word and Faulkner called the rallies alien and sinister—although they had been choreographed to be familiar and reassuring. The remainder of the loyalist community applauded or refrained from comment. Still, thousands signed up with the movement, even if no one was quite sure in which direction Craig was moving.

On March 18 between fifty thousand and ninety thousand loyalists, many drawn up in military ranks, listened to Craig at the Ulster Vanguard rally at Ormeau Park in Belfast. Observers assessing the cheers felt that the rally indicated primarily the continuing opposition of all things republican, most particularly unity. There was little discernible sentiment for UDI or even for the Northern Parliament as such. Sentiment, as always, was negative, against. No Surrender meant No Unity. Everyone wanted the Stormont system as it had been, a return to old verities even if this was not practical. Very few loyalists were enthusiastic about reforms or London interference; but the driving force behind the marches, the organizations, and the rising paramilitaries was fear of the triumph of Irish republicanism led by the most brutal and alien of men in the North and in Dublin. To them it was No Surrender. For the rest the faithful had to hope for Conservative common sense—after all, Faulkner was going to London again on Wednesday, March 22. Craig might feel that direct rule imposed from London was betrayal but even direct rule was not Rome rule. So Vanguard had provided only a megaphone, not a new direction, not a meld of all sentiment, not, yet, a new party fashioned as a front. And as yet Vanguard had no capacity to affect events. The real power was in London or in the barrel of various guns. And as they had the most power so did the men in London have the most guns. London would move next. Vanguard might not even have a turn. It was, in fact, Faulkner's turn.

Faulkner on his arrival in London felt that despite all, direct rule was not inevitable. Why would London shift two months after Bloody Sunday, two months further on in the IRA campaign, where republican blunders had eased the Paras' contamination? Basically the reason for the delay was that Ireland continued to have a relatively low British priority. And there was no gain, national, political, or personal, to be had from the province. Faulkner was mistaken about British priorities. Some within the Conservative establishment had been following Scarlett O'Hara's philosophy from the last page of *Gone with the Wind* to think about such matters on the morrow.

Lethargy, keenly reflected in Maudling's attitude, was as much a factor as cunning or conscious timing. The imposition of direct rule, getting rid of the Stormont reputation, had been a real possibility since the failure of internment. The Conservatives tended, not unjustifiably, to blame the Unionists for the chaos after internment. They did not choose to recognize that their own interest in an initiative without great cost had led to the authorization of internment. Innocent of Ireland, London had taken the easy way out and so had Stormont. Faulkner had several times proposed relatively radical restructurings of the system but nothing struck London's fancy. Stormont was Stormont and a seat of the emerging Irish problem. The failure of internment, the escalating IRA campaign, the pause at Christmas, Bloody Sunday—all Irish events urged serious surgery. Times had changed, and after that since nothing much seemed to be working, it was best for London to cut free and take over security—which left Stormont so little that pride would force them to acquiesce in their own dismissal.

It was not only the disappointment with Stormont but also the gradual realization that the province had reintroduced the dreaded Irish question into politics that moved the cabinet to act. The steady nightly television news, bombs and murders and even an incident at Aldershot in England, made the war real. The maneuvers of the IRA were not just criminal, the dreadful acts of psychopaths, but also had political ramifications within the United Kingdom. The Provos' truce meant that the IRA had to be taken seriously as a rational player.

This thought was followed by the news on Monday, March 20, that while in Dublin Harold Wilson, along with his spokesman for Northern Ireland, Merlyn Rees, had met three members of the Provisional Sinn Féin (read Provisional IRA): Joe Cahill, John Kelly, and Dáithí O Conaill. Even though Rees felt the three talked only in terms of military victory, some could see that a time of political maneuvering had arrived and the Unionists were a burden. Certainly the Conservatives did not want Ireland to become politicized in London, did not want to face an Irish question, did not welcome more involvement. So, though reluctant even yet, even after Bloody Sunday, in March Heath decided something must be done to move the issue off stage.

What the British wanted was just what Maudling had indicated—an end to terror, peace, and a provincial accommodation. The Unionists could not deliver the first even with an escalating British army presence. If peace were impossible as long as the Unionists remained visibly in control, then so was an accommodation. No possibility of an accommodation meant no peace. And so on. Northern Irish politics in March 1972 was a vicious circle. Terror could only be eliminated with peace that was impossible to achieve because of the costs of eliminating terror. London was eager for a tolerable level of violence that could be defined as peace. With that London could fashion some sort of provincial consensus and so oversee normality growing and paramilitary attractions ebbing. Unionist Stormont alienated all the minority, thus encouraging the IRA. With Stormont there seemed no chance (and Stormont had been given a very long run); with the British in charge of security there was a chance. If the Unionists wanted to stay around at Stormont and watch, they could. If not, not.

On Tuesday, March 21, Faulkner arrived in London with his deputy, Senator J. L. O. Andrews, son of John Andrews, Stormont Prime Minister in the early forties; several senior civil servants; Sir Harold Black, cabinet secretary; and Kenneth Bloomfield, deputy secretary. They did not anticipate that the meeting the next day would be traumatic. It had been almost two months since Bloody Sunday, since Faulkner had come on February 4 in anguish, and there had been no visible change in Tory attitudes. The invisible world of the center of the Tory establishment, where much occurs and little may be said even over the port, had arrived at a consensus. Rumors and suspected leaks had drifted about among the chattering observers but only a few knew that at last Heath intended to move. When Faulkner arrived at 10 Downing, just before 11:30 in the morning, he anticipated four or five hours of talks. And the talks moved at first along the allotted path. Lieutenant General Sir Harry Tuzo, GOC Northern Ireland, gave the military assessment. Heath mentioned the internment issue. Faulkner agreed some might be released and elaborated on the success of the security forces. Heath, staring into space, listened for some time. Then he announced without preamble that in effect London was going to take over all security control. Stormont's powers, already eroded by the various reforms that shifted responsibility to local authorities, would be negligible. Faulkner could wait it out, impotent and ignored, in Stormont or not.

The meeting broke for a politely friendly lunch and resumed, and the details were spelled out. There was no give in the London position. Heath, Maudling, and the rest had decided. The Wednesday meeting lasted nine hours, to the increasing anxiety of those left behind at Stormont and to the despair of the Unionists at 10 Downing Street, who could not at first accept that Heath was resolved and then could only plead that their Stormont colleagues would resign. Heath did not seem alarmed; "Tell them anyway and see what they say." The Stormont delegation thus condemned to resign still ate a hearty dinner of Aberdeen Angus rib of beef and baked Alaska at the Carlton Tower Hotel amid much gallows humor before returning to Belfast shortly after midnight.*

The next morning at Stormont all of the Unionists realized that the end had come. Faulkner accepted that his optimism about the cabinet's intentions had been misplaced and that his proposals had been viewed in London as nonstarters. They would have to resign and with them went Stormont. Faulkner and Andrews, who had personally reported the details of the nine hours, then flew back to London on Thursday to arrange the funeral. The Stormont parliament would be prorogued for one year but everyone knew the body was dead, and by Faulkner's return to Belfast meant the spirit was dead as well. There were still posed pictures and set smiles at the door to Number 10, civility inside, and final handshakes. Faulkner flew back to Northern Ireland just after midnight on Friday and Heath made his Direct Rule statement at eleven the same morning in Westminster. His speech went over the recent history of the Troubles and the meetings with the Unionists during the week. In effect, Stormont was to be closed down. "The transfer of security powers is an indispensable condition for progress in finding a practical solution in Northern Ireland," he said. "The Northern Ireland government's decision [to refuse the transfer] leaves us with no alternative to assuming full and direct responsibility for the administration of Northern Ireland."

That Stormont's refusal had been factored into British policy was evidenced by the fact that Heath announced William Whitelaw would be secretary for Northern Ireland, with junior ministers Lord Windlesham, a Catholic, Paul Channon MP, and David Howell MP, and a commission to advise him composed of residents in Northern Ireland. If the promulgation had not been long in the works, there had been ample time to devise alternative institutions. Stormont was now history. That evening in a television broadcast Heath said that "what the government have done today is intended . . . to put the past behind us and concentrate on the future." The major player had moved, the leading actor read a new part.

On Tuesday, March 28, 1972, at the Parliament Buildings, built for a thousand-year empire, the assembly met for the last time. John McQuade and Desmond Boal resigned since they wanted no role in a nonfunctioning assembly. The others—Faulkner, the cabinet, and the backbenchers, without the representatives of the minority, who had withdrawn previously and were celebrating elsewhere—went through the final, gloomy rituals. Stormont thus adjourned for good, even if the last wistful hope of a Protestant people found its way into the adjournment, which set a date for the future that for Stormont would never occur.

*For Faulkner's account, see his *Memoirs of a Statesman* (London: Weidenfeld and Nicolson, 1970), pp. 151–53.

Stormont would be history—and so possessed of all the awful and often unalterable power of the past in Irish politics and thus capable of shaping the future: "Adjourned accordingly at fifteen minutes past five o'clock until Tuesday April 18th, 1972 pursuant to the Resolution of the House of this day."

10

The British Response,
From Stormont to the Truce:
April 1972–July 9, 1972

Not Everything Is Possible At Every Time.
Heinrich Wölffin

On the day after Prime Minister Edward Heath announced that Stormont had been prorogued, for most purposes the cast of the Northern crisis froze into set parts and persistent roles. None could maneuver without a significant escalation in talent or purpose. None in fact would so desire. Each player, great and small, was fueled by a driving and obvious purpose, revealed and imprinted in the years that had shaped the world of 1972. To change, even to want to change, posed massive difficulties. The snap and crack of the armed struggle, the flash moments of sheer terror, the sudden shots or the unexpected splits and schisms, the betrayals and conversions, were merely the sparkle on the glacier's surface.

Yet on the day after the announcement, most observers assumed that everything was in motion, that the fever had broken, that the times were at last changing—there would be a truce or an agreement or new institutions. No one wanted to consider a permanent crisis, institutionalized conflict. Even if there could be no return to the good old days, however defined, surely the British initiative would lead to beneficial change.

Change, if it came at all, would do so ever so slowly, through the imperceptible erosion of sureties, the fugitive shift of priorities and assumptions. Time tended instead to impose obstacles to fluidity. Unpleasant ideological postures became not only fixed but also inviolate and in time even presented the holder with secondary benefits as well as refined rationalizations for self-consumption. There would in the future be fierce, often unexpected, and at times novel action, but while the plot might thicken it flowed sluggishly between set walls, down runnels all too visible in 1972. The intensely involved did not so much want change as vindication or triumph. And the others further afield simply wanted to be left alone.

The Provisional IRA had immediately announced that nothing had changed despite the fact that many in the North, Protestant and Catholic, assumed that everything had changed. The Army Council felt that they had bombed away Stormont and that the weight of bombs to hand would bomb away the connection entirely. All that was left for the British to do was to discuss the final two points of the IRA September terms: withdrawal and amnesty. The IRA was winning and if not winning could not be defeated. Mac Stiofáin stressed that "the Heath plans came nowhere near our terms."* It was not a case of all or nothing but rather that the goals for which men had died and others had been killed had not as yet been achieved. When Britain announced an intent to withdraw, when the volunteers were out of prison, then there was real movement. Nothing else had changed.

Irish republican grievances were not easily snuffed out by reform undertaken in London so lethargically and so reluctantly by a government more sullen than delighted with the end of Stormont. The IRA Army Council remained stable, Mac Stiofáin dominated military events, gear was on the way, and the door was filled with new volunteers. In March 1972 the leadership remained assured and confident, and equally confident that their republican rivals, the Officials, had fallen by the wayside.

In this there was much truth, for increasingly politics instead of war attracted the Dublin GHQ. And the end of Stormont might open political avenues into the future, the dearest desire of the Dublin Army Council. Most still within the Officials saw a role for an IRA, but not necessarily the traditional one. Mick Ryan might still be dedicated to the gun in politics but his old friends like Goulding and Garland had reconsidered. And despite the resignation of Roy Johnston from the IRA as the nature and costs of an armed struggle became apparent to him, the influential within the center of the circle still sought to transform the movement into a party without quite giving up the gun. In the North, of course, the active service volunteers felt revolution would come through the existing armed struggle. Rarely, however, did anyone from Dublin appear to reinforce their assumption.

In Dublin the core at Gardiner Place talked as if revolution were a program and not a killing matter. And at Gardiner Place, although the end of Stormont was publicly discounted as an end to change, the enlarged Army Council and the Sinn Féin leaders, disconcerted by Northern events, could foresee soon an end to the shooting. The radicals felt that if Stormont was gone, they might play a Northern role, if not, not; there was much to be done in the South. They did not consider an increased military role but rationales for truce. The Official IRA was not so much changed by the end of Stormont as revealed.

Thus, Heath's announcement meant that all the Irish republicans found themselves on the right road: the Provisionals toward an escalated war and the Officials into politics. For years neither considered other options and then not without the risk of another schism. For republican ideals or directions to be transformed enormous pressures of time and place were required. At the core were the Officials with a new vision and the Provisionals with the old. Revealed truth is not easily changed and not often calibrated to objective reality.

On the part of the British little had changed either. Patience had been

---

*Seán Mac Stiofáin, *Revolution in Ireland* (Edinburg: Gordon Cremonesi, 1975), p. 241.

exhausted, toleration of the Unionists eroded. Stormont had become a liability. The cabinet wanted to achieve sufficient peace through firm security measures to allow room to fashion a provincial accommodation. London wanted a quiet future with an acceptable level of violence administered by a devolved six-county authority: the middle ground. London's faith in the middle ground was as absolute and unchanging in 1972 as the IRA's in the ultimate Republic. This unchanging assumption arising from British experience meant that while the army and police imposed order, Whitelaw and his colleagues would begin a new and more modern political process. Power must be shared, not used to hurt. Far into the future the British would pursue this policy, seeking an acceptable level of violence and the devolution of authority by all sorts of means often unimaginable in March 1972: assemblies, constitutions, royal visits, plebiscites, promises, money and threats, truces and talks and talks about talks, and always hints of more to come. The more British policy changed the more it stayed the same.

The betrayed loyalists too learned nothing and forgot nothing. Denied in London, they sought vengeance at home. The anger of the remaining Unionists was no consolation, no vengeance. Politics had failed. The "defenders" had no effective defense, only an abiding anger. Faulkner was gone. Craig might want to soldier on, Paisley cry in the new Orange wilderness as orator and man of the cloth, but the everyday people wanted *something* done. The most militant loyalists knew at once what had to be done: what had always been done. They were emboldened because now violence would not simply be spoken from a podium, threatened by men in tailored suits who would go home to sherry and silver cutlery, but would be tolerated.

There had been no change in fundamental Protestant attitudes. The few and violent, the disconsolate, those for whom Craig had rationalized killing, would kill. They, the new paramilitaries, turned naturally upon those who were vulnerable: them, the others, Catholics, nationalists. The Protestant paramilitaries began killing those who should be, could be a danger, who might be in the IRA. They sought as target any vulnerable Catholic male: a transient worker in a border zone, a lonely farmer in a loyalist area, a postman or taxi driver in the wrong place, a man going home to a Protestant wife—whoever was easy to find. And killing was enough. The sadists did so brutally, the others with some enthusiasm. There was no need for proclamations or claims. The dead body in the ditch would do. It always had. Quite unwittingly and certainly inevitably Heath had unleashed the loyalist gunmen, made partially legitimate by the general anguish of the moment. The militants would no longer deny themselves. The killing began.

And for a time the killing was ignored, denied, filed under crime, under mystery, under best forgotten. The republicans did not want to believe their fellow Irishmen would murder solely for denominational reasons. The nationalists preferred to glide over a threat they had always feared, had incorporated into the folk memory of horrors and chose now not to discuss. To name the evil would make it real. The authorities did not want to think of their own as vigilante murderers, no matter the clues, no matter the evidence. The loyalists' habits made denial easy. The paramilitaries were content to kill, kill the guilty Catholics, kill the traitors from within, and let the bodies speak for them. They, unlike the IRA, existed in a half-world of patriotic gore, fearful of criminality, proud of the gun, part soldier touched with a murderous lust, part pilgrim in an uncertain crusade. So the bodies were recovered and listed as accident, as murder unsolved, untotaled, unwanted.

The very first death, on Sunday evening, March 26, was a Protestant. Ingram Beckitt, thirty-seven, was murdered by William Spence and John Thomas Boyd, both later killed by loyalist assassins. His body was dumped on Conlig Street off the Shankill after a final bullet was needed to finish him off. It was a brutal, pointless murder of a man who had done no more than criticize some defenders as "a bunch of thugs and gangsters" and threatened to go to the police. No one could betray defenders. Not Heath, not Beckitt. And the work of the defenders began in April with three murders.

In 1971 there had been five murders all told. In January 1972 there had been two, then one in February and two in March, but after Stormont was prorogued, the butcher's bill grew. In May there were ten murders. The first was actually an Official IRA man, Victor Andrews, brutally stabbed at least fifteen times by a Tartan Gang and dumped dead in an entry off Baltic Avenue on Thursday, May 4. He was one of the few IRA people so unlucky.

The sectarian killings were explained in various ways. On Friday, May 12, another Roman Catholic, Patrick Joseph McVeigh, this time without IRA connections, was killed by a burst of automatic fire apparently from plainclothes soldiers. The IRA could and did blame British army special operations, condemned many Protestant paramilitary killings as the work of British agents. And some of the killings could be hidden as crime or IRA feuds or special cases. In June five more Catholics were killed and the direction of events became more apparent.

The loyalist extremists, ill-organized, badly led if at all, usually incompetent, often with drink taken, were in Belfast determined on murder. Tens of thousands enlisted in the UDA or other organizations intended to defend, came together in country pubs or met as Tartan Gangs; only a few hard men went out to murder. Their example encouraged a few psychopaths, butchers driven to slaughter without politics or reason. Their example did not lead to a grand and open paramilitary war or even to pogroms and public violence. The killing simply added to the horror and indicated that, despite London's optimism, those in the middle ground might be targets, not examples; the integrity of the conflict had been untouched by the removal of one symbol, only intensified.

Those most reluctant to accept that the end of Stormont meant a continuation of the worst of the old ways rather than a beginning were the moderate politicians. The firm Unionists were still in shock. At Stormont on Friday, March 24, forty-seven members of the Unionist Parliamentary Party had pledged themselves to noncooperation. They remained, however, uncertain about their future role. The majority clustered around Faulkner but the old Unionist Party had been transformed. The elite had lost its role.

Their opposite numbers, the Irish nationalists, knew exactly what that role should be: a part in a new, parliamentary play that would corrode the image and attraction of the IRA while isolating the Orange extremists. The new play would be about politics, about power sharing, about a future without the gun. Like the British cabinet and the Alliance Party, the Irish nationalists, North and South, SDLP, Fianna Fáil, Labour, and Fine Gael, their voters and advocates, wanted to believe in a middle ground, a commonality of Northern interests, an interim accommodation. They wanted a piece of the action and this seemed to be what Heath offered. Thus, the prorogation of Stormont should have been an opportunity, a change in direction, a beginning of the end. So every significant politician—John Hume and Gerry Fitt, Jack Lynch and Liam Cosgrave of Fine Gael, the powers that be in Dublin and Derry, along the Falls and in Cork—welcomed the initiative.

By the spring of 1972, Dublin was as set on its course as the others. The national issue, ignored if possible, should as time passed inevitably attract fewer simpleminded patriots complete with historic remedies for a divided island. To assure this transition to realism, every effort should be made to contain militant republicans—in jail if need be—and to encourage nationalist political gain in the North. Whatever replaced Stormont—everyone assumed something must replace the Parliament—the politicians wanted the new to be attractive, an arena for the conventional, a reward for their own, an opportunity. The end of Stormont should mean the end of vengeance.

The prorogation thus seemed to most involved in politics and to much of the populace a major change. Rather, the end of Stormont should have led to major change, to reform, agreement, civil peace, tranquillity. Dublin, like London, wanted the North normal and marginalized. The Northern nationalists wanted normal politics, ideally Irish politics or island politics but in the meantime any politics that did not involve shooting. The end of Stormont might not bring back the dead, erase the horror of Bloody Sunday or the humiliation of internment, might not rewrite the irrevocable past or lead to unity; but it would open practical avenues away from chaos and conflict. Short views are vital in democratic politics and the nationalists thus expected that soon events pushed again from London would shift their way.

One of the difficulties for the Irish politicians was that the British were apt to ignore the impact of London action and attitudes—or often assume the Dublin establishment sympathetic to the IRA. On April 19, when the euphoria of the end of Stormont still existed, when the Irish government had high hopes of an amelioration of the crisis or at least the violence, Lord Widgery's report was released. Bloody Sunday was replayed with the report accepted by many, including many in Britain, as a cover-up. There were too many witnesses. Efforts to plant weapons on the victims or find forensic evidence proving the dead had recently fired guns or detail IRA attacks convinced few in Ireland but were generally used by the British media to clear the books, place the blame on the Irish, move on to other matters.* The Irish government could not for the time being show too great an enthusiasm for British initiatives, but the interests of the Irish Republic and the United Kingdom were convergent.

In various configurations the decent Dublin view of the Northern crisis was set.

---

*Twenty years later the RTE documentary on the events indicated that the scraps of forensic evidence presented could be explained in various ways. In fact, by then forensic evidence presented at the trials of those accused of IRA bombing attacks in Britain had been discredited and the convictions overturned. As for the Widgery report, it became a classic example of Britain as Perfideous Albion, and not only for the Irish nationalists.

Militant nationalism was dangerous, not worth the sacrifice, irrational, counter-productive, and ultimately in the hands of gunmen. Unity could only be bought at a blood price that no one, certainly in Dublin, wanted to pay. And such unity was not real: An unpartitioned island would still be a divided island, a Republic denied by Protestants would not fashion a single people with the common name of Irish, but instead would instigate revolt. Those who continued to pursue such an end were a danger to the Republic of Ireland.

Increasingly the decent Dublin view began to dominate the international response. The Northern actors on long acquaintance had grown complex, often unsavory, seldom the stereotypes of old. The Western media increasingly became aware of the terrorist problem, a new focus of horror and despair as the Vietnam visuals ran down. It was more difficult for the IRA to remain freedom fighters and good guerrillas. Che was dead and the Palestinians increasingly seen as fervid killers. The IRA bombs were indiscriminate, the punishment shootings repellent, the armed struggle increasingly dubious. The civil rights people had been transmuted into shrill radicals. Burntollet Bridge had led to abandoned bodies in back lanes. And now the loyalist gunmen were engaged in sectarian murder. The media were tired of and dismayed with Ireland. The Left had new doubts, even about the Officials, and the traditionalists in the Irish diaspora grew concerned with the old sureties and the new murders. NORAID here and there found a new reluctance to contribute to the militants.

All this was gradual, not so much change as acceptance that the crisis had grown complicated and lethal. Dublin at least appeared to adapt to the new realities, to move with the time, to avoid the old clichés. Unity might come some day—a unity of peoples, not just an island one color on the map—but in the meantime the Irish in Dublin wanted peace and quiet, justice in the North, devolved government, and an end to IRA pretensions and Orange institutionalized bigotry. And was not this what all reasonable people should seek?

So in Washington or Paris, on the NBC news or on RAI in Rome, politics began to edge out secret armies and in time even the photogenic bomb spectaculars. Neither Ireland nor the action nor the observers had changed much, only the price of familiarity. The long, slow erosion of the North as media crisis had begun. Without solution, without a final moral, without clear lessons or a proper end, the Troubles had fewer takers. Democratic senators, ABC television producers, Swedish journalists, transient stringers and visiting dignitaries regarded the end of Stormont as the end of one Irish adventure. Those in Ireland who persisted in their old ways aroused less sympathy. The IRA kept bombing but with less international impact. The demands of the majority repeated yet again aroused no interest. Partition and unity and civil rights and all the old watchwords had worn smooth, pebbles tossed away as the TV crews moved into Beirut or the Munich hostage crisis. The distant wanted an end to Irish history—and the prorogation of Stormont should be coda.

The withdrawal of intense international scrutiny was hardly noticeable. In fact, the reverse seemed to be the case as the media arrived for the final act. The footage sent home by the crews, the interviews in the front rooms of terrace houses, the statements of the leaders and movers still had play. When the new Northern Secretary arrived he faced an aggressive and knowledgeable press corps. The IRA bombed on schedule, increasingly dependent on car bombs to place their more sophisticated devices. The British patrols in the countryside were gradually pushing the action into sabotage and darkness. The new wave of Protestant militancy, seemingly, had crested in March, since the unclaimed murders went unnoted. And once again politics seemed to wait on events.

Whitelaw arrived for a whirlwind visit. He was not greeted by Faulkner—not a snub, said the new Secretary. The SDLP urged "those engaged in the campaign of violence to cease immediately in order to enable us to bring internment to a speedy end and in order to make a positive response to the British government's proposals. We also ask for an immediate cessation of political arrests by the British army and the RUC." The next day car bombs were parked at Markethill, County Armagh, and outside the Star Inn on Springfield Road, Belfast. The first detonated and the second was defused by the army. A complete ban on all parked vehicles in a large area of West Derry was imposed. There was a shooting at a club on the Falls Road and Ingram Beckitt's body was found on the Shankill Road. The gunmen's agenda was not that of the decent politicians of SDLP or the new British maneuvers of Whitehall. Kevin Boyle of NICRA urged a suspension of violence. John Hume said there could be no justification for continuing an active IRA campaign that would only play into the hands of the Ulster Vanguard.

On Monday, March 27, Craig addressed a Vanguard rally demanding a Stormont Parliament with real authority. There followed a two-day work stoppage by 190,000 workers and minor trouble in Portadown, Ballyclare, and Lurgan. On Tuesday, March 28, a hundred thousand attended a Vanguard rally at Stormont. To the innocent or the fearful Vanguard seemed the wave of the future, not Whitelaw, not the old institutions. Ian Paisley tried to stem the apparent tide: "The voice of Mr. Craig and the advice of Mr. Craig are the voice and advice of folly." Whitelaw announced that he would come to Ireland over "the difficult Easter period"—the republican marching season. In the House of Lords O'Neill said that growing moderate opinion was prepared to accept direct rule.

Faulkner, with some hedging, said he would cooperate with Whitelaw and that there should be no more strikes or a Protestant campaign of civil disobedience. In fact Faulkner, once the darling of the hard men, had been converted by power to the defense of parliamentary politics. If Stormont were gone forever, he would consider his parliamentary options inside the tent of governance not outside the door like Craig and Paisley and certainly not in the wilderness of the extremists or the withdrawal to retirement. Faulkner had not so much changed as mellowed.

In all the turmoil politically almost nothing had changed. The conventional parties, Catholic and Protestant, radical NICRA and fundamentalist DUP, sought a conventional role supported by London and Dublin. The hard men of the spectrum on the loyalist side—Vanguard—despite the rhetoric only proposed edging off into rent-and-rates strikes, protests, and boycotts, not murder. If murdering were to be done the two IRAs seemed determined to do so for the minority and the majority would be left with the invisible and lethal vigilantes of the defenders.

Before March 1972 these Protestant defenders had been conventionally institutionalized, yoked to the Stormont machine, required only to march in season and vote in bloc. They might join the B Specials, the Orange Order, or the crowds in front of patriotic orators, but they did not need to be concerned about the immutable order of things. The elite leadership handled such matters, despite the occasional intervention of the rough fundamentalists like Paisley. Any serious Catholic threat to the system was usually short-lived because of the prospect—not the reality—of pogroms. After 1972 the Stormont system no longer sufficed, gave neither visible evidence nor control nor the secondary benefits of domination. And what was left for the loyalists? Popular violence against Catholics was not applauded but was cause for arrest and prosecution. There was no point in voting. There was no satisfactory return in the threats of Paisley or Craig, repeated without punishing the locally disloyal.

When the most extreme and active fundamentalists decided to play a part, this signified not so much change as an intensification under new auspices. Stormont no longer supplied buffer and leash to those who wanted the tangible returns of domination. Most of the angry and thwarted Protestants were willing to ease their anguish by participation in the new rituals: attendance at a Vanguard rally or signing up with the Ulster Defense Association. Tens of thousands were involved in both new initiatives. A few of the most militant had from the first doubted the elegant establishment, more concerned with airs and graces than defending the majority. A few of these thus assumed that the right to defend permitted, encouraged, the practice of murder. These vigilantes-in-waiting were simple, cruel, often rough irregulars from a harsh background, stunted, violent, and rude. They were not the idealistic killers of the IRA, not the disciplined recruits of the British army. They were not unique to Northern Ireland, even if they had been specially warped by Northern Irish conditions and culture.

The Protestants who would kill under various titles, either paramilitaries or simple vigilantes, were men grown rank with hate and despair. They were men who believed the murderous clichés smeared on the walls, who could rationalize away the pleasures and power of killing with primitive politics grounded in rumor and conspiracy. Some were, indeed, sociopaths eager for any excuse to turn sadistic murder into respectable execution. Most were simply without empathy, all raw ego. They, if normal, were without even parochial sophistication, without prospects, and thus eager to impose their anger on events, on living symbols of the unpleasant world.

To conventionally humane people they appeared monstrous, raw, deadly without restraint or reason. Actually they were but narrow men, taught with hate, schooled by poverty and frustrated pride. As paramilitaries, made legitimate by need and uneasy toleration, they could act out murderous fantasies. The vast majority of the members of the new organizations were often well-meaning and decent, seeking an effective means to protect what they cherished. They represented a cross section of Ulster Protestants, biased, set in their fantasies, bigoted often, tolerant only to neighbors. Everyone had signed up, marched with the UDA or talked belligerently at the pub. This was less true as time passed and the paramilitary organizations like UDA grew smaller, confined to the working class, especially in Belfast. Even then most members were simply politically militant and at worst tolerant of violence used in their name by the organization's core of killers. Some were not unwilling to exploit the results. Some, very few, were eager to provide those results.

The recruits to the new, more lethal defenders were soon covered in self-awarded titles and clothed in secondhand uniforms bought at rummage sales. They were a tolerated lynch mob, a posse in aviator sunglasses and forage caps. Some even then in the company of killers and pub patriots were idealists, others were ambitious without formal qualifications; a very few were demented. The stayers of all sorts, however, found a career as paramilitary actor, a significance, a role for the ignoble, for those still important only through force or fear. They were given a gun by a friend and could for the first time act. The act was enormously powerful and patently dangerous. This was true even for men without imagination. Yet this appeal of therapeutic murder had few takers.

But even a few gunmen, determined on arbitrary targets, joined by the tiny number of psychopathic butchers, mostly unquestioned in the darkness of a primitive underground, could inflict major damage on society. A couple of dozen killers were too many. And especially so if society would not admit the pain and loss for fear that recognition would multiply the damage. Some fearful Protestants wanted the mysterious paramilitary killers as allies; some wanted them as neighbors and some did not; most wanted them quiescent, content if possible, unneeded, and if needed, then contained. What the silent majority of Northern Ireland wanted was peace and quiet—not at cost but by entitlement.

Whitelaw felt he could bring to the province a wind of change that would calm the waves of violence long enough to allow talking to take over from killing. The killing was apparently the province of the IRA, so Whitelaw and London focused their attention on the greatest din: the Catholic minority. The SDLP was to be persuaded to give up its boycott on politics. Its constituency was to be wooed by by phasing out internment (overt cancellation would have been to admit error). The British army was to continue the anti-insurgency policy that Tuzo felt should contain the IRA by April. In this he had the support of Faulkner, who noted that IRA talent was being eroded, own-goal bombs had resulted in fourteen IRA deaths in the first two months of the year, and violence was at a "generally" lower level made good only by the adoption of more callous attacks. The security forces were to keep up the pressure but not do anything provocative. And they were to stay out of the no-go zones.

Whitelaw began to order internees released, one hundred immediately and five hundred by June. Internment, especially for the nationalists, remained a crucial issue. The SDLP officially wanted no part of politics while the policy continued. Whitelaw dribbled out releases, thus building up credit. He also regularly pushed the majority politicians to come into talks, and this was in a sense pressure against an open door. The SDLP had immediately made every effort to replace the heavy hand of the IRA, urged peace and reconciliation and justice. "Give the initiative a chance," said Gerry Fitt. Cardinal Conway denounced the IRA. A peace movement was fostered and women marched in Andersonstown in Belfast and from the Bogside in Derry.

The problem was that in focusing on the minority the sense of grievance of the majority—*their* parliament had been dissolved—went unattended. Whitelaw personally made every effort to appear in the province, appear in Protestant areas, appear reasonable, open, fair, a decent Englishman. A large, rumpled, avuncular man with a red face and mop of white hair—he could have been cast by

Hollywood as a jolly Conservative politician—he was hard to hate, even in a haters' parish. He looked so decent that his accent did not offend, nor did his tailor, his Cambridge golfing blue, or his country estate in Cumberland. He was what he was; wealthy, privileged, Winchester, Scots Guards, former captain of the Royal and Ancient Golf Club, a politician without Irish connections or experience. He had been in the province only twice, once to attend a birthday party and then on a golf tour. Perhaps not a man for all seasons but a Tory with panache who might do for this most thankless of political offices.

He so clearly meant well that the majority was less restive than the fearful had supposed. For some he became "The Big Man" while for others he was a symbol that London had not forgotten the province. Not that he was not hissed and roughly handled at times, but then he was out on the streets in loyalist areas, where he could touch and be touched, not issuing statements from Faulkner's old office. The hard men were not softened by his charm, nor was the determination of the majority to have their way abraided by such Tory charisma. There was, however, no descent into civil war, no open pogroms—only the steady, silent toll of sectarian murder and the din of the IRA armed struggle.

Whitelaw wanted to exploit the trauma and opportunities caused by the end of Stormont, so he spent as much visible time in the province as possible. In fact, then and later one of the perpetual difficulties of the government ministers was that their constituency was in Britain, their political career in London, their home and family over the Irish Sea, and Northern Ireland was thus a sometimes place. Some would spend a great deal of time in the province, some less, but none went home every night to Malone Road or Seaforde. The other island was home and Ireland was a distant commute. There none moved without the panoply and appurtenances of high security. There none, at first anyway, was expert or comfortable. Still, Whitelaw made an effort and his presence counted. And for once the tides seemed to be running Britain's way.

On Sunday, April 2, the same day that Cardinal Conway had called for peace, Mac Stiofáin told the republican Easter commemoration gathering in Derry that if there were a truce, then "the fight of this generation will be lost and the suffering you have seen over the last three years will have to be endured again . . . Concession be damned: We want freedom." Whitelaw watched the speech from above in a British army helicopter.

In Belfast the day before, a group of women from Andersonstown had asked for a meeting with Whitelaw to discuss an end to the violence. They had been moved by resentment in the district after a woman had been shot dead during an IRA-army one-hour gun battle. Mac Stiofáin's reply indicated the obstacles that Whitelaw faced, symbolically above the battle in his helicopter, and the opportunity that existed to sap minority militancy. Peace and quiet had advocates but no one could determine the intensity of the desire or the intentions of the majority. No Catholic would opt for peace if a pogrom were in prospect. Then only the revitalized IRA would stand before them.

So Whitelaw, like others before him, would have to find a way to avoid the zero-sum game played in Northern Ireland, where giving to the minority was taking from the majority. And the majority by the spring of 1972 felt that there

317

must be an end to concessions, that the British and Whitelaw did not understand. Ulster Vanguard and particularly the UDA were attracting thousands. Rumors of the more violent UVF were rife. The new Tartan gangs of teenagers were worrisome to the RUC—and to the minority. And, still, the IRA wanted everything and any concession would be, therefore, pointless. The long-lived Protestant concept of "No Surrender" was not simply a bloody-minded veto but the only rational option to a united, Catholic Ireland.

None of this was clear from Whitelaw's helicopter on Easter Sunday. In fact, what the British hoped for was Irish policy as usual: Hold the fort, talk to all, find the middle ground, cobble together a devolved government, and get on to other matters. In the two months after the prorogation of Stormont an enormous amount of energy went into just such an effort. And because everyone else from the peace women to the Alliance Party steadfastly pursued the old ways, the more Whitelaw sought change the less could be found—except in British initiatives.

London tended to leave matters to Whitelaw and look ahead to talks that would produce a conference that would begin the process toward a devolved assembly. The relevant political parties in the province had proposed, most hastily, suggestions for future consideration, from Paisley's continuation of direct rule with a minicouncil at Stormont to the SDLP's All-Ireland Condominium. Frank McManus, a Stormont MP sympathetic to republicans, suggested a nine-county Ulster parliament; Faulkner's official Unionists desired strong regional government with a new parliament based on early proposals and reforms. No one could tell which were trial balloons, who was flying kites, what if anything London had in mind. Certainly there was evidence that a great many wanted something done.

The tides for peace seemed real enough within the minority community, affecting both the middle class and conventional on one cusp of society and the radicals and revolutionaries on the other. The peace women were simply a sign of the times and one that the Provisional IRA in particular took very seriously, perhaps even too seriously. The women, innocent of the structures and necessities of mobilization, without specific short-term aims, without certainty as to what was wrong, what should be done, expressed only a desire for better days. Their strength was that such an aspiration was all but universal except for the hard men of physical force. All this could only encourage the new Secretary. The response of the SDLP—open opposition to any armed struggle and support of the British initiative—indicated that the march away from the political boycott had begun. Fitt and company would be part of the long-sought solution.

Even the outraged loyalists, after settling down, did not seem so outraged. Faulkner, despite the defections from both sides of the party into Alliance and into Vanguard, was a politician, a conservative, a reasonable man. And Alliance wanted nonsectarian politics, and Vanguard, run by the alienated elite, seemed content to protest and might yet be wooed by ambition. The Orange gunmen were largely ignored in the din of the IRA armed struggle, which in turn might be diverted by negotiations if not closed down by the security forces. In April Whitelaw could have real hopes that the prorogation of Stormont meant the corner had been turned. The minority was showered with interest and concessions and the majority with firmness and promise.

The method obviously worked in that those dedicated to radical change, to the gun or the barricade, had to respond. Mac Stiofáin had to attack concessions at his Easter oration. Bernadette Devlin complained that releasing detainees should not be sold as reward, since such imprisonment was unjust in the first place. The Central Committee of Ulster Vanguard announced plans to establish an effective Parliament and government.

Concessions continued. The ban on marches was lifted and on April 27 an amnesty was granted for those who had violated it, including Devlin. The Scarman Tribunal's report on the disturbances of March and April 1969, ancient but contentious history, proved evenhanded, blaming extremists of both sides and agreeing that the RUC had made errors, but without being partisan: something for everyone but not enough for anyone. For a time the most interesting development was not found in the proclamations of the committed but in the aspirations of the women's peace movement. The media, eager for optimism, quickly focused on the marches and demonstrations, thereby exaggerating their impact.

Certainly the IRA felt the challenge dangerous. Their armed struggle inevitably proved brutal. Another woman was killed in Ballymoney in her own flat when a car bomb detonated outside. A woman in Derry was shot during an IRA–British army gunfight. A seventy-nine-year-old man was mortally injured by a bomb. A ten-year-old boy was injured when an IRA bomb factory exploded, killing three volunteers. Control of the no-go zones was not always a blessing: A pregnant woman from Ballymurphy in Belfast was painted, beaten, feathered, tied to a lamppost, and given forty-eight hours to leave her home. Whatever she had done, the impact of her punishment was counterproductive. If anything, the intensity of the campaign grew, despite or because of the Whitelaw initiatives. On April 14 the province was rocked by nearly twenty-four hours of bombing in Belfast, Newry, Castlederg, Sion Mills, Derry, and Ballymoney. The telephone exchanges in Kilkeel and Mayobridge were bombed too, while a Claymore mine was set off on the border near Newry. In all, thirty explosions were set off by the Provos.

Then the Officials were reactivated, their attention turned from politics. Joe McCann, a popular and well-known leader in the Markets, the Stickies' Belfast stronghold, was killed by British Paratroops alerted in Hamilton Street by a Special Branch RUC detective. The Officials claimed that he was murdered but the army said he had run from the challenge down Joy Street and only then been shot. The usual violence broke out in the Markets and escalated into gun battles through the night. At his funeral on Tuesday, April 18, Cahal Goulding, up from Dublin promised to retaliate: "In shooting Joe McCann, Whitelaw, Tuzo, and Heath have shown the color of their peace intiatives."

The Provos, of course, were not at all interested in peace initiatives, in any case not peace at any price. They had polled the volunteers and announced on April 6 that the volunteers were 100 percent behind the Army Council. In Derry on April 8 Martin McGuinness said, "We are fighting on until we get a united Ireland." So far in 1972 the fight had cost one hundred lives. There was no indication that the rest of the year would be better. Perhaps it would be worse. The IRA announced in Derry that they found a UVF file with photographs of two hundred Catholics.

Ever so slowly the Protestant backlash was emerging as a reality in the province rather than an oratorical threat or wishful thinking.

With the costs of the armed struggle going up in Northern Ireland and the prospect of peace thus more visible, the Provos were increasingly alarmed at the women's peace movement. The core idea of the republican movement since Fenian times had been the legitimate right to wage war against the British. The IRA, pretensions aside, was not an alternative government, not a broad-based liberation front, but a secret army engaged in a struggle to secure the Republic. To allow the tired and exhausted, the frightened, those at risk, those comfortable and conservative, the natural enemies of radical change, to erode the cutting edge of the armed struggle was potentially disastrous. Republican women were dispatched to harass such rallies. Some eight hundred women gathered around to hear Maire Drumm of Provisional Sinn Féin back the IRA. The peace leaders were pilloried as middle class or British pawns.

Certainly the proponents of peace included liberal opponents of Provo pretensions to be the legitimate heirs to Pearse and for the more orthodox IRA people to be the legitimate government of all of Ireland. On Friday, May 26, a twenty-four-hour vigil in from of the offices of both Provisional and Official Sinn Féin brought together those engaged in the peace movement: Brian Walker, chairman of the New Ulster Movement; members of the Northern Ireland Labour Party; representatives of the Women Together Movement; and Southern politicians like Conor Cruise O'Brien of the Labour Party and Garret FitzGerald of Fine Gael, decent liberals all with a tiny constituency in the North. The Provos were never concerned with the proper and self-righteous but only with their own, the people of no property, the people of the ghetto and small farms. So the elegant were ignored and the articulate damned.

The great numbers of women who appeared at the peace rallies mistook demonstration for mobilization. Unlike the civil rights people, who nevertheless shared many of the same illusions, made many of the same mistakes, and came to much of the same end, the women had no short-term goals that could be checked off—reforms, laws, concessions, way stations on the road into the future. They could offer nothing but momentary exaltation and an opportunity to act as witness for virtues. At least the civil rights radicals had won tangible concessions as well as admiration and euphoria. The peace women were a momentary phenomenon. Peace had many advocates but few pragmatic architects.

Everyone wanted peace. Cahal Goulding of the Officials wanted "peace on our terms" and Martin McGuinness wanted "peace with justice," which meant conceding the three IRA demands. The Protestants might be talking of marching and secret armies and no concessions to traitors but many yearned for peace during the spring of 1972 even as the province echoed to the IRA bombs. But there was a limit to marches and in time the peace women went home, the liberals exchanged views with each other, and the Troubles continued.

Then, the Officials' armed struggle ended. GHQ had already distanced the volunteers from Provo tactics and targets: The bombs were sectarian and the civilian casualties unforgivable. On Sunday, April 23, three hundred people attended a Republican Clubs rally where a resolution was passed condemning the IRA bombing of civilian targets. A similar rally against the "mad bombing" was called off in the Ardoyne after the Provos suggested it might not be "wise" to hold it.

The IRA feud had grown very bitter, with the Officials assuming their opponents were Green, sectarian Fascists and the Provos accepting that the Stickies were alien Pinks dedicated not to the gun but to making a deal with the establishment. In tiny Provo homes the children, often barely beyond babbling, were tutored in the evils of the Stickies nearly as often as in the sins of the Brits. In Official flats the Provos were a menace. Revolutionary feuds over the revealed truth are often deadly. Unlike similar revolutionary situations, the two IRAs did not compete in escalating violence, seeking thus the high ground of militancy, but rather to shape and hold their special constituency.

The Officials wanted to annex the Irish Left, creating a situation where the gun would no longer be needed in politics. The Army Council in Dublin assumed that the Irish people would support such a new direction despite the successes of the Provo organizers in the North and despite the refusal of the electorate of the Irish Republic to spurn membership in the neoimperialist Common Market. On May 10, in a national plebiscite, the Republic voted 1,041,890 to 211,891 for entry into the EEC, an enormous and unprecedented victory over both parochial concerns like the Irish language movement and also traditional class interests. The vote seemingly signaled that the frozen seas of Irish politics were warming. Times in the Republic were a changin', reflecting the concerns of the future instead of the rigid certainties of old quarrels.

Dublin GHQ was determined to change too, to move away from the gun, despite Goulding's bellicose speeches in the North after McCann's death. And the North suddenly presented Dublin GHQ with ample reason. On May 21 the Official IRA's Derry unit shot and killed William Best, a local boy home on leave from the Irish Rangers in Germany. Best had wandered freely about the Creggan visiting friends and talking about deserting. He was seized, tried, and executed by the officials "in retaliation for murders committed by the British army." Best was not some unknown Englishman but a local with family and friends and certainly not an enemy to Ireland.

The local population was outraged at the murderous arrogance and idiocy of the Stickies. Two hundred women showed up at Official headquarters in Derry to protest and demanded the Officials get out of Derry. The Provisionals also quickly asked the Stickies to withdraw from the Bogside and Creggan. On May 23, the day Best was buried, fifteen hundred women called as well on the Provos, asking for an end to violence. The women met with Whitelaw. Tom Doherty was announced as chairman of a committee of sixteen to seek a cessation of hostilities. McGuinness stuck to his peace with justice line and Séamus O'Kane of the Officials Command Staff insisted that a campaign of defense and realiation would continue to operate.

The end of the Stickies' war was, however, in sight. On May 28 six thousand people attended a Derry peace rally in the Shantollow area. At the same time some four thousand attended a republican movement march for peace with justice in the Creggan, where Provisional Sinn Féin leader Seán Keenan spoke. The Officials' move came the next day in Dublin, where the Official IRA GHQ at Gardiner Place announced an immediate cessation of hostilities, in accordance with the wish of the people they represented in Northern Ireland: "The over-whelming desire of the great majority of all people of the North is for an end to military actions by all sides." Although GHQ maintained the right of self-defense if attacked by sectarian forces or the British army, and although many within the movement felt that there was yet a role for the gun, the announcement was a giant step toward normal politics.

The Provisionals, on the other hand, had learned to live with tactical error, with volunteer blunders, with the cost of brutality, slaughter, and innocent death. The IRA "regret this as much as anyone"—which was certainly true; but there could be no denying—and the Provos did not—that the innocent were asked to pay a price for the armed struggle but that the goal made that price worth paying, even for the innocent. Moreover their Army Council and GHQ felt the movement was dealing from strength. The IRA had never been as large or as well armed. Rather than take the road toward peace and politics, the Provisional movement concentrated on arms and the armed struggle.

The Provos, like the Officials, had benefited from the great attic and garage search in 1969 that generated an arsenal of mismatched weapons. Almost from the first individual Irish-Americans had acted, bringing through customs, often under the blind eyes of officials equally concerned about their own in the North, more military odds and ends. For a time it seemed that every Irish-American was or wanted to be an arms smuggler.

Most of the new gear was World War II American weapons easily and legally acquired in states with liberal gun laws and mailed from Philadelphia or San Francisco, sent in the coffins of nationals returned for parish burial, in Aer Lingus luggage, in all sorts of not very ingenious ways. Given the risks taken and the ease of acquisition, the take was not enormously impressive. The result allowed a shift by some active service units from the Lee-Enfields of the great IRA arms raid of the 1950s that led to the border campaign, to M-1s and Garands. But this was insufficient for GHQ, and various initiatives were taken to secure a more impressive arsenal.

If the Provos were going to continue to be a major player through the armed struggle, arms were crucial. Without arms there could be no escalation and by 1972 every volunteer assumed that their army was on the crest of a wave, that the withdrawal of the British might actually be compelled. The IRA might win rather than succeed at the end of a protracted conflict when the British lost and had to make a deal. So far the campaign had depended on enthusiasm, gelignite, scavenged weapons, and the dedication of the volunteers. So increasingly GHQ wanted real gear.

The difficulty facing GHQ was that the IRA had neither experience nor assets in the arms game. Years of organizational penury made the involved reluctant to spend money on anything but hardware, so expensive false documentation and bribes were avoided. The methods that turned arms into machinery and thus moved it through customs barriers and British hurdles were alien. The IRA wanted guns for money. And they had no friends to help them. The disappearance of the British Empire and the transformation of the United Kingdom into a lesser international player meant that London had no virulent enemies. The Russians helped only those rebels whose activities could help Russia. So it went. No one cared about Ireland. No one considered the IRA challenge worth escalating. Mostly, despite assumptions to the contrary, diverse national liberation movements lack the inclination and assets to help their fellows. Thus, agents and friends sent to make a contact had little to report.

During 1972 the Libyan government of the eccentric and mercurial Colonel Mu'ammar al-Qaddafi, profoundly anti-imperial and at odds with Britain, became an outspoken IRA ally. On June 11, 1972, he announced at a rally in Tripoli, duly reported by the *Irish Times* the next day, "We support the Irish revolutionaries who are fighting Britain. . . . We have strong ties with the revolutionaries to whom we have supplied arms." He had agreed to have his intelligence chief, Major Abdul Salaam Jalloud, help if the operation was handled on the Irish end by someone they knew, that is, an IRA figure covered in the newspapers. This contact led to Joe Cahill arriving in Libya to arrange what became the famous and failed shipment on the arms vessel *Claudia* in 1973. The fashionable Palestinians, in particular Abu Iyad of Fatah, an organization replete with donated arms and money, would offer limited aid when an Irish agent arrived in Beirut. This contact for some remained a constant but had limited effective results. Other European initiatives failed because of inexperience, because of the duplicity of the suppliers, and almost certainly because of the activities of the British.

The Arms Crisis in Dublin, with John Kelly left standing in the dock and the Fianna Fáil cabinet in chaos, was only the first of a long string of IRA disasters and disappointments, for the Provos were mostly innocents in a cruel world. One potential dealer actually walked unknown into the front door of the Sinn Féin office on Kevin Street and talked to Dáithí O Conaill about a European purchase. At the subsequent Army Council meeting Mac Stiofáin, with some doubts, put O Conaill in charge of the operation. The adventure ended up on the front pages of the newspapers while O Conaill and his young and attractive aide, Maria McGuire, kept one leap ahead of various police forces. To some it had looked like a setup from the beginning and to most it indicated the penalties of inexperience.

Later in 1972, Mac Stiofáin did send an agent on a tour of the capitals of various potentially helpful countries. This resulted in the successful purchase, made possible by emergency donation from the Irish-American diaspora, of RPG-7 rocket launchers. These were flown into Ireland in the autumn of 1972. The Canadian volunteer pilot later lost his life when his plane went down over the North Atlantic on the way home. This success, however, was an exception in the GHQ efforts to acquire arms that for a decade tended to fail, fail publicly, fail painfully, and often fail as a result of secret British intervention as well as the traditional IRA incapacities. Each unwelcome revelation tended to discourage donors, who saw their money wasted, and sellers, who saw their goods seized and their names published. GHQ, however, never stopped trying, if always with the old ways. Mostly the various GHQ QMGs had to be content with very small purchases on the European market and scavenging.

The obvious solution to IRA problems lay in any case not with unknown European deals, hedged about by foreign intelligence services and British watchers, but as always with the American diaspora, the IRA's traditional supplier. There the key to the IRA arms problem evolved from existing contacts and resources to allow a back-door supply route that operated for a decade. The connection engendered American, Irish, and British suspicion, but produced until it was ended by the ultimate and fatal weak link. The major figure was an Irish-American, George Harrison. Born in Mayo in 1915, one of ten children in a very poor family, he had come to America and ultimately became a security guard. In many ways he was a typical Irish immigrant, a bachelor living in a foreign city—Park Slope in Brooklyn at first—with a menial job and set views, far more Irish than American. Harrison, however, was a radical republican, unlike most of his ilk, who had the most conservative social, religious, and economic views although they remained dedicated to physical force as a means to achieve the dream of an Irish Republic.

They were physical force men but not revolutionaries, wanted a nation once again but the same parochial institutions. And as they grew more prosperous, they grew less Irish, limiting their American connection to fiscal contributions and enthusiasm. Harrison was different, a working man of the Left, yet one who maintained his personal contacts within the orthodox IRA. And despite Harrison's public admiration over the years for most radical causes, a position hardly unique in Irish-American society in the thirties and forties but more so for the Irish republicans of the fifties and sixties, he was trusted by the old guard. George Harrison was sound. He was forgiven his exotic views, his involvement in radical causes, and his concern with worldwide liberation movements. These in the Ireland of the seventies would have made him a Stickie candidate and thus to the Provos a latent subversive. These in Irish America at the same period distinguished him from the principal Provo supporters from NORAID. So on the surface he seemed the odd man out for the Provos and their friends. This had never been the case—he remained a physical force man, a radical Fenian.

As soon as the IRA began to work toward a Northern campaign in the 1950s, Harrison had been contacted (the Dublin GHQ had very few American names on its list) and thus became involved in collecting and shipping arms to Ireland. He collected more than he shipped and what did arrive made little difference. At one stage in 1960 he was reduced to using the notoriously unreliable, if dedicated, playwright Brendan Behan to move a few suitcases. As might have been expected, given Behan's history, this ended in trouble, recriminations, and chaos. Shipping continued to be a problem for Harrison, so that he was left with more than the IRA had received. He was also left with IRA contacts that Irish quarrels and splits did not break.

In 1969, when the Troubles began again and when the astute within the movement foresaw a split, Harrison's name was still on the list. Early contact was made by a private emissary out of Dublin acting for those, mainly from Belfast, who would dominate the Provos. Radical ideas or not, affinity with the Officials' theories or not, Harrison, a pragmatic republican to the core, agreed to act. Gear was needed and gear would be found.

Unlike the last campaign there was going to be adequate money, although from time to time emergency fund-raisers would be needed. NORAID supplied legal money to legal ends, as well they might, since the FBI practically did their books and the Treasury Department's Bureau of Alcohol, Tobacco, and Firearms in time assumed a lead role in preventing arms from reaching the IRA. The new

Provisional IRA might have new supporters, more money, and Harrison's services but they also had the attention of a government opposed to terrorism in any form. The Provo supporters simply felt that their American government, like the government in Ireland, was misinformed about the Northern crisis.

Many of the same people who gave money to NORAID at the same time gave money that would go to purchase arms. And arms were easy to purchase legally in America, although major buys would alert the federal government. Harrison relied on his friend Liam Cotter, also a security guard in the same company, who was killed in an armed robbery at the New Amsterdam Theater in Times Square in 1976. The key man, however, was another Park Slope old boy, George De Meo, a Sicilian with reputed Mafia connections, who undertook the purchase, mostly in North Carolina, of both legal guns and those stolen and smuggled out of the surrounding army camps, especially Fort Lejeune. De Meo, a cunning local with no background in illicit arms, was essentially interested in money easily made. And the Irish had money and the risks were not great. If he had been more sophisticated and taken more care, he could have supplied ample ordnance for a real army. Others had and would. Still, an Irish secret army did not need a great deal, simply more than they had.

The key weapons for the IRA turned out to be the civilian version (Colt AR-15) of the regulation army assault rifle, the M-16, and the AR-180, with a similar look and performance configuration. The AR-15, sold as a deer rifle in America, was produced in Japan by the Armalite Corporation of Costa Mesa, California, and then, after the production run was complete, another fifty thousand were subcontracted from Sterling, a British arms manufacturer. Thus, the IRA had as a prime supplier Sterling of Great Britain. The .223 ammunition could be purchased in the United States legally or illegally stolen there or in West Germany.

The AR-180 Armalite became the standard IRA weapon. With a folding stock it could be reduced to two feet in length—"fit in a corn flake box, it will"—and its high muzzle velocity of 3,250 feet per second permitted the .223 bullet to penetrate both British body armor and the skin of the vehicle armor used in the North. With a flat trajectory and used as designed on semiautomatic, it was an ideal weapon for a less-than-expert urban guerrilla: In fact, the arrival of the Armalite meant that in Northern Ireland the IRA soldiers were better armed for their task than the British soldiers for theirs.

The Armalite connection ran through Harrison and Colter, who managed the payments to De Meo with the help of two other Irish-Americans, John Joe Martin and Tom Falvey. The Irish-Americans stored, cleaned, and oiled the weapons, usually in Harrison's apartment in Brooklyn, and then moved them to the Bronx and the next step. There the weapons were hidden in crates to withstand normal custom inspection in Ireland and finally turned over to the shippers on the docks. The appropriate papers and numbers for legal shipments had been arranged and the crates disappeared into legitimacy. The various steps in America were supposed to be separated but in effect were not.

On the arrival of the arms crates in Ireland, a second group, unknown to the Americans, and for that matter to all but one or two of the IRA command, moved the crates from the docks, through customs, and on to warehousing. This organization was recruited from friends and neighbors of a few long-neglected republicans, often forgotten by the police or never on anyone's list. Very considerable care was taken to see that the names never surfaced on anyone's list and that the people involved didn't fall prey to traditional IRA error. The IRA was only notified after arrival, when the shipments were ready to be picked up. No names were given to GHQ, nor were any details.

The Irish end of the conduit was kept clean. None of the people involved was ever caught or probably ever identified. The Dublin operation was a rare republican success, unknown, untouched, and effective to the end. And the end came in America not Ireland. Once within this Dublin organization the shipment then moved directly out of its legal fictions, out of the old crates, into the underground. The Dublin director used various stockpiles, mostly south of Dublin, through what was in effect the Kildare old boys' net. This complex was largely in the hands of an elderly and eccentric republican from Ballymore Eustace, Frank Driver, such an obvious candidate for illegal activity that, like George Harrison in New York, he was watched but paid no serious mind. From these hidden locations the Dublin controller had the arms moved to convenient sites, the end of the pipeline. These sites, different for each shipment, were revealed to the IRA QMG who had only to pick up the arms without knowing more. Thus, all the details were compartmentalized from the original buyers in North Carolina to the IRA volunteers with a truck and an address at the other end of Kildare. In theory no one involved knew the next step but in fact Harrison in New York and the import controller in Dublin knew the workings of the entire conduit and from time to time some on the IRA Army Council did as well.

In any case the result was that the Armalite conduit worked from 1972 until the end of the decade, when an unnecessary and careless telephone call from New York to Dublin by a new shipper innocent of proper procedure led to the unraveling of the network. Set up by De Meo, who had been caught by agents of the Treasury and made a deal, Harrison was finally arrested in 1981 and tried along with his various associates and NORAID bankers in New York.

To the amazement of all and the horror of the prosecutors, they were all freed when the jury accepted the patriotic and emotional explanation of the accused founder of NORAID, Michael Flannery, that all had assumed the entire operation was controlled by the CIA. The reputation of the CIA as the ubiquitous hand behind much that would otherwise be inexplicable was as prevalent in America as elsewhere. Flannery, an elderly and soft-spoken man of great dignity and sincerity, a paragon of Catholic and American domestic and national virtues, in his summation admitted all, and the jury effectively forgave all. Certainly De Meo was working for the CIA. The CIA must have had reasons. Certainly Flannery was convincing. At least the American government came away having closed down the Provo pipeline, if not for good at least for years, though this was probably small consolation for the prosecuting attorneys, who saw an airtight case dissolve after Flannery spoke.

According to the involved, the American connection produced approximately two hundred rifles and adequate ammunition each year of operation as well as an extra bonus in the autumn of 1977: six United States army M-60 heavy machine guns stolen by simple criminals from a Danvers, Massachusetts, arsenal the previous year and sold to Irish-Americans. These and their later replacements permitted some tactical escalation in the IRA campaign but still did not fill the need for an antihelicopter weapon. The search for ground-to-air missiles absorbed an enormous amount of IRA time and money and produced only disastrous exposures, mostly as a result of American sting operations. Thus, in the end the real solution to the Provo need for gear was the original arrangement with George Harrison, plugged into the independent Dublin receiver.

During the seventies the Libya connection produced mainly failure in that no arms reached Ireland, but there was compensation in that Qaddafi authorized funding for the IRA. Millions of dollars were transferred. Libyan agents would appear in prebooked hotel rooms in various European cities and turn over attaché cases crammed with one-hundred-dollar bills to IRA representatives whose lives had often been spent in jail, on the dole, or in jobs that paid weekly wages less than such a leather attaché case cost. This revenge of the bedouin arose from Libya's perception of the arrogance of imperial Britain in general and later that of Prime Minister Margaret Thatcher in particular. At what was a minuscule cost for Libya, the policy, really a special operation of low priority, did much to salve an IRA anguished over all the failed Middle Eastern arms ploys during the same period. Money soothes even revolutionaries engaged in the armed struggle.

With the growing Irish fiscal base created by all sorts of contributions as well as forays into the new Irish black economy, ranging from armed raids to taxi fees, there was new money. Diaspora money from NORAID and others, organization dues and internal sources, and extorted gifts added to the bottom line as the requirements of the movement escalated past all previous experience. Yet finances, always a revolutionary problem, were at least satisfactory. Political costs, publicity, personnel and welfare bills, all could far more easily be met, as could the demands of the military.

In the crucial armed struggle the active service units had for the foreseeable future adequate military supplies if not the tools for escalation. This fact tended to dominate republican thinking. The contrast with previous campaigns was clear. And the casualties that the secret army was inflicting began to dwarf those of the Tan War. The center of the IRA could contemplate winning—making the North ungovernable and the presence of the British army impossible. That most in London still considered the secret army to be little more than a residue of fanatical killers and misguided young men, their aspirations and pretensions ridiculous, and their prospects self-defeating, did not occur to the IRA. True believers can seldom imagine other perspectives. They lack empathy, often lack a sense of the possible—otherwise revolutionaries would never begin armed struggles.

In the late spring of 1972 the IRA believed armed struggle was about to drive the British to the bargaining table. In May alone the British army logged 1,223 engagements and shooting incidents and 94 explosions. Even the sanguine Tory politicians could not tolerate much more of the IRA armed struggle. It seemed incredible that men who a few years before had been clerks and bookmakers, bar boys and butchers' assistants, would replay the roles of Michael Collins and de Valera, deal with the destiny of the nation. Certainly the Dublin government was worried enough to make a move against them on May 26, when Ruairí O Brádaigh was arrested in Roscommon and Joe Cahill at the Sinn Féin offices on

Kevin Street in Dublin. Seán O Brádaigh was arrested the next day. It was a sign of earnestness on the part of the Lynch government, which felt edged into a corner. So the Army Council and the GHQ were actually encouraged.

Maire Drumm at Bodenstown on Sunday, June 11, had urged the huge crowd, largest in republican history, to make 1972 the year of destiny, the year of freedom. She and her whole family were republicans, had served in the IRA or Sinn Féin, had and would serve time in prison, were typical of the determined Provos of the North, ever ready with the faith and a hard word. When she came to Bodenstown, as a woman intent on peace with justice, she found a great hosting. Often the Republican Sunday in June was a reunion of the failed and bitter, old men who would not accept the waste of their youth, a few actives who could not quit, a scattering of volunteers, idealists, cranks, and malcontents. This year, 1972, there were thousands upon thousands, people of no property, tattooed lads, sunburnt small farmers, old men in rumpled tweeds, fat-faced babies in strollers, Cumann na mBan in uniform, and volunteers who had slipped into Kildare for the occasion. They were on a winner. The whole Derry staff was there, many of the commanders, most of four generations, and much of the visible movement. They truly sensed the tide moving out. Rumor was the British might want to talk. And if the British wanted to talk, why not? So much had happened already.

The Provos were determined, however, not to be stamped by a peace-at-any-price policy. They remembered the past, knew where talking could lead, had before them the example of Garland and Goulding and the once faithful. At their commemoration at Bodenstown the next Sunday, June 18, the distance the Officials had come was revealed when Seán Garland, hero of the border campaign, condemned terrorism. His life had been within the movement. He had fought in the North, been wounded beside Seán South, the martyr of Brookeborough, subject of ballads. He had undertaken any task and dedicated his life to the cause. And for many he was the paragon of his generation. He said that the republican movement, *his* republican movement, opposed terrorism, opposed bombs and the gun, did not want to bomb a million Protestants into a united Ireland. He had become a Leninist, a man of politics, convert to a new faith. The Officials would become simply another Free State political party. Some might keep a gun, but the armed struggle for them was over. Gardiner Place had given up physical force. And obviously Garland's oration was a planned counter to Provo dreams and Maire Drumm's year of destiny.

The Provos, of course, did not want to bomb Protestants into a united Ireland, they wanted their armed struggle to drive the British out of the island, the historic and traditional goal of any republican movement. So much for the Stickies, dangerous only to other Republicans, bought off by alien ideas and short-time radicals. The others, SDLP or Nationalist, Fianna Fáil and the Southern leaders, were as always politicians, all trimmers in troubled times. The physical force people thus had more evidence of the danger of conventional ambitions and politics, alluring as a fallen woman and as dangerous. Yet, the armed struggle had clearly led the Provos to a point where negotiations over the endgame would be needed. The British were not after eight hundred years likely just to pack up and go. Yet, talking had always contaminated.

On June 9 Martin McGuinness approached Mac Stiofáin and, two days before Bodenstown, suggested a press conference inside Free Derry with an offer of a seven-day IRA truce if Whitelaw would meet with Provo representatives. It would place the onus of peace now on Whitelaw, ease the IRA position in relation to the peace offensive and the general feeling that the republicans should respond to the end of Stormont, do no harm, and if successful be a triumphant breakthrough into diplomacy. Mac Stiofáin agreed. McGuinness, had come to dominate Derry by example, deeply concerned about his own and unswerving in his republican faith; if he wanted to try the press conference gambit, Mac Stiofáin would agree. On June 13, even before Garland could speak at Bodenstown, the press conference was held with O Conaill and Mac Stiofáin present, along with the Derry IRA and Sinn Féin people.

All through the Troubles the IRA maintained access into Derry through a net of poorly controled minor roads and with the skill of local drivers. One was driven at appropriate pace, at special times that constantly shifted in relation to the security forces, until the driver made a quick turn and was inside the no-go zone. The passage did not work every single time. In March Mac Stiofáin and Martin Meehan had been forced to creep about near a British patrol before they reached the no-go zone and the funerals of two volunteers. This time there was less trouble for Mac Stiofáin and O Conaill. Thus the media got the presence of two wanted men and a republican policy shift. The hard news went out. That evening Whitelaw issued a statement rejecting the offer, but the talking had begun, even with men of violence.

It had begun the same afternoon when the Northern Secretary had met with a three-man delegation from the UDA at Stormont Castle. The paramilitaries had arrived in masks, hoods, and wearing sunglasses. They looked not mysterious but childish. Still General Tuzo had arrived at the castle in his personal helicopter to join the talks, so the UDA, absurd or not, got the full treatment. Whitelaw told them that they would not be allowed to establish permanent barricades—but little else was accomplished other than to give the loyalist leaders a sense of their importance.

When the meeting became public at the same time that the talks with the IRA were refused after the offer of a truce, there was nationalist resentment. This resentment was sharper because of the IRA prisoners on hunger strike to achieve special, political status. On Tuesday the hunger strike leader, Billy McKee, the former Provisional leader of Belfast, was rumored to have died in Crumlin Road Prison. There were riots, and trucks were hijacked and burned for barricades throughout Catholic areas of Belfast before the rumor was scotched. At the same time the Tartan Gangs had set up barricades around the Ballymacarret district despite Whitelaw's insistence that there be no new permanent obstructions. On the next day the thirteen-man UDA Council met with Whitelaw over the barricades. The UDA was too formidable to be either illegal or ignored, with a membership of tens of thousands and seemingly in control over much of Protestant Belfast.

In the meantime the divisions within the majority political community continued: Sir Robert Porter resigned from the Unionist Party because Faulkner had criticized Whitelaw. The Grand Orange Lodge of Ireland called for a restoration of Stormont and support for Ulster Vanguard. Fifteen Presbyterian ministers from all parts of the province and one from Dublin joined those Shankill Road ministers who had criticized the UDA. And the UDA with or without the Tartan Gangs was still trying to put up some sort of barricade to balance the IRA no-go zones that the British would not crush. The UDA and much of loyalist opinion had no time for the killing-with-kindness approach. There had been too many reforms. There was nothing to be gained by further talking with the disloyal.

Whitelaw at least talked with the SDLP, increasingly eager to be a loyal opposition, the key bargainer for the nationalists. The SDLP seized as opening the IRA's truce proposal, offered without conditions. They felt their own boycott over internment could now be discarded without penalty. Their ideal was to involve the IRA, suspend the armed struggle, and get on with the everyday. On Thursday, June 15, Paddy Devlin and John Hume spoke with Whitelaw for two hours at the House of Commons after his Irish speech that called for a conference of the people of Northern Ireland. Devlin and Hume made sure that Whitelaw realized the offer of a truce was a serious one and that all sorts of opportunities might flow from talking.

In Northern Ireland there were various calls for Whitelaw-IRA talks, including one by twenty-one Belfast priests. On Friday Whitelaw issued a statement that, among other positions and suggestions, noted that "a ceasefire now would provide new opportunities for us all. Sanity and common sense must prevail before it is too late." Devlin and Hume met with Mac Stiofáin and passed on Whitelaw's offer to meet some lesser republicans at Stormont with the two of them present as observers. Innocent of politics as Mac Stiofáin, a military man, was supposed to be, he refused immediately. He had four conditions: (1) political status for the prisoners; several of the hunger strikers, including McKee, were in serious condition; political status would give the IRA immediate gain and get Whitelaw off the hook over the hunger strikers; (2) Mac Stiofáin would nominate the delegation; there was to be IRA gain in this since one of the nominees was a rising star from Belfast, Gerry Adams, then detained at Long Kesh; (3) Stormont Castle was out; there could be no atmosphere of the IRA as local petitioner; (4) no one but the IRA would be present; the Army Council wanted no politicians to dilute the confrontation.

The Provos were crafting a meeting that was not a photo opportunity or a UDA shuffle in dark glasses to be lectured on details. The Provos and Mac Stiofáin felt that they were entering history. Whitelaw, who sought authority from Heath and the relevant members of the cabinet, tended to regard the exercise as one more line in the sea. Innocent of Irish history, barely aware of the scope and seriousness of Provo ambitions, he felt that a meeting was at least worth a try.

Mac Stiofáin had come out of an English jail as the result of an arms raid, had no authorized talent or profession; his colleagues were bookmaker clerks, barmen, schoolteachers in provincial schools, obscure solicitors at best, the untutored and ignorant on average. Of course, de Valera had been a schoolteacher and Michael Collins a clerk, but that was long ago and far away—except, of course, for the Irish, who had forgotten no one and forgiven nothing. In any case Whitelaw, in for a penny in for the four points, agreed without quibbling. If talking would help end the killing, then he would talk. And by mid-June there had been a great deal of killing: 348 dead since 1969 and 142 between January 1 and May 29 in 1972.

On Monday, June 19, Whitelaw's office issued a statement that special steps would be taken to relieve the tensions within the Crumlin Road Prison. Somehow Lord Windlesham did not communicate the "terms of agreement" to the prison governor. This showed "an appalling degree of callousness," according to Paddy Devlin, who had some idea what each day was like for the prisoners. On the next day, however, the official word reached Crumlin Road, and the hunger strikers, some on their thirtieth day, ended the protest and began taking milk. A prison crisis was averted.

On June 20 an IRA delegation of Dáithí O Conaill, and Gerry Adams, who had been released, met with Whitelaw's representatives, Philip Woodfield and Frank Steele. The British, typically, could be seen as technicians; for the Northern Secretary considered the IRA approach important but a technical matter, a matter of talking to everyone, anyone, even terrorists. The IRA delegates represented the old and the new. By the summer of 1972 O Conaill was well known, notorious in fact, often the movement's spokesman, and many on the outside assumed he was its leader. He looked like a popular concept of a gunman—tall, lean, intense, habitually smoking—but unlike most active gunmen he had proved most valuable for the media. From an old Belfast republican family, Adams had become involved in protest politics even before leaving school. He combined his natural republicanism with his generation's dedication to radical change and made a certain impact beyond his own parish. Unlike many republicans he was open to discussion and preferred consensus. He possessed that rarest of commodities, a quiet charisma, and with it the trust of his fellow volunteers. He had risen swiftly through the ranks in the Belfast Brigade, dominated previously by Billy McKee, Joe Cahill, and Séamus Twomey from the forties or Ivor Bell and Brian Keenan from the fifties. Adams was a future leader and lost in Long Kesh. His release was pure gain. And, in effect, so was the whole diplomatic process.

A bilateral truce was agreed to with the Whitelaw meeting to follow in ten days. This was a formal IRA-British agreement, a breakthrough as far as the Army Council was concerned. The IRA Army Council agreed and on Thursday, June 22, the Irish Republican Publicity Bureau in Dublin announced that operations would be suspended from midnight, Monday, June 26, provided a reciprocal response was forthcoming from the British army. This was forthcoming: "The purpose of Her Majesty's forces in Northern Ireland is to keep the peace; if offensive operations by the IRA in Northern Ireland cease on Monday night, Her Majesty's forces will obviously reciprocate."

The Provos justifiably foresaw their historic confrontation with the British as a major breakthrough. The British considered it just a peripheral maneuver for minor gain. The republicans saw it as the culmination of the campaign and perhaps of fifty years of Irish history. They had bombed their way to the bargaining table. No Irish politician or party had managed as much since the treaty negotiations. Mac Stiofáin talked with a variety of people in Dublin about tactics and techniques; but all the republicans would arrive burdened and emboldened by history and constrained by their own limited experience in the outside world. As a group the IRA delegation tended to a seriousness of purpose and a suspicion of talk; decisions were to be made by unstated consensus. Only O Conaill was prone to discussion and he would be reined in by Mac Stiofáin and the Northern delegates. The British, elegant, sophisticated, deeply conservative, felt involved not in history but in a somewhat risky, tactical maneuver to touch all the Northern Ireland bases from the hard Orange gunmen to the IRA.

The Army Council wanted no letup in the armed campaign, thus showing the volunteers that there would be no sellout. Provo intelligence intercepts had also reported excessive RUC and British army optimism over the state of the IRA. Tuzo had regularly reported that the IRA would soon be on the run. Now the IRA turned on the pressure. In the three weeks before the meeting with Whitelaw twenty British soldiers were killed. The intensity of the operations continued up to the moment of the truce—the last British solder was shot and killed in East Belfast at 11:55 P.M. on Monday, June 26, five minutes before the truce went into effect.

Once the shooting had stopped, the Provos moved on the political front, producing a program for the future, Eire Nua, that envisioned a federated Ireland with a nine-county Ulster. This document, presented at a press conference on June 28 and in large part the result of work by O Brádaigh and O Conaill, indicated a political seriousness on the part of the movement. Although the manifesto was hardly likely to attract Northern loyalties or most of the Irish in the Republic, its launching just after the truce went into effect, a fortuitous circumstance arising from the lethargic habits of Irish printers, indicated that the Provos were more than gunmen.

Another British tradition surfaced at nearly the same time: their predilection for special operations in low-intensity conflicts. During the imperial wars beginning in Palestine in 1944, the British security forces had been deployed in conventional and familiar ways in both rural and urban insurgencies, but the commanders had favored often highly unorthodox units and operations: fake Mau Mau units, the countergangs fashioned by Kitson in Kenya, undercover military reaction forces in Cyprus or Malaya, the Special Air Service groups in Oman. In the North the British army and British intelligence had been relatively slow to respond across the spectrum. By 1972, with a real Irish low-intensity war, this was no longer the case. The internal intelligence wars involving the RUC, the army, and both external and counterintelligence, the agencies still called by most MI5 and MI6, continued to hamper security; but the net was increasingly in place, intense monitoring was the norm, and the black world of double and triple agents, false flags, informing, bribery and threats, agents provocateurs, absorbed considerable effort if as yet producing few hard results. The more military special operations began to appear, the usual rocks in the stream of British anti-insurgency

In May local people captured three men firing into a Protestant area from a car and found not only weapons but a military identity card and a British army radio. On June 22 four men were machine-gunned with a Thompson in the Glen Road, Andersontown, a Catholic area, by men in a car. The RUC investigation led to Captain James McGregor of the Parachute Regiment and Sergeant Clive Wilson, both operating as members of the Military Reconnaissance Force, an undercover organization attached to Thirty-ninth Infantry Brigade, commanded until a few weeks before by Kitson. But in the din of the IRA campaign, with car bombs taking down the center of Northern cities and sniping a constant, such activities were a minor matter.

During the truce these British special operations continued, indicating that whatever the intentions and inclinations of the politicians, the security forces had settled in for the long haul. Just as the army's reliance on the available anti-insurgency doctrine had in no small part contributed to creating an IRA insurgency, so too would special operations foster special, and for the British, not especially profitable returns. In the peculiar Irish conditions, undercover operations revealed often demanded enormous costs, and costs rarely paid by the army. And like the IRA the British army, the intelligence services, and even some politicians were increasingly willing to accept the cost of revelation and blunder, an integral component of covert anti-insurgency.

The Provos were more concerned about the stability of the truce, threatened by both the undercover British and the Protestant assassins. The Army Council's eyes were on London. The IRA delegation would include Mac Stiofáin, O Conaill, Séamus Twomey, Ivor Bell, and Gerry Adams. McGuinness would represent Derry, and the solicitor Myles Shevlin, who would make his way alone to London, was included as delegation secretary to have legal talent to hand. The others arrived for the first step in Derry on Friday morning, July 7. O Conaill and Mac Stiofáin had to slip out of the Republic, since they were now wanted men, while the others from the North had fewer problems. The delegation was driven along with Frank Steele from Whitelaw's office to a field, where a military helicopter lifted them to the RAF military airfield at Aldergrove, whence they were flown on to London. At Benson RAF station two large limousines with Special Branch drivers picked the delegation up and drove them to 93 Cheyne Walk, the house of Paul Channon, a millionaire Guinness heir as well as a Whitelaw associate, near Chelsea Bridge overlooking the Thames.

The IRA delegation had been prepared for a replay of the 1921 delegation and instead found that they were sitting in a large and elegant upstairs room, with antiques, carpets, a wall of books, exchanging pleasantries and oratorical clichés with several English gentlemen. It was not serious. There was no table, no note paper, no agenda. Whitelaw did most of the talking for the English and Mac Stiofáin for the IRA. There was not a meeting of minds, no cordiality. McGuinness disputed Whitelaw's aside that the British army would never shoot civilians and Mac Stiofáin the immutability of the Ireland Act of 1949, but in essence what had occurred was a presentation of the republican demands with an indication that such concessions like withdrawal might even be delayed even to 1976.

There was a break. When they met again Whitelaw indicated that the proposals would be put intact before the cabinet. After a second break Mac Stiofáin imposed a one-week deadline for an answer. Whitelaw no longer made any social effort to charm the Irish or ease their adamancy. The English had been exposed to what Mac Stiofáin called "a very determined delegation completely united in a solid policy," but the English thought the IRA delegation a group of preposterous gunmen seeking to schedule the dismemberment of the United Kingdom. There was no real assurance that a truce bought with such discussions was worth the price. The delegation was driven back to the airport in the same large limousines and flown on to Ireland.

On the flight Steele suggested that British casualties were not causing London problems: "We lose more men through road accidents in Germany in any one year than the losses you fellows are inflicting on us." Mac Stiofáin noted that he doubted if the British army had lost twenty soldiers to cars in the last three weeks and felt it amazing that Steele was so poorly briefed. What was amazing was that none of the Irish grasped how the English worked, how minor and irritating the Irish Troubles were, seen from London—an embarrassment, a tricky dilemma, but hardly the stuff of grand crisis. Such matters were not at the dictate of limited and ignorant gunmen with stark, staring eyes and blood on their hands. Whitelaw would take the truce if offered and move on to more congenial discussants, the politicians and the principled. There simply had been no middle ground or compelling force in the upstairs room on Cheyne Walk.

The meeting at Paul Channon's house would be the high point of the IRA's armed struggle, the closest the movement came to power. And even then, it is unlikely that either Whitelaw or the cabinet anticipated anything solid from the meeting. Talking to everyone seemed a good idea. Talking was better than killing. It was, of course, a high-risk discussion for the British government, since the loyalists would be outraged, as would many in Britain who still did not believe in having tea with traitors and terrorists. The IRA delegation had for so long clung to their luminous, almost transcendental dream, expressed mundanely as their basic nonnegotiable demands, that conventional negotiations were impossible. The entire movement had long been warped by the disastrous historical example of the 1921 treaty negotiations and the subsequent civil war that had made diplomacy, negotiations, even politics anathema to the men of physical force. Mac Stiofáin had sought advice from various individuals before the meeting to prepare; but no republican could really be prepared to compromise a dream, slice bits from an ideal.

A broad-based front might have produced dissent and discussion; but the core of the Provos, old or young, proved uniform in response and attitude. They had come not to negotiate but to arrange a timetable for British concession. The British had come out of curiosity and flexibility. They discovered grim men without graces or even guile, without give, who spoke memorized parts. The Irish delegation could not convince the British that they were shrewd or reasonable, could not do more than demand all and thus get nothing.

Even if something had been offered beyond the continuation of the truce, the inherent suspicion of British duplicity and the weight of republican tradition would have made the movement hold out for more, for all, for the ultimate Republic: at worst on the installment plan, preferably immediately. The delegates were not so much ignorant, which was the British impression, as innocent. They came burdened with patriot history and revealed the old simple republican dream intact and thinly clothed with the three demands and the concept of Eire Nua. The British found no reason, no reality, no flexibility, only arrogant, self-taught ideologues, a cut above the cartoon commanders of the UDA but still not in the end serious.

It was an impression that never changed. Years later Whitelaw would say, "The IRA leaders simply made impossible demands which I told them the British government would never concede. They were in fact still in a mood of defiance and determination to carry on until their absurd ultimatums were met." White-law had already decided that the IRA were terrorists and that "agreement is anathema to the terrorist mind." The IRA would not deal away the dream, would insist on conducting their "murderous campaign," and could not be persuaded to compromise or concede. The Provos, sooner or later, for Tory and for Labour, would be a given in any London equation: a violent negative, a veto to be eroded by the security forces, by the lure of peace and quiet, by the shifting loyalties of their constituency, by reality and a different reading of history.

While London would show enormous flexibility and often great cunning in dealing with the involved, the terrorist mind in Ireland as it had been throughout the empire remained alien. And it might be remembered that more often than not during the dismantling of the empire the British had found congenial politicians to manage the transfer of power, had outwitted the gunmen of EOKA in Cyprus or the Communists in Malaya, had transformed the forces of darkness and death into members of the Commonwealth's old boys' network, made prison a finishing school in imperial diplomacy. In Ireland the London reaction was little different: Isolate and ignore the gunmen, co-opt the moderate, try anything or everything to find a formula guaranteeing shifting British interests, unstated, often even unrecognized. And in Ireland what the British wanted was to be left alone in nominal control, at minimum cost, of the six counties.

All that had emerged from the negotiations seemed to republican advantage: The prisoners had political, or at least special, status, Gerry Adams was out of Long Kesh, the British had formally met with the movement, and the truce had not eroded IRA capacity. The British, on the other hand, had escaped with minimal costs from the dilemma posed by the hunger strike, had let one prisoner loose, and had discovered that the IRA could not be counted as a participant in any crafted accommodation. The latter was worth learning. And there was the truce. The IRA Army Council assumed that negotiations would continue, that the truce would continue, that the next act had opened. In a sense this was true, for the truce was both coda and prologue, the bridge from Britain responding to the Irish events to Britain shaping Irish events.

The IRA had hoped that negotiations could be broadened to include the militant loyalists. Instead the sectarian killings continued and the UDA went over to the offensive. The UDA leaders felt they could pressure "their" army to permit the symbolic barricades, although there was no real security need to wall off Protestant areas, only a jealousy of the minority no-go zones. On July 1 these defensive barricades were announced as UDA policy. On July 3 Whitelaw had already indicated that the British were not going to allow permanent UDA barricades when he authorized General Ford to have the army shoot at a confrontation at Ainsworth Avenue after the loyalists had erected barricades in the Shankill Road, Oldpark, and Woodvale the day before. The Ainsworth barricades would have enclosed fifty Catholic families and ensured a serious sectarian crisis. Rising from his dinner with Sir Robin Kinahan, a leading industrialist, Whitelaw over the phone gave Ford his order. The general in turn revealed his intentions to the UDA, who accepted a "compromise" and indicated to the British that the Orange gunmen did not want a shooting war with their own army.

As for shooting "guilty" Catholics, each as good as a volunteer in that other secret army, the truce had been goad to murder. In two weeks there were eighteen killings, more than one a day, and each quite visible now, without the din and smoke of the IRA armed campaign. One soldier had been shot and seventeen civilians. Not all were Catholics killed by Protestants. Some were retaliation killings, not recognized IRA operations but still murders by Catholics. Whatever hopes the republicans had of exploiting their London trip, the atmosphere in the North was poisonous.

Every effort was made by the IRA to keep the truce. Some volunteers, of course, wanted to continue the armed struggle, but GHQ kept all in line. In Belfast Séamus Twomey saw to it that not a single shot was fired or a single bomb exploded. The truce had driven the gunmen of majority to vent their anguish and frustration in killing and the people to the construction of ritual barricades. The British army had in republican eyes been lax in maintaining the truce. Special operations were rumored, evidence of intelligence forays found, favoritism to the Protestants thought to be pervasive. The IRA did not trust the British army, did not see long-term benefits from the truce, and anticipated entrapment and betrayal. In both Derry and Belfast there were all sorts of rumors. And in Belfast there seemed to be evidence that the British army was manipulating the UDA to the disadvantage of a minority left defenseless, with the IRA closed down by the truce. The IRA needed reassurance and there was none. On July 8 two volunteers were arrested by the army and two days on the hot line to London produced no release. London felt little was to be gained from the Provos. If the truce held, it would be to advantage. If not, plans were under way to shift the Northern balance by closing down the IRA in the no-go zones and opening up the political options. So London felt no urgency.

On Friday, July 7, in West Belfast the UDA sought to keep displaced Catholic families out of the mixed Lenadoon housing estate, where they wanted to move into houses deserted by Protestants. Lieutenant Colonel Mike Tomlinson, whose permission for the move was needed, in effect overruled the Northern Ireland Housing Executive. For the sake of peace, he ordered a twenty-four-hour delay after negotiations chaired by Tom Cromey, head of the Public Protection Authority, along with the UDA, the IRA, and local residents. The UDA was threatening violence. The Provos insisted they would move the families into the houses if the army did not. On Saturday, July 8, Provos Twomey, Séamus Loughran, the adjutant First Battalion, and Gerry O'Hare met with Tomlinson to find a means to end the stalemate. The next day still another meeting was held, at eleven in the morning, and Tomlinson still refused to allow the Catholics into the houses. Matters were carried no higher. London was out of touch and the truce was in danger.

The Catholics felt Tomlinson was in effect taking orders from the UDA. The Provos felt that with the truce in effect the British had unleashed the Protestants. Twomey gave the army until four that afternoon to carry out the policy of the Northern Ireland Housing Authority Executive. A large, hostile Catholic crowd gathered. Twomey felt the IRA could not back down as the people's defender nor could the British army take dictation from the UDA. The truce was in jeopardy and no one in London or Belfast, within the British government or the IRA Army

Council felt sufficiently strongly to defuse the Lenadoon confrontation. At five that afternoon, facing an increasingly hostile crowd of three thousand, the British army prevented a truck loaded with furniture from driving onto Horn Drive, Suffolk, so that the Catholic families could move in. The crowd began to stone the soldiers. The army fired rubber bullets and CS gas at the demonstrators. Twomey, who was present, told the army commander that the British had broken the truce. Shooting started and the British took up defensive positions as they counted over three hundred incoming rounds.

The IRA Army Council throughout the afternoon had tried to contact the authorities in London on their hot line. Heath could not be contacted at all. Whitelaw was out of touch over the weekend in Cumberland. Finally late in the afternoon someone in London finally came on the line about the collapsing truce: "Oh, well, it's a pity it's going to break. Perhaps we'll see you sometime." By then there was shooting in Lenadoon. At nine there was a statement from the Republican Publicity Bureau at Kevin Street: "The truce between the IRA and British occupation forces was broken without warning by British forces at approximately 5 P.M. today at Lenadoon Estate, Belfast. Accordingly all IRA units have been instructed to resume offensive action."

Just before midnight the Derry unit detonated six bombs in the center of the city. In Belfast a car bomb exploded in Skipper Street. In London Whitelaw made it clear that the "British troops were fired upon and only returned fire when under attack. . . . The incident was set up by the IRA." No one wanted responsibility for the end of the truce but no one was surprised. The IRA immediately revealed the London talks, but Whitelaw was forgiven by his own if not so easily by the loyalists in the North. On Monday he explained all in Westminster, detailing the IRA demands that "would be unacceptable to any British government." Heath decided no sacrifice was necessary. Whitelaw stayed as Northern Secretary.

If there were grumbles from hard Tories in London the outrage in Protestant circles in the the province was massive. Faulkner noted that "these talks were the logical conclusion of the policy of appeasement which Direct Rule has initiated. But they represented pragmatism gone mad." At least the midsummer madness appeared to have run its course in London and the province. Matters could have been worse for the cabinet. The gunmen had been flown over at a total cost of £540 to the Exchequer and some political embarrassment to the government, but nothing ventured, nothing gained. And little had been risked beyond Whitelaw's neck and they had gained two weeks of a truce, an insight into the nature of the Irish republican mind, and a satisfactory rationale for ignoring the gunmen in the future.

With the IRA entanglement and the truce behind him, Whitelaw was ready to move. Everyone, in fact, anticipated moves and maneuvers and advantage in the immediate future. Everyone had begun to position himself for what many felt would be the final run at a permanent arrangement. The Protestant paramilitaries had already started killing to clear the ground around their position and soon the IRA would begin again to underline the cost of lethargy and innocence.

11

Operation Motorman to Power Sharing, the Gun and Politics: July 1972–June 1973

Every Country Has the Government It Deserves.
Comte Joseph Marie de Maistre

The intention of the IRA was simply to maintain the pressure and once again force the British to resume bargaining. The trip to Chelsea had been a beginning. The impact they had made, however, and the cost of the maneuver in loyalist outrage meant that the British government, the British conservative establishment, and in time the entire establishment discounted the Provisionals as political players. And because it was a foregone conclusion that the IRA could not win militarily, the burden of any London response to the Provos was to fashion an acceptable level of violence while the future of the province was determined elsewhere. If the IRA wanted to see that violence escalated to even higher levels so that politics would have to include them, the British wanted Northern Ireland governed without undue cost—preferably by the Northern Irish.

While on Monday, July 10, Whitelaw was explaining in a statement at Westminster the rationale of the Chelsea meeting, eight explosions, including two car bombs in Belfast, rocked Northern Ireland. Counting the weekend deaths the 1972 total reached 206. Saor Éire announced mines had been placed in Belfast Lough. Meanwhile, Ulster Vanguard claimed that a Protestant army of sixty to seventy thousand could be mobilized within hours. Some more militant loyalist gunmen were already operating—during July, after the truce ended, thirteen Catholics were killed by sectarian assassins. And the Tartan Gangs, youth gangs wearing plaid scarfs in memory of the three young Scottish soldiers killed in March 1971, seemingly ran amok, set fires, threw stones, caused trouble—delinquent violence rationalized as politics. The chances of the renewed violence escalating into real civil war was not missed by the Northern Ireland Office. Worst of all, the end of the truce had come at the height of the Orange marching season.

The Glorious Twelfth of July marches began in Belfast with a fifteen-year-old Catholic boy shot dead by gunmen at his home. The body of a twenty-one-year-old Protestant who had been shot dead was found. In the evening at Portadown two more people—a Protestant and Catholic—were murdered. There had been IRA operations during the day but the pouring rain and the heavy security assured a peaceful demonstration to commemorate the 282nd anniversary of the Battle of the Boyne. During the demonstration Craig pointed out that "we do not propose to sit back idly and see our country destroyed." And certainly the province continued to be shaken by loyalist, sectarian murders, by the IRA armed struggle, by the gun instead of politics. On July 13 there was an exchange of threats. Whitelaw said that if the IRA returns to its campaign with ferocity, then "we will retaliate with the same ferocity." And the bombing and shooting continued throughout the province. At least by the summer of 1972 the British-IRA confrontation fit a pattern, however bloody, had conventions; it did not engender the same dread as did the unknown Protestant assassins who, worst of all, might speak for the majority. Certain militant loyalist spokesmen showed no evidence that they would deny themselves guns; rather, the reverse.

Each IRA operation now only seemed to provoke additional murder. And there was no evidence that the IRA would hesitate despite the killings. In the first eight days after the truce the British army lost fifteen killed and over a hundred injured. On Thursday, July 20, the Belfast IRA Brigade command met as always to consider the next day's operations. With the renewed war two weeks old, it was not thought by the involved to be a particularly significant meeting. The chief of staff and the Army Council wanted escalation, with a concentrated sabotage offensive for the next day, Friday, July 21. The intention was to detonate car bombs throughout the province. In Belfast at the meeting the brigade allotted operations to the relevant battalions and moved on to other matters. The major responsibility fell on the Third Battalion, whose volunteers would place fifteen devices. At midday Friday, July 21, the warnings began to be telephoned in, and just after two o'clock the bomb blitz was launched. There were too many bombs. There were too many warnings, three per bomb. The warnings shifted crowds from one danger spot to another or came too late or were not acted upon at all or in time. There were a large number of hoax calls as well. The Provos had overloaded the system with twenty-two bombs in Belfast. The Provos said the security forces did not make proper efforts, had ample time, failed to act. They would show little remorse.

Between 2:15 P.M. and 3:30 P.M. the explosions killed nine people, including two soldiers, and injured about 130. Two explosions did the most damage. At the Oxford Street Bus Station a bomb killed six people, including two soldiers of the Welsh Guards and two teenagers. On the Cavehill Road three civilians were killed, including a boy of fourteen. Those present and those at a distance would remember the impact of the bombs rather than the details. A corporal from the First Paras said, "I saw the consequences of those IRA bombs—twenty-six explosions in the city centre within an hour. Eleven people killed at the bus station waiting for a bus. I'll never forget that."* Details haunted those who cleaned up: "A little shoe, the bits and pieces, we had to put them into plastic

*Max Arthur, *Northern Ireland Soldiers Talking* (London: Sidgwick & Jackson, 1987), p. 87.

bags." The IRA would note both their warnings and the point that among the nine dead were two soldiers, an RUC reservist, and a member of a Protestant paramilitary group, but even then five of the dead were civilians, "and our attitude was that it was five too many."*

Almost everyone else was horrified at the downtown slaughter and not placated by explanations about warnings given or soldiers killed. The bomb blitz became Bloody Friday. The Dublin *Irish Independent* was fairly typical of Southern opinion: "We fostered the men who planned the murders of innocent men, women and children in Belfast on Friday; we fed these people with propaganda; and we took advantage, when we could, of their exploits." British opinion was unanimous, surpassed only by loyalist outrage. The Northern Ireland Office on August 2 published 150,000 copies of *The Terror and the Tears,* documenting the events of Bloody Friday, and another 100,000 on August 11. Whitehall now had all the excuse he needed. As Whitehall informed Parliament, "Our first objective is to destroy the capacities of the Provisional IRA who terrorize the community." Bloody Friday was ample justification for Operation Motorman to end the IRA sanctuaries in Belfast and Derry. The loyalists did not wait and began firing on individual Catholics.

The key to provincial security, the British felt, was the existence of the no-go zones in nationalist areas. These zones infuriated the loyalists and eroded British legitimacy. As soon as Whitelaw finished explaining away the meeting with the Provos, plans were made for Operation Motorman, the occupation of the Belfast and Derry no-go zones in such a way that there would not be full-scale war. The bombs of Bloody Friday simply introduced an additional logic to the move, which would allow a shift from security matters to the first steps in the political process. And a British army move would reassure the unionists and undercut the militant loyalists. Motorman would be the largest British military effort since the invasion of Suez, involving some twenty-six thousand troops, armor, Centurion tanks with steel plows instead of guns, air surveillance, a naval expedition, and a propaganda effort.

Mac Stiofáin had indicated that the IRA would defend their areas, supposedly filled with defenses—a yearlong bluff. "We had decided long before not to resist a serious reoccupation attempt by the British if it came.† And the British made every effort to guarantee that Motorman was no secret. Troops moved openly; the Saracens, still painted the sandy color of the desert, drove around in full view; all sorts of signs, signals, and speeches were given. The result was just as both had intended.

Motorman opened just before midnight July 30–31 when the Centurion bulldozer tanks were brought twenty-five miles up the Foyne estuary to Derry in

*Seán Mac Stiofáin, *Revolutionary in Ireland* (Edinburgh: Gordon Cremonesi, 1975), p. 296. Other observers felt that the Belfast Brigade must have intended to cause casualties, but a major reason innocents became victims was the inability of the IRA volunteers involved to take proper precautions or adequate care—after all, most were learning on the job. That casualties could be prevented was later demonstrated by McGuinness's operations in Derry, but elsewhere in Northern Ireland and especially in England either the level of skill was low or concern about indiscriminate results was equally low.
†Mac Stiofáin, p. 298.

four landing craft from HMS *Fearless* escorted by the minesweeper HMS *Gravington*. The Centurions came ashore over a trackway quietly laid by hand, cleared the barricades, and departed just before dawn, when the British troops moved into the Bogside and Creggan. The army shot and killed two men, a petrol bomber and a gunman. Some sixty Provisional volunteers had withdrawn into Donegal and others had gone underground. In Belfast there was almost no shooting at all. There were no casualties and no arrests. The total arms find for Motorman was small: 32 weapons, 27 bombs, 450 pounds of explosives, and 1,000 rounds of ammunition.

The most important aspect was that there had been no serious fighting. Yet the loyalists could be shown that no-go zones had been shut down and the IRA pretensions deflated at very little cost beyond deploying twenty-six thousand troops, a useful exercise in any case. In fact, gradually the army could see spin-off training benefits in exposing the troops to low-intensity conflict within the United Kingdom, not to mention the cheaper cost of keeping army units in Northern Ireland rather than on the Rhine. Certainly Motorman was a classical exercise by the army for political purpose—a confrontation avoided by both players for opposing reasons.

The IRA could not have won no matter how grand a stand had been made and would have been blamed for the inevitable civilian losses by the civilians involved. As it was they made the best of the situation. They lost their haven. They had to give up the symbols of Free Derry and liberated Belfast. And they had given up considerable tactical advantage. Worse, the momentum would go over to the security forces, although the battle was still fiercely joined and the IRA still could maintain their offensive at almost the same level.

On the same day as Motorman the ferocity of the struggle was underscored by an IRA operation in Claudy, a minor target at best, a small village some twelve miles south of Derry. An active service unit using local authority placed three large car bombs in a main street. They picked a foolish target and bungled the warning so that when the three explosions occurred no one had taken refuge. The village was devastated. Six people were killed at once and two died later. GHQ had not known of the operation, denied responsibility, and would continue to do so although an internal investigation by a member of the Army Council would detail what had gone wrong. Claudy, like Bloody Friday, became one of the arguments by nationalists grown weary of an armed struggle that promised a total victory only the faithful felt possible. The shambles of Claudy, the result of a vandalized public telephone that prevented the warning but still an IRA responsibility, was a bloody coda to Motorman, ample evidence of the cost of IRA persistence.

This IRA persistence became increasingly difficult to maintain as the British exploited their tactical and technological advantages. The end of the no-go zones gradually opened for the security forces a new world of intelligence. The most difficult challenge in anti-insurgency is to penetrate the secrecies of an underground composed of the faithful protected by their own. This had hardly changed simply because British patrols could move, if cautiously, through the Bogside or down the lanes off the Falls Road. What gradually evolved was an enormously complex intelligence-monitoring effort that in turn led to techniques, technical and human, to pursue rather than passively await information. None of this was easy or without tactical and political risk, and the entire process never had for long a single guiding hand.

When the Irish Troubles had spilled over into violence in 1969, a small, quite vicious war began within the British intelligence community. In the North the RUC had collected intelligence by osmosis, by being near the minority, by knowing names and attitudes and routines. The collapse of the old order had dried up these sources at the same time the intelligence consumers wanted more. When the army arrived on the scene, the commanders (often for good reasons) had doubts about the RUC's capacities, especially after internment, and in turn the RUC resented the military's attitudes and arrogance. Both were considered small time players by the internal (the old MI5) and external (MI6) intelligence services, each determined to shape Irish events to their institutional need. This was possible because Ireland was part internal and part external and hence up for bureaucratic grabs. Over the years to follow each of the major intelligence players had dominant days and fell on hard times, became involved in creating both elite units and bureaucratic linkages. Much of the struggle would remain classified, with only the most spectacular feuds surfacing and only the undeniable operational disasters finding a way into the public domain because of media interest or the revelations of the involved.

Belfast and Derry in particular, with the elimination of the no-go zones, offered the British immediate and obvious opportunity. The army began saturation patrols that led to the accumulation of all sorts of low-grade information. In time this monitoring process became far more efficient and ordered. The army and the police and their agents, the general public and the paid informers, all fed in everyday details. Observation posts, police barracks, watchers in the eaves and from high-rise buildings, produced daily returns. In time it was possible to tell not only who was who but also where they went and when, where they did not go, where they should have gone, whom they met. The British knew the milk order and the grocery purchases, the size of the electric bill and the content of the mail and the telephone calls, the family visits, the result of hospital calls, the borrowing and the lending. In time any vehicle could be tracked throughout the province by means of a central computer in Lisburn army barracks. The computer eventually played a significant role in IRA operational mythology. Good police work or informers were one matter, silicon chips another.

In time every shot fired in the province went through central forensics. IRA weapons could be traced as they moved from South Armagh to the Falls to the Short Strand. Police procedure, questions and answers, descriptions and crime statistics and investigations were ordered and filed in tens of thousands. In a sense the hard-core urban areas became carefully monitored concentration camps, not unlike very large, low-security holding pens: not Free Derry but a people's prison. The newly "interned" noted just this change after Motorman, on August 2, when the Bogside Community Association accused the GOC NI, Sir Harry Tuzo, of turning the Bogside and Creggan into an internment camp for thirty thousand people. That was in August 1972 and there were years and years of technical and tactical improvements to come that would turn night into day, conversation into records, movement day or night into police notes, shots in the dark into court-room evidence.

All this British activity was passive, waited on the action, monitored reality. Obviously any intelligence system wants to go on the offensive, penetrate the opponent, seek out intentions and capacities. And so the British ran their own agents into IRA areas, agents who merely moved normally as postmen or delivery boys, invisible listeners in hidden hutches in the eaves or more boldly as enthusiastic recruits to the movement. This was not easy. The arena was small, the players related or familiar, the alien easy to spot. On Monday, October 1, the Four Square Laundry van was ambushed in the Twinbrook Estate, Dunmurry, Belfast. The Four Square was a British front—one can learn a great deal from a laundry list or a laundry delivery—that a British army spokesman admitted had cost the life of one British undercover soldier. An IRA active service unit, engaged in one of three operations that day based on information smuggled out of Crumlin Road Prison, raked the van with fire, leaving fourteen holes, two ricochet dents, and Sapper Ted Stuart slumped dead over the wheel. The delivery lady, "Sarah," actually Lance Corporal Sarah Jane Warke, Provost Company, Royal Military Police, was passing out parcels at the time and escaped the attack by rushing out of 8 Juniper Place by the rear door. The IRA claimed to have killed five but the unit in its hurry failed to riddle the observer's hidden compartment in the top of the van. No one was killed in the other two operations. Still, whatever the score, the Four Square closed down.

Even more at risk were British agents; even Protestant civilians could not pass in Catholic districts, urban or rural; so an effort was made instead to recruit locals. This could rarely be done by finding a committed local; instead, agents were bought with reduced prison sentences, with money and promises, with hope of a distant haven after service, with threats, with blackmail, with all the nasty pressures available to government agencies. Much of the ensuing information was tainted—lies, exaggerations, rumors, hints, and guesses—and all had to be weighed and hidden if the agent, however inept, was to be protected. When several agencies are so engaged independently within a very small and enormously suspicious arena, failure is a given. And those who paid for error over the years were found dead on bits of waste ground and at the end of lanes, left on the roadside near the border in black plastic garbage bags, often booby-trapped for good measure. And some always paid because they had been betrayed, because of mistaken suspicions, because they foolishly wanted to be important, because underground armies are often as inept as intelligence agencies, and because, like the Four Square people, they blundered.

The cost, particularly paid by others, had never stopped the enthusiastic intelligence service, almost always engaged not in just seeking the best information out of the underground but adjusting reality. Most intelligence forces also play an active role in the drama through special operations. This was the case in Northern Ireland. It is a very small step from running an agent to betraying one, from betrayal as punishment to betrayal as a means to dispute and harm an opponent. Intelligence slips from knowledge to action in small, not always discrete steps. From the first, special operations appealed to the British intelligence establishment and would continue to do so despite the occasional disasters.

In particular by 1972 observers in the North had reason to suspect that the British army had undercover, elite groups at work not only seeking intelligence but also committing provocative acts to damage the IRA and perhaps the loyalist para-militaries.

The unionist population was not inclined to accuse their army; the few Northern journalists in place were dazzled by the violence and the complex politics and deterred by the constant rumor of conspiracy; and nationalist accusations in particular were thought politically motivated, wishful thinking. The nationalists and particularly the IRA did not want to accept Protestant killers and so preferred to blame the British army. But as time passed there could be little doubt that army personnel were operating in civilian clothing as a first line and seemingly had close loyalist contacts to operate at one remove. In time the suspicions would harden. The army operating in a war zone under pressure for results was one matter, while the other intelligence agencies pursuing provocative and risky special operations further from the action was another and more dubious enterprise.

In an unconventional war the center needs unorthodox means. In London Ireland was still mysterious and hard information difficult to acquire. And Ireland, gradually emerging within the British bureaucratic consciousness, also became an opportunity as well as a challenge. Those in possession of authority and capacity are often attracted to the irregular means as much as to the result, seeing in the unconventional a chance to play a greater, more pragmatic game, a real game. This was particularly true in a period in British intelligence, increasingly reactionary in assumption, when conspiracy theories loomed. Some, especially in MI5, assumed that the British political establishment, especially Labour, might be willing not only to sell out Ulster but also might be playing to Moscow rules. In such unusual times many intelligence people in London felt that unorthodox means had become standard. In 1971–72, MI6 became involved in one such unorthodox—and ill-advised—operation: the Littlejohn Affair, a classic disaster.

On the evening of November 21, 1971, Keith Littlejohn met with Minister of Defense Lord Carrington's army minister, Geoffrey Johnson-Smith. Littlejohn, who had served a term in Borstal in 1967, had arranged the meeting through Lady Onslow, a voluntary prison visitor, who knew Carrington and felt he might want to investigate Keith's elder brother Kenneth's claim to have information about the IRA. Johnson-Smith was impressed. Kenneth Littlejohn was charming, plausible, and seemed to have splendid and useful Irish contacts. Littlejohn, discharged ignominiously from the paratroops in 1958 and with a criminal background, had arrived in Ireland in 1970 as a fugitive from the police as the result of a thirty-eight-thousand-pound robbery that had jailed his brother-in-law. In Ireland as Kenneth Austen with a Dublin-based clothing firm, Littlejohn had lived first in Kerry as a jet-set businessman and then, when the firm ran into trouble, moved to County Louth, close to the border. There he followed IRA, particularly the Officials', fortunes. With his firm in ruins and faced with a summons from the Dublin High Court, he decided to use his nonexistent "IRA connections."

MI6 decided to run both Littlejohn brothers in Ireland with John Wyman, using the name Douglas Smythe. Why not pick up information where possible?

They mistakenly felt he had good contacts when what Littlejohn had was gossip and access to a few local unimportant and dubious Official volunteers. He did, however, have a winning way. The result was that in February 1972 the Littlejohns were dispatched to Ireland to collect information on the IRA and, more important, apparently encouraged, if not "authorized," to undertake a series of provocative armed robberies that could be blamed on the IRA. Kenneth Littlejohn also insisted that he was involved in plots to assassinate the republican leadership, whom he did not know and whose names he had trouble spelling; and in the case of the Officials they were individuals leading a group opposed to the Provisionals' armed struggle and eager to maintain their own truce.

The Littlejohn adventure was limited to the increasingly blatant robberies. Although they involved a few disenchanted Officials they were, as far as the Gárdaí were concerned, a private matter. Apparently the authorities were content to allow the Littlejohns to run loose, damaging the IRA, even if many of the Gárdaí would have preferred English thieves to be in an Irish jail. Between February and October 1972 there was no valid IRA information sent to London but twelve bank robberies, including one that returned seventy thousand pounds in Newry across the border in Northern Ireland.

On October 12 the spree ended with the robbery of the Allied Irish Bank on Grafton Street in the middle of Dublin's shopping district by a group of men who wore no masks, called themselves by military titles, and left thousands of fingerprints. Fourteen members of the staff identified the Littlejohns, who fled to the airport in Kenneth's car, trailing clues, and flew off to Belfast, Glasgow, and London before opening a planned restaurant in Torquay with the money from Allied Irish. This was the end. The brothers were arrested on October 18 at the request of the Gárdaí by Scotland Yard's Flying Squad soon after their final meeting with Wyman. MI6 did not protect them.

Both Littlejohns were returned to Dublin in March 1973, tried and convicted, Kenneth sentenced to twenty years and Keith to fifteen. Kenneth managed a brief flurry of interest when he escaped in 1974 from Mountjoy Prison and gave interviews to the BBC "Panorama" show and the London magazine *Time Out* before being recaptured. They were both released in 1981 on humanitarian grounds. In turn Wyman was arrested on December 19 with Gárda Patrick Crinnion, a sergeant in the Special Branch's C3, the terrorism and subversion division. Both were charged but only the count concerning attempting to obtain or communicate official information was pursued. Though found guilty, they were sentenced to only six months and were released, for they had already served the necessary time while under remand. By then Dublin-London cooperation was a dim prospect.

In retrospect MI6 had underwritten a loose cannon and tinkered to no purpose with the security force of a friendly country pursuing a parallel policy. Since many British intelligence people doubted even the loyalty of former and future Prime Minister Harold Wilson, it is no wonder they assumed that Dublin was an enemy—and a foolish provincial one that could be maneuvered to London advantage by such as the Littlejohns. What did happen, not to British disadvantage, was that many in the establishment felt that the Littlejohns indicated the necessity of moving hard against the Provos so that there would be no further

Littlejohns necessary—the provocative acts had convinced no one. The British willingness to underwrite such a special operation was credited to a sense of London political urgency rather than to an MI6 blunder or innocence on Irish matters. Dublin continued to assume that Ireland was greater in British eyes than was the case.

The urgency was actually felt in the Northern Ireland Office, where the purpose of all security operations during the summer of 1972 was to allow a political initiative that would involve as much of the center as possible. The Conservative MPs at least flew into the province regularly, had a sense of mission, and had a specific road to follow. Motorman had cleared that road into the future as far as Whitelaw was concerned. The way was visibly no less bumpy, as the Provos continued their campaign (though at a limited pace), but it was a viable way out of the chaos and toward, if not to, normal politics. In the meantime, the chaos continued.

On August 8 casualty figures showed that the death total since 1969 had reached 501. In the two weeks prior to Motorman there had been 111 explosions and 1,120 shooting incidents and in the two weeks afterward this had dropped to 41 explosions and 269 shooting incidents. It was no longer possible to build a car bomb or an explosive device quietly and move through the first stages within a secure zone. It was no longer possible to slip safely to a shooting site or a sniper hideout, blaze away until drawing return fire, and then withdraw without chase. IRA operations, almost daily, became more chancy and British saturation patrols more inhibiting. This was not always apparent to British squaddies worming their way through the mud of strange back gardens while women and children howled and beat bin lids and snipers blazed away from some distant roof. The same was true for army patrols creeping through alien green fields, fearful of snipers or land mines or trip wires and tricks, fearful even of the cows. Yet the numbers began to show military progress. Times were changing. And Whitelaw used the time to advantage.

The next big move was political. Seemingly the SDLP wanted to play if their boycott over internment could be surmounted. There was every evidence that the SDLP represented almost all Catholic opinion, short of the residues remaining to the Nationalists and the Northern Ireland Labour Party and the relatively few attracted to the nonsectarian middle-class Alliance or the Republican Clubs of the Official IRA. The SDLP wanted a return to politics, a share of the power in an assembly that would replace the old sectarian Stormont, and some sort of all-Ireland dimension to the ultimate accommodation. They, like nearly every other political player, wanted the Provos to disappear. Although the SDLP leaders could not give up the aspiration for a united Ireland, they could also hardly imagine an institutional form to achieve it. Thus, the SDLP would play for some power and a symbolic Irish component. So too would all those little center parties, in particular the Alliance of Oliver Napier, often the only party to be found in the middle of the road. The loyalists were another matter.

The moderates would play but the traditional fate of Unionist moderates was that they were gelded and put out to pasture. Practical and pragmatic Unionists had a short half-life once they failed to defend the majority's traditions, once they gave an inch no matter how obvious and compelling the reasons. The Unionists were, however, no longer a monolith. There were degrees of militancy, stages and opposing currents of the faithful. It was even growing hard to determine who was in the Unionist tent and who outside. Certainly outside were Paisley and the DUP, more likely to play a wrecker's role with any Whitelaw initiative than to go along with what London saw as reality and many loyalists saw as betrayal. Whitelaw's first problem was to begin a process that included sufficient players to disguise what might be a negative majority. Once the process was under way the magnetism of power and the charm of the game might attract a majority for what the Northern Irish Office had in mind: a devolved parliament with limited immediate powers, an Irish dimension just large enough to provide the SDLP with a fig leaf but not large enough to frighten decent loyal opinion.

On August 11 Whitelaw issued an invitation to the leaders of all the constitutional parties represented in the old Stormont Parliament to attend on September 25 a political conference in England on the future of Northern Ireland. The conference would be at the unused Europa Hotel just outside Darlington. It attracted immediate acceptances from the NILP, Alliance, and the Unionists under Faulkner. Whitelaw had hoped to include the SDLP, still frustrated because of their internment boycott but willing to be coaxed. Everyone wanted "something" in return for entering the game. Time was so short and the risks of letting Darlington slip away so great, Whitelaw felt he could not delay and so went ahead with the three early acceptances when he could gain no other immediate converts to the conference.

In the meantime everyone maneuvered for position. For example, on Friday, August 11, Whitelaw released eighteen men from Long Kesh, including Jim Sullivan, an Official and a former chairman of the Belfast CCDC, thus rewarding the truce and eroding the SDLP grievance on internment. On the same day the SDLP, after further talks with Whitelaw, decided not to go to Darlington, since internment still existed. There was a feeling with internment being wound down. The British were institutionalizing the emergency by other judicial means—Lord Diplock would soon become involved in preparing a report, ultimately released on December 20, on an alternative to the existing system. So the SDLP could still be picked up after Darlington. Paisley was lost, probably from the beginning, although his refusal related to his demand that Whitelaw launch an official inquiry into the shooting of two Protestants, killed on September 7, 1972, by the army during a UDA and Tartan Gang attack on the Tennent Street RUC station.

The attack was ample evidence that the extreme loyalists still had ambivalent feelings about their army. And their army had little time for them: "These were Loyalists, so-called Loyalists firing at British soldiers—great Loyalists, all Union Jacks and spitting in your face . . . we just went berserk, like Viking warriors. . . . We knew that they were going to kill us, that if we didn't fight like hell we could be overwhelmed."* The residents certainly felt that the Paras had gone "berserk." The army noted that shots had been fired at patrols in Argyle and Agnes streets before troops returned fire.

In any case Paisley had no intention of appearing at Darlington, even as a wrecker. In the North an axiom was that not only moderation penalized but also

*Arthur, p. 92.

did novelty, movement. The past paid dividends. The future might not. Paisley in particular was a master of articulate inertia, a critic of all change. Even if he suggested change, it was in tradition's name. He knew what he knew, articulated the fears and suspicions of his own, played only his game. And this was not always to the disadvantage of the advocates of cooperation. So Whitelaw was left with his three first acceptances. They were just enough to give legitimacy to the communiqué.

Darlington first persuaded the concerned in Northern Ireland politics to produce a party vision of the future, an exercise that attracted even those who did not attend. The conference opened with three delegates: Phelim O'Neill from Alliance, Vivian Simpson of the NILP, and Brian Faulkner. They agreed that Northern Ireland should remain part of the United Kingdom unless a majority decided otherwise, which was the legal position at the time and increasingly acceptable to the nationalist minority and to the Dublin government. They agreed that there should be some kind of provincial assembly and administration but not about how it should be elected, empowered, and controlled, all the crucial factors in devolution. And they agreed finally that there should be closer cooperation in social and economic matters with the Republic, a notion so vague that most loyalists would hardly flinch. The purpose of Darlington was not to alienate, not to offer a hard agenda, but to begin a dialogue that would arrive at answers very similar to those Whitelaw had in mind.

There was clearly a long way to go. Robert Cooper of the Alliance Party emerged to note that they had learned only that the Unionists had learned nothing. Still, no one had gone home. Darlington—four decent men and their advisers meeting in a hotel room in the midst of a deserted but closely guarded golf course—was a modest success. At a cost of sixteen thousand pounds Whitelaw had a bargain as well as a beginning.

The next stage was the dance leading to a promised Green Paper prepared by the Northern Ireland Office directed by Ken Bloomfield. This Green Paper would outline London's intentions: narrowing the nature of the Assembly, detailing the need and nature of the Irish dimension, and stressing the reality of the border pledge. For their part, most of the politicians still wanted either a reward in some form for participating in the process or advantage from a boycott. The something was often symbolic rather than tangible. The UDA, never before concerned with electoral structures, violently opposed promotional representation because, somehow, it might be to the other side's advantage. Many unionists wanted the border poll, a six-county plebescite on maintaining the province, a symbolic exercise, to come before the local elections so that they could display their loyalty and their domination over the minority. And the SDLP needed some return on their principled stand on internment, which blocked full participation.

Some loyalists were still looking for an alternative to Darlington rather than adjustment. On August 24 John Taylor, in his first speech since the assassination attempt, suggested that if the province was not to have its own parliament "then we must have an independent Ulster." In opposition Paisley and the DUP were dedicated to total integration with Great Britain. Vanguard called a rally for September 30. Many hard-line loyalists would appear under Craig's auspices.

Paisley, who suspected that Vanguard was flirting with UDI—"It is but a step from outright rebellion"—found no attraction in fronts he did not dominate.

The moderates refused to become involved. Faulkner would not come, nor would Enoch Powell, ever more concerned with Irish matters, nor would Heath. Ideologically the three nodes of attraction remained independence in some form, integration into the United Kingdom, or a variant of Darlington. The great strength of devolution was that this appeared a return to the Stormont past while both integration, supported by Paisley, was more of the present, and independence, suggested by Taylor and Craig, was a new direction and lacked tradition. No matter, for out of the rally came the Ulster Loyalist Council, announced by Craig on October 5, that included Ulster Vanguard, LAW, UDA, and various volunteer organizations. In London it was not yet certain, however, that the group could stay together or whether it would boycott the Green Paper. As Whitelaw told the Conservative conference at Blackpool, "No one over the centuries who had studied or had responsibility for Irish affairs has ever been unwise enough to claim any full understanding of them."

Certainly Craig's violent statement in London before the Monday Club meeting in Commons on October 19 did not fit English political practice or understanding. "We are prepared to come out and shoot and kill. I am prepared to come out and shoot and kill. Let us put the bluff aside. I am prepared to kill, and those behind me will have my full support." Craig, as many loyalists had and would, indicated that a constant in Northern politics was the assumption that recourse to the gun if frustrated or threatened was a given. Integrating Craig and his supposed army of eighty thousand in the Darlington game thus faced certain obstacles. So did tolerating Taylor's UDI option as realistic. Prime Minister Heath, speaking in the province in November, indicated that any such attempt would "bring about a bloodbath, but that were it to succeed, the British government would not pay one penny."

The narrow, intractable Provo gunmen fit the appropriate Irish stereotype and could be discarded, but Whitelaw still had to deal with "politicians" who called for killing and secession as a conventional response to dispute and opposition. Certainly the loyalists on the street had ready recourse to the gun. On October 17, and not for the first time, the army came under fire from Protestant as well as Catholic gunmen during rioting in several areas of Belfast. Whitelaw, however, persisted. The local elections scheduled for December 6 were postponed so that the poll of the border could come first. And then on October 30 came the Green Paper, "The Future of Northern Ireland," to be used as a basis of discussion. Essentially the Green Paper sharpened the Darlington points and indicated the direction of events. The result hardly received a wild reception. Taylor said it was a formula for a united Ireland. Paddy Devlin had doubts, even if Hume felt it contained the "first glimmerings" of reality.

If points were to be made in the final White Paper, the politicians would have to participate in the process. Faulkner and his Unionists, the Alliance Party, and the NILP were already involved and now the SDLP, who need not boycott a "process," could participate as well. The center could be covered and the goal was to entangle as much of the majority as possible. The border poll—"Do you want Northern Ireland to stay in the United Kingdom or join the Irish Republic?"—

was introduced at Westminster on November 1. On November 13, at Westminster, Whitelaw insisted that there could be no purely military solution to the Northern problem. That translated into an accommodation satisfactory to the minority represented by the SDLP. Whitelaw also said that integration was not on. That meant that an accommodation acceptable to the minority was the only path to power through politics. Whitelaw and London chose to discard both the loyalist politicians' rhetoric of violence and the reality of a call for UDI. In fact Taylor's suggestion that UDI could be made attractive to the minority only indicated that a new sense of reality had been introduced into loyalist thinking. And on November 14 the Unionist Party standing committee on the Green Paper voted against a Unionist veto eighty-six to thirty-seven; unlike in the recent past, the moderates controlled the machinery and thus did not have to prove their faith.

On November 27 Whitelaw announced that he would begin his round of talks with parties and organizations. On November 30 the Ulster Loyalist Council agreed to attend; with SDLP involved, almost all the relevant players were now in the game. Parallel to these very real political advances, the loyalist murder campaign had continued, spreading concern and dismay. Since July there had been seventy-four civilians murdered, forty-six Catholics and twenty-eight Protestants. Most of the Catholic deaths were at the hands of sectarian killers. Some of the loyalist acts were gruesome. On November 13 Anita Currie, the wife of SDLP MP Austin Currie, was attacked and beaten by armed men who broke into her home during the night. They carved the letters UVF on her chest.

Increasingly the UDA lost any credibility as a coherent force. The days when tens of thousands signed up as defenders had long gone. First the middle class left. The decent and proper withdrew. The political went into Vanguard or the DUP and the marchers made do with an Orange Lodge; the rioters needed no organization, could make do with a tartan scarf or a rock. And so the titles and rallies were left to the core, the men along the Shankill and in Woodvale, the clumps of rural righteous, the poor, the persistent, the Protestant activists without other home.

Most of those involved in loyalist paramilitary activities, however recondite their politics or crude their analysis, however close personal pressures might lurk to political motivation, were normal Belfast working-class men. They were not very different from IRA volunteers in age and occupation. They had limited prospects and narrow ambitions, were consumers not creators, sought to protect the psychological and real comforts of the past, a past fading for the younger militants into retold history. They wanted to play a part, wanted to serve, to defend, often at no greater level than an Orange march or the neighborhood riot. Some, the same lads that would volunteer for the paratroops or the Marines, wanted discipline, pride, a uniform, a role. In the UDA or perhaps the UVF, a more brutal grouping, they found pride of place and the rationale to take actions that observers found repellent: the arbitrary murder of random Catholics. Yet Northern attitudes transmuted murder at the front door into a militant and idealistic act with effective consequences, not the least of which was to punish the IRA. The IRA blew away innocent civilians, maimed dissent with a bullet in the kneecap, murdered for a mythical Republic. So in turn the loyalists in the UDA killed for an ideal.

No one would deny them, the volunteers of UVF or the military commanders clumped under the title UFF or Red Hand Commandos. And no one cared to mock the incoherent communiqués, the bizarre uniforms and military titles, the public threats to make a deal with the Russians or to outlaw the Catholic Church. In fact the media rushed to film commanders grouped around a table covered with an Ulster flag, men in camouflage suits, funny campaign hats, dark glasses, men with work-rough, tobacco-stained fingers, fading tattoos, unfashionable, almost undecipherable accents, who above the clutter of pistols spoke as commanders of their invisible troops, tens of thousands eager for action. The more talented, the more conventionally ambitious, the shrewd and articulate, wanted to use the paramilitaries as a vehicle for real politics, for personal advancement, as a respectable means in place.

Even the butchers could be transformed. Gusty Spence, responsible for the Malvern Street murder in 1966, had been impressed with the IRA prisoners he met. The Officials in particular with their tight organization, radical rhetoric, and dream of working-class unity had left a lasting impact. On the outside he tried to apply what he had learned to the new UVF that arose from the pubs of East Belfast and could be found in the loyalist heartland in the country, especially in East Antrim and Armagh. At its peak in 1972 the UVF may have had 1,500 members if anyone counted, and attracted those who wanted action, not display or ritual. It was, then and later, not so much an underground of cells or a secret loyalist militia as clumps of vigilantes willing to murder out of frustration and contempt for the papists. The UVF aspired to be a secret army like the IRA, but it was not. Nor were the moves to radicalize the working-class members successful.

Spence's effort would fail despite his aura. That is not what the men wanted. He was not alone in trying to make something viable out of the working-class loyalist structures. The toleration of the killers, the arrival of criminals to use underground authority and the toleration of the community for personal purpose, the difficulty of mobilizing an inchoate community seeking not so much power as the rituals of dominance, would have been obstacle enough even for the most talented.

For those who rose in the UDA, who were not killers, who were not criminals, who wanted conventional power and a real, not an imaginary, organization, there were rewards and opportunities—often prominence not power, often promises and possibilities rather than office—but still something. The real politicians certainly ignored the butchers and protection rackets, accepted the commanders in dark glasses as players, invited the leaders of the UDA or LAW on platforms, defended the UVF as logical and the sectarian violence as provoked.

The leaders, however, were often led by events, ignored by their followers, and unable to deliver either riot on request or numbers on demand. The paramilitaries could not organize effectively and play a regular role in the Whitelaw game; but they could provide cover for those who did not want to play but only to exert personally their dominance with a gun and who did not feel ashamed after carving initials on a woman. So Whitelaw, the security forces, even and especially the RUC, soon realized that such "loyalists" were criminal butchers first and foremost, not political actors. Whitelaw announced a special mobile "murder squad" on December 6. He and the conventional politicians still hoped to attract the real, if raw, loyalist talent, attract the fundamentalists if possible and if not at least maneuver them toward toleration of an eventual accommodation.

The fact that Craig's front, which included at creation the UDA and LAW, could meet on the Green Paper and look ahead to the White Paper was a positive step. It was not as crucial as keeping Faulkner's Unionists on board but it was still a good sign. In fact, the round of talks with party leaders was an end, not a means. The more they talked, the more they became involved in a procedure that would lead to normality, an acceptable level of violence, and an end to the Irish problem—and this was the dearest desire of everyone in London in any way involved with the intractable and mysterious Irish. And oddly enough, in Dublin the goal was the same, an end to a Northern problem achieved by decent means.

The Dublin strategy especially after the Belfast bomb blitz of Bloody Friday and Operation Motorman was to act on several levels. The British moves toward politics greatly assisted these Irish steps. Lynch therefore had welcomed the Green Paper, as he had Darlington; but he kept Dublin's desires muted. He wanted to encourage as far as possible political normalization within the North, in particular Whitelaw's maneuvers and the SDLP's responses, without provoking the Protestants. Second and consequently he wanted to put off any serious consideration of unity to a future time when such a course would be more attractive to the Northern loyalists. This could be achieved by an improvement in Southern economic viability (hardly an immediate prospect) and by a visible shift away from the appearance that the Dublin government was dominated by the Roman Catholic Church and was elected by a narrow, parochial, sectarian society. Thus, a variety of politics were sold in part as conducive to a united Ireland. For example, in supporting Senator Mary Robinson's Senate bill legalizing contraception on December 2, Conor Cruise O'Brien indicated that its defeat would be for Northern loyalists "final proof that Home Rule did in fact mean Rome Rule." Third, a real effort would be made in the United States and elsewhere to cut off support for the IRA. The Irish-American diaspora, where old slogans and old assumptions still had great vitality, was the crucial arena, since the United States supplied the major funding and, according to some, arms shipments to the Provisionals. In Ireland, drawing on the lessons and experiences of previous IRA emergencies just before and during World War II and again during the Northern campaign of 1956–62, the movement would be monitored, harassed, jailed if possible, intimidated if not, and always isolated from general opinion. Rioting in Dundalk—the border town where Provo gunmen like Dutch Doherty and Martin Meehan had been much in evidence—had led to republican supporters attacking a police barracks and to the concentration of minds in Dublin. The Provos were increasingly becoming subversives, dangers to the state, never again misguided patriots addicted to the wrong means.

So a meeting between Lynch and Heath was scheduled for London on November 24, where the Taoiseach would announce "a closer meeting of minds than he had ever experienced before." In the meantime Dublin showed every sympathy for Whitelaw's efforts. On October 14 Conor Cruise O'Brien of the Labour Party criticized the SDLP proposals for a New Ireland because they insisted on unity without the agreement of the Protestant community. The effort of the

Republic to appeal to that Protestant community had taken the form of a referendum, introduced October 26 in the Dáil, on deleting two subsections of Article 44 of the Constitution of 1937 giving a special position to the Catholic Church. As Jack Lynch noted, "The specific list of Churches was neither desirable nor necessary and should be deleted. . . . The proposed change would contribute to Irish unity." And so the vote on December 7 was 721,003 to 133,430 in favor of deletion—a triumph of reason, supporters felt. There were opponents, not so much militant republicans as contented citizens like the independent deputy Joseph Leneghan, who in the Dáil argued, "Why should they change the Constitution to suit a crowd of thugs in the North of Ireland? God grant that we shall never see that crowd of thugs come in here." The crowd of thugs that worried the government were not Protestants but Provisionals. On October 25 the Irish Minister for Justice, Desmond O'Malley, was in New York, appealing to Irish-Americans not to give money to NORAID because "much of what is collected gets to the Provisional wing of the IRA." It was that wing the Dublin government was determined to clip.

The moves against the Provisional IRA within the Republic had been a certainty for some time; only the time was in doubt. The adventures of the Littlejohns that ended in October had been in part tolerated for the same reason they had been initiated—to tarnish the IRA. And so other steps began. Dáithí O Conaill had been dismissed from his position as a schoolteacher in Ballyshannon, County Donegal, on September 22. On October 6 the Provisional Sinn Féin headquarters on Kevin Street in Dublin was closed for three months. Final impetus to turn the screw came during the last weekend of October, when men could still taste victory. Provisional Sinn Féin held its annual Ard Fheis in Liberty Hall on Eden Quay in Dublin. There O Conaill insisted that the conditions for another truce remained the acknowledgment by the British government of the right of all the Irish people to determine their own future. This meant British acceptance that the Northern loyalists had no majority, an announcement of intention to withdraw the British troops from Ireland, and finally, an amnesty for all political prisoners and wanted men. These still seemed viable propositions to the delegates who, like the military men, could still taste victory. The old faithful had never experienced the wealth of resources and support, could remember the tiny meetings in cold rooms and the long bleak years of tattered leaflets and a monthly newspaper; and the new recruits, innocent of past difficulties, were heartened by the end of Stormont, the thunder and toll of the armed struggle, the meeting in London, the feeling that they were part of history. And then Mac Stiofáin, creeping past the police, appeared to cap the evening with a rousing speech.

Mac Stiofáin's arrival also annoyed the government and the political establishment, who felt any lingering toleration was a mistake—the IRA man should be in jail—especially because on the same night a twelve-pound bomb was found in Dublin's Connolly Station and simultaneously four firebombs were detonated in hotels across town, although without great damage. Those eager to blame the IRA did so, for setting the bombs, for provoking the bombs, for bringing the war South. Those inclined to conspiracy felt the bombs were clearly placed for just that purpose by the British or the loyalists or even agents of the Dublin government. No matter, the war had again surfaced in the Republic and patience had worn thin. The word was out to find Mac Stiofáin.

His luck ran out on Sunday, November 19, when two Gárdaí detectives spotted him in the Dublin suburb of Malahide, being driven away from an RTE radio interview at the home of Kevin O'Kelly by Joe Cahill. He was stopped, questioned, searched, released, and followed until he made a break from the car. Picked up and held briefly in Malahide barracks he was taken to the Bridewell jail in central Dublin. He had decided immediately to go on a hunger and thirst strike although IRA policy was for commanders to go on a hunger strike only if there was no ground for the charges. Mac Stiofáin's intent was to pressure the government and attract general concern. To add a thirst strike meant that matters would be enormously accelerated since the impact.

Mac Stiofáin's trial indicated the nature of the Republic's response to the IRA underground. His arrest had been a muddle and he was then held, improperly without charge, for eight hours. His trial without jury before three judges under Article 21 of the Offenses Against the State Act for membership in an illegal organization indicated only that the prosecution had not felt the need to prepare a case thoroughly. It was hardly necessary, since the court was inclined to accept any evidence as sufficient for a membership charge. Even evidence would be unnecessary in the newly proposed amendment to the Offenses Against the State Bill of Minister for Justice Desmond O'Malley, which would allow conviction if a police officer merely expressed the opinion that the accused belonged to any illegal organization.

On the first day of the trial, Friday, November 24, Dublin was in turmoil. O'Kelly's interview had led to the dismissal of the RTE Authority, a nine-man board, on the same day. Conor Cruise O'Brien, Labour's spokesman on the North and a well-known liberal, felt that "it was more dangerous to leave these people in the shadows. . . . The autonomy of radio or television was as vital as the freedom of the press or Parliament." Garret FitzGerald of Fine Gael in the Dáil noted that "the real threat to the country was not the IRA but the threat to freedom of speech." On the next day O'Kelly refused to identify Mac Stiofáin's voice on the tape, thus largely destroying the government's case. Though O'Kelly was convicted and sentenced on that Saturday, he was released on bail for three months to appeal on Monday and was ultimately freed on that appeal. That afternoon, while Heath and Lynch met in London, the tape was allowed as evidence. Mac Stiofáin could be convicted because in the opinion of Gárda Kitt the voice was his, although the officer had not heard him speak for over a year and then only four or five times. Additional and at times inaccurate information was given by the arresting officer. No matter; the court operated under special rules and so Mac Stiofáin was convicted of membership and sentenced to six months, a foregone conclusion but ineptly achieved in a manner to outrage many. Mac Stiofáin left the courtroom and in a voice made rusty by his failing health shouted at the judges, "I'll see you in hell before I submit. I'll probably be dead in six days."

Some were not just outraged. On the following day an attempt was made to rescue him from the Mater Hospital. The attempt failed only at the last minute in a tussle between the IRA people, disguised as doctors and orderlies, and the police guards. Mac Stiofáin was flown by military helicopter to the army hospital in the Curragh Camp in County Kildare. There on Tuesday he broke his thirst strike because Father Seán MacManus persuaded him that his death would only provoke unnecessary violence. He continued his hunger strike for fifty-seven days, until ordered to stop by the Army Council; by then much had changed inside and outside the IRA.

Mac Stiofáin was not the only one swept up in the Republic. Maire Drumm, vice-president of Sinn Féin, had been arrested on November 5, and the president O Brádaigh, would be arrested on December 29 and sentenced to six months. Several other prominent republicans were also arrested for membership, including the Derry IRA leaders Martin McGuinness and Joseph McCallion in Ballybofey, County Donegal, the same day O Brádaigh was charged. Thus, at the same time that the British security pressure had tightened in the North during the second half of the year, the IRA guerrilla ocean in the South was being mopped up by the Dublin government.

The major visible step that the Dublin government intended was the amendment to the Offenses Against the State Act that in particular would allow conviction of membership on the opinion of a senior police official. Those who overtly favored the Provisionals were, of course, opposed on pragmatic grounds; but now the militant united-Ireland nationalists in the Dáil had become cautious in views that might appear to support the Provos. Fianna Fáil had been purged of such sentiments and of several members after the Arms Trial, so Fianna Fáil, the real Republican party, had no qualms about a firm law-and-order bill. The opposition was thus clustered around the assault on civil liberties with the few nationalists as a bonus. It was a bonus that if all kept to the book might well mean a defeat for Lynch and a general election.

Some in Fianna Fáil were delighted with the prospect. Some in Fine Gael were considerably less so; but Cosgrave, personally without any great enthusiasm, and the leadership had decided to oppose the amendment. As their spokesman on justice, Patrick Cooney, said, "How can [the Minister for Justice] come into this parliament and ask it to support a bill the like of which can only be found on the statute books of South Africa." So Fine Gael would vote against. So would Labour. So would they all.

While the Dáil was in session in Leinster House in the late afternoon of December 1, two bombs detonated in central Dublin, killing two CIE workers near Liberty Hall and injuring eighty-three others. Cooney said that his party had learned that the perpetrators "were revealed as fellow travelers of the IRA," although why this should be was unclear, as was the source of the accusation, soon forgotten. Cooney then announced, "We have decided to put the nation before party"; accordingly, Fine Gael would abstain, assuring passage of the antiterrorist bill. Those most apt to benefit from the bomb would be the opponents of the IRA. Those, then and later, who in Dublin noted this fact assumed that the bombs had been directly or indirectly a British special operation. One of the cars used in the bombing had a Northern registry and a warning had been telephoned into the *Belfast Newsletter* indicating a Northern origin. It did not matter. At four o'clock on Saturday morning, with Fine Gael abstaining, only Labour and a few independents or dissenters like Fine Gael's Oliver J. Flanagan (perhaps the Dáil's most conservative member) and Eddie Collins opposed the act. There would be additional police powers and an election, with Fianna Fáil running on a law-and-order platform.

Within Fianna Fáil many felt that Lynch had been undercut by the bombs as much as the IRA. He did call for an election on February 5, to be held on February 28. This time Labour and Fine Gael announced that if they won there would be a coalition, a real and principled alternative to Lynch, with a single program. Running against a party that after sixteen years had accumulated resentments and displayed a certain arrogance, the opposition had a real chance at victory. The poll was no revolution. The famous continued to lead the poll. Cosgrave received 13,054 first preference votes and Jack Lynch 12,427, and as a sign of the times, Charles Haughey edged out the party leader with 12,901. His Lazarus-like return to the top had been opposed without effect; in fact, one of President Eamon de Valera's last political acts had been to persuade his old colleague Frank Aiken to retire quietly rather than to withdraw loudly over Haughey's return. So Fianna Fáil won sixty-nine seats again; but only two independents reached the Dáil. Kevin Boland's Aontacht Éireann was wiped out, still another republican party shattered on conventional voting patterns and the national issue. Thus, Fine Gael with 54 and Labour with 19 seats could form a coalition with a majority of two, 72 to 70; Cosgrave became the coalition Taoiseach.*

Lynch took Fianna Fáil and Haughey into opposition. Even with Aiken retired, de Valera's term coming to an end, and some new faces in the Dáil, the Irish arena was much the same. After all de Valera, who had turned ninety on October 14, had been a well-known Dublin nationalist even before 1916, fifty-five years ago, and remained a potent figure despite his blindness and age. The new men might have tastes far from those living in frugal comfort in cozy homesteads, and so Fianna Fáil might be changing, but slowly. And so too Fine Gael under Cosgrave, a sound and honorable man, not without wiles, but without concern for image or display, had those who sought a new and better Ireland.

After the arrest of Seán Mac Stiofáin in November 1972 the IRA was slightly different. First the muted criticism of Mac Stiofáin circulated more freely. He had been too authoritarian, too closed to new ideas, unwilling to delegate authority—the reverse sides of virtues, of course. The feeling was, however, that since the North was fighting the war then the North should lead the IRA and that such leadership should be more flexible. The result was that the Army Council chose Joe Cahill as chief of staff, a Belfast man and not necessarily the one some

---

*The Irish had a complex system of proportional representation with the country divided into three-, four-, and five-member constituencies where the voter could display choice—first preference, second preference, and on down the list of candidates who were elected when the quota was reached—and then have their votes transferred to the next preferences, rewarding or punishing each of the constituency list. The speaker ran unopposed, and in an evenly divided Dáil, finding a member to take the chair was a complex matter. In any case, in the February elections signs may have pointed to a Fianna Fáil loss, but the party members felt that they were the party of governance and took any reverse for any reason as an affront and an opportunity to reconsider the leadership. Given the proximity of the Troubles, this, like most Irish elections, was dominated by personalities and local issues—only in moments of great emotion did the Troubles intrude and then only at a specific polling.

Northerners had in mind; but this proved a moot point. Cahill, as chief of staff, barely had time to monitor the chaos of Mac Stiofáin's arrest and round up the old GHQ staff when a unique interruption occurred.

Word came from Libya that the Libyans were going to make good on their earlier promise of aid and comfort. On June 11, in Tripoli, according to the *Irish Times,* Colonel Qadaffi had announced, if prematurely, "We support the Irish revolutionaries who are fighting Britain. . . . We have strong ties with the revolutionaries to whom we have supplied arms." Qadaffi's people, however, wanted someone who they knew to oversee the shipment from Tripoli and the only one they knew was Joe Cahill. His Belfast news conference after internment had become world famous and so had his face. Short, bald, an innocent's picture of an aging Irish leprechaun, he was easily recognizable and thus was for the Libyans the symbol of the deal to be done. So Cahill hurriedly left for Libya, putting J. B. O'Hagan in charge. Time proved to run as slowly in Libya as in Ireland and Cahill did not appear again until his arrest on the *Claudia* arms ship off Waterford in March 1973.

In the interim the center of the secret army was no longer dominant—the local commanders even more than usual controlled events. And gradually, as the older generation was arrested or retired, the class of '69 began appearing in army councils and on the Army Council. Still in Belfast Séamus Twomey would remain in command until brought down to the Republic in March 1973 to take over as C/S. Brian Keenan and Ivor Bell of the fifties had risen to prominence in Belfast, along with Gerry Adams. Derry had lost McGuinness, McCallion, and the freedom of Free Derry, so that reorganization there was far more severe than in Belfast, where size protected the volunteers, and the leadership provided continuity, even if the British repeatedly announced the arrest of Provisional battalion and brigade officers. In the country both Kevin Mallon and J. B. O'Hagan were in time arrested and leadership shifted to key commanders and smaller active service units. Large nationalist areas were bandit country, no-go zones in all but name, despite increased British army efforts at patrol and penetration. In the country the confrontation was almost a classical rural insurgency including the brutal sectarian murders reminiscent of the Greek-Turk intercommunal slaughter or the Arab attacks on Jews and their retaliation in the Palestine Mandate. In a real sense the IRA in the country remained traditional, very Irish, descendants of the rural agitators, night riders and ribbon gangs of the seventeenth and eighteenth century, except that the faithful, deeply committed to the Republic, had access to ample modern weapons and explosives. The rapid deployment of British anti-insurgency technology, each move punishing the volunteers until a means to cope could be found, and the improvement of British army techniques, gradually eroding IRA opportunity, prevented the dream of liberated zones but by no means made the roads safe or the fields secure.

As 1972 came to a close those who hoped for better days in the new year had to consider the persistence of the IRA, a secret army still confident of victory. The New Year message of the First Battalion of the Derry Brigade announced it was "determined to fight as long as the British maintain their control in Ireland." In 1972 the cost of that control for the British, the Irish, and the island had been enormous. The 1972 death toll alone was 467, and this meant 678 since 1969.

During most of 1972 that most crucial indicator of the intolerable had showed these deaths surpassing those of the automobile.

British army	103
RUC	14
RUC reserve	3
UDR	24
Civilians (includes paramilitaries)	323

Oddly, the number of British soldiers killed exactly equaled the number killed during the Easter Rising by the Irish volunteers, and the number of Royal Irish Constabulary killed in 1916 exactly equaled the number of RUC/RUCR. The twenty-four UDR were a bonus for the IRA. The numbers indicated that 1972 was as important a nationalist year as even the glorious 1916.* There was no telling what 1973 might reveal.

The Ireland of 1972, in particular the North, had experienced the most dramatic and deadly year since the Tan War, one that had begun with some hope and ended after unprecedented civil violence. Some had predicted chaos unless their particular agenda was enacted and some had predicted the course of events with remarkable accuracy. The IRA had escalated their campaign and seen Stormont go and the British government arrive at the bargaining table—all just as foreseen but, perhaps, not with just the results anticipated. The other nationalists had been delighted at Stormont's going, if not at the manner, but had not foreseen just how difficult a continuation of politics almost as usual would be. The Protestants had seen all their fears justified: their assembly gone, their army turned alien, their IRA enemy unchecked, their loyal institutions—the Unionist Party, the RUC and the security system, the Orange Order—and the privileges of domination, shaken, shattered, and denied. For the majority 1972 was a very bad year. And so all those who had foreseen a backlash unless their agenda was adopted had been justified, but in an unexpected way, for there was no descent into civil war, no Protestant militia in the streets; instead there were serial, sectarian murders by unknown killers. The establishment in Dublin also had its fears turned to partial reality, bombs in the street if not war in the North. And London, the major player, the game master, had made the expected moves if at half-speed: Stormont had been taken from the board, detention had been run down if not replaced, security had been elaborated and improved, and rather than any spec-

---

*The official casualty lists are often inaccurate in detail, but these details tend to cancel each other out—everyday murder taken by error as part of the toll of the Troubles, and political killing disguised by intent or oversight as accidental or criminal. The sum is the same. Thus, incidents may be subsumed under natural or criminal statistics by the authorities—an accidental drowning, a disappearance, a car crash—and not linked to the Troubles. Obviously, most of these incidents are closely held data in that those responsible prefer the death to be unlisted or ignored. As well various official casualty totals on occasion do not take into account incidents away from Northern Ireland, even those in the Irish Republic or England, much less on the Continent and further afield. The official Northern Ireland totals, however, are a sound indicator of the level of violence in the prime arena.

tacular initiative Whitelaw had sought to reintroduce the politics of devolution. Everyone had acted as might be expected, and as might be expected the results had been violent and without resolution. It was not, however, a case of the more Irish matters changed the more they stayed the same. History moved on and the North was different.

By design in a few cases, inevitably in others, but almost always haphazardly, the implications and imperatives of the events since 1967 were by 1973 being institutionalized—and to no one's pleasure. One of the persisting assumptions of most of the involved remained that the years of relative civil peace from the establishment of Stormont, years of discrimination, intermittent rebellion, penury and provincialism, were normal, the base line for all projects and comparisons. The North was different, the players were evolving, and their lives had been transformed. Just as the leaders of the IRA were different after Mac Stiofáin's arrest, so too was the entire organization different than it had been when crafted in the first Army Council meeting. The individuals involved had changed, their expectations and assumptions had changed, and their form, even with the old titles, was different. Not all was new, no more than all the others in Ireland were new, but they were different despite themselves.

Without planning or authorization the very demographic structure of Northern Ireland had changed. The greatest European population movement since World War II had occurred behind the back of the authorities for the most traditional of reasons: fear. Each tradition wanted to live with their own, be assured the neighbors would not turn deadly, felt the need for defensive quarters. So family by family, a street here, a mixed development there, the population sorted itself out into blocs and clumps. Some places in the country this was not possible; but even there the token other, even after generations, tended to move away. In Belfast in particular the British army, aliens always in a strange land, soon used maps with orange and green lines, the Prods and the Paddies blocked off so that the patrols would know the denomination of those firing at them, the likely escape routes, the streets to block, the houses to search.

Consequently, each community became more like itself, more concentrated and distilled, less vulnerable to experienced reality, and more open to assumption. Divided societies are very divided even when families live in adjacent plots, even when they shop at the corner store and drink at different tables in the same pub. Complete isolation, however, reinforces stereotypes. And the two communities simultaneously became concentrated; movement outside on the roads, to the center of town, journeys for shopping or on business, became rare. Many of the urban warrens had always been sufficient—the locals would not leave the round of wee store and pub, chapel and playing field but once or twice a year to venture into the center for Christmas shopping or some singular adventure. By 1973 this had become the norm for many working-class families, living within the isolation of ethnic estates or districts.

The comfortable might make their rounds as before (there were few bombs at the golf club or shootings at the zoo) but many less daring and less endowed stayed with their own. Children felt not less secure because of the violence but more, because they never saw an alien, local eyes always watched them, local habits were the only ones, local was safe. And it was in these heartlands, rural or urban, pure, limited in capacities and the quality of life, hedged about by danger and offering security, that the militants found favor and security.

Added to the many existing Irelands, rich and poor and North and South, the six counties of the North had divided into the normal mix of traditions and classes and the new islands of the defensive faithful in the Short Strand or mid-Tyrone, in Woodvale or about Ballymena. In the first province a visitor seldom noticed the new Troubles, passing through villages and districts that seemed unchanged, often as pure as the new havens, often (if affluent) still mixed; there were green fields, golf clubs, shopping centers, and only vestiges of violence. In the second, other Northern Ireland, if in Belfast or Derry, one entered a foreign country with gable ends painted for identity, with flags and banners and sullen men on the corner, with appropriate graffiti and army patrols; while in the country one farm looks like the next, each field as green, so that only the army patrols recognized the signs, the red glow of a sacred heart or an Orange lodge, the UDR lads at the pub or the Celtic crosses in the graveyard. And this spontaneous division, fashioned by fear, appeared irreversible. The Irish had united about their own in reality as well as in their hearts.

Many of the poorer districts had been cut off from any commercial center, had been discarded as customer or producer. And the violence had persuaded many within the government who supplied services, within corporations, or even as individual peddlers of nostrums or balloons, to look elsewhere. After a sufficient number of Ulster buses were burned, there were no more buses to burn, no means of transportation. After every streetlight had been shot out, there was no more light. While there was no money to be made in the sale of candles, there was money to be made in supplying alternative transportation: people had to get to work, to get to the center of the city, to reach a railhead or a pediatrician.

Thus, those with initiative introduced black taxis, tiny, sectarian transport, running mostly on set route. And within the paramilitaries those in charge of finance recognized an opportunity and began to license the black taxis. The result was an example of a new and enormously expanded black economy, always intertwined with the fiscal needs of the various secret armies and vulnerable to criminal penetration under varying banners. The IRA and particularly the UDA and Protestant paramilitaries were not averse to expropriation, extortion, or intimidation as a fiscal means. To these traditional revolutionary means were gradually added a myriad of others to fulfill needs unrequited. Drinking clubs were established and stocked, often by theft, serviced with fruit machines and snacks delivered by friends, and so turned enormous profits for their political owners or in some cases simply under their license. Televisions could be bought, furniture moved, films rented, electrical contracting arranged through the new economy. Overt and ideologically sound cooperatives existed along with protection sold for construction sites. Goods were moved without recourse to the appropriate authorities back and forth across the border, on or off the island, but always to the mutual benefit of the capitalist and his appropriate sectarian authorizers.

Deals were made across political lines and often across the sectarian divide. A great many deals had only the most marginal political content and then not always as expected. The UDA once attempted to open massage parlors, briefly a hot item, under their auspices in several fundamentalist Belfast areas. This was opposed by threat of violence by a group of more moral, everyday criminals who had assumed there was or should be a limit to greed. Thus the IRA, equally moral, became involved in supplying liquor, beer, and cigarettes but was adamantly opposed to hard drugs.* Gradually the funding of secret armies and less secretive political wings shifted from the traditional combination of faithful donation and armed expropriation to the taking of a vast medley of black businesses that replaced the conventional and eluded regulation. Much of this would be ignored by the analysts for a long time, money lacking the romance of blood in insurrectionary matters, until much later the new means were seen as novelties in the funding of terror. Not that the traditional donations of the faithful, special gifts from abroad, and the take from armed robberies were excluded. The finances of the secret armies were different but, like the army, not completely different.

The new local economy, like the new local paramilitary structures, reflected the growing need for self-reliance within the previously passive working-class communities. The Protestants had felt that their betters at Stormont, within the Orange Lodge, in the executive offices of Mackies or Harland and Wolff would see to their interests. The Catholics had no interests and few betters and so could but look South and endure. Thrown on their own resources, the deserted, beyond authority and without defenders, had to cope. Some found a new vocation as entrepreneur or political agitator or battalion intelligence officer. A Belfast republican housewife who would have hesitated to speak up in a pub on Saturday night might find that in time, with practice, she could stand on a platform before a thousand, speak to the point, and generate enthusiasm, conversions, and funds.

Denied by circumstances, many found profitable or useful careers, many not grand but nearly all unexpected. Violence, a decay of centralized authority, and the rise of new structures and organizations bred opportunities. A heretofore mute and inglorious Milton did not surface but editors and writers, bad poets and those who painted murals on gable ends, political instructors and graveside orators did appear in both communities. And so did chemical technicians, operational planners, bookkeepers and sales managers, not to mention the leaders of paramilitary or revolutionary volunteers and the organizers of riot and turmoil. Much was poorly done and haltingly, much existed by lack of alternatives, many could operate because competence and authority had disappeared; and just as a mural of King Billy was not likely to be accepted by the Royal Academy, the black economy or the paramilitary structures lacked elegance, market viability, and proficiency. The new structures and the new talents were, however, real, effective, and often ingenious.

Most of the new wave of skills, exploited talents, and novel structures was not

---

*This position has not stopped a generation of conservative British analysts from suspecting a drug connection, often summoning up wisps of possible evidence just as at every reported and often imagined international terrorist conference an IRA delegation is assumed. In Ireland a grip on the retail liquor distribution is connection enough for any secret army, especially one dominated by a social conservative leadership. Even at their most radical, most IRA volunteers see little point in international contacts unless money or arms are involved, and those who do find virtue in political advocates abroad are usually found within Sinn Féin rather than on the Army Council.

visible, was hardly recognized by the involved. What everyone saw, what touched each, no matter how transient, was the visible fact of the Troubles: the security presence. In an armed struggle one side is almost always invisible, discovered by graffiti traces, smeared posters, riot-used rocks in the gutters, and the sullen natives. The other side, possessed of tanks and planes and the assets of the state, is everywhere on view. In the North, especially in the cities, the great and visible change was the security presence.

Behind the Saracens and patrols, the huge, wire-festooned police barracks, the helicopters and barbed wire, the new institutions and attitudes of the locals were almost hidden. The security presence was the outward and visible sign of turmoil. A whole new architecture of authority was gradually created, often ad hoc and piecemeal, sometimes with enormous care and planning. Architects and security experts were brought in to design new military and police barracks to achieve security and, incidentally, the perception of dominance while the existing structures were elaborated and adapted to thwart attacks. Architects and security experts were brought in to design new housing developments to allow the deployment of armor and the limitation of armor, to cut off access to the others and limit the free flow of the subversives. The centers of the cities were hedged about with fences and gates and bright lights. On the night of Monday, November 6, 1972, the army without warning had moved into Belfast and erected an eight-foot-tall wire fence with forty-one permanent gates: People and so subversives would now be funneled through the inspectors, searched before arriving in the center, searched at each store, searched on the way out of a zone without parking and so without car bombs. In contrast the only sign of the IRA in the city was the boarded windows, evidence of failed security. Thus, anyone could see the layer of security, the no-stopping zones along border roads, the patrol emerging as from a war film in the country, the Para with a rifle darting between children and over back garden walls.

Supplementing the visible, a vast complex of procedures, overt and covert, had evolved from needs and failures. Like the surface of a pond suddenly freezing, the North found its governance transformed by security needs. In a real sense the old Stormont system authorized by the Special Powers Act gave the Minister of Home Affairs enormous powers as much to intimidate as to deploy. With Stormont gone, these powers had proven faulty and the security procedures of the past inadequate. With the arrival of Diplock's report, a new judicial system—directed against subversives, buttressed by existing practice, by the new prisons and procedures, and by the evolving and at times unauthorized tactics of the police, army, and intelligence—was added to Northern reality. A judicial machine was created that could remove the almost certainly guilty without recourse to traditional safeguards and procedure. Billboards urged potential informers to "Ring Belfast 652155 in Complete Confidence." The guilty, the subversives, could be identified, pursued, captured, and interrogated by novel means, a mix of technological capacity, tactical innovation, applied experience, and simple need. The competing and complex bureaucracies hampered the process, as did the loyalty to old norms, the political and moral cost of complete expediency, and the cunning of the vulnerable.

Yet the result was a new means to impose order and authority. And in time such a system became conventional: Bombers had their own ID numbers when they called warnings, informers knew the proper confidential telephone line to betray their neighbors, guilty suspects could anticipate entry into a system that would deposit them in an H-Block prison for long periods, shoppers knew what to do in a bomb scare, motorists during a roadblock search, hospitals after a riot. There were papers to fill out, forms to sign, lawyers to hire, roads to avoid, and questions not to answer. And all this, bit by bit, was absorbed and adjusted to local need. No tourist could see the H-Block system or even the fire lanes in the new estates any more than he could see the informers or the instructions on the yellow card that allowed a soldier to shoot. But unlike the other new institutions, security had the dominant visible face—the army helicopter over a country road, the stern-faced men at the edge of the waiting room at the airport, the police with submachine guns were indicators of a new and seemingly permanent Ireland. It was an Ireland only recognized as alien when the plane lands at Heathrow in peaceful England or the border is crossed going south on the Belfast-Dublin roadway and there are no more patrols or road blocks.

This new Ireland hardly appeared on day one of 1973; rather, it was the gradual adaption of a Western society to persisting political violence. In fact on day one of 1973, when Ireland and the United Kingdom entered the Common Market, entered Europe, the news from the North was, as ever, unsavory. A Catholic worker at the Rolls-Royce factor at Dundonald, Belfast, was shot and killed in his car in the first sectarian murder. A young couple were found shot dead near Muff on the Donegal and Derry border. The UVF complained about the treatment of prisoners. And Elizabeth McKee, a Catholic, became the first woman detainee under the new Detention of Terrorists Order of November 1972. There were Northern Irish names on the Queen's annual New Year's Honours List and a complaint to the commissioner for complaints about sectarian favoritism.

For the Northern Ireland Office, however, it was not just another awful January 1 but the beginning of a year that would be used to return conventional politics to the province. And despite the IRA's armed struggle, loyalist assassins, and the residue of the past, there was real hope that a corner had been turned during the five months of Motorman. And almost at once there was some indication that the horror and outrage generated by the sectarian murders had produced reconsideration. On January 4 a UDA statement warned all persons engaged in sectarian murders to stop now. Thomas Herron, the vice-chairman, unfortunately added that such murderers would be "eliminated," indicating that his paramilitaries had hardly given up killing as a convention. The UDA self-denial was a positive move, though hardly a reversal of form. On January 29 two young Catholics were shot dead on the Falls Road, one a boy of fourteen. The next day the IRA killed Francis Smith, accusing him of involvement in one of the previous day's murders. Tommy Herron immediately announced that the UDA consequently no longer wished to try to restrain Protestant extremists.

In fact during 1973 politics was not as usual in the province, for the IRA's campaign continued (albeit at a lower level), the sectarian murders and tit-for-tat killings were an irregular constant, and the loyalists again attacked the army and at times the police with fatal results. And there were still riots, ferment and tumult, threats, arsons, and violent crimes in various names and often simply for profit. There were accidental explosions and no-warnings bombs, malicious vandalism, and random violence. There was a steady toll of dead and maimed for all sorts of unpleasant reasons—in little over a year after January 1972 the Provos had lost thirty-nine volunteers through own-goal, premature explosions. And the aftereffects of the violence, the scarred and damaged civilians, the lost businesses and ruined careers, the lives warped or ruined, provided only dim, background murmurs to each new atrocity, every fresh murder. All of this violence, the Muzak of the North, was an offstage chorus to the party maneuvers, to the polls and programs, to the normal of political science texts, to Whitelaw's efforts.

Before long there were, however, factors to encourage Whitelaw. On January 11 Faulkner told the Unionists it was to Ulster's advantage to work with the British government and that the idea, proposed by Taylor, of some sort of loyalist-Catholic agreement on independence, was a nonstarter. On February 13 it was revealed that Craig, Taylor, Hume, and Ivan Cooper had met at Taylor's house in December; more important, the involved insisted that such a meeting was proper. In fact on February 15 the SDLP invited the United Loyalist Council to meet for discussions. The meeting did not take place, yet the possibility indicated a growing sense of unionist realism. And the SDLP was doing its share, looking forward to meeting with Craig, produced a program published in full-page advertisements in the *Irish News,* for the minority, and the *Newsletter,* for the majority. The real attention, however, was to the border poll, an unwelcome interruption for the nationalists, a necessary ritual for the unionists, a reward of Whitelaw's political process. Like much in Ireland, the event did not occur as planned.

The IRA had not simply been idly detonating bombs while Whitelaw beavered away at an accommodation that excluded them and their dreams. The IRA Army Council had decided to act upon the flow of political events by an operation with several purposes. Bombs would be set off in London on the day of the border poll, thus bringing the war home to an England apt to neglect Irish reality but also, and more to the point, indicating that the Whitelaw process was fundamentally at fault. There could be no "progress" without Irish consent, without involvement of the movement; the British would pay a prohibitive price along the way in a process that could only fail. The idea of bombs in England was always about. It had been an IRA option for generations, with roots in the Fenian era. In June 1972 Mac Stiofáin and the Army Council had discussed the matter, long before a border poll had been planned.

In general Mac Stiofáin was against "stunts" and had been unconvinced there was any need to operate in England. He was also keenly aware of the difficulty such operations posed. In 1953 along with Cahal Goulding and Manus Canning he had been arrested during the getaway of an IRA raid on an armory in the Felstead School in Essex and had spent the years to 1959 in prison. In 1972 the British Special Branch, originally established because of the Irish problem in the Fenian days, had thoroughly monitored Sinn Féin and Irish nationalist activity in Great Britain. There were few Provo IRA sleepers like Noel Jenkinson, who had managed the Officials' explosion at Aldershot in February 1972. Unlike the American diaspora, the Irish immigrants sought to disappear into the environment as rapidly as possible without stressing their Celtic connections.

Those loyal to the Provos were known and those not well known could not be trusted. This meant that British operations would have to be initiated with Irish volunteers dispatched for particular missions. In June at an Army Council meeting, Mac Stiofáin seriously contemplated a wave of sleepers sent over to open a new front but nothing came of the concept.

During 1972 the matter was explored. An advocate was James Brown, a twenty-six-year-old of the Belfast Brigade staff who had been released from the Lagan Valley Hospital by a team led by two young women. Brown, thus familiar with the capacities of the Belfast people, urged bombs for London planted by a special team, unknown in the North or England, that would be on the Aer Lingus flight to Dublin as the explosions occurred. Ultimately, with the loss of momentum after Motorman and with the prospect of politics as usual, in 1973 the operation was finally authorized by the Army Council.

As one of the volunteers, twenty-two-year-old Dolours Price (in charge of the team) noted, it was a highly structured operation. "A short, sharp shock, an incursion into the mainland, would be more effective than twenty car bombs in any part of the North. An operation that would destroy property, cause no death or injury, and gain worldwide publicity for the cause seemed to me like a good idea at the time." The result was much, if not exactly, as intended. The eleven involved took over four stolen cars, which were resprayed, equipped with false license plates, and loaded with explosives. On March 8 the cars were driven from an underground parking lot at Dolphin Square and by 8:30 in the morning were parked outside the Metropolitan Police headquarters at New Scotland Yard, the central army recruiting office at Whitehall near Trafalgar Square, the British Forces Broadcasting Services building in Dean Stanley Street, near Smith Square closer to Westminster, and the Central Criminal Court at Old Bailey. The bomb in the Ford Corsair at New Scotland Yard was discovered by a passing policeman and defused. When the warning was phoned in to the London *Times* the bomb in Dean Stanley Street was defused. The other two detonated on schedule, at the same time that eleven of the IRA team were picked up at Heathrow, including Dolours Price and her sister Marion. A combination of good police work, information filtered through from Belfast the previous day, and luck resulted in the arrests at the last minute, with three volunteers already on the plane.

The two bombs caused physical damage, as planned, but also killed one man and injured 180 people. The first detonated in the parking lot near the recruiting office and shattered windows in a pub, the Agriculture Ministry, and government offices along Whitehall. The other went off as police cleared people from the front of the Old Bailey. The British, as anticipated, were outraged and indignant that the capital had been bombed, civilians put at risk, the Irish wars brought to Trafalgar Square and the Strand. On the evening news and in the next day's newspapers, the border poll was neglected. The results, with the nationalists abstaining, were not a surprise: 591,820 votes for union with Great Britain and 6,464 for a united Ireland, 57.45 percent of the electorate voting. So the IRA bombs were the real news. And even the loss of the entire team would later put Dolours and Marion Price in a position to play a significant and effective role on hunger strike.

The London bombings were unusual not because there were casualties when not intended or because the volunteers paid heavily but because there was a tight cause-and-effect strategy in place. The operation had been planned in advance to alter perceptions and to achieve nonmilitary results. When the bomb had gone off in Aldershot after Derry's Bloody Sunday the linkage was perceived, not actual. Most operations are not as carefully crafted as academics or analysts, innocent of the very limited capacities and inherent incompetence of the underground, are inclined to assume. The March 8 car bombs, however, were a classic and effective example of strategic planning if not of tactical or technical skill.

The London bombs did not alter the fact that the border poll had taken place, had reassured the loyalists without unduly alienating the minority. Whitelaw had observed the polling and said, "I . . . was struck not only by the determination of the Protestants to vote but also by their obvious satisfaction in doing so."* Whitelaw saw loyal citizens pleased to exercise their democratic rights, pleased to make clear their loyalty. He saw what he chose, as did most in the Irish game. The minority saw more clearly that the voters could symbolically display their proper power over the others—voting as an Orange march, voting to indicate domination. Still, for Whitelaw's purpose the loyalists had received a treat first and would now be expected to become involved in real elections as the province moved on, bombs or no bombs, rituals or not, toward real elections and a devolved assembly.

Above the music of violence, the political news grew louder through each step: the White Paper of March 1973, the May 30 district council elections, and then the Assembly elections on June 28. The pace might have originally seemed hectic to the British but appeared lethargic to those Northern politicians eager for an accommodation. There was too much time for a negative majority to form, too much time for the men of violence to intervene. So the months after March 1973 were crammed with efforts to cherish and protect the center—and the center, if reluctantly, found sufficient common ground. Faulkner, Fitt, and Oliver Napier of the Alliance working with Whitelaw and his permanent secretary, Frank Cooper, persevered. It was not easy. The White Paper was released on March 20.

The three basics remained. The British connection was guaranteed through majority opinion, as the border poll had made apparent. The Irish connection was just real enough to provide the SDLP with a fig leaf in a Council of Ireland to discuss relevant matters. And finally an Assembly of seventy-eight members that would have committees whose chairmen would be members of the executive (i.e., share power). The Assembly would not yet have control of security or judicial matters still left to the Northern Ireland Office, whose secretary would replace the governor of Northern Ireland. A new loyalist group—Craig, Paisley, Orr and representatives of the Orange Order, UDA, and LAW—called for defeat of the IRA, the rejection of the Council of Ireland, and control of the RUC by the Assembly, which would have full parliamentary representation: no White Paper as it stood. None of the organizations entirely trusted the others or agreed on what they wanted—integration or independence, another Stormont or a majority concession to get an Assembly—but all agreed on what they did not want: a sellout to London, Catholics as partners, an end to majority domination.

*William Whitelaw, *The Whitelaw Memoirs* (London: Aurum, 1989), pp. 108–109.

On March 27 the Unionist Council of the Unionist Party, meeting in Ulster Hall, Belfast, defeated by 381 to 231 votes with about 100 abstentions a motion to reject the White Paper. In effect, the Unionist Party had split, but at least with Faulkner holding a majority of sorts. The hard men, Taylor, Craig, and the rest, not to mention Paisley, had not been seduced by the offer of real rather than negative politics. The base line for everyone was the White Paper published on March 28, a natural growth from Darlington and the Green Paper and London's intentions molded by the Northern needs. Alliance was for accommodation at nearly any cost. SDLP really had no place else to go as the party of the minority and would thus make concessions if driven. The official Unionists around Faulkner almost from the first had decided that a devolved assembly was crucial—something was better than nothing and nothing might be a disaster.

Faulkner in 1967 had been one more hard man on the benches of Unionism, with a greater ambition than his social station (the manufacture of shirts does not give entry to the gentry) might have then warranted. By 1973 he had recognized that the province needed politics that would only be permitted if the minority was involved. Without politics the province was vulnerable to all sorts of unilateral London moves, and like everyone else in the North, he did not trust the London establishment. So the official Unionists would go with the White Paper and try to attract all unionists. That the loyalists were divided on ultimate aims played into the hands of Whitelaw and Faulkner. The fundamentalist leaders, Craig and Paisley and Taylor and the new men of the UDA and LAW and the old Unionists like West—even Enoch Powell, the new loyalist sage—did not trust one another politically. They all spent considerable effort in protecting their flanks, watching the rear, rather than testing the slippery pole of power, which meant that Faulkner faced a quarreling dissent. Dissent was the norm in the province, crafted into a political art form by Paisley. Everyone knew what they did not want, but only Faulkner had a bit of paper with exactly what he wanted—as much as possible, given what London could afford.

London could afford more. The SDLP would have to stop dreaming of a united Ireland or a serious institutional connection, at least during the run-up to the Assembly elections. The SDLP would have to give up its support of the rent-and-rates strike called after internment. As always this was a symbolic matter, for the strike had never actually involved a majority of the Catholic, state-built, council houses and had only been used by nationalists and republicans as an example of people power and support for the politics of the moment. The high point had been in December 1971 when 24.9 percent of the Catholic council households had participated but had declined to 16.6 percent by June 1973 and would continue to decline. Nevertheless, the SDLP had to prove its respectability, largely to ease Faulkner's problems. And so it did but not publicly until December 28. The problems did not, however, disappear. And it was a long time between the proclamation of the White Paper and the local elections.

On March 30 Craig announced the formation of a new party, the Vanguard Unionist Progressive Party, to contest the elections. Supporting the new group were representatives of the UDA, including Herron, LAW, and DUP—a temporary allegiance for Paisley, Taylor, Harry West, and John Laird. Craig would resign from the Ulster Unionist Council but some would remain still opposed to

367

the White Paper. In fact the election campaign increasingly shaped up as a referendum on the proposal: a tryout in the local elections and then the Assembly vote in June. There were shifts, defections, resignations around the fringes, but essentially the major groups remained static: Assembly unionists and loyalists opposed to the Assembly, the SDLP for the minority, and NILP or Alliance for the middle. The others boycotted or played no significant electoral role. For observers the problem was sorting out the individual loyalist positions in the plethora of new configurations: VULC (Vanguard Unionist Loyalist Coalition) and DULC (Democratic Unionist Loyalist Coalition), the West Belfast Loyalist Coalition and the various independent candidates along with the official and unofficial Unionists and the reluctant DUP. It was very confusing. On the other side Bernadette Devlin and Frank McManus set up the Unity Movement to contest the local elections—bad news for the SDLP. The IRA would not play, of course, and at Easter the message was that their struggle would be brought to a successful conclusion "in our day." Certainly British security sought to see that the day never came and during the campaign took steps to reassure the loyalists if not to ruin the IRA. Kennedy of Republican Labour in Belfast complained that the troops were harassing, and threatened to boycott the elections. On April 21 McGurran of Official Sinn Féin, advocates of a truce and elections, was returned to Belfast after he landed at the Birmingham airport, and at Heathrow in London the Provisional Sinn Féin's Joe Clarke, ninety-two and a veteran of 1916, crutches and all, was refused entry and put on a Dublin-bound plane: He was absolutely delighted.

The militant loyalists wanted a good deal mre than explosions. To scotch rumors of an end to the RUC, Chief Constable Sir Graham Shillington, sent a personal letter to all 4,300 members insisting that the force would stay in being. All the maneuvers, however, did not placate those who really wanted everything and saw the Assembly as an evil temptation offered by Perfidious Albion. After all, the Pope had even made it clear that he supported the White Paper in his appeal for peace on April 22. In fact Paisley, uncertain as to the most effective wrecking tactic, nearly had his DUP boycott the elections but at the last participated.

The result of the local election on May 30, the first since 1967 and the first since 1925 to use proportional representation, greatly encouraged Whitelaw and the moderates, despite the complexity of the returns and the difficulty of assigning proper ideological positions to the Unionists. There were 1,222 candidates for 526 seats in 26 councils and no local issue was as significant as the big constitutional questions. The final count gave the Unionists 210 seats, DUP 13, and other loyalists 68; the SDLP won 82, Alliance 63, NILP 4, and the others were scattered: Nationalists 4, Republican Clubs (i.e., Official Sinn Féin) 7, Irish United 6, Independents 27, and no party 32, with a late election to come in one district. Not all the Unionists elected favored an Assembly but the results were for Whitelaw quite satisfactory. Alliance had done particularly well and Faulkner had not been denied. Thus the Darlington process passed another obstacle toward the crucial Assembly vote on June 28.

For much of the media, foreign and domestic, for those concerned with political events in the North, for the experienced observers and the thousands involved the renewed political process, the campaign for the Assembly dominated the news. Insurrectionary violence was loud, bloody, and often lethal, but boringly constant. Few beyond the involved grew excited about the campaign to restrict the use of rubber bullets, the death of a four-year-old shot in army-gunmen crossfire while playing in his back garden in Finaghy Park North, Belfast, the bomb in the printing works of the *Tyrone Democrat* newspaper, the Tartan Gang attack on a disco, an explosion in Bangor, or a rocket attack on the army post near the Vere Foster School in Ballymurphy. The Troubles, except for the victims, the gunmen, and the passersby, had become distant, statistics. On June 1 the death total reached 808, 130 since January 1, an improvement over the previous year. Since Motorman more than five hundred persons had been convicted and sent to prison for terrorist offenses but there seemed ample new recruits.

The secret armies continued as before. The UDA was racked in early June by further schism and expulsions and the murder of Michael Wilson, brother-in-law of Tommy Herron, and more trouble with their police and their army. There was another shoot-out in East Belfast on the night of June 10. The same day ten thousand Provo supporters gathered to defend the just war at the Bodenstown commemoration heard McGuinness, just released from a Southern prison, advocate the IRA position. On the same Sunday, the Pope called for peace with justice and Paisley claimed that the British intended to disband the RUC. And the bombs continued going off across the province even as each party produced on schedule an election manifesto. Much more than the local elections, the Assembly vote would make possible devolution. As the former Labour Minister James Callaghan said, "It is the majority who have got to decide their future. If they decide to wreck the Assembly and don't make it work, then I think the politicians, the people, and everyone in Britain will say—'Let's have a fresh look at the whole business.'" Harold Wilson agreed about an agonizing reappraisal if the Assembly failed, for the elections were a watershed in the history of the province.

On Thursday, June 28, a sunny summer day, the polls opened for the Northern Ireland Assembly elections throughout the province at 8:30. Bombs had already exploded in Magherafelt, County Derry, and Toomebridge, County Antrim. During the day a mortar bomb was fired at the polling station at the Kelvin Street School, Roden Street, Belfast. It was otherwise a quiet day. The lord mayor and members of the city council, MPs and senators, took time off to attend the funeral of Councillor Paddy Wilson, a forty-year-old Catholic who, along with a twenty-nine-year-old Protestant woman, Irene Andrews, had been stabbed to death in his car outside Belfast on the Highstown Road the previous Tuesday night. Polling ended at eight in the evening.

The results were not all that Whitelaw had hoped but, like the whole process since Darlington, were sufficient to continue. As everyone had realized, the key was the number of pro-Assembly Unionists. The nationalists and the center could be predicted but not exactly how the loyalists would vote—no one had quite figured out how they had voted in the council elections and there was no past record. The loyalists had never had to choose between ways into the future, heretofore charted out by the elite, supported or tolerated by all in the name of defense.

Of the 78 seats at stake the SDLP won 19, the Alliance 8 (a disappointment), and the Northern Ireland Labour Party 1. No Nationalist won and both the Republican Clubs and Republican Labour did poorly. There were thus 28 votes for power sharing; the Loyalist Coalition dominated by Paisley and Craig took 18 seats while 10 Unionists who were anti-Faulkner won, for a negative total of 38. Faulkner's Unionists won 22, less than the anti-Assembly loyalists, less than the nonloyalist parties, but enough to assure a power-sharing majority. Unless Faulkner could attract some of the anti-Assembly Unionists any future executive would depend on a minority of loyalist representatives. Still and all an Assembly was possible. The totals were as follows:

Official Unionist	24 seats	29.3% of total vote
Unionists	8	8.5
Democratic Ulster Loyalist Coalition	8	10.8
Vanguard Ulster Loyalist Coalition	7	10.5
West Belfast Loyalist Coalition	3	2.3
SDLP	19	22.1
Alliance	8	9.2
Northern Ireland Labour Party	1	2.6

Nearly all the famous names—Hume, Taylor, Fitt, Devlin, Currie, Harry West, and John McQuade—won Assembly seats. James A. Kilfedder in North Down, who had quarreled with Faulkner, led the poll with 20,684, while Faulkner received 16,287 in South Down and was elected on the first count. Paisley, elected on the first count in North Antrim with 14,533, came well ahead of Craig, 8,538, elected on the third count in the same constituency. Napier of Alliance and Bleakley of the NILP running in East Belfast got in on the eighteenth count as did Ardill in South Antrim. The individual statistics, except as indicators of local machines and popularity, did not really matter. What mattered was the stability of an Assembly directed by an executive that did not represent the loyalist majority, not even a "unionist" majority. It would be power sharing with a vengeance but it would be power sharing.

Whitelaw, the Northern Ireland Office, the Conservative government, London could feel enormous relief at the return of conventional politics to the province. Darlington to the Assembly election had been a long, arduous trek under constant harassing attack, a journey that displayed all the famed British political skills and patience and a grasp of the importance of symbols and perceptions in Irish matters—still largely mysterious. There was the assumption, not unwarranted given British experience, that the worst was over; a devolved assembly with power shared by both traditions sealed in overarching guarantees, the real with Great Britain and the symbolic with the Council of Ireland, was a return to the Stormont base line of March 1972 with the grievances corrected. The turmoil and the violence of 1972 was aberrant; British-style politics was the only reasonable option. In point of fact, the perceptions of the Irish players had changed. A reformed Stormont or a border poll would not put the genie back in the bottle.

The majority had failed to articulate and so to institutionalize the fundamentalist desire to fashion a governance that supplied the same psychic returns as the Stormont system. The hard men and the decent wanted reassurance, wanted admiration and a sense of worth, wanted personal pride and some unchallengeable power, items not easy to include in a White Paper or Green and items severely eroded over the previous several years. The loyalists felt betrayed and shamed and denied. The proper and decent in particular sought vindication without apology and without compromise. The Assembly did not do this. Stormont could not be resurrected. No politicians from the pragmatic Faulkner to the utopian advocates of independence offered an invigorating alternative. This boded ill for those who sought adaption to an Assembly arising from British assumptions about the nature of politics. Stormont had not been an unreformed, devolved assembly but an outward symbol of a system assuring the benefits of domination to a beleaguered but saved people. The new Assembly was about parties and votes and committees and, worse, compromise. It did not address psychic needs or eroded symbols or a people's worth.

As for those of the other persuasion, they could no longer be sold scraps or shunted aside. In 1967 the minority accepted their inferiority, a real and visible inferiority in education and profession, in prospects and housing, in most measures but ultimate salvation. They were the victim of history and their earthly salvation lay in history and in a future Dublin Free State. Events, year by year, had changed this. The civil rights campaign, not the results but the mobilization, and the IRA armed struggle, not the goal or the cost but the awesome turbulence, had shattered the unionists. Then the frustrations and failures of the majority, their schisms and splits and even their ludicrous attempts with the Vanguard to mimic in 1912, and with the UDA to copy the republicans, had left no single route into the future. Their provincial Catholic enemies seemingly had no such problem. Their new nationalist aspirations for the future were welded onto past grievance, and created an enormously effective mix that drew substance from not only the IRA armed struggle but also from the small gains of the SDLP. What the majority wanted was more. What the IRA wanted was everything. What the SDLP would take was something. What did the unionists want except the past back?

It was in fact a halting grasp of the new minority posture that tended to infuriate the majority, no longer dominant in their own eyes by right or by law, no longer sure of direction, no longer even sure what to defend. The British, however, were confident that the political process would provide sufficient opportunities for power and prestige, would erode majority anger and anguish and alleviate minority grievances. Dublin hoped so too; Dublin feared the spread of disorder and violence, longed for no trouble or Troubles at all. Thus the Assembly would have a great deal riding on it—and a great many eager to wreck it and with it convention, compromise, and concession.

12

Power Sharing and Protestant Power, the Northern Ireland Assembly to the General Strike: June 1973–May 1974

"He That Is Not With Me Is Against Me . . ."
Matthew 12:30

As usual the results of the Assembly elections were read by all the observers as so desired. And the winners read their wishes writ big. Merlyn Rees, speaking for London as well as the Labour Party, said, "There is not room for maneuver on power sharing at all. On this all parties at Westminster are agreed." After all, the center, if not the pro-Assembly Unionists, had won a majority. Still, the anti–White Paper loyalists of all shades had their moments as well—Jim Kilfedder, who opposed the White Paper, in North Down polled 20,684 first-preferences with a quota for election only 7,682. Paisley, with 15,553 votes and a quota of 8,907 in East Antrim, felt that in general and in his district in particular one could hear "the voice of freeborn Ulstermen saying to Messrs. Heath and Wilson, you will not push us into a united Ireland."

Then, again, others heard other voices. Hume's analysis was that "the IRA have now heard the voice of the people and it is time they listened." Brian Faulkner with 16,287 votes and a quota of 8,005 agreed in that the voters "have rejected violence. . . . This is very good."

Faulkner, as prospective Prime Minister in the new Assembly, had to worry about both his flanks while Hume (12,596 and a quota of 8,308) focused largely on his major competition. The Nationalist Party had died, the Northern Ireland Labour Party had returned to the wings, and only the Alliance Party with a mere 9.2 percent of the votes could drain the SDLP's domination of the minority constituency. The IRA boycott had not been effective and Kennedy of Republican Labour had run poorly in Belfast. The SDLP could rest content.

Most of the loyalists who played claimed to have won, or have won as much as could be expected. Yet, a few found that the political game was unkind: Tommy Herron of the UDA running as a Vanguard candidate in Belfast lost big. And some of his colleagues felt electoral politics should not be played at all, that he had delusions of grandeur. His paramilitary career came to a mysterious end when his body was found beside Glen Road, Drumbo, outside Belfast on September 16. No one claimed the murder and the RUC eventually assumed some personal motive. There had been one attempt before at his home on June 15 that killed his bedridden brother-in-law, Michael Wilson. There had been anger that Herron had the UDA providing protection to East Belfast pub owners—a Mafia-type operation according to authorities. In fact, some new full-time UDA leaders, like Andy Tyrie, thirty-two, a former machine setter in Mackies foundry from the Shankill, quiet behind scholarly steel-rimmed spectacles, hardly the image of a gunman, were as concerned with internal reform—easing out the rude killers—as with politics. Yet Tyrie, who became a familiar figure in Belfast, and others felt the UDA could and did have the power to act on events and to confront the British. They could not, however, assure paramilitary uniformity.

There was often trouble in analyzing loyalist killings, since discipline was so spotty and feuds so vicious, but those who would urge political means often alienated their own. Many loyalists were outraged at the radical ideas of some in the UVF or the talk of federalism or independence. Many wanted only to "defend." Others wanted more but lacked direction. Like the republicans before them, they found power hard to translate into votes. The division between shooters and populists had by 1973 become a Protestant paramilitary constant.

With the Provos the military still dominated the movement. So those who had not played in the election simply continued a different game: On June 30 three bombs went off in Derry and later that evening a bomb exploded at a UDA club in Buller Street, Belfast, injuring forty-seven people. Since the first of the year, 160 people had been killed, including 105 civilians. The Provos were hardly to blame for them all but their campaign remained lethal to the security forces, the volunteers, to bystanders and the innocent.

The election results (however read), the visible political process, the high-profile support of the Assembly in London, and the general desire for pause gave heart to those who wanted peace and quiet. On July 2 a paid advertisement in the *Irish News* by the CCDC told the IRA that "the crying priority today is peace." The real push for peace came with the political talks held the same day in Belfast between Whitelaw and Faulkner, Fitt, Paisley, Craig, Robert Cooper of Alliance, and David Bleakley of the NILP, and in London between Heath and Cosgrave. Later Cosgrave told a Conservative club that any push for a united Ireland would "dangerously exacerbate tensions and fears." He stressed that unity would wait and that Dublin would use that time to enact measures making any eventual unity more attractive.

This advocacy of internal reform was one of the major forces of the Irish response to the Troubles just as Whitelaw's tactical discussions in the political trenches made up one of Britain's. The drive toward normalizing the province's politics and isolating the gunmen was more visible, easier to grasp for all the involved: It was a very British response—reintroduce muddle and London fashions. The Irish position expressed by Cosgrave was different, a shift, an end to a half century of agitation and oft-expressed grievance, a willingness to wait on the future, to wait a long time while conditions were altered to unity's advantage.

A united Ireland thus remained a national dream but increasingly a distant one.

Cosgrave claimed there was no point in turning the majority in Northern Ireland into a disgruntled and alienated minority within a united Ireland. Increasingly, this Dublin position was not postured. Increasingly, those within the Irish establishment recognized that unity meant more than an island one color on the map. Associated with this shift was a rising grasp of Northern realities. Every time a bomb went off or an SDLP delegation came into town, trailing angst and alien attitudes, minds were concentrated. The North was not only different but also not as desirable. Mostly the Dublin government, Coalition or Fianna Fáil, wanted and had wanted for some time an end to turbulence and an end to the paramilitaries.

Yet neither the London conservative establishment (not all within the Tory Party) nor most of the Northern majority accepted the shift. As long as Dublin did not all but daily swear No-No-Never to One Ireland then the Irish nationalists had not really changed their agenda or priorities. It was obviously not to the advantage of many loyalist politicians and paramilitaries in the North to recognize that the ravenous beast to the South was no longer hungry. For the loyalists the Southern tiger must be real, not paper, and so no late conversion was convincing. And most, in fact, were honestly so convinced. Cosgrave was no different from Lynch or de Valera or the men of 1916, rebels, Irish nationalists. All were Catholic rebels who once in power had fashioned an Irish Catholic state complete with undisguised Rome rule.

Within the United Kingdom it was often easier and more congenial to assume that Dublin at least tolerated a secret army descended from their own faith and fathers, to assume that Northern problems, British problems, had arisen in great part in Éire. Many in the London establishment assumed Dublin could do far more in taming the men of violence and did not do so from grudging sympathy. So, over and over, the British chose to heed the devices and desires of their own hearts—the Irish in Dublin were at least in part behind Irish problems in the six counties. Cosgrave, a decent, almost dour man, deeply moral, a man of another generation, sought on that Monday to reach across to those whose views, if anything, were more radical than his own. Many listened and few heard. In Irish matters the secondary benefits of the past had takers in London as well as Ballymena and the Ardoyne.

In Belfast, with the elections passed and the anti-Assembly loyalists still divided, perhaps in disarray, Whitelaw had to shape the successful candidates into a devolved parliament where power would be shared. The details were enormously important, each concession bearing symbolic weight; and the involvement, as constructive critics, of the anti-Assembly loyalists was equally delicate and important. Just a Faulkner-Fitt majority might not serve if the cost was too great for either to persist or if the opposition engaged in wrecking tactics. And the anti–White Paper politicians had repeatedly threatened to wreck any Assembly.

One unstated asset for Whitelaw was that the players had, because of events in recent years, become inured to the din and clash of visible violence that shook the province. Imperceptibly the noise of the IRA's armed struggle, the revelations of more sectarian murders, the visible presence of the security forces, the ruins, burned-out buses, the graffiti, the ugly face that attracted the media and repelled the tourists, had faded into the everyday.

When Martin McGuinness spoke at the Wolfe Tone commemoration at Bodenstown on Sunday, June 10, with the present and past chiefs of staff in the crowd, Séamus Twomey and Seán Mac Stiofáin (Joe Cahill, arrested off the *Claudia,* was in Portlaoise Prison), he spoke with confidence of a victory in a just war. Once again there was a huge hosting, perhaps as many as ten thousand, and once again, a general confidence that the war could be won this year or next. The older republicans were still awed by the transformation of the old tattered conspiracy into a real secret army. The IRA was besieged by recruits, supplied by the American connection and occasional international contacts, funded by the diaspora, by foreign friends, by the old means and the new Northern black economy. And above all, the Northern volunteers had grown competent, effective, experienced, and sure of victory.

There was very little IRA concern, even privately, at the limitations imposed after Motorman, at the decline of all violence indicators from shots fired on an operation to casualties inflicted, and at the growing British intelligence and anti-insurgency capacity. None at the top seemed unduly concerned that the center had been adrift since Mac Stiofáin's arrest in November the previous year and that Twomey had barely begun to reassert control. There was then and later little dismay at the toll brought about by arrests. Mac Stiofáin, O Brádaigh, McGuinness and McCallion from Derry, Richard Behal, the movement's foreign policy specialist from Kilkenny, and Seán Meehan from Belfast were in the first wave. Then a tidy toll of commanders, particularly in the North, was arrested, with the loss during 1973 of key Belfast men like Gerry Adams and Brendan Hughes and then Kevin Mallon and O'Hagan from the country. McGuinness would be rearrested in 1974 and sentenced to a year. The movement was used to arrests, to volunteers shifting their arena of struggle into the prison. In fact, the movement was so accustomed to the bad old days that even the harder times of 1973 seemed heady. And the revived politics of the Assembly appeared an artificial creation by the British, a sham representing at best a snare for politicians desperate to get the gunmen off the stage.

So the Provisional IRA continued trying to make the province ungovernable. The shift in the armed struggle from escalation to persistence was not fully grasped by IRA GHQ. There were now IRA operations in Britain (the London border poll bombs had been harbinger) to compensate for the incident reduction in the provinces. And there was no unexpected bad news: Dublin was responding with the boot as might have been expected, the diaspora was organized and responding to need, and there were new radical friends abroad—even Qadaffi, unhappy with the loss of the *Claudia* (the IRA had been warned in Tripoli about their transport contacts), still gave money. So the military struggle continued throughout the year, not as far as the IRA was concerned as background noise to politics but rather the reverse.

But in fact, in July 1973 a great many outside the IRA felt that peace could be on the way. The talks in London between Heath and Cosgrave that would lead to the institutionalization of the Irish dimension that was needed for a Northern accommodation were heralded as the most important since the treaty of 1921.

The protest at the existence of talks by the Loyalist Coalition only underlined their significance. In Dublin Lynch supported Cosgrave and noted that the ultimate solution of unity, still an Irish aspiration but faint, would "take a a good number of years." The loyalists, however, wanted such an eventuality *never*.

On Thursday, July 5, a fifty-year-old Catholic from Andersonstown, Belfast, was shot dead at his business in Pembroke Street and the UFF claimed responsibility. On the political level, the anti-Assembly Unionists—Taylor, West, and the others—began to organize a bloc for the meeting of the Assembly, although to what end remained unclear. On July 26, Harry West was elected chairman and Captain Austin Ardill Secretary of the group. Paisley went his own way, threatening on July 28 that a five-minute limit on Assembly speeches was "a gag and a muzzle," thus suggesting that the anti-Assembly loyalists would engage in Assembly business.

Faulkner's Unionists, who could taste government, met with Whitelaw, as did Fitt and the SDLP, who could savor vindication and soon power to work out the procedures for the Assembly executive. In a sense Whitelaw's political process was as much in the doing as in the result, urging the politicians along separately so that details were discussed without need for major decisions—decisions that could only create discord among the various constituencies. On July 18 the Northern Ireland Constitution Bill received royal assent in Westminster and became law, with the first meeting of the Legislative Assembly scheduled for July 31. This early bird seemingly was nearly in hand.

As the North made its way uncertainly toward a return of provincial law, the security drive for order continued. The IRA South still acted at times as if these were still the glory days of 1972. On July 13 a press conference in a hotel at Dalkey launched the book *Freedom Struggle* and Twomey and O Conaill appeared. Many were outraged. On July 16 Patrick Cooney, Coalition Minister for Justice, said there would be "no slackening in the government's campaign to suppress subversive organizations." The major IRA culprits had disappeared underground so that the best that could be done was to arrest the editor of *An Phoblacht*, Eamonn Mac Thomais. And on July 19 the Littlejohns were convicted. On the same day in Belfast, the security forces swooped and arrested seventeen members of the Provos, including Gerry Adams, O/C of Belfast, Brendan Hughes, and Joe Cahill's brother Tom.

A series of such arrests would follow. These were particularly important because those arrested were the core and key of the Provisionals' armed struggle in Belfast. The fighting was in the North, the Northerners increasingly dominated the Army Council and GHQ. Adams along with McGuinness, free in the South, had been the best of the new generation. The Belfast losses boded ill for the IRA.

The IRA was as well gradually losing the struggle over interpretation—what was going on and hence what should be done. The explainers continued to explain according to their ideological imperatives but those without sharp interest in the province tended to adjust in time. This was particularly true of those paid to explain the complex in a few sound bytes, a minute of film, an editorial. As professionals they might exploit the violence, especially the convenient, visual violence of the Irish Troubles, but those not specifically politicized want explanation as well. And the old days of immediate certainties had gone without a sudden conversion to a single party line. Still, a consensus was in the making by the summer of 1973.

The British, especially in London, in large part out of conviction, sold the proposition that the British army was in the province solely to keep the two irascible factions apart and the duty of London was to urge reform, moderation, and devolved but fair authority on the locals. On December 2, 1972, Harold Wilson had complained that the situation in the province was rapidly becoming intolerable: "The writ of the law and order no longer runs. Mr. Heath should realize that there is a limit to what British people (taxpayers) will stand." He further outraged all opinion in Northern Ireland by indicating that Protestants and Roman Catholics were fighting each other and British troops were "caught in the cross fire."

This view that the British were neutral, long-suffering, and without interests beyond those agreeable to both sides in Northern Ireland became an article of faith in London and one easily sold to the distant. Such assumptions contained much truth—Wilson was expressing what many believed, not simply reading from a cunningly prepared script.

Britain wanted justice for all, stayed because the majority so insisted, and would pursue the dual mandate of ending terrorism and institutionalizing consensus. It was not as easy to see that this posture was a mix of the most contradictory, historically inaccurate, and politically improbable assertions, assumptions, and aspirations. It was quite easy to see (1) that many of the British seemingly disliked all of the involved, (2) that their presence represented, such as they were, law and order, and (3) that London appeared eager to disengage once a political accommodation could be reached. Only a few and those discounted were seen protesting (1) that Britain was if not the cause at least part of the problem, (2) that such arguments had been presented for staying in the Palestine Mandate, India, and Cyprus, and (3) that the Irish problem generated a variety of psychological and tangible advantages for the British. No, it was the British posture as the peacekeeper, advocate of democracy, and honest broker that most observers and most in Great Britain found convincing.

The varying governments in Dublin essentially built on the British view, contradicted nothing, but added a Celtic gloss, thus manufacturing the decent Dublin analysis that dominated all external opinion. Dublin accepted that London, the only player with the power to impose order, wanted an end to the Irish problem. The interim step—perhaps for some in Britain the ultimate step—was an acceptable, political accommodation and, most important of all, an end to IRA terror through an erosion of support and a firm imposition of order. At some dim and distant date, more distant for some in the Republic than others, once the Republic had been made desirable, the North would convert and a united Ireland would be possible. A united Ireland remained a national goal, an aspiration that could still exert a powerful draw on Irish emotions and an aspiration still held by many who could imagine no way toward the end. It was to the unobservant seldom clear that this "deathless dream," so reluctantly released, did not determine Dublin's Northern policy. The great difference imposed by Northern reality was the gradual acceptance in Dublin that dreams are not practical.

As the new President of Ireland, Erskine Childers, a Protestant, indicated on July 15, "The violence in the North has postponed the day of reunification." Even with reforms and a Protestant President, Dublin accepted that any such day was too distant for serious contemplation—would that all would accept this assessment. The adjustment that made this immediate renunciation of unity possible for Dublin—and not for the IRA—was the acceptance that the Northern majority should have veto power and the unstated, often unrecognized, distaste for the Northern minority and/or a potentially pluralistic united Ireland. The dream of 1916, sung on its way in every pub, still bright for orators and children's texts, on closer examination appeared a nightmare. And so Dublin could carp about the details, the harsh means used to impose order, the residue of institutionalized prejudice, the violence of the majority, the arrogance of London, but on the basics the two establishments were as one, traveling on parallel tracks for the foreseeable future.

The IRA, despite the shift toward politics by 1973 and the rising pressure for peace, remained a major player for observers. They were the rebels, initiated the violence, made the running. The gunmen of the UVF or the UDA lacked credibility. There were inarticulate men to be found in an upstairs room of a working-class pub, wearing funny caps and rationalizing atrocity. The paramilitaries did not supply easy material for academics, for analysts, for cameramen, all comfortable with the dogmas and doings of the republican secret armies. So the IRA could still attract the camera's eye but no longer write the script as well. The very accessibility that had drawn in so much of the media to what was admittedly a dramatic and even significant story undid them.

Wars, unconventional wars, are brutal, sordid, savage and coarse, a mix of blunder, terror, and random slaughter that seen up close contain no romance. The smashed and scattered bodies shot in ambush, the horrors wrought by glass slicing through a bombed pub, the look of roasted flesh or eyes popped out by the impact of a rubber bullet, the mess of an armed struggle on camera or off, erode enthusiasm. The memory of the bride who lost her legs at the Abercorn, the boy shattered by a bomb on Bloody Thursday, the howls of fright and the tears linger on, unerased by repetition.

So the media, no friend to causes, the academic tourists, the transient analysts, each an easy day tripper into terror, found the face of war and blamed, justly or no, the IRA. A liberation struggle, if that was the beast, was not worth the cost. All the IRA arguments, all the sacrifices and historical justification, all the grievances, all the long struggle for justice could not outweigh the blood. The arguments for liberation, in any case, no longer had the currency of 1968—the year of the guerrilla—and no longer maintained the purity of the old civil rights days. Too many had died unpleasantly and too many articulate explainers in London and Dublin and even in the North had proffered valid options.

Increasingly the IRA's argument that Britain was to blame for the island's ills, that a minority of loyalists on the island should not stand in the way of a nation, that the movement rode history's tide and that its armed struggle was just convinced mostly the faithful or the distant radicals marching to similar music. Each bead on the litany of blunder, the apologies for atrocity, the rationalizations for outrage, the very length of the undertaking devalued the IRA's analysis.

After all the chaos and din, the loyalists found their cause still tarnished, their arguments spurned, their community rejected. Once it had been the undeniable institutions of domination: Stormont and the B Specials, the RUC clubbing demonstrators in Derry, the refusal to accept reform, the sectarian orations and sermons, and the public postures long discarded in advanced democracies. Then after the reforms, after the end of Stormont, after the nature of the IRA became apparent, after consensus politics had loyalist takers, all the majority's potential assets were eroded by the brutality of the sectarian paramilitaries. A few men, tattooed with UVF and a Union Jack and willing to murder, contaminated a million. The fundamentalist oratory of Paisley and the indignation of the savage patriot outside a Shankill pub paled when compared to the slashed and maimed bodies of sectarian murder.

The rights of the majority and the loyalty to the British way of life were ignored. With the tit-for-tat killings, with the haphazard slaughter by the IRA, with the prospect of rule imposed by London, with the decay of order, tradition, and civility, the majority felt denied the fundamentals—life, liberty, and the pursuit of happiness. The majority, rich and poor, active and passive, Anglican and fundamentalists, were unhappy—the more so since their plight moved no one, their arguments went unheard, their grievances uncounted.

As for the disinterested on the ground or in distant institutions, they were difficult to find. The Irish diaspora played variations of the IRA position or accepted the wisdom out of Dublin. Increasingly the friends of the British accepted their explanations. Even if the British were condemned for an excess of vigor at Derry on Bloody Sunday or condemned for torture by the European Court of Human Rights, the NATO partners, the friendly Commonwealth nations, the majority at the United Nations accepted apologies and explanations. The United Kingdom no longer had a host of enemies eager to exploit any weakness. Instead, few governments wanted to criticize those who proclaimed they were engaged in an exercise to impose law and order, to seek justice for all, to oppose revolutionary violence.

Increasingly, as well, the distaste with the atrocities of the international terrorists expanded to cover the IRA, whose blunders killed the innocent as surely as did the fedayeen or Red Brigades. Even in the United States the traditional Anglophobia in Irish matters seemingly was dying. The elegant and elite from the State Department to *The New York Times* took Britain's word. There were no Irish issues, no congressional districts with an Irish majority, and no significant Irish politicians eager to oppose the decent Dublin view, even if they did not praise London. A few damned all concerned, a few faulted the British without embracing the IRA, but to a remarkable extent the decent Dublin analysis triumphed.

On July 31 the Northern Ireland Assembly met at Stormont and seemingly the British and the Northern Ireland Office, Whitelaw and the moderates, had triumphed. By the end of July the loyalist split was irrevocable, although those who opposed Faulkner and the Assembly remained divided in theory and practice. As early as July 7 Craig noted that the ten anti–White Paper Unionists could wreck the Assembly. They did, clearly, know what they opposed, as Faulkner underlined: "The struggle for power in the Assembly is an issue of the wreckers versus the rest—the wreckers being from any community, be it partitionist or the UDI, Vanguard or Democratic Unionists." Events at the first meeting, however, suggested that Faulkner had been too sanguine: The wreckers did not want power within the Assembly, they wanted no Assembly under existing terms.

Nat Minford, an Official Unionist, elected presiding officer by thirty-one votes to twenty-six (the SDLP abstained), became involved in a confused and heated debate during which he refused to accept a censure motion against him and refused to accept another motion calling on the Assembly to set up its own committee to draw up standing orders (i.e., to renegotiate power sharing). Amid general disorder, shouts, and boos, Minford adjourned the Assembly to a later date and left the chamber. His opponents stayed and organized a rump, sit-in session, electing the Reverend William Beattie, DUP, chairman, and passing John Taylor's motion of censure, twenty-six to zero. At the end of the day, William Craig and Ian Paisley led the dissidents in singing "God Save the Queen." The wreckers had wrecked the first session.

The next day Faulkner issued a statement that "no excuses can justify the behavior of Dr. Paisley's followers yesterday." Faulkner wanted the Assembly to get down to practical work. His loyalist opposites, not Paisley alone, wanted their opposition kept on a higher plane than practical work. The dissenters were united in damning Assembly procedures as a London dictate and those who accepted such a dictate as Westminster stooges who were thus on "a slippery slope to a united Ireland." Still, on August 2, ignoring Minford, who had "undemocratically" adjourned the Assembly, the loyalists turned in nominations for membership of the committee for the drawing up of standing orders. There matters rested for the moment as the committee—Paisley, Craig, Ardill from the opposition, SDLP's Cooper and Currie, Herbert Kirk and James Stronge of the Official Unionists, and Basil Glass of the Alliance Party—wandered off to various European venues examining other parliamentary procedures.

Besides the Assembly maneuvers and the paramilitary violence that absorbed so much media interest, there were the less visible politics of peace. In Northern Ireland, peace proved difficult to institutionalize. The churches seemed as much source of the problem as cure. There were few other effective social organizations focused on peace issues and even simple nonsectarian groups were thin on the ground. There were many groups, co-ops, committees, local initiatives, and Church programs; but all were small, special, and varied in purpose. One, the Corrymeela Community, founded by the Reverend Ray Davey in 1965 as a place of refuge and reflection, revealed the aspirations and limitations of all peace people. It was a considerable success but indicated the strategic problem. The more effective the organization, the narrower the focus and the less general impact the program had. The larger the mobilization the more fleeting the impact once enthusiasm evaporates, as it inevitably will.

There had been brief bursts of peace activity before but no institutionalization. Mother Theresa of Calcutta had come to Ballymurphy late in 1971 but on September 23, 1973, announced that she was pulling out her welfare mission, where her four Asian Missionary Sisters of Charity had been organizing community projects. Some in the church and out disapproved of missions to rather than from Ireland. And like most transplants and imports, Mother Theresa's effort was symbolic, not organic. Ballymurphy was not at peace, nor was Belfast, nor the province. On July 2, 1973, in Belfast, Brian Walker of the New Ulster Movement formed Peace-Point to coordinate some 180 organizations engaged in a rebuilding process and to produce a tabloid revealing the "better side of life" in the province.

On August 4 Peace-Point launched a week-long festival in East Belfast. The several hundred people who attended an open-air service in Victoria Park on reconciliation were witness to an aspiration rather than a gathering for a crusade or even a long march. Peace might be a "crying priority" but remained a minority, middle-class cause in 1973.

The politics of protest, the lever that had first tipped the Stormont system, had also become a minority pursuit and mostly, as always, a middle-class one. The paramilitaries, the most partisan political parties, the orators who could attract a crowd all made use of demonstrations and structured disorder. There were protests over the use of rubber bullets, over conditions in the ghettos, over the brutality of the security forces, over slights and for just cause. Like the din of bombs and the murdered bodies dumped in lanes, the protest ranging all along the violent spectrum from a few peaceful pickets to mobs armed with petrol bombs and backed up by snipers had become commonplace. As a result the radicals had faded back if not away.

In June NICRA's program for peace included an end to internment, a bill of rights, the withdrawal of troops to the barracks, and reform of the police and judiciary. By 1973 this was no way to quicken hearts or fashion a consensus. All during this period the radicals beyond NICRA continued their agitation but to fading interest. They deployed a variety of means, once trendy, now ignored. Radical politics without the gun had few Northern takers, as even the Official IRA was discovering. Bernadette Devlin had become dated. Their reforms seemingly could be best achieved by the conventional politics of the SDLP or even by the armed struggle of the IRA—protest was increasingly seen as adjunct to one or the other. Dated or not, irrelevant or no, they persisted.

On July 7 Michael Farrell and Tony Canavan, in Crumlin Road Prison serving eight months and six months for participation in a banned procession, went on hunger strikes demanding the status of political prisoners. Hunger strikes in prison are a traditional Irish remedy for the intolerable and at minimum attract considerable interest and sympathy. Farrell and Canavan, however, were not facing years in prison or grave injustice. Mostly such "protest" prosecutions had been delayed or dropped, but not in this case. Their imprisonment was thus unfair but did not attract great concern until the hunger strike had gone beyond the symbolic.

On July 27, on their twenty-fifth day, they were moved to the prison hospital and on the thirty-first day, August 2, moved on to a general hospital. There were protests and rallies. Two thousand came to a rally at Dunville Park held by the Political Hostage Release Committee. The rally collapsed into rioting, with youths stoning the Springfield Road RUC station and the British army firing rubber bullets. This was at the same time that the smaller Peace-Point service took place—the other cusp of politics as usual. On August 8 the two PD hunger strikers were released, along with about one hundred prisoners sentenced for nonterrorist activities. There was no question of amnesty. There were a few bonfires in West Belfast. There was no other great excitement. And the PD agitators were again on the street, a small point made. Increasingly, the radicals could make at best small points, organize small rallies, paddle furiously behind the whirling vortexes of violence and sectarian voting.

In fact Farrell and Canavan had been freed because the Northern Ireland (Emergency Provisions) Act came into force at midnight on August 8 and ended mandatory sentences under legislation such as the Public Order Act and the Criminal Justice Act of 1968. What the new act did was institutionalize the necessary emergency procedures as law. These procedures meant that the RUC and the British army could arrest on suspicion those thought to be engaged in subversive acts and be confident that the machine would carry the individual forward through a trial before a judge, not a jury—where intimidation might be possible or clan loyalty win over justice. With a judge, evidence acquired through an intimidated confession or the testimony of a paid informer or simply police work would result in a substantial sentence and subsequent imprisonment under rigorous security, usually at Long Kesh. Those so imprisoned almost always were guilty, if not as charged, but beyond the reach of normal procedures.

In order to maintain a semblance of judicial order, rather than arbitrary internment without evidence, the system had to rely on *some* evidence when none existed and so permitted and then encouraged the corruption of conventional justice for expediency's sake. This was to make the point that the province was not at war, that emergency justice worked, that murder was just murder. The system was set up not as much to camouflage security internment, a political debit, as it was to support the perception sold in London that the province was violent but normal. Order was maintained by law, not force; the IRA and the loyalist paramilitaries were involved in crime, not politics. The existing order required the sacrifice of law and the sacrifice was denied. Thus, those most articulate and uncompromising advocates of justice, even justice under law, the PD leaders, unexpectedly benefited by the Crown's justice shaped by expediency—the law distorted.

Such an interpretation would have had few takers at the time in London, where minds were sharpened as the IRA opened an arson and bomb campaign on the mainland. The small firebombs on August 18 at Harrods in Knightsbridge were first thought to be the work of someone with "a grievance," but the Irish Republican Publicity Bureau on August 20 claimed responsibility. The rash of small bombs, book bombs, firebombs, and letter bombs was simply a means of escalating the campaign as the security pressure escalated in the North. One letter bomb addressed to the military attaché exploded on the sixth floor of the British embassy in Washington on August 27 and blew off the hand of Nora Murray, the attaché's secretary. Other letter bombs were mailed to British officials in Paris, Lisbon, Gibraltar, Brussels, and Kinshasa. On September 23 the first fatality occurred with the death of an army officer who had been injured trying to defuse a bomb in Birmingham. Such a widening of the battle arena would become a convention for the Army Council, with plans under way by Brian Keenan and others to bomb Britain and thus again take the war to England.

But the major confrontation remained in the North, where security targets remained prime and economic targets acceptable. On the island, operations continued despite the obstacles, North and South, and the setbacks: The chief of staff, Séamus Twomey, was arrested by the Gárda Special Branch in a farmhouse in Monaghan fifteen miles from the border on September 1. Still, as always, the Provos persisted. A former British paratrooper, Eamonn O'Doherty from Tipperary, who was concerned with the war outside Belfast, took over as chief of staff. Despite the changes the IRA command remained fairly stable, with some in prison and some on the GHQ or Army Council and a few of the 1969 generation moving into responsibility. And with British pressure there tended to be too many volunteers on the ground and so no lack of talent. The Provos could still cope, even if the effort was greater and the number of bang-and-run or drive-and-bomb operations was way down.

On August 28 the Derry IRA finally blew away a symbolic target, the ninety-foot column overlooking the Bogside area from the old city that commemorated Governor George Walker, who had commanded the siege of the city in 1689—a splendid, never forgotten Protestant victory. The explosion that brought down the column did not damage the state of Walker, but the changed skyline emphasized the changes in the city, now Derry not Londonderry, now administered by an SDLP, not a Unionist, council. There were other symbolic events during the summer. On August 18 Lord Brookeborough, former Prime Minister of Northern Ireland, died in his sleep at age eighty-five at Brookeborough in Fermanagh—the symbol of Stormont was gone.

Prime Minister Heath announced that he would come to the province for the memorial service on August 28. He was heckled and booed on the steps of Saint Anne's Cathedral in Donegall Street in central Belfast. Craig was cheered on his arrival. But the address of the bishop of Connor, Dr. Arthur Butler, was less cheering to the fundamentalists: "It can be argued that if he had thought differently, if he had acted differently, Northern Ireland would not be in its present unhappy state."

In order to move the province from that state, Heath met with Faulkner and Fitt and the others urging the need for an Assembly Executive. The next day he repeated publicly his anxiety that the executive be formed as soon as possible. Craig refused to meet him; but after his departure, Whitelaw pushed ahead with the "delicate and divisive issues." In the South the government announced that after a two-day conference Dublin and London would exchange drafts on the structure and function of the Council of Ireland; Heath would next visit Cosgrave on September 17. This announcement produced the anticipated commentary, now ritual: Faulkner called it "worthwhile," the SDLP's Cooper called it a continuing process that should be welcomed; while Paisley denounced it as a "step toward an all-Ireland Republic" and Craig called it "unwise."

For Whitelaw and the Northern Ireland Office, a crucial factor was the aspiration of the Northern minority for an Irish dimension to any accommodation. Even as symbol such a formal recognition of reality—the involvement of the South in Northern events—was in 1973 a very difficult coda to add to the

Assembly arrangement. And there were practical matters to settle as well. The Assembly majority had not met together or begun to arrange the executive when Heath arrived in Dublin on September 17. Many of the details skimmed over in individual negotiation, from the rent-and-rates strike to the position, even the title, of the RUC, had to be made real.

Then Heath spoke out of turn in an interview with the BBC Northern Ireland political correspondent. The Prime Minister said that if the parties did not form an executive by March 1974, when the Northern Ireland Constitution Act would expire, it would be better to have integration with the United Kingdom rather than a continuation of direct rule. This caused an uproar in the province, indicating as it did a major, unexpected government shift and also the inability of British politicians to fine-tune their comments to an acutely sensitive Northern Ireland audience. Dublin protested, nearly everyone in Belfast was outraged, even Harold Wilson complained. The "suggestion" was withdrawn.

The nine hours of talks with Cosgrave the previous day, September 17, did, however, produce a joint communiqué on the Council of Ireland. The communiqué indicated that both men supported the council and would talk with Northern Irish representatives about its form and functions—assuming that such representatives appeared. As soon as there was an executive, Heath promised on September 19, he would call a tripartite conference on the Council of Ireland. But movement toward such a conference and such an executive continued to lack urgency. And Northern events had a tendency to erode optimism. The background music often dominated the play.

On October 5 Whitelaw at last brought the Assembly majority together to work out the details. The first meeting was uneasy. The majority and minority had known each other only as opponents across a chamber or on a ballot; Faulkner the Unionist or Devlin the ex-IRA internee were symbols, not people. And as people there were often more sparks than warmth. In Whitelaw the British had a chairman, tolerant of eccentrics and bores, a Conservative political necessity, patient, compassionate, and enormously painstaking, who understood the significance of details, the nature of the contradictory constituencies, and the delicate art of devising a formula. Nothing would have worked unless the SDLP and the Faulkner Unionists wanted it to work. And nothing would work for them unless it could be shaped into a form that they could sell to their own. Building on the first, Whitelaw moved meeting by meeting toward the second.

A Council of Ireland that had taken shape in Dublin had to be made palatable to both. The Unionists were desperate to defend the RUC and the SDLP to end internment. There was a need for a social and economic program. The result was a constant paper blizzard directed by Sir Frank Cooper that shaped formula to need, adjusting, amending and suggesting cunning ambiguities. It was a premier British political effort, enormously dull to all but the involved until it could be translated into cruder terms for the political marketplace.

The effort went on parallel to the clamor and tumult of the province. The most spectacular event was the Provos' great helicopter escape on October 31. A man with an American accent rented a helicopter and ordered the pilot to Stradbally, where two armed men boarded and the craft was directed to fly on to Dublin. There at Mountjoy Prison—late as always—the pilot had to put down in the prison yard. The guards apparently thought a minister was visiting the prison and watched, bemused, as Twomey, J. B. O'Hagan, and Kevin Mallon, the three key men the Army Council wanted free, rushed over and boarded. There was a bad moment when, heavily loaded and trapped in the closed yard, the helicopter hovered frantically just over the ground. The craft then soared off into legend as the Provo Birdie.

Twomey, back on the GHQ staff under Eamonn O'Doherty, gave an interview to *Der Spiegel,* further outraging Dublin. O'Hagan went back to the border but Mallon lasted only to a GAA dance at Portlaoise, where he was arrested at a motel on December 10. The Wolfe Tones' pop record "The Helicopter Song" sold briskly, some twelve thousand records in the South by November 22. The novelty of the event, no one harmed and the lads away, helped obscure for a moment the reality of shattered bomb victims and bodies at the end of the lane. The reality of the North during the autumn of 1973 was all too unpleasant, even as the favorable comparisons to the toll of 1972 were made.

On October 12 Whitelaw said that the security forces could be proud that the courts had heard over six hundred terrorist-type cases and more than four hundred people had been convicted and sent to prison for a total of two thousand years and there had been ten life sentences as well. There were always numbers to measure out trouble. The total number of deaths since 1969 was 893 by the end of October, with 201 assassinations reported since 1972. Up to November 13 the total killed for the province during the year was 225: 152 civilians, 54 army, 9 UDR, 7 RUC, and 3 RUC Reserve. And when the statisticians of violence had added on the latest figure, the total for the Troubles reached 903. There were similar running figures for security losses, for houses searched, for finds of ammunition and guns and explosives and bombs, figures for bombs defused and bombs exploded, figures for IRA volunteers killed claimed by the authorities and admitted by the Provos, figures for victims of sectarian assassins varying with the source, figures for compensation paid and buses burned and cars stolen, figures for hospital admissions, for punishment maimings, for arson and armed robbery and intimidation. There were now forms to fill out after searches and after bombs and after shoot-outs. The Troubles were being institutionalized by the clerks of contemporary government.

And any single special day could indicate how fragile such bureaucratic order could be. On the evening of Thursday, October 25, one hundred vehicles were hijacked and used to block roads all over the province. Bombs and bomb scares disrupted traffic and there were explosions in Rostrevor, Cookstown, Dungannon, and Belfast. A land mine exploded in Derry's Bogside and other bombs damaged premises along the Strand Road. Twenty-five Derry vehicles were hijacked and many burned. The province was in turmoil, normal life in many places had to be postponed, the paperwork over the following days was enormous. No one was killed or seriously injured. No conventional military ambush or urban shoot-out took place. In the Northern Ireland Assembly the members agreed that seating should be in the form of a horseshoe. Sometimes the political dimension seemed to lack reality. With enormous effort, many tried to ignore the chaos and get on with politics. Getting on required, however, not only ignoring the din but also discovering common ground. And every step on such ground posed fatal political risks.

The SDLP had to show symbolic gains and real advantages but could show them to a nationalist community largely united behind the party, even in some cases true for republicans who would favor their party as well as their army. The SDLP now represented all Catholic opinion, city and town, moderate and radical, if not every Catholic resident. They had organized the urban working class, a group not unlike their British coevals except for the constitutional issue, the fragile lower middle class of rising businessmen, clerks, and shopkeepers, and the small and scattered middle class of professionals and teachers and a few business-men. It was largely a party of the nearly poor and the almost destitute. There was no gentry, no upper middle class, few rich, and but a handful of demonstrably successful, usually in the law. Mostly upward mobility was represented by a carpenter turned contractor, a grocer moving into wholesale produce or local delivery, a pub owner with a dance hall and a chicken-processing business—or simply a university education and a desk. All had in common the grievances of the minority, the sentimental attraction for the Irish Free State and ultimate unity, their religion, and now their party.

This type of cohesiveness no longer existed on the other side of the divide. The constitutional issue divided the loyalists. It was not the long-noted differences of class and caste, of fundamentalist religion and advanced ideas, of town and country, gentry and the others, or the quarrels of doctrine that had destroyed the old Unionist Party, but the constitutional issue. Now what divided Taylor and Paisley and Faulkner was the shape of the Northern Irish system—integration or independence, federalism or power sharing, a return to Stormont or a boycott of all initiatives—each had advocates. No one wanted a united Ireland or even a more united island; but they could not agree on the shape of the future since the past had been denied. The SDLP could and did give on various details, since they were dedicated to something and symbols. Faulkner, on the other hand, could give very little without being harried by his loyalist enemies. And when faced with options, being a politician and a practical man, he tended to demand reality over symbolism, police powers over an Irish dimension.

The final hurdle was reached on Monday, November 19, when an agreement would have to be made on the composition of the executive and the retention of the name Royal Ulster Constabulary for the police. The other points could be adjusted. At the end of the day there was no agreement. Faulkner would face an Ulster Unionist Council, his party's leadership, meeting on Tuesday evening and could not offer concessions to either Whitelaw or his party colleagues. On Tuesday, November 20, before the meeting in Ulster Hall, Belfast, he stressed the four main points: the SDLP must condemn the rent-and-rates strike, support and acknowledge the RUC, concede a majority of Unionists on the executive, and deal with the Council of Ireland only on qualified issues. On this platform he scraped by 379 votes to 369 with the defeat of John Taylor's motion repudiating power sharing. A ten-vote victory for the leader was not a victory at all. The Unionists were finally firmly split and no power had as yet been shared.

On the next day a marathon session began at Stormont. Whitelaw had already telephoned Heath early that morning in a depressed mood and said he would return to London that afternoon, probably to report failure. To encourage the wayward, Whitelaw had his helicopter flown in and out twice. The clatter of the rotors from the lawn outside the windows indicated how close failure and the Secretary's flight to London really might be. And as always failure was averted by a formula and the reluctant acceptance of the other's limitations.

The SDLP would give on the rent-and-rates strike, quietly in December, a symbolic step long in the works; they would also accept the name RUC, a necessity, as Whitelaw pointed out, for the Conservatives as well as the Unionists. The RUC was a sticking point that symbolized more to the majority in 1973 than to the minority. The devout loyalists had been shattered by the end of the B Specials and an end to their RUC. An RUC with a new Catholic chief constable, James Flanagan, would be opposed by the entire majority, who depended upon the police to protect them as well as their interests. The RUC stayed and the wise knew that after Flanagan, a stolid and conservative career man, probably would come Kenneth Newman of the Metropolitan Police, who had been appointed senior deputy chief constable. He was a keen reformer with RUC experience, acceptable to a wide Northern spectrum.

Faulkner was determined not only to protect the police but, if possible, also to regain control for the Assembly. There would still be a Council of Ireland and both partners could explain that as they might. The Council was more important to the SDLP, who had to have an Irish dimension, than to the Unionists, who only had to oppose a united Ireland. So the Council meant much or little but had to exist. The real test was the executive, where the numbers could be counted. And Whitelaw and Cooper and cunning arranged a two-tier executive that satisfied, just, the SDLP and the Unionists.

At the end of ten hours the politicians had scraped through. Whitelaw helicoptered off on his way to London to relay the good news. The others motored home to begin explaining their famous victory. Although from time to time Northern politics would generate real surprises, November 1973 was not one except that few observers realized what a close-run thing the agreement had been, since a devolved power-sharing assembly seemed so logical. And if the agreement came as a surprise to the involved, the reaction was fully predictable.

The involved, from Heath and Cosgrave and Whitelaw down through the SDLP, Unionists, Alliance, and NILP, and out to the bastions of decent opinion and peaceful people had naught but praise. Cosgrave on RTE television summed it up: "We are on the road to peace now. The road ahead is not going to be easy; patience, understanding, generosity, and trust are needed. That is the role of the true patriot today." A great many patriots felt otherwise. For the DUP it was a "betrayal" and for Craig unacceptable to the majority. The radicals on the other side of the divide agreed. Bernadette Devlin McAliskey, who had married Michael McAliskey in April 1973, and Gerry Fitt, who felt a "total and absolute irrelevancy," insisted that the executive "would not work and should not be allowed to work."

At the Official Sinn Féin Ard Fheis in Dublin on Saturday, November 24, the five hundred delegates rejected the idea of a Council of Ireland. The Provisional IRA announced that it would destroy the new Northern Ireland executive as it destroyed the old Stormont—the SDLP were collaborators. On Friday,

November 23, an IRA unit opened fire on Austin Currie's home, hitting an RUC guard car and underlining the reality of the Provos' opposition. And the final tripartite conference had not even met.

Outside Stormont November had been much as October. The security forces, North and South, tightened the screws on the IRA. There were more arrests and some successes. One of the premier border Provo guerrillas, Michael McVerry of Crossmaglen, was killed on November 15. Another outstanding Provo gunman, James Bryson, who had escaped from the *Maidstone* prison ship and Crumlin Road Jail, had died in September after being shot in the neck by a British army sniper in an ambush in Ballymurphy, Belfast. Each such loss was more important because of the disappearance of a known hero rather than of an irreplaceable volunteer. Some of these heroes were too well known to the security forces and often not very good guerrillas—undisciplined, untrained, violent—but they were famous. And famous is useful for there were ample competent replacements.* Despite the figures and the growing effectiveness of the security forces, the Provos had more trained volunteers than they could use and more volunteers than they could train. And even those volunteers in prison were not lost; nor were the dead, who could be transmuted into martyrs.

In England the border poll bombers had been sentenced: nine of them to life, one to fifteen years, with one acquitted. They had requested transfer to a Northern Ireland prison and refused to act as prisoners. They had in effect gone over to the offensive. The most visible and long-running maneuver would be a hunger strike by the two Price sisters in support of their application to be moved to Armagh Women's Prison. Almost before the authorities realized what had happened they faced confrontation. On December 6 the Home Secretary in a parliamentary written answer stated his reasons for denying the request of the eight prisoners: "It would not be for the public interest." The transfer had been declined, perhaps without due thought, but as a general British response to hard-core IRA prisoners. As long as the IRA continued the war, their prisoners would be given a hard time, moved constantly and to inconvenient prisons, given no privileges, harassed by warders and the criminals, punished in all the little ways that a bureaucracy can fashion without directive or responsibility. No one in prison or out loved a bomber.

The Price sisters were not alone in the hunger strike, even though four of the volunteers ended their strike on November 26; but the two became the most visible—attractive, articulate, they were determined to be of use to the movement even while locked up. And for 206 days they posed a serious and unexpected problem for the authorities who did not want the responsibility of their death nor the onus of concession. After thirty-nine days the authorities introduced forced feeding, a vilely painful and unpleasant experience that each time the tube is forced down the prisoner's throat could be fatal, as it was with the Irish martyr Thomas Ashe in August 1917. Not only humanitarians, who felt that force feeding was torture, but also many in both Ireland and England became con-

*For a more detailed account of the nature of gunmen, see J. Bowyer Bell, "Career Moves: Reflections on the Irish Gunman," in *Studies in Conflict and Terrorism*, Vol 15, pp. 69–88, with a more extensive, general treatment scheduled in Irish by Coisceim in Dublin.

cerned at the ill treatment allotted to the Irish women. The strike dragged on month after month. The protest in Ireland and England continued. There were as well those with no love for bombers who felt the sisters, allowing themselves to be manipulated by the godfathers of violence, had brought on all their own discomfort. At the end of 167 days of forced feeding, the authorities devised a face-saving formula that saw the Price sisters in Armagh Prison.

As was always the case, the Irish understood the point made and many others were impressed—such a sacrifice in no small manner compensated for the atrocities of the gunmen. All could not be wicked and evil and mad nor their cause foolish and futile if such a sacrifice could be offered freely by two young women, bombers both, imprisoned forever, isolated from control and communication, who, day after day, with no end in sight, had their jaws pried open, a tube stuffed into them, and gruel forced down; they endured humiliating anguish inflicted to no schedule and with little compunction. The British authorities were mainly concerned with getting the Prices out of the news and not in heeding lessons from Irish history or the play of perceptions in an unconventional war. So they made a deal and said they did not. The sisters had been used by both sides and were now out of sight and mind in Armagh. Enough.

The IRA Army Council had received from the two not only the border bombs but also a prison coup. It was counted as another victory. There seemed no reason why there should not be more conventional military victories as well. There had never been as many trained volunteers, too many to deploy. The American arms connection was firm and though the *Claudia* had failed there was still no real shortage of gear. This meant that the Army Council continued to pursue the armed struggle with enthusiasm, if not always tight control. Those within the movement who were tempted by politics had to compose themselves.

The other gunmen, the loyalists, enjoyed no such stability of command as the murder of Herron hinted. No one, not even the visible commanders of the UDA, could speak for their members and often even the local units, UDA or UVF, could not impose discipline over those who wanted action, wanted to kill Fenians and not be troubled by programs and causes. Even efforts to improve the discipline of the underground militias like that undertaken by Lieutenant Colonel Edward James Augustus Howard Brush with his Down Orange Welfare, a country vigilante militia with a book strength of five thousand, really created forces with no more than ritual purpose. The really hard men could direct intimidation, impose levies, and kill on the sly but not fight a war. The leaders often shifted tactics—now a cease-fire, now a threat, a spurt of killing and then a pause.

No one understood the internal dynamics and so the loyalist violence was often truly frightening—random, often vicious, murder done with torture. On October 18 the UVF announced a forty-three-day cease-fire to begin on November 18 that would last until the end of the year but it would "resume its military campaign against selected IRA activists and targets" if firm guarantees were not given that Northern Ireland's links would be maintained with the United Kingdom. Even within the UVF, considerably more violent and indiscriminate than the UDA's gunmen, there were those who wanted to hit only "IRA activists," although many were content to kill any male Fenian. Even the more discriminating had a very broad definition of "activists." And who knew if the UVF had actually given up killing: on Monday, November 26 a fifty-eight-year-old Catholic was shot dead on his way home from work in the Ardoyne.

There was never any doubt about the IRA's kills. In Derry on the same Monday the Provos claimed responsibility for killing two soldiers at the Rossville Flats in the Bogside on Sunday. The next day they set up thirty roadblocks throughout the province. Two men were killed when their car smashed into one near Ballygawley, Tyrone. Another was shot dead by soldiers at a block in Coalisland. Two hijacked vehicles exploded. There was a shooting incident in Aghalane, Fermanagh. Fog and mist kept the army from clearing the roads once the sun went down so that the blocks were not clear until the next day, when bus service to the Falls and Ardoyne was withdrawn after vehicles were hijacked and burned. The bad news was a constant, not even reported in London and Dublin unless spectacular.

Instead, informed observers watched the tripartite meeting that opened at the Civil Service Staff College at Sunningdale, near Ascot, Berkshire, on Thursday, December 6. The gunmen and their spokesmen, republican and Orange, had been ignored. Sunningdale was for moderates. It was Whitelaw's final piece. But he had been taken to his reward—Secretary for Employment back in London—and replaced by Francis Pym on December 3. It was one more example, if example by December 1973 was needed, of London's priorities. The Heath cabinet was falling on hard times and needed Whitelaw back, not pursuing Celtic accommodations. Pym could finish up the details.

Sunningdale was an ordeal, not a simple walk through agreed concessions. Pym had to learn on the job, hurriedly tutored by Cooper and the Northern Ireland Office secretariat on Irish nuances. He coped. The Unionists stuck on devolved police powers and making much of the Council of Ireland. The SDLP focused on the Irish dimension, a symbolic need. Only an all-night session and a compromise by Heath on the police issue produced agreement. Faulkner and the others knew that if too much were conceded at Sunningdale, the hard men would run roughshod over those who had given a great deal more than an inch. On December 9 a ten-page communiqué was issued shortly after 8:00 P.M. after fifty hours of discussions. There was, as usual, something for everyone.

The Dublin government fully accepted that "there could be no change in the status of Northern Ireland until a majority decided it." The British government announced, again, its respect for the wishes of the majority, even if they wanted to become part of a united Ireland. There was agreement on the structure and scope of the Council of Ireland and for the immediate bringing to justice by the Dublin government of those accused of violent crimes in Northern Ireland, "however motivated." And there would be an appointment of a Police Authority by the Irish government and cooperation by both North and South on police matters through the Council of Ireland.

All this meant that London had gotten Dublin's acceptance of the legitimacy of Northern Ireland and cooperation in pursuit of IRA subversives. These were gifts to Faulkner as well, and were no surprise to the SDLP. As for the nationalists, they had a Council of Ireland, whose most immediate purpose did seem to be a more united Ireland but still was an all-Ireland institution with great potential. Thus, the SDLP could sell the Council as a means and Faulkner as an empty gesture made to achieve real concessions: the Dublin acceptance of the North's constitutional position and the Dublin agreement to hunt down the IRA—however phrased in the agreement.

In fact, the only problem for the SDLP and the official Unionists (the NILP and the Alliance were taken for granted, their constituency would be satisfied with any gain labeled moderate) was that the selling of the Sunningdale settlement had to be done in public. The nationalist minority could hear Faulkner trumpeting the deal as a grand one for the unionists, discounting the Council, polishing the Dublin concessions. In turn the unionists could hear the SDLP going on about an Irish dimension that would use the Council as the first step on the road to a united Ireland. When Faulkner, chief executive designate of the Northern Ireland Assembly, said, "I believe the agreement heralds a new dawn not just for Northern Ireland but for the whole of Ireland," many loyalists feared just that: The road from Sunningdale was a slippery slope to the Republic.* And many nationalists feared just that: They had been sold out to the majority in return for a mirage called the Council of Ireland.

The rest of the month was a political anticlimax, as the Sunningdale details were worked out and the expected reactions and resentments continued to surface. Paisley felt it was a confidence trick. Cosgrave thought it a good settlement. The Provos felt it contributed nothing, so, "The struggle for freedom will continue until a peace, based on justice, is secured." Cardinal Conway and Lord O'Neill urged acceptance; but Neil Blaney in Donegal, now an independent Dáil deputy, felt that Stormont was on the way back—an analysis lost on Senator Edward Kennedy in Washington, who felt that Whitelaw deserved the Nobel Peace Prize for "his towering success in the cause of peace." For those abroad concerned with Irish matters, only the NORAID supporters and militant Orangemen disagreed with Kennedy, with Sunningdale and the promised Council of Ireland.† It appeared that peace with justice was well served.

Yet peace with or without justice had yet to come to Northern Ireland, not before, during or after Christmas. On December 13 Faulkner discovered the wreckers were waiting in the Assembly for him: "I come here to speak in the Assembly and I find that his crowd of disloyal wreckers, led by a demon doctor who goes around the country preaching sedition, are preventing me. It is diabolical." While the Assembly debated the Sunningdale Agreement for eigh-

---

*Increasingly Sunningdale divided the old unionists' monolith, all loyalists, into two vague groups. On the one hand, there were the loyalists who sought the past in any future arrangement and at their most extreme were paramilitaries, but the vast majority simply voted for one of the dissenting majority parties, usually Paisley's. On the other, there were those who, recognizing existing realities, sought an accommodation that would most benefit the majority and voted for the descendants of the Unionist party. Thus, in a sense, all the later unionists were more loyal than many avowed loyalists, who would even advocate Ulster independence if necessary to maintain their system. There were class distinctions as well, the unionists more likely to be middle class, the loyalists more apt to be working class, with the paramilitaries almost entirely so. To complicate matters, the involved often continued to use the two terms interchangeably; none wanted to be disloyal and nearly all nearly always favored the union.
†While there were both Masonic and political contacts made in America by loyalists, the most fruitful for the paramilitaries in Northern Ireland were either directly across in Scotland or in certain Canadian areas, an Orange diaspora of sorts.

teen hours on Friday, December 14, an RUC constable was shot in the back and wounded on foot patrol in Newcastle. On the following day a former RUC member, Ivor Johnston, who the Provos claimed was an undercover agent, was found shot dead near Keady, Armagh, and an IRA volunteer, James McGinn, was killed by his own bomb at Clady Bridge on the border with Donegal.

The same day the Dáil passed the Sunningdale Agreement with a majority of five after three days of debate. Lynch said Fianna Fáil mostly supported the agreement. Dublin had done its part. On December 18 three car bombs exploded after warnings in London, injuring sixty-three people. The Provos had done their thing once more, communicating by bombs the cost of any Irish accommodation without their imprimatur.

Efforts to put on a holiday face had a limited impact. Pym announced the release from Long Kesh of sixty-five detainees, all but two of them republicans, including Séamus Loughran, who had taken part in the Lenadoon talks in Belfast in July 1972. This left 662 detained, too many for the SDLP, whose spokesmen complained on December 21—and complained about the Sunningdale talks being sabotaged by "violent men" as well. On Christmas Eve, two armed men were killed leaving a public house in Monaghan Street, Newry, as was a customer. On the next day, Christmas, a sixty-three-year-old woman was wounded when shots were fired in the New Lodge Road at no particular target. Shots were fired at troops in the Ardoyne. The next day a nineteen-year-old prisoner was found dead of injuries in the loyalist compound in Long Kesh. The same day a public house at Clogher, Tyrone, was destroyed by a suitcase bomb.

On the evening of Thursday, December 27, a small IRA group, angry at the Price sisters' sacrifice and acting without battalion or brigade permission, kidnapped Thomas Niedermayer, honorary West German consul in Belfast and managing director of the Grundig Company. Almost as soon as he was taken from his home at Suffolk near Belfast, he collapsed and died. The IRA continued to deny all knowledge of the kidnapping despite all sorts of pleas, including a television appearance by his wife. It was one more painful and unnecessary tragedy in a long, sad year.

The 1973 statistics indicated how sad: 250 killed—170 civilians, 58 army, 10 RUC, 3 RUC Reserve, and 9 UDR. It was not a very happy Christmas, despite the UVF truce and the Sunningdale success, and New Year's brought only the year-end numbers. On New Year's Eve, in an end-of-term ceremony at Stormont, Pym presented the eleven members of the Northern Ireland executive and four members of the administration their warrants of appointment. In 1974 the Northern Ireland Assembly—despite everything and because of British skill and patience—would become real, with a real executive: Faulkner, chief executive; Fitt, deputy chief executive; Napier, law reform; John Baxter, information services; Roy Bradford, environment; Currie, housing, local government and planning; Paddy Devlin, health and social services; Hume, commerce; Herbert Kirk, finance; Basil McIvor, education; and Leslie Morrell, agriculture; with the four second-tier members, Ivan Cooper, Robert Cooper, Major Lloyd Hall-Thompson, and Edward McGrady.

The Unionists were mostly new names to those outside the province. The famous unionists were retired, O'Neill or Chichester-Clark offering at best unheard kind words, or were loyalists on the outside, Paisley and Craig and West and Taylor, crying treason. These *real* loyalists were still determined on principle not to give an inch, play a spoiler's role. The SDLP at least had the nationalist household names. In any case the known and unknown would share power under Faulkner. On the next day, January 1, a Tuesday, these agreed powers would devolve on the Assembly. As its first act at the close of 1973, the new executive asked that 1974 be the Year of Reconciliation. In Belfast on the last day of the year, guardsman Alan Daughtery was shot dead by an IRA sniper in the Falls Road, number 250 for the year, 928 all told.

Events in Ireland moved violently into the next year: Early in the morning of New Year's Day 1974, for the first time a public holiday in the province, a twenty-four-year-old Catholic man was caught in a cross fire in the Ormeau district of Belfast and shot dead. If there were to be any sign of progress then it would have to be the fact that later in the day the Northern Ireland executive took up duty meeting at Stormont. The meeting was reflected by William Whitelaw's name on the New Year's Honours as a companion of honour.

Francis Pym, as the new Northern Ireland Secretary, was in place to see the new Assembly ratify the Sunningdale accords and move forward into power and responsibility. Another of the institutions of an Irish accommodation, the Anglo-Irish Law Enforcement Commission, with four British and Northern Ireland and four Republic of Ireland representatives, announced the next day that the first meeting would take place on January 16. By the optimistic it was taken as a harbinger of better days, as was the Republic's arrest of fifteen IRA suspects in Dundalk on the same day and the meeting of RUC chief constable James Flanagan and the commissioner of the Gárda Síochána on January 3.

To the advocates of the Assembly, the new departure appeared vital and now viable. As Faulkner noted for the forthcoming meeting of the Ulster Unionist Council, "If, out of fear, out of misunderstanding, out of suspicion, we were now to reject the very principle of friendship and cooperation, then indeed we would be condemning this island to strife without end." Taylor, whose resolution rejecting "the proposed all-Ireland Council settlement" would be before the Unionist Council, the anti-Assembly Unionists, the recalcitrant loyalist politicians, most of the hard loyalists, and increasingly more moderate general loyalist opinion did not agree with either Faulkner or the implications of a Council of Ireland. London had London's interests at stake, where increasingly the government, under pressure, was focusing on the prospect of elections, British concerns, personal agendas, not the historic challenge to Ulster's security.

The Provos had in their New Year's message announced, "We look forward with confidence to 1974 as a year in which the British rule in Ireland shall be destroyed and the curse of alien power banished from our land for all time." And their volunteers continued their armed campaign in the province and even in England—during the first week in January bombs exploded in Birmingham, England, and in Madame Tussaud's wax museum and the boat show at Earl's Court in London. These were trial, one-shot bombings as Brian Keenan of GHQ probed the mainland without the need to fret about politics or solutions. The Provos knew what they wanted.

Increasingly the loyalists were not at all sure what, beyond a return to the past, they wanted or would even accept. Some Protestants like Desmond Boal, formerly DUP Chairman and MP for Shankill, might be attracted by the lures of a federal Ireland; some political innocents like the UVF paramilitaries toying with politics between assassinations might praise his honesty and courage. The UVF, heretofore thought hard men without ideas, had curiously entered a "political" phase just as loyalist opinion had hardened. They had trekked south to meet the Officials, Goulding and Tomás Mac Giolla, president of the Official Sinn Féin, and even contacted the Provisionals in the Republic and went on to fashion a no-conflict agreement within the prisons before the new departure collapsed. Long afterward Gusty Spence, admirer of the Officials still, blamed devious and unenlightened publicity, petty sectarian attitudes from local politicians, and deliberate government obstruction for destroying "an important breakthrough." The UVF initiative, momentarily fulfilling the dearest Irish radical dream of the conversion of the Protestant workers, was an anomaly, a temporary aberration.

Nearly all loyalists simply ignored the innocent UVF gunmen and judged Boal by his advocates: Who welcomed his proposal? Paddy Devlin, old IRA man, Kevin Boland, friend of IRA arms smugglers, the IRA itself in the form of Ruairí O Brádaigh, all had kind words. For the real loyalists Sunningdale, the Council of Ireland, and a power-sharing Assembly remained anathema.

On Friday evening, January 4, in the Ulster Hall, Belfast, Taylor's resolution opposing the all-Ireland Council contained in the Sunningdale Agreement of December 1973 came to a vote. The Unionists supported Taylor 454 to 374, a majority of 80, later adjusted down to 53 but still a majority against the leader. Taylor announced that if Faulkner was an honest man "he would now resign leadership of the Unionist Party." And on January 7, Faulkner resigned. The historic Unionist Party, long rent by schism, had at last shattered. Most of the moderates stayed with Faulkner, all in the Assembly delegation except James Stronge and Herbert Whitten from Armagh. Some, disillusioned, drifted out of politics. The intransigents under West and Taylor considered themselves to be the Official Unionist Party, a point accepted when Faulkner moved his offices from the Unionist offices on Glengall Street to Malborough House in Victoria Street on January 9.

The bleak implications were simply ignored by all those tied to Faulkner's future: those who would share power, the SDLP, Alliance, and NILP; those who had negotiated the accommodation in London and Dublin; those who were daily involved in provincial governance in the Northern Ireland Office; and even and particularly those Irish and British civil servants preparing for the February conference to ratify the Sunningdale Agreement. What had happened transformed the Assembly majority: Faulkner's delegation no longer represented either the Unionist party or the majority community. There might be private public opinion polls that would show huge support. Professor Richard Rose of Strathclyde University, for example, published a poll on April 18 that indicated 69 percent of the people of Northern Ireland favored giving the executive a chance to rule and 74 percent in support of power sharing. There might be statements of support from the powerful on and off the island praising the Assembly and the province and the moderates. The reality, however, was that now the moderate Unionists were in a minority and their advocates and allies declined to notice.

Yet the rising militancy of the unionists, apparent well before the vote in the Ulster Unionist Council, indicated a most general disquiet concerning the Council of Ireland, the Assembly, and the direction of events. After all, the Unionist members of that Council knew their constituents as well as their own inclinations. They could hear Faulkner and the others selling one line and the Irish nationalists another. They suspected that all London wanted was quit of the province, had got that from Whitelaw, whipped him back to London as companion of honor and ornament of the cabinet and sent their Tory whip from the House of Commons, Pym, out to the province to oversee the results. Heath and the Conservative cabinet had to cope with a miners strike, with rising discontent, a winter of woes and power cuts warmed only by election rumors.

The loyalists wanted reassurance; instead, London used old formulas. For the Heath cabinet Northern Ireland was largely a distraction, a bother. Westminster politics were closing in on the cabinet. There was less time for Faulkner, for Pym, for the Assembly. So Faulkner was voted down and thus out and Taylor told a rally in Portadown, "We are out to destroy the Sunningdale Agreement." Cosgrave and Faulkner might meet with Pym's blessing, as they did at Baldonnel airport outside Dublin on January 16. The Anglo-Irish Law Enforcement Commission might meet at Hillsborough, as they did the same day. The work of the Northern Ireland Office and the new executive might continue, as it did. The loyalists simply ignored the polls and moderate Unionist politicians, for they felt they had the momentum for a change.

The means to express fundamentalist loyal opposition, however, had changed little, either in form or in effect. Paisley held protest demonstrations to Save Ulster. A loyalist petition was initiated by West, Taylor, and Craig, who hoped for 400,000 signatures. A bomb was found just before an SDLP meeting and there was weekend rioting in East Belfast on January 18 and 19 for indeterminate cause or purpose. The UDA accused the Tartan Gangs. A Catholic was shot dead at Carrickfergus.

The Provos at least supplied superficial novelty. An IRA spectacular was organized on January 24 by an English woman, Dr. Bridget Rose Dugdale, the thirty-two-year-old daughter of an English millionaire landowner, and a romantic recruit to Irish republicanism. Dugdale, with an erratic Provo gunman, Eddie Gallagher, and two others took to the air and dropped two milkchurn bombs on the Strabane RUC station from a helicopter hijacked in Gortahork, Donegal, and abandoned in Cloghan. The milk churns did not explode and the security forces soon knew the perpetrators, who moved south to the Republic and more adventures, to the dismay of Provo GHQ.

The most awful incident would come the next month in another Provo single-shot attack, no longer novel but grimly spectacular, in England on February 4. This time a fifty-pound bomb, slipped in with the soldier's luggage in the baggage compartment, detonated in a coach carrying army personnel on the M62 motorway from Manchester to Catterick Camp, Yorkshire. The blast shattered the coach. Eight soldiers and one woman with her two children were killed. The two IRA people involved escaped but not the innocent suspect, an

English woman, Judith Ward, who was arrested, tried, convicted, and sentenced to thirty years. Mostly, however, the IRA violence was pedestrian—car bombs and patrols ambushed, arson and trip mines.

All this was viewed as normal, background music to the real politics of the Northern Ireland Office. The executive published its social and economic program on January 21. The first meeting of the Assembly would be held the next day and there was little that the opposition could do inside Stormont or out. Protests, petitions, ritual riots, sectarian murders, threats, and promises could be ignored. And so on the night before the Assembly meeting, Paisley insisted that "direct action must be taken on the floor of the House and by the people through withdrawing their consent from government."

On the next day the direct action by those Assembly loyalists opposed to Faulkner certainly indicated not only a withdrawing of consent but also a refusal to allow government to proceed. The executive had anticipated parliamentary protest and complaint but assumed patience and moderation would win through. The loyalists, however, had exhausted their patience. Few democratic legislatures had witnessed such orchestrated chaos culminating in violence with the arrival of the police. This was not a matter of banging desk lids or shouting down the unpalatable but a concentrated effort to bring the Assembly not just to a stop but to disrepute.

The loyalists entered at 2:30 in the afternoon, prayed, and rushed forward to seize the seats designated for the executive. There were shouts and howls. Some climbed up and danced on desks. Other loyalists leaped upon the table beside the dispatch box, removed the mace, and began a parade about the chamber. Professor Kennedy Lindsay danced upon the speakers table and shouted, "We have driven the money changers from the temple." He then chained and padlocked himself to a bench. There would be No Surrender. The chaos continued until the police were summoned and the protesters forcibly removed. Faulkner later complained that Professor Lindsay had spat at him while being dragged from the chamber—a symbolic gesture according to Professor Lindsay. The speaker during the seventy-five minutes of chaos adjourned the chamber four times and finally had recourse to the police to remove the demonstrators, without undue force, according to the RUC statement, although five constables had been injured.

The entire exercise had become gesture and one that indicated the depth of opposition to Faulkner and the power that the executive held, for after the loyalists left the debate continued for ninety minutes. The more general question was whether the executive could continue to operate under such opposition. On January 23 the protesters walked out after ten minutes and debate continued without interruption. The following day they orchestrated an hour-long series of points of order to prevent parliamentary business. The executive struggled on patiently. The advocates of the Assembly and Sunningdale saw the protest as disgraceful, disorderly, puerile, unrepresentative, and futile. The Assembly would survive.

There were loyalists who felt that parliamentary displays were playing to the opposition's strength, that direct action might more easily be taken by the majority outside governing institutions. Heretofore those so inclined were to be found within the paramilitaries, who, when tired of the now ritual displays, protests, petitions, and riots, murdered the vulnerable. Their murders, shaming the moderates and distressing much of the loyalist community, had produced no visible effects on the major players who had fashioned the Assembly. Even the widespread and violent IRA campaign had not made the province ungovernable, only dangerous and costly.

Those loyalists who felt that the province could be snatched from Faulkner and the Northern Ireland Office by direct action—by simply closing down Ulster with a general strike—were largely invisible, unknown men, poorly dressed, inarticulate, who belonged to the various emerging and disappearing loyalist groups bubbling up in Belfast. They were far more obscure than the new paramilitary commanders who, in garish uniforms and reeking of cordite, had attracted the media. These others, shop stewards and workingmen, were united only in their grasp of the mechanics of labor unrest and the vulnerabilities of the provincial technological infrastructure. Unlike English Labour leaders honed in union organization, social mobilization, and ultimately parliamentary politics, the Irish came directly from the shop floor and the small, ill-attended meetings held in back rooms without form or agenda. They distrusted the politicians as well as the paramilitaries; they felt they were both radical socialists and true loyalists, and were certain that they had a means to effect events. That is what made them important.

These few not especially remarkable men, long on the fringe of loyalist organizations, had for some years discussed the potential of a real general strike focused on provincial vulnerabilities. They knew from experience that a strike for political purpose should not focus on penalizing owners, as in an economic strike, and not on a ritual display of support for a day or so, as had been the case with Craig's previous orthodox political stoppages. Rather, they focused on the nodes of technological control. Heretofore political strikes, called by politicians, had been holidays for rallies, short-term spectaculars and short-term failures, criticized by the authorities and even by the advocates of direct action. They led to ineffectual violence or simple ritual. Nothing else happened. When he called a strike, Craig wanted the streets filled with strikers, the air thick with rhetoric, results that were congenial and controlled by politics. That was sufficient, evidence of support, nothing more need happen.

A cunning workingman could make something happen or rather stop the crucial machines so that very quickly nothing normal would happen: no power, no lights, no energy, no petrol, no food, no communications, no movement. For years some loyalist workingmen had talked about the possibility. The key figures, known in 1974 only to each other, had moved through the Workers Committee for the Defense of the Constitution, founded in September 1969 as part of the Belfast loyalist mobilization, and into the Loyalist Association of Workers (LAW), represented by Billy Hull. The key figures along the way were Harry Murray, a shop steward at the Harland & Wolff shipyard; Hugh Petrie, the man behind Hull, a precision engineer in Short Brothers and Harland and a member of the Amalgamated Engineering Union; Billy Kelly, a power station worker and union convener from the Belfast East power station; Jim Smyth, an unemployed union man; and another middle-aged shipyard worker, Bob Pagels.

By 1973 LAW had splintered under Hull's domineering leadership and

Murray, Smyth, Petrie, and others met first as Loyalist Workers, then as Ulster Workers, and finally in January 1974 as the Ulster Workers Council. For most of the years of turmoil these workers had been invisible. Their small, unknown organizations would not have made good copy if any journalist had sought them out. Except for the rotund and eager Billy Hull, who liked speaking for LAW, there was nothing for the media. The workers did not have uniforms or titles, the skill to agitate before a crowd, or an interest in images and perceptions. Even in 1974 there was nothing to show but a few meetings in small, back rooms, the odd plan not even on paper, nothing very concrete: contacts made, details for a general strike checked, talks with the politicans and the paramilitaries but no agreements. The scheme seemed a hobby rather than a practical proposition.

But the proposition was very practical. This practicality gave such a loyalist strike its charm. All the powerful and grand, all the politicians, all the elegant and articulate did not seem to realize how vulnerable a technological state can be to industrial sabotage at key choke points. Loyalist workers could cut off the power. Loyalists could encourage or enforce key stoppages, interrupt communication, close down the province. The past strikes, the capacities of the loyalist street organizations, their own findings and contacts were real. An effective general strike was a possibility. The loyalist workingmen who did not see this possibility were hampered in part because of the very magnitude of the plan. They knew they could close down the province with a little help from their friends. And this prospect for a few everyday people seemed too large a project for such a committee of innocents to control.

Yet no one else seemed to be doing anything right or rather anything that worked. Petitions, protests, spitting on the opposition did not stop the Assembly or the decay of the loyalist position. Other everyday people had risen to challenges—even in Belfast the Provos had indicated what could be done. And so if the Provos could organize a secret army, then surely the loyalists could organize a general strike. Murray, Pagels, Petrie, and the rest did not really trust the politicians to run with the ball or the paramilitaries to discipline their own. But the help of both would be needed, the politicians to give a gloss of authority and the paramilitaries to assure compliance. So in time both were included in a twenty-one-man executive. In this coordinating body were Murray, Petrie (who was also leader of the Ulster Volunteer Service Corps—Craig's bodyguard), and Kelly, as well as their colleague Tom Beattie, a power station worker from Ballylumford. The politicians, Paisley, West, and Craig, would be co-opted.

At the first meeting a cross-section of hard-edged loyalists were present: Glen Barr, the Derry Vanguard man in the Assembly who was also a UDA officer; Andy Tyrie, as the UDA representative; Ken Gibson, who stood in for the UVF; Lieutenant Colonel Brush for the Down Orange Welfare; Bob Marno for his Orange Volunteers; and Bob Greene for the former B Specials, organized as the Ulster Special Constabulary Association. The key people, however, were not the famous politicans or even the appointed commanders of private armies but those like Jim Smyth who had been ready to go for six months.

The prospect of a general strike had been put on hold because a far more attractive option had opened up while the Assembly had soldiered on toward an acceptance of Sunningdale. In London Heath had decided that a general election sooner rather than later offered the best chance for his besieged Conservative government. Both Pym, even with only two months' exposure to Northern Ireland, and Whitelaw in London were deeply concerned about the impact of an election on the Assembly's prospects. There had been no time to show the benefits of power sharing, no time to make the SDLP presence in Stormont acceptable and conventional, no time to allow the displays and outrages of Paisley, Craig, and West to discredit such opposition. The Assembly was new, weak, ineffectual, and vulnerable. The Northern Ireland Office was wont to make this obvious by initiating policy and programs without consultation with the executive. Faulkner was made responsible for everything and granted no resources, often no warning. And the situation with Sunningdale and the Council of Ireland was still not set in stone, thus creating a volatile situation with apparent prospects for major adjustment to all aspects of the accommodation.

It was for Whitelaw's creation the worst of times for an election—the vote against Faulkner within the Ulster Unionist Council had indicated what an uncertain and emotional electorate might do. The Northern Ireland Assembly was for the Conservative cabinet but a penny on a scale heavily weighted on the other side by political necessity. Neither Whitelaw nor Pym had the leverage to delay a general election timed to what was thought Conservative advantage. No single issue could dissuade a party under threat, no single individual could have argued Ireland as more important. On February 7 Heath announced that a general election would be held on February 28.

In a flurry of conferences and bargains those opposed to the Assembly decided to make the general election a referendum on power sharing and Sunningdale by presenting a single slate, one candidate from a United Ulster Unionist Council (UUUC) under the slogan "Dublin Is But a Sunningdale Away." The *real* loyalists had not even been asked to Sunningdale and now they could make their distaste known. The Faulkner Unionists on the executive decided that their Stormont duties would prevent them from running for Westminster seats—all but Roy Bradford, Minister of the Environment on the executive, who went forward before a largely middle-class electorate in North Down. Already uneasy with the rising loyalist resentment, he began to distance himself further from Faulkner once the election results were tallied. The pro-Faulkner Unionists had to face the prospect of the big names—West, Paisley, Craig, Kilfedder, Harold McCusker in Armagh, the DUP's Robert Bradford—and the tangible unease of an electorate, unhappy in general about the tenor of Northern events and in particular about Sunningdale.

The result was often a free run for the UUUC. Even Faulkner noted in his own constituency that he would abstain rather than vote for a pro-Sunningdale SDLP candidate against an anti-Sunningdale Unionist. The great sectarian divide remained. The pro-Assembly Unionists on their side of the divided society would be forced to explain. Explainers under constant attack no matter how keen their defense have problems at election time. The Sunningdale slogan tended to overshadow any small wonders wrought by the Assembly. The Faulkner Unionists had very little to show, not even a full slate of Assembly loyalists. Much of the defense of power-sharing would be left to the SDLP, who ran a candidate in each constituency but were damaged by a split nationalist vote in two constituencies.

Yet even the SDLP was unhappy with the returns from the Assembly—Pym had not released enough internees, detention was still in place, the party had been forced to oppose a Catholic squatters movement and urge the payment of rates and rents. For many nationalists no tangible gains were apparent: What had the Assembly wrought, except posts for politicians? Still, the SDLP and much of the Catholic vote was committed to the Assembly but not so totally as to deny the radicals and critics sufficient returns to assure UUUC wins in narrowly divided constituencies. The crucial vote would be on the other side of the divide.

The election was for the Provos only a diversion. The Stickies might plan on three candidates on a Republican Club ticket, but this was only further evidence that the Officials had sold out. Thus, the IRA armed campaign continued, as did the sectarian murders by the loyalist paramilitaries. Provisional Sinn Féin did use the opportunity to demand that the British government transfer Irish prisoners in Britain to Northern Ireland, revoke the ban on Sinn Féin in Northern Ireland, and guarantee an end to harassment by British forces so that a free election could be held. As far as the Northern Ireland Office was concerned, the Provos had ceased to be a political player; the Assembly was the hope of the future. During a speech in Linton, Cambridgeshire, the Northern Secretary Pym did suggest on February 16 that Provisional Sinn Féin and the UVF advance their views "through the democratic processes," thereby linking the two groups of violent men with nondemocratic means. Otherwise the IRA was largely ignored as politically irrelevant, part of the problem, not the solution. The Provos in turn responded on election evening at about nine with a wave of bombs, twelve in Belfast and several out-of-town detonations. It was, however, a sideshow. Provincial attention was focused on elections, not bombs, on the inadvertent referendum.

Almost no one in Northern Ireland thought of the election in any other terms. Heath and Wilson, Labour, Conservative, strikes and United Kingdom programs and agendas meant nothing. Ulster voted for Ulster purpose, not British. And loyalist Ulster voted for the UUUC, whose candidate received 50.8 percent of the total vote on February 28 and returned eleven candidates, thus making it the fourth largest group in the new House of Commons. The total of anti-Assembly votes was 59 percent. The pro-Assembly Unionists, formed on February 4, managed only 13.1 percent, a precipitous decline from the Assembly election. The small parties and independents were marginalized—Alliance received only 3.1 percent and the NILP 2.1 percent. Although the SDLP received a respectable but hardly exciting 22 percent of the vote and Fitt held his seat in West Belfast, the vote in scope and timing was a disaster.

Almost incidentally, in Northern Ireland the other Westminster returns were considered—the election the rest of the United Kingdom thought to be the real contest. There the results were not so clear-cut. Edward Heath in a narrow election lost his majority. The Conservatives had won 300,000 more votes than Labour but four fewer seats. After a pause to explore stitching together some sort of coalition with the Liberals, he tendered his resignation on March 4. Harold Wilson and Labour would come to power but with an unsatisfactory parliamentary base—another election was probably on the way. So Northern Ireland would see new faces if not a new initiative. No observer imagined that in Irish matters Labour would be more congenial to loyalist complaints than the Conservatives.

These complaints had been made manifest in the vote. The Northern Irish electorate had used the Westminster elections to reject Sunningdale, the Assembly, and Faulkner. On March 1 he indicated his assessment of the results: "It represents the fears of the Unionists, basically the Unionists of Northern Ireland: fears about the unknown and the unknown expressed in that term Sunningdale. People know what the power-sharing executive is. They have seen us working and I haven't heard in the whole campaign any criticism of what we have been doing or what we are prepared to do." Give us time was his plea; surely Wilson would, if not Craig and the rest. Fitt, too, felt that the election had come "much too soon for the people of Northern Ireland to really begin to understand what Sunningdale really means." Give us time to produce was his request, and surely Wilson would. Time was a wasting asset at best, for the advocates of the Assembly had largely lost the mandate to rule a province divided once again.

Faulkner had listened only to his own heart's desire, not to those who condemned the Assembly root and branch, just as Fitt missed the implication of fundamentalist criticism that any power sharing, whatever the results, whether sooner or later, was anathema to the loyalists. The UUUC knew what they did not want: Sunningdale, the Assembly, an executive, Faulkner. And after February 28 they demanded elections to follow on their triumph that would return power to the real loyalists. The others could not rule for long if the people would not have them.

Their triumph, however, had brought Harold Wilson to power again and neither Labour nor Wilson were even as marginally sympathetic as the Tories. Wilson had on his own hook in 1972 as leader of the opposition gone to talk with the Provos, and he was, of course, a firm advocate of Sunningdale and the Council of Ireland. On a local television show on March 5 he said, "Nothing could be more harmful or more calculated to cause disorder and loss of life than to start changing a policy which has a broad measure of support throughout this country." The loyalists felt it did *not* have a broad measure of support in their country; nor did the announcements that Merlyn Rees, MP, fifty-three, former Labour Party spokesman on Northern Ireland Affairs, would be Northern Ireland secretary and Stanley Orme, MP, fifty, Minister of State. If Rees was no friend of Ulster, Orme, a Labour ideological crusader, was most likely an active enemy, for he had been vice-chairman for the small Democracy in Ulster organization and former chairman of the Northern Ireland group of the parliamentary Labour Party and as such an advocate of "reform." Thus, in the unexpected baggage deposited by the election was an unsympathetic Northern Ireland Office whose leaders would, once more, have to take a crash course in contemporary Ulster politics—even if their minds were closed, which some loyalists suspected.

This assessment was, like much else stowed in the loyalist knapsack, inaccurate and self-serving. Except for a very few Conservative mavericks like Enoch Powell, the British political establishment was still as one on the Irish issue, agreed down to the details of the agenda and the tactics. Wilson might well have met with the IRA (so, too, did the UVF) but, like Whitelaw later, he came away unimpressed; they were military men without sophistication, politics, or a place in the future. In fact Merlyn Rees, present at the Wilson Dublin meeting in March 1972, had also met again with the Provos, disguised as Sinn Féin, in Wilson's home in

Buckinghamshire on July 18, 1972, after the collapse of the truce. Those present had included Joe Cahill and Myles Shevlin, who had acted as secretary to the delegation that met Whitelaw. From this exposure Rees, a Welshman now Labour MP from Leeds (who made no secret of his dislike for Shevlin) came away, like Wilson, convinced that the Provos were beyond compromise.

Far from being an innocent, Rees, married into Irish Catholic connections, had long been Labour's shadow Northern Secretary. In many ways he was very typically Labour: a schoolteacher for eleven years, the son of a Welsh coal miner, sensitive, intelligent, tolerant but far less doctrinaire than many of his party colleagues. He had long been interested in Ireland. His father had served there before being gassed in France during World War I and had maintained an interest. Rees had been exposed in school to the enthusiasm of one teacher and then his marriage brought him the Irish Catholic connection. He was sympathetic to the concern within the Labour Party, where members like Orme, Paul Rose, and Kevin McNamara had sought Stormont reform. He was a British political rarity, like Orme, in his early interest in Irish matters, but his Labour career had been elsewhere.

Rees had been Labour Under Secretary of State at Defense and then at the Home Office before becoming opposition spokesman on Northern Ireland. He would arrive knowing a great many Irish players and postures personally, knowing the details of Conservative and previous Labour Irish policy in detail, and knowing the workings of the military and the Home Office. As an added bonus he had served as a squadron leader in the RAF during World War II with Frank Cooper and thus would have a head start with the secretariat. And unlike Whitelaw and Pym and others later, Rees wanted the Irish job. He felt he could make a difference, end internment, encourage moderation, fashion an accommodation.

Orme at least more closely fit the loyalist profile of a fuzzy-headed Labour man simply because he had long advocated Northern Ireland reforms. And Orme had little sympathy for the hard loyalists, who reminded him of Fascists. The comparison was hardly unique to Orme—many journalists found Vanguard rallies disturbing, found little attractive in the UDA or UVF or Paisley or most of the Orange establishment. With the very rare Conservative or anti-Catholic Irish exception, everyone in British politics, Conservative or Labour, Liberal or independent, radical or Celtic nationalist in Parliament or out, lacked empathy with the loyalists opposed to Faulkner. No one wanted a return to Stormont.

Nearly everyone wanted Whitelaw's initiative to succeed. Rees was as one with Pym and not at all unsympathetic to the Unionist people under IRA assault. He seemed to fit the Northern Office's need: a military man in a country devoted to military service, a politician with the Prime Minister's ear, intimate with both Defense and the Home Office, who had an old friend as Permanent Under Secretary. He knew the players, knew the details of the recent past, was pragmatic without a taste for the mysteries of covert Irish politics—the details in Dublin of the Sinn Féin meetings he found "very unpleasant"—or the trappings of national security concerns that arose from the IRA challenge. Most of all he wanted the job.

The job in March 1974 was no different from Pym's the month before: Buttress the Assembly. Once the flurry of political statements came out of London, Dublin, and Belfast explaining how the election results were to their advantage, a round of talks and conferences and contacts with the new people began.

Dublin sought to make clear that any united Ireland was a matter of Northern choice, not a real issue; London argued that the way forward was the same whether Pym or Whitelaw was Secretary; and the pro-Assembly people said that it would be government as usual and Sunningdale would be approved after democratic debate. In sum, nothing had changed for Dublin, London, or the Assembly. The anti-Assembly individuals and organization paid no attention. The loyalists followed their same road: clamorous opposition within the Assembly, protests and petitions outside, and a chorus of threats as background music. The new voice in that chorus came from the Ulster Workers Council, a grouping that few observers had noted.

On March 22 the UWC, directed by the new co-opted executive committee, announced that if Westminster policies were imposed on the Ulster people "grave industrial consequences will ensue." The threat was little noted but would long be remembered. Within the UWC Murray, Petrie, and the rest had opted for a strike if and when the Assembly accepted Sunningdale. Such an Assembly vote—and Faulkner had the votes—would provide a good symbolic starting point. The strikers could defend against unwelcome change, Assembly betrayal. Despite the paramilitaries, who would delight in recourse to intimidation in any case, despite the doubts of the politicians, who would have to go along in any case, the unknown organizers were set on a general strike, a strike that was by April ready on short notice. On April 2 the speaker of the Assembly postponed until after the Easter recess any vote on John Laird's motion to renegotiate Sunningdale. Tomorrow might be a better day for the Assembly. Events could wait on Easter.

Other events after the general election proceeded apace, with all sorts of flurries, alarms, and incidents but little that was unexpected. The IRA's armed campaign escalated with a spring wave of arson attacks and bomb explosions throughout the six counties. On March 7, for example, a five-hundred pound bomb in a hijacked van that had penetrated the security area detonated in central Belfast in front of the Grand Central Hotel, which was used as headquarters for the Royal Horse Artillery. The huge explosion devastated the entire area. On March 28 an additional £750,000 damage was done when the operation was exactly repeated, again within the tight security zone, this time with a six-hundred pound bomb in another hijacked van.

The Provos kept up British interest with single attacks in England. On March 26 there were two small bombs timed with two Japanese Coral alarm clocks detonated in Claro-Deverell Barracks in Ripon, Yorkshire. They had been left by Peter McMullen, the deserter from the Paras in Derry just before Bloody Sunday, and Englishman Joe Gilhooley, originally from Moss Side in Manchester. McMullen, along with his English contact, Marian Coyle, returned to link up with the helicopter duo, Rose Dugdale and Eddie Gallagher, in the Republic. On April 6 a series of fourteen bombs exploded in London stores and shops; two more went off in Manchester and three in Birmingham. On April 9 the center of Armagh town was partly destroyed by incendiary bombs that burned down ten shops in Market, Scotch, and Thomas streets. On April 26 Dugdale and company stole a collection of paintings from the home of Sir Alfred and Lady Beit near Blessington in County Wicklow, bringing the war south again, to the dismay of the Provo GHQ. On May 4 Dugdale was arrested with the paintings in Glandore, Cork, and general attention again turned to more conventional and more violent IRA attacks. And the chronicle of death and destruction went on through each successive week despite massive and more efficient security efforts.

The Army Council and GHQ had certain administrative problems that to a degree were eased when Twomey returned as chief of staff with Brian Keenan as the crucial GHQ operations officer, although the center of gravity for control was for some Northern commanders still in the wrong place. In Belfast there had been a series of Provo losses through arrests. The security forces had improved their doctrine and capacities, improved their intelligence capacities, and, relying on routine rather than intuition or novelty, began to see returns. Gerry Adams had been arrested in July 1973.

His replacement as O/C of Belfast, Ivor Bell, was arrested on February 24, 1974, escaped on April 15, and then was rearrested April 28. The new O/C, Seán Convery, lasted only until his arrest along with Frank Fitzsimmons of the First Battalion on March 8. The new O/C, Brendan Hughes, who had been arrested with Gerry Adams in July 1973 but had escaped on December 8, 1973, moved his key people into very quiet, very safe middle-class houses in Protestant areas. The police and British army were left behind in the old arenas around the former no-go zone with their old routines and practices while the IRA donned middle-class cover. Hughes was also able to set up safe stockpiles in respectable quarters at the edge of Catholic districts and even spend some time preparing strategic plans in case of a doomsday situation: an armed Protestant backlash.

The damage caused by a British sting operation within prison using double agents was contained. The gear was available from the stockpiles in the South. Money, if tight as always, was there, the usual mix of dues, profits from the black economy, expropriations, diaspora funds, and foreign contributions. The countryside was still solid and so the Provos could feel that they were ready for another push. But just when Belfast felt matters were in hand, Hughes, posing as Arthur McAllister, toy salesman, in turn on May 10 was arrested in the Myrtlefield Park flat along with Denis Loughlin, "company director." The Belfast Brigade had to regroup again.

Most of the security successes continued to arise from rote, from the institutionalization of counterinsurgency, from good police work. In the province on any given day five thousand automobiles were stopped, the driver questioned, and often the vehicle searched. This meant that, for example, in the year between April 1, 1973, and April 1, 1974, security forces searched 4 million cars, seized 1,600 weapons, sixteen tons of prepared bombs, and nineteen tons of explosives. In that year 1,292 individuals were charged with terrorist, criminal offenses. The vulnerable points were guarded, the center of towns and cities often fenced and patrolled. General and particular information was collected daily, ordered, and filed, month after month, by 1974, year after year.

What was true for the IRA, the prime target, was also true to a lesser degree for the Protestant paramilitaries. Neither the army nor the police had any love for secret armies, no matter the banner. Those relatively few loyalists who killed were avidly sought, for they were a danger to the legitimacy of the entire community. Thus, the RUC, an overwhelmingly Protestant force, and the UDR, a Protestant militia, over the years tended to seek terror where it was to be found; unsympathetic to Irish national grievances in most cases, hard on Irish republican suspects, the security forces as disinterestedly as possible pursued order under congenial laws and let justice wait on the politicians.

Some antiterrorists, more determined and eager than others, continued to seek out and destroy the unconventional Provos by special means, tricks, ploys, disinformation, false flag arrangements, and the use of new military and police covert organizations engaged in very special operations. SAS (Special Air Service) instructors were brought over to train the Fourteenth Intelligence RUC–Special Branch. The army had various special units, including the Military Reaction Force that had surfaced previously in plainclothes operations. In a covert, dirty war such units, however great the risks and however difficult the matter of control, were considered a necessary evil by the orthodox police and military and a wondrous opportunity, at times misused, by the romantic or unconventional.

These special operations of the security forces became a continuing thread in provincial life. Increasingly it was obvious to everyone that the British used undercover means, usually (and usually inaccurately) credited by republicans to the SAS. Some incidents during this period were obviously organized by undercover army personnel—ambushes or intelligence probes or simple rural patrols. The regular newspapers had reports, sometimes actions led in time to trials or official statements, and the IRA or civil rights organizations or interested parties announced disturbing findings from time to time. There were as well unexpected disclosures: On March 20, on a country road at Mowhan, Armagh, ten miles from the border, two soldiers of the Fourteenth-Twentieth King's Hussars were killed in the early hours when the RUC fired on unidentified men in plain clothes. Tales of army-RUC shootouts, with the army deploying weapons favored by the IRA, entered the folklore. The suspicious suspected the army was involved in provocative acts, shootings to cause sectarian trouble, bombings to gain sympathy or intimidate politicians, acts that went beyond tradition and were often as disturbing to loyalist opinion as to nationalist.

Certainly there was suspicion in many quarters, including again firm law-and-order Protestants, that the army and intelligence special operations needed control, were contrived to provoke sectarian strife and at times involved murderous paramilitaries and dubious agents. There were hints and mysteries and not only in the six counties: The SAS or at least British soldiers and Protestant paramilitary men were rumored to be involved in cross-border raids; the Little-johns' trail had led from Dublin to London; and then on April 13 Kenneth Lennon, a thirty-year-old Newry man used by the police as an informer, was found shot dead in a lane in Chipstead, Surrey, just two days after he had given the National Council of Civil Liberties a six-hour oral statement on his career as an informer. Even a formal report clearing Special Branch published on November

28, 1974, did not dispel the mystery. It was a "whitewash" claimed the National Council of Civil Liberties.* Over the years there were other unsolved mysteries.

The romance of the secret and the lure of conspiracy tended to escalate the significance of the seamy side of what was all too obviously a very dirty war, like most unconventional wars. Amid the squalor and misery of a war of attrition the covert fed the province's need for conspiracy, for explanation. And the covert has an appeal to those within the orthodox security forces who assume that secrecy permits all, allows an end to morality as well as expense accounts in three copies. The theoretical charm about special operations is that they are special, secret, so much more alluring than routine, rote, and authorization in triplicate. Except in Ireland there seemed as many revelations as secrets, as many triumphs by routine as by stealth, and as many losses of varying kinds as victories because of dirty tricks. Yet, as time passed, as the IRA armed struggle and the Protestant paramilitary low-intensity backlash continued year after year, these exposures produced not an end to the secret and authorized subversion, not even official lethargy, but institutionalization. The unconventional became conventional. The revelations did not surprise anyone, especially not the covert opponents of order, only disappointed those who felt the state this time, at last, was beyond recourse not to the secret (such means were crucial in a war against secret armies) but to the illicit. The dark side of the unconventional as conventional, the erosion of legitimacy in defense of the realm, was another price of an irregular war paid by all of the conventional.

The conventional politicians continued to pursue their ends in the spring of 1974 almost as if there had been no thunderous detonations in front of the Grand Central Hotel in Belfast, no bodies shrouded in black plastic bags found on country lanes, no dirty war, no unknown men in scruffy uniforms possessed of the truth who could speak for the people, as if there were no shuttered stores in Armagh town or armor in the Derry streets. Only the foreign photographers stopping on their terror tours noticed the patrols along the Falls, spoke with the intimates of gunmen, snapped their own picture of a child by a soldier, and moved on. No media vita or expert's portfolio was complete without an Irish entry, a visa for Northern violence, easily renewed with three days at the Europa. The politicians had to stay, had to accept the conventions of conflict, had to seek a formal structure to satisfy their own.

The British assumed that in the Assembly enough of the moderates could be so satisfied and so the general election could be ignored, along with the usual loyalist and IRA threats and menaces. In fact in Dublin, the Irish Minister for Posts and Telegraphs, Conor Cruise O'Brien, often a step ahead of everyone, recycled threats and menaces in moderation's name on April 1, when he told BBC's "World at One" that if Sunningdale were to fail it would mean civil war. This would become a set piece for O'Brien and others: Accept my analysis or the heavens will fall. It

---

*Cf. Geoff Robertson, *Reluctant Judas: The Life and Death of the Special Branch Informer, Kenneth Lennon* (London: Temple-Smith, 1976). There is a substantial literature critical of British covert actions in Northern Ireland, mostly based on open sources and speculation and the occasional memoirs of the involved, balanced by various military histories and memoirs, no less limited in detailed sources.

was a piece played over and over again until at last no one believed. In 1974, however, civil war seemed real enough—the IRA, never a font of strategic thinking, had even drawn up their doomsday plan with such an eventuality in mind. No matter that the politicians, the bureaucrats, the explainers and enumerators circled and talked. Wilson talked with Faulkner, the SDLP talked with Cosgrave, who met with Wilson and Rees, who talked with everyone. The Prime Minister came to Ireland on April 18 for eight hours to announce to a press conference, "We stand by Sunningdale. We want to see it become a reality." The journals published articles, the producers did chat shows, the watchers watched and turned in reports. No one much noticed the UWC, another acronym, more menaces, tatty unknowns with desperate nasal accents and no coherence.

On April 8 Rees and Orme had met with the UWC, whose grievances were long and tempers short. Their position on Sunningdale was clear but their other complaints haphazardly presented, and general truculence did not impress the British. The conventional Northern politicians were difficult enough, but at least they arrived with an agenda and displayed coherence. The anti-Assembly Northern politicians, Unionists, Vanguard, and DUP, organized formally since April 3 into the UUUC, shared the British doubts about the UWC but not so much because of their inexperience as because of their novel militancy: Craig, Paisley, and West preferred the old ways of petition, protest, and public display orchestrated into militant campaigns. Their people were collecting signatures to a petition (308,410 names would be on display by April 11), their parties issued statements, and they hammered away in public. They announced a three-day conference at Portrush in Antrim, April 24–26, when their favorite British politician, Enoch Powell, no longer at Westminster, would speak.

The UWC was invited but something of an unwelcome guest, like a stray cat dragging in a general strike under the mistaken assumption that praise would ensure. The UWC presented a list of six demands they felt the politicians should take into account. It was a mixed bag and was hence not taken seriously.

1. Dissolution of the executive; Secretary of State reassumes powers.
2. Assembly elections before September.
3. Constituencies reduced in size.
4. Parties on ballot not listed alphabetically but by random selection.
5. Council of Ireland rejected—even as a subject of discussion.
6. Secretary of State, after new Assembly, loses power of veto.

The thrust of the demands was to fashion a new loyalist assembly where the small parties would have a chance, the British no control, and the Council of Ireland no part. The politicians listened to the demands and went their own way.

When the loyalists arrived at Portrush, the paramilitaries and the UWC, the direct-action people, had been shunted aside. Instead there was Enoch Powell, whose analysis was one with theirs, although his advocacy of total integration was not.

> The conflict in Northern Ireland is not about law and order; it is not about civil rights; it is not about peace and security; it is not about participation, community relations and all the rest of the new-fangled claptrap expressions; it is not even about religion. It is about nationality.*

And this is just what the loyalists always believed—the Irish nationalists wanted Ulster.

The Portrush conference published on April 26 a coherent six-page policy document that listed the eight UUUC objectives, ranging from an additional ten seats at Westminster (an Enoch Powell favorite) to a call for a general election. The last point, opposition to a Council of Ireland, loomed largest.

Sunningdale was the first step toward a united Ireland, whatever Faulkner and the rest said. Once the camel had its nose under the tent wall, once a Council was in place, all that was left was the timing. Yet despite the results of the general election and the seeming unity of the loyalists at Portrush, there was little good news on the horizon. The IRA campaign continued unabated, despite promises from London and the Northern Ireland Office. On April 10 a popular retired UDR officer, Colonel George Saunderson, headmaster of Derrylin Primary School in Fermanagh, had been shot and killed in the kitchen of his own school by the Provos—a murder that even more than the Belfast bomb blitz brought the violence closer. And there was no sign of a changing tide. The Anglo-Irish Law Enforcement Commission's report on April 16 simply underlined the futility of appeasing Dublin when the members divided North and South over extradition, which was seemingly prevented by the Republic's constitution as well as political climate. There were over thirty wanted murderers free in the South and no legal means to reach them.

In the midst of their deliberation the Labour Secretary of State for Defense, Roy Mason, during a speech at Newcastle-under-Lyme, suggested that there was rising pressure for the government to set a date for the withdrawal of troops so that "the leaders of the warring factions could get together and hammer out a solution." It was just as the loyalists suspected—Labour London intended to abandon them to a traitorous power-sharing Assembly and the implications of the Council of Ireland. Mason, speaking vaguely, had never thought of the implications of his suggestion in Ireland. The Ministry of Defense swiftly issued a statement saying that there had been no policy change. The British spent a week explaining but the damage had been done.

For the loyalists April had been a bad month. On April 11 the *Belfast Telegraph* published the names of the one thousand dead and no one doubted there would be more. The IRA campaign had escalated; and there was evidence that they had new American weapons—two Armalite 180 rifles had been found in Lurgan, Armagh, on April 2. The British response had seemingly been the announcement to legalize Sinn Féin two days later on April 4, with the UVF thrown in to reward their apostasy. No one had been impressed with their 308,410 names. For the UWC, petitions were pointless. They decided on a strike for May 8. Paisley leaked the plan to the press and the strike was called off. The UWC, ignoring the

*Richard Ritchie, ed. Enoch Powell speeches, *Enoch Powell: A Nation or No Nation* (London: B.T. Batsford, 1978), p. 59.

coordinating committee, decided that there would be a strike and it would come immediately after the vote in the Assembly on Sunningdale. The politicians and the paramilitaries would hear the news when it was too late to interfere.

The Assembly vote was scheduled for Tuesday, May 14. There was a feeling that the moment would be crucial. During the days immediately before the vote a variety of events, carefully fashioned or quite unexpected, added to the tension. On Friday, May 10, Faulkner attempted to put to rest once again the loyalist fears of Sunningdale: "We state absolutely that a Council of Ireland: (1) would not be used as a stepping-stone on the road to Irish Unity; (2) would not develop into an All-Ireland Parliament; (3) would not have control of the Royal Ulster Constabulary." He too wanted more Westminster seats and control of provincial security. He convinced only those who already accepted the necessity of his policy.

On the same day the raid on Brendan Hughes's flat had presented Wilson with an opportunity to show the effectiveness of the security forces, a constant arena of loyalist complaint. On Monday in the House he released the IRA's doomsday plan in such a way that Protestant anxiety was increased, not eased, and sectarian tensions were heightened—were withdrawal and civil war on the way? Craig, ever ready with the hard word, had on Sunday during a radio interview on the RTE program "This Week" noted that the sectarian murders in the North were "understandable and excusable" if the Catholics were going to pursue the politics of the minority. For their part the republicans fielded Maire Drumm who in Kiltyclogher, Leitrim, announced that "1974 is the year of liberation." When Brian Faulkner deplored violence the next day at Sheffield University, condemned the IRA (chief enemy of justice and democracy), and underlined his hatred of the "whole rotten gamut of paramilitary organizations," he almost seemed to speak alone. Few uneasy loyalists wanted to hear his explanations. The British, however, were still attempting, despite the leaks and gaffes, to buttress the Assembly, the best, perhaps the last hope for Northern political moderation.

Rees on May 13 was in Dublin, meeting for six hours with Cosgrave and then Lynch, seeking support. The British thought that Fianna Fáil in opposition felt a renewal of patriotism so that the coalition government was overselling the Council of Ireland as if the loyalists did not follow every declaration. Rees's troubles were compounded by a Provisional IRA press conference on May 13 where O Conaill produced a copy of a 1973 letter of the Northern Secretary that said in part, "We have not the faintest desire to stay in Ireland and the quicker we are out the better." Bad news after the Mason gaffe. But all the fury of the last few days before the vote meant little. The UWC was going to strike.

On Monday morning, May 13, while Wilson spoke to the House and Faulkner at Sheffield, while Rees met Cosgrave and Lynch in Dublin, the UWC workers informed the politicians that there was to be a strike. Paisley, Ernest Baird (representing Craig and Vanguard), Austin Ardill, and John Taylor found the UWC men (Kelly, Petrie, Jim Smyth, and Andy Tyrie) determined. Kelly told them, "We've got the strike organized—it begins tomorrow at six when the vote is taken in the Assembly." Paisley was opposed. (He agreed at first but that evening issued a statement that the decision to strike had not been that of the UUUC.) Craig was opposed. There was argument but by lunchtime the decision was accepted. Baird agreed and Taylor came around. Ardill took notes as secretary and made no comment.

There would be a strike, regardless of the politicans, the UWC assured their agreement to be inevitable. The paramilitaries united in the Ulster Army Council were already drafting their strike statement: If Westminster is not prepared to restore democracy, that is, the will of the people made clear in election, then the only other way it can be restored is by a coup d'état. It was the very posture the politicians had sought to avoid. At least the UWC announcement that evening was pedestrian, simply threatening a provincewide blackout and perhaps a general strike: "If Brian Faulkner and his colleagues vote in the Assembly on Tuesday the 14th to support Sunningdale then there will be a general stoppage." Trivial to the end, the proclamation advised the workers' dependents to apply for Supplementary Benefit immediately. It was almost comforting after the paramilitaries' rhetoric—or would have been if anyone had noticed.

The assembled media, political observers, and the participants focused not on any subsequent strike nor on the Ulster Army Council's coup d'état but on the vote. The original motion put forward by John Laird read, "That this Assembly is of the opinion that the decision of the electorate of Northern Ireland at the polls on 28th February 1974 rejecting the Sunningdale Agreement and the imposed constitutional settlement requires renegotiation of the constitutional arrangements and calls accordingly for such renegotiation." It was the core political demand. Faulkner proposed an amendment to the motion that defended the executive's policy. At six in the evening, as expected, Faulkner's amendment passed the Assembly with forty-four votes to twenty-two; Faulkner Unionists, the SDLP, and the Alliance supported it, David Bleakley of the NILP abstained, and the UUUC opposed. Faulkner had won. The UUUC left glumly and gave no comments to the press.

A few minutes later, at 6:08 Harry Murray walked hesitatingly into the press room in the northern end of the Stormont building to face the media fresh from the Assembly vote. He was a small man with receding, mussed hair, wearing mismatched trousers and sport jacket. With him was Bob Pagels, a bit niftier in sunglasses and a gray suit and flash tie. Neither gripped the imagination. Murray stood before a small group of journalists and spoke above the press room din as the real story of the Assembly vote was called in to editors, producers, and copytakers. He talked softly in his hard Belfast voice about the work stoppage, wandered a bit, announced that production of electricity would be reduced from the normal 725 megawatts to only 400, and ended his short speech with, "It is a grave responsibility but it is not ours. It is Brian Faulkner's. He and his friends are ignoring the wishes of 400,000 people who voted against them in the general election and in doing so they must take the responsibility for this strike."

So there would be a UWC strike, maybe supported by the UUUC (not visible in the press room), maybe by the paramilitaries (the most inconsistent and disorganized of armies), maybe by the loyalist people. There had been no thunderous rhetorical lead-on as there had when Craig had called strikes. There had been no speeches, petitions, protests, no chapel meetings nor posters, no pamphlets on the street corners, no marches, nothing. The print journalists (press conferences by a man from nowhere, a man without authority or even much presence, do not attract the cameras) were bemused. No one had heard of Murray or much noticed Pagels, no one paid a great deal of attention to the strike announcement. Everyone filed the Assembly story, noted the strike announcement, and went home.

13

The Protestant Blacklash, the General Strike to the Convention Elections: May 1974–May 1975

"Fear and Hope are the Two Great Instruments for
the Governance of Men."

Jean-Jacques Rousseau

The general strike gave early indications that the UWC were, as they seemed, small men with a big idea, pretensions of control, and neither experience nor capacity. They feared the present and were without much hope for the future. They were not a mass movement, had not prepared the public or the strikers, had no control of the streets, only knew the vulnerabilities and key men. The paramilitaries had made no real plans and the politicians had been co-opted only to give the strike legitimacy. The result was that the province did not come to a standstill the first morning; in fact, over 90 percent of the province, farmers, industrial workers, druggists, and clerks went off to work as usual owing no loyalty to an invisible coordinating committee or a strike called at a press conference. The two most visible strike leaders, Harry Murray and Harry Patterson, had insisted on television Tuesday evening that there would be no intimidation. And at nine o'clock Wednesday morning there had been none: The roads were open and the people were at work. Kelly's men at Ballylumford station brought the electricity supply down to 60 percent and the Belfast industries began having difficulties.

Tyrie at UDA and UWC headquarters on Hawthornden Road realized that the workers were going in. The telephone calls began to arrive: "Some of the lads have turned up for work." This would not do—the strike broken before it began, and as much out of innocence and routine as reasoned choice. The paramilitaries began to spread the word while avoiding the kind of violence that would ruin the strike. Tommy Lyttle of the UDA, a thirty-five-year-old bookmaker's manager, emphasized that "you may have called it intimidation—but intimidation without violence is something very important." The most famous intervention involved the eight thousand workers at Harland and Wolff's, mostly Protestants, who at lunch break heard unnamed speakers announce that any cars in the employees' car

411

park at two o'clock that afternoon would be burned. The eight thousand workers immediately left the yard. Gradually the major industrial firms closed, often without any intimidation. Shops began closing, because of arson threats, because the neighbor did, because the word got out. The cross-channel ferries to Stranraer stopped running because the UWC had closed Larne harbor. Four-hour power cuts began. Soon 75 percent of the Derry area was without power. The Royal Victoria Hospital in Belfast had to use its emergency generator. Barricades began going up in Belfast and some of the towns. Bakeries closed down. Other shop owners or managers went home early.

No one in authority was as yet unduly worried. Much still seemed normal. There had been intimidation, reports came into the media, to the Northern Ireland Office, buses hijacked, workers threatened, so that the UWC sooner rather than later would be contaminated by violence. And the other strikes had not worked. The newspapers and the BBC anticipated a brief inconvenience. Robert Fisk of the London *Times*, who would become the historian of the strike, wrote, "It seems likely that Belfast will suffer no more than a slight loss of power during the daytime hours." There was no sense of urgency. Rees was in London. In retrospect the crucial time to prevent the strike occurred during the first day. But no one realized the urgency of the moment. If the RUC and the army had flooded the potential points of intimidation, if the Northern Ireland Office had realized there was a crisis, if and if. Instead there was pause and resentment. Faulkner in Belfast issued a short, harsh statement aimed at those who had abused the democratic process: "Where do they come from? Who elected them? What is their authority?" At 5:30 that afternoon Orme met with the political leaders (Paisley, Craig, John Laird), with representatives of the UWC (Bob Pagels, Harry Patterson, and Harry Murray), and with representatives of the paramilitaries (Lyttle, Tyrie, and Ken Gibson).

Orme felt he was dealing with sectarian Fascists, a political strike imposed by intimidation, and an effort to subvert democracy. He had no trace of sympathy for the strike leaders, the paramilitaries, or the loyalist politicians. Worse, he found the use of Labour's own weapon, a strike, somewhat traumatic, an ideological sin. Paisley, quick for the soft spot, noted his antistrike position was "a strange thing coming from an MP sponsored by the engineering trade union." Labour did find it strange to be in the strikebreaking business and so insisted, then and later, that the strikes that had led to the general election in February 1974 had been economic, not political, and had led in any case not to a Labour triumph but to an almost hung parliament. Labour strikes were different. Loyalist strikes were disreputable. It was still another example of the weight of British political baggage carried to Ireland. Orme saw Fascism and intimidation. Labour in particular and Britain generally would find the disloyal loyalists disagreeable. Their strike was not legitimate and so, perforce, must be imposed. The men Orme met were angry, bitter, grievance-ridden, intransigent, then and later swinging between petty wrongs and high policy; they were difficult opponents to esteem, whether the sleek Craig or the awkward, scruffy gunmen. From the first the British decided not to negotiate with the strikers; after all, "Where do they come from? Who elected them? What is their authority?"

In a very real sense several factors on Wednesday, May 15, the first strike day, had coalesced to assure an ultimate strikers' victory—if the committee kept its nerve and unity. The Protestant toleration of the British initiative, never great, had eroded. The executive was neither admired nor trusted. The SDLP sharing power denied to the loyalists was seen as subversive, a conspiracy in place in Stormont eager for a united Ireland. The Northern Ireland Office and the British government, particularly with Labour in place, engendered the usual ambivalence: a loyalty to symbols and devices of their own majority desires, not to actual governments and unpleasant policies. The loyalists were loyal to their perceptions, their reading of history, and their needs and desires. And for five years seemingly no one had cared about their grievances. The British had taken them for granted, made concessions to the others, allowed their province to be bombed away. So the UWC at an optimum moment presented an uneasy and resentful population an opportunity to act at minimum cost: Do nothing and watch them, the others, all of them, squirm.

By Wednesday night the vast majority of the Protestants had withdrawn their consent to be governed by the executive. Faulkner no longer had a loyalist mandate: Who was he now? Who had elected him? Whom did he represent? On Thursday, May 16, the barricades went up in Belfast, reinforcing British assumptions of intimidation.

The police with army aid could clear the major barricades and protect property, but they could not break the strike. The police, mostly Protestant, were mostly sympathetic to the strike but seldom had to face a conflict of interest. They did not even have to work to rule. They could not *make* people go to work. And no paramilitary man really defended the barricades or visibly intimidated civilians. The army, too, could not force normality had their commanders so desired, which they did not—strikebreaking, operations against civilians, were hardly popular military options for a regular army. They might have been effective the first day, but no one realized this at the time. After the first day, the workers were out by choice, by fear, through indolence or sloth, but out. They could not be made to work even if many tried and blamed their failure on intimidation. Anyway what could the army do, actually? More troops were flown into the province—troops with the United Nations in Egypt were even brought back—but soldiers could not operate the province or even maintain the power stations. Soldiers were a symbol and one the loyalists chose to ignore. They did not fear military intervention. Much of the Protestant bureaucratic apparatus of the province was in sympathy with the UWC. Most did nothing, which was something. Some leaked secrets or the plans of the authorities. Some simply stayed home, like the teachers and route men and boilermakers.

Those at the top might want to make the system work; but from the first they, and Rees particularly, recognized that compelling power did not exist. Even if the desire to use force within reason had existed by Thursday there were reasons not to do so. There was no longer any way, even treating the province as an occupied country, that the loyalists could be forced to accept British guidance. The Northern Ireland Office and London could seek to persuade, to intimidate, to threaten, to argue, to bribe, to compromise; but they could not effectively use force. All that was left was to encourage the executive, the keystone of the Assembly system, and hope the strikers would falter, divide, blink before the inexorable power of the Crown's stare. And London did have assets for the long haul. So London had hope but, as yet, no hope to offer the loyalists.

It became clear, as the days passed and the strike didn't weaken, that the province was in for the long haul. Fisk and the media, Rees and Orme and Wilson, Dublin and the SDLP, the minority, all had missed the dangers that a strike presented in the spring of 1974. The BBC became a striker asset, reported disinterestedly, shaped the strike as more economic than political, gave the UWC legitimacy, presented their demands and instructions, and tended to give credence to loyalist presentations. The articulate BBC made the inarticulate UWC coherent. The media foreign and domestic, radio or television, knowledgeable or not, also played to striker advantage. There was a sense of crisis. BBC and NBC and RAI thought the times historic. The Protestants, surrounded by heretics and knaves, were encouraged to believe they had embarked on an important adventure.

The British could do little about the lack of petrol, the barricades, the blackouts, the ruined milk and the starving cattle, the schoolchildren's missed exams, the gradually cascading economic effect as the province began to close down. And always they faced the threat that the power could be shut off entirely and so too viable life in the province. The army could not take up the slack, nor could the RUC, nor the British bureaucrats. London simply hoped the strikers would give up first.

So Rees refused to talk and waited. Dublin tended to suggest stronger British actions than viable. The SDLP, seeing the Council of Ireland snatched from them, loyal to the concept of the executive, not to Faulkner, impotent and internally quarrelsome, could only, like the British, hang on for better days, conferring with Dublin and quarreling with one another. The minority became little more than observers. Relatively little was done to them, except that on Friday evening, May 24, paramilitaries involved in intimidating Catholics at pubs in the Ballymena area shot the Byrne brothers dead at their public house at the Wayside Halt at Tannaghmore, Antrim. This atrocity led to the arrest by the RUC of thirty-three men, mostly from Belfast and Carrickfergus. Two were charged with murder, the others with aggravated burglary.

The strike committee was, like their opponents, often uncertain and divided. Yet they kept their nerve and coped, learned television manners, administrative practice, and the delegation of assumed powers. The great plan had worked. The paramilitary had acted as anticipated. The politicians had come aboard, even if Paisley had disappeared for a Canadian funeral at a key moment. The pivot was simply attrition: The executive and Northern Ireland Office, if they would not talk, could not wait forever. Increasingly the economic life of the province was authorized by the UWC, who from the first listed essential services, announced closing hours, permitted and denied, distributed passes and permissions, assumed governmental functions that the "real" government out at Stormont, cut off from time to time by blockades, could not perform. A workers' association began publishing a *Strike Bulletin*. They were actually running a coup on the installment plan. Barricades went up and came down. Shops opened and closed. Electrical power, the heart of the province's economic circulatory system, was controlled by strikers, and if cut entirely would assure flooding in Belfast streets and an end to coherent life in the province.

If violence was largely, if not entirely, peripheral to the strike in the province, the same did not prove to be the case in the Irish Republic. In Dublin on May 17, Friday, the third day of the strike, three car bombs, made from vehicles stolen in the North and driven south that day, exploded almost simultaneously at 5:30 in the afternoon, the middle of the evening rush hour. One exploded on South Leinster Street, off Nassau Street beside Trinity College on the south side of the Liffey. On the north side there were two blasts, one on Talbot Street and one in Parnell Street. The streets literally ran with blood, and bits of the maimed and murdered were scattered along the curbs, to the horror of those, stunned and deafened, who escaped the slaughter. Twenty-two people were killed immediately and over one hundred were injured, many severely. Two hours and eighteen minutes later, in Monaghan town, another car bomb detonated in front of Greachen's Pub on Church Square, killing five people and bringing the toll for the day to twenty-seven. Ultimately there would be thirty-three fatalities, the worst day of the Troubles.

Almost from the first it was clear that the explosions had been the work of Protestant paramilitaries. The motives offered in May 1974 were various but assumed that there must be loyalist and, perhaps, British advantage, depending on the proposed conspiracy theory. Subsequent investigations, years later, indicated that some fifteen to nineteen loyalists were involved and that, certainly at an initial stage, a British officer engaged in intelligence work in the border area. The later indication of British involvement and British special operations focused in part against the stability of the Wilson government does not make a rarionale much clearer. Perhaps the loyalists operated alone—certainly their names never emerged during subsequent revelations from loyalist informers otherwise forthcoming about nearly all other atrocities. Perhaps they were given a wink and a nod or help by military contacts. Twenty years later there would be those who claimed to know names, but motives were no clearer. Officially the 1974 Dublin bombs were still a mystery. Mostly the hard men needed neither winks nor nods nor very rigorous rationales for killing.

In the case of the Irish May bombs, it might not be unreasonable to suppose that it was an effort to punish the Republic, to reveal the cost of Sunningdale. This would be a congenial message to paramilitary men and, maybe, to some in British intelligence or the army. Certainly retired specialists in the Republic blame the British army for the bombs. The actual effect was horror, dismay, and anxiety. Cosgrave spoke that evening of "the revulsion and condemnation felt by every decent person in this island at these unforgivable acts" and said the bombing would "bring home to us here what the people in Northern Ireland have been suffering for five long years." This was hardly the response the bombers would have anticipated—sympathy for their province. And there was no policy change. The Dublin establishment still supported Sunningdale, still urged stronger action on Rees to break the strike, but after the bombs they did so with a greater sense of Northern reality.

Beyond the rewards of vengeance the bombs returned little to those involved. All that could be said for sure was that the single worse day of the Troubles took place in the Republic for uncertain purpose but with dreadful results. In the

North, amid the strike confrontation, the concern of the involved was hardly deflected by the bombs to the South. One painful exception was a comment by the UDA press officer Sammy Smyth: "I am very happy about the bombing. There is a war with the Free State and now we are laughing at them." Mostly, however, the loyalists had their own concerns, with lines forming outside bakeries and green-grocers and with milk, petrol, and animal feed in short supply. On May 18 Rees, after a meeting with the executive, said that there could be no negotiations under duress. On May 19, with electricity supplies dwindling, Rees declared a state of emergency. On May 21 the Labour government recruited their own to turn the tide: Len Murray, General Secretary of the British Trade Union Congress, led a back-to-work march to the Belfast shipyard. To bring in an Englishman, a Labour leader, to break their strike was a dreadful error: Only two hundred hardy people showed up for the march and an angry crowd hurled rotten vegetables at the little group. And on May 24, with some island admiration, the *Irish Times* said, "The Labour lads on the other side of the water are no match for the corner-boys of Belfast; those who held hands and sang 'The Red Flag' at the end of their party conference have been routed by genuine proletarians." It was a painful time for Labour when Orme's Fascists turned out to be good union men, if marching to an Orange drummer.

By May 24 the British were running out of initiatives. After a series of confused meetings on May 22 a new scheme was proposed that would allow Sunningdale to be phased in with a second step only after a test of opinion at the Assembly elections of 1977–78; without negotiations with the strikers, the Sunningdale package would in part depend on elections. It was a neat concession involving agreement to elections without agreeing, postponement of Sunningdale in whole but not in part—a splendidly designed watch without a mainspring.

In fact, it was so elegant that the SDLP almost balked, claiming that Britain was forcing them to decide during the strike, that Sunningdale was not the issue of the strike, and that agreement would damage the party at election time. The SDLP, a diverse coalition, had no loyalty to Faulkner and his associates and did not as yet fully identify with the executive; individually and collectively they were still shaped by the long years of exclusion and opposition. During the strike many spent much time in the South, seeing, as had the old Nationalists, the Dublin government as their ultimate protector. This was an attitude that only further alienated the loyalists. And Dublin's suggestions that Rees should use the British army only irritated both the Northern Ireland Office and the Labour cabinet. Neither felt Dublin or the SDLP should give them trouble, only support on demand, as such was in their interests. Finally the SDLP under Fitt's guidance came around.

Faulkner read the agreed statement at Stormont. Sensing further concession, the agreement had no loyalist takers. The agreement was "a lame attempt to bluff people into a united Ireland" suggested Paisley immediately. Articulate, sincere, and adamant opposition to the strike from the Labour government, from Heath and the opposition, from Dublin, from the SDLP and the Assembly Unionists, from the moderate and decent, had no more effect than the new statement on Sunningdale. As Tara, one of the more unsavory paramilitary groups, said in their *Belfast Newsletter* advertisement, "Sunningdale, the Council of Ireland and power-sharing must be destroyed. . . . It is better we suffer a little now than be slaves forever!"

Wilson's patience ran out. He proposed a nationwide broadcast on Saturday evening, May 25. The contents had been discussed at Chequers with Faulkner, Fitt, and Napier, along with Rees, Defense Secretary Roy Mason, and Attorney General Samuel Silkin. Then and later he was persuaded to adjust some of the language but the Prime Minister felt justifiably aggrieved. The army could not run the power stations and the eight hundred members of the Electrical Power Engineers Association had voted to walk out if they tried. The loyalists had arrived at a strategy whereby they proposed cutting their own throat unless they had their way: your money or my life. For the responsible in London such provincial suicide was out of the question. So Wilson spoke on Saturday evening from weakness and exasperation.

> British taxpayers have seen the taxes they have poured out, almost without regard to cost . . . going into Northern Ireland. They see property destroyed by evil violence and are asked to pick up the bill for rebuilding it. Yet people who benefit from all this now viciously defy Westminster, purporting to act as though they were an elected government; people who spend their lives sponging on Westminster and British democracy and then systematically assault democratic methods. Who do these people think they are?*

These people, of course, knew just who they were—*loyalists*, loyal to Queen and to Crown, loyal to democracy and the majority system, loyal to all those regiments and ships down through Britain's wars and campaigns, the Somme and Burma, Palestine and Jutland, devout, Christian patriots, loyalists all damned by a bland, sleek Labour man who neither understood nor grasped their resolution and faith in the realm. The next day the streets were crowded with those wearing bits of sponge pinned to lapels and jumpers and frocks. Spongers all.

By the time Wilson spoke, Faulkner had accepted that his time had run out. The leaders of the strike had not split, the people had stayed out. In fact more and more of his own, the middle class, the solid farmers, even his own back bench, insisted that he must talk to the strikers. And he could not. The Northern Ireland Office would not and he had nothing to say. Rees, Wilson, and the others might stand firm. They had hopes that the arrests of those responsible for the Ballymena violence and the death of the Byrne brothers on Saturday night, coupled with the

---

*Harold Wilson, *Final Term: The Labour Government, 1974–1976* (London: Weidenfeld and Nicolson, and Michael Joseph, 1979), p. 77. The Prime Minister, instantly and enormously unpopular with the loyalists, was at the time in Britain suspected as traitorous, a KGB spy, by the far right, especially certain people in intelligence circles. Cf. David Leigh, *The Wilson Plot* (New York: Pantheon, 1988). Some of this suspicion existed among intelligence officers in Northern Ireland, especially those involved in covert operations who suspected not only their own Prime Minister and his policies but also the intentions of the Dublin government. The province has always abounded in conspiracy theories, and, in fact, real conspiracies, so that the official covert events during this period, including the Dublin bombs and collusion with loyalist paramilitaries, remain murky. Recent unpublished work indicates British army involvement.

announcement on Monday that the troops would take control of the distribution of petroleum products as (part of a contingency plan to maintain vital services drawn up by Hume) might turn the tide. On Sunday Rees met with Fitt, the army commander of Northern Ireland, COC Sir Frank King, and James Flanagan of the RUC, then flew off to confer with Wilson at the Culdrose Naval Air Station before returning to Belfast. During this, the most crucial day so far, Roy Bradford, who since the February election had been distancing himself from Faulkner, announced that he opposed using troops to break the strike and supported talking with the UWC. Paddy Devlin and Ivan Cooper, in the Irish Republic after talks with Foreign Minister Garret FitzGerald, claimed they were unable to return the next day because of loyalist crowds. The RUC denied this. As far as Faulkner was concerned the SDLP had spent too much time in Dublin, thus substantiating the loyalist fears that the Catholic party was a tool of the government of Irish Republic. Adding a dash of reality, the leader of the Alliance Party, Oliver Napier, said that the executive now existed on an hour-to-hour basis.

On Monday morning Rees could announce the new plan for the petrol stations and emergency services; the UWC announced their own plan, an exact replica, fashioned through leaks in the Northern Ireland Office bureaucracy, where telephones were not safe nor minutes secret as the province's Protestants had united behind the strikers. This was the final affront, the last penny on the scales. The UWC at eleven announced the withdrawal by all workers from all industries. Rees asked them to pull back from the brink. The electricity supply began to dwindle. One after another areas of the province lost power. The UWC spokesman, Harry Murray, said, "We will break this regime up at Stormont. The executive has to go because we're not going. We're staying put and we will win."

By Monday the UWC had won. On that day Nelson Elder of Faulkner's Stormont Unionist MPs resigned and the rest of the backbenchers called for a meeting the next morning. On Tuesday morning Roy Bradford resigned from the executive. At the meeting of backbenchers held at Stormont, the decision was taken that there must be a dialogue with the strikers, despite Faulkner and Rees. The executive met at eleven o'clock in the morning for ninety minutes and decided that negotiations with the UWC must begin—Fitt, Hume, and Currie abstained and Napier supported the Unionists. Faulkner then met with Rees, who replied that the British government would not negotiate under duress. Faulkner tendered Rees his resignation. Five minutes later Faulkner reconvened the executive at 1:20 P.M. and indicated that the end had come. There was some futile last-minute effort to save the executive but Faulkner was correct: The end had come.

Rees announced shortly after two o'clock in the afternoon that Faulkner had resigned, along with the Unionist members in the Northern Ireland Assembly, and under the terms of the Northern Ireland Constitution Act of 1973 there was no statutory basis for the executive. Rees would be responsible for the preservation of law and order. Direct rule had returned and the Assembly, the power-sharing executive, and the Council of Ireland had become a matter for historians. The Assembly, which lingered on in theory, ended its last session with SDLP explanations and contentions: "Power sharing has worked and the idea of power sharing has worked." Outside, the long road up to Stormont was crammed with a vast tractor traffic jam to demonstrate farmer support for the strike. The loyalists were already rushing into the streets in celebration. As Paisley said, "Keep the English politicians out. Keep Dublin out. Let Ulstermen face to face work out the future of Ulster."

Each and all, the traditional spokesmen, the appropriate politicians, the old names—West and Fitt, and Kennedy in America and Cosgrave in Dublin, the Provisional IRA and the president of the nearly defunct Nationalist Party—said the appropriate things, comments as predictable as the bonfires in loyalist districts. Everyone learned what he or she chose to learn. Dublin still felt that somehow the strike could have been ended, sooner rather than later, by recourse to coercion and by a counter to intimidation. The loyalists had their faith in the power of the streets reinforced: Ulster will strike and Ulster will be right. The SDLP and most of the minority believed that British timidity and loyalist intimidation had snatched away the power they shared.

The British at least learned the necessity of adjusting to Irish reality. Since Whitelaw, London had sought to impose accommodation on the province by negotiating an Irish dimension with the Dublin government and a Northern Ireland devolved assembly with the moderates. There could be no moderates, minority participation, without an Irish dimension that in turn assured much of the majority's alienation.

Rees had noted what he called a rising Ulster nationalism, a concept many in London found both alien and dangerous. The people did not fear London sanctions. Still, as the options were considered—and nearly every option would be discussed, from turning over the province to the Dublin government to structuring the province as if it were Sussex—there was a consensus in London that it might be wise to let any accommodation arise from the province. Let, as Paisley suggested, Ulstermen face to face work out the future of Ulster, with the British providing more encouragement than guidance. What did the loyalists hope?

The need for some next step did not suddenly loom on Tuesday, May 28, when the executive vanished; as the strike continued even (and perhaps especially) Rees could imagine the likely results. In fact, the results were less disastrous than might have been imagined. After the bonfires and booze, the UWC and the loyalist politicians were content, and sought no immediate election or instant concession. There were rallies and provincewide demonstrations. The power went on, the farmers drove their tractors home, the barricades came down, and the workers would move off to Mackies and Harland and Wolff and the power stations once the celebrations were over. Faulkner and the Assembly Unionists were assigned to history's boneyard, along with O'Neill and Chichester-Clark. The sectarian killing continued, as did the IRA's muted campaign. The army was run down to fifteen thousand, the lowest figure since operation Motorman. The cost had been enormous. The Northern Ireland Finance Corporation estimated the strike had cost in monetary terms £225 million in direct costs. Fortunately the cost in blood had been far less, the Byrne brothers, a couple killed when their car ran into a barricade, and the peripheral deaths related to IRA activity. No one in the North wanted the responsibility for the deaths from the car bombs in the Republic. The strike had been political, waged with a minimum of violence, and had won a famous victory, almost without cost to the leaders, if not to the province and the government in London and the innocent dead in the Republic.

Everyone for years had anticipated a Protestant backlash—a violent expression of that Ulster nationalism—but nearly everyone had imagined either a vast pogrom that might include agencies of authority, the police, the bureaucracy, even some of the army, or else an armed struggle the mirror image of that of the IRA. The hard men had formed themselves into replicas of the Provos or Officials. Yet when Protestant power took to the streets, it was not organized by gunmen. The leaders were often the same kind of men to be found in the paramilitaries and certainly were workingmen uneasy and suspicious of the political elite, but they did not seek to use guns. West and Craig and even Paisley articulated their basic demands, gave cover to the strikers, ran up more appropriate banners, yet all this led to nothing. There was no secret army or vast mob to use for political purpose; instead there was a tiny, independent core of activists and a provincewide willingness to stay home, participate by negation.

In any pantheon of unconventional political successes the UWC strike was a splendid tactical achievement. It was not as deadly or permanent as the Provisional IRA's success in fashioning an armed struggle but it was still a major act. The general strike against a Labour Northern Ireland secretary was, if fortuitous in the nature of the Labour cabinet, advantageous in many ways. Strikebreaking produced all sorts of moral and legal problems for the British Labour Party. There was little violence. The ability of the dangerous paramilitaries to assure compliance with almost no resort to visible violence was more than could be hoped—any sensible analyst could have predicted the path of the loyalist politicians who, once the strike was in place, had no options and almost no role. The UWC anticipation that the province would support the strike was vindicated. The UWC had a far more accurate reading of loyalist opinion than the polls that elicited the decent and expected answers or the organs of opinion that shaped desire to reality or even the anti-Assembly politicians.

The UWC knew (1) what was wrong—the betrayal of the loyalists through the machinations of the English and the Faulkner compromisers; (2) what was wanted—an end to the Assembly, sooner rather than later; and (3) what was to be done—nothing, stay home, strike. The UWC leaders like other loyalists, did not know what should come next if the past could not be reclaimed intact. They had only lashed back at a specific and vulnerable construction, a symbol of unhappy times. They assumed certain subsequent developments. And they assumed correctly. They won. The Assembly and the executive collapsed. The Northern Ireland Office, the Labour government, the Dublin government lost. The Northern Assembly moderates lost. Once the symbol was shattered on Tuesday, May 28, the UWC became irrelevant. Their victory was specific, symbolic, and indicative of a mood—negative—rather than a beginning of a process. The Northern politicians rushed back into the void with plans and proposals and schemes, options, alternatives. In Dublin and London there were agonizing political reappraisals. And in the end the major players in London, the cabinet, and Rees in the Northern Ireland Office felt that much of the debate, many of the decisions, and the major responsibility should be left to those concerned. There was, however, some sense of urgency by those particularly concerned with Irish matters because almost certainly another British general election loomed, probably in the autumn; it would be better to put a plan in place before a new and perhaps different government came to power in London. Labour soon suspected that the Tories were tilting away from bipartisan Irish politics in view of the value of any Unionist Westminster seats after a close general election. Rees, Orme, Cooper, and the others rushed from the crisis and chaos of the strike directly into the construction of suggestions and proposals for institutions of accommodation that would arise from the ruins of the Assembly.

On Monday, June 3, an emergency two-day Westminster debate on Northern Ireland took place. Rees gave the cost of the province over the previous five years: 257 soldiers and UDR, 52 RUC, and 717 civilians, a figure that included 250 sectarian murders, mostly by Protestants; the cost of United Kingdom finance and loans; the cost of keeping the army in the province. There was no mention of profits. The *Times*, on June 3, the same day Rees addressed Parliament, noted Westminster's record:

> Since 1969 it has destroyed three Prime Ministers of Northern Ireland and one Chief Executive by forcing the pace of reform and a movement towards the Irish dimension that stripped them of majority support. It has virtually ruined the Ulster Unionist Party. It has suspended the Stormont Parliament that existed for 50 years; imposed Direct Rule; created an Executive that could not live and an Assembly that has been suspended, and has now restored Direct Rule through two fairly junior and inexperienced Ministers.

No wonder the Protestant majority did not trust Westminster. No wonder Labour began to doubt Tory support in the election run-up. As Rees told Commons, "We all need time." Yet he ended with the warning that "time is not on our side." And there were all the old problems overshadowed by the strike emergency. From the declining provincial economy with its enormous unemployment to the bodies found in waste ground, the Northern Ireland Office had no ready answer.

There was another difficult problem—actually an old problem still in the news: the Irish hunger strikers—the Price sisters and the two other London bomb blitz republicans, Hugh Feeney and Gerard Kelly, along with Martin Brady, Frank Stagg, and Michael Gaughan, who had been refused transfer to Northern Ireland prisons. This was the normal course for long-term inmates. Home Secretary Roy Jenkins said, "I must not be forced into a decision about their future location or an unwarranted promise as a result of any intimidation, however harrowing may be the consequences." So along with their armed struggle the Provisionals had become involved in a hunger strike campaign that could only be to their advantage.

By June the British government had painted itself into a corner. At one moment the IRA prisoners were simple criminals and the next moment they were political terrorists, whichever was to London's advantage. Rees, a sensitive and astute man, felt that "the Provisionals wanted their London-based team back home where its members could bask in political status."* This was certainly true in part but the British refusal was a political act indicating that the prisoners were not simply criminals. The system was not going to make life easy for car bombers, but it would hardly admit to being vindictive or admit their special status. The Irish should have been transferred if normal procedures had been followed, but once the strike began the government felt it could not be "intimidated"—admit error. The result was a rising tide of support for the hunger strikers, particularly as the brutal nature of forced feeding became public.

On June 3 Michael Gaughan died on the sixty-fifth day of his strike, after contracting pneumonia. Hugh Feeney had been on strike for 200 days and force fed for 175. Frank Stagg was "very ill." Gerard Kelly was reported to have gone blind. The Price sisters in Brixton Prison were weaker. Their father, Albert Price, pleaded for his "wee children" on television. Telegrams and petitions began to arrive in London, mostly from Irish nationalists, republican groups, and civil rights organizations. The British remained outraged that convicted bombers demanded anything. Forced feeding was ended—a decision that later became policy for all British prisons—but that was all.

A hunger strike has a special Irish meaning. The powerless when denied justice have only recourse to self-destruction, a procedure that in ancient times brought shame on the mighty as the poor man sat starving at the gate. No one starves over weeks and months, suffering excruciating pain and humiliation, simply as a cunning tactic; it must be done out of enormous conviction. Such suffering resonates deeply in the Irish. Even Harry Murray, UWC chairman, said, "I do feel deeply for these girls and the condition they are in, despite the evil deeds they committed."

Murray was something of a special case, soon forced to resign from the UWC on July 9, despite continued UDA support, after his criticism of loyalist politicians following an elegant, all-star weekend conference of the British Irish Association held at Oxford. Consorting with the famous, Rees and Orme, Conor Cruise O'Brien and Garret FitzGerald, had produced delusions of moderation in Murray that were still politically deadly. Those higher up the political feeding chain, O'Neill or Chichester-Clark, lose only position and power; but those nearer the dangerous edge of loyalist politics may risk more by dissent. Murray, who was gravitating toward the peace movement in any case, was fortunate at mere outrage. And his comments on the hunger strikers were somewhat acceptable to the paramilitaries.

Many loyalist hard men were in prison, familiar with the uses and costs of hunger strikes. There were then real pockets of loyalist concern about British prison practices. These could be found in paramilitary catchment areas as well as in the solid nationalist districts. The nationalists were as always sympathetic with the plight if not the cause. So there was growing concern even among those who abhorred the gun in politics. And the fact that there were women involved made matters more poignant. Paddy Devlin was in London pleading their case repeatedly with the Home Secretary.

*Merlyn Rees, *Northern Ireland: A Personal Perspective* (London: Methuen, 1985), p. 115.

Stagg grew weaker. Eventually the formula was found to satisfy both Jenkins and the Prices on June 7—they were given "clarification" that they would in time be transferred. In fact on June 13 Jenkins indicated that he planned a transfer in the course of the year. On June 7, the same day as the Price agreement, Gaughan's body was moved off the Isle of Wight to London by the republican movement. His casket was accompanied by eight men wearing black berets and dark glasses acting as an honor guard.

The return of Gaughan to Ireland and the interment in Ballina, County Mayo, was a long ritual, transforming a volunteer into a martyr, played out before the media and the people. Conservative British opinion was outraged watching a uniformed IRA honor guard for a convicted terrorist left untouched in England and then in Ireland. All the Irish prisoners came off the strike on June 8 on IRA instructions. The whole affair managed to focus at least some attention on the Provisionals and their aspirations even amid the analysis of the UWC strike. The entire affair was a net loss for the British government, still ignorant of Irish custom and the cost of hypocrisy.

The most specific outcome of the collapse of the executive was the need for an alternative to direct rule, and as soon as possible. Direct rule was hurriedly organized and the administration strengthened. There were all sorts of pressing details, new officials, new forms, new procedures and problems. These were administrative matters, crucial but temporary. Rees still accepted the power of positive thinking, that the rising tide of what he felt was Ulster nationalism would supply an effective base for a self-generated Ulster structure. Such a structure must be congenial to Westminster and the United Kingdom and must offer fair shares and some sort of Irish dimension.

Rees was picking up the same pieces scattered by the strike and handing them over to the provincial politicians. The civil servants had already supplied him with options and there were "no nice, elegant solutions lying around like a Sunday morning editorial." What emerged was a White Paper outlining a proposed convention that had emerged as a prospect even as the general strike continued. Rees, Orme, Cooper, and Philip Woodfield, leaning on the work of the civil servants, drew up the White Paper that touched on both history and the present reality from finance to law and order but keyed in on the convention, where the "people of Northern Ireland must play a crucial part in determining their own future." There would be a process of discussion and consultation and four weeks' warning of an election for the convention. Discussion and consultation began even before publication. Rees and Orme talked as well as drafted. Wilson received an early copy. Cooper had gone to Dublin early in June and Rees talked with FitzGerald on June 14, so the planning had an Irish dimension as well as cabinet support.

On July 4 Rees presented, along with the necessary legislation for direct rule, his new Northern Ireland White Paper—*The Northern Ireland Constitution*—to the House of Commons. His proposed constitutional convention would have an independent chairman and seventy-eight elected members for the twelve Northern Ireland parliamentary constituencies, elected by a single transferable vote. The convention's report sought a Northern Ireland devolved government, acceptable to a broad section of opinion in Northern Ireland and to the people and parliament of the United Kingdom. The convention would be dissolved on completion of its report or after six months from the date of its first meeting whichever came first, unless the secretary intervened—a provision that was meant to sharpen political minds.

Immediately and as expected the responses began to arrive. Rees orchestrated efforts to encourage those involved in the province. On the next day he had informal talks with FitzGerald on Anglo-Irish security and discussed extraterritorial courts in the Republic. The loyalists always felt Dublin could do more and so Rees subtly underlined the value of an Irish dimension. FitzGerald, for example, had met John Taylor on June 30 and on the next day held informal talks with various loyalist politicians in Belfast, where he was told forcefully that the Unionist Party saw no role for the Southern government in any future institutions for Northern Ireland—a statement the Irish Foreign Minister found "curious." Certainly the Taoiseach, Cosgrave, had done his part, for early on June 13 he indicated that the people in the South were having less and less desire for unity with a people so deeply imbued with violence. It was hardly a kindly comment on the North but it had the weight of truth. And on July 6 he gave his support to the initiative, with the usual qualification on power sharing and an Irish dimension. There was never much doubt about London and Dublin; the crux was the province.

There were early harbingers of goodwill. Although the IRA continued its armed struggle, at Bodenstown on June 16, the principal speaker, Séamus Loughran of Belfast, had said that "the Republican movement will not be found wanting in its willingness to talk." At the other end of the spectrum, beginning on June 17 the Protestant paramilitaries had met with the conventional politicians during a three-day conference at Vanguard headquarters in Hawthornden Road, East Belfast, that some hoped would ease the hard men into politics. The UVF, legalized on May 15, had announced the formation of the Volunteer Political Party on June 22. Glen Barr, Chairman of the UWC coordinating committee, indicated in an RTE program "This Week" that "concessions would have to be made. We are prepared to be good neighbors with Dublin." On July 20 Andy Tyrie said that "we feel we can sort things out now by getting Protestants and Catholics together."

Certainly the mainstream SDLP, sadder if not necessarily wiser, was reunited for a second try at devolved government; and the Unionists, now largely clumped in West's party, for without an executive and with a prorogued Assembly Faulkner's troops scattered, had never been averse to talking, if not to listening. Thus, as much as might be expected, the attention of the extremes had been attracted. Increasingly the British hope for the militants of whatever flavor was not involvement but quiescence. Neither paramilitary conglomerate had either the political talent or the vision, much less the experience and inclination, to play a constructive role. The two major political groups, the real players as far as the British were concerned, were again united and cohesive as the SDLP on one side and the UUUC alliance of the Official Unionist, Paisley's DUP, and Craig's Vanguard on the other. Cosgrave and FitzGerald in Dublin were helpful, if Jack Lynch was in opposition, just as the British Conservatives, anticipating the election, seemed willing to distance Fianna Fáil ever so slightly from the orthodox convention thrust, noting the case for later unity and power sharing.

So Rees and Co. had what appeared to be momentum but decided to delay any convention elections until 1975, after the Westminster general elections. Both the SDLP and the Unionists decided they needed time. Instead, therefore, Rees decided to publish a series of discussion documents. The first would appear in September as a Green Paper, *Northern Ireland: Finance and the Economy.* The British were given no time to shift through options at leisure or even concentrate on the coming convention. Despite the occasional note of moderation and the buzz created with the renewal of provincial politics, Rees found that the summer of 1974 was long and hot, filled with turmoil and fury. There were new, unexpected issues like the long wrangle over the formation of an antiterrorist Third Force of citizens that awakened all the old arguments about the B Specials and led to advocacy of private armies.

The old issues resurfaced and the old tumult escalated. There was massive nationalist resentment at the continuation of internment. Rees wanted it phased out but those in Long Kesh were still used as hostages; releases were dribbled out far too slowly for the minority community, who wanted no internment at all. And, hardly unexpectedly, the Provos moved into new bombing sweeps, mailed off letter bombs, and kept their active service units busy with a series of attacks in England—one bomb detonated in Westminster Hall in the Houses of Parliament on June 17, causing extensive damage. The IRA made the country roads unsafe and everywhere imperiled the security forces. At times it seemed that there were no longer sufficient targets for the Provo bombers, three years into an intense campaign of destruction. Between urban renewal, highway construction, and the IRA, some areas were hardly recognizable. In Derry, according to the *Guardian* in May, 5,200 houses had been destroyed or badly damaged, and 124 business premises, mainly offices and shops, had been destroyed. The Guildhall often had shattered windows, and old monuments had been turned to rubble. And Derry was a small city; five thousand houses meant very extensive destruction.

The violence had new watermarks. On July 23 a bomb was discovered on a British Airways Belfast-London flight of a Trident aircraft with William Craig and RUC Chief Constable James Flanagan and his wife on board when it landed in Manchester after a telephoned warning. Two days later the Europa Hotel in Belfast was bombed for the twenty-fifth time. Then on August 15 a new issue arose when the Provisionals claimed that Paul Magorrian, who had been warned by British troops that he would be killed, was found shot in the back at close range. Further evidence of a shoot-to-kill policy occurred on September 4 when two wanted men were shot and wounded in a parking lot on the south side of the border by British troops. Like detentions, British dirty tricks entered the nationalist litany of grievances.

As the weeks passed, the Provos ignored the politicians and pushed on with their campaign. This cost the defenders and the innocent enormous sums, no matter who did the figuring and who ultimately paid. In Belfast on June 27 two IRA proxy bombs exploded at Academy and Upper North streets causing an estimated £400,000 damages to shops and industrial premises. (Later that day the UFF set off incendiary bombs at the Ulster Timber Company in the Docks area that resulted in another £200,000 damage: £600,000 in one day.) The same day a Belfast security man on duty at the Club Bar was wounded and the Jolly Roger Protestant Social Club on Alliance Road was hit with two incendiary bombs thrown in the front door. And this was Belfast on one day, the day after Liam Cosgrave in Dublin claimed that the entire emergency had cost the republican government £40 million in security forces and compensation for destruction of property. In November Orme, in a parliamentary reply at Westminster, listed the costs of paid-out compensation as £95,531,690 for the period April 1, 1969, to October 31, 1974, and this was but a part of the Troubles' bottom line in sterling for the British government.

A summer that saw almost steady-state bombing in the province and England, several loyalist bombs in the Republic, and a return of the sectarian tit-for-tat shootings hardly indicated an acceptable level of violence. On July 25 Orme noted that since 1972 there had been 250 sectarian killings in the province, 170 Catholic victims and 80 Protestants. This facet of the Troubles grew more ominous by the end of the summer. The proxy bombs, kneecapping, and ambushes in the country were background noise to the alarm of anyone being murdered as symbol. By autumn the sectarian killing had, if anything, increased. Rees would report at the end of November that the total killed since September 16 was thirty-eight. He gave Westminster a taste of a province murderously divided:

> At twenty-one minutes past midnight the following night, the body of a man was found lying in a field off the Hightown Road, Glen-gormley, with wounds to the head and back. A taxi cab was found abandoned near the scene of the murder. At 11:48 on the Saturday night, a customer found the bodies of a man and a young woman in a store at the rear of the Edenderry Filling Station in the Crumlin Road. Both had been shot through the back of the head. The man was the manager of the filling station. On the same day, the owner of the Arkle Taxi Company in Clifton Street arrived at his premises and found his wife shot dead. A customer was lying dead in the waiting room.*

Such crimes were alien to British experience.

The Provos were willing to deploy on as many fronts as possible to stretch British resources, as the hunger strike campaign indicated. They continued their popular campaign against internment. Rees, a former critic of Long Kesh, was pilloried when he showed reluctance to release those whose colleagues were still bombing away the province. Still, the Provos gained credit, since not only the nationalist community was adamantly opposed to internment but also the Northern Ireland Office hoped to phase it out and replace it with some other effective practice. Internment still paid Provo benefits. There was also a long struggle over control of the electricity in Newry that led to a compromise

*Rees, p. 142.

satisfactory to Rees after two weeks of a power outage reminiscent of the general strike.

A traditional IRA arena was the prison, where volunteers served with no less dedication, only under different conditions. There were always escape plans, although those in isolated high-security facilities had little hope. In Long Kesh in July Gerry Adams was caught trying to leave in a visitor's place. There was always a pushing at the edges, often with legitimate complaints, often by prisoners who saw injustice where distant bureaucrats did not. There were disputes over food, over privileges, over conditions, over the law, over any loose end of control. The summer and autumn of 1974 was filled with such complaints, first by the Provos and their friends, then by the loyalist paramilitaries. These culminated on October 15 when the IRA prisoners rioted, ransacked the prison, and burned down many of the buildings, leading to further complaints and accusations, to demonstrations and riots in the other prisons, to barricades in the streets and complaints to Rees. Nearly as spectacular, on November 6 thirty-three republicans escaped through a sixty-five-yard tunnel: twenty-nine were recaptured within hours and three more that evening in Andersonstown, Belfast; one, Hugh Coney, was shot dead by a sentry.

The most dramatic escape took place on August 18 in the Republic at the Portlaoise Prison, where on June 30 a tunnel *into* the prison had been discovered. This time the IRA prisoners went the other way. Using tiny amounts of smuggled gelignite, nineteen prisoners blew their way out, to the confusion of the guards and the prisoners' outside contacts. There was a mad scene of racing prisoners disappearing into commandeered cars, back gardens, and the town's streets. No one was hurt and the country teemed with delighted rumors of hitchhiking gunmen, volunteers disguised as priests, famous commanders unrecognized at steak dinners laid on by admirers. Many in the Republic were amused by an escape-adventure amid the lapses and blunders and alarms.

Cosgrave and the Dublin government were outraged. There had been the growing general anguish with the Troubles spilling over into the Republic. The Irish army and Gárdaí had to be increased in size and deployed to monitor Northern violence. In the twelve months up to December 1974 the army had assisted the police in setting up 15,900 checkpoints and carried out more than three thousand patrols. There had been violence anyway. There were the bombs in Dublin; the summer bombs; the adventures of Rose Dugdale, the former instructor at London University and convert to Irish republicanism, that ended with her receiving a nine-year sentence for stealing the Beit paintings when she pleaded "proudly and incorruptibly guilty"; and the June 4 kidnapping, apparently for bargaining purposes, of the Earl and Countess of Donoughmore by a free-lance Provo group, which soon released them. Too much violence was brought south in Ireland's name. Cosgrave was a solid and pragmatic Taoiseach, parochial, even narrow; he had no trace of nationalist sympathy other than the general assumption that unity was inevitable, not like the rain and death and taxes but rather akin to universal peace; but it was not a matter for politicians or Irishmen. Those who sought it through violence were an affront. Those of whatever persuasion who carried that violence into his country were vile. In his Ireland he wanted no spectaculars, no rising security costs, no bombs set by the overswill of turmoil.

Whatever sympathy the Provisionals might find in republican figures like Boland and Blaney, the Cosgrave government offered none.

Conor Cruise O'Brien, appointed Minister for Post and Telegraphs by Cosgrave to isolate him, on June 30 on RTE's "This Week" said that he was not working for unity, since it was not practicable. O'Brien was impossible to isolate. Post and Telegraphs would be used as an antisubversion bastion. O'Brien would ride point for those who would dismantle the one Ireland dream, demolishing with erudition and logic the ideals and assumptions of generations past and do so with such apparent relish that he alienated his own allies and eroded his old commitment to civil liberties. He abhorred the Provos, their stunted pretensions, and their crude supporters. In his slashing and cutting campaign to rewrite Irish mythology as rigorous history he became a treacherous monster for committed nationalists but helped the country revise patriot history and present prospects.

Even more telling than an ebb of support for unity was the work going on in Washington to convince the Irish-American community that the Provos were not fighting Ireland's battle, that they were Marxist and undemocratic gunmen using money raised in the United States to kill Irishmen, endanger the Irish government, and set back unity for decades. The Irish embassy in Washington, with the most limited resources and aided by the excursions of John Hume, gradually began to have an effect.

Coupled with a firm approach to law and order arising from the government's distaste for the Provisionals and the violence in general, the Republic by the summer of 1974 was a wasting nationalist asset and increasingly a willing partner in the British effort to shape a decent accommodation within the United Kingdom. Lynch and Fianna Fáil had curtailed rhetoric that might raise expectations; Cosgrave's government stressed that such expectations were not only futile but also dangerous. Evidence regarding the effect government attitudes had on popular opinion was scarce. The Market Research Bureau of Ireland stated that in an opinion poll commissioned by the RTE program "Seven Days" only 36 percent of the Irish electorate were "very much in favor" of a united Ireland; on the other hand, only 11 percent wanted to delete Articles Two and Three in the Constitution that claimed jurisdiction over Northern Ireland. But the direction of the government's policy was clear—and Cosgrave as a shrewd politician felt he had read his own.

As an English politician Rees increasingly felt the necessity to be in Leeds; the crucial general election had been called for October 10. In Northern Ireland no one paid the slightest attention to United Kingdom issues. If anything the level of violence rose, and with it local consideration. In September the Provos assassinated—as "legitimate targets"—Judge Rory Conaghan and Magistrate Martin McBirney. Even the British were appalled when on October 5 the violence again spilled over onto the mainland. In Guildford, Surrey, no-warning bombs exploded at two pubs popular with off-duty soldiers. The explosions killed two servicemen, two servicewomen, and a civilian and injured fifty-four others. The latest atrocity had little effect on the election, and only further angered and alienated the British. The Irish and Ireland had few friends.

In Northern Ireland the vote would not be affected by any level of violence, any United Kingdom concern. The poll was used to determine the pecking order within the two communities—could the gains by the UUUC be maintained and could the Catholics find agreed candidates who might win in the marginal districts? The UUUC gained intellectual ballast when Captain L. P. S. Orr withdrew in South Down, one of the nearly marginals, in favor of Enoch Powell. Most of the radical and independents withdrew in favor of the SDLP or Frank Maguire, an independent, in Fermanagh and South Tyrone. The Officials' Republican Club candidates did not withdraw, running five members. So the total candidates came to 12 UUUC, 9 SDLP, 5 Alliance, 5 Republican Clubs, 3 NILP, 3 Communist Party of Ireland (Marxist-Leninist), 2 Unionist Party of Northern Ireland (Faulkner), 1 Volunteer Political Party (UVF), 1 Derry Labour and Trade Union Party, 1 Independent Unionist, and 1 Independent.

The UUUC lost only to Maguire and Fitt. With Powell taking South Down with a majority of 3,567 and John Dunlop with a majority of 4,667 defeating Ivan Cooper, the UUUC took seats that the SDLP felt might have gone their way if the Republican clubs, who took only 3 percent of the vote (21,633), had not intervened. At least Harry West had been defeated, replaced by James Molyneaux as UUUC leader at Westminster. And Faulkner, as everyone had accepted, was finished, gathering fewer votes than the Officials (20,454). The marginality of Alliance (5.1 percent) and NILP (1.6 percent) was reinforced. The UVF had shown as little drawing power as the Official IRA: Paramilitary strength was not through the ballot box, a positive move but through people's toleration, where nothing needed to be done. So the electorate was basically divided between the UUUC with 57.4 percent and SDLP with 21.7 percent.

At the end of the day with all counted out, the province also took note of the fact that Labour had won in the other island. Rees and Orme and Wilson would maintain their roles. One could assume that the convention would be pushed, grievances like detention corrected, and order maintained by the army and police, as always. There would be (and there were) further rounds of meetings during the autumn, with moderation articulated by all. No one anticipated anything but more of the same.

Actually a new, unarticulated strategy was evolving. Rees, almost like a sleepwalker moving along a corridor, realized that the center of balance needed to be moved to the six counties by an introduction of the normal. He favored a series of responses on various levels that looked like a conscious and cunning strategy of imposed stability. Instead, it was a typical British response: no theory, only practice, unarticulated values, personal experience and self-interest shaped by an Irish exposure. Rees wanted an accommodation, an end to turmoil. What was normal and sound—order, civility, democratic reform, justice—must be encouraged within the context of the province. Britain should not be seen to act to British advantage. If possible Britain should not be seen at all in a future world where appropriate power would be properly devolved on the province to be fairly distributed and used rather than maintained through British agencies. British policy should encourage a return to routine and the regular, or at least a partial approximation of the normal. The burden of British policy should be to shrink the conflict. He came to this conclusion by exposure to Irish reality, not through a theory of anti-insurgency.

Aspects of such a theory could easily be found in some of the work on low-intensity conflict in the enormous library arising from the anti-imperialist struggles culminating in America's involvement in the Vietnam War. The message was to run the armed struggle down. Such a concept of minimum force was not universally accepted: Some generals preferred to rely on steel and numbers. Some analysts wanted all the visible institutions—justice, the bureaucracy, the police, the local government—fashioned under one leader to impose order. Other specialists opted for the erosion of grievances and attitudes that led to violence.

In theory and later in fact, the advocates of normalization wanted to transform an internal war into a nonpolitical affair of tribal conflict or civil disorder, a matter of greed or crime: There were no guerrillas, only bandits, no terrorists, only lunatics, no need of an army, only recourse to the paramilitary police, no internment, only arrest and trial. The arena, cosmetically at first and then in practice, would be molded to everyday. Whenever possible minimum force would be deployed: Less was more. Whenever possible conventional institutions would be used. The major focus of the rebel is first to persist and then to escalate, so the aim of the legitimate center should be to act as if there were no armed struggle: Erode persistence, deny escalation, pretend all is normal. Since coercive force could not impose the normal, every effort should be made to fashion the impression and then the reality of the routine.

Later this "strategy" could be teased out of the chaos of events in 1974 and 1975 following the general strike, but at the time British policy was simply a variety of responses to immediate problems: the need to jettison internment that led to the appointment of a committee under the former lord chancellor, Lord Gardiner, to consider the Northern Ireland (Emergency Provisions) Act of 1973; the impression that rising Ulster nationalism made on Rees as he contemplated convention options; the natural withdrawal of extra British army units after the end of the general strike; the purely criminal nature of some of the tit-for-tat sectarian killings; the gradual reform of the RUC; an increase in the size of the RUC Reserve; and, despite Catholic fears and complaints, the success of the UDR. And later there would be the rising unease about the corruption of British forces as they resorted to the covert, dirty war.

All these facets of Ulsterization were emerging immediately after the elections but would be recognized only later, for during the autumn of 1974 the situation in the province seemed to decay without any clear direction. Atrocity and conflict, the sectarian murders, the English bombs, and the violence sucked up attention, not Gardiner's commission or the size of the RUC Reserve or any strategy of order.

The Provisionals, responsible for much of the violence if few of the sectarian killings, had by no means given up hope of negotiations. As always in a secret army, however, the military priorities dominated. Despite the decline in incidents the capacities of the volunteers had grown. The gear was coming in from America: Along with the first Japanese-made Armalites the QMG was now receiving new American-made Armalites. There was still the money from Libya. In fact in November a Provo delegation to Tripoli discovered to their horror that the loyalists had arrived in the desert with the appearance of Glen Barr, Tommy Little, and Andy Robinson and Harry Chicken of the UDA. The paramilitaries were there to discuss financial matters and, improbably, offshore oil and gas resources. The Libyans, intimate with anti-imperialist insurgency but still ignorant of the intricacies of Ireland, found all this puzzling. The loyalists came away empty. As for the Provos, their Northern units, despite the losses through arrests, were never more potent. There were still too many volunteers in the South. And there were now under Brian Keenan's GHQ guidance effective if small active service units in England.

There were some old problems. In November the shooting feud with the Officials in the North was renewed in Belfast. The feud did nothing for Provo support. In December the Stickies would suffer further losses when at last Séamus Costello took his friends and followers out of the Official IRA and Sinn Féin and formed the Irish Republican Socialist Party (IRSP), which attracted many Northern radicals, including Bernadette Devlin McAliskey. Simultaneously and secretly Costello formed the Irish National Liberation Army (INLA), another secret army, even secret for some time from its political wing the IRSP, thus cloning the traditional republican form. All of these splits, schisms, and feuds, little understood by those outside the underground, did little to engender support for any of the involved. Still, for the Provos, untouched by the Official-IRSP split, their necessary support was still high, the committed still committed, the fearful still dependent on their defenders.

There were certain problems and changes at the Provos' center, hardly a rarity or unexpected. Tight control from the center was always difficult and sometimes not even desirable. In 1974 the GHQ, under pressure from the Dublin government, was often out of touch with operations, but that was almost normal and the units in the six counties could cope. In October Eamonn O'Doherty, the chief of staff, still little known, was arrested in the South when the police stopped his car driven by mistake into a dead end. The Special Branch did not know who they had swept up, only who they missed. His companion, Dáithí O Conaill, still the most prominent Provo and assumed to be chief of staff, escaped from them on foot. The Army Council met and Séamus Twomey returned as chief of staff with Brian Keenan as his most important aid. O Conaill remained as spokesman and front man and O Brádaigh as president of Sinn Féin.

Each adjusted Army Council was much like the last. Unlike the Protestant paramilitaries, there was consensus on policy and tactics, and always the power of the dream now at work in a new generation. There was considerable adjustment to be done since O'Doherty had been a soldier rather than administrator and so was difficult to locate at times. Both Twomey and Keenan, open to the novel, wanted the English campaign to continue: It cost the British, at little IRA investment, sharpened London political minds, and might lead more swiftly to concession than the constant violence in Northern Ireland. What the English campaign produced, however, was another atrocity to go with the Guildford pub bomb that instead sharpened IRA minds already considering a novel opening to the British through independent mediators.

On Thursday, November 21, 1974, at 8:11 P.M., a man with an Irish accent, using the proper code word, "Double X," called in bomb warnings to the *Birmingham Post and Mail* indicating that the tax office in the Rotunda, a glass high-rise tower dominating the center of the city and a previous IRA target, was to be bombed. Another bomb, across the city near a bank, was defused. In the Rotunda a two-man IRA team had left bomb bags in two pubs close to the tax office. The choice of targets, which ran grave risk of civilian victims, the timing of the warning, the entire event indicated the ineptitude and callousness of the volunteers involved. They were incompetent and without the capacity to imagine the dangers to the innocent and to their own cause. Bombing pubs to hit off-duty soldiers was haphazard, deadly, certain to kill and maim the innocent. Any symbolic bombing ran risks of error or oversight. The IRA had always been willing to put English civilians at risk in England, but the Birmingham bombs gave every indication that the British civilian population was the target. Six minutes after the warning, while the police were clearing the Rotunda, bombed twice so far in 1974, a violent explosion occurred in the Mulberry Bush Pub and was heard in another pub, the Tavern in the Town, just before a bomb exploded under a bench there. The butcher's bill was horrific: 21 dead and 162 injured.

The British response, hardly surprising, was outraged indignation. There had already been some fifty English bombs before Birmingham. Everyone had been uneasy. With Birmingham the worst had happened. All the Irish were blamed. There were nasty incidents in several cities. The fact that the police almost immediately arrested those they claimed were the bombers, as they had after the Guildford explosions, failed to calm public opinion. In Parliament as well as in the country there was a demand that something be done. And so with haste and in anger, Parliament in forty-two hours rushed through the Prevention of Terrorism (Temporary Provisions) Act of 1974 (PTA). Although fashioned for special purpose the act was similar to the Prevention of Violence (Temporary Provisions) Act of 1939 and the Northern Ireland (Emergency Provisions) Act of 1973. Such legislation had already been discussed. The Home Secretary, Roy Jenkins, accepted the act as unique for a nation not at war: "These powers are draconian. In combination, they are unprecedented in peacetime. I believe they are fully justified to meet the clear and present dangers."

The IRA was to be banned in the United Kingdom. Suspected terrorists could be arrested without warrant and powers of detention were extended. Individuals could be excluded or expelled from Great Britain—that is, exiled to Northern Ireland or deported. In fact, within twenty-four hours the Special Branch had produced a list of people to be subject to exclusion orders. The key provision, however, was the power to detain anyone who might be "suspect" without any reason for a period first of two days and then up to a total of seven days. It was an exceptional power that the police used repeatedly, if often to very little effect, seemingly detaining Irish citizens only to annoy. Clearly with their list of exclusions the police welcomed the new powers, which became permanent as the PTA was repeatedly renewed. In effect the PTA could—and often was—used to criminalize political opposition, to harass suspect groups, to probe where conventional criminal law protected the individual. The PTA, therefore, generated enormous opposition from civil libertarians of various persuasions; but, certainly in November and December 1974, the act was enormously popular, indicated that something had been done.

Meanwhile in Northern Ireland some people had increasingly felt that conciliation instead of coercion had a role. There had been a renewed interest in peace demonstrations and petitions. On November 17, shortly before the Birmingham bombs, 2,500 people had attended an interdenominational peace service at Belfast City Hall organized by the Witness for Peace Movement. In fact, there was a secret interdenominational initiative to involve the Provisionals in a dialogue. The Provisional Army Council had the matter under advisement and the horrendous fallout of the Birmingham bombs simply accelerated the process. The entire spectrum of Irish and British opinion had condemned the bombings. O Conaill had appeared on television, ITV's "Weekend World," on Sunday, November 17, four days before the Birmingham bombs, to announce, "We strike at economic, military, political, and judicial targets." The consequence of war would be felt on the British homeland. Many assumed he had then ordered the pubs bombed to make his point.

No one believed the Provisional disclaimer on November 23. It would be eleven years before the IRA would admit to the bombing. No one believed O Conaill's interviews in the *Sunday Press* that the six men charged with the bombing were not in the IRA. No one believed him when he insisted there would be an internal investigation to see if the IRA had been involved and had violated operational policy. Nearly all tangible opinion remained set: The IRA had targeted the innocent. As Sammy Smyth of the UDA said even before Birmingham, "I could have shot every Roman Catholic without a shadow of compunction. They have nurtured this serpent." And so believing, loyalist paramilitaries continued killing without compunction, especially after Birmingham.

If the cycle of violence could be broken, then surely the peace people felt a place to begin was with the Provisionals. The first result was a meeting at 9:30 on Tuesday morning, December 10, at a small hotel at Feakle, County Clare, between the Provisionals and a delegation of churchmen. The Provisionals sent O Brádaigh and Maire Drumm, president and vice-president of Sinn Féin; Séamus Loughran, who had spoken of talking at Bodenstown in June; Twomey, the new IRA chief of staff; Kevin Mallon; and O Conaill. Only the last three supposedly represented the IRA. The churchmen were Dr. Arthur Butler, Church of Ireland bishop of Connor; the Reverend A. J. Weir, clerk of the Assembly of the Presbyterian Church in Ireland; the Reverend Eric Gallagher, former president of the Methodist Church in Ireland; the Reverend Ralph Baxter, secretary of the Irish Council of Churches (ICC); the Reverend William Arlow, deputy secretary of the ICC; the Reverend Harry Morton, general secretary of the British Council of Churches; the Reverend Arthur MacArthur, moderator of the General Assembly of the United Reformed Church in England and Wales; and Stanley Worrall, a former headmaster of Methodist College, Belfast, and former chairman of the New Ulster Movement. The churchmen were a distinguished selection from mainstream Protestantism, not fundamentalist bigots or street corner itinerants. They were decent, talented, determined, and without a trace of sympathy for the dreams and means of the Provisionals in particular or the postures of liberation struggles in general.

They felt that nothing but good could arise from a dialogue with the Provisionals. For their part the republicans were not averse to exploring an end to the armed struggle—and such an exploration could begin as easily at Feakle as elsewhere. Whatever the optimism of the innocent, the Provisional leadership knew there could be no military victory, only a British decision to cut their Irish losses, losses of all sorts, not just blood and sterling. If this were to be done on the installment plan or under cover of hypocrisy or even through real negotiations, the Provos would talk. Perhaps the July 1974 Chelsea meeting had been too clouded by memory of the Treaty, by delusions of grandeur, by a need to give not an inch. At Feakle it was made clear that the Provisionals were open to talks about peace. These were almost closed down as the Gárda Síochána Special Branch, tipped off by someone, suddenly arrived just as the three wanted men, tipped off by someone else, had departed. By then a process seeking first a truce and then substantive British-Provisional agreement had been initiated. On December 11 the leaders of the four main Christian churches in Ireland announced a Joint Campaign for Peace in Northern Ireland, and the Feakle talks were revealed as part of this campaign. The Feakle meeting came as a greater surprise to the British than the invitation had to the Provos. Whatever the risks, such a step, given the widening call for peace, seemed shrewd, despite the military risks of a truce on IRA security, for the volunteers were apt to take fewer precautions. There had been other Christmas truces and this one might move the ball into the British court. O Brádaigh indicated that Provisional Sinn Féin wanted "to see a peace that would endure and that must be based on justice." The other responses to Feakle varied.

On the following day, in a widely published newspaper advertisement, the four churches appealed, "For God's sake let Peace begin in our land this Christmas." The British, despite the Birmingham bombs, felt Feakle was a hopeful sign, as was the rumor that the Provos had contacts with the loyalist paramilitaries; but those responsible wanted to move carefully. The IRA had called for peace with justice, so as long as justice was not closely defined, peace was in business. The clerics met with Rees on December 18 and gave him their five-point list of suggestions, their ideas about conditions that might lead to a truce, and the Provos' reply. The republicans still focused on a long view, a culmination of two centuries of struggle. They wanted an all-Ireland assembly, a British army withdrawal within twelve months, and their prisoners freed. They wanted the Republic, not concessions, and so a cease-fire was only a first step. Still, on December 20 the Army Council announced a unilateral truce from December 22 to January 2. They feared negotiations, British duplicity, hoped rather for some small advantage.

With the Feakle meeting the Army Council entered a two-month period of direct, indirect, and peripheral negotiations focused on a permanent cease-fire. The clergy at first acted alone as intermediary but long before the end Belfast, Dublin, and even London seemingly abounded with agents, emissaries, well-meaning legates of peace. Soon both the Provisionals and the Northern Ireland Office entered a careful dance, seeking as much surface as substance.

The partners in this often clumsy shuffle were singularly ill-matched, driven by at best differing purpose. The Provisionals were led by narrow, intense men in the grip of an almost messianic vision that legitimized their use of the gun and made them indebted to the sacrifices of generations past. They wanted to move down the road to a Republic, a luminous, transcendental vision. Gunmen dreamers, killers caught in a universal, were commonplace in much of the world if not in the experience of the Northern Ireland Office, worldly third-level specialists, sophisticates in the country of the saved. The Provisional Army Council was willing to try on a truce if it came away with as much as possible or at least something. The British were urbane, sophisticated, versed in the structure of formulas whose words would entrap the involved in practicalities that would lead to mutual advantage and their nations' immediate needs. They neither understood nor liked zealots, especially those without appropriate experience or skills. They had not understood nor liked the UWC, with impossible accents and a muddled agenda, either. But this distaste for the Provos, limited, incompetent men with seedy ideas "inexperienced and not up to their task" was in the end irrelevant. The Provos were involved because they had the power that comes from the gun not because they had the tongues of angels or the talents of the Foreign Office.

As the process stretched out it became possible for the Provisionals to imagine more and more from less and less as the British negotiators offered little but a willingness to listen and to recast official policy. The Northern Ireland Office was willing to risk negotiations again. The British could not risk too much for fear of the potential dreary fallout from the loyalists, hard and soft, from the bypassed SDLP, from the critics in London, where the echo of the Birmingham bombs still reverberated. Rees was willing to allow his people to talk with Provisional Sinn Féin (not the IRA) and so for the British, James Allen, Frank Cooper, and others opened a dialogue. The British offered potential, possibilities, comments and asides; they passed phrasings and language written on bits of paper with no heading and no context across the table. The British position was that a cessation of violence would offer a new situation and new opportunities for everyone. The Provisionals wanted details.

The ensuing process was sufficiently detailed, complex, and open to interpretation that an academic dissertation could be elaborated on the maneuver. There was not simply a clash of cultures and intentions but a meeting of the simple faithful with complex pragmatists unaware of their own imperatives. The pragmatists wanted to tease an agreement out of the gunmen that would entangle them in a process away from violence. This Rees felt, would give him an opportunity to abandon internment, one of his goals, and get the Provisional Sinn Féin into politics. Neither prospect placed high on the Provos' agenda; both were seen as entrapment.

For Rees, internment was an atypical British response to coercion in the name of order rather than justice. He wanted an end to this incursion into British liberties that the Gardiner report would make possible. The Provos felt that internment was a mere facet of the British coercion machine, not atypical but intrinsic to the British control of Ireland. The republican prisoners who might have been involved in violence and could again be involved in violence were held until there would be no violence to tempt them. They were hostages. Rees could not imagine such an interpretation. "Detainees are not held for their political views but because of their involvement in violence."* No violence, a truce, then the end of internment.

*Rees, p. 148.

The Provos, seeing hostages held without charge or proof beyond suspicion, often well-founded suspicion, assumed that if the truce did not lead to the Republic, if violence began again, there would be internment again under some other name. Getting rid of internment was not a real step on the road to the Republic, only a cosmetic device. The Provos' assumption of British bad faith and hypocrisy was bottomless and founded on long experience. It was an assumption shared by almost all the rebels who had dealt with the British Empire. As for an "opportunity" to participate in electoral politics, this had even less charm for men committed to an armed struggle, who deeply suspected all such attractions that had lured generations down a blind path, who had no faith that Britain would ever keep to the political rules in Ireland if imperial interests warranted otherwise. Rees, who most certainly meant well, believed his offer true and valid. He saw the truce leading to real and desirable temptations for gunmen. The Provos saw such temptations as snares for fools, sold as lures by a Welsh gillie.

In public Rees had said only that the proposals had been received but no formal undertakings would be given. He did, however, make the very significant point that "a genuine and sustained cessation of violence over a period would create a new situation." O Brádaigh indicated that the cease-fire would continue if the British army did not take advantage of the conditions. And in private the maneuvering began. All was vague but hopeful except to the many who did not trust the IRA and for that matter often doubted the British.

The truce appeared to many loyalists a ploy, perhaps a ploy by the British, but a development that entailed great risks to the integrity of the province. The SDLP was not happy. For the general public, for those of goodwill, there was guarded hope and caution as the year ran out. Despite the truce, there was still sporadic violence, perhaps by the new IRSP or the Officials or undisciplined Provo militants, perhaps by the loyalist paramilitaries. As Rees soon made clear to the Provos, a new situation hardly existed when "someone" tossed a bomb into the house of former Prime Minister Edward Heath's house in London. The Provos closed operations down more tightly in order to keep their truce options open.

Rees also pushed the value of the coming convention, nearly forgotten in the rising violence and the Feakle fallout. "It would be foolish of me to express too much hope on the horizon and it's now up to the people themselves," he said. In fact, British interest in an IRA truce was focused largely on creating a stable environment for the convention rather than on some unlikely solution so many were seeking. The events of the autumn, the Provo bombs, especially in England, the return of the Protestant paramilitaries to sectarian killing, the feuds fought out on the streets between the Stickies and Provos and in hit jobs by the loyalists, the demonstrations and barricades, the prison tumult, all the noise of the Troubles had been turned up too loudly to permit political dialogue. If matters would stabilize at an acceptable level of noise, the convention could take center stage. Even if there was no agreement on the institutions of provincial government, even if the people themselves had no answers, the process was an enormous improvement over the erratic chaos that had only begun to taper off with the Provo truce at the end of December. What more visible sign of the times than a Provisional Sinn Féin peace march in Dublin on December 31 from Parnell Square to the British embassy to hand in a petition urging a positive response to the truce?

In Belfast between December 22 and January 17, Rees announced fifty-two releases from detention. This sign was received grudgingly not only by the Provos but also by most nationalists, who wanted everyone released. In his New Year's message the secretary stressed that "if a genuine and sustained cessation of violence" occurred, the government "would not be found wanting in its response." It was a hopeful ending to a year that, despite the horrors, had a small but real decline in the incidents of violence in the province: for example, 214 dead (down from 260) that included 15 RUC/RUCR and 11 army/UDR. The shootings were at 3,206, down from 5,018, and armed robberies dropped to 390 from 1,154. The bureaucratic statistics did not, however, include the dead and maimed in Dublin and Monaghan, Guildford and Birmingham, did not include the extension of the Troubles first to the diaspora and then other foreign parts. It had not been a good year. A negotiated truce would surely be a good beginning for 1975.

The complex negotiations involved members of the Northern Ireland Office, Frank Cooper, James Allen, and others, meeting with representatives of Provisional Sinn Féin, a legal organization in the province; the messages and commentaries transmitted by agents, largely the clergy; and the resonances and echoes provided by those brought into the process by the British. Given the enormous differences in intentions, agendas, expectations, and experience, given the volatile atmosphere of the arena, any success was unlikely. In the end the misperceptions of the involved made possible a truce that meant various things to various people. The negotiations, almost always at cross-purposes, indicated no apparent mutual benefit, but the British gave a little, hints and guesses and perhaps promises, and the Provos decided they had received enough for further probing. The IRA Army Council announced on January 2 a fourteen-day extension of the cease-fire.

Rees was encouraged that on the previous day the Provos had mentioned "ultimate withdrawal," which indicated some sense of reality. He had hopes for using the phasing out of internment as an incentive, for the lure of political participation, for a sudden lunge to practicality now that so many hopes had been raised. "'Can there be peace?' The people of Northern Ireland say 'yes.' The Government have responded positively and will continue to do so. We await a similar response from the Provisionals and the other paramilitary organizations."* On their part, the Provos wanted more visible signs of British concessions than public statements and bits of paper pushed across a table. The Provos' cease-fire ran out without agreement. There was renewed if low-level violence. There were large peace marches in Belfast and Dublin on January 19, with others planned in Derry and Newry for the next week. Rees said the situation was fluid. Privately he felt that the Provos' list of "reasons," a mix of real and imagined grievances, a mishmash of excuses, indicated the difficulty of dealing with devious and dubious gunmen. He would, however, still deal if there were advantage.

Both the Provisionals and the British talked past each other, barely aware of the nature of the dialogue. The Provos complained that they had not been given a pass

*Rees, p. 166.

to allow delegates through British army posts. Rees felt that this showed just how little the Provos understood the complexity and priorities of the security forces and the Northern Ireland Office—bits of paper handed to soldiers on guard allowing free passage was a childish request, impossible. This was true, of course. The Provos, on the other hand, felt that a great deal was possible, including such passes, if the British so desired: If it were in British interests a pass would open the gates of Buckingham Palace, much less convince an army patrol. This was true as well.

In the end the details did not matter. The British delegates offered just enough that could be made visible to allow the Provos to accept the hints and suggestions. There would be a truce. There would thus be a new situation that would permit the British to respond to the Provisionals' concerns, especially in the matters of internment, the signing of custody orders, the releases, and army harassment. After all, without the Provos' armed struggle there would be little need for internment or army harassment. The Provos got an outward and visible sign of their power with creation of incident centers to monitor the truce. There would be centers for the Provisional Sinn Féin to oversee the truce in North and West Belfast, Londonderry, Newry, Armagh, and Dungannon—their heartlands. These were merely technical matters, hot lines to keep the peace, as far as the British were concerned, a first step to assure compliance, not a concession at all but a necessary part of a cease-fire. To the Provos—and to many in Northern Ireland—the centers were evidence that the British accepted Provo power.

Rees, in fact, had to spend time calming all the other excluded players. In the process of truce negotiations he had a blistering verbal tussle with Paisley on January 7 at Stormont that delighted all of Paisley's many detractors. Now the secretary had to ease the suspicion of everyone else; the SDLP, bitter Sinn Féin rivals, the Unionists, the loyalist paramilitaries, the British Conservatives, his own party, the Dublin government, the lot. He explained away any anticipations that the Provos might have cherished after those bits of paper had been pushed across the table, after the winks and nods; but the incident centers remained. Many, like Paisley, believed that the British were intent on withdrawal.

More than most polities Northern Ireland was a cauldron of conspiracies. The loyalists in particular had placed their faith in symbols that were in the hands of the distant and distracted without concern for a part of an outer island. The British government might at any moment, by intent or neglect or even from pique, betray their trust and loyalty. As Paisley would say, "The only thing Protestants are legitimately afraid of is a dirty, underhanded deal done behind their backs."*

They year after year sought evidence of plots in London to match those of Dublin and Rome. The simple reasons for a cease-fire—to reduce the violence, to allow the free play of conventional politics, to move toward the normal—were unconvincing for many. Rees, the Labour government, London must be up to something more cunning. The Reverend William Arlow after his attendance at Feakle had even told John Taylor that he would go public on any British cabinet

---

*Padraig O'Malley, *Biting at the Grave: The Irish Hunger Strikes and the Politics of Despair* (Boston: Beacon Press), 1990, p. 175.

move to sell out Northern Protestants. The only advantage of the cease-fire conspiracy might be that the loyalist politicians would sense a need for moderation once elected to the convention. For, whatever the complex parsing of the truce, the slackening of violence did permit electioneering to reemerge.

The level of violence was still high but not unacceptable. The political process could move on toward the convention elections scheduled for May. The process, however, would move forward accompanied by turbulence and violence. Just as Rees had feared, the fractious secret armies other than the Provos rushed to fill the gap in gunfire. Worse, many of those involved in the continuing feuds and random murders were beyond institutional discipline. The intrinsic dynamics of underground organizations drove the remaining small secret armies into schismatic violence. The loyalist paramilitaries still lacked a coherent, positive ideology. They were driven by loyalty to a Crown whose representatives they did not trust and by fear and anguish disguised as arrogance and domination. Without a hard core, a messianic dream at the center, the appeals of personality, unrealistic ambition, self-interest, and the lure of easy money assured schism and faction, often barely disguised as politics. The loyalist paramilitaries shot each other over the raw possession of power and prestige, over personal affronts and the main chance: aspirations that assured repeated cycles of violence but not the discipline for permanent, armed schism.

The Irish republicans' struggle, perhaps contaminated by many of the same narrow factors, perhaps not, was lethally fueled over possession of the dream. Those who leave the old are heretics, worse than avowed enemies, for they deny the truth of those left behind, whose orthodoxy and vehemence increases in proportion to the defection. The actual reason that the Provisionals and Officials divided, that the advocates of Costello left the Officials, was a dispute over how to escalate, how to achieve the republican dream. He wanted an armed campaign in the North. They did not. The possession of the dream brings legitimacy, so within the movement the idealists punish the unfaithful.* The republicans killed for the faith and the loyalists because they lacked it.

Although the Officials and Provisionals came to shooting again in November 1974, the first time since the 1969 break, the enormous military superiority of the Provos, and most of all the antimilitary direction of the Stickies, tended to minimize the shooting. On the other hand Costello based his new movement on Official incapacity, their irrelevance to real revolution. This attitude attracted, especially in certain core areas in Belfast and the six counties, people who believed the gun had a place in politics. Costello's charisma and his exhilarating speeches drew those eager for a fresh crusade free of old quarrels. Many converts, especially in the twenty-six counties, assumed the IRSP was to be involved in radical agitation, with the gun a minor asset, necessary given the turmoil and the power

---

*In time many of those at the center of the Officials converted to the Marxist-Leninist ideal that allowed the postponement of any Irish armed struggle, a heresy as far as the Provisionals were concerned, no different in kind from those earlier republicans who had accepted the Free State, followed Fianna Fáil, or become involved in conventional politics. The IRSP in large part withdrew from the Officials because of the erosion of the republican dream, but the ensuing lethal feud indicated that the Officials had yet to give up their claim on the gun merely because the movement was being transformed into a Marxist-Leninist party: There was still power in the gun, still a use for the republican ideal.

of the orthodox. Some others, like the political figures Ronnie Bunting, son of Paisley's ally Major Bunting, and Miriam Daly, felt comfortable with the INLA, a secret army controlled by Costello that dominated the movement, an arrangement that in time led to Bernadette McAliskey's resignation.

The Officials thus faced a drain of their militants, the opposition of their own over the way into the future, and a series of provocations. They had a very serious quarrel with Costello that would help determine the fate of the new crusade. The break came over INLA volunteers taking their gear with them—a cardinal sin and a conscious provocation. The killing began on February 20 when the Officials shot dead Hugh Ferguson of the IRSP. The shooting moved south and the national organizer of Official Sinn Féin, Seán Garland, was shot six times (but not killed) as he stood before his front door in Ballymum in Dublin. Garland had led the raid in 1957 that produced the movement's greatest postwar martyr, Seán South of Garryowen, had been the quintessential republican for a generation, and had now been gunned down by two republican gunmen. On April 28 the Official O/C of Belfast, the popular Billy McMillen, was fatally shot down next to his wife of nine weeks on the Falls Road.

Efforts to organize the murder of Séamus Costello in retaliation failed although he barely scraped through a machine gun attack on his car outside Waterford by two Stickies on a motorcycle on May 7. The shooting eventually sputtered out. The INLA was too strong to crush and the Officials did not want to persist in the military game. So the IRSP was safe from its own and dominated several small areas—Divis Flats in Belfast had so many INLA men in place that it was known as the Planet of the Irsps. The INLA volunteers sought to prove their virility by becoming more lethal than the Provos. Just as Rees had feared, the splinters and fissures assured violence, whatever the Provos did.

The loyalist quarrels had long been as lethal as any in Ireland. They arose unexpectedly for uncertain motives between friends and neighbors, pretenders and commanders. The various competing loyalist secret armies were clumped around charisma and owed first allegiance to their neighborhood, often at first seemingly to their local, the pub headquarters. Over the years some members sought to introduce ideas, radical socialism, federations or independence, Ulster roots, but such excursions seldom lasted long and also led to internecine quarrels. Effective talent in the early years had organized and enlarged the core but had not constructed a positive ideology. The differences that counted seemed to be in the uniforms not the ideals.

The UDA wore recycled military camouflage jackets, floppy field hats, and the old UVF badge. The new UVF preferred black leather jackets, berets, and Sam Browne belts for commanders. The Orange Volunteers chose U.S. Army jackets but could not be mistaken for the UDA because they had a badge with a roundel, a red hand of Ulster and a crown. On media demand everyone wore dark glasses or hooded ski masks. The actual killers of the inner core, the Red Hand Commandos or the Ulster Freedom Fighters, wore civilian clothes on most operations. Most of the members were not killers, simply a militia eager to defend; there were fewer of them each year as defense seemed to involve atrocity. At unpredictable times the killing was not so much defending the loyal as eliminating the opposition.

On January 6, in the midst of the Provo truce deliberations, Charles Harding

Smith quit the UDA Inner Council dominated by Tyrie. Andy Tyrie was a loyalist paramilitary popular with the media. He was honest, mild-appearing in granny glasses, and ready with a quip or a quote. He had none of the brutal, intractable aura of the neighborhood hard men, crude, tattooed, rough bigots, more at home in pub brawls than television interviews. At times it seemed that no British politician or journalist had ever been exposed to their own working class, much less that of Belfast. The Provos, the UWC, the UVF were all so rough, so limited, so narrow. So Tyrie was a relief. He, however, had his moments. On January 14 unknown gunmen wounded Harding Smith. He held on amid his friends. On February 6 unknown gunmen tried again and Harding Smith decided to withdraw from power stakes and leave the province.

For most of the determined murderers, those not driven solely by the pleasure of the killer trade, the prime target remained the Catholics, who had been the principal victims during the last months of 1974. A Provo truce simply encouraged a tit-for-tat response by idle IRA volunteers. On April 5 a bomb was thrown into a Catholic bar in the New Lodge area. Two people were killed. A few hours later a bomb was thrown into the Mountainview Tavern on the Shankill Road. Five Protestants were killed. With the feuds and the random murders, retaliation and bodies scattered without claim or purpose, Rees's fears had become reality. The campaign for the convention was overshadowed. On April 29 the secretary warned that if the horrifying violence went unchecked rational political debate could become impossible.

Of course, rational political debate had never been a provincial specialty. Sectarian tirades and appeals to bigotry only encouraged violence and did not set bombs or pull triggers, but this was cold comfort. Rees and most of the politicians involved had, whatever the results with the Assembly, seen debate between the communities in and out of the chamber. If power sharing had not worked, politics was still nearly everyone's favored option—provincial politics, power politics, even, for the moment, convention politics. The random killing, the tit-for-tat murders, the lethal feuds had sharpened the minds of many, even if they had converted no one to moderation.

The convention election would have appeared, like the provincial elections of old, a referendum on faith. The two poles, the UUUC, still maintaining the uneasy alliance of Unionists, Craig's Vanguard, and Paisley's DUP, still bound by mutual enemies, shared suspicions and self-interest even while absolutely divided on policy; the SDLP, still an uneasy alliance of old and new, country and city, radical and conservative, Belfast and the west of the Bann, whose members and supporters, like the loyalists, grudgingly accepted the advantages of unity as the price of electoral success. Whether electoral success would translate into power was not clear in 1975.

Voting in Northern Ireland had long been frozen into support of one's own, a candidate often chosen by the controlling elite. The voter casting a referendum vote on the national issue often was even denied electing a friend to power, very little power in the case of the Nationalists. And there was little tangible return for the loyalist voter as well, for the controlling elite only rarely need be troubled by the economic or social needs of the Unionist voters. The collapse of the old Unionist monopoly, the rapid shift of loyalist elite control through the gentry and the mercantile class to those Protestants, rich or poor, skilled or not, who mobilized, had meant a period of majority uncertainty. Then the emergence of the tripartite UUUC represented a division of personal loyalties, fundamentalist preferences, and habits into new forms. The loyalist paramilitaries—once bitten, twice shy—did not become involved. The Nationalists too disappeared, and their voters, joined by a new generation and many previously inactive, appeared on the SDLP books. Both communities would still vote for their own (or, like the Provisionals, not vote at all), finding little attraction in the conciliation politics advocated by Alliance and to a degree by the NILP, or in the class politics advocated by the Republican Clubs, People's Democracy, and to a degree by the NILP. The astute could predict, nearly as easily as they had in the sixties, the outcome of the convention election.

Rees had known since the Westminster general election that he was going to move into 1975 with a hard-line Unionist majority, an uneasy Provo truce, and continuing sporadic and random violence from which only exhaustion might bring relief. And nothing much could be done. At least the SDLP had decided to run, if reluctantly, postponing disaster. The truce-as-conspiracy might be believed but seemingly did neither harm nor good. The Reverend William Arlow before the election indicated that he had been told by O Conaill and a member of the British cabinet that the Provos had been given a firm commitment that the British would withdraw if the convention broke down. Arlow revealed as much on the "Today" national television program on May 26. In the Republic the government tried to help, as Conor Cruise O'Brien noted, by keeping a low profile "to avert the emergence of a loyalist majority in the convention elections." Nothing apparently mattered a great deal. On May 1 the votes were cast as predicted.

The UUUC took 58.4 percent of the vote and 47 seats, a solid majority that would control the convention. The Official Unionists had 19 seats, Vanguard 14, and the DUP 12; an Independent UUUC had 1 and an Independent Unionist 1, for a total of 45 out of the 76 seats. For the excluded middle the moderate Unionist Party of Northern Ireland received 5, Alliance 8, the NILP 1; there were fifteen thousand votes but no seats for the Officials' Republican Clubs. The other 17 seats, 2 lost from the old Assembly in strong republican areas, went to the SDLP, whose leaders felt the party had done as well as expected. All the parties had done as expected. The intransigent loyalists had a solid majority. The eroded middle survived without promise. Faulkner scraped into the convention on the ninth count. The minority politically organized as the SDLP maintained the faith.

The British offered hope for politics in the form of a new devolved assembly. There would be a convention, but few could suppose how such a body would establish institutions that would fulfill British requirements to be acceptable to the minority through adequate power concessions and an Irish dimension. Power sharing and Sunningdale were the very core of loyalist complaints, not the aspirations of their convention delegation. And if O'Brien, no longer keeping an uncomfortable low profile, believed that the Protestants might be obliged to accept power sharing—a statement quickly repudiated by his Prime Minister—no one could imagine how to oblige the loyalists into positions they detested. After the general strike the loyalists did not fear any British recourse to force, nor did they have any great hope for the new convention. Rees, through conferences and contacts during the electoral campaign, through papers and reports, through copies of other "solutions" from Newfoundland to Australia, had sought to indicate means ahead. The UUUC did not want to move in such directions. Their people had voted for majority rights. The majority in Westminster did not "share power." The majority in Northern Ireland had voted to be British. The province of Northern Ireland was not a foreign country and did not need any special relationship to a foreign country. As Rees noted, as all but those distant from the arena or swayed by their own desires had known, "It was the loyalists who had held and still held the key to the link with the United Kingdom."*

*O'Malley, p. 197.

14

The Mold Sets,
the Convention to Direct Rule:
May 1975–August 1976

The Formula "Two and Two Make Five" Is Not Without Its Attractions.

Fyodor Dostoyevski

As the convention spring moved into summer, the nature of the province after years of raucous turmoil had congealed in most perceptions. The participants, their aspirations and intentions, their organizations and actions had become all too familiar. Even those in London, easily distracted, generally felt that the provincial currents were adequately charted. And alas, those currents tended to erode both patience and enthusiasm. Those with good wishes and high hopes, those charged with reporting the events, those eager for novelty and glitter, those attracted to crisis grew tired of the relentless provincial pursuit of contradictory interests.

Thus, even the decent players grew less congenial to the outside observers; and many did not seem to be decent at all, and certainly not reasonable. The Northern Ireland political game continued to be played with sullen intent and murderous results despite all the advice and proffered solutions, despite the maps on ways out of the impasse, despite threats and good sense and self-interest sold as accommodation. The players simply refused to play to others' rules.

Most grew tired of the province and its problems. It seemed that no one there learned anything, forgot anything, remembered anything. No one found useful the experience or wisdom of others, the efficiency of grand ideologies, or the certain returns of simple conciliation. No one seemed to pay any attention to the well-meaning, to the concerned and caring. So, spurned, the distant grew bored or angry. Many observers, many of the responsible, had adjusted their original, Irish stereotypes once and no longer saw advantage to distinctions and diligence in analyzing the Irish problem. Further concern was fruitless. Rees had immersed himself in Irish matters and to what point? Why bother?

The only thing out of Northern Ireland was the latest atrocity, the horror of the moment. The secret armies waged wars few could imagine succeeding and few could support. Politics led nowhere, had led nowhere, often existing apparently solely to frustrate compromise and accommodation. The political parties, led by household names, whether decent men or bigots, were little more than labels for tribes without many redeeming features. There were no heroes, only villains, faceless murderers, and everyday people shunted aside to minor roles. Moderation offered only a ticket to irrelevance and frustrated retirement. Those who persisted could manage only, like Hume, isolated from real power. To have power and then deploy it in moderation's name was to fritter away a career almost overnight. Even to so threaten, even to appear to so threaten, was often sufficient to be discarded by the purists, by one's colleagues, by the electorate, and thus by the people. The problem in Ireland remained that there was no solution.

The adventures of the young radicals, the cruelty of the establishment, the fleeting, photogenic glamour of the urban guerrillas no longer attracted. Even the most callous journalist wanted, if not a happy ending, a moral, a lesson to be taught, a meaning, not simply one more example of human truculence. Henceforth the long war in Northern Ireland could attract attention briefly by acts of escalated violence. What observers wanted was a final act. By 1975. Nearly all observers had given up on conciliation and had tired of violence.

In the Republic the residue of historical nostalgia for unity existed, often found in the politics of Fianna Fáil, but rarely in the priorities of the voters. London, still baffled, seldom cared to hear details. Rees had become an Irish specialist, sincere, inventive, but a bore. He had been captured by his department, spoke of complexities and conundrums that meant little in the corridors of Westminster or Whitehall and less to the public in Great Britain. The Northern Secretary repeated himself, as did the province. In the United States the great shift away from the IRA as liberator to a posture congenial to the Dublin consensus had continued. The western political establishment, generally without interest in Irish political concerns, tended to accept the wisdom of the Dublin government: Do nothing. No one much cared about Northern Ireland now but those made to suffer or those whose fate was involved.

The major player remained, as always, the British, the responsible party with the capacity to act on any level; but the British were not in a position to devise an accommodation incorporating the contradictory goals of the involved. Such preordained failure using the existing form tended to produce ennui in British policy circles. Almost all small and seemingly realistic initiatives failed with the regularity of the Irish rain to win general approval. There was never a consensus; each gain was always seen at another's expense. Any initiative, however well-meaning, however slight, produced only complaint. The big moves had foundered as well. A few of the British offered unconventional strategies, special operations, disinformation, unilateral withdrawal or even immediate integration. These too led only to controversy. So after 1975 Great Britain paid attention to Ireland only during the reverberation of atrocity. The specialists and those locally responsible could tinker with the dilemma, but the establishment and the populace on the main island was not interested.

Those sent to Northern Ireland often grew distant from their colleagues in Britain, became irrelevant as specialists in enigmatic tribes and dynasties. In 1975 Rees would return to London as to a strange country, his old colleagues ignorant of the snarls and tangles along the Falls or within the DUP. Caring little from the first, the British cared less with time. This lack of interest was to prove irreversible. The closer the violence (the Birmingham bombs), the more the English public demanded coercion rather than compromise. Righteous indignation was the convention and ennui the norm otherwise. Let the specialists handle the matter, let the Irish on their island, North or South, sort out matters. The new Troubles were their fault.

Most of those in Britain who thought at all on Irish matters accept as fact the useful proposition that the involvement in Ireland was as an act of goodwill and fidelity to law and order and even justice. Britain was there to separate warring and restlessly hostile factions, not out of self-interest. The cartoonists over the years showed the two sides, IRA or UVF, Catholics or Protestants, decent people and terrorists, as contenders, with the security forces and the British state as peacekeeper. No one told the British cartoonists what to draw. They drew as they perceived. The Irish were divided and at odds. It was their problem, and Britain's unenviable responsibility. The essential nature of British perception, a meld of sloth, innocence, arrogance, historical editing, realism, decency, and indifference, changed little over the years, only hardened. Moreover, because it was propagated often without overt malice, related well to perceived reality, and was articulately disseminated, a great many accepted the premise. The Irish were intractable and the British disinterested.

One of the more impressive of all British political achievements arising from the Troubles was to sell this view at large with the collaboration of the Dublin government and in time the Irish people. It was even more impressive given the long British imperial record of "disinterested" involvements in others' quarrels— Jew and Arab, Greek and Turk, Hindu and Moslem—involvements that were firmly grounded in self-interest. Still, the concept of Britain as referee had been firmed up by the aura of British historic decency, the articulate defense of London's policy of the moment, and the general Western distaste for terrorism. The perception was more easily sold because everyone else found burdensome a crisis without resolution or heroes. Let the British soldier on, carry a burden inherited from centuries past. The result was foreign reassurance for British policies. It was hardly surprising that the many abroad assumed that such analysis was accurate. What other course was there? Northern Ireland was not Algeria or Palestine or even Wales. What else could be done? So in London everyone took narrow and short views, supported technical adjustment, decent investment, and the officials in place, abhorred the slaughter (not great in raw numbers), and paid attention to other matters.

In Dublin the original response of Lynch in 1969 had been articulate and comforting inaction plus the adjustment of the old patriotism. This remained the Irish reaction. The rising British distaste for the Northern Irish crisis began to be paralleled in the Republic, if for different reasons. Year by year, bomb by bomb, the wonders of immediate unity evaporated within the public psyche. This was a slow and often unnoticed process. Unity might still be a general aspiration but could no longer be a simple slogan. Unity became at the very least complex. Loyalty to the Northern Catholics, especially but not exclusively in the form of the SDLP, continued for the short term. Dublin still saw the Protestants as

446

Orange bigots. The constitutional republicans, especially within Fianna Fáil, were still attuned to the oratory of old, but they were aging and adjusting. The ruthless violence and radical aspirations of the Catholic working-class gunmen and their friends frightened many in the Republic, including those in Fianna Fáil. The SDLP might be congenial and fit the old stereotypes, but the Provos did not. They offered trouble in Northern Ireland, still and again, and a resurgence of the old subversion in the Irish Republic. Militant republicans had always been a deadly enemy to de Valera's republican Fianna Fáil party and nothing there had changed.

Efforts to buy into the IRA in 1968–69 had been minor and tentative and disastrous. The Dublin establishment detested the Provos. They might not be as sweeping or as logical as Conor Cruise O'Brien but their distaste was as real. The Provos were easily denied by many conservatives—Communist terrorists killing Irishmen—but their aspirations were not. Unity could still be proclaimed as the goal if violence as a means was eschewed. But short of the conversion of the Orange, violence was the only potentially effective means.

Consequently, most of the Dublin establishment would have liked to have been as distant and disinterested as the London establishment, but could not. Some did not want to be, and clung to the dream of one Ireland that was daily denied in the butcher's bill from the six counties. Dublin had not yet fully come to grasp the dynamics of a North, even if the dangers to Irish stability were more apparent. There was no trouble with the pretensions of the Provos—the state had suffered through that challenge before—but other than peace and quiet, no Southern party had a rigorous Northern policy: peace with justice and no final closure or unity. Some still had hopes of unity somehow. Others would take peace without justice and an end to the fixation on unity. And the number grew despite, rather than because of, the advocacy of Conor Cruise O'Brien, who would allow no fig leaf of romance nor recourse to sentiment, who wanted a vocal end to the old dreams. Dreams die silently in cold hearts and not through the exercise of argument. In the Republic the heart too long denied grew yearly cold, chilled by the violence of those just to the north who still lived out the logic of their dreams. Year by year the winds of change were at work on the national issue.

To the north gradual change seemed unlikely to all. The province had been battered and bombed, the old unionist institutions lay wracked and ruined, the army was in the streets, the future in the hands of the ignorant and the violent. And why? The loyalists knew, as always, betrayal and alien ignorance. It seemed obvious to all of them, sophisticated or primitive, that their case was just and their analysis valid. The majority indeed, had a reasonable case, but it was irrevocably ruined by the historical record, by the character of the advocates, and by their strident presentation. Who wanted to be lectured at by Enoch Powell, however brilliant, a crank and an accused racist, or shouted at by Paisley, a primitive bigot? Who could be convinced that the B Specials had been good citizens or the UDA a citizens action group? So no one listened to the unionists.

The unionists' two key points were reasonable. Northern Ireland was a part of the United Kingdom, no different than Wales or Sussex. There was thus no reason for any interference from a foreign country: Norway had no say in Scotland nor France in Kent. So why should there be an Irish dimension to the province? And within that province if there was to be devolution, then the majority elected should have the majority control. This was the case with any democratic government. This was the case at Westminster, where the first-past-the-post electoral system at times produced minority governments and only a few seats in return for a massive third-party vote. Why must the provincial winner share power not earned by the minority? Why should that minority, whose leaders refused to accept the reality of the United Kingdom or the legitimacy of its institutions, be rewarded with power that would be denied in Wales or Sussex? Why should such citizens have political access to a foreign country? Since no one paid any attention, the loyalists tended to intensify all the old defense mechanisms that prohibited flexibility: Not an Inch. Why give an inch when the only return was not thanks but a demand for more, presented with bad grace.

The loyalists then suspecting that their base was eroding remained determined to husband every grain remaining. While confession of past error has, according to many, great rewards, few involved in the Irish crisis felt guilty, felt any need for atonement. The loyalists had done only what was necessary and reasonable to protect their way of life. In turn the nationalists, North and South, had been engaged in no more than a crusade for immediate justice with the expectation of the inevitable triumph of a national goal no different from that of all other nations. The British too had no cause to be concerned about old grievances and historic decisions. They only sought an accommodation to the advantage of all. Elsewhere, without responsibility or experience, the observers could hardly be blamed for innocence, ignorance, and reporting what they saw. No one felt at fault and the closer to the crisis the greater the sense of threat, a threat fashioned by others through no fault of one's own.

Ian Paisley was not to be blamed for the scarlet power of an aggressive Rome. The British cabinet was not to be blamed for the truculence and violence of the citizens of an unprofitable province. The IRA was not to be blamed for their clearly defined responsibility as guardians of the national dream. The politicians were not to be blamed for urging attractive policies. The bigots were not to be blamed for their hearts' desire. No one accepted blame. Each read the past as rationale, the present as trial, and the future as eventual redemption.

Simply because none of the parties involved in the Northern Ireland crisis had proved remarkably magnanimous nor the election results for the convention congenial to optimism did not necessarily doom the latest British initiative. Something might emerge. Rees felt that those in the province would have to find their own way. Britain, with the convention, had presented a playing field. It was quite possible, even likely, that the teams intended to play by the rules that might prohibit a game. The British had, foolishly, hoped that power sharing and the Irish dimension would not play a part in the electoral campaign. Instead the old Assembly had been the single issue. And the uncompromising loyalists had won—fair and square—on a platform of intransigence, and saw no reason to fudge. The SDLP insisted that such fudging—power sharing and an Irish dimension—was part of the game. The others in the convention and in the Northern Ireland Office devoutly hoped that a formula would be found. After all, a power-sharing assembly had existed with an Irish dimension, so another assembly was not a hopeless nonstarter. If a devolved assembly was to emerge—as all Northern Irish parties seemed to want—then such a formula must exist. Rees felt it was up to the provincial politicians to find it at the convention.

The convention in fact offered little of delight to the new members. Each received £2,500 and traveling expenses but not the rights and privileges of a real legislative assembly, a denial that confused some members. The convention was chaired by the chief justice of Northern Ireland, Sir Robert Lowry, assisted by two senior civil servants, John A. Oliver and Maurice N. Hayes, with Ronald Blackburn as clerk. Where the last time London had set the rules, this time the members would do so. Britain would urge moderation but Ulster would be left on its own devices. At worst it would be a chance for the politicians to occupy center stage instead of the gunmen.

When the convention opened, Harry West noted, circumspectly, that the loyalist majority would not take advantage of the minority; but Gerry Fitt for the SDLP felt that he could not look forward to the deliberation "with any degree of optimism." * Optimistic or not, the SDLP entered into the deliberations, which moved slowly through May and June, focused on procedural matters. There were also wider discussions at Stormont since Westminster seldom debated on Irish matters, although Rees supplied ample information from the dispatch box to keep the province informed. Mostly, however, the convention plodded on without a breakdown, finishing at midnight on July 3 after a final three-day debate on Fitt's motion concerning "the structures and systems of government designed to deal with the immediate human, social, and economic problems of Northern Ireland." In London on the same day Rees had warned his cabinet colleagues on the subcommittee on Ireland that if the convention failed, a real possibility, then the only option was continued direct rule. Rees felt that the three months of leisurely discussions had not been wasted despite some ructions: Glen Barr had stalked out, not to return, as a protest over loyalist prisoners in Scotland, and Robert Overend had expressed pleasure at the police batoning Gerry Fitt in the past and his desire to squeeze Paddy Devlin's neck in the future. Still, West, Fitt, and Napier had spoken against direct rule and for a devolved assembly. At least the discussions had only attracted attention away from the gunmen and not generated strife. When the convention recessed for six weeks the parties, again encouraged by the Northern Ireland Office, engaged in direct and private discussions.

The shift to convention politics had by no means eroded the level of violence. In fact provincial violence had during much of 1975 taken a peculiarly nasty turn. Up to the Provisional announcement of a cease-fire there had been a war of sorts, with rules of engagement and an apparent rationale for what often seemed to many as mindless sectarian atrocities. The Provos were engaged in an armed struggle against the security forces and were often as well opposed to the loyalist paramilitaries, who sought victims more indiscriminately but often at understandable moments of crisis or concern. There was random violence and occasionally a murder without political reason, the background music of the crisis, but this did not drown out the war drums. After the cease-fire matters shifted unpleasantly.

*Merlyn Rees, *Northern Ireland: A Personal Perspective* (London: Methuen, 1985), p. 198.

449

Almost from the beginning the truce lacked allure for many within the Provos. This number grew as none of the anticipated benefits emerged. Much had been based on hints and guesses, notes and nods, possibilities and sureties given without evidence. In retrospect there was the feeling that the movement had been led up the garden path by sophisticated and pernicious negotiators. Much had been given and little returned. Thus, from the first, local commanders had felt it proper to react to provocation and as time passed to initiate operations that to all others seemed a violation of the truce.

On July 7, Detective Constable Andrew Johnston was killed when he touched a booby-trapped desk in a burgled school in Lurgan. What seemed to the IRA a proper response to continued RUC harassment hardly seemed so to the RUC, still under daily threat during a truce unhonored. In fact, many of the IRA target rationalizations convinced only the faithful. Many operations appeared not only "military" but sectarian. Shooting an unarmed farmer off his tractor because he was a part-time UDR militiaman was taken by Protestants as sectarian, just as a trap bomb was taken by the RUC as violation of the truce. And as the authorized IRA target lists expanded even the neutral felt the truce had failed.

In turn the Army Council was reluctant to deny their own, to punish an aggressive spirit, to impose control from the top on popular and effective locals responding to local needs. Authority within the center circle of the Provisionals was in any case shifting, for all sorts of reasons, and the situation was both fluid and new. Compounding the uncertainties were the renewed feud with the Officials and the arrival of Costello's IRSP and INLA on the scene.

The other republicans also had entered a fluid period. The Officials in the Dublin center wanted an end to the Northern wars, the IRA run down and ultimately stored away out of sight. The military option could be retained for defense in a risky province and to expropriate funds. The lure of easy money always had its charms, despite the desire to change the Official Sinn Féin movement into an official workers party. The internecine feuds with the Provos and the new INLA were unwelcome but thought necessary as a militant example. To do less would be to have their organization shot off the streets. Nevertheless, by 1975, three years after their unilateral truce, the Officials had turned sharply toward radical politics and in so doing tended to exercise less control over the remaining IRA units. Mostly, except for a few like Mick Ryan and for a time Seán Garland, the military option was a declining asset, soon to be closed out. For another year Goulding would be chief of staff, until replaced by Garland, but their secret army was less an army each month and more a company of bodyguards and illicit funders. By the time Garland took over the remnants of the Official IRA, an organization that the party claimed no longer existed, little was left—and this was as intended. Thus, just because the Officials were moving away from military violence, they became involved in street battles, adding to the din.

The loyalists did not need republican feuds to believe that the IRA was alive, well, and virulent. Rather they believed the IRA might well be on the lip of triumph. Deserted by their own politicians, who were once again parading about Stormont talking to the SDLP, once again content with a sterile political agenda, the hard men had been abandoned. The glory days of the general strike had gone. Their self-appointed leaders had gone back up to Stormont. Worse, the British were rumored to be ready to leave if those loyalist politicians did not do as they were told up on Stormont Hill. On May 26 the Reverend William Arlow, involved since Feakle in the truce talks, had claimed that the British government had given a firm commitment to the IRA that British troops would withdraw from Ulster if the convention broke down. The British government denied this. The loyalists did not believe London. This was exactly what they had assumed: London would betray them, given any chance. The convention was bound to fail and the British to leave. The result was, as in the past, a rising militancy that led to further sectarian killings, and a vicious internal debate concerning options that led to further feuds and gunfights.

What grew more worrisome to all was not the feuding within the various paramilitary groups but the nature of the sectarian killings, which were blatant, spectacular, and often without explanation. On June 3 three Northern Ireland Protestants returning home from a dog show in Cork were ambushed and killed at the border. The murders were sufficient evidence that the IRA and the Irish were fully engaged in a war to drive the loyalists out of the province, a conviction that needed no further evidence. Later that month an effort was made in Kildare near Sallins to bomb a train filled with three hundred Officials on the way to Bodenstown. The attempt failed with the death of one of the men involved. Then the most spectacular of the summer's atrocities occurred at the end of July in County Down.

At three o'clock on the morning of July 31, the Miami Showband, an Irish pop group, was returning to the Republic from an engagement at the Castle Ballroom in Banbridge, a Protestant town. With varying personnel the band had been in business for thirteen years, although this was their first performance at the Castle Ballroom in four years. In a minibus were five of the six band members. The other had driven alone to his home in Antrim. Brian McCoy, the trumpet player, was driving toward Newry as the bus approached Loughbrickland, not far out of Banbridge. He saw swinging red lights ahead. Joint UDR–British army patrols were common along the border area, and he slowed to a stop. Instead it was a ten-man UVF action group disguised as an official army patrol. The UVF men moved the five Miami members out of the van beside the road while two men pretending to search the bus secretly attempted to place an explosive devise with a timer set to go off after the band men were released. The explosion would come when the minibus was on the road.

The loyalists were convinced that much cross-border showband traffic was carried out for the IRA. It was simply one more of the prevalent illusions of conspiracy and assumptions of IRA intrigue. The explosion would thus eliminate five typical targets—male, Irish Catholics in a vulnerable area—and in so doing prove that such cross-border dance bands really worked as a conduit for the IRA smuggling arms and explosives over the border. Didn't their own bombs kill them? The five Miami members began to become uneasy by the side of the road. The patrol asked curious questions, seemed odd. Des McAlea, the saxophone player, assumed that the patrol was a joint UDR–British army affair but still wondered why he was asked his date of birth as well as his name. Strange.

Then unexpectedly the UVF bomb detonated inside the minibus, set off by the static electricity from the band's loudspeakers. The explosion destroyed the van and killed both the UVF men inside. The explosion knocked the band members down near the roadside ditch and stunned them. The UVF men were stunned as well. The cunning two-stage operation had literally blown up in their faces. Two men had disintegrated along with the bus. In the glow from the burning vehicle and the fires set on the verge, the loyalists began firing into the sprawled band members. After a couple of heavy bursts of fire, they fled.

McAlea escaped serious injury and ran for help. Stephen Travers, hit by dum-dum bullets, also lived. McCoy and the two others were dead, shot repeatedly as they lay on the ground by the ditch. The UVF men had left their own mangled and burned dead behind and escaped into the night. One mutilated body was in front of the minibus and the other ninety feet to the rear. Debris from the wreck was scattered for a hundred yards. There were shell casings, filled magazines, a .38 caliber pistol, discarded berets, and a human arm tattooed with the inscription "UVF Portadown." Not a neat and tidy operation at all. A bungled massacre. Still, within twelve hours the UVF claimed responsibility for an edited version of the event. The general revulsion could not be so easily edited out of the act.

Not only did the fate of an innocent showband have particular horror and poignancy, but also the murders underlined the universal nationalist fear of the UDR and the British army. Any patrol of uniformed and armed men on the Northern Irish roads had become not haven but danger to the minority. The fact that the RUC followed up on the clues until there were both arrests and a conviction of some of the involved did not reassure many Catholics. A set of spectacles with a rare prescription was traced by sound police work and led to one UVF man, and a special Star pistol led to the assassins of IRA volunteer John Francis Green, murdered in the Republic in January 1975. Two of the killers had been in the UDR and this is what was remembered—collusion and sectarian murder on the Northern Ireland roads, not the perpetrators pursued by the police.

And the sectarian killing did not end but continued on and on, a long bloody blur with victims forgotten and atrocities overtaken by others; yet few had the impact of the July 31, 1975, Miami Showband. Those murders by the UVF maintained over the years a place in the atrocity standings, if below Bloody Sunday and Bloody Friday.

On August 13, a Provisional IRA active service unit under the command of Brendan "Bic" McFarlane planted a bomb in the Bayardo Bar on the Shankill Road in Belfast that killed five and injured forty clients. The bar, as was the case with many IRA targets, was supposedly a center of loyalist paramilitary activity and thus, according to the system's rationale, legitimate. To the vulnerable the IRA was engaged in killing Protestants to intimidate the rest, to punish the UVF or the UDA, to drive the majority out of the province. Linking a victim with the paramilitaries and the paramilitaries with the British security forces as imperial pawns convinced very few not easily convinced. And from time to time there was no such effort. Tit-for-tat killing along the margins of the core areas, random murder of random victims, was a tactic of armed men of both persuasions. The Army Council, meeting over the border, or even the O/Cs nearer the killing, either put the best military light on the act or ignored it when possible. The Provisional IRA leaders did not want to be involved in sectarian killing, nor did many volunteers—but few of them would sit idly by when retaliation was possible. The leadership also did not want to discipline aggressive and effective volunteers; if action could be rationalized, as the Bayardo Bar, fine; if not, not.

The security forces in the midst of the "truce" found a rising tide of sectarian killings, vicious and violent paramilitary feuds, and constant IRA action. The talking at Stormont may not have engendered further division but the violent edges of that division were all too apparent. At least one substantial security initiative was under way during the run into the convention, when Chief Inspector James Flanagan, the first Catholic to direct the RUC, initiated formal contacts with the Gárda Síochána. Early in 1974 the Gárda commissioner, Patrick Malone, had visited Flanagan in Belfast. The visit had been returned and the formal contacts grew in intimacy until they led to a political agreement, signed at the Baldonnel Irish military airfield outside Dublin, that set up formal panels on intelligence exchange and coordinated ground patrolling on the border. By the time Flanagan left office in 1976 as Sir Jamie much had been done although the two forces hardly acted as one.

The fact was that most of the Gárdaí increasingly saw the Provos as enemy and the Northern security forces as ally. Once the IRA undertook armed robbery south of the border, shot the Gárdaí who interfered, organized violent military prison escapes, challenged legitimate authority at every level, the Gárdaí's historic distaste for the RUC, the British army, and the agents out of London dissolved. Individually there had often been contacts, but after Flanagan there would be a steady current toward cooperation.

This was made easier by the continued effort at the top of the RUC to create a fully professional, nonsectarian organization. If the process was often lost on those in the nationalist ghettos, who wanted to toss stones and shout insults as well as receive police respect, the intention was real. The intention was often mistaken for the reality as one apologist after another would announce the end of the old RUC with the arrival of each new leader, each new reform, each real triumph. And there were successes. The RUC wanted to apprehend the UVF or UDA killers and see them tried, convicted, and punished, even when many on the force understood their motives. For those nationalists arrested on suspicion, harassed on the street, stopped at roadblocks, the RUC was still an arm of the Orange system, dangerous, unrepentant, neo-Fascist. Most of the Catholics would not notice the sometimes subtle changes in attitude and discipline. The RUC, Protestant or otherwise, were police and were appalled by any murder. Few kept paramilitary sympathy long: Most, nearly all, were loyal to law and order. The minority Catholics still felt the RUC was alien. The Gárdaí, with the same deadly enemies as the RUC, with similar jobs, had more sympathy; they saw the RUC put both the UVF and the Provos in jail, saw policemen, not bigots.

For their part the RUC recognized that the Gárdaí were not allied to the IRA, not tolerant of atrocities, not part of the problem, whatever the unionist politicians thought, but part of the solution. On July 9, for example, Dáithí O Conaill was arrested at Coolock, north Dublin, and held in the Bridewell Prison under Section 30 of the Offenses Against the State Act. O Conaill was the most prominent IRA man on the run, often a spokesman on policy matters, readily available to journalists, often mistakenly identified as the chief of staff. Free, he was a constant outrage, a loose villain for many in the United Kingdom. His arrest was viewed by the police North and South as a triumph: no more interviews or banned speeches from O Conaill for a while. On July 25 he was tried and convicted of membership in the IRA and sentenced to twelve months in prison—a success for the Gárdaí.

So cooperation remained a constant. Even when spokesmen in London or politicians in Belfast shouted about collusion between the IRA and the Dublin establishment, the security forces knew better. Even when more nationalist politicians in Dublin or the everyday Irishman complained about the sectarian RUC, complained about their shooting on sight and beating confessions out of suspects, there was no shift in the Gárdaí. The police in the Republic knew that their lives were put at risk by the Provos, by the new and ruthless INLA, and even by the Officials' fund-raisers. A team of radical revolutionaries had killed Gárda Richard Fallon during a bank robbery at Dublin's Arran Quay back in April 1970. There had been shoot-outs and armed raids and gunmen trouble ever since, worse since the IRSP appeared. In September 1975 Noel and Marie Murray, self-proclaimed revolutionaries, would kill Gárda Michael Reynolds during a raid. Both would be sentenced to death but receive life sentences. Thus by 1975 the police were more regularly at peril. The Gárdaí knew the risks police ran in a politicized society. Armed raiders were doubly dangerous if validated by a patriot cause. So the common gunman enemy canceled out much of British-Irish historical animosity and made formal and informal police cooperation a constant, despite bumpy instances.

The summer of 1975 dragged into the autumn with a series of rough and unpleasant moments. The convention delegates had spent their time in a constant round of talks that even Rees recognized had led down the same blind alley. The Unionists were not going to compromise the principles that had won them election, and the SDLP, assured of Westminster's veto, were not going to accept less than was just. There were leaks, disruptive press conferences, rumors, and reports of plots and conspiracies: the usual clutter of Ulster political discourse. The convention meeting had to be postponed to September 9 so that the talks could continue. The delay only allowed more disagreement, more suspicions. Rees had made up his mind that the convention would collapse. Then, at the very last moment, and from a most peculiar source, came the long-awaited formula for accommodation.

For some while Hume and Austin Currie had bruited about the idea of a temporary, voluntary coalition. In August William Craig, the Vanguard's hard man, felt that the constitution could include a clause that permitted, in an emergency, the majority to accept a coalition cabinet. He could replay Edward Carson's role in the creation of Stormont and take over the leadership of a devolved government. This coalition could run for four or five years, not unlike the Churchill Coalition in 1940–45. This would be power shared through an authorized, emergency government. It had charm. The Reverend Beattie of the DUP was agreeable. The dreaded words power sharing did not appear. Paisley had once said to an adviser, "Give me another word for power sharing."* Emergency coalition might be the answer. Craig could hardly be accused of being a moderate. Everyone wanted a real assembly. The SDLP would have to come into an emergency executive if offered seats or deny its public posture. The UUUC seemed ready to move. A policy document began to circulate. Craig was ready to follow Carson's example and move forward into power. At the end of August there seemed hope at last.

On September 1, gunmen, claiming later to be from an unknown South Armagh Republican Action Force but assumed to be local IRA people, burst into Tullyvallen Orange hall near Newtownhamilton in County Armagh, opened fire, and killed six Orangemen. Both the Provos and the INLA denied responsibility. Those interested blamed Costello's lot but such differences mattered little to most loyalists. Protestant opinion throughout the province was once more outraged, no place more strongly than in Paisley's own church. Another IRA atrocity and their own Unionist politicians were talking coalition. Talking to former IRA people like Paddy Devlin, to republicans like Fitt. Paisley demanded that security be improved, that Rees act, or the DUP would withdraw from the convention. Coalition was not on. On September 8 the UUUC overwhelmingly repudiated the idea of coalition.

Only Craig still supported the idea. He resigned as leader of the Vanguard Convention Party, now shattered on the rocks of coalition. Ernest Baird led a breakaway group of nine convention members called the United Ulster Unionist Movement, while leftovers as the Vanguard Unionist Progressive Party struggled on until February 1978, then reverted to the title Ulster Vanguard, structured as a pressure group. The only support Craig received was on September 10, with a public announcement from the UDA, still engaged in a lethal feud with the UVF. It was hardly the aid or comfort needed.

On September 18, after the failure of interparty talks, the UUUC rejection was confirmed. No emergency coalition. No compromise. Not an Inch. Craig was now isolated, preaching reason to the intransigent. On September 26 he said that it would be madness and unjust and dishonest to exclude the SDLP from a voluntary coalition. Craig—of all people—had swerved to the center and followed the route of his old enemies, the moderates, each harder than the last: O'Neill, Chichester-Clark, Faulkner. No one had ever accused Craig of brilliance but he had always had an acute sense of his own, the hard men of politics. In the summer of 1975 he was deceived by words, by the prospects at the top of the greasy pole. Unlike the others, who had unexpectedly counseled flexibility, he did not receive office for his conversion to moderation, if a voluntary coalition was moderation and not simply a move toward power hardly shared. No matter—Craig soon reached not the top but the bottom of the pole; his party splintered; the faithful turned elsewhere.

A month of maneuvers led no place. Craig's explanations were unconvincing. The Alliance's complex formulas were not wanted. On November 7 the convention met again and the UUUC voted in favor of their heart's desire, a return to

*Barry White, *John Hume: Statesman of the Troubles* (Belfast: Blackstaff Press, 1984), p. 180.

majority rule with no power sharing, by forty-two votes to thirty-one. The loyalists wanted the Ireland Act of 1920 that an earlier generation had spurned. The majority knew this would not meet Westminster's terms but it met their own: vindication even if the heavens fall. The SDLP replied with their standard line: "No peaceful solution of the Northern Ireland problem is possible without power sharing in government and an institutionalized Irish dimension."* The other minority reports from the Alliance, Brian Faulkner's Unionist Party of Northern Ireland, and the Northern Ireland Labour Party, would be of concern to political scientists but not to Rees, since they did not appeal to the UUUC. Yet Rees, persistent beyond the end, did not bring down the curtain on the convention. He wanted to continue discussion and then at a future date reconvene the convention with a specific remit. In the meantime, "political change and security policy had, as always, to move hand in hand."†

During much of the year Rees had been balancing the provincial violence with discussions of political progress and security policy reforms. The violence had been constant, internecine feuding among the paramilitaries, the recrudescence of IRA sectarian killings, random murder. There were constant political complaints, including those of Gerry Fitt, that the Provos were exploiting the truce, demands from the unexpected loyalist quarters that rumors of betrayal could best be countered by the crushing of the IRA. The political progress had been confined to the persistence of the convention. Security policy at least showed marked change.

The new Northern Ireland Emergency Provisions Act went through the Westminster Parliament without trouble; all accepted that the Irish emergency required special laws. And Rees in particular, who continued to release detainees, was determined to keep his promises to end detention and to introduce new emergency legislation. The new legislation was in part shaped to shift responsibilities to the province as well as to move toward normalcy. Both initiatives, so innocent and decent in intent, in time produced bitter fruit. In the summer of 1975, however, Rees could feel considerable satisfaction concerning security policy. Actual provincial security was another matter. And in the autumn it grew worse, not better.

The IRA Army Council had never felt that the truce really extended to the ongoing operations in England, once again under the supervision of Brian Keenan, who was released from his one-year sentence in July 1975. The small active service units, with shifting memberships and varying support structure, staffed primarily by unsophisticated, untrained volunteers who sometimes seemed devoid even of common sense, indicated just how vulnerable a complex society was to random violence and how difficult it had become for conventional policing to cope with a terror campaign. The volunteers tended to live in seedy rooms located in marginal areas and spend their time making long lists of potential targets drawn from old reference books, maps, and newspapers. The operations tended to be bombings at first; but the key London group eventually took to shooting up imperialist haunts, usually first-class West End restaurants.

*White., p. 207.
†Ibid., p. 210.

Only tenuous rationalizations could be drawn between an armed struggle and explosions in pubs or gentlemen's clubs, explosions without proper warnings, shots into restaurants aimed at no one in particular, at anyone who could afford the menu. And only the IRA accepted those rationalizations.

The bombs fecklessly placed in public places, as at Guildford and Birmingham, had taken a fearful toll not just of English life but also of Provisional legitimacy. Most of the English, including a great many Irish immigrants, by the summer of 1975 saw the Provos as ruthless, brutal terrorists, without restraint, humanity, or prospects, who murdered the innocent. Almost all loyalists had so believed for years and increasingly so did the Irish south of the border. The killers were mad dogs run amok in a civilized society. Those caught and imprisoned belonged there, isolated from decent society. Those who felt English perfidy and past Irish grievance was ample reason for a bombing campaign steadily dwindled to only the most irreconcilable.

The Provisional Army Council marched to its own orders. Unconventional war was by nature unpleasant, so the qualms of the many were to be expected, discounted, and ignored. GHQ felt that an English campaign was justified because it would stretch security and, more important, bring the problem home to the English people. So 1975 was hardly a year of truce. A bomb exploded in Caterham in Surrey and the next day an explosion in Oxford Street in London injured seven people. On August 29 a bomb on Kensington Church Street killed a bomb-disposal expert. On September 2 a bomb placed in the London Hilton by a four-man active service unit detonated, killing two and injuring seven. The Portman Hotel was attacked and one person killed. The Green Park tube stop was hit, killing another.

Bombs were placed in restaurants and under cars and in easily accessible public sites. Small units sent over from Ireland could, if careful, operate almost with impunity, despite the extensive security net. The volunteers holed up in lodgings spent their time waiting to place a bomb in an establishment club or a Wimpy's or whirl through the streets firing shots into imperialist five-star restaurants. They had no local contacts, touched base rarely with GHQ, kept up the pressure, and outraged the British. The shooting and bombing included a spectacular assassination in London on November 27. Ross McWhirter, coauthor with his brother of *The Guinness Book of Records,* who had campaigned for the introduction of the death penalty for terrorists and offered a £100,000 reward for information to "Beat the Bombers," was shot dead at his home in Middlesex. For the Provos he was a "felon setter" and a prominent establishment figure; for nearly everyone else he was, with his record book, a celebrity, not a target. In the autumn of 1975 he was another name on the butcher's list. And as the English names were added, tension rose. The convention had led nowhere. There was no political progress. And security was not on top of matters in the province or in Britain. The cease-fire had apparently become a farce.

The war in Northern Ireland had sputtered off and on through the cease-fire, but the IRA operations never ended entirely and neither did aggressive security measures. The bombings and shootings in England often triggered loyalist retaliation in the province, as did simple opportunities grasped by local IRA commanders. On September 23 the Provisional IRA detonated eighteen bombs

457

throughout the province. The Army Council in a Dublin announcement denied, however, that the truce had ended. There was still advantage to be wrung from the truce, from the Sinn Féin incident centers. Two days later the Provisionals again complained of British army harassment and promised that action would be taken against such violations of the truce agreement. With the acceleration of such IRA action the truce was no longer relevant. On November 12 Rees finally announced that the incident centers set up to monitor the cease-fire were to be closed—the cease-fire was meaningless.

By then the republicans had once more fallen to feuding. On October 29 the Provisionals attacked the Officials, leaving one dead and seventeen injured. The sporadic shooting continued until November 13, when a cease-fire was negotiated. The final total of the autumn shooting was fifty wounded and eleven killed, including Séamus Osguir, O/C of the Provisional New Lodge Incident Centre. For their part, the IRSP-INLA lost eleven prominent politicals who resigned. These felt the movement had become "objectively indistinguishable from either wing of the Republican Movement and possibly combining the worst elements of both."* Many had signed up with Costello aware of his military credentials but innocent of his military intentions. When the INLA-Official feud had broken out, Bernadette Devlin McAliskey had insisted vehemently that the IRSP had no military wing. By December 1975, the IRSP people found themselves enlisted as political handlers for a secret army under orders from invisible commanders. The shooting with the Stickies had come as a shock. The very existence of the INLA had come as a shock. Some radicals had left, some had stayed; few additional had been attracted. On the other hand the INLA picked up Provos, who wanted action and not a cease-fire, and a few new people. This armed struggle continued to worry the politicals. It was not radical politics. It was a killing. And the INLA's supposed associates in the IRSP pointed out publicly that Costello's new army seemed to use radical language to profess the sterile nationalism of republican tradition. So they resigned. The hard-core IRSP settled down to act as political front for an armed struggle, the few and determined associated with a few of the most lethal and ruthless. The IRSP never took off as a front or as an expanding political presence. The INLA group remained small, limited to a few core areas and subject to the erosion of time but dominated by Séamus Costello's purpose and example. At the end of the year the IRSP-INLA still had hopes of playing a significant radical, republican role.

The loyalist paramilitaries had hardly spent the convention months quietly. The feuds and sectarian killings had long since become a part of the violence of Belfast, often spilling over into the rest of the province. Rees and the security forces were losing patience with the Ulster Volunteer Force, no longer an illegal organization, where the Belfast gunmen seemed to be in the ascendancy. The UVF was still a loose conglomeration of hard men and private gangs often united by no more than titles and a common need for legitimacy. Dark glasses, a UVF pin, and a gun were sometimes enough to make an Ulster soldier. All but a few of the most ruthless or most depraved needed further rationale for sectarian murder.

*Michael Hall, *Twenty Years: A Concise Chronology of Events in Northern Ireland from 1968–1988* (Newtownabbey [Northern Ireland]: Island Publication, 1988), p. 60.

458

While any Catholic might do and at any time, although the killing peaked during seasons of anxiety and focused on vulnerable males, the Protestant paramilitary men wanted proper recognition. They acted like vigilantes but yearned for uniforms. Any political reason was adequate for most, but someone had to tend to the structure and ideology. Few did. The loyalist paramilitaries never managed to put their own house in order. They lacked the dynamism, idealism, and skills of their Irish rivals in the secret army business.

Reluctantly, the more observant recognized that the Catholics just across the way had fashioned a real movement, disciplined, highly motivated, organized with a compelling ideology. These Irish republicans arose with the same limitations, from the same ghettos and marginal rural slums as they did. And the Protestants did not have a secret army or a transcendental ideal or history or proper credentials. They were "defenders" and they wanted to be soldiers—their gravestones were carved "soldier"—but they were not. They were rough killers shambling on uncertain missions and some were not simply brutal but depraved, psychopaths who had found a vocation within the Troubles.

Curiously, by the summer of 1975 the one place that the UVF most nearly resembled the hopes of the leaders with aspirations and ambitions was in Long Kesh. There a strict prison regime coupled with discipline imposed by long-term inmates with local influence produced a camp of war prisoners. There were titles and authority and punishment. Duties were assigned. And largely under the influence of Gusty Spence, still influenced by the example of the Official IRA and their class-based arguments, efforts were made to shape an appropriate ideology. The UVF must resemble an army, act as soldiers, have a purpose beyond the murder of vulnerable Catholics, instill discipline and respectability in the ranks. Spence often preached to the truculent and deaf, those who had neither the mind nor the inclination for "politics" but only the will to kill.

While Spence and the UVF officers ran a taut military camp, stifling dissenters and disciplining the lax and murderous, their allies outside had come under siege by those who wanted action. The tit-for-tat killings had reached the stage to alarm not only the IRA but also the UVF men in Long Kesh, who persuaded Rees to allow a conference in April to take place in the prison between the loyalists and republicans. The loyalists negotiated an end to the killing of off-duty RUC and UDR members in return for an end to their random attacks on Catholics. The IRA felt these were legitimate targets, members of the security force, while the loyalists were killing any Catholic. Discarding the soldier image, a UDA leader from Belfast, Sam Smyth, announced—over the protests of the UDA leader from West Belfast, Jim Craig, sitting next to him—that whether a child of three or an old woman of seventy, all Catholics were legitimate targets. The Provos took note. Nevertheless, both sides agreed to continue killing each other and to exclude civilians from the war.

Outside Long Kesh the UVF Brigade staff had been taken over by those who still found any Catholic an appropriate target. Their view in the volatile times had many takers and was reflected in the movement's magazine, *Combat*: "There are no humane methods of warfare, there is no such thing as civilized warfare; all warfare is inhuman, all warfare is barbaric; the first blast of the bugles of war sounds for the time being the funeral knell of human progress." In September "Activist," preparing the UVF for renewed killing, wrote in *Combat* that "there is no humane or civilized way in which to fight that war." The decision to fight fire with fire had been made and a big push announced for October 2.

The result was one of the worst days in the history of the Troubles. The UVF carried out a provocative series of bombings and shootings that left twelve people dead, including three women, and more injured. None of the incidents had been planned with military precision or with great care. There was no need. The bombs and guns were handy and any target would do. An operation often consisted of little more than a meeting for a few drinks in the usual pub, the distribution of guns, a short ride in a hot car to a vulnerable target (a wandering pedestrian in a Catholic area, a nationalist pub or store with easy exit ways, an isolated house), a blur of violence, a quick, exhilarated ride back, the stolen car abandoned, and ample time for further drinks. Sometimes the result was merely one more body on the edge of the Falls or down a country lane, a small article in the daily newspapers, a funeral, a statistic. On October 2, however, the big push could not blend in with the usual provincial din of random death. The UVF's push had been too big.

The most brutal incident was carried out by nominal members of the UVF acting under the direction of a recently released prisoner, Lenny Murphy, a violent psychopath who had gathered around him a small core of bigots, misfits, and petty criminals. Marginal even to West Belfast, failures for the most part, drifters who wanted to belong, to be important, they were attracted to Murphy, a fearsome and fearful man with a lethal reputation—he had killed a man in prison, he had defied authority, he had killed outside prison, and he would clearly kill again. Suave, interested in the ladies, elegant in leather coat and scarf in a seedy and scruffy neighborhood, he dominated even the brutal. Murphy manipulated them all—his own volunteers, the UVF leaders who feared to challenge him, the system. He was cunning, familiar with the law and the police, and unrestrained in his lust for murder, for blood; his chosen method was to slit the throat of the victim. His "unit" would become known as the Shankill Butchers. They were responsible for more killings than any other mass murderers in British criminal history.*

On October 2 his operations, in association with but not authorized by the UVF, almost—but not quite—escaped special notice in a day of brutality. The RUC sensed a special malevolence, just as they would in the next killings. The Butchers, even in a killing zone, were special. Murphy had decided to ignore any instructions from the leadership and to kill the staff of Casey's Wholesale Wine and Spirits, near the Belfast city center, in the Millfield area, convenient to the Shankill. He told his unit—driver William Moore and two brothers, William and Noel Green—that the motive was robbery, although the timing—ten o'clock in the morning—suggested no concern with accumulating the take from drink sales. His gang never questioned him in any case. And once on site he acted with ruthless dispatch. On the premises were two married sisters, Frances Donnelly, thirty-five, and Marie McGrattan, forty-seven, and two eighteen-year-old boys,

---

*A detailed account can be found in Martin Dillon's *The Shankill Butchers: A Case Study of Mass Murder* (London: Hutchinson, 1989).

Gerald Grogan and Thomas Osborne. The two boys were kept with Moore in the storeroom while Murphy and William Green went upstairs with the sisters. Noel Green waited in the stolen car. When Murphy could not find any money he forced the two sisters to their knees and shot Marie McGrattan in the head with his .45 Colt semiautomatic and made sure that Green shot Frances Donnelly the same way. Downstairs Moore held the two boys, now frightened by the gunshots, at pistol point until Murphy arrived. He paused only long enough to make sure that both were Catholic and then shot them both. The sisters and Grogan were dead.

Thomas Osborne was still alive. Spurting blood from a wound in the neck, he staggered out and stopped a car. (He was rushed to the hospital but died three weeks later.) The four UVF men by then had returned to the Shankill area, set their stolen car on fire to eliminate fingerprints, and hidden the guns. The Green brothers were arrested but, fearful of Murphy, told only part of the story, which by then was submerged in other atrocities. And Murphy had moved on to further butchery.

The UVF's last vestiges of politicization disappeared in the October 2 din. The UVF under the hard-line Brigade staff was back in the killing business. Those eager to be UVF soldiers moved against these hard men but the damage had been done. The UVF was still legal, a maneuver by the Northern Ireland Office to try and tame the wild men. Rees and the police had already given up on this ploy. Obviously conciliation had produced no lasting effect. UVF volunteers had continued killing Catholics, often under the name of the Protestant Action Force, and feuding with the UDA and their own dissident volunteers. October 2 had simply been the culmination of UVF commitment to murder. The next day the organization was proscribed for a second time by Merlyn Rees, who had intended to act in any case. Like much else, however, the proscription looked forced, reactive, rather than part of a long-term policy. Events seemed to be running beyond control of the Northern Ireland Office or any authority.

The loyalist gunmen simply accelerated their campaign. Although a more moderate UVF Brigade staff emerged in Belfast after the October events, the politicals were still not in control of the hard men, much less those like Murphy who killed for pleasure. Tension increased when on November 12 Rees announced that the incident centers to monitor the truce were to be closed. The cease-fire was coming to an end and the IRA armed struggle began to escalate. Then the UDA-UVF feud broke out again on November 15 when a UDA man was shot and killed. On November 23 and 24 four young British soldiers were murdered in South Armagh by the IRA and Murphy had his excuse to kill. At 12:30 A.M. on the night of November 24–25 Murphy and his unit picked up a Catholic man walking home along Library Street, near Belfast's main thoroughfare, Royal Avenue. The victim was brutally beaten while the stolen car was driven back to an alleyway off Wimbledon Street in the Shankill district. There his unconscious body was dragged out of sight of the roadway and Murphy hacked his throat open, splattering blood over himself and much of the waste ground. He waved the knife—"the ultimate way to kill a man"—after nearly severing the head. The slaughter in the back alley alerted the police that this killing went beyond everyday terror. "We're looking for somebody more brutal than the average terrorist and we'd better get to him." Eventually they did but by then a great deal of butchery as well as average terror had occurred.

In fact terror seemed to be on the rise all through the autumn, more brutal, more extensive, less disciplined. The loyalist campaign, for example, again moved south. On November 29 two bombs exploded at the Dublin airport, killing one man and injuring five other people. On December 19 there was a pub bomb in the center of Dundalk in County Louth that killed one and injured twenty, three seriously. A few minutes later, ten miles away across the border in Silverbridge, County Armagh, another loyalist bomb was tossed in another Catholic bar and killed three people and injured five. On February 13, 1976, there were bombs in Dublin again, a large one at the Shelbourne Hotel on Stephen's Green and eight incendiaries in department stores and shops, the first attack in the center of the city in twenty-one months.

The loyalist incursions were not the only spillover from the Northern troubles to roil stability and sensibilities in the Irish Republic. In fact, on October 3 one of the more spectacular sagas of violence began, an adventure that transfixed the media and the public, embarrassed the authorities and the nation, and assumed an importance beyond the crime. The Shankill Butchers were hidden in the regular slaughter of the North. In the Republic the next drama played out before a watching nation. Dr. Tiede Herrema, the fifty-four-year-old Dutch manager of the Ferenka factory, part of the huge transnational AKZO group, at Annacotty, County Limerick, was kidnapped. He was nonpolitical, well liked by all, including the workers, manager of a company that gave needed employment. He also happened to be vulnerable, living on Monaleen Road, near Castletroy Golf Club, about four miles from Limerick City, foreign, and visible to one man looking for a hostage.

Those responsible were a small group of rogue Provisionals who had originally clumped around the Englishwoman Rose Dugdale, imprisoned in Limerick for her part in the theft of Sir Alfred Beit's artwork at Russborough House, Blessington, and the helicopter bomb in Donegal. When she was arrested the key was Eddie Gallagher, one of the premier hard men from Cabbrey, Ballybofey, in Donegal. He was former O/C of a fifteen-man unit in Donegal, and long on the run in the South. A heavyset, five-foot, six-inch, dapper man, dark, with a handsome Zapata mustache and a real presence, at thirty-two he held very firm republican convictions but had little formal education. He had been fascinated by Dugdale and she by him, opposites attracting. And so he began to act more independently of Provisional discipline. He wanted Dugdale freed. Several IRA volunteers had been involved in armed raids to raise money and not all of the money found its way to GHQ, as Gallagher pepared for more independent but still republican action. As a result GHQ began to consider him a rogue. His priorities had become personal.

Over the years a variety of hard men had for varying reasons acquired delusions of grandeur—thought of themselves as premier guerrillas, Irish Guevaras—or had personal priorities like one of Gallagher's friends, Peter McMullen, who had deserted from the British Paratroopers just before Bloody Sunday in Derry. McMullen, however, fell out with Gallagher over money matters. Gallagher was only interested in getting Dugdale out of prison, along with two other prominent republicans, Kevin Mallon and James Hyland. This became more important than GHQ operations or orders. Gallagher began looking for a suitable hostage. He was on his own.

All secret armies have problems with discipline at a distance; local priorities and individuals with obvious skills and special priorities are difficult to control effectively. Men like Gallagher don't report every day and often operate independently. And in time some no longer feel the need for the formality of GHQ while others, never tightly held, run to their own scents: the lure of easy money, the pleasures of private wars, the personal use of force, and most dangerous of all, dedication to a better and more effective armed struggle. McMullen, keeping money Gallagher felt was his, fled Ireland, wanted by both Gallagher and the IRA GHQ. He eventually found sanctuary in an American prison, giving interviews filled with dubious revelations. Gallagher was another matter. More than McMullen, he confused his priorities with those of the Republic.

Schism may be no more than an internal matter of discipline, a warning, or a body dumped by the roadside. Schism may also be the movement shattered—the Provos, the Stickies, and the INLA all emerged from ideological mitosis. Since 1970 several small private armies like Saor Éire arose, operated, and for varying reasons disappeared. Gallagher was thus a danger to the Provos, as example at least, even if his strategic capacities were limited. And he was a danger to the state. In a stable, democratic society a very few deploying violent means can cause disproportionate trouble, public anxiety, outrage, and indignation.

Gallagher felt that the Irish government would concede rather than suffer the trouble arising from a major incident. He felt that with his funds and a few friends he could snatch an international hostage and secure the quick release of Dugdale, Mallon, and Hyland. Gallagher depended almost entirely on one partner, a young, striking, darkly attractive woman from Duncreggan, Derry, Marian Coyle. At twenty-one, although quiet and almost shy, she was also an intense young woman, not content with an auxiliary role. From a family of twelve, she too came from a limited but republican background: secretarial school at sixteen, a favorite uncle killed in rioting in June 1970, and a brother sentenced to six years in prison for possession of a gun. Gallagher depended on her and two or three old friends plus the odd republican contacts, men who would think little about Gallagher's spectacular, agree to help as a matter of course, agree to steal cars or drive hostages or keep a man on the run, agree to political crime without deep thought. Their number might be eroding in Ireland but there were still many.

So Gallagher easily arranged his operations using Brian McGowan, twenty, from Clontarf Road in Tullamore and John Vincent Walsh, twenty-six, from just north of the same city. There would be others connected to the safe houses, but Gallagher and Coyle were the key. At first they had no problems. Their man was taken, moved to a safe house, and the demands dispatched. Despite the ease with which Herrema was taken, planning had not been very thorough. Gallagher did not know a great deal about the man or the foreign company, confused Dutch with German, and assumed everything would be over in a few days. All that he had gotten right was that the kidnaping would have an enormous impact.

The government had no intention of releasing prisoners under duress and so desperately wanted to trace the hostage. Ireland was turned upside down. The army was out, as was half of the nine thousand Gárdaí. Military helicopters were up, informers pulled in and queried, house-to-house searches undertaken, republicans questioned, promises and threats made. Intermediaries, two real ones and others potential, volunteers for publicity and participation, all sorts eager to be a part of the action appeared, along with special operations specialists for hire, mediums and psychics, experts and troops of journalists; the whole spectrum of terror groupies and professionals flooded the country. Conventional police work intensified and paid off. No volunteers or special help were needed. The Gárdaí found the trail. Ireland is a small country and the secret army was not fully secret. On October 21 the police and army nearly scooped up Gallagher and Coyle.

With negotiations dragging, Gallagher and Coyle had moved their hostage, ending up in the tiny bedroom on the upper floor of 1410 Saint Evin's Park, Monasterevin, County Kildare, on the Cork Road southwest of Dublin. Herrema was kept secretly and securely in the bedroom in the end house in a terrace of the new council housing until the authorities arrived downstairs eight days after the three had moved into the house. After a burst of wild shots from Gallagher, the three remained trapped in the tiny room, surrounded by circles of police and army and journalists and the curious. The siege of Monasterevin lasted until November 7. One Special Branch detective was shot in the hand while unwisely standing on a ladder outside the bedroom window, but there were no other crises. Gallagher lost hope and remained only long enough to maintain his pride before surrendering, to the enormous relief of the authorities and the country at large.

Herrema was treated as a hero. On December 11 he and his wife, Elizabeth, received the highest honor the state could confer, honorary Irish citizenship, awarded only once before, to the great art benefactor, Sir Alfred Chester Beatty. The Dutch government awarded the Orange Nassau medal to the Minister for Justice, Patrick Cooney, and the Gárda commissioner, Edmund Garvey. On March 11, 1976, after republican speeches from the dock, Gallagher was sentenced to twenty years' imprisonment and Coyle to fifteen. Neither was repentant; both with remission served their sentences. Soon after her term began, Rose Dugdale had Gallagher's son, Ruairí, in prison. Martin McGuinness, former Provisional O/C from Derry, was godfather and Marian Coyle was godmother. She, too, along with the other two, became a celebrity of one more spectacular crime generated by the Northern Troubles.*

It was in fact the general public reaction to such an "unnecessary" and embarrassing crime that gave the siege of Monasterevin its significance. The revulsion at the kidnapping was a sign of the disenchantment within the Republic at the cost of the national issue as pursued by the Provisionals—one Provo being like another, one IRA the same danger as the next. All brought with them bombs and death, confusion and humiliation, costs that most did not want to pay and many would now decry publicly.

All during the turmoil of Monasterevin and the escalated violence in Northern Ireland the IRA's English campaign had continued. In Dublin Séamus Twomey, who had taken over as chief of staff from Eamonn O'Doherty, had continued

---

*A contemporary journalistic account of the kidnapping may be found in Colm Connolly's *Herrema: Siege at Monasterevin* (Dublin: Olympic Press, 1977).

foreign operations under Brian Keenan. Keenan as early as 1974 had decided to put in a secret, sleeper active service unit unlike the one-time insertions that had involved the Price sisters and later the bombs at the Tower and Claro barracks. This time he chose volunteers with limited records from the South, women as couriers, and targets of local convenience. There were in 1974–76 also other IRA English units, some directed by Irish exiles, most sent over for the campaign, but the key unit would operate in London. To the innocent eye that active service unit was devoid of talent, sophistication, experience, and so capacity, a group of provincial young men innocent of the expected urban guerrilla skills. The core of the unit was composed of Harry Duggan, 21, from Feakle, County Clare; Joseph O'Connell, 21, Kilkee, Clare; Edward Butler, 24, Castleconnell, Limerick; Hugh Doherty, 22, Glasgow and Donegal; and for a while William Quinn, a rare Irish-American volunteer who had left his post office job in San Francisco to be part of history. The O/C was Brendan Dowd, 24, from Tralee. All were hard and determined—Harry Duggan had already shot his way out of a police raid on a safe house in Charleston, Mayo; but none had much formal education, formal training, or mechanical skills, and none had operated in London. No matter—they bombed and shot their way into the headlines once the campaign began.

Once more it was amply demonstrated that a few can cause disproportionate turbulence in a stable society. Then in a dramatic final act, the authorities closed down the campaign in another spectacular siege. The unit kept London in turmoil during much of 1974 and 1975. In December 1974 the din had been constant. On December 11 bombs exploded at the Naval and Military Club and the Cavalry Clubs. Also on December 11 there was a shoot-out at the Churchill Hotel. Three days later bombs blew up at three telephone exchanges. On December 19 a bomb was left outside Selfridge's and the next day at Aldershot railway station. On December 21 there were bombs at Harrods. The next day there was a failed assassination attempt on Edward Heath. This phase of the London season ended with seven bombs on February 27.

Phase Two began on August 27, 1975, with a time bomb at the Caterham Arms, Caterham, Surrey. In the autumn of 1975 the IRA London attacks were so frequent that the police had plotted the unit's likely attacks in the West End and thrown a radio-controlled net around much of west-central London. When the unit struck on Saturday night, December 6, the net collapsed upon them. O'Connell, Duggan, Dohety, and Butler were trapped in a small flat in Balcombe Street in London, with an elderly couple as hostages. They decided to hold out in hopes someone would clear out their safe houses.

The police, with Sir Robert Mark, the commissioner, in attendance, waited them out—no bargains, no deals, the only place the Irishmen were going was prison. They were wanted on thirty-eight charges, including the death of Ross McWhirter, as well as those of Professor Gordon Hamilton-Fairley, killed when a bomb detonated under the car of Hugh Fraser, a Conservative MP, and of Captain Roger Goad, a bomb-disposal expert. The siege of Balcombe Street, heavily covered by the media, lasted for 128 hours until December 12, when the four surrendered. The public, the media, and the police were delighted. A film was made and Sir Robert Mark was welcomed everywhere as guest speaker on coping with terror. It was a final, grand security triumph in a year that had turned sour.

In Northern Ireland in November and December there had been seventy-two explosions, sixteen attacks on police stations, and ninety shooting attacks on security forces. Six soldiers, three members of the UDR, and three RUC men had been killed. The provincial death toll for the year was 217 civilians, 14 members of the army, 11 RUC, and 5 UDR; the total of 247 was up from the previous year's 216. As was the case with each year's toll there was also the violence out of sight, the spillover and the psychic damage, the erosion of general liberty, and the daily price of terror paid in anxiety, limited options, inconvenience, insurance premiums, and higher taxes. And there was no Christmas truce, no hope that the various party talks during November would lead anyplace, and no sense that another meeting of the convention would be very productive, despite Rees's intention of trying again.

The new year opened disastrously. On January 4 loyalist paramilitaries killed five Catholics in South Armagh. All along the troubled areas of the border there had long been a private war as the isolated population, Protestant or Catholic, came under attacks. Whatever the theologians of the armed struggle or the ideologists of random murder had to say in their weekly newspapers or press conferences, the war on the border seemed shaped solely by sectarian passions. The IRA targeted the UDR in uniform and out, the RUC Reserve in uniform or out, Protestants all—but members of the security forces and so legitimate. Shooting a Protestant farmer on his door stoop while his daughter stood in the door was a military operation to GHQ and religious murder by Catholic rebels to the victim's community. The slaughter of the Miami Showband was a military operation to cut IRA supply lines for the UVF and religious murder by bigots determined to rule to the minority community. Both assumed, not without cause, that the other sought dominance, if not in the whole province then surely in their own patch and parish. Thus, while all were horrified that five Catholics were killed, they were not surprised. The same was true for the immediate reaction of the wronged. On the next day twelve gunmen of the Republican Action Force, apparently a cover name for the IRA, stopped a busload of workmen near Kingsmills, South Armagh. The men were taken off the bus and lined up along the verge. The only Catholic was told to step aside. The gunmen then shot and killed the ten Protestants.

The minority had made it abundantly clear that those in the majority simply presented more targets, did not possess more power to kill. They also demonstrated that minority patience and ideology had worn out: If there was to be arbitrary killing then the majority would pay too—arbitrarily. Whether this had a specific impact on the potential killers is by no means clear. The UVF-UDA militants were short on reflection and analysis and long on anger and violence. What did appear for the moment to occur was an end to a rising cycle of retaliatory violence—whether through Protestant reflection or not is unclear. Certainly the Catholics wanted no credit for intimidating the Protestants through recourse to terror. Perhaps they wanted the security that might accrue from the killing, but not the responsibility. IRA GHQ and the Army Council, too, as in all cases of tit-for-tat murder, did not want to think about the implications, could not risk disciplining units or organizing an investigation. Such retaliation was popular, or at least acceptable, and all but inevitable—and might, as noted, even work. It was, however, a clear violation of republican principles and often of IRA orders. A bomb in a Protestant bar might be covered, if scantily, by citing the target as a paramilitary meeting place and the paramilitaries as British agents. A UDR man shot in his garden was still a member of the security forces and a tea boy killed for serving soldiers had been aiding the armed enemy. Shooting ten arbitrarily chosen hostages in retaliation for sectarian murder was not so easy to rationalize. So GHQ accepted the Republican Action Force as real since they did not want to admit that Provo volunteers killed for sectarian purposes. No one else was fooled. Matters seemed to have gotten out of hand. Order could not be imposed by revolutionary terror.

In London Wilson felt he must act. There must be order. There was, of course, no act that would really have any great impact on Armagh reality. The UVF and the IRA were deeply embedded in society, grievances and prejudices were ancient, violence was an easy option. One active gunman was easily replaced because the lure of violence and the motivations for murder had not changed. The politicians of the convention had already demonstrated that there was no agreement, even in grievances, no prospect of concession: Politics was still a zero-sum game, as was the irregular war in the lanes and hummocks of the bandit country along the border. So something had to be *seen* to be done to calm British anxieties and the general provincial public.

On January 6 London announced that six hundred men of the "Spearhead" Battalion would be sent into South Armagh. A day later it was announced that extra units of the Special Air Service—the SAS of legend—would be sent into the area for patrolling and surveillance. Both Rees and the GOC knew it was a gesture more than anything else. Neither expected a few new soldiers to transform the situation. In point of fact the gesture was far more important than the authorities assumed, owing to the reputation of the SAS.

In a sense the SAS, supposedly never previously deployed in the province, had become a code word within the IRA and much of Ireland for those responsible for British dirty tricks. This had become true with Brigadier Frank Kitson as the military mandarin behind the theology of anti-insurgency, the dirty war. And in a dirty war it was hardly surprising that there were dirty tricks, special units, covert operations, and a world beyond the ken of the Northern Ireland Office or the GOC for that matter. In an atmosphere of constant conspiracy and worst-case scenarios, all the Irish, loyalist or rebel, Protestant or Catholic, North and South, assumed there were complex and cunning maneuvers by the authorities; they sought and found evidence of trickery, guile, and betrayal on every hand. If elected politicians had no difficulty seeing a legal party as a front for killers or, in the case of the brilliant and erratic Enoch Powell, an American CIA plot behind devolution, then the far less sophisticated lived in a world of mirrors, all reflecting malignant enemies and evasive friends. The SAS's formal arrival had been preceded by years of rumor, years of revelation, years of suspicion about the dirty tricks of all those involved.

The various conspiracy theorists were not always wrong. British intelligence since the end of World War II had been a disaster area. Covert organizations were often run by incompetent old boys, limited men of limited views, prejudiced and divorced from the conventional who were beyond top secrets and moles and plots.

They were regularly betrayed by their own to the Russians and by their implausible assumptions in reading reality. The new and effective recruits to the intelligence system often found the shoddy in charge and prospects poor. At least in Ireland there was action instead of betrayal, rumor and doubt, and humiliation by the American cousins at every turn.

The two major British agencies, MI5 and MI6, had waged a jurisdictional dispute over control that in the end had gone MI5's way. Talent, logic, and bureaucratic cunning had by 1975 won through despite the old boys' problems. In the process military intelligence and the RUC had fashioned their own special baronies. None really trusted the other very far or very often. Once policy became secret the obscure could become powerful, the army's information office could become involved in disinformation campaigns, and the individual officer could create his own net, his own paramilitaries. And so some did. Thus, the media could be told that the IRA was shooting dogs in target practice when in real life the British army was shooting dogs they feared would give away their patrols: a chip of disinformation tossed on the Irish board by small players—not a very serious matter. Rumor long before 1975 had indicated very lethal dirty tricks regularly deployed by those who need not answer to authority or often even to their superiors. These dirty tricks killed and maimed, produced bodies in ditches and reputations in shreds. They even threatened the Prime Minister. The atmosphere in London had grown poisonous. Discredited files, old rumors, and nasty speculation circulated in some intelligence circles as analysis. Wilson in fact had a direct confrontation with the head of MI5, "Jumbo" Haley, on August 7, 1975, about the department's failing. If he had pursued matters he would have seen revealed just how disloyal were the involved and how bizarre the fantasies.

The Labour Northern Ireland Secretary was not privy to such fantasies or to the covert Irish adventures of intelligence officers and special operations people; nor, for that matter, was the leadership of much of the security forces. In a world of nods and winks, understandings and unwritten orders, much can evolve even when discipline is strict. And discipline was not always strict. Who had authorized the Littlejohn escapes or the infiltrators that showed up on the IRA doorstep? Who had really planted the Dublin bombs in 1972 and 1974 or blown up the Alliance Party headquarters in Belfast? What was a British officer doing singing rebel songs in South Armagh pubs? And who had really shot the IRA man John Francis Green with the revolver found at the site of the Miami Showband massacre? In 1976 one of those who claimed to have been involved in a British army disinformation campaign, Colin Wallace, would even write Prime Minister Wilson, to no apparent avail. Irish dirty tricks seemed a long way from London. The answers from the advocates of conspiracies were discounted by the pragmatists and the realists. Some paranoia, however, is justified and some of the conspiracies were real.

In 1976 there was little evidence but enormous suspicion. Over the next decade such suspicions would in some cases be confirmed, in very few denied, but would always poison an already noxious atmosphere. British dirty tricks—the IRA and the loyalist paramilitaries lived in a dirty world as the norm—more often than not ruined the game of accommodation. They would prove enormously costly. One gunman shot on sight, on suspicion, one dead multiple murderer with bloody hands had to be paid for, sooner or later, at enormous political cost and, worse, with erosion of the general civility. The price of operational pragmatism, the cost of vengeance without the law, had to be paid by the system with a decline in legitimacy. So the arrival of the SAS was not seen in much of Ireland as a simple military move, not as political response to an impossible regional problem, but as recourse to the irregular. And this was (this time) not really the case. The SAS commitment to the province was always small, very small, often limited to training, and the regiment's special operations were simply effective techniques in a rather conventional, guerrilla war. The presence of competent, small units patrolling Armagh had an effect. In fact only eleven members of the SAS went in directly, followed by others who brought the total up to about sixty—hardly an arena flooded. Still, sharpened patrolling and standard military practice had an effect in what was a war zone. The bandits could not stroll their country at leisure. The SAS, the horror at the tit-for-tat killings, and the implications of IRA retaliation did ease the situation. But this was hardly noticeable for a time— forty-eight people died violently in the province during January alone.

During January while the killing went on outside, the politicians were again engaged in mutual and almost fruitless talks. Rees continued to encourage discussion—certainly better having the party leaders in the same tent talking than outside shrieking into the winds of rage. The convention was to meet in any case, agreements or not. And there were no signs of agreement. Rather, there was the ritual repetition of formal positions, logical or no, the exchange of rumor, and the belief in conspiracy that made up the matrix of Northern Ireland politics. As Rees noted, "The level of discussion was remarkably low; it was all a pathetic performance."* There was, of course, no reason that the province should produce philosophers or statesmen in elected officers or that those chosen should reveal a sudden bent for accommodation. There was inevitably a tendency of the involved, near and far, to consider Ireland major, a country whose politicians should equal Yeats or Joyce, whose officials should equal those in Westminster or Washington in competence, vision, and sophistication. The province was small, the pool of talent limited, the opportunity for ingenuity and initiative circumscribed. Ireland actually had more talent in office or running secret armies than most comparable entities. Rees and others had found the Provisional IRA, for example, not to be the equal of the Imperial General Staff or men of great skill and vision. Why should they be? They could, however, persist, run their armed struggle despite the skills and elegance of the United Kingdom. Rees and others had found the Northern Ireland politicians limited, narrow, quarrelsome and truculent, not the equal of Parliament. Why should they be? They spoke their clients' mind and refused any offer to betray their principles. They may have spoken clumsily, refused for contradictory and unconvincing reasons, but politics is often a crude game. While the British were not dealing with a county council, they were involved with adequate representatives of the province. And those representatives in the weeks before the recall of the convention vented their prejudices, repeated their election pledges, and refused to follow English guidance—the worst sin of all.

*Rees, p. 262.

In January, before Commons, Rees indicated his continued hope for a "solution" to the persistent problems—it was difficult even for Rees to accept that in 1976 the problem was that there was no solution.

> Far too many of the solutions of the past have come to nothing. Anglo-Irish History is littered with the handiwork of those who have failed, although they thought that they had the solution. There is no easy way out of the enmeshed and intricate problems of Northern Ireland, and those who think that they have a solution should reflect upon eight hundred years of troubled history. The solution to six years of violence and a community divided by the facts of history must be worked out slowly and surely with Northern Ireland and have a firm base in the support of the people of Northern Ireland. It would certainly be a mistake now to think that a final solution will come immediately. It would be a mistake also to think that we could impose or enforce a constitutional system and expect it to work.*

The convention talks had involved all aspects of devolution: the Irish dimension that absorbed relatively little time, the British dimension that focused on extra seats at Westminster for the province, a move Rees opposed if the province was to have a devolved government, and mostly on a formula, if such existed, for power sharing. On February 3 the convention reconvened with no hidden agreements and with no change in the UUUC or SDLP agendas. Although the Council of Ireland and the fear of an all-Ireland current had played an enormous part in loyalist consideration, the refusal to accept the SDLP as a partner, to share power as a necessity rather than as a majority promise, ended deliberations once the formal talks began. All the interesting proposals and trial balloons lofted by friends and minor parties were intriguing but useless.

On February 12 Fitt asked, "Is it right to say that the UUUC, either in government or in opposition, would never cooperate with the SDLP?" The loyalists hedged and so Hume asked if it were true that "there are no circumstances in which the UUUC would serve in cabinet with the SDLP?" Harry West replied, "That is right." And that was it. No power sharing whatever the name or formula. No power sharing, no Westminster approval. No approval, no devolution, no solution. Direct rule would return. Rees would explain to the Commons. The convention would meet for the last time on March 3 amid nasty final speeches, insults, and crude allegations. The convention was formally dissolved on March 6.

March was a month of endings. Devolution, with the end of the convention, was on hold, and provincial politics was without prospects. Local councils could cope with the very local and for the rest the members at Westminster would be available, twelve members belonging neither to the Conservatives nor Labour, representing not so much specific constituencies as their people, wherever resident. And the scene at Westminster would change as well, for within the Labour

*Rees, p. 265.

Party it had been known since the end of the summer that Wilson wanted to resign before another general election was necessary. He had been in Commons since 1945, in his first cabinet position in 1947, had led the party to four victories in general elections, and had grown tired of the game. Better to quit while ahead, while in office, while at the top of the pole. And so he would announce publicly on March 16 that he was stepping down. After a short campaign within the parliamentary Labour Party he was replaced by James Callaghan, who had first sent the British army into Derry and Belfast in 1969. The resignation meant that the Northern Ireland Office would undoubtedly be in transition until assignments had been finished up later in the year. The changes had already begun in the province.

On March 1 special category status was phased out so that any prisoner convicted of offenses after the first of the month would be treated as an ordinary criminal. Long Kesh was divided into two separate prisons: the Maze (Compound), made up of Nissen huts known as the Cages to hold the dwindling special category prisoners convicted before the cutoff date, and the Maze (Cellular), the newly constructed complex of buildings designed in the shape of an H—the H-Blocks—to be used for the new wave of inmates. This was a major part of Rees's effort to return the judicial system to normal, to end internment, and in so doing shift more security responsibility onto the provincial forces. It was also a crucial aspect of any anti-insurgency policy: criminalization, treat political crime as ordinary crime, deny the legitimacy of revolt. Rees anticipated, properly, trouble when the switch was made: The paramilitaries, republican or loyalist, defined themselves by motive, by vocation, not by the statutes. They were soldiers, volunteers, defenders, political activists, not ordinary criminals.

At the end of February there was the anticipated violent rioting protesting the change. Vehicles were hijacked and burned as barricades. Traffic was disrupted, roads blocked, bomb threats called (they were hoaxes). No one was killed. Nineteen people were arrested. Rees was both adamant and angered. "The vicious murders in South Armagh in January were still fresh in my mind as an example of the true nature of paramilitary killings. To treat the perpetrators of such crimes as special, politically motivated people was morally and legally wrong."*

Rees had become more deeply involved in Irish matters than any other British politician before or since. He had immersed himself in the details of Northern Ireland, learned the names and numbers, charted the currents, and heard out each cold heart. If he had not enjoyed the Northern Ireland Office, he had felt neither isolated nor exiled. Not fulfilled, surely, but fascinated. But despite his fascination he was, when all was said and done, an English politician, even if from Wales, and with an Irish connection. He had been sent abroad by his Prime Minister to cope with the unruly and ungrateful, the violent and the dreadful, to do the best for the everyday and decent. Murder, whatever the motive, was murder for Rees, for the British authorities, and for almost all of the British people. Few understood the Irish as well as Rees and few cared to do so. They were to be judged by British standards. No matter that certain murderers were specially treated, specially arrested

*Rees, p. 277.

and questioned, specially tried and convicted and sentenced, specially imprisoned—murder was murder. And so it was, but nothing was more apparent in the British acceptance that some murderers were special and thus were treated differently. Whatever the loyalist signs proclaimed, Ulster was not British.

Many who killed in Northern Ireland killed not out of personal passion or from greed or in the pursuit of gain but for an ideal, even and often, a flawed, warped and discredited ideal, even an ideal denied by the supposed beneficiaries. Such murderers, often protected by their own, proud in their vocation, are different and were treated so. Consequently, when Rees claimed that to treat them differently was morally and legally wrong, he criticized not the killers but the authorities, the British. He chose not to note that the paramilitaries were treated differently, always, one way or another. There were the SAS to hunt such murderers down, special prisons to keep them endlessly of remand, postponing their trials time after time, then the new Diplock Courts for the trials with no juries and special rules, and special camps where prisoners were in a special category in February 1976 but suddenly not so in March 1976. They were still, of course, kept in a specially built prison, under special guard. With the army at the door and the rates not paid for political reason, with the province in siege, the British would insist that all was normal. For the NIO, for the cabinet in London, murder was just murder, crime only crime: just like the rest of the United Kingdom. Northern Ireland was not Kent or Wales, and this was the problem. To call it so was not the solution, not even morally proper, certainly not legally possible if there was to be any order at all. If you had war, then shoot to kill, put the captured in camps, fight a dirty war but decently. But if there were no war, then "special courts" and "special prisoners," all the pragmatic but hypocritical measures to deny the present in order to reach a desired future were grounded in need not law. You cannot have it both ways but for generations Perfidious Albion has tried to do so, angered and disturbed at charges of hypocrisy against a nation dedicated to justice and fair play.

There were no political murders in Britain, had not been for centuries. That there were in Northern Ireland indicated how alien the province was to British norms: There the national issue was killing, there religion was lethal, there loyalties came with guns and martyrs. There each British scheme founded on assumptions honed by centuries of practice on the main island failed, as they had failed elsewhere on the island. To introduce criminalization because it was a practical maneuver was one matter; to do so because murder was *just* murder was another. Both criminalization and Ulsterization were good practical moves that, as moral initiatives, contained dangers to the British desire for the easy life. Institutionalized lies eroded British governmental legitimacy—and not only in Northern Ireland. Rees meant well; as a civil libertarian he wanted to end internment and return to conventional jurisprudence. As one who saw the need for local solutions to local problems, he favored Ulsterization. He meant well—and what options were there? Internment was ineffectual in practice and abhorrent in theory. Imposed solutions were unacceptable in practice and alien in theory. Yet if murder was to be murder, then London had to have the power to make it so through a conventional criminal justice system operating with a general consensus of approval. Such power does not come entirely from the barrel of a gun. Such power had never existed in Northern Ireland, where the morality of murder was not so clear, where power often emerged from grievance denied rather than the force deployed. Terence MacSwiney, who had died on a hunger strike, had said, "It is not those who can inflict the most, but those that can suffer the most who will conquer." This was not a British theme.

That such a theme could still play in the Irish arena despite the tide away from past positions in the Republic was made clear just as the convention dissolved. Frank Stagg, a member of the Provisional IRA, died on February 12 in Wakefield Prison after a sixty-day hunger strike. It was not his first strike. He had been involved in the long 1974 strike at the same time as the Price sisters, when Michael Gaughan had died in Parkhurst Prison on the sixty-fifth day. A hunger strike in an English prison, isolated, wasting, amid malice and temptations, is enormously difficult, a severe moral challenge maintained in a decaying body. Hunger strikes are not, even en masse, easy, not even, sometimes not especially, for the hard men. The talents of denial are unevenly distributed, no matter how firm the commitment. In 1976 very little was known about the nature of hunger strikes that had not been passed about among republicans. What was known in Ireland was that such a deed had a long history and a high moral content, and brought shame on those who denied the petitioner justice. Alone, far from home, Stagg, a justly convicted criminal, without power or means of petition, sought fair prison conditions by recourse to self-denial. When he died he was seen by many of the Irish as cleansed and admirable. He had harmed no one but himself and shamed no one but those who had denied him justice.

This interpretation was for all authority as deadly and dangerous as it was widespread in Ireland. In Britain Stagg was an IRA man who deserved his sentence and his conditions. The state could not, would not, concede what the demonstrably guilty demanded. So the state did not concede. Roy Jenkins had given up forced feeding after the Price experience, had moved them to a prison in Northern Ireland; but there was a limit. Soon any prisoner would skip lunch to intimidate authority. A state cannot be so coerced. What the British government did not recognize and the Dublin government did is that a state may not be coerced but can be shamed. Stagg had completed the first act of martyrdom that could not but rebound to Provo advantage—as he had intended, as they recognized. The Provos would use Stagg, more effective dead than alive in prison, as a historically valid sacrifice to hide the new brutal realities of the sectarian killing and random bombing.

Recognizing the challenge and reacting effectively were different matters. The coalition government in Dublin, descendants of those who had no sympathy for militant republicans of any shade, bungled. On Thursday, February 19, the plane carrying Stagg's body was due at Dublin airport, where a large republican contingent waited to escort the remains in honor through Dublin. In the past the patriot dead had been trooped across the island, often attracting enormous crowds. Stagg had asked to be buried across the country in the republican plot at Ballina. There at the graveside would come the ritual, now inviolate, of a martyr to republican Ireland. Not this time; the government had the plane diverted to Shannon, where the police waited. Authorized by some of the family, they removed the casket and rushed it to Hollymount cemetery, where Stagg was buried in a simple ceremony. He was seemingly safe under a concrete crypt and out of republican hands. On February 22, Sunday, there was a republican memorial service at Ballina over an undug grave. Joe Cahill spoke to ten thousand gathered from all over Ireland. Accused of subverting the wishes of the dead, intimidating the survivors, body snatching, blasphemy, and harassing the mourners at Ballina, the Dublin government showed no remorse. They were the government, elected representatives of the people, and their power was not to be eroded by recourse to old rituals by contemporary subversives. Better to have bungled on the harsh side than to have allowed the morality play to go on. Ultimately Stagg was secretly reburied by the Provos in the republican plot as he had wanted.

The Republican government increasingly felt that the problems of Northern Ireland were aberrant, troublesome to the peace and quiet most in Dublin wanted. On March 31 the great train robbery had taken place at Sallins and the confrontation with the IRSP and the civil libertarians, who suspected the police of running a heavy gang to force confessions and close down Costello. On April 25 the Provisionals' Easter ceremonies brought ten thousand people to a meeting in front of the GPO but there was no violence—only the evidence that support for militant republicanism still existed. On May 8 British SAS members armed but in civilian dress were arrested south of the border. New procedures concerning intrusions meant that they were kept and tried publicly, to the annoyance of the British authorities, to be fined and released. The criticism of Irish justice was more annoying than the discovery of the SAS south of the border.

There was later similar, if muted, British annoyance at the Dublin government's pursuit of the charge of torture during internment brought before the European Commission on Human Rights that ultimately reported in fourteen volumes on September 5. The commission decided that the British policy was not torture but was inhumane. Still, the commission decided that internment was not unjustified nor applied with discrimination. Rees and the British felt that their act had long been cleaned up. There were the Compton report, the Parker report, compensation paid, Heath's actions to stop the recurrence, apologies all around, and the practice of the present Labour government. Rees and London felt that Dublin should not have persisted. Olden times were better left to olden times. Dublin, however, as often is the case with the gored ox, felt differently, even four years after the event. Angering Britain further, Dublin continued the same case before the European Court, which finally reached an innocuous decision in July 1978. London always had problems accepting Irish priorities, often so different from their own, often so difficult to rationalize. So a bit more grit went into the gears of Anglo-Irish cooperation. Mutual interests in many matters could hardly erode old Irish grievances or persuade Dublin to operate to British tactical advantage every time. Yet both governments, both establishments, wanted much the same thing, if often under differently labeled banners. Even the oppositions (the Tory Party, since the previous year under Margaret Thatcher with Airey Neave as Northern Ireland spokesman, assumed by Irish political opinion to be more unionist in posture, and Fianna Fáil under Jack Lynch with Charlie Haughey and George Colley in the wings, assumed by British political opinion to be a bit more republican than the coalition) wanted peace and quiet and a formula of accommodation. Each recrudescence of the old responses to "provocation" caused problems, particularly because all the militants of whatever flavor sought such responses, acted when possible to impel the present into past molds.

For the Dublin government one of the most appalling challenges to any Anglo-Irish cooperation occurred on July 21 with a Provisional IRA operation against the new British ambassador. Christopher Ewart-Biggs took over in Dublin as the shake-up in the Northern Ireland Office continued after Callaghan replaced Wilson. His appointment, already on the books, appeared to some a cunning move by the British establishment: a substantive ambassador instead of an old boy sent to graze before retirement, a man with intelligence connections, a spy in the heart of Dublin. Ewart-Biggs was to others simply a bizarre Blimp, a man who wore a smoked glass monocle (he had lost an eye at the Battle of Alamein), wrote detective novels banned in Ireland, and had a beautiful wife, a quick tongue, and a splendid war record. At a press conference on July 20, he felt the need to tell the reporters in Dublin that he was not a caricature, a cross between Wodehouse and Kipling. To many he was simply an interesting chap. His colleagues thought he was an exemplary taskmaster, a keen negotiator, and an enlightened friend. He had served in Algeria during troubled times, where he had been threatened by the OAS, and elsewhere in the Middle East, as well as in Paris: a man for all seasons. The Provos' GHQ intelligence officer felt that Ewart-Biggs, ambassador or no, was a member of British intelligence. He was a legitimate target and, more important, indications were that he would be vulnerable. Twomey agreed—certain operations (usually any operation desired by the Army Council) could take place in the Republic despite standing army orders. The intelligence officer's report was accepted as basis for a Dublin operation. Twomey had his director of operations put together a small active service unit drawn from the available volunteers, mostly men on the run in the Republic.

The intention was to use the conventional methods of the border country in a Dublin suburb: a road mine or culvert bomb unlooked for by British or Irish security, who concentrated on escorting the limousine, not on clearing the road. On the morning of July 21 Ewart-Biggs was to drive from his residence in the southern Dublin suburb of Sandyford to the Embassy with Brian Cubbon, the new Permanent Under Secretary of the Northern Ireland Office, down from Belfast to confer with the new ambassador. Rees had not been able to make the trip as planned, thus missing the morning's events. The two had breakfast, came outside, and got into the 4.2-litre Jaguar, the ambassador on the left side of the back seat and Cubbon on the right. In the front Judith Cooke, Cubbon's private secretary sat, on the left of the driver, Brian O'Driscoll. There was not much worry about security when the ambassador moved by car, and it was thought better for him to commute to a secured house than live in a more visible one near the embassy. At the house, as his wife Jane noted, the "security arrangements made on our behalf—or rather Christopher's behalf—were oppressive. Gárda officers roamed the garden night and day, the entire house was brightly illuminated during the darkness hours, and Christopher shadowed by security guards wherever he went on foot or by car."* There seemed no need for worry.

The dark blue Jaguar turned left out of the grounds of Glencairn onto the Murphystown Road, followed by an escort car of the Irish Special Branch. The ambassador had been in Ireland fifteen days. The two-car convoy was under observation by the IRA active service unit, ASU, who had already stuffed two hundred pounds of commercial gelignite into a culvert a hundred yards down the Murphystown Road. The culvert bomb was to be triggered by an electric detonator operated by the armed volunteers from some bushes one hundred yards away. The site was too far from the Embassy to have attracted attention. No one had yet noticed the men in the bushes. Suddenly there was a tremendous roar and a bright flash. The Jaguar was tossed into the air, flipped over, and crashed back into the smoking crater. Such road mines tend to kill on the down drop when the vehicle is smashed rather than from the explosion as it is thrust intact upward. The left side of the ambassador's Jaguar hit first, crushing Judith Cooke and Ewart-Biggs. She died instantly with a fractured skull and broken ribs. He, with his neck broken and sternum smashed, was dying by the time the detectives from the escort car could reach the car. Most of the force of the explosion had gone out the sides of the culvert, but there had been enough lifting power to toss the Jaguar over on the left side. O'Driscoll and Cubbon were injured but would recover.

Two men carrying rifles were seen leaving the area. Actually the active service unit was larger and had a variety of weapons that proved unnecessary. The gelignite had done the job. A huge police and army sweep through the area found no suspects and few useful clues. An intensive hunt for the killers, with the usual suspects lifted and interrogated, led nowhere. Everyone knew those responsible if not by name—but they had been on the run for years and were not available. Not until September did an unidentified republican spokesman accept responsibility, but by then other matters had intruded; no single violent act could long hold center stage. And the assassination muddled off into scandal. The Gárdaí proceeded to bungle the investigation, leading to a scandal over misrepresented fingerprints and a cover-up. The entire incident had been a disaster for the coalition government. In an effort to shore up the state's legal defenses, already extensive, the government oversaw the Dáil and Seanad declaration that "a national emergency exists affecting the vital interest of the state" because of the armed conflict in Northern Ireland.

All through the summer that low-intensity but lethal conflict had continued as the Provos probed and maneuvered, seeking vulnerabilities. It cost an enormous amount in money and men and mostly in time and concern to reply to that armed struggle, to defend the innocent, to maintain the essential, and to support the normal. The constant security effort of the RUC and the British army even in the most dangerous zones was one long preparation for a single shot or the sound of an explosion. Regiments would come briefed, prepared with simulated training and proper warnings, and perform for several months in constant tension, always at risk. There was rarely an enemy. A few hits were claimed, some arrests made, a

*Jane Ewart-Biggs, *Pay, Pack and Follow: Memoirs* (Chicago: Academy, 1984), p. 201.

terrorist body recovered after a firefight. The soldiers were never at ease, never safe, and always a few soldiers were killed or wounded, shot from out of the ditch, bombed by strange devices—always targets, even at rest. And then the regiment would be withdrawn from the province for conventional assignments in Germany or Britain or Cyprus, even later for a conventional war in the Falklands. Northern Ireland seemed always there, no safer, no less challenging. This was not completely unwelcome to many in the British army. Soldiers enlist for adventure, for wars. Officers train for battle. Armies exist for wars and the low-intensity war in Northern Ireland was the only one available; nasty, brutish, and long, it still offered an arena for professional competence.

Of all the Northern arenas one of the most notorious was South Armagh and of all the British regiments the most notorious was the British Paras. From April 15 to August 17, the Third Battalion of the Parachute Regiment was responsible for supporting the RUC in South Armagh. For four months with red berets, blackened badges, clean faces, and weapons at the ready held in the Belfast cradle, they responded to provocation and if possible forced the pace rather than simply keeping a low profile. Nothing big happened, no Miami Showband, no big kills or long battles. More shots were heard but not noted, more explosions heard but not discovered. More people died but not for any clear purpose.

Tens of thousands of army hours went into the effort, great care, careful organization, and in the end no little action: 1,137 rounds of 7.62 rifle and general purpose machine gun ammunition were expended, along with 15 rounds of 9-mm. submachine gun ammunition. Mostly the guns were aimed at terrorists, barely seen, and rarely were they used effectively. One IRA man was hit and arrested latter in a hospital in the Republic; only the dead or some of the severely wounded IRA end up as statistics. The SAS killed one IRA volunteer on the Third Paras' first day, a volunteer they had already captured who then tried to escape. In their four months the Paras could claim no kills, nearly par for the course where, as always, irregulars are most elusive: fire and run, bomb at a distance, skip and hide. Lots of work is required for security, with no results. There were twenty-three hoaxes and seventeen confrontations, along with eight successful armed robberies to balance off 233 arrests, some planned, some speculative, and some after hot pursuit. Just numbers to go with the twenty-two plastic baton rounds fired and the eight 84-mm. rounds used against suspected IRA explosive devices and even the eighty-five color smoke-grenades used to attract helicopters. The numbers of futility during a quiet tour.

All this was not much ammunition expended for four months and it was expended to little avail. Despite the high professional skills and initial hopes, the tour did not turn out well. In fact at the end, Third Paras' preparation and painstaking conduct produced a dim and dreadful record. A few seconds here and there that could not be taken back, someone else's panic, a misunderstanding, a few lapses, and all that would be remembered from South Armagh during the summer of 1976 were the resulting blunders and losses.

The tour began when a Wessex helicopter came under IRA small arms fire, and then was damaged by an RPG-7 rocket and forced to limp to a landing. The IRA's greatest tactical desire was for antihelicopter weapons. At least on April 15 the IRA active service units had scored. And with the imported American M-60 machine guns and improving IRA skills the level of combat had increased. The British army helicopters would have to take more care. They would still fly but, like all the rest of the security forces, would require faster reactions. The challenges in the countryside meant the need for improved tactics, different training, better equipment, innovative response: The war did not stay still. The British army, professional, long skilled in small wars, drawing on the resources of the state, gradually fashioned a refined and effective anti-insurgency response. In 1976 this process was under way. It was a process that never ended as the long war dragged on through stages of improved competence for all in unconventional killing. Because the war was irregular and the IRA enemy was in possession of real assets, and was unpredictable, often unprofessional, yet intimate with the arena, the escalation of competence was never on the side of the army alone. All the skills of technology and battle schools made life more complex for the IRA but did little to shift the balance of assets. The IRA found it difficult to operate and the security forces impossible to impose order. Tour after tour, despite the increased British capacity, the war continued, no more visible to the innocent eye, no less dangerous to the involved.

All wars kill and in South Armagh the little war in the Irish countryside killed, but not always the right person. In their four months in 1976 the Third Paras found more wrong targets than right. Private Hastings shot himself in the foot and Private Evans shot himself in the stomach. An incident in a bar after drink had been taken ended with a lost pistol and Private Lee shot in the shoulder. The Third Para troops shot and killed an innocent motorist, a belligerent RUC constable, and on August 13, their very last day in the area, a twelve-year-old girl, Majella O'Hare. The IRA hit civilians as well, a Mrs. Jennings hit in the arm in the Market area of Newry, a civilian wounded in Warrenpoint by flying splinters, and an employee of Fishers Timber Yard in Newry, who was standing next to UDR Major James Henning during an attack. There were security losses inflicted by the IRA as well—the most notable when a radio-controlled bomb in a bicycle exploded in Crossmaglen and killed Private John Borucki instantly. Another Para barely escaped a booby-trapped flashlight. Duty in South Armagh was a high-risk operation for all, the civilians, the IRA, and the security forces—during the Paras' four-month tour, members of the RUC and UDR were hit and RUC Sergeant James Hunter was killed, as were two soldiers. In a real war this hardly equals the toll of training or moving troops about, and even in South Armagh half of the fatalities were accidents. The attrition hardly upset British army duty rosters. There were no real shoot-outs, a burst of machine gun fire once, no known IRA fatalities except Peter Joseph Cleary of Belleek, shot dead after capture by the SAS on the Paras' first day, April 14, in what were—of course—disputed circumstances. So in spite of the Paras' skills and determination, despite the care and professionalism, the tour was no net gain for order or for the British army. In fact the period was remembered mainly because of the death of Majella O'Hare and the arrest by the Gárda of several SAS men who blundered across the border. As the Third Para O/C was later to write, "I was just saddened that so much good and so much really hard work had been tarnished by a few unfortunate occurrences. Added together the thinking time which resulted in the death of two innocent people in two separate incidents was no more than 10 seconds and probably much less, but it was those seconds which tend to eclipse the other 10.7 million seconds of the four months."* Those ten seconds and a few others ended up counting, for the Third Para had others lapses and disasters during their tour. Nothing went well in South Armagh.

Nothing else seemed to be going well for any government. Summer talks by the politicians once the convention phase had passed produced nothing. In London Callaghan was intent not on Ireland but on creating his own government. Rees assumed, accurately, that he would be replaced in the Northern Ireland Office, perhaps by Roy Mason, a quite different type. Mason indicated to Rees that if he were in the province he did not fancy immersing himself so deeply in Irish matters. It might be better to stay outside the minutiae of the province, the names and foibles and predilections, the schismatics and splinters, the world of mirrors and minor prophets that had so intrigued Rees. Few wanted office in Northern Ireland because there seemed so little to gain, and that far away from the London center. And for London Ireland was foreign. So when Rees left in September for the Home Office—a step up politically—and Mason took over on September 10—hardly a promotion—there was greater concern expressed for British interests and initiatives than for Irish complications. Mason not only had no great interest in knowing the number of the floorboards on the Irish stage, but he also accepted that there was to be no immediate rewriting of the plot. Direct rule was the order of the day, not intricate convention negotiations, a lunge toward a Council of Ireland, or power sharing. All that had foundered. All that was left was a hard slog to impose order. And with his experience at Defense, Mason felt more comfortable with the military than with Rees's concerns about civil liberties denied by detention or with moves to find a political accommodation arising from local agreement. In a sense the locals had blotted their copybook, North and South, loyalists and nationalists. There could be no liberty, no politics, no progress while license in the form of gunmen and terrorists ruled the streets. If the politicians would not play, then they would have to wait on the sidelines.

Rees would leave the province with little reward. Detention had ended but so had special status—and all that might imply. The Provos had already started shooting prison warders in retaliation. Ulsterization had failed politically with the end of the convention but might work as an aspect of security—and all that might imply. In 1976 the police lost twenty-three killed, up from eleven the previous year; and the losses of the UDR went from five to fifteen dead. Nothing was free in the province. All Rees's lavished interest, his toleration of the often intolerable, his care and concern, had come to naught. No one had benefited from his tenure. And there were many to point to the collapse of Sunningdale and power sharing as his own contribution to provincial chaos: He could have closed down the loyalist strike, saved the Assembly, done better. In retrospect this is surely unfair. Even knowing the implications of the general strike on the first day (and no one did) a harsh response would not necessarily have brought a return to

---

*Brigadier Peter Morton, *Emergency Tour: 3 PARA in South Armagh* (Wellingborough [Northamptonshire], 1989), pp. 218–19.

work the next day. The general strike worked because in general it was supported by loyalists. If the RUC or the British army had scattered the paramilitaries, there was no guarantee that the loyalist workers would have trooped back. No matter, the past cannot be replayed. The Assembly had collapsed and neither Rees nor anyone else had found a means to build a successor: The loyalists' center of gravity had settled in a seemingly permanent intractability on both power sharing and an Irish dimension, so the proper minority politicians could find no mutually beneficial common ground. There was nothing left for the moment but a concentration on shutting down violence—and this seemed to satisfy Mason.

The RUC too got a new head in Kenneth Newman, who, at forty-nine, took over as chief constable on May 1, 1976. If in Ulsterization the RUC was to assume a greater role, then the police had to be both more efficient and more acceptable to the Catholics. Since 1969 this had been the intent of all involved—as long as such reforms did not truly alienate the majority, who felt a proprietary interest in their police. Newman, from the London Metropolitan Police, was seen as a new and nonprovincial broom. He replaced the Catholic Flanagan, who had been fortunate to last the course, since the IRA missed him twice. The most spectacular attempt had been on the flight on a British Airways Trident jet that left Aldergrove Airport in Belfast for Heathrow, London, on July 23, 1974, with Flanagan and eighty-two other passengers. A two-pound bomb on board had failed to go off because the paint left on a drawing pin prevented the current from making the loop through the watch hand.

Newman would need luck as well as skill in what was surely policing's most difficult job. Once again observers dated the reform and rehabilitation of the RUC from the arrival of the new man. One of the constants for a generation had been the unveiling of the new RUC, now—it was announced—acceptable to the minority community—except for the Provos. Each official report detailing the shortcomings and errors of commission and omission had been welcomed as a corner turned. Each new chief constable's tenure had been welcomed as the final culmination and capstone of transformation. At first those convinced tended to be limited to those who had imposed the change or written the report or appointed the commissioner. Gradually, however, the increasing professionalism of the police (who often acted as if murder was just murder done either by Catholics or Protestants), the lack of alternatives, and the priorities of moderate Catholics did, indeed, meld into a consensus that the RUC, if not revolutionized into a conventional police force, had improved sufficiently to warrant more general support.

In 1976 this day had yet to arrive. At the end of 1975 all but twelve (5 percent) of the delegates at the SDLP Convention had voted to withhold support from the RUC. The RUC, then and later, despite its apologists and supporters, was never a conventional police force: First, most of its resources, many of its priorities, and the entire thrust of its responsibilities focused on political terror; second, the force, except for a few token Catholics, remained overwhelmingly Protestant. The Protestants were largely loyalists—loyal to the state, their employer, and their own—even when under attack by their more militant colleagues. A few constables did associate with paramilitaries and more made little secret of their distaste for republican subversives. What was remarkable was that so few became involved with the UVF or the UDA and that so few allowed often justified suspicions of the minority to shape their work. Their visible attitude was a result of the fact that they were at risk on duty or at home, everywhere a target. They were reviled by those they must protect, often unappreciated by their own, and usually detested by the minority. The latter often supported or spawned the gunmen and the bombers, delighted in police losses, publicly displayed their hatred, at times contrived at murder. They saw the constable as state killer, oppressor, blunt end of the British truncheon. And so, filled with venom, they acted. The RUC's lot was not an easy one.

Because in Northern Ireland a kind word rarely turns away wrath and is so rarely given, the constables often made their displeasure or distaste clear, especially in the centers of Provo support or in the bandit country along the borders. Searches and seizures, road checkpoints, observation at an IRA funeral, traffic duty beside a Sinn Féin march—all contact with those most likely to mean them harm produced an inevitable grating of unsubmerged anger. The RUC was not everyday except where the rules of everyday ran, the middle-class communities or the peaceful patches of the countryside or among the ordinary decent criminals selling rum share certificates or stealing from the back of a lorry. The province had remarkably little serious crime unconnected to politics: The joy riders of the ghettos, the private armed robbers, the arsonists for hire, or the extortionists selling protection ran the risk of being mistaken for a terrorist when out for a ride or pursuing the lure of easy money. The others, the regular criminals, the lost tourist, or the man who had lost his dog, found the RUC filled with conventional constables. Everyone else found what was expected: one of their own or one of the others, a kindly eye or a hard word. The RUC could not be but what it was, more than the sum of the inevitable individual prejudices but less than a conventional force.

In fact no one had an easy time during the summer of 1976, with every heart's desire seemingly frustrated. There was to be no devolution, no reward for loyalty, no prospect of victory in the armed struggle, no politics, no peace for the decent nor profit for the wicked. Everyone was frustrated and many were bitter—Rees was lucky to leave for new responsibilities, a clean stage. Nothing at all came of the talks Hume had with the loyalists, the Reverend Martin Smyth, head of the Orange Order, and Captain Austin Ardill. There seemed no place for discussion. Brian Faulkner announced his retirement from public life on August 14, a historical figure by then as the province squeezed out another moderate pip from the Ulster lemon.

In Belfast the friends of the Provos turned on Gerry Fitt, once Republican Labour, now, as far as the militants were concerned, an apologist for the Brits. There never had been much future in the middle of the Northern Ireland political road and the Provos were inclined to view all not with them as part of the enemy—including Fitt. As the leader of the SDLP, Fitt increasingly had a hard word for those republicans who tolerate none but their own. On August 9 a mob tried to burn him out, bursting into the house and frightening his wife and daughter. He produced a pistol and forced them out. It was an ugly and divisive scene, not unexpected where rancor and bitterness, frustration and fear had become everyday emotions. Politics was hard to ignore for those trapped near the grating edges of the two communities, hard to ignore even by those who could only hear the echo of the downtown bombs from their gardens. Everything had been tried once by someone but never satisfied everyone. Paddy Devlin, who had been both Communist and IRA volunteer, had discovered the advantages of an independent Northern Ireland, a posture at times in 1976 held by Protestant paramilitaries with Devlin on their target list.

The most distressing aspect of provincial politics by 1976 was that there seemed no way out of what nearly all felt was an intolerable present. Neither war nor politics returned useful rewards, neither majority nor minority had a useful consensus or trusted their own. Nothing added up to a satisfactory conclusion; two and two came out five, and for most this, by 1976, had no attraction. One awful event followed another. The province without hope was gripped with a public apathy and a private agony. On August 8 Maire Drumm, vice-president of Provisional Sinn Féin, in a violent speech threatened that Belfast would be pulled down stone by stone if the prisoners were not given political rights. She was arrested. There were more hijackings the next day. If it was not one killing issue, it was another.

Two days after the Drumm speech and the ritual violence that had commemorated the fifth anniversary of internment, there was one more agonizing, inexcusable, useless violent event. At exactly three o'clock in the afternoon Anne Maguire was walking along Finaghy Road North with her four children, Joanna with her bicycle, baby Andrew, six weeks, in his pram, Mark, nearly seven, and John, two and a half. A few yards behind her, her sister, Eilish O'Connor, was accompanied by her children. Her eldest child, Michelle, had been killed eight years before just a hundred yards down the same road by a frightened motorist fleeing a riot. A minute or so earlier they had heard gunfire, no novelty in West Belfast.

The shots had come from the Tullymore Gardens area of Andersonstown, where a British army patrol had come under Provo fire. The two IRA men missed, then escaped in a stolen sky blue Ford Cortina. The soldiers radioed descriptions ahead and two army Land Rovers converged on the two men in the Cortina, which continued speeding down Stewarstown Road and into Finaghy Road North. The British opened fire on the Cortina. Just as the two women with their children reached the iron gates of a schoolyard the blue Cortina appeared on the street, still racing toward the center of the city and followed by the two British army Land Rovers. In the stolen Ford the driver, nineteen-year-old IRA volunteer Danny Lennon, shot several times, suddenly slumped over the wheel, dead. His companion was still alive but, shot through the stomach and legs, barely conscious. The Ford lunged, rode up over the curb, and smashed into the group.

Eilish O'Connor pushed her children out of the way but saw the Ford hit her sister's group. Andrew and Joanna in front were killed instantly. John, gravely maimed, died the next day in the Royal Victoria Hospital. Mark was not injured. Anne Maguire had both legs and her pelvis broken and suffered a severe concussion. She did not regain consciousness for weeks but survived. The Royal Victoria has one of the world's great trauma units, for obvious reasons. The British soldiers, surrounded by a hostile Catholic crowd, had immediately called for the military ambulance and set about freeing the victims from the wreckage. The victims were removed, the soldiers withdrawn. A tow truck took away the mangled blue

Cortina. The mangled bike and pram were left on the sidewalk for the photographers.

An IRA man dead, three Catholic children dead, a mother mangled, her surviving child injured, and no one to blame but the Troubles. On the spot a small altar was set up beside the twisted iron gates: a small statue of the virgin, some flowers, a candle, a rosary. Now and then someone knelt to pray. There did not seem to be much else that could be done. A pile of wilted flowers, a gutted candle, a garish, plastic statue, a few bent heads, a string of beads, and private grief. It was one more atrocity, one more horror, and nothing to be done.

But this time something quite unexpected happened: A spontaneous peace movement spread out to encompass both Catholics and Protestants, involving many who had not previously mobilized, a movement that overshadowed the end of politics, the changing of the guard at the Northern Ireland Office and the RUC, even the din of the armed struggle. Just when nothing seemed to be happening, peace appeared where least expected, in the banners of amateurs and innocents: Mairead Corrigan, the aunt of the dead children, Ciaran McKeown, a journalist for the *Irish Press* out of the radical student movement of 1968–69, and Betty Williams, a housewife from Andersonstown who had witnessed the accident. The Peace People had come to Ireland. Perhaps two and two could add up to five, perhaps there was a simple answer after all: peace.

15

Peace and War, a Time of Persistence: August 1976–December 1977

It Is Not Necessary To Hope In Order To Persevere.
William of Orange

On the evening of August 10, as the news of the tragedy on Finaghy Road North was covered by radio and television, the condemnations began to be broadcast. Deploring violence as senseless or brutal had become a ritual. Nearly everyone could condemn the Maguire incident, although the culprits favored varied. Mostly, however, the ritual condemnations focused on the men of violence, on the armed struggle, on those who pursued an urban guerrilla war condemned by much of the articulate population: newspapers, priests and preachers, politicians, the prominent, all again damned the violence that slaughtered in passing, senselessly, innocent women and children. Not for the first time, the conventional, reflex protest was underscored by a spontaneous reaction on the part of those without access to the media. Demonstrations for peace were by 1976 not unknown, just ineffectual.

This time the Catholic women of Andersonstown, still a hard-core Provo area, came out on the next day with their baby carriages, a thousand women spontaneously demonstrating not against violence but for peace despite the IRA. It appeared, even to many of the involved, an anti-IRA rally. At six o'clock that Wednesday evening, during a program broadcast on the Ulster BBC affiliate, Mairead Corrigan, Anne Maguire's sister, an aunt of the three dead children, dissolved into tears on camera. She continued to speak of the cost of violence despite her obvious grief. She had heard the dreadful news on her way home from a holiday on Achill Island and arrived in Belfast to identify the dead children and find her sister unconscious in the Royal Victoria, the very personal returns of violence in Belfast. She had agreed to appear on local television, where her calm appeal through her tears had a profound impact. She said, "It is not violence that the people want." She condemned the people who wanted "this slaughter."* The

*Richard Deutsch, *Mairead Corrigan Betty Williams* (Woodbury [New York]: Barron's, 1977), p. 4.

484

highly charged interview had an immediate impact. It was an emotional challenge to the IRA and a plea for peace. BBC picked it up and broadcast it twice on the national evening news. By the last showing few on the island had not seen or heard about it.

One who saw the interview, Betty Williams, a Catholic housewife in the Finaghy Road North area, asked her neighbors the next day, "Do you want to have peace?" The response was channeled first into a petition haphazardly collected on scraps of paper, pages from notebooks, bus tickets, whatever was handy: a plea for peace that spread across Belfast that evening. Something was being done. Protestant women joined in the protest against violence. Forty-eight hours after the deaths, Betty Williams could read over local television a petition that contained six thousand signatures. She asked for more, for help, gave her telephone number. She said she represented a group of Andersonstown women who wanted peace, an end to the IRA campaign. "I've always been afraid of the IRA. I am afraid of it at this very moment. But at least we are trying to do something . . . someone must do something . . . these three children must not have died in vain."*

That Thursday afternoon Danny Lennon was buried in the republican plot of Milltown cemetery. The next day there were sixty-eight obituary notices in the Catholic daily, the *Irish News,* for Lennon, a volunteer of Company B, First Battalion of the Belfast Provisional IRA. The IRA did not feel Lennon was responsible. The Maguire children were British victims at one remove. The IRA "sincerely regrets the death of the Maguire children and deplores the fact that this tragedy is being exploited by British propagandists and pro-British elements including some religious groups, the press and political parties."† Although there had been no organized protest and there was no visible structure, the IRA had immediately sensed that among Catholics there existed an untapped desire for peace and quiet. Only the most faithful, the most militant could accept the sacrifices of the continued armed struggle with equanimity. There was not yet an indication of erosion in the faith, but obviously peace without price, without sacrifices, without even definitions had takers.

Mothers feared for their children, their sons as volunteers, their toddlers as victims. Families did not want life to revolve around war. The constant din, the shooting and bombing, the soldiers, the riots and decay of toleration and decency, affected all. Why couldn't there be peace for a while? Why couldn't the IRA call a halt? And how could the Army Council explain that the British were to blame, and that the desire for peace and even the dead children had become mere pawns in the authorities' maneuvers? And beyond the first wave of emotion for peace, for a respite, lurked the most dangerous of all threats: the withdrawal of toleration, the denial of legitimacy.

This had happened back in the 1956–62 campaign, and it would close down even the existing armed struggle, so much greater, so much more intense, so much nearer success. So the IRA from the first feared the worst, exaggerated what was perceived as a real threat even before those who sought peace had really organized. The IRA did not want to wait for their people to realize that little had

* Deutsch, p. 6.
†Ibid., p. 9.

changed, that the minority still needed defenders, that the armed struggle was legitimate, essential, inevitable. Instead the IRA feared that the immediacy of "peace" would dilute their support and allow a cunning British intervention of some sort, a political concession, an offer difficult to refuse, promises, reforms. There could be no peace without justice.

On Thursday evening, August 12, a thousand women gathered at the accident site, where Father Malachy Murphy of the nearby Church of Saint Michael led the rosary and scathingly criticized the IRA. One woman told a reporter, "All that we want is for the IRA to go away and leave us alone. We want to have peace." The crowd sang "Hail, Queen of Heaven" and went home, ignoring the leaflets handed out by People's Democracy that placed the blame for the Maguire deaths on the British army. The Maguire funeral took place on Friday, August 13, after a procession from their house at 13 Ladybrook Crescent, past the spot where the accident occurred, to the Church of Saint Michael. The church was jammed. Betty Williams was there at the invitation of Mairead Corrigan.

After the ceremony the funeral procession moved onto Millbank, past the saluting RUC and to the graveside. It was no ordinary funeral. The television interview, the dreadful accident, the petition and demonstrations for peace had struck a chord. Good news from Ireland for a change. Many were moved. One so touched by the three tiny white coffins was the journalist Ciaran McKeown, who went home after mass to his own children and a rising sense of urgency. Something might be happening. As a pacifist he was hopeful, still not soured and cynical after watching the North as a journalist, the vocation of pessimists. Others, including journalists, saw events as a means to an immediate end. The London *Daily Express* featured Betty Williams on the first page: "Why I must stop the IRA."

Obviously the event could be used to thump the republicans. Rees, as Secretary of State, was more practical about the Andersonstown peace women: "They have shown the way. It requires courage to speak out, to accuse, to become a witness in a court of law, to become involved in law-enforcement. . . . The terrorists can be beaten only with the cooperation of the entire populace."* For Rees, it seemed, peace was to be obtained by betraying the republicans. Peace for the British equaled suppression. Just as the IRA had feared. Others, especially abroad, were supportive of peace, wired or wrote, dispatched greetings and offers of aid, sent congratulations. The mail began to pile up in Betty Williams's house, and in Mairead Corrigan's. The media remained in mass. McKeown could not get any time at Williams's house in the midst of the circle of journalists but was to meet the two that evening at the BBC studio. And by then he had already made his estimate of the situation. Before the RTE program he disputed Paddy Devlin's prediction of the events as a nine-day wonder: "I don't think so Paddy: I think this is the real turning point."†

The two women finally showed up downstairs after the program had been broadcast. McKeown offered Corrigan and Williams his aid. In a sense and appropriately, the peace people were created at the bottom of the stairs of a

*Deutsch, p. 9.
†Ciaran McKeown, *The Passion of Peace* (Belfast: Blackstaff Press, 1984), p. 141.

television studio by two distraught housewives and a journalist who had lost his "objectivity" in his spontaneous commitment of peace.

The conversation was consolidated soon by an agreement among the three to dedicate themselves to the cause. McKeown, a pacifist with experience in community work, soon left his position with the *Irish Press* to become a full-time organizer. Despite the inevitable quarrels and criticisms his complete dedication and rapidly honed skills proved crucial. He knew or learned how to run giant rallies, maintain files and correspondence, set up press conferences, and exploit foreign contacts. Neither Williams nor Corrigan, who were nearly the same age, thirty-three and thirty-two, with little formal education, were typical Belfast housewives. Williams had struggled to raise her family, a teenage boy and a girl of four, spent time in Bermuda, and had an inner toughness that compensated for a lack of sophistication. Corrigan was personal secretary to the managing director of Guinness in Belfast, no mean accomplishment, and had an intense interest in theology.

The three developed almost from the first an empathy that made the tribulations of the peace movement easier at the top. And the three indicated that a wealth of talent existed in Belfast, in Ireland, untouched by formal education or by opportunity, unsophisticated, shrewd, absorbent, capable of enormous sacrifice, eager for challenge: The IRA had already discovered the pool and now with the peace movement a troika would carry the dream further than most could have imagined.

They, especially the women, became the focus of the most intense concern, a core of a cult of peace that could not be denied but made them uncomfortable. Still, the three had begun rolling the rock, rolling it not without hope; but like everyone else they were startled at the avalanche: A rolling stone may gather little moss but have massive effects just the same. And the three proved more than capable in riding the avalanche if not in directing it to an appropriate site as foundation for a stable future. Mostly they, like all the others, were swept up in the movement, the sudden sense of motion in a static society. Each day brought more excitement, more motion, seemingly more opportunities.

The next day, Saturday, August 14, was a revelation to the doubters and confirmed McKeown's suspicions that this time was different. On a calm, sunny summer day ten thousand people came to Finaghy Road North for a peace rally. Most important, several busloads of women arrived from the Protestant Shankill. It was a mixed crowd, mostly but not entirely women, many with children, still simply and largely standing as witness. The emotion of the accident, the television interview, the excitement of the media had not evaporated.

And the Provos had a response to any peace without justice: the organized harassment of many of the women. A large group of Provo supporters, mainly young men, shouted and cursed. There were tussles, screams, howls: "Whores! Traitors! Brits Out! Provos Rule!" The media were properly horrified: gunmen against peace. The Provos from the first tended to overreact to the provocation of peace, unwilling to wait for the inevitable internal contradictions of the peace movement to remove the threat to their armed struggle. They would always defend their territory remorselessly, regardless of their image in further, less important arenas of provincial and world opinion. First, keep the base, then worry about an image: Image building from the time of the three Scots had not been a crushing priority. Waging war always was first priority. And the war depended on the people. And the people could not be permitted an easy, unchallenged drift to a British-encouraged "peace," could not be allowed to march behind the Judas goats, innocent and politically ignorant women. Neither had politics. Corrigan had left school at fourteen and Williams had taken a secretarial course. They were two simple women wracked by grief—and so dangerous.

If anything the crude harassment of the Provos in Andersonstown actually increased the peace movement's allure. If the gunmen were concerned, then the demonstrations must be effective. It was not only the Provos who felt the Peace People should adjust to provincial reality; everyone had suggestions. The three leaders decided simply to push on their own way. On August 21 twenty thousand people gathered for a peace rally in Ormeau Park in Belfast. The first real challenge was planned for the next week: a march up the Shankill. Peace was not just about the IRA and not just a Catholic responsibility. On August 28 the Women's Peace Movement (later the name Peace People was adopted), twenty thousand strong, marched up the Shankill while in Dublin thousands more marched through the center of the city. In Belfast there were all sorts of reports. McKeown was told by a UVF man that if the women were left alone "the trouble would be cleared up in no time." There was a sense of general euphoria. Catholic nuns were embraced by Protestant bystanders.

No one had a hard word. Tommy "Tucker" Lyttle, spokesman for the UDA, agreed that "I don't suppose it'll do much harm." Many became convinced that day that it would do much good. The media rushed about documenting the transformation. The marchers ended with speeches, and "Abide with Me," and Betty Williams leading "When Irish Eyes Are Smiling." The idea was viable. The next week there would be a symbolic double march in Derry, with Catholics and Protestants meeting on the Craigavon Bridge. A new and different marching season had begun.

The Irish autumn of 1976 was dominated by the great peace marches and monster rallies. It had been a long time—seven years—without good news that did not harm someone. Peace seemingly could be everyone's victory, no one's defeat. Rees's office had even before the arrival of the peace movement prepared a campaign with SEVEN YEARS IS ENOUGH signs that the IRA swiftly transformed into SEVEN HUNDRED YEARS IS ENOUGH—no one gains without someone else's pain. The IRA wanted not just peace but peace with justice, their kind of peace. Few noted the need to define *peace.* Now one could march in a parade for peace that might do some good, that showed a commitment to decency and the future and to an end to the evils of the Troubles. And so many drove to Derry or Londonderry and walked across the bridge with the locals, or the next week attended the Ireland-wide rallies that spread the word and the opportunity to participate: Antrim, Coleraine, Strabane, Craigavon, Dungannon, Newtownards, Ballynahinch in Northern Ireland, and in the Republic at Drogheda, Waterford, Dundalk, Longford, Kilkenny, Ennis, Nenagh, and Gorey. There were more rallies, and the geographical spread continued: Betty Williams was in Liverpool on September 18 and Mairead Corrigan in Glasgow on September 25.

Each rally attracted a different crowd but all were the same: a march, the media, a great clump of people, some from far places, listening to speakers bring the word, a generalized word without political message or visible agenda, then general delight followed often by singing. There was often the visible display of the enthusiasms of the charismatics—the hugging and smiles and bliss of the born again into fellowship and friendship. And then everyone went home to the everyday, invigorated, inspired, with life enhanced.

The new Northern Ireland Secretary, Roy Mason, had arrived on September 10 to find the island in turmoil, but for a change the excitement arose from a seemingly general desire for stability, order, and tranquillity. This sudden lunge to peace could hardly be helped by the Northern Ireland Office without contamination. So the authorities tended to adopt a policy of faint but real praise while urging all others to rally behind the movement. In Britain there was less restraint in supporting the development. Good news from Ireland was rare even if the entire population did not as yet support an end to violence. If there was not, as Mason and the authorities noted, a universal desire for peace, the nature of the opposition merely validated the movement.

Some of the opposition was politically irrelevant. There were those already at work on conciliation who, if yet quietly, resented the newcomers and their media train. Some of the disgruntled did not yet oppose publicly and often cooperated with the marches. Peace was big enough for everyone. Others continued to see "peace" as oppression hidden behind the delusions of the innocent, three blind pilgrims on a road paved with British intentions. These saw such peace as a danger to the cause. And the Northern Ireland Office saw this opposition during the autumn of 1976 as politically profitable for British policy. Sinn Féin held a counterdemonstration at Derry but managed a crowd of only 150. The DUP felt the movement was counterproductive. On September 14, the Peace People attempted to stop a hijacking on the Shankill and attracted a crowd of young people who pelted them with eggs. All during the season of the marches some of the Peace People came under such fire: Two daughters of Women's Peace Movement members were beaten in a Shankill bar on October 5 and three Peace People leaders were attacked and their cars wrecked in the Turf Lodge by a crowd protesting the death of a thirteen-year-old boy hit with a British plastic bullet. No one noticed that the three were critical of the British army—they were assumed to be on the other side.

One had to be on one side or the other in 1976. On October 23 Provisional Sinn Féin attacked a Peace People march on the Falls and after the melee sixteen people were hospitalized. These attacks only added spice and danger to the lure of the marches. Such highly visible and easily condemned violence meant that the movement was important; the marches were more than ritual and the rallies were not just an arena for euphoria.

Certainly the euphoria was widespread. From the first the detailed media coverage and the very existence of the movement had engendered major interest abroad. The peace establishment was ecstatic, and rightly so, for this was a spontaneous and effective mass movement arising from years of intractable conflict. The general public was encouraged: Good news has takers as well as bad. Congratulations came in and camera teams. Money was dispatched, and invitations to speak, and even more.

In Norway, on reading McKeown's *The Price of Peace,* written in August, a group convinced that nonviolence was tactically right for Northern Ireland gave the movement a People's Peace Prize that was worth £201,000 by the time the three peace leaders arrived to accept it at the end of November. Two major events were, by the time of the announcement of the Norwegian peace prize project, firmly scheduled: a London march from Hyde Park to a rally at Trafalgar Square on November 27 and on December 5 a riverside rally at the Boyne, near Drogheda, where King William's triumph had long been the symbol of the division in modern Ireland into the Orange and the Other.

The Peace People tended to dominate events, push politics and the para-militaries out of sight. Northern Ireland politics in any case had largely closed down as a result of the return of direct rule. The interparty discussions had led nowhere, and no one had any immediate suggestions for a new direction: The loyalists would not accept power sharing or an Irish dimension in any form satisfactory to the nationalists or Westminster. Every formula to hide the ensuing gap had proven ineffectual. London wanted a long recess and so there was a recess.

The loyalist paramilitaries, when the thinkers had time to consider, were no more united than the Unionist parties. While the UDA continued to attract those militants concerned with politics or welfare or neighborhood action rather than tit-for-tat murder, often well-adjusted, dutiful young men from decent families, those who killed also attracted recruits. Some killers, like Lenny Murphy and the Shankill Butchers, were depraved. Others were simply crude, cruel, limited men of violence, intimidating and fearsome. Some, however, were the mirror image of their IRA coevals across the peace line, neither psychotic nor prone to violence. Most of the killing was done by a mix excluding the disturbed whose presence complicated operations. And by 1976 the community at large had doubts about the necessity of such a "defense"—the IRA armed struggle was still real, provocative, and deadly after the truce but neither new nor likely to intimidate London.

One result was that each new Orange horror eroded support and silence. Murder for many of the decent was not defense but murder and they dropped a word, mentioned a clue, hinted to the RUC—still *their* police. The RUC under Newman, while still Protestant, had become more professional. And the RUC, even in the most sectarian days, had no love of violent crime. Shooting any stray Catholic, slaughtering the innocent hostage, blowing away a showband seemed, even and especially to policemen, criminal: murder the worse for the flag of politics. While it was possible to claim that IRA murder was murder, their armed struggle, often in the hands of the brutal and ruthless if rarely the demented, was a low-intensity war. Everyone in security so acted, from the soldiers on patrol to the RUC in jeopardy. The more brutal Protestant killings, however, could be and often were thought of by the constables as murder, not simple murder but certainly a crime and so amenable to pursuit and arrest and prosecution. Thus, the RUC response both to the Miami Showband killings and the Shankill Butchers became visible evidence that the force was not a sectarian tool but a law enforcement agency.

On October 18, 1976, the first major court case arising from Newman's law-and-order RUC strategy came, with twenty-eight members of the UVF in the dock. There were fifty-five indictments for murder, attempted murder, and charges related to robbery, explosions, shootings, and illegal possession of fire-arms and explosives. The case, however, had arisen from the evidence of a threatened UVF member that led to the arrests in October 1975 in Operation Jigsaw. The entire UVF apparatus in East Antrim—the Carrickfergus-Larne area—had been closed down, suspects arrested and brought to trial. For the RUC, Jigsaw indicated clearly that the Protestant paramilitaries were not immune, were not *their* paramilitaries but merely criminals.

This also was a sign that the attraction of the Protestant paramilitaries had eroded. The UVF had become a dangerous and vicious legion of the rear guard, not overnight, not completely, but times changed even if the butcher's bill would grow no shorter. As long as enough toleration existed to permit the very few to kill with impunity, and if the killers took care to avoid the RUC, then tit-for-tat murder remained an Ulster institution. And so it did. Some unionists would simply deny the crime, others would avoid consideration, some would find rationalizations, and a very few loyalists would proffer advocacy. The mix proved ample for a generation of vigilante murder.

The most dramatic and most focused paramilitary operation during the autumn of 1976 was the assassination on October 28 of one of the Provisionals' most visible and detested spokesmen, the vice-president of Sinn Féin, Maire Drumm. Fifty-six years old, she, along with her husband, Jimmy, who had spent much of his life in prison often without charge, was an absolutely dedicated republican. Their twenty-year-old daughter, Marie Theresa, had been jailed in November 1975 for eight years for possession of a loaded revolver. Maire Drumm had been convicted in July 1971 of encouraging people to join the IRA. In the previous August had come her threat to tear Belfast down stone by stone. She had a gift for the hard word and the provocative display. She had recently been arrested and convicted of illegal marching, spending more time in prison. Many Belfast republican women had for generations run up prison time in service of the faith. Loyalists charged her release was a disgrace: She was a harridan and a visible demon to them.

On October 3 she entered (for cataract treatment) the Mater Hospital in North Belfast, between the republican New Lodge district and a Protestant area. Her confinement was noted in the Belfast newspapers. On October 18, at the annual Sinn Féin Ard Fheis, her husband read her resignation as a candidate for vice-president. The announcement cited her health but promised that she would return soon to the "thick of the fray." She planned to leave the hospital on October 30 and move to a nursing home in the Irish Republic. In the meantime she was vulnerable. There was no special security at the Mater or near her room.

In Belfast most activists, Protestant and Catholic, IRA or UDA, were protected because they were unknown or, if notorious, hidden deep among their own. The Drumm house at Glassmullan Gardens, Andersonstown, was not only deep in republican territory but also a focus of British security interest. Close by was a British army post behind a corrugated metal fence and barbed wire; the soldiers were constantly on watch, would turn on a spotlight to check out any night visitors and dispatch a sentry to take down license plate numbers. Inadvertently the resented army post supplied an inner security ring; the outer ring was provided by the nationalist people of Andersonstown. At the Mater there was little protection but the aura of normality.

On the evening of October 18, 1976, two young men entered the hospital during visiting hours, between 7:00 and 7:30 P.M., and then disappeared. No one noticed them again until too late. At 10:30 P.M. a dark blue Ford Escort pulled up and parked opposite the main hospital gate. Inside the Mater, Maire Drumm was standing at a small six-bed ward, next to ward 38 on the second floor. Two young men in white coats pushed into ward 38. One drew a revolver and without a word shot her in the chest three times. She collapsed on the floor. The two turned and disappeared out of the ward. The Ford Escort started up and drove off into the night. Mrs. Drumm crawled several yards across the floor and then collapsed again. She was rushed into the operating room, where doctors found there was nothing to be done. Ten minutes later she died on the table.

Searches and checkpoints all over the city produced nothing. No gunmen were found. In Belfast operations there is only a brief moment of vulnerability. Withdrawals are quick and carefully planned. After a drive of a minute or two the stolen car can be abandoned near a clean vehicle or a warren of friendly houses. A sound alibi is then always available at the pub, at the house, at home. Even camouflaged security blocks across likely routes seldom hit lucky and did not this time. Maire Drumm was isolated and vulnerable and so dead. The overtly political figures among the Provisionals were always particularly vulnerable, since they had to appear "normal," whatever their actual assignments, show up for scheduled meetings, drive through danger zones, shake hands in the street or walk in public parades. Most took very real precautions to reduce the danger but in the case of the Mater the fatal assumption was that no one would invade a hospital on the edge of the New Lodge. They had, and having murdered, disappeared. No one took responsibility for the killing. No name emerged even from the later revelations of the "supergrass" informers, who told the authorities much about loyalist activities in the city. Both the security forces and the IRA assumed that the UVF was responsible and had failed to claim credit to ease the heavy pressure against their organization.

Many loyalists felt that the operation was justified, that Maire Drumm was an odious, treacherous subversive. A spokesman for Ian Paisley's party said "that she died the same death meted out repeatedly to many hundreds of Ulster people by the Provisional IRA, whose so called cause she so uncompromisingly espoused, will be seen by many as a poetic irony. She was indeed a victim of her own hatred."* This time the loyalists had hit a real target. It was an act of vengeance made visible, not a randomly chosen, innocent Catholic wandering on the margin of danger, and not one of their own (the other major Belfast 1976 assassination had been the UDA murder of one of their own, Sammy Smyth). This time a symbol had been erased. And so as she would have expected Maire Drumm was buried in the republican plot at Millbrook Cemetery; and as she would have expected, the rites were observed by the British army and the RUC.

*Irish Times, October 30, 1976.

This republican loss was painful but hardly crucial. Even in 1976, with the glory days of the mass, almost open IRA of 1972 long gone, there were still more volunteers than slots, more talents than assignments, more troops than battles. In 1976 the Provisional IRA had undergone a sea change as the armed struggle began again after the cease-fire. Their opponents too adjusted. The British had imposed direct rule and so closed down politics and transformed security with a policy of Ulsterization. The British army GOC, Lieutenant General Sir Timothy Creasey, and the RUC chief constable, Kenneth Newman, would on January 1, 1977, formally sign an agreement that established police primacy in security matters. This would prove a crucial shift, more than just a security shift from one pigeonhole of authority to another. The British were in the province to stay and the victory of the Republic, once imminent, receded. The police, the normal arm of order, must thus be seen to have primacy. The army could be pulled back from safe zones, almost inevitably Protestant areas, often middle-class but sometimes large country zones where the IRA had not operated, and even the marginal gray areas where trouble was real but rare. In the black zones after 1976 the army was in theory, and in time in practice, deployed to support the RUC rather than to walk point on the entire effort. The effort had gradually eroded the IRA capacity to act with previous freedom.

The old IRA role of defender, a secret militia army of large battalions and neighborhood units, no longer fitted reality. The IRA had to be ready to defend, but with the offensive phase long under way the units also had to attack a prepared and skilled opponent as well. The IRA had to be readjusted to the long haul and to a more cunning opponent. British and RUC counterinsurgency tactics continued to improve. The SAS was more important as a trainer and even more as an example than as an operating unit. In fact the greatest contribution the SAS made in Northern Ireland for good or ill was the projection of an image read as ogre, as exemplar, as monster or elite defender. In the province the few soldiers of the SAS were transmutted into major actors. The everyday units mostly did the job, better each year but never good enough, given the arena, of closing down the Provos.

The ideas of Kitson were common currency even if the publicist did not evoke universal army admiration. The army tended to suffer from unit turnover, fragmented intelligence on the line (this year in Armagh, next with the Army of the Rhine), and the difficulties of adjusting anti-insurgency to police work. The wonders of modern technology came to Northern Ireland: radar and heat sensors, night scopes and advanced listening devices, computer banks and improved riot gear. One of those ubiquitous soldiers moving down a Derry Street wore specially designed boots, specially fashioned gloves, held his SLR rifle in the Belfast cradle, kept in contact with a tiny radio, kept one foot on the ground in a patrol (a brick) that moved along in shrewdly planned stages, up, down, eyes front, eyes back, children and venom ignored. They looked much the same as in the past but they were not. More cunning, more care, and more skill were now needed to kill a soldier.

More important, British intelligence gradually improved, through experience, exposure, and practice, through harsh interrogation techniques, through the gradual triumph of MI5 and the acceptance of RUC skills, through a net of informers, double agents, intimidated witnesses, and volunteers. There were all sorts of security problems in 1976–77, the excesses brought by the charms of the covert and the recourse to forced confession, but in general the IRA could sense the growing competence and changed arena.

Those intelligence officers, whatever their formal title, who thought Wilson a spy and their disinformation (the professional word for lies) gradually disappeared, through attrition and the revelation of excess; they were casualties of the bureaucratic wars. And those wars were never really finished—the case with nearly any intelligence system that can afford two offices. For a generation there would be rivalry, incompetence, and confusion, although matters would improve. In 1976–77 and later the army suspected the RUC, fairly or not, as ineffectual and the source of leaks, especially to the Protestant paramilitaries. The army suspected the Gárdaí in the Republic for much the same reasons, if the leaks went to a different set. The army preferred to keep itself to itself, the future disposition closely held, the paid informers secret. In turn the RUC, recognizing military arrogance, had doubts about the army, a passing visitor to a province on the edge of empire, not a resident with an intimate knowledge of the land and people. The RUC had slightly different priorities, a different set of informers acquired differently, maintained differently, exploited differently. And none of the uniform services and their plainclothes agents was intimate with the civilian intelligence people out of London, their minds awhirl with the big picture and alien tradecraft.

In each camp there were further divisions between the elite and the line, between special new units and disgruntled old ones, between one sector and the next. At worst, ignorant security specialists betrayed or killed the assets of their allies and shot it out with their own; at best, the trap would close on IRA active service units or major commanders would be lifted by intent instead of the usual accident. Most important, details organized for retrieval began to accumulate, so that the province, especially the core nationalist area, became a closed camp under watching eyes. By the end of the decade the system and skills were largely in place, but not in 1976.

The Provisionals began adjusting from the top down; as an inherently conservative organization, there was no radical surgery. Those with time to spare could in any case only be found in the camps and prisons, so that only there could a great deal of thought be given by the experienced to the future. The Kesh became an IRA think tank during this period. Outside those not rushing from one operation to the next could contemplate adjustment only hurriedly. Certainly Twomey as C/S was open to suggestion. The IRA moves on consensus and moves slowly, hence the organizational changes necessary had in many ways already occurred informally. The movement had moved without the usual bureaucratic papers and proposals but just as slowly. Irish reality had changed.

What had evolved was a war in the six counties that spilled over along the border. Nevertheless, it was a Northern war that could only be fought by Northerners. Historically the IRA GHQ had been based in Dublin from May 24, 1923, when Eamon de Valera had dispatched his stirring postdefeat message to the Soldiers of the Republic, Legion of the Rearguard, that "other means must be sought to safeguard the nation's right."* He meant politics. Others did not. Their means had been a secret army and the Provos still used the constitution written at the end of the twenties by Sean MacBride, Moss Twomey, and others. A previous generation of Belfast IRA men, including Gerry Adams's father, had established a Northern Command, but in the campaign years of 1956–62 the IRA had been too small to warrant a "heretical" partitionist form from the past. Now some in the North felt that GHQ, even with Séamus Twomey of Belfast as C/S, could not cope with the war on the necessary daily basis. Mac Stiofáin had vetoed any such structural change as arising from a Belfast nostalgia that would complicate command. Now Twomey, more willing to listen than Mac Stiofáin, recognized there might be a case for change.

GHQ was in effect Twomey and his operations officer, Brian Keenan, moving about in safe houses in Dublin. GHQ had always been in Dublin, even when the C/S took trips. Keenan ran the English campaign from Dublin and Twomey coordinated the war in the North but both were overloaded. Perhaps a Northern Command might work—and so in November Martin McGuinness took charge as the first Northern Command as increasingly the six counties dominated the movement. The Army Council never really found an appropriate role for most Southern volunteers, whose numbers continued to decline precipitously. The young joined an army and found no war. They could not be used in the six counties and many did not want to be involved merely in politics or welfare or rounds of training for uncertain purposes. And the Army Council increasingly found the IRA too large and too vulnerable in the six counties, especially in Belfast. So began a readjustment into smaller cell units that were in theory to be closed and secret but in practice in intimate neighborhoods were merely smaller, more professional, and more difficult to find. The ultimate form was largely based on a plan worked out in 1976 by Ivor Bell while in Long Kesh.

The secret army thus was shedding its structure as an all-Ireland secret army with a role as militia-defender in the six counties. In the process the influence of the earlier Army Councils and the Southerners faded. Some blamed them for penalties paid for the cease-fire and the elusive rewards. If the cease-fire had been a mistake, it had been a more general mistake however, one few wanted to repeat but one that had seemed worth the risk to many in the six counties. Many simply felt it was time for a change. The Éire Nua federated Ireland advocated by O Brádaigh and O Conaill no longer had many takers in the six counties. If there was going to be a long and costly war, then why opt for the Republic on the installment plan? Seeing little immediate ahead, why not ask for all?

There were also all sorts of tensions within the movement: between generations, between those in prison and those out—some aggravated by police plots and disinformation, some natural, between those in the active service units and those not.

At times during this period the prisoners in Long Kesh, where much of the talent had been supposedly isolated, supplied the ideas and possibilities. These prisoners included Gerry Adams, Ivor Bell, Brendan Hughes, Kevin Hannaway,

*Dorothy Macardle, *The Irish Republic* (New York: Farrar, Straus & Giroux, 1965), p. 858.

and Davey Marley. Even the basic text for all volunteers, *The Green Book*, originated in the Kesh. There is always tension between those inside the wire and those outside, even with the relatively rapid written communication and unmonitored visits, even with the releases and arrivals that kept the lines open. In all secret organizations communications are faulty, encouraging schisms, misunderstandings, and skewed priorities. And there were all the other tensions inherent in an organization with regional lures, several generations of diverse attitudes, and a proven and distressing record of failure on the movement's own terms.

All of these stresses, personality conflicts or considered theological postures, focused on tactics and techniques. There was no split in the faith or within the movement, only a grinding move to another phase. Some were more political, stressed a different order of priority. Some were concerned solely with military matters: All else would drag along in operations' train. Some worried about the losses that the increasing Northern domination would entail. The losses, not the domination, were the concern, since it had become a Northern war. Some were critical of the British campaigns or favored more such ventures. Some approved of the Twomey-Keenan core and some had doubts. All this was normal and only rarely open to external manipulation. Whatever else, the Provisionals were united against those without the faith. The secret army would soldier on in cells or under new commanders but with the same dream. The leadership often had very little empathy with others, cut-out stereotypes in their book of proclaimed enemies.

The IRA's constituency was odd—its own, who would tolerate almost any tactic sanctioned by the Army Council, and the Irish people, in particular those most sympathetic in the North but essentially all the Irish. Those of the Irish people who opposed them, who set up the government in Dublin or Belfast, Protestant or Catholic, loyalist or Fianna Fáil Republican, were simply damned as dupes or as dreadful and ignored. Thus, the murder of the British ambassador, Ewart-Biggs, was well received by their own, tolerated by many of the sympathetic (as anticipated), was damned by everyone else—the dupes—who had been ignored in the planning. The Army Council did not empathize with and had little understanding of the priorities and motives of their Irish opponents; they tended to find Fianna Fáil as mysterious and unsavory as the UDA. Both should be in step with history but were not. So both were largely ignored. The republicans made no concessions: The long war warriors would march over such obstacles.

This long march trampled across the sensitivities and the assumed legitimacy of the establishment in Dublin. The secret army was subversive, dangerous, and unrepentant, and the murder of Ambassador Ewart-Biggs during the summer was just one more provocation. The conditioned response to such provocation was improved and extended security measures coupled with threatening rhetoric. Some in the Republic still believed in ultimate unity and the evils of partition but no one had a kind word for the Provisionals, Fascist gunmen and killers, a threat to the democratic state.

On September 1 the Dáil and Seanad in Dublin declared that "a national emergency exists affecting the vital interests of the state" because of the armed conflict in Northern Ireland. It was not so much that more emergency legislation was needed as it was wanted as evidence of adamancy. The worries of the civil liberties people were discounted The mad dog Provos who killed diplomats in the Dublin suburbs and provoked the bombers to come south must be squashed. There was competition to do the squashing. On September 24 the new Emergency Powers Bill was signed by President Cearbhaill O'Dálaigh, but he then referred it to the Supreme Court to test its constitutionality. Some felt this was an unnecessary nicety. On October 15 a booby trap bomb exploded in a house that the police were searching in Garryhinch, outside Mountmellick, killing one young Gárda, Michael Clarkin, and injuring five others. It seemed ample evidence of the need for emergency legislation. President O'Dálaigh, in fact, signed the bill the next day, after the Supreme Court found it not to be repugnant to the Constitution, thus permitting detention for seven days of persons suspected under the Offenses Against the State Act. There were those who felt he should have acted more swiftly. In fact the Minister of Defense, Patrick Donegan, had already called the President a "thundering disgrace" and so initiated a crisis that led to O'Dálaigh's resignation on October 27 so as "to protect the dignity and independence of the Presidency as an institution." On November 9 Patrick Hillery of Fianna Fáil was elected President unopposed, since the other parties, assured of losing, did not want to make the running. On December 3 he was sworn in as sixth President of the Irish Republic, a reluctant "beneficiary" of Northern events.

Those Northern events, in fact, colored all Irish life, and not even the aura of hope flashing out of the Peace People and their monster rallies could engender general optimism. On November 7 a demonstration carefully planted exactly 1,662 small white crosses, one for each fatality, on the grounds of the Belfast City Hall. Everyone knew that there would be more. McKeown, Williams, and Corrigan might believe that the beginning of the end was at hand, but the IRA was restructuring for a long war and despite Mason's optimism so too were the security forces. The vitality of the IRA had been shown in the orchestrated response to the end of special category status for prisoners. Rees had anticipated this reaction but thought it would be worth the price to end internment. This did not prove to be the case.

Then and later the British remained trapped in a dilemma: Accept the reality of a war with the IRA and hence legitimize special operations and special procedures at the cost of also legitimizing a secret army; or refuse to admit that the six counties had anything but a troublesome criminal problem. The wavering, compromises, outright lies, and self-deceit that arose along the fault line continued to warp British efforts at suppression and accommodation for a generation. For the IRA, murder was not just murder but an act of war, done to the sound of trumpets. They never had a problem, even when the innocent were killed in passing, a necessary sacrifice. Their constituency would narrow on this matter but the key for the volunteers was the armed struggle as war.

The British could never really decide, either in declared policy or in their hearts. Often it was mighty like a war and at other times simple murder. Criminalization was a pragmatic move to impose normality by decree. Nothing about the procedure or the targets was normal. Any observer could see "criminalization" was a label, a means of punishment, a form without content that hardly reflected reality. And from the first Rees, determined that the end of internment was worth the price, had known that the procedure would be opposed. The British were going to call war peace and wage peace by decree.

The IRA could never accept criminalization and give up their right to make war. It was a historic position and a pragmatic one, sought and protected since Fenian days, arising from the allegiance to the Republic virtually established in the hearts of the Irish. Frank Stagg had already given witness to the seriousness of the movement's intent: None would admit to being criminals any more than they would accept a British court's right to judge them in their own land. On September 19, after long internal debate on tactics and details, the refusal to comply by the rules began with Ciaran Nugent, aged nineteen, arrested in May 1976 and found guilty of possessing weapons and hijacking a car. He was as typical a volunteer as could be found. In 1970 his best friend from Saint Peter's Intermediate School in Belfast was shot dead by a loyalist gang while chatting with him on Grosvenor Road. Nugent was badly wounded. He had seen the British army curfew on the Falls—the Rape of the Falls—in 1970 and decided that "the British would have to go. . . . I had been attacked several times by the security forces and I felt they had no right to be in the country."*

Nugent had watched the H-Blocks being constructed from the roof of his compound until he was released by Rees. Now he would be the first prisoner in the blocks, with a three-year sentence. When asked for his size so he could be fitted "'For a uniform.' I said, 'You have got to be joking.' I was the only one in the H-Blocks. They dragged me into the cell. . . . I lay on the floor all night without mattress, blankets or anything else. The heat was reasonable in all fairness and I slept."† The next day he received a blanket. He wore a uniform once in order to tell his mother not to expect another visit: "If they want me to wear a uniform they'll have to nail it on my back."‡ He wore only a blanket for three years and was soon joined by others on the blanket until the number reached two hundred men and women in various jails. They were all volunteers in a secret army, not criminals, no matter what British law might say. British law was merely an imperial means, just like guns or manipulated Protestant paramilitaries.

The early attempts to coerce compliance all failed. Every two weeks, for example, they were left for three days in empty cells and served only black tea, dry bread, and watery soup. There were no visits, no recreation, no possessions, nothing but the cell and the blanket. They were maltreated. The warders were enemies—and the IRA so treated them. The first warder, Patrick Dillon of County Tyrone, had been shot and killed on April 8, and over the next four years the toll would be eighteen. Naturally treatment in the H-Blocks did not improve over the summer and autumn as the number of IRA men convicted under the new rules showed up, refused prison garb, and took their blanket.

Thus, when Roy Mason arrived in September he had found a mix of crises and opportunities. His arrival, of course, signified little about London's concern on Irish matters. There was little except a British desire for silence. Rees had been

*Patrick Bishop and Eamonn Mallie, *The Provisional IRA* (London: Heinemann, 1987), p. 278.
†Ibid., p. 278.
‡Ibid., p. 279.

brought back and Mason sent over for Wilson's political purpose. Wilson seldom thought more than a few weeks ahead and almost never on Irish matters. In the Conservative Party the arrival of Margaret Thatcher as leader on February 11, 1975, had meant, if anything, even less interest in provincial matters. Her friend and colleague, the new spokesman on Northern Ireland, Airey Neave, took a hard line on Irish security matters. But then so would Labour's Mason, who had already indicated that he was no Irish dabbler like Rees and would be no advocate of Irish matters in London. Security would be the order of the day. And the need for security was obvious from day one of his tenure.

The very rainy day he flew into Aldergrove Airport to be escorted by a convoy of Special Branch officers to his new offices, the UDA had been operating a controlled operation of hijackings, roadblocks, and bomb hoaxes to protest the treatment of their prisoners. The army estimated the total bill for the mess would come to £200,000. Mason was most unsympathetic to the paramilitaries' sensitivities—and the Protestant paramilitaries had clearly peaked. They had no place to go except prison if they caused too much trouble. And he was no more sympathetic to the IRA's views on political status. Mason, in fact, was not unduly sympathetic to provincial matters in general. Unlike Rees he was not fascinated by the Irish scene but by the army—two years as minister of defense had made the ex-miner an army man, an unlikely convert. He had no intention of maintaining the web of contacts that Rees had established nor of following the intricacies of local matters. Politics were closed for repairs if not by popular demand. The focus was security and an enhanced economic situation. Whatever else, Mason was a former miner, a Labour man, and advocate of the welfare state. Security, however, was first priority.

Mason became a strange and common sight within the province and the security establishment, a short, stocky man, trailing clouds of pipe smoke, dressed in his own design tweed safari suit made in Belfast, bolstering army morale, praising the police, emphasizing that the IRA was on the run, reeling. In all cases the army was to be defended. When a thirteen-year-old boy and a pregnant woman were killed by plastic bullets it was the Provisional IRA who were "cynically trying to exploit a number of incidents in order to restore their waning fortunes."* In fact senior security people finally had to suggest to the Northern Secretary that his announcements of IRA incapacities were counterproductive, engendering only an intensification of the armed struggle. Mason rarely managed to restrain his enthusiasm, which was, indeed, based on real security progress. The IRA might not have been reeling by 1977 but the level of violence had begun to decline and the capacities of the Provos were narrowed.

The other prong of Mason's fork, the economy, did not prove even this tractable. In December 1976 the provincial unemployment rate was at 10.4 percent, the worst in thirty-six years. Such a rate meant that in the hard-core Catholic urban areas nearly every adult male was unemployed. Jobs might be available by leaving school but in time such messenger boys grew too old, were let go for cheaper young replacements, and thus faced a lifetime on the dole. Over a

---

*Desmond Hamill, *Pig in the Middle: The Army in Northern Ireland, 1969–1984* (London: Methuen, 1985), p. 203.

generation all the enormous investment in the province, often skewed for security purposes, crumbled away. The new high-tech manufacturing plants refitted to produce Lear jets or De Lorean luxury cars would become textbook disasters. The American John De Lorean, after long negotiations and substantial British concessions and grants, would announce on August 2, 1978, that the new plant would open. It did, to general acclaim—and closed six years later, with the money gone, the market for luxury cars gone, and De Lorean gone, back to America and other scandals.* The old standard industries did no better. The shipyards were saved but could not find orders. The workforce was run down, never up. The new small businesses could not take up the slack of the old dying industries, linen and tobacco. Parts of the province appeared prosperous. The dual carriageways were extended, the M1 deep into the middle of Belfast. The wreckers joined the IRA in leveling the old. And there were new houses and council estates. Of course, even with the new housing the House of Commons was told on December 3 that the housing situation was "certainly the worst in the UK and probably the worst in Europe." Still, there were new houses if not always quite as normal as they seemed. The estates in vulnerable areas were often sited carefully for security purpose: In the province, bad neighbors are made harmless with good walls. So the neighbors were walled off, especially in Belfast; and the estates often had as well, Catholic residents assured visitors, roadways that were designed to take armor, and access routes that would provide military fields of fire. This was invisible, unlike the cages and guards around the Belfast center or the net-draped sangars and rocket-protected police stations that for many visitors canceled out any reports of economic progress. Neither the focus of the Northern Ireland Office on the economy nor the RUC's new community-oriented policies could hide the Ferret armored car at the corner or the burned-out buildings.

But the rise of the Peace People transformed the image of the province during the autumn and winter of 1976–77. Mason came to bring direct rule not to a hopelessly divided, bitter, and embattled society but to one seemingly imbued with hope and charismatic enthusiasm—or so reported the media. The media—local, Irish, British, and international—continued to shape the perception of the events, even and often for those involved. For years, after the early days of black-and-white stereotypes, the province had then become one more stop on the world terrorist tour, depressing and bleak, with clouds of rain and recycled rhetoric sweeping over the visitor whose guidebook was already checked, underlined, and dog-eared with use. Actually, as British spokesmen were wont to point out, the province was relatively peaceful even with the paramilitaries. The murder rate for Belfast was 18.8 per 100,000 at the very worst, and that of Cleveland, Ohio, was 35.6. In fact twenty-five American cities had a worse rate than Belfast. This was what the numbers said. What the pictures said, what the visible evidence said, what nearly every observer said, was that the province was wracked

---

*On June 19, 1992, a court estimated that De Lorean received by fraud $8,500,000. The judge said that if De Lorean had been before the court, he would have sentenced him to ten years in prison, but existing legal arrangements between the United States and Britain prevented extradition.

with dreadful and visible killing violence. And there was no end in sight, only the same intractable lethal stalemate.

Now the Peace People had given both the reporters and their viewers reason for hope: The good guys appear at least, even if they have not won. In fact the Peace People, despite the anxieties of the Provos and the hopes of the British, had very little impact on the day-to-day violence: Tit-for-tat murders continued, republican feuds continued, the Provos' armed struggle and the new British security initiative plugged right along, leaving behind bombed and burned-out buildings, the lengthening casualty list, the cost in money as well as the cost in blood and ruined lives. A British soldier standing in the draped Baruki sangar, named for the soldier killed by the Provo bicycle bomb, looking out over the scruffy central square of Crossmaglen, ninety seconds from the border, looked across an arena where seventeen British soldiers had died. Nothing was quite like Crossmaglen, absolutely without architectural distinction, economic prospects, or cause for a tourist pause, a tiny, marginal market town deep in the countryside, if also the capital of the IRA's invisible but real Republic of South Armagh: And nothing was hopeful there. The British army, except on patrol, was trapped in its cramped base where, for fear of IRA snipers, even the garbage was removed by helicopter. It was a grim if challenging posting reached only by helicopter. One new company used 2,336 tubes of camouflage cream their first month. The war was endless, and the peace marches, some only a few miles away, were in another country.

The security struggle in Crossmaglen, in Belfast and Derry and the towns, in the countryside went on and on, even as the cameras focused on Corrigan and Williams, on the banners urging Peace Now. There was no more peace in real life than there had been before Danny Lennon's stolen car crashed into the three children. Even the changes in the war were halting. The IRA shift to the problems of the prison in response to criminalization was as slow and uncertain and as deadly as was the British move to police primacy and hence Ulsterization. These moves, even the perpetual motion of Mason in his tweed safari suit, were not as spectacular as peace made manifest by parades and rallies—something between the Pied Piper and a pilgrimage. And as everyone asked the leaders, What next? "Where do you go from here?"* As the year ran out the answer was uncertain; but surely 1977 would be an improvement.

The year-end total of the costs of the Troubles was high, whatever the murder rate in Cleveland, Ohio, or the claims of Mason. Some 245 civilians had been killed, 14 members of the British army, 13 RUC, 10 RUCR, and 15 UDR. The beginning of Ulsterization, however halting, had shown up in the reserve figures of the police and army. The same shift could be noted in the murder of prison guards as a response to the new criminalization policy. The civilian total included the victims of the sectarian murders, a rising total that compensated for a decline in innocent victims like the three children killed on Finaghy Road North. The end result was a death total of 297, up from 247 the previous year, but still well shy of the horrendous 467 total of the premier year for violence, 1972. Despite the

*McKeown, p. 215.

totals and the atrocities, the end of politics, the all too visible sectarian strife, the year ended on a hopeful note almost entirely because of the peace movement. Mason might clamor about security successes, but it had been the marches and rallies that had attracted the eye. Even if nothing had really changed, and very little had, any hope was worthwhile.

In the case of the Peace People hope was still strong but the sensible realized that a rally has to go home. On January 6 the Peace People in their *Strategy for Peace* suggested a no-party assembly for community groups that would elect an executive. They wanted to bring in community politics through the back door of an unofficial initiative. It was an all-purpose option to Hume's non-Stormont assembly, a concept that attracted few. The constitutional convention was bad enough, a forum for a debate without the rewards of power, but these other private initiatives could simply not create institutionalized power tightly held by the Northern Ireland Office and at Westminster. The leadership, however, felt that the peace movement had to do something visible if not dramatic. And those at the top had kept the faith. Over the next several months, as the killing and bombing continued, Ciaran McKeown on April 3 could actually take heart from the turmoil: "We should be prepared for worsening violence . . . acts of violence will probably become more desperate than even those we have seen so far. . . . We have turned the corner, and the war is beginning to disintegrate."* He could see the trouble staggering on for a couple of years. But more and more vicious violence now meant peace later. It was an analysis that convinced few but his own, and they grew fewer as the year progressed without the euphoria of the marches or the excitement of the rallies. The carousel had gone around and around and was slowing.

While the peace movement began to run down and Mason's new security policies geared up, the province continued to suffer through the same old realities arising from increasingly tattered myths. The Provos promised on January 20 that they would tear down Belfast brick by brick if necessary to remove the British presence. Down in Dublin three days later, the Stickies continued their long march away from revolution: The Official Sinn Féin formally became Sinn Féin–the Workers Party. Very few new recruits came in despite the first half of the name, which had been retained to spite the Provos and to allay the suspicions of the more republican adherents of the new party. The old Officials, especially in the six counties, had continued to suffer erosions, first because of the decline in the urgency for defense and second because Costello's INLA attracted the military types.

There had been ideological blows as well: the decline of the central position of the national question; the early attitudes favoring the reform of Stormont that evolved into a less than revolutionary posture of political accommodation in the province; the shift to orthodox Moscow-oriented, Marxist-Leninist assumptions that alienated many self-proclaimed followers of Trotsky (no small matter in the tiny far Left circles of the North); and simply the increasing sense of distance from Dublin and the old ways.

*Michael Hall, *Twenty Years: A Concise Chronology of Events in Northern Ireland From 1968–1988* (Newtownabbey [N.I.]: 1988), p. 65.

By 1977 Goulding, Garland, Mac Giolla (still President of Official Sinn Féin), Malachy McGurran, and Dessie O'Hagan from Northern Ireland, and in Dublin Seán O'Cionnaith and Proinsias De Rossa, as well as others, had decided to gradually close down "the movement" and replace that decayed, amorphous, and curious institution with a modern party. The new vehicle would be slick, tight, efficient, based on rigorous ideological principles and run through democratic centralism. As a result Northern Ireland was considered intrusive, interfering with the future by upsetting the agenda. In 1975 Garland had referred to the "imbalance that the Six County situation creates in the entire country."* In Boston Mac Giolla said it served "to smother all progressive ideas, to weaken the forces and the left and to strengthen the right-wing parties."† This attitude hardened because schism tended to drive the parties further apart and hence what the Provos wanted must be wrong, counterproductive.

This drift away from the centrality of the national issue, from the postures and positions of historical republicanism, even from the past examples of radical republicans who also had focused on economic and social issues, attracted new converts. These often had no qualms about force in politics—after all they opposed regimes that carried weapons—but sought other means to alter history. Some were radical republicans returning to the fold like Eamonn Smullen, who served five years in Portlaoise Prison during World War II, retired, and then rejoined the IRA and was arrested in England in 1969 in an arms transaction. Others were without movement background but attracted because Official Sinn Féin was the port of last resort on the radical Left of Irish politics. Gardiner Place thus attracted a set of ideological recruits who could see the party as a vehicle for change and their own political ambitions—the Roy Johnston option retaken.

Eoghan Harris, a producer at RTE, appeared from the Wolfe Tone Society— the old halfway house for those with ideas attracted to the IRA—to galvanize the still uncertain Official ideology. Abrasive, arrogant, very bright, and enormously energetic, he had studied under the revisionist historian John A. Murphy at University College Cork and within Sinn Féin turned Murphy's conclusions—an attack on patriot history from the Right—on its head through the newly founded Research Section. Research Section became more dynamic than the quartermaster general. The new people had not signed up to be soldiers. They, like the student Eoin O'Murchú, who later joined the Communist Party, the rebels within the civil service, particularly RTE, and many militants in the labor unions, were tired of clientele politics from stolid old men: They wanted political action, programs, progress. There were still in the Officials firm republicans and sound military people (Mick Ryan at Dublin GHQ was both), but the future lay in conventional politics: the capture of the Irish Left. As a result the role of the Stickies in the North grew circumscribed; events there, where the Republican Clubs fought a lonely battle, were a distraction.

In Belfast there was still another feud with the Provos, the strains of diminution seemingly being nearly as great as those of escalation. On April 10 a

---

*Henry Patterson, *The Politics of Illusion: Republicanism and Socialism in Modern Ireland* (London: Hutchinson Radius, 1989), p. 152.
†Ibid., p. 152.

ten-year-old boy was killed and a teenager lost a leg when a bomb went off at a Republican Club meeting. The dead boy's uncle was shot dead by three gunmen on the way to tell the parents. The Provos were blamed. The Provos then attacked Republican Club marchers in Milltown Cemetery—the Provo's had nothing but scorn for the Officials' new Free State Party and so were outraged at all the lingering signs of the true faith, names and banners and rituals that were being daily betrayed in Dublin by Goulding and Company. And the Officials in Belfast and Newry and a few other places were far from ready to give up the gun or tolerate Provo provocation. The feud died down in the spring but revived on July 27. Four people were killed and nineteen injured before a cease-fire could be put in place. Six more people were injured before the truce took.

Whatever Dublin's attitude, Belfast could still defend its own militarily, and the purpose of the Northern units had become self-defense. Defense proved necessary because for some time there was tension and trouble around the edges. Even after Gardiner Place finally dropped Sinn Féin from their title and claimed that their IRA was disbanded, a gradually decaying Northern IRA remained to defend members and interests and a few others in the Republic remained to expropriate funds.

The disappearance of the Official IRA was a matter of perception. The Dublin ideologues knew it was being closed down. Some Officials thought it still existed. A few knew that volunteers were available but denied the fact. The authorities in Dublin and Belfast had their doubts but were willing to encourage any such signs. The Provos noted that the Stickies still were armed in the North and someone was doing armed raids all over Ireland—not them, and not always Costello. There was as well continuing tension between the Officials under whatever banner and Costello's INLA people, often provocative and more ideologically competitive than the Provos. By the end of the summer all these unwanted feuds had been patched up. Dublin GHQ with Garland as C/S and Mick Ryan as Director of Operations had made it clear that the shooters' day had ended: Narrow defense and revolutionary expropriation would be the future order of battle—and the fewer battles the better.

In fact with the example of the Peace People dominating the scene, the killers, whatever the cause or explanation, had sticky going. The North was tired of explanations and apologies, denials and rationales. In March one UDR victim had been shot dead in front of his two children and another man from the Ardoyne had been shot four times in the back while trying to shield his four-year-old son. The UDA still insisted they hit only IRA gunmen even when grieving families denied it. In turn the Provos were unmoved by opposition from their declared enemies. War was war. As Mason's security forces hardened the old military targets, as the soldiers became more skillful, the bases, camps, and sangars better protected, and the police more evasive, the IRA widened the ring. The IRA focused on local security forces, using a variety of explosive devices. There were booby traps, double bombs, trap bombs, pincers bombs, devices triggered by twine and by motion. The quartermaster general introduced homemade mortars, often lathed and tooled in the Republic and then moved north to be installed on flatbed trucks parked at measured distances from the target. If these were not accurate, they were still a fearsome threat. In February the IRA attacked capitalists. Volunteers shot dead the head of the DuPont Corporation in Derry and hit two more businessmen in the following weeks.

In all cases those executed by the IRA played a prominent role in the effort to stabilize the British-oriented six-county economy. GHQ announced that civilian searches at checkpoints were "part of the British occupation forces." GHQ had already announced that immediate families of policemen were "legitimate targets." In March an active service unit shot and killed the sixty-three-year-old mother of an RUC Reservist. These additions to the target lists were not always well received within the movement outside the hard-core militarists, and they were regularly criticized in the community at large. The complaints had an effect. The IRA would come back to capitalists at a later date but henceforth security families were killed by mistake or in passing rather than as prime targets. As Ciaran McKeown pointed out in April, these acts looked too desperate. And they were too brutal to have any desired effect.

The IRA had no option but to seek softer British targets or expand the battlefield. So far the prison protest over criminalization was considered secondary at best by GHQ, a cause for complaint, a means to involve the less militant or more liberal supporters in protest. And there was no viable political stage. The previous several months had seen an effort by Seán MacBride, former Irish Foreign Minister and head of the republican Clann na Poblachta, Nobel and Lenin Peace Prize winner, the most respectable of the militants, and the Belfast loyalist barrister Desmond Boal to seek out a middle ground between the paramilitaries. Both were illegal, both banned from conventional politics, both united in opposition to the end of special category, both without prospects in the scenarios planned by Mason. The meetings were secret and the results limited. The Prostestant militants, if not the loyalist paramilitary ideologues, had decided to force their way into the political arena with a return to the general strike.

None of the political factions in the province was happy with the vacuum that direct rule brought. Nothing was on the agenda except local elections in May. There was consequently a tendency to want more, since nothing was possible. The SDLP Convention in December 1976 had barely voted down a demand for British withdrawal. Some of the members instead opted for independence, although Hume, back from an American trip, and others beat this down. There was not much to offer instead. Sinn Féin had the gun and the prison protest and MacBride secretly at work. Alliance had kept the middle ground that no one much wanted. On the other side of the divide the various orthodox Unionists were quiescent—direct rule, if without advantage, did not humiliate. Paisley and his DUP were not for quiescence at any price. The leader felt that the pot could be stirred to advantage and at least excitement returned to Ulster politics. In the sense that something was needed he was joined by Andy Tyrie of the UDA—a revolution and independence was what Tyrie had on his wish list—and by some of the leaders of the 1974 general strike.

The problem for the militant Protestants determined on a general strike was that they had not seriously analyzed 1974 nor paid heed to the events of the last three years: Times had changed and had been misread. Paisley, Tyrie, and the others had watched the 1974 strike fall into place without a sense of the preparation that had been taken, the long hours of talking that had coalesced into a general consensus. The first day had looked spontaneous, with the paramilitaries rushing to the fore to intimidate waverers, but the keys were in place. The call for a strike in May, a call spearheaded by Paisley, not the anonymous and unthreatening self-selected worker-leaders of 1974, immediately alienated his own loyalist opponents and the many who felt he was once more howling to hear his voice rather than taking a principled stand. Neither he nor the DUP nor the United Ulster Action Council nor the UDA came up with a convincing reason for a strike—a protest against a lack of a security offensive against the IRA.

In the spring of 1977 matters actually seemed to be improving for the majority. The Northern Secretary was following a hard policy, harrying the IRA at every speech, cheering on the police and army, chasing the gunmen into their lair. With incident levels everywhere down and the IRA hurting itself with horrendous murders of old ladies and children, a protest against security policy, with no alternative program was unpersuasive. There was no united opposition against a Council of Ireland or power sharing or any other viable target. The 1974 strike had demanded one simple step—an end to the Assembly—and Faulkner and the Assembly had been vulnerable. A protest on security was not timely. The minority was doing the job for the majority: The IRA was feuding and murdering their rivals; the SDLP had nearly voted for treason in December; Dr. Edward Daly, Roman Catholic bishop of Derry had announced on April 10 his opposition to any attempt to change the character of Catholic schools. He claimed the Troubles were the result of centuries of injustice inflicted on his own because they refused to give up the faith.

Daly was in most ways very conservative, parochial, and deeply suspicious of republican pretensions. The Irish bishops still found opposition difficult and the Church's difficulties with the radical republican movement were long-standing. Thus, for loyalists Daly was a good symbol of Roman Catholic arrogance and intransigence, the Pope's advance guard, while his criticisms of the IRA over the years could be ignored—no problem for the unionist mind. In any case Daly's comment indicated no goodwill and toleration and pluralism from the Church, just the hard line. So too with the SDLP and the Provos. Why bother protesting? Let Mason handle it.

The Official Unionists under Harry West, already at odds with Paisley because of the Martin Smyth–Austin Ardill talks with the SDLP in 1976, chose not to support the strike, as did Vanguard and various Orange Order leaders. The UUUC alliance fell apart. Paisley and Baird were on one side, for the display; the rest refused to be led into what seemed a futile move. Most important, the shipyard workers on April 29 voted not to support the stoppage. There was no promise that the power workers would not follow their example. Paisley did not care, overestimated his hand, and announced the next day that if the Ulster people did not back the strike he would quit politics: "I did not choose political life. I went into it because of the call of the people. . . . The strike will not be called off. It will not be for twenty-four hours—it will be on until we get victory." And everyone was ready. The bakeries turned out bread in extra shifts every two hours. The security forces were primed and set to maintain order and open streets.

The strike began on May 3 and many of the factories stayed open. This time Andy Tyrie's paramilitaries did not sweep up the doubtful but were instead clashing with the police in East Belfast. Tyrie had a confrontation with the RUC outside UDA headquarters. Worse, the strikers failed to get the support of the Ballylumford power station on May 6. Ulster was not going to be closed down by the workers and the UDA did not have the resources to force a closedown. The strike was defeated but dragged on as the leaders looked for a way out. Paisley on May 13 found an exit: He announced the strike had been a success, was now over, and so he would continue in politics. There was no more talk of the security forces going in to root out the IRA.

The May 18 district council elections underscored what the collapse of the strike had indicated: The divisions within the electorate had firmed up; the small players were edged out of the center of the circle. The Official Unionist Party polled 29.6 percent of the first preference votes and the DUP, down a bit since the convention, 12.7 percent. Alliance held the center with 14.4 percent and the SDLP dominated the minority community with 20.6 percent. The other votes were scattered. The big four were for the moment players in a small field but one with the collapse of Stormont that encouraged council coalitions instead of the either/or politics so long familiar to the participants.

If the May 17 Northern Ireland elections indicated continuity, those for the Dáil in the Republic, held on June 16, brought back the party of government, Fianna Fáil and Jack Lynch, in a sweeping triumph, one of the most smashing in Irish political history: Fianna Fáil, 84 seats; Fine Gael, 43; Labour, 17; and 4 others. There were those who saw the win in Northern terms as putting a more republican presence in Dublin. After all, Charles Haughey of the Arms Trial returned to the front bench as Minister for Health and Social Welfare.

In January, perhaps anticipating an election, Lynch had called for British withdrawal (no date), and a united Ireland (no details). As early as an October 1975 by-election Fianna Fáil had taken a Brits-out line. The national issue could, thus, not be discarded so quickly, especially if it were seen to have electoral value. Others noted that in matters of subversion Fianna Fáil had never been reluctant to come down on the IRA with the boot. At least Conor Cruise O'Brien, the republicans' bête noire, the hard-line, increasingly antinationalist spokesman on Northern Ireland for the Coalition, was no longer a minister, no longer even in the Dáil. Still, just as in the case with the SDLP in December 1976, there was within Fianna Fáil more than Fine Gael or Labour a residue clearly nationalistic that might bode ill for a tranquil six counties. Thus, Lynch's government might turn out to do no harm but few in London or Belfast suspected that it would be as useful as the coalition in seeking an accommodation in common ground short of the mythical unity that had been the nationalists' lodestar for so long.

There had been the others trying to find a common ground between the Northern Ireland extremes. In the case of Boal and MacBride the talks had progressed to conclusions and complications—a complex formula that included a role for the European Convention on Human Rights to protect Catholics in the North and Protestants in the island as a whole in a mix that included Northern independence and a loose all-Ireland federation. The formula took advantage of some loyalist groups' rising interest in a unilateral declaration of independence. Independence had a certain charm as some loyalists sought their special Ulster roots, envied the IRA's ideological assets, and sought a future beyond "defense" and sectarian murder. Much of this discussion had been limited to the very few with political interests in the loyalist paramilitary units and from time to time a few politicians.

In fact the talks had the advantage that they had bypassed the conventional politicians so often distrusted as selfish and ambitious by all varieties of paramilitary opinion. The concomitant disadvantage was that those politicians did not spring up without representing a real constituency. The politicians might pander to popular delusions or represent the worst aspects of their voters, but they did really represent them—elections had indicated that those who moved beyond certain bounds were discarded, often quickly. Their party colleagues followed the same policy, for example, with O'Neill in the beginning and, recently during the convention, William Craig. Thus, however cunning the MacBride-Boal formula, any plan drafted in part by a former chief of staff of the IRA, Nobel Peace Prize or not, was going to be unwelcome in most loyalist quarters, where Boal, an unsound maverick, had few friends in any case. Many might talk of independence but the great longing was London backing of a British Ulster, security, reassurance, respect, not the dangers and responsibilities of novelty—certainly not a novelty that came with MacBride's imprimatur.

On May 17 both the Provos and the UDA denied involvement in the MacBride-Boal talks that had led nowhere solid. As Peter Robinson, a rising star in the DUP, announced, "The people of Ulster have only one message for the IRA. We seek your elimination. No one who talks to the IRA represents the loyalists of Ulster." And no one was talking to anyone in Ulster during the summer of 1977. On July 13 Gusty Spence in the Maze said loyalist politicians were a "sick joke" and suggested a summit conference of paramilitaries. His UVF colleagues outside said his views were his own. On July 23 John McKeague, soon associated with the new Ulster Independence Association, said that the British were going, that the days of the Orange Order and the Orange card were over, that everyone should get round a table. No one did. No one paid much attention.

The only cheerful item on the agenda was the planned visit of the Queen. Over a decade the British had tried every avenue of approach short of walking out, so why not a royal visit? And so there was to be one: two days in August, carefully monitored, no great risks but some display, all in the hands of the RUC—Ulsterization—with the army on alert.

All the IRA managed in reply to the arrival of the Queen on August 10 were a few riotous demonstrations out of sight in Belfast and a small, harmless bomb with a time detonator in a garden. At the beginning of the year there were still those within the Provisionals who felt that the British were weakening. Ulsterization was taken as a running down of the British army. The lack of investment indicated London's intent to cut British losses. Mason's indifference to Irish subtleties showed a general erosion of concern with the province, now but not forever a security matter. The bad news was thus filtered away. The volunteers behind the wire and the commanders who had been responsible for gearing up the army after the twilight truce that had seemingly eroded capacity were not as sanguine. The arrival of the Northern Command, the switch in Belfast to small units, and the narrowed operational options in the country that called for fewer activists, while arising from a different combination of factors, collectively indicated that the IRA was to be smaller, more skilled, less visible, and hardly the van of a wave to sweep out the British. Many in the new 1969 generation felt that change must come by expanding the battle arena to involve republicans in social and economic issues, incorporating the people as well as the sniper and bomber.

The new departure would require time and there at least the Provisionals had ample. This analysis meant that there would be a long war that must be expanded to become a people's war, a protracted, unconventional conflict, not just an armed struggle arising from the minority's vulnerability and toleration. The first public indicator of the slowly emerging consensus came at Bodenstown when Jimmy Drumm, a most conventional and conservative Belfast republican, gave the oration. The speech was a tribute to his martyr wife and to his own long service but as well it was a case of bringing in the old to authenticate the new. The new had arisen from a variety of sources and interpretations but ultimately centered on the articles that Gerry Adams, as "Brownie," had written in Long Kesh since 1975. Published in the *Republican News,* these distilled Northern IRA thinking.

The *Republican News* was symbol of the changes in the North. It was edited by one of the new republicans, Danny Morrison, who, with his ally, Tom Hartley, and the help of an old republican, Frank Card, had replaced Seán Caughey as editor. Morrison, Hartley, and those still in the Kesh wanted some realistic analysis of an armed struggle that left much to be desired. Many blamed the cease-fire. Some had special culprits. The devout, however, wanted not scapegoats but a new way forward and one that need not leave the road behind littered with discarded, old comrades.

Before Wolfe Tone's grave in Bodenstown Sunday in June, Drumm was to give the new word, now accepted by the Army Council. On the run in the Republic, Chief of Staff Twomey, a man of Drumm's generation, could see daily the problems, even if he had less concern with the nonmilitary solutions that appealed in Belfast. Noting that the British were not withdrawing, Drumm called for a struggle not based solely on the presence of the British army, the hatred and resentment of occupation, not solely on Ulster, but on a mobilization of all the Irish workers—a call for an all-Ireland focus on one hand and for a long war on the other. Both were novelties and both were to be the pillars of the future. In the summer of 1977, however, the future was not as clear as previously.

There was a tendency within the movement to blame—mistakenly—the truce for the growing military frustration of the IRA, a frustration that came in considerable part from the growing competence of the security forces. This security improvement continued to return dividends, if haltingly, until a state of equilibrium was reached. In 1975–76 it meant harder times for the Provos. GHQ had to make adjustments. The RUC vulnerability over mistreatment had at last been exploited. More to the point, guidelines for volunteers taken prisoner were issued: Silence was essential. The armed struggle was by no means winding down but the costs over the years had begun to add up. And there was less toleration in the Republic, which was a constant, each year no less difficult than the last and sometimes worse. There was a general exhaustion and the consequent and constant erosion of support.

People grew tired of a crusade with no visible end. Most people wanted peace and quiet, not sacrifice, not the guilt that denial caused, and so the IRA was blamed as much as the British. No armed struggle likes to admit a flagging of the faith, a gradual betrayal by the people, or the growing skill of the oppressor: easier to blame the immediate past, the old leadership who led the movement into the present. Those at the center of the circle were less inclined to finger individuals but all agreed that the truce had disappointed.

There were other disappointments as well. The greatest single one did not come in a wrapped package although in a sense the most unpleasant contents could be viewed on Saint Patrick's Day, March 17, 1977, when four famous Irish-American politicians, New York Senator Daniel Patrick Moynihan, the governor of New York, Hugh Carey, Senator Edward Kennedy, and the Speaker of the House, Thomas P. "Tip" O'Neill, issued a statement asking their fellow Americans "to renounce any action that promotes the current violence or promises support or encouragement for organizations engaged in violence." They meant, and said they meant, IRA violence, Provo violence, not that of the British army. The IRA had lost the battle for America, actually long lost it for lack of assets to deploy, for lack of talent, for reasons quite beyond remedy. Lost it was, however, if Tip O'Neill and the others rode roughshod over them on Saint Patrick's Day. The Four Horsemen would ride again on other Saint Patrick's Days, but 1977 indicated a compelling triumph of Dublin diplomacy, a triumph that had been building for years.

The previous Saint Patrick's Day Taoiseach Liam Cosgrave had been in Washington, speaking before both houses of Congress and urging that no succor be given to the IRA. He joined a long line of Irish representatives who had attempted to bring the new realities to America, especially to the powerful and those Irish-Americans prone to support the IRA efforts through NORAID. Out of reflex and innocence many Irish-Americans were thought by Dublin to donate as an act against partition and for unity, a historical gesture. Some did. Some gave to NORAID in hopes the money would be spent on guns, not on welfare, as was promised. Some knew that those shot by the IRA were likely to be Irish—RUC or UDR—but the wrong lot. Whatever the intention, the Dublin government wanted the flow into the republican movement stopped. And every official and many official visitors brought the word.

In the year after Cosgrave's speech the Irish campaign to influence the American establishment as well as Irish-Americans had continued with enormous help from John Hume, a shrewd and convincing enemy of the Provisionals. He had from the first cultivated American contacts and opportunities, had traveled in America, had met with Senator Edward Kennedy in 1974. Many American politicians would have agreed with Kennedy in his 1969 telegram to the Northern Ireland civil rights chairman: "Today the Irish struggle again, but not alone. Your cause is a just cause. The reforms you seek are basic to all democracies worthy of the name. My hopes and prayers go with you." By the mid-seventies times had changed and Hume, when he was able, had kept his American friends informed of those changes. He found American politicians willing if innocent listeners, even the Irish-Americans, often particularly the Irish-Americans adrift between the Easter Rising and civil rights. Hume and others insisted dollars to the Provos meant deaths in Ireland. To sop up some of the dollars for "welfare" the Resurgent Trust was founded by Tony O'Reilly, vice-president of Heinz in

Pittsburgh and an Irish success story in America. Mostly the rich and comfortable were attracted.

The famous Provo money was hard to find, hard to raise. Provo money was little money, bake-and-buy sales, dances in suburban motels, a five-dollar bill in a jar. Little people were the target, those thought innocent. Hume, and increasingly Dublin, not neglecting the little people or the money to be found with the rich and successful Irish-Americans, focused on Washington, on the politically powerful.

With the collapse of the convention Hume had found a temporary home in 1976 at Harvard's Center for International Affairs through the good auspices of Kennedy. The senator had been a prime convert to the decent Dublin view. This analysis, focused on the evils of the IRA in particular, was urged by Hume in Cambridge, in Boston, and Washington, in seminars, over lunch, at a series of meetings, formal and informal. And his work, independent and unsponsored, paralleled the work of the Irish Embassy. The embassy, with a paltry budget, no real leverage, little entry, and only a sound case to argue, managed still to convince much of official and unofficial Washington that all was not in Ireland as the Provos' advocates claimed. An enormously effective lobby can be created, as Greek-Americans demonstrated over Cyprus, with great conviction, a good case simply made, and persistence.

Directed out of Seán Donlon's Anglo-Irish section of the Foreign Affairs Department, the few officials concerned created a new presence in Washington and throughout the United States. Money helps, a national net of some sort is a prime asset, and a few good men at the center. The Embassy did not have a national net, rather the reverse in NORAID; but the times and the approach were appropriate, and the diplomats persisted— the press officer at the New York consulate, Michael Lillis, was moved to Washington as political counselor in 1976 to oversee the effort. He had created the Four Horsemen beginning with O'Neill, a real coup. In 1978 Seán Donlon became ambassador and intensified the effort. He was well prepared and utterly serious, as was appropriate for one who once had intended to enter the Church and had been trained at Maynooth, where he had known John Hume.

Donlon could be witty, wry, effective in public, bound upon the stage and take over the audience. He could sing, play the piano and the genial Irishman but with a cold heart—cold at least as far as romantic Irish-American Republicans were concerned. Not American Republicans, however, for these he wooed to effect. President Ronald Reagan came to the Embassy twice, and those in the administration then and later accepted Dublin's views on Irish matters, on the Troubles, on the IRA. At least President Jimmy Carter had pushed the British to make a move toward accommodation—with American money promised. Reagan and the Republicans did no pushing, nor did a growing number of Irish-Americans. The Friends of Ireland, who came to the issue after the first Kennedy St. Patrick's Day declaration was signed by the other three horsemen, were no friends to NORAID or the traditional Irish-American nationalists but took their lead from the Irish Embassy. They were, in effect, being asked to do nothing, letting Dublin handle matters, although money was always welcome. And so romantic Ireland no longer flourished in the American diaspora except among the NORAID faithful. Dublin had put the right people in the right place to win the Irish-Americans from Reagan down. The Americans were impressed by the seriousness of purpose of those involved. Hume, Lillis, and Donlon were practical men talking sense. They had an effect.

The British helped where they could. In Ham Whyte, the director-general of the British Information Service and deputy consul-general from 1972–76, they found an effective voice in New York, center of the American media. He and his huge staff of ninety were worth more than the more formal diplomats or heavy-handed strategists. As Sir Hamilton Whyte he was back with the British United Nations Mission from 1979–81. By then the Irish battle was largely won except for rationalizing the inevitable problems of an internal war within a democracy. As for Ireland, the British did not as did Dublin sell what was good for Ireland but what was good for the Western alliance; and they emphasized how awful were the gunmen. In any case Ireland was not a vital matter in the Anglo-American special relationship and increasingly was not even an irritant— after all, Dublin was mostly happy with the American posture.

The crucial factor in the seventies was that amid the uncertainties of the Carter administration, there was little interest in Ireland. This policy continued under Reagan despite his brief journey to find his problematical roots. If Tip O'Neill, a Democrat of the old school, a Boston Irish-American traditionalist, used his position and prestige to condemn IRA violence, Dublin had done quite well indeed. This American political consensus position had come after great effort by very few and at no real cost. The Irish Embassy could convince not only those who might as well buy the British case but also Irish-Americans who might have been prone to heed the Provos' argument, cleaned up for American consumption.

Those who wanted to believe in the IRA as a Marxist-Leninist threat to NATO could do so. Those who wanted to believe in the IRA were first brought to question the IRA's motives and then their intentions. Nothing helped the Anglo-Irish effort more than the reality of the IRA means. The cost of the armed struggle trickled in sporadically over the evening news with television tape of bomb explosions and weeping women, reports of dead civilians, the tales of the gunmen and the echoes of the explosions and slaughter in London and Birmingham. The IRA was seen as cause, not victim, ruthless, brutal, and unrelenting— and the British had a major effort going to see that this was the image that reached America. The bombs, the costs of the armed campaign, the atrocities, too often repeated, tended to drown out the concerns of those early friends of Irish nationalism in Washington.

These early spokesmen in Congress, not unmindful of the Irish vote in their district, had been convinced first that the civil liberties issue was prime and the British were at fault, and then that the British remained at fault and at bottom were imperialists facing a risen people in part represented by the IRA. Congressman Mario Biaggi, a much decorated former policeman who knew little of Ireland, provided a hearing for this view and ultimately established the Ad Hoc Committee on Ireland in September 1977. By then Congress had lost an early interest in civil rights. Some in Congress and in Washington, however, stayed with the civil liberties agenda, which was constantly renewed by fresh violations and novel usurpations by London and at times Dublin. They stayed with it far longer than the Irish Embassy felt warranted and far longer than the British government felt reasonable. So too did Biaggi, until his career foundered on other matters and he ultimately ended in jail.

There were as well those advocates who pushed the more traditional view of British imperial intentions, in particular the Irish National Caucus, formed in 1973 by Father Seán McManus, a nationalist priest from a republican family in Fermanagh. McManus remained sympathetic to the republican view despite the usual movement feuds and disputes over his efforts. NORAID people had very little impact outside of their own believers once the early days had passed and ultimately were registered as agents of a foreign power to counter federal pressure. Once the arms smuggling cases began to surface, federal law enforcement agencies took a keen interest in any group not vetted by Dublin, especially NORAID. This concern led to the arrest and trial (but not the conviction) in 1982 of several NORAID people, including the elderly Michael Flannery—who had admitted the "crime" proudly but insisted that he assumed the CIA was behind the operation that handed over $16,800 for the purchase of arms for the IRA. Beyond the hard core of NORAID were the sympathetic, who in time largely preached to the converted and made life difficult for the British but converted few and influenced fewer. The conglomerate of pressure groups sympathetic to or involved with the Provos never had much of a chance despite the regular British blunders and the traditional Anglophobia in some American circles.

They were amateurs rowing a leaky boat upstream. The trendy radical times had passed even as Ireland became a complex issue not a matter of black and white hats. The American establishment tended to listen to fellow politicians. The British connection was old, valuable, and compatible. Finally, most IRA supporters lacked sophistication, tact, a grasp of the possible within Washington, and access to the mighty; and they all suffered from lack of funds. There were a variety of contributing factors operating in the America of the time: (1) The impact of international terrorism gave armed struggles under whatever auspices a bad name; (2) a small, democratic Irish government of decent men, politicians and statesmen, colleagues, claiming the gunmen were evil and even Communist proved most effective; (3) the presence within the American establishment of several emissaries and visitors had a profound personal effect on key individuals; (4) the rising tide of conservatism that swept away President Jimmy Carter and brought in Ronald Reagan in 1980 had no sympathy for Irish rebels; and (5) there was a concomitant rise in general admiration for Britain and increasingly after 1979 for Prime Minister Margaret Thatcher. On any scales the United Kingdom would weigh more heavily than Ireland, but after 1969 Anglophobia of the Irish-American community was for a time no longer refreshed with new emigrants since a by-product of the Kennedy reform emigration bill's nonethnic quotas reduced the legal Irish influx. And the position of the Dublin government convinced many Irish-Americans that the old posture was no longer valid.

The Irish Republic took a posture not unlike that of the United Kingdom, one amenable even to Irish-American politicians. Few of them depended on an Irish vote and they sympathized with their Dublin friends under gunman threat. Still, it was the specific and carefully orchestrated efforts of the Irish government that transformed the historic American reflexes on Irish matters, especially within certain blocs of opinion. The Embassy led the many from a suspicion of imperial Britain through a distaste for partition to an understanding of London's problem. Others proved quite sympathetic to London's strategic analysis, but most Americans bought the Decent Dublin Analysis. And almost everything the Irish republicans did strengthened this purchase, atrocity by atrocity.

The specific intent, then, of both the British and Irish governments was to cut off IRA funding and arms sources in the United States. Doing so they sold their interpretation, which was bought largely intact by those with little knowledge about "Ulster," and even by Irish-Americans who had only a nostalgia for the old sod. Those most nostalgic were likely to be those least sympathetic to radical gunmen, which was an immediate Dublin-London asset. In London, especially within Conservative circles, the IRA was a Communist threat. They felt this especially about the Officials, who retained a place in the pantheon of enemies longer than their role in Northern Ireland would have indicated; but often, particularly after the rhetoric of the *Republican News* and *An Phoblacht* became more radical, they felt the same about the Provos. The strategic analysis was that the IRA was a rerun of Castro: a small red island off the shores of Europe, a threat to NATO, a potential seat of international terrorism, a serious danger to the West. The fact that this view, dearly and often sincerely held on the far Right in Britain, had few takers did not inhibit the salesmen. The IRA-as-Communist was generally bought by those convinced of London's priorities in any case. Thus, the Provos were Fascists to the radical Left and Communists to the militant Right.

Much more telling was the Dublin argument, seconded by London, that the IRA was undemocratic, unrepresentative, and was killing Irish people. In time instead of being "Communists" the Provos were transmuted into "Fascists." Democratic politicians could understand this easily. No one wanted to back the gun in politics. Thus Dublin sold an Irish body politic riven by IRA subversion and murder as opposed to the IRA's claim of a war of national liberation. London too, caught as always between the necessities of a low-intensity war and the advantages of criminalizing the struggle, if only in rhetoric, tended to stress the same themes.

London, however, chose to believe that much of the Irish trouble was a direct result of American money and arms—just as many in England felt that if the Dublin government *really* wanted to shut down the gunmen it would be possible. Thus the British had real short-term goals: NORAID crippled, the fugitive gunmen extradited, the covert arms trade ended. And they found a sympathetic response in America at all levels of law enforcement and with most regional and national officials. These were often real crimes, not political problems, and so the British managed real returns. One was the reluctant realization that the FBI and the Treasury Department's Bureau of Alcohol, Tobacco, and Firearms were not going to solve the Irish problem. For a long time London was like all those who blame outside agitators for internal problems: Much would be well if NORAID were frustrated, all American help to the IRA ended, the fugitives sent home. Then all that would be needed would be to close the border with the Republic, another dream, especially of those who had never seen the border. So the British in Washington were very serious about the worth of the American connection to the IRA.

Dublin, on the other hand, felt the Irish-Americans of NORAID and their friends only aggravated the situation. That was not the key. The key was to acquire the support of the American establishment for Dublin's interests. Whatever happened to the IRA contacts, American support for Dublin's view might be crucial to the fashioning of any ultimate, congenial accommodation. This was the real prize, not putting Michael Flannery of NORAID in jail. Dublin wanted Washington on their side, including the Irish-Americans stripped of any lingering fondness for the romantic IRA or even any distaste for British strategic interests in the island.

With Ireland a minor matter, certainly in Anglo-American relations, London wanted mostly specific help in isolating Ulster: no arms, no money, no refuge for fleeing gunmen, no kind words or chiding editorials, no haven for the enemy. And Washington did what it could and continued to do so year after Reagan year and on into the Bush administration, an indication that the American establishment stayed convinced even if the isolation of Northern Ireland brought no end to the crisis.

Dublin wanted understanding—their understanding—of Irish reality and in time aid in meeting the cost of any accommodation—and took as a sign of American support many of the specific steps that so interested the British. It was easy for those in authority in America to listen to the Irish, who wanted only that they learn the truth as written in Dublin, a truth all politicians and any wise man would accept. It was congenial to the United States authorities to oppose the IRA as terrorists. The British wanted the FBI to intervene in arms cases, NORAID penalized or circumscribed, fugitives returned—wanted them because the IRA was a threat to the West. It was easy to agree in a time when terrorism was a priority and effective counterterrorism so elusive. So Britain got real help: Even if no one believed the Provos were Fascists or Communists, they certainly acted like terrorists—and that was more than good enough.

Washington accented the official view from both Dublin and London almost before the two recognized their own mutuality of interests. The Anglo-Irish effort was an effective two-prong attack. Each was independent, each had different priorities and different arguments, and both were effective. The wavering and sensible could accept Dublin's view with minimal costs and the convinced and the determined could continue on the road that pleased the British. The strategy worked by 1977 and the posture of the American establishment on Irish matters remained an acceptance of the decent Dublin view and a willingness to facilitate British demands. It was a diplomatic triumph over ancient loyalties, considerable prejudice, fading fashions, and the not too impressive propaganda efforts of the republican movement.

None of those involved was at first aware just how irrelevant the Irish issue was in Washington power circles: a small country far away that evoked nostalgia, not detailed knowledge or great strategic concern. Some Americans retained a concern for any infringement on the civil rights of Northern Catholics. Few were aware of the vulnerability of either Northern Protestants or citizens of the Republic. Many Irish-Americans still felt partition was unfortunate and unity a proper goal. Few saw that the United States had any real role in condemning the first or seeking the second. America had no real strategic interests in the island. Let Britain handle its own. Certainly the United States had no interests of any sort in the internal affairs of the Republic or the province of Northern Ireland but only a disinterested concern for peace, accommodation, decency, along with a willingness at some future time to contribute financially to that end. As President Carter said on August 30, 1977, "In the event of a settlement, the United States government would be prepared to join with others to see how additional job-creating investment could be encouraged, to the benefit of all the people of Ireland."

The details, schisms, atrocities, and outrages that seemed unbearable in Belfast or Tyrone barely received newspaper space in the *Washington Post* or *The New York Times* unless they were especially dreadful. There was always space for novel and spectacular Irish news. In 1977 the involvement of an RUC constable in the kidnapping of a Catholic priest, Father Hugh Murphy, on April 23 in retaliation for the murders of RUC constables Millar McAllister and William Turbitt the day before by the IRA was not even a one-day sensation. Those interested in Ireland responded as was their wont: more evidence of RUC complicity in Protestant terror or a rare example of the pressures on the police under constant attack by gunmen. Most Americans were simply not interested in Ireland. Those who might have differed on matters of Irish nationalism were those found making the running for compromise and conciliation rather than unification. If the Four Horsemen were public enemies of the IRA, then the armed struggle would never find comfort in America.

Increasingly this was the case: Arms were caught, shippers stopped, boats trapped, fugitives extradited after years in prison as the Justice Department appealed and appealed. Sinn Féin speakers were banned, sympathizers placed on the FBI's list. Scathing editorials in *The New York Times* regularly accepted British views. Scathing editorials in most newspapers were horrified at each newly reported major atrocity. No new radical recruits came to the IRA's cause; there was no rush from the more affluent Irish-Americans, no volunteers as the seventies grew more conservative. Times grew slowly harder and less promising. America was too big to close down as refuge and armory but there would be no help, no toleration, no diplomatic aid or comfort. It was a grievous loss that went a long way to assuring that Ulster would not be internationalized, would remain an internal issue on a small island with consequences only for the involved and the nostalgic observer.

The Provisionals tended to focus on the American assets, preach there to the converted, adjust the exported political line to the conservatism of their supporters, and take the money donated for welfare openly or guns secretly. In 1977 the gun problem was largely solved, given the combination of a declining need by the smaller active service units and the steady flow of American weapons arranged in New York and Dublin. No secret army ever has sufficient arms and the IRA would have dearly loved to have acquired more elegant and more advanced weapons, in particular ground-to-air hand-held missiles to hit helicopters. They did acquire American military M-60 machine guns that could and did damage helicopters and replacements for the RPG-7 rocket launchers, but mostly they made do. In some cases the local product was very effective indeed: the truck-bed mortars, grenades that stuck to the target, and a firebomb made by mixing crystallized ammonium nitrate with aluminum filings and fixing it to cans of petrol. In fact there was a mini-industry within certain republican circles on the island that continued to produce the components for explosive devices from local material or from chemicals, and at first this industry did not worry the authorities. So the IRA could persist with a limited but effective armory.

The persistence throughout 1977 was at a lower level than in 1976 but still deadly. The great decline in the death total was a result of the tapering away of the sectarian killings. The failure of the convention, instead of driving the militants to guns, seemed to have the opposite effect. Direct rule was in the end British rule. Mason's enthusiasm for security matters, unlike Rees's concern with political ones, proved reassuring. The Ulsterization policy meant that the RUC, *their* RUC even if reformed and transmuted by Newman and the others, was again in the forefront of the province's defense. Increasingly on the street if not in the newspapers in 1977 rumor had it that the security forces were willing to be the boot in, and no place more effectively than during interrogation. Internment might be out but conviction on confessions was just as effective. The republican complaints of ill treatment never reached an audience beyond their own publications until Keith Kyle's "Tonight" program on BBC on March 2, 1977. Then the alleged treatment especially at Castlereagh barracks became a national issue. Mason criticized BBC as "one-sided," but even the *Belfast Telegraph* expressed concern. By the end of the year complaints against the RUC had risen to 2,000; those who alleged assault during the initial interview rose from 384 in 1976 to 671 in 1977. The result was a propaganda struggle, a fight over statements in courts, efforts by the RUC to respond with reforms to allegations they tended to reject. As Newman noted on June 24, it was the IRA's intention to damage the RUC in any way. In this case one benefit was a new front to exert pressure on a system that had provided evidence, however rationalized, that the end of detention was not an unalloyed blessing. And as observers pointed out, the introduction of a variety of reforms to protect prisoners indicated at the very least previous maltreatment. Mason and the RUC felt that this storm over Castlereagh had been weathered and could not hide the growing statistical proof that the security forces led by the RUC were narrowing the Provos' armed struggle. So month by month 1977 was proving a satisfactory year in contrast to what had gone before.

The IRA, as always, soldiered on—their great strength was persistence. For the Provisionals much had not changed. The British, the source of all political evils, were still in occupation. This occupation, despite all the clamor of reforms finished and evils corrected, still grated, for there were too few reforms to placate the minority and too many evils apparently beyond correction. Thus, while the armed struggle narrowed, the move to republican welfare politics on a parish level escalated. It gave those of the faithful without a military future a role and promised that the struggle could be carried to the South, where military means were severely circumscribed, and it fed on real grievances. If Belfast had the worst housing in Europe in December 1976, the same was true in 1977 and 1978. There were too many years to make up and too many errors, like Unity Flats and

Divis Flats in Belfast, high-rise horrors that would grow more egregious as the years passed. In July 1977 the unemployment figures were as bad as ever and as always Catholics suffered disproportionately. Those on the street corners, those who had never really worked, those who would want a first job this year or next or the year after could see no progress and cared little for reasonable explanations. Nearly ten years on and there was no provincial politics, no inevitable unity, no real purpose in the one vote, no new housing, and no job. Ten years of frustration did not yield to the conventional politics of the SDLP, despite the sensitivity and anguish expressed in their various ways by those like Fitt and Hume and Devlin. Paddy Devlin in fact left the SDLP because it was insufficiently radical. Sinn Féin, engaged in a revolutionary armed struggle, eager for absolute social justice, was ready not with textbook socialism but with new ideas and old means to force the pace of change.

During 1977 the movement shifted toward the ideas and means of Costello's IRSP-INLA, an ideological congruency eased by the growing disdain for the Stickies. Logically, perhaps, the Provos should have absorbed Costello but instead he was allowed to operate on the Left of their ecological niche to advantage. The IRSP competed ideologically with the Officials not the Provisionals and thus John White of Derry went with them where he was not attracted by the McGuinness Provisionals. Only later did the Provos lose some of their militants to the INLA, but even then it was a minor matter. And the INLA, eager to reveal militancy, took risks and structured operations with less restraint: The spectaculars would add to the noise at no cost to the Provos' more conventional supporters. Thus the INLA armed robberies in the South had already provided cover for the Great Train Robbery at Sallins—in fact, so did the Officials' armed expropriations, which the Gárdaí could not prove but were certain originated with Gardiner Place.

It was, in any case, difficult to amalgamate two such militant republican organizations when there were real advantages to separation: more recruits with two nets, more room for Séamus Costello to demonstrate his skills and independence, another option for the ideologically inclined who found Provo traditionalism, even if fading, unattractive. More important, rebel organizations develop an internal dynamic that becomes exclusive. A family is reluctant to adopt grown children or rebels other rebels: Fronts are often fabrications. A whole meld of individual characteristics, past associations, neighborhood loyalties, political attitudes, family ties, and often the luck of enlistment created a cohesiveness, especially for the Provisionals. The INLA operated outside the Provos with their own core areas of strength. Thus, the entire Official IRA unit in the Divis Flats went INLA. The grim high rise, a hard-core arena for grievance, every urban failure well represented, thus had become the Planet of the Irsps. There for a decade the INLA would have precedence, even as the movement eroded.

A danger for small groups in the underground is the vulnerability to being smashed at one go. The risk is that one or two bad operations will wipe out all potential, as in the case of Che in Bolivia—the entire *foco*. The INLA-Official feuds frightened off militants dubious about an armed struggle. The IRSP stayed small, as did the military wing, which survived both the Stickies and the British but became not a national liberation army but a small net of cells strong only in one or two places and so inclined to mix their volunteers in special operations. Their radical rhetoric found them friends in Paris and the Middle East, and so they garnered small arms shipments. And the INLA could only use small shipments.

Costello's charisma helped maintain the IRSP as an overt party, and he remained the dominant figure, the magnetic and dynamic center to his movement. In 1975, at a special meeting organized by the Committee for Irish Forum at the University of Massachusetts in Amherst, held between August 28 and September 3, he had made an enormous impression on the Americans. His presentation had run three hours instead of two, to the listeners' delight, and he had been asked to speak again. He and John White had put the IRSP on the map. The Provos had been denied visas, while the visiting Orangemen, even UDA representatives, had been noted as much as a rare species as real actors. Costello had stolen the show and he continued to dominate the IRSP-INLA. He was dynamic, manipulative, ruthless, secretive, and efficient. Often enigmatic or distasteful to others untouched by his charm or suspicious of his motives, he inspired mistrust in many republicans and in his enemies real distaste. Even within the Provos the response to him was mixed. Still, he was not taken as threat but as a potential asset. The INLA niche to the left of the Provos proved small and the attraction of the IRSP limited, North and South, so Costello's ambitions to play a major radical role, one his followers assumed was assured, came to grief. He would be a highly visible but minor actor.

The fact that he was highly visible and charismatic put him at the top of the Officials' enemies list, made him a target. He had escaped harm during the feuding but not for lack of trying on the part of the Officials. On October 5 his luck ran out. One of the premier Official gunmen, a small core of active service people clustered around Dublin GHQ kept for military needs, was Jim Flynn, one of the hard men from South Armagh. He was limited, violent, and resistant to discipline; Dublin GHQ had to keep him on a very tight leash. He could be counted on to perform but he enjoyed the exercise of power. His was a deadly revolutionary sin: He enjoyed the nasty part of the armed struggle. He liked the psychological power that came with a gun. And as the Officials closed down their war, his chances declined. What Flynn really wanted was to use the gun to achieve more general fame.

He settled on the idea of killing Costello and so entering Irish revolutionary history. His problem was simply that the feud was over, so killing Costello would be counterproductive as far as the movement was concerned. Dublin GHQ warned him off but he persisted and got what he later claimed was authority from Cahal Goulding—a nod, a wink, whatever. There was no problem in the planning. Costello now followed a regular, if cautious, routine and parked on Dublin's north side most days. His police minders were often careless and at times absent. Flynn took a double-barreled shotgun and waited on Northbrook Avenue off the North Strand Road in Dublin until Costello drove up, parked his car, and started reading the newspaper. Flynn walked up, shot him, and walked away. He appeared a few minutes later at GHQ and let the Stickies get rid of the gun and smuggle him out of the city. Costello was dead on arrival at Richmond Hospital. In order to be famous, Flynn talked; and the INLA killed him. The INLA then had to find its way without Costello, who had fashioned the movement around his analysis, his ambitions, and his assets. Without Costello the IRSP in time became a minor political splinter but the INLA, even smaller, became a very violent cadre that persisted in the armed struggle with less restraint and in time with less ideological purpose.

In October Costello's death was seen by many Provos as a loss to the armed struggle; many attended his funeral and few felt that his legacy, the INLA, would be a threat. Then the war continued. The security forces felt that the corner was about to be turned, that there might be light at the end of the tunnel. Mason certainly so believed. The army had doubts about the RUC and the RUC about the army. The intelligence situation still left much to be desired even if those who had tinkered with dirty tricks had left. Some would never leave. The most famous case was that of Captain Robert Nairac, who, operating apparently independently as a liaison officer attached to the army's Fourteenth Intelligence Unit, took extraordinary risks in his work around South Armagh. On May 14, 1977, he was kidnapped outside a border pub by the local IRA and, after being brutally questioned, was killed. His body was not returned. For a former member of the Grenadier Guards officer who had served openly in Belfast to assume as cover that of a local was foolish. For Nairac, who in most ways was an exemplary officer, it was an arrogant blunder and ultimately fatal.

The British, however, repeatedly had probems in Northern Ireland with those who found the charms of intelligence too great for caution, restraint, or common sense. In 1977 only a beginning had been made on centralizing and extending intelligence. Given the dangers inherent in covert work and the bureaucratic rivalries over personality, power, and policy differences, there was under Mason, as there had been under Rees, a flawed intelligence effort. Too many people were still minding the store. There was no unity of purpose and too much intrigue disguised as initiative. At least elsewhere Mason and so the cabinet, despite worries, could see tangible evidence of security progress.

What was achieved on the military front was hardly matched elsewhere. The Northern Ireland Office was not interested in provincial politics and so there were no initiatives: Direct rule might concentrate minds. The failed loyalist strike in the spring was good news but the loyalist paramilitaries remained as a latent evil and one particularly bothersome for the RUC being shaped by Newman into a real police force instead of a friend of the Protestant defenders. And in 1977 what should have been the latest triumph of the Peace People was recognized locally, if not among the media or the foreign peace establishment, as its last hurrah.

The effective end of the Women's Peace Movement, the Peace People, mass reconciliation, the influence and even the acceptability of Mairead Corrigan and Betty Williams, came at the very moment of greatest recognition. On October 10, 1977, the wire services reported in Belfast that the Nobel Peace Committee had just announced that Corrigan and Williams were winners of the Nobel Peace Prize for 1976, with the 1977 prize to go to Amnesty International. It was like hitting the global lottery, the image sweeps. But the first response from each finally produced for the begrudgers and opponents, long isolated by the difficulties of attacking "peace," a place to fit the wedge. Mairead, after bursting into tears, spoke, and among other comments said, "What am I going to do with the prize money? My mother always told me I'd never have any money." Betty Williams in London explained immediately when told of the award that "Mairead and I are not going to spend it, as many people think! We are going to put it into our trust [Peace People Trust]." This was what everyone had assumed: The prize went to the two as a symbol and the money would be used for peace. It seemed a wondrous moment in a year that had revealed the difficulties of organizing that peace. The great herd of the international media returned, attention was refocused on the wonders of peace and the accomplishment of two women in giving Ireland hope. It was the culmination of a laudatory book, *Mairead Corrigan Betty Williams*, by French journalist Richard Deutsch, keen observer of the Northern Irish scene, whose enthusiasm for peace shadowed his perception of Irish reality. The prize and the book are the last grace notes of a crusade that soon wound down. Everyone so wanted good news from Ireland that the Peace People had become not just trendy but a cause—Joan Baez wrote the introduction to Deutsch's book. Yet the Nobel Prize was the beginning of the end. Betty Williams decided to keep her half of the money. And horrified Mairead Corrigan, to maintain a solid front, kept her half too. The stories about fur coats became the reality of peace money in two pieces, one for Williams and one for Corrigan. And so the Nobel Prize was the beginning of the end.

Ciaran McKeown was ignored by the Nobel Committee. Then he was ignored by Williams on the money matter, which he did not pursue. It was too late. The damage was done. The movement's increasing problems in 1977 were ignored by the media. No one wanted to know that the movement had crested. The yea-sayers had an investment in peace, reported the good news for a change. From the first the Peace People had problems with their opposition to the IRA. Their general condemnation of violence seemed to distinguish between paramilitary violence, dreadful, and British army violence, not so dreadful. The call for the withdrawal of toleration for members of the various secret armies—the advocacy of felon setting, aiding the police, even informing, in Irish society—cost the movement further support but not yet among its advocates. Then the province had to be for or against the Queen's visit in August 1977; any position was sure to alienate some. And so it did. The two ladies spoke with Queen Elizabeth for twenty minutes. More people were alienated, few were attracted.

The number of those unhappy with the movement grew, sometimes out of sight, sometimes not. The irritation of still unnoticed social workers and community people who had long toiled in the vineyards of goodness attracted no cameras. The anger of Northern politicians, most particularly Paddy Devlin, accused by some Peace People of being the cause of the Troubles, did receive coverage, albeit hardly sympathetic. All the province's politicians, even the most cantankerous and militant, had invested much time and risked real danger in what they saw as a vocation that was now damned by housewives who created Peace People by television. Like many other isolated and divided people, many preferred to be divided in private, away from the television cameras that followed every move of the Peace People. Finally and especially, Ireland was always filled with begrudgers.

Mairead Corrigan, Betty Williams, and especially Ciaran McKeown had long been targets of jealousy, malice, spite, and even fair criticism that appeared in adversary newspapers, during pub gossip, and over cocktails at the university. There were complaints about the long foreign tours. McKeown was in Norway. The ladies were accepting degrees at Yale. McKeown was in Israel. They were accepting an award in Berlin. Everyone went to America. President Jimmy Carter was an admirer. Peace de luxe. There seemed to be delusions of grandeur in the new worldview. And the mean squabbles and rivalries at the top, real or imagined, were common currency in Belfast, in Northern Ireland. Prominence and so power meant, inevitably, naturally, criticism, fair and cruel. There were rumors of sin and photographs of fur coats. There were rumors of quarrels, not all baseless. Few of these were found in the enthusiasm of the television producers, newspaper editorial writers, or foundation program writers.

The grave difficulty of turning enthusiasm into an effective institution of change was ignored. The Peace People Assembly did no more than occupy those eager to participate but unable to see the way to act on events. The Peace People no longer had either a significant constituency or a clear mission. Yes, peace was popular, but then? Then the movement began taking stands that alienated, fashioned forms that had to compete, became part of the main, no longer a lightning rod for frustration. And what else could they have done? March on forever?

The peace marchers had gone home after the Boyne in 1976, leaving the leaders in the large Peace House at 224 Lisburn Road in Belfast, purchased with the Norwegian money, to sort out the future, if any. Papers, assemblies, programs, the journal *Peace by Peace,* the conferences and prizes were real, often literally saved lives, but somehow not the same as the marches, the wonder of standing among thousands on the banks of the Boyne or in the mean streets of Belfast united by zeal in good cause. The glory days were gone. The Peace People were, however, still good news in a bad news arena. So during the autumn of 1977 the first signs of the slow disintegration were ignored by the media—and by the Peace People— while the march to Oslo and the prize was covered in detail.

After Oslo the inevitable decline in euphoria occurred, accelerating when the prize did not go to the movement but only to Williams and Corrigan, not even McKeown; and when the money did not go to the movement either, the mandate of the media and the goodwill of many evaporated. The two women had the right to keep the money, of course, but to do so alienated many, perhaps most of those who had tasted the euphoria of the great marches. "They took the money" was what the begrudgers needed. In April, despite a prediction of worsening violence, McKeown said, "We have turned the corner and the war is beginning to disintegrate." Instead, after the Nobel Prize the movement disintegrated.

Increasingly the movement's grand purpose evaporated in everyday difficulties. A Peace assembly was just one more assembly, nothing like the exhilaration of the early days. A meeting was a meeting, raising money and making telephone calls and still no peace. Caught in the center of a web of enthusiasm and admiration, the leaders took a while to realize their act had been closed, if to glowing reviews. The media was reluctant to let go, the peace establishment and foundations kept the faith longer, but in the end the quarrels and violence of the province edged out peace. The Nobel Prize was the end of an extraordinary moment, oversold and overreported but still real.

There were fewer takers to wage peace. The months ran by and a year and another year and everyone nearly had forgotten but the involved and their neighbors. In 1978 the three founders withdrew from the executive. There was less money. Far from living in luxury, McKeown was in debt. And the organization was an emotional drain as well. The problem of special status for prisoners—the H-Block issue—caused dissension. All outside issues produced division. Morale declined. Money stopped coming freely, often at all. There was talk of returning to the old days, reorganizing as a women's movement. There was a wrangle in 1979 over the chairmanship. The disagreement at the top became intricate, interlaced with outside political arguments and personal differences. At the bottom, almost everyone had gone home.

In February 1980 the movement had irreconcilable if inexplicable divisions at the top. The chairman, Peter McLachlan, resigned. Betty Williams resigned for family reasons and moved to the United States in 1982. Ciaran McKeown had gone back to journalism but ended for a time as a typesetter and until 1988 associated with Belfast's Lyric Theater. Mairead Corrigan remained as chairperson until 1981, when she married Jack Maguire. His wife, Anne, Mairead's sister, unreconciled to her children's death and the continued Northern violence, had committed suicide in 1980. Mairead Corrigan-Maguire remained an executive member of the organization, now concerned with a group called Youth for Peace, a five-a-side Catholic-Protestant soccer league, bus trips to prisons, and religiously mixed holiday tours. These were programs of the long haul, community programs, small, effective, obscure. When Mairead Corrigan-Maguire toured the United States in 1992, she would be asked on an Irish cable program to explain who she was "so people would know."

The Peace People's movement that trailed off into posthumous fame and strategic futility, into recriminations and resignations, did not so much disappear as come full circle. There was no peace on a grand scale, no general euphoria, but only incremental reforms, individual successes. By no means an absolute failure, the organization persisted, although by 1986 there were reputed to be only two hundred members. It drew money from abroad, especially Norway.

Then, especially in the first months of 1976, the general desire for an end of violence (if at no clear cost) had been demonstrated by a great many in Northern Ireland and supported abroad by both the well-meaning and the self-interested. The Peace People had orchestrated these longings into visible marches and demonstrations. The province wanted peace. All this was good to know but of little practical use. In fact the entire movement had lacked reality, had been constructed on an ill-articulated but very pressing emotional desire for an end to the murder, threats, violence, and humiliations of all sorts arising in a society under internal siege.

Peace was simply, if at all, defined as an absence of the unpleasant and deadly. It was to be achieved by witness and declaration, afternoon outings, demonstrations and displays. Those who organized those demonstrations and displays, their friends and advisers, those who gave all of every day to the structure, to licking stamps and making phone calls and scheduling arrangements, mistook the act for the deed, for the power to impose peace, their efforts as an organization that could effect events. Instead they, like the radical civil rights people before them, were engaged in mobilization: raising the consciousness of those prepared for enthusiasm, considering commitment.

It was a dramatic first step but only that and only if elaborated into effective action. When the leaders began to organize, publish a paper, take positions on less ethereal issues, propose institutions and spend money, they found turning the gold of enthusiasm into spendable coin another act altogether. In a revivalist tent, amid the glitter and drama, the charisma of the preacher, it is exciting and rewarding to make a commitment, to be born again. It is, of course, more difficult to keep the faith on a daily basis. And if this faith requires sacrifices and painful adjustments then attendance at chapel may begin to lag. Gospel shows often become just shows—a few saved and many entertained. The faithful are encouraged and the lost are tempted.

The Peace People could encourage, could entertain and attract, could in the moments of mass euphoria exhilarate, but the long haul is made by those absolutely transformed: true believers. The less novelty, the fewest adjustments, the easier it is to propagate the faith. The IRA, for example, had arisen on unarticulated community convictions and existed on toleration. No great act was required, no participation, no attendance at events, no real change. The reward was being defended. It thus could "work" on a provincial basis but do nothing to change even incrementally the day-to-day attitudes of the involved. The broader the scale the less "peace" worked until only a haze of good feeling spread over the island. The Peace People had to compete with deeply held, if often unarticulated, individual and community beliefs. This was obscured by the euphoria of the moment.

In the early days acts were events. There was no need to shape reality, only to appear as witness. There was no enemy and no incremental returns in power or lasting returns. One marched in the good cause and went home. The Peace People proved to be a children's crusade, charged with emotion, dramatic, a trek across the Irish arena by the decent and often desperate, a journey watched uneasily by all those with real power and practical agendas. Such enthusiasm could lead the frustrated to other faiths, to other commitments, into affecting the future in uncertain ways. The practical could not tell if such enthusiasm could be harnessed to their disadvantage or harnessed at all. An era of good feeling may write no legislation, change no law, erode no long-held bias, despite all the media coverage. To what were the marchers committed beyond "peace"?

If the commitment required denial and sacrifice of existing assets—time, money, a lust for vengeance, power or prestige, the faith or the past, secondary or primary benefits of society as organized—then attrition began. The civil rights people had discovered this earlier. To attract there must be a role that could return minute but real dividends, returns that would allow the construction of an organization to structure both the sacrifices and rewards while maintaining an overarching sense of purpose. This could be done, euphoria and all, at a community level, even with primitive organization, as the women who came to mark the accident site discovered. Big, however, did not mean better but diffusion. The Peace People, like the radicals, had a dream—peace, which for them meant essentially the absence of a strife that arose from real, long-lived, seemingly intractable differences that would remain untouched. They, like the radicals, marched. They, unlike the radicals, could not produce tangible returns.

The Peace People at first did not organize to erode the causes of violence, only to propose an end to it. The paramilitaries caused violence and should stop doing so. The Peace People offered no means to that effect only an exhilarating opportunity to display an aspiration. Such display led only to more displays and the erosion of enthusiasm. Few but the IRA openly opposed them. Yet they had nothing to offer that would make the incremental changes necessary to erode grievance. A peace person was not born again into an all-encompassing faith, found no formulas for the future, only attended at little cost a charismatic moment.

Nearly all the Peace People returned to their same circumscribed lives, hedged by assumptions and axioms that tolerated a present that included institutionalized violence by most of those with power. The Peace People proved that there could be a consensus in the province but not one that could be exploited in any pragmatic way. Any step beyond the parade route evoked contention and schism. Peace could not be achieved but in pieces. None could find the proper master plan or all the pieces. No one could organize such a process of agenda especially with the existing mix of priorities. The years of assemblies, conferences, and programs were neither revolutionary nor any more effective in producing peace than had been the case with those who had always pursued small goals. For a brief, glowing moment the Peace People had seemingly gone for everything—rather like the other marchers in 1968 and 1969.

The civil rights radicals had mobilized minority opinion: Something could be done about existing grievances. And they had offered a way: Bypass the intractable impervious system by appeal to opinion, particularly British opinion. London had power to effect change and that power could be tapped with moral suasion. The provocative march was the means. The unhappy and disgruntled could act. The minority was persuaded that they could demonstrate and that such demonstrations would lead to the amelioration of grievances. Mostly, in 1968–70, the minority did not demonstrate, but stayed in and watched on the telly, observed from the pub or the front room. The minority, however, first tolerated and then supported those who did demonstrate. This support was crucial in 1969, but it was not the same as participation. The minority was mobilized but only haltingly organized: That would come later, with the parties and paramilitaries, would take years, and would rupture the previous consensus about ends and means.

Since the movement had dealt in attitudes and emotions, none could easily apply the apparent lessons: the desire for peace and quiet, the need for legitimacy for all Irish actors, the potential of the many untapped by the conventional, and the enormous difficulty of structuring change in a society thought to be in the midst of a radical transformation. The old attitudes, the lure of secondary benefits, the existing faiths had been confronted but not eroded. The legacy of the past inhibited the implementation of simple goodwill in a meaningful general way.

Such goodwill had a long and productive role in the province but neither a highly visible one nor a generally effective one. Particular effects, despite the persistence of violence, perhaps because of the persistence of violence that attracted so many alien eyes, from the media to the historians, could be achieved on an individual and community level. Doing good paid returns but only in small groups. And when such reforms, mainly directed at the injustice arising from a divided society, were raised to a provincial level they generated opposition that did not exist when the good was so obvious in the lads' camp trip, the bus to Long Kesh, or the football team.

Ideologically the assumption that the province's problems came primarily or solely from a divided society, the analysis sold effectively by London, was anathema to those who found in the British the never failing source of Ireland's woes. For many the erosion of difference did not address the real problem. And those who cherished differences, their way of life or their faith, and distinction saw only danger in any ecumenical move. Even toleration was not considered a civil virtue by many—it might lead, would lead, to subversion, treason, heresy. And even when toleration existed, the two communities, however intimately entangled, at heart lived apart, ignorant of the dynamics and faith of the other.*

Provincial politics was mostly a simple reflection of the competing and exclusive faiths. Those who had organized the Alliance Party in 1970 and to an extent those who sought class political bases sought to offer another way, a middle way. They had arisen as a means to end the divisions in Northern Ireland society. Most of those divisions arose from tenets cherished by many. Thus the nonsectarian, moderate parties soon had their constituents slotted into the sectarian society. Certain members of the tribe would vote Alliance or Labour but they were still members of the tribe, perhaps not even lapsed although obviously remiss. And the tribes, Protestant or Catholic, usually had little interest in even disinterested overtures. Whatever the Officials might claim about working-class unity, the orators were seen as fronts for gunmen of the IRA, worthy of emulation but for opposite purpose. Those who chose the Alliance were easily spotted, middle-class, without the fundamentals of the faith, who could vote as they chose because they had the assets to protect their way of life.

The provincial political arena proved too demanding for most who sought real returns from nonsectarian efforts. The political ground had been plowed, sowed with mines, soaked with blood. Any advance had to be over old ground against adamant foes in possession of the high ground. This was what the Peace People found as they marched about the border of the battlefield, fearful of entering and with no other tactical goal but movement. Some moderates felt that a valid approach was to nibble at the edges of the arena, restricting the room for battle, winning converts to decency one at a time.

Small efforts to erode differences were constant. As the years passed there was a long and honorable parade of those who belonged to interchurch groups, worked in the inner cities, invited children for nonsectarian vacations, started small schools, ran seminars or pleaded for nonviolence in Sunday school lectures or at the university, ran conferences, or established tiny groups with intimate contacts in the most militant centers. The peace establishment made Northern Ireland,

*The finest short introduction to the complexity of the divided Northern Irish society can be found in Rosemary Harris's "Anthropological Views on 'Violence' in Northern Ireland" in Alan O'Day and Yonah Alexander (editors), *Ireland's Terrorist Trauma: Interdisciplinary Perspectives* (New York: St. Martin's Press, 1989), pp. 75–100.

particularly Belfast, a stopover on the crusade toward conflict resolution. There were guest speakers and go-betweens, poets and painters who would not take sides, printers who skipped costs for peace pamphlets, and solicitors and barristers who gave free services to the decent. There were all sorts of groups and initiatives and approaches and eventually even institutions.

Some of this activity by many of the groups became ritual, acts that made the involved feel noble or decent or even relevant, an act that seldom cost serious investment or entailed great risk but might, indeed, do good. A stand against sin and for justice or peace or both could hardly do harm. As the Peace People had demonstrated, a great many people did want peace of some sort and would provide witness to that effect. As all the seminars and conferences indicated, everyone was to some degree at fault and everyone could to some degree aid in a move toward toleration, accommodation, an end to the slaughter. Very often the conclusions of the involved could be disputed only by those deeply involved in furthering the violence.

> We do not want to put forward messianic solutions to our problems, but we believe that the lack of agreement over political structures on the island inhibits the development of a whole range of normal social relationships. One of these is employment, the creation of which is seriously hampered by the energy and resources devoted to the containment of violence. The relationship of Churches to each other, respect for different traditions and for human rights, the rights of minorities, all of these also suffer in the context of violence. We believe change is possible, that things can be better than they are. We believe future generations will be puzzled and scandalized at our failure to forge more just and respectful relationships, and to pass on to them an island on which political structures are less contentious and on which there is less needless poverty.*

Who could disagree? And what did it mean? What was actually to be done? Much of this work recycled past efforts. The conclusions were a mix of cunning code words and proper positioning enormously important to the involved but irrelevant beyond the seminar room or the conference hall. Such exercises were effective as small-group encounters by those favoring conciliation, encounters that encouraged the participants, perhaps involved the marginal, worked one-on-one, but hardly indicated means to the undeniably desirable end: tranquillity, justice, a decent life for all, an Ireland to hand on with pride. Unlike the Provos, for example, the Peace People could not agree on what was the matter with Ireland—except the present, the violence, the poverty, the misery—and these were effect, not cause. Nor could they agree on what was to be done, except love thy neighbor and follow the precepts of the Gospels. They had no vision of an ultimate Ireland except an improved model of the present.

The power of the men with guns was that they knew a means, historically valid,

*Interchurch Group on Faith and Politics, *Towards an Island That Works: Facing Divisions in Ireland* (Dublin: Interchurch Group on Faith and Politics, 1987).

seemingly functional, that paid all immediate satisfaction if at some cost. And most gunmen came with a dream: yesterday recreated, an Irish Republic, the proletariat in power—sometimes speaking Irish and at other times under Orange banners, but always in power. The seminars were reasonable and articulate; after a generation they were polished and often elegant; they were always sincere, the product of decent men in an unpleasant world. They rarely, however, produced more than published results. Others wanted more than marches and footnotes, even as they marched and noted. Many found in the theory and faith of the scholars, sociologists, anthropologists, psychologists, the clerks of nonviolence and conflict resolution, the needed foundation to begin, to begin with a few, at the beginning, to work with individual hearts and minds in the community. Some, like the Peace People, had needed no analytical foundation: Like McKeown, they thought they sensed which way the wind blew. And on a community level there were fresh breezes, even if they tended to fade out over the province and were almost always overshadowed by the persistent and visible war clouds: War was still more photogenic than peace; a bomb, no matter how rare, was more newsworthy than seminars or children's camps. The summer camps did work, the seminars might not, and even the peace marches did no harm. The rule seemed to be that small tangible programs worked. What was difficult was to make each one a little better each day on a provincial scale. Reinforcing what people were— members of the Orange Order or republicans—could be managed by provincial rituals, but changing everyday unionists and nationalists into people without the old prejudices and fears was not so easy. It had to be done one at a time, over time.

One of the more famous efforts at reconciliation and peace proved to be Corrymeela, the "Hill of Harmony," which began as a student movement in 1964, before hint of the Troubles, and became a "place of peace and tranquillity away from the troubled areas where people from both sides could rediscover their humanity and relate once again to each other as human beings."* The core had been Christians, Presbyterians mostly but not exclusively, who wanted an activist role for religion—service, not complacency or tradition. Early on the community decided to be Christian in the widest sense. This decision was unpopular among the warring and often exclusive fundamentalists of the Protestant clans, but it proved enormously useful as the Troubles escalated and Catholic children as well as Protestant from Belfast, fifty-five miles to the south, came for programs and holidays. At a ceremony in 1971 a replica of the Cross of Nails, a symbol of reconciliation from the ruins of Coventry, was received. Readings were given by four members of the community. The local Catholic priest led prayers for forgiveness and a Presbyterian minister said prayers for peace.

By 1976 Corrymeela had founded other communities in London and Dublin, where there is a reconciliation center at Glencree, and the center was better known in the world of Christian activism than in the province. In the province Corrymeela had supplied the Peace People with their office, a first home, for nine months—a most appropriate alliance between the local and the general. Most initiatives from Corrymeela were local, short, and practical. Most important,

*Alf McCreary, *Corrymeela: Hill of Harmony in Northern Ireland* (New York: Hawthorn, 1976), p. 11.

however, those involved felt, beyond the individual good of principles in practice, Corrymeela had proven that at a grassroots level the churches did not have to be part of the problem but could work toward a solution.

Corrymeela was more visible than but typical of numerous programs arising from individual concern and seeking incremental adjustment. Such small successes encouraged, unduly encouraged, the advocates of conciliation: Violence might be persistent but dedication and organization could work in the community, in small projects, in individual lives. And so it did and so encouraged those on the ground. And so it was that the lasting, effective impact of the Peace People, other than the fashioning of a nostalgic moment of hope, could be found in the miniprojects, largely directed by a few with imported funds. These worked, month after month. And they were merely some of the many initiatives, local and alien, that did so.

There was no central clearinghouse for the concerned and caring but there continued to be those who were concerned and did care, despite the daily sacrifice, despite the small returns in power or perceived change, despite the risks and discomforts. In a religiously divided society many of the most effective of such exercises arose from the concerns of the churches. The contradictions of the province could be seen in the interfaith groups, the halfway houses to toleration, the meetings in the church hall balanced against those who established lay schools or organized nonsectarian conferences. The decent saw no contradiction, for the great consensus of all those involved was the transformation of the hearts and minds of the people, one at a time, in order to achieve a tolerant society with justice for all. So individuals of all sorts and conditions tended to turn to the small, to focus on one at a time, and to hope for a cumulative effect, later.

Later in politics is often never. Later, for those with millenarian faith, is preordained. Later, for those who want a return now, this afternoon, during the next confrontation, when the time to march comes, is too late. Incremental returns are not satisfactory. Even the returns are doubtful, except that the very effort rewards the involved. Progress is not highly visible. This is just the opposition of close encounters, small groups, the charisma of the tight community. There participation rewards—and the distribution of the returns of the optimism so generated across a large group on a lasting basis had proven an elusive goal nearly everyplace. It is difficult to maintain a whole army of believers unless they remain together on the march. And this was understandably beyond the power, if not quite the vision, of many in the movement. The province remained, after as before the Peace People, divided, whoever was to blame. Those who toiled in small vineyards continued to do so without general acclaim or much notice.

There was some encouragement for those eager for a greater provincial flexibility to be found in the district council elections on May 18, 1977, the first voting under direct rule. For the loyalists the relevant issue was the failed general strike. The scattering of loyalist votes would mean that the old one-party domination of councils would give way to alignments and alliances. Those who had emerged strong from the collapse of the old convention order kept their vote. The SDLP (at 20.6 percent, down from 23.7) and the two unionists groups dominated the returns; the Alliance also did well, with 80,011 first preferences and 14.4 percent of the votes (up from 9.9 in the 1975 Convention elections), to remain a major player. The great coalition of the UUUC failed to survive the refusal of the Official Unionists Party (OUP) to back the general strike, which alienated both the DUP and Craig's Vanguard dissident Ernie Baird, whose UUUP ticket received 3.1 percent. The loyalist Vanguard (VUPP), with 1.5 percent, and Faulkner's Unionists, as the Unionist Party of Northern Ireland (UPNI), with 2.4 percent, became irrelevant. The hardening of loyalist divisions into DUP and OUP, with the SDLP keeping much of the Catholic vote and Alliance the middle, meant marginalization for the NILP (0.8 percent) and the Republican Clubs (2.6 percent). There were again independents from both the Unionists and the nationalists whose votes tended to evolve from local rivalries. Politics, in fact, had become very local and less interesting: The vote was off by 10.2 percent from the 1973 council elections. The real result was that what electoral politics existed under direct rule would for some be found in the quarrels and maneuvers of the local councils, a descent from the aspirations of the convention or in the positions of the twelve Westminster members.

There could be no politics as usual. Under Mason at the Northern Ireland Office this was felt necessary, a long pause to concentrate minds while the security forces imposed order. Mason assumed the role of overseer of the thrust for security and pacification, a role that required less an intimacy with the devices and desires of Irish hearts than a grasp of the possible means to secure the province. And with his experience in the Defense Ministry and his lack of interest in Irish subtleties, Mason was well placed. He was also enormously unpopular, representing the unpleasant face of London's presence and a lack of concern with provincial sensibilities. Especially for the nationalists and particularly the Irish republicans he was the team leader of repression, constant in his assurances that the corner had been turned and the IRA defeated, that there was light at the end of the tunnel, that a British-imposed solution was practicable—soon.

Soon never quite came, although the mix of British tactics and techniques changed the intensity of the violence, the structure of the paramilitaries, and the prospects for conciliation. Mason sought to smash the IRA's armed struggle but instead achieved an almost acceptable level of violence; only the occasional spectacular atrocity created the perception from time to time in London that all was not well in Ulster. So Mason's tenure established a pattern for the province under direct rule: steady-state violence that erupted into the evening news from time to time. More was wanted but with the IRA contained new initiatives might have more running room. What no one foresaw was that, almost despite themselves, the IRA would do the running, not by recourse to more physical force, their dearest aspiration, but through unconventional political means, a far lesser option and one often ill understood.

Mason by December 1977 in his end of the year summary felt that the year had been a success in security terms. The IRA was on the run. Mason always thought the IRA was on the run. In November Lieutenant General Sir David House was replaced as GOC Northern Ireland by Lieutenant General Sir Timothy Creasey, who was to oversee the move to RUC primacy. Creasey was Mason's kind of general, making it clear that the army should stop "messing around and take out the terrorists."* In Oman, where he had served, the terrorists had just disappeared; but it was pointed out that Belfast was not an endless desert and so hiding disappeared terrorists would be a more serious public relations matter. In fact Creasey had to trim his enthusiasm. This Mason never managed. At the end of the year he gave a jubilant interview to the *Daily Express:* "We are squeezing the terrorists like rolling up a toothpaste tube. We are squeezing them out of their safe havens. We are squeezing them away from their money supplies. We are squeezing them out of society and into prison."† The army had to suggest that even if this were true, and there was evidence to that effect, it was not judicious to tempt fate. The IRA had a tendency to respond to Mason as to a Pavlovian stimulus, striking out at his confidence.

In fact a major blow had been dealt the IRA not by Mason's men but by the Gárdaí in Dublin, who arrested Séamus Twomey on December 5 on their way to Martello Terrace, Sandycove, to arrest Séamus McCollum, who had been involved in one more failed IRA smuggling attempt, this time out of Cyprus. Thus the Irish police collected two Christmas presents. The IRA then through the agency of the Army Council passed into younger hands. For a decade Gerry Adams and Martin McGuinness, as chief of staff and/or O/C Northern Command, in tandem or alone if one were in prison, directed the movement. Beginning in 1978, then, the IRA balance had shifted permanently to the North. Dublin became a stop on the tour, not the site of GHQ. The new emphasis on the Republic and its people as a resource came simultaneously with the arrival of the Northern generation of 1969 to power. No one complained greatly in the movement because the move was seen as natural—it was a Northern war—and because even the new radical program could hardly deeply alienate colleagues who were all men of no property. The guard changed out of sight of Mason and company and the long war continued, one year not greatly different from the next.

Certainly Mason's good year in 1977 had been a less violent year but still barely acceptable. Chief Constable Newman felt the police had made the effort, saying, "1977 will undoubtedly stand out as [a year] in which the police with the support of the Army, made an enormous effort to reduce violence."‡ The official figures indicated that in some part the effort had been productive. Provincial deaths were down from 1976's 297 to 112: British army, 15; RUC, 8; RUCR, 6; UDR, 14; and civilians, 69. The biggest drop was in civilian casualties. There were few sectarian murders and IRA bombing was more discreet. Also, shootings drooped to 1,181 from 1,908, explosions to 366 from 766, and armed robberies, despite the interparamilitary competition, declined to 591 from 813. So Mason had cause, if not for jubilation, at least for confidence that the tide was flowing his way: The IRA armed struggle was declining in intensity, the Officials were into politics, the INLA was beheaded, the Protestant paramilitaries had been frustrated in their general strike and were appearing in court, the RUC was taking the lead, and the army was in capable hands. It had not been a very good year but it certainly had been better than 1976. There might be hope in persistence.

*Hamill, p. 221.
†Ibid., p. 221.
‡Ibid., p. 221.

16

A Time of Attrition:
January 1978–December 1979

To do nothing is sometimes a good remedy.

Hippocrates

There was a general assumption in January 1978 that the new year would be one of only incremental change, although specific predictions varied. No one could see a ready direction, a means of accelerating events. The IRA was settling in under Adams and McGuinness for the long war without many options but the military one. Organizing a people's war was different from declaring one. The SDLP, disapproving of the armed struggle, without a provincial forum, and with growing internal quarrels, faced only irrelevance. Hume looked increasingly to Dublin, Fitt to London, and Devlin to class politics. The Protestant paramilitaries were divided between the few and militant who favored UDI and the many who wanted only to defend what they thought the British had taken from them—the old Stormont system. Their legal betters in the political establishment had little to offer beyond intense support for harsher security measures and a longing for provincial devolution at some date. The second general strike had only revealed the inherent divisions in Unionism. The other parties, NILP, Alliance, and the Republican Clubs, had to wait on events. The antagonism among variants of loyalism remained.

Novelty was thus in 1978 at a premium. The new Irish Independence Party, organized in 1977 by former Unity MP for Fermanagh–South Tyrone Frank McManus and Fergus McAteer, Derry Nationalist (son of Eddie McAteer, former Nationalist leader), with the Protestant nationalist John Turnly as a founding member, raised early hopes but eventually appeared to be a local phenomenon. McManus, brother of Father Seán McManus of the Irish National Caucus in the United States, had no leverage outside his home areas and not much to offer that the SDLP could not more aptly organize. The Irish Independence Party, in fact, offered only an alternative Catholic party and an indication that minority politics and/or Irish nationalist opinion had not been monopolized by Fitt, Hume, and Company.

From London, with Mason and Creasey in charge, there was once again little interest in Ireland, in Northern Ireland politics, or in novel approaches. Direct rule would allow order to be restored and in the meantime the government could move on to more urgent and interesting matters. Irish matters were urgent only to the Irish and even then not always in the South. There were those in Belfast and London who felt that Lynch and Fianna Fáil were drifting back into a more nationalist stance, out of conviction, perhaps, or habit, or for political gain.

Any Dublin tinkering, however, arose from the remaining residue of the appeal of unity without pain. The continuing appeal of the nationalist case was clear when the Roman Catholic primate of Ireland, Tomás O Fiaich, said for a newspaper, "I think the British should withdraw from Ireland. . . . I think it's the only way which will get things moving." O Fiaich was from South Armagh, a dedicated Irish-speaker, a man absolutely opposed to violence but obviously not to the unity of the island. And his idea of "moving" was not that of the authorities or the majority.

Tomás O Fiaich's interventions in 1978 and later grated on British sensibilities and outraged Northern Protestants, strengthening their belief in an Irish-nationalist-Catholic conspiracy. The fact that the Standing Committee of Irish Catholic Bishops conference said on February 25 that the overwhelming majority of Irish people wanted the campaign of violence to end immediately had no compensating effect. Evidence of only one kind was sought by the majority, or by much of the minority for that matter. All the churches were always against violence but differed on the root causes.

For loyalists and the British government, being against violence was not sufficient; comments had to favor pacification and accommodation, largely on British terms, to be credited as useful. The IRA should be crushed and the Catholics should so agree. There was always concern that Dublin was not serious about suppressing the IRA. On January 5, in an RTE radio interview, Lynch suggested that the government might consider an amnesty for republicans in the event of a cease-fire; perhaps it was a carrot offered in an effort to begin an endgame; perhaps it was no more than an aside, unrelated to a considered Irish policy. That Dublin, like O Fiaich, was of two minds was underlined on January 18 when the European Court of Human Rights in Strasbourg ruled on the case brought by the Republic concerning the interrogation methods used on internees in 1971. The court called the methods "inhuman and degrading" but not torture. The British felt the case should have been withdrawn; it was an old grievance that would only complicate future accommodation.

All of these signs of the vitality of Irish nationalism or the refusal of the Irish state to act in tandem with British security forces irritated London. The arrest of the SAS men who blundered across the border on May 5, 1976, was repeatedly recalled as unnecessary. The Republic felt it was too blatant an example, one of an estimated three hundred British army intrusions a year with not an arrest. In London the solution for some, often innocent of Ireland, was still to seal the border, isolate and destroy the IRA. It was not so much that Dublin and London clashed on specific issues, thus complicating their mutual interests, as that it was difficult for either to grasp fully that those mutual interests must cancel out old attitudes. Suspicion and distaste have a long half-life in politics.

Those in Britain or Belfast, those responsible, particularly those at a distance from Irish nuances and with the need for simple targets, found a visible one in Dublin or in O Fiaich or in all those who deplored violence but raised matters or took views not amenable to advocates of order, even before law. Comments made on March 12 by Northern Secretary Mason about the role of the Republic in terrorism produced outrage in Dublin. On their side, Irish nationalists, even those in the Republic who really did not want six more troublesome counties or to join some jerry-built, united Ireland, still found a draw in the old ideals. They hated terrorism, feared the dangers and instabilities brought by the IRA, and no longer accepted the simplicities of patriotic oratory. They did, however, feel a united island would be somehow splendid, if really united in all senses. This, however, was a dream.

Unity was, nevertheless, still a dream, not yet a nightmare. It might have electoral advantage. There surely remained a pool of Anglophobia even when there was a community of interests with London over most matters, even most security matters. No one in the Republic was ever sure how many of the old loyalties and attitudes remained. Even those who now detested the Provos found the British irritating. Times were changing, but how fast and to whose political advantage? The Easter Rising was long ago and different, dead history, not living precedent, except for the IRA. Present violence was wicked, unlike that of the old IRA. Still, there was an Irish dimension to the problem: Even the British had accepted this with the aborted Council of Ireland.

The nature of the Irish dimension took on a quite different hue in the eyes of militant loyalists who felt their devotion to London spurned and sought a more congenial policy. In January 1978 the militants, after talks with Andy Tyrie, founded the New Ulster Research Group, with Glen Barr from Vanguard as chairman, and staffed by the UDA. In May 1979 the Research Group would propose an independent Northern Ireland, which they insisted would be acceptable to both sides of the province. They suggested an assembly, with ministers chosen by the elected President, his deputy, and the Prime Minister. During the run-up to the 1979 proposal there was interest in the Ulster dimension within the UDA and within some parts of the loyalist community, but ideas and even politics were for most very secondary matters. The UDI flag had been flown before by those like Taylor; but many of the concerned, ultimate institutions were immaterial, the UDA exercise grandiose, and the real problem still the IRA and Irish Catholic nationalism.

The UDA was established to defend and to punish and to act, not to propose accommodation acceptable to the minority. Many suspected politics and some of the more powerful understood only the returns of force in their wards. The UDA still lacked the coherence and direction of their minority rivals. With Andy Tyrie as chairman, the UDA was dominated by an eight-man inner council made up of Tyrie and the seven commanders of the various military districts: Belfast, North, South, East, and West, Southeast Antrim, Derry County, and Mid-Ulster. The center could rarely impose on the parts, and promotion was still secured by force, charisma, and fear. Discipline was hardly military and each commander controlled most operations, from sectarian murder to armed expropriation as well as the defense of local interests, pubs, clubs, taxis, protection of building sites, collections—the whole growing black economy of the Troubles. The new money lured careerists into all the paramilitary organizations, but the Protestants had special trouble keeping funds away from private uses without engaging in internal war. Sections of the UDA were in the process of evolving into rackets run for local profit, which was often not shared even with all the local members. Skimming from the top assured feuds and suspicions and decay of avowed purpose. Crime paid no political dividends.

The Catholics were no more honest but the IRA was far more effective and far more disciplined. The New Ulster Research Group indicated that some of the Protestant paramilitaries wanted more than murder. The IRA had indicated what a working-class movement could accomplish, the general strike in 1974 had indicated the power of the Protestant workingman. For some the UDA was a vehicle for class advancement, for political and economic betterment, and for aspirations beyond defense and vengeance and personal gain.

Local power tended to remain with those who could deploy force, control income, and express the power of the gun in their own presence. The motives of such men varied enormously but they tended to be raw and intractable and local. Their organization was highly personal and focused not on daily rituals, training, or lectures and meetings, but on operations. Contacts were constant and social until a mission was needed, money had to be collected, or discipline imposed. Some UDA members did not work at regular jobs but only a few, like Tyrie, were full-time organizers or operators. With unemployment high the successful managed their interests, drank in the clubs, and intimidated their followers—the time of the cowboy killers was passing. Tyrie had a very long run as head of the UDA because his acute sensors allowed him to both fashion consensus at the top and avoid confrontation with local power at the bottom. He did not so much lead as represent. He spoke rather than acted, and skimmed the real political froth off the top of the UDA pot.

UDA politics was always a spin-off item on a narrow agenda, a facet of interest to those with the capacity and concern but rarely the talent to mobilize the entire movement. The UDA was still in many ways a militia-mob dotted with hard men for the hard jobs, very much a free association of defenders in Ulster. For most involved, its major—often only—task was "to defend." A few volunteers might bomb in the Republic but for Northern reasons. There were foreign contacts in Britain, Canada, and even in Libya in 1974, although the Libyan connection led to nothing. In June 1979 eleven Scottish UDA men were given long sentences for acquiring arms and ammunition and furthering the aims of the Ulster Freedom Fighters. The UDA remained an Ulster player, one that engendered violence in response to provocation—IRA atrocities, British betrayal, Dublin statements, the Protestant politicians' compromises—but no more.

This violence was more than enough for the victims, for the RUC, who increasingly under Newman responded as would conventional police, and for the British army, who had never been fond of loyalists tossing bricks at the Queen's regiments. Just as Mason urged a hard line on the IRA by the security forces, so too was there little sympathy for the Protestant paramilitaries, except where they could be manipulated in the dirty war against the Provos. It was always apparent that the loyalist gunmen were a lesser threat. They lacked the skills and organization, they were trapped by their loyalty, and they were more prone to be tempted by private gain. Thus, the UDA was not proscribed until August 1992, even though everyone recognized that the Ulster Freedom Fighters did not exist except as a cover name. The UDA might be a special threat to random Catholics, sometimes to their own who could be exploited, or to each other, but not to the state, not to Britain. The IRA, on the other hand, waged war against the United Kingdom, killed soldiers as a duty. Hence those who ran the very special British operations used the Orange gunmen as agents provocateurs and so kept the Crown at a slight distance from the murder of suspects, the bombing of civilian targets, and the dirty war.

The UDA men, recruited individually or taken in groups a bit more formally, were not loath to act, did not feel manipulated, but part of a joint effort to defend. The underground world they entered was a miasma of covert operations, paid informers, turned gunmen, agents operating under false flags, criminals on the make, the passing psychopath, and undercover people from intelligence, the military, the police, the paramilitaries of all persuasions, all pursuing special agendas, many ruthless, a few deadly. The British were running false gangs, a mix of turned and usually marginal IRA people, willing Protestants and assigned agents. The Protestants rarely minded the atmosphere or the operations. Military operations in an alignment with the British army were what the volunteer had always wanted, not a chair at a roundtable discussion, membership in the New Ulster Research Group, or a chance to vote for it or for its 1981 successor, the Ulster Loyalist Democratic Party.

By 1978 the British army was moving away from lax control at the top that permitted a great deal of free play in the black world. It was not a smooth process and reduced but by no means ended covert military actions. These ranged from plainclothes soldiers in classical ambushes on through to intelligence officers running informers, gunmen hired with a slogan, and criminals in and out of prison. In a society prone, often for reason, to conspiracy theory, much was accredited to British cunning: paid murder, politically motivated bombing, atrocity, and theft. Even loyalists, especially those from conventional backgrounds, were appalled at the evidence of special operations credited, often with reason and evidence, to the British military operating in a dirty war. The military, in turn, cleaning up its own act, felt that no other regular army could have responded to the situation as well, as decently.

During the Ulsterization process the army in Ulster was reluctant to hand over control to the RUC. General Creasey and others had doubts about the RUC. They probably would have had doubts about any police force coping with what appeared to the military to be a low-intensity war. The troops were now spread too thin. What many felt was needed was the central control that Kitson had called for in his new book, *Bunch of Five,* although the book did not mention Northern Ireland directly. Kitson wanted everything, including the judicial system, to be adapted to the needs of the campaign. The army felt that this had not been done effectively and that the IRA would exploit the police in their new high-risk profile. Sooner or later, the army felt the RUC would slip up.

On February 17 the Provos had as target the La Mon House, a hotel-restaurant-conference complex near Comber, outside Belfast, in north County Down, the heart of Unionist territory, and planted two of their new petrochemical firebombs on a window of the function room. The mix, ANFO, of crystallized ammonium nitrate and aluminum filings, alongside gasoline, produced a huge fireball when it exploded. The choice of La Mon was made on narrow operational grounds: lax security, easy access, easy withdrawal; it was a hotel, and one in "safe" Unionist territory.

The hotel was very much a soft, economic target. The IRA had chosen Friday night, when the main room was filled with over three hundred people. Many guests were members of the Northern Ireland Collie Club at the annual prize night or of the Northern Ireland Junior Motor Cycle Club. The IRA warning was inadequate. The first roadside phone was vandalized. Before the volunteers could reach the next phone they were stopped and questioned by a UDR patrol. Delayed, they could give the RUC only a nine-minute warning. There was not time to evacuate the building.

The IRA repeatedly failed to plan for delay or confusion, failed to foresee problems, and most distressingly failed to select targets, even soft targets, so as to keep civilian casualties down. There was no sign that competence had in any way improved beyond a decline in own goals and a rising sophistication in construction. The volunteer operations were still roughly planned and the bombs hardly state-of-the-art, even if lads no longer rushed shouting into a shop carrying an infernal device.

At La Mon House shortly before nine o'clock in the evening the two devices detonated and the blast was followed by a fireball that burst through the main room, searing to a crisp many in its path, setting others afire, gutting the hotel. Patrons staggered out of rooms lit only by flickering flames and filled with choking smoke and still burning bodies. When the surviving staff and customers struggled outside, some were aflame, many were burned, and all were stunned, then and later. Twelve people were killed; some of the charred and shrunken remains had to be identified by the dental records. Many more were injured; twenty-three were maimed and very badly burned. The inside of the La Mon House had been transformed into an inferno.

The outcry was horrendous. Ten thousand posters were soon on the streets showing the twisted, charred bodies. There was little defense. Many republicans thought the target foolish and the volunteers callous. There had been eighty IRA bomb attacks in the previous six weeks, each carrying high risks. Even the IRA statement issued by the Republican Publicity Bureau indicated that a dreadful mistake had been made: "There is nothing we can offer in mitigation bar that our enquiries have established that a nine-minute warning was given to the RUC. This was proved totally inadequate given the disastrous consequence. . . . All killing stems from British interference and from their denial of Irish sovereignty."*

*IRA statements are released through the Irish Republican Publicity Bureau, an invisible conduit between the secret army and the Sinn Féin office in Belfast or Dublin. The statement may be generated by the relevant GHQ staff or come out of the Army Council—reactions to events often lag behind publicity needs because the appropriate authority cannot be reached. Only rarely and usually with great care is a Sinn Féin statement critical of IRA policy or actions, and even then the Army Council may be involved in drafting that criticism. Obviously an overt political party like Provisional Sinn Féin generates its own agenda, but in theory and usually in practice the republican movement's public reaction is seamless: All the involved are

GHQ tightened up control over local units, insisted that targets that endangered civilians—commercial buildings, hotels, trains, and buses—be chosen more carefully. In the next ten weeks there were only twelve bomb attacks, none high-risk. The next day, Saturday, long before GHQ had responded to La Mon, an active service unit bombed the Ulster bus depot in Derry city, destroying sixteen buses and doing some £500,000 of damage—a swift, clean, effective operation. No one noticed because of the continuing fallout from La Mon. Such a disaster made a people's war all that much more difficult because Protestants were horrified and most Catholics were equally appalled, even republicans. Why a hotel? Why a dog club? Because it was there, vulnerable, part of the "artificial economy of the six counties" did not seem sufficient reason to put at risk innocent lives.

On top of the La Mon bomb and the subsequent effort by the Army Council and GHQ to tighten operational control, Gerry Adams was arrested in the wave of arrests following the bomb and charged with membership in the IRA. The security forces assumed that he was a leading figure not only in the open politics of the new departure but also in the closed world of the secret army. Adams was kept seven months on remand before being released. His incarceration gave him an insight into prison conditions that would prove useful, but removed him from the center of the circle. He was replaced as chief of staff by Martin McGuinness, who remained after Adams was released so that the two continued on in tandem. Ivor Bell, a physical force man from the fifties, had moved into control in Belfast and as O/C Northern Command would direct one key area while increasingly part-time, experienced activists took over in the countryside. Few full-time people could exist for long. Yet the cunning and careful could operate undercover for years. In the countryside the IRA had produced a generation of increasingly skilled guerrillas, even in 1978 some full-time guerrillas.

Despite reluctance by the purely physical force people, the new direction was assured: Only the means remained uncertain. How to integrate an army into a politically active movement? How to move ahead? The truce had sorely disappointed some, like Dominic McGlinchey, who would move on into the INLA. He was credited by the British with a string of ruthless and brutal killings and became a most wanted man. Others merely reduced their visibility and paid little attention to GHQ: In the IRA the distance out to the pointed end can be very far, command and control difficult, communication rare. Most active volunteers knew what to do without being told and did it better as time passed.

In Bellaghy, Derry, a small divided farming village, one of the new breed of rural guerrillas was Francis Hughes. A success in the field, he rose to O/C of South Derry and then had to give it up because he was on the run, continually seeking targets while pursued. The RUC and British credited him, like Dominic McGlinchey, with a string of killings. What made the conflict in the area particularly bitter was that the RUC, the RUC Reserve, and the UDR were made up of his neighbors; everyone knew everyone, if not very well. And casualties

---

true believers, all accept the ultimate authority of the Army Council at the core of the movement, and for a generation all have supported the armed struggle.

touched everyone. In the Maghera UDR barracks five men were killed during Hughes's time. The Protestants suspected all Catholics of complicity in murder. Close to the border many Protestants suspected their neighbors were involved in a conspiracy to drive out Protestants, take over the land, redress history. In turn most of the Catholics had little confidence in the authorities, one day the sectarian B Specials and the next the UDR. The result was a bitter and unforgiving civil war that first divided the community along sectarian lines and then increasingly divided the Catholic community into those tolerant of the IRA and those violently opposed to violence used in their name. Hatred, hidden but real, festered. No one knew whom to trust, who was the real enemy. The ancient arrangements allowing the two traditions to coexist were strained.

Hughes saw himself, as did his associates, in a quite different light, not a sectarian killer but an Irish rebel guerrilla. He admired the heroes of the Tan War, Tom Barry and Dan Breen, and sought a romantic career, not to murder from a ditch. "I don't want to be shooting them. I want them to bloody go home in the morning. But what other way do I have to protest, can you tell me? . . . I hate what I'm doing. I really hate it. But I'm going to keep doing it—that's the funny thing about it."* He had joined the Officials, strong in the area, but left when they declared a cease-fire in 1972 and formed his own unit, the Unrepentants, which was incorporated into the Provos in 1974. His career as a guerrilla had dash. He spoke to his RUC opponents on the phone, walked through roadblocks, became a legend as the Boy from Tamlaghtduff, intimate with the countryside, sleeping rough in a potato field, escaping army patrols, hitting and running and dropping by home for Christmas dinner. It was a military style soon out of fashion—the long odds favored the security forces. The times could not support a career as a full-time guerrilla—the end of the decade would see units composed of those living at home, sometimes joined by a few specialists from across the border, but no guerrilla columns, not even one-man shows like Hughes.

On a moonless night, March 16, 1978, at a quarter past nine, Hughes and one other volunteer moved through Barney Cassidy's field near Ranaghan Road, Fallylea, two miles northwest of Maghera. In the same field was a two-man SAS surveillance post hidden near a manure pile. There had been information that Hughes would be in the neighborhood. The two IRA men were in paramilitary uniform. Hughes wore an IRA black beret, a green army combat jacket with an Ireland patch on the sleeve, and olive green army trousers, and carried a Garand M-14. The SAS men thought he was British army. They blundered, broke standard operating procedure and challenged the IRA men as the two came to within twelve feet of the hide. They did not want to shoot their own. It was a fatal mistake. The two IRA men immediately opened fire. Their slugs tore into Corporal David Jones, knocking his SLR out of his hand and fatally wounding him in the stomach, lungs, and liver. The second SAS man was hit, knocked on his back but not disabled. With Jones screaming and the IRA men firing, he managed to open up with his submachine gun, firing one long automatic burst of twenty-six rounds, hitting both IRA men, smashing Hughes's thigh.

*Tom Collins, *The Irish Hunger Strikes* (Dublin and Belfast: White Island, 1986), p. 56.

Sending away the other volunteer, Hughes, much of the time crawling, got across Ranaghan Road and up into the fields, struggled into a tiny culvert screened with gorse and shielded with whitethorn and blackthorn bushes and whin. He could hear the arrival of an ambulance and the Quick Reaction Force of Gloustershires from Kilrea, radioed in by the surviving SAS man. The British were looking for three IRA men. In the dark no one found him. The dogs lost the scent. Hughes lay in his ditch, covered with moss and bramble, bleeding and waiting. At about noon on Saint Patrick's morning, March 17, the soldiers discovered him. He should have been dead but was still defiant. After a couple of hours waiting for the ambulance, he was moved, gravely ill, to Magherafelt Hospital. Ten months later, on January 24, 1979, he was formally arrested in the hospital. He was tried in February and convicted on five counts, including the SAS shooting and a bomb at Coagh, County Tyrone, in January 1977. Hughes received a life sentence for killing the SAS man and eighty-three years on the other counts.

He was moved to Long Kesh in February 1980, where he joined the prison community, one leg nearly two inches shorter than the other and his convictions unchanged. He went on the blanket and joined the dirty protest. He had by then become a legend in an organization ever mindful of history. A real guerrilla from the hillsides of Derry, even in prison, was an asset, and in time he became the subject of the inevitable poem, which ended, "I'll never see the likes again of my brave Francis Hughes." He was an expiring breed. The war no longer had much room for the columns in the hills. The Provos did have columns along the border created by bringing together from six to ten volunteers for single operations, leaving their tail back in the Republic. While they seemed to be old-style flying columns, what Hughes had wanted, they were far more transient and far more professional.

The Republicans, as always, moved ahead on more than one front, seeking vulnerabilities, seeking to stretch the authorities' capacity to react. Even the purest physical force republican, descendant of the Fenian dynamiters or the rural night riders, approved of confronting the British wherever possible. In 1978, however, the military option was first. Despite the new departure heralded in Seán Keenan's Bodenstown speech, almost all political and social work was still directed at supporting the secret army. With O Brádaigh as president of Provisional Sinn Féin as well as a member of the Army Council, politics was integrated into the armed struggle but as a support mechanism: to protest, to aid and comfort, to fund the families and dependents, to organize the sympathetic, to parade, and to disseminate the policy of the movement. Sinn Féin was not a party in any conventional sense but rather an integrated aspect of the republican movement; not a front, not really a tool of the IRA, but a facet of the organized assets. The party, of course, took on a vitality of its own; many workers were not military, certainly not members of the IRA, and at times barely aware of the mysterious nature of the movement. They had joined out of belief, worked out of conviction, and seldom found contradiction between their party, their perspective, and that of the movement and the army. There was, however, a strain on the balance of the purely political and the narrowly military, a difference in agendas and priorities. La Mon obviously caused problems—an image was damaged and the fact that many volunteers did not care especially about their image did not repair it.

All those involved in the movement were supportive of the armed struggle as the key—the republican movement was not a constitutional one even if Sinn Féin was legal. All accepted that the secret army came first, even when the secret army pursued policies that hampered Sinn Féin goals. Many could wish the army more tidy, more efficient, but it remained the engine for ultimate change. With the example before them of the Stickies' slide into conventional, parliamentary politics, most still detested the existing systems and institutions, alien except as convenient arenas of battle. Elections were to demonstrate support, engage the many, not win seats as a means to power. In 1978 the battle was still largely fought by the volunteers engaged in the long war while a new role for the new departure was being shaped haltingly by Sinn Féin.

Ultimately, republican policy was determined by the Army Council. The Provisional Army Council co-opted new members when there were arrests, resignations, or losses; it was felt that war conditions prevented the meeting of the Army Convention, the elective body of the entire IRA. So Adams lost his place on arrest and on release had to wait for slots to open up. There had always been this continuity. As long as there were seven republicans (and sometimes even when there were not) there was an Army Council. This core of seven, the true government of the Republic according to the traditionalists, inheriting legitimacy from the Second Dáil according to the very faithful, ruled through consensus. Rarely were orders given and then rarely without surety that they would be obeyed. In a relatively small, tightly knit band of true believers long intimate with each other and their reading of history, much could be taken for granted. And much was: History, the movement's accumulated wisdom, standard operating procedures, and mutual experience produced answers and options in most situations. Divisions came as they were wont to do in revolutionary organizations when escalation presented choices—and after a decade the primary concern of the Army Council had been to maintain momentum, to persist without a visible end to the campaign. Increasingly the consensus was that the truce had been a disastrous error but had indicated that pursuing only a military option was not productive.

Politics, votes, elections, seats, had long been seen as co-option into an illegitimate system that would hardly cede the power to destroy itself. The Officials had chosen a road that seemingly offered two tracks, political and military, but the Provos had always felt that politics as a prime means operating on the system's terms would corrupt the faith. And year by year they could see this in the attitudes and policies of the Officials, who had now formally closed down their military option. The movement could use the institutions of the state but could not, should not recognize them. They must abstain from taking seats in illicit assemblies like Westminster, Stormont, and the Dáil. Thus, politics for the Army Council had been limited to Sinn Féin as auxiliary, O Brádaigh and O Conaill with seats on the Army Council and access to the media were vital cogs in the movement but not dominant ones. What the new Northern people wanted, especially Gerry Adams, was a movement structured through Sinn Féin that would reach more people for more reasons and thus increase republican control, support, and presence. A long war was a people's war and a people's war required the people to be organized and incorporated. The more radical IRA reformers would include more conventional politics, like the Officials, but did not want to pay the cost in discarding faithful republicans. Others felt that as long as the new direction did not lead down the same road taken by the Officials, a people's war would be advantageous. O Brádaigh and O Conaill and the rest were enthusiastic and anticipated that sooner or later those from the six counties who were fighting the war would also want, as seemed right, to direct the political struggle. The older republicans would have no trouble following as long as principles were not violated—and abstentionism for many remained not only sensible but principled. Increasingly as the past was raked about for examples, the younger men were particularly critical of the truce. The movement was by no means divided but as always contained various traditions and local attitudes—Francis Hughes was very different from Gerry Adams or Dáithí O Conaill. All in 1978–79 sought an effective means into the future within the movement. Politics could be another face of war.

There were for Provisional Sinn Féin two inherent difficulties. First, how participate in an electoral process that would produce very little real power? Untaken seats are only symbolic assets, except on a local level. Second, how to structure a course that permitted both support of narrow IRA military goals and of more general and often conflicting political policies? What was good for the IRA might not be good for Sinn Féin. The Army Council largely ignored both dilemmas: In 1978 abstentionism remained dogma and militarism pervasive throughout the movement. Adams, McGuinness, Danny Morrison, Tom Hartley, and the others might see a great change in the making, but it would take time to seep out through the movement. Even with a change in focus, North and South, support and especially votes were uncertain. The Irish had given sons but hardly ever votes to the republican movement. In the Republic, votes were to be translated in theory, if not in fact, into leverage in Dublin—what did Sinn Féin offer? In Northern Ireland the whole direction of events for a decade had been for the minority to wrest more from the system—and what more could Sinn Féin offer than the SDLP?

So the party had a problem in appealing for more voters who would want more than an opportunity to express support for the armed struggle by casting a symbolic ballot. One means was to redouble the involvement at the bottom, focusing on neighborhood matters, housing and welfare and medical advice and jobs and all the details of a local government that hardly functioned in some areas. The key areas at the beginning were those mainly controlled by the IRA—there was power in the street of the old no-go zones and the movement began to pick it up. It was a real but halting process, slow spadework with slow returns. And the very control that made it possible tended to operate against the IRA: The use of force, beating minor offenders, maiming criminals with a bullet in the leg, intimidating the reluctant might be a necessary adjunct to maintaining order but it alienated many. One lad shot because of a grudge, one man beaten by error, one contribution used for drink had a disproportionate effect on the perceived morality of the movement. And working with the people required different talents and different priorities —many volunteers wanted to be soldiers, not welfare workers or part-time policemen, although some could switch back and forth between roles if need be.

Such problems were far down on the list of the Army Council's priorities, for there was a war to be waged. At the top, at the Army Council or GHQ, a nonmilitary issue had to be seen as a wedge to drive into the British power structure, not a shovel to turn over a seedbed. The shovelers could keep at it unless they were needed to dig trenches. Ever so gradually the shovelers of Sinn Féin, especially in Belfast, with Adams's enthusiasm, became involved in local matters.

In 1978 the concerns of those who focused on the vulnerabilities of the Brits—where to hit, preferably with physical force—and the assets of people politics began to merge on a traditional issue: the prison struggle. The Army Council had always been attracted by the opportunities that prison presents. When an IRA volunteer goes into prison, he is not removed from the struggle but merely transferred to another arena. As a prisoner of war he has traditional responsibilities to his new unit, to general prison policy, and to the IRA. Some volunteers may opt out of the movement, go through prison as individuals and emerge without convictions or contributions to the movement, discarded volunteers. As the years pass some long-sentence prisoners make their lives within prison, a special, permanent, and undemanding environment, not harshly unpleasant for conformists. A few remain adamant and unrepentant, even alone in an English jail, far from a unit, isolated and harassed, individually continuing the fight. The Price sisters and the other hunger strikers in England were, as prisoners, in action as much as they had been when they planted bombs. Many more, however, went into prisons or camps dominated by their own.

There they served in a variety of ways: Policy may indicate doing hard time, constantly confronting the system, or soft time, cooperating for later purpose. Every effort may be focused on plots to escape, even with a minimal chance of getting away; or no escapes may be authorized without assurance of success. In 1974 the prisoners in the Kesh had burned down the camp around themselves and at other times most of the volunteers had been cooperative. The writ of the GHQ runs and IRA prison rules are valid. A prison IRA unit may have little impact on GHQ or considerable but maintains behind the wire a certain independence and local dynamic. Policy inside can arise from inside priorities while GHQ is focused elsewhere. Prison life can be very full, even rewarding. There are classes, republican history to learn, future policy to contemplate, protests to organize, and often escapes to prepare. The IRA's response to the prison arena was so organized and so effective that in detail it was copied by the Protestant paramilitary prisoners, eager to be a real secret army too. And the authorities were regularly driven to readjust even their grand strategy of criminalization. The prison produced seasoned republicans and opportunities to punish the authorities even from a cell, at times especially from a cell.

In the Northern conflict both the British and the IRA continued to seek the advantages of war and peace. The IRA wanted all the rights of a simple citizen and the privileges of waging war. The British wanted to respond to war with war but deny that more was at stake than a rise in crime. The IRA went out to shoot and kill from ambush in pursuit of war and when ambushed in turn expressed outrage that the state would so kill. The state in turn denied, if at all possible, that such deaths were casualties of war but rather merely justly slain criminals, a danger to civil order. In prison the same struggle over definitions, shifting postures, and legitimacy took place. Criminalization meant that there was no political crime, no political prisoners, certainly no prisoners of war; the IRA volunteers were nothing special except dangerous.

The difficulty was that the entire law enforcement system from the soldier walking point in a brick in the Bogside to the terms of release treated the IRA volunteer specially. Even the one prisoner in an English jail, without allies, friends, or much hope of escape was not forgotten by the system that treated every IRA man or woman as special, dangerous, incorrigible.

The hunger strikers in England had sought to be treated as normal prisoners and moved closer to home. Before that Billy McKee had gone on a hunger strike in 1972 to be treated specially. He had won that concession from Whitelaw. In the Republic the hunger strikers at Portlaoise Prison in 1977 had failed to do so. Dublin, all too familiar with IRA prison tactics, had held out, refused, and the strike had collapsed. In Long Kesh the IRA was not dependent on a few as in England but on the many who were dedicated and eager to punish the British, not just confront an Irish government that had to be treated with ambivalence to maintain the Southern sanctuary. The IRA had assets in the Kesh ready, eager to be used. In turn with criminalization the authorities had decided, knowing the cost, to break the IRA asset: the control of the inside of the prison for republican purpose.

The British were willing to create enormously attractive prison conditions—50 percent of any sentence remitted, splendid new facilities, privileges, and kindness—as long as the IRA gave up special status, accepted the sign of criminality that a prison uniform implied. The British could and did arrest without sufficient evidence, force concessions, try before Diplock Courts with special rules, imprison for terms unrelated to those given in non-IRA cases, and house the volunteer within a system filled with restrictions, harassment, and punishment, with surrender the only option to achieve concession or leniency. It was a conveyor belt into a cage or a cell where official intimidation ruled. But not if the prisoner would accept criminality; for London and Belfast denied that those trundled to prison were in any way special: Criminals were criminals. Later the *Irish Times,* uncompromisingly antirepublican, would indicate the apparent hypocrisy of the British position in that the British Government claimed that the issue was a matter of principle so there could be no special category. Yet everything was special about the prisoners in Long Kesh. In fact, the whole state of Northern Ireland was special and was set up to be special.

This was the point of the Northern prison struggle for the republicans: Their volunteers were prisoners of war and to make them into criminals would also make Northern Ireland into a normal part of the United Kingdom. The argument was not really over conditions or details but over sovereignty, over the cause of the armed struggle. The Irish resistance was a public and private commitment to the reality of the Republic. Not all prisoners went on the blanket or took part in the protest; some conformed, some shifted back and forth; but as long as there was substantial resistance, the British had failed. As Nugent had said, they could not nail prison clothes on the back of the IRA.

The first stations on the conveyor belt were the major police and military stations (Castlereagh RUC station and Palace, Girdwood, and Fort Mona army centers), where suspects were held for questioning. By 1978 there were some who suspected that the security forces were permitted to eliminate suspects even before they reached the first stage—knock them off the border in ambushes, forays over the border into the Republic, in shoot-to-kill rather than arrest situations. Between December 1977 and December 1978 the security forces shot dead eleven people in what critics called most dubious circumstances. On December 24, 1978, for example, Patrick Duffy, an auxiliary member of the IRA in Derry, had entered a room staked out by the British army after an explosives find. Unarmed, he was shot and killed. The British soldiers involved claimed they felt threatened. Critics felt that they had murdered Duffy—perhaps commendable in war but hardly a proper procedure against a suspected criminal.

Each of the killings was isolated, surrounded with special circumstances and often doubts, and emerged only gradually and often only then as a pattern to those who sought one. Certainly the British army made use of ambushes, a killing zone for anyone who walked into the field of fire. From time to time the innocent walked into an ambush as well. On June 20, 1978, an IRA active service unit carried out an operation to bomb the general post office telephone exchange depot on the Ballysillan Road, Belfast, and walked into a SAS-RUC ambush. The SAS used Armalite rifles the RUC man a Sterling. Although the reasons for the stakeout were never clear, what occurred is clear. The SAS set up the ambush on adequate intelligence. The three-man IRA unit walked into the killing zone and were shot down, along with one innocent civilian, a Protestant pedestrian, William James Hanna, while one civilian witness, also a Protestant, escaped to report in his statement that the four had been killed without warning. This is again conventional practice if at war, not so if the writ of law is to run. The authorities sought to minimize and shape the event, reporting an exchange of gunfire when the IRA men had no guns and claiming that a warning had been given when the surviving witness heard none. There was clearly a contradiction between public posture and private procedures. And this moral and legal gray area remained.

The events at the various barracks surrounding interrogation were a different matter: Hundreds of incidents of maltreatment to secure confessions could not easily be denied, explained away, or categorized as random overenthusiasm. The suspects were in the hands of the law, they were not bombers or gunmen on a mission. With no internment the authorities might often arrest those in the IRA known to be guilty, often guilty of specific crimes, but lack conventional evidence. The authorities needed either a solid witness or a confession, the second being more convenient than the first. And so the suspect was isolated, intimidated, often threatened, and regularly physically maltreated. Questioned in relay for long hours by those who swore vengeance against his family or contact with the sectarian killers or resorted to brutality, the suspect might eventually sign anything. Usually this was the case for IRA suspects and often the same procedure was used on Protestant paramilitaries. It was never used on ordinary criminals— they were not special.

The word of maltreatment, just as it had after internment, began to seep out during 1976 and 1977. Castlereagh became notorious before there was proof, before any disinterested investigation could begin. The republicans complained. The authorities denied all—if there were bruises they were self-inflicted, the IRA suspects would, of course, lie. Civil rights workers complained. Three Catholic priests, Fathers Denis Faul, Brian Brady, and Raymond Murray, released dossiers on the extorted confessions. The Diplock Courts simply accepted the confessions. Between July 1, 1976, and July 1, 1978, 2,293 people were charged in Belfast with scheduled offenses and the bulk of the evidence was obtained by confessions. The SDLP issued a statement accusing the police of "illegal, inhuman, and obscene" behavior toward suspects. The *Sunday Times* on October 23, 1977, had published a report undertaken by the Law Department of Queen's University Belfast which said that 94 percent of the cases before Diplock Courts produced convictions and between 70 and 90 percent of convictions were based wholly or in part on admissions of guilt made to the police during interrogation. The Queen's lawyers were not alone; the UDA released their file the same month on mistreatment by the police. Thirty solicitors who worked in Diplock Courts wrote to Mason stating that "ill-treatment of suspects by police officers, with the object of obtaining confessions, is now common practice. . . ." Ultimately an Amnesty International Report on June 13, 1978, confirmed that "maltreatment of suspected terrorists by the RUC has taken place with sufficient frequency to warrant the establishment of a public inquiry to investigate it."

The report of the Bennett Commission's investigation was made public on March 16, 1979, long after the procedures in the police station were common knowledge. A week before, Dr. Robert Irwin, forensic medical officer, had claimed on London Weekend Television's "Weekend World" that detainees he had seen during the course of his work at the Castlereagh interrogation center bore evidence of physical ill treatment by RUC detectives. He had estimated that he saw 150 maltreated prisoners. The authorities compounded their problem by leaking material about an attack on Dr. Irwin's wife by a soldier that might indicate his prejudice—a pointless exercise, since the official Bennett report would accept that there was evidence of maltreatment. Mason promised safeguards. By then more elegant but still no less intimidating interrogation methods had been instituted—and the IRA had given classes in the means to resist such interrogation that made the criminal justice system work for special criminals.

Once convicted (and most of the suspects in Northern Ireland were indeed guilty if not always on the evidence or of the particular crime in question), the prisoner was most likely dispatched to the new Maze—the prison built next to the old holding camps. In Britain matters ran differently for the crimes were fewer, more spectacular, and seemingly capable of conventional proof in court. The Birmingham Six bombers or the Guildford Four had been convicted on real evidence, including confessions, and their claims of mistreatment were discounted by the British establishment and most of the public. There had been a rush to conviction, but only those suspicious of every British court felt them obviously innocent. Even in Ireland many, perhaps most, assumed them guilty. The IRA knew, however, that English justice had once again convicted the suspects because they were Irish, not because they were guilty. Nothing could be said until the volunteers were not at risk: Why admit the Great Train Robbery or the Birmingham bombs and have the police on the trail of the IRA men involved? When the Balcombe Street people appeared in court in May 1976 they were willing to admit their responsibility. One IRA man had already made a statement accepting responsibility for a bombing at Woolwich. He later indicated involvement in the Guildford bombing. This was not welcome news to the authorities nor could it be completely ignored although the confession was quickly labeled spurious, a ploy.

The courts apparently did not want to hear, nor did the police, the British establishment, or many in Ireland. The bombers were in jail, where they belonged. They were unpopular criminals and their cause still limited in appeal. Yet without much help from the republicans (a dubious advantage in Britain), without resources, those prisoners who claimed unjust convictions in the courts as a result of doctored evidence, maltreatment, and systemic prejudice began to attract support. Between July 20 and July 29, 1977, a leave to appeal the convictions in one of the bombing trials, that of the Maguires, was heard. There was growing unease about the convictions by some in Britain who followed judicial matters, but there was no general public concern as yet. And so there was no surprise that leave for any of the Maguire household to appeal against conviction was refused. Those who believed in the innocence of the Irish prisoners did not, however, give up hope, for even in cases of injustice in simple criminal cases, the British judicial system had been loath to admit error. The prisoners would have to wait on new evidence or the times or the unexpected, but they would not have to wait without hope. They, too, had been caught up in the conveyor belt system that adjusted justice to secure convictions—a few in England, many in Northern Ireland.

For most of the convicted IRA members, the H-Blocks were the last stop of the conveyor belt. The new Maze prison might be splendid and shiny (the finest such facility in Europe, according to government spokesmen), and the rules in Northern Ireland on remittance time might be lenient and sentences shorter than in Leeds or London; but the system was intended to force compliance. Prison was not to rehabilitate but to impose costs on rebellion. Repentance would be rewarded after it was coerced. Defiance would be punished. With Rees gone and Mason in favor of focusing on security, not politics, the prison became one more battleground in criminalization.

The first prison engagement had occurred when Ciaran Nugent had refused to wear prison clothing. The authorities, keeping to the rules that they fashioned, began to punish all those who resisted—the expected struggle over the legitimacy of the war. They were punished every fourteen days with a strict regime. They were locked in their cells, fed poorly, and denied their three privileged visits a month. Because they were not allowed to appear naked, they lost their one statutory visit too. They were denied radio, television, books except for a Bible, pen or pencil or writing material, and parcels and letters. They lost 50 percent of their remission time so that their sentence doubled. Rules were adjusted to prison advantage. The prisoners had to go out of their cells to wash. The IRA volunteers went wrapped in one of their towels. This was a violation of the rules. If they wanted to wash, they would have to do so in their cells. And there, as far as the prison authorities were concerned, they could sit—cold, naked, bored, alone, apparently impotent in their boxes.

The prisoners were not actually alone nor without power. Even segregated in cells they lived among their own, often intensely so, their minds concentrated on defiance. A prisoner had twenty-four hours to contrive defiance, seek escape; nothing else clutters the mind. A political prisoner knows that, unlike the criminal, he has a great network of friends and contacts outside who will publicize his plight, come to his aid, help him over the wall or to pass the time. It is rare indeed that a prisoner cannot devise a means to construct and send a message out and receive one back within twenty-four hours. In the Kesh it was sometimes possible to get same-day service. And with nothing, no clothes, no possessions, no schedule to meet nor debts to pay, no car to wash, nothing to do and nothing to lose, the prisoners can make enormous sacrifices beyond the capacity of the guards or the authorities to match. Thus, every day the authorities may face staged riots, no matter how brutal the suppression, may face naked and angry men who spit and howl and refuse the simplest order, disobey the most logical rule, men willing to be brutalized on schedule rather than concede anything at all. Pain and humiliation become the rewards of confrontation, not the penalties of disobedience.

In the end death but not discipline can be imposed purely by force. The prisoner must acquiesce to some orders, cannot be forced in everything. Perhaps a single person, isolated in solitary for years, can be coerced, but not a group determined on resistance as the purpose of living, even at risk of death. So each order is sign for further resistance at any cost. And the costs are not always paid by the prisoner; for guards can be shot on their doorstep, fingered as traitors, bribed with promises, intimidated, and at the very least shamed by rules meant not to regulate but ruin. IRA prisoners are always dangerous, often rebellious, seldom predictable. Even when escape seems impossible—the H-Blocks were built to be escapeproof—and resistance largely isolated in solitary cells, the dedicated can defy authority. They can intimidate: "Who will walk your daughter home from school?" They can bribe from the outside, frighten families on the outside, slander on the outside—leak to the UVF which guards are the IRA's agents, thus making them targets. They can have their gunmen kill on the outside. They can simply say no. Like the Fenians lying in chains for years on a stone floor, badly fed, poorly clothed, forgotten, they can deny the system: persist. Keep the faith. "It is not those who can inflict the most, but those that can suffer the most who will conquer." The more that is inflicted, the greater the injustice. The more that is suffered, the greater the ultimate victory. Republicans thus do not make easy prisoners. They can bring the prison down around their own heads merely to frighten the authorities with the noise: Their values are skewed in that they are willing to suffer much to inflict very little. And the greatest return for IRA prisoners in 1978 was to inflict humiliation, to make the system admit the hypocrisy of criminalization.

In the H-Blocks, isolated in solitary cells, without physical weapons, the IRA prisoners refused compliance, would not accept an imposed system. They resisted searches and procedures. Locked in cells, they destroyed the furniture. When the furniture was removed, they sat on the floor after breaking the windows. In the midst of winter the windows were broken again and again. The guards taunted. Prisoners would not obey, would not cooperate. When their slops were spilled intentionally, they spilled them as well. Their cells were filthy, the floors slippery with waste. They fought searches as unnecessary humiliation. They were forced to comply, and beaten for security reasons. The harassment over toilet facilities, spilled slops, and warder insults finally brought on the dirty protest. The slops were tossed out the window, not in the toilet. The windows were sealed and the slops were then thrown on the floor, on the walls, into the corridors. The prisoners were naked, living in excrement, the walls smeared with waste, the floors slippery with feces and urine. They still refused to bathe. The guards forced them into vats of water. Each time there was violent resistance that put prisoners in the hospital and left most bruised after beatings.

They stuck it out and more joined, living by choice defiantly in reeking squalor that no number of chemical cleansing by warders in protective suits, spacemen forced to enter a foul cave, could remove. All this took place in isolation, word gradually spread out of the H-Blocks first to other republicans, then to other prisoners, finally to the public. The men on the blanket had escalated the struggle. In time the women prisoners in Armagh would follow their example, but most attention was focused on the H-Blocks.

Outside in the province, there was, as always, protest at the entire law enforcement treadmill. Rumors of harsh treatment on arrest had spread, with the documented evidence from the internment period as indicator. The Diplock trials and some of the sentences were public evidence. And the concept of criminalization had been opposed by both Catholics and Protestants. The republican resistance would make the blanket men heroes and in time the dirty protest a drama. All these protests tended to fall into two camps: the involved, who sought to use their legitimate grievance as weapon against the authorities, and the disinterested, who feared that the authorities would warp the system, deny justice, corrupt the law in pursuit of order.

The republicans, the IRA, and the Army Council had doubts about those outside the faith. The radicals, the civil libertarians, the progressives and the decent were not part of the great crusade, had other priorities, marched, as it were, under their own banners. The faithful have always found it difficult to march in step with others, even on the same road. The republicans in 1978 also had quite different priorities: The first was the armed struggle. The liberals and the lawyers wanted instead to maintain or perfect a system the IRA sought to destroy. The Army Council was at one with them in attacking the conveyor belt, the criminal justice system. Yet there were so many protests; seemingly, the worse things were militarily the more protest issues appeared: the use of plastic bullets against protesters, the excesses of the security forces during searches, during arrests, during their allotted rounds, the brutality of interrogation, and the H-Blocks.

The authorities, as usual, found the distinction difficult to make and the case against the system lacking in merit, not to mention reality. The IRA or People's Democracy or the civil liberties lawyers were up to no good, caused trouble, did not want order at all. No one outside the hard men at the point, a soldier with a bomber or a warder under threat, wanted recourse to naked force, but most of the involved—elderly judges, officers in the Green Jackets, RUC Special Branch detectives—felt that armed subversion needed special responses. Criminalization had merit because it buttressed the legitimacy of the state—there is only crime, no war, no political offenders—and it punished the rebellious. Those in the H-Blocks were guilty of subversion, had only themselves to blame, refused to obey the rules, preferred confrontation over routine details, chose to go naked, to smear themselves with excrement, to live like animals. So be it. By summer 250 prisoners were on the blanket, on dirty protest.

The authorities accepted no blame. Life for all republicans, especially the unrepentant and incorrigible, should be made unpleasant, if not to punish then surely to dissuade others. Who would volunteer for years crouched, rank and naked in an empty cell smeared with feces—no glory there, no delirium of the brave. The H-Block campaign should deter the bold volunteer. And since 1976 the time between entry into the IRA and arrest was often only a matter of months. One operation or two and then a chance to wallow in filth in a frigid cell for years, for the cause, for Ireland. Almost from the point that the IRA's armed struggle began the authorities had sought to make service in the republican crusade painful and costly for the volunteer, his family, and often his neighbors. From the very first everything was blamed on the gunmen, all the troubles, all the searches, all the delays to remove bombs, all the barricades and border closings. All these were their fault. There were over thirty thousand searches a year in Northern Ireland, the ghettos were treated like enemy territory. The suspects were stopped and harassed, questioned and threatened on country roads, in their farmhouses, on the streets of Strabane or Newry. The RUC was hostile. The UDR seemed little more than the B Specials in army uniforms. The army was thoughtless and often brutal. All sorts of nationalists were hassled. Mothers were warned about their children. Pubs were raided and the drinkers scattered. Disruption and intimidation were constant. At the other end each prisoner was hostage; the privileges, the sentences with remittance or without, the visits and the facilities, everything that touched the hostage, were used to break the pure and reward the penitent. A prisoner in England might be moved without his family being informed. A rare and costly visit ended in a bleak office with notification of a recent transfer. Prisoners were moved constantly and erratically as a security precaution, left vulnerable to maltreatment by other prisoners, who were generally angry with the IRA—mad bombers. They were watched and warned and kept from their own. Life was not intended to be easy but special, especially unpleasant.

No place did the authorities seemingly have more power to punish in all matters than in prison: Compliance could be forced. The very degree of coercion attracted the support of the movement and of those enlisted in the cause of justice. So from the first there had been protests organized by Sinn Féin, organized by ad hoc committees, organized by the parties of the Left, even organized by friends of the Protestant paramilitaries, uneasy allies in the prison wars. There were marches, petitions, requests for outside investigation, appeals to Dublin, to the United Nations, to human rights groups, to anyone with such concerns. There were meetings and posters and tracts with only the focus changing: internment, deep interrogation, Diplock Courts, police brutality, miserable prison conditions, regulations as punishment, and finally, criminalization. Much of the protest was effective only with the convinced. Much was simply ignored by the Irish public. There was no general sympathy and little interest but a constant background din of complaint.

The IRA Army Council had very little time for much of this and left matters to O Brádaigh and Sinn Féin or to the committees. One of the spin-off benefits of the Troubles was an intense level of community activity by those previously muted by habit, low expectations, and lack of training. The Protestants, the Peace People, and since the civil rights days the Catholics, had all been exposed to community organization for community purpose. Thus, on January 22 a thousand people gathered in Coalisland for an "antirepression" conference organized by Bernadette McAliskey and held under the auspices of the Tyrone Relatives Action Committee, which had been formed in 1976. It was not a big meeting nor much noticed. Anything Bernadette McAliskey did got a few lines but the H-Blocks were no great draw. In the Republic no one knew what they were and in Britain and much of Northern Ireland no one wanted to know. McAliskey hoped that the issue could revive the glory days of 1968 and the great radical protests. There was little sign of this. These local action committees that had arisen in response to the H-Block problems of special status concentrated on marches and petitions on behalf of the prisoners. Women, mothers, sisters, friends, marching at the head of a raggedy column nude except for blankets was worth a picture or two but not much more.

This protest was, as far as the IRA was concerned, all to the good—republicans took part—but peripheral to the movement. McAliskey, who was sound on the national issue, was still too young (even after ten years), too radical, too independent for many republicans, especially older republicans more comfortable with tight discipline and conservative habits. Devlin was fine as a symbol, less so as a leader. Sinn Féin people came to the Coalisland rally but had doubts about any broad-based, united front as proposed at Coalisland. The IRA did not like fronts, preferred control, had other priorities. At the very first banned meeting way back in 1967, Betty Sinclair had pointed out how difficult it was to work with republicans—and as a devout Marxist she was familiar with ideological intransigence. The IRA Army Council was focused on the army not the streets.

The *Republican News* said on February 4, "Any public campaign against torture and for political status needs to be pointed firmly in the direction of 'Brits Out,' and needs to recognize the necessary methods for this aim. For status and torture in reality cannot be isolated from the Brit presence, a presence which cannot be removed without the armed struggle." The Army Council and Northern Command doubted that the movement had the resources to concentrate on amelioration rather than elimination. Who needed "the lunatic fringe, the castoffs, and rejects of the political spectrum?" This view was hardly different than that of the authorities for the civil liberties current that was running parallel to republican concern. Loonies and gunmen were concerned with the H-Blocks; and for much of the spring, the gunmen had other, more important matters on their menu. Sinn Féin, in fact, in a statement published on May 18, felt that the H-Block campaign was an "issue deliberately created by the British regime to direct people, time and energy, from the main goal of national liberation." A secret army may be surrounded by a vast, uneven, and thin nebula of support that contains all sorts and conditions but the purpose is to maintain the center, the military. There should be a struggle in the prisons, there always had been, but the prisons should operate largely on their own resources.

What changed the Army Council's priorities and analysis was that the prisoners were generating real action, creating very considerable sympathy, and, most important of all, the outrage and indignation of the authorities, criticized for what was seen as a necessary if unattractive duty. If the Brits were angry, then protest had advantage. On July 30 Archbishop O Fiaich visited the H-Blocks and what he had to say truly transformed them into a central issue of the Troubles—to the outraged indignation of the authorities and for uncertain purpose for the IRA. There in the fetid, stinking cells, he found naked men, all bones and bruises, with long, tangled hair, wild eyes, and high spirits. The prisoners taught each other Irish, one shouting lesson to the next, and scribbled poems on the walls with toothpaste. Their situation was the fault of the intractable authorities determined on criminalization. He found the most appalling conditions and so reported.

> One would hardly allow animals to remain in such conditions, let alone a human being. The stench and filth in some of the cells, with the remains of rotten food and human excreta scattered around the wall, was almost unbearable. In two of them I was unable to speak for fear of vomiting. Several prisoners complained to me of beatings, of verbal abuse, of additional punishments (in cold cells without even a mattress) for making complaints, and of degrading searches carried out on the most intimate parts of their naked bodies.*

The authorities could hardly deny the conditions, but they could deny responsibility—the prisoners were to blame, according to the Northern Ireland Office.

> These criminals are totally responsible for the situation in which they find themselves. It is they who have been smearing excreta on the walls and pouring urine through cell doors. It is they who by their actions are denying themselves the excellent modern facilities of the prison. They are not political prisoners: more than eighty have been convicted of murder or attempted murder, and more than eighty of explosive offenses. They are members of organizations responsible for the deaths of hundreds of innocent people, the maiming of thousands more and the torture by kneecapping, of more than six hundred of their own people.†

The authorities had caged those who murdered and maimed, broke every law, shot to kill. They were criminals treated differently only because they were more dangerous: could suppress evidence, intimidate witnesses, organize escapes. O

*Michael Hall, *Twenty Years: A Concise Chronology of Events in Northern Ireland from 1968–1988* (Belfast: Island, 1988), p. 70. O'Fiaich's impressions were widely reported and noted far beyond Ireland and Britain.
†Hall, p. 70.

John McMichael and Andy Tyrie of the Ulster Defense Association in Belfast.

The Reverend Ian Paisley in West Belfast, assuring the loyalist people that the 1977 unionist strike could continue until all the aims were met.

Peace People demonstration at Woodvale in Belfast in 1976.

Taoiseach Charles Haughey and Prime Minister Margaret Thatcher in 1980.

H-Blocks, the Maze Prison.

Bobby Sands, who died on
Tuesday, May 5, 1981, on the
sixty-sixth day of his hunger
strike.

Sands's mother on hearing of his death.

*INLA Color Party at the funeral in Derry of Michael Devine, the last of the hunger strikers,
who died on August 20, 1981, on the sixtieth day.*

The ruins of the Grand Hotel, Brighton, after a Provisional IRA bomb detonated on October 12, 1984, during the Conservative Party conference in an attempt to kill Prime Minister Margaret Thatcher and members of the cabinet.

Plainclothes policeman and British army personnel at the scene of the shooting of Sinn Féin. president Gerry Adams in 1984. Three gunmen were arrested.

IRA *mortars after the attack on the Newry station that killed seven male and two female constables and injured thirty others.*

Provisional IRA mortars before use against the Royal Ulster Constabulary police station in Newry, County Down, on February 18, 1985.

The signing of the Anglo-Irish Agreement on November 15, 1985, at Hillsborough, County Down, by Prime Minister Margaret Thatcher and Taoiseach Garrett Fitzgerald. Standing, left to right: Dick Spring, Irish Labour Party and Tanaiste (Irish Deputy Prime Minister), Tom King, Northern Ireland Secretary, and Sir Geoffrey Howe, British Foreign and Commonwealth Secretary.

Reverend Ian Paisley speaking during a massive loyalist demonstration at the Belfast City Hall against the signing of the Anglo-Irish Agreement. Peter Robinson, Deputy of the Democratic Unionist Party, is on the left and James Molyneaux, leader of the Ulster Unionist Party, is on the right.

Provisional IRA Army Council statement being read in public by a masked volunteer flanked by two armed guards.

Provisional IRA masked color party.

Above and below: Aftermath of protest demonstrations.

Loughall RUC station after the Provisional IRA attack was ambushed by the SAS and eight volunteers were killed on May 8, 1987. The IRA panel truck is in the left foreground. The RUC announced that the weapons captured had been used in seven murders and nine attempted murders over the previous two years.

One of the British army surveillance towers on the border of the Irish Republic.

Scene of the Enniskillen explosion, when eleven people were killed at a Poppy Day ceremony by a Provisional IRA bomb, November 8, 1987.

The site of the Enniskillen bomb near to the War Memorial.

Burning vehicles in West Belfast on March 7, 1988, after rioting in reaction to the shootings of three IRA volunteers in Gibraltar by the SAS.

A policeman halting traffic immediately after an IRA bomb exploded on June 15, 1988, in Lisburn, killing six British soldiers whose bodies still lie in the burning rubble.

Ian Gow's ruined car after the Conservative MP's assassination by the IRA on July 30, 1990, in the driveway of his home in Hankham, Sussex.

Margaret Thatcher walks across fields on the South Fermanagh border with County Cavan at Kinawaley during a helicopter tour of fortified British army post in November 1990.

January 1991 IRA mortar attack on Downing Street while Prime Minister John Major held a special cabinet meeting.

The debris from a Provisional IRA bomb in April 1991 that detonated near the Baltic Exchange, killing three people and injuring ninety. The resulting damage was expected to cost the insurers 800 million pounds—a cost greater than all claims put together for similar attacks in Northern Ireland since the beginning of the Troubles. As a result, the British government agreed in December 1992 to help insure buildings against such damages.

The smashed van at the Teebane crossing on the Moagh-Cookstown Road where seven construction workers were killed in an IRA attack on January 17, 1992, because they had been targeted as aiding the British army.

Members of the Ulster Volunteer Force in the countryside. During 1992 Protestant paramilitary killing increased. This led to further concern about intelligence leaks from the security forces and, coincidentally, the banning of the Ulster Defense Association in August by the new Northern Ireland Secretary, Sir Patrick Mayhew.

Fiaich acted as if the terrorists were martyrs. And the prisoners seemed determined on martyrdom, stressing not their deeds but their motives, not the violations of the law but the illegitimacy of its enforcer.

Neither the republicans nor the authorities would listen to each other; neither would admit any logical flaw in an absolute position. Empathy is rare in Ulster. And both would insist that the supposedly disinterested—a Roman Catholic primate, a man of peace—accept the one interpretation. There was no dialogue, no argument, not even logic, eventually. Both simply repeated with growing anger their convictions. They spoke from a different reality. The two sides, however, as O Fiaich's reaction indicated, were not equally appealing. The prisoners were both special and criminals and the records demonstrated that they would not have been the latter unless they were the former. They had and were treated specially. And the state was supposed to be more responsible instead of less. Thus, not only did the prisoners' case appear stronger if not fully convincing, but so too did their condition appear more appealing—the weak and naked and dirty confronting the state had a universal attraction. And increasingly during 1978 and 1979 the media were attracted and the coverage was so presented, further engendering official indignation. On September 2, 1978, fifteen thousand showed up for an H-Block demonstration. Bernadette McAliskey was moved— the past seemed recreated. Sinn Féin felt that "every drop of publicity had been hard won." The republicans had been won over to deploying their own prisoners as an asset—while not neglecting the armed struggle, never neglecting the armed struggle.

The anger of the authorities was intensified proportionately to the size of the H-Block crowds. The IRA was exploiting the issue, twisting reality, demanding unjustified rights and assuming moral positions their gunmen did not deserve. The killing was continuing even as the television tracked women in blankets and wives in tears. The IRA campaign, although run down, no longer a matter of big battalions, wild gunfights, and steady-state bombing, continued to chop away at the security forces. On June 25, 1978, the *Sunday Times* reported the views of a senior British officer: "Provo morale, equipment, intelligence and strength are all OK from their point of view. They are pacing the war." This was not what Mason believed or Creasey wanted to hear. Warders were shot and killed. RUC men were booby-trapped and ambushed. Bombs were being detonated in waves. On September 21 the Provos bombed Eglinton airfield in Derry and destroyed the terminal building, two hangars, and four airplanes. There was still toothpaste in the tube. None of the hard-core areas was any safer. Every tour of duty in South Armagh or Tyrone seemingly guaranteed British casualties.

It was the only game in town. Politics was low key. Dublin was annoyed with Mason, but Lynch and Prime Minister Callaghan smoothed matters over at the Copenhagen European Community summit on April 19, 1978. Callaghan, in fact, in a switch of Labour policy, pushed legislation to increase the number of Northern Ireland seats at Westminster—without Stormont the province was underrepresented. The only sign of life was in Britain, where there were various suggestions that London should withdraw from Ulster: The British were bored and annoyed with the province and the Irish and disgusted with the violence. Each call for "Brits Out," no matter how far to the Left, how irrelevant, caused shivers in the loyalists: This month's Troops Out trendies might be next month's Labour. In August the *Daily Mirror* called for the government to announce a withdrawal to be completed within five years. The English were part of the Irish problem. The rest of the English newspapers and none of those responsible for the province would agree. On September 22 both Mason and the Conservative spokesman for Northern Ireland, Airey Neave, Margaret Thatcher's friend and one-time mentor, issued simultaneous statements attacking this call for withdrawal. The army felt that there "would be anarchy if we walked out, and a tremendous victory for an illegal organization. The Rule of law must win." The British army had to pay the cost elsewhere; in August eight army bases were bombed the same night in Germany. Still another front had been opened.

In the province the SDLP concentrated on the Irish dimension and relations with Dublin, a move away from Fitt and Westminster as source of change that had begun in 1976. Paddy Devlin had already left in September 1977 and there were other feuds and conflicting ambitions. Paddy Devlin and Séamus Mallon, of the SDLP, had wanted to talk with the Provos, always a risky proposition and often to little purpose, since the republicans had habitually been opposed to compromise or accommodation. An internal settlement did not look promising; Callaghan and Neave were as one on direct rule, and Dublin would listen but had nothing to offer. The loyalists were no better off. The unionists could not unite; no one trusted Paisley but his own. And Paisley sought confrontation, not a way forward. There was more talk of a new paramilitary force than of new political initiatives. Vanguard had evaporated and Craig was isolated. The UDA's political ventures were marred by the continuing feuds and shoot-outs.

The distance traveled in Ulster politics to no terminal was apparent in October in Derry. There on Sunday, October 8, Provisional Sinn Féin marched to celebrate the civil rights demonstration of October 5, 1968, when Stormont began to crack. Protest had in ten years been captured by Sinn Féin and reduced to displays in aid of the armed struggle. Demos were for prisoners of the armed struggle, victims of the armed struggle, martyrs of the armed struggle. At least in Derry the demonstration was an exercise in nostalgia. The event did not go off quite as planned. By the end of the day sixty-nine RUC men in Derry had been injured when the DUP staged a counterdemonstration. The times had changed, however, in that only two of the RUC had been injured by republicans; the other sixty-seven had been injured by the loyalists. The DUP came back with a protest march on October 14, rioting, as expected, occurred near Guildhall Square, considerable property was damaged, and another thirty-two policemen were injured. Politics was protesting protests.

Politics for the SDLP was projecting a wish list. On November 14 the SDLP annual conference voted that it was "desirable and inevitable" that the British withdraw. Why not seek everything since they were getting nothing? The SDLP urged the British and Irish governments to call a conference involving the two Northern Ireland communities. In December the party launched a "New Ireland" campaign that indicated the only solution was within an all-Ireland context. This was the very prospect that frightened all the unionists and a course of action that had no appeal in London, where Irish matters were still an intrusion. Ulster would get more seats at Westminster and less time from the establishment. The loyalists could not fashion a united direction, or any direction. Direct rule at least caused less anguish than any move to accommodate the minority. So unionist politics protested the IRA armed struggle, minority ambitions, and Dublin interference, and waited on London.

The IRA kept right on with the armed struggle. On November 14 bombs throughout the province injured thirty-seven people. The Provos had, as well, a traditional response to the H-Block confrontation. On November 26 Albert Myles, deputy governor of the Maze, was shot dead in his North Belfast home. GHQ had recognized that Northern Ireland operations were becoming more difficult: Bombing easy targets was insufficient and the security forces were no longer as vulnerable. Improved British technology, tactics, and intelligence had to be countered even to maintain the same level, much less escalate the campaign. Twomey had always favored spreading operations to England, where one bomb counted more than a dozen detonated in Ireland. And Brian Keenan had again set up active service units: Again, a very few people tied to GHQ, not to English assets, could cause disproportionate concern and attract English attention. On December 17 and 18 the IRA units in England launched bombing attacks on five British cities. Car bombs exploded in London. The IRA was the Christmas news.

The Provisional IRA had welcome news from a quite unexpected source. In England a criminal who had been involved in the robbery of a post office van discovered amid the takings a report, stamped SECRET, entitled "Northern Ireland: Future Terrorist Trends." It had been written by Brigadier Glover, and was complete with scribbled readers' initials. The robber dispatched the report to the Officials as well as the Provos. It was read with delight, shown to friends, and then in May 1970 to the press. It seemed a real coup, Irish luck on the IRA's side for once. It was a middle-level analysis that indicated not so much secrets as British army thinking on the IRA and Ireland. It bore little resemblance to Mason's analysis, indicating as it did that the Provos were engaged in a war of attrition that seemed likely to continue at the same level for the next five years, with increasing professionalism. Some of the estimates on IRA financing were shrewd if not exactly accurate; others, such as the Irish Republic's role as safe haven, were more conventional if not true exaggerations. For the IRA readers the analysis, with its prediction of a trend toward greater professionalism, indicated just how serious real British officers thought their secret army had become: a far cry from the haphazard scramble in 1970 to defend the threatened with a handful of mis-matched weapons.*

Yet nothing much had changed at all. The acceptable level of violence, the politics of protest, the everyday life of the province were irregularly interrupted by serious incidents, not just women marching in blankets or heavyset men with red, white, and blue rosettes throwing stones at "their" police, or the army rousting teenagers against a wall smeared with streaky letters appealing for all to Break the H-Blocks. These incidents, however, were seldom sufficiently serious to maintain the interests of London politicians or even the international media. Bombs in London had a short half-life of interest; bombs in Ireland were passé. To

---

*The report can be found reproduced in Seán Cronin's *Irish Nationalism: A History of Its Roots and Ideology* (Dublin: Academy Press, 1980), pp. 339–57.

bring in the foreign television cameras hard news had to last more than twenty-four hours. Instead the province became a regular stop for terror-and-violence footage taken on the way to Beirut or other killing grounds. The Troubles by 1978 had even been institutionalized by the international media.

In 1978 there was less optimism at the December summing up. Mason and General Creasey were still confident that the hard line was working, both would have preferred even more stringent measures, neither was convinced even yet that the RUC under Newman could cope with the IRA. The numbers, however, were not bad if still horrific: 14 army deaths in contrast to the 15 the previous year, 7 UDR (down from 14), 4 RUC (down from 8), 6 RUC Reserve (the same), with 50 civilians (down from 69). The death total was 81, in contrast to 1977's 112 and 1972's 467. The total for all other indicators—injured, incidents, weapons captured or searches made—were as encouraging—not yet acceptable but an improvement.

There had been real if not always visible improvements for the security forces. For much of the seventies the IRA had benefited from the American arms connection, which produced about 250 assault rifles and appropriate amounts of ammunition a year—enough to replace those lost by the active service units, caught in dumps, stolen, or lost. The civilian versions of the American M-16 had become the basic weapon of the IRA although as the size of the cell units decreased some individuals preferred other models: the NATO SLR used by the British army, items from the Heckler and Koch line or more specialist items from other sources, the Gewehr G-43 rifle or the Beretta submachine gun. Still the Armalite was the IRA weapon and the American connection was the sure source.

Efforts by Keenan and others to bring in weapons through the Palestinians, new American connections, and illicit European purchases had mixed results, mostly bad. Séamus McCollum, who had been arrested with Twomey in Dublin in December 1977, had failed in Cyprus when weapons acquired from the Palestinians had ended up with the Belgian police in December 1977. Five Irish-Americans, including Vincent Conlon from the 1956–62 campaign, were arrested in Philadelphia in December 1977 for shipping M-1 and Lee-Enfield rifles illegally. Even the Royal Canadian Mounted Police had gotten into the act, breaking up an IRA ring in 1975. There were friends elsewhere as well but always serious problems. Several antiterrorist intelligence sources in the Middle East and Europe had fashioned highly professional safeguards that were rarely penetrated by the IRA agents, who were innocent of clandestine tradecraft or, in some cases, of even rudimentary precautions. In Europe IRA operations in the mid-seventies were handled first in Belgium and Holland by Paul Kavanagh and then by others. These were ideal sites, between France and Germany, with border restrictions easing as trends to one Europe increased for tourists ahead of police cooperation. Small shipments through the ferry ports, Schiphol Airport, and the major harbors showed up in Ireland in dribs and drabs: SKS assault rifles, Beretta submachine guns, M742 Remington Woodmasters from the United States, as well as electronic equipment, cordite, small amounts of plastic explosives (no one liked to deal and to transport explosives, no matter how inert), advanced long-delay timers, and commercial detonators. All this was encouraging, but neither the

QMG nor the operators abroad could get a big European shipment through to Ireland.

Still, enough arms were purchased. The most famous and deadly proved to be seven M-60 United States Army heavy machine guns taken from the National Guard armory at Danvers near Boston in 1976 and smuggled to Ireland by 1978. The last M-60 was captured in Derry in August 1982, after the weapons had caused ten deaths and nineteen serious woundings and downed at least one helicopter.

The American connection collapsed as a result of simple police work. On April 11, 1976, a seventeen-year-old civil servant, Ann Loughlin, was arrested in the Ardoyne with a Finnish Valmet semiautomatic 7.62 rifle down the leg of her green slacks and twenty-one rounds of ammunition in her pockets. The serial number, 146325, was passed on to the American Treasury Department's Bureau of Alcohol, Tobacco, and Firearms and traced to the New York gun dealer George De Meo and from him to the B & B Guns store in Wilson, North Carolina. Two more IRA weapons, an Armalite AR-180 used by the Balcombe Street Provos unit in December 1975 and a Gewehr G-43 rifle seized by the Gárdaí in Buncrana, Donegal, on January 15, 1976, firmed up the connection. De Meo, who was a dealer, not an idealist, offered information for leniency—in 1980 he was given ten years. By then the authorities had traced 703 IRA weapons to the United States and made sufficient arrests to break the connection. The last blow was the natural death of a crucial link in New York. His innocent replacement made one unnecessary telephone call. On November 1, 1979, the Irish Gárdaí seized a shipment of 156 guns, including an M-60 machine gun, on the Dublin docks. No one showed up to claim them, and the papers, all in order, led nowhere. The Dublin end never came unraveled but the pipeline was broken and the QMG had to look elsewhere.

Very few weapons were actually needed by the Northern Ireland active service units, and these were kept in dumps and moved when needed as replacements from the outer fringes of the combat zone toward central Belfast. British ballistics could often trace the career of single, popular weapon over the years. Losses were very large except for closely held weapons in the countryside, where private dumps were possible. So the IRA QMG was always seeking more. In January 1979, with De Meo out of action—ample proof of a unity of purpose among Irish, American, and British law enforcement authorities—the security forces could feel progress on one front.

A second front that always seemed disappointing but improved was intelligence. All the old problems remained, although the conspirators and disinformation buffs had been weeded out in several organizations. There was no central control. There was rivalry among all the agencies, especially between the RUC and the military, and between MI5 and everyone else. There was still too much room for private initiative in the field that, like the loss of Captain Nairac in South Armagh, was counterproductive. There was neither guidance from London nor any great interest in the product. Nevertheless, by 1979 the product had improved enormously despite the problems, despite the turnover of military personnel in particular, and despite the continuing innocence of many regarding Irish matters. There had been lessons learned, codified, included in texts, and taught to those sent to the province. Files and categories had gradually been accumulated: the habits of the suspect, the routine of the dubious, the careers of the known subversives. The December 1977 raid that had lifted Séamus Twomey in Dublin had produced all sorts of IRA documents for the British. The repeated raids in Belfast particularly produced a growing midden of material. Very early on Newman had, as well, set up a special detective squad under Chief Inspector George Caskey to probe the relation of the IRA and Sinn Féin; more evidence was still needed for a charge of conspiracy. Few believed that Sinn Féin was an independent entity but then it was not just a creature of the IRA Army Council either. Mindful of the need for more texts and of the conspiracy case, in December 1977, security forces raided five Sinn Féin premises and the houses of twenty-nine suspects. In April 1978 three hundred police constables took part in raiding the two headquarter offices of Sinn Féin, local offices, activists' homes, and a printing works at Lurgan, where the weekly 13,500 copies of *An Phoblacht/ Republican News* were produced. The RUC assembled eight thousand potential exhibits for their case, including the five-thousand-word Maze document, "People's Assembly," that called for a broadening of the war machine through community politics: the new departure. Many of these documents were more theoretical than the police imagined, and certainly many were read by more security personnel than IRA volunteers. There were always more papers to read as the raids continued. In June 1979 a revealing find indicated that the IRA was just as busy reading RUC intentions from stolen communications. In any case, much IRA business, even the most important, is done by unarticulated consensus and tacit agreement, word of mouth, not by the exchange of correspondence or the management of files. Few of the older commanders talk much, few commanders want to know anything but what they need, and operational officers often keep their contacts in their heads. This was especially true with certain cunning planners like Séamus Costello of the Officials and INLA and Brian Keenan of the Provos. This is what makes a secret army secret.

The British, however, were finding Ireland and the IRA far less secret. Paper does talk and people and experience is not all lost, even with shifting personnel. Combined with the constant stream of detailed reports from patrols, the police, informers, mechanical devices, roadblocks, public records, spies, the Gárdaí, from all manner of sources, this paper helped produce an enormously detailed mosaic. Every operation was the font of detailed police work. Every bullet was traced, every document filed, often every witness questioned. The computers worked overtime; and if there were many unturned stones, many stones were on file, certainly all those that had been thrown.

The guerrilla sea was being poured into a fish bowl—not that this seemed to disturb the fish greatly, for the IRA coped, took precautions, shot informers, intimidated those who might talk, perfected their own tradecraft, gave up the telephone, became more professional. By 1979 the whole conflict had become more professional, whatever the lapses and lacks on either side. If the British had clipped the American connection by the end of the decade, the IRA still had ample arms. If the British intelligence was coping, especially in monitoring the hard core, this did not prevent operations. If the IRA could still operate, there had been no escalation. There had been no politics either during 1978, no progress, no lessening of tension or reduction of a general intransigence. The year had been a continuation of the recent past, troubled, violent, predictable.

On January 1, 1979, the IRA detonated bombs throughout the entire province. Brian Keenan, who was still directing foreign operations, had prepared to take the campaign abroad again, this time in an unexpected place. He had dispatched an active service unit to the Continent, where the easy border crossings, large number of foreign tourists and guest workers, and the novelty of the arena offered considerable promise. On March 22 two gunmen shot dead the British ambassador to Holland, Sir Richard Sykes, along with his footman, while they stood beside his Rolls-Royce parked outside his residence at The Hague. The two gunmen walked away and IRA sources in Belfast conceded that the Provisionals might be responsible. The assassination ushered in a minor but continuing second front in Europe, with volunteers shuttling in and out over the next decade, rarely making use of any permanent diaspora and rarely operating with great efficiency. For some time various agencies assumed that an IRA unit had nearly blown away General Alexander Haig, the American NATO commander, by mistake when targeting the British commander's car. In fact a German group was responsible. Other IRA actions were often inept and counterproductive, hitting civilians, even women and children, by mistake. The tradecraft of assassination is not easily learned on the job or readily taught by men on the run. An attempt on the British ambassador to NATO killed a Belgian banker instead.

The presence of the IRA in Europe, however, cost the British Army of the Rhine and the diplomatic and intelligence service time, money, and concern, as security had to be increased, operations initiated, and habits changed. At the same time it eroded any residue of official support for the Provisional IRA in European countries. The Germans had the Red Army Faction and 2nd of July, the Dutch the South Moluccans, and the Belgians the CCC; everyone suffered from the Palestinians, then the Armenians; and so the arrival of the IRA was hardly welcome. Unlike the INLA, the Provos made very few local contacts but kept to themselves, posed as workers or tourists, ran operations until caught or forced to withdraw. Additional security might cost the British money and time but the repayment came as the IRA emerged as part of the "international terrorist conspiracy."

Actually the Provisionals had very few contacts outside their own diaspora. The Libyans, still annoyed about the lost of the *Claudia,* gave money at irregular meetings in European hotels over these years and kept in touch. The Palestinians were sympathetic to the occasional agents who made their way to Beirut. But mostly the Irish kept themselves to themselves. The efforts to buy arms usually aborted. One agent with drink taken misplaced twenty-five thousand pounds on one French trip. Agents were sent to safe houses that were no longer safe. Secure communications were only an aspiration. Anyway, the IRA Army Council did not feel that the armed struggle was going to be won in Belgium or Germany but at home. In Europe the risks were small, the cost mostly in money, and the returns could be high—a reasonable bet.

If there were to be really effective operations away from Ireland then the site was England, where every spectacular would have a far greater effect. The QMG continued to seek arms but seldom to any great effect. The various revolutionary legates to Europe and far places brought back little. The real war was elsewhere. Thus, what GHQ wanted were bombs in London and Manchester and British army bodies in Tyrone and Derry. Neither was an easy matter. In fact, on March 20 Brian Keenan was arrested. The RUC had stopped two cars, a brown Honda Civic and a yellow Toyota, traveling north on the main Dublin-Belfast road just beyond Banbridge in County Down and taken the occupants, three men and a woman to be questioned. One turned out to be Keenan. He was moved to England within two days, to stand trial in June 1980, on the evidence of fingerprints found at two of the bomb factories of the Balcombe Street group. The British blamed him for the three-month wave of bombing in which 9 people died and 113 were wounded. He was found guilty and sentenced to eighteen years.

Whatever his virtues, Keenan was not a tidy administrator nor very forthcoming. Much of what he knew went into prison with him. Over the years the most successful IRA operators abroad had made use of private individuals and avoided their own. Keenan was no exception. Both his talents and his contacts were gone—a loss that GHQ tried to make good by dispatching a rescue team to England to try another helicopter escape.

The operation was typical. The volunteers were chosen because they were sound and dependable rather than discreet and sophisticated. All were well known to the security forces in Northern Ireland, their faces on file, their movements checked when possible. The mission was blown from the first. It is not easy for senior active service people to pull out without a whimper. It is even more difficult to send them off to a largely mysterious city where Belfast accents and inexplicable movements are likely to attract attention. In any case the four—Gerald Tuite, who had been involved in the 1978 bombing campaign; Bobby Campbell and Bobby Storey, the senior active service people; and an older republican, Dickie Glenholmes—were arrested in a flat in Holland Park, London, and, except for Storey, eventually ended up in Brixton Prison, the target of the helicopter escape.

If Francis Hughes was the old model, town-and-country guerrilla, then Bobby Storey's career choice as a new urban guerrilla made him very contemporary. And heretofore he had been very successful. He was ruthless, cunning, streetwise, parochial, bold, and best of all, lucky. His older brother Séamus, at home in Riverdale, West Belfast, in 1971, was arrested but escaped with nine others on rope ladders thrown over the prison walls, stayed out for a year, but was recaptured and sentenced to three years. Bobby Storey, the younger brother, had "come under notice" although he was not interned until his seventeenth birthday, on April 11, 1973. He was not released until May 1975, when internment was phased out. He returned to West Belfast totally committed, a professional in attitude and employment.

Several factors motivate a gunman in Northern Ireland. There are real economic complaints. One-third of the members of Sinn Féin are unemployed, in contrast to only 13 percent of the SDLP (still no small number); the housing is truly poor and so are the prospects. Most affected are the permanently unemployed in the urban areas. At best some manage either casual labor or entry-level jobs—messengers, bar assistants, and stock clerks—until a new generation is hired. Thus there is a pool who can foresee nothing but the dole or emigration.

Such a pool of the young, active, and resentful, renewed with each new school class and laced annually with those who finished secondary school to no avail, cannot help but be a fruitful source for the gunman recruiter. In fact the IRA turns away many who would volunteer, to prevent a guerrilla overload. And those most likely to seek entry are often those with an experience of personal or at least family humiliation or harassment. This is hardly a special event in the hard-core nationalist areas—most of the young have similar experiences. Some have as well a republican family or close friends, most display a mix of idealism and a sense of adventure, and all are influenced by the polarized atmosphere of the particular day.

These factors hold true, however, for practically everyone coming of age in the intensely nationalist areas. Not everyone has a republican family but most have relatives involved, most have been hassled or harassed, most know someone who is imprisoned, often for cause but always for the cause, and nearly everyone has been exposed to the riotous times: rituals, protests, incidents, army blocks and searches, the searing oratory of the loyalists, the immediate memory of the great events: August 1969, internment, Bloody Sunday. Storey was no different than most, including many who did not become volunteers. No one ever really knew who would volunteer, not priest or parent or friends. Storey was typical except that he had been active almost always—a child stone thrower, a teenage messenger, and as soon as possible, a volunteer.

On paper Storey was an unprepossessing IRA agent, a young man well known to the authorities, with no education, no exposure to a world beyond West Belfast, and no skills, and at six feet, four inches, highly visible and easily recognizable. He was screened, monitored, and yet active. His operations were rumored and as far as the authorities were concerned real as he moved up the steps in operational skills. He was suspected of bombing the Skyways Hotel at Aldergrove Airport— how many six-four IRA bombers could there be? The judge was not impressed with the evidence ("unsatisfactory and unsafe") and so Storey was released. On March 11, 1976, he was apparently involved in a killing in Dunmurry but again he escaped punishment, although his teenage companion was convicted of murder. Storey was now famous—the RUC called him the Brain Surgeon because of his reputed "head jobs," murder by a single shot in the head—but his luck held. He was arrested again for the murder in Turf Lodge of a member of the security forces in December 1977, and the charges were dropped. In May 1979 he was released from another charge of ambushing and wounding a soldier in a house in Lenadoon. Put on the Keenan escape by the IRA, he was watched by the authorities until his arrest on December 14 of that year in Holland Park. He denied everything. Tried but not convicted, retried and found not guilty, he left Old Bailey in April 1981, the ideal urban guerrilla, deadly, dedicated, cunning, capable of evading the system of protection and punishment, just as Francis Hughes had used his environment to continue operations. Both had been over-used. Bobby Storey, with his height, his limitations, and his record, had had a remarkable run that should have persuaded the Belfast Brigade to use him sparingly. Good gunmen are hard to find. He was arrested in August 1981, convicted of possessing a firearm, and sentenced to eighteen years: his first conviction after a career of nearly ten years. It was a triumph for the RUC and the

British army, who recalled that once he resisted one shift after another of interrogators for sixteen hours a day for seven days, staring at the wall, saying nothing, not even hello—a technique that became standard IRA procedure after arrest. In the Kesh he was as troublesome, breaking out in a great escape in 1983, although he remained free only an hour and was picked up wading the Lagan River trying to evade the cordon. When the Army Council lost Keenan who better to get him back than someone like Storey? He was not elegant, not sophisticated, not even unknown, but he was good and sound. So they sent him for Keenan.

What Keenan had done was carry his address book. The British found it when he was arrested. Seemingly no one in the IRA is ever arrested without carrying revealing, usually most damaging, papers. For a secret army that kept few records, the IRA volunteers always seemed to carry "something" written down. Keenan was no exception, although something was salvaged because his notes were, like his contacts, personal. The loss of Keenan did not interrupt the IRA's campaign in the province but it caused severe difficulties once some of the entries in Keenan's coded address book were unraveled. (In fact, it is likely that a more cunning code would have been unraveled even more quickly.) Keenan depended on notes to himself, initials, and references that continued to worry his colleagues for months once they realized the British had the book. In the meantime the security forces moved on what they had. On June 15, after a period of surveillance, three hundred police and one hundred soldiers raided three houses in Coolnasill Park, Andersonstown, at Dunmurry, and near Lisburn.

There was an enormous haul of documents to add to the growing file. And the RUC found in one attic a command post filled with radios, unscrambling equipment, sophisticated monitors, military-style transmitters, position-fixing devices, telephone taps routed through the British Telecom network from sophisticated leads. The entire high-tech complex had been equal to that of the security forces. Even more disconcerting, the security forces found the transcripts of Operation Hawk, the most sophisticated and comprehensive surveillance operation ever mounted by the RUC. Hawk had been tracking the IRA leadership, feeding in new data, using Keenan's notebook—and all the while the IRA had listened in and adjusted. Belfast GHQ Intelligence/Officer had even moved their IRA commanders about in order to discover their code names—one gunman was disconcerted to learn he was listed as "Chicken." Breaking Hawk had made it possible for the IRA to cancel a large operation just before Keenan's arrest. Two ten-man Provo squads were to penetrate the petrol tank farm at Sydenham, in the midst of the Belfast docks, and plant forty-two bombs made with a 420-pound cache of explosives that had been smuggled into the Markets area of the city early in March as the RUC had watched. Instead of another killing SAS ambush, which was in place, the IRA lost only the explosives. And they plugged more leaks that had been exploited by the British. Intelligence played both ways.

After the collapse of Hawk following the three-house sweep in Belfast, the British were no longer so ready to chortle over the IRA's incompetence. This was the "Paddy Factor." This produced their own goals when IRA bombs killed IRA volunteers. There were stories and examples and fables: one incompetent IRA bomber who, traveling in the underground stayed on the Circle Line, in London, going around and around and never reaching the end of the line, where he was to leave his device. There were volunteers who forgot to wind clocks or left the detector back at the flat, gunmen who called home to Belfast, got drunk at the wrong time, blundered about with ancient equipment and little clue. The Paddy Factor was the British professionals' assumption of Irish incompetence. Some of those who had been in South Armagh or patrolled off the Falls were not as sanguine but there was a general agreement among analysts that the IRA lacked operational elegance, international contacts, or technological skills. The end of Hawk was not a complete end of innocence for the security forces or of IRA blunders but it indicated that both would subsequently be on a higher level. Even after ten years, however, the IRA lacked sophisticated talent, remained a working-class organization in a middle-class world. But they coped: On-the-job training, concentrated minds, persistence, and a little help from friends went a long way. The debacle of Hawk was evidence to that effect.

The IRA, operationally conservative to a fault, relied on the old ways, tested and true. If operations were moved to The Hague, the killing was still personal and close up, two gunmen on their own far from GHQ. And there were always the errors. On March 3 a Provo bomb-ambush in County Armagh caught a group of boys on their way to a dance in Keady. In the explosion two sixteen-year-olds were killed and three others injured, one losing an arm. The IRA could only offer its "deepest sympathy" to the families and explain that "tragically the youths, and their position on the road, were mistaken for the movement of soldiers, and the bomb was set off." Over the years the necessity for such apologies was such that the cynical suggested that the Republican Publicity Bureau and Sinn Féin could use a form letter. The British army, after their own errors and mistakes, tried to stress that the violence was initiated by the IRA—the troops were just responding. Their spokesmen too were sorry about the civilians caught in ambushes or hit by stray bullets.

The violence in the province was revealed again during 1978–79 to be in a way responsible for other, even more unsavory, horrors. On February 20 the loyalist murder gang known as the Shankill Butchers, responsible for nineteen killings, were sentenced at the Crumlin Road Courthouse in Belfast. Justice O'Donnell passed forty-two life sentences and terms of imprisonment totaling two thousand years on the eleven defendants. Dominated by the single depraved and cunning serial killer, Lenny Murphy, the very private army using UVF colors had killed for pleasure, for fear of their leader, as a matter of little concern, killed again and again in such a way that from the very first the RUC felt matters other than politics were involved. Murphy, in prison on a fourteen-year sentence, escaped the murder charges because his colleagues still feared to testify against him—he had poisoned one witness inside prison and had had two others badly beaten. The reports of the murders, only some sectarian, were gruesome. On February 3, 1977, the Butchers had abducted Joseph Morrisey off the Antrim Road and dumped his ruined and disfigured body in a parking lot at Glencairn a little later. His teeth had been torn out, his fingers broken, his face smashed with a hatchet. There were forty slash wounds and his head was nearly severed from his body. The RUC detectives, hardly novices in bloody violence, had never seen anything like it. Politics, even the most brutal vigilante politics, had little to do with such killing. The most awful Protestant murders were relevant to political purpose, often carried out by limited but dutiful young men eager to defend, with victims who were traitors, rivals, or symbols—Catholic men.

The Shankill Butchers hid behind a loyalist screen and killed and tortured for pleasure and their own sense of purpose. The Butchers' tale was not finished until Lenny Murphy was released in August 1981. Within twenty-four hours he had killed again, a stray alcoholic derelict, a Protestant innocent, Norman Alexander Maxwell, who crossed his path at the Rumford Street Loyalist Club. Maxwell was beaten into the ground and then killed by Murphy driving a car back and forth over the body. There was no reason except the opportunity to kill. The next victim, Brian Smyth, a UVF member from Bangor, simply wanted money owed on Murphy's secondhand Rover car. Murphy was seen as a danger to everyone. The atmosphere had changed. Neither the UVF nor the UDA wanted mad murderers disturbing their arrangements and clearly Murphy was without restraint. After yet another murder, Murphy was killed on November 16, when he arrived to visit his girlfriend at Forthriver Park, by a team from the Provisionals. The IRA had been acting on intelligence received from their sources in the UVF-UDA community, which would finger their own for their own purposes. Murphy was just one of several prominent members of Protestant paramilitaries who were given to the Provos.

The sentences given to the Shankill Butchers again indicated that the RUC was more professional and conventional, for those who were eager that the police shed the lingering traces of the bad old days. Newman, who had become Sir Kenneth in 1977, would finish his term on December 31, 1979, and could feel that the RUC was a transformed force. In a sense the RUC was whatever the beholder desired. Some saw and would continue to see the RUC as sectarian, because it was largely Protestant and oppressive, and because it was both paramilitary and also unsympathetic to nationalist aspirations. Others felt it was a highly competent, brave, and dedicated law enforcement agency, which, if not like every other British police force because of the special situation in Northern Ireland, was still worthy of praise. There would never be agreement in the province although the opponents of the RUC grew fewer.

The Catholics and their parties would perceive the RUC as more professional not because this was the case, which it often was, but because the political climate required nationalist accommodation with the authorities. Newman had done much that was real but mainly he had begun and his successor, John Herman, had continued to improve the professional quality of policing and ease the hard edges of official sectarian arrogance. The RUC was still a Protestant police force. The majority attitudes could not be removed and often caused problems—the interrogations at Castlereagh took place during Newman's tenure. There was no hope to make a Protestant police force under daily threat of violence, largely from the Catholic minority, behave as if a dirty war did not exist. So it was still possible to sell the old image to eager or even innocent buyers. Thus, on August 2 the U.S. State Department, not unmindful of the Irish-American lobby, refused to license an export order of three thousand M-1 carbines and .357 magnum revolvers, to the outrage of the authorities. On the same day the IRA killed the three hundredth soldier, which added to the authorities' indignation. The State Department seemed to equate IRA gunmen with the RUC in refusing them both guns. The NIO felt it was an outrage—but these were certainly the wages of past sins.

For the most part the RUC in 1979 concentrated on its new posture, which was required by Ulsterization. The British army remained skeptical: The army saw insurgency and found it difficult to imagine how policing, however professional, could cope. The police were not sufficiently aggressive, not hard enough, not familiar with the appropriate techniques to winkle out the IRA. The RUC tended to treat the IRA as an extraordinarily effective criminal menace, while the army responded to them as occasionally competent guerrillas. The army's response, despite all the denials over the years, had gone far to create the IRA as a real secret army by playing the guerrilla game, while the RUC treating crime as crime sought order rather than a war. Since the Northern Ireland Office never was able and never sought total command and control of the thrust for order, the two responses continued to run free and more often than not canceled each other out.

Whatever the structural problems the security forces faced in 1979, the same old IRA kept on the pressure of the long war. Thus, while the Labour government seemed to be winding down in Britain, the news in the province was more violence. On March 23 the IRA set off twenty-four bombs across the province. Mason still felt the Provos were reeling and in a sense this was true; the IRA could persist if not escalate. The time of the protracted campaign had come. IRA operations tended to be traps or bombing operations difficult to prevent because of the huge number of targets. Some traps would work and many would not; a few waves of bombings could be organized but a constant attack could not. The province did not have so much a level of tolerable violence as a series of tolerable incidents.

The unending creeping violence in the province, as had been the case for a decade, scarcely attracted the attention of the London establishment, fixated on the far more crucial matter of the decay of the Labour government. James Callaghan had replaced Wilson with a quite splendid vita—Chancellor of the Exchequer, Foreign Secretary, and Home Secretary—when his 1969 intrusions into Irish matters had seemingly offered hope and accommodation. Genial, competent, and if need be cunning, he ruled as a result of a Labour-Liberal pact with a very small and uncertain majority by the summer of 1978. He had also ruled not as well at the top of the greasy pole as he had given promise on the way up. Increasingly he had problems with his own, the unions and their demands.

Ireland was the least of his worries. Rees had been concerned with such matters, unheeded in Westminster; his replacement, Mason, was concerned not with politics but with order, reflecting a cabinet that only discussed Irish law and order, never Irish policy. The Northern Ireland Office was left to cope, the Foreign and Commonwealth Office had little to say, very few in or out of government had any Irish interest (Rees was safely back at the Home Office), and any Labour advantage had already been taken. Ireland was of concern only because

Callaghan, in return for more Ulster seats at Westminster, secured the votes of the Ulster Unionists, assuring his majority over the winter of 1978–79. The logic of the seats did not mute some concern of some Labour people that they had been sold for time in office, a bad bargain. Time to cope with the economy was, however, crucial to Labour, for an election would be required by October 1979.

In any case the Conservatives showed as little interest in Irish matters as Labour. Douglas Hurd, as Tory front bench spokesman on European affairs, had visited Belfast in February 1978 to prepare for a local BBC TV "Spotlight" program on British perspectives and had spoken to Andy Tyrie and then Gerry Adams and Danny Morrison. Adams was not impressed with him lecturing when he should be listening. Then again, Hurd and the establishment were unimpressed with most Northern Ireland figures, and republicans in particular, thinking them limited, crude, narrow, intransigent, and tainted by the gunmen. The Unionists were furious when they found out about the meeting and complained to Margaret Thatcher. No one in London cared much one way or the other.

The voices that felt Labour should not be vulnerable to Unionist pressures were muted, while all attention focused instead on a series of disastrous strikes and pay agreements that produced the Winter of Discontent in 1978–79. There was talk of an emergency and there was evidence that Labour's time had run out. The prospect of an earlier election was obvious.

Labour had hoped to straggle through and face the Conservatives, led by Margaret Thatcher, with some semblance of order. She was still, as a woman, a novelty, although her time in opposition had been spent well and her competence could not really be doubted. Her party was moving to a position clearly opposed even to that of Heath, who accepted many of the assumptions and arrangements with welfare in Britain as inviolate. James Prior, a Heath heir, continued, on the other hand, to dominate much Tory domestic policy, representing a posture greatly in alignment with Labour assumptions. Thatcher began to be more clearly opposed to a generation of state socialism and establishment compliance with the welfare state. She wanted an election that gave Britain a clear choice, not more of the same, Heath or Wilson, Callaghan or Prior. "Choice is the essence of ethics."* Her more radical right advisers were considered an abomination by Labour, and her own ideas considered reactionary. But by 1979 the Labour record did not inspire great confidence, and even running against a strident woman, a hard Tory, would not be a sure thing.

Whatever the plots and conspiracies of British politics, there was never an Irish issue. No one worried about an Irish vote or the impact of a general election on Ulster. Yet the Irish played a vital role in setting the stage for the advent of Margaret Thatcher. In January the strikes grew worse, as the water workers, truck drivers, and public service workers went out. The railroads stopped, the hospitals closed, schoolchildren had no schools. Union behavior on the picket lines in February became aggressive and by March all pay claims had escalated as the government seemed to waver. The government moved from day to day until a

*Hugo Young, *One of Us* (London: Pan, 1989), p. 123.

vote of censure by the Scottish nationalists took place on March 28. Labour could put together one more majority if the Liberals held, if some of the small parties gave votes, if the Irish helped. Two Unionists, John Carson and Harold Mc-Cusker, voted with Labour; the other eight voted with the Conservatives. The break was not unexpected. The Irish who really did not help were in the end two who "naturally" should have been Labour: Gerry Fitt and Frank Maguire. They abstained. Maguire was mostly an absentee member. His constituents saw little advantage in any English combination. But Fitt was a natural ally. His vote indicated just how reactionary Callaghan's Irish policy appeared on the Falls: bought Unionist votes, Mason's law and order, the snubs, the years of last remembered, first forgotten. Labour fell by one vote, 311–310. Polling day would be May 3.

Almost before the campaign began the Irish issue arose once more in a peculiarly lethal manner. Costello's descendants in the INLA-IRSP had not faded away; instead, they had evolved into a small, hard-core group with contacts in Europe and ambitions to compete with the Provos in an armed struggle. As with many other groups limited in resources and numbers, their first choice was spectacular individual terror. On March 31 Airey Neave, Conservative spokesman on Northern Ireland and friend of Thatcher, got into his car in the parking lot of the House of Commons at Westminster, the heart of the establishment. Under the blue Vauxhall INLA had attached a two-stage bomb that had a timer, using a wristwatch, which was already on and run down to zero. The detonator was live. The second stage would go off as soon as the car was no longer level. Neave shifted, drove up a ramp, and hit a small bump. The mercury tilt switch in the explosive device affixed to the bottom of the vehicle under the seat clicked and the bomb detonated. The explosion tore up through the seat and ripped off both his legs. A policeman rushed to his side and looked into the shattered car. Neave's face was blackened, his body ruined. He died thirty minutes later, just after reaching the hospital. The bomb announced that the INLA was back in the killing business. Their communiqué claimed Neave was a rabid militarist who called for more repression of the Irish people. His murder shocked the British but did not put Ireland into the election as an issue.

Thatcher was running to transform British society, not to worry about Ulster terrorists. Oddly, several of those close to Thatcher—Neave, Ian Gow, and Enoch Powell—*had* been concerned with Ireland, a rarity in the party and among British politicians. Neave supported devolution, although with some doubts—direct rule had advantages. Gow and Powell preferred to integrate the province, let normal politics arise. Powell, no longer a Conservative but an uneasy recruit to the Official Unionists, pushed not only integration (especially in London, away from his colleagues, who wanted a return to Stormont) but also a perplexing conspiracy theory that lost him friends and followers and convinced few that the CIA, the Americans, the Foreign Office, and others were involved in a plot to bring a united Ireland into NATO. Thatcher had revealed almost no interest in the Irish problem or the special positions of Neave, Gow, and Powell. If she had any interest in Ireland, it arose from a conservative bent and a natural sympathy for the unionist position. The Conservative Manifesto had simply called for a regional assembly—devolution. Some in the party, including Gow and Sir John Biggs-

Davidson of the Northern Ireland back-bench committee, continued to favor total integration. This position had some support in the party and the charm of simplicity. Treat the province like Devon and soon it would be like Devon and the Provos would give it up. The Conservative "integrationalists" were the only real alternative to the agreed policy of direct rule based on imposing order. The question was best left to the Northern Ireland Secretary of the moment (and few had any complaint about Mason, a sound man, a hard man) and the security forces. All supported the army and the police, decent under dreadful provocation, a credit to the kingdom.

Most Conservatives simply had little serious interest in the province, a distant, strange, and unpleasant place. A bomb on April 17, in the midst of the campaign, that killed four RUC constables at Bessbrook, Armagh, just reinforced this view. Thatcher, too, saw the Irish issue as one of law and order and not one of accommodation. Her concern was to make Britain great, "to change our ways and our direction"*—except in Ireland, where no novelty was needed until order was restored. The real battle was over making Britain great, reversing a generation of the welfare state, bringing back initiative. In the spring of 1979 something was obviously needed as the country teetered on the brink of an emergency brought on by greed and Labour compliance. The Conservatives offered another way, one worth the risk. On May 3 Thatcher and the Conservatives won a majority of forty-three seats.

The election campaign in the province had moved down the allotted path of tribal politics. The same people ran in the same districts, made the same speeches, received the same votes. Yet, because of the splits in the various parties, there was a sense of change and uncertainty and gain for the extremes—only the DUP took new seats. In East Belfast, Craig, running as an Official Unionist, after his swerve at the convention barely lost his seat to Peter Robinson, the rising young man of the DUP, in a near dead heat, trailing by only 15,994–15,930, and in North Belfast John McQuade also won for the DUP over the Official Unionists. James Kilfedder resigned from the Official Unionists and won as an independent. The SDLP declined from 20.6 percent in the 1977 local election to 18.3. The DUP, despite the wins, dropped from 12.7 to 10.2. The OUP was the apparent gainer, with 36.6 percent, over three times the vote of Paisley and company. Alliance hung on with 11.8 but the Republican Clubs and NILP got smaller. The UDA had announced in *Beyond the Religious Divide,* which came out on March 29, for negotiated independence, but would put forward no candidates until the council election in May 1981.

Mostly the Westminster election had been a testing for Northern Irish tribal leadership that in the marginal districts risked a loss to the others if the test split the vote. In the June 7 elections for the European Parliament a provincewide vote indicated more closely the tenor of political opinion and the powers of the organizations in the first count—Paisley won on the first count, Hume on the third, and John Taylor on the sixth.

*Young, p. 130.

Paisley	170,688	29.8%
Hume	140,622	24.6
Taylor	68,185	11.9
West	59,984	10.0
Napier (Alliance)	39,026	6.8
Kilfedder	38,198	6.7
McAliskey	33,969	5.9
Bleakley (Community)	9,383	1.6
Devlin, Paddy	6,122	1.1
Cummings, E. (UPNI)	3,712	0.6
Brennan, B. (Rep. C.)	3,258	0.6
Donnelly, F. (Rep. C.)	1,160	0.2
Murray, J. (U. Lib.)	932	0.2

In an election that could be seen as a poll that would not reward the candidate with much relevant power but would provide great prestige and a wider stage, the loyalists voted first for the most visible and articulate spokesmen of their grievances. The Catholics voted for their leader, the coming head of the SDLP, as Fitt and his London-centered posture became irrelevant. The others voted for their own, for unionists and nationalists, for Bernadette or Hume or even a few for Paddy Devlin and the Officials' Republican Clubs. If there was any message at all it was that Ulster loyalists were unyielding and unhappy and the SDLP was a closed monopoly looking away to Dublin. The loyalists were likely to be even more intransigent and unhappy if prodded for an accommodation with an Irish connection. Two provincial elections in two months, of only marginal interest to anyone but specialists, indicated no change, certainly not for the better.

The next month everything returned to normal. On July 18, at the European Parliament at Strasbourg, Ian Paisley, who had complained the day before that the Union Jack was being flown upside down in front of the building, was shouted down when he sought to interrupt Jack Lynch, the European Council president. Paisley would pursue Ulster's own agenda even in Europe. Tomás O Fiaich returned from Rome as Cardinal O Fiaich to announce that his invitation to Pope John Paul II to visit Ireland had been accepted. Everyone in the Republic seemed delighted. All the Northern Ireland Catholics appeared equally delighted. The novelty of a Pope, a Polish Pope visiting Ireland delighted all, the pious and the curious. Despite the erosion of secularism the Irish Catholic church was still an enormously powerful and pervasive institution, securely based on the faith of millions on the island. Even the sophisticated, in some cases especially the sophisticated, thought the visit grand, a brilliant concept. The cunning hoped the Pope would be against violence and would say so publicly. Everyone practical saw opportunity in the visit. Paisley called for the Pope to be banned from Northern Ireland. The Church of Ireland's bishop of Connor, Dr. Arthur Butler, deplored Paisley's attitude and indicated that he was pleased for the sake of the Roman Catholic community. The Presbyterian moderator, Dr. William Craig, was unwilling to meet the Pope "not from any personal feelings or animosities, but from theological convictions." Paisley disapproved on all these grounds and claimed, as leading June vote catcher, to speak for the province: "I have the right to speak for the Protestant people of Ulster, for I have a mandate from them while these clergy have only ecclesiastical officialdom." And the dispute dragged on, involving all with an opinion to offer or a criticism to make. Paisley had to be told his bullying days were over. The proper did so throughout the island. The Bible-thumping parson was a recruiting agent for the Provos. The fundamentalists defended their long-held ground. The Grand Orange Lodge criticized the visit and regretted "that the occasion should promote the unacceptable face of Romanism." There was one oddity in the barrage of predictable responses: The radical Protestants of the UDA assured Cardinal O Fiaich that the Pope could visit wherever he liked. In any case, the Pope was scheduled for September and it appeared that he would visit Armagh.

All the fuss, the reflexive animosities and posturing, the matters of principles displayed as trailing banners, the opportunity to take high-minded and popular positions at no cost, often to be found in the province after one more atrocity when violence had to be deplored, tended to erode whatever shreds of patience that remained in the province. The same flurry of provocation and Pavlovian reaction occurred on August 11 when an Irish National Caucus delegation indicated in Belfast that it planned to make Northern Ireland a major issue in the United States elections. The authorities and the loyalists in Northern Ireland were dead set against Irish-American tinkering or any American involvement at all: The Americans were distant, ignorant, and probably the friends of the Provos. The good work that Hume and Dublin had done among the Irish-American politicians and the American political establishment in general was ignored. Habitually America had meant trouble for Britain in Ireland. On August 22 the new Northern Ireland Secretary, Humphrey Atkins, rejected the suggestion of Governor Hugh Carey of New York, one of the famed Four Horsemen, that Carey should preside over New York talks involving Atkins and Irish Foreign Minister Michael O'Kennedy—an SDLP dream event. It was also a quite unlikely eventuality as far as the British were concerned.

Prime Minister Margaret Thatcher had indicated her priorities when Humphrey Atkins, a handsome man with well-cut suits but no Irish connection, who had worked with her in opposition, was on May 5 dispatched as Northern Secretary of State, the third Tory whip to be sent to Ireland, after Whitelaw and Pym. He came to Ireland not apparently for the benefit of the province or to pursue a special policy but as exile and reward. Rhodesia was to receive far more attention from Number 10 Downing Street than Ulster, where direct rule and imposed order through stringent security measures were matters for technicians, to be overseen by Atkins and neglected by all others engaged in transforming British society. The Irish could go back to their interminable feuds and follies. And so they did.

At a little after 11:30 A.M. on Monday, August 27, the twenty-eight-foot cruiser *Shadow* V moved out into the waters off Mullaghmore in Sligo on Ireland's west coast. On board were Earl Mountbatten and five members of his family: the dowager Lady Brabourne, eighty-two, mother-in-law to his daughter; Lord and Lady Brabourne; and their twin sons, Nicholas and Timothy, Mountbatten's grandchildren. The boat was piloted by a fifteen-year-old boy from Enniskillen,

Paul Maxwell. Mountbatten was near the end of his vacation. He had been coming to Classiebawn Castle at Mullaghmore for years. And for years he had been watched by the IRA intelligence people in the west of Ireland.

From the beginning of the Troubles in 1969 there had been thought of exploiting his presence. He was a royal, the queen's cousin, an international figure who, as the violence continued, seemed to feel, like many other English visitors, that a cheery greeting by the locals meant acceptance. Ruairí O Brádaigh had felt that the house might be "sequestered"—seized by republicans—for the refugees fleeing south in the summer of 1969 but nothing was done. The I/O in Fermanagh had brought various schemes to GHQ, unwanted by Mac Stiofáin and his successors. The focus was on the six counties and the British army, not assassination. There was inherently nothing wrong with targeting Mountbatten but the units in the area never came up with a firm plan. In 1978, by the time matters seemed to be in hand vacation time was up. There would be another go in 1979, this time using a bomb carefully tested in Louth and carried out by a small group brought in especially for the mission. He had been carefully watched. There were the usual Gárdaí assigned to him but little real security and no interest out of Belfast. On August 27 two Gárdaí watched the boat through binoculars from the shore.

On that Monday and most days the easiest access to Mountbatten was the boat. In 1979 IRA intelligence indicated that the Monday run around the lobster pots might be the last chance. This time there was a bomb in place and a radio-controlled detonator. If an attempt was to be made, it would have to be on Monday and the presence of the others would have to be ignored. The local O/C with authorization to carry out the operation did so. He was after a symbol. Mountbatten, at seventy-nine, was an ornament of the British establishment, honored for his war service and for his direction, as viceroy of India, of the last days of the British raj. He was honored by his birth (no merit there) and by those who loved elegance and tradition. Earl Mountbatten of Burma, the uncle of the Queen, the symbol, was what the Provos detested: British arrogance personified. He was not a visible enemy of Ireland, not a figure with any real power, not personally hateful. He was, however, an imperial symbol and his violent removal would have a profound effect—rather like the murder of the British ambassador Ewart-Biggs in Dublin. In this the Army Council was mistaken. Even in Dublin not one in a thousand people could have named the British ambassador, although most people knew there was one; but worldwide tens of millions of people had heard of Lord Mountbatten. The impact of his death would be far greater than the Army Council or GHQ imagined.

When *Shadow V* reached the lobster pots Paul Maxwell brought the boat to a slow stop and moved to the side to pull in a pot. When the pot reached the surface, there was a roar and a huge flash. The boat disappeared in a burst of smoke as a blast wave shook the shore. Mountbatten, Maxwell, and Mountbatten's grandson, Nicholas Knatchbull, fourteen, were killed outright. The elderly Lady Brabourne died the next day. Lord and Lady Brabourne were seriously injured. The news came through almost at once, even if details were sketchy. Few had any doubt from the first that the Provos were to blame. It fit their style.

Even before the bomb detonated, a thirty-one-year-old carpenter, Tommy

McMahon, an IRA explosives officer in South Armagh who lived in Carrick-macross in County Monaghan, along with Francis McGirl, a gravedigger from Ballinamore, County Leitrim, had been stopped and arrested at a roadblock by the Irish Gárdaí on simple suspicion. The two were kept for questioning. Once the word on Mountbatten came in to the police, they had further suspicions. McMahon was found to have paint from the boat on his shoe. He was a man with no republican record except for being briefly detained several years before when an IRA constitution was found under his bed. And here he was involved in the murder of a lord. Short, fat, red haired, a teetotaler and nonsmoker, he hardly looked the part of the diabolical assassin. He was in many ways a typical IRA volunteer from the border area, disciplined, self-taught, determined. He told the police little, was convicted of the crime on November 23 that year and sent to prison. Francis McGirl, a distant cousin of the Leitrim republican leader John Joe McGirl, was acquitted. Long before the arrests were even known, the impact of the bomb off Sligo had swept across Ireland and Great Britain to a wider world.

The London newspapers the next day had cleared their front pages for Mountbatten's death: THE BASTARDS screamed one full-page headline. The television readers went on at length about Mountbatten's life, his service, his importance. In fact the eminence of Mountbatten, the focus of all concern, the hero and royal, masked the death of an Irish boy, an old lady, and an innocent grandchild. At first everyone focused on the lord. Everyone, suitably horrified, had nothing but good to say about Mountbatten, who became a major twentieth-century figure over-night; and all had nothing but condemnation for the IRA murderers. Many in Ireland were well and truly horrified: all the Protestants, as usual, all the conventional and decent and their religious and political spokesmen, as usual, and a great many everyday people who saw no point in killing an old man, even an English lord. Too many innocent people were being killed as well. The IRA did not care: Their constituents in America and Ireland were delighted and many who condemned the act secretly had no time for English lords—or so they assumed. The symbol had been smashed and the English, the British, everyone had been shown what the cost of staying in Ireland would be.

Then at teatime on the same day reports began to come in from Radio BBC Ulster of another IRA operation. Casualties seemed to be high but at first the numbers were not firm—six or eight or more dead. The total seemed quite high even for a successful trap-bomb. Then the authoritative reports were broadcast. On the northern shore of Carlingford Lough (the south shore is in the Republic), a modern, divided highway connects Newry with the village of Warrenpoint. The road runs beside a canal. Near an old lodge close by is a spot called Narrow Water. There in 1972 IRA volunteers had fired three thousand rounds at the British army from an old farmhouse across the water in the Republic, safe from return fire. After that nothing much had happened in the stretch of County Down on the east side of Newry.

Several days previously the local IRA unit had buried a five-hundred-pound bomb, operated by a remote control device, under a stone archway of the derelict lodge. It was a good site and if not immediately discovered would give the volunteers a double threat, for the primary bomb would be hidden in a hay wagon parked by the side of the road. Intimately familiar with likely British responses, the IRA had buried the bomb on the spot that the British would use as a defensive fire base and rescue site once the hay wagon exploded next to their passing convoy. There was an old castle on the water side of the highway and an ideal lay-by off the main road on the land side. It was a natural defense spot for anyone under attack along the road. It was also a trap.

An enormous number of trap-bombs trapped nothing. No target appeared and the bomb had to be abandoned or removed. Sometimes the target appeared at the wrong time, sped by too quickly, or appeared accompanied by civilian traffic. Sometimes the unit was caught going in or the bomb was discovered by patrols. Only rarely was there free time to work unobserved by local Protestants or even wary Catholics, unnoticed by patrols or helicopters, unmarked by all sorts of technological devices. There was always something, a leak, an informer, a sign left on site, a rumor, something. At Warrenpoint on August 27 there was nothing.

Soon after 4:30 that afternoon a platoon of the Second Parachute Regiment appeared in a convoy: first a lead armored Land Rover, then two four-ton trucks. They were on their way from Ballykinler Barracks, County Down, to Newry. The IRA had a line-of-sight view and a control device constructed with a model aircraft radio. As soon as the trucks reached the hay wagon a pulse would be sent. The convoy drove straight on. The lead driver noted the hay wagon but kept going. It was the country after all. "Obviously the guy who detonated the first bomb must have been experienced, to take out the rear vehicle. It was the old classic ambush technique: take the back vehicle out to cause the maximum confusion, and then a second bomb waiting for the backup."*

The signal was sent and five hundred pounds of explosives in milk churns in the hay wagon exploded beside the last truck, turning it into a twisted, blackened hulk smoking in the grass strip in the center of the highway. Burning straw was thrown over the road. Some of the paratroopers lay smoldering. One crept out of the rear of the truck, his uniform on fire. The air was filled with black smoke and the highway with bits of truck and bodies.

> Everything went black, and this noise: the only thing I can equate it with is thousands of gallons of water rushing, sort of roaring like a waterfall. I must have blacked out for a bit because I then clearly remember sitting in the road feeling bitterly cold—not cold like in cold weather, but like I was encased in a block of ice. It was too cold to imagine: I felt so bitterly cold, it was as though I was entombed. I sat holding my left arm, in the road, swaying a bit. Obviously there must have been all sorts of carnage around, but none of it registered, just the bitter cold. Then I must have blacked out again. The next thing I remember was being lifted into what I thought was an ambulance, but evidently was a helicopter.†

*Max Arthur (editor), *Northern Ireland Soldiers Speak* (London: Sidgwick & Jackson, 1987), p. 133.
†Ibid., p. 135.

The other truck and the Land Rover skidded to a halt. The platoon had lost at one go six dead and two critically wounded. The survivors were rushed back along with the other Paras to a defense position four hundred meters away at the wide entrance to the old Narrow Water Castle, where there was shelter in the granite gateway from incoming fire. The defense position was exactly on top of the IRA's buried bomb.

The air was still black with smoke. Two Land Rovers from Second Para on patrol in Warrenpoint sped toward the site. Reinforcements began to be helicoptered in. The commanding officer of the Queen's Own Highlanders, Lieutenant Colonel David Blair, and his radioman, Lance Corporal Victor McLeod, had landed in a Gazelle helicopter to evaluate the situation before moving in the reaction team. Blair spoke with the Para commander, Major Peter Furseman. The Paras had taken some incoming fire and were responding. A Wessex helicopter slipped down into the defense cordon to remove the wounded and then began to lift off. Then there was a second enormous explosion that tossed the Wessex about and covered the road with a second cloud of black smoke. The pilot righted the chopper and the Wessex clattered off, leaving a sudden silence on the road.

There was the snap and twang of incoming small-arms fire and the survivors this time fired back into the Republic across the water. They had no targets but sprayed fire anyway. They hit none of the IRA men, who were soon gone, but British fire did hit and kill one young man, a British tourist, a queen's coachman whose parents lived in the Royal Mews in London. Twelve more had died in the second explosion, including a major and Lieutenant Colonel Blair, and two men had been severely wounded. Some of the bodies were so badly mutilated they could only be identified by their boots and socks. It was the single most disastrous day in Ireland for the security forces, the worst for the Second Parachute Regiment since it had been dropped on Arnhem in World War II. "Any soldier would admit that as an operation it was very well done. But, nonetheless, we were of course very angry at the losses we had taken, which naturally the battalion had to learn to live with. It's never easy to take that number of casualties."* Eighteen dead soldiers and Mountbatten was the toll for the Provos on August 27—and the British had shot a royal coachman and not made capital of the dead civilians off Sligo because an uncle of the Queen was too important.

The impact of the day was shattering, even and especially in London, where Prime Minister Thatcher had her first Irish crisis. There was nothing that could be done about Mountbatten but eulogize him. In Ireland General Creasey, no advocate of moderation, who believed that terrorism could be beaten, was outraged. His army was shaken and also outraged. Somehow it was the RUC's fault. They had not coped as promised. On August 29 Thatcher flew to Northern Ireland to show personal backing and support. At the tiny operations room in the Crossmaglen post where the Prime Minister had been helicoptered with great secrecy, the local army brigade commander tossed down the metal epaulets that had belonged to Lieutenant Colonel David Blair, and said, "This is all that's left of one of my bravest officers." The brigadier pointed out the map where each pin

*Arthur, p. 137.

marked a security casualty in bandit country. The map was prickled with little pins. The army wanted a single security chief, an army man at the top. The RUC could not cope.

The army continued the push for control and a freer hand at a lunch at Mahon Barracks, Portadown, so that by the time Thatcher met the RUC chief constable, Newman, at Gough Barracks, at Armagh, Thatcher had doubts about the RUC's capacity to cope. Newman indicated that a return to army supremacy, an army chief, would be a step back. It was the only way to reach the Prime Minister, who was as outraged and angry as the army and as little inclined to moderation as the grieving soldiers. Margaret Thatcher did not want to take a step backward and so Ulsterization was accepted as the way forward still. On August 30 the British cabinet decided to increase the RUC by one thousand. Thatcher had listened to the army plea for control at the top and on her return appointed an old intelligence maven, Sir Maurice Oldfield, the MI6 spymaster who had run the Special Intelligence Service from 1965 until his retirement in 1977, to coordinate intelligence.

Oldfield set up shop, with RUC Assistant Chief Constable John Whiteside and army Brigadier Robert Pascoe as local experts in place. Oldfield's reputation was excellent. A civilian with a career in intelligence, he was a capable organizer. A key player would be Colonel Richard Lea, commanding officer of the Twenty-first Regiment SAS, as GSOI Intelligence/Security Group. To sort out intelligence, to end rivalries, private ventures, and institutionalized blunders would have almost been worth August 27. In practice, however, Oldfield was apparently a mistake. His health was very poor; in fact he had stomach cancer, and his energy was limited. Worse, his career had always been in jeopardy because of his homosexuality, known to too many and ignored by the old-boy network for too long. In Northern Ireland his luck ran out, his denials on security forms were no longer accepted and he lost his clearances, his job, and then his reputation as all sorts of stories entered the public domain. He left Ireland in six months, largely discredited, a figure for mockery, and died in March 1981, still under a cloud.

His legacy in Ireland was not scandal but the foundation at last of a coherent British intelligence effort, despite the damages caused by special operations where no one planned for failure or could cope with revelation, despite the inherent problems of rivalry and cross-purpose, where mistrust was intractable. This Northern Irish effort was buttressed by integration with work in Britain and in cooperation with agencies abroad. Most attention was focused on the Provos. The Officials, who as Marxist-Leninists were the favored enemy of the conservatives, had become instead an example of effective co-option; the Protestants were largely a matter for the RUC alone, truly a criminal matter; and the various small schismatic groups could be pigeonholed with the IRA.

Despite the awe and horror of the public at the events of August 27, nothing else of note happened. O Fiaich in Rome felt the ground crumble under him as the death toll at Warrenpoint came in, and agreed that the Pope should skip Armagh. The SDLP was still looking for an Anglo-Irish initiative but no one seemed interested. The Provos got more money from supporters, who had been previously despondent or distracted. The Dublin government got further evidence that the IRA was an internal security problem. Everyone resented being blamed for

Mountbatten and for the bombs set off at Warrenpoint from the Republic. Mostly the Irish politicians, however, were fixated on the fading of Lynch's popularity—a big winner in 1977, his star had faded. This especially concerned all the marginal deputies who were worried about reelection. So the succession stakes began early. The June European elections had clearly shown a drop in the Fianna Fáil vote and so the rumors began that Lynch would go. On September 10 Síle de Valera, a green Fianna Fáil deputy, criticized Lynch's Northern policy. In October British overflights were raised as another point of attack. The critics had no alternative policy. No matter, Lynch was on the defensive, especially after Fianna Fáil lost two by-elections in Lynch's Cork, one in his own constituency after he had campaigned personally. The front-runners, Charles Haughey and George Colley, really began running and they were neck and neck.

The Pope did not come to Armagh, but he did come as far as Drogheda. There, on September 29, before 250,000 people, John Paul II spoke to the Provos: "Now I wish to speak to all men and women engaged in violence. I appeal to you in language of passionate pleading. On my knees I beg you to turn away from the paths of violence and return to the paths of peace. You may claim to seek justice. I too believe in justice and seek justice. But violence always delays the day of justice. Violence destroys the work of justice." So London, and for that matter Dublin, could not have asked for more: One month after August 27 the Pope in Ireland asks for an end to violence.

Irish republicans were no more moved by a Polish Pope innocent of the island asking for an end to violence (no mention of British violence) than they had been by Irish bishops innocent of nothing. Ireland had been conquered by force, partitioned by force, and by force it would be saved. On October 2 the Provisionals issued a statement saying that the British presence could only be removed by force. This statement confirmed Thatcher's view, that of the army, and the view of much of the police. Many loyalists, however, felt the great risk was treason, not open defeat.

There were other issues in London, too. Thatcher had to run her British revolution and even bloody epaulets could not shift her priorities. The British army got Oldfield, the RUC got primacy. The Northern Ireland Office had doubts about a simple continuation of the policy of direct rule without a parallel political initiative. Atkins and the Conservatives certainly did not want any Dublin involvement, as envisaged by Hume, or a rerun of the Sunningdale story that had foundered on the general strike: An Irish dimension assured disaster. What was needed was some sort of small step to go with the imposition of order. On October 25 Atkins announced that he was inviting the OUP, DUP, SDLP, and Alliance to Stormont to discuss a possible political settlement. The OUP rejected the invitation out of hand. Down in Dublin, Lynch, with his own position decaying, said that the Northern Ireland problem "continued to be as intractable as at any stage in the last ten years." Two days later the SDLP at its annual conference urged a joint Irish-British approach—the Irish connection line pushed without adjustment. Fitt felt the SDLP should accept Atkins's suggestion. The DUP and Alliance, always willing to talk, had not said no. The SDLP people other than Fitt were focused on the Irish connection. This was not what Atkins or the British had in mind. They wanted to start small, talk about local politics with local people, ease out of direct rule or at least move beyond absolute concentration on security.

On November 20 the British government published a consultative document proposing a Northern Ireland "constitutional conference." It would be a nice, small, baby step toward devolution, a show of politics amid all the pressure for force. Gerry Fitt thought it a beginning and said so. Hume and the powers that be in the SDLP did not. It was too narrow for the SDLP—if no Dublin and then no SDLP. On November 22 Gerry Fitt resigned. He had long been out of step with Hume, the Dublin option and the country nationalists. By November he felt the party's attitude disastrous and completely misguided. His focus on Westminster and on the decency of the Labour Party, coupled with his opposition to the pretensions of the Provos, had begun to erode his base in West Belfast as well. There many saw few benefits in politics and none in a Labour Party that had sent over Mason and was sure to be out of power for years. At last rid of Fitt, who in the past had done heroic work but who, the new men felt had long outlived his usefulness, the SDLP anointed Hume as leader and Séamus Mallon as deputy leader: no one from Belfast, everyone for an Irish dimension.

The focus of Northern Ireland politics—and after two years there was provincial political movement—became the prospects of the constitutional convention as proposed by Atkins. The SDLP decided to play, thus catching the OUP and its new leader, James Molyneaux, who had taken over from West in 1979, by surprise: The Unionists may have said no too soon and too firmly. On November 23 the OUP executive gave Molyneaux as their leader overwhelming support for spurning a conference that was "booby-trapped" with the Irish dimension. On the other hand, the DUP had decided to show up—Paisley, too, could see the advantage of keeping the OUP outside the circle. Alliance was always a sure starter in any accommodation stakes. So Atkins at least had both communities if not the orthodox Unionists, whom he dearly wanted, the fringe parties, who did not matter, and the paramilitaries, who were now absolutely beyond the pale. Thatcher and company had no intention of taking tea with terrorists. All previous attempts had led nowhere but to embarrassment, and all reports of the capacities and limitations of the gunmen indicated that further effort was futile. So Atkins announced that his constitutional convention would convene on January 7.

It would clearly be a year with a new cast: Thatcher and Atkins, not Callaghan and Mason, Hume, not Fitt, Molyneaux, not West, in the wings, the new IRA–Provisional Sinn Féin leadership running the armed campaign. No one could figure out the shifting power structure of the UDA under Andy Tyrie—at least he would still be there to interpret. In the Republic there was an old face in a new office: Jack Lynch had unexpectedly gone. Lynch had simply looked vulnerable. The loss of the two Cork by-elections and a trip to the United States that allowed full-scale plotting in Dublin had produced a crisis. He resigned on Wednesday, December 5; he had planned to go in a few months anyway. So there would be a new face in Dublin as well.

The narrow favorite was Charles Haughey, an evil totem for the loyalists and an enigma for the nationalists. All agreed on his ambitions and political skills. Haughey had counted his votes, overestimated his assets, not for the last time, and won, not for the last time, with a forty-four to thirty-eight vote of the Fianna Fáil Dáil party over George Colley. It was thought the greatest comeback since Lazarus or at least Richard Nixon. His arrival was greeted with despair by those who voted for Colley and with distaste by Fine Gael, whose new leader, Garrett FitzGerald, referred to Haughey as a man with a flawed pedigree. He was someone who had been mixed up with the Provos, someone morally unsound. The Arms Case was not forgotten—there were newspaper photographs of the Provos' John Kelly celebrating on Haughey's return to the top. Haughey had a different perspective to nationalist matters: "I condemn the Provisional IRA and all their activities." The Provos should have expected no less. Fianna Fáil in power had no love of the IRA. If there was profit to be made for nationalism or from nationalism, the Taoiseach would handle such matters, not subversives. Not that he would, like Atkins, ignore the subversives, who might hold a veto over progress toward a solution of the national issue. On December 16 Haughey even met members of the UDA's New Ulster Research Group in Dublin. Times seemed to be changing.

The events of the last several months of 1979, with the apparent return of politics, had not culminated with a marvelous success for either Ulsterization or police primacy. To assure Ulsterization the Northern Ireland Office was increasingly engaged in a confrontation with the republican prisoners, which had spread to the streets of the province and become a more general issue. To assure police primacy only the last-minute intervention of Newman had deflected the army from assuming control again, so that Oldfield was handy as coordinator but the RUC were still riding point. And neither the army nor the police had closed down the Provos. The extent of opposition by the proper people in Ireland, Catholic or Protestant, to the Provos was indicated on October 15 by an opinion poll published by the Economic and Social Research Institute in Dublin. Only 21 percent of the people in the Republic gave any support to the Provisionals and only 3 percent expressed strong support. The Provos, of course, did not heed surveys but only their historical legacy. So there were still all the usual manifestations of the long war: the increasingly professional country ambushes; the new groups operating along the border in bandit country and the long-lived, above-ground units in rural areas; the regular but each time unexpected bomb blitzes; the single snipers in Belfast and the towns; the cell structure; and the shifting targets.

The shift in 1979 had been the tactical implications of criminalization for the Provos. On November 26, in the midst of the maneuvering about Atkins's conference proposal, the Provos hit the province with a blitz of bombs—twenty-four were detonated in Belfast alone. On December 3 the IRA shot and killed outside his home the second-in-command to the governor of Crumlin Road Prison. He was the sixteenth member of the prison service to be murdered in retaliation for the denial of political status.

While the gunmen kept busy, a new campaign had been launched on October 21 by a more general spectrum of supporters, including Bernadette McAliskey: the national H-Block/Armagh Committee. The prisoners, the men in the Kesh and the women in Armagh, had five demands, not political status by name but more by degree. They demanded the right (1) to wear their own clothes, (2) to refuse prison work, (3) to receive one parcel and one visit a week, (4) to associate freely with one another, and (5) to have the remission that was lost during the dirty protest returned. The demands could easily apply to all prisoners, as the involved pointed out. In fact the demands could easily be seen, if from a distance, as proper prison protest applicable everywhere. The demands were seen by the authorities as little more than a ploy by the subversives, for the real issue remained the use of criminalization to smash the legitimacy of the IRA: Who ruled, the British Crown or the Irish republicans?

During 1979 the Crown had faced the same old problems, always grown more complex, skewed and twisted by new currents, compounded by error and contingencies and always by the unforeseen. The year had ended on a political up despite the boycott of the OUP and had seen a Protestant paramilitary turn toward politics, even if in advocacy of independence. The worst sectarian killers had been sent to jail, a reward of RUC professionalism and primacy. And the Provos had gotten no worse if not any better.

The year-end figures were not really alarming at all and would have been impressive if it had not been the one evening at Warrenpoint: 38 army dead and 10 UDR, 9 RUC and 5 RUCR, with 51 civilians, for a total of 113 compared to just 81 for the year before. The biggest difference was the 18 soldiers killed on August 27. The figures, like those in 1978, were a long way from the horrendous totals of 1972, but indicated that the long war was not being won if not being lost. The number of injured was down a little, to 914 from 1,052, shooting incidents declined to 728 from 755, and explosions to 422 from 455. There were even 5 fewer armed robberies, with a 1979 total of 434.

Most people in the province, most of the time, lived as if there were no Troubles; few any longer paid much attention to the ubiquitous security presence, the wired-off center cities, the handbag searches, the patrol outside the window. Many areas rarely had problems or patrols outside the windows. The ritual riots, the bomb blitzes, the shootings were momentary and localized.

Long wars are so low in intensity that hardly anyone paid attention in Dublin or London until some momentary horror brought swift confusion and the media for a day or so. The next year would be for the new faces a window of opportunity—maybe present exhaustion and the cost of attrition would lead to accommodation. The new year for the old campaigners would be more of the same, searching and killing, bombing and dying. No one seemed to be doing anything new. And doing nothing had not proved the remedy for the Troubles. Actually the new year would eventually see novelty once more arise unexpectedly from the closed world of the prisons. There was always some new horror out of Ireland and in 1980 it would be the struggle within the closed cells of H-Block between the old Irish and British antagonists—another arena but the same battle.

17

Unconventional Conflict, the Hunger Strikes: January 1980–October 1981

Persuade him to eat or drink? . . .
while he is lying there,
perishing there, my good name in the world
is perishing also. I cannot give way.
because I am King; because if I give way,
my nobles would call me a weakling, and, it
*   may be,*
the very throne be shaken.

William Butler Yeats, *The King's Threshold*

In Northern Ireland, January 1980 started as might have been expected. In Belfast, at a British army checkpoint on Whitelock Road, a joy rider, sixteen-year-old Doreen McGuinness, was shot dead and a boy wounded; only the driver escaped. The young stole cars and ran roadblocks as a lethal lottery that, unlike most adventures, sooner or later assured tragedy. The troops were turned into an obstacle course for the rites of passage, more evidence of the increasing institutionalization of violence.

No one was really surprised at the year's beginning. Everyone who cared had just read the year-end statistics of the deadly Irish quarrels. January was also a time for beginnings. It was the month that the Northern Secretary sought to piece together some sort of political structure, an assembly. The cynics in Belfast and London assumed the move was intended to calm any American concern during the presidential election and to indicate good faith. Two years of Mason and hard security as policy had led only to Warrenpoint and Mountbatten, confrontation in the prisons and murder on the streets. Maybe a political option for the local players would shift the emphasis away from the IRA. Any political arena would have some attraction. The SDLP, after the resignation of Fitt, had reluctantly agreed to talk to Humphrey Atkins though not formally to anyone else. Matters of security and relations with the Irish Republic took place in a parallel conference that led nowhere. The nationalists wanted power sharing embedded in any settlement. They also wanted an Irish dimension and the loyalists did not. The Official Unionists simply refused to take the exercise seriously and did not appear. They were willing to pursue a reformed local government without a devolved assembly, which the nationalists were not. Paisley was, apparently, willing to enter the discussion in order to dominate the stage not to make policy. Only the Alliance Party was really keen. The Alliance Party was always keen for any move to accommodation, even if the talking was limited to Paisley roaring on stage, the SDLP whining in the wings, and no sound at all from the Official Unionists offstage.

On January 6, the eve of the constitutional talks, a land mine explosion near Castlewellan, County Down, killed three UDR men and injured four others. This brought the death toll for the Troubles to two thousand, hardly a harbinger of goodwill for Atkins. The Northern Secretary still intended to push his proposal for devolved government, published in November 1979 as *A Working Paper for a Conference,* that would be followed on July 2, 1980, with *Proposals for Further Discussion,* based on the futile discussions held between January and March. Contemporary crises move ahead on seas of paper rising from the hard work, research, conferences, reviews, learned speculations, the contribution of consultants, and the wisdom of very bright bureaucrats. The end result, shaped to contemporary need, not unmindful of political desires, is the very purpose of much of government, a purpose often (as in this case) futile because reality is not addressed. These papers were like a finely tuned, many jeweled watch without a main spring. The British suggested three possible ways of minority participation: some form of proportional representation in choosing the executive, weighted voting, or a bicameral arrangement providing checks and balances. In a purely formal sense it was ingenious, a delight to political scientists or constitutional lawyers but not to Irish politicians.

During the conference Atkins had talks with the DUP people that, he indicated, on no firm evidence, had revealed remarkable moderation. The SDLP did not understand how a refusal to consider either an Irish dimension or power sharing could be a basis for "moderation." In any case the DUP could only maintain propriety briefly and reverted to type and to their basic demands in basic language. The imagined moderation evaporated. There was no hope to tame Paisley, to involve the Official Unionists, who still thought London was play-acting, or to co-opt the SDLP. But it was better to have the focus on the legitimate leadership of the province instead of the activities of the paramilitaries.

There were two major difficulties facing any who would define an institution of governance to incorporate all those in the province. The first was that at base what was truly wanted but seldom articulated by each party could not easily be shaped to constitutional requirements: a rewriting of history to present advantage. Second, it was a continuing fact that intransigent strategies paid electoral dividends: If we cannot have much of what we want then let us ask for all and oppose anything. Consequently, any formula of accommodation would fall short of the emotional needs of the committed. Any politicians could gain credit simply by appealing to those emotional needs over the hard-won specifics of some cunning constitutional structure. It did not matter to the loyalists what the Sunningdale Agreement actually said but only what it meant emotionally:

betrayal, step one. The argument that worked was the emotional one that touched each Protestant identity, the uncertain product of a long historical process. So, too, the minority's desires for an Irish dimension taken as revealing history's judgment, just as the loyalists feared, step one to the vision of unity, a triumph of Irish Catholic nationalism.

Paisley had been particularly successful in building a career and a party on this historical Protestant fear so often expressed in arrogance and domination. Hume once pushed him as to what he really wanted, since protection of the Unionist-stated position was built into the Sunningdale Agreement with a veto in the Council of Ireland, and the status of Northern Ireland was written in as well. What did he want, what was his position? Paisley replied, "It is very simple. I'm loyal to the Crown as long as it remains Protestant."* It was not a direct answer at all and not simple either but quite revealing. This was the position of the loyalists—provisional loyalty to the British Crown, absolute loyalty to their way of life, ideally to be structured so as to remove fear of betrayal. So there could be no surrender on details and there must be a constant defense from real and imagined enemies. The loyalists could never be reassured sufficiently, would always assume any concession the first of many. Hume, Atkins, and all the political scientists were talking about constitutional details and adjustments while Paisley, eliminating the polemic, was seeking the reassurance of history rewritten.

They were at cross-purposes. No accommodation, even a return to the Ireland of 1921 or 1967, could reassure the fearful loyalists. And no accommodation, even in some complex federated structure like the Council of Ireland, could abolish the sense of grievance of the nationalists, who also wanted history rewritten so that they would, as proper, win in the final act. The closer agreement came on a given detail the higher the anxiety level for the involved. The loyalists conceived "giving" as a historical defeat and the nationalists "taking" as a historical right. The minority, assuming they would win in the end, could give more easily than the majority, who assumed they would be betrayed in the end. The nationalists would, therefore, always have a better case in disinterested eyes, and the loyalists, recognizing their dilemma, would compound their problem by redoubling their intransigence in reaction. Atkins wandered in without fear of treading on disaster, offering, like some British magician at a pageant run once too often, goodwill, sweet reason, and promises. None had takers. The OUP would not inspect the goods at all and the SDLP only at one remove. On March 24 the conference adjourned without effect or agreement—the least effective initiative to date.

Hume at least managed an end-of-term meeting with Atkins and his permanent secretary, Ken Stowe, at Hillsborough on April 18, where he pushed the need for a London-Dublin approach. Hume had various analogies and ideas that involved a federal Ireland, intimacy between the islands within a European context, the examples of Benelux and the Nordic Council, all sorts of wonders that would evolve out of a great Anglo-Irish initiative instead of the small Irish six-county initiatives that had attracted interest since the collapse of the power-

*Barry White, *John Hume: Statesman of the Troubles* (Belfast: Blackstaff, 1984), p. 214.

sharing Assembly. Hume sought an Irish accommodation—there could be no solution given the perceptions of history but there might be effective arrangements that would not deny the dreams and ideals involved. This could not be managed within the six counties, where only the two dreams existed, monitored by the power of London. Gerry Fitt, now sitting in Westminster as an independent Republican Socialist, a party of one, had looked to London for redress of grievance; but Hume felt that the Irish Republic must be brought into any accommodation to balance the equation.

What was needed was an accommodation on a large scale, larger even than Ireland, where the old dreams would have new competition. In the old days the British Empire had offered if not Ireland then many Irish a new role, new opportunities. In 1980 many in Ireland looked to Europe for a new and broader role. Hume hoped to dilute the six counties in Europe, to extend the solution even beyond Dublin and London by bringing in the outside world to redress the bitterness of the old quarrels. The Americans had been persuaded to his position. Washington could offer money, goodwill, power, prestige, pressure to come when needed, and enthusiasm on the world stage. The Europeans were increasingly touched. The exposure to Paisley in Strasbourg, the murder of Mountbatten, the IRA and the civil rights leaders, the Troubles as news, all had introduced through television a greater world to the Irish problem, to a need for a reasoned and rational accommodation that all could support. And what Hume wanted to see was a moderate accommodation involving London and Dublin, American enthusiasm, and a European future. It was in everyone's interests except those whose particularist dream was too vivid to deny—alas, this was apparently a majority in Northern Ireland, the one great weakness in Hume's policy.

No one paid an enormous amount of attention to the SDLP's demand for an Irish issue, which was taken, as Fitt had indicated the previous November, as a Santa Claus request. The Council of Ireland had caused the downfall of the power-sharing executive and repeated insistence upon it would continue to assure a majority boycott. This was true if the majority had the capacity to veto, if by no other means than a boycott, any or all institutions of accommodation in the province. Thus, London could not impose an assembly with an Irish dimension—and Hume apparently would not play without one. Actually, what Hume wanted was not Dublin involved in the province's affairs but the province as a factor in Anglo-Irish agreement. In 1980 this was not clear. What was clear was that Atkins's constitutional conference had failed and all the old difficulties and disasters bubbled up again, some minor but symbolic, some poignant, none pleasant.

On January 19 a letter from the prisoners was read at the Provisional Sinn Féin Ard Fheis. It said that commitment to the blanket protest was high but they could not hold out forever. The Army Council was still, as always, primarily concerned with the armed struggle. Two days before, a firebomb being transported on a commuter train had detonated and killed an IRA volunteer, Kevin Delaney, and a civilian, and had injured five other people. Once again there was general pressure about recklessness and innocent deaths. The clergy refused to allow Delaney's body into any of the churches of West Belfast. Eventually mass was said in his home and the IRA went back to the war. On January 26 a

Ballymurphy IRA unit used an M-60 machine gun to kill a British soldier, Errol Price, twenty-one, of the Duke of Wellington Regiment. Two civilians were hit when the soldiers returned fire and more were antagonized when the army rioted in the area.

A second response to the British, other than that of the traditional physical force, arose from the Delaney death, when women on protest in Armagh Jail decided to wear black tokens and hold a ceremony. In a harassing search to find the berets and tricolors the women prisoners were mauled when they tried to return to their cells by sixty male and female warders, some drafted in from Long Kesh for the day. One uproar followed another, with later accusations of provocation and brutality. The war was in the prison. And in February thirty-two of the Armagh women went on dirty protest. If anything, the new battleground was the most desperate. If someone did not make a move to ease the confrontation, matters could only decay.

The common wisdom insisted again and again that someone would have to make a move. No one did and the protest ground on week after miserable week. There was enormous frustration within the Kesh and within the republican movement. The H-Blocks as an issue had gradually become prominent but not enough to affect the authorities. After years on the blanket, after the beatings and filth of the dirty protest, after the institutionalized humiliation of the system, the prisoners wanted action. Provisional Sinn Féin, the IRA GHQ, and the Army Council had no real assets to play. The orchestration of protest was difficult. The habitual nationalist enemies of the republicans, the SDLP and the Church, would play no part except for specific reasons. General support would come only if the cause could be made general. Many republicans did not even want to play the protest game, disapproved of the confrontation or the dirty protest: How could living in filth—"just like the Irish"—win the war? There must be an appealing rally point for protest to work. And there was none in sight. So the republicans found January a cold month.

On January 21 Anne Maguire, the mother of the three children whose death on Finaghy Road North sparked the Peace People movement, committed suicide after returning from a failed attempt to make a new life in New Zealand. Soon the remnants of the peace movement split publicly, with the resignations of Betty Williams on February 1 and the former chairman, Peter McLachlan, on March 5. The media had kept the peace movement alive long after the fuel of hope had been spent. By the spring of the year there could no longer be any pretending and the movement stabilized as one of many welfare organizations, doing great good with small programs, out of sight, out of mind, a historical fragment. There never seemed good news from Belfast, from Northern Ireland.

On February 1 the Belfast Welfare Rights Poverty survey indicated that Northern Ireland was the poorest region in the United Kingdom, which was hardly a surprise. In June a study called *Ends That Won't Meet* was published by the Child Poverty Action Group. It ran through the problems, all without easy solution: unemployment—two thousand jobs recently lost, sixteen thousand in jeopardy, and thirty thousand at risk; low wages; higher prices; severe housing problems; and larger households. The news in January that the government intended to raze two blocks of the Divis Flats was too little, too late—the community wanted the whole horror complex demolished. And West Belfast was simply the most visibly afflicted area.

Despite the very considerable investment in the province, the amount like all else being adjusted by politicians and statisticians to immediate purpose, despite new houses, new roads, new social facilities, the six counties continued to come in last in any United Kingdom table of accounting. There was always bad news: The new industries did not replace the old, the new houses were not sufficient, and the previous efforts like Divis Flats were worse than the terraces they replaced. The burned-out buildings, derelict cars, the graffiti and the giant republican wall murals, the waste ground and British patrols, the joy riders, the idle poor and the mean streets had become the backdrop for tens of thousands of photographs, for television tapes, for films and novels. The landscape was a media convention that actually hid the province's seemingly intractable social and economic problems.

Rural poverty was not photogenic. Much misery could not be seen along the Falls or during riots. The invisible costs counted in bad health, alienation, poor teeth or none, alcoholism, destructive behavior, despondency, wasted talents, wasted lives. All this hardly showed up in the statistics, much less on the evening news. The loyalist urban poor, except in the marching season, lacked charm for the media. The country misery was hidden in green fields. And most of the deprived had no place in the news. They simply did the best they could; often, unless in the hard-core areas, they were untroubled by much of the violence, and concentrated on surviving with small pleasures.

The poor uninterested in politics, the vast majority, did not march or protest, throw stones, contribute to the UVF, or buy *Republican News*. They never wanted more than peace and quiet and a job, perhaps a wee house and money for the pub, a new coat, a turkey at Christmas. They had narrow, everyday lives, dreaded that their children would volunteer for a dirty war, lived in quiet desperation or emigrated to other miserable prospects but without the army on the street. In Northern Ireland they made do, eking out happiness on a bad diet, valium, and too many sweets. They filled the small houses, enjoyed their children and the telly, had a dog, went to the pub, had a flutter on the pools, had small hopes, short views. They coped. Decent, more cheerful than conditions warranted, they knew they lived in interesting times but like most would have settled for dull days. They were loyal to their street, their bit of the Shankill or the Ardoyne or the Creggan, were Belfast proud or Derry people, had no apologies for the times or the Troubles. They went to church and the films, saved pennies, had old friends and set routines, read the papers, lived as quietly as possible. A focus on the small, the one lane, the old parish almost always indicated everyone coping. There was a residue of toleration and goodwill; these were not the best of times but not the worst. Only the big issues, the prominent concerns, caused trouble.

The most prominent factor for the new year, a factor long in the making and one that would again bring the Troubles into the dull rounds of daily life and not in the province alone, was the hovering H-Block problem. On March 3 Cardinal O Fiaich and Bishop Edward Daly of Derry made a visit to the Kesh and saw the decay in conditions firsthand. The British had not been happy with O Fiaich. He was too much an Irish nationalist, a conservative Irish Catholic and yet not sufficiently conservative on Irish matters for the British Conservatives, and less so after he revealed how horrified he had been at the state of the prisoners. Conditions were, indeed, horrific. The prisoners were battered, dirty, thin, foul and naked. They lived in filth, in the cold, existing in inhuman conditions. Photographs smuggled out showed strange wraiths with hollow chests, great halos of hair, long beards, and huge staring eyes—icons of suffering. The guards and warders, personally and as policy, would give not an inch, were brutal not just to restore order but to humiliate. With the IRA gunmen outside shooting prison officials and guards, there was little government sympathy for their colleagues in the cells. The prisoners insisted on fighting the system, provoking authority, breaking the rules. The Northern Ireland Office had regularly pointed out that the prisoners' condition was self-inflicted. The prisoners were condemned criminals seeking rights nowhere else granted, certainly not in the Republic of Ireland, where such "rights" are granted unofficially except in times of confrontation. The British, seeking to break the republicans, intended to make such conditions an official issue, one more aspect of treating criminals as criminals, not a civil rights issue at all.

The British position had been supported by a report on February 6 by the U.S. State Department that exonerated Britain of any human rights violations in Northern Ireland—symbol of the Reagan-Thatcher special relationship on "terrorism" according to the republicans, disinterested analysis according to the British. The prisoners were at fault. They had brought on their own misery as a means to punish the authorities. Their misery was self-inflicted, not a British responsibility. The authorities, like the prisoners, were self-righteous, possessed of the whole truth, uncompromising.

Self-inflicted or not, the protest had very gradually come to the attention of a broader audience, spreading out through Irish republicans to those concerned with civil liberties, and then on to the disinterested, and at last attracting the very interested media. Dirty men in blankets made a bit of a story, not big but continuous; they made interesting news. Sympathy lay with the prisoners, the weak, the naked and dirty; but nonviolence required photogenic confrontation to be most effective; issues had to be reduced to stark coloring. And so the H-Blocks were not yet big news, not even in Ireland. The Northern Ireland Office did not want big news, did not want any news. They wanted the republican prisoners to act like ordinary prisoners. Then the media might take an interest, but not before. The prisoners were simply causing trouble for themselves and to no useful end. And with rare exceptions British authorities would continue to blame the prisoners for failing to comply with reasonable rules that would guarantee more than most prisoners received and more than the IRA gunmen guaranteed their victims.

Those victims of the IRA were gradually becoming more difficult to find. The arrival of Oldfield to coordinate intelligence and the passage of time for the army and police had meant that the new men—Lieutenant General Sir Richard Lawson, a "political" general dedicated to police primacy, and the new RUC chief constable, John Hermon—had more security tools available. There would, of course, never be perfect intelligence, an ideal military response, or a conventional police force in the province, but the tide had begun to turn. In Ballymurphy, for example, a quick reaction had been devised that allowed a helicopter to hover over a suspected IRA firing spot traced by sight, by on-site radar or infrared tools, by night sights, and by intelligence sources, thus summoning in a flood of patrols. The result was that the IRA sniper team instead of thirty minutes' grace had only a minute or so. It took the active service units a week to compensate but the lead time continued to diminish. The days of banging away were gone, the days of two shots went, and in time ambushes had to be meticulously planned, with a long chain in and out, to permit only a single shot. In 1980, however, there were still IRA ambushes with the M-60 machine gun, still snipers operating with limited backup, still urban guerrilla war in Belfast and some of the towns, with more traditional confrontations limited to the rural areas.

Belfast was slowly being transformed into a gigantic camp, where the hard-core nationalist areas were isolated, all in and out traffic monitored, all residents filtered and filed, and all movement watched. The computer system grew grand at a cost of £300 million—people, vehicles, letters, telephones, social welfare, licenses, all sorts of data were fed into the memory banks. The areas were surveyed by television cameras, by army observation posts both overt and covert, by regular and irregular patrols, by watchers in the military barracks and police stations, from vehicles and from helicopters, from reports of informers, from friends and overheard conversations. There were agents and turned subversives and spies, criminals who would bargain with information, the fearful who would inform on their mates if protected—some murky people indeed. There was a need, once interrogation at Castlereagh and other barracks had been cleaned up, to find confessions another way, and in the twilight world of agents and assets, informers began to drift around the margins of the paramilitaries, attracted by easy money, the prospect of pardon, the fear of betrayal. After Oldfield the use of informers became the major engine of the conveyor belt to the Kesh: In the eighteen months after Oldfield's arrival thirty informers gave evidence that led to the arrest of three hundred suspects. An apparently related benefit was that within two years murders and bombings were reduced by half.

The informers involved were mostly dubious, marginals, petty criminals, opportunists, the weak. Several had considerable operational knowledge and in the case of the INLA could do very serious damage to a small organization. No great classical IRA informer on the inside appeared, certainly not in court. Those who did testify indicated the nature of life in the twilight. On August 3, 1980, Anthony O'Doherty was arrested and on October 29 pleaded guilty to forty-seven charges ranging from robbery and blackmail to three attempted murders of police constables. He had long worked for the army and the police, perhaps from as early as 1969, had undergone special training, been given weapons and instructions, and given a long leash. He had been involved in IRA attacks, one resulting in the wounding of two UDR men, but it was his free-lance criminal activity that led to his arrest. He confessed to all the crimes except one murder charge and in so doing implicated his handler, RUC Detective Sergeant Charles McCormick, who in time was convicted on three charges but had his twenty-year sentence reversed on appeal and went free. The two had lived in a world of authorized crime and played both ends against an uncertain middle. Many of the new informers did not even hope for gain. Confused, uncertain, they had drifted into actions with high penalties and then were attracted to the out offered—to "grass" on their friends—by the authorities. Few, Protestant or Catholic paramilitaries, ever came forward out of conviction. Some were more fearful of their own than of the authorities, some faced long terms in jail, and all had lived in the twilight world of subversion and fear. They were offered a day in court, a period in custody, and a new life promised elsewhere.

All of this was made elegant by the most advanced technological means—even the Americans were impressed with the exercise. In the center of the net was the Ulster Security Liaison Committee (USLC). After Oldfield left it was under the control of Sir Frank Brooks Richards, and it moved to RUC Belfast Headquarters at Brooklyn, where MI5 was located. There would always be friction between those involved, especially at the pointed end of the stick where "sharing" sources was anathema and tragic misunderstandings inevitable.

And there would never be any final adjustment to the capacities of the IRA, who, despite limited resources and talents, despite the tiny arena, despite all the problems inherent in covert organizations, managed to adjust and persist. In 1980–81 the movement had exhausted most conventional resources. Money was short and old republicans had to be tapped. There were too many demands—the prisoners, the dependents, politics and protest, the payroll, and the needs of the quartermaster general, QMG. NORAID funds were static or declining, Libyan money was there but no one knew for how long, and traditional sources in Ireland had narrowed.

The war was gobbling up assets, but the IRA persisted. It was a low-intensity, relatively low-cost war. In some cases the war became ritual, the conventions of the unconventional: The IRA used one strategically placed house so often that the cost of repaying the glass broken each time at four pounds a shot resulted in the householder offering to have a key cut—better the lads in the front room than another cold draft in the kitchen until the trip to the glazier—glaziers did well out of Belfast, unlike nearly everyone else.

The rewards of the Belfast black world accrued to the British that spring when the M-60 group became prominent. On April 9 the group lured an RUC squad to an ambush site with a bogus report of a break-in at the local library and killed one constable and wounded two. The squad, once again enlarged, managed its own transport, communications, dumps, and safe houses. They used fringe contacts, like the taxi driver James Kennedy, whose girlfriend had two brothers in the unit. On May 2 four volunteers—Joe Doherty, twenty-eight, Angelo Fusco, twenty-four, Robert Campbell, twenty-seven, and Paul "Dingus" Magee, thirty-three—had taken over a house on the Antrim Road. The RUC was alerted to their presence. An eight-man SAS patrol in plainclothes arrived. When they leaped out to surround the house, the IRA men opened up and killed Captain Herbert Richard Westmacott and forced the SAS to withdraw but not far enough for an escape. After a short siege with more and more security forces deployed the unit surrendered. Four volunteers and one of the few M-60s were lost. The British kept up the pressure to the extent that the IRA began to suspect an informer. Kennedy had already been questioned in October and November and was again under suspicion. The unit got another M-60 but the pressure continued. He went to Dublin, returned, was questioned by the Ballymurphy IRA, panicked, and went to the RUC. Most of the M-60 squad known to Kennedy were picked up and charged. He was guaranteed immunity from prosecution and safe passage out of the country. Between those who would grass and those who could not cope with the rising level of British skill, the authorities could see an acceptable level of violence in the not too distant future. Of course, the tolerable level had gone up by exposure over the decade. Nevertheless, as the months passed, the IRA's armed struggle, still deadly and unpredictable, was a known. The security forces increasingly felt that they could cope.

What many felt was that the British had—perfidiously as always—changed the rules and kept flying the same colors, just as they had with political status. There was an undeclared war filled with ambushes and patrols, snipers in the city and bombs in the trunk; but even such wars have rules. If the British wanted to deny such a war in order to pursue criminalization as an anti-insurgency policy, this made sense, had a conflict logic, but in 1980 the security forces apparently had decided to escalate the unconventional war into a dirty war—break the old rules that seemed to be to IRA advantage. The IRA preferred to fight a war where civilian rights had force, where criminalization was at times to criminal advantage: Those suspected of crimes are not shot on sight, need not fear walking into an ambush, can surrender on demand, anticipate jail and trial and at worst time in a cell.

The visible leadership of the republicans, those involved in legal politics, operated outside the laws of the battlefield and could only be approached through legal means: The RUC arrested Sinn Féin people suspected of being in the IRA like Gerry Adams not because of their political activity but because of their assumed association with the IRA. Putting people in cages on suspicion had been counterproductive, but by 1980 there were thousands in cages, most because of real crimes, not just potential attitudes. Some were there for the wrong crime, some were serving disproportionate sentences for the wrong crime, but most were properly assumed guilty once they had been tossed on the conveyor belt. The IRA also demanded the right to define their enemies. The first circle consisted of uniformed opponents, even if not in uniform, even if on vacation or home in bed. Then came government officials, even if only civilians, even women, far from the battle. Then came those who helped the core, builders or drivers or train drivers. So Mountbatten and Margaret Thatcher were targets, and so were recruiting officers on holidays, and so were barmen in Protestant pubs used by the UVF— agents of the empire. The loyalist paramilitaries often published enemy lists but seldom had to fret about uniforms or positions—the province was filled with nationalists.

The victims were chosen asymmetrically. Each actor had an ill-defined menu of appropriate individuals and categories. The target list of the authorities contained in theory only those who broke the law and resisted arrest with arms; the IRA's list contained those, armed or not, who actively oppressed the Irish nation; and the loyalist paramilitaries targeted any vulnerable Catholic Irishman, although those visibly guilty would be most attractive. When anyone added a target, especially with limited rationale, the rules were broken and the victims outraged, no matter how illogical this may have seemed from afar: The rules in an unconventional war are not reasoned, not necessarily rational, hazy at best, but real enough for the involved.

The British apparently had decided to adjust the rules once the INLA people had killed Neave. The assassination was provocative, brutal, and because it occurred at Westminster, intolerable. Action was needed to ease outrage as much as to punish the guilty. The guilty would have to pay, of course, but a major target of any retaliation was conservative British opinion: those who wanted their own back. There is no one so bloodthirsty as an Englishman who feels unjustly maimed. Killing with a dirty bomb a war hero, an honest politician, an Englishman at home in the Houses of Parliament was intolerable. Very considerable care and cunning was deployed so that vengeance was taken cold, at a distance, and without prospect of direct penalty. It was thus possible for even the involved much of the time to deny responsibility: The operations had evolved out of normal contacts within the covert world of the Protestant paramilitaries, where there was no need to fashion false gangs, as had Kitson in Kenya, but only to scatter hints and clues, prospects and details. The loyalists, isolated from the real IRA, were enthusiastically attracted to visible Irish nationalists: spokesmen and politicians and H-Block advocates.

Most of the potential victims were involved with the Provisionals and so assured of protection; few left safe areas, most had barricaded homes and circumscribed lives. Belfast had become the center of a do-it-yourself security industry: Little houses had reinforced doors to thwart those who would batter their way in using sledgehammers, and inside, wire screens to slow assaults, and finally, sealed doors and rooms on the second floor. Getting to the prominent, even with intelligence, was difficult. Maire Drumm had mistakenly depended on the traditional and unstated neutrality of hospitals, a mistake not likely to be repeated. The other prominent Provisional Sinn Féin people took care. Those not with the Provos had fewer potential guards or, at a distance from the armed struggle, apparently had fewer enemies. The IRSP felt it should be treated as a party, like the Provisional Sinn Féin.

This turned out to be a fatal assumption by the leaders of the IRSP. The lack of sufficient INLA defenders permitted access by loyalist gunmen that was denied in the case of the Provisional Sinn Féin leaders. And it was assumed, with some justification, that in the case of the IRSP people the distance between politicians and operational planners was slight. At least some of the Sinn Féin people were only interested in politics. This distinction was wasted on the loyalists, who considered all radical, vocal, and organized Irish nationalists as dangerous. The H-Block Armagh Committee or the PD, the IRSP or the Stickies, were all responsible for the turmoil, for subversion, for Neave's death and Mountbatten's and the rest.

At eight o'clock on the evening of June 4, 1980, John Turnly was gunned to death on his way to a public meeting at Hamill's Hall in Carnlough. A Protestant, a former British army officer, he was also an Irish nationalist and a founder of the Irish Independence Party—an apostate as far as the loyalists were concerned. When Turnly stopped his car, another car pulled up beside it. The door of the other car was thrown open, banging into Turnly's door, and two gunmen opened up with a submachine gun and a pistol while his Japanese-born wife, Miyoko, and his sons watched in horror. He was hit nine times, killed on the spot, and hunched over in his seat as the assassins drove off. The hit was swift, brutal, well-planned, and successful—except that four UDA men were arrested and charged with the murder and a fifth with hiding the weapons. One of those convicted claimed that he had been working for the SAS and had been given two army-issue Sterling submachine guns, forty-eight magazines, and three thousand rounds of ammunition. He named names and claimed that various republican targets had been discussed. There were other curious aspects of the case—documents destroyed, suspects released, the murder on August 23 of an IRA man released from the Kesh; but in the end not enough details to prove a grand plot.

On June 26, 1980, Mrs. Miriam Daly, a lecturer at Queen's University Belfast and a well-known member of the IRSP, was found by her ten-year-old daughter in a bloody heap, face down in her front hall. She had been tied to a chair and shot without the neighbors noticing. Miriam Daly, who had been prominent in the H-Block campaign, was assumed to be one of the visible faces of the INLA—and with such a small organization, not an innocent face. There had been a heavy army and police presence around the time of the shooting and physical evidence that the murder had been carefully planned and effected. There was general nationalist suspicion that the killing had the signs of an operation directed by John McMichael, South Belfast UDA commander since 1979, who had both close intelligence connections and a desire to operate like the SAS.

On October 15 Ronnie Bunting and Noel Lyttle were shot dead in Bunting's house in a cul-de-sac in Downfine Gardens, Andersonstown. Bunting was a Protestant, the son of Paisley's old 1968–70 ally, Major Ronald Bunting; he had been involved first with the People's Democracy, then with the Officials, and had gone into IRSP-INLA at the split. He was an advocate of the armed struggle, an apostate, an H-Block leader. He and Lyttle, IRSP and an H-Block campaigner, were obvious targets. Bunting, in fact, had been threatened when questioned at Castlereagh Centre in August and had taken the threats seriously, making a formal complaint. At 3:15 A.M. the threat became real as the sound of the front door being smashed. The two murderers were "cool and calm and knew what they were doing" according to Bunting's wife, Suzanne, also a Protestant and H-Block campaigner. They went right to their targets and shot them repeatedly. Suzanne Bunting was shot in the shoulder when she tried to pull one gunman away as he fired down into her husband's body. On his way out he turned and shot her again in the mouth, leaving her bleeding on the floor. Her husband, hit seven times, was dead, and Lyttle was dying, with the children standing about screaming.

Again there was evidence of very good intelligence—the men knew which doors to sledge and where the targets would be in the house. There was also evidence of unusual British security activity in the area, indications that the investigation was less than thorough, more concerned, for example, with the Buntings' documents than the spent cartridges. The unexpected eyewitness related that the two killers were of medium height, wore khaki ski masks, khaki corded sweaters with suede shoulder pads, and khaki trousers tucked into military boots—British army work clothes; but, of course, such clothes were available to all. It did not seem an appropriate covert costume but the Protestant paramilitaries had a fondness for military decor, and the UDA a great admiration for the SAS.

Then on January 16, 1981, another UDA assassination attempt, planned in a room above a pub in Lisburn owned by John McMichael, turned into a spectacular act of vengeance denied. This time the victims were Bernadette Devlin and her husband, Michael McAliskey, shot repeatedly in front of their three young children in their home in the Derryloughan townland near Coalisland. Two of the UDA men smashed their way into the house with sledges at 8:15 in the morning, shot McAliskey four times, leaving him on the kitchen floor, and then in the bedroom shot Bernadette Devlin eight times.

The three UDA men involved were caught, tried, sentenced, and imprisoned; but again, as Bernadette McAliskey pointed out, there were unresolved questions: Why were four paratroopers on hand immediately? Why not the Argyll and Sutherland Highlanders stationed locally? Why didn't their radio work? (The phone lines had been cut.) And why did they leave without giving medical aid? It took twenty minutes for the Argylls to arrive and this was barely in time to save the two. Perhaps it was simply one more UDA murder from beginning to end, but the nationalist community felt that the string of killings that began with Turnly had all the hallmarks of the UDA, obviously an enthusiastic ally, manipulated by the British, seeking out the vulnerable. For many it was taken as fact that they were SAS killings, British killings, and protests were made at various levels and in varying degrees of intensity to the British authorities. Certainly each killing during the period added further to an already dreadful confrontation that had moved out of the closed cells of the protesting prisoners into the streets and, by the recourse to the ultimate weapon, the hunger strike, into a two-year battle transmitted worldwide by the media.

As early as March 26 the British had sought to defuse the H-Block problem, once more in the news after O Fiaich and Bishop Edward Daly had visited the Maze on March 3. Atkins had announced concessions on March 26 that would permit prisoners to exercise in sports clothing and to receive one extra visit a month. The prisoners rejected the concession. There were usually between 360 and 380 men on protest at any one time, some coming on and some going off for varying reasons. The hard-core fought it out, getting through each day. On April 1 O Fiaich and Daly met with Atkins on the prison issue. There was no new concession. The British publicly were adamant: no compromise, no deal with the criminals.

Repeatedly in statements and in print the Northern Ireland Office stressed that the prisoners were criminals who were denying themselves access to one of Europe's most splendid prisons. Every effort had been made to keep the Maze "in the forefront of modern prison practice." The prisoners had brought on their own misery and could end it at any time. The British position was no different from that of any state—the Republic of Ireland had broken the hunger strike in 1977 and did not recognize political status. No one recognized political status. In fact, the tone of the authorities during the blanket protest and the dirty protest had been one of indignation that any blame for the confrontation might accrue to the system, a system under the threat of the gun on the outside and the unending rebellious protests on the inside. All this turmoil was designed not to secure justice or even imagined rights but to damage the legitimacy of the Crown, to harm Britain. The H-Block protest was merely an aspect of the IRA armed struggle.

If there was interest at all in the prisons of Northern Ireland it was channeled into old prejudices and attitudes. The Protestants of the province delighted in harm coming to the republicans if a few of the paramilitaries had second thoughts about their own special status or lack of it. The rise of police professionalism had meant hard times for the UDA and UVF, especially when brutal murder or simple crime was involved. The majority, however, supported their government, their prisons, and the rules that the IRA opposed. Outside republican circles only strong Irish nationalists were H-Block people although increasingly there was a general nationalist desire that the wretched conditions could be eased, either because the protest was embarrassing to public figures or because the conditions of the prisoners aroused sympathy, regardless of the issues involved. In 1977 Father Raymond Murray, an advocate of prison reform, wrote, "Whatever the past deeds of the men in H-blocks may or may not have been and whatever the justice or the injustice of the sentences, one has to admire their courage, fortitude and endurance against impossible odds."*

This was the very response that the British did not want. They wanted the struggle isolated inside the Maze, at least inside the province. And after two years this had remained largely the case. Even in the Republic there had been little interest; many had no idea what the word *H-Blocks* splattered on country walls meant. On May 21 Taoiseach Charles Haughey arrived in London for a summit with Thatcher. Both were on their best behavior. Haughey, supposedly the Greenest of Irish leaders, the one most likely to exploit the national issue, wanted to calm British fears, charm the Prime Minister, lay the groundwork for an accommodation that seemingly must arise from the ten years of the Troubles. Surely Dublin and London could see a way into the future that would incorporate in some form the residue of the great dream of 1916. Thatcher, surely the most pro-Unionist of any recent British Prime Minister, knew little and cared less about Easter 1916 and all of that, wanted Ireland out of the way, and so was willing to spare Haughey the time, time invested in diverting Dublin's attention from more embarrassing matters. Haughey went out of his way to be charming and charming he could be, and Thatcher was not diverted by argument, disputation, or lecture. In the communiqué the Irish government expressed its wish to secure unity "by agreement and in peace," accepting that any change in the constitutional position of Northern Ireland could come only by the consent of the people of Northern Ireland.

To Irish nationalists it appeared that Haughey had not only been agreeable but had negotiated away rights embodied in the Irish Constitution of 1937; he had given up the historical claims of unity and accepted a formula not unlike that advocated by the British Parliament. It was only a postsummit communiqué, but it caused a real quiver in the heart of formalists and disappointed the H-Block people, who had hoped for more from Haughey. But he was content to have

*Padraig O'Malley, *Biting at the Grave: The Irish Hunger Strikes and the Politics of Despair* (Boston: Beacon, 1990), p. 23, quoting from one of the numerous works published by Denis Faul and Raymond Murray on the injustices arising from the Northern Ireland crisis: *H-Blocks: British Jails and Irish Political Prisoners* (Northern Ireland: Dungannon, 1977). As the date indicates, they were often first at the barricades of revelation and protest.

prepared the ground, displayed his charm, and got the Irish issue off ground zero. The H-Blocks were low on his worry list.

It was the first setback for the prisoners. Republicans could never quite believe that Dublin would let them down, or rather let the nation down, despite the past record, the experience of the movement, and the evidence of their own eyes—often gained in Free State prisons. The second disappointment came on June 19 when the European Commission on Human Rights unanimously rejected the case of the protesting prisoners. Basically with a nod to misery the report substantiated British contentions:

> The protest campaign was designed and coordinated by the prisoners to create maximum publicity and to enlist public sympathy and support for their political aims. That such a strategy involved self-inflicted debasement and humiliation to an almost sub-human degree must be taken into account. . . . The Commission must observe that the applicants are seeking to achieve a status of political prisoner which they are not entitled to under national law or under the [European] Convention.*

The British were obviously and vocally delighted—they could not have written a better report themselves.

The problem was that the prisoners were unmoved, and what began to attract the many to their cause was not justice but misery—the self-inflicted debasement and humiliation that required the participation of the authorities. Just being judged right by the European Commission did not mean that the confrontation would go away. Other standards and norms were at work as well.

Fortunately for the British, these forces remained weak. Haughey was intent on placating Thatcher and focused on his own political future; a national election would be needed to authenticate his role, his place in history. The Northern politicians, having spurned Atkins's constitutional conference, showed no interest in his second-round suggestions, published on July 2. The nationalists wanted to move up to an Anglo-Irish dimension and so welcomed the London suggestion. The unionists wanted to move back to a form of Stormont and so opposed Atkins's partial step, opposed anything Haughey suggested, opposed all movement not in their direction. So nothing was happening—other than the steady-state killing spotlighted on occasion by the spectacular assassinations of H-Block leaders or a major IRA attack. The prisoners increasingly felt that their protest was going to fade out. By autumn there were approximately eight hundred or nine hundred republican prisoners, the numbers changing nearly daily: One set of figures gives on one day 1,365 prisoners; of those who did not have special status were 837 republicans, and of these 341 were on dirty protest. The IRA leadership was firm and morale was still high despite the lack of British concessions and the difficulties of maintaining the protest. In January 1979 the authorities had foolishly concentrated all of the most incorrigible IRA prisoners in one wing of cell block

*European Commission on Human Rights, *Decision of the European Commission (1980)*, Strasbourg, ECHR, 1980.

6, thereby setting up a Provo university that concentrated on future strategy. In September the authorities compounded their error by moving the thirty-two men back into the main protest blocks, thus inserting fresh, skilled leadership. By the summer of 1980 this leadership felt that the only option remaining was a hunger strike. Brendan Hughes and Bobby Sands had felt that this was the only course when the meeting between O Fiaich and the Northern Ireland Office had led nowhere in April. There was no place else to go, although a hunger strike was always a dangerous risk if not a novel one.

During the Troubles the results drawn from hunger strikes had varied. Billy McKee had won political status for Northern prisoners, mainly because Whitelaw and the Northern Ireland Office was involved in various negotiations that might lead to accommodation and could not bear the weight of McKee's martyrdom. The Price sisters had come off after two hundred days of forced feeding with only vague promises but had in time been transferred to Armagh Prison and forced feeding had been discarded by the authorities. In 1976 Frank Stagg and Michael Gaughan had starved to death and in the following year the strike at Portlaoise had failed. Other hunger strikes, such as those of Thomas Ashe in 1917 and Lord Mayor Terence MacSwiney at Brixton Prison in 1920, had produced martyrs, not concessions; the great republican hunger strike by antitreaty prisoners had failed in 1923. In Ireland in September 1939 Patrick McGrath, a 1916 veteran, was released by Eamon de Valera after forty-three days but then the government stood firm, first against Tony D'Arcy and Jack McNeela, who died in 1940, and Seán McCaughey in 1946. As de Valera said in 1940, "The government has been faced with the alternative of two evils. We have had to choose the lesser, and the lesser is to let men die rather than the safety of the whole community be threatened." It was also an Irish government always faced by men who maintained that they were the legitimate heirs of 1916, the true faithful, the real Irish—a position with sufficient logic to harden most hearts against them.

Most other hunger strikes in Ireland had been symbolic, often without intention of the ultimate confrontation: Mac Stiofáin had come off a hunger and thirst strike to prevent violence and then a hunger strike at the orders of the IRA GHQ and, fairly or not, disappointed those eager for the ultimate confrontation. Other strikes were brief, often unauthorized, and mostly irrelevant to the problems of the Kesh. Each, however, drew on historic examples and the Irish tradition, reworked from legends and rumor, and involving a vocation to sacrifice, to suffer never unmindful of the lure of martyrdom. While the hunger strike was hardly Irish alone it was in a sense very Irish, very Irish Catholic, very much a nationalist tool, where the powerful could be shamed by the self-sacrifice of the weak: The process of starving was triumph, not the concessions wrested from authority.

Both Sinn Féin and the Army Council had enough problems without managing the H-Block protest as well. Thus, while intermovement discussions continued in the summer of 1980, the prisoners in the Maze unexpectedly had the mixed blessing of two new hunger strikes as evidence and case studies. Neither of the new strikes had been foreseen and neither strike had unencouraging results. In May 1980 Gwynfor Evans, sixty-seven-year-old president of the Welsh Nationalist Party, Plaid Cymru, threatened to start a hunger strike to the death on October 5 unless the government honored a pledge for a Welsh-language station on the fourth television channel. On September 17 Home Secretary William Whitelaw, who had conceded to McKee in 1971, conceded to Evans. Evans never began the strike and thus could not have extorted concession; Whitelaw had merely made an appropriate administrative decision. In the meantime a well-known IRA man, Martin Meehan, enraged at his conviction on dubious evidence, went on an unauthorized sixty-six-day hunger strike, terminating in a thirst strike, and then came off when Cardinal O Fiaich intervened. Evans might have shown that the British under special circumstances would concede; Meehan had provided the authorities with a test run.

The most detailed studies relevant to hunger strikes were probably the studies of the medical impact of starvation in the German concentration camps—not a pleasing parallel—and the impressions of those involved in previous cases. It had never been a very interesting focus of rigorous research, no more than torture had been until institutionalized in certain authoritarian countries. But the act was a relatively common rebel strategy: In the decade 1972–82 there were at least two hundred strikes in fifty-two countries, with twenty-three deaths, mostly Irish, in ten countries. There were as well strikes in closed prisons and camps that could not attract public notice. Each took place within a special culture and had historical and cultural resonances not found elsewhere. Each, however, despite the great differences in individuals followed a common pattern, as the body devoured itself with predictable physical and psychological results.

For the IRA leaders in the Kesh, their own movement's experience, the nature of the British opponent, and the anticipated physical costs were simply background music for the key theme: the absolute dedication necessary for a strike. Mass strikes failed because hardly anyone could predict their own, much less everyone else's, conduct further into the strike. Each single striker had to be prepared to continue to the end. After years of the most brutal and desperate protest, the naked, dirty years, the Kesh leadership had no doubts. Once on they would stay the course, die for their friends and for the dream. In a sense the real lure of the strike by the autumn of 1980 was the call to action: The protest was fading and the prisoners were left with failure, misery, and years to serve without an ideal, without a fight. With a strike they could act, albeit by doing nothing. This act embodied all that the movement admired, all that the prisons had taught, and all that could be done before acquiescence and humiliation.

The Army Council and the GHQ outside continued to be far less sure about such an adventure. The H-Blocks had already soaked up much of the military effort, engendered more sectarian killings, perhaps with British army involvement, and required a major adjustment for the movement in its association with the H-Block protest movement. And a mass hunger strike would make new demands of the inherently conservative Provisionals. A hunger strike was traditional and traditionally no one knew the end until the drama was played out. The leadership was thus caught between the two poles and dithered—also a tradition.

The republicans' view of the British remained static: perfidious, duplicitous, cunning, heartless, and intransigent, evoking a high moral purpose and acting on the most cruel regulations of power. The British view of the Provos was as absolute. The Provos were wicked, immoral, without principles or flexibility, godfathers of violence capable of manipulating and murdering for the slightest gain. The two sides were not mirror images of each other; they were Irish and British, incomprehensible, uncompromising. The actors spoke from different scripts and were involved in different dramas, although on the same stage and taking cues from each other. The hunger strike meant far less to the British and thus they lost by it far more; they missed the point of the play and had to pay double entry. The act of the strike was vital to the Irish. The sacrifice paid, not the results. When in the olden times the aggrieved and powerless sat starving outside the castle gate the mighty lord was shamed. The final act might or might not be concession and justice but the play by beginning had paid dividends, although at great risk. The British, pragmatic and rational, stood firm against the extortion of criminals. London was right and did not need to make either substantive concessions or a generous move that would only be misunderstood. They misread the hunger strike as a contest decided in the endgame, when a refusal to concede would bring a victory, while the Irish knew that on the island the long, bitter game would give a victory not as sweet as a British concession but just as real. It was not who won or lost at the end that would be remembered but how the game was played. That was in Ireland; in Britain, games have clear winners at the end of time.

For the game to begin at all for the prisoners, their friends on the outside asked for more time to get their forces appropriately deployed. The Provisionals' H-Block campaign already had struggled through troubled times. The crucial difficulty was that as true believers possessed of the truth the movement found external associations difficult and politics and protests divisive. Republicans had long been suspicious of conventional politics, and no recent commitment to people's politics arising mainly from the ideas and ideals of the new generation of Northern radicals was sufficient to erase the attitudes and assumptions of generations. Modern Irish history, republican experience, and personal exposure had led to the existing analysis: Participation in bargaining politics had produced betrayal and disappointment; the 1921 Treaty had been negotiated and accepted—politics over principles—and efforts to correct this by recourse to a parliament, whether the Dáil, Stormont, or Westminster, had failed the Republic—but not the politicians rewarded with power. And from de Valera to Seán MacBride and on to Goulding and Garland, good republicans had been content to organize one Free State Party after another, to accept titles and honors instead of persisting in the true course. Efforts by the radicals on the Left, by hard men and visionaries from George Gilmore and Peader O'Donnell in the thirties up to Tomás Mac Giolla's Official Sinn Féin turned Workers Party and the Northern radicals of 1968, had produced no Republic, much less a revolution. Politics within an illegitimate system, radical politics, parliamentary politics, politics at all, corrupted and ruined. Even an alignment with professed H-Block allies was difficult. The republicans anticipated control. The victims were their people, purity of principle—the ideals challenged were their own. A protest controlled by republicans would not involve the faithful in the dangers of accommodation, compromise, and adjustment so necessary in politics so dangerous to the faith. Republicans viewed politics as a scarlet woman, tempting, attractive, and in the long run sinful. Republicans, somewhat like the Church, protected their own from sensuality by a denial praised beyond measure as principle, by military vocations that insured against temptation, and for the everyday by warnings of the risk of involvement for any reason but narrowly defined and momentary gain.

With the H-Block issue the Provisionals had a narrow focus on the needs of the prisoners both as individuals under enormous pressure and as unarmed but potent players in the armed struggle. Bernadette McAliskey or even O Fiaich might seek justice; but the Provisionals wanted, if not a victory, then at least a tangible gain, not something for nothing, not something as justice, but something taken as a right by sacrifice. The IRA had from the first targeted the personnel of the prison system. For the IRA GHQ, protest did not mean replacing the gun but adding to the agenda of the armed struggle. The republicans continued to set their own priorities, march to their own drum and at their own pace. Again and always what the movement did not want was advice, the well-meaning giving direction, the outside imposing other standards and other strategies. What the center did not want was the hunger strike to take on a life of its own that would warp their agenda, their armed struggle. Already the H-Block protests had caused problems and returned uncertain benefits. There was advantage to be taken but no sure means. And always the prisoners were a weight on everyone's mind. Adams had been in the H-Blocks, knew the pressures, felt the draw of the desperate, naked, and dirty men in their cells. Through much of the protest time in 1978 and 1979 the organizers had moved uphill, hassled with their allies, won interest abroad, even in the Republic, slowly. There was a growing momentum but nothing to keep the media in residence.

When the H-Block protest began the republicans had been as difficult as always. But increasingly, as Gerry Adams and his associates controlled the protest campaign on the outside, an effort was made to listen to others, to seek consensus, to cooperate and coordinate and avoid the imposition of the party line. Not that ultimate control was yielded or a compromise of principle was tolerated; but the arrogance of certainty was less, if not the certainty. A new era of soft words, acquiescence to disputation, and allies as assets evolved during the two years of struggle. By autumn the republican center around Adams could build on the prisoners' determination, on the work of two years of protest, and on the new tactics of conciliation; and they could count on the British to be intransigent in public and conciliatory in the inevitable secret negotiations (perfidious as always). The advantages of some sort of accommodation to the prison confrontation for all seemed apparent to republican planners. A strike need not lead to death—recent history from Evans to Billy McKee and the Prices indicated that arrangements could be made even if not admitted. Besides, the prisoners could not hold out forever without hopes of escalation or concession—and the prisoners would not concede, could take matters in their own hands. Cardinal O Fiaich on September 24 claimed to be "hopeful of progress," but the prisoners knew better. There would be a strike.

On October 10 the prisoners announced that they were commencing a hunger strike on October 27. After the announcement on October 23, the Northern Ireland Office announced that prisoners would be allowed to wear civilian-style clothing provided by the authorities. As was the case with the offer before the April meeting with O Fiaich, the prisoners rejected the proposal as "meaningless"—another poisoned concession, too little to be acceptable but a sign of decency for the approaching confrontation. The strategy was hardly detailed, nor were the plans for protest firm. The H-Block protest organizations would pursue the same five crucial demands made for and by the prisoners: (1) no prison clothes, (2) no prison work, (3) permission to organize with one weekly visit, one letter out, and one letter and one package in every week, (4) free association with fellow prisoners, and (5) entitlement to full remission of sentences. The prisoners would demand political status. "We claim this right as captured combatants in the continuing struggle for national liberation and self-determination. . . . Our widely recognized resistance has carried us through four years of immense suffering and it shall carry us through to the bitter climax of death, if necessary."*

The question of the legitimacy of the armed struggle, the efforts by the authorities to break the prisoners and by the prisoners to secure their rights, was the foundation of the confrontation but not the visible battle. The issue for the public was the five points—decent demands denied. As for these five points, most any prison reformer would have advocated them as a policy for all prisoners. It was, however, in October too late for the British to agree without appearing to concede to extortion. As for political rights, a great deal had happened since McKee's strike way back in 1972 and Thatcher had no intention of giving in on what had become a matter of principle, and a principle supported by the European Commission on Human Rights. That report had also called for flexibility and generosity, both notably lacking in the prisons.

Inside the Kesh preparation by the IRA O/C, Brendan Hughes, had gone on all autumn. Letters for publicity were churned out, options were discussed, and strikers were chosen out of seventy volunteers. Hughes would join them; Bobby Sands, another Belfast man, unnoticed outside as a volunteer but inside intense, dedicated, and determined, would take over as prison O/C. The seven would be Hughes, a dominant figure since his arrival, John Nixon, Seán McKenna, Raymond McCartney, Tommy McKearney, Tom McFeely, and Leo Green. All were in good health, with the possible exception of McKenna, and all eager to begin.

On October 27 the seven refused meals on the first day of a fast to the death. On October 28 Margaret Thatcher announced publicly and unequivocally that there would be no concession, no political status. The lines were drawn. There were 342 prisoners on the dirty protest in the Kesh and 33 in Armagh. The focus, however, had switched to the seven, and the two years of H-Block protests had provided a foundation for an escalating response. Provisional Sinn Féin and the radicals were out drumming up support, picketing John Hume's house, complaining about SDLP inaction, marching and meeting. On November 2 there were organized demonstrations throughout Ireland and Ruairí O Brádaigh announced that the strike was "a showdown with imperialism."

As always in Northern Irish matters, real and imagined intermediaries sought a compromise or a vocation as diplomat. Demonstrations grew. One in Dublin

---

*Liam Clarke, *Broadening the Battlefield: The H-Blocks and the Rise of Sinn Féin* (Dublin: Gill and Macmillan, 1987), p. 123.

attracted over ten thousand people. Nationalist opinion remained divided. Fitt adamantly opposed concessions just as he opposed Provisional pretensions and the damage that O Fiaich and Daly did by encouraging the protesters. Cardinal Basil Hume in England appealed for the government to resist pressure. The SDLP dithered. Returns from the Republic were mixed, divided almost down the middle on political status according to one poll and equivocal as far as public statements by politicians went. There was agreement that the confrontation was undesirable, and soon all the Dáil parties were backing an effort by Hume to use the European Commission's report as a means to get some minimum British concessions on the five points. On December 1 three women in Armagh Prison, Mairead Farrell, Mary Doyle, and Mairead Nugent, joined the hunger strike. On December 4 Atkins publicly spelled out British opposition to concessions on the five points that would "legitimize and encourage terrorist activity" but noted that he was willing to "discuss the humanitarian aspects of the prison administration in Northern Ireland."

This seemingly indicated that there could be no give at all on political status but a deal of sorts on the five points. There was not, however, a great deal of negotiating room. Nor were there proper intermediaries or much time. The seven strikers had been segregated for medical monitoring on December 1. One unanticipated prospect had opened up when the Anglo-Irish summit came to Dublin—Haughey might use his influence, if any, to accelerate negotiations. From time to time he had indicated his continuing nationalist concern and his star was certainly in the ascent. On November 6, in a Donegal by-election, Clem Coughlan of Fianna Fáil won and thus so did the Taoiseach—a general election and five years of Fianna Fáil beckoned. Haughey had rebuked Síle de Valera for accusing the British of callousness, which might be taken by the British as a sign of his moderation. Rather, it was a move to maintain control of the issue. Haughey might ride the wave to a deal with Thatcher and get everyone off the hook. On the eve of the summit two thousand people in Dublin demonstrated for the prisoners.

Haughey had a far grander vision than five points or the prison conditions of subversives. He hoped for a grand solution to what must seem to the British a costly and pointless plod through a quagmire. If there was to be a settlement, as Haughey felt necessary and possible, if it was to have an Irish dimension, as Haughey and the SDLP felt vital, then there would have to be an Anglo-Irish understanding—and the earlier the British were made to understand the importance of the issue and the mutuality of interest in fashioning a solution, the better. Anglo-Irish understanding meant in the real world agreement between Haughey and Thatcher if something was to be done in the increasingly volatile Irish political climate, with Síle de Valera making nationalist speeches and the Provos and their H-Block campaign making the running. So Thatcher, without any great commitment, came to Dublin to meet Haughey on December 8. She brought along Humphrey Atkins, of course, but also the Chancellor of the Exchequer, Geoffrey Howe (money matters, of course), and the Foreign Secretary, Lord Carrington. The media in Dublin speculated that Carrington's experience in Rhodesia might be relevant, that something might be in the air. They did not consider that Ireland was being graced by a high-level descent, with the appropriate personnel on display—Ireland was, after all, a foreign country. Thus, even before the meeting the Irish teacup had been whipped to a speculative froth, not the least because the Taoiseach clearly did have grand ambitions. He had always had grand ambitions and after a year in power he wanted to achieve something more substantial than office.

The meeting between Thatcher and Haughey brought together two very special people similar in nothing but ambition and language; superficially consummate politicians, neither had ever displayed the conventional skills and virtues such a calling required. Both could attract a devoted, often fawning, retinue and an inviolate bloc of votes; both had a gift for the hard word; both had a singular egotism; and both represented a new wave wearing designer clothes and urging old virtues. Both alienated their own more conventional supporters, horrified the opposition, and as often as not became the issue instead of the advocate. Neither suffered fools gladly, especially those foolish enough to disagree, and the closer the dissent the more brutal the response. Neither had second thoughts and both possessed enormous sensitivity to the nuances of party. Haughey had refined the gifts for far longer than Thatcher but he operated in a far smaller and far more intimate arena. Thatcher was on the path to world prominence while few outside Ireland could pronounce the Taoiseach's name. When they met in December, however, they seemed more of a pair: ambition triumphant, power achieved, the future open, and both at the height of power deployed.

Haughey had risen from the bottom of the old middle class to wealth and political prominence with a mix of raw talent, shrewd judgment, desire, and the best of Irish luck, not to mention a good marriage and a grasp of the possible. He had come to dominate the party of government when it was devoid of ideas. The party of de Valera had fashioned a rural, pious, provincial Ireland, isolated, narrow, dominated by the beneficiaries of the national movement—clerks, teachers, publicans, bureaucrats, and country solicitors—and by the ideas of the Church and the rural secondary schools. The great ideas and radical instincts had played out in censorship, national pieties, and the smug assurance of survivors.

Haughey arrived with the advent of real money, money acquired through speculation in association with government, the nation's one great industry, which manufactured entitlements, regulations, paper, and positions. The new money was teased from ticky-tack housing developments, state projects, real estate arrangements, and the destruction of Georgian Dublin—Ascendancy Dublin—that was exchanged for tasteless but glittering new Irish office blocks. This new, often jerry-built Ireland allowed some to ride to hounds and own yachts, fashioned a new consuming middle class from those previously content with lace curtains, and ignored the poor and the emigrants. The new power elite was no more dreadful than elsewhere. They were a curious breed of politicians who, despite their mohair suits and German cars, were still rooted in much of the old Ireland. Haughey had early been exposed to the national struggle at the bottom, not the top. In 1969 he had seemingly been led astray by sentiment, ambition, and a misreading of history that led to the arms trial—and by a flawed pedigree, according to FitzGerald. Now, on the eve of a new decade in power, he seemingly had an opportunity to find an accommodation on Northern Ireland by deploying logic, intimacy with the issue, and charm.

The object of his intentions, Margaret Thatcher, was misread from the first.

She knew all she wanted to know about Ireland—intimacy was unnecessary once one had stood in the stark and crowded command post at Crossmaglen and looked down at the bloody insignia of a British officer killed by terrorists. As for Anglo-Irish relations, Thatcher had no interest in the Republic except as Dublin appeared recalcitrant in pursuing gunmen. To come to Dublin was imposition enough. Time was better spent on the revolution in Britain and the entanglements of Europe. What Thatcher wanted from Ireland was what every British Prime Minister had wanted for half a century—nothing, an island Wales, if with less Celtic spoken, that flew a tricolor bunting and acted like the English. Most in London still knew more about Nigeria or Oman, strategically vital spots, than about Ireland. And as for Haughey's charm, the British impression was quite the opposite. Small, with a curious shock of hair, a pliable face, and an alien accent, he appeared, if not a crook, certainly not a charmer. Thatcher liked tall, well-dressed, modestly charming Englishmen of a certain age, not small, dapper, presumptuous Irishmen who many in London felt had terrorist connections.

The British Prime Minister, a guest in a strange house, was warmly polite, put on an interested face, listened. She had arrived as a convinced unionist who saw the Irish problem as a matter of imposing order, an order that might or might not be assisted by a Haughey administration. The H-Blocks were a minor matter. The Taoiseach mistook Thatcher, a figure quite out of his ken and his own manipulative skills.

So the delegations met, Thatcher, Carrington, Howe, and Atkins for the British and Haughey along with Brian Lenihan, Minister for Foreign Affairs, the Taoiseach's man and a ubiquitous minister, and Michael O'Kennedy, the Minister for Finance, one of the successful new generation. It was a real summit, the first such meeting with senior ministers. And it was in Dublin. It would be a triumph if nothing went wrong, and nothing went wrong. The meetings lasted all day and included a private session of seventy-five minutes between Haughey and Thatcher. There was general agreement and no painful problems.

The joint communiqué mentioned that their talks were "extremely constructive and significant"—which meant in diplomatic language that no one had shouted or raised impossible demands. They agreed on "the need to bring forward policies and proposals to achieve peace, reconciliation and stability." This had been basic policy in Dublin and London for a decade. And there would be joint studies covering a range of issues, including possible new institutional structures, citizenship rights, security matters, economic cooperation, and measures to encourage mutual understanding. In sum, it was a nice necessary meeting with a vague end-of-term communiqué and no sign of specifics. Haughey chose to read matters differently. He indicated at a large press conference that there had been a "historic breakthrough"; but he did not, since he could not, elaborate further. The Irish cabinet then entered upon an exercise to indicate the reality of this interpretation with off-the-record winks and nods implying that the entire Anglo-Irish constitutional problem was open. Brian Lenihan, his master's voice without the need for propriety, appeared for an RTE interview and said that he anticipated an early end to partition. It could well have been that he did.

The immediate impression of both the British and old Haughey watchers was that a concerted effort to manipulate the conference and the media response into a triumph had been launched. Either the wish fostered the deed or else the Taoiseach's overweening ambition had driven him to a momentary "triumph" that assured subsequent distaste in London. The latter seemed to be London's view. Thatcher announced that there was no intention of altering the constitutional position of the six counties, but not in time to stop the loyalists, led by Paisley, from rushing into the street to demonstrate through the province. Paisley cut into Haughey, an old hate figure, praising his own Protestant ancestors who were cutting "civilization out of the bogs and meadows of this country while Haughey's ancestors were wearing pig skins and living in caves." Pig skins or no, Haughey had very little to wear once the wishful thinking and pretensions had gone, along with Thatcher's sympathy and interest. On December 15 he called Northern Ireland a "failed political entity," but this was to cover his domestic flank, for he still hoped that something would work out with London. The next year, in the Fianna Fáil's annual Ard Fheis, he spoke of his hope that a year would see the end of the road.

By then the muddle and debacle of December 1980 at the Dublin summit had long been overshadowed by other matters. The events of December, however, reinforced London's impressions of many Irish politicians and much of Irish politics—sleazy charm, narrow ambitions, duplicity, and the word more vital than the deed. It was not Thatcher's kind of world at all. For the Prime Minister, no was no and the sooner said the better. Those who disagreed were discarded if allies or castigated if in opposition. In the case of Ireland there was rarely time or need to be concerned. As for the H-Blocks, she had said no. There was nothing more. Her advisers and bureaucrats might find a formula that would allow the strikers to avoid death but that was a detail.

The details of a solution proved more elusive than the various parties had imagined. Many conduits were in place; the clergy and prison officials were involved, John Hume was on call, and John Blelloch, the civil servant in charge of prisons, came and told the strikers that the reforms were available once they came off the strike. Hume, in fact, felt that he was near to an arrangement that would get the prisoners much of what was needed on the matter of association and clothing. A continuing difficulty, however, was the uncertain lines of communication. All sorts of people wanted an accommodation but few knew the strikers' intentions. As for the illusion that the Belfast Sinn Féin people were running the strike for specific advantage, this was by no means the case. Gerry Adams had already indicated the position: "We are tactically, strategically, physically and morally opposed to a hunger strike."* Sinn Féin would, however, back the strikers while urging reason on them. Adams and the rest felt they could not order moderation or concession. So the men in prison ran the strike and could be approached only through their own.

One problem was that Seán McKenna's condition was causing concern: The inevitable impact of starvation moves through allotted stages but at slightly varying speeds and may accelerate if there is inherent weakness. By December 12, when six UDA prisoners embarked on a parallel hunger strike to achieve

*White, p. 219.

segregation of loyalist and republican prisoners, McKenna's condition had visibly deteriorated. The loyalist strikers meant that a deal need not be focused specifically on republican demands. McKenna's condition meant that any deal had to be made soon to save him. With negotiations under way—O Fiaich was to see Atkins—the prisoners feared that McKenna might die almost simultaneously with an offer of acceptable concessions on the five points. Atkins was to speak to Parliament and O Fiaich felt that a moderate tone, coupled with some give on the five points, might persuade the prisoners, whose minds had been concentrated by McKenna's condition. To keep up the pressure and distract Atkins from using McKenna as leverage, as a means to give the strikers less, twenty-three more prisoners went on strike on December 15; and with McKenna fading seven more were announced for December 16.

Atkins now postponed his statement so that the strikers could read it first. The speech came into the prison on December 18, the fifty-third day of the strike, with McKenna given only twenty-four hours by medical opinion. When McKenna, during one of his lucid periods, was told he had only one day to live, he expressed his determination to continue. The Atkins statement began, "The seven republican prisoners, who were in the fifty-third day of their hunger strike today took food." There were accompanying documents on conditions arising at the end of the strike: "Within a few days clothing provided by their families will be given to any prisoner giving up his protest so that they can wear it during association and visits. As soon as possible all prisoners will be issued with civilian type clothing to be worn during the working day. [They will] become entitled to eight letters and food parcels and four visits. Prisoners will be able to associate within each wing of the prison blocks in the evenings and weekends."

There it was. The strikers had been addressed as republicans not criminals. Heretofore Atkins had always referred to them as criminals. There were the concessions, not ideal but real. And a senior civil servant was on the way from London to explain them in detail. And there was McKenna. If they waited for the details he might die. And for what? The man from London was held up by a delayed flight. The prisoners came off the strike on December 18. The six were in good shape and high spirits. McKenna was moved first to the military wing of Musgrave Park Hospital, where he learned the strike was over, before being transferred to intensive care at the Royal Victoria Hospital because of a potassium deficiency. The women at Armagh came off the strike and the UDR men at the Kesh. There was rejoicing in nationalist areas of the province and it was announced that Bobby Sands as O/C of prisoners was to meet the Maze governor, Stanley Hilditch.

It was a very momentary rosy glow created largely by the republicans' public assumption that they had won concessions. Other republicans in the Kesh and out could see none and so reported that the hunger strike had failed. Refusing to be responsible for McKenna's death, the republicans had stepped back at the last minute for hints and small gestures. When substance was sought, there was none. The first euphoria evaporated. Crucially, they would not be supplied with their own clothing before having to wear prison-issued clothing. They would still have to don prison garb. Those who had rushed to join the dirty protest in support of the strike and in anticipation of concessions began to conform. Those involved were crushed and none more than Bobby Sands, who felt that he had been outwitted, had swallowed promises, had led the men to a defeat that could only be recouped by another hunger strike in far less promising conditions. There appeared no other way and this time he would lead from the front, determined that promises and guile would not be sufficient to end the protest.

Outside, the leadership did not want a strike, insisting that the best move was to claim victory, marshal public opinion to that effect, and await a British response. Adams insisted that although the strike had been a victory, it would be well to remain vigilant, alert, and patient. Patience had eroded in the Kesh. Sands had to wait while under increasing pressure from Patsy O'Hara, O/C of the thirty INLA prisoners, who threatened his own strike for political recognition. Governor Hilditch's policy of dealing with prisoners one on one reduced Sands's authority and led to the growing trickle of conforming prisoners. By the year's end, morale was shaky.

For the authorities it had been a better year than many could easily recall but still too violent and too dangerous. The arrival of Thatcher and Atkins had meant no real shift away from Mason's assumptions, a commitment to order first. The double blow of Warrenpoint and Mountbatten had seemingly given the 1979 game to the Provos. The 1980 death numbers were far better: 8 soldiers instead of 38, 9 UDR instead of 10, 3 RUC instead of 9 and only 1 more RUCR, 6 instead of 5, with a grand total of 76 instead of 113. Shooting incidents were down to 642 from 728 and explosions to 280 from 422; bombs defused, malicious fires, armed robberies, and all the other indicators were down but still very high. Atkins's constitutional conference had failed but no one had placed great hopes in the exercise and at least it had kept the politicians talking. The talking had moved on to summits in London and Dublin that led not to the major changes imagined by Haughey but at least to a sense of purpose on the part of the legitimate institutions. It had not been a bad year, had not been without promise; and for the authorities it ended on a grace note with the end of the hunger strike.

In retrospect it would be clear that the conventional response of the authorities, in particular the Northern Ireland Office, to the end of the hunger strike lacked elegance and anticipation. Instead of exploiting the end with concessions that could easily have been made to all prisoners, adjustments that could have been phased in over time on the five points while holding firm on political status, the authorities sought to pursue the tactical victory on to a final demonstrable crushing of prison resistance. The Northern Ireland Office, as always, had misread the prisoners and their own assets. Determined not to give an inch, they could not tolerate the republicans claiming a victory that did not exist nor the chance to erode prisoner morale. The authorities assumed that, having won, they could now reap the benefits in the form of visible humiliation: the prisoners in prison garb, criminals all. So Sands, and the republicans outside, found that the hints and nods had led nowhere, that they had been fooled by British duplicity. In this small victory over the prisoners the British were not magnanimous but mean. So instead of inducing despair and defeat, the British response led the prisoners to a greater resolve and determination. Sands, who felt responsible for the December debacle, and the others could not be diverted, even by their own outside prison. The

British had made the traditional hunter's error of confusing the wounded with the dead.

Outside, attention moved elsewhere. The toll of assassinations—Turnly, Mariam Daly, Ronnie Bunting and Noel Lyttle, and then the attack on January 16 on Bernadette and Michael McAliskey—had finally upset a wider audience. Bernadette McAliskey was still a figure beyond the province, beyond Ireland. Her attack overshadowed the others. It overshadowed the murder on January 21 of Sir Norman Stronge, former Speaker of the Stormont Parliament, and his son by the IRA, who then bombed down his house, Tynan Abbey. Bernadette McAliskey was news, not the ninety-six republican prisoners who on January 27 demonstrated against the refusal of prison authorities to issue them with their own clothing by breaking up cell furniture and smashing windows. Devlin was news, not the British soldier shot dead in the middle of Belfast on January 24 or the twelve people injured in an IRA bomb blitz two days later.

That kind of violence was mere muzak to the occasional spectaculars that drew in the media. Devlin's narrow escape drew in the media for a day or two of hard news; then other interests in other places called. The international media were thus a reasonable barometer of the intensity of Irish events but each passing year required a greater storm to shift the barometer. In Irish terms, good news or bad, this meant that the Troubles had become static, worse pliable, malleable so that after each spectacular the integrity of the old quarrels and positions reemerged hardly changed. The situation was not frozen hard, where a cunning blow would shatter the form, but remained stable, always able to transform any news into the expected. Nothing changed the basic configuration. On March 11 the Ministry of Defense would begin building a permanent brick wall to divide the Falls and the Shankill—a "Peace Line," according to the army public affairs officers. To many it was an outward sign of the intractable inward divisions of the city. The whole province was walled off and ignored except for coverage of the dreadful, the novel, and the sensational. And for the media, fixated on novelty and sensation in any case, Ireland could by the new decade offer only sensation. Nearly everyone sensed, accurately or not, a game being replayed, the tape run over and over at slightly varying speeds but without further development.

Not even good news, like the first meeting, on February 2, of the senior British and Irish government officials in the joint studies sessions agreed to at the Dublin summit, had an effect. Good news had never led to local effects in the province before. All hopes had been disappointed, all political initiatives or novel movements had failed from the beginning; the concessions to the civil rights radicals, the reforms at Stormont and the closure of Stormont, power sharing, the Peace People, Atkins's constitutional conference, which was no more alluring at the beginning than the constitutional convention of 1975 had been at the end. And bad news was the news mostly. There may have been fewer murders in 1980 but no one expected murdering to stop. Next year there would be a spectacular atrocity or two to go with some heralded political maneuver—the usual. The international media had become cynical on any proposed accommodation, as had most British politicians and many in Ireland. After a decade of the Troubles novelty was not easy.

On February 6 Ian Paisley slipped five journalists out of Belfast to a remote hillside in County Antrim, where he spoke to the men of Ulster, five hundred strong, who would be a third force resisting to the death the process of all-Ireland integration from the Dublin summit. Paisley was following the example of Carson; he sought the leadership of the province under threat, sought prominence after a year that had not given politicians and spokesmen much coverage. The five were then taken back to Belfast to spread the word. There was a lack of seriousness in the entire exercise. No one now believed that Paisley would cross the far line of agitation into action. Everyone, government officials, the Northern Ireland Office, other party leaders, condemned his display. Everyone assumed that the hastily patched-up ritual of the Carson trail meetings (the first was in Omagh Orange Hall on February 13) would lead nowhere. There was Big Ian waving a bandolier—not a gun—and calling down the wrath of Orange ancestors on those who would betray the chosen people. Few were impressed. Sir Edward Carson's son was annoyed: "I dislike intensely the way my father's name is being used." Certainly the other unionist parties who saw the exercise as a DUP effort to seize the majority initiative, not unlike the failed general strike in 1977, had little but scorn for the march. None of their lot was taken in; nor were the nationalists, who had gradually accepted the Reverend Mr. Paisley as an inexplicable act of God, like the rains, to be suffered and ignored. The Northern Secretary announced on February 25 that there would be no "sellout" of the Union in the Anglo-Irish talks. So much for Paisley. What more could he do? What new could he do? There was now a precedent for nearly everything. He kept right on marching and by autumn had announced a Third Force that none could find. No matter—by then there were other ploys available to stay near the front of the stage. Some acts, no matter how often offered, are still bought by either the media or the faithful.

Certainly when the republican press officer in Belfast announced that there would be a new hunger strike beginning on March 1 there was a general sense of déjà vu. One strike, which had indicated that the British would not concede, no matter what, had just ended in December. And there were no visible new factors and fewer hopes for any republican novelty: The protests had exhausted enthusiasm, the failure had exposed the sterility of the ultimate weapon—the British were beyond shame, unlike those lords threatened by ancient hunger strikers. So if Paisley was out on the Carson trail to no visible purpose or result, the republicans seemed about to replay their failed act. On March 1, five years to the day after special status had been abolished, Bobby Sands began the new hunger strike.

This time the plan was to have a staggered start to allow waves of threatened strikers to reach a danger zone. The British would thus be faced with recurrent strikers at risk if they denied Sands. The director of the operation would be the new O/C of prisoners, Brendan "Bic" McFarlane. Once destined for a religious vocation, McFarlane had instead volunteered for active service in Belfast, where he had been involved in the bombing of the Bayardo Bar. Because this attack, claimed by the IRA as an operation against UVF agents of the Crown but seen as a sectarian retaliation by many, might be used against him, it was decided that McFarlane would not join the strikers but would coordinate the events. Sands would go first, joined next by Francis Hughes, from Derry, where the authorities now claimed he was responsible for the death of twenty-six members of the security forces. They called him the Bellaghy Butcher. Hughes imposed his presence on the strike despite his potential lack of appeal to the general public. He had lived despite his fearful wounds because of the same determination. He insisted, and he was a hard man. Sands had always been the obvious first choice, still guilty over the collapse of the first strike; he now felt he must lead from the front.

Sands was neither the guerrilla in the classic mold of Francis Hughes, a taciturn, hard man with limited vision, nor a famous or important urban figure like Brendan Hughes or Bic McFarlane. His career had been short, unremarkable, and so typical. Most volunteers did not last the course to become notorious or important. Born in 1954, he had come from an equally typical background. His father worked in the post office; there was a hint of Protestantism in the background, although the family was as Catholic as most. In fact they moved from a Protestant area because of it when Sands was seven to Rathcoole, where, in June 1972, they were intimidated out of their home again and moved to Twinbrook. The expulsion made a deep impression. He had been a Belfast boy keen on sports, no great scholar, very ordinary in recollection even when splendid traits were later easy to imagine. Early married, he was still only eighteen when he was arrested six months after he joined the IRA—pistols were found in the house where he was staying. He spent his time in the cages enthusiastically involved in republican prison life. Gerry Adams was O/C of his cage, number 11. Prison brought out his talents, imposed discipline, and rewarded his dedication and enthusiasm. His energy was like lightning in a bottle and the narrow arena of the Kesh fitted his talents.

Released in 1976, he joined his wife, Bernadette, and his three-year-old son, became O/C of an IRA unit in Twinbrook, and took an active part in community activities, bringing in the black taxis, publishing a republican newsletter, establishing a Sinn Féin cumann but still attracting no great attention. Within six months he was back in jail, caught with three others in a nine-man bomb attack on the Balmoral Furniture Company. His interrogation was harsh; and, although the authorities could not prove his link to the bombing, he received fourteen years for possession of firearms after eleven months on remission. He was sent back to the Kesh in September 1977 and immediately went on the blanket and dirty protest.

Again he blossomed in prison, where the intensity of the confrontation magnified his intensity and his dedication. Outside he lived in a somewhat broader world but one that had not offered a vocation, only opportunity. In the Kesh his dedication and drive could make a difference—one man counted. Sands found a role, as had so many others during the Troubles, that allowed him to exploit his natural assets. Poorly educated, limited, and provincial, he thought in clichés and stage symbols drawn from his Catholic faith and his grasp of republican principle. He continued his Irish studies, wrote propaganda, letters, and poetry, shaped the caged lark as his symbol. He had memorized the romantic historical novel *Trinity* by Leon Uris and called out the story down the locked corridors of his H-Block. Even those passing through caught his intensity; slight, eager, absolute in his republican vocation, he suspected, in a sense knew, that to be effective his hunger strike would have to be to the death: a death he saw in terms of those figures and symbols he knew, a martyr's death, the death of the patriot dead, all those failed dead heroes of the cause, the death that comes to the faithful of the Church.

All armed struggles arise from simple, easily expressed ideas that, no matter how rigorous or rich for the philosophers, can be written on banners or sprayed on walls. All struggles offer stereotypes and symbols; most of all they offer an opportunity for the young absolute in their commitment, emboldened by their own dedication, to sacrifice. This is one of the enormous attractions of a life underground—not the gun or the power, not even the risk or the danger, but the sacrifice—even unto death, especially unto death. And so it was for the Cypriot Greeks of EOKA or the Jews of the Irgun and so it is for the Palestinians or the Muslim Brothers or the Basques. Each acolyte arrives in a different context with a different historical and ideological baggage, shaped by special cultural forces and personal predilections, but all come absolutely dedicated to their faith and to the chance to sacrifice to redeem the ideal. Sands was simply the typical pared down to the intense and burning core. Slender, naked, and dirty, with a long mane of blond hair, sharp eyes, and a quiet tongue, he was no real poet, not a grand talent or a great guerrilla, but rather one of the best of his ordinary generation who chance had put at the center of the stage. He was equipped with great resolve, burning intensity, and a simple faith simply expressed in the transcendental Republic.

For Sands and for those who would come later, the strike would not really be about the five demands, political status, or the legitimacy of the movement and the armed struggle; it was to pit the will of the just against the power of empire. For the republican to win the British would have only to take his life, would have only to refuse to act and thus show their shame. And he was sure that Britain would act to character, hold firm, and so lose a moral struggle. This was to the strikers a great moral struggle between Irish justice and British oppression that would be so recognized only when life was given and taken. The criminals would be revealed not by a declaration by Thatcher, not by the courts or judges, but by a trial of spirit within the H-Block cells by men alone with their faith. Hughes and the others might not recognize the inevitable but from the first Sands did.

The murals that went up on the gable ends deployed the imagery of Catholicism, garish colors, elongated bodies, saints and the saintly, Christ down from the cross, painted not like the naive works of the Orange murals or the splattering of the untrained but with the truly stilted realism of the secondary school art student, awkward, inept, but because of the emotional charge still moving, more moving than polished realism. There, in giant illustrations, done not so much to be seen as to be done, the church and the movement joined, the men of Easter, the lily and the lark made one with the older iconography. The pious—and many republicans were pious—could feel at home, and many of the pious who detested the Provos were moved by the reality, their reality, found in the mural, in the sacrifices of the Kesh. The strikers were seen by many as Catholic martyrs as well as nationalist ones. The nation's history of denial and suffering because they were Catholic and Irish was recalled and refashioned. It was not a response anticipated or, on reflection, desired by much of the clergy who opposed the republicans. Reflections on such matters came much too late: The strike was perceived by Irish nationals, by Irish Catholics, as a traditional response to power displayed and deployed. Beyond the Falls and the reach of the murals was a people waiting to be touched by the old faith.

Recognizing what was needed and fashioning the rituals for general consumption was easy—what the republicans lacked was an enthusiastic audience. The Irish had suffered through the first strike. The authorities had won through once and saw no problem with a repeat. The sympathetic were tired. Haughey had his own agenda, a general election built on the Donegal result and a deal with Thatcher. The SDLP and Fitt and the others wanted no part of the protest; Fitt wanted the strike to fail. London had other interests—Ireland was boring.

Then on March 5 Frank Maguire, the Westminster member for Fermanagh–South Tyrone, died unexpectedly of a heart attack. There would be a by-election. The H-Block people saw an ideal opportunity—run Sands as a symbolic protest candidate and so generate interest and enthusiasm and support. The Sinn Féin people moved almost immediately to clear the field for a one-on-one election.

The SDLP (hardly for the first time) found itself in a nasty corner. The party posture as the Catholic party, modern, trendy, and inclusive rather than a conglomerate of partisan issues united by religious affiliation, meant that every election should be contested. Sometimes, however, the partisan interest wandered off as had Gerry Fitt, now sitting at Westminster as an Independent Socialist, or stayed out, as had Frank Maguire. If there were two minority candidates in a nationalist district, the split vote would and had given the seat to the tribal enemy, the unionists. This had happened in Fermanagh–South Tyrone in February 1974, letting Harry West win for the OUP, but not during the second election that year, when the SDLP relented. In fact the SDLP tended to relent when the prospect of tribal disapproval was intense. It was embarrassing but inevitable, one of the costs of politics in the province. The combination of the Provos involved, desperately involved, in exerting pressure within the province, and the emotional appeal of the Sands candidacy gave Hume very little room to maneuver. The SDLP constituency, especially in the country, particularly after the departure of Paddy Devlin and Fitt, overlapped the natural one of the Provisional Sinn Féin people. And this was going to be a national issue election, a one-issue election if Sinn Féin got the nomination for Sands. Many nationalists abhorred the violence and pretensions of the Provos, but the historic loyalty to the tribe remained. A vote for Sands was a vote against them, the Protestants, the British, the others, more than a vote for the Provos. What the SDLP feared was simply that their voters would be dangerously indignant if a Unionist were elected because of a split vote. The SDLP would dither but they would accept reality and not run this time, this once; so Austin Currie's name was put forward and then withdrawn.

The other natural candidates—Maguire's brother Noel, the Irish Independence Party's Frank McManus, and Bernadette McAliskey—were all subjected to intense pressure. This pressure was more intense since person, not party, was involved. Currie had an easy out—the SDLP was standing aside—but he might sneak back; but neither McAliskey nor McManus wanted to ruin Sands's chance or their future prospects. Noel Maguire insisted he would run no matter what. He did not even manage a graceful withdrawal from a seat that by local rules might well have been his. The Provos were, if anything, less than graceful. Pressure from the locals, from the province, even from the United States was exerted to be sure that Sands had a straight run against West despite Sinn Féin attitudes. On March 20, thirteen minutes before the deadline, an angry Maguire withdrew his nominating papers as his daughter and niece sobbed outside. Sands would have his clear run. And Currie, who had decided to have a go as an independent, did not get the word because time ran out before a call could reach him from Maguire's pub that would let him register his papers at the very last minute.

It was very hard to stand against a man who was in a prison hospital, had lost over seventeen pounds, and was the focus of parades, protests, petitions, and the most emotional appeals. Currie had run against the IRA in the constituency before but running against a starving man was another matter. It was unfair competition so only Harry West was left in the way and the vehement opposition of anti-Provo nationalist voters, no small force, who might stay home but would not vote for a loyalist. The key question was how solid the tribal vote would be—would the Catholics come out and vote for an IRA man, starving or no, in proper numbers? Would the unionists vote in sufficient numbers? The unionists had their own problems with a Paisley loyalist candidate who finally withdrew after causing maximum anxiety. The key would be who stayed home on election day, April 9. The H-Block group would have to bring out almost all of the usual nationalist vote to win and the usual nationalist vote was not a sure thing. And the Sands people had very little experience running a slick electoral campaign even with the help of their radical friends.

The Sinn Féin people out from Belfast (Fermanagh was a very long way from Belfast) were taken aback to discover the hatred and divisions within the constituency. They were used to the comforts of their West Belfast republican ghetto, not to the civil war conditions of the countryside, where many nationalists blamed the Provos for most of the Troubles. As the campaign continued the hunger strike broadened as planned. Francis Hughes joined Sands on March 15, and the next day they were joined by Raymond McCreesh from South Armagh and the INLA's Patsy O'Hara, who resigned as prison O/C in favor of Micky Devine. There were now four lives at stake.

Sands was run as an H-Block candidate, with no reference to local issues, with endorsements from all (including the disgruntled nearly candidates), and with an appeal to vote against West and Paisley because "His life and his comrades' lives can be saved if you elect him."* West did not run a shrewd campaign, letting slip the chance to attract some of Currie's 10,786 anti-IRA votes garnered in 1979, and the Sinn Féin people learned how to run a campaign on the job with both the imported radicals and sympathetic locals. On the eve of the polling day all the locals could say was that it looked close. On April 9 there was a high turnout (86.8 percent) for the by-election. Sands won over West with 30,492, a majority of 1,446, down from Maguire's 3,541. It was a triumph. The international media began to arrive. Harry West was shocked: "I never thought the decent Catholics of Fermanagh would vote for a gunman." The SDLP had been afraid they would and now Sinn Féin was on the cusp of a wave of sentiment to save Sands.

*Clarke, p. 145.

The pressure of violence during the campaign had been building up. A British businessman, Geoffrey Armstrong of British Leyland, was shot and wounded while giving a lecture at Trinity College in central Dublin; a UDA councillor, Sammy Millar, was shot and wounded in his Shankill Road home by the INLA; there were a pair of INLA-UDA tit-for-tat killings in Belfast; an RUC constable was killed by a booby-trap bomb in his car; a Derry woman collecting census forms was shot dead. Protests spread across the island, slowly at first. H-Block posters began to appear in windows in the South. The issue was hot. The British establishment was as disconcerted by the vote as Harry West, and the security forces were troubled by the decay of order. There was, however, no give at the top from Thatcher: "A crime is a crime is a crime." And Sands was in prison as a criminal.

Once Sands was elected, many Catholics anticipated movement on the hunger strike. There was none. Never meant never as far as Thatcher was concerned. There were riots following celebration parades in Belfast, Lurgan, and Cookstown. In fact in Belfast there were daily riots and the IRA began moving more freely. Many were reminded of the good old days of the no-go zones. And there was the usual results of a hard army response. In Derry a fifteen-year-old boy was shot and mortally injured by a plastic bullet on April 15 and then two teenagers were killed by an army Land Rover on April 19. Moderates felt that something had to be done.

The longer the confrontation the stronger Sinn Féin seemed. The province was fixated on a deathbed vigil. Sands's condition was the first news. Rumors were rife. Conspiracy theories abounded. There was fear of pogroms and killings to come by many Catholics. The minority community wanted leniency and their leaders from Hume to Cardinal O Fiaich felt there must be a means to conciliation, to save Sands and get everyone off the hook. In the South Haughey postponed elections until matters clarified. In London there was no sign of give. In Belfast a stream of visitors and intermediaries began to appear, including Síle de Valera and her fellow Euro-MPs Neil Blaney, who had backed Sands's candidacy, and Dr. John O'Connell. Hume urged intervention by the European Commission of Human Rights. Father Daniel Berrigan and former United States Attorney General Ramsey Clark were turned away at the prison gate. On April 22 Haughey spoke to the British ambassador, Sir Leonard Figg, immediately after a harsh Thatcher statement refusing to meet de Valera, Blaney, and O'Connell, whom she called "MPs from a foreign country." The papal nuncio to Dublin indicated he would be willing to go to the H-Blocks. The Taoiseach met with the Sands family and had them sign an appeal to the Human Rights Commission. Was there a chance? Was Haughey just playacting for points? Could anyone help?

Despite all the movement there was no momentum toward an accommodation: The five points were still on the table and Sands had been on the strike longer than McKenna. There was not a lot of time. The European Commission did not work out. The Pope's personal secretary, Monsignor John Magee, spoke with officials and then saw Sands on the fifty-eighth day. The Church was united against violence but not necessarily as one on the hunger strike. Already the British Cardinal Hume had condemned the hunger strike as violence, a position backed by the papal envoy to Britain, Archbishop Bruno Heim. Magee found he could do little. Sands was very weak and had almost died a few days before. The last outsider to reach Sands was Don Concannon, the Labour spokesman on Northern Ireland, as a Northern Ireland minister one of those responsible for criminalization. He spoke to Sands on May 1. There was no give inside the prison and no sign of compromise from the Northern Ireland Office. As Sands had suspected from the first, he would have to go all the way. All the talks, intermediaries, commissions, and back channels had produced nothing. The IRA and Sinn Féin had suggested Sands's election on April 9 would permit an end to the strike without loss of face, but the strikers would have none of it.

The movement outside had always been opposed to the strike, fearful of the risks and the lack of control. Even the undeniable benefits accruing to the movement from the Fermanagh–South Tyrone by-election were not sufficient reason to continue. The republican movement creeps ahead on consensus, often tacit, unarticulated, gradual, rather than on set orders: Very few orders are given without assurance that they will be accepted. Sands and the others were determined; they had been willing to delay but not to give up the ultimate weapon. It was not just about the five demands, not the problem of political status, but the wider thing that could be won from the great confrontation, that mattered. Dying would be victory and so too would living if the demands were accepted. Sands had always been prepared for the worst. And since the British would give a bit but not sufficiently Sands would allow his life to be taken for the risen people. On Tuesday, May 5, at 1:17 A.M., he died.

The Northern Ireland Office, hewing steadfastly to the orthodox version of events, issued a statement: "He took his own life by refusing food and medical treatment for sixty-six days." For the British he was a dead criminal who had wrought his own ruin. Others felt he had done so as a result of the machinations of the IRA godfathers of violence. Somehow the subversives had devised a strategy of leverage that allowed them to win by losing—and those who lost refused to be labeled misguided, pawns used by the Army Council. It made life difficult for the orthodox, all varieties of the orthodox.

Father Denis Faul, an advocate of prison reform who had lost his enthusiasm for the hunger strike along the route, now felt Sands had mistaken his role. "He saw himself as the Messiah, Christlike, and he was determined to go ahead." Father Faul had no time for establishments, the prison authorities or the republicans or even at times his own hierarchy. What concerned him was that Sands and the republicans had created their own spiritual world without need or recourse to the Church. The people were even demanding that the Church intervene to aid the strike and the strikers. The Irish church was not comfortable with any criticism nor with the pretensions of republicans who could do without their formal blessing. The republicans had transformed the old rituals, made use of the taught virtues, tilted the faith to their own use. Many in the English Church simply seemed to respond as English nationals, damning the strike as violence, damning the strikers as terrorists. The Irish establishment was in a more difficult position both with their parishioners and their own reactions. Mostly, however, the strike engendered suspicion and distrust by the orthodox—not, as the Protestants and many British imagined, support.

The Protestants' harsh attack on the H-Block strikers—let them all starve, fewer IRA killers, "another bastard dead"—was at times both uncertain and ambivalent. Some of the paramilitaries sympathized with the stand on political status and had even gone on hunger strike themselves; but most, like their more political figures, were troubled by the transformation of a defeat, a death, into a victory by an alchemy alien to the loyalists. There was a trick to wishing ill to an enemy who seemed bent on doing ill to himself somehow at your expense. In a way this unease was more troublesome than the fact that thirty thousand good Catholics had voted for a gunman. That was expected of Irish Catholic nationalists. The massed international media was sympathetic to Sands—but no one understood the loyalists anyway. The tide and interest seemed to be running for the Provos. No one cared about Paisley posturing on the Carson trail or about Protestant opinion. It was nice that Thatcher and the Northern Ireland Office had held firm. So the most avid cheered Sands's death but few were cheered by it.

That ritual began with the word of his death beaten out by the bin lids of West Belfast, a long, dreadful clanging that went on and on as the little streets and lanes filled. The riots that began on May 5 became a constant in Belfast and Derry, simmering down and breaking out again. On May 5 the casualties included a milkman and his fifteen-year-old son, Protestants killed a few streets from their home in Tiger Bay. A retarded man overexcited by the turmoil threw the first stone and then their milk delivery van was bombarded with bricks and crashed. An IRA sniper killed a policeman. The next day the toll was more typical—a policeman was shot dead and an INLA member was killed by his own bomb. On May 7 Sands was buried and the violence put on hold. Seven hundred media people were in the city to cover the event. It was a memorable funeral, the greatest of all for the republicans; a crowd of one hundred thousand watched the funeral cortege pass by. The son Sands never knew, eight-year-old Gerald, trotted along with the family, the mother who did not want a dead son, a wife made martyr too. And many followed on, marching endlessly to Milltown, while the entire British security force was on full alert: 7,000 RUC, 5,000 RUCR, 11,000 British army, 7,000 UDR. The British flew in six hundred extra troops of the Spearhead Battalion. At the Busy Bee shopping center the procession stopped. Volunteers in black berets and masks appeared and fired a volley. The authorities could do nothing. The IRA men disappeared into the crowd. The march began again. Then there followed the rest of the tradition, the honor guard, the flag, the oration, and the great crowd straggling home as the young broke off to riot.

It was a huge pageant, a real life drama transmitted worldwide by satellite, watched by millions who could understand little but the fact that a man had starved to death for justice on a faraway island, a man so important that the British Empire had sent an army to watch him into the grave. Sands became not just another name on the Milltown republican monument with martyrs chiseled on back to 1798, not a movement hero, not even an Irish hero, but a universal, a coin to be spent for the deprived. His simple poems filled with the republican clichés of belief, the symbols of the church and patriot history, circulated in cheap editions. One could pick up Mercier Press's *Skylark Sing Your Lonely Song*, published in Cork in 1982 at many news vendors in Ireland, at Irish shops in London or San Francisco, find his poems known to rebels far off in Beirut or Berlin who could hardly find Ireland on the map or knew what Erin meant.

614

Oh! star of Erin, queen of tears
Black clouds have beset thy birth,
And your people die like morning stars,
That your light may grace the earth.

But this Celtic star will be born,
And ne'er by mystic means,
But by a nation sired in freedom's light
And not in ancient dreams.

Sands's name was painted on walls in famous cities, sympathy was voted by groups no one in Belfast knew, in cities, often countries, that no one recognized. The ayatollahs named the boulevard in front of the British Embassy in Teheran for him. Many wore a lark pin for the caged lark that had been his symbol, many added his name to the generation of rebels, the last name perhaps in a world where the rebel vocation was no longer trendy, and many would remember a victory won through denial, not with a gun.

The drama was not over but the death of Sands had shaped the future. London had already paid an enormous price for intransigence, a price that had only barely become apparent to those certain their posture was proper. What else could they have done? Concede, give in to extortion, treat with terror? London might give a bit around the edges, secretly; but the only course left was to hold firm. The other strikers still trapped in the cells had realized gradually that the British were going to let them die. They had let a member of Parliament die. And closed into the intense and intimate fellowship of the II-Blocks, steeled by Sands and transformed by the weeks on fast to seek that other thing, not just the five demands. The next three remained determined. Sands was replaced by Joe McDonnell, who had been arrested with him after the attack on the Balmoral Furniture Company. There was now a second wave on the way.

The stages of deprivation became commonplace—the impact of chemical changes, the decay of various systems, the ebb and flow of lucidity dependent on predictable biochemical factors. The men were dying by the numbers and all the negotiations, initiatives, petitions, and anguish on the outside filtered through to them from a different, louder world that had almost been forgotten. There were no concessions and no drawing back. Their families came to watch them die. And they did. On May 12 Francis Hughes died on the fifty-ninth day of his fast. Another great funeral in his little parish was transmuted in "The Boy from Tamlaghtduff" by Christy Moore. There were the riots and the anguish. The IRA stepped up their operations. On May 19, near Bessbrook in County Armagh, five British soldiers were killed when a land mind blew up their armored car. On the same day an eleven-year-old girl from Twinbrook, Belfast, was mortally injured by a plastic bullet. On May 21 Raymond McCreesh and Patsy O'Hara died, both on their sixty-first day. The first four were gone.

Life went on. Not everyone was obsessed with the hunger strikes. London still had other priorities. On May 28 Thatcher came to Belfast and said that "faced with the failure of their discredited cause, the men of violence have chosen in recent months to play what may well be their last card." It was not only a remarkable misreading of recent events but also indicative of British determination not to give in to gunmen. There were certainly a lot of gunmen about at the end of May: On May 29 an off-duty RUC constable was shot dead near Newry and in Derry two IRA men were killed in a gun battle; two days later an RUC Reservist was shot dead while guarding a patient in Belfast's Royal Victoria Hospital and an army bomb disposal man was killed by a car bomb near Newry. This Fetch Felix was the seventeenth bomb disposal man to die in the Troubles. So the deaths went. And so too did politics go on. In Dublin Charles Haughey announced on May 21, the same day the two hunger strikers died, that a general election would be held on June 11; he slipped the contest in between H-Block crises and before the momentum signaled by the victory in the Donegal by-election was lost. In Northern Ireland there was a long-scheduled local government election.

In the highly polarized Northern Ireland these elections on May 22 did not produce any clear indicator of direction. The moderates were damaged, but the only very clear winner was Paisley's DUP, slipping past the OUP as the largest party, 176,816 votes to 176,342, although the number of seats was only 142, to 152 for the OUP. Alliance did poorly, down to 8.9 percent from 14.4 and the SDLP went down from 20.6 to 17.5 mostly because of the competition from a variety of small nationalist and republican parties, although the Officials' Republican Clubs–Workers Party lost half of its six seats and took only 1.8 percent of the vote. The IRSP and PD each elected two and the Irish Independence Party did best of all with 21 seats and 3.9 percent of the vote. The shift in nationalist priorities was shown in the loss of Gerry Fitt's seat on the Belfast city council after twenty-three years. West Belfast had changed but not Fitt. It was about what might be expected in difficult times—a defensive shift, small but real, to the extremes. Mostly the province was still traumatized by the Sands election, which would have to be run over again in August because of his death. The local elections simply indicated, as always, little change in the balance of the divide and this time a small decay in moderation, actually less than might have been expected.

Not expected were the results of the general election in the Republic, for Haughey had from the beginning of his tenure great confidence in his capacity to unite the party of government and win a general election. He was undone by his own image and the seepage from the H-Block crisis. The Taoiseach aroused very considerable distaste in many Southern voters, including some in Fianna Fáil, but that party had no other viable candidate and yet that candidate intensified the opposition. The result was a Fianna Fáil disaster for Haughey only in power because Lynch did not look a winner and he had. Fianna Fáil won 78 seats, down from 84, while Fine Gael moved up with 22 additional seats, 65 instead of 43, and Labour lost two, garnering 15 instead of 17.

The most deadly blow to Haughey had been the victory by H-Block candidates in two constituencies that should have returned Fianna Fáil. The Provos had not been impressed by the Taoiseach's aid and comfort for the hunger strikers and so ran prisoners in those areas along the border where serious support might be found—and they came within a few hundred votes of winning a third seat. Sinn Féin victories with nationalist protest votes in Dáil elections were hardly unknown. The president of Provisional Sinn Féin had been elected an abstentionist member of the Dáil in 1957 in a general election that had seen three other Sinn Féin candidates returned (Monaghan, Sligo-Leitrim, and South Kerry) out of nineteen and a total of 65,640 first preference votes.

This time Fianna Fáil had underestimated the H-Block impact and overestimated their Taoiseach's attractions—who could have imagined 65 Fine Gael victories. Fine Gael's new leader, Dr. Garret FitzGerald, formed the next government on June 26 after Haughey lost the first vote, 83–79 with three of the independents, Jim Kemmy, Noel Browne, and Joe Sherlock, all of the Left, voted against. Kemmy voted for FitzGerald and the other two abstained so that the final vote was 81–78 and the Fine Gael–Labour coalition took over with Dr. John O'Connell as speaker.

Historically Fine Gael had been slightly less nationalist in display and Fitz-Gerald was far more conventional than Haughey, almost academic, a practicing writer and economist with a love of statistics; genial, kindly, at times vague, he made few enemies and was known to the media as Garret the Good. Whatever permanent views Dublin might have on Northern Ireland, the new government, with a tiny, vulnerable majority, could only be less contentious. FitzGerald and most of the establishment in Dublin wanted nothing more than an end to the H-Block crisis that had disrupted the pattern of events—somewhat to Fine Gael advantage in that the two seats that went to the H-Block people in June might have kept Haughey in power. Mostly the news from the North was bad.

The IRA, making good use of the turmoil, had escalated their campaign. On June 10 the Belfast Brigade had an unexpected triumph when seven of the M-60 IRA prisoners, and one other IRA man in Crumlin Road Prison shot their way past the guards' cars, dashed to waiting getaway cars under fire, and were whisked away free and clear. Those who escaped were Gerry Sloan and his brother Larry, Michael McKee, Paul "Dingus" Magee, Peter Ryan, Robert Campbell, Angelo Fusco, and Joe Doherty. There was a week of celebrating in Belfast and Dingus Magee walked openly in the Bodenstown parade, spoke to the republicans, and escaped the charge of the police. It was a fleeting triumph, however, for six of the volunteers were arrested in the Republic and put on trial for the escape (a law that evaded the historical onus of extradition) and another, Joe Doherty, was picked up by the U.S. Justice Department and became a cause célèbre as he fought successfully year after year against extradition sought by the British and the Reagan and Bush administrations, allies in the struggle against terrorism. Not until 1992 did the United States Attorney General get him extradited back to Northern Ireland.

In the meantime, however, the IRA units kept up the pressure, each H-Block crisis releasing a violent protest that could be used as cover for the snipers and bombers. In the summer of 1981, the overriding issue in Ireland remained the H-Block dilemma and only incidentally the armed struggle. The strikers seemed determined; in public and in private they could not imagine that the British would not in the end, as always, prove flexible, duplicitous. Prison, despite the steady flow of visitors and communications, is a very closed world, intense, narrow, a close drama with vital roles for all. The agenda of the strikers was not that of those in Belfast and London, their priorities and assumptions were too parochial. They could not direct events and by midsummer could hardly influence them. Yet, the island was seething. Black flags had appeared, twisted around lamp posts and hanging from windows. No matter how isolated the country road a bit of black cloth could be found tied to a telephone pole or fluttering by a barnyard gate. From the day Sands died some wore a touch of black as mourning. The proper and the conventional resented the black, the mourning, the power of the gunmen showing up across the country. While Sands's death awakened old loyalties, it also revealed hidden divisions. Despite Protestant fears and British suspicions, many of the Irish-Irish had nothing but contempt for the Provos— animals, killers, wicked, violent men draped in colors they shamed. One school-teacher with a black armband could divide the faculty and students where before none had suspected the existence of the national issue. The island was riven, again, still.

There could be no easing back to the regular until the pressure eased off in the Kesh. There certainly could be no normal politics as long as the strike continued. Hume had been to London on May 13 to urge moderation on Thatcher but without effect. O Fiaich had warned the British on May 21, when McCreesh and O'Hara had died, that London would face the wrath of the whole national population if its rigid stand went unchanged. As Thatcher wrote, the British posture was simple: "The Government will not negotiate terms for ending the hunger strike either with the prisoners, or their representatives."* The riots had gone on nonstop, the IRA had escalated the armed struggle, the international media had transmitted the hot news: The H-Blocks had become the issue of the moment. But as the weeks passed the British held on. The strikers did not understand: "What sort of people are we dealing with? It appears they are not interested in simply undermining us, but completely annihilating us. They are insane—at least Maggie is anyway."†

As the weeks passed the next wave of hunger strikers moved into the danger zone. They were minus Brendan McLaughlin, taken off the strike on May 26 because of a perforated ulcer, but by July others were at risk. On July 4 the prisoners issued a statement that they would welcome the introduction of the five demands for all prisoners and made no mention of political status. It was a sign that nearly any deal would do. The leadership in prison, however, felt they needed something in return for the dead and the hopes of the nationalists. And despite the hectic and almost continuous backstage negotiations that the H-Block people felt showed a secret British flexibility, nothing happened.

On July 8 Joe McDonnell died on the sixty-first day of his fast. On July 10, on the day of his funeral, his young son, weeping, clung to the coffin, trying to hold it back as it was lifted to be carried out of the house. There had been fewer in the streets at the news, fewer protested across the island, fewer marched behind the coffin to the grave. In Dublin only four hundred had turned out, and fewer in Sligo, three hundred instead of the eight thousand for Sands. McDonnell had almost won a seat in the June elections and now he had been forgotten. There was seemingly no more awe and horror and indignation. Yet Belfast had turned out again, and the security forces used the occasion and tried to snatch the honor

*David Beresford, *Ten Men Dead: The Story of the 1981 Irish Hunger Strike* (London: Grafton, 1987), p. 263.
†Ibid., p. 72.

guard after the final volley. The helicopters stayed over the cortege, replaced as the need to refuel occurred, the Land Rovers were near. When the cortege stopped again at the Busy Bee center for the volley, the police and army moved in, directed by the choppers. The guard fired the volley but was tracked running away. In the melee Patrick Adams, Gerry Adams's brother, a member of the honor guard, was shot and captured. At the grave John Joe McGirl of Leitrim, wanted in the province, gave the oration; the ritual was inviolate.

On July 13 Martin Hurson died—the sixth. Those on strike and in line to go on strike refused to quit without some gain. The republican leadership had pushed an end after Sands had won the election, had pushed an end after the first four had died, had sought any means out. The families wanted an end to the strike—most had never wanted a beginning.

Father Denis Faul, a regular visitor in the H-Blocks who was famous for publishing scathing attacks on abuses within the criminal justice system, had returned from a vacation taken after the first four deaths to find the strike still on, more dead to come. He met with the families on July 28 and then with Gerry Adams, who felt that only the prisoners could end the strike. Adams was sure that an order sent into the H-Blocks would at best split the movement and more likely would simply be ignored. Faul, however, wanted an end to the strike he had once supported and worked on the relatives, to the anger of the strikers and the republicans. He became the enemy for the republicans, for he blamed them for the strike, for the deaths, for the failure to achieve tangible gain. And he took his case to the families, working on their anxiety. The call by relatives two days later for Adams to end the strike, coupled with Garret FitzGerald's statement on July 31 that the IRA could end the strike, increased the pressure.

The unionists and many of those in authority tended to agree that the IRA was to blame and could end matters. Father Faul, with the backing of nearly all of the clergy, felt he had found a way to end the strike through the families. He began to ride point, a position that suited his temperament, on the drive to end the protest. He had wide support from the clergy, the conventional, and the authorities. And so all those who despised the Provos massed against them: It was their fault, just as the Northern Ireland Office had said. But the prisoners who had discussed breaking could not bring themselves to do so.

Everyone urged flexibility. From America the Four Horsemen—Kennedy, O'Neill, Moynihan, and Carey—urged Thatcher to give. She would not. On July 1 Cardinal O Fiaich had met the Prime Minister and Humphrey Atkins at 10 Downing Street for a lecture, but there was no dialogue, and the meeting ended after the cardinal's own lecture with cold, polite exchanges. There would be no face-saving concessions. All during the public stalemate there were intense negotiations, some in Belfast through a backdoor channel to the Foreign Office in London that seemed potentially productive and others initiated in Dublin or through private individuals. Efforts out of Dublin were crippled because the Irish government was urging a moderation on London that had not been shown to republican strikers in Ireland. So nothing resulted. Thatcher was not one to give and all the secret talks simply could not disguise her "Never." She would not listen, no matter the credentials of the explainer. Atkins at the Northern Ireland Office had no real leverage, no influence over the Prime Minister. Much of the secret negotiations had to be carried out in the shadow of her intransigence. No one now would or could give an inch least of all the hunger strikers.

Their families could, however, intervene, gain something tangible, a life. On July 31 the relatives of Patrick Quinn, who was dying and unconscious, asked the doctors to resuscitate him. He woke in his mother's arms. "Now Paddy, aren't you glad to be alive today?" she asked. And he answered, "I don't know whether I am or not."* She had no doubts. "He was screaming and struggling. The lack of oxygen to his brain was causing terrible epileptic fits. I couldn't bear his suffering."† She had talked with Faul. After that some of the involved knew that Father Faul and the families had found a way to end the strike: Wait until the man could not protest and have the doctors snatch him from the grave. Some families had promised not to break the strike. Others had not. The INLA people threatened to pull out. The others were holding firm. It was too late for Kevin Lynch, absentee member of the Irish Dáil, who died on August 1 on his seventy-first day. His mother had promised not to intervene. Kieran Doherty died the next day, his seventy-third day. There were now doubts, even from a few of the hard-line advocates.

Eight were dead and there had been only hints from the secret Foreign Office man and anguish from supporters. Outside the H-Blocks there had been costs as well: 51 dead, including 10 policemen and 13 soldiers, with over 1,000 injured and 1,700 arrested. There had been trouble in the Republic: A riot at the end of a march on the British Embassy on July 18 resulted in injuries to 120 Gárdaí and 80 demonstrators and £1 million in damages; then a bomb exploded in a power plant in Monaghan, and there were attacks on Gárdaí stations. It was a strange summer, with the flags on government buildings flown at half-mast for the dead Dáil member, hunger striker Kevin Lynch, while inside the responsible sought means to act against the subversives without arousing popular indignation.

A pause was expected after the two deaths for the next men to come on line but on August 8 Tom McElwee unexpectedly died on his sixty-second day, before the family was ready to act. Momentum had ebbed. Others were replacing the dead but many now expressed doubts. The parish priest, Father Michael Flanagan, at McElwee's funeral in Bellaghy on August 10, demanded an end to the hunger strike. Bernadette McAliskey walked out in protest. The next in line, Micky Devine, had made it clear that he felt the strike should end but somehow the logic did not extend to him. He told McAliskey to walk out of his funeral carrying the coffin if the priest spoke against the strike. He would hold on.

In the meantime the British government announced the Fermanagh–South-Tyrone by-election to replace Sands would be held on August 20. The British had voted new rules through Parliament so that there could be no hunger striker as candidate. Still, in many ways it was a replay of the first election, but this time with the advantages on the H-Block side. The SDLP felt the seat should be theirs but stood aside for the same reasons the second time as they had the first. Sands's election agent, Owen Carron, stood as the anti–H-Block candidate, not without the usual tensions with the protest allies, in particular the INLA. This time,

*Beresford, p. 359.
†Clarke, p. 188.

however, the Republican Clubs–Workers Party had an entry. On April 24, 1982, the Officials would at last drop Sinn Féin and become simply the Workers Party but they had long been a vitriolic opponent of the Provos. All their arguments were crafted in neo-Marxist language but in part their position arose from old feuds and old clashes. The Workers felt they had moved on, moved on so far that positions once identical to those of the Provos had been forgotten in the new ideological purity. So harm could be done to the Provos and the voters could be given a choice. The Alliance too wanted to give the voters a nonpolarized option. There were a couple of minor independents, a Peace Party and a General Amnesty ticket, but the real opposition came from the OUP's Ken Maginnis, a Dungannon councillor, major in the UDR, former B Special, a loyalist true blue. Any smart money would have bet that Carron, an ordinary member of Provisional Sinn Féin with four competitors to draw off votes, would not match Sands—Maginnis had a chance.

The result on August 20 was that Carron got more votes, 31,278 to Maginnis's 29,278, and thus a majority of 2,230 contrasted to Sands's 1,446. Alliance received 1,930 and the Workers 1,132. The two independents were way back, with General Amnesty at 249 and Peace at 90. It was a surprise, and seemingly put new life into the strike just as the logic of breaking it had become compelling with McElwee's death on August 8. On the same day Micky Devine died, firm until the end. In a sense it canceled hope. The families would act. Few wanted to sign up for a pointless sacrifice. Time was running out even before the tenth man died. And Carron's election did no good. Thatcher would not see him nor FitzGerald. The end was in sight by then.

When Micky Devine, the tenth man, died on August 20, 1981, there were not as many mourners to stream out of the mean ghetto estates as there had been for Sands or the others. There were fewer television minicams at Micky's funeral, fewer minutes on the nightly news in Bonn and Paris, fewer inches in the New York newspapers. The agony of Irish prisoners starving to death, once almost eerie, an alien Celtic ritual, had almost grown commonplace.

The British realized that somehow their strategy had aborted, their righteousness paid no dividends, but still did not know how this had been done. In any case, it did not matter in Birmingham or Manchester. The Irish could do as they chose, die as they wanted. The government waited out the skeletal bodies, the ritual IRA funerals, the regular flurry of bad publicity: By August they had paid full entry to the patriot game and by then additional dead Irish rebels, common criminals in law and practice, did not add a penny to the scales of calculation. As far as Thatcher was concerned, they could all die. This was a sentiment supported by the loyalists in Northern Ireland who, despite some UVF-UDA ambivalence about political status, abhorred the republicans' pretensions, had watched the confrontation from the sidelines, ignored, misunderstood, unhappy as always. Anyway, it was all going to be over soon. The families would intervene if not the IRA or the Church or common sense.

So Micky was last, lucid, mostly conscious to the end. Water that his system could not absorb dribbled out of his mouth. His head slid off the pillows. His nose was too thin to hold his glasses. He drifted asleep. When awake he was unable to lift his head. He forgave his estranged wife—for what, she could never imagine—

and announced he would hold firm to the end. He went blind, and soon after a mumbled Hail Mary during his final communion he lost the strength to speak. At two o'clock in the morning on Thursday he vomited and sank into a coma. Just before eight that morning the cardiograph beside his bed suddenly showed no peaks or valleys, there was a beep, and that was all. Micky Devine was dead—the last, a volunteer of the INLA, O/C of prisoners before the strike, his most responsible posting in the smallest, most radical, most ruthless of the republican constellation of secret armies, now a martyr for Ireland, a victim, a momentary hero, a Derry boy dead.

Micky Devine had been born in 1954, the same year as Sands, a world away from the H-Blocks and the new Troubles, back in the worst of times. Times were always bad for the poor Catholics in Derry, that small city run by small-minded Unionist bigots. The loyalists had held the few jobs close, allotted the few council houses, gerrymandered the election districts, and in the marching season organized parades to commemorate anniversaries remembered no place else. In 1968 they had in their intransigence, in their belief that history had frozen, brought their old world down. Before that, for the likes of the Devines, there was little hope but emigration. To stay meant years on the dole, years that would be narrow, mean, dirty, and humiliating. They had only the scraps of life, no savories or graces. Families were ruined with access to the meager comfort of the Church, scratch games, and small, cheap pleasures. Some could be happy at times, at home, love the city and their own. Few could be fulfilled. There was the drink for some and despair for most: penury, shoddy housing, rain, the cold, the damp, a bleak, used world of greasy cloth caps, nasal voices, bad teeth, stunted children, dank walls, dirty puddles, rough pubs, and a way out only for the few bright ones and the solicitor's son. The civil rights marchers seeking votes or justice or jobs could hardly put this litany on their banners but the reality of Derry city was such that many wanted a revolution, not reform, and vengeance, not simple justice.

There Micky grew up, a round-faced lad with thick glasses, freckles, and splayed feet, a lad who avoided games but spoke with a sharp tongue. He was nothing special, had no charisma, was no hero to his own; he was one of the many. And for a bit he had it better than many. He went from school to a good job as a bright, well-dressed Catholic lad moving up in the world of shop assistants to the center of the city at the Diamond in Austin's furniture store. He married Margaret Walmsley in a necessary rush and they had two children. He developed an interest in politics, became "Red Micky." And then there was the drink and the Troubles. The marriage did not stand up to the pressures and the job did not last—after three years he gave it up for politics.

Micky had been stunned and radicalized by Bloody Sunday. "I will never forget standing in the Creggan chapel staring at the brown wooden boxes. That sight more than anything convinced me that there will never be peace in Ireland while Britain remains." And there was no more peace for Devine; he joined the Official IRA and then in May 1974, twenty years old, he moved over to Costello's side in the feud and in time into the INLA. Other than a few shots fired from ambush for the Stickies, a rite of passage for most Derry youths, he was not a gunman. He could not see well enough to shoot. He did not raid banks to raise money for the cause or make speeches or edit the newspaper. He appeared hooded a couple of times for the television people and was recognized by his own because of his feet—no secrets in Derry. Mostly he did as he was told. Much of the time he scrambled for a living. His marriage was gone; the divorce proceedings were forwarded to him in the Kesh. Margaret was gone, along with the two children, Michael and Louise. She had stopped visiting long before. Outside, he had a drinking problem. He was not a success, was not promising anymore. He was simply one more Derryman, self-educated, radical, and adamant, an almost tubby boy with a round face, black-rimmed eyeglasses, red hair, and a gift for the hard word.

In September 1976 he was arrested after a raid on an arms dealer in Donegal across the border had led the local security forces to the haul. It was a botched job. Prison was another rite of passage for many in Derry, a service not a disgrace. After nine months in Crumlin Road Prison in Belfast he was transferred to the Kesh, where he went on the blanket and then the dirty protest. In time for the strike he was O/C of the few INLA prisoners until in June 1981 he went on the strike: "A death with dignity is infinitely preferable to indefinite torture."*

By the time Micky Devine died in August 1981, a great deal was known about the process of voluntary starvation. The scattered medical histories had been collated, the exposure to previous instances analyzed, and the H-Block case histories elaborated. It was possible to trace with some accuracy the schedule of dying despite the great individual differences. The body decayed at a set rate, one stage after another, each signaled by a physical change, some unpleasant, some a relief, but all certain. It was a death more predictable than the weather, death one day at a time, sure, sign—posted. The wastage was scheduled right to the final coma and the last ping of the cardiograph. And after the flat line ran came the ceremonial disposal, the transformation of the man into martyr.

There was a great crowd in Derry—not as large as for Sands, nothing would be—but a grand crowd still. There was the guard of honor from the INLA, the Irish tricolor and the movement's Starry Plough flag, the thud of muffled drums and the sad skirl of pipes. He was buried above Derry town with the other republican dead, tenth and last H-Block martyr home at last, himself, alone. As the years pass and the others are forgotten, how many will remember Micky Devine and his orangey hair, scooping beans out of a tin, serving customers in a furniture store, dying by degrees? Who will still care about the lad who sent an open letter to Cardinal Hume on the nature of British violence, one-time sniper at the British army post beside a Maxol garage at the end of the Brandywell, failed husband, lost father, dead volunteer?

He was simply an everyday rebel. He was not a poet or a planner, no hard man, no gunman; he never planned on dying by choice. He volunteered, did the necessary, chose the hard road, and died for himself, his friends, for the INLA, for Derry and Ireland. Who will remember? His wife, who left him in prison for another man, Séamus MacBride, an ice cream seller, and has other children, lives on counseling. Sometimes it seems most of the Derry women live on counseling and chemicals, waiting even after twenty years for better days. His wife remem-

*Tom Collins, *The Irish Hunger Strike* (Dublin: White Island, 1986), p. 569.

bers, cannot understand what she did that he forgave her for on the last visit with the children. She called each new baby Devine though. And remembers. Fewer Derry people do remember each year. There have been so many to remember, after a time so many patriot dead clutter the mind. The families knew there would be no concessions. Why add more numbers, another, and another, someone's son, someone's husband? What was there to prove? That the British were shameless and the Irish brave? The British and their friends had thus placed enormous pressure on the relatives and lovers to save the doomed, end the strike, close down the province and the Kesh as morality stages. The British might have steeled themselves to pay the media price but they did not like it, felt ill-used, and wanted an out as long as there was no visible compromise. So the family became responsible, not the militant hunger striker or the British authorities. So at the end, when consciousness slipped away a day or so before death, the family, the waiting mother, the sister, would authorize an end. Patrick McGeown's family took him off the same day Micky Devine died. On September 4 Matthew Devlin's family requested medical intervention to save his life. Having salvaged one, none was safe and so none should die. Others came on to replace the dead, but as gesture. The strike was formally ended at 3:15 on the afternoon of Saturday, October 3, after 217 days.

For Devine and the other nine the pipes have been played and the volleys fired over their own patriot graves. Their names are chiseled in marble and sometimes mentioned in ballads sung by those filled with pints and pub sentiment. Still, a ballad is something, and a name chiseled in stone is better than being tumbled into a shallow grave. And Sands was more than that. His name on a Paris wall and his poems read aloud in a Mexican university—these are no small matter. And for Micky Devine, there was a republican funeral, the single great ritual of Celtic glory on an island short of present glory: the sad pipes and the pacing of the honor guard, the banked flowers and an oration, and then the sharp crack of shots over the grave, a special pageantry, rough-edged and real under the circling British helicopters, before the cameras of the Special Branch detectives. This is the final reward available from a secret army without grace or great gifts, without medals, without chevrons, pensions, or prospects. There under a low Irish sky for a moment the incandescent Irish Republic becomes alive, all the crowd, red necked and rumpled, friends and enemies, are touched. And then everyone goes home again certain only that one way or another the Irish Republic will touch them all again. So Devine was dead and buried as patriot, special for a while, the last of the ten, perhaps soon forgotten, perhaps not, a simple life turned revolutionary asset in an H-Block battle that in the end went to the weak.

One of the peculiar aspects of all armed struggles is that a triumph means the weak have persisted over the strong, the will won over tangible assets. All such contests are asymmetrical and most result in the reasonable, the predictable and the conventional, in the expected victory of the orthodox, usually quickly but in most cases eventually. The big battalions win at war. The victory of the rebel, so much rarer, is so much the sweeter and always of great analytical interest. How were the conventional observers wrong? What crucial assets did the rebels have that were not immediately visible? What weakness existed in the arsenal of the orthodox? What has always been curious about Irish republicans is that defeated, as expected, they have unexpectedly continued, neither losing for good nor winning for all.

The Irish republican movement has managed to persist despite visible defeats: the most protracted armed struggle of modern times, two centuries of disaster, betrayal, and frustration. Instead of being merely protracted, the struggle became institutionalized. The republican assets savored and cherished were perceptions, not guns or money or foreign friends. These were seldom available, while the dream was always there for the taking. The movement transformed the everyday volunteers attracted by the purity of the vision into the faithful who would, decade after decade, despite, perhaps even because of temporal failure, sacrifice. Sacrifice was sufficient, not salvation. The purpose was to keep the faith, to bear witness, to maintain the conduit through which flowed legitimacy and meaning, to struggle. The purity of the ideal compensated for the failure in the field, a purity passed on unsoiled by failure, by the corruption of politics, by compromise, a faith in both the patriot dead and the integrity of the cause.

Thus, when Sands and the others confronted the British, who had only to remain steadfast to assure a conventional victory, they could win in their own, republican terms and in the terms understood by many in Ireland simply through their grace in persisting. This was a clearly defined responsibility. The act of being denied would be victory, not a concession of the five points in some arcane formula, not even political status as a right. What the strikers sought was certain if they remained steadfast. And so, like the opponents, they did. And so each won what had been sought and each was rewarded in kind—the British with the trappings of a conventional triumph in what had been a spiritual war and the Irish with a triumph of the spirit willing to suffer all. This Irish republican victory was perceived as such not simply by the wretched and angry of the Third World or the Catholic Irish attracted by the atavistic traditions of old but by many who perceived the confrontation as one of will against power. The British may have taken the marbles but that was another game. The Irish game was different and none could count the returns although all could count the cost.

If the will lasted to the final breath, this spiritual victory could not be denied: The game was in the playing, not the winning. The ten died and so suffering won. They had their lives taken for their friends and for the ideal, the dream. This the pragmatic, confident, and conventional missed, especially the British, as they had always missed the values of the island so different from their own. The authorities had maintained the rules that they had imposed, denied extortion, and thus "won"—but even to the most intransigent Tory just what had been lost in the winning was clear and yet inexplicable. Somehow the Irish had created out of murder and extortion, out of suicide, out of violating sense and rules, a victory with distressing implications. The Irish had not played the British game and so had not lost. No one in power ever quite understood how this was done. Why was justice, as traditionally defined, not better served? Why did murder and extortion undergo a Celtic sea change and become acceptable, admirable? And if the victory was hollow, what had really been lost? So London claimed victory.

On an everyday tactical plane the hunger strike ended the prison confrontation between the two immovable opponents, both convinced of their righteousness and the other's intransigence. The republicans called off the dirty protest on the day the strike began to allow all to concentrate on the real battle. When concessions were granted, no dirty protest would be needed—and the prisoners were certain that concessions would be made. The Northern Ireland Office's pursuit of absolute victory proved ill-advised—not so much advised as a policy continued. After the hunger strike ended, there was no intention of repeating the error. This time sufficient, if secret, compromises would be made on the five points to prevent some other unknown horror. The strike then technically and tactically for both meant an end to the dirty protest that concessions, sooner or later, on the five points would assure. The prisons would no longer be the site of a continued confrontation. The war in the Kesh would be run down as fast as face permitted.

Tactically the British had not conceded political status but had admitted the special status of the prisoners and drawn back from the commitment to break the republicans. Tactically the prisoners had found a way out of their dilemma, institutional misery that would in time, without hope of reform, erode all but the dedicated. Political status could be claimed even when such claims continued to be denied by the authorities. Most of the rewards of political status were received because the rules had been changed: a British specialty. And the British could deny that they had done so: another British specialty. What had been arranged was a variation of the unspoken arrangement that allowed two different societies to exist in the province at the same time, clashing only ritually, ugly and violent only under pressure at the edges. Each side simply ignored the unacceptable assumptions and perceptions of the other. In the Maze or the Kesh, whether criminals or patriots did not matter as long as no one made the other acquiesce in the opposing reality.

In the prisons, the end of the hunger strike meant an end to confrontation. Both sides claimed their perception was real, neither forced the issue. The prisoners were unbroken and unrepentant. The authorities had conceded nothing. And this result was almost certain once Sands had decided on the first day, March 1, that this strike would last all the way. He would persist. This meant that at the end there would be an accommodation no matter what the result, a reality hardly apparent to either player so focused on his own move, his own determination.

On a higher strategic level, the strike and the concomitant outpouring of sympathy and support had solved the Provisional Sinn Féin's dilemma in shaping a people's program, in widening the battleground. The movement would continue the armed struggle but in conjunction with the party's participation in politics, so exploiting the new support. This support encompassed both those who would give votes or time or money and those who for the present would tolerate the movement because the ten deaths had indicated the nature of the volunteers. Such young men and their cause could not be without merit even if misguided. In the Republic many did not change their politics or their opinions about the Provos, yet they found at the end of the day that their criticism ended with the word *but*. Their goals are impossible, out of date, their methods are abominable, immoral, and ineffectual, but their commitment to the death, their luminous vision denied the practical, their lives and sacrifice must mean something.

What this meant for the republicans was a pool of toleration that would inevitably be eroded by the inevitable brutality of a dirty war and by the passing of time. Still, the pool of those who would really help gave the republicans a foundation to widen the war without stealing from their military. The Provos won this way into the future hands down while the British received nothing but more potential trouble and no special route out of their Irish bog.

Off the island, the impact of the strikes, shown on color television, blurred by distance and local perception, reported as spectacular, was fitted into all the existing preconceptions. Sands and the others became martyrs in an anti-imperialist struggle that engaged the poor and the rich, the Third World and the developed world, the North and the South, the rebels and the rulers. All the proper trendies, all the radical regimes, all the far revolutionaries were as one with the Irish republicans, but so were those who did not need more grist in their propaganda mills. Obviously the Irish-Americans on one end of the spectrum and the Libyans on the other would support their own. Obviously contemporary history's weak and wretched (or at least their elite rulers) would identify with those weakest of all, naked prisoners in empty cells suffering for their cause. Sands and the others, however, touched a great many without politics, without ulterior purpose, with only the news of the starving time, the drama and the deaths, to consider. Thus, on a broader plane, beyond the checks and balances of prison tactics or the weight of Irish political advantage, the global battle went to the Irish.

It was not so much a victory over the British or imperialism or the rich and powerful as a victory for the dedicated, those who in an apparently reasonable cause were able to give each day part of themselves, a real and continuing example unto the end of dedication. In a sense the cause, Irish nationalism, did not really receive many converts nor did the opponent, British imperialism, engender great opposition; but the individuals and thus the Irish gained admiration. For the distant, the hunger strike was tragedy, the deaths almost inevitable, necessary, the details and conditions faded in the act and the suffering. Bobby Sands was transmuted through the electromagnetic spectrum into a presence felt in quite alien climates, his name given to streets, scribbled on walls, added to votes of commemoration, memorialized by those who could not find Ireland on a four-color map. It would not last, of course. The street signs would rust and fall off, the graffiti fade, the proclamations be put away in drawers. On May 5, they still march in Belfast. The ten are not forgotten yet, not by those who loved them, those who admired them, those who were touched by them or hated them. The names have faded, they are history to the young, but the movement has always been able to cherish the patriot dead long past reasonableness. What also lasted if not as long was the residue—the Irish rebel willingness to suffer in a good cause and die in good time. It was wasting capital whose spending was not easy to manage. Whatever the problem of cashing goodwill into rebel currency, there could be little doubt that the Irish republicans had in this matter as well won.

So in the end the British had been maneuvered into a seemingly defensible and legitimate position that guaranteed disaster. To concede would be to lose at the beginning. To hold firm was vital at any cost. And the costs came due. In the asymmetrical clash of perceptions, the events of 1981 meant very different things on the steps of the Carlton Club than they did in a Sinn Féin office on the Falls or even in a television producer's office at RAI or NBC. And so too differed the perception of the costs paid by the involved. Fortunately for the peace of mind of many in the London establishment, the disastrous costs could be denied because these were an eventuality outside the usual British rules. Who cared for the graffiti scrawled on slum walls or protest marches in distant capitals? What does transitory opinion matter in the face of facts? Criminals in prison may not extort concession. And they had not done so. They had not won. Even those within the British establishment who knew that the victory over the hunger strikers had real costs soon turned to other matters. Those who thought the hunger strikers had "won" did not understand reality. In holding to this demonstrable fallacy, Thatcher and company proceeded apace, having conceded nothing, learned nothing, and forgotten nothing; and so they lost not a whit of their composure or assurance, lost only the day. There would, however, be other days.

18

The Return of Politics, Sinn Féin, the Assembly, and the New Ireland Forum: September 1981–May 30, 1983

Vision is the art of seeing things invisible.
Jonathan Swift

Once the families began to intervene the end of the hunger strike was a matter of scheduling. There was no point to wait, one after the other, for kidney failure, coma, and family intervention. For a time during September the strikers held on, but for the others it was time to move on. Symbolically, Humphrey Atkins moved on when Thatcher appointed James Prior Secretary of State for Northern Ireland. Once more the post was used for British political purpose, this time as exile for one thought too ambitious, too "wet" in his enthusiasm for the new Thatcher direction, too close to the old pooh-bahs of the Tory Party of Heath. As Employment Secretary, Jim Prior had been at the center of power, apparently tolerated by Thatcher. He still had outside but real hopes of the very highest office, but he had been maneuvered into a corner when he hinted that if offered Ireland, he would refuse, so it was offered, and he at the end had to climb down, accept. The Thatcher government had no place for wets. Northern Ireland was as far away as Prior could be sent without exile to the back benches, which was clearly a matter of time. He thus appeared in Belfast, with flawed credentials, to mop up after the hunger strike and his own dashed hopes. With Northern Ireland and Prior out of the Prime Minister's mind, those responsible could only seek moderation instead of a continuation of confrontation by their own devices.

Prior was joined by the new Prisons Minister, the elegant, aristocratic Anglo-Irish Lord Gowrie, who had lectured at Harvard and who was not unmindful of Irish sensibilities or attitudes. He spoke with the relatives, alleviating their sense of powerlessness. Something would be done. Prior talked with Cardinal O Fiaich and Father Faul on specific matters, remission and prison clothing. Faul suggested a 100 percent restoration. After dithering, 50 percent was agreed and the crucial concession concerning "own clothes" made. Thus when the strike was called off on October 3 the strikers had something tangible that might as easily have been offered in July after the death of the first four. In July, however, the strikers and Thatcher controlled matters. In September it was Faul and Lord Gowrie, O Fiaich and Prior, those who drew no strength from adamancy or sacrifice. Instead all hoped that the trauma of the strike might concentrate minds on conciliation. The bitterness remained.

Most who had suffered through the 217 days felt that one of the great watersheds of provincial history had occurred, that the massed minority at Sands's funeral was as significant as Bloody Sunday, although to what purpose was not clear. Nothing could be the same and questions of remission were irrelevant to the enormous store of bad will and alienation generated during the strike. The republicans would seek to consolidate their gains, turn sympathy into influence. The loyalists would seek to prevent poststrike concessions. Why pander to murder? And while the ten men had died by their own decision, thirty members of the security forces had been killed by the IRA. The British would seek as always peace and quiet without great commitment—London was not bitter and alienated, Thatcher seemingly had won. Won or lost, London and Dublin and the few shell-shocked moderates in Northern Ireland wanted to recess from crisis.

There was always tension and crisis in the province. Thatcher had become the symbol of all that the nationalists detested across the water: arrogant and ignorant, mistaking power for righteousness and intransigence for courage. Thatcher moved to the very top of the Provos' enemies list; but far more important than vengeance, the Provos' agenda had shifted. The international impact of the strike, the by-elections, the enormous popular support, had given the movement a means to extend the as yet theoretical people's war. The Northern republicans, especially those in Belfast around Adams, had been exposed to both conventional and unconventional politics and discovered firsthand that all power does not come from a gun. The need for political initiatives, mindful of publicity, the role of the media, and the reaction of allies, were clear. The money that had poured in for the H-Block campaign was largely spent, the enthusiasm and dedication had seemingly been rewarded with ten deaths and a triumphant Thatcher. Within the movement the hard men of physical force still had little interest in politics but the old republican political advocates, O Conaill and O Brádaigh and the others in the Free State, somehow seemed passé—voices from another time, faithful, true, and irrelevant. Their Éire Nua was not the real new Ireland of the hunger strikers, the armed struggle, the radical ideas of a people's war.

Two years before there had been no Sinn Féin political organization. The movement had even boycotted Bernadette McAliskey's European Parliament campaign as an H-Block candidate in 1979, when she received nearly forty thousand votes. In 1979 politics was suspect even in coalition with friends. But the new men in Belfast felt in 1981 that the mass support shaped from May to August could transform the province and so the island's political balance. It was crucial to establish Sinn Féin not simply as a six-county party but rather as an all-Ireland movement, everywhere appealing to Irish interests. The times were promising if the Provisionals responded effectively.

From the first the nationalist moderates, the spokesmen for their church, the men who deplored the gun and suspected the radical, had feared that the polarization of the province, the alienation of the minority, and the legitimization of the republicans would be a disaster for law and order, for the conventional, for the British, and a disaster for them. And just as Hume and O Fiaich had predicted, the moderate nationalists had been squeezed. The SDLP had been offered no choice. To betray the strikers meant to lose the claim to be the legitimate minority representative. There was no way to win, no way even to control the losses. There was no choice, since to opt for the first assured the second in any case. The SDLP stood aside and would have to struggle not against an obsolete and ill-organized Nationalist Party but a resurgent and dedicated Provisional Sinn Féin rising on Catholic resentment. Whether the Provos could be politicized was not clear but there was every indication that Adams and Morrison and the rest were going to make the attempt.

In Britain there was only a small residue of concern about a distant problem: Something might be done to instill normality in the province. Few felt any enormous urgency. The only Conservatives who cared were a tiny minority in favor of integration into the United Kingdom. The Prime Minister was not interested, knew only enough about the province to stand firm—the SDLP was not a Unionist party and thus could expect no concession. Labour was little better. At the Labour annual conferences there had been no full-scale debate between 1969 and 1981 and no debate at all in 1973 and 1975. The Northern Ireland Committee—Callaghan, Roy Jenkins, Denis Healey, Richard Crossman, Lord Gardiner, and the like—showed concern but not much more, certainly not with Thatcher seemingly in place for the long term. Ireland, even Ireland of the H-Blocks, was just not a pressing priority. There were a few concerned people in the Northern Ireland Office who urged Prior to seek political accommodation. He began to look about for a formula that would ease matters. On September 29, when the British Labour conference voted to "campaign actively" for a united Ireland by consent, a shudder went through the Unionist community. In reality the British Labour Party had never shown enormous concern with the Irish issue and did not look likely to come to power soon. Certainly, more than before, there was a current in London flowing toward taking some sort of action, though not immediately, and not one that required any great expenditure of capital or concern. It was not a very strong current, often lost to view in the riptides of normal politics and pressing issues, but direct rule could not be forever. The common wisdom was that a recess might suggest a direction, if a direction were needed. The difference between Irish urgency and anguish and British quiescence was never more obvious.

At the Northern Ireland Office the first few weeks of the Prior administration had quickly exposed the tangled strands of provincial events. Prior, inserted into a difficult situation far from his old office or interests, began thinking about devolution of some sort, partial, timed and staged, something to get conventional politics moving. He early on decided that the concept of integration—treat the province no differently than Sussex or perhaps Wales and soon the province would be like Sussex or perhaps Wales—was a nonstarter. Those Tories who supported integration (a mix of those concerned with the pressures against London in Scotland and Wales, those who wanted the province above all else to be British, and Enoch Powell, who remained convinced of a CIA plot to integrate the six counties into the twenty-six for NATO purposes) were only a tiny group, articulate but atypical. Most Tories were not interested at all.

Certainly the province went right on with the accustomed deadly games. The IRA's armed struggle kept right on running up the year's toll: At the Mid-Ulster Hospital in Magherafelt, an RUC reservist was killed after visiting his wife, who had just had their second child; an RUC constable was shot and killed in a public house in Killough, County Down, and another was killed in a rocket attack on his Land Rover; and a UDR man was shot dead as he walked out of Mackie's factory in Belfast by the INLA. And the loyalist paramilitaries were back in the sectarian killing game. On October 8 Belfast independent councillor and H-Block supporter Lawrence Kennedy was shot and killed; on October 12 the UFF shot a Catholic man while he sat in his living room; and on October 19 the UDA blamed the RUC for shooting dead one of their men at a checkpoint. All told, sixty-four people had died during the seven months of the hunger strike, and the killings continuined without interruption. There were, along with the deaths, bits of good news. On October 6 Prior had announced the new prison rules on clothes, remission, visits, and association in the H-Blocks. There was the hope that conciliation would allow reconciliation.

There was instead evidence that the republicans planned to build on their ten martyrs. The continual rioting after Sands's death, which had merely tapered off in the early autumn, had produced still another nationalist grievance: the plastic bullet. In 1973 the plastic bullet had replaced the rubber as a means of riot control. Supposedly painful but harmless, an improvement over rubber, the four-inch by one-half-inch plastic projectile, shot from a distance at 160 miles per hour, was meant to bound about in a riotous assembly. Shot directly at a target from close up, it could be and was deadly. Up to 1982 plastic bullets had killed thirteen people in the province and proven more deadly by several factors than the old rubber projectiles. In 1981 some 29,601 rounds had been fired, according to the RUC, causing 203 injuries. There were ample horror stories of wanton discharges, close-quarter shootings, and the use of the plastic bullets during "technical riots" (i.e., any victim was technically rioting even if no riot could be found). The result was one more grievance, one more campaign to add to all the others. Thus, the Prior-Gowrie concessions on October 8 were diluted by the continuing crosscurrents whipped up as a by-product of heavy security and riotous display. It would not do any good for the police to note the massive decline in plastic bullet incidents in 1982, for the nationalists were convinced that the bullets were used only against the Irish, the nationalists in particular, and used often wantonly to maim. There was such evidence, it was felt, in 1981. Why worry about ups and downs? Maiming and murder by plastic was still maiming and murder.

On October 11, less than a week after the agreement on H-Block conditions was announced, the IRA moved to England again with a nail-bomb attack outside Chelsea Barracks in London that killed one woman and injured forty-six other civilians and soldiers, one teenager fatally. On October 17 Sir Stewart Pringle lost a leg after a bomb attack at his home, and on October 26 a police bomb disposal expert was killed by a bomb in Oxford Street. These attacks, planned earlier, indicated that the IRA response to the British adamancy on the hunger strikes was to extend the military campaign. IRA operations cannot be finely tuned, especially at a distance, so that the tendency of the media and the analysts to read the text of incidents is often inaccurate.

The London operations did not relate to October Irish events but to previous attitudes and options on the part of the Army Council. When Keenan had been lost as GHQ Operation Officer, new preparations in England had been put on line. When the H-Block campaign escalated, the British card was played. And there was never any reason to cancel. The thrust to broaden the battlefield by deploying Sinn Féin did not mean limiting the armed struggle. Operations in England at the very least joggled the British public and kept Ireland a live if unpleasant issue.

On November 1, at the Provisional Sinn Féin Ard Fheis, the new direction began to take more practical form, displaying assumptions arising from an interpretation of the events of the year of the H-Blocks. The rise of a new generation of Northern radical republicans who bore the brunt of the war and thus should have the major say had been building and was not really opposed by the old guard, North or South. There were real differences in attitude, priorities, and experience, but all were republicans, one on the faith. O Brádaigh and O Conaill had no interest in splits or retaining power. It was a matter of timing. In theory this was the case, one like generation growing into power without need of confrontation. In practice there were real differences. The Northerners now felt that the Éire Nua federal Ireland policy had served its purpose as a temporary explanation of republican aims that would conciliate the Protestants and impress the media. O Brádaigh and O Conaill tended, as time had passed, to believe it was a way forward, not an expedient or a compromise.

At the Ard Fheis the delegates voted to remove it from the party manifesto but failed to get a two-thirds majority. This was achieved the next year with the emphasis on an all-Ireland state. The old federal policy no longer sat well with the militant Northerners, some of whom saw it as an unnecessary concession to intransigent Unionist opinion. The Stickies had followed a pro-Protestant line up a blind ally, calling for workers' unity that never occurred. Wolfe Tone and his call to unite the whole people of Ireland was all very well but it was better to assert the independence of the country (and these were not mutually exclusive aspirations). The Éire Nua vote was an outward sign of the passing of a generation. This was not an easy affair. A great deal of commitment and concern had gone into Éire Nua, although the issue was a tactical one. Still, the loss hurt.

The process of change thus tended to generate sharper differences than had existed. The old , being replaced, were blamed for old failures. Their long service was at times seen not as a sacrifice but as a burden on a movement eager to effect events. The republican movement has never been long on gratitude. The traditional reward for past service has often been a broken heart. The new felt compelled to criticize the old—because the old had not always been right, because the Republic had not been achieved, because the new needed to be different and right and on the way to the Republic. In particular the 1975–76 truce and the ensuing erosion of IRA strength it was assumed to have induced gradually became a key complaint, even by those who had not opposed that truce.

This issue, however, was minor in 1981. Another factor discussed only in private was the rising prominence of Belfast. The Belfast people were parochial. Some volunteers had never seen a cow and others discovered the rest of the province only when running for office. This was hardly novel but the characteristics of the Belfast republicans often grated. Their accent was harsh, their assurance considerable, their city ways hardly touched by the old republican traditions of Kerry or West Limerick. Even the GHQ and the Army Council meetings had moved out of Dublin and north, along the border. The chief of staff came into Dublin once or twice a month to check with various officers and friends—a visitor.

Thus, as always, there was resentment between those who seemed as one, all neighbors on a small island, to those unaware that more than miles separate the Falls from Mid-Tyrone or South Armagh from West Kerry. When those not at the center of the circle felt ignored the very prime intent of Adams and the others to make a thirty-two county movement was threatened by the perceptions of those they would involve.

The specific differences in 1981 were not as significant as the proposed directions. The delegates voted to contest elections and to take local seats in Northern Ireland; this was not an end to abstentionism at all and not ideologically revolutionary, but it was an indicator. The older generation was obviously deeply suspicious of any move on abstentionism, which was regarded by some of the radicals as a tactic, not a principle. The purists, most republicans in 1981, felt that participation in illegitimate institutions gave acceptance to usurped authority. There was no difference between refusing to wear prison garb and sitting in the Dáil at Leinster House in Dublin, or at Westminster, or at Stormont in Belfast. Protest politics, the deployment of the mob or the picket, the use of petition and public disputation, was a proper republican weapon. Using elections as leverage, as had been done in Fermanagh–South Tyrone, was proper, a means deployed since 1918. Taking local seats was tolerable, allowing Sinn Féin people to act on the ground without involvement in illicit institutions. If there were ever to be a division within the Provos, it would surely come on the degree of conventional political participation the leadership felt legitimate. Too much participation and another generation would follow the Officials into Free State politics and disaster, just as had previous generations: Seán MacBride and Clann na Poblachta and even de Valera and Fianna Fáil. Too little participation and the armed struggle would be isolated from the people, as had happened with the 1956–62 campaign. Thus, there was a little tremor caused by the exhilarating speech by Danny Morrison that encapsulated the direction of the movement: "Who here really believes that we can win the war through the ballot box? But will anyone here object if with a ballot paper in this hand and an Armalite in this hand we take power in Ireland?"

On both cusps of the movement, those physical force men who trusted only the gun and those purists who suspected all politics, not always the same people, there were small and secret reservations. The physical force people were encouraged by the word that the IRA would escalate the bombing campaign in England and the purists that abstentionism was not in question (at least outside the secret seminars of the Belfast radicals). And beyond the tea seminars of the new generation, the campaign kept right on killing.

Increasingly during the autumn the loyalists felt that, as usual, they had been ignored. Paisley had threatened his Third Force, but no one believed his threats. No one paid much attention. Too many people paid attention when on September 27, in Dublin, Garret FitzGerald launched a crusade to alter the sectarian and parochial sections of the Irish Constitution of 1937, largely an Eamon de Valera draft that all knew had been approved by the Archbishop of Dublin, Dr. John Charles McQuaid, and contained sectarian articles. This FitzGerald maneuver was seen as a step toward unification and so was opposed immediately by James Molyneaux for the OUP, who was immediately criticized by William Craig, who felt the move very significant; and thus Craig for many loyalists maintained his standing in the line of discarded moderates. There was no way and never would be a way that Dublin could transform their way of life so as to make it palatable for Protestants. For unionists anything that moved toward unity was bad. As Paisley said on November 6, the meeting of the Anglo-Irish Inter-government Council, organized at the second Anglo-Irish summit, confirmed his worst fears. London was contemplating a sellout. Certainly London and Prior and the security forces were not taking the measures necessary to end IRA violence. As the Reverend John Batchelor said on November 12, after an RUC reservist had lost both legs in his booby-trapped car, "The time for talking has passed; we cannot allow one more death. I call upon the British government to use the manpower that is available and to legitimately mobilize a third force to smash the terrorism in our midst. The IRA must be put down like the animals that they are." No new moderation there but the old loyalist demand for harsh measures—just how harsher measures would work was not made clear, but at least Batchelor indicated faith in a Third Force and putting the IRA down like dogs. This is what many wanted, had always wanted. Whether it could be done was far less important.

This growing loyalist anxiety that had built up during the hunger strike and been unappeased by the autumn's events—Prior's moderation, Paisley ignored, FitzGerald's crusade, the Anglo-Irish council meeting—was by mid-November a visible tide away from the satisfaction that had been gained from "one more bastard dead." Then on November 14 five IRA volunteers walked into a community center in Finaghy to kill Robert Bradford, a former Methodist minister and an Official Unionist MP, who was meeting constituents. A strident loyalist, a friend of Paisley, a symbolic sectarian Unionist, he had been chosen as a target to punish the Unionists for their behavior during the hunger strike and for their murders during the autumn: IRA preparations had been made to defend against any loyalist backlash and ideological explanations readied for what was essentially a sectarian operation against a political opponent. The IRA felt that there was little point in making overtures to those who had made clear they were going to keep their privileges. Such people, UDA or Official Unionists, were thus agents of the Crown, legitimate targets, Irish or no, shot because of their alliance with London, not their religion. Bradford might be a bigot but to the disinterested he was an Irish bigot, a politician, neither a paramilitary gunman nor an off-duty serviceman. For most republicans, however, he remained a legitimate target, as had Taylor or Sir Norman Stronge or any of the others. Restraint concerning such targets was induced by fear of a backlash, not by the nature of the victim. In the case of Bradford, precautions had been taken. The defenses were up. So the volunteers shot and killed both him and caretakers who got in the way. The deed would sharpen loyalist minds. And the loyalist mobs did not appear. The mob was about all that did not appear; the province suddenly lurched toward a civil war just as the tension created by the hunger strike seemed about to fade into all the old familiar issues.

The peaks in sectarian murders credited to or claimed by the Protestant paramilitaries have tended to come during visible and public frustration within the community. The frustration tends to arise from an inability to act on events during a period that Protestant control is demonstrably scant and even Protestant opinion goes unheeded, often unasked, by London. Since the onset of the Troubles the militant Protestant community has fed on its own historic fears and suspicions, occasionally in a frenzy. The proper and conventional middle class was seldom if ever in a frenzy, although often in despair. Generally they had accepted the need for change, supported the initiatives from London, more assured than the militants that their way of life would not be seriously endangered; they deplored the violence of the militant fundamentalists as crude, cruel, inappropriate, and dangerous. Paisley or the UVF were the unacceptable face of unionism. Uncertain as to the extent of their Irish component, shocked to be Irish in England and British in Ireland, they nevertheless identified with the British establishment, largely with the Conservatives. The *Belfast Telegraph* supported the Northern Ireland Office. The elite in pulpits or from boardrooms supported authority. Some, like BBC Northern Ireland, might query the dictate of the Northern Ireland Office, but most indicators of opinion revealed a lack of militancy, a desire for effective authority, and an opposition to all thought of a united Ireland, as well as a nostalgia for the olden days, a persistence of bias in assumptions and attitudes about the minority, and a tendency to do nothing in times of stress. At worst the middle class explained the cause of déclassé violence in such a way as to encourage it, but more often they sought every means to moderate the provincial turmoil.

The moderation of the provincial establishment evoked only suspicion in the poorer parts of the Protestant community. The toleration for even the most unsavory acts, often performed by the child of a neighbor, a friend's lad from across the road, created a mist of acceptability. This environment encouraged a persistent militancy within the Protestant community, especially within Belfast, that allowed not only the mob to act when provoked but also individuals to act in the name of the mob or the loyalists. The grand motivations of Protestant reaction, made visible with bodies left on the province's fault lines, are often no more than individual predilections, a few driven by a few special motives easily enumerated but difficult to predict. How does one fit the Shankill Butchers into the formulas of reactive violence? When do the occasional killings become a wave, feeding off the cycle? When are the occasional killings simply an occasion taken beyond the events of the day, the politics of the month? Certainly, the republicans in November 1981 anticipated a strong and violent loyalist reaction and so prepared. Certainly as not general violence but individual murder became increasingly visible, all the provincial voices expressed fearful concern.

Especially in killing matters, opinion is not easy to gauge until the mob is at the door or the body left in the garden. Almost no one admits, if asked, to favoring violence. An enormous number understand the motives of the violence and thus rationalize it even while the killer may feel no need to explain. Many in the province regularly predict violence—a case of wishful thinking for those who are selling a remedy or a program but also a means to urge action on others, provide alibis for others. Whatever he believes in his heart of hearts, Ian Paisley standing before hundreds of men possessed of arms crying for the extermination of the IRA seemed to many nationalists to be expressing a desire for an action many loyalists would applaud but few would advocate publicly. Opinion, thus, is hard to weigh because the means of approach alter the subject, because the subject can be contradictory, transient, even unrelated to action: How many know what they will do when the knock of an unknown man on the run comes at the front door? In November in the province the fading of the H-Block issue, divisive, deadly, spectacular, simply seemed to permit the same old polished stones of anger to be thrown again. All was to have been changed and nothing changed.

November was a very bad month although no one could quite explain why not October or December or what were the special factors. Certainly the loyalists felt that somehow they had been bypassed by the hunger strikes, had lost out. Certainly many needed very little encouragement from their own to kill. In the end, however, prediction, especially about the future, is difficult: No one saw that the IRA would seek to punish the loyalists by murdering Bradford, not even most republicans; no one foresaw the splurge of November killings, perhaps not even the killers. And once the killings began no one had any idea how to turn off the murder other than by the now traditional appeals to reason, decency, and propriety, appeals that had failed to move the gunmen every time in the past.

On November 15, Hume had claimed that the IRA intended to provoke a civil war. The next day the Reverend William McCrea seemingly called for one: "We owe it to our children, even if we have to die, to fight the rebels with a Holy determination and never to sheathe the sword until victory is won." He, as yet without sword, was at Enniskillen with Paisley, who announced his despair at any acceptable change arising in Westminster and reviewed the first appearance of his Third Force: five hundred marching men. He called for a day of action on November 23. The ministers, as in the past, were not unmindful of the sedition and firearms laws, so for the moment the Third Force was limited to rhetoric, a rhetoric the responsible feared as much as the marching men.

Secretary of State James Prior, invited to the Bradford funeral at Dundonald by the family, where a seat was reserved, felt he must attend. He went with a heavy RUC guard. He was booed by the unruly crowd on arrival. He had to make a dash for the door. Inside on the porch, Paisley met him and announced, "You've no right to be here." Inside the filled church he was hissed. It was pointed out that the flag on the coffin was the flag of Ulster, not the Union Jack. Britain had failed the province again, failed as always. The minister called for a return to capital punishment. On coming out of the church Prior was pushed and kicked by a tumultuous crowd. Unionists were shouting, "Kill him! Kill him!" and tossing pointed umbrellas like javelins. It was the fault of the British that security had been lax, that Bradford had been killed. It was Prior's fault. And for him it was a macabre day that ended with isolation on the top of Stormont hill. He said later, "It was not an experience I would ever wish to live through again."*

There were provincewide memorial services, tributes read, moments of silence, threats read as sermons for those "who are prepared to fight and if need be to die to save Ulster from the IRA terrorists and the treachery of the Thatcher administration." A Catholic man was murdered in Craigavon as evidence of intent. The British army announced that six hundred more men would be arriving. Despite the fact that this particular Protestant tape had been run through the provincial echo-machine so often it tended to whine, the authorities felt the threat was real, this time, again, always. There was the same repeated demand for strong action against the IRA demon. The faithful loyalists longed for internment, mass arrests, shoot-to-kill orders, state terror, sealing off the border, the works.

That the "works" would merely escalate the crisis—assuming London wanted to fund the cost of state terror regardless of any moral qualms—was ignored. The loyalists, no less than Prime Minister Thatcher, did not want to hear what they did not want to hear. Any restraint, even in the name of practicality and efficiency, was bad. To move the border posts back a hundred yards was surrender. To remain within the rule of law was foolish when law was under threat. One of the things they did not want to hear was the stern warning by the RUC chief constable, John Hermon, that no armed Third Force would be tolerated. The militants had always had trouble with "their" police force and "their" army insisting on primacy and often on enforcing the law as written. Still, antirepublican militancy was for many loyalists natural, desirable, a matter of belief.

Most of the militant majority wanted "all political restraints and handcuffs taken off the security forces and a real war carried out against the IRA" so that the forces could "flush out the Republican enclaves." They wanted not just vindication and vengeance but history adjusted, but as the the years passed they came to doubt this could happen. The result was an escalation in rhetoric that each time eroded loyalist viability in such matters: threats and whines and Paisley marching up and down hills. The nature of such rhetoric persuaded the decent and moderate not to become involved. One exposure to the wrath of the righteous was usually sufficient. So many good and moderate people did nothing rather than embark on what would be seen as a treasonous crusade, a crusade against the majority's way of life. On November 18 Paisley claimed that Thatcher would be taught a lesson, that the full orchestra had not played. On the same day the UDA withheld their support from any day of action and the IRA killed a former UDR member. There were those more militant than Paisley.

On the next day another UDR member was killed in Strabane in what seemed one more in a series of IRA provocations. The Workers Party claimed that the IRA was producing a river of blood in a campaign to drive the Protestants out of Northern Ireland. The Workers, now dedicated to parliamentary democracy, North and South, and internally to democratic centralism and the received tenets of Marxist-Leninist philosophy, had become the most severe critic of the Provisionals. The Workers sought not a revolutionary war but means that would

---

*James Prior, A *Balance of Power* (London: Hamish Hamilton, 1986), p. 149.

permit the effective play of class politics, presently corrupted by sectarian currents unleashed by the Provos. And the Provos obviously intended to use those sectarian forces to cloud the minds of the Workers. This analysis had a widening number of takers in the Republic, where the party was trying to seize the high ground on the Left, in competition with the bourgeois Labour Party for the workers' vote. Matters did not go as well in Northern Ireland, where tribal politics dominated first loyalties and the Workers' support for the transient but necessary institutions of the state, a required stage in the dialectic, was misunderstood or perhaps understood too well. On the island the Workers, despite having become, as some said, the only Western Stalinist party, were an admired example of discarding the gun in politics, accepting parliamentary reality, and going forward without littering the road behind with bodies. The hard Left ideals, the curious foreign ideological alignments, the elevation of the party as absolute exemplar, would have alienated a conservative society that had usually expelled the few radicals, except that the Workers were sound on the national issue as defined by all the constitutional parties and always sound about the evils of the Green Fascist Provos. Who knew better? And who better to point out just where the killing was leading in November 1981 than much of the leadership of the Workers, who had been there at the beginning? The Workers on the far Left had become respectable. Their private IRA by 1981 was a Northern bodyguard and a few men still involved in expropriation, a residue irrelevant to the new purposes, unknown to most of the new members. All from sound ideological bastions were as one on the attacks on the Provisionals, cause of Northern conflict that prevented the province from moving on as the dialectic indicated.

In this they were joined by the nationalist leaders in the North, including Cardinal O Fiaich, who said, "What we need now is an end to violent deeds before the whole population is engulfed in an orgy of death and destruction." He was supported by nearly all of opinion in the Republic. As time passed, the clergy's advocacy of peace increasingly alienated the republicans in the North, driving the church to more extensive condemnations. None of this was new except to the individuals involved. None could admit it was a struggle between faiths rather than over definitions and politics. And it was a rivalry simply ignored by Protestants, who preferred their Irish rebels to be devout and typical Irish Catholics in form and theory.

As the month of November dragged on, the major problem seemed to observers concerned about the province, to be the loyalists, not the provocative IRA killings, actually no more than the continuation of the armed struggle, but a sectarian war. Everyone had expected a loyalist backlash during the hunger strikes, but the usual level of riot and turmoil was so high that escalation was hardly noticed. Now, in November, when matters should have settled down, the fear of a Protestant backlash became the anguish of the moment. Yet there was no real rise in Protestant violence. The only escalation was the widening of the arena with an INLA bomb at a British army camp in Herford, West Germany. The INLA, ideologically attractive to the European Left, had made a few good personal contacts on the Continent, where operations were actually easier than in Northern Ireland. Anyway, the INLA was in Germany and the UVF and UDA were around the corner.

The loyalist threat, however, seemed to consist of the old potential, made evident by a few random killings, and Paisley. Despite Paisley's effort his old opponents showed no inclination to join his parade. The UDA was opposed and there was no support from the labor unions, no support from the industrialists, no support from his political competitors. The OUP held a separate rally at Belfast City Hall in competition with the DUP on the Day of Action. The Third Force was apparently only the DUP in old army fatigues. On November 21 guns were produced at a Third Force rally at New Buildings, County Derry, and two days later there was a mass demonstration of the Third Force in Newtownards, with the usual violent rhetoric: "The killing of the IRA is over as far as Ulster is concerned! We will exterminate the IRA!" This had been the promise of William Craig a decade before, when he was the point of the loyalist lance instead of the 1981 voice of moderation within the loyalist community. Exterminating the IRA was not so easily managed. On November 28 an RUC constable with only a few weeks' service was killed by an IRA bomb detonated at Unity Flats in Belfast. Then it was December and the days trickled by with no new horrors. There were little incidents—rocks thrown, shots fired—but as the holiday moved closer there were no IRA bomb deaths or tit-for-tat killing.

At this time the RUC in Belfast was deeply involved in turning a former small-time IRA volunteer, Christopher Black, arrested on November 21, into an asset, not just as an informer but as a potential witness against his former colleagues. He agreed to testify in return for immunity on November 24 and began to talk. Cell structure or no, Black knew a lot and, if protected, was willing to talk before a judge, heretofore not a good career move. Now the RUC guaranteed him safety. They sensed big cases, lots of IRA people on trial, a breakthrough. While he was engaged in producing a sixty-two-page statement, a convoy of police and soldiers drew up before his home in Ballyclare Street. His wife and four young children were hustled into a car. The contents of the house, everything but the blinds in the windows, were loaded into a furniture van. The house was locked. The convoy pulled away and drove to a temporary accommodation for the Blacks inside the married quarters of a heavily guarded army barracks outside Belfast. Black was for the authorities a "converted terrorist" but for everyone else in Ireland he was the first of the supergrasses: those who traded their associates for leniency and security. The importance of Black was not immediately apparent, for informers had testified before, and had put away the IRA M-60 group and the UDA in East Antrim; but this time the authorities would elaborate the technique by concentrating on the weak in secret armies grown too large. Haltingly, a new era of supergrasses had arrived—one more riptide in the Northern Ireland pool.

The IRA hardly noticed. With its new cell structure in Belfast and its improved country units, often controlled from across the border in the Republic, the army was down from an organization of thousands in 1972 to a core of full-time active service members, paid twenty pounds a week when there was money, constantly on the move, dropping in at home from time to time or ringing up. In fact, Black's early testimony allowed a sweep to lift several hard-core volunteers who hid out in various safe houses at night but by ten in the morning had breakfast with the family. Then, too, sons did not like to go too long without seeing their mothers or their children or a few of the old lads. It was difficult to impose absolute discipline on those who were on the run, especially for those with the same predilections. The men and a few women IRA soldiers were comfortable in their environment, bold, often foolhardy, fierce, and erratic.

The RUC knew many by name: The tall Bobby Storey was hardly unique in being on every list, his picture on each barracks wall. Beyond the mix of men on the run and men in place (not all of these known by any means) were those who waited to fill a slot, who marked time or carried messages, arranged for cars or flats or meals, kept the gear, moved fertilizer to be used in bombs, stayed out of sight. Even if the core four hundred were lifted, a long-lived dream of the authorities, there would have been only a short recess before the new generation of hard men took over. The Provos had too many guerrillas and gunmen for the terrain: British security was so effective that only a few could operate. Once the riots of H-Block were over, the IRA had to cut back, plan each strike more carefully; even the foolishly bold who telephoned home every night and drank in the same club knew that operational caution was a requirement for longevity in the gunman's trade. So by December caution canceled turmoil, if only for a time. The Protestants did not run amok. The IRA killed no one. Prior was able to talk politics, if to no great effect.

In Dublin, still on his crusade to make the Republic fit for Protestants, Garret FitzGerald on December 9 suggested that new links with Britain might reassure the Unionists. He had a letter from President Reagan, sent on December 4, offering support for increasing such Anglo-Irish contacts, surely a good sign. The use of American good office to support the decent Dublin position had long held attraction for a variety of figures in the Republic. And now the American president supposedly had a special relationship with Thatcher, a new conservative too.

The unionists were not reassured by all of this, but the reverse. When the Taoiseach said the Republic must sacrifice its wish for immediate unity, he was thought to dissemble or at best simply to postpone until tomorrow what he could not manage today. His wish to rewrite Articles 2 and 3 of the Constitution, so daring in Dublin, was irrelevant for loyalists in Northern Ireland. A bit of paper labeled Constitution would hardly change the nature of a state composed of Irish Catholics, a state that had from the beginning sought the six counties as right. Garret the Good and his proper Dublin friends might be willing to delay the inevitable, might be willing to tidy up the rough edges of their Republic, but the loyalists would never agree to forgo their way of life by absorption within an Irish Ireland. If the British betrayed the Unionists, then loyalty would be given to their own, even, as some had suggested, if they had to go it alone. FitzGerald and the others were engaged in a publicity exercise. And in this the loyalists had allies in the Provos, who saw constitutional reform in the Republic and acceptance of a loyalist veto first by Haughey and then by FitzGerald as a move not toward unity but away from the national goal.

Politics were put aside for Christmas, and while there was no IRA truce, there was no IRA killing either. Suddenly it was the last week and then New Year's Day and December had passed without a death due to the Troubles, the first such December in ten years. The 1981 statistics were not so cheerful; the IRA campaign during the hunger strikes had upped all the totals. The overall deaths were up from 76 to 101, with 10 army and 13 UDR in 1981 instead of 8 and 9, and 13 RUC and 8 RUCR instead of 3 and 6. All the other indicators were up too; the injured rose to 1,434 from 878 and armed robberies to 587 from 412.

The security forces were not, however, disheartened. The H-Block crisis was over; the prisons were again prisons, not battlefields, and not the cause of escalated violence elsewhere. The investment in the technology of control, the increasing professionalism of the police and the army (despite rotating service), and the response to IRA activity in the Republic by the Gárdaí, in England by the police and army security, and in Europe by the various national services would produce results in time. The RUC received very considerable aid and comfort. In 1981 an additional £34 million was budgeted to bring the annual police total to £350 million. There was an increase in the RUC of 500, with 300 more slots in the RUCR and 336 new civilian employees, bringing the total force up to 8,000. Most important, a new means to secure convictions and intelligence was evolving out of sight with the use of informers (the supergrasses) who could be persuaded to reveal the inside workings of the paramilitaries and testify against their former colleagues. In December it was too early to tell if the supergrass ploy would work, but the signs were hopeful. All told, 1981 had ended on a high note for the security forces. And on the first day of the new year the chief constable of the RUC, John Hermon, was awarded a knighthood.

By the end of January matters had returned to normal. A gunman walked into John McKeague's stationery shop and shot him dead. McKeague was a bitter and unpleasant man, a homosexual who surrounded himself with attractive young men in uniform, to the horror of most of his macho loyalist paramilitary associates. Most of these had deserted McKeague and many suspected he had been murdered because of his involvement in a long-lived scandal concerning the misuse of the young inmates in the Kincora boys home. The Kincora scandal involved all sorts of official figures, produced all sorts of conspiracy theories about Stormont bureaucrats, the RUC, and British intelligence figures, and dragged on until 1986 without happy resolution despite recommendations for reform. On October 28, 1983, Sir George Terry, former Sussex chief constable, would report that there was no evidence that civil servants, police, or intelligence figures had tried to suppress the case or had been involved in homosexual activities. The scandal hung on with a remarkable half-life and in 1982 the idea that McKeague was involved seemed reasonable to the fascinated; after all, he was a cunning and deadly paramilitary pervert and hence should have been involved.

McKeague had long been at the cutting edge of sectarian hatred. He had since the beginning of the Troubles been a focus of attack. His mother had been burned to death when his shop and flat in East Belfast had been set on fire in 1971 by "the enemies of Ulster." He was thought to be the founder of the Red Hand Commandos and in 1971 was one of the first persons to be accused under the Incitement to Hatred Act, although the first jury could not agree and the second acquitted him. Over the years he had not mellowed, nor had his habits become less discreet. He was murdered simply because he was a famous bigot and so a significant target for the INLA people. The INLA could not afford to be less deadly than the Provos and certainly McKeague had long been considered a world-class bigot. So they dispatched a gunman who killed him without unduly disturbing the loyalist community.

For the Northern Ireland Office, with a broader vision, such matters could now be left to the security forces. The office sought more extensive adjustments with the end of the H-Block protests and hunger strikes; the easing of the November crisis meant that Prior's tentative plans for some sort of devolution could be sharpened and take form. The idea was that devolution could be achieved piecemeal, the politicians fed crumbs to work up sufficient appetite so as to swallow the bad with the good, power sharing with power, perhaps even a tack-on fig leaf labeled the Irish dimension near the end. The Northern Ireland Office would encourage a move toward a provincial assembly by offering a growing collection of minor agreements and concessions. The Northern Ireland Office felt that the more extreme options were nonstarters; both integration into the United Kingdom or withdrawal were out and continuing direct rule was really an expedient, not a permanent arrangement. Something should be done that would get the province back on the road to devolution and its own assembly. Prior talked to all but could only afford to listen to what he wanted to hear. What he and London wanted was devolution.

The Prior plan would be fashioned so as to make participation along the way attractive. The politicians and parties might be involved incrementally. And so the suspicious might find themselves knee-deep in the devolution bog before noticing. It was not new (little in Ireland was); in fact, it had been the subject of an article by Dr. Brian Mawhinney in the *Guardian* in March 1981. This time it was for real. Prior chose, as had others in a similar position before him, to discover, if not wild enthusiasm, at least toleration for his plans during talks with the unionists and nationalists. In fact, everyone listened, everyone talked, and no one said anything final. The SDLP, looking to Dublin, wanted an Irish dimension to go with power sharing. If Prior would not bend to this, Hume told him, then the SDLP would not sit in the assembly. And the unionists all wanted no Irish dimension and the power that should be justly theirs. Only the optimists of the Alliance were enthusiastic.

The only potential arena for agreement was the division of assembly power, thus opening a field of play for the theorists and political scientists. The NIO began to put together another White Paper, another accommodation that this time would offer more than Atkins's aborted constitutional conference. Even if the SDLP, the DUP, and the OUP were unhappy, they had not said never. And like the Northern Ireland secretaries before him, Prior believed in the absolute virtue of talking, even talking to no purpose. After all much of politics was talking, passing memos, reading the papers, and having coffee. This at least could still be done at the Northern Ireland Office.

By focusing on a small arrangement, made in and for the province, acceptable to London and, for the moment, beyond the reach of Dublin, Prior ran against the inclination of Hume and the SDLP. Hume wanted Dublin involved to redress the balance and he wanted the United States to use its auspices to ensure at least real British interest in the Irish problem. Matters did not work out quite as expected. On January 28, the day before the first meeting of the Anglo-Irish Inter-Government Council, the visible sign of the Anglo-Irish summit, FitzGerald's government lost a vote on the budget proposal, and fell. No one was very surprised. The Irish seemed to have embarked on a series of elections to see if Haughey could put together a solid Fianna Fáil majority or fail and let in a coalition. London had preferred FitzGerald because he was not prone to sudden lurches toward the old nationalist postures. Haughey seemed willing to revive talk of a united Ireland. Thatcher, of course, had little time for anyone tinkering with internal United Kingdom matters and less for Haughey, who seemed to grow greener by the month. On February 11, 1982, the Irish electorate went to the polls but returned no clear verdict. Haughey and Fianna Fáil could not manage a majority, nor could the opposition shape an effective coalition: Fianna Fáil won 81 seats, Fine Gael 63, Labour 15, Sinn Féin–Workers 3, and independents 4. It was at least undeniably good news for the former Officials, who formally became the Workers Party on April 25, but for hardly anyone else.

Haughey, the master craftsman, first managed to beat back a Fianna Fáil challenge to his leadership with Desmond O'Malley riding point on February 28 and remained as Taoiseach with a minority government resting on the support of the Workers and independents, who were promised a variety of concessions. The most visible was a large packet of inner-urban proposals worth £91 million that had wooed the independent TD from Dublin-Central, Tony Gregory. As far as Prior was concerned it meant that, once again, Haughey, the most nationalist of Irish politicians, was in power on February 9 as the new Taoiseach; his acceptance of a Northern unionist veto of a united Ireland was forgotten or at least forgotten for the moment. Events in the Irish Republic were not thought helpful at the Northern Ireland Office, other than the fact that the Provisional Sinn Féin candidates did very poorly. The Anglo-Irish entente was put aside along with the Council.

Ireland no longer had the same appeal with Haughey in power, no longer seemed as firm an ally against Provo pretensions. There was suspicion that even the charge on March 6 against the IRA man Gerard Tuite, who had escaped from prison in London and been arrested in Ireland for causing explosions in England, had no great significance. The Tuite case was the first time a person was charged in the Republic with a crime committed in Great Britain, but Dublin still opposed extradition. Many in the British establishment remained suspicious. Dublin was still regularly blamed for providing the Provos haven. All the cross-border cooperation, the rising distaste of the Irish army and police for the IRA, the general public abhorrence of the Provos, were ignored by many politicians in Britain and nearly all unionists in Northern Ireland. One Haughey mention of a united Ireland and many of the politicians in Britain and nearly all the unionist ones in Northern Ireland blamed Dublin for any security problems.

The Provos, like Prior, were still at work. On March 2 an attempt was made on the life of the province's chief justice, Sir Robert Lowry. There were more bombs and a spectacular ambush on Crocus Street in Belfast when an active service unit using an M-60 killed three soldiers. The Armalite still had the major role on the island. And as long as the IRA stayed on the island and kept the killing total within reason, hardly anyone in London paid much attention.

On April 5 the British government published the expected White Paper on Northern Ireland—Prior's proposal on rolling devolution. It was welcomed with at best tepid praise, except for the expected enthusiasm of the Alliance Party—Oliver Napier told his party conference on April 24 that rolling devolution might be the last chance for the province to solve its own problem. Mostly there was only grave suspicion in the province and modest praise from the British media. John Hume had already called the plan "unworkable." There was to be an elected assembly of seventy-eight members, one more devolved assembly. A proportional representation system would be used and, more important, once in place the members would reach an agreement on how devolved powers would be exercised. The real key was that for any power to be devolved 70 percent of the members would have to agree. In other words, unless the Catholic minority was agreeable, it was unlikely that the assembly would receive anything from London.

London was no more enamored of the proposal than the Irish. Thatcher had little interest in Irish matters that did not reflect a concern with order and maybe law. On March 17, 1982, Haughey was in Washington urging Reagan to urge the British toward Irish unity. Since he could not have unity (Thatcher had made that clear), the Taoiseach was staking out the green for his party. The rumor that unity was no longer an Irish priority, was dependent on Northern consent, was no longer very impressive. Reagan had told him the people in Northern Ireland must find the solution—so much for Dublin dictation when it ran counter to the special relationship. Haughey might keep beavering away on Irish unity but his moves were minor. On May 10 he would appoint two from the province, Séamus Mallon of the SDLP and John Robb of the moderate New Ireland Group, to the Irish Senate. It was a ploy tried previously by Seán MacBride. The gesture only resulted later in Mallon's being disqualified as a member of the Northern Ireland Assembly. All of these gestures when noticed by Thatcher only stiffened her resolve to ignore any Irish dimension.

Thatcher had warned Prior not to make the edges of his paper green; she thought, it was said, that the proposed bill was a rotten one but would let matters go. On March 25 the cabinet approved rolling devolution. Let Prior push the bill through while the government focused on the Falklands. What Prior did in Ireland really did not matter much even if her parliamentary secretary, Ian Gow, seemed to think so. Thatcher was an emotional unionist when asked. Most knew better than to bother her by asking. She did not want to be bothered. The cabinet did not want to be bothered. Prior had been sent to Belfast to get him out of the way, out of the center of the circle. He announced on April 16 that the Falklands war would not delay rolling devolution, nor would Haughey with his revived Green nationalism. Anyway the whole matter was technical, an assembly to set up six committees to monitor Stormont departments under paid chairmen and deputy chairmen and then, after a period of party cooperation, proposals for devolved powers acceptable to the 70 percent—all very theoretical and dull. The whole business was not only dull but also irrelevant, for the White Paper appeared two days before the Argentine invasion of the Falklands. Like most nations and most governments, one crisis at a time is the rule; the spectacular drives out the ordinary or even the previously urgent. The Falklands engendered the most intense British national response since Suez and this time there was minimal dissent as the country focused on war in the South Atlantic. Margaret Thatcher, formerly under political siege, growing a bit tatty around the edges, was transformed into a Churchillean figure, the state of the armada sent to the Falklands was of daily concern, the presence of a royal, Prince Andrew, at the war fascinated the evening press, and the war swept away the provincial and pedestrian. The Lion was rampant and Thatcher iron in determination. Even Prior, the discarded wet—too liberal for the Prime Minister—isolated at Stormont, was impressed with the Prime Minister: "She took risks which not many of us would have been prepared to accept: there was a large bill to be met, but no one can doubt that she had her place in history. The army came home on those great troopships to a moment of patriotic fervour."*

What mattered Ireland, a closer island without a splendid war? Ireland did matter. The Dublin government did not support Britain's war, not with enthusiasm, not at all. Instead, unlike most of Western Europe, the EEC, NATO, and the United States, the Fianna Fáil government, taking what London felt was an anti-British attitude, abstained in United Nations votes and created a very obvious anti-Irish backlash in a deeply patriotic United Kingdom. On May 3 Fianna Fáil Defense Minister Paddy Power had called Britain the aggressor in the war. The British establishment would take some while to recover from this unexpected Irish posture. In London some journalists and analysts were quick to point out that if Britain was willing to send troops thousands of miles to the South Atlantic to protect 1,400 Falkland Islanders, how much more would be sacrificed to maintain the connection with the unionists in Northern Ireland? Thatcher would make this perfectly clear when she informed the British ambassador in London in July that the United Kingdom had no need to consult Dublin on Irish matters. So Ireland's attitude was noticed and remembered for some years, and Haughey was blamed personally for not falling into line to resist Argentine aggression. Haughey had already made it plain, in any case, that he wanted nothing to do with rolling devolution.

Prior's bill moved ahead through the various stages with almost no notice except for the handful of integrationalists who talked and stalled and upset no one but the Northern Ireland Office. All this left traces for administrative historians but little impact on events. Events in Ireland were as expected. There was an IRA bomb blitz on April 20 that hit Belfast, Derry, Armagh, Strabane, Ballymena, Bessbrook, and Magherafelt, killing two, injuring twelve, and doing £1 million of damage. Police were shot and soldiers killed. IRA agents were caught in the United States in June trying to buy ground-to-air Redeye missiles. Bombs were found in Donegal. And then there was another spectacular, this time on London, when British attention was focused on the South Atlantic. On July 14 Prior had announced that the Assembly elections would take place in October and then had gone to the United States to sell rolling devolution and to counter Haughey's influence. The war in the South Atlantic was still a hot topic. No one was focused on the IRA.

The Provisional IRA's GHQ had set in motion another English campaign that sputtered on as the few volunteers acted and disappeared. On July 20 the active service units in London at last had everything in place. As the Queen's Household

*Prior, p. 149.

Cavalry trotted alongside Hyde Park in Knightsbridge for the changing of the guards, a car bomb detonated beside the parade. The men and horses were smashed across the street; two soldiers were killed and several wounded; torn and dying horses hobbled through the haze of cordite as the stunned summer crowds watched. Almost at the same time a device in the bandstand in Regent's Park detonated underneath an army band, scattering the musicians, black and bloody, in front of the shocked audience. The grand total for the two events was eight dead soldiers and fifty-one people injured; three died later.

Bombs in London always produced horror, righteous indignation, and a wave of anti-Irish sentiment. This time not only were English boys dead but also all those beautiful horses. The one horse that survived became a hero, an evening newspaper star, while the photographs of the lovely dead animals, tossed along Rotten Row on the edge of the park, were a grim reminder of the other war across the Irish Sea. In a way the horses seemed to bring home the horror more than the dead soldiers or the thunder of bombs in the West End. The English, while they might love a soldier, truly loved horses, and so, correspondingly, hated the bombers. Not since the Manchester-Birmingham massacres had there been such emotion. This time, however, there were other priorities and no need to rush through legislation or riot in the streets; the horses and the soldiers barely lasted as nine-day wonders.

Back in the province matters ground along with the expected steady-state violence, noted only in the papers and on BBC Ulster. All the news tended to be bad despite individual sorties against the inherited ills of the province. On February 19, as predicted, the DeLorean Motor Cars company had gone into receivership. Fifteen hundred workers were laid off on May 31. This was hardly the end of DeLorean's long-running disaster, which cost the taxpayers some £77 million and culminated eventually with DeLorean being acquitted in Los Angeles on a drug charge on August 16, 1984, because he had been entrapped by the FBI. The DeLorean car became a collector's item and a symbol of industrial development gone bad. Prior had one more unexpected problem to sort out. And the statistics of misery indicated that times were worse: The 1981 census, released in July, indicated that 133,727 people had left the province in ten years, so that the total population was down for the first time in a century, to 1,509,892. The only surprise was that so few had left; but then, new legislation had cut off the United States as haven, and the population, Protestant and Catholic, was enormously loyal to their wee country, their parish or bit of the city. They should have left—the housing was still awful and between redevelopment razing and the IRA bombs most urban areas still looked like sets of World War II films.

This perception was not really accurate. Generally, housing might be bad, but new houses were being built; the wretched, year by year, were being decently housed. Five thousand new houses a year was a lot, would rehouse the province in time. There were community centers built, and sports centers, and even a few new glass buildings. The security requirements created a small industry—one under threat from the IRA but one that offered opportunity nevertheless to the daring and in the end often to the army. There was private building, if not much, and there were new factories, if not many. Belfast from time to time glowed with seasonal prosperity. The old Bogside in Derry was gone and many in the country no longer lived in hovels without water or light or prospect of decency. Times might not be good but in many ways and in many places they were better.

Many saw only the awful, the failings, the outward signs of a troubled province. Some of those who lived in new council housing and benefited from new government schemes still felt deprived. And many were deprived and far too many were unemployed. There might be less misery and that more evenly distributed, but times were still hard. The Catholic ghettos were still the worst. A private Flax Trust report published in January 1983 indicated that in the Ardoyne, among a population of eight thousand, male unemployment was 54 percent, with serious deprivation; 28 percent of the families lived in overcrowded conditions and 35 percent of the homes lacked basic amenities. In Ballymurphy the local cooperative effort had failed, the building turned into a military fort. Security did all right out of the Troubles but not the poor, especially not the poor Catholics.

For many of the poor the only visible new building was a brick wall that cost eighty thousand pounds between the Falls and Shankill roads. The city would be crisscrossed with these brick peace lines—good walls made not good neighbors but secure neighborhoods. The access roads in and out of the ghettos remained a danger, where killers in stolen cars sped down from their safe neighborhood to shoot the victim of the week. In time there would be very few such access roads left, and those who seldom saw, even at a distance, one of the other persuasion except in the center of the city, would never see them. And who wanted to leave to go to the center through gates and checks and under the eyes of the television cameras, the British soldiers, the police, the informers and spotters into a neutral zone where an enemy might appear? And from time to time such a gunman did appear to shoot a soldier in mufti, an informer, or a late customer at a Catholic bar. Belfast, despite the assurances of the Northern Ireland Office, despite the decline in city center bombs, despite the lights and low military profile, was not Leeds or Brighton. It could be gay and upbeat and well decorated for the holidays, but there was still the wire, the army, the men with guns, and the taste of tension. Some liked this (who wants Dublin, where every day is the same?), but most simply stayed home on the dole, waiting for a better house, better days, the next spectacular.

In fact there were various approaches to adjusting the Troubles in Belfast to advantage. There was money about and opportunities to make more. The lack of authority established a free-market zone where taxes could not be collected, the paramilitaries became involved, and old services were supplied by new people and new services offered by the cunning. The government was eager to spend in some areas for varying purposes and could be encouraged or, if need be, bilked. All sorts of industry flourished: Glaziers did well out of bombs; construction could be adjusted to security needs, from police stations to new locks on the front door; building sites needed guards to guard against promised sabotage, needed workers who were amenable, needed a protector. Someone had to seek goods across the border to everyone's advantage, handle the new videos, assure that deliveries would be made and repairs undertaken. Northern Ireland in general, especially Belfast and the border, became truly free enterprise zones as a whole class of mini-entrepreneurs arose from working-class homes, with the skills of clerks and ambitions of merchants. Some could just make ends meet and some could soon afford a Mercedes and a Spanish holiday. The Troubles did not trouble all equally.

Certainly the British were spending money to secure order, not just money on the RUC or the army but also on the new police stations and security structures, state-of-the-art buildings, bomb-proof with integrated communications. These sleek facilities were often grotesque from the outside. The function determined the form: huge, lowering, omnipotent, and mysterious buildings that exuded a vague sense of menace. Many were bleak, reinforced concrete blocks lightened only by watch towers and the froth of nets, decorated with coils of razor wire and a Disneyland of aerials. Some checkpoints were garish in yellow and black. All were intrusive, interrupting the traditional streetscape or lowering in the green countryside. The RUC tried to compensate for the harsh image by opening police-sponsored Blue Light discos for the young people but had not dared try this in the hard-core republican area where a blue light over a station door was target, not welcome. In republican districts the governments could not even repair the streetlights or protect phones or public transportation. There, in what were still largely no-go zones, any government intervention was monitored by the IRA, any security presence as mission entailing real risks. Still, a very real effort was made to improve matters, if not to win the hearts and minds of the nationalists, simply because in the United Kingdom it needed doing. Money was spent on new housing and new sports complexes, on the highways out of Belfast, on road schemes and utilities. Whether or not this was an investment in winning the hearts and minds of the dissidents, it meant jobs and money and was a sign that all was not bleak. This investment, however, did not deny those who operated for good or for ill, for private gain or for the public good, in the vacuum left when authority withdrew under threat.

Some, like the churches, the Peace People, the political parties, and inspired individuals created welfare programs, gave advice, found jobs, counseled on schooling, provided transportation for prisoners' dependents, ran club rooms, and sponsored poetry readings and original drama. Some, like the finance officers of the paramilitaries, encouraged black taxis as a source of income, established drinking clubs, controlled slot machines or security on building sites. These all made profit—profit for the party, profits for people, racketeering as an industry. When conventional capitalists withdrew, stopped running buses or sold off the pub, the ambitious supplied the service and took a percentage—and paid no taxes and sometimes paid no supplier. There were failures. Ballymurphy Whiterock Pictures struggled along for ten years until 1983, when it went into liquidation, leaving only a huge military fort in what had been the Whiterock Industrial Estate.

In Ballymurphy, a dissident and radical priest Father Desmond Wilson, established with a committee the Springhill Community House, which sought to reach into the community, working class, isolated, besieged, denied most services, dependent on their own. In November 1982 he set up the Conway Mill Community Education Centre, which sponsored the traditional menu of seminars, readings, classes for pleasure and classes for state examination, debates, and dialogue. Across the city in Protestant Rathcoole a self-help group was set up to provide facilities for the young among the fourteen thousand people who did not

649

have a single community center. The Troubles, in fact, inspired the rise of new people, some of whom found careers in subversion, where not only gunmen were needed but also self-taught accountants, radio technicians who learned the trade from manuals, import-export experts, Irish speakers who could teach what they had taught themselves, social workers and editorial writers. There were also many who simply did good, filled a need with what was available. New people built their own centers for their own neighbors with their own plans, filled them with their own programs, serviced the locals, and then expanded the net.

As always, the view depended on the location and the perception of the involved. While Father Wilson was busy in the Springhill Community House, a less benign campaign was also under way in Ballymurphy to use the rules of government welfare to local advantage. There had been in Strathclyde in Scotland a local campaign to see that every resident received all the proper entitlements. In Ballymurphy such a campaign engendered great enthusiasm: They *were* entitled and it cost nothing and the government would have to pay. The campaign spread over much of Belfast, returning unanticipated funds. Between April 1982 and March 31, 1987, figures from the Falls Road Office of the Department of Health and Social Service indicated that the Upper Springfield area that included Ballymurphy had received in Single Payments alone (furniture, fuel, clothing) £8,378,900. The natives had invented a welfare industry, one that kept right on producing for them. Driving by the old terraces or the huge bleak estates, the ruined redevelopment sites or the grim high-rise Unity or Divis Flats would not give a clue to the intense activity on the ground. For every cluster of sullen men in shoddy clothes huddled by the closed door of the pub, waiting to spend money better used on milk or the rent, there was another group around a deal table in a borrowed room planning a campaign to start a children's play school or publish a newsletter on civil rights or demand an antidrug program. There was much to do that was only marginally related to the great political dispute, the armed struggle, or the need for local defense. In their way even those who collected black taxi money or arranged that the UVF would oversee security were engaged in a world that required initiative and skills not previously found along the Falls or Shankill, where the bosses had made the decisions and the times had been managed by others.

The country towns were somewhat different, more normal. The countryside could visually hide the violence. In the towns there were signs that in time could be ignored: the security center, an army barracks, an RUC station, huge concrete structures draped in antirocket netting, topped with razor wire and aerials, with guards at the door, armored vehicles in a protected parking lot, the tracking television cameras and the soldiers hidden behind the next. Most else was everyday, the few Ferrets, the armed police and soldiers, twenty years of patrols and burned-out buildings, and no one noticed. The local butcher shop was the same, the supermarket, the pub with new paint, the crowds of schoolchildren in uniforms, the clerks rushing back after lunch to the courthouse, the Japanese cars in the street and the signs for Poppy Day or appeals for Saint Vincent de Paul, the same routines. There were new factories as well as closed businesses, tourists still came, the fish ran and the pubs served lager. Members and guests came to the gold clubs and never noticed the boarded buildings in town. Everyone went to church on Sunday and walked the streets and lanes without much thought.

There were inevitable changes. There were fewer old men in cloth caps, fewer bikes, and more traffic, but an unfocused, local eye saw the landscape as normal. Tomorrow was remarkably like yesterday. Occasionally there was a fresh ruin, the IRA striking at hotels or stores or RUC stations, but mostly ruins were tidy or replaced, and ignored. Life ran relatively smoothly between local spectaculars, and those were more evident on the evening news than at the side of the road. There was milk to be picked up, exams to take, girls to meet, and old women to bury. Life and death in the countryside, except for those whose first priority was the Troubles, and even then, moved along much as it had the year before and would the next year, despite the shrill sermons, the bombed hotel, the television terrors. There had always been hellfire sermons and tragedies and some sort of terror on the radio or television.

During 1982 there was an escalating but not surprising challenge to the authorities from republicans committed to the gun as means and radical rhetoric as rationale as the INLA competed with the Provisionals. The province now had two republican secret armies and the smaller appeared more virulent. The shift in focus, if not in deployment of resources, by the IRA during and after the hunger strike permitted those involved in the direction of the INLA to escalate their own campaign, attract the purely physical force people as well as those more comfortable with the revolutionary analysis of Costello's successors. Some recruits simply found the Provisionals or their local unit uncongenial, the wrong family, the wrong people, and in a sense too confining—IRA discipline, like British army anti-insurgency, improved, if erratically, over time. The intensity of feeling of the H-Block crisis was reflected in an escalated INLA effort.

Tolerated by the Provos as a schismatic but hardly competitive group, the INLA had sought prominence by recourse to more ruthless and less restrained violence. The political leadership had been eroded by resignations, arrests, and murder. There had been heavy pressure in the Republic after the Great Train Robbery and no reason for radicals to enlist in a seemingly flawed crusade. In the North although Dominic McGlinchey had arrived to give operational coherence, there was no longer a very effective IRSP outside the GHQ and almost no real political analysis within. Volunteers often knew the jargon but were far more concerned with local predominance, the details of operational matters, and adventure. Too small, lacking in great vision or middle-class talents, increasingly covert and illicit, the INLA had to escalate or decay.

In a single revolutionary environmental niche there is room for only one species—the more dynamic. While INLA had no aspirations to replace the Provisionals, a rock-solid aspect of the Irish terrain, the leaders did want a real part of the action. So the INLA had escalated their way and let other matters ride. On May 20, 1982, a bomb was defused in the home of the Reverend William Beattie of the DUP. If the Provos could kill Bradford then the INLA would have a go at one of Paisley's lot. On September 1 they were somewhat more effective, shooting and wounding Belfast DUP councillor Billy Dickson in his home. On September 16 a bomb in the Divis Flats killed a British soldier but also two boys, one eleven and one fourteen—one more gunman's mistake. Four days later the southern INLA contingent blew up a radar station at Schull in County Cork—an ideologically satisfactory, nonlethal operation against an imperialist target that resulted in still more pressure from the Dublin authorities. On January 5, 1983, the INLA would be declared illegal in the Republic. Only a scattering of activists was left, the visible in the small IRSP and a few of the INLA people in Dublin and Cork and a few pools like West Limerick.

In Northern Ireland Sir John Hermon assured the people on September 23, 1982, that the INLA and IRA were reeling. There was no doubt that the army and police were more effective but this hardly was the impression of the vulnerable, and in a secret war impressions count. Rather than reeling the two were still pursuing operations with vigor throughout the province and were involved in a bitter round of shootings around Armagh. On November 7, 1981, seventeen-year-old Trevor Foster was killed, mistaken for another member of his family who was in the British security forces: another gunman error. On November 10, 1981, a former UDR man was shot dead. In Armagh on January 24, 1982, a young man was killed by British security forces, apparently during a burglary in disputed circumstances. Then there was a pause in the killing, if not the attempts in the area until on August 27, 1982, Wilfred McIlveen, a former member of the UDA, was killed in a booby trap explosion. On October 7 Private Frederick Williamson was shot and died when his car crashed and prison officer Elizabeth Champers was also killed when her car crashed as well. There were unofficial responses. An out-of-uniform UDR group tried to kill the reputed INLA man Raymond Grew at his home in Armagh on September 22 and on October 25 an out-of-uniform UDR man along with several other loyalists murdered a republican ex-internee, Peter Corrigan. Over in Enniskillen on November 9, Detective Constable Gary Ewing and a civilian were killed by an explosive device attached to their car outside the Lakeland Forum. Two RUC reserve constables were shot and killed on November 16 at Markethill near Armagh.

For Protestants it appeared as if the IRA was striking out at local Protestants as well as the police. On October 18, for example, an INLA gunman burst into a classroom and shot and wounded a sixty-one-year-old headmaster as his class of ten-year-olds screamed and hid under their desks during the attack. The headmaster was vulnerable and had been in the UDR six years previously—sound reason for an INLA eager for targets, but a Protestant shot down in front of children to intimidate the rest as far as the Protestants were concerned. The gunmen seemed determined on terrorizing the loyalists with sectarian killings disguised as attacks on the security forces—retired or aged UDR men, reserve policemen digging in the garden, everyday people claimed as paramilitary, and the occasional gunman's mistake. No wonder the UDR and RUC showed little moderation in seeking out the killers and bombers. For nationalists it appeared that the Protestants were using their security positions as cover for the murder of Catholics. Loyalists felt that the Provos and the INLA were making an effort to drive the Protestants out of the country. What could not be denied by anyone was that the anger and tension generated by the violence in Armagh had grown throughout the autumn of 1982 and culminated in an IRA operation on October 27. The Provisionals had placed a land mine at the Kinnego rotary near Lurgan and detonated it when an RUC armored Cortina passed: Sergeant John Quinn and

Constables Alan McCloy and Paul Hamilton were killed. The locals were no more outraged than RUC headquarters in Belfast. Something would have to be done.

In fact, this time something was done. The republicans seemed again on a crest, with the successes of Sinn Féin during the Assembly elections and the recent wave of killings. When the bomb went off the RUC had in place a prepared response, a Headquarters Mobile Support Unit (SSU) that had been set up under E Department of the Special Branch. There were two units of twenty-four policemen who had been trained in part by the SAS, not unlike an earlier Bessbrook Support Unit that had operated in cooperation with the SAS and Gárdaí along the border in 1979. There was a willingness by the RUC to take more active measures, the British army had long complained privately that the police were not sufficiently aggressive, (i.e., did not act like an army). On November 11 the RUC shot and killed three unarmed IRA men near Lurgan. At least 109 shots were fired. The three, Eugene Toman, Seán Burns, and Gervaise McKerr, had been fingered by an informer (who received two thousand pounds) as the men responsible for the Kinnego rotary bomb. The RUC men involved in the shooting were later charged with the murder and acquitted absolutely. The RUC announced the three had been shot as they broke through a routine police checkpoint. The nationalists believed the IRA men had been under surveillance from an E4A intelligence agent in an unmarked Japanese car and then ambushed by a special RUC antiterrorist team.

On November 24 a seventeen-year-old Catholic from Lurgan, Michael Tighe, was shot dead when he walked into an ambush set at an IRA explosives store. His companion, Martin McAuley, was seriously wounded. The police had been told by their paid informant that this was the dump for the explosives used in the Kinnego bomb. The hide had been bugged and the ambush taped in a nearby surveillance vehicle. No one had expected Tighe. The IRA man was another matter—he was thought involved with the rotary bomb as well. In any case the RUC was ready with an explanation that did not include the bug, the tape, or the surveillance vehicle and did include informer information added to the file that the boy had been in the fringes of the IRA, which was not true. Again the nationalists felt that the RUC had been involved in another trap ambush, another example of shoot-to-kill without warning.

The next incident hit the INLA. On December 12 two RUC armored Cortinas were sent to Séamus Grew's home in Armagh to be joined by a British army red Granada to await the expected arrival in Armagh of Dominic McGlinchey. Grew and Roddy Carroll's yellow Allegro had been followed all day by an E4A inspector in a Peugeot. He had crossed the border, ridden back from a funeral for a family friend, and picked up McGlinchey, who was then dropped. The inspector managed to telephone Armagh but the ambush stayed in place—just barely. There was a mixup and an army private crashed his car into a RUC Cortina, breaking a constable's leg. Everyone leaped out and milled about. Grew drove past with only a glance at what seemed a simple accident. No one glanced at him. Suddenly the Peugeot screeched to a halt and the inspector shouted that Grew had just driven by. An RUC SSU constable, John Robinson, leaped into the Peugeot beside the inspector, who took off after Grew's Allegro. The inspector whirled past the Allegro, cut Grew off, and stopped. Then Robinson threw open the door and stood up beside the Allergo. He was armed with a pump shotgun and a machine pistol. He opened fire on the two men. Fifteen shots splattered into Carroll and the car. Carroll was killed instantly. The RUC man ran closer to the Allergo and fired again. Grew tumbled out onto the road. Robinson stood over him and continued to fire. Grew was hit several more times, once in the back of the head. The inspector hurriedly drove the Peugeot off and the police took over the scene. Robinson faded into the background. The RUC reported another attempt to run a roadblock, one that had injured a policeman and resulted in the death of two INLA men. The inspector's Peugeot was reported on duty elsewhere.

There was, as had been the case with the other shootings, a call for an inquiry. Again the original RUC explanation collapsed and a different story emerged. The RUC agreed that there would be an inquiry. Nothing was heard of the results. The judicial system took over. Robinson was charged, tried, and acquitted. Critics complained that vital evidence in such trials had a way of disappearing, that the RUC closed ranks and covered up, that the courts took the official word as gospel, that such justice was no more than a closing curtain on murder by authority. On December 14 Prior had admitted that there were special antiterrorist squads in the RUC but denied that they had been given license to kill suspects. There was no shoot-to-kill policy.

The nationalists did not believe him. Even the statistics looked odd. There had been a great many shootings in disputed circumstances; of these, seventeen incidents had led to trials that produced one manslaughter conviction of a soldier, overturned on appeal, and one sentence of twelve months' detention in a young offenders' center for manslaughter, suspended for two years. There was one conviction for murder but the British soldier was released in 1988 after serving two years and three months and later returned to his regiment. It was not a convincing record given the details available.

Much later, in September 1988, Chief Constable John Hermon would say in the *Times* that there was no such policy as shoot to kill, it was a misnomer, and the shootings in Armagh had not alienated the nationalist community. Actually he was right in that the security forces always were trained to shoot to kill once they shot. The question was instead, Should they be setting killing traps if the IRA were simply criminals? Hermon in 1988, as in 1982, had no intention of getting into a detailed argument: His RUC was doing an impossible job well.

By 1988 not even other matters and the passage of years had buried the issue: The RUC entry into the dirty war in Armagh that culminated in the killing of the two INLA men generated one more current of protest that in time would become an international issue. This time operational incompetence—as both the INLA and the IRA knew, shooting to kill and effective bombing are not that easy—and authoritative arrogance based on the assumption that control of the evidence, the legal proceedings, and the ear of the media would be sufficient, would give the republicans one more unexpected propaganda triumph. The issue would not die and the murder of the investigation by Superintendent John Stalker, as crude and unrepentant as the shootings, would only cause further turmoil. What might be deplorable if traced to gunmen—after all, shooting on sight was not only their trade but also a historically justifiable guerrilla means—was simply unacceptable if a state was responsible.

In a study hardly sympathetic to government positions the editor Anthony Jennings included at the beginning two quotes that clearly defined the cusps of the difficulty.* One by Frank Kitson, included in his 1971 book published and repeatedly quoted by both republicans and advocates of protecting civil liberties, is the bald statement of a soldier fighting a dirty war:

> The law should be used as just another weapon in the government's arsenal, and in this case it becomes little more than a propaganda cover for the disposal of unwanted members of the public. For this to happen efficiently, the activities of the legal service have to be tied into the war effort in as discreet a way as possible.

In contrast, Lord Lowry, no friend of subversives, spoke for the security forces: "This war is being waged by organizations which style themselves armies and observe military procedures, but it has not invaded, and will not be allowed to invade, the courts. The rule of law has prevailed and will continue to prevail there." The problem for Judge Lowry, who knew all too well after the attempt on his life in February that the war could come to the courts, was that if justice did, indeed, prevail it was not seen to do so by observers. Many, perhaps most, nationalists no longer believed in British justice. Not only had the system been bent to convict suspected republicans, but it also relegated the Irish Catholics in general to the status of suspects. At its best the system did work but often it seemingly worked only in that the allotted steps were followed without reference to logic, reality, or justice. It was hardly a novel challenge for a state under subversive, armed challenge; but it was especially crucial for the one state that had more than any other crafted the laws of justice over centuries of sacrifice. Of course, to the militant Orangemen justice was intended to punish the traitorous and if the system failed to do so—and it often did—then justice was denied. Surely a purpose of the law is to maintain the necessary order for the loyal, to reassure the endangered and threatened. For this it need not be tempered by either mercy or by concern for the sensibilities of scholars and civil rights advocates.

To many in Ireland and out, Kitson's quite pragmatic advice seemed to have been shaped by the British into the rules of "justice," lies accepted as truth, perjury as fact, and the rules of evidence skewed by prejudice. Although the British government tended to ignore the tremors that problems in the province caused in the international arena—the province was an internal matter—over the years there were investigations by a variety of organizations and calls for remedial action by distant governments. Often ill-informed or simply spiteful, these critics were joined by both specialists and the sincere who sought the rule of law. Especially after the hunger strikes had scattered the issue worldwide, the British government had to be aware of, if not amenable to, distant critics. Even in minor matters like the use of plastic bullets, the European Parliament called for a ban

*Anthony Jennings, ed., *Justice Under Fire: The Abuse of Civil Liberties in Northern Ireland* (London: Pluto Press, 1988). The first quotation is taken from Frank Kitson, *Low Intensity Operations* (London: Faber and Faber, 1971), p. 69, and the second from R. V. Gibney (1983) in the *Northern Ireland Judgement Bulletin*, pp. 7–8.

throughout the European Community on May 13, 1982, and in October the British Labour Party conference, taking the cue, urged a ban throughout the United Kingdom. Britain, however, continued to exploit the advantage of the Thatcher-Reagan friendship, enhanced on Irish matters by the work done by Hume, Seán Donlon, and the others in the United States, and by the rising European concern with international terrorism. Still, no RUC constable could fire a plastic bullet, certainly not in front of television cameras, without sending out far ripples. With an assured Prime Minister like Thatcher, such ripples hardly determined policy, but in times the certainties of the nationalists and the concerns of the disinterested created doubts, doubts found even in London among the establishment.

It was not only in the evolving shoot-to-kill cases that there were these doubts (including doubts among those who found the Irish republicans abhorrent) but also in the earlier English bombing cases, where there had been a rush to judgment. Gradually British justice in Irish matters came under growing pressure. Justice was not seen to have been done. The legitimacy of the center was eroded, the more so because the explanations and rationalizations of the authorities were so flimsy. Spokesmen did not even feel the necessity to lie well, craft realistic explanations and alibis; when caught they simply quashed further investigation. The end result of the shoot-to-kill incidents in 1982 and later was a net gain for the gunmen. The government's defense of the Prevention of Terrorism Act, the Diplock Courts, the full panoply of emergency powers often proved less than convincing. And the government did not really seem to care. As long as the gunmen murdered then order was necessary.

In the meantime in 1982, the INLA kept at the killing game. The group had no great trouble making good the attrition caused by the security forces, although their lack of political skills was hampering the escalation of the movement. In fact there was ample evidence in December that the INLA was as capable and as brutal as ever. On December 6 the INLA targeted a public house and disco at Ballykelly, a small, quaint, almost English village between Coleraine and Londonderry, set in open, tidy farmland near the British army Shackleton Barracks. British soldiers for forty years had found recreation and relaxation in the local area. Some of the pubs and stores in the area were off-limits to soldiers, but not all—not the Droppin' Well at Ballykelly, where the Monday night Razzamataz Disco drew in a crowd, mostly from the adjacent barracks, men and women, married and single. It was dour, a single-story building roofed with a concrete slab, made appealing by surface glitter and the drink and music inside. On Monday night, December 6, there were about 150 dancers, many from the Cheshire Regiment. Two couples, hardly remembered, sat near the wall for a while over a drink and then left; behind them under the table they left a holdall containing a five-pound explosive device with a time-switch. Thirty minutes before closing time the device detonated. This time the luck of the Irish worked to British disadvantage: the explosion jarred back the outside wall and the entire prestressed concrete roof slab crashed down on the crowd. It took most of the night to dig out the survivors. The bleak white arc lights were brought in and the police and army spent hours sifting through the ruins. Twelve soldiers and five civilians were killed and sixty-six others were injured seriously. The INLA planners, like many of the IRA operators in England, had targeted the soldiers and ignored the civilians, locals who fraternized with the troops. Within days on December 12, the shooting of the two INLA men in the trap-ambush in Armagh seemed to be a direct security response to the Droppin' Well bomb. One atrocity engendering the next. Four years later the RUC, using more conventional police methods, would trace and arrest the four from Derry who brought in the holdall. They confessed, were tried and convicted, and jailed for life for the seventeen killings; the daughter of one of the women, who had helped in the reconnaissance of the disco, received ten years for manslaughter. In December 1982 the Droppin' Well disaster was in sharp contrast to the previous quiet December of 1981, a month without incident. Not only was there no recess in violence but also on the same day of the Droppin' Well, the trial of Christopher Black, first IRA supergrass, the Crown's converted terrorist, opened in Belfast with thirty-eight people implicated by his testimony. The revelations would play on in the courtroom until August, after 120 days of testimony. By then the strategy of the supergrass had become central to the security forces, a matter of the most intense and divisive debate, involving not only the vulnerable republicans and the civil rights advocates but also many within the security apparatus.

In fact, the impact of witnesses purchased with promises contained the seeds that would blossom and choke the INLA. The organization was vulnerable not to the gun but to informers. Despite the supposed cell-structure, Ireland being Ireland, any volunteer, even one kept at the margins, soon would know the names and some of the records of a substantial number of the members, perhaps all locally and many others who were in touch. In the Provisional IRA the informers were dangerous and for a time debilitating, but membership was large and the losses could be absorbed and even used to advantage in some units. With the INLA there were only fifty or sixty still active and no waiting second wave, only a few possibles drifting on the edges. In 1980 and 1981, with no clear lines of control and succession, Gerry Steenson and Gerald "Sparkey" Barkley, with the help of Harry Kirkpatrick, had attempted to dominate the INLA. They were opposed by Seán Flynn. The rivalry led to the murder of Barkley. Although by 1982 there seemed to be some sort of order, with Dominic McGlinchey in control, in fact the INLA was more an alliance of suspicious local units, not unlike the UVF. The traditional pressures of schism and paranoia were increased by the informers.

Once a supergrass began to talk the authorities would have an insight into the units involved and would know names and what to do with their suspicions. Even if the information did not lead to show trials, it did lead to harassment, arrests, ambushes, and the decay of INLA options. The INLA was not crushed immediately but the "converted terrorists" did what the shoot-to-kill strategy could not. So the INLA men began to talk. John Grimley's revelations led to twenty-two men charged, Seán Mallon's to three, Jackie Goodman's to thirty-six, Robert McAllister's to eleven. The most important was Harry Kirkpatrick, who was arrested in 1981. He had been previously named by the other three. A leading Belfast figure, his revelations beginning in 1983 led to thirty-eight INLA people being charged. Kirkpatrick was no marginal figure but a key player in the INLA, which was already torn by internal power struggles that involved those in prison as well as those on the run. Kirkpatrick as informer was a devastating blow. Those few INLA people still free acted to control the damage by snatching hostages. Kirkpatrick's wife, Elizabeth, was kidnapped in May 1983. In August his stepfather, Richard Hill, and his thirteen-year-old stepsister, Diane, were kidnapped. The latter two were rescued by the Gárdaí from a house in Gortahork, Donegal, and his wife was released and sent back to her parents in Belfast when it became clear that Kirkpatrick was going to give evidence no matter what. Still further threats were made but to no avail. The courtroom itself became the site of a riot. At the end Kirkpatrick's evidence convicted twenty-four INLA men. These convictions, unsound for a variety of reasons, were ultimately overturned in 1986 by a court of appeals and the convicted were released on December 23, 1986. This effectively ended the great supergrass ploy. By then the INLA had disappeared into a quarrel of gunmen, some violent and unrestrained killers, over irrelevant labels—INLA-GHQ or INLA–Army Council or Irish National Liberation Organization, tattered banners often flying over pathological shooters. The INLA finished in a spate of murders as the survivors killed each other. There were a dozen deaths in a few weeks, including McGlinchey's wife, shot while giving her children a bath. It was a classic example of the decay of purity, the power from a gun corrupting especially the limited and the weak. All that was left was a few gunmen with titles and little restraint.

But in 1982–83 the INLA was still a factor, still cemented by old ties, external enemies, mutual suspicions, and the advantages of the name. There was very limited capacity, little operational restraint, and little left of IRSP. Still, the INLA would be sufficiently driven to undertake one more ruthless and dreadful spectacular on November 21, 1983, and sufficiently conscious of the republican responsibilities to hide the act by attributing it to the "Catholic Reaction Force." INLA gunmen threw open the door of the Darkley Mountain Gospel Lodge Pentecostal Church in Armagh during Sunday service and opened fire. The crack of the guns, the moans and scuffles, the sounds of an atrocity were caught on a tape being used to record the service. In the end the INLA gunmen had killed three elders and wounded seven other parishioners. The church had been chosen because it was known to the gunmen, isolated, vulnerable, and most of all Protestant: Catholic retribution by neo-Marxist primitives. On December 27 McGlinchey indicated that the INLA had been indirectly involved, an admission that surprised few. The name Darkley became synonymous with republican sectarianism, the ruin of Wolfe Tone at a Sunday service in Armagh. The INLA had become rogue, a grouping of gunmen without restraint, without ideological or operational discipline, a few faithful and most living on their nerves and the high provided by danger and death. The era had come of Mad Dog and Dr. Death, bodies left on the roadside, mystery murders and schismatic gang wars led by crude men with elaborate titles.

The most striking security event in the period 1982–83 was not action in the field, although there too problems occurred, but in the courtrooms, where the long-running saga of the supergrasses took place. From 1969 on the conflict between peace and war in maintaining order generated tension: Special conditions, required special actions and institutions, tolerable in a war, intolerable during peacetime. In a war, strip-searching prisoners, lying to the media, shooting enemies with plastic bullets, suborning witnesses, killing on sight would have caused no note. In peacetime such actions would have meant prison for the involved, horror by the responsible, and an end of these violations of the norm. In Northern Ireland there were no easy answers, certainly none supplied to the soldiers on little cards or imposed by a judge in the Diplock Courts or announced as policy by the prison authorities.

The security forces, the responsible, thus had problems from the point of the exercise out there in the twilight war searching for live gunmen at great risk. At each stage from open conflict, capture, interrogation, remand, trial, conviction, sentencing, imprisonment, release, and subsequent harassment, there was criticism. Everything was in dispute as the opponents of the state sought to use the normal standards to protect their own, keep their momentum, and destroy the system. The authorities sought to keep the standards as normal as possible while protecting their own, imposing order, and defending the system. The asymmetrical conflict was particularly poignant because the confusion was not simple hypocrisy on either side. Both the illegals, the secret armies, and the legals, the authorities, the not-as-secret armies, believed in the grand tenet of a liberal society. No one much argued from simple pragmatism: Killing works, a dirty war is best, justice should be corrupted if necessary. When someone did there was general horror.

The efforts to impose law and order indicated an insurmountable conflict, a contradiction in terms that gave the establishment as much trouble as the gunmen. The era of the supergrasses was as one with all the other conflicts between law and order, internment, heavy interrogation, and the ongoing shoot-to-kill controversy. The authorities felt that they could not convict normally, even with the Diplock Courts. There were too many Bobby Storey types or too many republican suspects who never got to court at all. Sir John Hermon noted that although in 1981 918 people had been charged, this was a drop from the 1,308 charged five years earlier. Murder charges were down from 313 to 48 and of the 985 murders recorded in 1981 only 26 had been cleared. 1982 was not greatly different but Christopher Black's arrest in November had opened up a new possibility: informer witnesses. Use of the converted terrorists began almost simultaneously with the more blatant policy of murdering suspected gunmen instead of arresting them. And even if arrested there were still charges of brutality. There had since 1969 been other problems further up the line if or when the suspect reached the courtroom. The system could not, or believed it could not, get convictions under the old, normal system. Internment was needed. When internment was replaced, hard interrogation was used. The confessions speeded the conveyer belt to the Kesh. The courts seldom released the suspect. Bobby Storey was living evidence, however, that the courts at times tried to be fair, whatever the record of convictions that indicated corruption and justice.

Yet it was difficult to convict without confessions, even in the Diplock Courts; thus, Christopher Black as supergrass filled a real need: a legitimate means to put much of the active IRA away by turning the marginal and fearful into assets. It was thought prudent and desirable to put away the worst of the UVF and UDA in parallel cases. They were gunmen as well, if no threat to the state. The most notorious loyalist supergrass trial, between February 16 and April 11, 1983, involved the evidence of Joseph Bennett. It was so ineptly presented under cross-examination that the prisoners' friends and relatives had already rented a room for the post-trial celebration. To their horror, fourteen of the sixteen were convicted. The republican analysis that this was a show of being nonsectarian was reinforced when a review of results indicated that by September 1985 not one loyalist remained on remand or sentenced on the uncorroborated word of a supergrass. By then, however, the republicans had been badly shaken by the process. The process was relatively simple: A vulnerable suspect was offered leniency and subsequent protection in return for testimony (uncorroborated) that would convict his associates. There was little money involved—a small allowance, the family taken in, and a future life promised. Informers informed out of the most narrow self-interest and without much thought to the morrow. Only one informer (Kevin McGrady, transformed by a born-again religious experience in Amsterdam after leaving the IRA) volunteered to testify.

In many of these cases the witness was a weak and marginal man trapped between a certain sentence and the discipline of the republicans. Testimony was a mix of lies, rumors, recollections, hard facts like raisins in the pudding, and inherent confusion. Few did well under cross-examination. Many had criminal records stretching back to childhood. Some had been encouraged by their handlers to commit further crimes. Several had been in RUC pay for years. They lied, forgot, lied about the lies. Few were happy. On the stand they looked and felt foolish, used and shamed before everyone. Some began to withdraw their evidence, fearful of vengeance. A few, however, were men who had been near the core—not in most cases important but simply knowledgeable. There would be thirteen Provo supergrasses, only a few of them important or even knowledgeable members. It only took a few to destroy the INLA. For the Provos the most dangerous supergrass seemed to be Robert "Bido" Lean of the administrative staff of the Belfast Brigade GHQ. He had been arrested in 1981, 1982, and again in September 1983. This time he had agreed to testify. His family was moved out by the RUC.

Lean's common-law wife, Geraldine Coleman, and her five children stayed in protective custody for twenty-four days and then they fled. She pleaded with him—the families of the witnesses were at risk, everyone was all too aware that some had been kidnapped, others threatened, and all harassed and insulted by their own. To inform was in Ireland a fearful sin and for a real volunteer, one who had kept the faith, to turn on his own was the most dreadful crime of all. He and his were smeared forever and (in theory only) no harbor was ever again safe. Whatever the myth, the fear was real and the fate of local informers, if caught, was certain—brutal interrogation and a bullet in the head, the body left in the lane, the name ruined and the family shamed. There was no easy way to count the toll of executed informers, since some murders were not claimed, some took place in the Republic, and some seemed random, a bar brawl or a car accident; but the prospect of vengeance was a shadow over those who might cooperate. Lean, not really the important Provo the RUC announced, still knew names. He gave them rumors, guesses, hearsay, and facts. Some twenty-seven names were involved and there might be more.

On October 19, 1983, Lean switched. He escaped from his minder, turned up for a Sinn Féin press conference, and renounced his testimony. He was not the first. The combination of dubious individuals, appallingly inept testimony, the lack of any but uncorroborated testimony from avowed murderers and perjurers who even lied under oath as they spoke, the enormous cost and great length of the trials, the mockery of observers, the outrage of the international legal community, and the fear of worse—all together resulted in a reevaluation. Convictions so achieved were costly, risky, and, as Harry Kirkpatrick's case indicated, not necessarily the end of the exercise. So, like confessions achieved by hard interrogation in 1976–79 or deep interrogation in 1971, or like internment instead of conviction in 1971–76, or like a meld of other nasty techniques arising from the dirty war, the use of supergrasses was discontinued.

Interrogation techniques had improved, crude violence was no longer as necessary, security achievements were more effective. The dangerous hard core of the Provos was more elusive. By the mid-1980s the prime IRA suspects had been reduced to a few hundred, those carefully monitored, and as a result the tools of the treadmill to justice could be more refined, less visible, and, if not much more effective, far less likely to engender legal outrage. The supergrass project was the last effort to build a generally effective net to scoop up suspects without heeding the historic restraints on the authorities.

The cost of the supergrass strategy, one way or another, proved prohibitive, given the results. At first the results looked promising. The statistics indicated that in eighteen months some 500 people had been arrested and charged with 1,500 offenses. In some areas violence was down by 60 percent, especially in the black areas of Belfast. The INLA was dormant, as were the UFF and the UVF. There had been an enormous intake of intelligence. In 1982, 1983, and 1984 the costs were only gradually apparent and the returns were clear: no better evidence than the shrill and angry response of the republicans and radicals. The RUC felt the entire balance could be turned by a real push, a huge effort, massive show trials. The result was an enormous investment resting ultimately on the word of confessed perjurers, the character of self-declared murderers, on the most dubious members of the dark side of society. RUC ambition would overleap itself, but not at first.

In 1982, at the very beginning of the supergrass system, with Black arrested in November and his trial underway on December 6, the violence figures had remained relatively static: 97 deaths, down from 101. The British army figures were 21, up from 10, with the RUCR at 4, down from 8. The republicans had murdered 71, two more than the year before, and only 71 because an operation against the RUC band playing at the graduation ceremony at Queen's University on July 9 failed when the group, after playing, took a different route in their two minibuses and bypassed the IRA car bomb. The Provos' active service unit of seven was convicted of sixty terrorist offenses and the three volunteers who had planted the car bomb received sentences between thirteen and eighteen years for conspiracy. Other operations, of course, aborted without visible signs; in fact, it was increasingly difficult for the IRA to mount effective operations, especially in Belfast, although by no means impossible. The killing trade was not an easy one, certainly not in contrast to the glory days of the no-go zones or even the long riots of the hunger strikes.

The year-end figures tended to indicate what had become a trend often obscured by the public clamor over the triumphs of Sinn Féin or the evils of the supergrass system: The IRA had been curtailed by the security forces, incidents had been reduced, operations had become very difficult, low-level events were not worth the effort, and targets, especially high-profile categories, were secure from all but the most cunning assault. It was not so much that security was winning—winning and losing in such a war are largely matters of perception—but that the security forces, deploying advanced technology and the experience of years crafted to the locale, and playing on the ugly image of terrorism and the decay of the national issue in the Republic, had narrowed the field of battle. And on that narrow ground the IRA could only operate effectively on occasion and with great risk. This led GHQ to search for other military options or other means to reach the desired target. This was often not the major priority of a movement where a broadened battlefield appeared to exist already in the new success of Sinn Féin. It thus produced strains between those with varying priorities, those dedicated to political escalation and those who felt physical force was the most effective weapon of change. These strains had always existed, but the rise of the party as a real factor produced stress as well as gain. What was good for the IRA was not always good for Sinn Féin, but all movements, most parties, have tensions, blocs, currents, internal squabbles. Many, often most, active in Sinn Féin were not in the IRA; they realized they came under Army Council discipline but few of them felt uncomfortable about this as they pursued party interests. And the party interests were not always the same or even parallel to those of a secret army. Two nets might be better than one but at times they fouled each other, disturbed the single catchment area or tangled as both sought the same fish.

The disagreements, while real, were by no means as important as outside observers were inclined to believe. Sinn Féin, being more visible, was assumed to be more important, a miscalculation often made by its members and its advocates, who were not always aware of the dimensions and dynamics of the republican movement even after a lifetime of service. Some crucial players had never signed a declaration, bought a newspaper, or spoken in public or in private; they had provided only a blind eye, a deaf ear, a nod, and a smile—but enough of these and no police force could operate effectively, nor could any election indicate the secrets of the heart.

In fact, it was the elections that broke the hopes of Prior. His rolling devolution had been supposed to dominate the news, give a new direction to Ulster futility. The year 1982 was supposed to be the year of the Assembly,* not of gunmen murdered by special RUC squads, not of dead horses and dead soldiers scattered on a street beside Hyde Park, not the year the pub roof collapsed on the Cheshire

---

*A detailed account of the transient Assembly can be found in Cornelius O'Leary, Sydney Elliott, and R. A. Wilford, *The Northern Ireland Assembly, 1982–1986: A Constitutional Experiment* (London and Belfast: Hurst and Queen's University Bookshop). The various ingenious efforts at devolution over a generation offered political scientists and lawyers not only a subject of comment but also a chance to offer policy options. The result is a remarkable and extensive literature of formulas and formulations. In part some reached fruition in the form of government action. The play of options continued during the spring of 1992 Mayhew round of talks with, among other proposals, a federal variation on European practice suggested by the SDLP.

Regiment in a little Derry village. Prior's initiative would have been lost anyway in the midst of the Falkland extravagance, but Northern Ireland always seemed good for a horror to crowd the decent off the evening news. Prior had shepherded the bills through Parliament with the only interest arising from the carping of the integrationalists. In July he announced that the Assembly elections would take place in October: The SDLP was opposed to sitting in the Assembly, Alliance was enthusiastic, and both DUP and the OUP would contest the elections but expressed no enthusiasm. The only novelty was that Sinn Féin, with the Armalite out of sight, would ask its supporters to turn to the ballot. No one had a clue how they would do. This was not a Save Bobby Sands campaign. This was a regular election and Sinn Féin knew little of regular elections and had little practical to offer the electorate. The unionists had been shocked at the thirty thousand Catholics who voted in Fermanagh-Tyrone for a gunman and his agent, but that had been a special case, sentiment and tribal loyalty over sense. For years the British and the authorities had expressed as faith the proposition that any support for the gunmen was extorted, toleration imposed by the gun. The IRA was a small, isolated, unrepresentative, and pretentious gang of criminals. If the nationalists had a representative it was the SDLP, much too rural, much too nationalist, without the steadying urban hands of Fitt and Devlin, who in resignation had become quite proper people in British eyes: good Labour types, union men if not unionists, and certainly antirepublicans. So the SDLP was the key, if there was to be a nationalist key, in the Assembly, and the SDLP was more nationalistic then Hume.

Hume was trapped in his party's refusal to support the new effort at devolution. He and his did not believe it would work or that any small devolution isolated at Stormont would work. He placed his hopes still in a grand settlement: Dublin-London imposing a formula rather than a London formula or a Northern Ireland formula. Haughey's 1982 nationalism was not a help; FitzGerald had a better press, a sense of the possible, an inherent moderation, no political need for patriotic oratory, and a good rapport with the British. Haughey seemed more interested in asking for all than in getting nationalists something real. Still, there was going to be an Assembly and an election.

In that Assembly election the new model Sinn Féin would run. And rather than leave the field open to the hated gunmen, Hume and the executive decided that the SDLP would run candidates but not sit. This was a surprising reversal—the SDLP as abstentionist with Sinn Féin as the real opponent. Both ran on an abstentionist platform, using the election to judge popularity. By September the campaign was under way. The approaches were traditional, appeals to tribal loyalty, with the real campaign focused on the break of the inviolate blocks of vote: Would Paisley gain or the SDLP hold firm? Both the big Unionist parties favored a devolved assembly without the need to share power. The unionists now had two Unionist parties. The DUP was slightly more enthusiastic about devolution, but the Unionist vote would swing on personalities and organization, not issue. The real novelty was supplied by Sinn Féin. Many observers doubted that the Provos, running in only seven of the twelve districts, could transfer their special vote during the hunger strikes into electoral support. Adams, McGuinness, Danny Morrison, and the rest were gunmen's advocates at best, and most likely real gunmen in electoral mufti.

The result was another and most depressing surprise for the Northern Ireland Office and most especially for the SDLP. Sinn Féin received 64,191 first preference votes, 10.1 percent of the total, for five seats, to 118,891, 18.8 percent, and fourteen seats for the SDLP. The vote was read as indicative of a real and permanent Sinn Féin hold on the nationalist community. In point of fact such a vote was not unique, not unexpected, and not even at the expense of the SDLP, which had received an even smaller percentage (17.5 percent) in the 1981 district council elections. Still, there were SDLP losses, down five seats from the 1973 Assembly and three from the 1975 constitutional convention. On the other side of the divide, the DUP lost its lead position, garnering 23 percent to 29.7 percent for the OUP. In the middle the Alliance came out well with ten seats from 9.3 percent. The Sinn Féin people thus joined the same old Northern Ireland faces, Paisley and Hume and Molyneaux and Kilfedder. Craig was gone, defeated in his old stronghold, and Faulkner's Unionists had nearly faded away. Both results were expected. Everyone did much as expected except the small parties—the nationalist vote in effect went to Sinn Féin and the unionist to the two major Unionist parties. Paisley, with the lingering taint of the Third Force disaster still about him, was disappointed as well, but that was (as always) a passing phase.

When Prior's Assembly met on November 11 it was a collection of Unionists dubious of their mandate and doubtful of the utility of the exercise. They were at Stormont as much by reflex as by intent. Almost at the moment that James Kilfedder of the OUP was being elected speaker, the RUC was shooting dead three IRA men who had driven through a checkpoint near Lurgan in Armagh. On November 16 the IRA shot dead two reserve RUC constables in Markethill, Armagh, evening the score somewhat. On the same day an IRA operation in the Frontriver Park area of Belfast was received for once with satisfaction of varying degrees by nearly everyone in the province: Acting on a tip from the loyalist paramilitaries, two Provos shot and killed Lenny Murphy of the Shankill Butchers. On November 24 came the shoot-to-kill ambush in the farmyard in Lurgan that killed Michael Tighe. At least for the Northern Ireland Office, November apparently brought some good news in that the unstable minority government of Haughey collapsed on November 4 and a new Dáil election was held on November 24. FitzGerald came back as coalition Taoiseach on December 14 with 86 seats, 70 from Fine Gael and 16 from Labour, which, under its new leader, Dick Spring, agreed to go into a coalition on December 12. Fianna Fáil was down to 75, the Workers Party had 2, and there were 3 independents. This time a majority looked sound enough to last. The "good news" in Dublin was treated as largely irrelevant for the moment by the NIO far more concerned with cost of the bomb at Droppin' Well on December 6 than with the musical chairs game in Leinster House.

The dead of the Cheshire Regiment cast a pall over a year that, unlike 1981, did not end quietly but with a vicious bang. Yet and again the Northern Ireland Office felt there was reason to hope, despite a great many frayed ends. The shoot-to-kill controversy had for the moment ended the RUC's involvement in anti-insurgency. There was far more hope—and there were far greater resources in place—arising from the supergrass strategy. An informers strategy had recently had remarkable results in Italy, although for quite different reasons, and the use of informers was an age-old ploy against subversives everywhere. What the RUC hoped was to transform the technique into a major tool now that imposed reforms had disrupted the judicial conveyor belt to the Kesh. At least the end of the hunger strikes had brought a slackening of riots and confrontations and so lessened the need for plastic bullets and the police and army on the streets. December, in fact, was neither the beginning nor the end but simply when the yearly statistics of the various deadly quarrels were closed, closed on a year much like the previous. At year's end all the armed robberies and malicious fires would fade, along with the elections, the spectacular disasters, and the scandals; the exhaustion of one more troubled year would remain. Margaret Thatcher made a Christmas visit to Northern Ireland on December 23, indicating that London had not forgotten the province during 1982. But it had not been the best of years.

The Northern Secretary pushed ahead into 1983. The Assembly was at least a place to begin, in place, filled with reluctant Unionists and ever-hopeful Alliance people. But the new year brought more of the same: On January 6 two RUC men were shot dead by the IRA in Rostrevor, Down, and ten days later County Court Judge William Doyle was murdered at the door of a Catholic church in South Belfast; judges, especially Catholic judges, were as much a target as the police. Off and on, GHQ or the Army Council would add vulnerable categories: prison wardens, recruiting personnel, construction workers on army projects, judges, and businessmen. There would be several incidents and often the campaign would fade away, the judges or workers safe for the moment. Increasingly, however, targets had to be soft. The security forces were difficult to hit and especially difficult in Belfast, where the armed campaign had to compete with the new role of Sinn Féin.

It was not the persistence of the IRA campaign that frustrated Prior; the consensus at the center had long been that the IRA could be eroded, forced into a secondary role, circumscribed but not defeated. When the loyalists (or Tory politicians) called for absolute defeat, they really wanted a psychological triumph over contemporary reality, not a good body count. The real crux of the Northern Ireland problem in January 1983 was the political process, long stalled. On January 30 the SDLP annual conference reaffirmed the Assembly boycott.

What politics did exist seemed to arise from Sinn Féin's efforts to exploit their success in the Assembly election. Suddenly founded on the moral capital of the hunger strikers, the party was legal, if not quite respectable, and sounded trendy to the radicals. It was tolerable to many in the Labour party—and a group of unrepentant gunmen to many in the Northern Ireland Office and most Unionists. On February 26 Ken Livingstone of the British Labour Party flew to a two-day meeting arranged by Sinn Féin in Belfast, a meeting often in doubt because of IRA activity, and always contentious. Ken Livingstone was symbolic of the hard Left (the Loony Left for the Tories): provocative, outrageous to his enemies, shallow and intent on publicity and provocation, but still a thorn in Thatcher's side. Now he had taken up the Irish question, accepted the republican line, raised an issue better left to the Northern Ireland Office. The government in London was displeased. The Northern Ireland Office was displeased. The Irish Unionists were outraged that Red Ken would associate with Sinn Féin killers.

All three were equally annoyed with Labour's opposition in Parliament to the Prevention of Terrorism Act in its present form. No one in power wanted to have the statistics read out that indicated thousands questioned or harassed and few arrested and fewer convicted or to hear of the infringements of civil liberties. Thatcher felt Labour was simply causing trouble. With the rarest exceptions, Irish policy had been above politics—in fact, the opposition to the Assembly bill had come largely from within the Conservative Party, and the civil libertarians within Labour had proven as stern as their Conservative colleagues: Callaghan had sent in the troops, Roy Jenkins as Home Secretary had tolerated the forced-feeding of the Prices, Roy Mason had been a hawk as Northern Secretary, everyone had backed the Prevention of Terrorism Act or any other measures. All had accepted that the IRA and Sinn Féin were criminals that survived through intimidation and murder.

The sensible in the Northern Ireland Office and in London had, thus, been taken aback by the Assembly results. Too many Catholics had voted for Sinn Féin to allow the well-used argument that all IRA support was extorted. Too many Catholics had voted for Sinn Féin to ignore. Many had argued that the republicans must try alternative means to the gun—and now they had. The result had driven the SDLP into a boycott and the unionists into a rage. And here came Livingstone taking advantage, ignoring the murders of Droppin' Well, consorting with terrorists. On a grand and ethereal scale, the NIO faced the options of encouraging the Sinn Féin political venture and so alienating the Protestants or ignoring Sinn Féin politically and relying entirely on the security forces to maintain order. The security forces alone were not an attractive option. Dealing with Sinn Féin was unattractive, no less so because Labour seemed inclined to do so. On February 17 the Westminster Labour Party would decide to oppose the existing form of the Prevention of Terrorism Act, evidence that the government's unchallenged initiative was slipping. From abroad even more annoying interference came when the European Parliament's political committee inquired if Britain could use economic or political assistance in solving the Northern Ireland problem. The Conservatives in general and the government and Prime Minister in particular were outraged. The Irish Republic had already on February 1 sent the Foreign Minister, Peter Barry, to London to express to Prior doubts about the usefulness of the Assembly. No one seemed to understand that there was little that London could do—or wanted to do.

In fact, in the Republic Garret FitzGerald's government was under pressure from Haughey and Fianna Fáil to take some positive action on the Northern Ireland issue. Out of office it was easy for Fianna Fáil to seek to outflank Fine Gael on the nationalist issue, focus more closely on the needs of the Northern minority. On February 27 in Dublin, Haughey, reconfirmed in his leadership, told a Fianna Fáil audience that the British and Irish governments should organize a constitutional conference as a first step in an ultimate British withdrawal from the island. Hume and the SDLP certainly wanted an Anglo-Irish agreement, an Irish dimension to any Northern accommodation, but they had doubts about a British willingness to discuss the province in the context of withdrawal. Fine Gael considered the Haughey initiative a political ploy. In London the establishment in general and again in particular the Conservatives, accepting that any withdrawal was not in the cards, was in fact an Irish pipe dream, found confirmation of all their suspicions about Haughey and Dublin. The unionists of all flavors had renewed evidence that Haughey was the point of the lance—an unrepentant Irish nationalist.

Despite all the froth and contention, the surface turbulence was hiding a more serious approach to the Northern Ireland political stalemate increasingly advocated by Hume and so much of the SDLP. Hume, exposed to both American and European examples, well traveled, moderate in manner and approach, felt that in order to achieve effective devolved government in the province, there would have to be some sort of Irish dimension, whatever the formula. The European experience, especially—the Benelux or Nordic unions, the Common Market and European parliamentary institutions—and even American federalism, offered working examples for an ultimate accommodation. Without an Irish dimension of some sort, the SDLP would find it difficult to participate in a Northern assembly just as the Unionists had found themselves vulnerable to the loyalists during the general strike in 1974. Since the Unionists, stabilized as the Official Unionists and Paisley's DUP, were equally aware of the fate of the Sunningdale Agreement, any Irish connection could not easily count on their support. In any case the British government, doubtful about any special relationship with Dublin, even a Dublin with FitzGerald as Taoiseach, and little interested in the political needs of the SDLP, was caught between Sinn Féin and the uncompromising unionists. In London Parliament voted in favor of a new Prevention of Terrorism Act. The Conservatives seemingly had done with Ireland for the moment.

The SDLP, out of the Assembly, out of mind for Britain, out of reach of friends in Europe and America, would be soon out of business unless there was political movement. In Dublin there was a feeling on the part of the coalition government that something could be done, should be done, for SDLP and about Northern Ireland. At least if something were seen to be done, Haughey would be outflanked and the Northern Catholics reassured. Haughey, of course, felt that nothing Fine Gael could do would outflank his seizure of the nationalist issue—the opposition could always be more militant without responsibility for action. All that the coalition could do was act and any act would fall short of what Fianna Fáil would claim was needed. Hume knew that what was needed was at the very least visible movement. In January he had settled on a Council for a New Ireland. There all those democratic politicians committed to a new Ireland could discuss the options. This FitzGerald was willing to proffer, a conference open to all Irish political parties about the future: Talking about talking was becoming an Irish political institution. FitzGerald's own strategy to adjust the Irish constitution to appease the unionists had failed both North and South. There was nothing more to offer the SDLP but a conference.

For the SDLP it was a case of survival as well as shaping a vision of the future. The British had talked but not really listened, strung Hume along while attending to more serious matters. The Protestants, the majority, the Unionists had no real interest in a new Ireland, in a vision that did not offer the charms of the past. For them and all militant loyalists an Irish connection remained anathema, as for Britain it remained irrelevant. For Dublin, however, it would be the main thread of the tapestry of a new Ireland. On March 11 the government in Dublin announced the formation of an all-Ireland forum on the lines suggested by the SDLP.

For those anticipated to be the beneficiaries of any forum conclusions, the people of Northern Ireland, the majority had not only no interest in such a vision but also no intention of playing the SDLP game. Hume and the rest had boycotted the new Assembly: Let them wander in the Dublin political wilderness. On March 24, the Official Unionists, the Democratic Unionists, and Alliance rejected FitzGerald's invitation to the all-Ireland forum. Provisional Sinn Féin was obviously excluded from such a forum, and even the Workers, well on the way to becoming a conventional political party, declined to participate on March 29, so the Northern Republican Clubs would not be represented. The vast majority of the North was opposed to the Forum, so from the first the exercise was flawed. Any vision of a new Ireland would be shaped by the conventional parties of the Irish Republic in conjunction with Hume's SDLP, not by those most concerned. The avowed purpose of what became the New Ireland Forum was not, however, the major intent of Hume and FitzGerald. They saw any forum as just that, an arena to present visions, an exercise in public relations, a sign and symbol that Northern nationalist politics was in good and active hands. While the New Ireland Forum might and in time did become a fact, take on a reality for the involved, the original idea was both sound and cunning and most of all limited in scope.

That the New Ireland Forum was such an exercise seemed clear to all but those who became involved. The Unionists pointedly ignored the whole process. More to the point, the Unionist members of the Assembly sought to find agreement on some form of devolution. Unhampered by the presence of the SDLP, scorning the aspirations of the republicans, the Unionists discovered as time passed that agreement was elusive. The Unionists' aspirations could not be reassembled into a single agenda by a single assembly once the mold of the old Stormont-Orange establishment had been shattered. On May 10–11 a long, all-night session could not produce even an agreed approach on devolution. And then the focus of politics moved again. At Westminster the attention was soon focused on a United Kingdom general election that absorbed as well the politicians of Northern Ireland. Thatcher and the Conservatives sought five more years and Ireland was on the margin of their minds. There were seventeen seats at stake in Northern Ireland, mostly sure to be Unionists', but the Tories assumed they would not be needed for they all hoped to win big after the Falklands triumph. For the Unionists it was again an opportunity for the two major contenders to seek a dominant position within the province—the real elections continued to be within the two communities and so often to the advantage of the other side if the vote split properly. Thus the majority in the province had other priorities—an election, an armed struggle—and so scant interest in a talking shop in Dublin.

Sinn Féin and the IRA had their own problems, their own agenda, and as always their own vision. In fact the Provisionals found problems without viable solutions. The informers and supergrasses had played havoc with the organization. The fact that the Protestant paramilitaries suffered too, that many civil libertarians were outraged at the trials, that the confessions might not stand scrutiny for long did little to ease the panic. Many in the IRA feared that too much cover would be lost, that the secret army's secrets would be discovered. One informer frightens a great many even while revealing the names of only a few. Every informer is also an apostate, has denied the power of the faith. Nothing is more deadly within a revolutionary organization with a revealed faith than the realization that betrayal is possible, the faith not absolute. Thus, the whole Provisional movement had been put under pressure.

There was as always pressure on many fronts. In New York the leader of NORAID, Michael Flannery, was to be Grand Marshal of the Saint Patrick's Day Parade, but in response the Dublin government sent no representatives. The American-Irish political establishment was increasingly opposed to republican maneuvers and was outraged at the capture of the parade by gunmen's friends. So the quarrels and boycott by the Irish-American politicians indicated the erosion of support for the IRA that Flannery was to have symbolized. President Reagan on March 17 announced that those who supported terrorism were no friends of Ireland. And Senator Kennedy, one of the Four Horsemen, while calling for Irish unity in the Senate, had long made it clear that the IRA was anathema. Certainly in America a long, slow decline in hard-core support began after the end of the hunger strikes. The money flow slowed but never ended. The faithful stayed faithful and were at times reinforced by those from the new tide of illegal Irish immigrants, many from the North. The Irish-American community in general, however, had lost patience with the long war. There was general distaste with the brutality of the IRA, with those who seemed more akin to terrorists than freedom fighters. The emotions aroused by the hunger strike dissipated and the gunmen were left in full view.

The republicans had much the same problem in the six counties where the dirty war could be seen more clearly as brutal, where the involved lived down the road rather than merely appeared on the television news or in the lethal statistics of the deadly quarrel. Thus on April 3 the Army Council Easter Statement indicated that there would be no more punishment shootings—kneecapping—that, depending on the seriousness of the alleged offense, might wound or maim or clumsily kill the victim. This new self-restraint was only temporary but indicative of the cost of running an armed struggle. No one liked the shootings, but no one within the IRA could see how discipline could be maintained or control over certain areas ensured without resort to force. The state had jails and judges, but the IRA had to make do with threats that at times must be made good. Enormous goodwill was lost not only because of the violence of the act but also because the punishment often did not seem to fit the crime or was related to matters that were not a crime at all. As with all phases of the IRA's armed campaign, familiarity bred distaste even and especially among those most loyal.

This did not stop the killing or the horror. On May 10 a woman shielding her soldier husband was shot and killed by the Provos in Derry. The death toll showed little indication that times were improving, that the Provos lacked sufficient support, whatever happened about the Dublin forum or the Saint Patrick's Day Parade. On May 24 a one-thousand-pound bomb detonated outside the RUC station in Andersonstown, causing a million pounds of damage and indicating that after a decade the security forces were still vulnerable, that all the pressures against the Provos had not deflected their armed campaign.

The New Ireland Forum was not even intended to deflect the Provisionals, hamper the Sinn Féin political front, but rather was shaped to attract attention, to offer a future where the militant republicans might even find a place. The republicans did not want any such place nor did the Unionists nor the British. Each pursued the future with a special vision and often one difficult to articulate. Only a few people in Dublin, perhaps not even Hume, seemed to believe in the reality of a new vision, the possibility of the new. Certainly Hume and the SDLP believed that it was politically expedient, generally wise, useful, and potentially practical to discuss such a vision.

19

The Anglo-Irish Agreement, the Triumph of Politics: May 30, 1983–November 1985

Practical politics consists in ignoring the facts.
Henry Adams

Even before the grand opening of the New Ireland Forum in Dublin Castle, real politics of a sort had returned to Northern Ireland in that Thatcher, riding the crest of the Falklands war, had called for a general election on June 9, 1983. As always, the election had nothing to do with Northern Ireland, nor did Ireland have anything to do with the election. The province would simply be polled again to see how the solid blocs split: Was Sinn Féin a passing fancy, and what was the state of play for Paisley's DUP? The only recent contest, the Armagh by-election to fill the seat vacated when Mallon was disqualified by accepting a Senate seat in Dublin, gave no hint because the SDLP had boycotted it. The Workers Party candidate received 4,920 votes, and the remaining 26,907 of a poll of only 34.1 percent went to the Official Unionist Party candidate. The June Westminster election was closely fought and closely watched. Everyone was out and running, especially against their own. Fitt, now vehemently anti-Provo, ran against Adams, with an SDLP candidate as well. Owen Carron was running in the famous Fermanagh–South Tyrone constituency against both a Unionist and an SDLP candidate.

On June, however, the big winners were the OUP, which swept aside the DUP (34 percent to 20 percent, eleven seats to three, with one seat to the Ulster Populist Unionist Party, James Kilfedder's vehicle), and Provisional Sinn Féin, which took a solid 13.4 percent of the vote, in contrast to the SDLP's 17.9 percent (only down from 18.8 percent in the Assembly elections). Gerry Adams, with 16,379 votes, won Fitt's old seat in West Belfast. Fitt, as an independent, polled 10,326, and the SDLP's candidate garnered 10,934 in a three-way race. Hume won in Derry, as expected, despite Martin McGuinness's 10,607 Sinn Féin votes, and Owen Carron lost in Fermanagh–South Tyrone to Ken Maginnis with a majority of 7,676 because this time the SDLP ran a candidate who took a crucial 9,923 votes. No matter, Sinn Féin was sufficiently delighted with their percentage and Adams's victory in West Belfast not to harp on the SDLP betrayal. So Paisley was damaged, the Provisionals and the OUP were encouraged, and the SDLP stayed the same. The others, including Alliance (down to 8 percent and its leader, Oliver Napier, not elected) were almost irrelevant. In the real election across the waters Thatcher triumphed as expected and Prior stayed as Northern Secretary.

The results had seemed to mean very little for the province—almost the same faces, the same distribution of power. Gerry Fitt's London friends were disappointed by his loss: The more determined his opposition to the Provos had grown the more popular he had become in the Westminster corridors and club rooms, where he was heralded as the best type of Irish politician, sincere, decent, amusing, loving a drink, always there with the wry word. He had savaged the IRA, attacked the SDLP for lack of courage when no candidate was put forth against the hunger strikers, and ultimately would urge a vote for the Workers Party instead of any of the nationalists. In Belfast he had become anathema to many—his home was burned down in an arson attack on July 4—but not across the water. And so on July 21, 1983, Gerry Fitt, father to the Miss Fitts, former soap boy in a barbershop, former merchant seaman, and onetime republican, became Lord Fitt. It was an improbable fate, unimaginable long ago, when he had stood alone in London, a Belfast hero to many in the province and a help to more.

Fitt as a lord boggled the imagination of Northern Ireland. Times had changed. For Fitt Irish nationalism had been captured by Green Fascists, killers with an Easter lily on their lapel, and so he had ridden point against them, to the applause of those in London who understood neither the risks nor the motive. In 1983, unrepentant, he was driven off the political stage into the House of Lords by Gerry Adams. The others, the longtime players, remained, the SDLP down in Dublin at work on the Forum report and the Unionists in Stormont or Westminster intransigent as ever.

Whatever happened at Westminster or at Number 10 Downing Street, in the province what politics remained stayed focused on the Assembly, with its uncertain mandate and truncated membership. The OUP returned in February and stayed until walking out in November 1983, after the Darkley massacre, in protest over security, not returning until May 1984. The party was never enthusiastic about the 1982 Assembly bill. The DUP in particular was sincere about devolution but would not accept even the minimal requirements of Westminster. Instead the members were inclined to wander from their brief debate in a vacuum, but at least they were willing to keep the institution alive. Since the Assembly adjourned from July to November 1983, the political focus shifted south to the Forum in Dublin. There too the sense of irrelevance and artificiality was dispersed by the concerns of the moment: After all, 80 percent of Ireland was represented. Everyone was impressed with the work, noted that Northern opinion played a major part, by which they meant the SDLP representatives, "their" Northerners, and so hid from the reality that the majority in the North was unrepresented.

The Forum was composed of the chairman, twenty-one members of the three large Dáil parties, including FitzGerald, Haughey, and Dick Spring, leader of the Labour Party, and five SDLP members, including Hume, Mallon, and Austin

Currie. There was a secretariat, evidence was taken and presentations were made from all sorts of bodies. As time passed the significance of the Forum grew in the perception of the involved: so many bright people, so much material, so serious an effort, and after so long a time a real attempt to shape the nature of a new Ireland. The Taoiseach had for some years proposed various interim steps that might lead to a convergence of the two traditions. He wanted the Republic more clearly pluralistic, the constitution adjusted and the laws altered. During the election campaign in November 1982 he had suggested all-Ireland courts and an all-Ireland police force to counter terrorism. In January 1983 he had urged a tolerant, just, and compassionate society in Ireland. Persuaded by Hume that the Forum might define that society, he had talked with Thatcher in March and then in May had overseen the Forum. Haughey was less compassionate, more traditional, and yet willing to engage in the Forum debate. Thus there grew in Dublin the feeling that a new future, a new Ireland, might emerge from the investigation first accepted as no more than a sop for Hume and the SDLP.

The old Ireland in 1983 kept moving right along, innocent of the complex details of the Forum, isolated from the Unionist scuffles in the Assembly. There were no immediate elections in prospect until the one in June 1984 for the European Parliament, an election often used as a popularity contest in Northern Ireland and a means of reward in the Republic. Without elections, without visible results emerging from either the Assembly or the Forum, the remainder of the year was left to the violent and the everyday. There was a revival of the death penalty issue, a tradition among hard Conservatives who wanted to see the IRA gunmen hanged; the debate ended with a Westminster rejection with a majority of 116 on July 13, the same day the IRA killed four UDR soldiers with a land mine in County Tyrone. Increasingly it appeared that the IRA was shifting the focus out of Belfast and into the country. This was not so much policy as practicality. Belfast was difficult.

Belfast was more difficult partly because the testimony of the supergrasses, a strategy in full flower in the summer of 1983, had not been totally composed of lies, exaggerations, and rumors. On August 5, at the end of the long trial, of the thirty-eight IRA suspects implicated by Christopher Black, sentences totaling more than four thousand years were given to twenty-two guilty defendants; four defendants were released and the others received mainly suspended sentences. The authorities were delighted, particularly the RUC. In September Prior would defend the tactics, unmindful of criticism of the nature of such evidence and the tenuousness of such convictions (in 1986 eighteen of the twenty-two would have their convictions overturned by the court of appeal). In August, however, it appeared that a new, effective, largely painless means had been discovered to sweep up the subversives. More monster trials were in the works.

While the security authorities concentrated on the supergrasses and the politicians on their Assembly and Forum, the Provisionals went their own way. Once again operations in the Republic complicated their supposed safe haven and added a sense of urgency to the Forum talks. Although IRA policy, as embodied in the famous Army Order 8, was not to pursue military operations within the twenty-six counties, increasingly this had been adjusted to need and opportunity:

The assassinations of Ewart-Biggs and Mountbatten had been against British forces.

This was not true as far as the steady, often hardly noted, series of armed robberies that helped the perpetually empty treasury. GHQ only wanted significant expropriation—each one alienated the state, regardless of size, so why do so too often or to too little purpose? Certain local units, however, became engaged over the years in small-time robberies of post offices and stores that made West Limerick or the border the site of criminal subversion. The Gárdaí had trouble with those crimes because a large movement with good intelligence, even when using rather limited volunteers, has a far better chance of success than everyday criminals.

One result was that by 1983 the Irish police and army considered the IRA the number-one enemy and so they increased their cooperation with the Northern Ireland authorities and reduced their toleration for the gunmen in the South. This was particularly true when spectacular operations were undertaken, such as kidnapping for large ransom. In November 1981 Ben Dunne, heir to the largest chain of department stores in Ireland, had been kidnapped at Killeen, just outside Newry in Northern Ireland, held for six days, and released, although the family denied paying a huge ransom. In August 1983 a five-man gang tried to kidnap the wealthy Canadian businessman Galen Weston, whose Adams Foods controlled the Quinnsworth supermarket chain. The attempt collapsed and the five were arrested. At Weston's home outside Dublin the gang had walked into an antiterror squad police trap. Later in the year the long kidnap saga of Don Tidey, an English employee of Weston, ended with his rescue unharmed on December 16, the arrest of two of the involved, but the escape of four and, most important, the death of a soldier and policeman in a shoot-out. This was a deadly high spot of the spreading blot of crime linked, if not to the IRA, often to those involved in the Troubles.

It was not always clear who was responsible for some of the crimes, everyday criminals, rogue IRA units, or authorized volunteers. Everyone immediately speculated that when the race horse Shergar was stolen, the IRA must be involved. Shergar was never found and the IRA denied involvement. What concerned the authorities was that as times changed, crime, especially political crime, grew violent in the Republic. The IRA people would shoot in order to escape, had shot and killed. The result was an embittered Gárdaí and army with no sympathy for the gunmen, and an outraged government determined to end such threats to the law. Some indication of the anger could be found in the gradual progress toward extradition. The problem had been eased with legislation that allowed trial in the Republic for crimes committed in the United Kingdom, thereby removing the pressing need to hand over IRA people to the British authorities. From time to time the Dublin government had done so since the days of de Valera: Escape from a Northern prison might lead to a swift one-way ticket back. The British, of course, wanted formal extradition, a procedure agreed to by most members of the European Community, as an outward sign of Dublin's cooperation in the war on Irish terror. In a sense Dublin had simply been waiting for an appropriately unpleasant case to use as an example.

In January 1982 Dominic McGlinchey, the INLA man, had been arrested on a warrant seeking extradition to Northern Ireland for a particularly unsavory murder. In March 1977 Mrs. Hester McMullan, sixty-seven, was shot and killed by gunmen who also attacked and wounded her RUCR son at Toome Bridge, County Antrim. In December 1982 McGlinchey's plea of political exception was denied by Irish Chief Justice Tom O'Higgins, an exception made obsolete since terrorist violence had no political content. The McGlinchey case did not end either his career or the extradition issue but indicated the direction of events. McGlinchey had a run as chief of staff of the INLA, was extradited at last on October 11, 1985, but with a legally faulty prosecution he had to be released in Northern Ireland and returned for trial to the Republic: extradition to the extraditer—only in Ireland. He ended up in Portlaoise Prison.

On July 31, 1984, Séamus Shannon, who was accused of murdering the former Speaker of Stormont, Sir Norman Stronge, and his son, James Stronge, was extradited. Tides were shifting, if slowly. The old national assumptions were no longer valid in contemporary Ireland. And the old nationalist support of the IRA suffered a steady decline. All indicators of popular support declined as a result of criminal violence in the Republic, the intrusions by Northern paramilitaries, and the IRA atrocities in Northern Ireland and England. The constant din of the Troubles shamed the nation.

In September the IRA had at least one clear triumph with a minimum of horror in what became known as the Great Escape. On September 25 thirty-eight prisoners broke out of the Maze Prison and nineteen stayed out. It was the largest and most successful prison escape in British history. One guard, James Ferris, was stabbed and killed. Two key men, Larry Marley and Bobby Storey, did not get away, but some of the famous did, like Bic McFarlane, O/C during the hunger strikes, and Gerry Kelly, who had helped plant the first London bombs in 1973 and had made several escape attempts since then. Both would finally be arrested years later in Holland after involvement in various continental operations. The size of the breakout and the success of the nineteen who stayed out, hiding in the North for days before dribbling south to stay on the run and in the IRA, overshadowed the one death. The Great Escape had all the necessary ingredients—daring, good luck and bad, notorious IRA men freed and others recaptured—to attract maximum publicity and considerable sympathy.

It also had an unanticipated impact on the IRA. The men chosen to escape had generally been the best lost in recent years, eager to continue, capable of aiding the struggle. Given the security pressures in the Republic all had to go on the run, and maintaining badly wanted men is an expensive affair, not so costly in money as in time and planning and the use of resources. On the other hand, the IRA suddenly had an injection of trained talent to revitalize the entire organization. The escapees did not run and hide but ran and worked twenty-four hours a day. They could not go home again. The IRA became their world just as much as the Kesh had been. There was a grim attrition rate. Not only were McFarlane and Kelly caught in Holland smuggling arms, but three were killed by the SAS and others were arrested in Ireland and Scotland. After five years eight of the original nineteen had never been caught; one got bail on escape charges; one got rehabilitation parole; the three were killed; and the rest were arrested.* Those who had lasted the course within the IRA on the run, truly full-time, had made a real difference in refining and polishing an underground organization that barely resembled the untrained, enthusiastic volunteers of Mac Stiofáin. The new model IRA was shaped for a long war.

The armed campaign, if not as spectacular as the Great Escape, was a constant amid the elections and debates. The 1983 statistics of violence indicated the slackening of the pace: Total deaths were down to 77 from 97; British army losses were only 5, the lowest since the first death in 1971; the UDR was up a bit, from 7 to 10, while the RUC, the cutting edge of Ulsterization, lost 9 killed, up from 1, and the RUCR lost 9, up from 4. The only remaining spectaculars for the gunmen came in November, when a bomb in the Ulster Polytechnic in Jordanstown, County Antrim, killed an RUC inspector and a sergeant and wounded thirty-three others. The Darkley murders on November 21 overshadowed the year, as had the bomb at Droppin' Well the previous year. Thus, the murder of the OUP Assembly member Edgar Graham by the IRA at Queen's University Belfast seemed almost conventional, one more dreadful death, condemned by all proper people, a victim like all the others, soon forgotten except by those close to him. As an RUC widow had said about the hunger strikers, "After they die, they will be forgotten, just as those policemen and soldiers who died are forgotten after a while, except by those who loved them."

On March 14, 1984, Gerry Adams and three other Sinn Féin leaders were shot and wounded by the UFF as they drove back to the Falls Road after a court appearance. For the loyalists all Sinn Féin people were targets, the more famous the better—and Adams was the most famous.† In a sense there were no innocent people in Northern Ireland. In some killer's eyes no one was innocent. On May 17, 1984, the Northern editor of *Sunday World*, Jim Campbell, was shot and seriously wounded by the UVF in his North Belfast home. Someone did not like what he wrote. Some victims neither wrote nor spoke but simply drank in the wrong pub or walked up the wrong street. The more fearful of all were those not chosen as individuals but as representatives of *them* gathered in some symbolic arena. Everyone in the province and everyone in England thus became one of *them* for someone. On December 17 an IRA car bomb exploded outside Harrods in

---

*In June 1992 in the United States two more, Kevin Barry Artt and James Joseph Smith, were taken into custody on passport offenses in California. Cf. Jim Cusack security correspondent of the *Irish Times*, June 8, 1992. The six still free are assumed to be living under cover, perhaps outside Ireland, probably in the United States.

†In 1992 revelations about British army involvement with the loyalist paramilitaries indicated that the information that made possible attacks on Adams and others had been given to the gunmen as a matter of anti-insurgency tactics. On the other hand, during the trial of Brian Nelson, a former UDA intelligence officer and British army agent, his handler, a senior British intelligence officer identified as Colonel J., under questioning reduced his estimate of the numbers of lives saved by Nelson from up to two hundred to two examples—and one of these was Gerry Adams. Of course, Adams has remained on every loyalist hit list for nearly a generation and so takes great care even within his home territory, making any leaked information especially valuable—in one case the fact that the revelation that the roof of his automobile lacked armor coupled with his presence at a Belfast court made access and vulnerability available to loyalist paramilitaries.

Knightsbridge, killing five people, including an American, and injuring eighty others, a dreadful and deadly Christmas present.

Once again the Army Council had authorized English operations without firm rein on the targets and without great remorse when the bomb detonated. In Ireland, and mostly in England, the IRA killed civilians by error, through callous incompetence, by outrageous, unforgivable neglect, but not by intent: Informers, builders on security sites, judges and passengers in police cars were not really civilians. In England, however, the volunteers were less discriminating, thus making it increasingly difficult for the movement to deny the terrorist label. After all, terror was a well-used recourse—why else shoot men in the knee, kidnap informers' wives, or bomb pubs used by paramilitaries? Those sent were often feckless in operation and feckless in evasion, leaving behind fingerprints, maps, and lists, and attracting attention; and yet, despite their blunders, they persisted. The police might delight in the "Paddy Factor" but each new wave of IRA English operations took a toll, stretched the authorities, outraged opinion.

As always, of course, the IRA pointed out that the British had carpet bombed Germany in World War II as a patriotic duty and without compunction, so why were the little devices of the IRA so evil? Yet evil they seemed, certainly to the British and increasingly to many with no stake in the island. A dirty war fought before television cameras has an awesome intensity that was not the case when cafés burst apart in bomb blasts in Algiers or bodies floated down the Seine. This was not the same as the maiming in far-off Aden or Malaya, not when the ruins of horses and people came into the house on BBC while the cordite still hung in the air. So the names of the victims might soon be lost in the shuffle, but the cumulative effect eroded any sympathy for the republicans or the Irish. If the IRA had sought to nauseate the English so that they would withdraw from the sickening Irish, then indiscriminate bombing might have a rationale. This did not seem to be the case. Very little strategic planning occurred at the meetings of the Army Council. The pressure of the armed struggle must be kept up; the English must not be allowed to ignore just grievances; new targets, vulnerable targets, visible and impressive English targets must be found. And so a few men reassured by their faith bombed Harrods.

With Darkley and Harrods the year came to an end. Margaret Thatcher even flew over on Christmas for a six-hour tour, met with shoppers in Newtownards, Down, and talked to the army and police in Armagh and Tyrone. Three weeks later Cardinal O Fiaich called her visit to the carefully chosen UDR base in Armagh "disgusting" because several of the UDR men there had been accused of murdering Catholics. The UDR had become a Protestant militia with only a tiny Catholic representation, more professional in outlook and training, far more so than the old B Specials, but still Protestant, still integrated into the loyalist community. The Catholics did not trust the regiment—one slur, one rumor that a UDR man was turning over intelligence to the UDA killers, one taste of bigotry, and all the old fears were justifiably awakened. And from time to time there was actually evidence that UDR members were involved in paramilitary activities, did help out the UVF or UDA, did harass Catholics because they were Catholics. What was remarkable (from a distance) was that the UDR had grown into a far more professional force than its Protestant nature would have indicated;

the military training and supervision, the presence of British officers, and the indoctrination had not made the officers and soldiers disinterested but rather restrained. The UDR was a sectarian force, like the police, and would always be; but by 1984 the regiment was also highly professional, deeply committed to the defense of order and so their community, fully opposed to the IRA, often justifiably suspicious of the nationalist community (i.e., local Catholics). There were always incidents, as critics like O Fiaich were apt to point out, that did not always result in the retribution that the minority demanded. The authorities were loath to punish their own for an excess of zeal. A Private Ian Thain went back to his regiment after twenty-seven months in prison as a result of his conviction for murder. There were later awards for those who directed troops on Bloody Sunday. No politician in London wanted to consider that their army was involved in dirty tricks. No unionist would admit that the UDR was anything but an instrument of justice. On June 5, 1984, Lord Gibson, while acquitting three RUC men as "absolutely blameless," publicly praised them for shooting to kill and asked that "the finding should be put in their record along with my own commendation for their courage and determination in bringing the three deceased men to justice, in this case to the final courts of justice." This was British justice and all the instruments of the system were faulty, none more so than the almost entirely Protestant UDR, successor to the B Specials. In any case the UDR as grievance was once more noted because Thatcher had made a special appearance—a symbolic touch not lost on any of the involved. *All* of the elements of British authority were to be supported.

In Dublin the government announced that it could not agree with Cardinal O Fiaich's statement. The Irish government was eager for the anticipated Forum report to arrive in a benign climate. On March 15, 1984 Taoiseach FitzGerald explained the Forum to a joint session of the United States Congress. American support would, of course, be welcomed, an aspect of moving an accommodation out of the bog of provincial politics. In those provincial politics the Northern Ireland Assembly limped along, one eye on ancient quarrels and the other on the Forum. There was no real change in attitudes and no flexibility; the new was adjusted for the old convictions. On January 6 a group of DUP Assembly members returned from a visit to Israel and suggested that the border with the Irish Republic be sealed with a wire fence and protected by electronic surveillance equipment, their lesson of the day from the Holy Land. But despite two periods of OUP boycott, once at the beginning and then for six months after the Darkley massacre, the committees were functioning, the debates were lively if traditional, and Prior's hopes could flicker along.

The Forum Report was finally released in Dublin on May 2. Hume called it "an extraordinary day in the history of our island." The debate on the future could move, as FitzGerald and Hume had planned, onto a new plateau. There had been twenty-eight private sessions, thirteen public sessions, and fifty-six meetings of the steering group of the party leaders and the chairman. There had been over three hundred submissions and oral presentations from thirty-one individuals. The report rested on a year of hard work, investigation, staff studies, and rising enthusiasm.

Essentially it explored the possibilities for a desirable future Ireland. The present had become the problem and that problem rested on a divided island containing a divided society. The problem was no longer assumed by Dublin nationalists to be imposed by British interests and nourished by British power. Times had changed and the problem was indigenous. The solutions, however, remained constant. The New Ireland would arise from an internal accommodation to a selection of national possibilities. It was a blueprint of a framework. There should be, most important of all, the principle of free consent. Both traditions, Catholic and Protestant, should be recognized, and everyone's religious and civil rights should be protected. There should be security structures with which both Unionists and nationalists could identify. The key was the form. There was the most desirable option, the one Haughey and the Greener nationalists pushed as proper, although no general agreement had been found. This was a unitary state. Two other forms were also proposed as options, a complex federal-confederal state and a system of joint authority. There was enormous satisfaction in Dublin.

The original suggestion had been made by John Hume, a capable, experienced, and moderate politician with extensive Irish and international contacts, the very best of Irish politicians in establishment terms. He was sophisticated, articulate without charisma, and cautious to a fault. There could have been no better advocate for an Irish Forum. It was not unreasonable to assume that such a confluence of concerned opinion could perform a variety of more general tasks as well as delineating a new Ireland that might emerge in any future accommodation. It could keep Northern Ireland politics alive in nationalist terms while isolating Sinn Féin. There would be an impression, perhaps even the reality, that movement on the issue existed. Something political was being done. The field was not being left to the gunmen of any persuasion. The very act of discussion was policy. And such discussion would as a second facet engender the basis for future action. If a goal, albeit an ideal, was shaped, then the road forward would be more apparent. And the very shaping of such a goal would present the involved an opportunity to display their skills, skills that would contrast with the more primitive responses of the fundamentalists or the republican recourse to violence and the unconventional that had displaced political discourse. The Irish parties would be attracted, and involved; and those responsible in London, prone to nodding off except during the aftermath of disaster, would have to take note.

With the Forum in action, London, Northern Ireland, and the Irish in general could see a seriousness of purpose and a competence displayed by those edged from the stage by the hunger strikers. And what could be lost? Nothing else was happening—and nothing was dangerous, dangerous to the stability of all political systems, dangerous for those denied an opportunity to act on events. It had seemed a reasonable time to take stock to advantage.

There was now a generation no longer responsible for the old postures and presumptions increasingly isolated from Northern reality. De Valera's generation was gone, his presidential term ended in 1973. Erskine Childers, son of his martyred republican colleague, had been elected in May 1973, and de Valera retired to private life. He would die at the age of ninety-two on August 29, 1975, at the Linden Convalescent Home, Blackrock, Dublin, a monument to ages past. The new men were half his age, cut off from the old quarrels by death and time.

Once, de Valera had been handcuffed to Desmond FitzGerald; he did not know FitzGerald's son, whom he first met only in 1973. All the Irish were intimately tied to the Republic's immediate past, a past in one way or another shared by all, the political families and the new men; but the ties had frayed.

Liam Cosgrave's father, William T. Cosgrave, once the president of the Executive Councel of the Irish Free State, had died in 1965. Garret FitzGerald's father, Desmond, the first Foreign Minister in the glory days and in Cosgrave's cabinet as well, was dead even earlier, in April 1947. Charles Haughey's father-in-law, Seán Lemass, at the GPO in 1916, was dead; his only son, Noel, had died in 1976 at forty-seven. Most of the old IRA were dead, if not their legacy. Many of the new men did not have famous fathers, had risen on their own. Hume was such a new man, a replacement for the old Nationalist Eddie McAteer but no radical. There were few political radicals in the Republic in any case and despite the bitterness of past quarrels there was a general consensus on many issues. Nearly everyone wanted a united Ireland but not at any great cost. Even, then, the reality of union was beginning to grate: The ungrateful nationalists, the republican gunmen, the Protestant fundamentalists, the Northerners all did not appear worth the trouble.

So a real and in time enormous gap began to open between what was theoretically desirable—a dream based on nostalgia, wishful thinking, illusion, and patriotic history—and what was practical. There were still strong nationalist feelings about the "presence" of Britain on the island, the existence of "the border," the charm of one Ireland, but these resentments and aspirations lacked the intensity of the old quarrels. No one but subversives would kill for them. Once this had not been the case and the result was decades of bitter and unforgiving quarrels. For years Irish politics had been about the national issue, and in quite different terms than in 1983.

Foreign observers were often baffled by a political system that still divided on a vote taken in 1921 on the Anglo-Irish Treaty, a system that had absorbed none of the more fashionable ideologies or adjusted to the winds of political change that elsewhere blew. The new Ireland still seemed filled with old men and old quarrels, but this was in part illusion. The old quarrels had not been resolved but the advocates were dying away. The old quarrels were based, not as had been assumed, on the verities of history but on poorly crafted illusions and assumptions, often on well-meant lies. The true course of Irish history, the plain tale of events over which the parties clashed and clattered, had been thrown up as base for a new state, a new nation needing legitimacy. The divisions were relevant for the old days, fifty years before, but had become dated, attenuated in substance, irrelevant in interpretation. The world and Ireland had not stopped in 1916.

There were those who, as they came to power, sought new positions, if not at the expense of the old. All those of what FitzGerald called the New Ireland could more easily examine the future with less luggage to tote from the past. The verities of the past had, indeed, been raw, the stuff of political church gate speeches. The fault lay not in Ireland but in the English. For eight hundred years justice had been denied to the Celtic nation and after 1916 and all of that, only the last step remained for London to accept geography as reality. It had been sold so often and bought so easily that the nature of the North had remained quite alien and irrelevant to Southern patriotism. This simple text had to be adjusted, was being adjusted, to include the reality of a divided society in the North as well as the nation. And so the Irish electorate, if more slowly, was changing, too, and would not punish innovation. Much could be questioned, adjusted, discarded. So the time and the personnel were right and ripe.

The time was particularly ripe because the crisis had come to the Republic not as alien bombs exploded as special operations or sectarian vengeance, border intrusions ignored, spectacular terror on the television, but as tremors within the electorate, within the nation. The hunger strikes had raised old emotions and presented unpleasant possibilities. The H-Block people had received real votes rarely given by those who husbanded theirs to ensure an agent in the Dublin power center. While the loss of the Dáil seats to the H-Block independents had only a temporary if real impact on the course of politics in the Republic, the implications were serious. A return of the national issue with the orthodox politicians and parties idle except in repressing the radical republicans was not a cheerful prospect. The fact that the Provos had not yet capitalized on the start made during the H-Block campaigns did not mean that they would not or could not. No one really knew how strong the old loyalties might be. In any case it was unwise simply to ignore the matter, although this was nearly everyone's first choice. The national issue had to be not defused but addressed.

The Northern problem had, as far as possible, been ignored after 1971 and before 1981, except in matters of internal security. Unable to act upon events, increasingly ill-disposed to all but a few of the Northern minority, innocent by choice of the complexities of the province, the Southern politicians preferred to think on other matters. No one could say so but that was another country, and if not far away, more the pity. The old, unquestioned positions and old animosities might remain, but they were quite isolated from a reality not well understood. From time to time there was a flurry related to the threat of the Provos or to the horror of the moment, but in general the South was isolated from the Northern Ireland game. Dublin had been as satisfied with the Council of Ireland as its advocates, an outward sign of hidden isolation and ineffectuality. No more had been needed. More had been asked from time to time, and everything—a united Ireland—was still on the never-never agenda, enshrined in the Constitution and patriotic oratory, to be found in many hearts, and for most a matter for another generation. Little, however, had been expected because little could be secured except as gift. Dublin's writ did not run in the province, Dublin had no veto and increasingly limited influence even among its "own," and most of all Dublin was isolated from the game. Visible impotence in politics is deadly and Dublin was impotent. To pretend would be foolish, to intervene would be futile. And although partially hidden, the alarms and excursions of the hunger strike crisis had revealed the Dublin establishment as foolish and futile and most of all impotent.

The government's seeming impotence was perceived, rightly, as a danger to the long unchallenged stability of the nation. Dublin must at least seem to be involved, active, effective—not because of a general need for those in responsibility to be a defender of the national faith and those in the North but because such an image was necessary to be perceived as viable at home in the twenty-six counties. The government, the establishment, isolated, impotent, irrelevant, had to appear virile, a player acting on events.

The involved took to Hume's proposal because it would permit a play within the play. The Irish actors could fashion with skill and craft an agenda for a New Ireland, the options and the adjustments, and in so doing set the pace of the crisis (or appear to do so) for those who mattered, the Irish, the nation. The New Ireland Forum was not a swindle, not *simply* an exercise in public relations, not indoor relief for politicians and bureaucrats, but a real effort to reenter the game by manufacturing playing chips with the only available materials: words, ideas, and images. The problem came when such images were taken as real. The results thus reflected the perceptions of the political establishment and indicated, not to the involved but to the alien eye, just how isolated from Northern Ireland the Republic's establishment had become. The Southern Irish did, now, recognize there was an Irish as well as an Anglo-Irish problem, but the desired solutions were the same. Those involved did not consider their options as wishful thinking because there was no one to contradict them in Dublin; they did not note the reality of unionism on the island and failed to understand at all the workings of the London establishment. If cynicism be excluded, it was evidence only of continuing innocence. London was not the only place that had chosen peace and quiet over serious analysis and old emotions over recourse to reality in Northern Ireland matters. The Forum report was thus based on the seemingly undeniable reality as perceived by the Dublin establishment moderated by Hume and the SDLP.

Those who did deny it had not been consulted or seriously considered: the unrepresented Northerners and the British establishment, especially the Conservatives. One by one the Unionist parties produced a rejection of the Forum and then a proposal for a future unrelated to Dublin aspirations: The OUP had already produced *The Way Forward* in April and then came the DUP's *The Unionist Case: The Forum Report Answered*; there was to be an Alliance party paper on devolution on June 25. None favored any of the Forum options.

Somehow the Irish nationalists, despite "understanding" their fellow Irish people way up there, felt such opposition only a matter of historic truculence. As Séamus Heaney, quoted on September 13, in the *Irish Times,* indicated, they were after all Irish—and what else mattered?

> Culturally and psychologically, they have to be constantly welcomed on the land. Their collective political machine must, I think, be rebuked and broken if possible. As a power group, they have never collectively yielded a damn thing and they have to learn to be a bit better-mannered towards their Catholic neighbors. But I think that anything that excludes them from being Irish, anything that makes them feel unwanted, is not called for. The writers should welcome them and the politicians should punish them.

So there it was in the plain, poets being more open than politicians: The Unionists needed to mind their manners, shape up their act, and then they could come down and be real Irish, like us. This is exactly what all the Unionists assumed the Forum options indicated, what the Republican establishment intended given a chance, the very reason for renewed dedication to Unionist principles. And their attitude attempted to make this clear to the blindly optimistic carrying Forum banners.

Despite this, there was a feeling that a new chapter had begun. This was particularly true because Taoiseach FitzGerald hoped to persuade Thatcher of the wisdom of moving toward a new Ireland. On March 15, during the annual Irish pilgrimage to the American celebrations of Saint Patrick's Day, he had used his speech before the United States Congress to urge American politicians to call for British acceptance of the Forum proposals. Bringing in the New World to counterbalance the British, Hume's dream, was not that easy. Haughey had made his possession of the national issue clear in that only a unitary state was acceptable.

On May 25 in Washington, both the Senate and House voted unanimously to back the Forum report. Such votes would have little currency in London, where the Prime Minister had a very special relationship with her fellow conservative in the Oval Office. The administration and Reagan himself cherished the special relationship with Thatcher, seen as a new conservative too, and so when Reagan made his four-day visit to Ireland in June, he told the Dáil and Seanad in Leinster House that he opposed violence and that, though he admired the Forum report, current American policy was not to interfere in Irish matters.

Even more problematical was the unrequested support of Labour's leader, Neil Kinnock, for the Forum report and Irish unity by consent. There was a fear in Dublin that whatever Kinnock favored Thatcher might oppose. And it was to Thatcher that FitzGerald would have to take his case, a Thatcher triumphant in the Falklands war that Ireland had not supported, assured of tenure with the sweep in the previous year's June elections. She was a unionist at heart, and, ignorant of most Irish matters, appalled by the "nationalist" violence set loose within her United Kingdom, within a province not different from her Finchley constituency.

There was in fact no great surge of interest in the Forum report except among the involved. In the North the European Parliament elections to be held on June 14 captured most political interest. Such an election was for the province a great popularity contest watched for hints of shift. This time Paisley recouped previous losses, leading the poll with 230,251, 33.6 percent, a personal triumph, the voters using his name as banner for No Surrender. Hume, the Catholic candidate, came next with 151,399, 22.1 percent, a good show but, as expected, not up to Paisley. Then the orthodox Unionists gave Taylor 147.169, 21.5 percent, like Hume a good show but not what had been hoped for after the success of the Westminster elections the previous year. Danny Morrison did not move Sinn Féin to new heights but did take 91,476 first-preference votes, 13.3 percent, indicating that the republicans were in for the long haul, not an occasional protest; but very few votes shifted to Morrison on the subsequent counts, indicating a polarized minority community. Alliance faded to 5 percent and the others—the independent Kilfedder, the Workers, and an ecology candidate—trailed along behind, irrelevant to the results. And the results seemed to indicate little change. In the Republic there was a low turnout and a split result: Fianna Fáil, eight, Fine Gael, six, and one independent. Then it was summer without the Forum for news.

683

Northern Secretary Prior made it clear on July 2 at Westminster that the British government rejected the proposals of the New Ireland Forum report. There was no surprising support from Northern Ireland—Gerry Adams and Sinn Féin felt the suggestions no more than a bag of dolly mixture candy produced to comfort corrupt politicians. Dublin was a preserve of unprincipled careerists seeking ministerial Mercedeses. On July 12, the Glorious Twelfth celebrating the Battle of the Boyne, Orange Order resolutions condemned the Forum report. It seemed fitting that Boyne had also been in the news four days before, when fifty thousand people had assembled at Slane Castle to hear a Bob Dylan concert and one man fell into the Boyne and drowned. If anything was blowing in the wind for the Forum it was not visible—the flag hung limp. Not much was to happen in the summer but the inevitable twists and turns of violence and confrontation that made up the Northern Ireland news. This news was increasingly filtered through ennui in the Republic, where detailed coverage was no longer as good, where the restrictions of Article 31 of the Broadcasting Act on allowing Provo subversives to appear in any form on television hampered investigation, and where editors and producers yearned for positive news. The Republic had grown tired of the Troubles.

And there were always new troubles. The Northern Ireland Office had banned the expected appearance of Martin Galvin, an articulate and charismatic American leader of NORAID who was scheduled to appear in the province. Banning an American who had done nothing and was under no indictment from the United Kingdom was a blunder. Sending the RUC out to arrest him at the site of his anticipated speech in Belfast after his surprise Derry appearance on August 9 was a second blunder. It was a most unpopular order as far as the police were concerned: It almost guaranteed a riot on camera. Not only did the cameras tape the riot but also the police provided a killing, live, in color, close up, personal, as a constable shot and killed Seán Downes of Andersonstown on August 12. Prior admitted that a "bad mistake" had been made, the RUC was again damned as brutal and sectarian. The outraged protested in parades, the mobs appeared, the violence spread, stones were thrown, rioters appeared as on cue, snipers appeared on Shankill Road, and the tape of Downes's death played on and on, over and over. A bad summer, indeed, with the revelations of "grave irregularities," concerning the RUC's shoot-to-kill cover-ups surfacing at the same time. Prior at least was out of it, replaced on September 10 by Douglas Hurd.

Thatcher and FitzGerald had met the week before, on September 3, for a brief exchange to schedule a formal summit on November 19. There the full attractions of the Forum could be unfolded and a beginning made. Prior, who had discarded the three options, was gone, if not Thatcher and the government; the Orangemen were back in their Masonic halls, representing only the past; Sinn Féin, representing despair and gunmen, should play no part in a new Ireland; and so the Unionists would have to come around. Dublin wanted them to come around, to agree to participate, to recognize that their rights and concerns were addressed and protected. None of this came up in London. It was merely a preparatory meeting, little more than a photo opportunity between the Prime Minister and her preferred Irishman. FitzGerald was thought far more acceptable than Haughey, who by then trailed a cloud of sins and failings in London eyes.

In November FitzGerald could make his case for the Forum. Thatcher might listen, an activity she tended to find painful, to Irish matters, a subject she tended to find dreary. Still, the Forum option lived and would go on the road in November. The events of the autumn, once more spectacular, tended to increase the need for action. The shoot-to-kill issue, coupled with the revelations of the supergrass trials, kept a variety of security issues on the boil. Then, on September 29, the Irish police seized seven tons of arms on the *Marita Ann* fishing boat off the coast of West Kerry. The shipment had started off from Boston in the American *Valhalla* and then been transferred to the Irish boat at sea. It was a coup for the American authorities, close to the arrangements, which were carried out largely by a tiny independent group in Boston, and for the Irish, who scooped their end of the transfer with ease.* Any reduction in IRA potential and capacity was welcome. And for some years the quartermaster general had too often come up dry on forays on the Continent and to America. Libya was still shut, or at least the IRA was not trying there, satisfied for the time being with the funds coming in from Tripoli. The Palestinians preferred the recognition of the Irish Republic to IRA solidarity and nothing else was on the horizon. Yet, even the loss of the arms returned publicity and public concern. Thus, despite the return of politics made possible by the Forum, despite the falling indicators of violence in the province, once again the IRA caused trouble and display. However far away the six counties might be from Westminster, the Carlton Club, and Whitehall, they were much too close to Dublin for the Irish government, spilling over in perception and all too often in reality.

One of the IRA's most spectacular moments did not so much interrupt the slow pace of Anglo-Irish negotiations over the Forum as it concentrated British minds. And only the British could make a move. The other players could only refuse to play. Unexpectedly, the IRA was able to indicate the penalty for delay and the potential costs of an Irish problem without promise of solution, without even prospect of serious negotiation.

The events that accelerated history occurred very early on Friday, October 12, when an IRA bomb detonated in the bath of Room 629 of the Grand Hotel in Brighton during the Conservative Party's annual conference. The explosion had a devastating effect, putting at risk the entire British government. The IRA, since the hunger strikes, had intelligence officers in Britain checking the Prime Minister's security. All British security had been tightened after the Neave assassination and presented the IRA with a classic dilemma: When the target's location was known, there was no access; when there was access, there was no target. Even a suicidal assassin would have difficulties. The solution came when the IRA realized that the QMG possessed a bomb that could operate with a long lead time. This advantage had been used to lengthen escape time and even to place a small symbolic device in the garden near the Queen's route on the Belfast visit. If a window of opportunity could be found, as had been the case with the garden, for access to an area that the Prime Minister would later use, then the problem was minor. The bomb could be detonated by a timer set, not hours in advance, but

---

*Cf. John Loftus and Emily McIntyre, *Valhalla's Wake: The IRA, MI6 and the Assassination of a Young American* (New York: Atlantic Monthly Press, 1989).

weeks or even months. Making use at first of television timers and gradually more sophisticated electronics, the IRA bombers could by 1982 plant bombs with a specific detonation date even years in the future. The chance that the device would not work increased slightly over time, but if properly set and undisturbed the chances were tolerably small.

The IRA intelligence officer in Britain knew that in 1982 Thatcher had attended the Conservative Party conference in Brighton, where it was easy to mingle but not so easy to hit the prime target. The next year the show moved to Blackpool, and then back to Brighton in 1984. The IRA I/O thus knew that Prime Minister Thatcher, barring an unexpected election upset, would be in Brighton and would stay at the Grand Hotel. He even had her room number from the previous Brighton meeting. Two IRA people checked out Blackpool in 1983 but nothing was done. Brighton had advantages. All that was needed was to rent an appropriate room, remove a bit of the wall, and then place the bomb, set the timer, and plaster over the cache. After that the bomb would detonate as scheduled.

On September 15, 1984, Patrick Magee checked into the hotel. He had been born in Belfast, raised in Norwich, East Anglia, and, after a record of petty crimes, had returned to Belfast and Unity Flats in 1971. He was soon in the IRA and then in custody until November 1975. In 1978 Magee had been assigned to England and with Gerard Tuite had planted some eighteen bombs in five cities. The Brighton bomb would be his most ambitious. As Roy Walsh (a memorial, the name of one of the IRA team that had bombed the Old Bailey in 1974) he checked into the Grand Hotel for three nights with half board. It was £180 investment. He had requested a sea view, anticipating being given a room higher in the hotel which would attract less security interest and might be closer to Thatcher, who would not want to be on a lower floor if the disgruntled miners out on strike tried to occupy the premises. He secreted twenty or thirty pounds of commercial explosives, heavily wrapped in plastic to hide the odor, behind a panel in the bathroom wall. He attached the timer, which would make the connection at 2:54 A.M. on Friday, October 12.

If the luck of the IRA had held, the Grand Hotel would have collapsed upon the entire British government; as it was the impact was enormous. The bomb detonated on schedule in Room 629 just as the occupant of Room 628, Mrs. Jeanne Shattock, the wife of the chairman of the Western Area Conservatives, was running a late bath. She was killed instantly. The couple in 629 were mangled; Donald MacLean, a senior figure in the Scottish Conservative Party, survived, but his wife, Muriel, did not. The blast also broke the central chimney stack, collapsing it into twenty-eight rooms below, and the hotel shuddered.

The main structure held but the damage was extensive. Much of the hotel crumbled, bringing many of the guests with it, including leading Tory politicians. The Prime Minister narrowly escaped harm but four people were killed that day: Sir Anthony Berry, fifty-nine, MP for Enfield and Southgate; Eric Taylor, fifty-four, chairman of the North-West Area Conservatives; Roberta Wakeham, forty-five, wife of the Government Chief Whip; and Jeanne Shattock. Muriel MacLean died in a hospital on November 1, and a sixth victim, Mrs. Gail Scanlon, a leading Conservative Party member, died at thirty-eight in 1985, a year after the bombing, crippled by a back injury sustained at the time. Among the thirty-two injured were Norman Tebbit, Secretary of State for Trade and Industry, and his wife, Margaret. The dreadful reality of the bomb was underlined for the average news viewers because the rescue teams of police and firemen used the television crews' lights to dig into the heaped ruins of the hotel and extract the victims. It was very close, live and personal for an enormous audience.

No British minister would ever again slam a hotel door without a second thought. No British political or military figure would ever again move as freely. One of the costs of the Irish Troubles was troubled English men and women who could no longer walk as free on their own island. But the Prime Minister had been lucky, as always, had survived.

> The IRA claim responsibility for the detonation of 100 pounds of gelignite in Brighton, against the British cabinet and the Tory warmongers. Thatcher will now realize that the British cannot occupy our country, torture our prisoners and shoot our people on their own streets and get away with it.
>
> Today we were unlucky, but remember, we have only to be lucky once. You will have to be lucky always. Give Ireland peace and there will be no war.

The fact that Thatcher both escaped and appeared the next afternoon to give her scheduled speech drew attention away from the dead and the shattered and maimed survivors. Thatcher was the news. There were those who had not wanted her to make the speech but, firm and determined, she appeared with the hard word to hand: just what the British expected and wanted to hear.

> We will never give up the search for more effective means of defeating the IRA. If the IRA think they can weary or frighten us, they have made a terrible miscalculation. People sometimes say that it is wrong to use the word "never" in politics. I disagree. Some things are of such fundamental importance that no other word is appropriate. I say once again today that the government will never surrender to the IRA. Never.

The assumption in Ireland was that the effective means the British and the Prime Minister had in mind would be escalated special operations against the IRA, less concern with the niceties of civil liberties, a return to the bad old days not unlike the series of killings that had devastated the INLA after Neave's death—effective, ruthless, professional, mysterious, and explicable most easily as vengeance achieved at one remove. The IRA and INLA anticipated a security response, as did most in Ireland—and in a sense they were not disappointed. Certainly the authorities invested an enormous amount in finding the individuals responsible for the bomb. And beginning in 1984 British special operations in the province appeared to be more frequent and more ruthless.

Patrick Magee, who had planted the bomb, was traced through his fingerprints found in the room, his identity established by the antiterrorist squad, who managed to attach a trace on him. They discovered that not only had he not been withdrawn from the English campaign but also that, under the instructions of Gerard McDonnell, one of the September 1983 escapees, Magee was involved in a bombing blitz to begin in July. In June the police arrested Magee, McDonnell, and two women, Ella O'Dwyer, a middle-class, university woman from the Republic with no republican connections, and Martina Anderson, a former beauty queen who had joined the Derry Provisionals in 1982 at the age of twenty. They also arrested Donal Craig, Seán McShane, and Peter Sherry, a very active IRA man who had, nevertheless, run as a Sinn Féin candidate in March 1984 in a by-election for the Dungannon council. It was a strange team, with experience, dedication, and obvious weaknesses. Craig was a drinker who immediately led the police to a safe house filled with explosives. Magee was the subject of extensive Metropolitan Police extradition efforts even before the Brighton bomb. McDonnell, as participant in the Maze escape, was most wanted and most photographed. The use of a Derry woman, complete with past associations and pronounced accent, and a middle-class type from the Republic showed the operational need for deception but no great cunning.

The police, of course, were delighted that they had caught Magee and all those involved with the new campaign plus an escapee in part because of the traditional lack of Provo fieldcraft. Just as the operational people had been willing to use the well-known and highly visible Bobby Storey in England, so had they sent over a Kesh escapee and a mismatched crew because they could be trusted. The use of a proper Southern Irish woman was the only novelty—and something of a shock in Ireland, where the Provisionals were assumed to be working class to a man. Certainly the Provisionals had limited middle-class talent, and much of that covert, but the remarkable aspect of the various English campaigns over a generation was that little was learned and yet much damage was done. And most of the volunteers ended in English prisons, even when they had to be brought all the way back from San Francisco, as was William Quinn after years of extradition proceedings. An American from California with an Irish father and Mexican mother, Quinn was deployed in the English campaign, one of the few non-Irish volunteers used during the armed struggle and one who was charged with, among other matters, shooting a police constable in London and so was badly wanted. The Provos assumed that the real response to Brighton would be not English antiterror moves and arrests, but vengeance.

Thatcher had rejected the ideal of any "sudden new initiative." What the sensible if not optimistic FitzGerald anticipated was nothing but the SAS. Instead, what occurred around the Prime Minister was a concentration of minds not attuned to vengeance but to the need for an effective policy response. What was needed was an arrangement to put Ireland back in the box, not authorization to snip off a few prickly points. The SAS would not do this, nor would internment, nor fiddling with provincial politics. Thus, with the Grand Hotel still heaped in a Brighton street, some of those who mattered began to consider means to get rid of the Irish issue. Certainly not Thatcher, not yet; but that might come if strength could be required and not concession. In the meantime preparations were tidied up for FitzGerald's arrival in London in November, a minor matter for the British, a crucial one for the Irish now wedded to the Forum report as key to the future.

On November 1 the small team set up by the British Irish Association under the Scottish judge Lord Kilbrandon published a report suggesting not the Forum options but rather other approaches, including that of the Protestant majority. The Unionists, forgotten in the Assembly, paid little attention to any options and more to their own existence: The "clapped-out old bus" of the Assembly, celebrating its second year on October 20, had, according to the DUP's youngest member, Jim Wells, "found itself a new engine."* Polls indicated that over half the Roman Catholics believed that the SDLP should give up the Assembly boycott. The way forward might be through the supposedly discredited Assembly that the DUP at least thought could be shaped to resemble Stormont with a few cosmetic changes. Then came the London summit and a reappraisal for all.

FitzGerald had been so deeply involved in the Forum that he was inclined to tunnel vision, a fifty-year malady of the decent in Dublin if hardly unique in political misfortunes; empathy is always rare and even interest is to be commended. Often in Irish politics either empathy or understanding would have simply complicated any attempt at political accommodation at all; ignorance, lack of communication, even innocence could be adjusted to agreement. To accept the reality of the zero-sum game was to give up the game of compromise, of politics. So FitzGerald came to Chequers, talked with Thatcher, and agreed to a communiqué that communicated very little except that the Forum had not found ready welcome. Both governments had abhorred violence, recognized the two communities of Northern Ireland and the necessity that their rights be reflected as well as safeguarded in provincial governmental structures, and that security cooperation should be maintained and improved. There would be another summit later. There was nothing of a new Ireland, nothing new. Thatcher had done her duty and as was her wont explained her position, her government's position, the position of the United Kingdom, which was changeless, seamless, and intractable. FitzGerald might have listened and persisted or resisted, but he had to accept the bland result that arose from minds not meeting and wait for another day and another chance. More American pressure, more reason, and time would work wonders; Ireland was not built in a day. But in a day, the same day, Margaret Thatcher, when asked about the Forum options, answered honestly. She felt the summit had been a "'full, frank, and most realistic meeting." As for the Forum report:

> I have made it quite clear—and so did Mr. Prior when he was Secretary of State for Northern Ireland—that a unified Ireland was one solution that is out. A second solution was confederation of two states. That is out. A third solution was joint authority. That is out. That is a derogation from sovereignty. We made that quite clear when the report was published.

That was it. No fiddling around, no weasel words, no maybes, and not even a kind word for the Forum's exertions. FitzGerald was left naked to his enemies.

*Cornelius O'Leary, Sydney Elliott, and R. A. Wilford, *The Northern Ireland Assembly, 1982–1986: A Constitutional Experiment* (London: Hurst, 1988), p. 186.

Haughey struck on November 20: "To the Taoiseach I say: You have led the country into the greatest humiliation in recent history." In London, FitzGerald had no effective comment to make. What could he say? "The outcome of the summit is not to be underestimated." It wasn't only the astute in Ireland who thought him ruined by it. He had abjectly capitulated to British intransigence. His hopes were in ruins and the Forum was a farce. In the North, James Molyneaux, speaking in Newcastle to the Official Unionists, said that it was like "a people walking in the darkness who had suddenly felt the sun in their faces." Not an Irish sun obviously but one rising in the east over Number 10 Downing Street, a Unionist sun. The garden trail had ended with a lecture by the wicked witch to a dumbfounded Paddy. It was humiliating.

Thatcher's response had come as an incredible shock to the Irish political establishment. Almost as an aside she had reduced thousands of hours of work, enormous hopes, and reputations and assumptions to political rubble. It was out, all of it: The research, the composition, the drafting, the arguments and compromises, the shrewd formulas, the investment—all bore only the most marginal relation to reality. In fact the entire concept of Hume was that a new Ireland structured by consent was always an aspiration, not an available political goal to be reached by specific acts. Such an Ireland would require that the majority in the six counties be transformed, born again into a new polity. As long as they were them, they would not consent. So then what? The Forum had been taken in Dublin as a means to put substance into a dream, to address realistically the nature of a future supposedly inevitable and certainly the hope of most Irish nationalists.

Those involved had been led deep down into a cul-de-sac of their own making, dribbling away rationality and pragmatism in the engagements of the moment. Begun, if by some unconsciously, as little more than an exercise in public relations, the Forum had seduced the involved into assuming that the exercise had a reality beyond a complex and elegant wish list. At any stage reflection would have indicated that options, however carefully honed, that were satisfactory only within the bounds of orthodox Irish nationalism could play little part in any real resolution of the Northern problem. For years the analysts and academics had indicated that the problem in Northern Ireland was that no such resolution could be found. The problem had remained there was no solution. No one could craft a formula that would allow the majority and minority to work in tandem in the province. The province would not agree to an Irish dimension, so how could it agree to incorporation under any label? And if so incorporated how could a new and united Ireland emerge that would encompass a bitter and angry unionist population?

In point of fact, the real Northern dimension was singularly ignored by those engaged in writing the report. The presence of the SDLP, whose more conservative members shared not Dublin's assumptions but their aspirations, was welcomed as representative of the Northern opinion. The SDLP, no less than the Nationalists before them, could readily be seen as the Northern branch of Irish politics. Their particularism, deepened and sharpened by exposure to the turbulence of the North, could be and was easily eroded in the congenial atmosphere of the Republic, their constituency was assumed monolithic, their dreams realistic, and the events of the past decade no veto. As time passed the Forum simply ignored the wishes and desires of the Northern gunmen—to recognize the gun would be to legitimize the gunmen while ignoring the intentions and capacities of the Northern majority, who would come around to Southern reality. The Forum seemingly knew little of the depth of the Northern Unionist commitment to the British connection, knew little of or about Northern Protestants, factored them in with pro forma concessions and promises. The SDLP was filled with people who lived next to Protestants, across the street from unionists; but proximity in a divided society is nothing. They understood their Northern neighbors differently than their friends in the Republic but no better. And the Forum group also ignored the policies and postures of London in general and the Conservative party in particular. The members of the Forum were often brilliant, shrewd, and pragmatic, and through long exposure to politics, were not foolish optimists, but almost all assumed that, speaking for 80 percent of the Irish people, the proposed options could be realistic for the entire Ireland. No one wanted to think too long on the fact that Northern Ireland was represented by those who spoke only for the SDLP in the six counties. The Forum did not really address the Northern Ireland problem at all.

The New Ireland Forum report was a Southern Irish solution to a Southern Irish problem. Highly detailed, cunningly phrased, beautiful as an artifact, it was a triumph of the drafter's art. All involved in the Forum had followed the devices and desires of their own hearts. No one cried stop. No one asked why a million Unionists would see their future in such options, such adjustments by the Dublin establishment. Unionists saw the Republic as Roman, a monolith, and no constitutional tinkering, no referendum on a confessional constitution, no promises of any sort, would be adequate. No one in Dublin wanted to weigh the depth of loyalist hostility. Goodwill and good intentions would prevail. No one asked if the British government had somehow been transformed so as to make London receptive to what had never so far been acceptable in practice or in theory.

What did Dublin expect? There had been the DUP's George Seawright, Scotsman and loyalist, urging on May 30, less than a month from the publication of the report and just before President Reagan's visit, that all Catholics be incinerated, a position sufficiently radical that he was expelled from the DUP at the end of the year: "Fenian scum . . . taxpayers' money would be better spent on an incinerator and burning the whole lot of them. The priests should be thrown in and burned as well." What kind of one-Ireland under a Forum formula would have a place for him and his? Northern Secretary Prior at the other end of the unionist scale on July 2 rejected the conclusions. The republicans just thought the exercise was a farce. And Margaret Thatcher, never one for the soft word, whacked it down on November 19. FitzGerald reportedly and not unreasonably felt the Prime Minister had been "gratuitously offensive." She had certainly been abrupt.

Oddly, all was not lost at all. In fact, much was gained, and much that in the very beginning had not been foreseen. Hume's idea of an investment in what a new Ireland might mean had absorbed so much concern and had led to such a detailed accounting that regardless of the conclusions everyone involved felt the need to respond in kind. Even Thatcher would be convinced by the more prudent that something at last had to be done. Thus, the New Ireland Forum, coupled with the revelation of the vast and lethal passions simmering under the surface of the province during the hunger strikes and the consequent political implications for all, not just sharpened minds but for the first time in a decade moved Ireland nearly to the top of the British political agenda, introduced a reality into Dublin politics formerly lacking, and so crafted a larger arena with more amenable major players.

The bomb in Brighton and the press conference at Chequers indicated the cost of simple persistence no matter how just the long march. The British all wanted something inexpensive done about Ireland that would put it in a box where it could not get out. There had hitherto been no solution because a multiple veto existed on the ground. And whatever attracted substantial support also assured an absolute refusal by those whose acceptance was thought necessary. Someone, usually the more militant, could always veto moderation. The loyal fundamentalists, without political skills or experience, had ended one noble experiment with the general strike, just as the radical students, an irrelevant band of young people, had with alien tactics touched profound grievances and begun the collapse of Stormont, and the secret republican armies had drawn bounds and limits in blood and bombs. The everyday voter had denied the center. The Orange sectarian killers had put paid to many of the well-meaning and posted the cost of minority gain—each group, some very small, some very unrepresentative, had effectively played the zero-sum game. There was no reason to assume that they would change in the near future. Yet if the detailed and provocative New Ireland Forum engendered a direct response from London, then the focus would not be on microapproval but on general principles. There was thus a multilevel response to the crisis as raised by the Forum, not so much to the report itself, despite subsequent rationales to that effect, but to the need for momentum away from the abyss, away from the structured anarchy of the street.

If there were to be peace and quiet and a move to more appealing matters, then something had to be done about Ireland. The Foreign Office arrayed its specialists and influence to advocate an accommodation. The lead was given by David Goodall, seconded to the cabinet, a serious Catholic who had some idea of the Irish, the Unionists, and had worked with the Prime Minister during the Falklands War. In this he had an ally in Thatcher's Cabinet Secretary, Robert Armstrong. These forces were strengthened when Prior, seemingly a burned-out case, left politics to be replaced by Douglas Hurd, a more serious player by this time. Although Thatcher might have kept Prior about, his career, like so many others, had finished in Ireland where he could be easily forgotten. Hurd, however, arrived to tidy up loose ends, not as a loose end. He would stay only until September 1985, when he would be replaced by Tom King. Then Prior, who knew it well, noted that "the Northern Ireland Office is always regarded as a dustbin." For Hurd, however, it was not. There was this once a chance to do something about the province, for the province could do nothing in return.

If the provincials would not share power, then London and Dublin could arrange an Irish dimension over their heads; they would defuse the issue except in the six counties and there depend on direct rule, the imposition of order, and time to concentrate political minds. There would no longer be an Irish problem but rather a matter of defining the nature of devolution—a provincial matter best left to provincial minds. In order to manage this exercise, Thatcher had to be brought along slowly with the evolving structure of agreement, since she was apt to revert to sentimental unionism if hurried. Still, the process had begun. With luck the circle could not yet be squared but could be rolled off into a Celtic corner. This was the first choice in London and not such a bad choice in Dublin, where the dream of "one Ireland" was eroding.

On the evening of the Thatcher "Out, Out, Out" statement, none of this was apparent; rather the reverse. Any sensible person would have assumed that Thatcher, a sentimental unionist, who had stood down the extortion of the hunger strikes regardless of the cost, who preferred the hard line and the hard word, who had escaped an IRA assassination attempt, who had seen through the pretensions of the Forum, Hume, and FitzGerald as she already had Haughey, now would stay the course. There was no need to stitch together even a temporary arrangement. The Unionists would prefer something of their own choosing now that all the nationalists' options had been trashed, but direct rule would do. Enoch Powell and the other Tories might hope for integration, sooner or later, but they too could wait now that concession was no threat. The provincial Unionist politicians, in fact, quite delighted with events, began to shape a Stormont option: Hume would have to give up the Forum strategy and come back to the Assembly sooner or later or risk electoral defections. Westminster might now accept a more reasonable formula for the future Assembly's devolved powers. Thatcher had spoken, thrown out the Forum, and opened the way for a Unionist structure to be erected on the ruins.

Instead those surrounding her, both within the Conservative establishment and among the mandarins of Whitehall, saw no advantage in the triple "out" for British politics and no possibility of a return to Unionist rule. They were steadfastly loyal to the principle of the Union but not to most of the Unionists, who were one way or the other mostly unpleasant and occasionally appalling. The "loyalists" had not really been loyal to the government of the day, not even to Westminster, and would not be to the Crown if need arose. They were loyal to their interests, which were not those of Britain. Every effort to find an accommodation had been damned as treason by those who swept away moderation in radical speeches and the toleration for their own gunmen. They were not, of course, as awful as the subversive and deadly IRA gunmen, evil criminals, but they were rarely decent and even then were always whining about loyalty and betrayal, when they did the betraying and regularly showed no loyalty to the requirements of Westminster: Police had been stoned, soldiers shot, laws flaunted, and motives impugned for years. Political debate was childish and scandalous, the private armies intolerable, the whole establishment obsolete and obstructionist. Even a formerly sound man like Enoch Powell, Thatcher's old mentor, had been transformed into a crank. In point of fact, they did not even recognize their own best interests, which for Number 10 Downing Street should be much the same as those of Finchley. Nevertheless, they were British of a sort and Thatcher was a unionist of a sort, so that in an arrangement to remove the province from contention their interests would be safeguarded, if not paramount.

The Unionists within Northern Ireland could hardly imagine the busy minds in London contemplating the implications of the November summit. What the province saw was *real* support, a humiliation for the Irish Republic, a window of opportunity to shape devolution as a mighty fortress. On November 24 James Molyneaux could tell the Official Unionist Party that Mrs. Thatcher had slapped down the plotters. Enoch Powell, suspicion incarnate, sensitive to every potential conspiracy, often disappointed in Margaret Thatcher, this time felt she had broken out of a vicious spiral planned to create an all-Ireland state—the plotters were thwarted, the CIA at bay. After all, Bishop Cahal Daly, the day after Molyneaux's statement, said that the failure of the Anglo-Irish dialogue would be too calamitous to contemplate. That was just the calamity the Unionists wanted on the heels of Garret FitzGerald's "greatest humiliation." That is what they feared would be denied them. There was no real and further assistance from the Northern Ireland Office or from London and in turn no real initiative from the Unionist establishment.

The discussions in the Assembly simply ran through the same well-plowed ground, old prejudices, old grievances, old arguments. On December 4 the new Northern Secretary, Douglas Hurd, spoke to the Assembly. It was to be his only appearance and to the fearful Unionists it did not bode well. To begin with, there was a hostile display by the former DUP member George Seawright ("the Protestant candidate for a Protestant people") in the gallery, ample evidence that nothing had been learned, nothing forgotten. Seawright might be the most virulent loyalist but one such would do for all. The fundamentalists were still for the Northern Ireland Office undigestible and unappealing. Again a loyalist had bitten the hand that might feed him, feed them all. And for what? How could someone screaming in a deliberative assembly engender affection or admiration or even understanding? Obviously sentiment would not be a Unionist asset to any exposed to such a display—and Thatcher could be touched only by mutual prejudice or vestigial sentiment if policy advantage was not obvious. In Dublin on the same day she turned her hard words to soft use in replying to a question about her response to the Forum: Her weakness was "giving a direct answer at a press conference to a direct question." This was hardly a weakness admitted, but it indicated that Dublin might still be in the game. To the north, Hurd's speech had been prepared previously and was thus cold: Terrorism would be worn down (not smashed as the loyalist dreamed), development schemes for Belfast and Derry were mentioned (development was splendid but pie for the morrow and not the real meat of the meal), and the third part of the presentation, constitutional matters, was a mere recitation of the historic position. This was never enough. Worse, the Anglo-Irish talks might still be in the cards, a deal behind the backs of the Assembly and beyond the reach of the Unionist veto. What the Unionists wanted was not to hear about the continuing interest in the Anglo-Irish dialogue but rather the reverse.

The reverse was not what the Unionists got. They got rumor of talks, talks about such talks; on January 20, 1986, Northern Secretary Hurd would indicate that machinery was being constructed with an aim to facilitating regular and systematic consultation with Dublin. The only time that the Unionists received satisfaction on the British connection was at the press conference after the November summit, and the euphoria was soon gone. By the time Hume spoke to the Assembly and Thatcher arrived on the same day in Dublin for the European

Community summit, less direct responses were being crafted away from Number 10 Downing Street but with the Prime Minister's authority.

This quickening political current could be dated from December 4, when the first public signs emerged. All other public signs in Northern Ireland matters were the usual—depressing, violent, shameful. The previous year had ended with the Darkley killings but 1984 sputtered out with minor murders, an IRA man and an SAS soldier killed in Drumrush, Fermanagh, on December 2 and on December 6 two IRA men shot by the SAS in Derry. The new supergrass strategy, never wise, always erected on the character of the dubious, liars, killers, paid or trapped informers, and habitual criminals, began to fall apart under the strains, the size of the investment, and the evidence of the open courts. On December 18 in Derry thirty-five local people held on 180 charges were released by Lord Chief Justice Lowry in the trial of Raymond Gilmour, the IRA man from Derry. The supergrass option was not dead by the end of the year, but the authorities' original high hopes had clearly been misplaced. On Christmas Eve the court of appeals quashed the convictions ("unsafe and unsatisfactory") of fourteen men jailed on the evidence of the UVF supergrass Joseph Bennett. In fact December was a vintage month for the advocates of judicial fair play in that on December 14 Private Ian Thain was the first soldier to be convicted of murdering a civilian while on duty in Northern Ireland. (He would serve only short time and then return to his regiment: Not everything was changed.)

Thain's conviction was a Northern Ireland event and then his round trip back into his regiment tended to moderate any enthusiasm for a new era of justice. So his case only served as a nationalist grievance against the entire judicial system that permitted policemen to shoot and kill and be judged innocent, that encouraged habitual criminals purchased by the state to send men to prison in supergrass trials, that always opted for the system. On December 23 Cardinal O Fiaich insisted that alienation among Northern Irish Catholics was at an unprecedented level. The year seemed to drag to a close trailing all the old quarrels and uncertainties. At least the annual death toll for the first time since 1970 did not seem very important. The murders had to be spectacular to be noticed and the toll had to be huge to engender interest. Instead, over the year losses had been for the province moderate and down: The total was 64 instead of 77; British army, 9, UDR, 10, RUC, 7, and RUCR, 9. This was dreadful but in a sense a tolerable level of violence, background music to the new political symphony being written out of sight by the bureaucrats in Dublin and London. With any luck the cunning felt the next year, for a change, at last, would be a political year.

The Unionists were all too aware of just what kind of politics might be involved as the evidence of an Anglo-Irish deal began to pile up. Besides the ill-fated Forum exercise, the Kilbrandon report that had been sponsored by the British Irish Association and drawn up by a committee opened up another set of potential arrangements. These were denounced promptly by the few who bothered to examine the text, especially by republicans who saw a revived Stormont, and especially by Unionists who seized on a suggestion concerning increasing the RUC at the expense of the UDR. The Kilbrandon report, which appeared and quickly disappeared, at least extended the debate, even if it managed to unite in opposition most shades of Northern Irish political opinion—and that too was a harbinger. The key advisors in London accepted as a given that neither coercion nor sweet reason was going to win Ulster hearts. As Fitt said in Lords in December, "It is a reasonable document—that is why it is not accepted in Ireland: because the more unreasonable you are over there the more success you are guaranteed electorally." The early signs were hardly encouraging. Hume's attempt to talk the Provisionals into politics collapsed after a few minutes because they had brought a video camera with them to be sure everything was on record. And, of course, the armed struggle continued with a security disaster. On February 28 an IRA mortar attack hit the Newry RUC station. IRA mortars were usually fired off the back of a truck, and although they were improving technically they were still inaccurate. This time the salvo cleared the blockages and landed to dreadful effect: Nine officers were killed, the greatest single RUC loss so far. Ireland had seemingly changed little in the new year. Yet 1985 did develop as a political year.

During much of 1985 it appeared two independent processes were at work to reach an Anglo-Irish accommodation. The two governments were in regular and secret contact shaping a final agreement that would be acceptable to both a Unionist Prime Minister in London and a Dublin government monitored by the nationalist hawks of Fianna Fáil and the aspirations of the SDLP. Whatever the agreement it would have to be shaped so that it could be swallowed, sooner or later, by the Northern Unionists. Unionist sentiment within the Conservative establishment was slight and so Thatcher, who at least three times apparently balked, proved to be the key; sentiment had to be shaped to reality, her virtues directed to the desired end, a text written that had no flavor of concession but rather of potential, easily read as British magnanimity. FitzGerald, with much less leverage, wanted the potential to sell to his own, to the SDLP, perhaps to Fianna Fáil, but certainly to Ireland the long-sought Irish dimension. London could operate largely without reference to political restraints, but FitzGerald had to be sure that enough was in the text to make the venture worthwhile. It would undo the humiliation of the November 1983 Thatcher press conference without engendering nostalgic nationalism on the part of Fianna Fáil. On February 21 Thatcher had told a joint session of the United States Congress, an ideal venue for an Irish comment, that, she and the Taoiseach would "continue to consult together in the quest for stability and peace in Northern Ireland." On March 22, 1985, Douglas Hurd and Foreign Secretary Sir Geoffrey Howe met Taoiseach FitzGerald and Foreign Minister Peter Barry for talks at the top on a new formula.

So the potential and then the text moved between offices; paragraphs and items were added and subtracted, conferences held, delegations dispatched, and research done in the long, complex, essential process of drafting that intrigues only the involved and the subsequent analyst. All of this went forward in secret, indicated by occasional official comments and asides that led the shrewd to suspect the process if not the details. On April 17 Hurd said in Belfast that he might, indeed, proceed with a new political formula for Northern Ireland even if there was not agreement among the local politicians. There was, of course, no such agreement in sight. Prior's rolling devolution had spread over a barren beach, leaving only the bleak Assembly as evidence. In any case the formula was already in the drafting.

The original raw grist for the mill was the two governments' basic assumptions about the Irish problem. Civil servants usually bring these to the table but not written into the agenda. Instead they had at the beginning a general outline of what an Irish dimension might be—the necessary postures and positions requiring incorporation, the new institutions that might be required, and finally the existing experience and suggestions. These, after nearly a generation were legion: the entire Stormont experience and parallel structures elsewhere, the Sunningdale drill, the various efforts at provincial accommodation—conventions, assemblies, debates, and proposals, the Forum, theoretical and comparative examples, and the useful from the evolving public debate. All of these had to be shaped and refined and this was accomplished with remarkable discretion beyond public gaze.

The public debate that was useful and positive in the procedure was not the traditional clamor of grievance, outrage, and paranoia that made up much of the debate of Northern Ireland politics. Nor did it comprise the presentations of most politicians. The drafters were only too aware of the historical record, the past wars and the cherished assumptions of the involved. Instead, they examined the more theoretical suggestions that had begun with Kilbrandon—the Forum was part of the problem, not the solution. Finished in May 1985, *Ireland: A Positive Proposal* by Kevin Boyle and Tom Hadden, both Northern Irish legal scholars long concerned with the province, displayed a variety of possible options, including a stress on the necessity for a Dublin-London agreement on the constitutional problem of the province and the need for any powers granted to Dublin in the province to be reciprocated for the United Kingdom in the South. In other words, Dublin was going to have to amend its wish list if it wanted access to Northern Ireland events and Britain should no longer operate without regard to the Irish dimension. Boyle and Hadden went on in detail, including potential structures for devolution that were of less interest to the hidden bureaucrats. In normal times few bureaucrats but the specialists would have been interested at all. In normal times such theoretical proposals would have been at best read, noted, praised, and then filed, but times were not normal. There had been quite literally thousands of analytical works on the Northern Ireland problem, and nearly every facet of any potential accommodation had been explored. In 1985, however, real people were secretly at work producing a real text. Thus, Boyle and Hadden came to print at an ideal time to allow public debate and private consideration of a good book grounded in Irish reality.

The direction of the debate was increasingly apparent, gathering the support of the decent and the distant. On June 11 Pope John Paul II encouraged the dialogue for peace. Such encouragement only deepened growing Unionist concern. As Paisley said, "The Pope would be better off excommunicating those members of his Church who are butchering the Protestants of Ulster." It did not ease their growing anguish and outrage when on July 19 Cardinal O Fiaich announced that "90 percent of religious bigotry is to be found among Protestants, whereas the bigotry one finds among Catholics is mainly political." That Catholic political bigotry seemed to the Unionists increasingly likely to be rewarded. Everyone had suddenly started drafting agreements and accommodations.

In July 1985 a committee under Lord Donaldson that included Shirley Williams and David Alton, MP, sponsored by the two small parties of the British political center, the Liberals and the Social Democrats, produced Northern Irish proposals in *What Future for Northern Ireland?* Here too the Dublin role was stressed—there would be no solution without an Irish dimension. There was the usual insistence that there were two traditions, the majority should control the British connection, and power must be shared in the province. There was nothing really novel except in suggested Anglo-Irish institutions, a British-Irish Parliamentary Council and a British-Irish Security Commission that had been foreshadowed in the Sunningdale Agreement.

Almost all of the proposals tended to rest on similar unstated assumptions, sometimes actually stressed for the slow of wit. Ireland was different. Ireland was a divided island. The six counties in the North were of concern to the rest of Ireland. Those counties housed a divided society. Such a society, then, must have an all-Ireland dimension and be governed locally if at all possible through structures that protect the minority, the other tradition. Most analysis concentrated then on the nature of the Irish dimension and the structure of provincial authority. Something had to be done, for the province simply could not be left to its own devices. British withdrawal, supported by some of the Labour Left and the Irish republicans, would assure more violence and thus would be irresponsible. Some who predicted such violence may have indulged in wishful thinking, but most simply assumed vast civil strife would begin with more dreadful results than the long, slow killing that had heretofore been acceptable. Britain had a responsibility to act, and in 1985 Britain wanted to find an accommodation that would remove the issue from the agenda. An "issue" that at Brighton had nearly resulted in the violent destruction of the entire government could not be treated simply as a minor matter. It was to British advantage to act in such a way as to reduce the prospect of violence, involve the Irish government, and open a road for decent provincial government, if not now, then later.

The analysts assumed that the existing arrangement of direct rule with no Dublin involvement was artificial and ineffectual and should go. Those who wanted it to go by treating the province as integral to the United Kingdom and thus obviating any need for Dublin were few, to the right of the Conservatives, and so discounted. Those who wanted no Irish connection and rule for the majority in provincial matters—most Unionists—were doubly discounted because they ignored geography and the historical context of the problem and ignored the previous distressful record when power was not shared and legitimacy was lost. Neither group seemed to accept that geography—island Ireland—was destiny, that as a result Ulster was different and must be so treated. So the British had the responsibility of adjusting this strange province to existing institutions and aspirations. The adjustment would be judged successful if stability could be produced and so cause the disappearance of an Irish issue.

The various proposals all accepted in some degree these premises, including the capacity of the British government to act, the advantages for most in it so doing, and the two keys that had already brought down Sunningdale: power sharing and an Irish dimension. Each proposal focused on potential institutions and laws, confederations and condominiums, joint committees, federal bodies, enumerated rights and privileges, the tiers of local government, the text that must be adjusted to perceived reality. The civil servants thus were given throughout 1985 a whole menu of potentialities that, if they had been offered a year before, would have been forgotten except by learned colleagues, department chairmen, and the authors.

Amid all this offstage bustle and visible analysis the Unionists grew increasingly uneasy. On February 7, 1984, the Assembly had authorized a Devolution Report Committee that lethargically but seriously addressed its brief, appointing a specialist adviser Professor Harry Calvert, a constitutional lawyer from Cardiff University, holding meetings, accepting presentations, following from a quite different perspective the Forum precedent. Although the SDLP was absent and the Catholics were unrepresented, the OUP had returned and the committee was taken seriously by those involved. On February 19, 1985, the committee presented the Assembly with its second report, in two volumes, which indicated no consensus but showed that much ground had been covered. Hurd had shown some interest in the results but few expected the Unionists to discover an acceptable form of power sharing. The committee continued on with six meetings between February 25 and October 7 but to little effect. On October 7 an outside mediator, Sir Fred Catherwood, an Ulsterman who was MEP for Cambridge and North Bedfordshire, was brought in to find an "acceptable scheme of proposals for devolved government in the Province."* He produced the Catherwood proposals on devolution on October 28, the eve of the anticipated Anglo-Irish agreement, which he did not want to disrupt. There was a debate the following day but the third report of the committee was, according to the Parliamentary Under-Secretary of State, Nicholas Scott, "a doubtful starter." Paisley felt the comment was flippant but it was accurate: The Assembly horse was dead, not a starter at all.

In January 1986 the proposals were withdrawn by an Assembly that by then many had forgotten existed and on March 13 the Devolution Report Committee was dissolved, although as a grace note a fourth and quite final report was published. In a real sense the work of devolution, although futile, indicated that Unionist politicians, including the most intransigent and outrageous, could do sound parliamentary work. The process, the procedures, and the reports, if of no interest after the event except to historians and of little interest at the time, were evidence of a seriousness of purpose and a dedication to detail worthy of admiration. The Unionists could not find an agreement in time simply because they did not agree on the nature of devolution.

The failures of Irish politics on many levels, often in full public view, came because there was no consensus, not only on the most basic and, as it developed, lethal issues but also often on simple matters of degree. A polity shaped by unarticulated psychic needs, dreadfully dangerous historical assumptions, divided loyalties, paranoia, and irreconcilable cleavages is apt to produce disagreement, even by those most likely to agree—in this case, Assembly Unionists. To accept that these inherent schisms were inevitable and that agreement was impossible would mean, in truth, that the Northern Ireland problem was that there was no solution. This was not what London wanted or what Dublin preferred. Thus, from the time of the London summit of November 1984, the specialists and experts had been at work to devise a formula that would be, if not

*O'Leary et al., p. 154.

acceptable, at least capable of being imposed. While this exercise proceeded in secret, accompanied by the public reports and debates, those involved in the Troubles plodded on mostly unmindful not only of the scribes at work but also the everyday Irish world.

During the course of the year Northern events, the usual events, tended to be considered as further evidence that an Anglo-Irish agreement that would ease the stress was necessary. It was not so much that the news was bad, as usual, but that the usual news was bad. Paisley claimed in March at the DUP Conference that the Irish government, the SDLP, and the Catholic hierarchy had a vested interest in IRA atrocities. The government failed to rescue the Northern Ireland gas industry in April. Four RUC officers were killed by an IRA bomb at Killeen on the border in May—the same month that the Lear Fan aircraft company announced the closure of its plant. The district council elections on May 15 gave ample evidence of the dimensions of the problem that thus needed a political initiative. The OUP, keeping with the trends, improved its position, winning 29.5 percent of the vote, up from 26.5 in 1981, to the DUP's 24.3 percent, down from 26.6 percent—a net gain for moderation. So was the SDLP's slight improvement in its first preference votes, from 17.5 percent to 17.8 percent, despite the competition of Provisional Sinn Féin. But Sinn Féin's 75,686 first preference votes, 11.8 percent, indicated the persistent appeal of the republicans—gunmen to all moderates.

As the marching season approached, the Protestants increasingly felt that this secret agreement, probably being negotiated by those without concern for the majority, would be shaped to help the SDLP and so harm the Unionists. The Orangemen in July rioted against any bans on their marching through Catholic areas: the annual triumphant parade of domination that had grown ragged over the years. On July 12-13 the rioting in Portadown between the RUC and members and friends of the Orange and Royal Black Institution parades—parades that had previously passed through the Tunnel area and were now confined behind walls put up for the occasion—persuaded Protestants that the times were troubled. Those who sought cheerful sectarian news might find it in the censorship later in the month of a BBC-TV documentary and the ensuing hubbub. They could on August 30 look to the meeting of Molyneaux and Paisley with Thatcher at Number 10 Downing Street to protest the Anglo-Irish talks. But Unionists during the summer of 1985 found little comfort and much trouble. The IRA was still bombing and shooting. The Belfast magistrate's court was damaged by a van bomb and two accused informers, Gerard and Catherine Mahon, were shot dead in East Belfast. Even the supposed monster Dominic McGlinchey was sent back to the Republic. It was a troublesome summer for the majority and so too for the moderates.

Only the IRA and Provisional Sinn Féin seemed to rise on the tide created by the London-Dublin negotiation. Active service units were still active. In fact the strategy of the Armalite and the ballot box had put hidden strains on the republican movement. Again what was good for the gunmen was not necessarily good for the candidates. An armed campaign produces horror, error, atrocity, and brutality, and must be waged ruthlessly. An informer shot and dumped for the dustmen, a lad from the neighborhood shot and maimed for petty theft, a bomb that collapses a building on a pedestrian, are simply incidents in a war. They do not help Sinn Féin candidates get elected. Such candidates need not only positive news but also money, time, enthusiasm, and commitment that many in the IRA felt should be focused—if not solely, then mainly—on the military push. In Belfast, Ivor Bell, who had been chief of staff and had dominated the Northern Command for years, felt the campaign was being run down, if not by intent (and there were those who so believed), then by too much politics on the part of Adams and company. The movement had a failed campaign on its hands, he told the Army Council, and resigned, insisting that the other six do likewise. Bell wanted a special General Army Convention (there had been no General Army Convention since 1970) and a reaffirmation of the war. Adams closed the door on Bell and three others so that they would play no further part in the movement. Bell was court-martialed and retired to private life, as a plasterer, along with his republican associate Ann Curry Boyle. This might have solved the immediate problem, but the inherent conflict between war and politics remained to trouble the movement. As usual, much of the quarrel took place entirely in secret, then and later, and for observers it appeared that the IRA simply kept on making trouble.

Increasingly the population of the Republic had given indication that the Troubles wearied them. It had all gone on too long. There had been too many alarms, too much violence, too much asked for no return. Coverage in the media did not so much decline as grow less intense, less focused, less inclusive. RTE still did television specials but through each a ribbon of distaste for the Provisional IRA could be found, and many said such distaste was required: The state wanted it, the producers, often friendly to the Workers party, wanted it, and apparently most of the people accepted it. Besides, there were many more interesting local matters: In Kerry the long run of the Kerry Babies scandal fascinated. A young woman, sinful, misguided, foolish, innocent, ignorant, was accused of killing her newborn illegitimate child (or was it children or was it not?). The scandal touched on juicy issues from police incompetence to women's rights, everything playing the old Ireland against the new. There were the visits of the prominent. There had been President Reagan himself the year before on his roots pilgrimage. Then in 1985 Tip O'Neill came from America—a grand and popular man, the O'Neill who had introduced Thatcher to Congress as Prime Minister of Great Britain, no mention of Northern Ireland. There had been Crown Prince Akihito and his wife from Japan, and the President of Israel, Chaim Herzog, born in Dublin. There were the now traditional wrangles in Haughey's Fianna Fáil: Desmond O'Malley was expelled and plotted a new party. There was a murder mystery involving a curate in Roscommon. The Post Office, An Post, was to run a national lottery. There was a new archbishop of Dublin, Dr. Kevin MacNamara. Religious statues of limited aesthetic merit were reported to be moving before the eyes of the faithful, and the most faithful Monsignor James Horan, had finally organized an airport in the wilderness for the Knock shrine to Mary that had long attracted the pious to the wilds of County Mayo.

These were more interesting, more comforting, and more exciting than Northern horrors. There was all sorts of excitement in the Republic that did not involve the IRA or Paisley or a divided society. Irish society, real Irish society in the twenty-six counties at least, seemed to be doing quite well while the politicians beavered away on the agreement.

And so it was for the prosperous and for the content, many of whom still assumed that all must be well so that the Republic of 1985 could prove attractive for a united island, as foundation of a united Ireland. Those pleased with the nation saw royal visits, the statue at Ballinspittle in Cork, and Kerry scandals as peripheral to the major concerns of the nation, the fodder of the media, not the reality of the day. The real Irish day looked cheerful from Dublin 4, from the Taoiseach's office, from the proper pubs and French restaurants. It looked fine to those who drove to work in BMWs and raced boats on the weekend. And it often looked promising to those less well endowed, employed civil servants, school-teachers after a raise, the new workers still at the new plants, and the salesman with his first car. People who had never had lace in the window could afford whiskey instead of a pint of stout. Those in residence, those visible and not stacked in high-rise council flats or hidden out in country hovels, were easy.

What Ireland needed, this Ireland, their Ireland, the New Ireland, was simply to rasp off the rough edges of a parochial society. Change the confessional Constitution so the North would not be offended. Add modern laws on birth control and divorce and perhaps abortion so the North (whose Protestants, as conservative as any, did not seek such changes) would not be offended. Improve the fiscal stability of the state so that the Northern Irish could be part of the new prosperity. The old quarrels could thus be subsumed in a new, rich Ireland integrated into Europe. As Cardinal O Fiaich told the *Guardian,* on August 25, 1986, "If we remain the last Catholic country in western Europe, that is because we have been remote, rural and poor: all these things are passing." It was the duty of the government to hurry that passing and so to welcome unity. This strategy, advocated in particular by FitzGerald and opposed on occasion by those who felt no concession need be made to the Black Northerners, who should be punished for bad manners, posed certain problems.

One of the persistent illusions of both the rich and the class bound is that money matters most: The Unionists could be bought. One of the persistent illusions of all democratic politicians is that conflict can be transmuted by formula: There is a text to transform implacable reality. Both combined in grand Republican strategy: Sell the charms of the New Ireland, the new reality. As Fitzgerald said, "Our nationalist hopes and aspirations must take second place to providing a stable, peaceful society for those citizens in Europe, of both traditions, in Northern Ireland." For Northerners, the country, rich or poor, was Catholic, and that was indigestible, whatever the laws or the text of the constitution. And besides, Ireland was hardly a green and pleasant land.

The reality in 1985 simply left for many much to be desired.* The everyday,

---

*J. J. Lee in *Ireland 1912–1985: Politics and Society* (Cambridge: Cambridge University Press, 1989), produced a scathing and highly detailed survey of the Irish failure, especially but not solely the economic failure, in contrast to the achievements of the other European polities, often those with fewer potential advantages. Because Lee wrote as an indigenous historian, a patriot, he could not be lumped with the neo-Marxists, external critics, and political naysayers;

the lack of housing starts and the fudged building permits, the primitive debates in the Dáil and the decay of the cities, became evidence in the competition over the future. The dream had been an Irish Republic that would be beacon and comfort to the Northern Protestants, Irish really, Unionist only because of the lack of options, loyal to the Crown as guardian of interests that an all-Ireland Republic could cherish as well. First prosperity had come to the Republic, and there were repeated efforts to transform the confessional state. By 1985 the new model Republic should have revealed the shifts in Southern Catholic priorities, indicated a prosperous and tolerant land eager for steps toward the culmination of history's plan—one Ireland. There was no pluralism but rather a preference for being more pious, more Catholic in matters of divorce, abortion, and the special place of the Church. There was less prosperity, and ample evidence that the money generated had been ill spent. Ireland was no splendid beacon but almost a burned-out case itself.

Once the royal visits, the new pubs and glitter-glass buildings and U2 concerts were weighed against the failures, the Republic had less to offer than when poor and pure. The economy might, of course, strengthen, but in matters of money two factors apparently remained constant. First, the Republic could not maintain its population—emigration continued for those without prospects and for those who found the atmosphere too narrow. Second, the Republic, in contrast to all other western European countries, had a flawed economy that, despite vast improvement, penalized the poor, the old, the very young, heavily taxed the salaried, and catered to special interests, especially those with political clout, large farms, or substantial business interests. Only the foreign and the rich found ease in Ireland. Why should those in Northern Ireland seek membership in a historically flawed state?

The prosperity that had greatly reduced emigration, spread money into the countryside, and brought in foreign businesses and manufacturers had been unevenly allotted and included painful costs for the quality of life. Some of these costs were inevitable: Housing had to be built on green land, roads had to cut through fields, fine old buildings had to be razed or adjusted, the little farms were really not viable, and the many pubs could not last in a competitive society. The old was often replaced with horrors. The successful often were without social responsibility, or vision; they were certainly without good taste, experience, or restraint: The newly rich in a capitalist society are often universally dreadful on first acquaintance, and Ireland had few old rich to dilute the primitives. Aspects of the new Ireland grew so awful that even the pop stars had qualms. Rock musician Bob Geldof, at the civic reception in his honor in Mansion House, Dublin, was scathing about the city:

> It used to be one of the prettiest in Europe and now it's a shambolical mess. . . . Not only is the city increasingly brutalized but the people in it have lost their old openness and that has a lot to do with the destruction of the city. Please stop destroying Dublin.

---

therefore, his rich and closely reasoned work, replete with charts and graphs, came as an unpleasant package to a remarkably complacent establishment.

It was not what the establishment wanted to hear from someone from Black-rock, a South Dublin suburb, who had made it big. Pop stars should go for long cars, blond ladies, and Hollywood houses, not social criticism. The new Dublin establishment wanted kind words. Many of them thought that the vast, tacky estates, the ugly glass buildings, the endless bright white villas along the previously unspoiled coast, the roads slashed through old districts were splendid. And all of them, council estates out of sight or Mediterranean cottages in Galway (all too much in sight), had made someone many a pretty penny. The chattering critics complained about the destruction of Dublin, the building scandals, the ruin of Viking Dublin for the benefit of the bureaucrats' new concrete bunkers, the impossible tax system, the suburban sprawl. These were the carps of collegians and belted earls, easily spurned as not real Irish by the cute men in from the country. The others—the radicals who complained that the country had a drug problem, children were in need, social legislation was primitive and welfare service stark, old people suffered and hospitals were closed and grants went only to the comfortable and foreign firms that always closed sooner rather than later—could be ignored as subversive, not really Irish, by those with access to the Dáil and a Mercedes. Some of the successful were responsible, some of the Catholic money was old and decently spent, but the feel of the country was tawdry. The establishment and a great many who managed to stay in the country either accepted or advocated this, their New Ireland, an Ireland with a future.

The future for all unionists was seen as separation from the Republic, not to a new Ireland, but the old loyalties. That London seemed about to endanger this future through some sort of betrayal, some sort of agreement with the Republic, became not only increasingly obvious throughout 1985 but excruciatingly pain-ful. Unless they did something they would be savaged by their own—"yesterday's men" according to Molyneaux on October 30—but what was to be done? Whatever Garret the Good, Taoiseach FitzGerald, suddenly an English favorite, said, Séamus Mallon of the SDLP on November 10, at an SDLP conference in Belfast, was making no high-minded denial of his aims, his party's aims, their aims, Catholic aims: a united Ireland: "We cannot, will not and must not put this aspiration on the back boiler. We cannot make liars of ourselves, we cannot leave it in suspended animation for any length of time." And so on November 14, when Enoch Powell at last learned for certain that there was to be an Anglo-Irish agreement beyond reach of the loyal, he reminded Thatcher "that the penalty for treachery is to fall into public contempt." On the next day Garret FitzGerald and Margaret Thatcher signed the formal agreement at Hillsborough Castle, Down, on behalf of the Republic of Ireland and the United Kingdom.

The new Anglo-Irish Agreement would be sent on to Westminster and the Dáil. The text had the peculiar charm that those who shaped the words sought not reality but a satisfactory vague formulation filled with potential. This meant that much could be read in or out, much might be accomplished or evaded by appropriate reference. In part by necessity, surely at times by intention, the document was shaped to be excruciatingly vague, a precise formulation of uncertainties and possibilities as much as a hard-edged blueprint of the future. The fact of the treaty was more important than the details, the medium was the message. The formal text contained twelve articles:

Article One recognized that the change in the constitutional status of Northern Ireland, which was not desired presently, could only come by agreement and the subsequent legislative arrangements then necessary.

Article Two indicated that the context was the British-Irish Intergovernmental Council, BIIC, that the Irish government might put forward proposals but that there would be no derogation of sovereignty.

Article Three noted details of the BIIC, that it would meet regularly and have a secretariat.

Article Four was crucial, indicating the aims for the conference as a framework to accommodate the two traditions, to promote peace and stability and prosperity, to devolve power on the basis of a widespread acceptance, and, in the language of the text, to accept modalities of bringing devolution about—the Irish government would propose schemes on behalf of the interests of the minority community.

Articles Five to Ten listed the concerns and functions of the BIIC—that included matters that the Irish government could put forward—human rights and elections, flags and discrimination and a possible Bill of Rights, the composition of various bodies, including the Police Authority and Police Complaints Board; aspects of security, legal matters including the possibility of mixed courts in both jurisdictions; and cross-border security, economic, and social matters.

Article Eleven called for a review after three years if requested.

Article Twelve reiterated the possibility of an interparliamentary link between London and Dublin, first suggested in 1981.

The Agreement was thus rich in potential, seemingly opening all areas to dual concern, extending by treaty Dublin concerns into all aspects of Northern affairs, stressing the need for further and satisfactory institutions and means of cooperation. The text, however, was aspiration, a call for cooperation without compulsion or even indication of agreement on any of the topics so briefly touched. It was a modest beginning, but it was more than some had thought possible, and so presented as a major step.

The involved could thus, justly, read much or little into the text, find comfort or horror in both the details and the entire venture. Unionists could only assume that the Conservative government in London (Labour would be worse), representing the elusive British political opinion, accepted that all Ireland was different and that the Unionists were a part of Ireland, beyond the prime concern of Great Britain. London must assume that Northern Ireland was different. Northern Ireland, as different, must be treated separately in many matters but aligned with British practice devolved. The Northern Irish must display a mature and agreed, agreeable, political balance. In the meantime, the natural course was for London to arrange the Irish dimension with Dublin and to let time impose a political sense of reality on the involved. There would not yet be an abandonment of direct rule. The deployment of the security forces would be untouched, but open to the potential of review of the Irish government. Much, maybe all, seemed to be the same but might be different because Dublin could be involved. No one yet indicated *how* involved.

Many of the British assumptions seemed in London and in Dublin obvious and were not questioned, but they would be taken as dreadful threats to Unionist assumptions and pretensions. Why was loyalty different in Northern Ireland? Why, indeed, was the province different from any other part of the United Kingdom? Why should any part of that kingdom have the "right" to opt out for membership in a foreign state—a united Ireland shaped in Dublin? Why should a geographic term Ireland have such a compelling political hold on the British imagination? There had never been a united Ireland except in the dreams of violent rebels. And those dreams had never really been supported by the Irish, not the Catholics and certainly not the Protestants. The first republicans of Tone, the Irish nationalists, the Fenians, the Easter rebels had no island vote of confidence. The 1918 election was not fought on an independence platform by Sinn Féin. The Irish people tolerated but did not endorse the IRA in the Tan War and might have accepted the results—an Irish Free State—as least troublesome but hardly as the heart's desire of a united people. Inevitable Irish unity was as false a concept to the Unionists as London's perpetual advocacy of the special nature of the province. Geography should not be destiny. Especially geography read from an Irish Catholic primer by the English should not be the basis for an island accommodation. And this would be seen to be the case. The British had accepted a self-fulfilling assumption: Since they are different, part of one island, treat them differently—and see that they act differently. Because Ireland is naturally a single unit we in London, at Dublin's prodding, must from time to time see if the unnatural loyalist community wants to, is ready to, cut loose from London. Anyone could have foreseen that the Unionists would feel that all the potential crafted in the Anglo-Irish Agreement was actual betrayal. The Irish-Irish did not, they were so immersed in their own illusions. Many in London counted on time to erode unionist fears, instill a sense of the possible even in loyalists, and reveal that the agreement did no harm to a Northern Protestant future. What neither Dublin nor London foresaw was that the Unionists would within the province seize on the issue and try to freeze politics. In so doing they prevented "progress" as foreseen in the agreement but also isolated and institutionalized the Troubles within the six counties. They became a constant, a bore, a parochial matter like the rest of the province. In its own curious and Irish way, the Anglo-Irish Agreement neither punished nor rewarded, neither brought the future closer nor killed the past, but instead engendered a violent stability not unlike the immediate intention of the drafters.

20

The Institutionalization of Turmoil: November 1985–December 1989

The important thing is never to hope.
It is hope that brings turmoil, destruction.
Acceptance, resignation, stoicism—yes!
    But never hope.

John Hewitt at Corrymeela, September 1985

There they were at the traditional press conference after the signing of what was being heralded by the minders and associates as the greatest step in Anglo-Irish relations since the Treaty: the Anglo-Irish Agreement of 1985 (AIA). All smiles, Garret the Good and the Iron Lady stood for photographs. There was to be fame for all who were involved in producing an accommodation, a way forward, a splendid and carefully crafted formula to remove the Troubles from crisis. Everyone was smiles. The agreement had grown out of the effective Thatcher-FitzGerald chemistry and become a grand collaborative enterprise drawing forth the best of both peoples, all the skilled civil servants, savants, and statesmen involved. There was something for all, no infringement of sovereign rights, no denying Ireland has a formal voice for the first time in Northern Irish matters. There was no way to gainsay that the Irish Taoiseach who spoke that first day in Irish to *all* the Irish had accepted the unionist veto on the march of the Irish nation. Everyone had given, and everyone on both islands could take heart.

If there were not already quibbles, this first long orchestrated drumroll of public euphoria over the agreement would have caused tremors of doubts in the pragmatic and cynical. Enoch Powell, irrevocably wedded to the grand conspiracy, had already found FitzGerald not wondrous and good but "smarmy and ingratiating"—too nice by half. For the other Unionists, for all loyalists, for the majority in Ulster, nice made no matter. They did not need to read the fine print—hardly anyone inside or outside Ulster read the agreement at all. Any deal done with Dublin, done behind Ulster's back without Ulster's consent, was forthwith against Ulster's people, evil. Imagine the arrogance of the man from Dublin and the Dáil speaking to Ulster with the words *Tá sé chuspóir againn comh-aitheantas agus comh-urraim a bhaint amach don dá fhéiniúlacht i dTuaisceart Éireann.* Down in Dublin they still thought that Ulster would allow itself to be gobbled up in some provincial Catholic ministate complete with a language no one understood but everyone must learn. Not Ulster. And not because of the new treaty. And the attempt was all the worse for being done by the very Tory who had shouted, "Out, out, out" to Irish-Catholic-republican pretensions arrogantly presented as options, a foul and publicly poisoned dish offered by gunmen's children.

The response had been evolving over the past month as the direction of events became clear. On November 2 a campaign had begun to set up loyalist Ulster Clubs (the originals had been formed to protest changes in Orange route marches) in every district council area so as to be ready for the worst, ready to protest. By January 1986 the clubs claimed to have eight thousand members in forty-eight branches. By January 1986 protest had come a long way from the autumn of 1985. Then the protests had escalated once the signing took place. This immediate response of the Unionists only added to the fulsome praise for the AIA elsewhere. If Paisley and Powell hated the result, something good must be between the covers. Rarely had so many at home and abroad been united on any facet of the Irish Troubles. Everyone had become exhausted with Ireland, with the Irish—including those very Irish. All yearned for good news and so escalated the chorus of huzzahs. Both the Irish and British diplomatic and media mills settled down to sell the AIA within the Western world, sell what they and many others devoutly believed was a splendid product. The result over the next year was an amazing triumph: Outside the six counties very few had a harsh word and many were convinced. It was a triumph almost equal to that of the Dublin government in undercutting the Provisionals in the Irish-American diaspora. It was a triumph of hope over experience. The huzzahs were in any case often spontaneous rather than induced—everyone wanted an end to Ireland.

These huzzahs broke over a rather modest proposal that solved several British problems and gave the government a worldwide presentation cover: "There may be murder on the streets, prisons filled with Irish patriots, curtailment of rights, and horrors galore, but see, we have negotiated an agreement." So Thatcher and the Conservatives and the British were ever more tightly webbed to an agreement that was but a list of possibilities and prospects and needed only one side reluctant so as to evade the details. For Dublin, from the beginning without real markers in the game, it completely erased the Forum venture, quieted the SDLP and most nationalists for the foreseeable future, and allowed the country, once convinced, to return to more tractable matters. The Irish people, like everyone else exhausted by the Irish issue and fearful of involvement, now looked forward to promised peace and quiet.

So the parties needed to do no more than sell the agreement to ensure tranquillity. On November 27 the agreement passed Westminster at the end of a two-day debate, 473 votes to 47, one of the largest majorities on a division in parliamentary history. Only the Irish Unionists, a sprinkling of Tories, including Ian Gow, who idealistically resigned as Minister of State at Treasury in protest, and the odd Labour One-Ireland advocate voted against. At Leinster House Fine Gael, Labour, and the Workers Party favored the AIA while Haughey and Fianna Fáil had nationalist objections that actually eased acceptance in Conservative and Unionist quarters. Haughey, fairly or no, was seen to be intent on capturing the high ground of the national issue as an asset for future elections rather than being deeply concerned with the details of the agreement. The Dáil approved the AIA on November 21 by eighty-eight to seventy-five, a party vote, although Haughey said that he would not oppose devolution that was to Northern nationalist advantage. No one could be sure that there was capital to be made from opposing the agreement on nationalist grounds, so Fianna Fáil hung loose on the edge of opposition. Thatcher held no brief for Haughey anyway. Matters progressed. An Anglo-Irish secretariat was set up at Maryfield outside Belfast. Nothing was left but the remnants of opposition in London and Dublin—and the outrage of Ulster Unionism.

Thatcher had no great interest in maintaining any momentum toward resolution of the Irish problem. She had no great interest in Ireland. She had finished with Ireland, drafted the most radical response to the intractable issue in generations. That was that ragged end tied up. Dublin could be content with formulas and formalities even while the doubts about the agreed wisdom of an eventual united island spread. Haughey might find his high ground a swamp. Thatcher was finished. The international community, engaged in more pressing matters, could take Ireland as over—thank God, one less trouble, one more gleaming example of justice achieved by goodwill, reason, democratic governments, and decent people. The Anglo-Irish campaign merely reinforced a natural tendency. The United States was tapped for money, $250 million through a special vote by Congress on March 11, 1987, in time for Saint Patrick's Day. And there matters rested except in Northern Ireland, where the real struggle had barely begun.

The response of the entire spectrum of unionist opinion was the same: horror and anguish. Betrayed at last. Just as they all had always thought would be the case, just as they had always foretold, just as they had predicted and promised and warned, the other British had sold them out, given away their birthright. Generations of forebodings had in the Anglo-Irish Agreement been made manifestly real. And that foreboding would never stop, validating each new disaster: The chosen people had been betrayed, somehow, by someone. At last their paranoia had proven justified, their angst founded in reality.

It was as if the flimsy nightmares so long sold as substance had before their eyes been transmuted into monsters. There it was in the long, gray paragraphs of the civil servants and the politicians, there bound by Her Majesty's Stationery Office in Belfast, there in real life. And there was thus almost relief as well as the promised anguish. All wallowed in a grief and despair that all felt, a grief and despair that thus went beyond all bounds of reason, beyond the dry and not so dreadful clauses of the agreement. It was a *nostalgie du traison*, almost an ecstasy of justifiable misery long awaited. Harold McCusker before the House of Commons expressed his own bitter anguish at both the document and the endgame of the humiliation of the Unionists:

> The agreement deals with my most cherished ideals and aspirations. On three occasions in the week prior to the signing of the agreement, on the Tuesday, Wednesday and Thursday, I stood in the House, having been told in essence by foreign journals what the agreement

contained, and it was denied to me that an agreement existed, or had even been reached.

I went to Hillsborough on the Friday morning . . . I stood outside Hillsborough, not waving a Union flag—I doubt whether I will ever wave one again—not singing hymns, saying prayers or protesting, but like a dog and asked the Government to put in my hand the document that sold my birthright. They told me that they would give it to me as soon as possible. Having never consulted me, never sought my opinion or asked my advice, they told the rest of the world what was in store for me.

I stood in the cold outside the gates of Hillsborough castle and waited for them to come out and give me the agreement second hand. It is even more despicable that they could not even send one of their servants to give it to me. . . .

I felt desolate because as I stood in the cold outside Hillsborough castle everything that I held dear turned to ashes in my mouth.*

There cannot be the slightest doubt that McCusker and the loyalists felt, not without justification, humiliated. There cannot be the slightest doubt that their hopes and fears, often indistinguishable, seemed to have taken form for them in the pages of the Hillsborough agreement in an especially cruel way. They in fact read the text as an intention rather than as it was written, read implications, possibilities, and potential as all realized. They had been bypassed through negotiations with the Irish Republican government in Dublin, negotiations that Ian Gow, who resigned from his friend Margaret Thatcher's government over the issue, insisted arose from the armed struggle of the IRA:

Our fellow countrymen from Northern Ireland will perceive—and will not be wrong in perceiving—that the agreement would never have been signed unless there had been a prolonged campaign of violence. The agreement will be perceived as having been won as a result of violence. The Irish National Liberation Army and the Irish Republican Army will believe that their violence is succeeding.†

Gow felt the IRA would continue its long war emboldened by the agreement. McCusker felt that the agreement had in fact delivered him into the hands of that IRA, which had for fifteen years "murdered personal friends, political associates, and hundreds of my constituents." The Anglo-Irish Agreement, whatever else, did not by word or implication turn the majority over to the IRA, much less the minority in Northern Ireland. But the Northern loyalists equated any accommodation with total defeat, and any member of the other community with all members of the IRA. They expressed their resentment with truculence, exaggeration, and intransigence before the House of Commons, in subsequent speeches, during the long campaign against the AIA. A lament at humiliation was one

*Antony Kenny, *The Road to Hillsborough* (Oxford: Pergamon, 1986), pp. 102–103.
†Ibid., p. 113

matter, but the response of McCusker and the Unionists seemed one more delusion of persecution by a majority, one more shrill and exaggerated whine over any concession to anyone but their own. The first wave of protest—too anguished, too extreme—reinforced the image of the loyalists as intractable, unrelenting reactionaries.

When the Unionists went on to focus all their efforts on negating the agreement, they did so with minimal outside support. Ian Gow and Enoch Powell, whose analysis suggested that loyalty to the Queen did not presuppose loyalty to Commons, were different. They argued, did not whine. They were exceptions. And as such in November and December 1985 they were irrelevancies in Irish and British politics. Both had become Irish cranks. Unionist complaints, again, still, did not seem to be addressed to reality but to dreadful conspiracies and most improbable worst-possible-case assumptions. Yet even the orthodox and the experienced felt betrayed by the Hillsborough agreement. The fact that Tony Benn, Joan Maynard, and other Labour members would vote against the agreement in Westminster because it was *not* a step toward a united Ireland appeased few Unionists. Haughey's complaints that it traded away national assets appeased few Unionists. Molyneaux declared the agreement a sellout. Paisley declared the agreement a sellout. They all declared it a sellout.

On November 17 a special session of the Assembly called for a Northern Ireland referendum on the agreement and if the British government refused, then the DUP and OUP members of Westminster should resign and force province-wide by-elections on the single clear issue that the majority opposed a form fashioned behind their back with the connivance of a foreign state. It was not an unreasonable position, but it was so unreasonably presented as to disappear amid the turmoil and truculence of oratory that often seemed on the lip of treason. Not an Inch had enormous psychological power, may in war even have snatched victory from grave difficulties; but in a democratic system such intransigence seldom pays adequate returns. A Unionist policy of shrill and uncompromising rejection returned again psychological benefits but isolated all the majority politicians and parties, restricted politics to others, and ushered in an era of stalemate, where talks could only be about talks. The Unionist posture did, for them, have the virtue of emasculating minority political life. Without power there could be no sharing, could be no conventional politics.

For the unionists, there could be the politics of majority protest. This was most congenial to be involved, where the returns from a negative stance and a siege mentality could be paid in psychological tender if not in power. There had not been much conventional political power available in Northern Ireland for some time. Direct rule was London rule. The Northern Ireland Westminster members were simply ignored. Local councils existed but for very local things—and even there the arrival of Provisional Sinn Féin transformed the little clubs into arenas. Thus the Unionists and the loyalists (when there was a difference) shaped a congenial strategy of negative protest. The existing governing institutions—the Assembly, Westminster, the contrived by-elections, the local councils—were co-opted and used to attack the AIA. What could be done was made manifest on January 11 by the forty-foot banner stretched across the Edwardian City Hall in the center of Belfast by order of the Unionist members of the city council: "Belfast

Says NO." It was put up at the taxpayers' expense, the first step in a bitter minor struggle over local government rights and privileges waged with great intensity over the new symbol. The Unionists deployed their assets, their experience, their symbols, and their indignation in appropriate and often effective ways that captured and controlled almost all provincial political life.

Protest, agitation, display, and ritual had long been natural in provincial politics: marches and countermarches, banners and boycotts, sit-ins, disruptions, staged riots, the whole panoply. As Paisley said in the Commons, "There is a crisis in our land. The only thing that will steady our people is the opportunity to do something." So the loyalists began, everywhere and with every means to hand. They challenged the law of the land even though on November 25 the High Court in London had refused leave to Unionists to challenge the legality of the AIA. They were no longer loyal to London, Westminster, or the cabinet, but to themselves. On November 20 the Northern Secretary, Tom King, had been assaulted by an angry mob when he arrived for a luncheon at Belfast City Hall. On November 23 the first massive demonstration had gathered from 40,000 to 100,000, depending on the politics of the enumerator, before Belfast City Hall to hear Ulster's grievances. Attempts to get ahead of the Unionist leaders produced complications: Tom King in Brussels unwisely said that the AIA meant the Irish government accepted that there would never be a united Ireland. This was just what Provisional Sinn Féin and the militant Northern nationalists had suspected, but what King should not have said. He apologized on December 3, thus giving the loyalists more ammunition. No one could be more loyal than they, certainly not a Northern Secretary.

When the first session of the Anglo-Irish conference met at Maryfield on December 11 two thousand loyalists showed up and attacked the police at the gate. On December 17 all the Northern Ireland Westminster members resigned so as to force by-elections as a referendum on the treaty. The referendum campaign began immediately. It was announced that a special loyalist protest march would begin at the end of the month at Derry and would end at Maryfield.

All the action in the province was being initiated by the Unionists. The British simply continued to rule directly. Security was the prime issue, especially because the supergrass strategy was coming frayed in public. Still, on December 18 twenty-five of twenty-seven INLA men were convicted on the uncorroborated evidence of Harry Kirkpatrick, not a marginal criminal but a famous gunman. Such convictions only brought unease to many observers and most nationalists. There were attacks on the use of emergency legislation, plastic bullets, prison conditions, and the use of informers; and finally there were leaks and hints about how the dirty war had been fought by the British army and MI5. The unionists felt their security eroded by all this criticism. The IRA often seemed to slide way down on the urgent list. In fact this was actually the case, for in an armed struggle perception matters and the IRA was perceived as a side issue to the battle over the AIA.

The year-end figures for 1985 on violence underscored this. The death total was down to 54, the lowest since 1970. RUC losses were up to 14 from 7, and RUCR losses to 9 from 2; British army losses dropped to 2 from 9. The UDR lost 8, compared to the previous year's 4. These were an acceptable level: unfortunate, but a vast improvement on the old days. The assumption was that a mix of improved anti-insurgency tactics, the impact of informers and the supergrass trials, exhaustion, and the requirements of the Provisional Sinn Féin had eroded IRA offensive capacity. This indicated something of an unwarranted optimism in that the Provos welcomed in the new year a few minutes after midnight with a bomb that killed two RUC constables. Some in authority continued to believe that the AIA would edge the IRA gunmen further from the stage and undercut Sinn Féin. In fact on December 28, when eighteen members of Sinn Féin had been arrested, Adams claimed that the SDLP and the government of Ireland were responsible for the arrests—anything to harm the Provos. So the treaty was taken as a nationalist victory to isolate the Provos, to force them into politics or oblivion, except the loyalists still saw the IRA operating and security measures criticized.

Politically the agreement had given the SDLP no role. Direct rule was still direct rule. There was still no provincial power to share and the SDLP was a provincial party. The SDLP was reduced to the parish pump, the inevitable quarrels over priorities and personalities, the disadvantage of organization without the returns of office. Only the occasional intervention of London interest kept up SDLP hopes that devolution, power-sharing, had a future. Any unconventional protest was risky for a conventional party. The edge of violence and the contamination of the Provos was too close. The Provisionals scorned the agreement as merely one more concession, not progress toward an all-Ireland republic. The Protestant paramilitaries or at least the Ulster Freedom Fighters, the pointed end of the UDA, announced that members of the joint conference and secretariat would be legitimate targets.

In the end an Agreement arising from the political turbulence of Northern Ireland attracted there the grudging support of most of the SDLP, some other Catholics, and the few nonsectarian moderates, but nearly three-quarters of the Northern Ireland electorate vehemently opposed it. The next stage of the crisis was cluttered with the maneuvers of the involved to move the center of gravity back to Northern Ireland. First it was necessary to wait for the Unionist protest to die out. While the protest, boycott, and sullen political withdrawal continued, the Provisionals, balanced between the needs of Sinn Féin and the primary call of the IRA, readjusted for the long war. And the military campaign, if not renewed with vigor, gave evidence in the province and on the island that the armed struggle was far from over. GHQ also and again exported their campaign into England and onto the Continent. While the IRA regrouped in the train of the AIA, the SDLP looked for more movement, many moderate Northern Catholic politicians began to move into Southern politics. The Protestant militants, politicians or paramilitaries, must perforce repeat themselves but for the declining purpose. Talks about talks would come to the point of talking in earnest, and then the majority would have to swallow the reality of the agreement. Everyone said so. And they, from moderate Unionists to paramilitary loyalists, couldn't or wouldn't.

So 1986, with the reverberations of the IRA midnight bomb still about, began with the arrival at Maryfield on January 4 of the OUP-DUP march from Derry. The gates were wrenched apart amid scuffles. The OUP dissociated themselves from such violence but the rising star and deputy leader of the DUP, Peter Robinson, didn't. The AIA conferences kept meeting (the third was on January 10, in London) and announcing results: There would be discussions on extradition and the Flags and Emblems Act; the RUC would accompany UDR patrols. The agreement was at work without Unionist support. Then on January 23 came the fifteen by-election results: 418,230 Unionist votes, short of the hoped-for 500,000, and the Newry and Armagh seat lost to Séamus Mallon with a majority of 2,583. It was still a massive endorsement of the Unionist position but a propaganda exercise that gave the SDLP a seat at Westminster. The election also showed a decline in the Sinn Féin share of the nationalist vote from 41.9 percent to 35.4 percent. So, as promised, the agreement helped the SDLP, hurt Sinn Féin, but isolated the Unionists, who could and did point out that the vote for candidates favoring the agreement came to only 21.9 percent of the province. No one cared. Tom King had already said that they "cannot go on saying no. They must say yes to something."

They did not say yes for a very long time. McCusker and Robinson announced on January 26 that they would not take their seats at Westminster, since the Unionists were boycotting local government in the province. In fact the Unionists were still busily engaged in using the government available as a means to protest. Court cases were begun, eighteen Unionist councils refused to give a tax rate, the Assembly was used as a forum, meetings were held, negotiations opened; McCusker called for a tripartite meeting and momentary euphoria was engendered by a meeting at Number 10 Downing Street on February 25 between Thatcher and Paisley and Molyneaux. New institutions were established in the loyalist Ulster Clubs under Alan Wright, whose father had been killed by the INLA, to secure self-determination for the Ulster people. There was a return to the symbolic general strike on March 3 that involved a paramilitary presence, the threat of a permanent boycott by the Ulster Clubs if stores stayed open, and the complaint that the RUC had failed to prevent intimidation despite forty-seven injured policemen by the end of the day.

That the RUC, defended by Sir John Hermon on Irish RTE, had incurred loyalist wrath was made clear by attacks on RUC homes that forced fifteen families to move. The Protestant police now too often faced an aroused Protestant people. Crowds threw silver coins at the Judas police who had sold out to American money once the congressional vote of aid to Ireland was reported on March 12. In the first two months of 1986 some two hundred police had been injured in the clashes that arose from loyalist protests. In March the British sent in an additional 550 troops, bringing the army to the highest level in three years. Attacks on RUC constables and homes continued and culminated on March 31 in a riot in Portadown after the march of the Apprentice Boys of Derry was banned. In the riot thirty-nine policemen and thirty-eight civilians were injured. On April 4 fourteen police homes were attacked.

Paisley hurriedly returned from the United States and condemned all such attacks. Every effort was made to leash the loyalists attacking *their* police. The loyalist attacks began to taper off. One advantage for the authorities was that the paramilitaries had largely remained quiet, not so much out of conviction but because the nature of the organization had changed. Even then a traditional response might have been simply to kill random Catholics, as had been done in 1972. But it was not 1972. For even the hard men in the UVF and the UFF to see great advantage in sectarian terror to take the risk, there had to be a perceived need, a threat. If the Catholics were not sharing power, if the Provos could not escalate, if the great betrayal had come and gone with the agreement, and nothing had happened, why start to defend by killing Catholics? There had been direct British rule before the agreement and there was direct British rule now. The inarticulate loyalist gunman in his dim pub corner had intuitively grasped what was not as obvious to the politicians—nothing had changed in the province. In any case the actual motives of the killers have always been difficult to discern even through conversation with the involved. In 1986 and for some years the UDA and UVF, especially in Belfast, had decayed in political purpose and paramilitary structure as the remaining leaders turned to more personal interests. In 1986 what was more important than profit, personal gain, and the institutionalized benefits of the covert social world that would bring out the killers? Not the agreement. And so they showed up for the strike and attended the riots but had no need to "defend," since nothing could be seen to be under attack. Still, it was an appropriate time for action and a few men with guns ran loose on the margins of the Catholic areas, so there was a brief resurgence of murder, particularly in North Belfast; but there was no provincewide paramilitary action as in the past.

In fact, the ones most under attack seemed to be the RUC, for even with Paisley's intervention, the loyalist militants only quieted gradually. Trouble flared up again. On March 31 loyalist gangs attacked Catholic homes in Lisburn with stones and petrol bombs. The RUC defended the Catholics. The loyalists continued the attack. There were riots on Easter Monday at Portadown, and Keith White was fatally injured by an RUC plastic bullet—the first Protestant killed by the riot rounds. After his funeral the mobs of Protestant young took to the Belfast streets despite appeals for calm by Unionist politicians. Police were attacked with guns and bombs and rocks, millions of pounds of damage was done. This time the RUC were the first target, not just in the way of attacks on Catholics. The police seized arms and ammunition from loyalist centers and the loyalists responded with riots the next day in Portadown. There had always been Unionist unease with the paramilitaries, but at least they appeared organized, wore uniforms, had self-given ranks and avowed aims. What the Unionists saw in Belfast was the mob and in Belfast the mob could be truly deadly if released. A killer in dark glasses and beret addressed as Commander was awful enough, but an anonymous crowd, armed, angry, drunk on pints and the thrill of murder, a mob howling in the streets, put everything and everyone at risk. On April 23 the Unionists used the Assembly to call for a twelve-point package of protests that included a "day of deliverance" as well as an appeal to the RUC not to enforce the agreement; these stratagems, it was hoped, would keep the lid on the city. The politicians urged that the first Orange march of the season at Portadown be canceled.

Sir John Hermon focused not on the peaceful intentions of the politicians but on their long record of public militancy and their attempt with the Assembly document to put the RUC on the side of protest. He publicly attacked the Assembly appeal as a step to create disaffection within the RUC—"bordering on subversion." In the first six months of the agreement the loyalists had made three hundred attacks on police on duty and three hundred on RUC homes, forcing the rehousing of fifty police families. And the Northern Ireland marching season was about to begin—1,200 parades, each a police problem.

The advocates of the agreement had faced problems as well in that the selling points for one side had to be hidden from the other. Security cooperation, which both Dublin and London wanted, had to be shaped to different constituencies. Irish authorities did not mind sending back mad-dog Provo murderers to British justice. But extradition to British justice was assumed to be politically risky, was not thought to sell well in the nationalist Republic. This was because British justice had often seemed to be a contradiction in terms, and when, unfortunately, between the H-Block crisis and the problems over the convictions of the Irish bombers in England, fair play could still hardly be assured. No southern politician wanted to advocate extradition too fervently, even when eager to see IRA gunmen in prison. The British and the loyalists, avoiding the real enthusiasm in the Republic for security cooperation, made the public attitude on extradition more important than private practice. When at last the Republic agreed to extradite prisoners to the North to stand charges, the British authorities blundered and bungled, not once but time and again, in seeking to extradite with flawed requests. A blunder in March 1986, the fourth such British error, simply emphasized the problem. Evelyn Glenholmes, wanted in the United Kingdom for offenses in 1981 and 1982, had been released once in Dublin because of errors in the warrants. Then on March 22 she was released again because the second set of warrants was invalid. By the time the third set reached the court, she had disappeared.

In the House of Commons Sir Eldon Griffiths criticized the Director of Public Prosecutions, noting, "There is a painful contrast between the detailed and careful and often dangerous work of the police service of the Irish Republic and the Metropolitan Police and the RUC in undertaking to obtain the information, sometimes at the risk of their lives, and the slipshod and careless way in which that was dealt with within the DPP's office." The loyalists of the North did not want to hear praise of the police who kept the hated agreement nor criticism of the British prosecutor's office seeking out terrorists but sought the guilty in Dublin. There the courts—again—had taken refuge in a technicality to release a terrorist. It had happened before, when McGlinchey was extradited to Northern Ireland and convicted and then had to be re-extradited to the Republic after he was acquitted on appeal. Séamus Shannon had been acquitted of the murder of Sir Norman Strong and his son in January 1981 at Belfast Crown Court in December 1985 after being extradited from the Republic. In Dublin, in the same month, Brendan Burns, wanted for the murder of five British soldiers, walked free from a court because the RUC extradition warrants were quashed in Belfast by the chief justice of Northern Ireland. The escape of Evelyn Glenholmes in March 1986 that outraged Unionists had no basis in Dublin complicity, but this did not matter.

During much of the year any evidence of any sort was marshaled as ammunition against the agreement. There was, of course, no unity among Unionists on every tactic. On May 6 the Belfast City Council had voted twenty-seven to twenty-three to resume normal business and so end adjournment policy; the agreement could best be fought by using the council. On the sixth-month anniversary on May 15 there were more demonstrations, the telephone switchboard at Stormont was seized by the DUP, there was a work stoppage at Ballylumford power station, and lots of new posters were put up. During the first six months the Unionists had moved forward on many fronts. They had boycotted existing institutions and manipulated them. They had called for talking if the agreement was suspended and had been refused, first by King on March 10 and then in a letter by Thatcher on March 24. A rate strike was announced on April 23. Speakers in the Assembly warned of a bloodbath on May 14. The Official Unionists had angrily cut the special relationship with the Conservative Party, which dated from the nineteenth-century struggle over home rule. On June 2, two weeks after the six-month demonstrations, Molyneaux felt the agreement was crumbling. No one could see why.

Two days later Ian Gow and others launched a pro-Unionist Union in Britain. In fact the agreement inspired a variety of action groups in both England and Northern Ireland to marshal all shades of Unionist opinion: Friends of the Union organized by English friends like Gow and Biggs-Davison and Lord Moyola and the Charter Group of Northern Ireland composed of unionists. There was as well the by-invitation-only Ulster Resistance, initiated in November 1986 by Paisley, Robinson, and the Reverend Ivan Foster—a structure that was said to have had nine "battalions." And some within the "battalions" of Ulster Resistance were intent on a more military approach than even the more militant loyalist politicians could support. DUP sympathy for the Ulster Resistance creation declined markedly when in the summer of 1987 the police found arms similar to those seized from the UDA at Portadown and the UVF in Belfast—someone was planning real resistance. Most of the organizations, however, offered traditional political action, not violent but often strident protest. Then came the end of the Assembly, and more trouble, and more attacks on the RUC. In 1986 there were five hundred loyalist attacks on the RUC. And with the rising heat of the moment, not only logic was lost but also restraint. Even the most militant began to fear that the long, hot summer of marches would find the province in chaos.

Oddly enough, the July Orange marching season saw no widespread violent backlash but was not without incident. On July 6 much attention was focused on the RUC effort to monitor who could use the Tunnel route in Portadown, which previously had been used to take the drums and fifes, banging and tooting, by the Paddies' Obin Street homes. There were few more egregious examples of the use of the parades to intimidate and by 1986 such exercises were not only counterproductive within the province but also lost the loyalists any residue of remaining support from the outside world. The marchers, of course, had always so marched and they didn't care what anyone thought: "It's to hell with the future and live on the past." Their leader, George Seawright, the most militant of men, was barred by the police from the Tunnel area. The RUC "compromise" on only routing the Portadown march around Obin Street still outraged the Catholics. There was no peace for the weary police. From July 11 to July 16 there was trouble again in Belfast and Portadown, and on July 14 Catholic homes in Rasharkin, Antrim, were attacked by fifty loyalists with clubs and hatchets—"the nastiest and most vicious" attack so far, according to King.

The protest, if real, had been against a symbolic humiliation (the most real of all) that could not be assuaged by negotiation or concession. Once the anger, in part engendered by the outrage of the public politicians, had been spent, and spent more quickly because the target of opportunity had haphazardly turned out to be *their* police, the drive against the agreement could be channeled into appropriate protest. Much of such protest was not crafted to ensure riot and violence, not even organized so that violence might occur. In fact, all Unionist-loyalist action for months had been protest but using many institutional forms, courts, local councils, Westminster elections. The process wore on everyone after a while. The NIO decided to close up the Assembly. Only the DUP and OUP attended and thus the Assembly had no evident value, so on June 23 it simply dissolved, with no further elections planned after October, when the membership reached the end of term. Maybe it could be resurrected in the future. Maybe not.

But it was not as easy to "dissolve" as the Northern Ireland Office assumed. Outside Stormont two hundred loyalist protesters ultimately inspired a police baton charge. Inside, twenty-two of the remaining members, mostly DUP, would not leave, stayed the night, and were dragged away by the police the next morning. A rump Assembly was established in Belfast City Hall. There the old Assembly continued, pretending nothing had happened, month after month, without Speaker, committee structure, staff, or, after a while, public interest. Attendance dwindled, debates went unreported, and finally in November the sessions were discontinued. The Assembly, one of the more curious constructions of Northern Irish constitutional life, had proved a holed bucket waiting for the water of agreed devolution that never came. After Paisley, called the Uncivil Warrior by the *Times*, had snatched the corpse of the Assembly from the authorities, he went after the seat of real power. On July 10 Paisley and Robinson and four thousand loyalists took over Hillsborough in an early morning protest. Increasingly, the marches and the riots dominated the stage.

The rest of the summer's news was startling but had the effect of tranquilizing the loyalists, if for the wrong reason. Just as Dublin had been blamed for the repeated failure of extradition warrants, now the Republic was held up as an example that unity on decent terms was impossible. FitzGerald's strategy to turn the Republic into a prosperous, nonsectarian magnet ran afoul of Irish political complexities. The Taoiseach would have preferred to get rid of Articles 2 and 3 of the Constitution but opted for a referendum on divorce, a surer winner.

The entire campaign was confused. FitzGerald's strategy, Haughey's national posture, uncertainty as to political advantage across the spectrum, and the difficulty of voting on what many, perhaps most, saw as a moral issue, not a political adjustment, mingled. There was no consensus on the issue. Some equated a vote for divorce as a vote for contemporary values, a posture that attracted both advocates and opponents. Some voted against the future or against the past, against the Church or as the parish priest suggested. Some preferred to be more pious than more practical. Many simply opposed such a fundamental change. Haughey, neither interested in piety nor opposed to change, felt later that the referendum would not take "away one iota from progress toward a united Ireland." He felt that the divorce referendum should be judged on its own merits, not as a means to end partition. This is largely what occurred. Haughey did not see that the referendum was relevant, since "no matter what we do down here, if we were to elect the head of the Orange Order as president of this Republic, the Unionists would still find we are doing something dishonest, deceitful, and totally unacceptable to them."

The polls indicated victory for the referendum, formed as the Tenth Amendment to the Constitution. FitzGerald felt it would be the first giant step to adjust Catholic Ireland to the modern world, general practice, and European example. The polls were wrong. The vote on June 26 was "no" by more than three to two, 63 percent against and 36 percent for. Many voters thought they were simply being asked what they wanted on the matter of divorce, and they had answered: The people simply opposed it. They had not been asked to vote on the structure of an eventual Ireland but on a moral issue. Other voters felt that because they *had* been repeatedly told so, that the referendum vote did indeed relate to Northern Ireland. Hume had said that he hoped "the people of the Republic will cast their votes for an Ireland that will respect the rights of conscience of all its people, Protestant, Catholic, and dissenter." By 1986 a great many in the Republic had become dissenters on the North. Seeing the national issue here smuggled into the Republic as divorce, and having had enough of all *that*, they voted their conscience and be damned to the North. This might even indicate a confidence that the Protestants would have to come into a united Ireland on the Republic's terms. Or it might not. Maybe it was a vote for a little Republic but a pious one. No one knew, although there were lots of post-election explanations.

What mattered a great deal in the summer of 1986 was that the Northern unionists took it to mean that no one could ever force them into such a sectarian state that remained defiantly Catholic in law and habit. Paisley on July 1 felt that the referendum "has brought us back from the brink, because I believe that if it had been a success the British government would have been pushing us with more vigor down the united Ireland road. I would say that the civil war, which I believed was almost at hand, has receded as a result." The Republic, whatever the reason, had voted against pluralism, derailed FitzGerald's unity strategy, and postponed union for the immediate future. The step back from the brink might simply have needed a public excuse. The mob was in the streets and so the politicians needed reasons for the mob to go home. In the referendum they found a reason.

The second boon for order arose from the fallout of Manchester Deputy Chief Constable John Stalker's investigation. He had begun work on the undercover operations of the police in the Armagh shoot-to-kill allegations of June 1982. There had been rumors of obstructions and of revelations to come, and those concerned with conspiracy were busy at work on theories. Stalker's inquiry, the rumors, and reports of an investigation into the career of Stalker's friend in Manchester, Kevin Taylor, began to circulate. The plot thickened on May 29, when Stalker was told by Colin Sampson, chief constable of West Yorkshire, that he had been "removed forever" from the Northern Ireland investigation and was to stay home. His friendship with Taylor was compromising, if quite unrelated to his work in Northern Ireland. No one in Ireland believed this for a moment. On June 6 it was publicly announced that Colin Sampson would head the RUC Northern Ireland investigation.

The Stalker Affair grew. There were revelations about Stalker's troubles with the RUC, with his Manchester police colleagues. There were revelations about the lack of evidence against both Stalker and Kevin Taylor and rumors of a cover-up reaching into very high places. Stalker was cleared on August 22 but the rumors continued. It was a long-playing media delight, generating books, films, and Stalker's resignation from the police, and a very considerable scandal without resolution.* In Northern Ireland among loyalists, the interpretation was that the province and the police were immune to busybodies. The RUC might well have shot to kill—many loyalists certainly hoped so. The RUC might well have covered its tracks with a cooperative judicial system at first and with the old boys' network when Stalker appeared after the fact. Many loyalists certainly assumed this to be the case—but wasn't that grand?

So the Irish Catholics had blotted their copybooks in voting down divorce, opting for piety, revealing the reality of their sectarian state. The RUC investigator Stalker had been turned back. And who cares what the television says or the newspapers report? The province had been brought back from the brink of a civil war that Paisley had foreseen. There was still ample action and excitement, for the loyalists had hardly finished protesting against the agreement. Peter Robinson with five hundred loyalists invaded Clontibret just inside County Monaghan on August 7, assaulted two members of the Gárdaí, and marched through the little village in military formation. At the end of the day he was arrested. Robinson was an apt deputy to Paisley, all agreed. As usual the subsequent legal fallout was used by the DUP to push their protest. Still, as Harold McCusker of the OUP said, the agreement was not worth fighting for, much less dying for, and so increasingly the protesters avoided the streets and pursued their aims through less dangerous channels. On November 1 Paisley and Molyneaux launched the campaign in Britain at an Orange rally in Glasgow. The British, a few Masonic friends aside, were not interested in Ireland. There was no swelling tide of sympathy, only ennui at all levels. On November 7 Belfast Lord Mayor Sammy Wilson barred Northern Ireland Office ministers from Remembrance Day service at City Hall. Northern Irish loyalists were not interested in association with those who could not remember past loyalty. On November 10 an Ulster Resistance was formed at a closed meeting to take direct action against the agreement. Increasingly direct action was limited to words, pickets, and proposals, although the crowd did run riot after a huge Belfast delegation on November 15, the anniversary of the AIA, damaging and looting some seventy shops. The fact that a year had passed with no sign of compromise in London tended to take the edge off loyalist protest. There were limits to saying no, although there was no real end to the posture.

The next big push started at Belfast City Hall on January 3, 1987, when the OUP-DUP leadership announced a monster petition to the Queen. It was to be delivered to Buckingham Palace on February 12 with 400,000 signatures appended. In fact the direction of protest began to shift ever so slightly toward what might be done instead of what had been done wrong: Most unexpectedly, a beginning was made when the UDA published *Common Sense*. Returning to politics after the internal purge by murder, the UDA suggested a constitutional

---

*John Stalker's story is contained in his *Stalker* (London: Harrap, 1988). There is as well a small library of books and articles—even a 1990 feature film, *Hidden Agenda,* inspired by the affair.

conference, a devolved assembly, and a coalition government based on party strength. The internal loyalist paramilitary competition, however, pushed ahead as habit dictated. On February 7 the Ulster Freedom Fighters claimed they had planted eighteen incendiary devices in Donegal and Dublin. This was a week before the petition arrived at Buckingham Palace and indicated that the long wave of political protest had ebbed.

The Unionist protest had been a triumph of techniques and tactics rarely bettered in a democratic society. With limited leverage but great popular support, the leadership had deployed supporters through the entire spectrum of activity and influence. Westminster and its electoral machinery were used. The provincial Assembly was used, particularly after its dissolution. Local governing bodies were used or boycotted or adjusted to purpose. The courts were used in London, in the province, even in time in Dublin. A referendum was manipulated without recourse to permission and another was urged. New organizations were established, like the Ulster Clubs, and old organizations sympathetic to the cause were given new roles. Those aligned with Unionist orthodoxy—Orange Orders, veterans groups, demobilized B Specials, country militia, moribund support groups—were used. There were marches and demonstrations, crowds on the spot and mobs promised. There was not always coherent central direction but often none was needed: Protest created its own imperatives and agenda. The campaign was carried to Great Britain and the DUP invaded Monaghan. The conventional and moderate unionists often had qualms about the degree of violence and the potential of the mob, but violent agitation was as Ulster as the Giant's Causeway, the scenic volcanic outcrop on the northern Antrim coast, so that generally violence was structured, even when mobs were in action. In the province riots tended to run to rules. Not always. The attacks on the RUC were foolish and were restrained by the politicians when the penny dropped, and it was recalled that they were *our* police only as long as they identified with *us*. This was not easy for the RUC to do when their houses were being burned.

The Belfast summer riots also concentrated minds—a mob like that is no one's friend—and an imposition of discipline on those who would run riot was begun by loyalist political leaders. Ritualized riots and a few broken heads or burned-out Fenians might pass in most of the province, but Belfast held more dangerous substances, contained the critical mass that might go off—a chain-reaction with no lead bars to snatch out in time, a chain-reaction that could lead not to a pogrom down that lane but unrestrained and lethal sectarian civil war. The beast could be a valuable ally in the arsenal of protest, but was not easily discarded once aroused. Once again by midsummer 1986 the beast long on the chain of practicality had been encouraged to lunge and snarl by years of public threats, patriotic incitement, and rationales for the approaching Armageddon. There was real fear that the collar might be slipped. Never in all the years of oratory that incited to violence did the politicians themselves move beyond the hidden white line of legality: Secret armies might be used as a threat, future murders might be explained, violence might be suggested; but no arms were carried and no legal offenses were committed.

So riotous behavior was used, misused, promised and threatened, summoned up, and when grown too big was hurriedly crammed back into the bottle.

Generally, however, the gates were smashed, not the gatekeepers. Action ranged from peaceful sit-ins through riots. There were as well the unwanted but related sectarian murders in North Belfast. These killings, however, were done by the few, not the mob, and by 1986 were almost traditional. The Unionist tried to ignore the killings and rely on politics. Persuasion was used on the highest level, meeting at Number 10 Downing Street, intimidation during the one-day strike at every shop door, pamphlets were printed and posters put up and sermons given. Taxes were briefly withheld and symbols manipulated. There were hard words by rabble-rousers and reasoned oratory by proper gentlemen. In the end, the agreement remained not only untouched but also untouchable. Margaret Thatcher had even indicated that the advent of the hated Haughey as Taoiseach would bring no relief. So all the enormous investment in protest, the splendid array of techniques, the cunning and craft and care, did not succeed in doing more than absorbing the interest and energies of the Unionist and loyalist dissenters within the province. Those who would learn the ways of democracy, the nature of power, and the limits of protest could learn by turning to the record of the Unionists between November 15, 1985, and November 15, 1986. In the end the agreement, as planned, was beyond loyalist reach, beyond their arguments, and most important of all, was too benign to warrant the enormous emotional charge the loyalists brought to bear.

The Catholic civil rights workers had cared about something that mattered. What mattered, really, about the Anglo-Irish Agreement to those other than unionists? Again the disproportionate and violent response to a slight, the gross reaction arising from only suspicion, alienated the alien. Why were innocent Catholics killed in North Belfast? Why were decent constables' homes burned down? Why was an entire establishment so violently unhappy with march routes that they killed over them? The IRA was fighting a nationalist armed struggle, brutal, murderous, perhaps counterproductive, surely with little hope of success, but explicable. British counterinsurgency, even the brutal arrogance of the Orange bigots who often turned to vigilante murder, were explicable, if detestable. Not so all the violence arising from an agreement that was modest in scope, modest in language, and ineffectual in practice. What, then, was the matter with the Unionists, the loyalists, to stir this inexplicable outrage?

Just when everyone thought that there were no surprises, once more Ireland produced a novelty that fortunately threatened few and ultimately faded away. At best it was a window on a people's psyche, a splendid case study in political protest action; at worst it was an example of a cankered society incapable except in dominance. Back in January Tom King had said, "They cannot go on saying no. They must say yes to something." What King and others missed was that there remained enormous secondary benefits from saying no. These psychological benefits were not fully satisfactory but, like a great many secondary benefits in Northern Ireland, they tended to dominate any dialogue. The most the Unionists could imagine was discussing reasons not to say no while the benefits of obstruction continued. And militant loyalists were not even interested in discussion.

Gradually a few Unionists began to realize that the agreement was not to be destroyed by protest or protest alone. On November 26, 1986, OUP councillors had voted not to resign from district councils despite party leadership support for the proposals. The members saw sense in keeping what tiny power still existed in small offices. What had a year of sweeping protest accomplished? The agreement was still in place and even if it was hateful it had very little impact on daily life or political life. The agreement was just there, frustrating to those who protested but no bother to the everyday farmer or the solicitor's clerk, not a daily matter at Mackie's or along the Shankill. Paisley was expelled from the European Parliament on December 9 after repeatedly interrupting Thatcher's speech. It was grand, spectacular, distant protest, the hard word in front of people who thought Ulster a raincoat and could not easily find Ireland on a map. And where did it lead? Thatcher came over again at Christmastime, on December 23, and reaffirmed the government's commitment to the agreement.

It was not as if events had been limited to the unionist protest or solely shaped to their needs, only that the unionists had made the visible running. The same old dreary problems lurked out of sight. In January 1986 unemployment in the province had been 21.6 percent and by October was up to 23.1 percent. There was an appeal for state action to aid industry—or else violence would be encouraged; even in Irish economic reports violence had a role. A report showed improvement but still too few Catholics and women in the civil service. Divis Flats in Belfast and Rossville Flats in Derry were to be demolished, the Northern Ireland Office and the Provos combining to transform the skyline of the province. One of the accepted rituals of the Troubles had become the "review." And no matter what special events or particular initiatives had occurred since the last review, there were constants. The toll of dead crept upward, past anniversaries and special numbers—one thousand dead, two thousand dead; and the grievances—economic, social, judicial, political—remained statistically visible. Unemployment was high and always worse for the Catholics, amenities were short, housing was poor, facilities were not the equal of those in Britain or Europe and were always to Catholic disadvantage.

There were mixed returns on the security front as the long-running problems of extradition, shoot-to-kill, British justice, and prison conditions continued, intensely involving the concerned and mere background music for the rest. The supergrass system was coming to an end amid releases and recriminations. From the South there was good news for those who sought evidence of Dublin's aid in the struggle against terrorism, and insufficient progress for those who doubted such a commitment. The Republic announced an intention to sign the European Convention on the Suppression of Terrorism, which included extradition provisions. Not until November 1987 would an extradition law pass the Dáil—the concept of extradition was more troubling for Irish nationalists than the practice. In any case there was no great evidence that the agreement had produced an easing of the more unpleasant aspects of Northern security or brought the Irish Republic into harmony with United Kingdom policy and programs.

The AIA Conference's first meeting in Dublin on October 6 did discuss border security, but Dublin found no easy "concessions" to offer the electorate when Thatcher, on November 4, in a confidential letter to FitzGerald, rejected the demand that the Diplock Court judges be increased to three. Concessions were not Thatcher's way and no one in London wanted to hear again how unfair the Diplock system was while IRA gunmen were still at work. Dublin had hoped that the British would clean up their judicial act a bit so as to sidetrack island complaints about British "justice." The London establishment virtually ignored reports from Amnesty International or the Standing Advisory Commission on Human Rights, much less complaints from the victims or their friends. Once the agreement was in place, most British interest focused on security matters as the route to the normal: no gunmen, no Diplock Courts; no interfering Irish-Americans, no one shot dead with plastic bullets; no bombs, no prison protests; and no IRA, no Orange murders. Ireland had again become simple.

The republican movement, the focus of British concern, had, like all other Irish factors during the post AIA period, been neglected—except at the moment of atrocity or as rationalization for actions by others. The Provisionals had adjusted to loyalist turmoil, paid little attention to the agreement, continued and expanded their own armed campaign, run Sinn Féin in the "referendum" elections with a small but worrisome decline in votes, and survived a major schismatic threat with minimum damage. In fact the republicans finished 1986 with great confidence. What outsiders saw as a quiet year the knowledgeable knew was an important milestone.

The annual summing of the cost of the year once again attracted little interest; the butcher's bill seemed to indicate that the Unionist protest had absorbed much of the militancy while the IRA had simply maintained the pace on their part. The death total was slightly up, to 61 from 54, a difference that mattered if you recognized a name on the list but statistically a minor matter. The army lost 2 instead of 4 and the UDR 8 instead of 2, the RUC 10 instead of 14 and the RUCR 2 instead of 9. These were grim again if personal but hardly more than a bad week of automobile casualties in the United Kingdom. In the same year, 1986, there were 128 homicides in Phoenix, Arizona, and hardly anyone noticed, even in Phoenix, where it was a record toll. In less than two years more people are murdered in New York City than were killed in twenty years of the Troubles. The Irish total was awesome by any standards, but society found automobile deaths easily tolerable—and always more numerous. Yet anyone killed in the midst of social conflict, especially if innocent, is one too many. And even one killed spectacularly can have an exaggerated effect on civic stability. And the lethal toll crept up; incremental misery. On July 12, 1989, twenty years after the first fatality, Francis McCloskey, sixty-six, a Catholic knocked down and killed by the RUC in Dungiven outside an Orange hall on July 13, 1969, the grand Northern Ireland total reached 2,763 and was used as the title of an analytical work on the distribution of death by Michael McKeown. The statistics of deadly quarrels had become a minor speciality. Professors at American universities received grants to collate them into conclusion, journalists kept a running record, and the state provided the necessary legal certification.* What was clear in December 1986 was that the Protestants had not run amok after the agreement and the IRA's armed campaign had not, perhaps could not, escalate.

One sign that security targets were difficult to find had been the extension of the authorized list. On August 5 the IRA, in a new warning, identified people

---

*Michael McKeown, *Two Seven Six Three* (Dublin: Murlough Press, 1989). Even those statisticians who factor in the lives lost in Britain, the Republic, and the Continent tend to come up short since some, a few, deaths are not obviously or easily attributed to the Troubles.

holding a wide range of positions relating to security. In the previous year five people had been killed for providing services to security forces. This meant that those who accept contractual repair on police stations, laid bricks on an army base, perhaps even those who refilled Coke machines at army laggers could be "legitimate" targets. There were the individual decisions on contracts and Coke machines, an occasional attack, the protest of the moderates and authorities, and life moved on. The crisis, was static even if, as a few of the cynical indicated publicly, the AIA was not the final accommodation but merely a formulaic facade.

As for the IRA, from the underground matters appeared quite different. The quiet 1986 was important not as sign of slackening but the reverse—or so the Army Council assumed. The assets invested after the H-Block campaign had been largely political and these, producing good returns in Northern Ireland, needed to mature in the Republic, where the cause had been neglected for years. In the North direct rule meant that there was little real political power available through election. The local councils were worth the trouble and could be used without violating the old republican principles of abstentionism; the seat in Westminster was not worth a split. But in the Republic power was in the Dáil and if Sinn Féin were to seek power, the absolute and ultimate purpose of a revolutionary, through elections, then the way to Leinster House had to be opened. The movement did not anticipate a majority, did not need a majority, for they represented not numbers but the ultimate Republic established in every Irish heart and so had the right to wage war. In waging this war against the British enemy, seat of all Irish troubles, a twenty-six county advocacy was necessary that could be achieved in part, and only in part, through political means. For the struggle, the long war, a twenty-year war if necessary, to succeed then a Sinn Féin presence in the Republic was crucial and so a way into the Dáil must be opened—and if opened assured that a certain number of the traditionalists would not be swayed that this was a violation of principle.

According to traditionalists, to be legitimate the movement *must* deny the Dáil as a matter of principle. Adams, McGuinness, Morrison, and others of the new Northern Sinn Féin did not agree, although they understood the position. The issue was delayed for argument, to shape consensus, to underline the penalties of going and the necessities for staying, to wait on events. Adams, more than most republicans, sought consensus—but in the end, there would be a split. The traditionalists who had watched Adams and company take over the IRA, take over Sinn Féin, take over the movement, accepted that the North should run the war, that a new generation was in charge, and that changes would be made. But they would not bend principles. These traditionalists were mainly the Southerners who had rushed to start the Provos in 1969 to 1979. O Brádaigh, O Conaill, and the others; but they had support in the North as well. They did not, however, have as much support as they first assumed, not when it came to a vote. Their generation had aged and many were out of the movement. Many of the new members (there were as many who had been republicans since 1969 still alive as there were who had been republicans during the rest of the century) were not as moved by their argument on principles. Most important the Army Council, the Army Executive, the IRA in action and in prison, all supported the Adams-McGuinness leadership, more so actually than did the thirty-two-county Sinn

Féin. And out beyond the actives, in that nebula of the faithful, some active, many available, all concerned, the Army Council mattered most.

The IRA was not going to split. If the faithful left, they would have to leave the army and the prisoners behind and in so doing leave behind many who really would have preferred to go with the old abstentionist principle, deny the bastards a nod. Not this time, however, and so the pure republicans could only count on themselves—and not on all of those who agreed with them. Some would stay who might have gone and some would not take sides and the time to take sides had come by the autumn of 1986.

Not only had Adams gotten rid of Ivor Bell, who, as chief of staff after McGuinness stood down before the Assembly elections, had pointed out the failings of the campaign; he had also spoken for those who suspected Belfast and/or Sinn Féin of going political. These, the physical force men, often traditionalists, the country soldiers, also traditionalists, were convinced by the Army Council that the war would be pursued. For a generation the major indicator of IRA military strength had been the store of matériel: There were always volunteers, money could be found, legitimacy seemed beyond fatal compromise, and the republican world was constantly renewed—the problem was gear. This problem in turn arose from the lack of IRA friends and sources and the concomitant lack of useful British foes. The IRA lacked the appropriate skills and political and strategic assets to acquire arms illicitly. And no one hated the British sufficiently at the appropriate moment to come to their aid. Post-imperial Britain rarely had enemies useful to the IRA—the residual holders of anti-British sentiment saw no point in alienating a major power because of nostalgia. And when the opportunity might have arisen, as in the case of the Falklands war, there was no Belfast man to be found in Buenos Aires. There was, consequently, a persistent need for more gear, better gear, any gear, especially matériel that would allow escalation: refined explosives, sophisticated small arms, electronic devices of all sorts, advanced fuses, next-generation firearms, and particularly missiles.

At the beginning of an armed struggle very little can be elaborated into major impact: A king can be killed with a dagger; the Zionist Stern Group killed Lord Moyne in Cairo with two previously owned revolvers; Grivas managed EOKA with one small boatload of oddments and revolvers sent into Cyprus by mail; the Mau Mau made their own guns. Later, as the rebels move toward irregular war, their irregular armament becomes regular, their organization a counterstate, their war more conventional. The IRA had started with next to nothing but goodwill and junk. This almost traditional problem is without a solution. The lack of arms engenders ingenuity in procurement, cunning in operations, care in target selection, and enormous costs in time and planning—usually for reasonable returns. As the number of weapons rises the rebel commanders find a rich menu of options, a temptation toward the conventional, a decay of the virtues of poverty (thrift, maintenance, pride in possession, caution, and a sense of limitation), and, perhaps, not so much delusions of grandeur as aspirations to legitimacy. The more armament one has the more one wants. For a rebel there can never be too much—except in the case of enormously shrewd rebels, who grasp that within the underground too much is more dangerous than not enough. How would the IRA use tanks? If delivery could be guaranteed, the Army Council would probably authorize the shipment. Some rebels do, indeed, need more conventional weapons, for as they move out of the underground they face conventional war; this was true for Menachem Begin's Irgun and for the Vietnamese. Yet, in the underground, while less is not necessarily more, too much is a dangerous temptation.

The IRA Army Council had almost never had to spurn such temptation. They lacked the contacts and sources for modern weapons; they lacked the experience and skills of purchase and shipment; they did not even understand the mechanics of the trade. Consequently they were dependent on their own, especially in America, or on those who learned on the job, learned haltingly if at all. In September 1984 seven tons had been lost when the *Marita Ann* was captured off the Kerry coast. The load was contaminated from the first. No one but the Irish would have persisted with drops from small boats—even thrillers gave up this method long ago.

Illicit arms shipments, those without a government at one end, are a tiny and irrelevant part of the trade. One refurnished obsolete main battle tank costs more than all the arms that the IRA acquired or lost in twenty years. Illicit arms are small potatoes and shipped as such. Arms are disguised with paper, cargo manifestos, dockets, insurance certificates, all bought and paid for. They are acquired with paper, bills of lading, sales slips, end users' certificates—and money. They arrive documented as used agricultural machinery, Bulgarian home appliances, electrical generators, even bulk chemicals. They have become on paper something else and are so treated. Inspection is the least of the problems of shipment, since the purchased paper tells all. With money hard to come by— armed robbery, even for political purpose, does not guarantee a steady income— the IRA had always been reluctant to spend money on paper. They wanted the gear and so they smuggled. They often did so without realizing that a lack of governmental friends meant a plethora of government enemies directing agencies to monitor covert shipments. Arms transported without a government sponsor, even a covert sponsor, are at very great risk. They usually end up, like those on the *Marita Ann*, in the hands of the wrong people—money wasted, volunteers imprisoned, arms gone.

The Provos were regularly sold out at the beginning or discovered along the way and delivered to the authorities—Irish, British, French, Dutch. They had enemies that they never knew in Israel because of their contacts with Palestine, in Washington because of the global antiterror campaign, in certain struggles because their inept operations ruined more serious illicit trade, in contacts that were not what they seemed, more likely to end in London than Sofia or Berlin. And thus had almost no allies and did not make any. Where they operated against the British in Germany, Spain, the Netherlands, and France, they alienated the locals, who were sufficiently burdened with the usual transnational terrorists and local subversives. This did not stop the IRA trying, nor did it cut off everything, nor did it curtail Irish ingenuity. Items were bought off the shelf or sent into the island in bits and drabs. If rockets and missiles could not be bought, the IRA funded research and development in America by sympathetic individuals, just as the old IRA had done with the Thompson submachine gun and the Fenians with the submarine. There was always a problem, never a solution, but the QMG somehow coped and the volunteers had what was needed if not what was desired.

Since little was needed to fuel the armed struggle and because much of that was available through the Irish-American diaspora, the small European markets, or domestic production, little proved ample. The Army Council and the various QMGs always wanted still more and especially certain weapons of escalation, in particular hand-held ground-to-air missiles—the ideal operational would be the very simple fire-and-discard tubes that would put all British army helicopters at risk and give second thoughts to all those involved in United Kingdom air traffic. Even a few missiles would change the pattern of British military response in the countryside, and it was in the countryside that the war was being most effectively fought.

Increasingly Belfast resembled a vast concentration camp with the Catholics penned in under watchful guards monitoring their moves. They were prisoners with considerable local freedom, experience, cunning, and familiarity with the physical and ethnic landscape of the arena; they were able to operate once, but rarely regularly without enormous risks. So it was in the country where the imposition of control was not as effective—despite a line of great, spindly watchtowers stretched along the border, dogs, the latest technology, and elite troops increasingly familiar with Ireland, and despite the assets of the dirty war, informers, bribes, threats, extortion, intimidation, and murder. The countryside needed weapons to escalate and Belfast to persist. The volunteers had long ago become professional guerrillas, urban or rural, within the narrowing arena. In 1970 the IRA launched 191 attacks for each member of the security forces killed—an era when each killing did not matter much since the total was much higher—and by 1984 the figure was nineteen attacks per death—an era when killing soldiers mattered a great deal and was much harder. So with Northern Ireland closing down despite IRA skills, the expansion of the war elsewhere was logical. Sophisticated weapons would help.

Those within the movement who were concerned about such matters were also inherently suspicious of the movement's center, now Belfast, once Dublin, and the contamination of politics. Thus, when the Army Council produced a flood of new weapons, including a great store of Semtex explosives, the coherence of the movement was assured. Any purists' split would leave behind the weapons, the wielders, the prisoners, and so the IRA—and this time, unlike the toleration shown Costello, who had split after all from the Officials not the Provisionals, there would be no other IRA. One war. One IRA. The Army Council made this clear.

What had happened was that the IRA had reopened the Libyan connection that had petered out into transfers of money. These funds had been an enormously welcome and important matter to the Army Council and but a few crumbs on troubled waters to the Libyans. The IRA had not been able to turn this money into arms—or very many arms. In 1984–85, Libya—in effect the maximum leader, Colonel Mu'ammar al-Qaddafi, and his second-in-command, Major Abdul Salaam Jalloud—had once again found reason to tinker with the IRA as a small aspect of their ongoing war on imperialism. This consisted of supporting revolutionaries, monitored more closely as the scene of the action came nearer to Tripoli: Ireland was far, far away. The Libyans were, in fact, rather open about their arrangement with the IRA. On June 17, 1986, Major Jalloud told visiting

German members of the European Parliament that his country planned to renew aid to the IRA. The Libyans were particularly concerned about an incident in London in 1986, when Libyan diplomats were expelled after a woman constable, Yvonne Fletcher, was shot and killed from inside the Embassy—an incident that outraged the British government, the media, and nearly all of the people. The use of Britain the same year as point of origin for some of the American planes that attacked targets in Tripoli as terrorism sites had simply exacerbated matters. The Libyans did not care for the British Empire anyway.

The IRA-Libyan contacts over the years had been erratic and Libyan knowledge of the struggle, even after years of exposure, was slight. There is no great international terrorist network but only men who make telephone calls from creased address books, often to discontinued numbers, to set up a meeting in some anonymous room over tea to see if something can be done. This year one set of telephone numbers, that year a friend in a government office, the next year a trap ambush and no report back to headquarters. The door-to-door salesmen of revolution—Irish revolution, Arab revolution, any irregular war—lead lives of covert desperation that sometimes produces the gear but more often frustration and once in a while death.

None of this mattered, for the Libyans agreed to allow the IRA to pick up, pack, and ship out gear—mostly small arms and Semtex explosives but perhaps later some small missiles. The phone call had been made by luck at the right moment. In effect the IRA were told to take matériel from that building and so they did. Eschewing paper, they depended on small boats run through Malta. The project was outrageous in its daring: Libya was closely monitored by several anti-IRA intelligence services, Malta was filled with British citizens, the seas between Libya and Ireland might look empty but were constantly monitored by all sorts of unseen eyes, including American satellites. No one imagined they would be needed, that the IRA would persist in ancient procedures—so the worst player proved more effective than a real contender. In time the Irish news media would reveal in detail what could be learned about the Libya-Ireland connection. Those arrested certainly told what they knew. In August 1985 the first boat, the converted yacht *Casamara*, arrived at a rendezvous off the Maltese island of Gozo, met the Libyan *Samra Africa,* took on ten tons of weapons, and arrived off the Clogga Strand south of Arlow, a small Wicklow town south of Dublin, in September. The yacht was charged and captained by Adrian Hopkins, former owner of a Bray travel agency. Hopkins had republican sentiments, financial problems, maritime experience, and only one Irish crewman aboard. This shipment contained five hundred crates of AK-47 assault rifles, pistols, hand grenades, ammunition, and seven RPG-7 rockets. In October the *Casamara,* now named the *Kula,* returned to the Mediterranean. The second shipment, which included heavy Soviet machine guns, "Dushkas," left Malta waters on October 6 and arrived safely off Arlow. In July 1986 there was another shipment of fourteen tons, including, according to the authorities, two SAM-7s. In October 1986 there was still another large shipment of eighty tons, which included one ton of Semtex, reportedly ten SAM-7 missiles, more RPGs and AK-47s, and hundreds of thousands of rounds of ammunition. This arrived on another ship, the *Villa,* also bought and captained by Hopkins. The boats would anchor jurisdictionally between the Irish navy and the Gárdaí, just beyond customs and outside general notice. The matériel would be moved ashore and trucked away, divided, and moved into dumps, some old and some brand-new, some North and some South. No one noticed.

There were some rumors within the IRA about big operations to come, so that the prospect of any militant volunteer leaving an IRA receiving serious gear was slight. The Army Council had achieved two major goals: gear and gutting internal opposition. With a little luck they would have gotten their hearts' desire: effective SAM-7 ground-to-air missiles; but so much stuff was coming in that Western intelligence agencies noted the fact and the conduit was snapped shut. In October 1987 the Irish-manned *Eksund* sailed for Ireland with a cargo that included even more gear than anticipated; but on November 1 it was taken in a French customs ambush in the Bay of Biscay. The ship was seized so quickly that the crew could not sink it. The French reported that the *Eksund* was loaded with a 150-ton load of arms, AK-47s, heavy machine guns, SAM-7 missiles, Semtex, and ammunition.

It was the last direct shipment from the Libya connection, not that the connection was broken. On April 1, 1988, Colonel Qadaffi would again pledge aid to the Provisional IRA and two weeks later would announce that he was setting up support centers for both the IRA and PLO. By then Ireland had been turned upside down looking for his earlier shipments. The Gárdaí, using various lists of possibles—the usual suspects, the old faithfuls, Northern exiles, the doubtful, Sinn Féin types, no Officials but any doubtful household—scoured the countryside in the Republic. Beginning on November 23, 1987, in Operation Mallard, at least twenty-five thousand and perhaps fifty thousand homes were searched. Not to have the house turned over was an insult for any of the faithful. To be searched, on the other hand, was an outrage for those mistakenly on the list, and a dreadful surprise to families who thus discovered their children had heretofore hidden Sinn Féin politics. Some wanted IRA men were found—including two Maze escapees—but no great arms hoard. Empty bunkers were found dug under farm buildings and at the corner of fields, small dumps with new weapons were found, and a large dump was found on a beach near Malin Head in County Donegal. Estimates were that the IRA had thousands of AK-47s and the needed ammunition, and perhaps some SAM-7s. The police, North and South, said the missiles were in the country. In point of fact, the Provos did get their missiles at long last, but after three attempts to deploy them despaired. Either the missiles were faulty or had been damaged in transit or the volunteers could not cope. They were dumped. In any case, there was Semtex, which made the most difference of all.*

*In Tripoli the authorities were again unhappy that the IRA had been caught with Libyan arms, a replay of the *Claudia* debacle, but the good opinion of the West was rarely a high priority. The American air strike in April 1986—an air strike in part launched from British bases, after Washington accused Libya of organizing a bombing of an American club in Berlin—did indicate that there were penalties in dabbling in special terror operations. When the Americans accused two Libyans with complicity in the mid-air bombing of Pan Am Flight 103 over Lockerbie Scotland with the loss of 259 lives on December 21, 1988, Tripoli sought both to evade responsibility and to keep the two out of Western hands. One Libyan maneuver

Most of the weapons were kept in the Republican dumps, but the new explosives began to show up. The first use had already come on October 28, 1986, when an IRA mortar bomb that failed to explode on a British army observation post at Drumackavall, South Armagh, was found to be filled with Semtex. The explosive gave the IRA teams far greater operational flexibility, especially in the escalating campaign off the island. The rest of the shipment gave the IRA more arms than volunteers. The AK-47s turned up only slowly because the active service people remained loyal to their old weapons—some were as familiar to the Belfast ballistics office as to the owner. But the IRA had the gear, and so those traditionalists who would—understandably but unfortunately—stand on principle could stand down.

On November 1, 1986, at the Mansion House in Dublin, the six hundred delegates of Sinn Féin gathered at their annual Ard Fheis knowing that a decision on abstention would be made. Delay to build a consensus had diminishing returns. For the traditionalists it was a vote on long-established principles. The sole surviving member of the legitimate, long-ago Second Dáil, Tom Maguire, had just told O Brádaigh that in his opinion abstentionism was a basic tenet of republicanism, a moral issue of principle. Abstentionism gave the movement legitimacy, the right to wage war, to speak for a Republic all but established in the hearts of the people.

Gerry Adams felt that legitimacy was not a matter of such artificial institutions and principles but the legacy of history. Abstentionism was a means to an end and a means that no longer served the movement but hindered the long march to the Republic. And he could speak from strength, knowing that three weeks earlier an Extraordinary General Army Convention of the IRA, the first army convention since 1970 (war conditions had been used to avoid meetings), had backed his new departure. The IRA had—as in 1969—been polled first, captured by the Army Council and GHQ.

> I can understand that some comrades view a change in the abstention policy as a betrayal of republican principle. Some of you may feel that a republican organization making such a change can no longer call itself 'republican'. If there are delegates here who feel like this, I would remind you that another republican organization has already done what you fear we are going to do tomorrow.*

This time, however, much of the ill-defined republican movement, the inactive, the attached, the great haze of the faithful that circled around the visible IRA–Sinn Féin center, had been brought along as well. This time, with a war

---

was during meetings in 1992 in Switzerland with British officials to hand over details of the old IRA contacts to win favor with the West. However useful these details might have been, no state likes to betray—and betray publicly—covert contacts, thus inhibiting future operations, but for the Libyans the IRA was expendable. The Provisional GHQ had to assume that the Libyans revealed all that they knew—which was not much more than the British probably knew by 1992—and thus might put at risk certain volunteers.
*Patrick Bishop and Eamonn Mallie, *The Provisional IRA* (London: Heinemann, 1987), p. 356.

continuing, the delegates and most members felt matters were not as in 1969–70. They had not come full circle and would the next day keep straight on in solidarity with the IRA and the armed struggle.

November 2 came and two-thirds voted against the traditionalists and for dropping abstentionism: 429–161 of the 628 present. Ruairí O Brádaigh, Dáithí O Conaill, and about one hundred others walked out to form Republican Sinn Féin (RSF) at a previously hired hall in a hotel outside Dublin. They felt, as did many, perhaps many who stayed, that a struggle based on expediency would corrupt the cause. They took fewer people than they had intended. And they were warned by the Army Council that there was to be no competitive IRA. The core of the new RSF was from the old Southern Provisionals who, unable to play an effective role in the armed struggle, had gradually been edged from the center of the stage by Belfast. The RSF also included those traditionalists from everywhere. Once more, the commemorations and prisoners fund, the structures abroad, were set up. In the United States a struggle was waged for control of diaspora resources, usually in the hands of traditionalists like Michael Flannery in New York. RSF kept their contacts with those still Provos but who had doubts about the military staying power of Belfast. The purists, however, did not try to organize a competing secret army. With Republican Sinn Féin waiting in the wings, the movement—not necessarily the visible structure of Provisional Sinn Féin— would have to maintain a real military momentum. There was a flurry of military operations in and around Belfast during the remainder of the year in part to indicate to the country militants that the city was not a center of politics. A six-hundred-pound bomb went off in the Lisburn Road and a number of hotels were bombed. Key military events, however, were elsewhere.

The Libyan shipments, especially the Semtex, and the presence of a guerrilla overload in Northern Ireland that released volunteers for overseas missions meant that there was a shift in IRA emphasis and structure. The actives and those on the run were attached to GHQ or regional units under the command of Kevin McKenna as chief of staff. The Army Council was little different from the previous year, for it changes slowly and mainly as the result of arrests. The losses to RSF did show up on the Army Executive, but most of the IRA stayed in place. Yet the purists had a hard case to answer for many republicans. What had the whole movement been about? Why had so many died, suffered, ruined their lives rather than accept imposed institutions? What had all modern history proven but acceptance meant co-option and corruption? Look at de Valera and Seán MacBride and then the sad sequel of the Stickies, now the antinationalist Workers Party content with a few Dáil seats while praising the RUC and denouncing the Provisionals. Why rerun 1969? And what was so different about the practical need now, 1986, that required the jettisoning of proven principles?

Many traditionalists, including J. B. O'Hagan, Joe Cahill, and John Joe McGirl, stayed with the Provisionals. In fact McGirl, from Leitrim, at seventy a well-known and enormously useful figure, had spoken at the Dublin Ard Fheis directly to the point: "Today we have an army that has been fighting for sixteen years and will continue to fight until British rule is ended." There were those, then, who would have liked to go but could not, could not split in the midst of war. And they stayed, stayed with the army and the arms and the prisoners.

Equally important, many of those outside the center of the circle did not rush to support the new direction. They kept the barn door open for a dump, lent money or a car, kept the support systems operating. But they kept their faith in abstentionism as well. They were unlikely to have to sign an oath or go into the Dáil anyway. And as a bonus for the reluctant Sinn Féin electoral returns postponed most problems, perhaps indefinitely. There was no longer a Northern Ireland puppet assembly, even Gerry Adams had not taken the oath in Westminster, and in the Republic matters did not work out as Sinn Féin had hoped.

Sinn Féin electoral support in Northern Ireland, once it bottomed out, remained reasonably solid, largely immutable to IRA atrocities or SDLP pleas or to the erosion of time. In the Republic everything was different and more depressing. In 1982, after the hunger strikes, the Provisional Sinn Féin vote had not held in the 1982 Dáil elections. Nothing much could be done about the general election on February 19, 1987, that led to Haughey returning as Taoiseach. Abstentionism had only recently been discarded and the campaign was hasty. This was the excuse. It convinced few, certainly none among the watching Republican Sinn Féin dissidents, who saw their predictions come true: No one in the Republic was interested in voting for the Provos. And they did not. The defeat was catastrophic, with the party getting less than 2 percent of the vote. It was possible to plead lack of time, lack of preparations, the united enmity of the conventional parties, and the fallout of the split in November 1986, but there was still the miserable fact that less than 2 percent had voted for the Provisionals. Most hopes turned to dust as the traditionalists nodded on the sideline. Instead of a thirty-two-county political effort, the leadership had only political trouble. There were problems in Northern Ireland but not such devastating results as in the Republic. In the by-election referendum poll in January 1986, in the four constituencies where there was a Sinn Féin–SDLP race, there had been that small loss, a 6 percent swing away from the party. In the Westminster general election on June 12 that returned, not unexpectedly, Margaret Thatcher and the Conservatives to power, Sinn Féin dropped to 11.3 percent from 13.4 percent in 1983. This was still 35 percent of the nationalist vote and Gerry Adams kept his seat in West Belfast. SDLP, with its vote up 3.2 percent, won three seats—Eddie McGrady defeated Enoch Powell in South Down and Mallon and Hume won. The Unionists running on an abstentionist platform—a republican tactic—saw a drop of 2.3 percent, for there were those who felt that the institutions should be used, not shunned. Sinn Féin felt, given all, that they had lost ground, as might have been expected, but still held the fort in the North. The Republic was going to be more difficult than imagined.

The SDLP in turn felt a corner had been turned with the erosion of the Sinn Féin vote, and they also had hopes that with IRA activity down, the republicans could be tempted into normal politics. There was the problem that there was no normal politics in Northern Ireland since the agreement. The Unionists—OUP, DUP, and James Kilfedder as UPUP—were boycotting Westminster. The whole Unionist establishment was focused on boycott, protest, and demonstrations, on demands for an end to the Anglo-Irish Agreement while London and Dublin went their own way. There was as well a growing interest in options, a need to do something other than say no. The Charter Group, headed by Harry West, sought a return of devolved government and ultimately produced a policy document in 1987. Some were interested in opening the province to regular British parties. Many wanted something other than direct rule—once the agreement was set aside. And until the agreement was set aside nothing much was happening.

Still, isolation and ennui had not stopped the SDLP from moving to Dublin for the Forum and ultimately helping to shape the AIA. So Hume and company waited for an opening if the Provisionals moved toward conventional politics in the six counties. There were real signs. The Provos had put together a policy document, *Scenario for Peace,* for the 1987 Westminster elections that indicated a willingness to play by the rules, even if the Unionists could not believe such intentions. In the local councils they would not talk to the Sinn Féin members, and they did recognize the few Sinn Féin chairmen. In general the British establishment, after years of pleading for the republicans to enter mainstream politics, tended to react with alarm when this happened, closing down options and hampering Sinn Féin, still seen as a front for terrorists. Thus, Sinn Féin speakers were banned from Britain and not allowed to speak on British television. They could *appear* but not speak. In an interview reported in the *Times* on October 26, 1988, on the ban on radio and television appearances, a government spokesman insisted that "in order to beat off your enemy in war, you have to suspend some civil liberties for a time." When a war was needed to rationalize contradictory Northern Ireland policy, a war was declared.

What the SDLP wanted was peaceful competition, which they were sure they could win as the conventional Catholic party; what they could not dent was the Provos' war support: those who voted for defenders or voted against the Brits and the Orangemen in the most extreme means available or those who voted Provo because they belonged to the republican universe. As long as Britain kept fighting the war this constituency would not get too much smaller, and this would limit SDLP growth. Hume and Adams met regularly for nine months beginning in January 1988, although without tangible results. In fact, throughout the island, the watchers, the media, those who misunderstood the nature of the republicans, sought signs that peaceful Sinn Féin would triumph over the martial secret army. Certainly there were signs of strain between the Armalite and the ballot. There were also problems with bungled IRA operations, innocent people killed who should not have been at risk, tactical curiosities like the attacks on the Dublin-Belfast railway. Those attacks seemingly united the country, angering passengers and risking ultimate closure of the line. Attacks on marginal working people engaged in construction on buildings used by security forces were dubious too. On August 19, 1985, Séamus McAvoy, a businessman from Coalisland, whose firm manufactured portable buildings often purchased and used by the British army as temporary accommodations after IRA attacks, was shot dead in his bungalow in Donnybrook, Dublin. But the campaign against IRA-defined collaborators continued into the next decade, despite criticism. The IRA was sure that collaborators were legitimate targets. In fact, killing such collaborators by making them drive car bombs was later defended as well.

The whole question of legitimate targets—generals and their civil servants and then those driving civil servants or building garages for those cars—caused serious problems for the IRA. Targets had to be seen to be valid. This was not always the case, despite IRA satisfaction or subsequent rationalizations. One of the more notorious cases was the murder of a Pakistani tea boy at a British army canteen in Silverbridge, Antrim, in April 1974, often remembered long after more brutal killings were forgotten. Shooting an Irish manufacturer in Dublin not only upset the Irish Republican authorities but also many who felt the man was a civilian. Shooting Northern Irish, some not young, none political, for driving a bulldozer or laying brick upset a great many people. On August 4, 1988, for example, as part of the campaign against subsidiary targets, two elderly Protestants were sprayed with at least 150 rounds of automatic rifle fire as they returned home from repairing the Belleck RUC station. They were blameless and defenseless men making their way home after a hard day's work, according to the *Belfast Telegraph*. Their murder provoked the Belfast loyalists to kill two Catholics the next day. This was not one of the IRA's best operations as far as most observers were concerned. The IRA rarely made excuses for such operations. Excuses were saved for demonstrable mistakes. The two old men were two Crown agents at security work.

Any shooting upset those eager for tranquillity. And the IRA had not only to shoot the security forces but also often the locals in order to maintain a grip on their support areas—the old no-go zones—and to eliminate informers. A few car thieves left in a lane with their knees shattered, splattered in blood, their mothers weeping at the hospital door, or the wee man next door dumped dead, shot in the neck for talking to the army, might be necessary, but the acts were brutal and so costly. This was particularly true with punishment shootings: No one ever felt his leg was justifiably ruined or their son maimed for good purpose. And the evidence that power and personality had played too great a role cast a shadow over any neighborhood legitimacy. How could a secret organization that without evidence or trial maimed and mutilated also speak through Sinn Féin like any other party? Not easily was an answer given.

The pursuit of a dirty war while voters are canvassed can never be managed without stress and dispute. What did remain a basic was that the movement was committed to the use of physical force because the leadership believed on good evidence that no other way would be at all effective. The intention was to push the war in the country, where British security vulnerabilities existed, and to move again in Britain and the Continent. Foreign operations required very few volunteers but long planning and considerable money. No one, of course, planned for Continental failures. But no matter what, the republican dream was shaped to an armed struggle. To that purpose conventional politics could be shaped, must be shaped in an all-Ireland context. This was why the traditionalists were cut adrift.

At nearly the same time the other republican option still active in the armed struggle, the INLA-IRSP, finally imploded. The INLA gunmen had suffered a disastrous sea change once the supergrass strategy began, for while the Provos could suffer very considerable losses, the smaller group could not. The betrayals, especially of Harry Kirkpatrick, broke the remaining bonds of faith. The IRSP-INLA had been Séamus Costello's creation. When he was shot and killed by Jim Flynn on October 5, 1977, the movement never again found a way forward. His successors within the political formation of the IRSP were weakened by the erosion of the Great Train Robbery arrests and the feuds with the Officials and finally the assassinations in the North.

The INLA, always the core, fared better in that the gunmen survived, held on to key assets, grew both more professional and more ruthless. In order to play any part in the drama they had to kill spectacularly; increasingly, these displays were divorced from any political content. The volunteers had the words memorized but were deaf to the music of the game. Still, they ran operations, participated in the hunger strikes, kept the faith. But the INLA proved too small, too deadly in tactics, too ineffectual in strategy, and at last the tradition was betrayed. The INLA had no place to go, the Provos were uncongenial, the Officials out of the killing game, and the purpose of the organization had died with the killing. And the killing took away the experienced volunteers as well as the politically aware. Those who escaped often went into exile, drifted away to the South, or disappeared from sight.

When Dominic McGlinchey, no strategist or radical thinker, was arrested, leadership fell to John "Big Man" O'Reilly, a rough, coarse, unrestrained man who would give political motives to his angers and whims. He savored the power of the gun. McGlinchey—the famous "Mad Dog" of the journalists—seemed elegant in contrast to a leader who not only committed atrocities as a matter of course but also did not recognize them as such. Leadership fell to other locals. And the residue was wracked by feuds. There was little restraint, and radical politics found little place in the killer's trade. The arguments and recriminations reached even into the prisons, and the revelations of the supergrasses merely made matters worse. Relatively quickly the INLA broke into several factions that only avoided lethal feuds because the most determined were often in prison. The feuds soon enough became deadly both outside and inside prison. When the INLA people were released on December 23, 1986, with the collapse of the supergrass system, the leadership of what was left was sorted out with violence. The players were hard to follow. There were no teams, no program, no numbers, no script. There was no longer an INLA. There was, instead, the INLA–Army Council, dominated by Gerry Steenson, who began to call himself (for good reason) Doctor Death, and Jimmy Brown, formerly of the IRSP in Belfast, who felt that the end had come and resigned. There was something called the INLA Revolutionary Council. The biggest group comprised those associated with O'Reilly in the new INLA-GHQ. After 1987 an Irish Peoples Liberation Army Organization (IPLO) organized the leftovers. All were small, each a tiny group of full-time active service people living on their nerves. All the names and shifting alignments could not disguise the fact that the small INLA group had shattered into a few strong individuals seeking a role along with a scrap of legitimacy or at bare minimum someone to cover their back in a gunfight. The aberrant and unstable, the marginal republicans or simply those who liked the trade, the power, and the killing were attracted. These volunteers had become corrupted, attracted to killing. They were truly gunmen, deadly pilgrims in an idealists' crusade they used only as cover.

As could have been predicted the shooting started at a peace conference. Who easier to shoot than your own, close, unprepared, and rivals in the trade? In January 1987 a meeting was arranged at the New Rossnaree Hotel, a mile outside of Drogheda in the Republic, between O'Reilly INLA-GHQ people and their

INLA–Army Council rivals. "Ta" Power, thirty-four, was the honest broker. At 5:20 in the afternoon, while Power, O'Reilly, and two other Northern men, Peter Stewart and Hugh Torney, sat over tea and sandwiches, they were attacked. Power- -the neutral—was shot dead by error and collapsed on the table over the spilled tea and blood-soaked sandwiches. Stewart struggled away from the killing zone. The key man, O'Reilly, was mortally wounded but managed to stagger out into the parking lot before falling dead. In Belfast two other O'Reilly men were not at home and so escaped the purge. Dr. Death had struck.

With O'Reilly gone the sides were even and so opened a final burst of a dozen killings. One shoot-out followed the next, to the delight of the security forces and the dismay of most republicans. Dr. Death was killed in Belfast. Mary McGlinchey, Dominic's wife, was at home in Dundalk on January 31, 1987, bathing her two children, Declan, seven, and Dominic, six, when two gunmen pushed into her house and through to the bathroom. They stood in the door and shot her in front of the screaming children, watched as her body tumbled into the tub. They left her behind in a bloody bath with frantic children, her murder the brutal burnt-out end of the ideal. It was the death of the INLA and Costello's dream. The INLA was not a secret army but gangs of rebels turned murderous butchers. A few with no place to go soldiered on in the IPLO, ran a few operations without authority or purpose, like Dessie O'Hare, an undisciplined, unwanted local republican gunman, along the border. Others shot and killed George Seawright. An IRSP still existed on paper—but only on paper, for the old INLA had gone.

The ruin of the INLA and the withdrawal of the traditionalists into Republican Sinn Féin brought no actual gains to the Provos. In the Republic they found hostility to them as a Northern party, as subversives, as competitors for scarce votes that belonged elsewhere. Southern voters were used to electing an advocate for entitlements, an agent in place, not a parliamentarian involved in national issues, especially the dreaded national issue that asked but never gave returns. The great pools of discontented young people poorly housed in vast estates outside the central cities, in endless council houses without amenities, grass, or trees, without pubs or markets or much in the way of public transport, should have bred grievance and radical votes. These pools of resentment and thwarted ambition that spread once Irish prosperity spluttered out in the eighties were, however, emptied by the drain of emigration to Britain and illegal emigration to the United States. Tens of thousands of potential dissenters left each year from all over the country. Some simply sought to better themselves, and these might have voted conventionally; but many were the stuff that had made the Provos in the six counties and so were lost. Those who stayed were not converted to the republican vision. No defenders were needed, the national issue did move the many. They were living in free Ireland, and the conventional parties offered a program that promised returns, not radicalism. Provisional Sinn Féin did attract the idealists, the national radicals, those alienated by the democratic centralism of the Workers, those who saw a need for radical change that would not come at the hands of Fianna Fáil or Labour and should not be shaped by neo-Stalinists. They were not very many. Thus the dreams of an all-Ireland constituency sufficient to affect events collapsed before Southern reality. So few voted for the Provisionals in the general and local elections that even the republicans, the greatest repository of unwarranted optimism in Europe, grew pessimistic.

The island had been horrified by the INLA feud, consoled only by the fact that one set of gunmen were killing the other. Increasingly in the Republic, the overspill from the North had destroyed any residue of concern for the national issue. The police had known for years that the Provos used armed robbery in the Republic to raise money—some very crude crimes by very marginal volunteers without talent or training or much sense. Along with the spectacular kidnappings and the quiet killing along the border, these robberies made life difficult for the authorities and, most important, dangerous for the police and army. And the habits of violence and the rationales of the killers contaminated Southern society.

The most spectacular evidence was the short and violent career of Dessie O'Hare, the media's Border Fox, who was a sociopath, a limited and unstable man on the margins of the IRA in South Armagh who frightened his own, frightened his wife, frightened anyone who came in contact with him: a seething, angry man ready to kill and maim for little cause. With the IRA he had been involved between 1976 and 1979 in a series of wild gun battles that endangered the organization, and he was edged out after he was arrested in 1979. His life had been a mix of armed robbery, killing operations, idleness, and drift. On his release in 1986, he floated on the fringes of the INLA in Dundalk until every gun was needed. He took part in the INLA feuds. He was also reputedly responsible for the killing of Mrs. Iris Farley during an attack on her son, a UDA member in Armagh. With the INLA fracture he had his fifteen minutes of command before the killing destroyed the organization, including his splinter in Dundalk. He remained undisciplined, brutal, and violent, shooting up a pub with his wife inside in a fit of pique before taking off on his final spree.

The opportunities of civil disorder had opened a world of power and violence for a very limited man and he in turn increased the turmoil of the times. In October 1987 he brought his fantasies and guns with him to the Republic. He surrounded himself with other rejects and discarded gunmen, and in October 1987 kidnapped a Dublin dentist, John O'Grady, wrong victim, and later maimed him, cutting off a finger. He imagined a Revolutionary Brigade and a political motive, and with his equally inept gang led the police on a long and dangerous chase during which officers were shot and innocents held hostage. In November a police ambush trapped him in County Kilkenny. His companion was shot dead; he was wounded, captured, charged, tried, convicted, and sentenced to forty years. He gave a bizarre ten-minute speech from the dock, as if he were patriot and not a criminal: "Justice for the oppressed of Ireland can only come through the barrel of a gun. Victory to the universal enemies of Britain and especially victory to the Irish Revolutionary Brigade."

O'Hare was visible proof of the overspill of violence that brought not only guns into the Republic but also transformed the police and army into users. Everyday bank robbers would be shot down in the main street by police fearful of a raid by a secret army, as much casualties of the Irish Troubles as those shot down for the same reason by an RUC-SAS squad in Belfast. Crime was contaminated by politics, the national issue meant killing as well as patriot songs sung in pubs, and the authorities in the Republic got the worst of all possible worlds. The Provos gave Southern lawmen a bad conscience and brought bad news. But increasingly the conscience grew clean —the Provos were, if not O'Hares, worse: cunning and crafty gunmen. They should be in prison like O'Hare or in the Black North where they belonged.

It was not just the Provos; the Irish increasingly voted against all involvement with Northern Ireland. The national issue had no takers. Haughey came back as Taoiseach with a minority government on the speaker's vote on March 10. The election on February 17, 1987, had seen the rise of the new Progressive Democrats under Desmond O'Malley, essentially an anti-Haughey, anti–politics as usual coalition that had taken fourteen seats. Fianna Fáil, with eighty-one seats, fell short of an overall Dáil majority. Haughey had kept the nationalist card, perhaps out of faith but certainly for political purpose. Now it had no real worth on the electoral board. No one cared enough about the Anglo-Irish Agreement for it to be worth pushing as an issue or later demanding a renegotiation. The Provisional Sinn Féin entry had indicated that the hunger strike vote was unique. Ireland had done with the national issue. The decline of prosperity, the reasons for the recession, the allocation of sacrifice, and the means to revival determined electoral politics and specific issues. The parallel current was the domination of all issues by Haughey; cunning in opposition, often ineffectual in office, but always confident, even arrogant, he was what Fianna Fáil had to offer. He generated fierce loyalty and absolute opposition, never quite managing to achieve sufficient electoral success to rest easy. His presence split his party when Desmond O'Malley left and others withdrew to the back benches or the wings, sullen and spent.

All through the 1980s Haughey would seek to fashion a powerful Fianna Fáil majority—and fail. He concentrated on the recession and prospects for development. On the national issue Haughey spoke as an Irish statesman, made judicious appointments of Northerners to the Senate, yet grew moderate on the problem, even if alert to any British slight. Like many he expressed an interest in unity, someday, somehow, without violence. He showed concern about the divided society—now as trendy as partition once was an issue; and he showed himself, as was to be expected from the leader of Fianna Fáil, hard on security matters and on Provo pretensions. Whatever his own national aspirations, as a consummate politician he was aware that the nation was exhausted with the Troubles, spiteful and tired, so he sensibly focused on the pressing issues within the Republic.

No one, if possible, paid much attention to the Northern Ireland issue. The Troubles, many hoped, had been shunted aside with the agreement; so they had been told. The media hurried over the details, the newspapers did not report each bit; more information could often be found in the new London *Independent* than in the *Irish Times*. Haughey during his time in power was part of the trend, accepting the agreement and just as easily accepting that the problem was not an Anglo-Irish confrontation but Anglo-Irish cooperation. The mutuality of interests was frayed in Ireland only because of the occasional resentment that due deference was not shown to Dublin sensibilities by London—a result of the low priority given the island in Britain, the historic incomprehension there of the Irish other, but not of malice.

Those who were concerned were often punished: the potentially "subversive" homes searched after the *Eksund* seizure, the harassment of those even marginally involved in republican activities, hard words everywhere for republicans. There was no longer a need to maintain the wonders of 1916—in fact it was difficult for Conor Cruise O'Brien, who had become a Southern unionist and had even contemplated the virtues of internment, to keep ahead of those who would attack the Provos. The bitter recriminations of the Workers, who now had understanding words for the RUC and the Supergrass ploy, had become common currency. The Provos were mad dogs. The Republic wanted no part of the Troubles, no part of Northern Ireland in whatever guise.

In the presidential elections of 1990 the Fine Gael candidate, Austin Currie, selected after public fumbling, was treated as an alien with a funny accent and could not even hold his tribal Fine Gael votes. He might have been elected to the Dáil but that did not mean he could represent the Republic. So much for the North; better a radical Labour Party woman, Mary Robinson, backed only by her own party and the Workers. She was aided by the Fine Gael confusion, a dispute over whether the Fianna Fáil candidate, Brian Lenihan, had lied and to whom and when, and Haughey's bungling over that dispute. So she was elected over front-runner Lenihan, and better Robinson, better anyone, than one of them. The electorate seemed tired of old issues, old faces—and more than ever of the Troubles. Thus, Provisional Sinn Féin found that their political momentum from H-Block days was long gone in the South. The war could escalate only a little and the ballot box had not filled up either. The movement was stalled.

If the republican movement gradually reached an impasse, too strong to be ruined, too limited to escalate, then the fate of the Protestant paramilitaries was even more dire. Their very absence from much of the great Unionist protest against the agreement indicated that matters had changed since the glory days when tens of thousands marched about the streets of Belfast for the cause of the moment at a word from the UDA Supreme Council. The paramilitaries had not disappeared, but the loyalist organizations had fallen on very hard days. They were never well organized, never for the long haul, only coalescing around individuals and neighborhood ties. No coherent ideology developed. No political initiative attracted any but kith and kin. There was never a call for constant killing or a structured "defense"—defense was a psychic need not an underground militia.

Thus those who had become used to local power that came from a gun transformed themselves into petty warlords collecting extortion, receiving deference by their locals, and turning a more sophisticated penny in rackets that kept individuals funded, if not movements. More often than not the cobbled-together uniforms, the titles, and even the killings were the front for organized crime that was not very organized but often beyond easy reach of the RUC. The supergrass trials badly disrupted the organizations, in particular the UVF, which was small and contained those involved in criminal activities and so was more prone to police pressure. The lack of political sophistication also meant that the organizations had been penetrated by informers and agents who increasingly found less of political interest.

Without much available as political rationalization and with no real mission to defend during the months of anti-agreement protest, penetrated by British intelligence and with few friends in the UDR or the RUC, the individual warlords concentrated on the prospects of easy money. In the eighties the UDA and UVF became criminal organizations without a single, effective command structure, without limits except those imposed by charisma, fear, and arrogance. The paramilitaries entered a long period of feuds, betrayals, and corruption that eroded almost all of their volunteer support. The UDA's Andy Tyrie stayed in place, in part because he did not oppose the local commanders, who had become bandit kings. The locals lived precarious lives of luxury, were apt to be sold out by underlings to hired murderers, to the republican secret armies, to the police and the army, to each other. They were replaced by clones lured by easy money.

The most obvious result was a war of attrition, a very dirty war, that saw the murder of the more prominent Belfast loyalists. Several were undoubtedly set up for the Provisionals, who counted sectarian killers appropriate targets; others were killed by rivals. Not all the murders were credited or claimed and the dead were often praised by those who, close up, smelled of cordite. In 1983 Lenny Murphy of the Shankill Butchers had been shot on his girl's doorstep by the Provos. He had thus been one of the first to go and the one least missed. After that there was steady attrition.

One of the key figures was James Craig of the UDA, who kept his bodyguards with him on European holidays. As a UDA commander in Long Kesh he had made contacts with Official IRA prisoners who later became involved in organizing their movement's fiscal structures in Belfast. In time these arrangements served as a model for Craig: Extortion, licensing rackets, building site fraud, theft from the system for political reasons became for Craig lucrative income. In 1979 he met with four IRA Officials over a Stickie shot as a Provo by the UDA. Two of the four later went with the INLA and Craig kept up these contacts as well as modernizing his own arrangements. Soon there was a clearing out of UDA warlords, murdered by persons unknown but in circumstances that indicated inside intelligence. First had come Lenny Murphy, then two UVF commanders, Frenchie Marchant, suspected of carrying out the Dublin-Monaghan car bombs of 1974 with the help of British agents, and Fred Otley. Both killings were credited to Craig and the losses devastated what was left of the UVF.

In January 1987 the UDA had published their new document, drawn up by John McMichael and entitled *Common Sense*. It proposed a devolved government: "We all share the responsibility for creating the situation, either by deed or by acquiescence. Therefore we must share the responsibility of maintaining good government." The declaration of moderation and the threat to investigate UDA corruption had done him no good among his own. Whatever the virtues, especially the timing, *Common Sense* emerged from the internal confusion of the UDA as cover for the problem of corruption. Why should McMichael, a long-serving UDA hard man, stir up trouble now? Craig certainly did not need an investigation of corruption. An enormously influential television program by Roger Cook, "The Cook Report," had revealed the actuality of UDA corruption, in color, on the screen, before everyone. The viewers could see a defender demanding money with menaces, money that was most obviously not going to the cause. There had already been criminal trials and various revelations of UDA extortion, bribery, theft, and intimidation.

So far Andy Tyrie had not risked such an investigation. Now McMichael, the presentable public face of the UDA but also at times O/C of the UDA murder squad, the Ulster Freedom Fighters, seemed to be a clear and present danger to the Belfast rackets because he sought to probe the charges. Everyone knew where that would lead. Craig used his contacts. On December 22, at his home in Lisburn, McMichael, who was still second-in-command of the UDA, was killed in the ruins of his blackened car, destroyed by an IRA booby trap. The Provos had taken him out as a sectarian killer, leader of the UFF, ally of British imperialism. He had been set up by Craig and his friends, who were not interested in politics but profits. So McMichael was gone. He had, however, a concern with politics as well as with murder. His cross-community concerns, like those of similar working-class Protestant militants Ernest Elliot, Sammy Smyth, and John McKeague, were what the eulogies remembered. The republicans and most nationalists remembered instead the bigotry, the incitement to violence, the killing. Any UDA politics had long been smeared by corruption. The Protestant paramilitaries had become criminals, deserved no eulogies, no fine send-off by other warlords who had passed on the data necessary for their deaths.

If the UDA was to survive, changes would have to be made. Belfast being Belfast, a UDA commander appearing anonymously and seen in silhouette on BBC 2 "Newsnight" announced that Andy Tyrie must go. Tyrie called for a vote, lost it, and finally resigned on March 11, 1988, four days after a bomb had been found attached to his car. After fifteen years the UDA had no Tyrie, who had grown stale as the organization decayed into crime. He had been too many years too close to corruption for those who hoped to reintroduce politics into the UDA nexus. The media hardly knew what to do without Tyrie. Wry in a lethal business, an unlikely paramilitary, short, tubby, asthmatic, with a Zapata moustache, first a landscape gardener and then a machinist at Rolls-Royce, he had risen to the top of the UDA as the more powerful were murdered. He stayed on top, surrounded by his brigadiers, the local barons, and the psychopaths.

The new men began an investigation of Craig that led to information from Belfast received back from UDA people in London. This made it clear that McMichael had been set up by Craig. The UDA and UVF were worried about the growing number of dead. John Bingham, Marchant and Otley, and finally George Seawright, the virulent anti-Catholic who had wanted the papists burned and had been shot on November 19, 1987, by the splinter Irish Peoples Liberation Organization: a "popular hit." Seawright, vehement, unrestrained, and provocative, had been the firebrand at work during the dangerous Orange marching season. As a Scot he seemed to feel that he had to be more Orange than the Irish. And he had so attracted republican attention. He even suspected that he was on the IPLO hit list. There were very few hit men in the IPLO and none with politics beyond a patina over bigotry so that Seawright was ideal: most bigoted of all and nearby. There was a growing loyalist fear that this list and other republican lists were being supplemented by intelligence on their movements. Seawright had suspected a conspiracy. The Protestant paramilitaries were letting the republicans do their killing. Seawright's suspicions did him no good. He died on December 3.

All had been killed deep inside loyalist territory with an ease that only local cooperation would have made possible. There was evidence that Craig was the Provo source. Not much evidence was ever needed in such cases. On October 15,

1988, Craig was lured to a meeting of the UDA in the Castle Inn in East Belfast, where two men in ski masks entered the bar and shot him. He fell dead on top of his drink. The UFF had decided he was too dangerous alive. His death did not end corruption within the UDA or the UVF; the rackets ran on to others' benefit. But a more reasonable percentage went to the organizations and for arms. With the failure of conventional politics, replaced by boycott and discussion, the loyalists no longer had assets to wager. They had lived on killing and credit and when the credit was withdrawn continued the rackets if possible and the murders if angered. They were angered by provocations real and imagined. Arbitrary, unpredictable, and lethal, the killers simply kept on and on.

Spokesmen claimed, as they always had, that the victims were republicans. Scandal resulted when those spokesmen revealed official documents listing suspected IRA people (ergo, we the UVF or the UDA have names). Yet those killed were still not IRA people. On March 14, 1988, at a UDA press conference a message from the UFF was read claiming that "innocent Catholics" had nothing to fear from the organization. The next day the UFF shot and killed a Catholic trade union official. There were no innocent Catholics. The principle, especially in Belfast, was, Why bother? The murders became steady state, background music, accepted, deplored, and forgotten. The UDA did, however, reorder their organization, return to constructing a military option. A liaison between the UVF and the Red Hand Commandos, still tiny and on occasion lethal, was established. The three cooperated in a bank raid in Portadown that netted £325,000 spent on arms that arrived early in 1988. The RUC had seized most of the arms. At the end of the decade the paramilitaries were still a fact of Northern life. They still killed. Some groups tried for known or suspected republicans. Mostly they killed no one important, not like the arranged INLA and Maire Drumm killings. Mostly any male Catholic would do, just another murder symbol, a dead Fenian, nothing changed except one family, a funeral, a bitter sermon, and all was as before.

From January 1, 1989, until February 10, 1991, the loyalists killed twenty-one people out of the total of seventy-eight violent deaths in the province—their contribution to the Troubles was still by no means minimal. Most of the dead were Catholics and Catholics without connections to the republican movement. Twelve were killed by the UDA, none with links to the republicans. The UVF did kill two men with republican ties and the paramilitaries claimed the small incendiaries placed in Clerys of Dublin and seven other stores and claimed more that were not found. These small firebombs were the first operations in the Republic since the protests over the AIA—a long way from the murderous bombs of earlier days.

In the country the small paramilitary groups, tied into Belfast by personal association rather than organizational structure, had not been corrupted nor, for that matter, very active. When they were active efforts were often made to find real republicans, Sinn Féin people or their friends, suspected IRA men. The nationalists felt some people were "suspected" because UDR members gave out data. So to add to the long playing Stalker-Sampson affair went an extended investigation of the security of security forces, in particular the UDR. In time the investigation led to evidence of leaks, but not on a massive scale. The country vigilantes kept up the killing. This was not so much tit-for-tat famous in Belfast as a sudden burst of frustration at the impact of the IRA armed struggle. In Belfast time ran faster and response was more closely related to perceived provocation. The falling off of Belfast killings, however, had been largely a result not of external but of internal events—the purpose corrupted, the vigilantes at play in a slough of easy money. The return to politics after the era of corruption meant that criminal activities were more carefully monitored, corruption was curbed, and the ritual murders continued.

The Northern Ireland Office, under the slowly lessening din of the agreement protest and the echo of IRA and Protestant paramilitary gunfire, had as well the continuing everyday political problems arising from direct rule. Responsibility for everything official was British, the Assembly was closed, many of the local government councils did not work, devolution was an aspiration. Most of the problems were long-running. There was still trouble over extradition and Father Patrick Ryan found on the Continent with seemingly incriminating documents and wanted in England, ended up in the Republic of Ireland, safe for the moment. It was one more fuss about local matters turned grand, this time with a wayward cleric who yearned for a career as a conspirator—but one in the limelight. A quite different and more serious foreign problem (not that extradition was not considered in London an important matter, only that Father Ryan was not a key republican player) was waged over the MacBride Principles. Here, as so often was the case in Irish matters, the British had been maneuvered into the wrong not by themselves but by their enemies. In an effort to stress the continued failure of the British in general and the Northern Ireland Office in particular to end discriminating against Catholics in employment, Seán McManus came up with a petition that would seek to end American investment in the province unless the suggested rules were followed. The principles were quite reasonable and were used to persuade a variety of American state legislatures to vote in favor of them. The principles bore MacBride's name, and he was not simply a famous liberal lawyer, winner of both the Nobel and Lenin Peace prizes and a famous United Nations official, but a former chief of staff of the IRA. As Irish republicans, he and his were hateful to many Conservatives in London, so instead of signing up on matters that were favored as government policy, the British opposed the principles with all sorts of good and unconvincing reasons. The difficulty was that not only was there discrimination in employment, by both communities, but there was also no way that legislation could either fully eliminate it or satisfy the legitimate and greater Catholic grievances. The MacBride agitation made this clear and indicated that the fault lay with London.

British spokesmen and diplomats were forced to wage a war not against the simple minds of NORAID but against civil libertarians (or often some Irish-Americans so appearing) who sought reform, not revolution, in the MacBride Principles. Again the move spread Britain thin, cost time and money and effort. In California a concerted effort had to be made to persuade Governor George Deukmejian to veto the MacBride Principles in September 1989. As the Northern Ireland Office Economic Minister Richard Needham said, "I am very pleased the governor made this decision. I don't believe the passage of the MacBride Principle does anything to encourage investment in Northern Ireland." Britain had been forced to look more closely at continued discrimination and to take action, but those involved in the NIO and in London disliked the exposure of any such undemocratic vulnerability. There was new legislation, continued effort. The Northern Ireland Fair Employment Agency under Bob Cooper had been transformed into the Fair Employment Commission, which sought to eliminate discrimination without the need for lobbying secondhand through the American state legislatures. The MacBride Principles deeply offended many English Conservatives, who felt ill used about Ireland in any case—evidence was the *Times*'s vicious obituary when MacBride died. He had not been an active IRA man for half a century but his distinguished career gave his Irish view a prominence many Tories felt undeserved. He was once a gunman, and his principles were one more Irish irritant.

If this were not foreign problem enough, allocation of the American funds, first suggested by President Jimmy Carter, to be spent in the province and border counties, engendered various local criticism, at times self-serving and at times well-meaning. Even American money could not be spent without dissent and dispute. In any provincial matter, too many always sought ulterior motives, hidden agendas, even conspiracies. There were charges that the SDLP was taking American money. There were arguments on how European Community funds should be allocated. It was clear that not even free money could engender enthusiasm for either the agreement or the Northern Ireland Office. All of this, however, was better than the action generated by the Provos, who, despite the agreement, did not suddenly disappear.

The Protestant politics of protest kept right on too, still more visible than the IRA operations. Many at the Northern Ireland Office hoped that the IRA was, in fact, on a permanent downswing. The agreement seemed to have balked their killing, even if the Protestants were not convinced. On January 3 the Unionists had launched a petition calling for a referendum. They collected 400,000 names and handed the petition to the Queen on February 14 at Buckingham Palace. Bypassing Thatcher had no effect; there was no referendum. An OUP-DUP task force had been established on February 14 to find alternatives to the agreement. There was not much hope. Haughey had become Taoiseach in the Republic on March 10 but did not denounce the agreement—no help from that devil. The Day of Defiance on April 11 had a low turnout. The Unionists had turned again to Britain and launched an anti-AIA campaign with a press conference and a fifteen-thousand-pound advertisement in the *Times*. These steps had led nowhere. The June elections that saw Enoch Powell lose his Westminster seat passed without Unionist advantage nor indication that anyone in London was going to budge. The Queen's speech urged devolution—a prospect that, if associated with the AIA, was still opposed by the Unionists, especially the OUP. At last, however, Paisley and Molyneaux announced that they would use the results from their task force to open low-level introductory talks with the Northern Ireland Office. On September 14, 1987, after a nineteen-month boycott, the two finally met with Northern Secretary Tom King at Stormont for "talks about talks." And there the political dialogue rested.

The IRA in the meanwhile had increased its activity in the countryside. The newspapers and evening news did not report much but the roads were dangerous, the helicopter flights heavy, the indicators of border trouble high. The Protestants, as they had before, felt that the attacks on members of the UDR and RUC, often at home and those homes often on the margins of Catholic-controlled areas, were part of a coherent plan to force the Unionists out. The IRA denied they were waging a sectarian war and went on shooting the Crown's agents. On May 8, 1987, the British finally closed one of their trap ambushes to effect. The authorities were acting on information acquired. A variety of disinformation is usually released about what and when and how the authorities are informed, so as to cause maximum confusion within the IRA, already subject to considerable paranoia, some institutional, the by-product of underground life, and some arising from the supergrass debacle.* The British knew the target and time of a minor IRA operation, an attack on a deserted RUC substation in the tiny village of Loughall County Armagh on Friday evening, March 8. It would bring together a small IRA column, eight armed men in blue coveralls, balaclavas, gloves, and running shoes—the rural guerrilla costume of professionals. The Provos intended to hit the station soon after it closed at seven in the evening. The previous September a very similar operation had been undertaken against an RUC station at the Birches in north Armagh using a JCB digger. It was part of the campaign of smashing small rural stations and then intimidating any repair and construction crews, thus forcing the RUC out of the countryside. The group drove instead into an SAS-RUC trap—a killing ground set with crafted fields of fire to take out all the IRA volunteers. The unit traveled in a JCB digger and a blue Toyota van toward the station from the Portadown end of the town at 7:30, when it was still light. The IRA men had a bomb in the digger and were moving it toward the station. The digger arrived at the gate of the station. Several IRA men remained in the van, twenty yards away. Then the locals heard a long burst of gunfire (there was no warning), then a huge explosion as the bomb in the JCB detonated, and finally another long burst of gunfire.

The digger was a heap of metal and the RUC station was badly damaged by the explosion, one side in rubble, most of the windows gone. The blue Toyota diesel van was flat on the road, riddled by automatic fire, the front windshield pocked and shattered. Two IRA men were found dead in the back of the van, another in the driver's seat, one dead on the front right-hand side and two others on the front

---

*Later on May 21, the IRA attempted to abduct Colette O'Neill, thirty-nine from Ardboe. The telephone call authorized that the IRA attack on May 8 had originated at her house. Apparently the IRA thought she was involved in supplying the authorities with information. She evaded the attempt because the IRA abductors' car was stopped at an RUC roadblock. She was taken into custody and kept under police protection in Nottingham, England, from May until October. In September the Provos were finally willing to listen to her story. Quite homesick, she opened direct negotiations on October 5 with the IRA, which led to an understanding. In a complex arrangement she agreed not to press charges against the three men involved in her attempted abduction and the IRA agreed that she was not an informant. Like nearly every case of covert conspiracy, the story continued with echoes and ripples, warped images, rumors, and reports beyond verification. O'Neill claimed, in fact, that the RUC had spread a story through the nationalist *Irish News* that "a woman" had been traced by the IRA after the murder of two senior RUC officers in Armagh in March 1987 had led to the capture of documents. "They hoped it would blacken my name, make me turn and put the men down the line and let me know that I daren't go back to Ardboe, that my life was in danger." *Magill* Dublin, November 1989, p. 41.

left-hand side. One volunteer had tried to run forward and his body was found some twenty yards up the road, in front of the van. Another man had tried to escape by running back down the road, and his body was sprawled a hundred yards back down the road toward the town. The whole thing took less than ten minutes. The press speculated that thousands of rounds were fired. Eight dead IRA volunteers—it was a coup.

There was also a little trouble that proved hard to hush up, although the army tried. First, two local cars had driven into the killing zone as well. One, a white Citroën containing Anthony and Oliver Hughes, had been shot up, instantly killing one brother, the driver, Anthony, and badly wounding Oliver. A local, Mrs. Beggs, had a miraculous escape from her red Sierra when the rear window was smashed in by heavy fire and the car's body pocked with bullets. She scrambled out and crept away, badly shaken but safe. The security forces had come to kill everyone inside the killing zone and had only just missed. Second, there was no warning and no attempt to take prisoners; two of the IRA men had been shot down running away from fire. Shots had been apparently fired from close up, coup de grace shots from those standing over downed bodies.

No matter, it was a triumph: eight dead IRA for zero losses—except for the one dead innocent. The RUC displayed the weapons: six automatic rifles (three German Heckler and Kochs, one Belgian FN .762, and two FNC .223s), one Spas shortened, pump-action, 12-gauge shotgun, and one .357 Ruger revolver. None of the guns was new; all were well cared for, favorites. The guns had been used in a total of seven IRA killings, in thirty-three IRA operations. These IRA dead were practiced murderers, hard cases, professional gunmen, killed in action not murdered. It was war again in Armagh, not a police action. So far during the year twenty-two people had died, including the second most important judge in Northern Ireland, Sir Maurice Gibson, and his wife, Cecily, Lady Gibson, killed in their car as it passed an IRA car bomb just at the border at Killeen on April 25; four policemen, and one member of the UDR, and now the eight IRA men were dead.

The eight IRA men included several named by the authorities as senior operators. The most prominent was Jim Lynch, from Tully, near Monaghan, one of the more wanted IRA men in Northern Ireland, according to the authorities. He had been held in various prisons for ten of the previous fifteen years, but still had found the time to be an important figure in local republican affairs. He ran IRA groups along the border and had even attended the last Sinn Féin Ard Fheis, which had voted to end abstentionism. Padraig Kelly, an IRA commander for East Tyrone, who was married with three children and his wife expecting a fourth, lived across from his parents in a Dungannon housing estate. His father had not known he was in the IRA but was "proud of him that he went to do something about the plight of the nationalist people and died fighting for his country's freedom."* His son had replaced Peter Sherry from Lurgan, who was sentenced to life imprisonment for his part in the Brighton bomb conspiracy, as O/C of East Tyrone; now someone else would have to take over. Another of the eight, Patrick

---

The Sunday Tribune (Dublin), May 10, 1987.

McKearney from Moy in Tyrone, had been on the run since breaking out of prison in the Great Escape in 1983. He was one of the new, hard professionals who had transformed IRA capacity in the country.

Some of the dead were simply local men in their local unit. Four, all young, all unmarried, came from the little Tyrone village of Galbally. On one side of the road in the village is a grocery store and a large public house and on the other side a Catholic church with a graveyard, a credit union office, and a small string of houses; further down the road is a small housing estate and a public school. On the next morning in Galbally the telephone poles had black flags, twists of cloth; and the relatives and neighbors stunned, went to each of the four houses. "It's not the easiest thing to do." For others farther away there were demonstrations and riots, stones and plastic bullets; a bomb was thrown at the home of a county court judge, John Curran, in the Old Cave Hill section of north Belfast; vehicles were hijacked and barricades built and disturbances continued for a week past the funerals. By then the black flags at Galbally had tattered in the wind.

All of the eight volunteers became martyrs for the movement. There were arguments with the police over the republican funerals. Like everything else in the province, funerals became arenas of contention. The republicans wanted to choreograph the one great gift possessed by the movement in a martial moment in which the transcendental Republic became visible. The authorities deployed their forces to observe, to intimidate, to express anger that criminals were buried as soldiers. At times there were riots and often scuffles and once on March 13, 1987, the IRA retaliated with a bomb at the graveyard gate just before an RUC funeral. More than two thousand supporters, friends, and family came to James Lynch's ceremony, and dozens of wreaths were laid in the Monaghan Cemetery. In the North there was to be no talk of murder tolerated by any of the parents who saw their dead sons as soldiers who had died for the Republic—not, as some publicists might have wished for the Loughall Eight, the victims of British SAS killer gangs. The lads were on an IRA operation, soldiers who had died courageously for the Republic, and that was that. And so it was. They were buried as soldiers.

There was a sold-out concert in their honor on Parnell Square in Dublin, using the Christian Brothers auditorium; the performers, playing and singing, volunteered their talents, and the remaining faithful were drawn in. Only the hard core and a few more were likely to appear in public by 1987. Joe Cahill was seated in a car outside, nodding to friends. The felons of the forties were inside with the new young members of Sinn Féin. There were a few of the rich and famous, an American or two, and mostly the same faces checked off the same lists by the Special Branch police watching outside. Funerals and murder and martyrs by 1987 ran to rote and checklists, except for those grieved.

The funerals were not only those of the paramilitaries, dead defenders set up by their own, psychopaths attached to splinter groups, volunteers in a secret army that had left a trail of innocent dead; there were also funerals for those who died defending the state, a legitimate state, the system in place, the center. The security forces were often given official funerals, soldiers buried as soldiers, police with a flag-draped coffin; but often the funeral was private, the grief private, the loss not noticed nor turned into spectacle. The authorities were supposed to be in control, the state secure, society safe; elaborate funerals for soldiers and policemen would not reinforce that supposition. Thus there were often dark hearts but there were not black flags fluttering from telephone poles in some small Protestant towns. And there were always far too many grim processions behind a young man's coffin, pale and shocked children, shattered wife, parents suddenly old, anguished neighbors and those other young men, the colleagues, grim faced, trim in their best uniform, those who had volunteered to stand in harm's way, to serve their state, the state, and so to risk dying for the Queen.

Their life was as different from that of the gunmen as it is possible to imagine except at the end, except that the profession was joint, the risks mutual, and the result too often the same. The UDR were paid, promoted, promised pension—none worth the risks, for they had volunteered for duty, not returns. They were trained and deployed, placed on rosters, in uniforms, entered into the computer, and put out as defenders and targets, often in their spare time. They, like the RUC, were inevitably a sectarian force, but every effort was made to see that the force was fair—not that this could quite be managed or that the skeptical nationalists could be convinced. They formed the third leaf of the security trinity of army, police, and militia, and were the symbol of the majority's determination to stay, not be moved, stand fast in what in the country was seen as a Provo effort to capture the country, acre by acre, one dead UDR man and woman at a time, one abandoned farm at a time. Each year, every year, the UDR men and women were the new crop in a long killing season. It was not the steady toll of the combatants or even the spread of targets abroad that predominated in the perception of both the involved and the observers but the death of transients, spectators, the unlucky who had been on the way to the parade or bringing home a lamb chop, not sailing in harm's way with bravery, only going about the day's routine.

The killings that shaped the end of the decade were those not intended. For the IRA the end of the decade was a series of disasters, mitigated almost solely by British political and security blunders. Even at Loughall the British had managed to blunt the impact of the SAS by the murder of Anthony Hughes, an innocent civilian, a local, a Protestant, and the maiming of his brother Oliver. The IRA military successes too, had a tendency to appear ruthless and brutal rather than spectacular and dramatic. So just as the IRA managed to force the pace of the armed struggle, the cost of so doing came mostly from traditional incompetence, not British skill. The innocent were victims, often not the IRA or not even the security forces. The innocent were victims of inept IRA operations, callous volunteers, and inane planning; they were victims of a secret army that even after twenty years could not murder with competence and could not take care to protect the innocent.

The most dreadful of all the IRA errors came first with the Remembrance Day bombing—the Poppy Day Massacre—in Enniskillen in November 1987. There had been bombs that endangered Northern Ireland civilians before, but the IRA GHQ had made it clear that great care would be taken, henceforth, in target selection and timing. This apparently consisted simply of asking local units to be cautious. Local units are not in the business of caution and often rely on republicans without wit or experience or skill to plan and carry out operations. In

Enniskillen a bomb was placed in the speakers' platform. At the appropriate moment the local establishment, the veterans, soldiers, and all those who wanted a close view of events would gather there. There was no prospect of limiting any explosion solely to military or even security figures. The bomb was set to go off exactly at the moment of remembrance in a crowd that surely would have civilians, innocent of anything but location, as well as proper targets. It was as callous a placement as some bombs in England; but, unlike many of those, it was set off without warning. The bomb exploded in the midst of a group of civilians. The start of the ceremony, like the start of all Irish public events, had been delayed, and so no "real" target was killed, only eleven innocent people, six men, and five women. Sixty-three people were injured, all local. It was an unalloyed horror that generated one of the rare Sinn Féin apologies and vast contention within the republican movement.

The IRA offered "deep regret" at the results. At the Sinn Féin Ard Fheis in January 1989, Gerry Adams said that the accidental killings of civilians by the IRA must stop because they retarded the republican struggle. Enniskillen was the worst but by no means the last disaster. Almost no republican found excuse for the Poppy Day Massacre beyond the truism that war is nasty. The event was thoroughly covered by the media: the grief, the broken parents, the children, the ruin of normal lives for no reason. Gordon Wilson forgave those who murdered his daughter, urged reconciliation, became the hero of the massacre. And the massacre, real enough and horrid enough, was used as a bloody club to beat the Provos: mad dog killers. Poppy Day would join Claudy and La Mon and Bloody Friday as IRA atrocity. Enniskillen became not a place, a provincial town, but a bloody bead on the rosary of the Troubles.

The republican world collapsed inward on the core. Everyone else, even those previously sympathetic, were horrified. The result was a spontaneous coalition of all those who hated the IRA and hated all its friends, who hated violence, who often hated the Troubles and the shame of it all. Every facet of Irish society, North and South, took the opportunity to damn the IRA, damn Sinn Féin, and damn those who did not do so. The media, the church leaders, the spokesmen of the sensible and obscure, the taxi driver and the barman, the old enemies of the movement on the island and abroad, the new Workers Party and the old Tories, everyone had a hard word. And there was little that could be said—the blunder had been made and this time there was no compensating factor, no Warrenpoint to attract attention, no British coverup, no soldiers dressed as civilians.

Worse, the IRA moved on into a long series of blunders, gross errors, and operational bad luck over the next year that caused the movement vast harm, limited the impact of the successes, and attracted attention away from the blunders and stupidities of others. In December 1987 two pensioners were killed by a bomb intended for a police family. In March 1988, in an attack on a Fermanagh man mistakenly thought to be in the UDR, the IRA killed his sister. In July a trap-bomb in the Falls Road baths detonated and killed an innocent Catholic man and woman—dead for walking down the wrong road. The next month the Protestant Hannah family was killed on the Armagh border by a bomb intended to kill a judge. Killing judges had a mixed audience but to wipe out a young family because their car looked like the target was appalling. In August another booby-trap explosion that went off at the wrong time killed two Catholics, a sixty-year-old woman and a fifty-five-year-old man. In October a seventy-year-old Catholic woman collapsed and died during a mortar attack on a Fermanagh RUC station—so far the IRA had been lucky with the notoriously inaccurate mortars but persisted with the weapon. In October a Protestant man in Belfast was killed by a booby-trap explosion meant for the UDR. The next month a sixty-seven-year-old Catholic man and his thirteen-year-old granddaughter were killed in a van-bomb explosion outside the RUC station at Benburb, Tyrone. In January 1989 a Protestant former member of the RUCR was shot and killed while visiting his Catholic girlfriend—incompetent intelligence again or simple bigotry.

Even when operations were effective there would be too often an unexpected cost: An RUC car with important officers was blown off the road by a cunning trap mine that also killed a nun driving another car.* The gods of the armed struggle were absent. Just as matters were turning routine in Ireland, Continental operations then produced another highly visible series of blunders—women killed, a baby killed, tourists instead of soldiers killed. Because the errors went on and on, were scattered out over several years, and, with one or two exceptions, were similar to other blunders in the past, time eroded their effect. In the case of Enniskillen the entire spectrum of anti-Provo opinion had used the opportunity to attack the republicans and attack them effectively.

After Enniskillen the horror and outrage were real. Most people were tired of killing innocent people, certainly of killing innocent people without gain. The gain for the authorities, however, was frittered away in blunders elsewhere. The blunders of British justice, the refusal to prosecute the apparently guilty for reasons of security, the outrageous statements of judges or ministers, the reports of security misdeeds, seemed to arrive in a flurry soon after some IRA outrage. The attacks on IRA volunteers produced not SAS triumphs but state murders. Many, not just Irish nationalists, felt the authorities should not shoot to kill, engage in war and claim there was peace in the province. Such hypocrisy did not pay. The British army blundered, and the British government and the British courts. The same anguished voices could only be raised so often in despair over IRA atrocities, British special operations, loyalist murders, without growing hoarse and ineffectual.

Much of the outrage over Enniskillen was eroded in January 1988. The loyalist paramilitaries were caught smuggling in arms on January 8. The British announced on January 25 that no one in the RUC would be prosecuted as a result of the Stalker inquiry (eighteen people were eventually reprimanded). And on January 28 the Birmingham Six—accused IRA bombers—appeal was denied in a

---

*Those involved in the deaths (the killing of the nun particularly and especially outraged Catholic Irish opinion) were discovered, arrested, charged, tried, convicted, and imprisoned, but this came too late to appease the appalled, who always wanted immediate, not even swift, action. That the authorities often acted effectively in such killing, that many of the guilty were caught and ended up in prison as a result of either loyalist or republican paramilitary operations, did not really compensate for the horror of the moment. Nothing could be done instantly and so more recent atrocities and limited media coverage of the ultimate trial eroded the impact. Neither vengeance nor justice was seen to be done.

decision that few disinterested observers could defend. The case continued to collapse over the next two years. It would take a long time before Enniskillen and the rest could simply be forgotten; but Britain, too, was capable of blunder.

In the end the IRA operational blunders prohibited any real expansion of support but did not erode the core of the faith. The republicans on television rationalizing atrocity so enraged the British that Sinn Féin spokesmen had been banned, could be seen but not heard, a fruitless exercise. Once again the judicial response to armed subversion seemed to barter hard-won British assets, civil liberties, for the momentary pleasure of hurting the elusive republicans: Speaking was denied, suspects could be held without counsel for seven days, internal exile existed (no Gerry Adams in England), and the conveyor belt judicial system in Northern Ireland was used as a means to imprisonment, not to secure justice. All this upset many people in and out of the United Kingdom who had looked for justice to be done by the heirs to centuries of practice. And justice as practiced did not even return the benefit of stifling the subversives any more than did the occasional successful special operations of the security forces. The greatest harm done to the republicans seemed, like the British case, to be done by themselves.

The IRA, in fact, had always possessed the capacity to turn their disasters into triumphs: Easter 1916, a failed coup marred by blunders, began the most glorious moment of long struggle. It is in death, at the moment of interment, that a sacrificed gunman is transformed into the patriot dead. At a funeral, for a moment, the Republic exists and legitimizes the movement's capacity to make war. IRA funerals are the great secular ritual of Ireland. Policemen are merely buried as officers, amid grief, and soldiers by their comrades in a martial ceremony, but for an IRA volunteer the transcendental Republic is created for that moment when the illegal volley is fired over the draped tricolor flag. Funerals matter a great deal and so were used like all else as a battle area. And this in turn led to elaborate incidents that blurred the Poppy Day memories.

In Belfast a bizarre complex of events began with the war over funerals that had peaked with the bomb on March 13, 1987, at Roselawn Cemetery—an explosion accompanied by forty bomb scares and an IRA warning to RUC "ghouls." In April 1987 Lawrence Marley was shot dead at his home in the Ardyone by the UVF. He was one of the few real IRA people killed by the Protestant paramilitaries, famous in the movement for his role in the Great Escape. The authorities could either allow the funeral and the IRA presence, thus showing weakness, or seek to place a heavy presence on the ground to prevent the republican ritual— and thus be in alliance with Bishop Daly. The bishop had banned requiem mass at any future IRA funeral because of the volley fired over the coffin of IRA volunteer Gerard Logue by two men on March 24. As was often the case the RUC maneuvered themselves into the worst possible response. On April 6 the police flooded the area around the Marley home and the family postponed the event. Bishop Cahal Daly had also said, "Any unnecessary and disproportionate display of force undermines respect for the law." The IRA, of course, had no such respect: It was the audience of Catholics that mattered to them. It was not lost on them that the police had not appeared at the funeral of the Protestant paramilitary John Bingham six months before; only Unionist politicians had attended. Then the UVF was an inconvenience, murderous but not a threat to the state. The IRA ritual was such a threat. The Marley stalemate lasted through the next day, the family and the IRA refusing to force the coffin through the heavy RUC cordon while the television camera ran. The next day, after realizing the extent of the funeral crisis (millions were watching on television), the RUC pulled back a little and the procession made its way past the glowering police and often hostile crowds, pulling some five thousand mourners behind the coffin.

Nothing was more telling about the global, electronic village than to sit in Gaza in a room filled with young Palestinian nationalists watching the event live from a station off a satellite feed in South Lebanon. The use of provocation against a powerful, authoritarian foe, the mix of rocks, the restraint of the ritual riots, the use of the funeral—none passed without comment, all had been watched live, close up, personal, and in color. And it would not be long before Irish republicans could watch on ITV or BBC Ulster the lessons put into practice with the Intifada. Larry Marley's funeral may have been only a penny on the Palestinian scales, but it did play on Middle East television and it did indicate in Belfast the unending probing for vulnerabilities. One of the perpetual chinks in British surface armor came at the fault line between peace and war. For the state murder is just murder, and yet the authorities kill as if it were war, enact emergency legislation and call it normal, assume that because their friends are supportive the disinterested will accept the illusion.

The IRA inadvertently created an incident by error when one operation in the Continental campaign ended in failure, a failure that had various and curious spin-offs. On March 6, 1988, three IRA active service unit members (Mairead Farrell, thirty-one, Daniel McCann, thirty, and Seán Savage, twenty-four) were shot and killed standing on a street in Gibraltar by an SAS unit flown in for that purpose. The IRA had discovered that the security in Gibraltar, far from Northern Ireland, was lax. There had never been an IRA presence in Spain or Gibraltar, and first-time attempts are easier; consequently, the IRA had planned a car bomb to go off in the midst of the changing-of-the-guard ceremony. The target selection was reasonable but after that the ritual errors were made: The three people chosen were sound, responsible volunteers—and known to every security person in Belfast. Mairead Farrell, formerly a student at Queen's, had just served ten years for bombing the Conway Hotel near Belfast and was famous—on the scan screens in European terrorist filters she would have pride of place among women terrorists, with most of the Germans gone. Her street knew she had gone back with the Provos—and if they knew so did the British. McCann had served two years for possession of explosives and was a well-known IRA man. Savage had been charged with IRA membership and conspiracy to cause explosions but had been released. They were the kind of people kept under nearly constant observation. The British knew where they were and where they were not.

When the three showed up in Spain in November 1987, where they had not realized they would have to register if they used hotels, the local climate was hardly friendly because of the long-lived Basque ETA armed campaign. Many in Spain had long assumed an intimate connection between the ETA and the IRA that existed largely in the imagination of theorists. In any case, three people with Belfast accents, IRA records, and no clear vacation business were going in and out of Spain. The Spanish authorities, alerted by the British as to their suspicions, monitored their every move. The moves and intentions of all three were known to the British all the way up to the Prime Minister. On December 9, 1987, Home Secretary Hurd told the European Minister of the antiterrorist Trevi Group that the IRA was planning to make the attack. By February the target was known, and on March 2, 1988, the special SAS team was flown to Gibraltar.

The decision to trap the three inside a Gibraltar ambush had already been made. On March 6 the three had been followed by the Spanish and turned over to the British teams at the border. Standard operating procedure in such terrorist operations is to make sure that all the terrorists are dead. Once across the border, the three IRA volunteers were targeted terrorists. The SAS was not interested in the details. They had come to kill. It did not matter that the IRA team's car did not have any explosives aboard, nor that the three were not armed. Wearing summer clothing, the three wandered about under surveillance until the trap shut. Then all three were shot dead. Watching civilians saw no effort made to capture the three—it appeared that one or two even tried to surrender. They were shot without warning and without compunction. While this was standard SAS practice, it was not standard procedure in an arrest. What were the SAS doing in Gibraltar, killing terrorists or assisting law enforcement? The official story began to fall apart immediately. Rationales and justifications for the shooting had to be found. There were too many witnesses, leaks from everyplace. The necessity to explain—often inaccurately—at higher and higher levels sapped the euphoria for the kill. The operation was transformed into murder by the state.

Only the convinced Conservatives accepted the nine-to-two inquest jury's "lawful killing" as an end to the matter. For many, including many with no time for the Provos, the British had shot to kill, had lied, and had lost credibility as a result. The *Independent* on September 10 noted that by "employing military men rather than the police to cope with IRA bombers and gunmen, the state is encouraging their pretensions that they are engaged in war as opposed to crime." It was too late then to turn the war into a failed arrest. The Saga—Death on the Rock—stretched out, grew elaborate, involved television documentaries, witnesses who saw a frenzied attack, no warning, lies to back the authorities, the volunteers shot while on the ground, while putting up their hands—not at all what the British authorities claimed. The usual media circus grew grand on the scandal. And there were not only official lies and evasions but also the behavior of the British media. The IRA was first convicted on the front pages and the SAS was exonerated, witnesses were smeared—a bad job. Spanish displeasure leaked out. Finally the failed operation turned into an IRA bonus when part of the media revealed the nature of the killing and the attempted coverup.

In Belfast, even the conventional martyrs' ritual had unexpected and frightening twists. The authorities were still bitter about the struggles over the earlier IRA funerals that made them appear abroad just as ghoulish as the IRA claimed—and the authorities knew just how cunningly the IRA managed funerals. This time they decided to scale down the security presence, stay out of the cemetery, let the republicans alone, and so reduce media coverage of the ritual. The three were given a traditional funeral at Milltown cemetery in West Belfast. Because of their service and the Gibraltar operation fallout the funeral drew, as expected, the cream of the overt republican movement. They were all there as promised—Gerry Adams, Martin McGuinness, all the Sinn Féin people, many volunteers passing as ordinary, friends, family, all the enormous number required by custom to appear and a great many who were just curious.

Taking advantage of the event, a Protestant mixed up with the UDR, Michael Stone, sought to punish the traitors apparently on his own. On March 16 he arrived with four Russian-made grenades and a revolver. He threw the grenades to little effect but shot and killed three people and wounded several others. He performed live on television and became in certain circles a hero: A song was written (Protestants are Irish and like a ballad too) and graffiti went up on gable ends. After all, he had tried to wipe out the core of the republicans in public on television: Why not a hero? He had been in the Kesh, stayed inactive, returned as a free-lance, usually shunted aside in even the most violent organizations, for he was apparently a danger to have about, "a man who would do absolutely anything." John McMichael had used him but few others would dare. And so he showed up at Milltown, disturbed, dangerous, dull in aspect and in conversation, and shot into the crowd, killed three people he did not know, and went off to prison. "He's a hero to some people."

There was an immediate demand for an investigation: How had Stone slipped through security? Why was there no security? Why was it necessary for the crowd to run him down and capture him—nearby M1 Motorway—and where were the RUC? Many in Belfast, a city not innocent of conspiracies, suspected the authorities. Then on Saturday, March 19, 1988, at the funeral of Kevin Brady, one of the three killed by Stone, the anger and suspicion came together for one more horror. Two British army NCOs, Corporals Robert Howes and Derek Wood, uninstructed or incredibly foolish, drove into the funeral cortege. Many in the immediate crowd thought it was one more murder attempt. The crowd closed in on the car and dragged the two out. They were beaten, stripped of their clothing, and beaten again by a mob of the frantic. Several IRA men in the crowd did not care what had brought two army targets into the crowd. Using panic and the throng as cover they dragged the two away, propped them up against a wall, and shot them—Wood was hit six times and Howes five. Much of the brutal incident was filmed both by the television teams and the spy helicopter hovering over the funeral. The two deaths had an enormous impact not because they added to the murder toll or because they produced secondary struggles over use of the footage or long and complex trials of those indicted for the murders, but because massive, global television audiences could see murder done close up.* The audience saw the mob, the corporals' panic, the reality that lay behind all those numbers and the ritual complaints about violence. People who for twenty years had followed the events from Dublin or Tralee were touched and horrified by the real murder on their screen.

---

*Those who shot and killed the soldiers were never found. When those who had dragged the two from the car were convicted of murder by a Diplock Court and sentenced to life imprisonment, the Haldane Society in London criticized the procedure, the court, and the convictions, contending that there was no evidence of murderous intent by the confused crowd and the court had not taken into account the climate of fear in Belfast after the Stone killings during the funeral of the Gibraltar IRA volunteers. As usual the judicial establishment had no interest in such criticism, quibbling by Labour lawyers far from the reality of Belfast.

The Milltown killings, but for the television footage of live murder, would have settled back into obscurity, one more atrocity for no good cause, for no real cause at all. Even the footage was not as dramatic as might be imagined: Real life is not like a movie, with proper angles and close-ups, with editing and background music; in Belfast there was no one to dub in realistic sound or erase a blur. No matter—the corporals' deaths were on film and were for most realer than real. The Troubles were made actual for the first time for those who had never smelled cordite or seen a smashed kneecap. Now, courtesy of the minicam, they had watched the last dreadful minute of two more lives, two more numbers.

Sometimes it appeared as if the Troubles had been reduced to numbers, more dead, more talks, more time in prison or suspects arrested under the Prevention of Terrorism Act. There were lethal subfields: The Dublin *Sunday Tribune,* in July 1989, reported that the IRA had executed thirty-three suspects for informing. Like most statistics it was close enough; a few mistakes were included and a few names were missing. They went into the grand total—security forces, own goals, innocent Catholics, guilty Protestants; the whole was moving toward three thousand. These were not really world-class numbers but there was no end in sight. The refusal of the Unionists to accept any beginning as long as the AIA existed as the basis meant that the talks about talks had nowhere to go. The benefits of refusal that assured no one could outflank those leading the negative crusade, that assured a marshaling of political forces repaid not in office or power but in pride and prominence, were equal to any imagined culmination of talks. Talks would be to concede, accept the perceived humiliation of the AIA, unless those talks were arranged in such a way as to extract a price from the SDLP and Dublin. The point was not so much to win an agenda or a formulation as to punish the others. It was a hopeless Unionist position. On October 14–15 secret talks were held in Duisburg, West Germany, far from prying Orange and Green eyes, involving Jack Allen for the OUP, Peter Robinson of the DUP, the SDLP's Austin Currie, and Gordon Macwhinney of the Alliance. The difficulty was that the Unionists would not talk unless the agreement was suspended and the SDLP would not talk if it were. As a result of no visible politics, the initiative in the province slipped again into the hands of those who could act on events, those who did not wait on elections as an exercise in tribal loyalty or appear at meetings with the Northern Ireland Office that led to meetings with the Northern Ireland Office.

The hope that the IRA lacked the military capacity to continue the armed struggle and the hope that Enniskillen would erode their will both proved premature. Instead the IRA planted a bomb under a van carrying soldiers at a fun run in Lisburn—six were killed. On June 23 the IRA shot down a helicopter at Crossmaglen in Armagh. There was again serious talk of internment, certainly in the North and perhaps in the South. The Provos were active both on the Continent and in England as well as in the province. On July 23 the thousand-pound bomb that had killed the Hannahs and their son instead of the judge brought the total IRA mistakes to seventeen since November 1987.

Then on August 20, 1988, a bomb attack on a British army bus smashed the vehicle all over the road near Ballygawley, Tyrone, and killed eight soldiers. It was the worst attack since Warrenpoint and indicated the dangers of the roads.

Seemingly as if in retaliation on August 31 another SAS ambush closed on the Provos near Drumnakilly, this one baited, not just laid on. Three volunteers were killed, supposedly long-suspected IRA people, and so in small measure compensated for the Ballygawley bus. For much of the British public, fans of the SAS since the televised rescue at the Iraqi Embassy in London in 1980, the unit could do little wrong—South Armagh, Loughgall, Gibraltar, now Tyrone, all were justified; or, if there was fault it was without the politicians. The Irish IRA gunmen, however feral, were regarded as dangerous and deadly, without mercy, and thus to be treated without quarter. The Tyrone operation underlined just how really dangerous the seemingly pleasant green back country of small farms and tiny villages had grown as the IRA failed to disappear in the wake of the agreement. The SAS involvement, coupled with a failed trap in Belfast that killed an innocent taxi driver, once again revealed the war in the midst of peace issues. That there was a war was difficult to miss, even for the innocent. The general British public might prefer that the Irish be left to the Irish, but if not there was little sympathy for providing gunmen with the niceties of the law during an unconventional war. A new storm broke out over the British soldier, Guardsman David Holden, who shot dead a Sinn Féin election worker, Aidan McAnespie, on his way to a football match in the Republic. It was a replay of all the other arbitrary shootings—excused, soldier returned to duty. On December 17 there was a celebration of the three hundredth anniversary of the siege of Derry by the Apprentice Boys. The prologue is never past.

The new year was mostly a repeat. The agreement or its shadow dominated the options, reducing the politicians to talking with each other about matters discussed to tatters. One must not only be brave to enter Northern Irish politics—Austin Currie's home had been attacked thirty times—but also have an incredibly high boredom level. At least Paisley traveled over to the Continent from time to time to insult Thatcher or the Pope at the European Parliament. Most of the everyday politicians were reduced to talking to each other. King, encouraged by word of talks at Duisburg the previous October, began (through his junior minister, Brian Mawhinney, as intermediary) to set up formal talks about talks. This at least was an improvement over no talks, no politics but protest, and the steady rise in the toll of sectarian killings by Protestant paramilitaries, IRA soldiers, and the security forces. It all began again. The IRA sought to clean up its act. The Fermanagh unit, suspected of sectarian killing, was disbanded. Martin McGuinness said that it was a clear message to all that killing civilians was wrong: "We must not, in challenging British rule, be the initiators of further injustice." On March 7 two young children watched an IRA gunman shoot their father, supposedly a UVF man, and then in the confusion shoot two old men who had been with him. Another error. The UVF and UDA did not think killing Catholic males, especially any with Sinn Féin connections, was wrong, so their operations continued, and once in a while they even managed to hit an IRA man. On February 13 one of the province's best known Catholic solicitors, Pat Finucane, who defended republicans, was shot and killed and his Protestant wife, Geraldine, was wounded. As in so many cases, the brutal splash sent up far waves, for a junior minister, Douglas Hogg, had a month before criticized some Northern Irish solicitors for being "unduly sympathetic" to republican clients.

757

No matter what appears on television, how long the butcher's bill, how brutal the events, those away from the province seldom understand the dynamics of danger: Hogg hardly intended his words to kill. Nor do visiting professors grasp the danger of their in-depth interview, nor do the television people anticipate that their coverage may endanger even the innocent caught in one freeze-frame. The Troubles are often treated as normal. And after the long years, where each event has a tangled past and bleeds out into new problems, even those responsible grow weary. What did 1989 have to offer but horror, no political progress, the decay of hope in the agreement, and the same old quarrels?

By Saint Patrick's Day, twenty-four people had been killed in 1989 terrorist violence, with a spurt of twelve between March 7 and March 19, including a former UVF leader, Jackie Irvine, and a Roman Catholic grandfather shot in retaliation, along with a civil servant. The next day the IRA shot and killed two senior policemen, Chief Superintendent Harry Breen, the most senior officer killed in the Troubles, and Superintendent Bob Buchanan, as they returned to Northern Ireland after a meeting in Dundalk with the Gárdaí officers. It was a grave loss for the RUC, raised all sorts of counterintelligence questions, and acted as a counter to the IRA's previous mistakes. On April 12 an IRA bomb exploded early by mistake in Warrenpoint and killed a twenty-year-old woman. One of the IRA people had apparently brushed one of the detonator switches—another accident. Gerry Adams sent his sympathy to the family while the SDLP councillor in the town, Jim McCart, said, "Let us put the blame where it belongs—the Provisional IRA. Let there be no bullshit about warnings, it was sheer bloody murder." After regrets, the IRA intended to keep right on with the campaign. War is brutal. The British had shot McAnespie on his way to play football and covered it up "administratively." McAnespie was dead and the soldier was back with his regiment. Nothing was new. The shooting and the bombing continued, more troops were sent into Armagh, and then came the local elections.

There was for the center a modicum of good news. The DUP and Provisional Sinn Féin had their votes squeezed. Most notable was the DUP's loss of 6.6 percent, indicating the increasing troubles that Paisley had in keeping his troops in line. Republican Sinn Féin did not run. Provisional Sinn Féin lost votes but held the key areas and even won a seat in Enniskillen; the Poppy Day fallout had not destroyed their support, as many had hoped. Still, the party was badly hit, losing 17 seats, winning 42 compared with 59 in 1985. But because of a heavy vote in West Belfast the popular total was down only 1 percent. Alliance went up to 38 seats and the Workers Party stayed at four.

In the province the Workers remained marginal. Party leader Tomás Mac Giolla, TD, who had shepherded his party from the old straight-arrow, Second Dáil republicanism of the mid-sixties through to the edge of the nineties and a neo-Marxist-Leninist version, retired as party leader, leaving a legacy of hope and ambition in the Republic. The next generation arrived in the form of Proinsias De Rossa. He was not too new, having been a minor IRA man in the fifties campaign. But the transformation into an orthodox party was nearly complete. There were a few Sticky guns on the shelf in the North to protect their black economic interests; but armed expropriations were almost a matter of the past. Increasingly the party was dominated by those with no IRA background, attracted by present policies not old priorities. The Workers had managed that most difficult of feats, transforming an active guerrilla group into a conventional political party—and one that was enormously critical of those remaining republicans and surprisingly supportive of the Northern authorities, even the RUC's use of supergrasses. The local elections simply indicated again that the party had no real constituency in the province: The Catholic vote went either to the Catholic party or the republicans or was scattered on the fringes while the Protestant vote tended to divide between the proper and the Paisleyites. Alliance indicated that despite everything or perhaps because of everything there was still a center of sorts.

More general politics was merely a continuation of the agreement. London and Dublin issued a review and neither showed regrets. The Unionists could only talk on. Austin Currie had actually joined Fine Gael in the Republic in order to pursue his career in the June general election: No one could see a devolved Irish assembly any time soon. So, too, had John Cushnahan of the Alliance, who moved south like Currie and managed to win a Euro-seat, if barely, on the twelfth count. In Northern Ireland the Euro-elections had set results, a tribal popularity contest—only the number of votes the superstars attracted was in doubt. Paisley received 160,110 and Hume 136,335 while Ulster Unionist Jim Nicholson picked up his seat on transfers from Paisley. Sinn Féin's Morrison attracted only 48,914, 9.1 percent, contrasted with the SDLP's 25.5 percent, a party record. Alliance took 27,905, 5.2 percent. There was no return for novelty: The Conservatives, who sought to bring British politics to the province, a move opposed by many Conservatives who wanted no part of Ulster, got 25,789 votes for 4.8 percent; the Greens and Left did poorly. Paisley could feel he had recouped his local election losses and Sinn Féin that they still suffered from IRA "mistakes." The news from Dublin indicated that Haughey had failed to get a Fianna Fáil majority—his fifth failure—as the electorate shifted to the Left, taking away half of the PD's seats and even giving the Greens a seat. The result seemed to mean little for Northern Ireland because the feeling was that Haughey would find a way to stay in power, and if not, Fine Gael was even more dedicated to the agreement. The elections of 1989 indicated only that the more nothing changed the more depressing the Troubles were—to what end?

The killings went on elsewhere as well. Corporal Steven Smith of the Royal Tank Regiment in Germany opened his car door and was blown away by an IRA bomb in front of his wife and children—a mistake narrowly avoided. At least in Ulster the Orange marching season brought controversy but no violence in 1989. There was the continued steady-state killings and bombs that attracted notice only when especially brutal. In North Antrim at Rasharkin, on April 4, three UVF gunmen broke into the house of Gerard Casey, twenty-nine, with four children, and shot him dead in his bed next to his wife. The police were not surprised, having suspected the dead man of terrorist connections for some time. The paramilitaries kept on killing. And the IRA's armed campaign now had a whole menu of targets on order: the courts, the Dublin-Belfast railway line, the RUC-army security posts in the countryside, informers, contractors and collaborators working for the security forces, the UVF and UFF killers, the UDR, and always the army, anyplace, Belfast or Britain or Germany. There were also symbolic targets in England and individuals within the British imperial machine.

In May 1989 the IRA killed a British soldier and a prison employee, and issued a statement that indicated their position: "We remind the British people on this tenth anniversary of Mrs. Thatcher's government that the Irish Question remains unresolved and cannot be resolved by military policies." The IRA intended, of course, to continue their own military policies. On one weekend in May nine British soldiers were injured by two bomb explosions near the border. In response to the rising IRA presence in South Armagh Ulster Secretary Tom King sent in extra troops. The IRA summer attacks meant that again the countryside was more dangerous than it looked, even though there were long pauses caused by aborted IRA operations or security force successes. A bomb that killed a member of the RUCR in Strabane on June 27 was the first fatality in almost two months.

In September 1989 an IRA bomb in the military barracks at Deal in Kent killed ten army musicians and injured twenty-two. It was a soft target but a military one—marines first, musicians second, as Gerry Adams said. The twentieth anniversary of the arrival of British troops on the street had already passed with the media heavily represented but violence rare, with eager television crews urging children to demonstrate for their cameras. There was excitement during the summer in the Irish media over leaks from the UDR to Protestant paramilitaries, a constant in the North; there was less excitement about the annual appearance, often banned, of NORAID's Martin Galvin for internment commemorations. Thatcher showed her faith in the UDR, again, still, by another whirlwind visit: Her only concerns were about the troops and Dublin's compliance with security arrangements. Haughey, aware of the rumors about a new republican party, perhaps with Neil Blaney as leader, perhaps not, that would be established as an antiextradition group, had to move cautiously in the direction that was desired by both Dublin and London.

The republicans in Ireland and elsewhere still had to live with the dirty war while seeking political gain: It was no easy process. On September 7, 1989, at Unna Messen, near Dortmund in West Germany, an IRA gunman shot Heidi Hazell, the German wife of a British soldier, Clive Hazell, the intended target, as she sat alone in her car. She was shot fourteen times. The killer had not taken the step closer to make sure of his target. On October 26 an IRA unit in West Germany shot and killed a British soldier and by mistake his six-month-old daughter. Only the unexpected resignation of the Chancellor of the Exchequer at the same time divided media focus. Mistakes by others—the British army, the Protestant paramilitaries, the republican splinter groups like the IPLO, who killed an innocent tiler, Robert Burns, forty-nine, father of four, in November—did not cause the same ritual outrage. These killings were no danger to the state and in the case of the SAS or the regular army, the killings were committed by the state; it was the Provos that sought to destroy the center. And the center's supporters, the institutions of the legitimate, the media and the church and the parties, the decent and the moderate, all were at risk when the Provos killed. And all through 1989 they kept on killing. On December 13 a large active service unit attacked a border checkpoint at Derryard in Fermanagh; two soldiers were killed and a third seriously injured in the exchange, in which the IRA used heavy machine guns and grenades. The new Northern Secretary, Peter Brooke, felt that the two had died "in defense of ordinary decent people of Northern Ireland." He announced that the government intended to defeat terrorism in all its forms.

After twenty years the government seemed no closer to that victory. Tom King had come back to the province to announce that "we are going to win, sooner or later." It still looked like later. Certainly it was for King, who left the province in July and was replaced by Peter Brooke, who saw out the decade with his talks about talks and the Muzak of violence. The decade did end on a high note in that the fearful year-end summing up noted that 62 people had died as a result of the Troubles, the third lowest total since 1970 and nowhere near the over 180 killed in traffic accidents. In fact the violence indicators had been slowly declining throughout the eighties.

The decade ended as it had begun, with violence, stalled politics, and foreboding: Nothing good was on the menus and all concerned had seemingly exhausted the visible prospects even for serious change much less progress toward accommodation. There would be some new names, the old leaving the field. Fitz-Gerald was gone; Currie and Cushnahan were in the Republic. West had retired and Craig was irrelevant, last heard indicating that force might have to be used against the AIA. Sir John Hermon, who had been in the RUC since 1980, would not be around. He was to be replaced by Hugh Annesley, assistant commissioner of the Metropolitan Police in London. Hermon had been a hard, cantankerous, rough man who had made the RUC less provincial and far more effective. Violent crime was still relatively rare in Northern Ireland, so for ten years the police had been structured to stop terror—mostly the IRA's armed struggle but the violence of the others as well—and by 1990 the RUC was impressive indeed in all aspects of subverting the armed struggle, from cutting off financing to monitoring movement with television cameras. No one in London paid much attention—the British were, as always, bored with the Irish. Tom King had been brought back to London as Defense Minister, not a burned-out case at all, when he was replaced by Brooke in July. Brooke would continue talking about talks. The major external players were still in the game. Haughey managed to weave together against all past principles a coalition government with his old enemy, Dessie O'Malley, and so was still in place for the new decade. In London the Iron Lady seemed beyond challenge and she had no residue of interest in Ireland.

The boredom in the eighties had not prevented the appointment of able men as Northern Secretary nor the structuring of serious political initiatives, not only the fabled agreement but others as well; nor had boredom limited continued efforts in Britain and abroad to minimize the worst of the fallout. The Irish in Dublin had grown not bored but resentful, feeling a growing distaste for the national issue as defined by Northern Irish events. Austin Currie, elected to the Dáil, and John Cushnahan, to the European Parliament, did not indicate a new trend—political talent was not that thick on the ground in the Republic, which is, after all, a small country, and both had recognition value. They were elected in spite of the national issue rather than because of it. The British may have forgotten everything and learned little but those in the Republic in power and at the crossroads had used the ten years to reconsider the nature and cost of nostalgia, simple faiths, and rebel songs. In the province, more lost than ever, the Unionists and the more militant loyalists had chosen to kill rather than compromise when time from the returns of covert militarism made that convenient—the paramilitaries had been, not surprisingly, attracted by the lure of easy money but not to give up the gun. The IRA, having discarded the fair-weather faithful, mostly in the Republic, found that the political crusade had no new support, especially in the Republic, where in the 1989 general elections Provisional Sinn Féin took less than 1 percent of the vote. There were still those involved in the Troubles who had hopes in accommodation and votes and formulas. In October 1989 the British Tories had overwhelmingly authorized, over the leadership's opposition, a Northern Ireland branch, the North Down Model Conservative Association. It was a step to turn the province into an ordinary part of the United Kingdom, not Irish at all but, as the Unionists always said, British. There were those who still advocated devolution or independence or federalism. Nothing was truly new. There were only so many options, and most of them were now threadbare.

Everything somehow had ended on a negative note, not an inch given, no result from the talks on talks, no votes for Sinn Féin or end to the gun or novelty offered. Those abroad who had bought the agreement saw their enthusiasm misplaced; the final accommodation was one more oversold formula. Ireland disappointed the British again, as did the Irish. On the island the butcher's bill was static, an acceptable level of violence. The ripples now could be seen as regular on the Continent and in England, the Irish still troubling the distant. There was not even a new atrocity, just the same old IRA mistakes, UVF random murders, and British army dirty tricks, a long-running, twenty-four-hour serial with no hope of a novel episode.

21

The Next Decade, the Pattern Set: 1990–1992

Separation between past, present, and future is only an illusion, however tenacious.

Albert Einstein

As the decade came to an end, there was nothing special to celebrate and little hope of movement toward accommodation or conciliation, nor were new directions available to those still determined to pursue their lethal dreams. Few bothered to sum up the decade and few even bothered with the year-end statistics. Nothing was new. Everyone remembered everything, forgot no grievances, recalled nothing but failure. The scholars had found that there was still discrimination in Northern Ireland, each for his own, but that Catholics still had a poor deal although not as bad as before, and that the whole province suffered. Specialized action groups arose to point to problems that after twenty years still needed remedial work. Promises were made. No one but the involved paid great attention. The Troubles were no longer an aberration but were so protracted as to be convention. It was not the sort of condition that Western politicians sought or found acceptable, for they were inevitably optimistic, sought office to ensure beneficial change. And instead a pattern of persistent Irish violence, accepted by nearly all, had emerged that indicated neither a societal learning curve nor even a desire for compromise that might ensure enormous benefits. The secondary benefits had become institutionalized, primary. So with each successive year the themes and issues of the recent past emerged for a time and then faded away, replaced by another familiar motif.

The major actor, the only one with even partial control over the script, the British establishment, remained dedicated to both the easy life and a hold on Ireland—contradictory goals. British quality time was seldom given to Ireland. At an operational level, where politics and the security forces worked, the major problem for London and for the Northern Ireland Office in Belfast was how a decent, democratic society fought a war and called it peace or pursued peace without recourse to the potentially useful means of war. The use of the state's assets in an undeclared conflict regularly produced contradictions that could not easily be explained away. The explaining away generated, as it had everywhere, enormous anger at British hypocrisy. Yet, in so doing Britain received enormous psychological returns, unearned, drawn from old capital. Few nations doubt their righteousness; but few have had such a long run as the British in Ireland in transmuting rather dubious responses into self-assurances of goodness and disinterested sacrifice. The British feel that they are there not because Ireland is truly part of the kingdom but because of the call of a higher duty: the imposition of justice on warring tribes. If not wanted by the majority, the Irish, they will, of course, go. All the British want is that the Irish, Catholic or Protestant, who they do not especially like, be British. In persisting in Ireland—Ulster—for duty's sake, the British have regularly adjusted what they are doing, fighting a nasty, dirty war, to what they chose to believe: that Ireland is mostly normal, nearly at peace, and this year or next will be like the rest of the kingdom. This belief is denied and disputed with awesome regularity.

The prime axis of dispute runs from the pointed end of the stick, out poking around where murder is done (the SAS, the dirty war, the nightmare of informants and betrayals and ambushes) on through the open conflict, the capture, trial, conviction, sentencing, and imprisonment of those dedicated to a different dream; and it doesn't end even with the manipulation of a lifer's sentence, but follows on to the grave and beyond. Each factor in the process has moments of prominence that immediately spin off waves of complicated reactions and responses: The rise and fall of the H-Block issue was the grandest of all, but after a generation the foci of contention were still expensive: shoot to kill, deep interrogation, extradition, informants, more intelligence scandals. By 1990 there was even a new genre of dirty war revelations, men who had lied and stolen or plotted against Harold Wilson* or heard of killing by the army and then in print recanted; Colin Wallace, Fred Holroyd, Peter Wright. It was a minor literature contrasted to the Great Scandal, the treason, of Burgess, Maclean, Philby, and the rest, but it was still a nasty side effect of the Troubles. Those involved were small and narrow, men with grudges, not graces, who once thought it grand to plot against the Prime Minister over whiskey, to lie to the press and to press special operations as a symbol of pragmatic power. They were the drudges and the drones of the system, buffs and boys' own spies. Even before Thatcher came to power, the type had been edged out of Northern Ireland, although there were still activists to be found in the security establishment. The later revelations, more interesting to those seeking scandal than enlightenment, indicated only that Ireland had brought out the worst in the lower reaches of the establishment as well as at the top.

The British government under Thatcher and then in November 1990 under her replacement, John Major, seemingly had lost any residue of interest in the island. Major had no Irish interests; hardly anyone in the cabinet did except those

---

*A reporter from the London *Observer* revealed the details in *The Wilson Plot* (New York: Pantheon Books, 1988) concerning the ineffectual scheming against the Prime Minister. As far as Ireland was concerned, there was a feeling by some within the security establishment that harsh measures were needed that the London government did not want to grant and so individuals and groups undertook such measures—deception, penetration, black propaganda, simple lies, and special operations—within both the province and the Republic. Such acts were considered not only effective, pragmatic, and expedient but a counter to political timidity at best and treason at worst.

who had suffered in the Northern Ireland Office. The British response to Irish matters had settled into ill-humored ritual. Tom King had been brought back to a more interesting career as Minister of Defense after his years plodding on as optimism evaporated. With minimal impact he had overseen the institutionalization by default of the conflict. The new model IRA emerged. The Protestant paramilitaries did not disappear into crime but shaped corruption to lethal sectarian ends and so returned to killing as politics. The politicians grew sullen and truculent. The Dublin government went its own way, sometimes useful and sometimes, almost out of old habit, impeding British aims. It was not that nothing happened but that nothing happened to lead London to hope. Where was the boon of peace and quiet once promised by the agreement? Instead there were bombs in London, killing on the Continent, and the same old chaos in the province.

No one was really interested anymore. Neil Blaney had investigated the prospects of a new party arising on the extradition issue and found no interest. In 1989, twenty years after the British army arrived, the anniversary had been memorable only to those then involved who had hardly imagined so much time had passed. Callaghan with his bullhorn in Derry and Bernadette savaging Maudling in Commons and the tea for the troops had been as yesterday. Now the young radicals were middle-aged with teenage children. The young and the damned and the daring had lumpy figures, gray hair, and mostly more reasoned convictions. Now the killing was done by those who were children at the time, whose whole lives had been lived amid the Troubles. The babies pushed in strollers at Bodenstown or on the Glorious Twelfth had come of age. For them, Bloody Sunday was as Agincourt or Normandy, a long-ago, famous battle. Their battles were of the day. Paisley was an ancient, Rhonda's father, and O Brádaigh was too an old one with his son, Rory Og, at the desk of Republican Sinn Féin on Aston Quay overlooking the Liffey. The famous paramilitary prisoners were often frail, worn by years without a horizon and often without hope of redemption. Many of the Irish, however, came through the years equipped with their knapsack stuffed with history, often the same history their fathers carried and often the same history that now burdened their children.

The past replayed too often erodes even the endless capacity for sensation, so that even murder may not enliven. On September 29, 1990, 100,000 Orangemen showed up in Belfast to celebrate the three hundredth anniversary of the Battle of the Boyne, less of a spectacular than planned. It was one too many an anniversary—many felt as if they had already marched each of the three hundred times. They stayed home. And so the others marched to history's beat and nothing happened and they came home. Earlier in the year, in January, the nationalists of Derry had commemorated the civil rights march in Derry that had ended in Bloody Sunday. This time many wished they had stayed home, for history came alive, unexpectedly, unpleasantly, as has been the practice in Ulster for years. The IRA had placed a bomb on the wall near Walker's Monument, sure that on Sunday the police and army would be there watching the display. At 4:15 P.M. on Sunday, January 28, just as timed, the bomb went off; but, unexpectedly, it scattered debris and rocks on the crowd below. One stone fatally injured seventeen-year-old Charles Love of Strabane—a dreadful error, a freak accident, the luck of the Irish.* He was buried on the same day as the civil rights pioneer Brigid Bond, secretary of the Derry Housing Action Committee and chairperson of the Derry branch of NICRA. So there were two deaths, one after all those years of turmoil that had begun before the other fatality had been born. They were in a way casualties of the Battle of the Boyne, as interpreted three hundred years later. Ireland of the sorrows simply seemed to go on and on, boring but lethal.

Back at the beginning Richard Rose, the American professor of politics at Strathclyde, had said that the problem was that there was no solution. And so far there had been none, although not for want of trying. "Contrary to Rose's assertion that no such solution exists, there are a whole series of possible solutions."†Possible but not actual. Everyone knew there were possibilities. Some were excluded because they could not be imposed and others still had advocates. There were lots of solutions. The New Ireland Forum had served up the favorite three of Dublin and watched them tossed out. And more practically, over the years the British had, with or without the consent of the involved, launched several—conventions, assemblies, power sharing, and all varieties of devolution— to no avail. There were all sorts of solutions: incorporation into the United Kingdom or a unitary Irish state, more direct rule or a recreated Sunningdale with power sharing and an Irish dimension. There might be a federal state (the Provisionals with the discarded *Éire Nua* had shaped their variant) or a confederal Irish state with joint sovereignty. There were many varieties of power sharing on offer, codetermination, a consociational system and those who would build on dual citizenship or shared citizenship or joint authority. Some proposed repartition or devolution without power sharing. Some, now these and now those, advocated an independent Ulster, some through consent and others by unilateral declaration. There had been hope of a neo-Marxist class solution or a deal between the loyalists and republicans at the expense of the moderate and middle class.

There were many, many proposed solutions, but none that had the support of all or nearly all of the involved—that was the continuing problem. There was no acceptable solution.‡ Northern Ireland had become a small arena for great clashes between contradictory ideals, exclusive legitimacies, dreams that persisted with-

---

*In time the IRA explosives specialist who made and set the bomb was discovered to have been a British informer. He was kidnapped, interrogated for a tape record, and killed by the IRA. Some felt that the Derry bomb might have been placed so as to kill, but as with most Irish conspiracy theories, no one knew for sure, although many believed or denied with venom.

†Arend Lijphart in the Foreword to John McGarry and Brendan O'Leary, *The Future of Northern Ireland* (Oxford: Clarendon Press, 1990), p. vi.

‡In *The Future of Northern Ireland*, the contributors touch most of the available solutions that are not shaped mainly through future violence with a remarkable and persistent optimism. Arend Lijphart, a distinguished scholar, long concerned with Ireland, in his short introduction notes how politicians have been ahead of scholars in advocating consociational arrangements, mentioning Holland in 1917, Lebanon in 1943, Austria in 1945, Malaysia in 1955, Colombia in 1958, and Northern Ireland in 1972—not a list to convince gamblers in tranquillity. It should, however, be noted that only optimists would have urged democratic institutions on warring tribes originally, and accommodations have come, if not to Lebanon or Colombia or Northern Ireland, to many troubled arenas in the West and even to some of those in the former Soviet empire. If this could be the case even as a result of scholarly investment and commitment, the world would be a far more tranquil place.

out winners or losers. Those who did not benefit from this clash, those with property and without dreams, those with traditional skills, traditional ideals, those who possessed adequate capital of one sort or another and some idealists as well, found such a situation intolerable. Yet even then matters could be worse, for there were other routes to an absence of violence.

There were as well the unacceptable solutions achieved by force over resistance: an Irish Republic, an Orange Ulster, a simple British withdrawal leaving the island to cope or a British deployment of counterterror and an end to the IRA; perhaps there could be a flight of Protestants or Catholics (a society truly divided), perhaps a class revolution, or structured pogroms as a step in nation building—all sorts of violence in the future's name. No one had the power or the will to impose a solution. No one had the desire to impose a solution, although the more militant could imagine a future without the other, an Ulster free of papists or a united Ireland with only consenting and compliant Protestants remaining. Polls in the Republic always showed a large majority in favor of unity—someday, somehow. Few in the Republic favored violence as a means. Yet in Northern Ireland violence was deployed to defend what still existed or to create conditions that would permit an amendable accommodation. The republicans did not intend to erase the other tradition, nor did the loyalists necessarily want to rule over all Catholics. Both militant factions in a sense needed the other as much as the loyalists needed the British as symbol of the system and the republicans needed the British as monster cause of all Irish ills. So while they were violent solutions, none had the will or the power to fashion such an endgame. All were restrained by ethics, by policy, by psychic needs, by decency.

One of the most persistent patterns in the tapestry of violence in Northern Ireland has been the variations on justice—justice done or justice corrupted, justice in the midst of war and peace. The primary focus was on British justice although in many cases parallel arguments and responses took place in the Irish Republic. There evolved an enormous legal literature* on existing and proposed legislation, each new commission or act adding another printed wave. For example, the Northern Ireland (Emergency Provisions) Act of 1987 arose from twenty years of legislation and practice constantly examined by scholars. Thus, emergency legislation came under scrutiny, particularly acts concerned with civil liberties; critics noted that these acts arose as a political and psychological response to provocation, extended broad policing powers with too limited restraints, and were then used not only as a weapon but also in instances unrelated to the original provocation. The Prevention of Terrorism Act, generated by the anger and anguish of the 1974 bombs in Britain, gave the police powers that were readily used, mostly to harass Irish travelers, if rarely used to produce formal cases against Irish republicans, and also at times deployed against criminals and non-Irish terrorist suspects. In other words, the security and police authorities had benefited generally from a momentary political reaction but in Irish matters

---

*A relatively recent summing-up is in Gerard Hogan and Clive Walker's *Political Violence and the Law in Ireland* (Manchester and New York: Manchester University Press, 1989). One author, Clive Walker, had already elaborated his Manchester 1982 dissertation into *The Prevention of Terrorism in British Law* (Manchester: Manchester University Press, 1986).

to no great advantage. The number of Irish suspects questioned in relation to ultimate convictions of any sort thereby initiated was enormous and over the years consistent.

The restrictions on liberty imposed by the Irish emergency worried many: The right to remain silent was seriously eroded, the right to travel freely within the United Kingdom was restricted, and such limitations, taken as a matter of course in Belfast or Tyrone, found advocates for their transport to Leeds or Kilburn. The Irish emergency, seemingly alien, had emerged as an English issue. Those who were suspected of bringing it over in the form of subversive speech could be sent back as internal exiles and those with the wrong accents might be questioned for no other reason or no reason at all under the Prevention of Terrorism Act when they returned from holidays in another part of the kingdom. England was a less pleasant land. More disturbing was that the use of the act implied an anti-Irish bias in the British judicial system. Over the years this assumption grew within both Irish communities and the legal profession. In sum, the British paid for the momentary psychological benefit of the Prevention of Terrorism Act with an erosion of both British civil liberties and the concept of British fair play. In this very real sense, a cost was paid for with a slight but constant decay in the quality of British life and the integrity of British institutions. After a generation the cost was hardly enormous but still as real and distressing as the inevitable ripple effect into British life of other aspects of Irish violence.

One of the long-lasting, most public, and most unpleasant threads in this pattern arose in a way much like the Prevention of Terrorism Act in the aftermath of IRA bombs in Britain in the seventies. Three sets of suspects were arrested, tried, and convicted in a manner that indicated to many that British justice was systemically denied to Irish suspects. These observers, more British than Irish, felt that the nature of the British and their judicial organization was so warped as to deliver only the ends desired. They argued that no Irish person could get a fair trial; for the system was skewed even if the law was impeccably written, the form was followed without deviation, and every opportunity to challenge the procedures and results remained open. More practically, the argument was made that in these three cases, all similar, the system had not worked and refused to concede error. Even with the more narrow focus the system at large had much to explain. Could justice be done and if not could error be admitted? It appeared justice had not been done—at any stage. This was denied root and branch by the judicial profession, by almost the entire establishment, and, as well as could be determined, by the populace at large. All believed deeply in British fair play, British justice, the creation of *their* tribe. Other peoples relied on force, trial by fire, and the vagaries of the gods. The Irish were surely more like the others than the English?

The three cases in British courts dragged on as issues, often even after all legal appeals had been exhausted, dragged on year after year, into the next decade and out into the nineties. When the IRA bomb convictions were at last overturned, the judicial system had been savaged even though over the long haul the struggle for that reversal had been waged largely in Britain by the British. The three cases were neither complex nor difficult. The Maguire Seven, the Guildford Four, and the Birmingham Six were groups that had attracted the attention of the police immediately after IRA bombs detonated. They had been arrested, questioned— beaten into confessions, according to many of the involved—and convicted on a mix of evidence, confessions, circumstances, and technical presentations. Another unsustainable case was that of Judith Ward, convicted in large part on a confused confession. From a distance all the confessions had appeared doubtful, the circumstances more apt to favor acquittal, and the technical presentations unconvincing. The juries and judges and the appeals courts, however, had accepted the confessions, the circumstances, and the evidence, found no subsequent reason to adjust, and persisted in contending that the guilty were in prison. New evidence regularly turned up that eroded a belief in this assumption, even if some of the evidence could not be weighed by the system. From early on the IRA had indicated that all were innocent, but this only convinced some of their guilt.

In fact, the system felt that not only had equity been achieved but that through the appeals process great care had been taken to review justice done. An end to judicial review should come; the case had gone on too long and, as Lord Denning indicated, "It is a scandal that should not be allowed to continue." Still, the movement toward reversal had continued. Not, of course, fast enough to those who saw only injustice in justice denied and then the system praised for following form. The cases became year by year an international issue that finally put the British system on trial. The cases followed an almost traditional course. The victims knew no one of importance and were known to no one but their friends and the court. In time their protestations attracted concern. One of the journalists, Brian Gibson, who covered the Birmingham Six trial, published *The Birmingham Bombers* in 1976. In that book he wrote that he had "not doubted since the very early days that the police got the right men." Early general opinion, which wanted victims, assumed that the police had the right ones and simply ignored the flaws in the case. Only very slowly did doubters arrive. Small, smudged pamphlets appeared, notable defenders of victims of injustice were contacted, meetings were held in cold, smoky rooms, church halls, and school auditoriums, advertised by fliers, attended by radicals and ethnics. And with each new revelation the appeal moved upmarket, the significant were attracted, the money began to come into the cause, politicians had to take a stand, the posters had designers and the publications slick covers. The victims became the Six or the Four and the issue moved into the national news.

The longer the cases dragged on the more was at stake for the system. The Maguire Seven served their sentences out and so sought not freedom but vindication. The others remained in prison. Denning also said that if an appeal in the Birmingham Six case succeeded (and Denning felt them guilty, proven guilty by a sound system) it would be "such an appalling vista that every sensible person in the land would say it cannot be right that these actions should go any further." In November 1981 the House of Lords, the final court of appeal had upheld the judgment against the Birmingham Six. That should have been the end of matters but was not. Their defenders grew in number as the old evidence was shifted, as new evidence emerged, as the cases became celebrated. Many, both specialists and everyday people in Ireland and Britain, still believed the bombers guilty as found. But lurking doubts began to occur in high places, if for no other reason than that systemic error in the British judicial system—quite unrelated to Ireland or the IRA or racial prejudice—had not only occurred before but also had produced a most willful refusal by the establishment to contemplate error.

The system tended to hunker down and deny the obvious until no one was left convinced but those responsible for the injustice. Consequently, the outraged indignation of the authorities, the arrogance of professionals, the absolute assurance of the establishment did not serve the system well. The refusal to contemplate error in fact made increasingly uneasy even those who, not unlike Denning, feared the result of those radicals who insisted on justice though the heavens fall. The break-even point came in 1986 with the publication of *Error of Judgment, the Birmingham Bombings* by Chris Mullin, a novelist, journalist, and soon to be the successful Labour candidate for Sunderland South, and *Trial and Error, the Maguires, the Guildford Pub Bombings and British Justice* by Robert Kee, an even more successful journalist who, through his book *The Green Flag*, turned into a television miniseries, had become the English expert on the Irish. These books convinced many of the innocence of the bombers and even more that the system preferred to find means to deny previous error than to correct it. From this point on, the burden of proof—whatever the finer points of the law and the nature of the courts—rested with the system. By the time Grant McKee and Ros Franey published *Time Bomb* on the Irish bombers, English justice, and the Guildford Four two years later, the cases, Judith Ward's excepted, were famous and the reputation of British justice damaged by charges, widely accepted, that the Irish in general were at risk and that any error was likely to be denied.

The cases now began to cause Britain harm elsewhere. One spin-off disaster was that the repeated public judicial evasions seemed to come at times that proved advantageous to an IRA regularly under attack for ruthless incompetence. Flawed British justice provided the gunmen with a smokescreen. One Birmingham Six appeal was, as noted, refused in January 1988 with the republicans still devastated by the Enniskillen Poppy Day Massacre. Later the cases could be used for other political advantage, even in other judicial contests. The prisoners, none even close to the IRA, much less members, served the republicans better than many volunteers. As time passed and the cases remained issues, there was new evidence, the confessions were accepted as unacceptable, the police came under suspicion for all sorts of illicit conduct, the circumstances recounted were seen as unconvincing, and much of the evidence as presented proved faulty or improbable—and the ability of the judges involved to ignore the obvious could no longer be ignored.

When the Guildford Four case was declared unsound and the men released, two books soon appeared, Gerry Conlon's *Proved Innocent: The Story of Gerry Conlon of the Guildford Four* and *Stolen Years, Before and After Guildford* by Paul Hill with Ronan Bennett. These books kept up the Birmingham Six pressure and did little for the reputation of the British prison system.* The West Midlands police involved had

---

*One prisoner's book that received little notice—not the least because it was first published in Irish and then in Ireland—was Aíne and Gibhlín Nic Giolla Easpaig's *Sisters in Cells* (Westport [Mayo]: Foilseacháin Náisiúnta Teoranta, 1987). It details the imprisonment of two Donegal sisters involved in republican activities in Manchester and so snatched up on the fringe of IRA operations. In their case the police had some evidence that they were not entirely innocent, at

come into suspicion for criminal conspiracy as well as beating the suspects. The suspects' claim was called by Mr. Justice Bridge "most bizarre and grotesque." Many outside the judiciary no longer believed the West Midlands police or that beatings were bizarre. The judge appeared to have construed the evidence or the tatters remaining to protect previous positions, not to achieve even the pretense of justice. As Hugh Callaghan of the Six was to say, "It has been known for years we were innocent."

The judicial system, knowing this to be true, was refusing to face reality, since reality was too appalling a vista. Then a final bit of judicial arrogance was added by Lord Denning in an August 1990 *Spectator* interview: "We shouldn't have all these campaigns to get the Birmingham Six released. If they had been hanged, they'd have been forgotten and the whole community would have been satisfied." Elderly and foolish Denning, who had already criticized the release of the Winchester Three, accused of a conspiracy to attack Tom King at his home, in April 1990, spoke for the corruption of purpose that the Irish Troubles had brought to British justice.

In March 1990 a Granada Television show concluded that the Birmingham men were not guilty and named several of the IRA men who were. When in July 1990 the British director of public prosecutions felt that the convictions could no longer be considered safe, sixteen years of nightmare was nearly over. It was too late for Giuseppe Conlon of the Guildford Four, who had died in prison. Attention then switched back to the Birmingham Six, still in prison. On February 7 authorities discounted a scientific test that had become the key remaining evidence. Finally, on February 25, 1991, a prosecutor's office spokesman said that there was not enough evidence to support the murder convictions; it was all but certain they would be freed when the case reached the court of appeals in March. After another delay the end of imprisonment for the Six, finally, after sixteen years, came on Tuesday, March 14, 1991, when Hugh Callaghan, the oldest at sixty, Patrick Hill, Gerard Hunter, Richard McIlkenny, the youngest, William Power, and John Walker walked out from the Central Criminal Court, Old Bailey, to the cheers of their supporters and the news that a royal commission headed by Lord Walter Runciman of Doxford would recommend changes in criminal law and procedures. The British also promised payments for wrongful conviction of from £176,000 to £192,000 each. The coda to the Birmingham Six saga would all be to the critics' advantage despite adjustments to assure future British justice.

The Irish government expressed "relief and joy" and praised those who had so vigorously campaigned on behalf of the Six over the years—these did not include many Irish politicians of note until the case had already been made for the "IRA" bombers. Irish politicians, except for a few, had seen no advantage in involvement in British cases when there had been enough trouble with the IRA at home. No one much had wanted to admit, for example, that Nicky Kelly, not pardoned until the spring of 1992, and the other IRSP suspects might have been innocent

---

least in location, when a bomb went off during construction, but their Irish view of an English prison is much like those of the entirely innocent people in the three major cases.

of the Great Train Robbery or the existence of a Police Heavy Gang who used force during interrogations of subversives. Mainly what the Irish establishment wanted after 1985 was British justice seen to be done so that their partner in the Anglo-Irish Agreement would prove congenial to Southern opinion. Justice for the IRA had never been a high priority for the Dublin government, under constant threat by gunmen who denied the legitimacy of the state. The Republic had its own emergency legislation, its own judicial *cause célèbre*, its own problems—but the system could hardly be charged as inherently being anti-Irish. Bishop Edward Daly noted that the Birmingham case proved "the system in Britain has problems and it must face up to those problems" and pointed out that "poor people generally have a struggle to prove their innocence in Britain"—especially if they are poor Irish people charged with setting bombs, especially if convicted.

Justice was at last seen to be done, but grudgingly, after sixteen years and without grace. Justice had been denied because nearly everyone wanted culprits and because the system, rigid in self-assurance, could not imagine that those supplied had been snatched off the street for expediency's sake and dispatched to British prisons by those following the forms but not the substance of the law. The judicial system did not produce justice and, as Denning had justly feared, presented an appalling vista, became one of the walking wounded of the Irish Troubles. In fact the problems of justice arising from the Troubles were not limited to England alone. The Americans became entangled in extradition cases that appeared to involve a concentrated "political" effort by the Justice Department to cater to British interests by persisting in reinterpreting the law and reappealing the results (both quite proper, of course) not to achieve justice but to create specific results. In time American law did make it easier to extradite "terrorists," narrowing the political exception, sending William Quinn back for trial. He was the American citizen accused, among other things, of murdering an English policeman in London. The longest-lived and most controversial case, however, was that of IRA volunteer Joe Doherty, who in 1981 had been tried, convicted in absentia, and sentenced to life for the 1980 killing of Captain Herbert Richard Westmacott, a member of an eight-man SAS unit who had been hit during an IRA ambush on Antrim Road in Belfast. Doherty had been arrested and then had escaped with the seven other IRA men from Crumlin Road Prison just before the court hearing. He came to the United States illegally and sought covert asylum and a new life in the Irish diaspora. He was arrested at his work behind a bar in New York City and after nine years was still in the Metropolitan Correction Center in 1991. He had served the longest term for an internee except for some of the Mariolitas who fled Cuba in 1980. Doherty has been the subject of complex and Byzantine legal maneuvers for a decade, a famous case, a legal event, a man in a jumpsuit waiting out the years in a locked room. And like those in English prisons unjustly, he had served the republicans more effectively without a gun than he had as a soldier.

In June 1990 his lawyers won their eighth successive court victory that, as expected, led to the reopening of his asylum case and a criticism of the United States Attorney General, Richard Thornburgh, who "abused his discretion to reopen. We conclude that he based his decision in large part on the types of geopolitical concerns that Congress intended to eliminate from political asylum cases." Thornburgh had argued that United State–British relations would be damaged if Doherty was given the right to request asylum. In New York Doherty was still in prison. There he had turned out to be charming and cheerful, an asset to the republican cause if no longer an IRA volunteer. Caught in very military action, he had no taint of gunman, no terrorist bomber, and he has been philosophical about his fate, about the conflict, about the law. And the law has appeared in this case open to manipulation for American political purpose: Why is the man, guilty of no crime in New York, still in prison? Then in February 1992 the Justice Department at last managed to extradite Doherty—expelled and flown on a United States Air Force plane to Britain. He was returned to Crumlin Road Prison.

As the years pass, the fact that the mills of American justice were grinding fairly or slowly seemed more and more a contradiction in terms to those who care little about Ireland. To grind a man's life to bits for a decade was not fair, no favor at all but punishment. The system, as was the case in Britain, insists that the very length of the procedure indicated how fair matters actually have been: There is no quick shipment back to a British prison but every recourse is open to the gunman, more recourse than the IRA's victims receive. The few Irish gunmen involved in the American system, like Doherty, Quinn, and Peter McMullen, who ended up wanted by both the British and the Provos, and several hard men as well, have been bench marks of the efforts of the government to adjust the system to the perceived challenge of international terrorism and the resistance by civil libertarians—and some conservatives concerned about anti-Communist gunmen and rebels—to traditional liberties.

In Northern Ireland, of course, the judicial system had been transformed so as to produce convictions, not necessarily justice, except in the sense that most suspects were undoubtedly guilty of subversion, however denied. No one who has watched the Diplock Courts at work can be entirely comfortable with the system, even when no ready alternatives are at hand. In the process, from time to time, innocent people were imprisoned amid the IRA volunteers and UVF defenders, but mostly the mistakes could escape once the authorities were convinced that an error had been made—although often at a cost and often not soon enough. Amid the politicals there was always a mix of outright criminals, who might have existed on the margins of the paramilitaries and so were tossed onto the conveyor belt. There were as well those tossed on the antiterrorist belt as a convenience to the authorities.

At times there were those who claimed innocence and could not easily be released. The accused were subversives, the crimes real, but the means of conviction in special cases had seemingly been shown to be unsound. One continuing case in Armagh involved four members of the Ulster Defense Regiment accused, tried, and convicted for the UFV–Protestant Action Force murder of a Catholic painter, Adrian Carroll, on November 8, 1983. Their case, which raised reasonable doubts in some quarters, at least let the authorities privately contend that injustice was nonsectarian and judiciously applied to all, not just to republican subversives.* In fact, three of the four did secure release in 1992. All of the costs and inequities of such emergency justice produced again causes and articles, radical and reasoned protest, trouble for the authorities, reform and persistence in oppression; but—and it was a most important but—Northern Ireland, whatever the theory, was different. The province and the island had always been different. Ulster was obviously in the grip of an emergency that required special responses and special exceptions to general practice: So silence was a token of guilt, interrogation could be if not brutal most assuredly intimidating and without counsel, and members of the legal Sinn Féin could not be interviewed by television reporters (although the sound could be turned down and their words could be repeated as a voice-over: the wonders of the law made a fool twice). The questioning of the Irish tourist on the way by ferry to Belfast or the refusal to allow Gerry Adams to enter Britain or the expulsion of suspected republicans from Birmingham or Glasgow were seen as Northern Ireland problems.

These problems abutted but did not penetrate Great Britain. This was not, however, the case with the English bombers, for there, in the heart of the land of common law, injustice was seen to have been done, systemic injustice arising in part from simple prejudice. The combination of an awesome crime requiring some form of attonement and available throw-away victims—poor, Irish, convenient—proved too great. The system and all its supporters in this Irish matter chose what was amenable and immediately rewarding over the ideal that required patience and toleration. In justice the British chose the secondary benefits, primitive, real, and once primary in less elegant societies. The costs have accumulated over the years, compounded by a reluctance to accept their reality, and as such have indicated that peace and quiet and ignorance on Irish matters must be bought with a decay in the quality of British life.

These costs are far more obvious and painful in the response to the threat of violence rather than the elegance of the judicial reaction. Security can only be achieved at the loss of liberty, not just the liberty guaranteed under the law but also the liberty of ease that previously a tolerant and benign society offered to almost all. Violent crime was rare and ritualized, the streets were policed by unarmed bobbies, the land was green and pleasant. This image seemed real to those who benefited, was real to any who came from more tumultuous societies. In New York a single year's murders totals two thousand against just over three thousand for twenty years of the Troubles. In many countries the police carry submachine guns or the courts are forms to intimidate the peasant. In Britain the arrival of immigrants and the impact of incivility in class relations has again attracted scholarly and analytical attention to the long British history of civil turmoil, riots, arson, agitation, and injustice that, however real, pales before that of most other societies. British life for two centuries has been remarkably pleasant—stable, often genial, proper, even prim, whether in a Welsh mining village or a Glasgow council estate. The arrival in Britain of the Irish issue has made life less civil, less genteel, less safe.

---

*Ian Paisley, Jr., *Reasonable Doubt: The Case for the UDR Four* (Dublin and Cork: Mercier Press, 1990), issued not only by a traditional republican publisher but also with a Foreword by Robert Kee, who championed the cause of the Birmingham Six.

It has required only a few bombs scattered down the years from the Tower to the Grand Hotel in Brighton to generate a whole layer of protection: Improved and expensive security and police precautions have been taken. No one opens bulky unexpected mail from Belfast if wise. Everyone wonders about the Irishman who is buying a clock or the lads down the street with odd hours. There is abroad a vague sense of menace. No politician walks entirely free, slams a hotel door without second thought, sees a strange man by the car without a flicker of concern. No police constable can turn a dark corner without some marginal recollection of what other officers have found around some English corners. Some shoppers at Harrods or on Oxford Street or customers at any pub in Birmingham recall that every day need not be like the last. The British, especially the English, are, however, if not immune to the revolting Irish, now a phenomenon nearly two centuries old, at least largely resigned soon after each wave of justified indignation that follows the latest atrocity. Most of the people, according to nearly every poll published for a decade, would be delighted to break the Irish connection, get the troops out and let both tribes settle their differences on the faraway island. These Irish differences are never thought to be Britain's fault or British maintained. Most want only the Irish in Britain to be like everyone else, like them. The Irish as Irish are not up to standard. The Irish as gunmen are revolting and should be put down. The slippage between these postures has made the assumptions of those involved in the pursuit of justice appear to be less than just.

In the meantime most of the people want, like their government, to do as little as possible about the Irish issue. And the Irish issue usually emerges only to the blast of explosives, a bright flash and a burst of black and brown smoke rolling up a street with a foreground covered with debris and later one or two blanketed bodies: the atrocity of the month. Such atrocities now produce a ritual response—indignation, a determination not to concede to violence, a sullen, fading resentment, an acceptance of limitations imposed by security, and then very quickly a move to other matters, other events, real wars like the Falklands and Iraq, the election or Princess Di's marital troubles.

The year 1990 saw the continuance, as everyone expected, of IRA operations in the province, especially in the countryside. The security forces, with their vast intelligence network, their intimacy with the subversives, with the new and honed tactics and access to the cutting edge of anti-insurgency technology, had made the IRA's task more difficult. (The loyalists still found little problem in shooting random Catholics or vulnerable Sinn Féin figures.) The IRA difficulty was the hierarchy of targets: British military and prominent figures on down to innocents too close to a callous bomb. The more attractive the target the more likely the IRA could not get through. So England was the IRA's first alternative target. There the IRA active service units used their spare time to trace the secondary figures of the establishment, retired generals, minor politicians, civil servants from the Northern Ireland Office or the Defense Ministry, nearly famous policemen, those with the hard word for Ireland if no great power. There were lots and lots of targets, too many to guard. All of these could more easily be attacked in England than even a private soldier along the Falls—that is, if the volunteer wanted to live again for another day. So the IRA sought to take the war to England.

In 1990 the IRA looked for means to make their armed struggle more military while the British still stumbled when they waged war instead of peace. All such conflicts are asymmetrical. The first uproar came because of the application in Belfast of anti-insurgency tactics to criminal provocation. The security forces broke up a simple robbery on a bookie joint by responding to the incident as if those involved were IRA gunmen. The robbers did have on the traditional balaclavas, black hoods with owl eye holes, used by many of the urban gunmen at work, and they carried guns, whittled out to resemble the real thing, and worse, they may have given the early impression to informers that they were engaged in theft for a cause. They certainly appeared in the terrorist fashion of the moment for Belfast field work. And so, clothes making the terrorist, the three were shot dead in a trap-ambush: a British mistake, again, honest criminals done in as subversives. Their families were outraged and the community and the naysayers.

NIO Security Minister John Cope denied a shoot-to-kill policy, saying, "Neither the police nor the army set out to find suspected terrorists and kill them. It would not be right, it is not the proper way to enforce the law." It appeared, however, that if the terrorists came to the security forces, shooting was proper. One of the monitoring techniques in Belfast consisted of unmarked military cars cruising in the few remaining access streets. After an unexpected terrorist incident, the army might well have a car in the way of the escape route to the appropriate safe no-go zone. The terrorists might well come to them as the British army car with soldiers in civilian clothes and armed with automatic weapons cruised for offenders. This, indeed, happened when two loyalist assassins on a motorcycle shot and killed a Catholic on the street. Whooping and hollering, they made a U-turn and began their short escape run back to safe Protestant territory, only to run directly into an unmarked army car and a volley of shots. One killer was shot dead. The motorcycle smashed into the car and tossed the other man, wounded, into the street. He was hurriedly removed and little subsequently released about the incident, for "neither the police nor the army set out to find suspected terrorists and kill them." And if they did, by definition they were terrorists and so guilty, which is what made the three dead men scattered about the bookie shop so disturbing.

In the Republic the Irish police had opened up on bank robbers on the main street of the small town of Athy in County Kildare, fired without restraint, perhaps without need, without great control, and with disastrous effect: One robber was killed and eight people, including three policemen were hit, all hit by police bullets. It appeared that the effective ambush of Dessie O'Hare had given the authorities a taste for the gun. Each detective had an Uzi but not all had the needed skills. So there was a scandal, again, North and South, over extending war to peaceful criminals, especially on an island where almost all violent crime is political. The cost of the Troubles could easily be seen, was seen, as eroding Irish civility, even and especially the civility of the criminal class, who might soon take to guns in self-defense.

Those who had guns were often no more secure. On April 9, near Downpatrick, a UDR Land Rover passed an IRA culvert bomb on the roadside. The second Land Rover, with four soldiers, did not manage the passage. The detonation of the thousand pounds of explosives cored out an enormous crater, tossed the vehicle thirty feet away, and killed all four. Brooke responded, "I am absolutely appalled by events in Downpatrick and the loss of four UDR men. Actions of this sort are wholly senseless in that they will not deflect us from our intention to defend the community against these evil men." The IRA Easter statement announced that British troops would not be safe anywhere in "Ireland, Britain, continental Europe or indeed any part of the world."

Actually the year had been remarkably tranquil—the first British soldier was not killed until May 5, when a sniper hit Lance Sergeant Graham Stewart near Cullyhanna in South Armagh (the 423rd army fatality). And the overseas IRA actions were not impressive—the day before a sixty-pound Semtex bomb had failed to detonate at a barracks in West Germany. There was more concern over the rising number of sectarian killings in the province by loyalists than over a surge of IRA activity. A bomb in a van did kill a British sergeant and injure his colleague while they were driving through Wembley in England and indicated that the IRA had at least one team still in Britain. So when two RUC officers were shot down in front of shoppers in Belfast later in the month, the media was hardly interested at all in the nasty, distant event. The local reporters, of course, described the incident, quoted the witnesses. Those at risk cared. "It was a terrible sight. The blood was pouring down the back of their heads." The authorities in the province cared, but elsewhere there were other spectaculars. The World Cup was on. The Irish team returned on July 1 in triumph. And there was always other news more novel than bloody Irish spectaculars.

Some minor spectaculars are more dreadful than others. On July 24 the IRA set off one of its massive land mines under a main Armagh road just as an RUC car passed over the target zone. The police car was turned into the usual twisted, blackened metal wreck, bits and pieces scattered along the verge, and all three constables were killed. This time, however, a nearby car was smashed sideways as well just on the edge of the explosion. The social worker inside escaped but not Sister Catherine Dunne from Dublin, who was killed. This was the nun incident. The headlines read, "Three Police and Nun." She was the fist nun killed in the Troubles. The IRA lost the benefit of their proper target in another, if predictably brief, wave of outrage—even Catholic nationalists had second thoughts. The Pope in Rome called for peace, condemning "the injustice and futility" of violence. The IRA blamed it on "unforeseen and fluke circumstances." Nearly everyone else blamed it on the IRA. And, as noted, by the time justice was done, it was too late. The outraged always wanted instant vengeance.

The mistakes in Ireland (bad luck with the nun as much as negligence, apologists would note) were paralleled on the Continent, where luck could seldom be blamed. The return to Continental operations, where there were few victories of any kind, occurred for the traditional reasons: spreading the action, the closing off of targets in the province, and the perceived vulnerabilities of Britain. Early attempts had not been impressive, although the British ambassador to the Netherlands, Sir Richard Sykes, had been killed outside his residence in March 1979 and in August in Brussels an IRA bomb had exploded under a bandstand in Brussels, injuring seven bandsmen and eleven civilians. In December 1980 the attempt on the British European Community commissioner, Christopher Tugendhat, had failed and in August 1982 arrests had disrupted a bomb campaign planned for France and the Netherlands. There had been a pause but the invisible aspect of Continental operations—the acquisition of arms, the establishment of nets and contacts—had gone ahead, despite not only local but also British MI6 lures and traps. One of these had worked when, with British information, Dutch security police arrested Brendan "Bic" McFarlane and Gerry "Blue Boy" Kelly, two more Maze escapees and key active service personnel, at an apartment in a suburb of Amsterdam. There the police found identification, a mixed lot of currency, guns, and keys to a truck container parked on the docks and filled with drums of nitrobenzine explosives—all easily replaced, unlike McFarlane and Kelly.

Visible operations had begun again in March 1987, when an active service unit had placed a car bomb outside the British army's West German headquarters at Rheindahlen that detonated and injured thirty-one. The next year this had been followed by a series of attacks in the same area, one RAF man was killed and two wounded in a machine gun attack in Roermond, the Netherlands, on May 1 and simultaneously a car bomb in Nieuw Bergen had killed two RAF men and wounded another. Five days later in Bielefeld, West Germany, a bomb attached to a serviceman's car had failed to explode. On July 13, nine soldiers had been injured when a bomb detonated in Duisburg, West Germany. The attacks had been sporadic, perhaps the work of very few active volunteers, and only marginally effective. From January 1988 until June 1990 there had been seventeen IRA attacks; nine used Semtex to construct bombs that generally proved ineffectual; the other eight were shootings that tended to focus on the wrong target or to hit innocent transients. The cumulative effect of the Continental attacks, which may have stretched British security and did attract the media, had proved costly to the IRA. There was another list of blunders followed by excuses. And the Continental operations, costly in funds, had led to a series of arrests, ten in the 1988–91 period, mostly within the triangle of Germany, Holland, and Belgium, where the volunteers crisscrossed on their missions.

There was no transnational terror network to help, only a few friends on the ground (several of whom were discovered) and the cover of the great number of foreign guest workers in Europe. Except for money that could always be spent elsewhere, the IRA assets used were expendable—the IRA always had more volunteers than could be effectively deployed in Ireland, the arms and explosives were handy and available, the targets still soft. The arrests meant that the IRA did not get the benefit of the on-the-job training—no one involved would make the same mistake of not taking the final step beside the car window to see the target as more than a blur and so to avoid shooting a woman—but someone else might make the same mistake in a first operation. Kelly and McFarlane had learned on the job and survived. They could be replaced, but by the inexperienced who would also learn on the job. Killing close up is not learned from a book and every arrest removed some of the IRA memory and so capacity. The volunteers could and would be replaced by others who would learn as they practiced—the old-fashioned way. And these old-fashioned mistakes would be compounded by IRA habits.

The volunteers sent to Europe were often known to the British police. Donna Maguire, twenty-three, from a respectable Newry family, who was arrested in

June 1990 on the Continent, had been arrested in Rosslare, Ireland, in July 1989, coming off the ferry from Cherbourg. She was with a companion, Leonard Hardy, who was in possession of bomb-making equipment. Maguire had traces of explosives on her clothing, bomb-making instructions, false passports, and her address book. The last discovery led to three arrests in France by the local police who were tipped off by the Gárdaí. The address book was an almost traditional IRA lapse: Never plan for failure so always carry papers if about to be arrested. The events at Rosslare were hardly an example of cunning tradecraft. But Maguire was acquitted, and then used again by the IRA—a sound asset if a blown one. Only one of the four arrested in June 1990, Paul Hughes, had no known IRA connections. He was an electrician who lived with his parents on a small farm in Jonesboro outside Newry.

None of these and few of the other volunteers knew much of Europe or the skills that effective action requires. And their most notorious operation, according to the police, was the murder of two Australian tourists shot by mistake for British servicemen in the Dutch town of Roermond. Of course, almost exactly a year before, the IRA had killed two RAF men at Nieuw Bergen in Holland and one in West Germany. And these operations, successes and disasters, were made complex not only by IRA limitations but also by the effect of the cooperative European authorities. If anything the IRA, operating out of the Irish diaspora of guest workers and the drifting tides of foreigners in the northern European Community countries, could claim credit for the increasingly effective response of the European security forces to provocation and terror. Except for individuals and the odd radical, the IRA had no friends and no pool of sympathy on the Continent; only the size and the lack of local intelligence gave them opportunities to strike at British targets, but from the first the cost in volunteers and money had been greater than anticipated. GHQ is always too optimistic.

It had actually become easier for active service units to start to operate in Holland or Germany than in Britain, where the Irish overwhelmingly wanted no part of the IRA, had left Ireland behind them, wanted to get ahead, and were a risk not a boon. So that with pronounced accents, no easy cover, and public and security forces alerted by years of incidents, any active service people sent over to England from Ireland ran considerable risks, often ran them, kept free but had to be careful and cunning. And lucky. Much the same was true on the Continent—luck was needed as much as skill. And not only were the IRA volunteers abroad not always lucky, they were also not always sufficiently cunning and careful. While the three had been lost at Gibraltar and ten in Europe, an additional eight were arrested in Britain: a total of twenty-one for twenty-five deaths inflicted—and not always the right deaths or even appropriate ones. The loss of the volunteers could be made good but the secondary costs were high. The arrested could not be abandoned, nor did GHQ so intend, but the IRA was not structured to manage such matters on a daily basis and was often hard pressed for new funds to handle legal matters. The operational failures—mistakes—combined with the publicity of the arrests and the attention of Continental authorities produced only a limited final return for the campaign. The problem is that there was no solution: Operations had to be risked and the costs paid, again and again.

The IRA campaign in England had managed to avoid some of the more egregious errors if not to reach truly impressive targets. The bomb that exploded at the barracks in Deal, Kent, and killed ten soldiers was the most lethal and typical: very easy targets, very nastily done, difficult to defend against, and difficult to rationalize as military action except to the committed. The British authorities had found it easier to condemn as senseless, violent, and useless the attacks than to prevent them. A consoling factor was that most of the British successes during the British campaign so far had come as the result of that bad Irish luck, not brilliant British police work. In August 1987 Martina Shanahan, Finbarr Cullen, and John McCann had been arrested for allegedly spying on the Wiltshire home of Northern Secretary Tom King. Not the police but King's daughter had grown suspicious of the three. The Winchester Three were con-victed of conspiracy on what appeared scanty evidence—being Irish and lurking in the woods seemed, not unreasonably, sufficient for the police, but not, as it turned out, for the London appeals court that overturned the conviction in April 1990. It had been a net IRA gain.

In December 1988 a thief broke into a car watched by IRA man Patrick Sheehy, who then compounded the problem by shooting the thief. Sheehy was unstable, with limited capacity, sent along as an extra when he should have been refused entry into the organization in the first place. He returned to Ireland, became involved in low-level actions, and then committed suicide in January 1991. In any case the incident led the police to an IRA safe house in Clapham, in South London, provided by Nicholas Mullen, that contained 150 pounds of Semtex, AK-47 assault rifles, a photograph of one IRA suspect, Kevin Sheehy, and the traditional long hit lists that volunteers draw up to wile away the idle hours. Mullen, who had rented the flat, organized cars, arranged for banking facilities, and acquired valid driver's licenses and false identity documents—all the necessaries that make life in the underground so complex—was arrested, convicted, and sentenced to twenty years.

In order to ease the problem of safe houses (it was difficult for several men with no visible jobs to look normal month after month), the IRA reverted to traditional hides: holes dug into the countryside. These could sit idle for years and be ready when the next unit arrived. In 1989 three caches of Semtex had been found by chance in Stoke Newington, Hampstead, in London, and outside Scarborough, Yorkshire. Again, all were discovered by luck not by police work. Of course, an enormous amount of detailed and methodical police work focused on each suspect, each incident, all suspicions. The amount of paper produced by one bomb boggles the imagination. What is needed in a modern, complex society where political crime is relatively easy to commit, at least the first time, is a system that can take advantage of a lapse, the aberrant or the peculiar, and seize the chance. Everyone yearns for hard intelligence, an informer in place, a tapped line, a glimpse into the core, but ends by taking what bits and pieces turn up. In October 1989 locals had found a dump on the Pembrokeshire coast. The police set up a watching trap and pulled in two armed IRA men, Liam O'Dhuibhir and Damien McComb. Semtex was found in the flat in Luton rented by one of the pair.

Most of the rest of British successes were similar; long preparation and routine without effect, then unexpected luck or an IRA blunder, and revelation. In May 1990 Tyrone man Kevin O'Donnell ran through a red light in North London.

Police discovered not a spare tire but two freshly unearthed AK-47s in the trunk of his car. In October 1990 two alleged IRA members were arrested near Stonehenge in Wiltshire carrying out what appeared to be a surveillance operation on the home of Sir Charles Tidbury, former chairman of Whitbread, whose name had been found on an IRA target list. This time instead of congratulations there were complaints that the police had acted too quickly, failing to trail the two back to the safe house and the others involved and revealing that potential targets were now under security surveillance. Nevertheless, Sir Charles was safe and two IRA operators removed from the English scene.

In the summer of 1990 there were ample IRA operators still on the English scene. The toll of soldiers over the three years after the 1988 renewal of English operations was more impressive. The one big incident in 1989 was the bomb in Deal Barracks in Kent that killed soldiers, even if the British media labeled them teenage bandsmen. And in 1990 there were twelve bombs, one soldier dead and two wounded, and in addition the most important victim yet for the renewed English campaign. There the idea had been to vary the targets, vulnerable soldiers, military facilities, and seek out symbols and, if possible, major figures. Keep the Brits off-guard and raise the costs.

Ian Gow, MP, was Thatcher's friend and better known in Ireland as a friend of the Unionists, a man with the hard word, than he was in Great Britain. There he was simply the Prime Minister's former parliamentary secretary who had, seemingly foolishly, resigned as Minister of State at Treasury over the Anglo-Irish Agreement. His colleagues knew and liked him but few of the public outside Ulster would have recognized his name. On Sunday night, July 29–30, Gow's car in front of his house had been rigged with an ultrasensitive trembler switch bomb. On Monday morning, he came out, got into his car, slammed the door, and began to drive off when the switch trembled and the bomb detonated. He was killed almost instantly. The car blackened and burned, twisted metal around his smashed body. For the IRA and their constituency in the summer of 1990, he was an appropriate target. Gow was more famous, more important dead than alive. The establishment was horrified—one of their own had been killed. Haughey called it an "appalling and brutal assassination," which it was—but then, it was intended to be just that. Thatcher was stunned and outraged. Everyone was grieved—a decent, amusing, dedicated man had been killed at home (the "Dog's House") and for what? The famous came to the funeral and the media drifted away and Gow became one more item in the lethal statistics of the deadly Irish quarrel.

GHQ operations in Britain had for two years continued to shift among vulnerable British military targets (individual soldiers, barracks, the bottom of the power pyramid), symbolic targets like the Stock Exchange that in theory harmed no one, and real individuals at the top, like Gow. On September 18, nothing forgotten, the IRA shot Sir Peter Terry, former governor of Gibraltar. He was hit in the face and body but not killed, and his wife was slightly wounded in an attack at his home near Stafford. An attack on General Anthony Farrar-Hockley, former commander of Northern Ireland land forces, failed, as did a misdirected bomb attack on the home of former cabinet secretary Lord Armstrong. On the other hand an army sergeant, Bernard Cox, was hit and wounded in London. He was a bit down the major targets list but the Provos still had hopes.

781

An IRA spokesman pointed out to no one's surprise that Thatcher was still a prime target; but simple soldiers seemed easier to hit.

For some observers the most interesting target was a conference on international terrorism held in London at the Royal Overseas League club in October 1990. A four-pound Semtex bomb was found under the speaker's lectern seventy-five minutes before the conference was to open. James Gerard McGarrigle, a kitchen porter from Northern Ireland, was urgently sought thereafter by the police but was not to be found. Actually the IRA was after the speakers, William Waldegrave from the Foreign Office and Peter Imbert, the Metropolitan Police commissioner, rather than the experts. In a gravely overcrowded analytical field with more proclaimed terrorist specialists than functioning terrorists, the IRA thus did not help the rationalization of the discipline as a side product of one more assassination attempt directed at the rich and famous. Besides individuals as targets, the next year saw symbols and systems factored in as well.

For most everyone else the most dreadful IRA tactic was the return to hostage drivers. This time the drivers were also targets. This unexpectedly gruesome practice, even after all the previous horrors, attracted world interest. On October 24 the IRA forced three accused informers, lashed in place and fearful for their families, to drive three different trucks, which had been turned into enormous, mobile bombs, into British army posts. The human bomb, with a frantic and frightened driver tied to the seat, thus arrived in the midst of British troops who were unable to understand the danger. The one explosion that worked resulted in seven deaths, one informer and six soldiers. The second attempt, in November, indicated that outrage did not dissuade the operational officers. A 3,500-pound bomb in a truck was driven to an army checkpoint at Annaghmatin, near Newtownbutler, by a hostage driver. Tearing at his ropes, the driver shouted a warning. Freed, he and the soldiers watched as the IRA detonator exploded soon afterward but the bomb did not.

In between the two bomb incidents, the IRA continued provincial operations with the same mixed results, seemingly an inherent aspect of the armed campaign: On November 11 the IRA killed two RUC men, an inspector and a reserve constable, on the shores of Lough Neagh, but also killed two civilians accompanying them on a duck hunt. "The IRA savagery displayed today is only what we have learned to expect from these foul creatures," was the view of William Ross, Ulster Unionist MP for Londonderry East. The Northern Ireland Secretary again condemned the killings as needless and futile—the British could not be driven out by terror. He felt that the increase in violence and killings came from the "dark forces" of armed aggression and the evil of oppression still at work in the province. These forces and evils were exactly what the IRA assumed they opposed rather than represented. Someone was certainly responsible for the increase in violence (the Lough Neagh killings brought the year's total to sixty-nine, twenty-six of those since October 1). The IRA could claim a large part of the total, especially the growing list of police. The 1990 total for the RUC was eleven: shot dead in the kitchen, shot dead on a street, killed in a land mind explosion, abducted and murdered, shot down amid Saturday morning shoppers in the center of Belfast and now the two at Lough Neagh.

The British had their own problems with the persistent dark forces. The shoot-to-kill issue arose again with still another ambush, two miles from Loughall, that resulted in the death of two IRA volunteers, Desmond Grew, thirty-seven, from a well-known republican family, who was wanted in Germany for the killing of the British soldier and his child, and Martin McCaughey, a former Sinn Féin councillor. Grew's brother, Séamus of the INLA, had been the key figure in the earlier shoot-to-kill incident that led to the Stalker investigation—an investigation in 1990 still not buried. Adams at his funeral called Grew "a freedom fighter, a patriot, and a decent upstanding Irish citizen." Ken Maginnis, Unionist security spokesman and member of the Dungannon District Council, on the other hand, called him a "deadly killer. . . . Grew showed no mercy. He was a man with whom you could not take risks." And the security forces had not.

So the first year of the new decade moved along neither novelly nor tranquilly. Everything was good news or bad for someone. The new archbishop at Armagh was to be a long-standing vocal opponent of the Provos, Dr. Cahal Daly, who replaced Cardinal O Fiaich. The late cardinal often seemed too nationalist for the British. Then so seemed much of the Catholic clergy in the province even if they were no friends of the IRA. The IRA, of course, saw the clergy as a bitter enemy, allied to authority and so ultimately to the British system. In London, meanwhile, the IRA played their role as villain in the introduction of the new security laws in the House of Commons on November 19 that were to give the force of law to emergency legislation. This was "repression by reflex action" according to Labour, but it indicated that the Troubles, even in law, were no longer an emergency but a permanent situation. This would be legislation to ease the legal problems of the security forces not prospective suspects and subversives. Security was the problem in 1990 as it had been in the previous decade as far as the cabinet was concerned. Even as Thatcher arrived on her first visit since Enniskillen, the media seemed more interested in the leadership struggle back in London than in her Ulster itinerary. London seethed with political rumor—a real revolt in process against the Prime Minister was being noised about even in farthest Ulster.

The rumors were right. The big year-end news was the convulsion within the Tories that retired the Iron Lady for the unknown John Major, neoconservative acolyte and for Irish purposes a cipher. Haughey, in something of a reversal, three weeks later met the new Prime Minister in Italy during a conference of European heads of government and announced that Major did not have the "slightest doubt" that he supported the agreement. So Thatcher was gone with the year, to the regret of the IRA, who knew that devil well. She had been the ideal enemy—haughty, imperious, strident, and arrogant; and the IRA still had plans for her. She left to mixed reviews and then both the Conservative and Labour parties focused on the next election; for them her departure had risks and gains but no relation to Irish tastes.

No one much was focused on Ireland. The year's fatality total was 82, 76 in the province, about average, down a bit, and 6 elsewhere. The security forces' acceptable losses were British army 7, UDR 8, RUC 7, and RUCR 5, a fair balance of murder to go with 49 civilians in Northern Ireland and 3 outside: Ian Gow and the 2 Australian tourists killed by the IRA on the Continent by mistake to balance the 3 British soldiers killed. What made the numbers especially depressing was that, as Maudling had so long ago sought, they were "acceptable"—about what was expected for 1991, one or two atrocities, some shoot-to-kill victims, innocent civilians killed for loyalist purpose or IRA error, a few informers, the security forces, the IRA losses, and one or two particularly important individuals, an Ian Gow or a George Seawright. Most of the numbers would be forgotten except by those who grieved. Most in 1990 had already been forgotten by the end of the year. Who would remember William Sloss, shot dead on July 15 by the IPLO splinter group but denied by the UVF as one of theirs? Who would remember Dermott McGuinness, shot dead on October 16 by the UFF but denied by the IPLO as one of theirs? At least Fergal Caraher, a member of Sinn Féin, shot dead by the British army in South Armagh, caused a scandal. "With over 300 similar deaths in disputed circumstances and only one conviction . . . there can be little doubt that the British look after their own." But that was Gerry Adams at the funeral and what else would one expect? Everyone expected little new for 1991.

There was little new, change but little new. The IRA opened a firebombing campaign that, according to the authorities, cost the province jobs. This was not the concern of the IRA, long contemptuous of the practical problems of the artificial economy of the province. The most visible of all Provisional gunmen, who had gone with Republican Sinn Féin, Dáithí O Conaill, died unexpectedly on New Year's Eve—one old name gone. Paisley had doubtful comments to make on Brooke's talks about talks—the same old Paisley. And Brooke, no longer the new man at the NIO, was still at work talking. There was an interdenominational service for two killed on North Belfast's Murder Mile and 250 appeared, an important moment for them but for few others, which was often the case with moves for reconciliation that rarely outlived the event. Events in Ireland were in any case overshadowed by the focus on the real war in the Persian Gulf. Not that Iraq had no place in Northern Irish events—Gerry Adams condemned "the hypocrisy of those who while condemning the armed struggle of the IRA, support the use of wholesale violence against the Iraqi people." That was, of course, Adams speaking again. And Irish violence was different but as it turned out not so different. Even little wars make great waves if structured to effect, and despite all the bungles and feckless slaughter and dead volunteers, the IRA had amassed enormous experience in exploiting limited military assets. This they did, again, in the midst of a real war, snatching the headlines from the real armies in the Middle East replete with giant bombers, high-tech missiles, and multimillion-dollar tanks. One weapons load of an American Apache attack helicopter cost what the IRA had spent on their armed campaign over twenty years. Low-intensity war is low in all costs but lives and civility.

The culmination of the IRA's English campaign came on February 7, 1991, with an attack on Major originally intended for Thatcher. Thatcher as Prime Minister was the most appropriate target of all. Having been once unlucky simply meant that the IRA would try again, even if there was another Conservative Prime Minister. This time the assets of a first attack had been lost: The security surrounding the Prime Minister would be intense. Soon after the IRA became more active in England in 1988, the security at Number 10 Downing Street was increased at a cost of £800,000. The new police guard post was external evidence, resembling a similar box in the enormously popular sci-fi television series "Dr. Who." Once again the IRA operational officer found a combination of weapon and access.

This time, the IRA would use the mortars that had been used for years in Northern Ireland with mixed results—the most deadly attack had been the one on Newry on March 28, 1985, when nine RUC personnel had been killed. This IRA Mark 10 mortar was cunningly constructed from three oxyacetylene cylinders arranged on a rack with rubber collars at their base to cushion the impact. The propellant, made from sugar and sodium chlorate, would send the projectile, packed with forty pounds of industrial explosive, in a predetermined arc. The IRA operators would make their calculations but, as usual, in the end would trust to luck. The IRA weapon was probably not much more inaccurate than military models that could not be brought onto target without repeated rounds. The IRA could get only one big bang and hit or miss, mostly miss. Still it had distance and could be set with remote control, and it could be set at some distance from Number 10 Downing Street and outside the immediate security ring.

In July 1990 a van was purchased. The IRA could go over security from inside the van. The second part of the equation was found in a site open to the public where a van could be parked to let the mortars drop their shells into Number 10 Downing Street from the rear. To the innocent eye the spot did not even seem near to the heavily protected buildings, which were two hundred yards away on Downing Street and Whitehall, because it was a good way around on foot. But it was less so for a mortar. Unexpectedly in November 1990, in the midst of the preparation, Thatcher had been shuffled out of office and so out of Downing Street, replaced on November 28 by Major. None had been more disappointed than the IRA Army Council. No matter, the operation would go ahead, even if one British Prime Minister was not like another. Thatcher would still be a prime target, a cost for the state to guard for the rest of her life or until the end of the armed campaign. So Prime Minister John Major would do—and the cabinet as well if the IRA unit got lucky. The time for the attack had to come soon after the bits were in place, when the van could be parked, and when the cabinet was likely to be in session.

So on February 7 the prepared van, with the roof cut open, the mortars in place, and the timer ready, was driven through an unexpected snow to the site two hundred yards away, near the Defense Ministry. The driver parked beside the statue of Spencer Compton, eighth duke of Devonshire, who had moved the rejection of Gladstone's home rule bill in 1886. The driver got out into the snow, walked a few steps, and jumped on the pillion seat of a waiting motorcycle just after ten o'clock. The motorcycle was driven away. After eight minutes a policeman began to walk leisurely over to check the illegally parked van. At 10:08 the first mortar went off with a huge roar, followed by two more loud bangs. The van burst into flames as a preset incendiary device went off to destroy the evidence. The three rounds arched up and then down toward the target: Two rounds drifted away and crashed into a small park in front of the Foreign and Commonwealth Office near the front of Number 10. The other crashed into the rear garden behind the Prime Minister's residence. Sitting in the Cabinet Room above listening to David Mellor, Chief Secretary to the Treasury, discuss his visit to the United Arab

Emirates were the Prime Minister, Foreign Secretary Douglas Hurd and Defense Secretary Tom King, the two former Northern Ireland Secretaries, Chancellor Norman Lamont, Trade and Industry Secretary Peter Lilley, and the chief of the defense staff, Sir David Craig. It was, indeed, a star-studded target: the war cabinet for the "real" war in the Middle East, the core of the British government. With a little Irish luck the results of the mortar rounds could have been catastrophic.

The mortar shell smashed into a cherry tree and exploded with a huge blast, metal and wood spraying about the garden and into the surrounding walls and windows. A bit of shrapnel stuck in the chief whip's wood paneling at his house at Number 12 Downing Street and glass showered rooms in the chancellor's house at Number 11. For the war cabinet the crash of the explosion was muffled by the bombproof netting on the window, but still the room shuddered and flakes of paint drifted down onto the table. Glass was scattered on the floor of both the Cabinet Room and the Prime Minister's second-floor study. Major looked up, startled, and suggested, "I think we had better start again someplace else."

Almost at once everyone knew it was a bomb, probably an IRA bomb; both Hurd and King knew all about IRA bombs, and no one had forgotten Brighton. No member of the British cabinet can ever travel quite free of the Celtic menace, one of the costs of the little Irish war imposed by the IRA. The war cabinet then reassembled in a secure underground bunker while outside ceremonial troops wearing bearskins and carrying rifles with fixed bayonets flooded the area near the flaming van. For a moment in the gray flurry of snow it was a take from a comic opera war run for the television camera crews already arriving on the scene. The cabinet meeting continued—Irish events can at most postpone more serious matters, shift a venue not a policy. Outside police scurried about and the sirens of reinforcements shrieked closer. The two failed mortar missiles were burning on a strip of grass on the far side of Downing Street, just at the base of a statue of Lord Mountbatten, the IRA's most famous victim, sending up a cloud of acrid black and brown smoke. And even with the Iraq war the IRA mortars snatched the world's front pages. As the IRA statement announced, *their* war went on, their mortars had nothing to do with Iraq, only with Ireland. Even still, the Prime Minister at the very center of the net was vulnerable to Ireland—not politically, of course; as an issue Ireland was static.

In 1991 the IRA would shift to more traditional English targets with bomb attacks on Paddington and Victoria railway stations on February 18. These were the first strikes at what the British called "civilian" targets since the Harrods explosion in December 1983 that had killed six and injured ninety-one people. The IRA did not think of railway stations as "civilian" but as transportation centers that if smashed would disrupt English life. The Paddington bomb detonated at 4:20 A.M. when the station was empty and a general warning was then phoned in for all the mainline stations at 7:00 A.M. In what the IRA would call a "cynical decision," Scotland Yard's antiterrorist squad decided not to close the rail terminals. There had been too many false alarms lately. The Paddington bomb had not been a false alarm, but that event was over and the commuters were on their way to London. So forty minutes later the bomb detonated—a big blinding light and a wall of fire—in a trash container at Victoria Station during the morning rush hour, killing one man and injuring forty. The police then immediately closed the six mainline terminals and eight other smaller rail and subway stations, locking the barn door and crippling all London rush-hour traffic. Three hours later, after another warning by a man with an Irish accent, Heathrow was closed.

There were no further bombs, but considerable argument concerning the police reaction, especially after the Paddington bomb had given warning. Republicans countered the claim that Paddington and Victoria were civilian targets by noting that they did not understand why London railway terminals were "civilian" targets but Iraqi roads and bridges filled with truck and car traffic being bombed by the Royal Air Force were "military" ones. The British establishment and media did not see the parallel, they never had. IRA bombs were illicit and RAF bombs legitimate. There were always rationales by Irish republicans, always IRA suspicions that the police used warnings and the media used its coverage cunningly to British advantage, even at the risk of life. For most people in or out of London none of this mattered—bombs had gone off and innocent people had been killed or maimed. The dead man's wife, who wanted no retaliation, regretted that she had not said good-bye; a mother with children in the hospital was less forgiving: "If I ever get my hands on the animals who did this, I will rip them apart—they should see my children lying in hospital with tubes and drips coming out of them."

The victims in London, in England, and especially in Northern Ireland, as always, soon disappeared back into the mass, the dead buried after the traumatic hurried funeral. The maimed were forgotten: men without hands, ladies without legs, the savaged and scarred and broken with years to go, walking with canes, wheeled to the films, lying years damaged, dependent, their misery known only to the neighbors. The congenial, amusing Ian Gow, the cheerful bright man with a loving wife and family and a nice house by the sea, would be remembered, praised by his colleagues and friends, by the Prime Minister at the funeral. He was almost famous, more so dead. But who would care about the man burned, broken, and ruined on the platform at Victoria but Jane Corner, an early widow? It was a dirty war, and one the British pointed out had been initiated by the IRA.

In England the costs were as always painful—lives lost, key and symbolic targets smashed, civility eroded, justice at risk, and life even at the center made more unpleasant, so unpleasant because it all seemed so senseless. In the new decade there were a series of visible IRA successes: The attacks on British soldiers, bombs in the Stock Exchange and Carlton Club, the assassination of Gow, and then in 1991 the attack on Number 10 Downing Street and the railway terminals collectively indicated the cost to Britain of an Irish War. But the cost, despite the exaggeration of effect caused by elaborate media coverage, was easy to pay, and through repeated exposure was easy to minimize, even within the dynamics of the system. There were the usual ripples spreading out from the events, urging retaliation or vengeance, support for improved security measures, anti-Irish sentiments expressed to the dismay of the tolerant and the huge Irish diaspora long without the slightest sympathy for the "national cause." And there were the ritual announcements that terror was futile, democracy perpetual, and the IRA evil. And then the victim was buried, the stations cleaned up, the ruined van taken away to forensics, and the cabinet was meeting again in the Cabinet Room. No change. No concession. Very little concern. Everyone had been through it before. Ireland was replaying as a sequel without an audience, the plot was a bore, the characters shopworn.

Any week would indicate the patterns in the weave of the long chronicle. Soon after the London bombs, in mid-February in the province, came a remarkable bland week without an election or a major atrocity. It was as much as any an average week a generation on. Prime Minister Major made his first flying visit to Belfast in between the more important war cabinet meetings focused on the Iraq conflict. His attention had been attracted to the other war, one worth at least a flying visit. He found the IRA "contemptible." He also appeared at Foster's Mountain near Silverbridge, Armagh, beside one of the strange watchtowers along the border, a mix of corrugated steel, industrial steel lattice, and sci-fi aerials all protected on the ground with more corrugated steel walls and wire: something out of the East German frontier and Buck Rogers that loomed over the Irish fields as if ready to grind forward like a robot in some new *Star Wars*. It was a good time to visit. The next week a largish IRA active service unit dropped in two mortar bombs and fought a fierce fifteen-minute gun battle. Several hundred rounds were exchanged—almost like the glory days twenty years before. The Prime Minister had missed it. And in turn the new President of the Republic, Mary Robinson, who had suggested a rethink of the Anglo-Irish Agreement, was invited to come and talk with the Protestant people along the Shankill—a major security problem for the RUC but one that should prove surmountable, said a police spokesman. The UDA agreed to the visit "if that is what the people want." It had been a long time since Irish politicians had made flying trips to the Falls.

In England there had been another delay in the Birmingham Six case, one more unexpected bureaucratic delay before their inevitable release. There were the continuing complaints about the Prevention of Terrorism Act, this time led by Lord Colville, who said, "Any arrest made successfully under the Prevention of Terrorism Act could have been made under normal legislation." There were the complaints that transforming the emergency legislation into permanent acts had focused on security needs—always with the unstated assumption that Ireland was different, that there less liberty was necessary. There was the continuing trouble with extradition: IRA suspect Desmond Ellis had gone on hunger strike to stop the process that had still in time put him in England, where the charges had to be withdrawn (one more error), and then new ones were found as long as he was in place (one more Dublin political storm and the threat to adjust the law). In Dublin there were complaints about the Prevention of Terrorism Act, used for no good purpose to detain a pair of Irish boxers on the way to a competition in Birmingham. And the spread of the legal Troubles was indicated by the fact that Joe Doherty's lawyer was in Belfast to report on the eight-year fight against deportation. And in a court in the Netherlands four IRA suspects went on trial, accused of the murder of the two Australian tourists, Stephen Melrose and Nick Spanos, on May 27, 1990.

Murder went forward in the Troubles, even in a dull week in February 1991. There were all the usual tokens, appeals and hunger strikes, extradition and the Prevention of Terrorism Act to go with the visiting politicians and the gun battles. The IRA was active in Belfast with arson attacks, and someone had sent a booby-trapped letter to the wife of Michael Stone the loyalist killer in prison for the Milltown cemetery attack in 1988. Gerry Adams's brother, Seán Patrick, thirty-two, was jailed for fourteen years for an attack on a police station in 1989—some Belfast republicans were not involved solely in the ballot box approach, despite Mitchel McLaughlin of Sinn Féin criticizing civilian casualties in the English campaign. Danny Morrison, publicity director of Sinn Féin, was in fact on trial, accused of involvement in the kidnapping and interrogation of an informer. Ten people had been charged with abducting and conspiring to murder the IRA informer Alexander "Sandy" Lynch, who had been a police agent used against the IRA and INLA since 1983. The authorities were delighted to have netted Morrison, supposedly a Sinn Féin person. And the Belfast Unionists, who still saw little difference between Sinn Féin and the IRA anyway, were ruled out of order by a judge in their effort to prevent a Sinn Féin member from addressing the city council. Elsewhere, the SDLP felt that there was no hope of reaching a political settlement with Sinn Féin as long as the party supported violence. More direct measures against subversion were taken when a loyalist gunman shot a young Catholic man, whose brother-in-law had been shot dead by terrorists in 1985, and injured his three-year-old niece on the national Bawnmore council estate in Newtownabbey. The crowd attacked the RUC constables investigating the shooting and one officer had two teeth knocked out. Earlier in the week another Catholic man had survived a similar attack in his home on Durham Street, West Belfast, although he was hit in the arm, leg, and groin. All these were the usual local items seldom picked up by television or even the big newspapers.

As the year progressed, more violent than 1990 but without indication of either political or security advantage, the IRA campaign began to seem endless, pointless to all but the committed republicans. Even members of Sinn Féin from time to time seemed ready to talk rather than to back more killing. The attacks in England, the increasingly large bombs detonated in Northern Ireland, the steady toll of small incidents and small losses seemed to lead nowhere. The ever hopeful sought signs from Gerry Adams and Provisional Sinn Féin that a truce was a prospect, that a move to the political front had advocates within the movement: Certainly Adams spoke, as always, for peace in moderate tones but in the end without shifting from support of the armed struggle. And the optimists had to deal with the fact that the reorganized Protestant paramilitary organizations were attracting a new generation. And only a very few such gunmen outside the control of most loyalists and so far beyond reach of the RUC could cause enormous damage to a fragile society.

The IRA's campaign at least had logic and rules. And it apparently could be sustained indefinitely; neither arrests, security sweeps, betrayals, nor the skills of the security forces could close it down. In fact, IRA operations in England went sporadically with shifting targets, shifting means, and with no losses to the chagrin of the police in particular. In April there were incendiary devices found at the Preston railway station and ignited in seven shops in Manchester. On June 28 a bomb went off outside the theater where the Blues and Royals military band was playing, and two days later a bomb was found near the RAF–Royal Navy careers office in Fishergate, Preston. There were more incendiary devices in London in

August, but the first IRA losses did not come until November 15 when Frank Ryan and Patricia Black Donnelly, young, unknown to the authorities, the next generation of recruits, blew themselves up handling a bomb in a garage in Wanstead, East London. The British Home Secretary, Kenneth Baker, like most of the British, found only satisfaction in IRA losses and often only distaste in Irish events. Gerry Adams was saddened by the Home Secretary's "unconcealed glee," but then most in Britain thought of Adams as the head terrorist, a major factor in the continuation of the Troubles. Many might want the British out of the province where no one was grateful and many deadly, but few wanted to see any kind of IRA success. There, too, nothing had changed.

The loss of two volunteers did nothing to deter the IRA. There was a series of incendiary devices detonated or discovered during December, including one in the book shop of the National Gallery in London that did little damage but attracted attention to the campaign. It was a campaign run at small cost but with a few volunteers, which went right on into the new year with the explosion of a five-pound bomb at Whitehall Place near Downing Street. With minimal effort the IRA could disrupt commuter and rail traffic anyplace in England, bomb and burn if at a low level—this was made clear the next year on February 11 when a bomb in a telephone kiosk caused massive disruptions around Whitehall just as John Major was meeting in Downing Street with the leaders of the four major Northern Ireland parties.

In the province security problems were complicated by a revival of loyalist violence, and the loyalists tended to have better local intelligence than the security forces. Some nationalists felt in fact that the two collaborated against the mutual enemy. In any case, on Sunday, March 3, 1991, four Catholic men were shot dead in front of a pub in Cappagh, County Tyrone—it was a year before the IRA admitted that the loyalists had killed IRA volunteers. Mostly the loyalists, good intelligence or bad, still simply chose the convenient Catholic. On the next day, Monday, a Catholic taxi driver was shot dead in Belfast by his two passengers. The murder was as always condemned by all but the responsible but was to be repeated through the course of the year.

The year 1991 was not an auspicious one for Northern Ireland politicians. The IRA's English campaign was too low-level to impose a great sense of urgency on the Major government, but the violence in the province shifting gradually away from the IRA campaign to the sectarian murders of revived loyalist paramilitary organizations caused serious concern. At the end of March in a mobile shop at Craigavon, a loyalist gunman shot and killed two young women and a young man who rushed to help them. Responsibility was taken by the Protestant Action Force, the cover name used by the Ulster Volunteer Force for murders that could not be claimed even remotely as political. This time the gunman did not disappear into the loyalist mass. By April 5, two men were in court charged with the three murders, thus easing nationalist anguish and concern.

A tit-for-tat sectarian war would be even more deadly than the IRA armed struggle, and the politicians lacked a promising direction to distract public attention. Brooke's talks, which by the end of February had dribbled along for thirteen months, had promised at best very little, had been delayed by very small objections. As Brooke pointed out, the gap between the nationalists and Unionists was not very wide, only very deep. Into that gap for a generation had dropped every initiative, most hope. Mostly no one saw what was to be gained. In the meantime the sectarian murders continued, and these at least concentrated minds. Brooke announced that the scheduled talks under the Anglo-Irish Agreement would be suspended for ten weeks so that the Northern Unionist politicians could at least agree at last to meet with the nationalists with hated agreement "suspended," if not disowned as they had wanted. Brooke hoped North-South talks would then follow. Sinn Féin would be barred, for the party had not condemned violence or renounced the armed struggle. Few politicians, North or South, wanted Adams involved and so insisted on Sinn Féin making a formal denial. Seemingly the loyalist paramilitaries were not even, unlike Sinn Féin, interested in talking about talking.

Briefly there seemed to be a positive response in that the loyalist paramilitaries of the Ulster Volunteer Force announced a ceasefire. Within hours on April 17, a Catholic taxi driver, John O'Hare, father of five, was murdered by the Ulster Freedom Fighters—still the cover name for the UVF—when he answered a call to a house in South Belfast. His wife's first husband, Hugh Duffy, a brewery worker, had also been shot dead by loyalist gunmen in the early seventies. Two days later another attempt by the UVF on a taxi driver failed at Belfast Castle in north Belfast. With the sectarian incidents continuing despite the UVF truce and the head-to-head political talks finished, Brooke also had to postpone the first plenary session on Tuesday, April 30. Not good news at all. The parties involved, especially the Unionists, could always find reasons for delay.

Beyond the negotiations the same low level of stress and turmoil continued as before: riotous scenes in the Belfast city council, an RUC sergeant mortally injured in an IRA attack on a police Land Rover. On Sunday, May 5, thousands attended a rally in Belfast to commemorate the tenth anniversary of the death of Bobby Sands. There Adams criticized Sinn Féin's exclusion from the Brooke talks. Day by day the Brooke talks or lack of talks made the political news. No one party or individual, even those Unionists least interested, wanted the responsibility for their failure.

In the meantime, as always past incidents returned to complicate the present. On May 9 Sinn Féin publicity director Danny Morrison began an eight-year jail sentence for the false imprisonment of an RUC informer. This was received with enormous satisfaction by the security forces and the unionists. Many saw him as a key member of the republican movement at least and more likely a ranking IRA man. Justice seemed done. Justice in Dublin and London was rarely seen to be done or at least with alacrity. In England the appeal of the Birmingham Six had dragged on to the anger of the impatient, who felt their innocence proven. And those impatient included not only their defenders and much of Irish nationalist opinion but also most disinterested opinion. Delay was not thus judicious but seemed petty, malicious. In Dublin there was the visible shadow of the embarrassing case of Nicky Kelly, imprisoned on dubious evidence for the Great Train Robbery at Sallins, released in July 1984 but not pardoned despite the fact that the other three defendants had been declared innocent. Kelly had been cajoled off a hunger strike with the understanding that the Fine Gael–Labour government would allow his appeal through the civil courts—a prospect that, as Lord

Denning had suggested in the case of the Birmingham Six, opened "an appalling vista." Michael Noonan, Minister for Justice, felt that to release Kelly, despite the new evidence, despite doubts about the old evidence, would imply that the principal judges had "acted incorrectly or incompetently." So in 1991 official Irish criticism of British judicial practice had to be somewhat muted.

No judicial system likes to be found wanting, no government responsible for injustice, and no establishment cruel, and so it is always much easier to believe the subversives are at fault than one's own. The British had encouraged far greater difficulties for the government and the system by their judicious and undoubtedly legally proper delay in the cases than by daring to accept blame forthwith. At last on March 19, the Birmingham Six were freed. This left only one largely forgotten Irish prisoner, Judith Ward, who was released in 1992. In Ireland Kelly had to wait a little longer for his pardon. In the province meanwhile, the UDR Four case, Protestants accused of killing a member of a well-known republican family in Armagh in 1983, too, was causing more general concern. This case was ultimately referred back to the Court of Appeal on July 25, 1991, indicating that justice was seen not to be done properly for the majority as well as the minority. And indicating as well that the past was part of the present. It was not only the continuing famous court cases that caused trouble but the anniversaries, the bad news. On May 14 the inquest was held for Lord Kaberry of Adel, who was injured by the Carlton Club bomb in June 1990 and died nine months later, allowing no one to forget even after the rash of new bombs the toll of the old. On May 16 Dame Janet Gow said at her husband's inquest that he had held the IRA in contempt.

So there was the old bad news, the new bad news—eight people were injured when an IRA bomb exploded at government offices in Belfast on the same day as the Gow inquest—and the continuing bad news with the government, again on May 16, reporting a rise in unemployment statistics in the province for the fifth straight month, 13 percent, 99,010 people. There were always provincial economic statistics and most of them grim. Government compensation payments for personal injuries and damages to property were on the rise, the highest in a decade. By the end of the year compensation would reach a record of 57 million pounds sterling. There was as well repeated evidence that sectarian discrimination continued, usually to Catholic detriment. The bad news in 1991 seemed always up, troops deployed or security forces killed, sectarian incidents or complaints about hiring practices.

Increasingly, outside the province few seemed to care a great deal about Northern Ireland troubles about the Troubles. Except for an occasional patriotic outburst from the adamantly national, most in the Republic preferred local matters. No one wanted to hear about new Troubles. Attention was given to optimistic signs like the Brooke talks, but the background music of killing and contention interested no one. RTE seldom wanted to do specials or cover more than the hardest news. Major atrocities, traditional examples of British injustice, danger to the Northern nationalist community required or encouraged response, but for the most part opinion in the Republic, like that in Great Britain, if not content with a tolerable level of violence, had adapted to the Troubles.

So 1991 moved through the spring: three UDR men killed and fifteen others, including three civilians, injured at a British army camp in Armagh by a huge

IRA bomb, and three IRA volunteers killed in a trap ambush in Tyrone, car bombs and a Sinn Féin councillor shot dead. At least and at last the Brooke talks were finally on, scheduled to open June 17 after Paisley almost balked at the last minute over the choice of Sir Ninian Stephen, former British governor general of Australia as the chairman. There were to be talks not so much because there was something to talk about—the Unionists still agreed only on what they did not want—but rather because by nature politicians were inclined to talk. If Brooke was denied, what was left? So the talks were scheduled.

There was the cheerful news from Libya as Tripoli offered to give London information about contacts with the Provisional IRA. The British felt that Libya had much to answer for in that the arms shipments that ended with the seizure of the *Eksund* by the French authorities had overfilled the IRA's armory. The new stocks of weapons gave the IRA more guns than guerrillas, this despite the steady erosion caused by arms finds in both the Republic and Northern Ireland, and allowed the movement to auction off older weapons to supporters abroad to raise needed funds. The crucial addition proved to be the Semtex plastic explosives, which allowed the volunteers to increase the power and variety of their bombs and reduce the risk of premature explosions. These IRA bombs ranged from armor-piercing devices known as drogue bombs to booby-trap devices under cars that were used to kill at least thirty people in Northern Ireland by 1992. The Enniskillen bomb in November 1987 was Semtex-based, as well as those used in English operations, against Gow and the Royal Marine Band in Deal, and on the Continent. Libya at the very least had made the IRA more efficient and more effective so that a change of heart in Tripoli, while welcome, was not an initiative that sparked great enthusiasm in London. The damage had long been done by the time the Anglo-Libyan group met in Geneva.

Within the province meanwhile, the unpleasant-incident level remained stable, the toll of death and injury, ruin and devastation, rising at approximately the pace of the previous year. The INLA shot an informer. The IRA killed a leading loyalist, Cecil McKnight, chairman of the Ulster Democratic Party and a leader of the UFF-UVF. And then on July 3 the Brooke talks, so long in the making, ended simply because no one had anything new to say. Recriminations and accusations seemed more politically advantageous than talks continuing to no purpose, formalities that could lead no where all the Unionists could go. Thus the Unionists and loyalists entered the marching season united again on opposition to change. No one had surrendered or given an inch or gained an inch. James Molyneaux, leader of the Official Unionist Party, said that it was time to start "binding together this entire community," but all prospects indicated a continuation of unresolved aspiration and the recollection of past grievances.

Any initiative seemingly engendered immediate opposition in some quarter. The British announced that the UDR was to be merged with the Royal Irish Rangers. This was in part for fiscal reasons and in part to dilute the charge of sectarianism—one hundred members of the UDR had been charged with serious crimes, often political crimes, and seventeen were serving sentences for murder. That any militia contains criminals convinced few nationalists that the UDR was more than the B Specials in special uniforms or that a merger would change anything. The unionists had their own doubts. That many old regiments had to adjust to new strategic and fiscal reality convinced few loyalists that their UDR, their defense, was being taken from them by London fiat.

As for the summer, the usual was as usual. In Belfast the tiny Irish People's Liberation Organization was willing to engage in tit-for-tat killing, was unable to do much more than kill the most vulnerable and soon its own. The IRA, on the other hand, was still avowedly nonsectarian. From time to time IRA commanders were less restrained than republican ideology suggested. One Belfast O/C who had lost a brother to sectarian murder had been quite willing to strike back at the loyalists, but arbitrary tit-for-tat killing always caused enormous strain within the secret army. On the other hand, certain brutal killings were quite acceptable. The IRA had murdered a suspected farmer, Thomas Oliver, in Rivertown near Dundalk in the Republic. Although the armed struggle recognized the border, officially eschewed operations in the South, the exceptions were manifold. Suspected informers were never immune. The wave of criticism in the Republic was ignored—old enemies seeking fresh means of attacking the IRA. Armed robbery, murder, arson, intimidation, and all the functions of support and maintenance that fueled the war used the Republic as arena. Army Orders could be stretched in case of need just as they were in Northern Ireland and often in the case of the bombs in England.

The rest of the year was one long chronicle of the past repeated. British soldiers were charged with murder of civilians, not for the first time. Old cases reemerged to cause fresh dispute. And always vulnerable individuals innocent or guilty, Catholics or Protestants, republicans or loyalists, the unlucky, shot or bombed. From time to time there was a novel unpleasant event to attract, if briefly, the media. Otherwise the province struggled along making do. Some found no problem, they lived in pleasant areas, bought houses cheaper than elsewhere in the United Kingdom, seldom went near troubled areas, and ignored unpleasant matters, read the English papers, went elsewhere on their holidays. Even the killing grounds of Tyrone or Armagh *looked* normal.

In fact no place in the province was quite normal. This corner had tricolor-painted curbstones. Anyone in a passing car could see that rural wall with an orange UVF sprayed across the top. There were tattered election posters flapping on telephone poles in the country urging a vote for Danny Morrison or Paisley. And no one could miss the strange architecture of the security forces: the watchtowers along the border, the draped army checkpoints, and strange communication devices on police stations. It was possible to stay home, to avoid the news, to converse only on social matters, to drive quickly back and forth to work, a tunnel life. The province prohibited the truly normal. Many may have tried, but even then such a life was never really normal, quite beyond the helicopters or the rumble of the bomb, beyond rumor.*

Many, most, certainly tried to lead everyday lives. Poets might write poems about love and the landscape and the painters deploy international styles, but they also met in seminars and conferences to confront the appropriate responses to the

---

*Perhaps the most effective presentation of Northern Ireland as "almost" normal can be found in the photographs of Paul Graham, published as *Troubled Land: The Social Landscape of Northern Ireland* (London: Grey Editions, 1987), with texts by Declan McGonagle and Gerry Badger.

world beyond meter and geometry. There was the clatter of helicopters passing over garden parties and patrols plodding through the fields and even, from time to time, army patrols driving down the Malone Road past the upper-middle-class houses. That many hardly noticed this was not a sign of the normal but of accommodation.

There was always, always something that required adjustment, some new quirk of the abnormal. In August 1991 the IRA demanded that six young "hooligans" leave the province, a parallel to the more formal internal exile by the London government of certain "subversives" to Northern Ireland using the Prevention of Terrorism Act. In an attempt to impose authority in certain nationalist areas, the IRA had long resorted to maiming—kneecapping—a most unpleasant and brutal option that inevitably alienated as many as were intimidated. Exile at least was an improvement over murder or maiming. It was, however, nearly as outrageous to those involved, charged, tried, and convicted by hidden gunmen, to those who saw such a secret army as simple terrorists, to any who wanted the rule of law as well as local order. Three left; one negotiated a pardon but two took refuge in Newry Cathedral.

It was late-summer hard news. It was more attractive than the dreadful toll of the sectarian killings. On August 5 a Protestant was shot dead in Tyrone by the IRA. He was accused of paramilitary connections, and as was often the case, the charge was denied by the grieving family. On August 9 a Protestant loyalist was shot dead by the IRA in Derry. The next day on the Falls Road a Catholic shopkeeper was shot dead by loyalists. On August 12 a Sinn Féin member was shot dead in County Tyrone. Two days later two women were injured in a loyalist attack on a bus taking relatives to visit republican prisoners at the Maze. It was a dreary and deadly chronicle.

Thus the two men seeking sanctuary was more attractive, allowed protest against the IRA, promised confrontation without murder. On August 14, there were protests over the IRA threat to the six men in Newry. Outrage and indignation, the rush of antirepublicans to criticize the IRA, had never greatly affected the leadership and did not indicate to them a loss of support. Groups for peace, groups opposed to kneecapping, opposed to attacks on the Dublin-Belfast railway, arose and remained regular critics. The clergy always criticized their "violence" and too the conventional parties and all the majority and of course the cause of all Ireland's evils, the British. So the two accused of taking refuge in the Newry cathedral, the circling media, the outrage and editorials and the usual round of antirepublican statements hardly swayed the leadership. The two stayed eleven days, made statements, and fled into hiding, leaving their defenders without victims. The cardinal archbishop of Armagh, the recently appointed Cahal Daly, implacable enemy of IRA pretensions, felt the two had been "most ungrateful."

By autumn attention was again attracted to the real instead of symbolic confrontations. The sectarian killing intensified and this time there was not even the slight hope of political option to distract loyalist attention. And it seemed that there were now republicans willing to retaliate, kill openly for sectarian purpose. In the first week of September, two Catholics and one Protestant were murdered. On Tuesday, September 10, a young Protestant, John Hanna, was killed by the IRA, who claimed he was a member of a loyalist terror squad. It was the fifty-sixth death of the year. On September 14, a Catholic man, Kevin Flood, was shot and killed.

It was, however, the UDA that was causing the greatest concern, for a new generation had arrived to replace those corrupted by power and opportunity for criminal gain, corrupted by connections with the security forces and even the Provos. The old hard men had fine clothes and big cars and gangster ways, lived beyond the mean bars and short streets that fed the paramilitary kitty. They were killed or displaced. By the autumn of 1991, the new men had moved to respond in what was felt was an appropriate manner to IRA violence. On Saturday, September 18, Larry Murchan, a Catholic newsagent, was shot and killed in his shop by the Loyalist Retaliation and Defense Group. The Protestant paramilitaries were increasingly able to target republicans but relied much of the time on convenient Catholics. Just before midnight in a housing estate in Cookstown the RUC shot and killed Kevin Flood, a student who innocently stumbled into a police ambush.

The UFF announced that all members of the Gaelic Athletic Association, forty thousand in Northern Ireland, were legitimate targets. Other than to add to the tension, the threat meant little practically since the loyalists rarely investigated their victims beyond the necessary religious requirements. In any case, during October the sectarian attacks continued. The killing was intensified if anything by the IPLO, who sent a squad into the Diamond Jubilee bar and asked for the former loyalist prisoner Harry Ward by name. When he tried to flee through the pub's off-license liquor salesroom, they followed and shot him at least six times. What nearly everyone feared was that the few gunmen involved, a dozen or so Catholics and somewhat more Protestant loyalists, would drag their communities into a shooting war rather than the round of tit-for-tat murders. Such sectarian one-for-one murders were dreadful but tolerable. The horror was soon dissipated because of familiarity with atrocity and the limited numbers. The occasional and eratic killing was part of the acceptable level of violence.

In a sense on November 4 an IRA bomb detonating at the military wing of the Musgrave Park Hospital in south Belfast, which killed two British army medical officers and was universally condemned, returned the Troubles to the familiarity of past atrocity. Then the sectarian killings began again. The British deployed fourteen hundred extra UDR reserve troops on active-duty police patrols. Hundreds of police constables were working twelve-hour shifts. In the second week of November, five Protestants and two Catholics were killed in surprise attacks. The IRA claimed four victims. Loyalist gunmen of the UFF fired on a brother of an IRSP member. A loyalist roadblock claimed three more, two Catholics and a Protestant, in Craigavon, where security was less tight than in Belfast. In fact, the province was flooded not only with fear but also with security forces determined to prevent further decay in order. In 1990 there had been seventy-six people killed and already in 1991 the provincial total had reached eighty-four; thirty-six of those had been murdered by loyalist paramilitary groups, contrasted to nineteen the previous year.

The IRA, still concentrating on security forces, had killed eleven civilians, often claiming that their targets were not innocent but involved in the struggle in some way. A UDR man, for example, was kidnapped and killed in Armagh when he was making a delivery of soft drinks to a garage. The UDR was a "legitimate" IRA target and so the members were never safe. The UFF killed a Catholic while he made a delivery for a Chinese takeaway restaurant. The history of the province had become one long chronicle of cruelty. And there was only so much that could be done. Private homes could only be made so safe with bolted front doors, wire cages on the stairs, locks on bedroom doors—a series of barriers that would keep away gunmen battering their way toward the victim if the police answered the panic telephone call in time. Sometimes it worked. One set of loyalist gunmen fled from a new line of defense used in one house—two rottweiler dogs. Various barriers were in the house of every politician, most public figures, all those who might be a target. And for many there was no protection at all. Any taxi driver was vulnerable to any call for service, but there were hundreds of taxis in Belfast and the drivers simply depended on the odds. After all, more people were killed in car accidents and the toll in Belfast was small in contrast to the murders in Washington, D.C., or New York City. Still the year had been especially nasty because sectarian murder seemed more brutal than the long dirty war between the IRA and security forces, where there was pretense at rules and restraint. There were, of course, rules and restraints even along the provincial fault lines, but they had been repeatedly broken. Shooting a lad delivering a Chinese dinner or killing a man in a chips van or, worse, shooting children could hardly be done to the sound of trumpets, was simple murder often barely for political purpose.

The IRA bombed in central Belfast, devastating the Europa Hotel, once again, and the Grand Opera House. In 1991 IRA's northern command had focused on using Semtex and increasing the size of single car bombs, more blast in one basket. The RUC estimated that these bombs weighed one thousand pounds and were part of a new front. In response, in August the British had introduced the 40mm Luchaire rifle grenade, which could be fitted to the standard army SA80 rifle. This was supposed to give the army a weapon to hit IRA armored trucks carrying Semtex bombs. Most IRA mobile bombs were not armored except for military targets left parked and a warning given. Giving soldiers in Ireland what was immediately called an anti-tank weapon upset the locals, who saw the introduction as an escalation and a danger to civilians—the projectile had a range of 360 meters. Just as in the case of plastic and rubber bullets, the new device generated extensive if not long-lived controversy. The army insisted it gave them a capacity to respond to the IRA jettisoning large bombs in trailers from tractor units, pointed out that the IRA had killed eleven soldiers by sending trucks loaded with explosives into permanent checkpoints. How many of those trucks would have been stopped by rifle grenades was a moot point. Most nationalists felt it was merely another military quick-fix that endangered everyone but the British army. The device apparently was never used—IRA armored vehicles were, if not unknown, at least rare. Without notice the device was withdrawn from use.

The IRA kept on bombing and in all sorts of ways with all sorts of devices. In fact, volunteers had bombed inside Crumlin Road prison in protest over the British effort to merge loyalist and republican prisoners, part of the long-term British strategy of eroding the concept of political crime. The Provos made no attempt to moderate their violence for the approaching Christmas season. A two-thousand-pound IRA bomb went off on Friday evening, December 13, in an attack on the Craigavon RUC station, injuring seventy people. More than sixty of the injured were civilians, mostly from a nearby Catholic housing estate. On December 19 another massive IRA bomb detonated in the center of Belfast, close to the law courts, but no one was injured.

And so the month dragged on. The IPLO shot a man in a scuffle outside a bar, perhaps an operation gone wrong, perhaps a simple brawl. Even the Provisionals felt the IPLO schismatics had to be condemned and called for the group to disband. This was as far as the Army Council would go, public condemnation, private pressure but no shooting. The few IPLO gunmen went right on shooting, indiscriminately spraying a bar in a loyalist area, the Donegall Arms in Roden Street, with gunfire that killed two Protestant men. For the second year in a row, the IRA formally announced a three-day Christmas ceasefire. The last two deaths came on December 21, the same day as the attack on the Roden Street bar. William Johnston, twenty-eight, was killed at his girlfriend's house by loyalists, and there was another loyalist sectarian attack on a bar in Finaghy, which killed Aidan Wallace, twenty-two. The result was not only an IRA Christmas truce but also Christmas funerals and the traditional round of condemnation and pleas for moderation.

At three minutes from midnight on December 27 the IRA truce ended with a bomb on the railway line near Newry. Nothing seemingly had changed because of the truce except that sectarian attacks during the last days of the year failed. In fact, nothing seemingly had changed in Northern Ireland at all, certainly for the good, in the course of a year that saw political frustration and increased violence. It was not as if there was no change in the new decade, nothing but the long political stalemate and the odd violent spectacular. Rather the changes on and off the island simply did not seem to have any great impact on the essential immobility within the province. The talks about talks had led to talks that ended almost at once, seemingly the last flicker of British political ingenuity. The sectarian killing went on and on, the pace fitting no model; the incidents went up or down, at times for some specific reason or at times for no reason at all. The IRA's armed struggle went on and on, the security forces unable to impose a lower level of violence. The past was prologue with a vengeance.

The year 1992 began rooted in the violence of the past. On January 3, loyalists shot and killed a Catholic butcher, Kevin McKearney, in his father's shop in Moy, County Tyrone; an uncle was also injured, as well as a ten-year-old girl. McKearney was thought to have been targeted because of the death before Christmas 1991 of a student, Robin Farmer, murdered by members of the INLA. McKearney came from a republican family and that was sufficient for the loyalist gunmen. Two of the dead man's brothers had died in the Troubles. One, Seán, was killed when a bomb he was carrying blew up prematurely, and the other, Padraig, was one of the eight IRA volunteers killed at the SAS ambush in Loughgall. Another brother, Tommy, was still serving a jail term in Maghaberry prison.

On January 9, Philip Campbell, twenty-eight, was working in his mobile fish and chips van parked on the roundabout near Moira when a silver-colored car drew up and the driver waited while the UFF gunman fired through the open door and mortally wounded him. The UFF statement noted that "unlike the government, we have the will to take on republican paramilitaries and no amount of failed security force policy will deter us in our task in 1992." Twenty-four hours after Campbell's funeral, a car bomb detonated at Glen Road in Coalisland and killed a second Catholic accused, falsely, as was usually the case, of republican connections. It was a replay of the previous year, when ninety-four deaths were reported in the province. A Provo breakout at Crumlin Road Prison was discovered. The sectarian killings continued. The IRA was active still, bombing in both England and the province. In London the IRA active service units focused on sabotaging the train systems but had recourse to their usual car bombs and arson devices. And the security forces made little progress. And in the Republic the police suspected that the IRA was behind a major bank robbery. In the most spectacular armed robbery yet, two million Irish pounds had been stolen, automatic machine guns deployed, and a getaway car used that had a Northern Ireland registration number. The Gárdaí were still finding arms dumps filled with the returns of the IRA-Libya connection, but continued arrests and successes only indicated that the IRA still had strength in the Republic.

The old incidents often dragged on, 1992 not different from 1991, nothing ever finished. Two of the *Eksund* arms ship men released from French prisons were arrested at Dublin airport. At the end of January a spokesman for the RUC announced that the Director of Public Prosecutions would charge the two British marines with the fatal shooting of Fergal Caraher and the wounding of his brother Michael at Cullyhanna on December 30, 1990. It was a rare positive response to nationalist criticism of army actions. And the court case involving Brian Nelson, who as a member of UDA had worked for British intelligence, indicated collusion between loyalist death squads and British security agencies.

Republicans had long insisted that the British army manipulated the loyalist paramilitaries, sometimes indirectly, sometimes directly, leaked them information, set up targets, used them in their prosecution of a dirty war. Certainly events in 1992 indicated that the British had little intention of greatly limiting the security forces in that dirty war. In fact, the British intelligence component was reorganized not as a "reform" but partly in hopes of countering IRA operations in England. MI5 was to take over responsibility from the police's Special Branch, originally set up to counter the Fenians and so quite opposed to any such change. MI5 without subversive KGB agents to pursue had been given the IRA as alternative despite their lack of Irish experience and lack of skills in preparing criminal cases. Bureaucratic change would make the war on all sides no less dirty any more than amalgamating the UDR with a more conventional regiment would remove nationalist suspicions.

Still London pursued options to violence or despair. The Northern Secretary, Brooke, was still continuing his round of talks even if contact with the Dublin government was ended for the moment. He still had hopes, and talking was better than shooting. In fact, as a public-relations ploy, on January 19, 1992, Brooke had been cajoled into singing "My Darling Clementine" on RTE's "Late Late Show." At the same time an IRA bomb at Teebane Crossroads near Dungannon detonated beside a van carrying civilian workers from an army base—thus, IRA targets. The huge explosion killed seven men immediately and mutilated seven more. There, unfortunately, was Northern Secretary Peter Brooke, decent, well-liked, doing the best possible with a hopeless task, at the very moment, on Irish television singing away his remaining credibility with most unionists.

Brooke offered his resignation. Major would not accept it. The IRA was to blame. Across the province and in most of the island there was the same horror at the murder of simple working people, similarly expressed by all those in authority in Belfast, Dublin, and London—Major called it "odious, contemptible, and cowardly." There were the same demands for harsh measures from the majority and the orthodox—Unionist Ken Maginnis called for internment. There was the same persistence with British policy expressed by the Northern Secretary—"The IRA will not succeed by the means they are using. A democratic society cannot give in to the bomb or bullet." And there followed the horror of the victims at the Teebane Crossroads bombing, the grief of the living, the funerals, the condemnation of the churches, and, as the IRA intended, considerable private reflection on the dangers of assisting the security forces even as civilian workers.

Elsewhere the characters changed if not the Irish plot. In Dublin at the end of the month, on January 30, the seemingly indestructible Taoiseach Charles Haughey announced that within the week he would resign as Prime Minister. Time and a series of disclosures, political, fiscal, and party scandals, some that had not quite involved him, had collectively finally eroded his credibility within Fianna Fáil. For the Unionists the monster who had smuggled arms, sought an Irish role in Northern Ireland, temporarily even attracted Margaret Thatcher with his gift of a Georgian teapot, a united Ireland man at heart, would be gone. He had started before there was trouble. Lemass's son-in-law, back in the days when de Valera mattered and O'Neill was thought radical. He had lasted for a generation. He was replaced by Albert Reynolds, a deputy who divided the party the least and did not foreclose others' ambitions. Whatever else, Reynolds had none of Haughey's liabilities on Northern Ireland, if none of his skill and charm and cunning. Still, he might want to have a go, make his own mark.

With a new and dynamic President in Mary Robinson, who had long been sympathetic to the Unionists' concerns, the Dublin center was open to change, to British initiative. In the midst of the sweeping change at the top, the Workers Party came apart as the moderates sought to discard the old ideological Marxist-Leninist verities cherished by the core of republican apostates, Garland, Goulding, and many in the North. Mac Giolla, however, was the only one of the seven Dáil Workers deputies to stay with the party. A majority of the old party, including six deputies under Worker Party leader Proinsias De Rossa, sought a new alternative to the old party dominated by democratic centralism in a brand-new party. This new Democratic Left centered in the Republic had less attraction for the Workers in the Republican Clubs of the North or for those deeply committed to Marxism. In effect, the Workers Party was more or less back to the Officials' constituency of fourteen years before when the gun—except for fiscal and defensive purposes—went on the shelf.

At least Irish politics would be different, if not the Troubles. In Northern Ireland, there was merely more of the same. February was a bad month. Allen Moore, an RUC constable, crazed by the death of a friend in a domestic incident, had fired shots over the grave, been arrested, his police weapon withdrawn and then released. The next day he walked into Sinn Féin offices on the Falls Road and with his own gun opened fire indiscriminately, killing three people and wounding two. Then he simply walked out, escaped the security net, drove to the shore of Lough Neagh, and there shot and killed himself. The next afternoon five Catholics, two teenagers, were gunned down, murdered for sectarian purpose while standing in front of a bookmaker's office in south Belfast in the lower Ormeau area of the city. These murders at Sinn Féin headquarters by a demented RUC constable and in south Belfast by loyalist gunmen overshadowed the death of an IRA man in Fermanagh near the border, killed by a reserve UDR member. It was the only IRA attack so far in 1992. Most of the 1992 killing was in Belfast, and much of the city was in a panic that a new wave of tit-for-tat sectarian killings would begin.

Then on February 16, Sunday evening, four IRA volunteers were shot dead by the SAS in Coalisland during a Provo attack on the town's police station. The engagement engendered again, as always, the suspicion by many nationalists that excess force had been used. The loyalists were delighted and DUP press officer Sammy Wilson said that the deaths were a cause for cheers, not tears. There was certainly little else to cheer about. Twenty-six people had been killed during the first thirty-seven days of the year. The rise was due to the loyalist killings. Some Provos were known to be less reluctant to retaliate than others, and all republicans recognized the need to appear to be defenders of the nationalists. The loyalist killings and cheers might provoke civil war, not just tit-for-tat retaliation.

The North's Security Minister, Brian Mawhinney, told the House of Commons in a written reply at the beginning of February that 3,184 people had been killed in EC-wide incidents since 1968—a figure soon out of date with renewed killing in Belfast. The rising toll did not, however, bury politics entirely. At Major's bequest, Brooke opened talks with Reynolds, although whether they were substantive or cosmetic was not clear. What was clear was that Major had a place for Northern Ireland on his agenda at a particularly delicate moment both in the province and in the United Kingdom.

In London there had been speculation about political change. An election was required by July, when the new Prime Minister, John Major, attractive but hardly charismatic, would oppose the remodeled Neil Kinnock. The new model Labour Party, cleansed of the hard left and brought into the British mainstream, seemed to have an excellent chance. The Conservatives, with a new but not especially dramatic leader, years in office to accumulate resentment, and the burden of the persistent recession, appeared to many observers vulnerable. Major decided on an early spring election. The Westminster parliament was dissolved on March 16, with elections scheduled for April 9 and Labour a slight favorite. As usual, general elections meant little in Ireland except the opportunity for a display of party loyalty, often highly predictable but in 1992 perhaps of more general interest. If the election were close, if there were to be an almost evenly divided parliament, the Conservatives might need Unionist votes. Even if the experts predicted a close Labour win, and for a time the polls did too, the Irish politicians simply displayed their usual wares in the province, ran their usual candidates.

The results surprised many of the experts and not only in Great Britain, where the Conservatives, despite the recession and the new Labour posture, won an adequate if not sweeping victory with a majority of twenty-one. In Ireland the big news was that Gerry Adams of Sinn Féin, 16,826 votes, 42.1 percent, up 0.9

percent, lost his seat to Dr. Joe Hendron of SDLP, 17,415 votes, 43.6 percent, up 7.8 percent. He lost not because of demographic changes or defections but because of Protestant strategic votes. Instead of voting for their own, no matter if no Unionist could carry the nationalist constituency, sufficient numbers of Protestants had voted SDLP, as they once had in the past for Gerry Fitt. The loyalists in 1992 preferred to display their distaste for Adams rather than support their own Fred Cobain of the Ulster Unionist Party, whose share was 11.9 percent, down 6.7 percent from the previous election. The hard left hardly was visible—the Workers received 750 votes in the constituency. SDLP was in, Provisional Sinn Féin out.

Generally, there was a nationalist drift toward SDLP, but Adams was still head of Sinn Féin, still a major player, and his party had mostly held its own. The DUP slipped a bit as well, a tiny gain for the center because the Ulster Unionist Party made some gains as well. There was change, then, change that encouraged moderates and London. Major replaced Brooke as Northern Secretary with Sir Patrick Mayhew. Despite the renewed talks, Brooke had not regained his credibility because of the RTE appearance. Major decided on a new Northern Ireland team. Sir Patrick Mayhew was considered hard line in so much that as Attorney General he had refused to prosecute some of the RUC officers involved in the alleged shoot-to-kill incidents that had led to the Stalker-Sampson inquiry. The Stalker affair had never died. Northern Ireland being Northern Ireland, in April 1992 inquests into the deaths of the six men ten years before that had formed the basis of the Stalker affair was set to reopen. Mayhew also had reportedly annoyed the Irish government in his handling of the extradition issue. The past is never quite past in the province. Michael Mates, a retired lieutenant colonel who had served with the army in Northern Ireland, was appointed as the Northern Ireland Office security chief. Some Unionists sensed a hard line. Some nationalists and much of Sinn Féin thought the appointments were a sign of a stronger security line. Séamus Mallon of SDLP dubbed Mates "Colonel Blimp." No one could really imagine any sudden British policy change, but Northern politicians always fine-sifted any London move.

After a generation, advocacy of a hard security line by the responsible meant little in practice if much symbolically. If security went further, there could be little pretense of law applied and little hope of eroding Catholic commitment to Sinn Féin. Mostly the level of Irish violence had so far remained acceptable during much of 1992 after the January bomb at Teebane Crossroads. Any riffle through the newspapers soon after the general elections would indicate the gunmen at the same routine. In Armagh the IRA shot a Catholic man thought to be a spy for the UDR. In Belfast the Ulster Freedom Fighters shot a former loyalist paramilitary leader in a campaign against corruption and collusion with security forces. In fact by May the loyalist paramilitaries were outkilling the IRA by two to one in 1992. In April six were killed by the UDA-UVF and two by the IRA. There was an IRA car bomb explosion in the center of the city of London—two hundred pounds of Semtex went off, killing three people just hours after the election results were announced and an inaccurate warning had been given. Enormous damage was done. All the other indicators were much the same: Unemployment, discrimination, complaints about security harassment, any survey showed an unhappy province.

At least Major did not simply ignore Ireland, but to many's surprise, he sought to continue Brooke's talks. On Monday, April 27, he met with Taoiseach Reynolds in London along with the relevant ministers to discuss subjects of mutual interest under the Anglo-Irish Agreement. Mayhew and the new Irish Foreign Minister, David Andrews, was scheduled to meet and Northern Ireland political leaders got inter-party talks under way again on April 29. This was the major point of focus: not the murder of the young Catholic mother, Philomena Hanna, twenty-six, shot dead on April 28 by the UFF, who claimed she was a member of the IRA; not the killing the next day of Conor Maguire, who was connected with the Irish People's Liberation Army, shot in the head as he worked in an advice center in Ligoniel, dead despite his bulletproof vest by the Ulster Volunteer Force; and not the British soldier who died when the IRA bombed the border post near Newry on May 1. There was always enough bad news. On May 5 a Protestant pensioner was shot dead by the tiny but still lethal IPLO, which had carried out three such sectarian murders the previous year. The members, still crude, often undisciplined, unwanted by the Provisionals, incapable of the quiet life, found rationalization for action, for killing, for a moment of power that comes with a gun, by flying the last soiled tatter of Séamus Costello's radical banner over sectarian murder.

Such murder had to be especially savage and pointless to attract more than the conventional ritual protests and horror. Northern Ireland was immune to nearly all but the most savage and pointless but ever mindful of past grievance, past brutality. On May 11, Judith Ward, who had served eighteen years, convicted on the most scanty evidence for playing a part in three IRA bombings, was freed on bail and her appeal would be allowed "in due course." She was the last of the prisoners wrongfully convicted. The British judicial system, never eager to admit error in any case, had been shaken. Each conviction unwound slowly, publicly, painfully for the authorities, and rarely did the judicial establishment show remorse or magnanimity, rather the reverse when the convictions were found to have been without foundation. The net harm done to all the involved, victims and the security establishment, the families, the prosecutors, the judges, the systems' defenders, and not least of all, British society, was enormous and not yet apparent to those who felt the system adequate, splendid, self-correcting. A Royal Commission was set up and would suggest, probably by 1993, means to clear up any deficiencies.

The Republic did not show up much better. Kelly was finally pardoned but those in power were equally reluctant to apologize for past error. There would be no compensation and no inquiry. In an interview by the Dublin *Sunday Tribune*, Taoiseach Albert Reynolds was hardly effusive in his regrets. Thus, when on Friday evening, June 19, 1992, Kelly and Ward, along with Billy Power, Gerry Hunter, and Johnny Walker of the Birmingham-Guildford cases, met to celebrate in Boss Crokers pub in Dublin, the event was evidence for many that Irish justice was as flawed as British. Certainly there was no happy formula of justice available for application for a democratic state under armed subversive assault, but the Anglo-Irish cases indicated as well that the entrenched establishment was apt to choose order over liberty. Those within the system were likely to deny the possibility of error, defining any criticism on them as an assault on the heart of the state rather than a legitimate demand for justice. In fact, simply because the republican cases concerned subversion and major crimes, the system's defense appeared more valid than if the victims had been merely poor or simply ethnically alien. In fact, of course, only Kelly had real and radical politics, while Ward had at best muddled views. The others had been merely poor and, as Irish, ethnically suspect, subversive only in the eyes of the authorities who, unlike justice, were not blind but saw what they chose to see. This tunnel blindness that allowed the erosion of justice had oozed out from the Maze and Diplock Courts, the special operations of Northern Ireland, to become one of the most costly byproducts of the Troubles.

Many in Britain had little sympathy for the critics of the system, a system under attack by those who had been elected by no one, empowered only with the gun, Irish killers. There was no need to apologize or to explain, and there were still those who felt that to admit error, particularly in the matter of Irish bombers, was unthinkable. There were those who could not imagine that British justice had in many Irish matters, especially within Northern Ireland, become a tool of the security process, a means of vengeance and retribution. For many of the conservative and orthodox, British justice could not be imagined as any but a disinterested institution evolving from a long, glorious past, an ornament, not the parody, imagined by so many of the Irish, especially the victims of their family, friends, and advocates.

Many in Britain, and certainly not simply Tories or Blimps, had been repeatedly horrified by the IRA atrocities, by the murders on the Continent, by the endless killing not only across the Irish Sea but also within English towns. They found the loyalists nearly as revolting as the republicans. Many did not like the Irish and few understood them. Even the interested and concerned were shaped by unrecognized prejudices and old myths.* Yet withdrawal was, like most simple answers, no answer at all. The British public and many of their leaders certainly wanted an end to the Irish Troubles but not at any cost. And it seemingly cost so little to press order over law, to kill those who would kill, to treat the IRA as beyond the pale of British justice. The IRA operations could still revolt but not escalate in a cost greater than revolting the British public. The IRA's war was too low-intensity to do more than revolt.

The London government had always tried to avoid open war, at best use conventional means, and at worst hide brutal repression under the language of bureaucrats. To do otherwise, to release soldiers as soldiers, only tended to make matters worst—a generation of atrocities, outrages, revelations, and faulty convictions had, too, taught London the strange rules of the province. The security

---

*Denis Healey, a significant British figure with an Irish heritage and a concern with the Irish problem, reports in his memoirs, *The Time of My Life* (London: Michael Joseph, 1989), p. 342, his amazement that Protestants and Catholics can recognize each other on sight while he finds them physically indistinguishable.

rules were never really discussed publicly, for the line between peace and war even after a generation remained blurred. All the involved wanted the advantages of both—the British army, the RUC, the IRA, even the loyalist gunmen wanted to be soldiers, just as those of the IPLO splinter wanted to be volunteers and the crudest loyalist killer a defender. And all the politicians wanted peace, law, not order kept by killing, by a British army eager for action.

In fact, aggressive army security led to a serious incident in Coalisland, where a British paratrooper lost both legs in a mine explosion. The Paras were loved no place in nationalist Ireland, certainly not around Coalisland in mid-Tyrone. Each tour of duty tended to involve incidents engendered by their aggressive tactics: a response necessary, said their commanders, for survival in an area infested by the IRA; brute force without legal restraint, said the nationalist locals. When the Paras ransacked Coalisland in a confused medley of stolen weapons, riot, army guns fired, and general anger, there was a feeling by the nationalists, and not the nationalists alone, that the regiment for two weeks had not kept order but only harassed the locals. The Ulster Unionist MP Ken Maginnis from Tyrone, a former UDR major and his party's security spokesman, expressed his doubts about Para behavior. The result was a call for their withdrawal. A lieutenant in command of one patrol was suspended. Brigadier Tom Longland, who was in control of regiment operations in the Armagh-Tyrone area, was replaced much ahead of time. The shift in assignment—he had "not settled into" his role in Northern Ireland—was not in reaction to the incident, insisted the Defense Ministry spokesman. Few in the province accepted this explanation. Soon the Paras were moved to low-visibility duties.

While the London media noted the strain between the army and nationalists, the incident was hardly novel, no real change. What did attract wider attention outside the province was a new book, *Big Boys' Rules: The Secret War Against the IRA* by Mark Urban, a former soldier and defense correspondent of the London *Independent* in 1992. Urban's book indicated what most in the six counties accepted: The British army was authorized to trap and kill IRA volunteers within certain guideline, "clean kills." Those involved, usually the SAS and 14 Intelligence Company, had killed at least thirty-seven gunmen since 1976—all but one assumed to be IRA volunteers. Such operations indicated the nature of the Troubles as far as the British army and the relevant security authorities were concerned: a war with special rules. There had been other revelations and publications, not the least substantial works by Martin Dillon (*The Dirty War*) and Raymond Murray (*The SAS in Ireland*), but the first was by a journalist concerned mostly with Irish matters and the second by a civil libertarian priest long critical of the authorities. Urban's revelations, coupled with the incident at Coalisland, again focused, if briefly, British attention on unwelcome Irish matters.

Mostly there had been hope, especially with the failure of Adams to hold his seat in the general elections, that Ireland was an easing issue. Mostly, as always, British attention was focused on British matters: Major in for five more Conservative years. There had been as well a splendid Irish scandal with the Bishop of Galway admitting a long-ago affair and a seventeen-year-old son. The other new

Irish scandals had been complex, fiscal, about old lies and deals and no more worth British interest than the bank strike or the postal stoppage. So most of the Irish news, Coalisland apart, had been less jarring. There was a new Taoiseach with a new cabinet, a new Northern Secretary, new talks. If there was no new hope, there was nothing especially dreadful on the horizon. Atrocities could neither surprise nor long outrage anyone. The most worrisome trend during 1992 was the rise in the number of loyalist murders; by the year's end, their victim total would surpass that of the IRA for the first time. The grand total for the province of 84 was even with the addition of seven people killed outside the province, far less than the 149 Northern Ireland traffic deaths. Everyone involved rather tended to expect tomorrow to be somewhat like yesterday. Now the newspaper photographs of a devastated London financial district or the ruins of Lurgan, the reports of weekly sectarian murders, the revelation of judicial failures, the bombs on the London Underground or the Paras running loose were like the weather, bad but tolerable. Three years into the decade and the more changes there had been, the less the intractable structure of the Troubles had shifted.

Major was not willing to allow tomorrow to be like yesterday, actually intended to continue the Brooke initiative, which had been kept alive not simply as an election ploy but because the new Prime Minister felt there must be a political option. Thus, the Northern Secretary again approached the Northern parties on the need to renew talks. With Major in for five years and with the shadow of the sectarian killings over the province, the politicians were amenable to discussions. For seven weeks the Northern Secretary kept the four Northern Ireland parties talking about talks, again. Finally on Friday evening, June 12, after twelve straight hours of negotiations, all four Northern Ireland parties moved on to another stage, a meeting in London with Irish officials chaired by Sir Ninian Stephen to talk some more. There were to be later stages and ample opportunities to balk, to postpone the undesirable implications of any agreement, to find formulas to allow old positions to be adjusted. Even, as the British hoped, a formula for devolution could be structured. Still a return to normal, regional politics appeared far off, but as always, talking was a desirable alternative to conflict. Even the republicans showed evidence of restraint. On Sunday, June 21, at their annual gathering at Bodenstown, the oration by Jim Gibney from the executive of Sinn Féin, focused on politics and the willingness of the movement to suspend the campaign while the British were still present in Northern Ireland. And there was no Army Council statement read to the crowd—both signs of moderation that seemed more significant to republicans than to most political observers, who felt real progress would come from the formal talks that could lead to some sort of accommodation—and in November 1992 the talks collapsed again, if not forever.

Essentially, those doing the talking, the four major parties, agreed on certain matters, as did Dublin and London. Politics, not war; peace, not an armed struggle; stability, not violence. They agreed about wanting to erode the IRA's armed struggle and trying to prevent sectarian violence even if a divided society could not be made whole, a divided island one or the future reconstructed as the past. This could not be achieved by refusing to talk, so they agreed to talk: agreement through exhaustion. Devolution, however fashioned, appeared as the only political option possible to direct rule, no one's favorite option. If the obstacles could be evaded or eroded, a devolved assembly of some sort might be possible. If not, if the long process faltered or failed or if successful and devolution as in the past proved transient, nearly everyone in the summer of 1992 felt no harm was done in trying. And the crucial compromises and accommodation had yet to be made. So the talks would go on. The UDA would be banned. The moderates would urge peace and conciliation. The militants would have to adjust their agenda if nothing more. The cynics and realists would as always wait for one more failure. At worst there was hope of movement and at best a real chance that the beginning of the end had arrived.

22

The Troubles Without Final Conclusion: 1992

Everything is remembered. Nothing is forgotten.
V. I. Lenin

Prediction is very difficult, especially about the future.
Niels Bohr

History is something unpleasant that happens to other people, according to Arnold Toynbee, and for a generation Ireland has been involved in living, lethal history. For many generations the Irish had been engaged in fashioning their history to fit the present, to act as foundation for unfulfilled aspirations, as a tool. Much of Irish nationalist history, patriot history, was shaped as one long struggle between the oppressed and the empire, while the more scholarly saw Irish history largely as marginal to great events, as aspect of British history, a reflection of European currents, not special at all. The Troubles brought the Irish into interesting times, real history evolving on the streets and behind the closed doors of political exchange. "May you live in interesting times" is a Chinese curse and one now fully understood by most on the island, who have found history better read than made, better between covers than as rationale for the killing down the lane. Except for those few driven by dreams, true believers, most on the island would prefer that the times were normal, that crime was simple theft by ordinary decent criminals, that scandal was not about killing but about bishops or corruption.

Actually, of course, normal history ran its allotted course for much of the island. The Troubles did taint or touch everyone but not always and not often. The many, especially in the South, led everyday lives much of the time, engrossed in family quarrels and accomplishments, theater openings and football pool results; they sat exams, visited the pub and the family, ran the car and fretted about the children, commented on the weather. In the Republic life truly seemed quite conventional except for the few focused on subversion. Even the subversives did not really dominate daily life in the North. In fact, Northern Ireland was in many ways tranquil. According to European statistical studies, the province had little *but* terrorist crime, was otherwise remarkably law abiding. All the police and the army patrols, the intelligence agents, the complex technology that monitored armed dissent, the bizarre security buildings had arisen because of supervision. Without the political Troubles the province would have been little different from the peaceful Republic to the south. But these Troubles arose because irreconcilable aspirations could not be housed normally after 1968. When these aspirations could be ignored, the police and army ignored, the reports of incidents or the evidence of turmoil ignored, which was for most much of the time in 1982 or 1992, then the province seemed almost normal. The great violence of the seventies had passed.

There were plays and galleries, the zoo and the opera in Belfast, when the building was in shape. There were golf clubs and fishing waters and wild fowl and new restaurants good enough to be praised at length in the Dublin newspapers. A new Northern Ireland Tourist Office opened in Dublin during the summer of 1990—almost opposite the site of one of the Dublin bombs on Nassau Street— and elegant posters were distributed to catch the eye of visitors to the safe side of the border. Holidays were celebrated, birthdays that did not involve dead patriots or living legends, pints were lifted in pubs never bombed, milk reached the creamery and printouts the proper desk. Desano's and Rossi's sold ice cream and Derry football was the rage. All this was difficult to remember for those concerned with politics or focused on the Mayhew talks or the intentions of Provisional Sinn Féin. Most in the province wished politics gone, an old, awful story without a final chapter. Most hardly recognized the secondary benefits that came in the train of the Troubles or the psychological investment most had in the participants. Peace and quiet was advocated, but the voting patterns did not shift or the prejudices erode or the assumptions adjust to a new reality. And so the turmoil and the trouble continued.

Even the rich and isolated found that the violence changed their patterns of shopping, the shape of the landscape, the content of the evening news. The others without great resources who lived within a small arena kept to their own and out of harm's way; those without interests beyond the ledger, the lambing, or the comedies on television had to make an effort to shut out the conflict. And those close to the fault lines or living in the contested ghettos, whatever their resources or interests, could not even manage this. For them the Troubles were off the Falls or Shankill, down the road at the checkpoint, or in the rubble of the last bomb. Still, many refused to be dominated by the violence, by troubles not of their own making.

Many refused to be dominated by the conflict, not just everyday people but those dedicated to making the new—artists, writers, dramatists, and film producers. At the end of a generation of violence, at a conference on the arts in Belfast in the summer of 1990, foreign observers found that the most curious aspect of the Troubles was how determined many Irish artists were not to be so troubled. For many, art need not be shaped to terror's agenda or society's need. A poet need not offer solutions or a painter reconciliation. Those who sought the sound of political art, the clash of ideology, found mostly silence. The dog was not barking at gunmen or bigots. That was significant. No school of political art appeared, no Russian constructionists or Mexican muralists, no single poet became the voice of the Troubles, no single poem like Yeats's "Easter 1916" epitomized the era, no popular ballad or pop song lasted long. Some artists, of course, did do the Troubles, and all, even as they wrote ancient history or Irish plays, were shaped in some part by the Troubles.

There were, of course, real artifacts of the Troubles, some good, many transient, some awful. There was the new security architecture, not yet in the glossy monthly journals, the net-draped police stations, the monster towers stalking the borders, the estates designed for control; and there was the wry and vicious graffiti, constantly renewed, elaborated, updated on the walls. There were a great many transient efforts by locals and visitors to give form to the turmoil in bad novels, worse plays, crude pictures, and unsung ballads, but no recognizable school of the Troubles emerged in any field.

There were, in fact, one or two new directions, but no pearls were elaborated out of the grit of murder. In fact, as always, most involved in making things kept on making as before. A great many painters made pictures with no subject or only those traditional to the craft. Many poems were still about love, parents, sunsets, or the turning of the seasons. Conversely, much without visible contemporary political subjects had been enriched by the events, and some work, ostensibly on earlier matters or distant targets, was really very much about the present problem. Lots seemed to be made without a thought of gunmen or hunger strikers or emergency legislation. Along with the political plays there were the traditional dramas about family and sex and little hates; and songs shaped to teen dreams in tune with the beat out of film soundtracks and twelve-inch singles. There were great whirling paintings on religious themes on show across the gallery from reassembled junk painted garish. There were new piercing paintings not addressed to the issues of Ulster but, like the songs and the plays, to the traditions of the West.

Still, over a generation the Troubles had generated anguish expressed not just in overtly political verse or drama shaped for political purpose but also in all aspects of life. Many artists, poets especially but hardly alone, felt anguish that the killing was Irish, the quarrel so squalid; as John Hewitt wrote, "My Heritage Is Not Their Violence." It was, however, the heritage that, adjusted, had been used to rationalize violence, maintain the integrity of old quarrels. Some poets wrote to those quarrels, wrote in response to what would become for John Montague "an enormous seeping bloodstain," others would not bend at all, wrote on matters unforced by the zealots or the dreamers. On the island poetry still mattered, even beyond the educated, and a poet still had a real public. There are, given the numbers, a great many good Irish poets, new Irish poets for these times, no longer so young but still with a famous name to come outside the circle of many general readers: John Montague, Brendan Kennelly, Séamus Heaney, Derek Mahon, Paul Muldoon, Thomas Kinsella, Peter Fallon, Paul Durcan, Eavan Boland, and many others. Late and soon Ireland has bred poets and, if not another Yeats, who has? Some besides pedants and the family would read an ode and so odes on the Troubles were written and read and often dispatched to where good might be done: across the Irish Sea or to New York and beyond. There the literate can learn of a Belfast that demands that the poet inhabit "a world of sirens, bin-lids and bricked up windows." Many poets would not, and wrote to that effect or on other matters entirely. Some wrote in hopes of change although they had Auden on

Yeats before them: "Now Ireland has her madness and her weather still,/for poetry makes nothing happen? . . ."

Still there did remain the wishful, thinking that poetry might matter. It appeared, however, that such cunningly crafted correspondence and sullen art was mostly dispatched to dead letter boxes, there opened and read by academic clerks and the idly curious. The British, in any case, found no great revolutionary voice in Ireland, no Yeats to give pause, no O'Casey to conjure, no hero on the barricades, no cause that made English sense or Britain blush. Dirty wars have no heroes only victims. The gunman became cardboard thin, found in thrillers as terrorist, found in films as brutal pawn of sinister purpose. Che might make his way in *Evita* to Broadway but even Bobby Sands lacked star quality. Those who elevated him to hero, wrote his name on walls, and changed street signs admired the act, hated the authority, found little splendid in the boy who was limited by his talents to actor, not playwright. Ireland has had neither great poet to translate the great hatred to a learned room nor really a new heroic Cuchulainn, only the ravens of the dead, persistent, implacable.

In 1916 there was enough middle-class poetry by the leaders of the Rising to fill a thin anthology, but then there was Yeats as well. In the last generation the real and the complex poets took none of the involved to heart, wrote well for their own, and added the lines to the anthologies and pleasures of the readers.

> *He draws a helicopter after him*
> *His beret far below, a wine-red spot*
> *Swallowed by heathery patches and ling*
> *As he sweats up the slopes of Slieve Gullion*
> *With forty pounds of history on his back.*

And what more should one ask of Michael Longley or his paratrooper on reconnaissance? A lovely poem on a quiet moment in a war that has in Ireland grown up with the children. The man with the red beret hardly knows the country long and the poem never and neither can easily be fashioned to use for London or Dublin or Belfast. Whole anthologies, series of pamphlets, this magazine or that gallery, have focused on nothing else but the Troubles and others only on their own problems in making anything good at all.

Much is bad. And nearly all that has been badly written—bad thrillers, poor novels, patriot poems, butchered feature film scripts, hurried docudramas and historical novels—only uses the names and stereotypes for the usual purpose. The rebel ballads were quick and slight, new words to old tunes, and the new beat of pop wanted no rebel songs. Elsewhere on the screen or between pages the IRA gunman, a boy grown brutal, saved by a girl or killed near the end, is as ubiquitous as the guilty butler in the closed room. Violence has interpreters, explainers, those who would elaborate or transform, flawed alchemists; but mostly they are only those who exploit the Irish variant for immediate commercial or analytical need. So most that has been written is bad. This is always the case; but unlike Gresham's law, it does not drive out the good. Séamus Heaney has shaped Sophocles's *Philoctetes* to his needs as "The Cure at Troy," which addresses the Irish conflict with more hope than most:

Human beings suffer
They torture one another
They get hurt and get hard.
No poem or play or song
Can fully right a wrong
Inflicted and endured.

The innocent in jails
Beat on their bars together,
A hunger-striker's father
Stands in the graveyard dumb.
A police widow in veils
Faints at the funeral home.

History says, Don't hope
On this side of the grave.
But then, once in a lifetime
The longed-for tidal wave
Of justice can rise up,
And hope and history rhyme.

So hope for a great sea-change
On the far side of the revenge.
Believe that a further shore
Is reachable from here.
Believe in miracles
And cures and healing wells.

If hope and history are far, as yet, from one, there has still for art's sake, for history's sake and hope's, been much good written about the Troubles, written despite the Troubles and because of the Troubles. There has been nothing of course that would make the deaths worthwhile. Who would trade *Guernica* for a million Spaniards? Most of the poets and the novelists are not well known to the great public that is reached by streamer headlines and the evening news, who do not know as their own do Anne Devlin, Jennifer Johnston, or Benedict Kiely. A few are noted if not long remembered: the 1983 novel *Cal* by Bernard MacLaverty, which became a film, Benedict Kiely's *Proxopera*, which surely pleased no Provo. There are lots of good novels and many made on the mulch of the Troubles without need for banners and blood.

Poets write for their own and the novelists for the trade; but pop music is for the many, the very many, not profound but indicative, not for all time but now: *Sergeant Pepper's Lonely Hearts Club Band* speaks for much of a generation. And Ireland for a very small place by the mid-seventies began to loom large in popular music. Before then the era of the showbands was poignantly provincial, out of time. Irish pop took a fork. There was the traditional, across a spectrum of the old pub ballads well done, the Dubliners, the Clancy Brothers, the Wolfe Tones, who often sang rebel songs, republican songs or traditionally done in pubs like the

Chieftains and even Celtic rock. And there was Irish rock starting with Thin Lizzy focused on the traditional subjects of the era, flower power protest related to lost love and the evils of Vietnam and very rarely subjects more topical than alienation and acid. With the Boomtown Rats Irish rock moved big time in an international style beyond Christy Moore and Paul Brady, who mentioned the North, even beyond Van Morrison, so far the one Irish international star, to the very big time, to Ireland as the heart of pop rock, to U2 and the cover of *Time* magazine. There were the Pogues and Sinead O'Connor, the old Horslips and the new Hothouse Flowers, and the causes were those of the global electronic protest, the environment, the nuclear threat, American military power, racism, and the rest.

Northern Ireland even for the Irish was not inspiration, a place where the madmen lead the blind, not just cause mostly, just there, implacable and often hateful. On July 13, 1985, Bob Geldof's monster Wembley concert Live Aid, with satellites to the global village to aid the starving in Africa, displayed the new sensitivity and involvement of pop music and the world, and at the same time the Scot bigot George Seawright was marching his militant Protestant troops into the tunnel of Portadown to humiliate, once again, the Catholics, even if rocks had to be thrown at the RUC to do so. What was Live Aid to Portadown or Portadown to pop rock? Even the Northern Irish musicians were inclined to dream of an alternative Ulster. The real one was unpalatable, "police and priests, forty shades of green and sixty shades of red." For many there were no heroes, and no rebel songs, even and especially by U2 and especially about Bloody Sunday as commemorated by republicans. And, as always, there was the attraction of distant, and, to the innocent eye, less complex causes, new nestings for the wild geese of rock. It was apparently easier to scorn the Great Satan Reagan and his war machine, to stand against obvious evil or support obvious decency elsewhere than to make sense or music of the Troubles. So Bono of U2 probably has spent more time in Ethiopia and Central America than in Ulster under a blood-red sky and probably more wisely. All the Irish songs are sad and their war nasty. There are those musicians, however, concerned with that war: Ruefrex, Andy White (who went from Belfast to Cambridge and holds no brief for rebel gunmen), and Nigel Rolfe. They may be just names to those outside the trade, but are signs that for these troubles "Kevin Barry" or "Seán South of Garryowen" are not golden oldies but dangerous relics. The Pogues sing of the Birmingham Six as well as the drink on the ferry to Liverpool. Mostly rock spent the Troubles with other troubles, but one burden of a generation was an abiding suspicion of a present where the past pulls the trigger.

The plays, those directly or indirectly on the Troubles, were more frequent. They were produced in art centers—the Soho Poly Theatre Club or the Irish Arts Theater, at Symphony Space on New York's West Side, and at Off Broadway theaters. Sometimes they were quickly forgotten and sometimes revived. Many came and went to little notice, another exercise for a small festival or a theater in a basement, while others, even if not in grand arenas, were well received by the critics, who, gradually more knowledgeable, could contrast this treatment of the hunger strikers and Bobby Sands to a previous treatment of women prisoners in Armagh. And then there were the real plays in famous theaters attended not by the dedicated but by the public. Brian Friel wrote about the Troubles in *Making*

813

History, *Freedom of the City*, and *Translations*, and Stewart Parker and Séamus Finnegan wrote about them in *North* and the others. There is the wondrous title of Frank McGuinness's *Observe the Sons of Ulster Marching Towards the Somme* that appeared in 1985, and Graham Reid's *Remembrance* and Joe O'Byrne's *The Ghost of Saint Joan*. They all made plays that had a point, had relevance and had an audience, an audience in Ireland and for some in the West End or Off Broadway as well. Just performing, like Belfast's Black Taxi Community Theater, was often drama enough. The republican movement's plays and the patriotic historical plays written with the Troubles as foundation and the other works on paper often stayed unperformed, filed under fiction, not altogether forgotten. Some were shaped not so much by art as by political need, indignation, or hope of change. In Dublin in June 1990 there was a pageant along the Liffey for the Birmingham Six, candlelight and images on boats and the television teams present, a penny on the scales of British justice—better late than never. And there were twenty years filled with all those sincere plays done without money in church halls that sometimes, at best, appeared to scant audiences at the drama festivals, then disappeared, soon forgotten, like old posters, old protest marches, empty husks once hope had fled. Twenty years of unstaged plays read by the hopeful, read as far away as a stage hired by the hour in New York, or as nearby as the local pub, read to a few and forgotten, relics of indignation. There were the novels unread except by authors and the poems returned unpublished, the art confetti of the Troubles scattered in the air only to be washed away later in the day.

The films were different. Films have to be paid for, made for money, made for large audiences who seek entertainment. Five or ten million dollars is low budget. A million dollars scarcely buys film stock and rents equipment. Even a decent documentary costs an enormous sum if done from scratch. And no distributor wants home movies: Those are left for dedicated directors, who can take the results on a lecture or sell cuts to the networks. Money matters in films, determines if films are to be done at all. Someone must pay and the audience is to be entertained not enlightened.

The Troubles offer entertainment, stereotypes, and a stage set for vicarious violence. The films were rare and often tangential, a single scene from Ireland (a moment in the Irish *Eat the Peach*) or else the films were failures, the IRA as stock villain. In *Harry's Game* a good thriller by Gerald Seymour became a decent film—and had real Irish music by Clannad—with gunmen as nasty or dead or both. The IRA supplied stock bad guys except in *Hidden Agenda*, when the British establishment suffered—villains all, stereotypes each. Yet, more people saw *Hidden Agenda*, to the horror of official Britain, than anyone's official propaganda. More people read Leon Uris's *Trinity*, memorized by Bobby Sands and called out each night down the corridor of the H-Block, history as the prisoners would have it written, than have read all the works on the Troubles. A few films (*Exodus* or *Dr. Strangelove*) can make the complex simple, shift general opinion for decades but none has done so for Ireland as yet. By far the most successful has been the 1992 film *The Crying Game*, with a screenplay by Neil Jordan, who also directed. The film, a thriller involving the IRA, was a Golden Globe nominee and justifiably won a variety of other awards and nominations. Mostly, however, Ireland of the 35-mm. film has been backdrop. The green island is still inhabited on celluloid by the Quiet Man and Ryan's Daughter. The IRA gunman may again lurk in the cabinet of stereotypes but this was always so. Ireland and the Irish have not been transmuted yet by big films. Those who would make great films found no one to invest the money and those concerned with documentaries came away with less than had been hoped. It is very costly to do Ireland well without assurance of return.

Inexpensive images are best made with paint. Painters, however, like poets, were cautious about subjects dominating the medium.* Violence might provoke a sudden spurt of instant art, out of style, out of anger. Michael Farrell went first to Miss O'Murphy but then on to gentle wit and different subjects. Some (like Brian Bourke, Basil Blackshaw, Barrie Cooke, or Camille Souter) continued to paint what had always interested them. Louis le Brocquy does Beckett's head and even Robert Ballagh prefers to paint a portrait of Noel Browne as well as work for good causes. The regulars, the old men of Irish modern art, Patrick Collins or Tony O'Malley or F. E. William, do as they've always done. T. P. Flanagan made a set of sculptures out of Belfast, but for most the Troubles form no subject. The others kept to their last. Seán Scully went from thin stripes to international fame with thicker ones and Cecil King lived and died with the right angle. And enormous metal forms, small boxes, smears, and landscape had young advocates. Geometry or performance, postmodern approaches or the latest from Milan, the means of the real art world in New York or Cologne brought in glossy magazines and spread by word of mouth, mainly won the day among the young artists not just over means but also over the subject to be shaped. Abroad the Irish subject was filtered through distance and culture, shaped to special local needs. A California painter come to New York, Ann McCoy, concerned with Jung and symbols, in 1981 painted *Osiris* for the hunger striker Patsy O'Hara. There were over the years many works with Troubles titles and no more. Closer to the subject, Richard Hamilton, the father of English pop art, painted his *Citizen*, both subject and sentiment real, about the dirty protest in 1983 and later in 1989 painted *The Orange Man*—myth and politics, Hamilton's late concerns, made real. Many Irish painters continue to look elsewhere. Even the radicals were more inclined to repaint Goya and do Irish politics by marching, a form of Celtic performance art in any case. Brian O'Doherty in America, horrified by Bloody Sunday, became Patrick Ireland but kept on with white strings and fashions unrelated to Derry. Others dedicated paintings to the hunger strikes and painted as they had before.

The walls of graffiti, the gable ends, the lark ascending and the king on the white horse became symbols for others but never really generated international concern—and more than any other arts painting and sculpture are shaped by global concern; none seek to be an Irish painter only a famous one. So painters like poets were attracted to the great concerns, minimal sculpture or postmodern canvases. The Imperial War Museum Committee in London dispatched John Keane as an official artist for the Gulf War after seeing his Northern Irish work—art for history's sake. Ulster between peace and war has as yet no official artists. There and to the south, most artists kept to the concerns of the authorized

---

*The best and almost the only easily available treatment of art and the Troubles is Brian McAvera's *Art, Politics and Ireland* (Dublin: Open Air, n.d.).

styles but added gunmen in ski masks to neoexpressionist paintings where the driving force of the original was a new generation of German angst attenuated when transferred to Irish brushes. Such brushes were not actually inspired by the horrors of the North but rather by the swirling of the German paint. Some few Irish artists did at times take the Troubles as subject, do strange works on the bodies covered by newspaper in the Dublin streets after the bombs or, like Tom Bevan, assemblages out of the debris of turmoil. More conventionally Brian Maguire from Dublin and Jack Pakenham from Derry and the few other painters from Patrick Graham to Dermot Seymour added in the killings, took the image of the Troubles for the main subject. Yet feminism or the environment generate as much artistic concern. For the visual arts, the Troubles did not engender a fashion or a school; they only provided the odd and interesting singular response.

The new wave of conceptual art, politically correct, didactic installations so attractive in the trendy New York gallery world eager for popular causes and sensational presentations often found no Irish takers, where the old men painted as of old and the young looked to the Continent. In fact the most novel visual accomplishment of the Troubles were the eerie republican murals done by untrained hands seeking the realism of the religious calendar, the drama of the cartoon hero, making use of canned colors and real emotions. These republicans, unknown, unremembered, painted walls done not so much to be seen as to be done—Action painting. The message was in the doing. The style was soon set and rarely changed, one wall as faithful to the dream as the next. The act was sufficient, so the paintings were often abandoned or neglected almost as soon as they were finished. The sacrifice of making was sufficient, revealing briefly the garish guns in store-bought colors, the elongated martyrs and the poorly lettered battle cries, not at all art naïf, like the Protestants' King Billy, but art as act, art as the deed, leaving behind the painted traces like the scent of a secular mass completed.

The art of the times, the one medium that grasped the Troubles early on and exploited the possibilities to an enormous audience, was television.* These, said U2, are the times "when fact is fiction and TV is reality." Thus, television drama could not compete with Ulster reality. And with few exceptions the television of adventure series, macho made-for-the-medium films, or Irish westerns populated by central casting gunmen played only a small and peripheral role in either the industry or the conflict. One or two indifferent thrillers, a little group of sponsored teledramas on a divided society, a few specials with decent scripts— and the rest was for those who focused on the real. Documentary television, the nightly news, the investigatory film, the soft news beloved of the British industry (and therefore the almost satellite Irish RTE and RTE 2), especially the novel Channel Four but even the orthodox BBC, found a subject worthy of their mettle.

*The mass media's involvement with the Troubles engenders considerable analytical interest involving those concerned with communications, with propaganda, with civil liberties, and finally with the impact of terrorism on democratic societies. A selection of the response can be found in Bill Rolston (editor), *The Media and Northern Ireland: Covering the Troubles* (London: Macmillan, 1991), and for a comparative work, Joanne Wright, *Terrorist Propaganda: The Red Army Faction and the Provisional IRAS, 1968–1986* (New York: St. Martin's Press, 1990).

Ireland was easy, not too expensive, English-speaking, foreign, a quick one-day round-trip from London. There were guaranteed visuals, hate, and that special frisson that proximity to murder gives the journalist. There is nothing like the smell of cordite and the crump of a bomb around the corner to add significance to everyday film. By the time one lot had become blasé, caught Sinn Féin's act once too often, seen the same red eyes behind the UVF mask for a year, a new generation eager for the sharp end of the medium arrived. And there was always something, if not new, then better, something horrid out of Ireland: a new atrocity, a new crime, a new bomb: The names might change, though not often, and the script was hardly ever new. But like the circus, the similarity each year was enlivened by new acts and a novel costume on the old elephants.

The Troubles took place on television; for many they began with the footage of Gerry Fitt splattered with blood, and panned on through the images of the day, the jumble of bodies and the confusion of Bloody Sunday, the enormous flash and roar of a Belfast building bombed into the street on camera, the scattered, plastic-bagged bodies on a country lane, the British army patrols, the children with stones, and the Orange men marching. All went into the maw of the medium, viewed, recalled, stored, and rerun. The news. Television made the violence real—in the case of the two corporals killed at the funeral, made the violence seem truly real. Millions would grow to loathe Paisley on television, the voice of the lion in the zoo—and in Ulster the cages were often unlocked, adding spice to the taping. Millions would watch the reflective Gerry Adams, distinguished beard and quiet voice, explain the necessity for murder until his voice was shut down in outrage, speakers replaced by others for the state explaining their authorization for murder. Adams became far more interesting as a voice-over reading his apologies for bloody blunders as his lips moved soundlessly out of sync. Millions recognized the variations in paramilitary costumes displayed on television, could follow by television the hunger strikes from the bland Northern Ireland Office spokesmen in three-piece suits to the funerals in tiny country graveyards. Not everything was on television: not most of the killing, never the long, ruined lives, not the boredom of years in jail or the feel of pain, not even the tang of cordite, and certainly not a hint of the months spent over a clause in a housing act; but a great deal was on television. But the medium did not follow the cold news, the years without hands, the years with a ruined face or without a son or in a closed cell for an act long ago, forgotten. That was violence and turmoil taken cold, and the hot news ran on and on. Telly gave a great deal of hot news, some served cold and more than might have been expected: It was a television Troubles.

That Ireland, Ulster, often a few tiny enclaves, could become the arena for great issues and major causes. The major themes of the West as well as the private horrors of men meant that events in Pomeroy or Downpatrick could be elevated to the general—but on television this rarely was the case. The medium sought both novelty and sensation but also topicality: what had just happened, what was about to happen. There were looks back as the conflict stretched out—five years, ten years, and then twenty years of atrocity. But there was no special television wisdom or insight. The medium has been shaped to cover the moment, not probe the past, even the immediate past. And even contemporary probing proved troublesome for the involved, for all, even for the viewers. The intervention of the medium often became intimately involved in the problem, posing issues and probing where some felt quiet was most useful. The loyalists with a flawed case tended to suspect anyone with a camera or a question. The politicians at least had not been chosen by the cameras, so no television charismatics appeared. The young radicals at the beginning and then the republicans and soon most in the province, however, were intimate with the needs of the medium. After a bit, no one much blundered on camera as the medium was integrated into the events. And in London the government wanted understanding from the news, not trouble. No matter how timid, television that reflected the province gave trouble to those in London who only wanted to forget Ireland.

Thus the BBC's "Real Lives" that featured Gregory Campbell of the DUP and Martin McGuinness of Provisional Sinn Féin became an issue that the government seemingly mishandled by complaining about the focus on an IRA man. The Conservatives were angered that McGuinness, the IRA gunman, appeared not as a mad dog but as a politician, a charming and articulate husband and father. It was neither the first nor the last time the message of the medium cluttered the government's agenda. The appeals of the English bombers, the Maguires, the Guildford Four, the Birmingham Six, became a long-running serial of the eighties; there were the "Maguire Seven" and "Dear Sarah" and Chris Mullin interviewing the real bombers. Justice was hot, worthy of the medium; topicality was the rule. This was true even when the endless anniversaries turned up a moment for reflection, ten years on, twenty years on, a thousand dead, the next thousand. So most British and Irish television documentaries tended toward the crisis of the moment, Death on the Rock, loyalist corruption, or the IRA's next move. Often as not these half hours or hours became one with the problem, color tape manipulated or censored or revised, "Murder on the Rock" as important as the murder on the rock. Sometimes there was no need of revision or recrimination, no problem. In a miniseries of dutiful talking heads the former Northern secretaries came on, older, wiser it was assumed, reflective, often talking about events seemingly deep in the past. They seemed to find the past hard to recall in detail and those details not subject to retrospective change. The past was set as poured for we did the best we could. Like much of the television coverage it was not good enough but still a decent effort.

No one yet can be sure what effect the daily television ration of Northern Ireland and the spate of hour specials on the North has had on the viewers. Some caused trouble, added a penny on justice's scales for the accused bombers, did real harm to the corrupt Protestant paramilitaries; but the jury is out on whether Martin McGuinness as friendly family man is a plus for his party or a farce. And the often nightly presence of the Ulster voice—Paisley in full cry, the recriminations and insults, the funerals, the buildings tumbled in a cloud of smoke into the street under a camera's eye—what effect does all this have on viewers, on attitudes, on real politics? Abroad, the Troubles are a mix of images collected over the years, good for film at eleven on atrocity days but otherwise on hold. In the province the Troubles are the lead story that comes on each evening almost without fail. In the middle distance, in Dublin and London, where only news, often bad, and the occasional documentary reach an audience long reluctant for such news, the result is different, the impact sporadic but constant, all the players known, the plot followed, the series a regular—but to what effect? What has television wrought? In Texas or Sicily Ulster is a crisis, one with South Africa or Lebanon; in Strabane or Newry it is us, the daily dose; but in Cork and Coventry what has twenty years of coverage wrought?

Those most likely to tell what the medium has managed are those articulate in their certainties and focused on their own desires and devices. The polls in Britain and the indicators of opinion have for years demonstrated a distaste for Ireland, a latent British patriotism stirred by provocation and atrocity, but mostly an ennui and a desire for withdrawal. The polls and the election returns indicate that even the residue of nationalist sentiment in the Republic has been eroded by exposure to the cost of nostalgia. The participants in the conflict know that their acts can be exaggerated, their message made piercing if shaped to producer's needs; and so, they fine-tune their natural inclinations. Yet at the end the medium has not been a conduit constructed to corporate and national needs as much as another thread in the pattern. If Paisley appears on schedule so too do the BBC or RTE mobile teams. Television is integrated into the Troubles, not as observer but as regular participant, and at what cost and to whose advantage is by no means clear.

Nothing is very clear at the end. Art may elaborate and television may be part of the play but why has there been violence, conflict, a perpetual crisis at all? Who is at fault, what does it mean, and most of all, not what could have been done but what should have been done? There has been a generation of those who would seek to answer such questions: historians and social anthropologists, journalists with pretensions to grandeur and political scientists with rigorous tools of analysis. An entire cottage industry has arisen on the edge of the battlefield to report upon the results, to suggest modes of action, to seek roots and find appropriate accommodations.

John Whyte, professor of politics once at Queen's University Belfast and then University College Dublin until his early death in 1990, spent years collecting, sorting, and analyzing the product of that analytical industry. He had noted that seven thousand books and articles had been published and he undoubtedly overlooked some—and the spate continues.* It was possible for a while to cover the flood, though all sorts of contributions were unleashed at the beginning of the civil rights campaign. But gradually the tide washed away even the willing. It was like reality in that at first it was possible to know nearly everyone in a march and then most in the front row and finally there were too many marches and too many new faces and too much going on elsewhere—the particular dissolved into the general. And so with the analytical word. Very few can be intimate with all the immediate chaff, the newspapers, the magazines, the weeklies and monthlies and journals of opinion, the party papers and pamphlets, the tracts and appeals and long articles in the *Baltimore Sun* or *La Repubblica*. And how can one absorb the studies in social anthropology, contemporary history, political sociology, politi-

---

*Beyond the computerized bibliographies and major library catalogs available to most scholars, there is largely untouched a massive ephemeral literature of the Troubles, often in languages other than in English, usually by those deeply involved in their own politics. Thus the works published in Arabic or Swedish, much less Italian or Spanish, seldom figure largely in the bibliographies of the Troubles. And largely such work reveals more about the Arabs or the politics of Argentine radicals than about Irish matters.

cal economy, and political science, not to mention the studies in psychology? Most scholars and many readers are discipline-bound, many in one field hardly aware that survey research exists, or peace studies, or the law. Most disciplines are torn by ideologies, some exclusive. Fashions and methodologies and concerns of overwhelming importance to the involved shape the results. There is, hence, neither easy and absolute summation of the general investigation nor coherence in analysis.

There is instead an enormous literature that can and has produced bibliographies of bibliographies or, for those dedicated to the subject rather than the scope of the investigation, splendid chronologies, hundreds of pages to cover a year or so. Ireland has been an ideal subject, a small country wracked by great issues, a country with advanced statistics, an international language, a convenient arena filled with articulate combatants, local analytical talent, libraries of evidence, and willing subjects. It's true that there is still much not done; perfect knowledge has long been the analyst's dream. And everyone, it seems, has had a go, complete evidence or not. No discipline has been found wanting and often, it seems, few methodologies not deployed. The Troubles have been treated in the *British Journal of Sociology* and *World Politics*, in official histories and in the *Strathclyde Studies in Public Policy*. Seemingly few journals have been without an Irish article and few university courses taught without a bob or bow to the Troubles—a facet of political psychology, statistical analysis, contemporary history, and all the rest. And at the end, until now, there has been no summing up, no general text but rather the analysis of specials and a popular focus on the latest atrocity.

After any lecture, at the conclusion of any dissertation, the audience, general or specialized, wants to know not only what is going to happen but also who has been to blame and what should be done. Hardly anyone feels that the Troubles have been a blessing, whatever the secondary benefits to some. Nearly everyone feels, then, that there is fault to be allotted. And the optimistic assumed there is even a proper course to be taken.

If Whyte's four general topics of approach were taken (the religious, economic, political, and psychological aspects), not a consensus but a grouping around assumptions and conclusions would be available in each. But none of these answer what most people want to know: Why in Ireland, who is at fault, what will happen, and what can be done? Even the questions asked with deadly regularity to any assumed expert present the general assumptions that such queries should, if they do not, have answers. The answers given by the specialists, often as an aside to the particular task at hand, are as various and contradictory as the assumptions and programs of the involved. There is no consensus. The same highly detailed, rich evidence plowed by two honest and sincere seekers produces contradictory crops. Even when special pleading, faulty work, trendy methodologies, history written backward, and research planned from assumed results, when all the ills of any analysis are discarded, there is no consensus.

This in itself indicates the special and general nature of Ireland: The reality can be heard going off in the street but the nature of the event remains elusive. Ireland and so the Irish are special children of a particularly persuasive history that in large part shapes the present and divides the province, the island, and the isles. Everyone agrees on history. Nearly every general work begins at a distant beginning. The first lesson learned by each innocent journalist arriving at Derry's walls or the Sinn Féin office on the Falls is that he or she watches an old quarrel. Almost everyone agrees with the hard facts, the dates of the atrocities and the statistics of discrimination and the acres under cultivation. After that it becomes a matter of interpretations. These can be lumped and categorized as part of the problem: the nationalist variants and the Unionists, the neo-Marxists and those concerned with internal conflict, the spectrum of psychological cause and the many varieties of political explanation. Each of the groups involved, the British establishment and the Irish, the Northern nationalists and the Ulster loyalists, the republicans now and the republicans then, have their own history, their own data not to be denied, and their own interpretation, which is satisfactory to no other but substance to the converted. There is something for everyone and someone to buy it.

That this diversity remains after a generation and remains true for many disinterested investigators indicates that the Irish Troubles surely contain a nexus of factors not easily teased into convenient categories. In some primitive societies war and marriage are one ceremony. Ireland in analysis like Ireland in real life is simultaneously open to variant explanations. Many such explanations, even and particularly by scholars, are argued backward, so that future chaos is avoided only by accepting present policy based in theory on disinterested analysis. Many arrive with closed minds: Class analysis the only road to the future, or consensus is a mere matter of integrating education or applying the wisdom of the social sciences as practiced by the wise. Some explanations may be more compelling than others, but this has not so far dissuaded the others' advocates. Some explanations may be of little help to those who seek policy options—a belief in original sin may, indeed, explain much of the Troubles, but like fear of the mob, a useful factor is shaping constitutions, it is of no great use in determining what should be done now. That there has been no solution is not assurance that an accommodation cannot be found.

In fact the repeated question—What could have been done differently?—so beloved of the journalist, so much a matter of despair for the specialists, does not have an easy answer. Given the same characters, the limitations of the arena, the forces at play, even those key moments look difficult to fine-tune to the advantage of the player. Key moments for republicans are obviously not necessarily the same for the loyalists. What is needed is a single moment about which it could be said, "If only," and then history would have flowed differently. If Caesar had lived, if Pickett had not been sent on his charge at Gettysburg, if Napoleon had died early, then all admit that the immediate morrow would have been different. What most people want in posing the question is now an alternative Ulster, the existing child of recent history being too difficult.

One of the foci of concern has always been the loyalist strike in 1974 that ended Sunningdale and all its wondrously complex accommodations that in some form have been the most popular options ever since. The Anglo-Irish Agreement is simply a rewritten Irish dimension as the Assembly was simply an attenuated form of the power sharing. If the Northern Ireland Office and Rees had been blessed with second sight, could they have broken the strike on the first day or soon, flooded the key points with police, deployed the army more effectively, used the media to advantage? What could have happened? What if? In hindsight, Rees says no, but then he would say that. In hindsight many in the British Tory establishment feel this way a key moment and Wilson missed it, but then they would. The nationalists and republicans always felt more could be done, but then they would. Just as the unionists would and did feel that nothing could have deterred a risen Protestant people. In retrospect the power of what happened grows—the strike did work, history did happen, musing over options is very much a spectator sport but one with a lasting fascination. What could have happened to change the course of events on the first day of the loyalist strike? What?

Rees had a telling point: You cannot intimidate a people into desired behavior or not with the weapons that he had to deploy or was willing to deploy. So it comes down to whether the unionist community driven to the river would drink. The loyalist militants said not and so did not. In the case of the Anglo-Irish Agreement, one facet of Sunningdale was put in place beyond their reach. London decided that the loyalists, the unionists, the Protestants would not resort to force to oppose what was symbolic rather than punitive. And they did not. Did this mean that in 1974 for one day London and the NIO had a chance to intimidate the loyalists? The year 1974 was a long way back from 1985, and then that one day was not then seen as so important. And the key aspect of power sharing is voluntary sharing, so British intimidation then would simply mean more trouble later and so ruin any accommodation: One cannot, as Rees said, force cooperation within the United Kingdom. And once the spectator goes further back to seek points where the strike could have been prevented, it is like a chess player asking to go back four moves: Reality vanishes.

And if 1974 were not a turning point, then where does one look for an act that might change history? Many have proposed a single point in the past to approach with perfect knowledge and there adjust seamless history. Mostly, however, the direction of history in retrospect looks remarkably consistent with past practice. The civil rights people deployed a perfect weapon, given everyone's nature in 1968–69, to highly predictable results. The Provisionals in 1970–71 did what was natural and convenient to their assumptions to largely predictable results. The loyalist defenders responded to danger, as had always been their want after 1972, undesired but predictable by those who knew the province. Certainly the British establishment maintained a remarkably predictable course as did British public opinion. Over a generation in Irish matters the British have responded with a remarkable consistency, changing little and adjusting not at all since the old ways have returned new returns in secondary benefits. Over the long haul mostly what happened indicated deep trends that might have symbolic movements—Gerry Fitt's bloody head, Bloody Sunday, Sunningdale—but it was all of a piece: if not one head or one accommodation, then another similar.

What might have changed the pattern-predictable was not a single act, an assassination or the arrival of a new lion, no Cleopatra's nose a bit longer that would have put off the Roman Caesars, but an incremental change in attitudes, a willingness each day to shift a little. It was on this basis that so much conflict-conciliation work, cross-cultural programs, reconciliation movements succeeded, but only in places and in parts never in the province as a whole, where the deep currents continued. On a local level change could be seen—at this school, during this meeting, with these people. Stretched to the Peace People over the whole six counties, euphoria did not last, just as protest marches after August 1969 did not matter once provocation had unleashed a return to basic responses that had been hidden, not atrophied by time.

Incremental change works *in* Northern Ireland but at the same time fails to work *for* all Northern Ireland. And so, too, with most explanations, true at one level—not even for one set of facts, true for this moment or that, true where attention is focused and yet often contradicted at the same place, at the same time: ambivalent analysis. No one knows what step will be taken or not taken and asking only moves the moment of decision, not the contradictory assumptions. Many types of Irish ambiguity can be found simply on examination. Until the door is opened and the man on the run seeks shelter, the householder does not know the response—asked, he finally does know, and asked later, he does not know why. In Ireland over the generation of the Troubles reality was rich and contradictory, amenable to varying explanations, denying few—a wondrously vague microscope slide. Peer down at the problem and various realities come and go with the slight turn of the knob. Most turn quickly to their favorite setting, many take the image first seen. No one knows what to make of mutually contradictory images that come and go with the focus.

In one sense, then, Ireland in 1967 had evolved very slowly over the previous century, isolated, parochial, shattered by violence only briefly and at no enormous cost between 1916 and 1923. The old ways, attitudes, and assumptions lingered on year after year, only gradually eroded by the wonders of a pluralistic, consumer culture that after 1945 swallowed up western Europe except at the fringes. Just as the combination of the imperial opportunity and the gradual end of all grievances in the nineteenth century tranquilized the island, so too did the new opiates, television and trendy but disposable objects, decent health and welfare entitlements, macadam roads for the school bus, do so in the twentieth. In 1916 British blunders permitted the few to organize rebellion while the nationalist population endured: The great Irish nationalist virtue is persistence, no matter how great the opposition. Once the republicans had gained the outward signs of partial independence—and the Northern loyalists evidence of their danger—the slow absorption of the special and particular continued. The Irish diaspora almost disappeared. Americans like Ronald Reagan scarcely knew their roots and others in Britain could serve the Crown after a generation or so as English in all but blood. On the island the Irish-Irish were going, the language, on a government-supplied life support system, was comatose, and the republicans were relegated to dingy offices on Gardiner Place. The Orange state was obsolete and once adjusted by decent moderates would be acceptable for the foreseeable future. The loyalist killers were dying off, sullen, sour, unneeded—Malvern Street murder by marginal rejects. Soon Ireland would be a comfortable island with frugality at risk and the correction of the divisions a matter for the morrow. Ireland was easing into a present where the old dreams, Orange or Green, would have too few takers to matter. The present would be an array of consumer choices, commercial airs and graces, decency borrowed from the needs of the market. Ireland would move into Europe, integrate into the new West, become one with the postindustrial world of mass culture—a thousand shades of lipstick, designer cat food, still mass on Sunday but four hours of television indoctrination each day, no mysterious or atavistic faiths. The world is less real than certain segments of the electromagnetic spectrum. The future is available on the never-never in living color, available for all, and in 1967 was almost available for the Irish.

Then a 1960s generation more urgent than the times chose protest over flower power, just barely out of step with the times, a bit passé, a bit parochial; they marched instead of listening, provoked those not yet corrupted by things or general good but loyal to the perceived lessons of history. All then acted as was their wont. The Orangemen, equally parochial, resisted every inch, the republicans, marching to their own trumpets, moved to the second stage of provocation against the British, and the British delayed and compromised, made a muddle papered with articulate explanations and government papers into a policy. In Dublin the first sign of change, that the simple political tunes could not again be sung to advantage, was the acceptance at the top that the Republic had no power and after a year or so no interest in sacrificing. This had always been true. The republicans had even made a virtue of lacking power. Death could be more important than life. Not losing could be more important than winning. In protracted armed struggles these were essential for rebels without prospects. In fact all the philosophical assumptions of a century of armed struggles came out of or could be found in the Irish experience—the few were frantic for means to act and so seized upon their own inabilities. Dublin, then, gradually accepted that Ireland was not only a divided island but also a divided society and to incorporate the latter into the former was beyond power and desire. As the Orangemen said, six into twenty-six won't go; nor, felt Dublin, should it. This new Dublin in fact was truly representative of the Irish-Irish, who had never shown inclination to sacrifice. The majority still wanted unity but without cost and without complication. Most feared violence and the six counties were violent. The Unionists, most loyalists, too were fearful of the street and the mob. The orthodox Unionists in the OUP grew increasingly conventional if not in language. Paisley and the DUP represented fundamentalist loyalists who would tolerate killing, speak treason, but stay home and call it a general strike. Doing nothing seemed to mean that the center in London and Belfast and Dublin was soft. So the Irish idealists, the romantics and violent, the frantic and convinced, all the true believers, North and South, many with limited capacities and narrow vision, could act freely. They did. The advice that it is better to do evil than to do nothing had no moderate takers. The quiet stayed quiet, proper, spoke to themselves and the decent. Good men did not so much do nothing as limit their good works to their own while maintaining the same public face. The small changes in attitudes and assumptions that could play a real and effective part day by day in small groups disappeared out in the provincial ocean, where killer fish lurked. Until the small adjustments changed the temperature of the waters, the others, ever voracious, made the running.

The certain, the believers, took advantage of the powers granted the faithful, the toleration of their own, the predictable behavior of the others, and the freedoms of an open society to cause trouble, to assure the new Troubles. And hearts grew brutal. Generations had been fed on comforting lies, shaped by institutionalized injustice and authorized bigotry. This divided but shared past produced by 1970 the final wave of denial. The dream of the dangerous had shape only in the past, a past created in a patriot history that judged easily and thus offered solutions to be sewn on banners. It was a history formed with comforting legends, black villains and old grievances, a history made of sectarian tracts, folklore, and pub ballads. And it was a history that also contained facts and justifiable fears. These facts and fears were used to rationalize acts (called solutions) that destroyed order.

These solutions, so compelling and comforting to the convinced, had the legitimacy of the dead: The Fenians had won the right to wage war and those who signed the Great Ulster Covenant in 1912 the right to oppose the Crown in the Crown's name. There were no private armies, no lone gunmen, but rather those with differing credentials of legitimacy, rarely recognized but by the other faithful. Northern Ireland became a stage for conflicting perceptions, self-denying ordinances, contradictory legitimacies, all armed, all dangerous, and all offering the committed not simply future triumph but today's victory over history. This was a real and enormous psychological compensation, even while starving to death—particularly while starving to death. And most wondrous of all, in a pedestrian society glutted on consumption, these legitimations offered the opportunity to serve, to sacrifice, to act, to become someone, to become part of that history that had for generations been the only ethnic asset of peoples denied, threatened, isolated, humiliated, or shamed. To act meant to be and this was not a secondary benefit. No wonder the corner boy wore dark glasses and a beret and gave the BBC a few minutes of his time as commandant or commander; no wonder that misused, this alchemy produced Dr. Death, a marginal man twisted in the times and feared by all if respected by none. No wonder that the revolution has turned what others consider secondary benefits into primary ones. The logic found in London or New York, Oxford or Stanford, does not run in the Divis Flats or Portadown. In Northern Ireland risen peoples have received from history, as promised, a role offering rewards that their own admire and will not deny, and so a life lived with passionate intensity.

The decent nationalists, the decent Unionists even in opposition, provide the agar for the bacilli of the faithful. They have done the usual, the amenable, the normal thing, have kept not silent but too still too long. Everyone decent in fact emerges as witness to the cost of convenience. Everyday doing nothing overt, doing only what was natural not what was right or needed or difficult, could not and did not cancel the passion of the faithful, even when they were few or dreadful or brutal. In time the costs came due. All the decent had done was to follow the devices and desires of their own heart, fed on the comfortable old prejudices and perceptions. They never denied the real grievances and rarely appeared among their own as daily witness for moderation. Even with an act of will the transformation of perception is difficult and so decency is the last resort of moderation. The temperate deplore rather than destroy, criticize rather than act, stay home and off the streets, for they only feel the grievances of others, not their own. If sufficiently torn by guilt, not rare in the West if odd in Ireland, they may be transformed into advocates, often more shrill than the harmed. And why should Northern Irish moderates feel guilt over the small gifts of a brutal history? And how does one come into the street among mobs and madmen? What effective path is there for the proper and decent?

The British had long assumed that not only were they decent but that the deployment of the state's power (no need for the establishment to march or the middle class to conspire) would see that the center held. The threat was the Irish, an unsavory lot. The British find pleasure in their bias (which they seldom recognize), in their remaining displays of power and glory, in their righteousness and assumptions, so piercingly expressed by Margaret Thatcher. They are forgiving of those they have wronged, those who grieve over old, unhappy, far-off things and battles long ago, and are quite unaware that they secretly scorn the Irish they hardly know, those Celts who will not be them. Anyway, despite all that there were no other options. And what else could Britain do? More force would deny the foundations of the nation's system and less would assure further local violence. More concessions merely provoke those others who would rather deny than receive. Withdrawal would guarantee chaos, the degree depending upon the desires of the analyst, but certainly in the past the aegis of Britain imposed has assured violence removed. The Arabs and the Jews, the Greeks and the Turks, these Nigerians and those, the Moslems and the Hindus, all ran amok, so why not the Irish Catholics and the Ulster Protestants? So staying is the worst choice except for all the others, and returns at small cost great gains. The Irish have not won over British history, still need tutelage, still are insufficiently like us to trust alone; and so this Ulster duty grants imperial returns in assurance and reinforced pride. Why go when everyone received this reward for merely tolerating the revolting Irish as a horrid example? And why go when the cost is acceptable?

For Dublin the dream now is that the North could stay silent in the margins as it did for so long--unknown, mysterious, unredeemed, and forgotten but on patriot holidays. Now the prospect of the Black North as a Green province appalls all but the few faithful republicans and the romantics. Everyone can still be for Irish unity but a unity that, as all insist, is achieved without violence, a proviso that assures not only there will be no unity but also no need for sacrifice, so improbable is the conversion of the loyalists. So that tattered assumption, unity without violence, is the last illusion.

Once Britain and partition were the causes of every Irish ill. It has been painful to accept that this is not so. Now, at nearly as great a cost, the Dublin establishment may recognize that they are the problem, not the solution. The Republic, saved from Europe's chaos during a century of isolation, has failed to provide for all the Irish, failed to exploit opportunity and instead catered to only those who remain, failed to be an island worthy of either saints or scholars. Dublin's Ireland is small, mean, provincial, inefficient, home in the nineties to a new and limited elite personified by a Taoiseach's grandiose office that long overlooked decaying Georgian houses let go by a system that caters to the needs of the successful. The new men in politics and out have done well, raised others' taxes and bought yachts.

Their state has penalized the poor, the old, and those not readily fitted into the system, sent them abroad or stashed them in bleak housing estates on the far urban edges. This failed society cannot cope with its own much less with the chaos of the North; it cannot admit, yet, the failures of the present. Frugal comfort is denied to many, Ireland denied to many, an Ireland rebuilt as monument to first-generation greed and simple taste for glitter and expensive sheen. Why not? The Irish have been on short rations for centuries. Certainly the Ireland they have shaped is less of a green and pleasant land than the myths of the diaspora would suggest.

Perhaps, rather, this first elite, drawn from the *petite* bourgeoisie, without interest in thrift, is at fault in seeking entitlement for the winners and not opportunity for the Irish. The Orangemen and the republicans are as one in agreeing that the Republic has as little to offer now as Stormont once did: grand for the beneficiaries, adequate for the majority, but unjust and humiliating for the remainder. At least in the Republic emigration is a safety valve for the boiler. It gives the government time. And with this time, the new Irish direction, stripped almost clean of the old republican illusions, may yet cope. If not, then the Troubles may yet involve more than the six counties, more than an increase in armed robbery and the encouragement of armed subversion and violent crime. While the British have changed hardly at all on Irish matters (for Ireland hardly matters), the Irish have changed a great deal, nowhere more than in the Republic. The establishment may find taste and compassion and the necessary disciplined skills to keep their Republic free of frantic dreams from the six counties.

Those other Irish in the six counties, the Catholics and the Protestants, have both found their lodestars, Dublin and London, to be leaden failures. The loyalists have no loyalty to the AIA and no hope in London's long-term attraction to secondary psychological benefits from a marginal province. The Unionists will talk about an accommodation, may even move forward on the matter, but not with any enthusiasm. The Catholics, despite the Dublin affection for the SDLP, recognize that the agreement has no reality, and is a formula to satisfy those who want no real responsibility. Hume may have brought it back to Northern Ireland as triumph but life grumbles on, made more difficult partly because one of the great changes that has occurred in a generation is that the Catholics no longer feel inferior or the Protestants feel innately superior. On the evidence the Catholics have destroyed Stormont, created a secret army, imposed change, and become, if not rich and powerful, at least regularized; and so the Protestants feel not only threatened but denied as well. Northern Irish society is divided differently in ways no one can understand.

The confident nationalists have, for the moment, no place to go—the Irish Republic may be the end point of history but history has a long way to run. So far the IRA is slowing down history by the continued devotion to old goals and old means and old assumptions. A new model IRA that could intimidate all the loyalists and raise the cost beyond paying for the British seems unlikely and for most undesirable. So the IRA will stay, the believers, rejected by their own, elected by themselves, faithful and in the service of death (for did not the ravens defeat Cuchulainn?). Defeat can, as in the past, be transmuted into a foundation for the pursuit of the Republic. Yet many Catholic nationalists, certainly those who vote for the SDLP and refuse Sinn Féin, for different reasons than London and Dublin, want the same short-term goals—very little, devolution perhaps, peace and quiet, an end to the killing, all the same things the moderate Unionists want but at the expense of those moderate Unionists. And the Unionists do not want to share any more benefits, any future power, any Irish dimension no matter how feeble, because this would further erode their dignity. They, as much as the moderate nationalists, have to fear their militants, who still kill out of habit and resentment. The majority has gradually recognized that the minority is not quite as inferior as they thought. Still church-bound, the minority is not as feckless and foolish, and is far more deadly, than was imagined except by those who shaped the secret army as an ogre and bad dreams as politics. Those most aware are those most threatened, the loyalists at the fault lines, the poor Orange gunmen, often frantic that history seems to be dribbling away to the other side of the great divide in Ulster society.

The mutual toleration of the divided society then, adjusted for the Troubles, eased by the withdrawal into enclaves, offers hope, but not much, and certainly not hope for any formula that will change hearts or for any accommodation that will return the present to the past. Mutual toleration is a poor base for any structure that will certainly be attacked by the violent and supported only from a distance. The decay of moderate commitment to old sureties has not, then, resulted in a new willingness to sacrifice for decency. And it is hard to see the results of little, daily changes in attitudes. The totems of the tribe are still dominant, as every election indicates. Democratic accommodations have been achieved over a great many centuries of incremental change, accelerated by appropriate violence—the violence in Northern Ireland so far has been history's veto on moderation, accommodation, even agreement between nearly equals.

And those waging violence still have the running. The republicans are easier to dissect. In sum, as long as there is an overt British presence, as long as Northern Ireland is a province under the Union Jack, there will be those to pursue an armed struggle; this is both faith and reasoned politics. And given the givens in Ireland, these republican faithful will not be too few to maintain trouble at a distressingly high level for the involved. Since Britain does not want to act as long as the costs are low and the IRA still lacks the skill and talents to raise the cost, the future is most likely to see the present acceptable level of violence continued until a major player can move. The hope of republicans that the loyalists will move toward an Irish solution rather than toward the gun in defense of a domination now visibly dead has been as disappointed as that of the moderates who hope the virulent Orangemen will accept accommodation—power sharing and an end to sectarian murder.

Murder pays the Protestant paramilitaries rewards they cannot find elsewhere. If the threat to Orange society were greater, if the British withdrew or the IRA could escalate their capacity, then such sectarian murder would not serve as defense and could be countered by the IRA. As a traditional Protestant response, sectarian murder works to Protestant advantage only if there is no real war, only if the present stalemate continues. If the province goes up for grabs, hardly likely but not impossible, what matters most of all is that Protestant violence does not escalate. In a real civil war the UDR and RUC have the military skills to protect their own if not to slaughter all others, but what will really matter is not the number of guns but the Protestant assumptions of the threat. If in the unlikely event that London decides to withdraw, the majority will decide to stay or go without reference to capacity to harm but with an estimate of the odds on persisting. Any signs of disengagement will simply start the deciding on an individual basis—those with the capacity may decide to take their practice or their assets to Sussex or Midlothian. In Algeria the odds shifted, the Arabs and the FLN were perceived by the French not just as winners but as alien winners set to create an Algeria better deserted. This could, indeed, happen to the Protestants, not necessarily on a Tuesday morning but in changed conditions over the years. Over time a Protestant withdrawal without any violence and without much notice has in fact happened in the twenty-six counties. This has little to do with the killing capacity and a great deal to do with the mysterious ethnic psyche of the majority. While the republicans can continue saying no for the foreseeable future, the loyalists, under certain circumstances, cannot—on the island they are a minority and within the United Kingdom they are an even smaller minority. In the final analysis they, unlike the IRA, need outside help. By holding firm, by giving not an inch, the equilibrium can be maintained, if not local dominance. Deserted and alone the cohesion might go and loyalty to themselves prove insufficient. Certainly the IRA believes this the case and so too do many moderate nationalists. Few except the IRA, however, want to find out if this is the case.

In the end the Troubles came because Ireland was improperly synchronized; it was no one's fault and not easy to predict. The old values had not eroded and the new opportunities had not attracted. The time only offered means to act in congenial ways. It is easy to insist that the debased old dreams should be denied and yesterday's banners rolled and stacked, too easy when those banners led parades that ended in office for those in the front row, marchers who found the old words a comfort and their use no cost at all. The traditional rituals and rites seemed so natural, so easy. These ways offered great benefits, Orange and Green, often unavowed, often psychological, not economic or political, often to those denied elsewhere by the existing organization of society and the island. So there were always new and frantic believers suddenly converted to the past as the means into the future. Those who sought to act on events, to make history to history's patterns, had the legitimization of the past as authority. They needed only to rationalize on occasion, kill to the sound of trumpets. Elsewhere others were emboldened by Lenin's or Mao's example, by Allah's word or the people's need. The enemy was killed by the book. But in Ireland he was killed to history's tune and the blare of those unseen trumpets, audible always to the faithful.

In Ireland legitimacy was won from history, a legacy and a clearly defined responsibility. Behind the delirium of the brave and the bloody body on the front hall floor lay history's legacy that sent out men with guns and dreams to kill for a faith, broad or narrow, often mean, sometimes grand but always real. And the center did hold, reformed from London, reinforced by London, tolerated or advocated by Dublin, manned by locals at great risk. The center could not erode the ancient legitimacies that inspired the gunmen, or could it find the proper balance between war and peace. The best that could be managed was a series of formulas, from 1969's reform of Stormont through all sorts of proffered options to the Anglo-Irish Agreement in 1985. It was an accommodation that could not factor in the most militant dreams and failed in practice to secure even the minimum demands of the moderates on both sides of the divide. After that there was nothing to do but talk about talking. So Brooke and Mayhew talked. And so everyone had to accept second best, direct rule and an occupying army, an armed campaign that could not win, a divided island that reflected a divided society, six counties no longer just Protestant but still defended with a gun. Perhaps talking would produce a devolution, a stronger center, but the gun could not easily be talked out of Irish politics. So the Troubles went on and on and on. No one was to blame and everyone was at fault.

There seems no easy end. All those possible solutions exist but there is not a consensus on one and so there is no solution. The dedicated want not accommodation but the faith made whole. They gather in bleak rooms with hard chairs, a smell of rising damp, old Irish cigarettes, and Jeyes cleaning fluid, a room lit by burned amber light from small bulbs. There is always a small, suspicious crowd at the door, the filter to keep out the dangerous, the authorities, the spy. Such close, ill-lit, sour rooms are hatching pens for subversion—bleak, dour, deadly rooms with a fatal attraction for the idealists. On both sides of the divide, men and women in Ireland have been sitting for all of this century in those upstairs rooms across from second-run cinemas listening to grievances that have been unsolvable for decades.

If they don't come down the stairs into the back lane from this particular hall, this particular night, they may still be found at the rear door of a gritty country pub waiting for the others to bring the gear. They are both real and stereotypes. They have waited inside with a pint, men with crumpled, country clothes, heavy boots, red hands, and sunburned necks, with the eyes of gulls, unwavering, without remorse. These four or five taciturn men, farmers by trade, killers by choice or by necessity, will be dropped off afterward at home and one will call in a communiqué the next morning. It will be the morning after the four battered down a reinforced door with a sledge and burst into the small front hall of an isolated house. The driver will have waited down the lane, the motor ticking over, the exhaust a thin gray trace on a cold night, the windshield clean with the swish and swipe of the wipers. At the house the others will have raged up the stairs, smashed the locked door into a bedroom, and shot, over and over to be sure, one of them. The victim will have died, still dazed, next to his screaming wife, with the children howling through the wall and the chained dogs barking at murder done. And the killers will have gone, and the dead man will be buried in a day or two, to recriminations and pleas for reconciliation and rituals of despair. Buried in the rain or on an incredibly bright summer's day with a golden one-time sun, but buried in shock and horror—any weather for grief.

For any of the killings, there will be some ritual condemnations, and some bureaucratic responses as police file the evidence and the files are marked, and there will be some responses involving the victims. On an everyday level there will be organizations like the Catholic Silent Too Long to complain, and support groups to help, and petitions to seek protection, but the dead stay dead and the gunmen of destiny wait for the next time. For a generation they always have, as normal as the rain and never as rare as the one sunny summer day. For as far forward as one can see, there will be those who must walk in harm's way, dressed in the Queen's uniform or hidden in mufti but paid to put the killers away—or down.

And just as surely the British soldier who reaches out to touch the full whiskey bottle on the ledge will be added to the butcher's bill. And so, too, will the RUC constable who this once neglects to run the mirror under the new Volvo, locked all night in the garage and so surely safe, and leaves a wife to hear the dreadful crump that turns man and motor into blackened ruins, broken, burned, and then the explosion reverberating through the quiet street and the dogs barking on and on. These were paid for the risks, their survivors paid for their loss—no one need be a constable or enlist in the Royal Marines. Those in the secret armies are paid in a different coin, more valuable but less easy to weigh, and they too end up buried amid the grief of many who would have preferred not to be defended, not to have paid for a Republic that has come no closer. Those, the defenders and patriot dead, at least chose the risks.

The middle-aged woman, eyes wide and dazed, fingers opening and closing, her new dress splashed with blood, sitting on the curb in the middle of smashed jelly jars, did not choose to be near the bomb. The man-child in a flash jacket twisted across the wheel of the stolen car, the windshield pocked with high-intensity rounds, his eyes wide, bubbles of blood on his lips, too stunned to cry, was the one caught while joyriding. He knew there was danger but never for him—the teen dream of excitement at the roadblock had turned into a lung punctured, a body turned into a bag of blood. The clerk covered with white plaster dust cut with tears, the old man shaken by a random brick between his shoulders, the wife too frightened to cry, left on the floor with the cat after the killers have gone, finding the man at home; the lad who gets up in the morning with stubs for hands—these are the real faces of an acceptable level of violence. So are the ladies on sticks, the young men with petrol-broiled faces, the mothers who never come out of the bedroom, and the kids who sniff glue and ride their stolen car into the future past the roadblocks. It is not pretty in real life, puddled blood smells and so do fresh bodies, sweet faces above ripped necks, bones broken with hammers. And behind it are the blank eyes of practiced killers, assets who pull a trigger as a light switch, on and off and another ruin bagged in plastic and left out with the bins, another done for Ireland. And on the other side there is the ambush, killing by the numbers, or the high received when a single round thumps home in a target seen eerie green in a night sight. War can still be romantic, especially on the telly and at a distance. It is exhilarating to be shot at without effect, run past the roadblock, toss a stone, watch the town center burn; but it is not romantic to walk blind for all time or to hobble on stiff legs or to attend the wife's funeral with the children in hand. There is no acceptable face of a dirty, secret war.

Irish bodies, some under folded flags, many with only futile flowers, are still carried by shattered families under leaden gray skies to be buried by the anguished while the others watch with cool, dispassionate eyes, awaiting their turn in their plot of Ireland. Irish bodies, ruined or riddled, will be carried down Belfast streets and Tyrone lanes for the foreseeable future. Some who come to the island go home to be buried, go home in army coffins to no bit of Irish ground at all but only to a mention in the regimental annals and a note in the newspapers. The newspapers have newer typography, odd fonts, better pictures, new men writing the same old stories. Last time Brighton and before that Harrods and the Tower and this time Number 10 Downing Street and next time certain and maybe Irish luck will run and maybe not; it has not yet.

There are still at any moment men with guns standing by a tree, sitting in an upstairs bedroom or a parked car, waiting to kill for their cause. There are still many to die on the island because of one cause or another, at the hands of one army or another. Some will die swiftly, filled with Irish beer and Irish bullets, and some slowly, life dribbling away in a ditch on a soft day or in prison on a life sentence, no remission, no mercy. All these are the discards of the patriot game, soldiers or unlucky children, scattered pieces beside the board that now indicates not endgame but perpetual stalemate. There are still players, killers, rebel gunmen and loyalists who still believe. There are in Fermanagh and Down, on the dark Shankill or in the Bogside of Derry, men who risk their lives and families to see that the Queen's writ runs, the gunmen come a cropper; some have uniforms and others do not, only titles or sporadic stipends. The years pass and the Royal Victoria Hospital becomes renowned as a trauma center—the best place in the world to be shot is the Lower Falls—and Belfast becomes famous for intricate reconstructive knee surgery, the spin-off benefit of paramilitary discipline. Local security responses have grown cunning and few houses in risky zones can be forcefully entered without a sledge hammer and no one notices the gates into the Belfast city center when Christmas shopping, or the cleared zones along the roads near the border. Time makes all the artifacts of the Troubles conventional.

The Troubles go on, mostly just out of sight, around the corner marked "Up the Provos" or in the terraced house with the Union Jack. They go on beyond the wall topped with barbed wire, and in the pale faces leaving the cinema, one a killer and the others not. It goes on mostly inside the minds of men, the hardest arena for winning, the hardest to find, the last to yield to reason or to force, to concede to fair play or to admit resolved grievance. These Irish minds and even some in London have been shaped by Anglo-Irish history written by prophets and the faithful. Much in a generation has changed, patriot attitudes in the Republic, Protestant assurance in the North, the cost of change and the acceptable price of doing nothing. Much has not changed at all.

The IRA Army Council meets every two weeks or so, as it has for longer than the members care to remember, as it will next month and the month after. The republican faith is a clearly defined responsibility, shaped by history, real and imagined, by the sacrifice of the lost, by the cost already inflicted on the enemy and on the others, on the innocent and on the whole island. The loyalists remain, despite the muddle and the failures, resolute in defense of an assurance that after all these years is not so eroded as to be worth discarding; even after all the murder the determination to persist is gathered around the loyal like an invisible cloak, stained with blood but regal yet in their perception. But it is not stained with dragon's blood, for the loyalists read no minds, not even their own. It is a garment stitched up with fear and pretensions, not very useful to prevent the ague brought by the winds of change but still cover for killing. The British, whatever the persuasion, are still there, acolytes of Perfidious Albion, righteous, arrogant, assured, standing firm at the end of long centuries of certification read as history across the Irish Sea. And across the border, the other Irish stand on the edge of events that all profoundly hope will grow no closer, a wiser, wary Irish no longer so sure about history's inevitable direction, not even sure enough to hope for a much better day: A tomorrow like yesterday will do.

Ireland has always found hope in history not in the future. The national trait has been to persist, not, despite the republicans, to rebel, to change history. Even and especially William of Orange said, "It is not necessary to hope in order to persevere." It is enough to say no, no not in defiance but with guile. Those who control the past determine any future. Those prophets who whisper fearful change are denied. History is so written backward, a chronicle of winners as losers and losers as just and so the narrative's winners after all. History and reality exist only in men's minds. The future is another day, a gray day without the glory and the demands of the patriot past. The future is only prologue to the faith triumphant, triumphant over grievance, triumphant at the end of a long dialectic, the clash of opposites that this last time will let justice win and history end. And if there can be no victory, there yet can be revenge. History in Ireland has yet no end, no tomorrow, no date with hope, no final author. The war, such as it is, is not one that makes men grown fond of it. The last romantic gunman is long dead, in the grave or a cell. H-Block holds only pragmatists with bad luck. No one goes into the UVF or the IRA to troop the colors but to kill. No one believes revolution is magnificent. There is neither glory nor much hope in this war. Not in Ireland. Not yet. No further shore is in sight, none imagined by most. There are benefits but this is always so with wars and with any peace. Those advantages of the Troubles in Ireland are now conventions, the normal, not special gifts from triggermen.

So the months pass and the years and the Troubles remain; aberration has changed into institution. In the combat zone there are still bombs, and there are often bodies at the end of the lane. The army patrol with rifles in a Belfast cradle at the school crossing are no different from the lamppost to the transient child. The columns with black borders in the newspapers, the straggling parade behind a piper, theirs, ours, someone's, down the next street, the slow grind of the RUC Land Rover with aerials and guns, the annual commemoration for this horror or that triumph, the whole lot is like the weather, a given, the public face of the Troubles. And out of sight, some can hear the sound of trumpets that turn murder into politics, the past into the future, and the future into prologue. Only the faithful can hear those trumpets. On the island, still mostly peaceful, there are after a generation of Troubles still pilgrims from the past who would yet, despite all, because of all, sacrifice their own, themselves, and the others for a vision denied the pragmatic. Ireland still houses fantasies and faithful, lethal dreamers. The Troubles still turn up rough, hard men and women, not all without uniform, not all in mean rooms, some with school ties or easy manners, but all with simple answers to Irish riddles. There are those, then, who possess the absolute truth and are tinged with the smell of cordite. To the sound of unheard trumpets they have made violence conventional and the Irish Troubles all but permanent. There are years to go and butcher's bills still to pay. The many break stones of faith and the heart is still cold. Yeats knew. The Irish know. Now we all know.

> *And the trumpets all are burst,*
> *And the trombone, cried he,*
> *The trumpet and trombone,*
> *And cocked a malicious eye,*
> *But time runs on, runs on.*

And so it does run on, a generation, years of Troubles, no end suggested, the turmoil institutionalized and the killing acceptable. The Irish have not been condemned to the Troubles because they did not remember their past but because they have not yet adjusted it to present circumstances, have not been able to organize beyond the tribe or those who can be touched. So far accommodation by exhaustion has not occurred, nor has compelling power been deployed, nor has enormous harm been done. It is such a small, lovely island and they are such a grand people, and it is such a compelling, horrid war, every estate and all the ideas of the West twisted and at odds—a small, nasty, persistent, tolerable, and so awful war. There is trouble without resolution or revolution, trouble without sufficient cost to inspire effective response. Perhaps only the Irish could give us neither peace nor war nor promise, could so persist that the intolerable becomes an institution. Everyone is to blame, none emerge untainted. All smell of righteousness ruined. No one, the wise or the wicked, the scholars or the saints, have found an exit. Great issues have been fought out in a small compass but not to resolution nor to exhaustion. And so for the Irish Troubles a generation is gone and a century is running out, but not Irish persistence. The Irish, whatever else, are indomitable.

Sources, an Essay

Although every contemporary crisis generates an enormous literature, a wealth of conventional primary and secondary sources as well as the still available testimony of many of the involved, often in conjunction with extensive and available photographic, tape, and film coverage, there is much that does not emerge. Historians wrote and rewrote the history of World War II without knowing that the Allied generals could read vital German code traffic with the enigma device. And some documents, some secrets, may never appear. Lost letters of Napoleon still emerge and recently the files in Moscow and Warsaw.

Even after twenty-five or fifty years, many governments are chary about granting access to previously classified documentation. Private files are often closed or lost or destroyed. By then the attrition rate for witnesses has reduced recourse to those present at the event. Ultimately, the analyst, the scholar, will be left with the available public or private literature, special collections, and the work of previous scholars—the traditional ore of the historian. In the case of the Irish Troubles twenty-five years have elapsed since the first inklings of crisis and a few relevant government documents are appearing. Some papers in both London and Belfast are now at least in part open, although the more interesting documents, dealing with security matters, are likely to remain closed or inaccessible for some time. The covert activities of states often remain covert as long as the state controls the paper. Still, many of the involved are willing to give interviews, the primary source to substitute for the lack of official documentation and the often scanty private papers. As for some of the interviews, they look more relevant in the citation than in content. UVF gunmen or IRA commanders—or even famous politicians—may talk for the record but censor their comments. And, too, the private papers of many of the involved, the manuscripts, letters, diaries, proposals, and notes that are already being used by scholars, have yet to indicate substantial change in the accepted plain tale of events. To a degree some of the relevant Northern Irish past never reaches paper, and this is especially true of illicit covert organizations that keep few if any records. The paucity of official records and private documentation has never deterred the bold, the curious, the determined, the ambitious or committed—rather, the reverse. The material, available sources, as always, increase with time just as the living record dies off. There is never an ideal time to begin.

On Irish matters the years since 1967 have seen waves of investigation by all sorts and all disciplines despite the difficulties in the arena, despite the paucity of some sources, and despite the classical problems of contemporary analysis of perspective and access. Thus, for the Irish Troubles it is the best of times and the worst of times in the matter of sources: some official documentation, enormous amounts of paper, and most of the relevant actors.

A conventional list of sources includes, then, two general levels. The first level contains (1) primary evidence from direct interviews, (2) unpublished primary material, official, organizational, and private, and (3) published primary material, governmental, organization, and personal, including interviews. The second level is the entire spectrum of secondary work that fills the conventional library: contemporary newspapers and periodicals, books and articles, whole journals, chapters, and pamphlets. A generation ago a detailed analysis of the sources for the entire history of Ireland after the 1916–22 period would have made a short article. Now considerable shelving and a computer is needed.

Before 1967, the Irish, divided in the South by the agony of the civil war and in the North by religion, largely refrained from investigating the immediate past. There was some academic interest in Ireland as a new state but from abroad. There was none in Ireland. Thus, in my work on the IRA, the published sources, including some material before 1922, could be limited to a few pages. Even matters like election results had to be hunted down in old newspapers. There was no analysis, no history, often no secondary literature at all even about the most conventional matters. The contemporary Troubles, on the other hand, have generated so many published sources that there are separately published bibliographies, always out of date by the time published: For example, *A Social Science Bibliography of Northern Ireland, 1945–1983,* compiled by Bill Rolston, Mike Tomlinson, Liam O'Dowd, Bob Miller, and Jim Smyth (Belfast: Queen's University, 1983), contains 270 pages counting the index and lists five thousand items. For Ireland in general there is the even more substantial *Modern Ireland: A Bibliography on Politics, Planning, Research and Development* (Westport, Conn.: Greenwood, 1981), compiled by Michael Owen Shannon and now, like the social science bibliography, a decade out of date. As with the Troubles, there never seems to be a stopping point, an end to violence or to the books.

I tried to keep up with the emerging published literature after 1969 with a series of articles in the *Journal of Politics* and *Éire-Ireland,* republished in *The Gun in Politics: An Analysis of Irish Political Conflict, 1916–1986* (New Brunswick: Transaction, 1987), until exhaustion and editorial patience intervened. There is thus no real hope of detailing all the sources available. That would be another book and one with a short half-life, another drama without a final act. Even contemporary works on one aspect of the era have extensive bibliographies: books, interviews, pamphlets, dissertations, and documents.

One collection of invaluable sources has been several volumes of chronologies.

This means that the plain tale of events can, at least until the compiler's patience lags, be followed. The most useful and most famous work, drawn out of the Belfast journal *Fortnight,* a prime general source for the Troubles (see Robert Bell et al., *Troubled Times: Fortnight Magazine and the Troubles in Northern Ireland, 1970–1991,* published in 1991 by Blackstaff in Beflast), has been the three volumes of Richard Deutsch and Vivien Magowan, *Northern Ireland 1968–1973, Volume 1 (1968–1971), Volume II (1972–1973),* and *Volume III (1974)* (Belfast: Blackstaff, 1973, 1974, 1975). *Fortnight* continues to publish a chronology, and in the United States there is the *NINS* (Northern Ireland News Service), published weekly in Albany, New York. There are two interesting short chronologies. One is Michael Hall's *20 Years: A Concise Chronology of Events in Northern Ireland from 1968–1988* (Belfast: Island Publications, 1988), which often draws on local sources but, more important, indicates Belfast priorities. The view from Dublin with a quite different vision of island events is *Ireland: The Past Twenty Years, 1967–1986* (Dublin: Institute of Public Administration, 1986), edited by Jim O'Donnell. It is even possible to follow the more lasting comments in the appropriate pages of Conor O'Clery's *Phrases Make History Here: A Century of Irish Political Quotations* (Dublin: O'Brien, 1986), or follow the quotations at least up to 1986.

There is not a complete chronology, a Facts on File for the Troubles, nor certainly a single overarching work. The crucial data guide, however, has been *Northern Ireland: A Political Directory* by W. D. Flackes and Sydney Elliott, published by Blackstaff in Belfast in various editions beginning in 1980. There is a brief chronology, but the crucial section is the dictionary of people and organizations and even events supplemented all in one handy volume with election and security statistics, pocket histories, biographies, and details often found no place else. It is a first source for the curious, the student, the journalists, any investigator, all those who would sensibly avoid the enormous primary and secondary literature, who do not want a day-to-day account, who need facts, not historical narrative.

There has been until now no single history any more than there is a complete bibliography, nor can there be a section on sources that does more than indicate the nature of the available sources. Those who attempted to put the Troubles down on paper, even those who were engaged in the simple chronology of events, found that there never was a formal or satisfactory stopping place. Even the chronologies grew dated, new facts about old troubles emerged, and there was never an end in sight. Nearly everyone assumed that sooner or later there would be an end. In the interim it was possible to concentrate on events with beginnings and endings, to examine the evidence to date by varying methodologies for varying disciplinary purpose. There were special foci of concern: the laws relevant to civil liberties or the impact of the events on the media. There was thus no shortage of work that could be done, that was done, using an enormous mass of printed material and a great number of potential sources. All these sources, all the work was indicative of the part that paper as well as the gun plays in politics. The published usually became grist to the provincial political mills.

Even a focus of one discipline or one facet of the Troubles indicates an extensive literature and usually one still expanding. No bibliography that is not itself a book can do justice to the entire spectrum of material or indicate more than the reality of some ten thousand titles. John Whyte's estimate in his *Interpreting Northern Ireland*, of seven thousand serious items did not, as noted, include much outside English or much of the analytical paper that drifts off the edge of any great crisis. The figure does indicate that Ireland of the Troubles engendered a massive conventional literature of primary sources and secondary comment. The more sensible approach is to indicate here what kind of material is at hand or still hidden, to say where analysts have searched, to present some selections from those involved to give an indication of the foundations on which this particular text rests.

INTERVIEWS

Since my original and continuing analytical interest in Irish matters was focused on the contemporary IRA, a secret army that kept few records and published mostly for the committed, much of my time on the island has been spent talking to the involved, those within the republican movement, those responsible for opposing it, those concerned with its politics, and those with no interest in such matters at all. This Irish concern led to interviews formal and informal in my generation of travels. One never knew when an Irish connection would appear. The IRA had and has friends in strange places. The Irish are to be found nearly everywhere, especially everywhere. And everywhere Ireland was news, even on the edge of Eritrea or in the seminar rooms of Harvard. These distant arenas often reveal the activities of those involved abroad: at the United Nations, in American bars, in Beirut or with radical European parties, at international security conferences, during debates in Washington or London or among the leadership of the Palestine Liberation Organization. At times one could find Bobby Sands's name or the initials *IRA* scrawled on very distant walls. Even the agents of Ulster loyalists appeared in unexpected places from Libya to Canada or negotiating with South Africans in Paris. There have been a generation of interviews, many informal, some unexpected, all useful. Some individuals were sought out specially, formally—special trips to London to talk to a selection of those officials involved ranging from Merlyn Rees at Westminster to Sir Frank Cooper in his Rothschild office, a large office bare of any Irish memento. As the years passed, few in London or elsewhere found the Irish Troubles a pleasant recollection. There were interviews with exiles and the retired, in America or Germany or Italy, and with observers and scholars. There were thousands of Irish hours with or without notes taken. Those still involved were always eager to talk if permitted, but as time passed few others wanted to be troubled with the Troubles.

It is for the persistent, even those without connections, quite possible to talk with nearly anyone from the Irish Taoiseach to a UVF commander, to ask nearly anything and often to be told more than might be expected. So far and hardly unexpectedly, those presently or recently engaged in the dirty war, those involved in intelligence matters, those open to prosecution or to disgrace, have remained reticent and will probably continue to do so. All historians want to know everything until they discover matters better left hidden. And many of the secrets of the Troubles are intriguing but not especially important, particularly as time passes.

As time passes, even many of these hidden bits become public, appear in court cases, are revealed by aging gunmen, become club gossip in London or appear in memoirs. Mostly the motivations of the individuals and groups involved, the resources used, the reasons for deployment or the aspirations of the concerned can be deduced. The details of security matters, the intricacies of the IRA and especially the loyalist paramilitaries, some policy decisions by the responsible remain hidden. And much that is hidden is not really vital although always useful.

The only means to discover the hidden that may be of use well before any prospect of publication or public revelation is through interviews. Even the gunmen and the civil servant grant interviews—at times, often for their own purposes, but always adding to the vast accumulation of data. At times these interviews have been taped and printed by some scholars; at other times they can be cited but not reproduced, and often they serve only as resonances and redundancies—give fuller orchestration to the past. In my case tape recorders have never seemed wise and my notes are of use only to me, not to others. Yet the greatest single source for the text has been the accumulation of data arising from a generation of interviews, ten thousand hours of conversation.

PRIMARY SOURCES

Unpublished. One of the changes of the age is the gradual disappearance of private correspondence. Governments may still slide forward or backward on paper, generate miles and miles of records, often collated, filed, indexed, available for later, but the really interesting decisions, as always, are private but seldom, as in the past, noted in letters or kept in diaries. In the case of the Troubles the letters and notes and relevant documents with the aid of the specialist become published memoirs rather than the published letters, and the investigator often finds few private papers to use as sources. There are still private papers that can be used and cited, but rarely are voluminous records kept—and even more rarely by those new to organizational needs and political mobilization. The telephone calls may not be recorded. The fax, of course, may, if the records are kept, compensate. Conversations are often not noted or recorded or, alas, remembered.

The Troubles are in this matter especially troublesome because many of the involved have not been by nature record keepers but doers, simple soldiers, inarticulate gunmen, marchers and protesters, politicians, those without interest in the written record. Many of the politicians are, and properly so, provincial, without great interest in history's judgment or historians' needs. A wise actor on the scene might know that historians as well as he or she make history and keep tidy papers for future use, but not most members of the Stormont Assembly or the Dáil, not most strike leaders or paramilitaries. Possession of IRA paper, after all, is a prison offense and no wise gunman keeps a diary when even, as has often been the case, an address book alone can be deadly. In fact, the most interesting unpublished papers have been the communications smuggled out of Long Kesh, especially during the hunger strikes, tiny, tiny print on wrinkled toilet tissue available at times through Sinn Féin for certain writers.

Some archives will probably never be opened; most churches, some parties, many organizations and businesses will keep their secrets secret, their paper processes private. When surveying Irish archival sources, I found that many organizations assumed their records to be of no historical interest but closed in any case and others, especially churches, intended as always to keep themselves to themselves and so found any inquiry odd. Still, as always, there will be available, probably sooner rather than later, an enormous unpublished literature, letters and documents privately held, notebooks. And from this and recollection already have come the memoirs of many of the concerned. In time all that government and organizational paper will be opened to view. For now the concerned finds the correspondent easier to reach than the correspondence, but even now there are those private individuals whose letters over the years have reported on the immediate scene, whose papers are useful, whose records are conventional sources. Those who have already published often have additions and corrections to add or may be able to focus on other aspects of their past.

It is especially with the Irish, if not the British, in personal contact, not on paper, that real communication often occurs: Upon retirement Taoiseach Seán Lemass had no personal papers, unlike de Valera, who, with a keen sense of how history is made, saw that his were used to produce an authorized biography and then carefully ordered and put on file. Mostly private political papers have been used as always, first by the owner to produce the book, then by scholars looking into special subjects, and finally opened to the public in an appropriate setting. So far primary, unprinted documentation is rarely opened and what is available—often for the asking in private cases—is rarely consulted. The most interesting material is closed and the rest is easily ignored because of the wealth of printed matter.

Published. First come the governments. The various printing offices in Dublin, Belfast, and London continue to produce parliamentary debates, reports, special papers, committee findings, all the documentation vital to those concerned with public administration, housing, the social services, the unemployment rate in Strabane, or the number of voters in Bannside constituency. Some of these government publications have generated literally millions of words of comment—the Widgery Tribunal report on Bloody Sunday and the Anglo-Irish Agreement in particular. This has been true with other events as well. The shooting of six unarmed Catholic men, five alleged IRA gunmen, and one innocent transient in Armagh in August 1982 appeared to be carefully planned ambushes that led to the Stalker inquiry and all its subsequent ramifications. The killing of the three IRA volunteers on Gibraltar inspired libraries of material, reports, judicial records, comments, parliamentary debates, and comment from other capitals, from foreign organizations, public and private. Even a list of special reports on the more general aspects of the Northern Ireland Troubles published by Her Majesty's Stationery Offices in London and Belfast would run on for pages—all those now forgotten contentious documents, the Hunt report or the Parker report, the Green Paper, or even the text of the Forum. There are as well British government reports on all aspects of Northern Ireland economic and social life, in some cases no more detailed than would be those reports focused on Leeds or Scotland but usually read with more care by more customers. The material most useful can, as is usually the case, be found in the more specific and often more contentious reports and in the debates from 1968 on held at Westminster, in the various devolved chambers at Stormont, and in the Dáil, if rarely the Seanad in Dublin. Elsewhere other governments' concern with Irish matters has been limited, often limited to law enforcement authorities or the statements of the Prime Minister. The Irish problem has never played a great role at the United Nations, in part due to British skills, in part to the changing perception of Dublin, and in part because amid the global chaos, turmoil, and wars of the last generation the island has been marginal to great interests or to major trends. Still, Paisley brought Ulster into the European parliament, and deputies and representatives in distant capitals often comment on Irish matters even, if mostly, the Irish remain innocent of the fact.

What the island has been, however, is visible, spectacular, and a media target, so that while governments beyond those involved have published little, the crisis has induced much organizational interest on the part of civil libertarians, by those groups involved in peace research or community relations or radical revolution or whatever distant special interest that finds in Ireland a new arena. Mostly those so involved have published. All the political parties, groups, splinters, conglomerates, and schismatics do not really exist without proclamations, proceedings, party newspapers, published papers, and regular minutes. Even a small party like those descended from the Official IRA—Official Sinn Féin, Sinn Féin—the Workers Party, the Irish Republican Socialist Party, the Workers Party and now in 1992 the Democratic Left—have left a thick paper trail, sufficient in fact that Philip Beresford found enough material up to the year 1974 to write a Ph.D. dissertation at the University of Exeter in 1979.

All of this party publication varies enormously in content, of course, but also in style and impact: some elegant, slick, annuals with photographs, some run off on a mimeograph in fifty copies, distributed on a few streets and mostly lost by the next day if it were not for the Linenhall Library repository of even the most ephemeral scrap. In fact, some newsletters may exist only in typed copies as prison newspapers have or a single handwritten issue. Much of this may have narrow interest, few readers, and limited impact, but may be vital for an analyst. Some local history can be very local, making Ciarán De Baróid's *Ballymurphy and the Irish War* (Dublin: Aisling, 1989) seem vast in scope. Some organizations deeply engaged in matters arising from the Troubles may attract only the specialist's eye—trauma surgeons who specialize in knee injuries or small-arms experts circulating results from the field.

A typical example might be the Political Vetting of Community Work Working Group's *The Political Vetting of Community Work in Northern Ireland* (Belfast: Northern Ireland Council for Voluntary Action, October 1990), a publication that arose from the concern of some that the British government was exceeding reasonable bounds in deciding which community organizations were assisting paramilitary organizations—in this case the denial of a grant to the Irish language group Glór na nGael. This concern led to a general conference and on to the publication, slick, bright red cover, small circulation even in Ireland and almost none abroad. It is a useful insight for some future analyst but presently one more of the thousands upon thousands of organizational documents on the shelves. Some of these "documents" are not so primary, slip over into commentary, are secondary, not part of the problem but part of the analysis. It is easy enough to slot the report of the New Ireland Forum as documentary (government funded, government published) or even the Éire Nua program of Provisional Sinn Féin (party funded, party printed), but not easy when dealing with the hundreds of small groups—often, one suspects, parties of one—that distribute their proceedings. Wherever on the shelves such primary work is placed, there much space will be required.

Far more conventional are the published works of those involved in the politics of the Troubles, the individuals, not the organizations. These range from the childhood memoirs of Gerry Adams of the Provisional Sinn Féin, *Falls Memories* (Dingle [County Kerry]: Brandon, 1982), to Merlyn Rees' highly detailed account of his involvement, *Northern Ireland: A Personal Perspective* (London: Methuen, 1985). The returns in memoirs are mixed, nothing from Paisley but a work by his daughter Rhonda Paisley, *Ian Paisley, My Father* (Basingstoke [England]: Marshall Pickering, 1988), a woman who has, of course, entered politics herself. There is nothing from Jack Lynch or Charles Haughey, except published speeches, and perhaps now that the latter is retired, there's the promise of something to come. There is already a long autobiography by Garret FitzGerald. Generally the responsible Irish politicians or, if retired, statesmen in Dublin have found that the less written about the North, the better. In Northern Ireland Terence O'Neill offered *The Autobiography of Terence O'Neill, Prime Minister of Northern Ireland 1963–1969* (London: Hart Davis, 1972) to go with his earlier *Ulster at the Crossroads* (London: Faber and Faber, 1969), though neither was especially revealing in contrast to James Callaghan's or even Jim Prior's memoirs. Not all the Northern Secretaries or relevant British officials have produced: Ireland was not a major matter for most, as a glance through the index of any of the several biographies of Margaret Thatcher would indicate. Enoch Powell cared, came to Northern Ireland and so from Ireland to Westminster as representative, spoke on Irish matters and so published, but few others cared or spoke or published.

Still there are lots of memoirs. The prize would still go to one of the first on the scene, Bernadette Devlin with her *The Price of My Soul* (New York: Alfred A. Knopf, 1969), never out of print and still read by those with minimal Irish interests. A quite different work, one for the specialists, is the most useful *Working at Stormont* (Dublin: Institute of Public Administration, 1978) by John A. Oliver, whose recollections of forty years in the Northern Irish civil service will long serve scholars. In some areas of Northern politics scholars have been ill-served by published memoirs. Generally, the unionists, particularly the militant loyalists and especially the loyalist paramilitaries, have not shown any great concern with publishing beyond authorizing proclamations and issuing party statements. In fact, Northern politicians, almost all still engaged in the pursuit of power, have rarely published, unlike the civil rights leaders who often matured into analysts or scholars. Paddy Devlin surprised all with two short books on his recollections, but for the most part the fall of Stormont, the rise of the SDLP, or the career of John Hume have been left to others. Generally there has been more—or at least as much, given the Irish concern with the word—than might have been expected from those responsible for the law, for those engaged in politics, and for those who never expected careers that would be worth a memoir.

For those concerned with order, often with war, the problems of security have tended to limit publication—Ireland is not an old war and this is as true for the paramilitaries as it is for retired colonels. Seán Mac Stiofáin's *Revolutionary in Ireland* (Edinburgh: Cremonesi, 1975) is as interesting for what it does not contain as for any IRA revelations—details, yes, republican analysis, yes, revelations, indications of dissent, errors, no. Many of the latter—the errors as well as the gossip for a brief period in 1971–72—can be found in Maria Maguire's *To Take Up Arms* (New York: Viking Press, 1973), which is based on her time with the Provisional movement. Mostly, like most active rebels, the gunmen wait until the shooting is over to publish.

There are those observers who have come, often, usually, innocently, to Northern Ireland and after what seemed adequate exposure withdrawn to report on their time amid the Troubles. Most, if not all, transform the time into history, such as Kevin Kelley with *The Longest War* (London: Zed Books, 1984), or the product of their discipline, such as Frank Burton with *The Politics of Legitimacy: Struggles in a Belfast Community* (London: Routledge and Kegan Paul, 1978), secondary, analytical sources all, but a few write their memoirs, a genre not unlike travel books, stylists abroad in strange places, the curious among the exotic. In fact, Ireland's premier travel writer, Dervla Murphy, has written *A Place Apart* (London: Murray, 1978) to go with Ethiopia from a mule and by cycle to India. Two examples of work by those less prepared for Northern Ireland can be found in two texts by Americans: Sally Belfrage's *The Crack: A Belfast Year* (London: Deutsch, 1987) indicates more of the author's exposure to the novelty of the working class than about Belfast, and John Conroy's *War as a Way of Life: A Belfast Diary* (London: Heinemann, 1987), without analytical pretensions or artistic aspirations, only curiosity and opportunity, produces, as intended, an extended journalist's account of his year in Belfast.

Mostly such primary sources are more primary than source. Some of the best accounts by those involved cannot easily be accounted in a list of sources. The elusive give interviews, often taped, that then appear for varying purposes. Cahal Goulding's views may be found in Italian in an ephemeral tract of the radical left, or those of the Protestant paramilitaries may emerge translated into German or Spanish and published in newspapers or magazines seldom read by those most concerned with Ireland. And few concerned with Ireland are aware that there is a European literature of sorts that at times can be mined for useful nuggets. It hardly seems worthwhile, in any case, worrying about interviews in Swedish works when the involved are willing to talk in English to most of the interested.

Many of those who turn their time in Ireland into secondary analysis include large chunks of verbatim interviews, thanks to the tape recorder, in the final result. These memoirs at once removed are often contained in curious cartons. For example, the ethnographic exploration in Allen Feldman's *Formations of Violence: The Narrative of the Body and Political Terror in Northern Ireland* (Chicago: University of Chicago Press, 1991) may be of interest to those concerned with anthropology but has generated simple confusion in the many focusing solely on the Irish Troubles and so mine the work for the material contained in Feldman's fascinating interviews. And for varying purposes a great many direct interviews have been done and can be found by the keen who may be uninterested in first use but intent instead on their own purpose.

SECONDARY SOURCES

Those with the most general purpose want a text that simply gives a narrative history: what happened, to whom, perhaps why. The first printed sources for the contemporary historians are thus the newspapers of the day, a narrative chronology of the moment that others will later winnow down and print. For Ireland there are essentially the great newspapers of record that detail all, the more general newspapers of the time, dailies or weeklies, that indicate the nature of the news being disseminated, and the product of the involved, the party papers, the journals of special opinion, the committed papers, *Combat* or the *Billy Liar* in Belfast, *An Solas* in London or the *Irish People* in New York. Some neighborhood newsletters have a short half-life, some party publications tell little about what goes on in the party, most small papers are the province of specialists. Only the dedicated read student newspapers or ideological journals, seek out the true word published only in Irish and then intermittently subscribe to *Iris* or *Saoirse* or expect them to appear on time.

It is the real newspapers that provide most analysts with the plain tale. In Ireland this has been for much of the period the *Irish Times*, descended from the Anglo-Irish but now the nation's elite journal of record. The newspaper has maintained excellent Northern Irish and London contacts, but as the years have passed it has gradually been less concerned with the crisis. The other Irish newspapers, in Dublin the *Irish Press* and the *Irish Independent*, as well as their evening and Sunday editions, *Cork Examiner*, and in Belfast the *Belfast Telegraph* and *Irish News*, if not as detailed, are focused on local events. On Sunday from Dublin for over a decade Vincent Browne's *Sunday Tribune* has often had revelations and analysis in depth. In London, the great newspapers, *The Times, The Guardian, The Daily Telegraph*, and, on Sunday, the *Observer* and *Sunday Times*, with their particular postures and foibles, have followed the Troubles, but the new London *Independent* now has the best Northern coverage.

In Ireland the political journals, one a week, every two weeks, each month, regularly had analysis or revelation: In Dublin John Mulchay's *Hibernia* is now gone and the quite different *New Hibernia* did not last, then first *This Week* and then Browne's *Magill* ceased publication. In Belfast *Fortnight* is the last survivor and always the vital journal for Troubles: One could really avoid a generation of the *Irish Times* and settle happily with *Fortnight*. The British weekly journals, the *New Statesman* or the *Spectator* or all the rest, are most interested in how Ireland infringes on British politics, usually politics as seen from London. Rarely does the British regional press beyond Northern Ireland do more than reflect the London consensus.

Beyond Britain and Ireland, the world's media has been attracted to hard news, sends out teams or correspondents for the latest atrocity or sometimes, like *The New York Times*, to check on island events. Mostly the world's press, often the press in Dublin and London, depends on stringers and unsolicited telephone calls. Mostly what attracts the general media is as always novelty and sensation, the scandal for the moment. The correspondent on the spot is thus apt to write for various journals at various times. David McKittrick, after 1986 the Ireland correspondent of the London *Independent* and author of *Despatches from Belfast* (Belfast: Blackstaff, 1989), has been principally a correspondent for the *Irish Times* in Northern Ireland and London since 1973 but has also written for *The Economist, Le Monde,* the *Observer,* the *Sunday Times,* and the *Sunday Tribune* as well as *New Nation, Fortnight, Hibernia,* and the *Listener,* among others. His shift from the *Irish Times* to the London *Independent* simply indicates that even the major newspapers change their focus over a generation. The special journals of opinion, the party papers, those publications that are in a sense part of the problem, present even more turbulent a picture where much is hidden and revelation is rare.

Few but specialists and the police bother with the specialized newspapers of the parties and the players and few but academics involved in communication or public opinion need do more than read the *Irish Times* or the *Independent* in order to follow the plain tale of events. Reading twenty-five years of any newspaper is a more than sufficient chore even for the specialist determined to watch the Irish tale unfold on the page.

This Irish tale if it has had no end also has had no easy beginning. When did the Troubles begin? And what lies before that? Those who were dispatched to give the facts, tell the tale, found themselves operating without context, with no past to read, with no conventional sources. On an island where history mattered so much there seemed to be no history to read. Journalists dispatched to Northern Ireland to cover the crisis could not discover who was who, much less who had done what to whom in the immediate past. So at first with the first great wave of journalists in Belfast milling about the Europa lounge, efforts were made to write the history of the Troubles without quite having a last chapter or knowing where to begin. The journalists in particular had been left an empty playing field, no sources to absorb, no history to warp, nothing but the sounds from the street and the interest of publisher, producers, and the general public.

Irish events were perceived by all, even the least informed, as a crisis that had evolved out of a complex past. It was also assumed, even by the best informed, that the crisis would find an accommodation sooner rather than later, an accommodation that would free the commentators to move on to some other spectacular. The media people were largely astonished to find very little in print that would help them understand events nor many specialists who could be tapped. The recent past was a mystery, not to be absorbed with a quick read and a few telephone calls. There was no real written history, no reference books, no political dictionaries or chronologies, and no one to call up and ask.

In fascination at the events and in desperation, the journalists, the aliens and the locals, wrote their own books on the Troubles. Constantine Fitzgibbons, Max Hastings, Simon Winchester, the Insight Team of the London *Sunday Times* (the latter were primed with revelations by the Official IRA), Andrew Boyd, and others did for themselves and published the result. Coupled with these hastily assembled but often thoughtful and even adequate books were the television programs—British, American, Continental, and independent—the quick novels, the thrillers, the Troubles as trash, and works neither thoughtful nor adequate. Along with the media impressions there were the comments of those who had parallel political interests elsewhere, Italy or Germany or America, or who were engaged in investigating seemingly similar events elsewhere—nonviolence or secret armies or civil liberties. Most of the first wave arrived innocent of Irish matters and many of the Irish from the Republic were equally innocent of Northern Ireland matters.

Most of the early books, almost all the books, began with potted history, continued through the dramatic and spectacular events of 1968–73, and usually ended with the vague assumptions that an accommodation would, somehow, see a united Ireland and an end to violence. The good journalists, some Irish and some not, wrote interesting books and the hasty and superficial bad ones. Most of the politically conscious found what they sought, often only talking to their new friends. Many of the analysts collected another case study, often without leaving Belfast, and many journalists composed their reports from the gleanings of the Europa Hotel bar and the handouts at official briefings. In this Ireland was no different than any trendy crises, honey to attract all sorts.

Added to the efforts of the journalists and the first largely innocent commentators were the efforts of a few Irish scholars such as Liam de Paor, Conor Cruise O'Brien, or Owen Dudley Edwards, who sought to give depth to the history section. O'Brien has in fact not only continued to write extensively about the Troubles, often in the form of reviews later collected in book form, often sensibly if always with commitment to his own interpretation, but also has become an actor. He was a Labour deputy in the Dáil, spokesman on Northern matters, and later Minister of Post and Telegraphs, where supposedly isolated from the North he remained an active player. The same was the case after he left the Dáil to be editor of the London *Observer*. The same is still true, for he continues to pursue his own course, which arises from his long and often distinguished career, and castigate his enemies, who are legion. Essentially O'Brien arrived at a position not far different from that of a moderate unionist. O'Brien's position was always contentious. Never one to suffer ill-tutored Irish patriots gladly, he became for some radicals and many republicans the epitome of the failed liberal, a national apostate, an aging scold.

He, of course, was not the only one who doubted the wisdom and the reality of a united Ireland, however vaguely defined. And most outside the IRA could only vaguely define such an Ireland and made almost no suggestion on a peaceful means to achieve such an end. There were even at first a few published dissenters who did not see a united Ireland as inevitable or desirable, such as Patrick Riddell in *Fire Over Ulster* (London: Hamish Hamilton, 1970). Mostly the journalists and commentators found the Unionists unattractive and the radicals spectacular. And a considerable number of those radicals, eager to watch revolution in the streets of Belfast or Derry, soon wrote their own history, if seldom at length. They produced the appropriate analysis for their radical audience in London or Berkeley or Milan and soon works for a more general audience. In a sense the Troubles was virgin ground for analysis or even explanation, and the analysts of the left rushed in just as did the explainers of the medium, all but obscuring the few works of the prepared and tutored.

In 1967 when the Republicans held their tiny banned meeting in Belfast, the few they attracted were more than the total of the scholars and analysts in or out of the country concerned with Ireland since 1923. The few who had published on

Ireland had moved on from their work on the Commonwealth connection or the new constitution to other academic matters. The Irish academics chose not to publish. The ground had been left to a new generation, many in 1967 without even degrees in hand in most cases. Even then those prospective scholars involved in academic investigations, such as Maurice Manning, later to be a luminary of Fine Gael in the Dáil and Seanad, who was working on the Blueshirts, and Peter Pyne, now at Magee College, University of Ulster, in Derry, who was studying Sinn Féin in the twenties, were not concerned with really contemporary matters. Irish academic journals, Irish academic tutelage seldom went beyond 1916. Such matters were best left to journalists like Tim Pat Coogan in his *Ireland Since the Rising* (London: Pall Mall, 1966) or those on the *Irish Times* who did the work that the social scientists, not really a recognized Irish discipline, and Irish historians eschewed. In the sixties a few attracted to Ireland as a subject tended to be foreigners more interested in a special case study rather than in Ireland particularly.

By the time it became clear that the events in Ireland were a considerable event, most journalists were long in print and the academics were just beginning to appear in bibliographies, first in journals of opinion, those with a short shelf life, and then in the more conventional, the *Journal of Politics* or *Government and Opposition* or those with special concerns about peace or divided societies or insurgency. The few books that were published tended to have been long in the works, such as that of Rosemary Harris in social anthropology, *Prejudice and Tolerance in Ulster: A Study of Neighbors and "Strangers" in a Border Community* (Manchester: Manchester University Press, 1972), Richard Rose's bench-line poll results in *Governing Without Consensus* (London: Faber and Faber, 1971), Ian Budge and Cornelius O'Leary on Belfast politics, or, for that matter, my own work on the IRA, which was motivated like most alien scholars by a general interest—in the dynamics of revolution—and appeared in 1970 (London: Anthony Blond) to compete with Tim Pat Coogan's history, *IRA* (London: Pall Mall, 1970), which arose out of his chapter in *Ireland Since the Rising* rather than the impact of Northern events.

By the middle of the seventies, the first wave of journalists had departed, so the media often visited Northern Ireland but had other major interests, appeared for atrocities or to fill out comparative television treatment of terror or divided societies or the subject of the moment. The political activists still showed up but in sharply diminished numbers, and each then published while standing upon a growing heap of analysis, some by activists, much by scholars. Ideological quarrels in and out of academia now had to take account of years of existing work. And the existing work, increasingly as the years passed, included that of maturing generations of scholars. These scholars, too, often were attracted not by Ireland as much as by the nature of contemporary violence, yet gradually emerging in Ireland and Britain was a new generation of scholars who were coming of academic age in the midst of the Troubles, for them a constant, not a violent, interruption.

The Irish Troubles increasingly evolved during a time of terror, a decade of spectacular violence, that involved especially Germany and Italy in Europe but all the West. This was because of the transnational nature of some of the operations,

847

kidnappings, hostage seizures, assassinations, hijackings—particularly those of the radical Palestinians but also the Armenians or Croatians or South Moluccans, people forgotten by history and the West. Thus, the IRA or the UVF, the transformation of the Officials into the Workers, the impact of the peace people or community socialization attracted scholars without an Irish context, often without much Irish exposure.

Ireland remained a stop on the terrorist tour, a required chapter in books on political violence or necessary paper on most conferences on world order or civil rights. At the same time those scholars with less trendy concerns, often Irish or British, were attracted to the island because so little substantive work had been done; they began to winnow the past, not only the most recent past, but the old ground long watered only by patriotic oratory. The new scholars were often quite committed not so much to party or Irish principles but to specific methodologies, to the insights of the new Marxists or the techniques available to the social scientists.

For a variety of reasons the historians and political scientists came late to the Troubles, still a fertile field as case study, as ground for journalists' investigation or academic work done at one or two removes. Historians are prone to want time to pass before beginning, but as the years passed and the Troubles persisted, even the historians joined with the social scientists in treating Irish events as a proper arena for study, more than just contemporary example to add weight to theories or models. The result has been a growing literature, sound, often profound, sometimes comparative, but nearly always grounded in conventional academic approaches and means. Thus, there has been detailed work done on divided societies, children and violence, community mobilization, conflict resolution. There are as well scholars who pursue their interest in political parties or administrative practice despite, not because of, special Northern Irish conditions.

Coupled with the academic concern with Northern Ireland, there was a concomitant concern with Irish and Anglo-Irish history that in no way deflected the patriots and politicians from recourse to the old myths recycled to adjust to new realities. Many of the most committed read little in any case and what they did read was chosen from the orthodox cannon. Along with the new academic interest in Irish matters in general and modern Irish history in particular came a new trend in Irish publishing and political history: instant books, often paper-back, often transient, but in many cases most useful. Any scandal, spectacular atrocity, or election often produced a book: The fall of Stormont, the fallout of the train robbery at Sallins, the hunger strikes soon found their way into print. There were swift biographies, hurried memoirs, narrow academic analysis of election results, and the regular appearance of either sound work by journalists or considered work by scholars. And for those who prefer a few pictures to thousands of words, there have been almost annual collections of photographs.

Nearly every event is thus covered in one way or another and often in ways that indicate the concern of the authors or the catchment area of the contents. Thus, the killing of three IRA volunteers on Gibraltar engendered concern on the island by the majority Catholics about civil rights issues, a concern reflected in certain British quarters, and by the Protestant majority in Northern Ireland with the special operation's success, a concern reflected in certain British quarters, but in

Great Britain the key was the acrimonious dispute over the television coverage and real or imagined state intervention. In fact, the problem of censorship led to a second cycle of television coverage, a subject that fascinated the industry if not all viewers. Thus, the hunger strike produced a spate of publications on the island and often elsewhere but was not a major publishing consideration of Britain.

On the other hand, the culmination of the IRA English bombers' court cases in reversals, scandal, and acrimony everywhere produced many works—that of Chris Mullin, *Error of Judgment* (London: Chatto and Windus, 1986), had more than any other factor accelerated the move toward review. Once freed the prisoners added to the literature (Paul Hill, *Stolen Years, Before and After Guildford* [London: Doubleday, 1990], and Gerry Conlon, *Proved Innocent: The Story of Gerry Conlon of the Guildford Four* [London: Hamish Hamilton, 1990]), even before the legal scholars and political concern were well under way analyzing the implications for the judicial system. The former prisoners became transmuted into celebrities and their everyday lives, after years in prison, became grist for the British and Irish journalists; even film producers were attracted.

In any case nearly every facet of the Troubles is covered, by academics (Cornelius O'Leary, Sydney Elliott, and R. A. Wilford, *The Northern Ireland Assembly, 1982–1986: A Constitutional Experiment* [London & Belfast: Hurty and Queen's University Bookshop, 1988]), by journalists (James Adams, Robin Morgan, and Anthony Bambridge, *Ambush: The War Between the SAS and the IRA* [London: Pan, 1988]), by participants (John Stalker, *Stalker* [London: Harrap, 1988]), or their biographers (Colm Kenna, *A Biography of Gerry Adams* [Cork: Mercier Press, 1990]). There is something for everyone. Nearly everything is covered, if not well at least for the time being: the impact of violence on the family, the nature of peace keeping, the plight of victims, the evolution of republican ideas, the symbols of the ghettos, the nature of Irish terrorism, or simply the latest report, the last atrocity. There have been medical articles detailing work on gunshot trauma, sociological articles on torture victims, articles on territoriality and on children's games, on art of the Troubles and on the trouble of the arts in Ireland. Much of the work is peripheral to any narrative or the past generation that focuses on the conventional, the gun in politics, the plain tale of events. Yet even to note that there is a massive literature on discrimination, economic policies, housing the working class, or civil-military relations really is no help to the specialist or the general reader. There are a score of books on Irish "terrorism," usually collections, often useful to the scholar but rarely to the general reader.

Who needs to know, wants to know the details, the serried titles of all that work on the religious implications of the Irish crisis, the tracts and elegantly published volumes, the weekly newsletters, the sermons hastily printed and dropped through mail slots, the diatribes and screeds arriving through the mails without request, the printed faith distributed on street corners and at church doors of every denomination? None but the specialist and the faithful need write off to the American Protestants for Truth About Ireland in Gwynedd, Pennsylvania, to acquire the monthly issues of *Northern Ireland Human Rights Review*. Yet for the specialist and the faithful it is there for the reading along with the thousands of items, the hundreds of journals and newsletters and newspapers of the committed.

All this, the evidence of the faith at work, is hardly balanced in the end by the odd scholarly volume, unless one seeks not the facts but salvation, revelation rather than a disinterested history. And there are all sorts of efforts to produce history and analysis on the religious aspects of the Troubles, just as there is another literature on the economics of violence. There are books on Paisley and the Protestants on the Catholics and on the way to salvation and any number of Godly solutions to the Irish problem. What is apparent to anyone who goes beyond the daily newspaper or the nightly television, even as far as the bookstore, is that where once there was nothing much of anything Irish beyond poetry, now there is too much. There is something for nearly everyone, something published about nearly everything.

Thus, one concerned solely with the tribulations of the British army in Northern Ireland has not only the conventional sources of all contemporary history and in particular the specialized British military journals but the results distilled. There are regimental histories (Michael Barthorp, *Crater to the Creggan: The History of the Royal Anglian Regiment, 1964–1974* [London: Leo Cooper, 1976]) or military memoirs (Peter Morton, *Emergency Tour: 3 PARA in South Armagh* [London: Kimber, 1989]) and often some unconventional works as well, such as A. F. N. Clarke's *Contact* (London: Secker and Warburg, 1983), which gives a most unvarnished account of the brutality of a dirty war, followed up by a similar exercise by Michael Asher in *Shoot to Kill: A Soldier's Journey Through Violence* (London: Viking Press, 1990). There are specialized books on bombs, such as George Styles's *Bombs Have No Pity* (London: Luscombe, 1975) or Derrick Patrick's *Fetch Felix: The Fight Against the Ulster Bombers, 1976–1977* (London: Hamish Hamilton, 1981). There are books composed of memoirs—Max Arthur's *Northern Ireland Soldiers Talking, 1969 to Today* (London: Sidgwick & Jackson, 1987) is especially useful. There are the detailed four volumes compiled by David Barzilay, journalist, Scotland Yard spokesman, and public relations consultant, that end in 1980 and the more concentrated and conventional histories by former officers (Michael Dewar, *The British Army in Northern Ireland* [London: Arms and Armour Press, 1985] or Desmond Hamill, *Pig in the Middle: The Army in Northern Ireland, 1969–1984* [London: Methuen, 1985]). There is Chris Ryder's *The Ulster Defense Regiment: An Instrument of Peace?* (London: Methuen, 1991), to go with his earlier study, *The RUC: A Force Under Fire* (London: Methuen, 1989). There are works on the army of the Irish Republic and the Irish Republican Army, in particular that of Patrick Bishop and Eamonn Mallie, *The Provisional IRA* (London: Heinemann, 1987). Few, whatever the subject, are wholly disinterested and more than a few are very special pleading.

Thus, nearly any point of focus has been covered, the more specialized or those open to comparative analysis by scholars and those more spectacular or conventional to the involved, the individual, the simply interested. There is a text on *Violence and the Social Services in Northern Ireland*, edited by John Darby and Arthur Williamson (London: Heineman, 1978), and one on *Northern Ireland: A Psychological Analysis* (Dublin: Gill and Macmillan, 1980). And as the list of examples in this discipline or that area extends, it becomes clear that there is too much, even if only the scholarly, the recent, the most useful were to be included. How can Bob Purdie's work on the civil rights movement, *Politics in the Streets* (Belfast: Blackstaff, 1990), be neglected, and if included, what of the other works on the period, such as Paul Arthur's *The People's Democracy, 1968–1973* (Belfast: Blackstaff, 1974) or Eamonn McCann's, Michael Farrell's, Raymond McClean's, or Conn McCluskey's commentary finally out in 1989, and then James Downey or Frank Curran? And there is still the promise of more to come if Thomás Mac Giolla ever retires from active politics or Anthony Coughlan publishes as promised. The same bibliographic surfeit arises at each subject point.

Recently at least the reverse of Gresham's law seems at work, as the good has driven away some of the bad. There has been scholarly summing up, big subjects given disinterested treatment. The magisterial *Northern Ireland: A Comparative Analysis* (Dublin: Gill and Macmillan, 1987) by Frank Wright has been long in the making and quite worth the wait: dense, a highly detailed analysis by a scholar long at Queen's University in Belfast, now at Limerick, that, alas, will not be read by those responsible for Irish affairs who have most to gain. In recent years, beginning with Wright's book, there has already been a series of works that, if nothing else, indicate the change in Irish academic capacity and appeal as well as the persistence of analytical postures. Thus, the comparative studies continue, ranging from individual efforts to the collections. There is the committed work out of Zed Press. Townshend's shift from the earlier Irish Troubles to more contemporary matters is apparent. On such matters not long ago he appeared quiet amid the alien corn at the University of Haifa in Israel on the same platform with me as well as with Conor Cruise O'Brien and Owen Dudley Edwards, enough to drive a historian back to a more tranquil era.

Many relevant works do not focus on the years of the Troubles. General histories tend to begin earlier and stop sooner than the present. Many are more interested in roots than in the present conflict and others touch Northern Ireland only tangentially. Thus, the late Nicholas Mansergh's fine *The Unresolved Quarrel: The Anglo-Irish Settlement and its Undoing, 1912–1972* (New Haven, Conn.: Yale University Press, 1991) seeks to elucidate the long and complex trail that led to the collapse of Stormont rather than to illuminate any aspect of the Troubles. To even touch on much of the new history would be to enter a different forest, often filled with trees only marginally of concern to the issues of the Troubles if often containing most useful insights.

There is now a library of good history and turgid social science, dreadful history and rigorous social science. All this allows a new generation of secondary analysis that is not necessarily part of the problem, often undertaken by those who have spent decades on that problem. There is the result of a lifetime of contemplation on Irish matters by John Whyte, who tragically died just as his work on the interpretations of the Troubles by the multitudes was to be published. There is so much that Whyte can deploy categories of analysis and generalizations on interpretation. His bibliography of basic works runs to twenty-six printed pages. There is the optimistic survey of McGarry and O'Leary, who do not accept Richard Rose's early suggestion that the problem was there was no solution. An analysis that may not be eternal. The authors in McGarry and O'Leary indicate that there may be hope even as Rose's generalization yet holds true. If there is as yet no solution, neither is there yet an end to the analysis. And this is but a short selection of recent works that could easily be extended beyond all patience without need to tap journalists, the journals, or esoteric sources.

Charles Townshend, (ed.), *Consensus in Ireland: Approaches and Recessions* (Oxford: Clarendon, 1988)

Bob Rowthorn and Naomi Wayne, *Northern Ireland: The Political Economy of Conflict* (Boulder, Col.: Westview, 1988)

Adrian Guelke, *The International Perspectives* (New York: St. Martin's Press, 1989)

Arthur Aughey, *Under Siege: Ulster Unionism and the Anglo-Irish Agreement* (Belfast: Blackstaff, 1989)

L. J. MacFarlane, *Human Rights: Realities and Possibilities, Northern Ireland, the Republic of Ireland, Yugoslavia, and Hungary* (New York: St. Martin's Press, 1990)

John Whyte, *Interpreting Northern Ireland* (Oxford: Clarendon Press, 1990)

John McGarry and Brendan O'Leary, ed., *The Future of Northern Ireland* (Oxford: Clarendon Press, 1990)

Frank Gaffikin and Mike Morrissey, *Northern Ireland: The Thatcher Years* (London: Zed, 1990)

Joanne Wright, *Terrorist Propaganda: The Red Army Faction and the Provisional IRA* (New York: St. Martin's Press, 1990)

Gerald McElroy, *The Catholic Church and Northern Ireland Crisis, 1968–1986* (Dublin: Gill and Macmillan, 1991)

John D. Brewer with Kathleen Magee, *Inside the RUC: Routine Policing in a Divided Society* (Oxford: Clarendon Press, 1991)

Michael J. Cunningham, *British Government Policy in Northern Ireland, 1969–1989: Its Nature and Execution* (Manchester: Manchester University Press, 1991)

David J. Smith and Gerald Chambers, *Inequality in Northern Ireland* (Oxford: Clarendon Press, 1991)

Brigid Hadfield, *Northern Ireland: Politics and the Constitution* (Buckingham: Open University Press, 1992)

Before one becomes an entry in the list of finished texts, there are other steps that can be, often are first taken. There are several journals focused specifically on Irish matters, if not solely the contemporary Troubles: *Éire-Ireland*, published by the Irish-American Cultural Institute; the Field Day pamphlets; *Irish Political Studies*, the yearbook of the Political Studies Association of Ireland, an organization that in the regular *Bulletin* keeps up to date on the state of contemporary research; and the bilingual *Études Irlandaises*, which covers history and politics as well as civilization and literature. As for the enormous library of analytical journals, few in any discipline have not published at least once on the Troubles, most evidently those focused on contemporary politics, especially aspects of conflict, and thus those concerned with political violence, peace studies, ethnic and religious strife, comparative conflict, insurgency, and facets of divided societies. Thus, not unexpectedly, entire issues of journals like *Conflict* or *Terrorism* have been dedicated to Northern Ireland.

Beyond the published work in journals, there exists an entire additional and often productive sphere of academic papers, presentations, and unprinted seminar results, dissertations, and theses, the paper foundations in some cases of future additions to the literature and at other times only a scholarly exercise. There is now a Centre for the Study of Conflict at the University of Ulster and a new generation of scholars all too aware of the practice as well as the theories of the Troubles. The specialists can scan the lists of dissertations or receive the notification of works-in-progress from the various professional organizations. Those less concerned can wait for the printed result. The analysis, in the meantime, continues apace out of sight of not only the general reader but the average scholar. At the September 1992 meeting of the American Political Science Association convention, Cynthia Irvin of Duke University, who has done field research in Northern Ireland and the Basque country in Spain, turns up in a panel on media and conflict as well as a panel on expressing political opposition, while Robert F. Mulvihill of Rosemont College in Pennsylvania has a paper on "The Center Doesn't Hold: Political Violence in Northern Ireland," Mary E. Kazmierczak, from Madison, Wisconsin, has one on "The Anglo Irish Agreement and the Conflict in Northern Ireland," and Nathalie J. Frensley, from Texas, has one on "Rhetorical Transitions Across Conflict Stages: Propaganda Content and Style in the Northern Ireland Troubles." There are as well analytical reports done for various agencies, various governments, for banks and corporations, for foundations—reports on Northern Ireland or that include Northern Ireland as a key example. There exists more paper than can possibly be acquired and read for particular or general profit.

Amid all the analytical debris there are often most interesting bits, interviews or unexpected perspectives, information from a far discipline or found in a strange place. Much of this analysis with limited circulation, however, is based on general printed sources, on momentary concerns, especially academic, and on the need to include one of the era's major conflicts for theoretical contrast or comparison. If the work has general analytical value, if it can be of use at least to scholars and specialists, the results gradually move to the printed page and the general literature. Thus, John Whyte worked on Provisional Sinn Féin in Belfast for his dissertation in sociology; the first printed results appeared in journals—for example, Robert W. White and Terry Falkenberg White, "Revolution in the City: On the Resources of Urban Guerrillas," *Terrorism and Political Violence*, Vol. 3, No. 4, Winter 1991, pp. 100–32—and will emerge as a book published by Greenwood, a formal text entered into the enormous literature of the Troubles.

In sum there is both too much to read but too little that provides concise and coherent analysis, much less explanation, for the general reader. Much published is part of the Troubles, much is done to academic formula or for special purpose. Much has been done for a particular patron or for promotion. This is hardly novel.

Amid all that has been published, what is remarkable has been the shelf life of many of the entries, whether memoirs like Bernadette Devlin's or the early benchmarks like Richard Rose's *Governing Without Consensus: An Irish Perspective*. Ian budge and Cornelius O'Leary's *Belfast: Approach to Crisis, A Study of Belfast*

Politics, 1613–1970 (London: Macmillan, 1973) will not easily be supplanted any more than Tom Wilson's *Ulster, Conflict & Consent* (London: Blackwell, 1989), published fifteen years later. Where once Ireland in general was hardly served at all by historians and analysts, now there is a sound, often conventional, at times splendid secondary literature focused not only on Northern Ireland but also on all facets of Ireland illuminated by the contemporary conflict. Works of the involved like *Up Off Their Knees* by Conn McCluskey have brought back the history of the sixties, all but lost in the tumult of the civil rights demonstrations and the subsequent shooting. For those who care to read it, contemporary Ireland now has a history, and as William Faulkner remarked, "The past is never dead. It is not even past." And many have labored to see that the Irish past lives on on the page.

In the last few years, if there has been no effective movement to find an Irish accommodation, an end to the Troubles, there has been not only the continuing blizzard of pages and paper on the issue but also a series of substantial analytical works, mostly academic, that at minimum chronicles the evolution of the conflict and at times gives an insight into the nature of political reality, recent history, the Irish. After a generation where most comfort has been cold, an undeniable return can be found shelved: histories and surveys, thin volumes of poems and thick ones of numbers, charts, and graphs. It is a poor if extensive return for the cost taken by the Troubles, but it is a return, a net gain, and in an arena where most actors still are engaged in a zero-sum drama in seemingly endless acts, it is comfort of a sort.

Index